THIRD CANADIAN EDITION

Organizational Behaviour

Improving Performance and Commitment in the Workplace

Jason A. Colquitt
University of Florida

Jeffery A. LePine
University of Florida

Michael J. Wesson
Texas A&M University

Ian R. Gellatly
University of Alberta

Mc Graw Hill Education

Organizational Behaviour: Improving Performance and Commitment in the Workplace
Third Canadian Edition

ISBN-13: 978-1-25-909427-9
ISBN-10: 1-25-909427-8

2 3 4 5 6 7 8 9 0 WEB 1 9 8 7 6

Printed and bound in Canada.

Director of Product Management: Rhondda McNabb
Group Product Manager: Kim Brewster
Marketing Manager: Cathie Lefebvre
Product Developer: Tracey Haggert
Product Team Associate: Stephanie Giles
Supervising Editor: Jessica Barnoski
Photo/Permissions Editor: Marnie Lamb
Copy Editor: Rodney Rawlings
Plant Production Coordinator: Scott Morrison
Manufacturing Production Coordinator: Sheryl MacAdam
Cover Design: Liz Harasymczuk
Cover Image: John Fleenor/NBCU Photo Bank via Getty Images
Interior Design: Liz Harasymczuk
Page Layout: Laserwords Private Limited
Printer: Webcom, Inc.

Dedication

To Catherine, Cameron, Riley, and Connor, and also to Mom, Dad, Alan, and Shawn. The most wonderful family I could imagine, two times over.

—J.A.C.

To my parents, who made me, and to Marcie, Izzy, and Eli, who made my life complete.

—J.A.L.

To Liesl and Dylan: Their support in all I do is incomparable. They are my life and I love them both. To my parents: They provide a foundation that never wavers.

—M.J.W.

To my parents, Roy and Beverly, who taught me everything I ever needed to know about commitment, unconditional love, and achievement striving. To my brother, Duncan, who left this life too soon. Finally, to Belinda, who reminds me every day why two heads and hearts are better than one.

—I.R.G.

About the Authors

JASON A. COLQUITT is the William H. Willson Distinguished Chair in the Department of Management at the University of Georgia's Terry College of Business. He received his PhD from Michigan State University's Eli Broad Graduate School of Management, and earned his BS in psychology from Indiana University. He has taught organizational behavior and human resource management at the undergraduate, masters, and executive levels and has also taught research methods at the doctoral level. He has received awards for teaching excellence at both the undergraduate and executive levels.

Jason's research interests include organizational justice, trust, team effectiveness, and personality influences on task and learning performance. He has published more than 30 articles on these and other topics in *Academy of Management Journal, Academy of Management Review, Journal of Applied Psychology, Organizational Behavior and Human Decision Processes,* and *Personnel Psychology.* He recently served as editor-in-chief for *Academy of Management Journal* and has served on a number of editorial boards, including *Academy of Management Journal, Journal of Applied Psychology, Organizational Behavior and Human Decision Processes, Personnel Psychology, Journal of Management,* and *International Journal of Conflict Management.* He is a recipient of the Society for Industrial and Organizational Psychology's Distinguished Early Career Contributions Award and the Cummings Scholar Award for early to mid-career achievement, sponsored by the Organizational Behavior division of the Academy of Management. He was also elected to be a representative-at-large for the Organizational Behavior division.

Jason enjoys spending time with his wife, Catherine, and three sons, Cameron, Riley, and Connor. His hobbies include playing basketball, playing the trumpet, watching movies, and rooting on (in no particular order) the Pacers, Colts, Cubs, Hoosiers, Spartans, Gators, and Bulldogs.

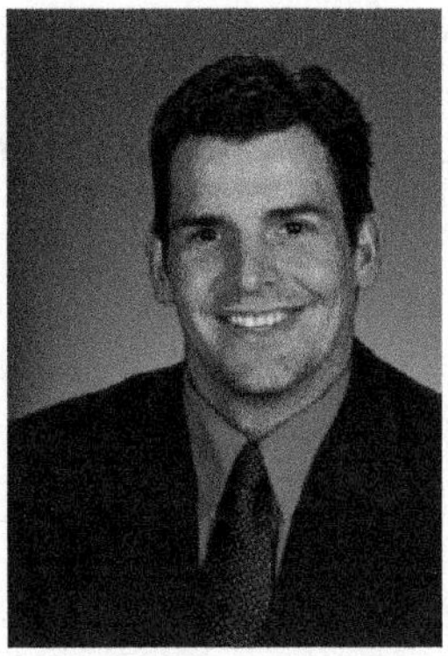

JEFFERY A. LEPINE is the PetSmart Chair in Leadership in the Department of Management at Arizona State University's W.P. Carey School of Business. He received his PhD in organizational behavior from the Eli Broad Graduate School of Management at Michigan State University. He also earned an MS in Management from Florida State University and a BS in finance from the University of Connecticut. He has taught organizational behavior, human resource management, and management of groups and teams at undergraduate and graduate levels.

Jeff's research interests include team functioning and effectiveness, individual and team adaptation, citizenship behavior, voice, engagement, and occupational stress. He has published more than 25 articles on these and other topics in *Academy of Management Journal, Academy of Management Review, Journal of Applied Psychology, Organizational Behavior and Human Decision Processes,* and *Personnel Psychology.* He has served as associate editor of *Academy of Management Review,* and has served (or is currently serving) on the editorial boards of *Academy of Management Journal, Journal of Applied Psychology, Organizational Behavior and Human Decision Processes, Personnel Psychology, Journal of Management, Journal of Organizational Behavior,* and *Journal of Occupational and Organizational Psychology.* He is a recipient of the Society for Industrial and Organizational Psychology's Distinguished Early Career Contributions Award and the Cummings Scholar Award for early to mid-career achievement, sponsored by the Organizational Behavior division of the Academy of Management. He was also elected to the Executive Committee of the Human Resource Division of the Academy of Management. Prior to earning his PhD, Jeff was an officer in the U.S. Air Force.

Jeff spends most of his free time with his wife, Marcie, daughter, Izzy, and son, Eli. He also enjoys playing guitar, hiking in the desert, and restoring his GTO.

MICHAEL J. WESSON is an associate professor in the Management Department at Texas A&M University's Mays Business School. He received his PhD from Michigan State University's Eli Broad Graduate School of Management. He also holds an MS in human resource management from Texas

A&M University and a BBA from Baylor University. He has taught organizational behavior and human resource management–based classes at all levels but currently spends most of his time teaching Mays MBAs, EMBAs, and executive development at Texas A&M. He was awarded Texas A&M's Montague Center for Teaching Excellence Award.

Michael's research interests include organizational justice, goal-setting, organizational entry (employee recruitment, selection, and socialization), person–organization fit, and compensation and benefits. His articles have been published in journals such as *Journal of Applied Psychology, Personnel Psychology, Academy of Management Review,* and *Organizational Behavior and Human Decision Processes.* He currently serves on the editorial boards of the *Journal of Applied Psychology* and the *Journal of Organizational Behavior* and is an ad hoc reviewer for many others. He is active in the Academy of Management and the Society for Industrial and Organizational Psychology. Prior to returning to school, Michael worked as a human resources manager for a *Fortune* 500 firm. He has served as a consultant to the automotive supplier, healthcare, oil and gas, and technology industries in areas dealing with recruiting, selection, onboarding, compensation, and turnover.

Michael spends most of his time trying to keep up with his wife, Liesl, and son, Dylan. He is a self-admitted food and wine snob, home theater aficionado, and college sports addict. (Gig 'em Aggies!)

IAN R. GELLATLY is a Professor in the Department of Strategic Management and Organization in the Alberta School of Business at the University of Alberta. He received his Ph.D. in Industrial and Organizational Psychology from the University of Western Ontario. Prior to joining the University of Alberta in 1998, Ian taught in the faculty of management at the University of Lethbridge. Within the Alberta School of Business, Ian teaches courses in organizational behaviour and human resources management at the undergraduate and graduate levels.

Ian's research interests fall within the field of organizational behaviour. His work has touched on many topics covered in this book, such as the antecedents and consequences of employee commitment (the separate forms of commitment and profiles of commitment), motivation, and employee withdrawal. Ian has published numerous articles on these and other topics in *Journal of Applied Psychology, Organizational Research Methods, Journal of Organizational Behavior, Journal of Vocational Behavior, Human Performance*, and *Human Resource Management*. He currently serves on the editorial boards of the *Journal of Applied Psychology, Journal of Organizational Behavior*, and *Journal of Personnel Psychology*, and is an ad hoc reviewer for many other journals. In addition to his teaching and research, Ian has served as a consultant to business and government.

Ian enjoys spending time with his family. His hobbies include squash, hiking in the Canadian Rockies, watching HBO, road trips, live NHL hockey (*Go Oilers!*), Sudoku puzzles, and epic fantasy novels.

Brief Contents

Preface xii

PART 1
INTRODUCTION TO ORGANIZATIONAL BEHAVIOUR 1

CHAPTER 1 What Is Organizational Behaviour? 1
CHAPTER 2 Job Performance 29
CHAPTER 3 Organizational Commitment 59

PART 2
INDIVIDUAL CHARACTERISTICS AND MECHANISMS 89

CHAPTER 4 Personality, Cultural Values, and Ability 89
CHAPTER 5 Job Satisfaction 135
CHAPTER 6 Stress 171
CHAPTER 7 Motivation 207
CHAPTER 8 Trust, Justice, and Ethics 243
CHAPTER 9 Learning and Decision Making 279

PART 3
RELATIONAL MECHANISMS 315

CHAPTER 10 Communication 315
CHAPTER 11 Team Characteristics and Processes 353
CHAPTER 12 Power, Influence, and Negotiation 403
CHAPTER 13 Leadership Styles and Behaviours 437

PART 4
ORGANIZATIONAL MECHANISMS 471

CHAPTER 14 Organizational Structure 471
CHAPTER 15 Organizational Culture and Change 501

Glossary GL-1
Chapter Notes EN-1

Contents

Preface xii

PART 1
INTRODUCTION TO ORGANIZATIONAL BEHAVIOUR 1

CHAPTER 1
What Is Organizational Behaviour? 1

What Is Organizational Behaviour? 3
- Organizational Behaviour Defined 4
- The Role of Management Theory 5
- An Integrative Model of OB 6

Does Organizational Behaviour Matter? 9
- Building a Conceptual Argument 11
- Research Evidence 13
- So What's So Hard? 15

How Do We "Know" What We Know About Organizational Behaviour? 17
- Moving Forward in This Book 22

TAKEAWAYS 23
KEY TERMS 24
DISCUSSION QUESTIONS 24
CASE 24
EXERCISE 26
OB ASSESSMENTS 27

CHAPTER 2
Job Performance 29

Job Performance 31

What Does It Mean to Be a "Good Performer"? 32
- Task Performance 33
- Citizenship Behaviour 38
- Counterproductive Behaviour 41
- Summary: What Does It Mean to Be a "Good Performer"? 46

Application: Performance Management 48
- Management by Objectives 48
- Behaviourally Anchored Rating Scales 49
- 360-Degree Feedback 49
- Forced Ranking 51
- Social Networking Systems 52

TAKEAWAYS 52
KEY TERMS 53
DISCUSSION QUESTIONS 53
CASE 54
EXERCISE 55
OB ASSESSMENTS 56

CHAPTER 3
Organizational Commitment 59

Organizational Commitment 61

What Does It Mean to Be "Committed"? 63
- Forms of Commitment 63
- Withdrawal Behaviour 72
- Summary: What Does It Mean to Be "Committed"? 78

Trends That Affect Commitment 79
- Diversity of the Workforce 79
- The Changing Employee–Employer Relationship 80

Application: Commitment Initiatives 82

TAKEAWAYS 83
KEY TERMS 84
DISCUSSION QUESTIONS 85
CASE 85
EXERCISE 86
OB ASSESSMENTS 87

PART 2
INDIVIDUAL CHARACTERISTICS AND MECHANISMS 89

CHAPTER 4
Personality, Cultural Values, and Ability 89

Personality, Cultural Values, and Ability 91

How Can We Describe What Employees Are Like? 92
- The Big Five Taxonomy 92
- Cultural Values 101
- Summary: How Can We Describe What Employees Are Like? 107

What Does It Mean for an Employee to Be "Able"? 107
- Cognitive Ability 108
- Emotional Ability 114

Physical Ability 117
Summary: What Does It Mean for an Employee to Be "Able"? 120

How Important Are These Individual Differences? 121

Application: Personality and Cognitive Ability Tests 125

TAKEAWAYS 127
KEY TERMS 128
DISCUSSION QUESTIONS 129
CASE 130
EXERCISE 131
OB ASSESSMENTS 131

CHAPTER 5
Job Satisfaction 135

Job Satisfaction 137

Why Are Some Employees More Satisfied Than Others? 138
Value Fulfillment 139
Satisfaction with the Work Itself 144
Mood and Emotions 151
Summary: Why Are Some Employees More Satisfied Than Others? 158

How Important Is Job Satisfaction? 159
Life Satisfaction 160

Application: Tracking Satisfaction 163

TAKEAWAYS 165
KEY TERMS 165
DISCUSSION QUESTIONS 166
CASE 167
EXERCISE 168
OB ASSESSMENTS 168

CHAPTER 6
Stress 171

Stress 173

Why Are Some Employees More "Stressed" Than Others? 175
Types of Stressors 176
How Do People Cope with Stressors? 183
The Experience of Strain 185
Accounting for Individuals in the Stress Process 188
Summary: Why Are Some Employees More "Stressed" Than Others? 190

How Important Is Stress? 191

Application: Stress Management 194
Assessment 195
Reducing Stressors 196
Providing Resources 196
Reducing Strains 199

TAKEAWAYS 200
KEY TERMS 200
DISCUSSION QUESTIONS 201
CASE 202
EXERCISE 203
OB ASSESSMENTS 205

CHAPTER 7
Motivation 207

Motivation 209

Why Are Some Employees More Motivated Than Others? 212
Expectancy Theory 212
Goal Setting Theory 218
Equity Theory 224
Psychological Empowerment 228
Summary: Why Are Some Employees More Motivated Than Others? 231

How Important Is Motivation? 232

Application: Compensation Systems 234

TAKEAWAYS 236
KEY TERMS 237
DISCUSSION QUESTIONS 237
CASE 238
EXERCISE 239
OB ASSESSMENTS 240

CHAPTER 8
Trust, Justice, and Ethics 243

Trust, Justice, and Ethics 245

Why Are Some Authorities More Trusted Than Others? 247
Trust 247
Justice 253
Ethics 259
Summary: Why Are Some Authorities More Trusted Than Others? 267

How Important Is Trust? 269

Application: Social Responsibility 271

TAKEAWAYS 272
KEY TERMS 273
DISCUSSION QUESTIONS 274
CASE 274
EXERCISE 275
OB ASSESSMENTS 276

CHAPTER 9
Learning and Decision Making 279

Learning and Decision Making 281

Why Do Some Employees Learn to Make Decisions Better Than Others? 282

- Types of Knowledge 282
- Methods of Learning 284
- Methods of Decision Making 291
- Decision-Making Problems 295
- Summary: Why Do Some Employees Learn to Make Decisions Better Than Others? 303

How Important Is Learning? 304

Application: Training 305

TAKEAWAYS 307
KEY TERMS 308
DISCUSSION QUESTIONS 309
CASE 309
EXERCISE 310
OB ASSESSMENTS 312

PART 3
RELATIONAL MECHANISMS 315

CHAPTER 10
Communication 315

Communication 317

The Communication Process 318

What Does It Mean to Be a "Good Communicator"? 319

- Face-to-Face Communication 320
- Computer-Mediated Communication 323
- The Communication Process: Potential Issues 328
- Summary: What Does It Mean to Be a "Good Communicator"? 333

Communication Networks 336

- Formal Communication 336
- Formal Networks 337
- Informal Communication Networks 340

How Important Is Communication? 342

Application: Interviewing 344

TAKEAWAYS 345
KEY TERMS 347
DISCUSSION QUESTIONS 348
CASE 348
EXERCISE 349
OB ASSESSMENTS 351

CHAPTER 11
Team Characteristics and Processes 353

Team Characteristics 356

What Characteristics Can Be Used to Describe Teams? 357

- Types of Teams 357
- Variations Within Team Types 360
- Team Interdependence 364
- Team Composition 367
- Summary: What Characteristics Can Be Used to Describe Teams? 375

Team Processes 376

Why Are Some Teams More Than the Sum of Their Parts? 377

- Taskwork Processes 379
- Teamwork Processes 382
- Team States 386
- Summary: Why Are Some Teams More Than The Sum of Their Parts? 388

How Important Are Team Characteristics and Processes? 388

Application: Training Teams 392

- Transportable Teamwork Competencies 393
- Cross-Training 394
- Team Process Training 394
- Team Building 395

TAKEAWAYS 396
KEY TERMS 396
DISCUSSION QUESTIONS 397
CASE 398
EXERCISE 399
OB ASSESSMENTS 401

CHAPTER 12
Power, Influence, and Negotiation 403

Power, Influence, and Negotiation 405

Why Are Some People More Powerful Than Others? 406

- Acquiring Power 406
- Using Influence 411
- Power and Influence in Action 415
- Negotiations 421
- Summary: Why Are Some People More Powerful Than Others? 425

How Important Are Power and Influence? 427

Application: Alternative Dispute Resolution 429

TAKEAWAYS 430
KEY TERMS 430
DISCUSSION QUESTIONS 431
CASE 432
EXERCISE 433
OB ASSESSMENTS 434

CHAPTER 13
Leadership Styles and Behaviours 437

Leadership: Styles and Behaviours 440

Why Are Some Leaders More Effective Than Others? 443
- Leader Decision-Making Styles 444
- Day-to-Day Leadership Behaviours 449
- Transformational Leadership Behaviours 453
- Summary: Why Are Some Leaders More Effective Than Others? 460

How Important Is Leadership? 461

Application: Leadership Training 464

TAKEAWAYS 465
KEY TERMS 466
DISCUSSION QUESTIONS 466
CASE 467
EXERCISE 468
OB ASSESSMENTS 469

PART 4
ORGANIZATIONAL MECHANISMS 471

CHAPTER 14
Organizational Structure 471

Organizational Structure 473

Why Do Some Organizations Have Different Structures Than Others? 474
- Elements of Organizational Structure 475
- Organizational Design 480
- Common Organizational Forms 482
- Summary: Why Do Some Organizations Have Different Structures Than Others? 489

How Important Is Structure? 490

Application: Restructuring 492

TAKEAWAYS 495
KEY TERMS 495
DISCUSSION QUESTIONS 496
CASE 496
EXERCISE 497
OB ASSESSMENTS 498

CHAPTER 15
Organizational Culture and Change 501

Organizational Culture 503

Why Do Some Organizations Have Different Cultures Than Others? 504
- Culture Components 504
- General Culture Types 509
- Specific Culture Types 510
- Culture Strength 513
- Maintaining an Organizational Culture 515
- Summary: Why Do Some Organizations Have Different Cultures Than Others? 518

The Culture Change Process 519
- Analysis and Diagnosis: Is There a Need to Change? 520
- Understanding and Managing Resistance? 523
- Change Interventions? 524
- Evaluating the Change Process? 528

How Important Is Organizational Culture? 529

Application: Managing Socialization 532

TAKEAWAYS 535
KEY TERMS 535
DISCUSSION QUESTIONS 536
CASE 537
EXERCISE 538
OB ASSESSMENTS 538

Glossary GL-1
Chapter Notes EN-1

Preface

Why did we decide to write this textbook? Well, for starters, organizational behaviour (OB) remains a fascinating topic that everyone can relate to (because everyone either has worked or is going to work in the future). What makes people effective at their job? What makes them want to stay with their employer? What makes work enjoyable? Those are all fundamental questions that organizational behaviour research can help answer. However, our desire to write this book also grew out of our own experiences (and frustrations) teaching OB courses using other textbooks. We found that students would end the semester with a common set of questions that we felt we could answer if given the chance to write our own book. With that in mind, *Organizational Behaviour: Improving Performance and Commitment in the Workplace*, Third Canadian Edition, was written to answer the following questions.

Does Any of This Stuff Really Matter?

Organizational behaviour might be the most relevant class any student ever takes, but that doesn't always shine through in OB texts. The introductory section of our book contains two chapters on topics not included as stand-alone chapters in other books: job performance and organizational commitment. Being good at one's job and wanting to stay with one's employer are obviously critical concerns for employees and managers alike. After describing these topics in detail, every remaining chapter in the book links that chapter's content to performance and commitment. Students can then better appreciate the practical relevance of organizational behaviour concepts.

If That Theory Doesn't Work, Then Why Is It in the Book?

In putting together this book, we were guided by the question "What would OB texts look like if all of them were first written now, rather than decades ago?" We found that many of the organizational behaviour texts on the market include outdated (and indeed, scientifically disproven!) models or theories, presenting them sometimes as fact or possibly for the sake of completeness or historical context. Our students were always frustrated by the fact that they had to read about, learn, and possibly be tested on material we knew to be wrong. Although historical context can be important at times, we believe that focusing on so-called evidence-based management is paramount in today's fast-paced classes. Thus, this textbook includes new and emerging topics that others leave out and excludes flawed and outdated topics that some other books leave in.

How Does All This Stuff Fit Together?

Organizational behaviour is a diverse and multidisciplinary field, and it's not always easy to see how all its topics fit together. Our book deals with this issue in two ways. First, all of the chapters in our book are organized around an integrative model that opens each chapter (see Figure 1-1, reproduced here). That model provides students with a roadmap of the course, showing them where they've been and where they're going. Second, our chapters are tightly focused around specific topics and aren't "grab-bag-ish" in nature. Our hope is that students (and instructors) won't ever come across a topic and think, "Why is this topic being discussed in this chapter?"

FIGURE 1-1

Integrative Model of Organizational Behaviour

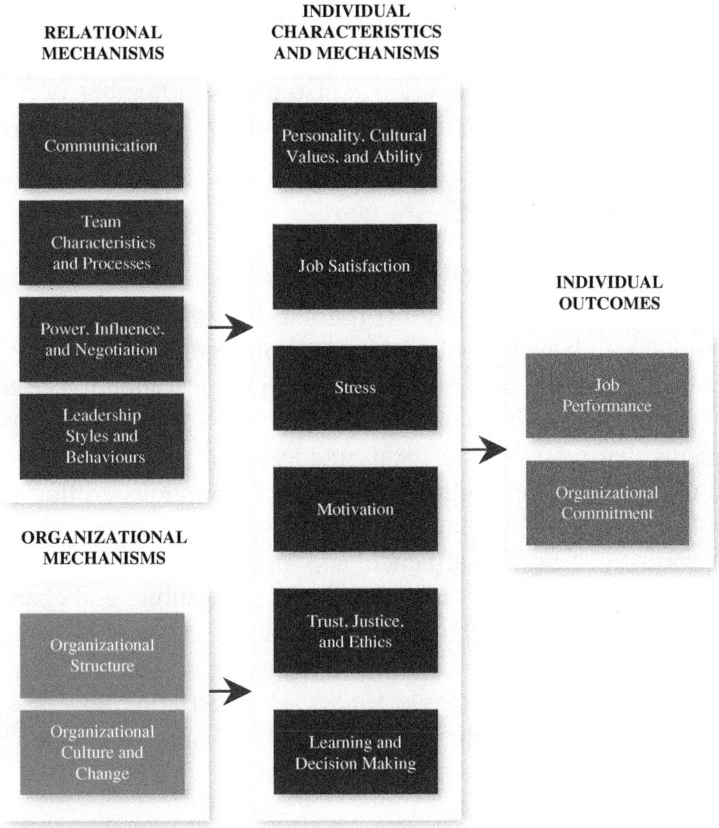

Does This Stuff Have to Be So Dry?

Research on motivation to learn shows that students learn more when they have an intrinsic interest in the topic, but many OB texts do little to stimulate that interest. Put simply, we wanted to create a book that students enjoy reading. To do that, we used a more informal, conversational style when writing the book. We also tried to use company examples that students will be familiar with and find compelling. Finally, we included insert boxes, self-assessments, and exercises that students should find engaging (and sometimes even entertaining!).

What's New in the Third Canadian Edition?

For this edition, we maintained the focus on employee performance and retention, and discussed the various topics in relation to these important work outcomes. We have included a new, stand-alone chapter on communication. We felt this was appropriate given that that so much has changed within this topic area with regard to technology itself (e.g., Web 2.0 applications within work settings) and the challenges faced by individuals, teams, and leaders who have to master the communication process. We have also strengthened our coverage of motivation theories and applications by including an updated discussion of how human needs influence effort levels and behaviour. There is extended coverage of the culture change process, emphasizing the important steps of problem diagnosis and evaluation, and an expanded section on how management practices can be used to bring about and support desired culture change. In addition, we have updated all of the cases and movie clips, and quite a few of the exercises and assessments. In each chapter, the opening vignette (featuring a Canadian-based company or a popular character or an organization that Canadian students will know well) provides context for the chapter and serves as background information for the chapter-ending case. We also continue our practice of bringing in many current examples from Canadian companies. Of course, the field of organizational behaviour has moved forward since the inaugural edition of this text, and we have attempted to capture and summarize the most up-to-date research findings in each of the content areas. In keeping with the research-based theme of the text, we also profile a number of new Canadian men and women who work tirelessly to generate the knowledge on which books like this are based.

Chapter-by-Chapter Changes

Chapter 1: What Is Organizational Behaviour?

New to this chapter is a revised integrative model (Figure 1-1). For pedagogical reasons we have reorganized slightly the schedule of chapter topics. Inspection of Figure 1-1 reveals that the two focal individual outcomes, job performance and organizational commitment (retention), remain unchanged. We then introduce and discuss a variety of topics that capture some of the more important individual characteristics and mechanisms that relate to the focal outcomes. In this regard, we now present the chapter on personality, cultural values, and ability earlier than in previous editions. A new category within our model, relational mechanisms, includes chapters on the following topics: communication; team characteristics and processes; power, influence and negotiation; and leadership styles and behaviours. The topics of organizational structure and organizational culture and change continue to be discussed as organizational mechanisms within the integrative framework. The chapter-opening vignette and chapter-ending case have been revised in this chapter, as has the exercise. The OB on Screen feature has been revised to focus on the movie *Moneyball*, illustrating how scientific data can be used to more effectively manage human capital. Throughout the chapter we have updated Canadian examples and content.

Chapter 2: Job Performance

This chapter begins with a new chapter-opening profile that features Oshawa-based GM Canada. This organization has been and is still in transition as it struggles with performance issues and ways to better connect with its customers. At the end of the chapter, a new case describes some steps the company has taken to create alignment of employees' performance with its new vision and set of core principles. The OB on Screen feature now centres on the movie *Flight* to vividly illustrate how dimensions of job performance may be related in unexpected ways. Throughout the chapter we have updated Canadian examples and content.

Chapter 3: Organizational Commitment

Our new chapter-opening profile features the popular retailer Costco, spotlighting all the things this company does to keep its employees loyal, even during tough financial times. The case also raises questions about whether Costco's turnover rate could conceivably be too low, given the need for fresh faces as it enters new markets with new competitors. The OB on Screen, about the film *Up in the Air*, illustrates the potentially painful (and liberating) process when committed employees are required to change organizations. Throughout the chapter we have updated Canadian examples and content.

Chapter 4: Personality, Cultural Values, and Ability

In this edition we again focus attention on Nexen, one of the largest oil and gas companies in Canada and a wholly owned subsidiary of China-based CNOOC Limited. This organization operates in a global context, and specifically in an industry that continues to face skill shortages in many technical areas.

Under the circumstances it would be tempting to hire anyone and "hope for the best." By adopting a more inclusive recruiting strategy and by considering a broader range of individual characteristics, Nexen has been able to find people with the right fit. The updated chapter-ending case encourages students to understand what "fitting in" means, and the kind of personal qualities it takes to work in a high-pressure, culturally diverse, team-based work environment. Other changes include a new movie in the OB on Screen feature, *Admission*, along with updated Canadian examples and content.

Chapter 5: Job Satisfaction

This chapter updates and extends a case that was introduced in the previous edition. It is a great example of how jobs not known to be particularly satisfying (e.g., customer service representatives within a call centre) can be transformed into highly satisfying jobs by altering the context in which the work is performed. In the chapter-ending case we see that the "weird" culture made famous at Zappos has now started to affect management practices within its parent company, Amazon.com. Other changes include a new movie in the OB on Screen feature, *Burn*, that illustrates for students the importance of facet satisfaction and the job characteristics model. Throughout the chapter we have updated Canadian examples and content.

Chapter 6: Stress

Believe it or not, healthcare professionals are among the most stressed-out people in the country. It is only fitting that our chapter-opening profile updates an innovative new Canadian program that was developed for healthcare facilities. The case at the end of the chapter has been revised and explores if and why nurses "eat their young." But this isn't just about nurses, and instructors will be able to use this case as context for a discussion of generational differences in the workplace. The OB on Screen now features the movie *Argo*, which provides insight into why people do work that's highly stressful. Throughout the chapter we have updated Canadian examples and content.

Chapter 7: Motivation

Our new chapter-opening profile features Netflix, the company that accounts for a third of all Internet traffic on a typical weeknight in North America. The case describes Netflix's "freedom and responsibility" philosophy, where employees have control over how they are rewarded while being held to high standards of accountability. The OB on Screen feature focuses on engagement using *Dark Knight Rises*, wherein Bruce Wayne begins in a disengaged, unmotivated state because Gotham City no longer needs Batman. It takes a new threat to give the Dark Knight a sense of purpose, the only question being whether Bruce possesses the competence to reclaim the mantle of The Batman. In this edition we have expanded our discussion of need theory and the role of human needs for motivational processes. Other changes include updated Canadian examples and content throughout.

Chapter 8: Trust, Justice, and Ethics

This chapter begins with a company profile that every student will be familiar with—Nike! The revised case highlights working conditions in some of its overseas factories—and the ethics of those decisions—as well as the difficulties of operating a global business where differences exist in terms of trust, justice, and ethics. The updated chapter-ending case shares a dilemma faced by senior managers at Nike. Instructors can also use this case as a basis for a broader discussion of corporate social responsibility, and the trade-offs that sometimes have to be made. The ethics section has been completely rewritten, and we have included a new exercise at the end of the chapter that deals with unethical behaviour. *Man of Steel* is the OB on Screen selection, the focus being on Clark Kent's concerns about trusting humankind with his identity and the world's concerns about the trustworthiness of a super-powered alien being living among them. Throughout the chapter we have updated Canadian examples and content.

Chapter 9: Learning and Decision Making

This updated chapter-opening profile includes a main character who is an accounting student working at KPMG Canada. The case at the end of the chapter provides opportunities for students to discuss and apply their knowledge of learning and decision making. The OB on Screen feature now focuses on *Star Trek into Darkness*, highlighting the differences between Kirk (instinctual) and Spock (logical) to bring out a discussion of the types of decision making. Throughout the chapter we have updated Canadian examples and content.

Chapter 10: Communication

We begin this chapter by featuring TD Canada Trust. This is large Canadian-based banking firm with operations all over the world. The company has recently adapted interactive, Web 2.0, social networking technology to help it manage communication processes and information flow within the overall organization. In the chapter-ending case, students will examine some of the issues associated with these new communication tools. We begin the chapter by reviewing the communication process, including a discussion of the different forms of face-to-face and computer-mediated communication. Then the chapter reviews some of the most important issues that facilitate or forestall the communication process. Next we review and discuss formal and information communication networks within organizational settings. Our practical application focuses on the job interview, and describes how students can learn to be more effective communicators. The assessments and the exercise have been designed to provide relevant application experiences with communication concepts covered in the chapter. Our movie feature is *The Wolf of Wall Street*, as we see Jordan Belfort skillfully using verbal and nonverbal communication to motivate his "killers." Throughout the chapter we used as many Canadian examples as possible.

Chapter 11: Team Characteristics and Processes

We begin with a new chapter-opening profile that features the Canadian Space Agency, in particular the astronauts who have to work together in crews to accomplish missions. The case at the end of the chapter describes a planned mission to Mars and some of the unique challenges the astronaut crew will likely face. We have also included a new assessment that requires students to consider three different types of interdependence within their project teams. The OB on Screen feature now centres on the movie *The Avengers* to illustrate the concepts of process loss and synergy. Throughout the chapter we have updated Canadian examples and content.

Chapter 12: Power, Influence, and Negotiation

Our chapter-opening profile features one of Canada's most venerable companies, Canadian Pacific Railway. Since mid-2012, CPR has gone from being one of the very worst railways in North America to being one of the very best, largely due to the leadership of turnaround ace Hunter Harrison. The chapter-ending case requires students to evaluate and discuss how Hunter has been able to acquire power and effectively use influence and negotiation tactics. Instructors may want to carry over this example to the next chapter on leadership styles. The new OB on Screen feature uses *Skyfall* to illustrate forms of power and the varying approaches to conflict management and when to use them. Throughout the chapter we have updated Canadian examples and content.

Chapter 13: Leadership Styles and Behaviours

This chapter updates a profile and case that was introduced in the previous edition. Steve Jobs is one of the most controversial and instantly recognizable names in recent history. Much has been written about the late Steve Jobs, and his phenomenal success at Apple, and the chapter-opening profile we briefly trace the leader's journey from the inception of Apple to his resignation in 2011 for health reasons. In the new chapter-ending case, students are asked to grapple with a variety of questions, including "How might we categorize Jobs's leadership style?" Although Jobs enjoyed much success over his career, was he an effective leader? The OB on Screen feature now centres on *Lincoln*, focusing on the movie's depiction of Abraham Lincoln's specific transformational leadership behaviours. The feature helps tie into the chapter's discussion on not only transformational leadership but also leadership in politics. Throughout the chapter we have updated Canadian examples and content.

Chapter 14: Organizational Structure

Our new chapter-opening profile features the Cheesecake Factory, highlighting the company's hierarchical and efficient organizational structure—something that isn't always apparent to customers. The case illustrates some of the pros and cons with any structure choice a company makes, along with bringing out some of the effective methods by which the Cheesecake Factory has maintained consistency across all of it restaurants. The OB on Screen feature now centres on the movie *The Company Men*, giving us a glimpse of the restructuring process through the eyes of those most involved. We see that implementation of rational business decisions, in some cases, comes at a terrible personal and emotion cost to managers and employees. Throughout the chapter we have updated Canadian examples and content.

Chapter 15: Organizational Culture and Change

Our new chapter-opening profile features Yahoo, and the well-publicized efforts new CEO Marissa Mayer has gone to in order to change certain aspects of its organizational culture. The case illustrates the public (no more telecommuting) and private (Mayer having to approve every hire) things the company is doing to create a shift as well as the power a CEO can have in the creation of a culture. In addition to updating the chapter with Canadian examples and content, we have extended our coverage of the culture change process, emphasizing the important steps of problem diagnosis and evaluation, and expanded the section on how management practices can be used to bring about and support desired culture change. In the new OB on Screen feature, a scene from the movie *Price Check* helps highlight how difficult it is for a leader to come in as an outsider and make changes to a culture, and how small things can make a huge impact (positively and negatively!).

Special Features: OB Focus Boxes

As you have probably noticed from our choice of cover, we see organizational behaviour—the good, the bad, and the ugly—at work everywhere. The OB focus boxes take OB out of the classroom and show students how the concepts in each chapter apply to so much more than just the workplace.

OB on Screen

This feature uses movie quotes and scenes from recent and classic films to illustrate organizational behaviour concepts. From *Moneyball* to *Star Trek into Darkness, The Wolf of Wall Street* to *Man of Steel*, Hollywood continues to offer rich, vivid, examples of OB in action.

OB ON SCREEN

This feature is designed to illustrate OB concepts in action on the silver screen. Once you've learned about OB topics, you'll see them playing out all around you, especially in movies.

Moneyball

You don't put a team together with a computer, Billy.... Baseball isn't just numbers; it's not science. If it was, then anybody could do what we're doing. But they can't because they don't know what we know. They don't have our experience and they don't have our intuition.

With those words, Grady Fuson (Ken Medlock) tries to show Billy Beane (Brad Pitt) the error of his ways in *Moneyball* (Dir. Bennett Miller, Columbia Pictures, 2011). Billy is the general manager of the Oakland Athletics (A's). After losing to the New York Yankees in the playoffs, Billy's been forced to trim a payroll that is already a third of what the Yankees pay. To the angst of his head scout Grady, Billy turns to Pete Brand, aka "Google boy," a recent hire with a degree in economics from Yale. Pete is well versed in "sabermetrics"—the scientific search for objective baseball knowledge begun by Bill James, with a nod to the Society for American Baseball Research (SABR).

© Columbia Pictures/Photofest

The film, based on the Michael Lewis bestseller,[25] shows how science can complement experience and intuition. For example, Pete's advanced analytics showed that "on-base percentage"—a statistic dependent not just on hits but also on walks—was a more valid indicator of a player's value than the home runs emphasized by traditional scouts. Ironically, the success of *Moneyball* caused a number of baseball teams to hire "sabermetricians," erasing some of the advantages that Billy's approach had given Oakland.[26] Indeed, the use of advanced analytics has taken hold in other professional sports, most notably the National Basketball Association.[27] Hopefully evidence-based management will allow organizational managers to do what sports managers are doing—test their theories of success with data.

OB for Students

Be they undergraduates, masters, or executives, everyone enrolled in an organizational behaviour class has one thing in common: They're students. This feature applies OB theories and concepts to student life. It examines questions like "What makes students satisfied with their university?" "What personality traits improve performance in student groups?" and "Should student grades be kept secret from recruiters?"

OB FOR STUDENTS

What does satisfaction mean for you as a student? After all, pay, promotions, and supervision are less relevant for full-time students than for full-time employees. One recent study examined the facets of satisfaction for students,[68] including:

- *University satisfaction.* Do students feel good about their university choice and experience, and would they recommend their university to others?
- *Housing satisfaction.* Do students feel good about where they live and the surrounding neighbourhood?
- *Leisure satisfaction.* Do students feel good about their social life, their leisure activities, and their friendships?

The results of the study showed that all three facets had moderately strong positive correlations with an index of overall student satisfaction. So students were more satisfied when they liked the university, liked where they lived, and felt that they were having a good time. In addition, the more satisfied the students were, the better they performed in terms of their grade point average (GPA). In other words, happy students tended to be better students.

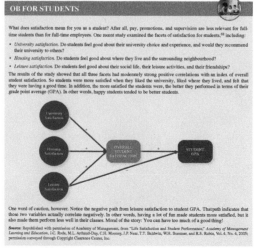

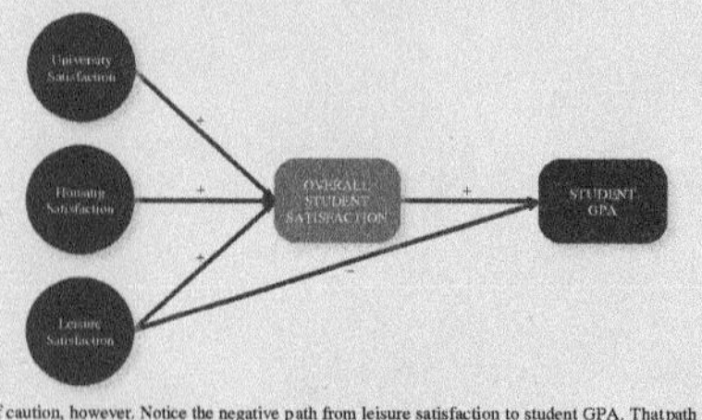

One word of caution, however. Notice the negative path from leisure satisfaction to student GPA. That path indicates that those two variables actually correlate negatively. In other words, having a lot of fun made students more satisfied, but it also made them perform less well in their classes. Moral of the story: You can have too much of a good thing!

Source: Republished with permission of Academy of Management, from "Life Satisfaction and Student Performance," *Academy of Management Learning and Education*, J.C. Rode, M.L. Arthaud-Day, C.H. Mooney, J.P. Near, T.T. Baldwin, W.H. Bommer, and R.S. Rubin, Vol. 4, No. 4, 2005; permission conveyed through Copyright Clearance Center, Inc.

OB Internationally

Changes in technology, communications, and economic forces have made business more global and international than ever. This feature spotlights the impact of globalization on the organizational behaviour concepts described in this book. It describes cross-cultural differences in OB theories, how to apply them in international corporations, and how to use OB to manage cultural diversity in the workplace.

OB INTERNATIONALLY

As mentioned previously, there is perhaps no more perilous journey for a company to take than merging with or acquiring another large firm. These problems are exacerbated when the two companies are from different countries. As few as 30 percent of international mergers and acquisitions create shareholder value.[91]

While global mergers and acquisitions have remained flat for several years, experts believe another upswing is coming.[92] Why? Hopefully, we've illustrated the inherent difficulties of trying to merge two different cultures even when the organizations are in the same country. These cultural differences can be magnified when international culture plays a role as well. Your college experiences have probably shown you that different countries have different cultures, just like organizations. People from different countries tend to view the world differently and have different sets of values as well.

For example, DaimlerChrysler bought a controlling stake in Mitsubishi Motors, thinking that a strong alliance between the two automotive companies would result in high levels of value for both. Unfortunately, the merger broke up, for reasons that have been attributed to the international culture differences between the two firms.[93] The Japanese managers tended to avoid "unpleasant truths" and stay away from major change efforts—a tendency that DaimlerChrysler never confronted but also could not accept.

There are many stories of failed international mergers, and one of the greatest reasons for such failure is that corporations don't recognize the impact of national culture differences (in addition to organizational culture differences). One such acquisition that doesn't intend to fall victim to this issue is the purchase of Volvo Car Corporation (Sweden) from Ford by China's Geely Holding Group. Although the relationship started out extremely rocky, with Geely executives storming out of an initial meeting in Sweden because they felt they were being treated like they were stupid, the two companies seem to have agreed to some compromises. Volvo, somewhat against their more safe and family-friendly culture, is now producing high-end luxury models to compete with Mercedes-Benz and BMW, which fit with Chinese desires. In addition, although Geely wanted to build three assembly plants in China to jump-start sales, the company is following a slower, quality approach at the behest of Volvo's CEO. For now, it seems that both CEOs are open to each company learning from the other.[94]

OB Research in Canada

An important theme in this book is to present and discuss concepts, models, and theories that have been tested and validated using carefully applied scientific methods. But who are the people behind the research findings? What is it about OB that captivates their attention? Why do they study what they do? In this edition, we continue to introduce a number of Canadian-based researchers who are recognized as experts in one or more of the topic areas we will be reading about.

OB RESEARCH IN CANADA

Dr. Travor Brown is professor of labour relations and human resources management in the Faculty of Bus Administration at Memorial University of Newfoundland. Before moving to St. John's, Newfoundland, Dr. Brown earned his Ph.D. at the University of Toronto. Dr. Brown's research interests are varied, but he has done a lot of work to advance knowledge of goal setting theory and how this motivational technique can be used to improve training effectiveness. Specifically, his work has looked at how best to set goals to improve learning processes (Chapter 9), teamwork behaviour (Chapter 11), and leadership development (Chapter 13). Asked how he got interested in the field, Dr. Brown replied, "I was a former competitive swimmer and a swim coach. The sports world's focus on coaching, development, inherent role of goal setting sparked my initial interest in organizational behaviour and remains today as I am just finishing my role as past president of Swimming Newfoundland & Labrador. As I often joke with my stude never left the coaching world—just moved from the aquatic environment to the workplace!"

Dr. Brown has published numerous articles in prestigious scientific journals, and has presented his work at Canadian, U.S., and international conferences. His academic background is coupled with extensive industry experience. He worked in the telecommunications and manufacturing sectors prior to completing his Ph.D. at the University of Toronto and remains active in the practitioner community. You can look him up at www.business.mun.ca/why-us/meet-o people/faculty-instructor-profiles/travor-brown.php.

Special Features: In-Chapter Sections

Throughout each chapter, we have included features that we feel will help facilitate learning, clarify concepts, and keep students focused on what is important in each chapter.

Learning Outcomes

To help students identify the key concepts being explored in the chapter, we have opened each chapter with a list of questions they should be able to answer at the conclusion of the chapter. These Learning Outcomes are then referenced at the start of their discussion in the text, so that students can easily discover where each topic is being explored.

LEARNING OUTCOMES

After reading this chapter, you should be able to answer the following questions:

10.1 What is communication, and how does this relate to organizational behaviour?

10.2 How does the communication process work?

10.3 What do face-to-face and computer-mediated communication offer?

10.4 What are some of the more important issues that can affect the communication process?

10.5 How does information flow within organizations?

10.6 How does communication affect job performance and organizational commitment?

10.7 What can people do to facilitate effective communication during the job interview?

Chapter-Opening Vignettes

We want students to be able to recognize organizational behaviour concepts at work, and the chapter-opening vignettes profile events and people in real organizations to encourage students to critically evaluate and apply each situation to the chapter content.

Canadian Pacific Railway

Since his arrival at Canadian Pacific Railway Ltd. in mid-2012, few would argue with Hunter Harrison's ability to influence how things are done within the company.

Canadian Pacific Rail

The history of Canada is closely tied to railway. Not long after Confederation, July 1, 1867, the Canadian Pacific Railway Limited (CP) was founded to connect Canada's emerging population centres in Ontario and Quebec with the vast potential of its relatively unpopulated West.[1] In spite of great political obstacles and the enormous engineering challenges associated with traversing the Canadian Rockies, the "last spike" was finally driven in on November 7, 1885 at Craigellachie, British Columbia.[2] Although the cost of construction nearly ruined the fledgling company, within three years of the first transcontinental train leaving Montreal and Toronto for Port Moody, B.C., on June 28, 1886, CP's financial house was once again in order.[3] Over the years, as CP grew so did the company's interest in non-railway ventures, such as manufacturing, shipping, hotels, airlines, natural oil and gas extraction, bus transportation, trucking, pulp and paper, and waste management.[4] Today, CP has divested itself of non-core businesses and is primarily a freight railway company, headquartered in Calgary. The company ownsroughly 22,500 kilometres of track all across Canada and into the United States, stretching from Montreal to Vancouver, and as far north as Edmonton.[5]

Recently, as in the beginning, the company has found itself facing great challenges. Throughout the 2000s, the company had been battling strong headwinds, and by 2012 CP was in very rough shape, sporting the worst operating performance among all the major North American railroads.[6] For instance, the company's operating ratio—a productivity index that represents operating costs as a percentage of revenue—was a dismal 80 percent, making it one of the least profitable railroads in North America.[7] Once again, the company was flirting with financial ruin.

Hunter Harrison, a seasoned railway executive and proven turnaround expert, was brought out of retirement to serve as the company's CEO in mid-2012. Harrison's vision for CP included longer, faster trains and better customer service at lower cost.[8] To achieve these goals, it would be imperative for him to introduce and implement radical changes quickly within an established bureaucracy so that CP could once again become efficient and flexible. Some of these changes would involve the elimination of surplus positions (mainly through attrition and/or voluntary turnover; reducing the workforce from 19,500 to 14,700 employees), the shedding of 400 older locomotives and 11,000 cars, dropping some terminals, and initiating disciplinary actions against employees who failed to comply with safety and working rules.[9] At the end the 2013, the company's operating ratio had dropped to 65.99 percent—*on a par with industry leaders* and a full three years ahead of schedule. As Harrison was recently quoted saying, "We're doing things that people didn't think were imaginable."[10]

Key Terms

Students often find themselves bombarded by terms and concepts, and it can be difficult to keep them all straight. To mitigate this challenge, we have highlighted key terms and placed the definitions in special text boxes, where possible directly under the paragraphs in which they are introduced. This way, it is easy to find where terms are discussed and students are able get to know the language of organizational behaviour.

Four other influence tactics are effective only sometimes. **Ingratiation** is the use of favours, compliments, or friendly behaviour to make the target feel better about the influencer. You might more commonly hear this referred to as "sucking up," especially when used in an upward influence sense. Ingratiation has been shown to be more effective as a long-term strategy and not nearly as effective when used immediately prior to making an influence attempt.[26] **Personal appeals** occur when the requestor asks for something on the basis of personal friendship or loyalty. The stronger the friendship, the more successful the attempt is likely to be. (The ***OB Internationally*** feature following shows that, as with other influence attempts, there are cultural differences when it comes to this kind of an appeal.) An **exchange tactic** is used when the requestor offers a reward or resource to the target in return for performing a request. This type of request requires that the requestor have something of value to offer.[27] Finally, **apprising** occurs when the requestor clearly explains why performing the request will benefit the target personally. It differs from rational persuasion in that it focuses solely on the benefit to the target as opposed to simple logic or benefits to the group or organization. It differs from exchange in that the benefit is not necessarily something the requestor gives to the target but rather something that results from the action.[28]

ingratiation
The use of favours, compliments, or friendly behaviour to make the target feel better about the influencer

personal appeals
An influence tactic in which the requestor asks for something based on personal friendship or loyalty

exchange tactic
An influence tactic in which the requestor offers a reward in return for performing a request

apprising
An influence tactic in which the requestor clearly explains why performing the request will benefit the target personally

The two tactics that have been shown to be least effective and might result in resistance from the target are pressure and coalitions; of course, this doesn't mean they aren't used or can't be effective. **Pressure** is the use of coercive power through threats and demands. As we've discussed previously, it is a poor way to influence others and may bring benefits only over the short term. **Coalitions** occur when the influencer enlists other people to help influence the target—peers, subordinates, or one of the target's superiors. Coalitions are generally used in combination with one of the other tactics. For instance, if rational persuasion is not strong enough, the influencer might bring in another person to show that that person agrees with the logic of the argument.

pressure
An influence tactic in which the requestor attempts to use coercive power through threats and demands

coalitions
An influence tactic in which the influencer enlists other people to help influence the target

Special Features: End-of-Chapter Sections

Chapters conclude with a series of features that provide a tie-in to the chapter-opening features or reinforce chapter concepts through additional experiential material.

Takeaways

Students are always asking, "What are the most important 'takeaways' from this chapter?" This section gives a point-by-point review of the Learning Outcomes found at the beginning of each chapter.

TAKEAWAYS

3.1 Organizational commitment is the desire on the part of an employee to remain a member of the organization. Withdrawal behaviour is a set of actions that employees perform to avoid the work situation. Commitment and withdrawal are negatively related to each other—the more committed employees are, the less likely they are to engage in withdrawal.

3.2 There are three forms of organizational commitment. Affective commitment occurs when employees want to stay and is influenced by the emotional bonds between employees. Continuance commitment occurs when employees need to stay and is influenced by salary and benefits and the degree to which they are embedded in the community. Normative commitment occurs when employees feel that they ought to stay and is influenced by an organization investing in its employees or engaging in charitable efforts.

3.3 Employees can respond to negative work events in four ways: exit, voice, loyalty, and neglect. Exit is a form of physical withdrawal in which the employee either ends or restricts organizational membership. Voice is an active and constructive response by which employees attempt to improve the situation. Loyalty is passiveand constructive; employees remain supportive while hoping the situation improves on its own. Neglect is a form of psychological withdrawal in which interest and effort in the job decrease

3.4 Examples of psychological withdrawal include daydreaming, socializing, looking busy, moonlighting, and cyberloafing. Examples of physical withdrawal include tardiness, long breaks, missing meetings, absenteeism, and quitting. Consistently with the progression model, withdrawal behaviours tend to start with minor psychological forms before escalating to more major physical varieties.

3.5 The increased diversity of the workforce can reduce commitment if employees feel lower levels of affective commitment or become less embedded in their current jobs. The employee–employer relationship, which has changed due to decades of downsizing, can reduce affective and normative commitment, making it more of a challenge to retain talented employees.

3.6 Organizations can foster commitment among employees by fostering perceived organizational support, which reflects the degree to which the organization cares about employees' well-being. Commitment can also be fostered by specific initiatives directed at the three commitment types.

Key Terms

This end-of-chapter list features key terms included in the chapter. All terms and definitions are also available in the Glossary.

KEY TERMS

ability (dimension of trustworthiness)
ability to focus
abusive supervision
affect-based trust
benevolence (dimension of trustworthiness)
cognition-based trust
cognitive moral development
corporate social responsibility
disposition-based trust
distributive justice
economic exchange
ethics
four-component model
informational justice
integrity (dimension of trustworthiness)
interpersonal justice
justice
moral attentiveness
moral awareness
moral identity
moral intensity
moral intent
moral judgment
moral principles
procedural justice
reputation
social exchange
trust
trust propensity
trustworthiness
whistle-blowing

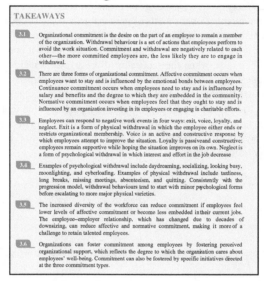

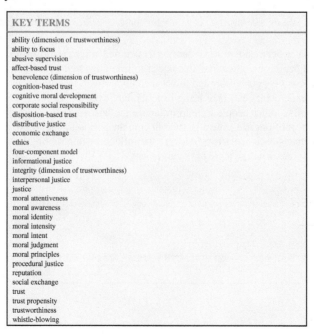

Discussion Questions

Instead of being only for review purposes, our Discussion Questions ask students to apply concepts in the chapter to their own lives and experiences.

DISCUSSION QUESTIONS

6.1 Prior to reading this chapter, how did you define stress? Did your definition of stress reflect stressors, the stress process, strains, or some combination?

6.2 Describe your dream job and then provide a list of the types of stressors that you would expect to be present. How much of your salary, if any at all, would you give up to eliminate the most important hindrance stressors? Why?

6.3 If you had several job offers after graduating, to what degree would the level of challenge stressors in the different jobs influence your choice of which job to take? Why?

6.4 How would you assess your ability to handle stress? Given the information provided in this chapter, what could you do to improve your effectiveness in this area?

6.5 If you managed people in an organization in which there were lots of hindrance stressors, what actions would you take to help ensure that your employees coped with the stressors using a problem-focused (as opposed to emotion-focused) strategy?

Cases

To help bring students full circle, a case appears at the end of every chapter, providing a follow-up to the discussion highlighted in the chapter's opening vignette.

CASE • ROCKET MEN (AND WOMEN)

NASA, in collaboration with the international space community, is planning a mission to send a crew of astronauts to Mars. Among other objectives, scientists are interested in the possibility of growing food in space, and there are now reasons to believe that Mars may be a good place to farm.[190] Although this mission isn't scheduled until the year 2030 or so, NASA has already begun to explore how aspects of the mission are likely to impact the crew's ability to function effectively.[191] You see, the assigned crew of six to eight will be living and working together in a noisy capsule about the size of an average kitchen for three years—it takes 6 months to get there, they'll stay for 18 months, and then there's the 6-month journey home.[192] Given the constraints of their environment, and the fact that the crew will beworking long hours under very demanding conditions, it's inevitable that they'll get on one another's nerves on occasion. There's literally no place to go to escape minor annoyances, and as frustration builds, the probability of emotional outbursts and interpersonal conflict increases.[193]

Of course, it goes without saying that conflict among astronauts in a small space capsule millions of miles away from Earth is not a good thing. Astronauts who fail to fulfill a responsibility because they're preoccupied with conflict could put the mission, and the lives of the entire crew, in jeopardy, and this is true whether the conflict is bubbling under or has risen to the surface. Hard feelings might hinder teamwork as well, and the failure to communicate an important piece of information or to provide help to a member of the crew in need of assistance, for example, might also lead to disaster. Unfortunately, however, the duration and demands of the mission are almost without precedent, and therefore the specific practices that need to be implemented to facilitate crew functioning in this context are unknown.

To address this issue, NASA has awarded grants to psychologists to study teams that have to live and work together in isolated, confined, and extreme environments for extended periods.[194] To help increase understanding of conflict and teamwork and how it can be better managed, the psychologists are working on technology that tracks the whereabouts of each crew member, and his or her vocal intensity and vital functions such as heart rate.[195] This information would be used to pinpoint where and when conflict occurs and to understand how conflict influences subsequent crew interactions. The crew will be given feedback so they can learn how conflict hurts teamwork and cohesion. This feedback could also motivate crews to take the time to discuss teamwork issues and to devise ways to manage conflict and other process problems.

Although it's impossible to anticipate all the issues that might arise on the mission to Mars, NASA believes that research on team process is necessary to enhance the viability and performance of the crew that is ultimately charged with the task.

11.1 Which team processes do you believe are most important to the crew of astronauts travelling to Mars? Why? Are there specific team processes you feel are relatively unimportant? Explain.

11.2 Describe additional types of information that could be collected by the psychologists to help crews better understand their interactions and how they influence crew effectiveness.

11.3 Discuss how team training could be used to build effective processes for the crew travelling to Mars.

Exercises

Each chapter features an OB-related exercise: Some we have created ourselves over the years, but we have also included tried-and-true "classics" that nearly everyone we know uses in class.

EXERCISE • GUESSING PERSONALITY PROFILES

The purpose of this exercise is to explore how noticeable the Big Five personality dimensions are among classmates. This exercise uses groups, so your instructor will either assign you to a group or ask you to create your own group. The exercise has the following steps:

4.1 Individually, complete the Big Five measure found in the ***OB Assessments*** box of this chapter.

4.2 Write your scores on a small white piece of paper, in the following format: C = _____, A = _____, N = _____, O = _____, E = _____. Try to disguise your handwriting to make it as plain and generic as possible. Fold your piece of paper so that others cannot see your "CANOE" scores.

4.3 In your group, mix up the pieces of paper. Begin by having one group member choose a piece of paper, reading the CANOE scores aloud. The group should then try to come to consensus on which member the scores belong to, given the norms for the various dimensions (C = 14, A = 16, N = 10, O = 15, E = 13). Keep in mind that group members may wind up reading their own pieces of paper aloud in some cases. Once the group guesses which member the paper belongs to, they should place the paper in front of that member.

4.4 Moving clockwise, the next group member should choose one of the remaining pieces of paper, continuing as before. The process repeats until all the pieces of paper have been assigned to a member. Members can be assigned only one piece of paper, and no switching is permitted once an assignment has been made.

4.5 Group members should then announce whether the piece of paper assigned to them was in fact their set of scores. If the assignment was incorrect, they should find their actual piece of

OB Assessments

We close each chapter with a feature designed to help students find out where they stand on key OB concepts covered in the chapter. Students thus gain insights into their personality, their emotional intelligence, their style of leadership, and their ability to cope with stress, which can help them understand their reactions to the working world.

OB ASSESSMENTS • ARE YOU AN ACTIVE LISTENER?

Purpose This self-assessment is designed to help you estimate your strengths and weaknesses on various dimensions of active listening.

Instructions Think back to face-to-face conversations you have had with a co-worker or client in the office, hallway, factory floor, or other setting. Indicate the extent that each item below describes your behaviour during those conversations. Answer each item as truthfully as possible so that you get an accurate estimate of where your active listening skills need improvement. Then use the scoring key provided in the Instructor's Manual for this book to calculate your results for each scale. This exercise should be completed alone so you can assess yourself honestly without concerns of social comparison. However, class discussion will focus on the important elements of active listening.

Active Listening Skills Inventory

When listening to others in face-to-face, telephone, or similar conversations, how often do you do the following?	Never or Rarely	Seldom	Sometimes	Often	Almost Always
1. I keep an open mind when others describe their ideas.	○	○	○	○	○
2. I organize the speaker's ideas while s/he is talking to me.	○	○	○	○	○
3. I ask questions to show I understand and am focused on the speaker's message.	○	○	○	○	○
4. I interrupt before the speaker sufficiently presents his/her views.	○	○	○	○	○
5. While listening, I mentally sort out the speaker's ideas so s/he makes sense to me.	○	○	○	○	○
6. I use gestures and words (nodding, agreeing) to show I am listening.	○	○	○	○	○
7. I let my mind wander when listening to people.	○	○	○	○	○
8. I try to visualize and feel the speaker's experience while s/he is describing those events.	○	○	○	○	○
9. I summarize the speaker's ideas to confirm that I understand him/her correctly.	○	○	○	○	○
10. I focus on what the speaker is saying to me even when it doesn't sound interesting.	○	○	○	○	○
11. I see the topic from my perspective rather than from the speaker's perspective.	○	○	○	○	○
12. I show interest while listening to others.	○	○	○	○	○

Source: © 2010. Steven L. McShane. Used by permission.

Student Resources

Available with *Organizational Behaviour: Improving Performance and Commitment in the Workplace*, Third Canadian Edition, is a comprehensive package of supplementary materials designed to enhance teaching and learning.

MARKET LEADING TECHNOLOGY

Mc Graw Hill Education connect®

Learn without Limits

McGraw-Hill Connect® is an award-winning digital teaching and learning platform that gives students the means to better connect with their coursework, with their instructors, and with the important concepts that they will need to know for success now and in the future. With Connect, instructors can take advantage of McGraw-Hill's trusted content to seamlessly deliver assignments, quizzes and tests online. McGraw-Hill Connect is the only learning platform that continually adapts to each student, delivering precisely what they need, when they need it, so class time is more engaging and effective. Connect makes teaching and learning personal, easy, and proven.

Connect Key Features:

SmartBook®

As the first and only adaptive reading experience, SmartBook is changing the way students read and learn. SmartBook creates a personalized reading experience by highlighting the most important concepts a student needs to learn at that moment in time. As a student engages with SmartBook, the reading experience continuously adapts by highlighting content based on what each student knows and doesn't know. This ensures that he or she is focused on the content needed to close specific knowledge gaps, while it simultaneously promotes long-term learning.

Connect Insight®

Connect Insight is Connect's new one-of-a-kind visual analytics dashboard—now available for both instructors and students—that provides at-a-glance information regarding student performance, which is immediately actionable. By presenting assignment, assessment, and topical performance results together with a time metric that is easily visible for aggregate or individual results, Connect Insight gives the user the ability to take a just-in-time approach to teaching and learning, which was never before available. Connect Insight presents data that empowers students and helps instructors improve class performance in a way that is efficient and effective.

Simple Assignment Management

With Connect, creating assignments is easier than ever, so instructors can spend more time teaching and less time managing.

- Assign SmartBook learning modules.
- Instructors can edit existing questions and create their own questions.
- Draw from a variety of text specific questions, resources, and test bank material to assign online.
- Streamline lesson planning, student progress reporting, and assignment grading to make classroom management more efficient than ever.

Smart Grading

When it comes to studying, time is precious. Connect helps students learn more efficiently by providing feedback and practice material when they need it, where they need it.

- Automatically score assignments, giving students immediate feedback on their work and comparisons with correct answers.
- Access and review each response; manually change grades or leave comments for students to review.
- Track individual student performance—by question, assignment or in relation to the class overall—with detailed grade reports.
- Reinforce classroom concepts with practice tests and instant quizzes.
- Integrate grade reports easily with Learning Management Systems including Blackboard, D2L, and Moodle.

Instructor Library

The Connect Instructor Library is a repository for additional resources to improve student engagement in and out of the class. It provides all the critical resources instructors need to build their course.

- Access Instructor resources.
- View assignments and resources created for past sections.
- Post your own resources for students to use.

Instructor Resources

All our instructor resources, which allow instructors to create a customized multimedia presentation, are conveniently housed on the password-protected instructor's section of Connect.

Instructor's Manual

This manual, prepared by text author Ian Gellatly, was developed to help with organizing your classroom presentation. It contains an extensive "chapter roadmap" with an outline, Teaching Tips (e.g., hints on how to handle difficult topics), suggestions on ways to maximize the use of in-chapter pedagogy and the usage of assessments/exercises in the text, and suggested resources for exploring topics related to the chapter content.

Test Bank

Our test bank, prepared by Colquitt Connect author Grace O'Farrell from the University of Winnipeg, contains a variety of true/false, multiple-choice, and short- and long-essay questions, as well as "scenario-based" questions, which are application-based and use a situation described in a narrative, with three to five multiple-choice test questions based on the situation described in the narrative. We've tagged each question according to its knowledge and skills areas. Designations aligning questions with the text's Learning Outcomes, difficulty levels, and page references exist as well. Multiple versions of the test can be created and printed.

PowerPoint® Presentation Slides

The PowerPoint® presentation slides, prepared by text author Ian Gellatly, based on instructor feedback, are designed to give instructors the flexibility to tailor their presentations to their class needs. The format leaves a significant amount of room on the slides for students to take notes, but still maintains the use of tables and figures straight from the book, as well as including some full definitions and descriptions for the topics covered.

Organizational Behaviour Videos

Available through online streaming from Connect as well as on DVD, these video selections are for instructors who want to incorporate more "real world"examples into the classroom. Instructor notes can be found in the instructor section of the Connect.

Manager's HotSeat Online

The Manager's HotSeat allows students to watch over 14 real managers apply their years of experience to confront daily issues such as ethics, diversity, teamwork, and the virtual workplace. Students are prompted for feedback throughout each scenario and then to submit a reporting critiquing the manger's choices while defending their own. The Manager's HotSeat is ideal for group or classroom discussion.

Acknowledgments

A great many people played a role in helping us put together the first two editions of this textbook. Truth be told, we had no idea we would have to rely on and put our success in the hands of so many! Each of these people had unique and useful contributions to make toward the publication of this book, and they deserve our sincere gratitude.

We are utterly indebted to Kim Brewster, our group product manager, for her encouragement to write the textbook and her support for our desire to write "a different kind of textbook." Thanks also go out to Tracey Haggert, product developer, who did her very best to keep us on track in terms of actually getting things done and who provided valuable feedback throughout the process. Special thanks to Jessica Barnoski, our supervising editor, and our copy editor Rodney Rawlings, who helped to pull all this together. We are particularly grateful to the following people who allowed us to showcase their work in our OB Research in Canada feature:

Natalie Allen, *Western University*
Karl Aquino, *University of British Columbia*
Ofer Arazy, *University of Alberta*
Silvia Bonaccio, *University of Ottawa*
Travor Brown, *Memorial University of Newfoundland*
François Chiocchio, *Université de Montréal*
Catherine Connolly, *McMaster University*
Arla Day, *St. Mary's University*
Michelle Inness, *University of Alberta*
Kai Lamertz, *Concordia University*
Kibeom Lee, *University of Calgary*
John Meyer, *Western University*
Kevin Tasa, *York University*
Christian Vandenburghe, *HEC*
Jia Lin Xie, *University of Toronto*

In addition to the initial feedback from the U.S. market, we have had the great fortune of having so many Canadian faculty members from colleges and universities around the country provide feedback on various aspects of the first three Canadian editions of this textbook. Their input made this book substantially better, and we thank them for their time and effort:

Wendi Adair, *University of Waterloo*
Stan Arnold, *Humber College Institute of Technology & Advanced Learning*
Akanksha Bedi, *Bishop's University*
Gerard Braithwaite-Sturgeon, *University of Ottawa*
Don H. Caplan, *Royal Roads University*
Dianne Cyr, *Simon Fraser University*
Angela Davis, *University of Winnipeg*
Jane Deighan, *Southern Alberta Institute of Technology*
Kelly Dye, *Acadia University*
Andrew Fergus, *Thompson Rivers University*
Barb Gardiner, *Southern Alberta Institute of Technology*
Isabelle Giroux, *Brock University*
Jai Goolsarran, *Centennial College of Applied Arts and Technology*
Sandy Hershcovis, *University of Manitoba*
Alfred Jaeger, *McGill University*
Scott Jeffrey, *University of Waterloo*
Dan Kazakoff, *University of Lethbridge*
Lisa Keeping, *Wilfrid Laurier University*
Mike Kelly, *Nova Scotia Community College*
Roy L. Kirby, *Carleton University*
Diana Krause, *Western University*
Joanne Leck, *University of Ottawa*
Doreen MacAulay, *St. Mary's University*
Teal McAteer, *McMaster University*
Lissa McRae, *Bishop's University*
John Pucic, *Humber College Institute of Technology & Advanced Learning*
Martha Reavley, *University of Windsor*
Kim Richter, *Kwantlen Polytechnic University*
Umair Shah, *University of Waterloo*
Lynne Siemens, *University of Victoria*
Stephen Smith, *Trent University*
Kathryn Taft, *Capilano University*
Simon Taggar, *Wilfrid Laurier University*
Innocenza Jay Tuason, *Kwantlen Polytechnic University*
Ron Velin, *Langara College*
Bryan Webber, *Vancouver Island University*
Shawna Weingartner, *Western University*
Diane White, *Seneca College of Applied Arts and Technology*

We would also like to thank our students at the undergraduate, masters, and executive levels who were taught with early versions of these chapters for their constructive feedback toward making them more effective in the classroom. Thanks also to our Ph.D. students for allowing us to take time out from research projects to focus on this book.

Finally, we thank our families, who gave up substantial amounts of time with us and put up with the stress that necessarily comes at times during an endeavour such as this.

Jason Colquitt
Jeff LePine

Michael Wesson
Ian Gellatly

PART 1

Introduction to Organizational Behaviour

What Is Organizational Behaviour?

CHAPTER 1

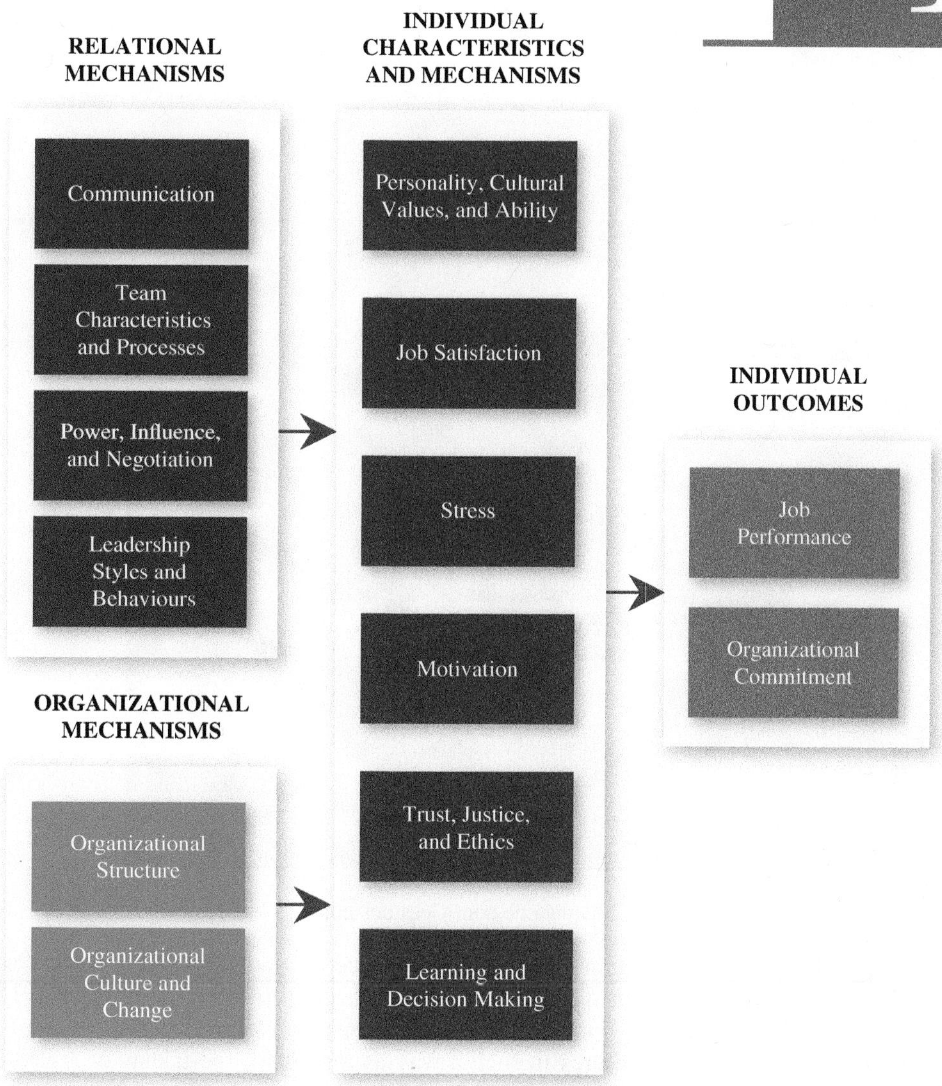

LEARNING OUTCOMES

After reading this chapter, you should be able to answer the following questions:

1.1 What is the definition of "organizational behaviour" (OB)?

1.2 What are the two primary outcomes in studies of OB?

1.3 What factors affect the two primary OB outcomes?

1.4 Why might firms that are good at OB tend to be more profitable?

1.5 What is the role of theory in the scientific method?

1.6 How are correlations interpreted?

Leading the Way

One of WestJet's greatest assets is an organizational culture that focuses its employees' attention on strong customer service and ways to lower costs.

Icholakov/Dreamstime.com/GetStock.com

What do an airline and a bank have in common? You would be correct if you guessed that both WestJet and the Royal Bank of Canada (RBC) were named along with a small handful of other companies as Canada's most admired companies.[1] Why were these companies chosen? In spite of being in different industries, all had developed their respective corporate cultures in such a way as to unleash the talents of their people to achieve important organizational goals.

According to Gregg Saretsky, President and CEO of WestJet, "our culture of care not only delivers a world-class guest experience, but our culture is fundamentally important to sustaining and growing our business in the longer term."[2] Commenting further on importance of culture, WestJet's Ferio Pugliese, Executive Vice-President, People and Culture, emphasized that "many organizations talk about the importance of values and culture. At WestJet we do more than talk—we LIVE IT! Our culture drives a superior guest experience that is brought to our guests consistently every day. That's because we have the right people on our team."[3] But it's more than having a service-oriented, caring culture. "If you walk around our airports or our airplanes, and you come in contact with WestJetters, you'll see they act like they own the place. And we're really okay with that because that's what we're trying to create here at this company," says Ferio Pugliese.[4]

For RBC, a winning corporate culture has meant openly valuing teamwork and ongoing learning and development, and embracing and harnessing the diversity of its employees. "Our strength comes from the combination of what we have in common, like our shared values, vision, and purpose, as well as what makes us different, like experiences and perspectives," says Gordon Nixon, president and CEO of RBC. "We recognize the value and power of tapping into the full spectrum of ideas and abilities that people possess. Doing just that has been a strong part of RBC's past success and is crucial for seizing the opportunities ahead. We are competing in a global marketplace, and we know that our growth will depend on an increasingly diverse and global workforce."[5] Without a doubt, "it is our people that bring our brand to life every day with our clients," says Zabeen Hirji, Chief Human Resources Officer.[6]

Both WestJet and the RBC are people-driven companies that have been able to find employees who are conscientious and intelligent, motivated and satisfied with their jobs, and committed to their organizations for a longer-than-normal period of time, and who perform their job duties reliably and enthusiastically. Simply put, both are leading Canadian companies that seem to be doing an excellent job managing organizational behaviour!

WHAT IS ORGANIZATIONAL BEHAVIOUR?

Before we define exactly what the field of organizational behaviour represents, take a moment to ponder the following: Who was the single *worst* co-worker you've ever had? Picture fellow students with whom you've worked on class projects; colleagues from part-time or summer jobs; or peers, subordinates, or supervisors working in your current organization. What did this co-worker do that earned him or her "worst co-worker" status? Was it some of the behaviours shown in the right column of Table 1-1 (or perhaps all of them)? Now take a moment to consider the single *best* co-worker you've ever had. Again, what did this co-worker do to earn "best co-worker" status—some or most of the behaviours shown in the left column of Table 1-1?

If you ever found yourself working alongside two people of the types profiled in the table, two questions would probably be foremost in your mind: "*Why* does the worst co-worker act that way?" and "*Why* does the best co-worker act that way?" Once you understand why they act so differently, you might be able to figure out ways to interact with the worst co-worker more effectively (thereby making your working life a bit more pleasant). If you happen to be a manager, you can formulate plans for how to improve attitudes and behaviours in the unit. Such plans might include how to screen applicants, train and socialize new organizational members, manage evaluations and rewards for performance, and deal with conflicts that arise between employees. Without understanding why employees act the way they do, it is very difficult to find a way to change their attitudes and behaviours at work.

TABLE 1-1

The Best of Co-workers, the Worst of Co-workers

The Best	The Worst
Have you ever had a co-worker who usually acted this way?	*Have you ever had a co-worker who usually acted this way?*
Got the job done, without having to be managed or reminded	Did not get the job done, even with a great deal of hand-holding
Adapted when something needed to be changed or done differently	Was resistant to any and every form of change, even when changes were beneficial
Was always a "good sport," even when bad things happened at work	Whined and complained, no matter what was happening
Attended optional meetings or functions to support colleagues	Optional meetings? Was too lazy to make it to some required meetings and functions!
Helped new co-workers or people who seemed to need a hand	Made fun of new co-workers or people who seemed to need a hand
Followed key rules, even when the reasons for them were not apparent	Broke virtually any rule that somehow made their work more difficult
Felt an attachment and obligation to the employer for the long haul	Seemed always to be looking for something else, even if it wasn't better
Was first to arrive, last to leave	Was first to leave, last to arrive
Million Dollar Question: *Why do these two types of employees act so differently?*	

1.1 What is the definition of "organizational behaviour" (OB)?

Organizational Behaviour Defined

Organizational behaviour (OB) is a field of study devoted to understanding, explaining, and ultimately improving the attitudes and behaviours of individuals and groups in organizations. The research findings of OB scholars in the management departments of universities and of scientists in business organizations are applied by managers or consultants to find out whether they help meet "real-world" challenges. OB might be contrasted with two other courses commonly offered in management departments: human resources management and strategic management. **Human resources management** takes the theories and principles studied in OB and explores the "nuts and bolts" applications of those principles in organizations. An OB study might explore the relationship between learning and job performance, whereas a human resources management study might examine the best ways to structure training programs to promote employee learning. **Strategic management** focuses on the product choices and industry characteristics that affect an organization's profitability. For example, a strategic management study might examine the relationship between firm diversification (when a firm expands into a new product segment) and firm profitability.

organizational behaviour (OB)

Field of study devoted to understanding, explaining, and ultimately improving the attitudes and behaviours of individuals and groups in organizations

human resources management

Field of study that focuses on the applications of OB theories and principles in organizations

strategic management

Field of study devoted to exploring the product choices and industry characteristics that affect an organization's profitability

The theories and concepts found in OB are actually drawn from a wide variety of disciplines. For example, research on job performance and individual characteristics draws primarily on studies in industrial and organizational psychology. Research on satisfaction, emotions, and team processes draws heavily on social psychology. Sociology research is vital to research on team characteristics and organizational structure, and anthropology research helps inform the study of organizational culture. Finally, models from economics are used to understand motivation, learning, and decision making. This diversity brings a unique quality to the study of OB, as most students will be able to find a particular topic that is intrinsically interesting and thought-provoking to them.

The Role of Management Theory

The theories and concepts found in OB have also been heavily influenced by the popular management approaches of the day. Over time our ideas about how best to organize, coordinate, and manage human work activities have changed, as have our view of cause–effect relationships. As you will see, many of the "modern" theories and concepts described in the text have their roots in one or more of these management theories or approaches.

Classical management scholars, such as Frederick Taylor (1856–1917) and Max Weber (1864–1920), put heavy emphasis on specialization, coordination, and efficiency. A major influence on the way people viewed and thought about OB was the work of Frederick Taylor, the father of **scientific management**.[7] As an engineer, Taylor was focused on designing optimal and efficient work processes. Using scientific methods (e.g., careful observation, measurement, experimentation), Taylor and his colleagues would study how to optimize performance of any task (e.g., by reducing the number of hand movements exhibited by bricklayers, and thus reducing fatigue, more bricks could be laid in a given time period). Once determined, these new work procedures would be taught to workers and encouraged with financial incentives.

scientific management

Using scientific methods to design optimal and efficient work processes and tasks

Another important contributor to the classical approach to management was Max Weber, most often associated with the term **bureaucracy**.[8] Rather than focus on specific work processes, Weber looked at the entire organization. For Weber, the bureaucratic form was a technically superior method of organizing, coordinating, and controlling human work activities (Chapter 14). Characteristics of bureaucracy included: (1) the division of labour with a high level of technical specialization; (2) a strict chain of command (authority hierarchy) in which every member reported to someone at a higher level; (3) a system of formal rules and procedures that ensured consistency, impartiality, and impersonality throughout the organization; and (4) decision making at the top of the organization. For the classical theorists, productivity problems, if and when they occurred, were likely viewed at the job level as the result of design flaws, failures to implement specified processes, or inadequate working conditions (e.g., illumination, not enough work breaks), and at the organizational level as the result of deficient structural characteristics.

bureaucracy

An organizational form that emphasizes the control and coordination of its members through a strict chain of command, formal rules and procedures, high specialization, and centralized decision making

In stark contrast to the classical approaches that stressed the importance of the formal organization and its functioning, the **human relations movement** emerged as management scholars began to recognize that the psychological attributes of individual workers (e.g., needs, attitudes) and the social forces within work groups had important effects on behaviours. A famous serious of studies, conducted between 1924 and 1933 at the Western Electric Company's Hawthorne plant, revealed the limitations with the classic approach to management and organization.[9] Originally these studies were designed to resolve the organization's productivity problems by applying popular scientific-management techniques. The irony, of course, is that a classical-approach application produced the foundation on which the human relations movement was built. The Hawthorne studies, although crude in comparison to the organizational research being conducted today, revealed the importance of many of the topics we discuss in this text, such as group values and norms, leadership, motivation, job satisfaction, and organizational culture. For the human relations theorists, productivity problems, if and when they occurred, were likely viewed as the result of worker alienation from the organization, failure of the work to satisfy important personal needs or goals, low organizational commitment, or workgroup norms encouraging low rather than high performance—in other words, very little causal emphasis on the characteristics of formal organization.

human relations movement

Field of study that recognizes that the psychological attributes of individual workers and the social forces within work groups have important effects on work behaviours

Today, contemporary management theory recognizes the dependencies between the classical and the human relations approach. We see this recognition reflected in a number of the theories and models of OB in which the consequences of situational characteristics (e.g., financial incentives, job design, assigned goals) are thought to *depend* on characteristics of the individual or vice versa. Fundamental to this "contingency" approach is the idea that there is no one best, universal principle. The same is true for OB. As you will see, OB—in all its forms—is the result of many different kinds of variables coming together.

An Integrative Model of OB

Because of the diversity in its topics and disciplinary roots, it is common for students in an organizational behaviour class to wonder, "How does all this stuff fit together?" In terms of this book, this means, for example, "How does what gets covered in Chapter 3 relate to what gets covered in Chapter 12?"

To clarify such issues, this textbook is structured around an integrative model of OB, illustrated in Figure 1-1, that is designed to provide a roadmap for the field of organizational behaviour. The model shows how the four different kinds of topics in the next 14 chapters—represented by the 14 ovals—fit together. We should stress that there are other possible ways of combining the 14 topics, and Figure 1-1 likely oversimplifies the connections among them. Still, we believe the model will provide a helpful guide as you move through this course.

FIGURE 1-1

Integrative Model of Organizational Behaviour

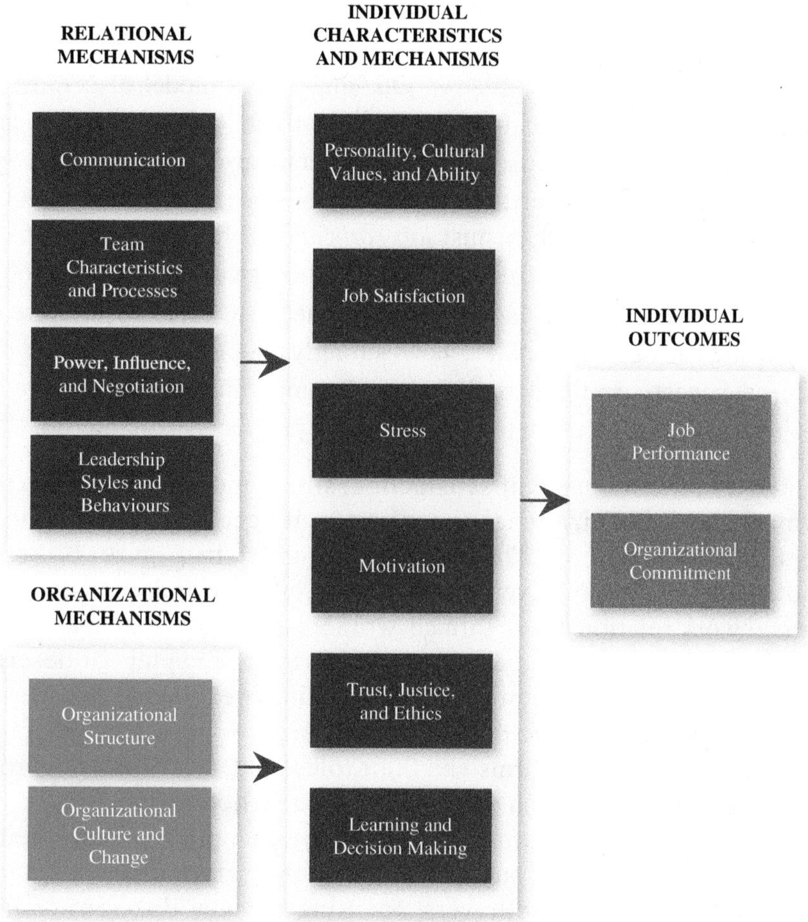

1.2 What are the two primary outcomes in studies of OB?

Individual Outcomes The rightmost portion of the model contains the two primary outcomes of interest to organizational behaviour researchers (and employees and managers): *job performance* and *organizational commitment*. Most employees have two primary goals for their working lives: to perform their jobs well and to remain members of an organization they respect. Likewise, most managers have two primary goals for their employees: to maximize their job performance and to retain these employees for a significant length of time. Chapter 2 discusses several specific behaviours that, taken together, constitute good job performance. Similarly, Chapter 3 discusses beliefs, attitudes, and emotions that cause an employee to remain committed to an employer.

This book starts by covering job performance and organizational commitment so that you can better understand these two primary OB goals. Our hope is that by using them as starting points, we can highlight the practical importance of OB ideas. What could be more important to an organization than employees who perform well and want to stay with the company? This structure also enables us to conclude the other chapters in the book with sections that describe the relationships between each chapter's topic—for example, motivation in Chapter 7—and performance and commitment. In this way, you will learn which of the topics in the model are most useful for understanding your own job performance and your own desires to stay with (or leave) your company.

1.3 What factors affect the two primary OB outcomes?

Individual Characteristics and Mechanisms Our integrative model also illustrates a number of individual characteristics and mechanisms that directly affect job performance and organizational commitment. In Chapter 4 we focus on several of key personal characteristics, *personality, cultural values, and ability*, and describe their relationships to performance and commitment. Then we look at a number of important individual mechanisms: *job satisfaction*, how employees feel about their jobs and day-to-day work (Chapter 5); *stress*, employees' psychological responses to job demands that tax or exceed their capacities (Chapter 6); *motivation*, the energetic forces that drive employees' work effort (Chapter 7); *trust, justice, and ethics*, how strongly employees feel their company conducts business with fairness, honesty, and integrity (Chapter 8); and *learning and decision making*, the ways employees gain job knowledge and use it to make accurate judgments (Chapter 9).

Relational Mechanisms Of course, if satisfaction, stress, motivation, and so forth are key drivers of job performance and organizational commitment, it becomes important to understand what factors improve those mechanisms. The integrative model in Figure 1-1 acknowledges that employees do not work alone but have to effectively interact and coordinate with others. We describe how critical work relationships, with co-workers and leaders, shape the individual mechanisms of satisfaction, stress, motivation, trust, and learning. Chapter 10 describes fundamental *communication* processes, and the factors that help or hinder exchange of information within the workplace. Chapter 11 describes *team characteristics and processes*, exploring the structure of effective work groups, such as their norms and their roles, and describing the processes at work in the behaviour of groups and teams, such as cooperation, conflict, and managing diversity. Chapter 12, on *power, influence, and negotiation*, examines how people leverage their relationships to attain authority and achieve desirable outcomes within organizational settings. In Chapter 13 we describe how leaders relate to their followers, focusing on how different *leadership styles and behaviours* impact the attitudes and behaviours of others at work.

Organizational Mechanisms Finally, our integrative model acknowledges that individuals and groups function within an organizational context. Every company, for example, has an *organizational structure* that dictates how the units within the firm link to (and coordinate with) other units (Chapter 14). Sometimes, structures are centralized around a decision-making authority; sometimes, structures are decentralized, affording each unit some autonomy. Chapter 15 examines *organizational culture and change*. Every company has, within it, shared knowledge about the rules, norms, and values that shape employee attitudes and behaviours; from time to time, these organizational cultures have to change, and we review this process.

The Value of an Integrative Model Each of the chapters in this textbook will open with a depiction of this integrative model, with the subject of each chapter highlighted. We hope that this opening will serve as a roadmap for the course—showing you where you are, where you've been, and where you're going. Some of you will be able to apply those topic areas to your current working life, whether you are working full-time or part-time and whether you occupy a managerial or non-managerial role. Of course, you might be a full-time student or between jobs at the moment; but it turns out that many of the same concepts that predict success in an organization also predict success in a classroom. We will explore some of those commonalities in our ***OB for Students*** feature, which appears in each chapter and illustrates how OB concepts can be applied to improve academic success.

OB FOR STUDENTS

This feature is designed to demonstrate the generalizability of many OB principles by applying them to another area of life: life as a student. Each chapter will explore how a particular topic occurs in the classroom. Some of the things you can expect in the chapters to come are as follows:

Job satisfaction (Chapter 5). How do students judge how satisfied they are with their university life? How do they weigh things such as where they live, how much they like their classmates, and how much they enjoy what they're studying?

Stress (Chapter 6). The working world doesn't corner the market on stress; juggling several classes along with life's other responsibilities can be quite stressful in its own right. We'll explore how various kinds of stressful demands affect student learning and class performance.

Communication (Chapter 10). Computer-mediated communication channels and social-media applications may have changed forever how students exchange information and acquire knowledge. We'll explore whether these new tools offer advantages over face-to-face communication, and some of the issues to watch out for.

Team characteristics and processes (Chapter 11). Several classes use team projects. We'll explore some of the important drivers of the effectiveness of student groups, in the hope that you can use this discussion to improve your own team's functioning.

Organizational structure (Chapter 14). What kinds of organizational structures do most students find attractive when they are on the job market? Do some students have different structural preferences than others?

Organizational culture and change (Chapter 15). How do new students learn about the culture of a university? Are there benefits of socializing new students in the same way that organizations socialize new employees? What would such socialization efforts look like?

DOES ORGANIZATIONAL BEHAVIOUR MATTER?

Now that we have described exactly what OB is, it is time to discuss another fundamental question: Does it really matter? Is there any value in taking a class on this subject, other than fulfilling some requirement of your program? (You might guess that we are biased in our answers to these questions, given that we wrote an entire book on this subject!) Few would disagree that organizations need to know principles of accounting and finance to be successful; it would be impossible to conduct business without such knowledge. Similarly, few would disagree that organizations need to know principles of marketing, as consumers need to know about the firm's products and what makes those products unique or noteworthy.

However, people sometimes wonder whether a firm's ability to manage OB has any bearing on its profitability. After all, if a firm has a good-enough product, won't people buy it regardless of how happy, motivated, or committed its workforce is? The answer is: Perhaps for a time, but effective OB can help keep a product good over the long term. The argument might be made in reverse: If a firm has a bad-enough product, isn't it true that people won't buy it, regardless of how happy, motivated, or committed its workforce is? Again, perhaps for a time, but the effective management of OB can help make a product get better, incrementally, over the long term.

Pop quiz about the automotive industry: Which automaker finished behind only Lexus and Porsche in a recent study of initial quality by J.D. Power and Associates?[10] Toyota? Nope. Honda? Uh-uh. The answer is Hyundai (yes, Hyundai). The automaker has come a long way since comedian Jay Leno likened a Hyundai to a bobsled ("It has no room, you have to push it to get going, and it only goes downhill!").[11] That turnaround can be credited to the company's increased emphasis on quality. Work teams devoted to quality have been expanded eightfold, and almost all employees are enrolled in special training programs devoted to quality issues.[12] Hyundai represents a case in which OB principles are being applied across cultures. The ***OB Internationally*** feature in each chapter spotlights such international and cross-cultural applications of OB topics in each chapter.

Hyundai's emphasis on work teams and training had increased the quality of its car.

© AP Photo/Dave Martin

OB INTERNATIONALLY

Changes in technology, communications, and economic forces have made business more global and international than ever. This feature spotlights the impact of globalization on the organizational behaviour concepts described in this book. More specifically, this feature will cover a variety of topics:

Cross-cultural differences. Research in cross-cultural organizational behaviour has illustrated that national cultures affect many of the relationships in our integrative model. Put differently, little we know about OB is "universal" or "culture-free."[13]

International corporations. An increasing number of organizations are international in scope, with both foreign and domestic operations. Applying organizational behaviour concepts in these firms represents a special challenge—should policies and practices be consistent across locations or tailored to meet the needs of the culture?

Expatriation. Working as an expatriate—an employee who lives outside his or her native country—can be particularly challenging. What factors influence expatriates'job performance and organizational commitment levels?

Managing diversity. More and more work groups are composed of members of different cultural backgrounds. What special challenges are involved in leading and working in such groups?

Building a Conceptual Argument

Of course, we shouldn't just accept it on faith that OB matters, nor should we merely look for specific companies that appear to support the premise. What we need instead is a logical, conceptual argument that captures exactly why OB might affect the bottom line of an organization. One such argument is based on the **resource-based view** of organizations. This perspective describes what exactly makes resources valuable—that is, what makes them capable of creating long-term profits.[14] A firm's resources include not only financial (e.g., revenue, equity) and physical (e.g., buildings, machines, technology) ones, but also ones related to organizational behaviour, such as the knowledge, decision making, ability, and wisdom of the workforce and the image, culture, and goodwill of the organization.

resource-based view
A model that argues that rare and inimitable resources help firms maintain competitive advantage

The resource-based view suggests that the value of resources depends on several factors, shown in Figure 1-2. For example, a resource is more valuable when it is **rare**. Diamonds, oil, Howie Morenz hockey cards, and *Action Comics* #1 (with the debut of Superman) are all expensive precisely because they are rare. Good people are rare as well. Ask yourself what percentage of those you have worked with have been talented, motivated, satisfied, and team players. In many organizations, cities, or job markets, such employees are the exception rather than the rule. This being so, the effective management of OB should prove to be a valuable resource.

rare
In short supply

FIGURE 1-2

What Makes a Resource Valuable?

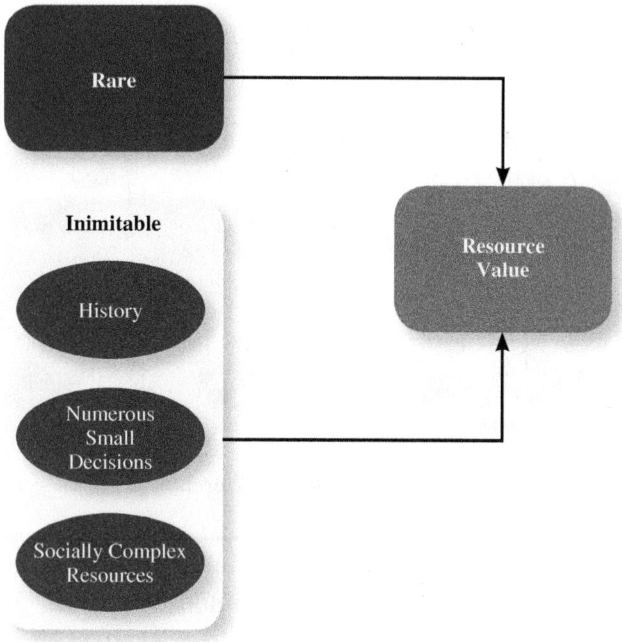

The resource-based view also suggests that a resource is more valuable when it is **inimitable**, meaning it cannot be easily copied. A new form of technology can help a firm gain an advantage for a short time, but what happens when a competing firm reproduces it? Many of a firm's resources can be imitated, even though it is sometimes expensive. Manufacturing practices can be copied, building layouts can be mimicked, equipment and tools can be approximated. Valuable people, in contrast, are much more difficult to imitate. As is illustrated in Figure 1-2, there are three reasons why people are inimitable.

inimitable

Incapable of being imitated or copied

History People create a **history**—a collective pool of experience, wisdom, and knowledge that benefits the organization. History cannot be bought. Consider an example from the consumer electronics retailing industry, in which Microsoft, taking its cue from Apple, launched its first Canadian retail store at Toronto's Yorkdale Shopping Centre in 2012.[15] The company hopes the stores will give it a chance to showcase its computer and mobile phone operating systems and hardware and gaming products; but it faces an uphill climb in the retail space, because Apple has a ten-year head start with almost 30 retail stores across Canada.[16] Microsoft's position on the "retail learning curve" is therefore quite different, and chances are it will grapple with many issues that Apple resolved long ago.

history

A collective pool of experience, wisdom, and knowledge that benefits the organization

Microsoft opened its first Canadian retail store in 2012. The look and feel of the Windows Store is very similar to that of Apple's retail outlets.

© Joshua Lott/Reuters/Corbis

Numerous Small Decisions The concept of **numerous small decisions** captures the idea that people make many small decisions day in and day out, week in and week out. "So what?" you might say, "Why worry about small decisions?" To answer that question, ask yourself what the biggest decisions are when launching a new line of retail stores. Their location, maybe? Perhaps their look and feel? It turns out that Microsoft placed their stores near Apple's, and mimicked much of their open, "Zen" sensibility.[17] Big decisions can be copied; they are visible to competitors and observable by industry experts. In contrast, the "behind the scenes" decisions at the Apple Store are less visible to Microsoft, especially those that involve hiring and managing employees. Apple seems to understand the inimitable advantage such decisions can create. A recent article in *Workforce Management* included features on the top human resources executives for the most admired companies in North America.[18] Interestingly, the entry for Apple's executive was cryptic, noting only that the company "keeps its human resources executive shrouded in secrecy and refuses to respond to any questions about HR's contribution to the company's most admired status."

numerous small decisions
Small decisions that people make every day

Socially Complex Resources People also create things like culture, teamwork, trust, and reputation, which are termed **socially complex resources** because it is not always clear how they come to be, though it might be clear which organizations do and do not possess them. One advantage Apple has over Microsoft in the retail wars is the unusual amount of interest and enthusiasm generated by products such as the iPad, iPhone, iPod, and MacBook Air, which have an "it factor" that brings customers into the store, and as a result Apple itself sits atop *Fortune*'s list of the 50 most admired companies in the world.[19] Competitors can't just manufacture "coolness" or "admiration"—these are complex things that people develop in mysterious ways.

socially complex resources
Resources created by people, such as culture, teamwork, trust, and reputation

1.4 Why might firms that are good at OB tend to be more profitable?

Research Evidence

Thus, we can build a conceptual argument for why OB might affect an organization's profitability: Good people are both rare and inimitable and therefore create a resource that is valuable for creating competitive advantage. Conceptual arguments are helpful, of course, but it would be even better if there were hard data to back them up. Fortunately, it turns out there is a great deal of research evidence supporting the importance of OB for company performance. Several research studies have been conducted on the topic, each employing a somewhat different approach.

One study began by surveying executives from 968 publicly held firms with 100 or more employees.[20] The survey assessed so-called "high performance work practices"—OB policies widely agreed to be beneficial to firm performance. Thirteen questions asked about a combination of hiring, information sharing, training, performance management, and incentive practices, and each question asked what proportion of the company's workforce was involved in the practice. Table 1-2 shows the questions used to assess the high-performance work practices (and also shows which chapter of this textbook describes each practice in more detail). The study also gathered the following information for each firm: average annual rate of turnover, productivity level (defined as sales per employee), market value of the firm, and corporate profitability. The results revealed that a one-unit increase in the proportion of the workforce involved in the practices was associated with an approximately 7 percent decrease in turnover, $27,000 more in sales per employee, $18,000 more in market value, and $3,800 more in profits. Put simply, better OB practices were associated with better firm performance.

TABLE 1-2

Survey Questions Designed to Assess High-Performance Work Practices

Survey Question About OB Practice	Covered in Chapter:
1. What is the proportion of the workforce whose jobs have been subjected to a formal job analysis?	2
2. What is the proportion of the workforce who are administered attitude surveys on a regular basis?	5
3. What is the proportion of the workforce who have access to company incentive plans, profit-sharing plans, and/or gain-sharing plans?	7
4. What is the average number of hours of training received by a typical employee over the last 12 months?	4, 9
5. What is the proportion of the workforce who have access to a formal grievance procedure and/or complaint resolution system?	8
6. What proportion of the workforce are administered an employment test prior to hiring?	4
7. What is the proportion of the workforce whose performance appraisals are used to determine compensation?	7

Source: From M.A. Huselid, "The Impact of Human Resource Management Practices on Turnover, Productivity, and Corporate Financial Performance," *Academy of Management Journal*, Vol. 38, pp. 635–72. Copyright © 1995. Reproduced with permission of Academy of Management via Copyright Clearance Center.

Although there is no doubting the importance of turnover, productivity, market value, and profitability, another study examined an outcome that is even more fundamental: firm survival.[21] The study focused on 136 non-financial companies that made initial public offerings (IPOs). Firms that make an IPO typically have shorter histories and need an infusion of cash to grow or introduce some new technology. Rather than conducting a survey, the authors of this study examined the prospectus filed by each firm. (Reporting rules require that prospectuses contain honest information, and firms can be liable for any inaccuracies that might mislead investors.) The authors coded each prospectus for information that might suggest OB issues were valued. Examples of valuing OB issues included describing employees as a source of competitive advantage in strategy and mission statements, emphasizing training and continuing education, having a human resources management officer, and emphasizing full-time rather than temporary or contract employees. Five years later, 81 of the 136 firms included in the study had survived (60 percent). The key question is whether the value put on OB predicted which did (and did not) survive. The results revealed that firms that valued OB had a 19 percent higher survival rate than firms that did not.

Every year since 2005, panels of prominent Canadian business leaders have been asked to evaluate some of the nation's largest companies on criteria such as, vision and leadership, cultural alignment with the organization's strategic goals, reward and recognition practices, financial performance, and corporate social responsibility.[22] On this basis, annual awards are given to those top ten companies who demonstrate that they deserve to be one of *Canada's Most Admired Corporate Cultures.*[23] Only a handful of these top winners have consistently reached this elite level (Table 1-3). Not only are these winners drawn from a range of industry sectors, but it clearly shows that firms with very good OB practices also tend to be some of the most successful organizations in the country—in both good and difficult economic times!

TABLE 1-3

Canada's Most Admired Corporate Cultures

Top Award Winners (listed alphabetically)
1. Four Seasons Hotels and Resorts
2. Royal Bank of Canada (RBC)
3. TELUS
4. Tim Hortons
5. WestJet Airlines
6. Yellow Pages Group

Source: "Canada's 10 Most Admired Corporate Cultures," Waterstone Human Capital website, www.waterstonehc.com/cmac/hall-fame, accessed August 2014.

So What's So Hard?

Clearly this research evidence seems to support the conceptual argument that good people constitute a valuable resource for companies. Good OB does seem to matter in terms of company profitability. You may wonder, then, "What's so hard?" Why doesn't every company prioritize the effective management of OB, devoting as much attention to it as they do accounting, finance, marketing, technology, physical assets, and so on? Some companies do not do a good job managing their people. Why?

Work by Jeffrey Pfeffer provides one possible answer. He has written extensively on the OB practices that tend to be used by successful organizations. According to Pfeffer there is no "magic bullet" practice—one thing that, in and of itself, can increase profitability. Instead, effective management of OB requires a belief that several different practices are important, along with a long-term commitment to improving those practices. This premise can be summarized in what might be called the **rule of one-eighth**:

rule of one-eighth

The belief that at best one-eighth, or 12 percent, of organizations will actually do what is required to build profits by putting people first

> One must bear in mind that one-half of organizations won't believe the connection between how they manage their people and the profits they earn. One-half of those who do see the connection will do what many organizations have done—try to make a single change to solve their problems, not realizing that the effective management of people requires a more comprehensive and systematic approach. Of the firms that make comprehensive changes, probably only about one-half will persist with their practices long enough to actually derive economic benefits. Since one-half times one-half times one-half equals one-eighth, at best 12 percent of organizations will actually do what is required to build profits by putting people first.[24]

The integrative model of OB used to structure this book was designed with the rule of one-eighth in mind. Figure 1-1 suggests that high job performance depends not just on employee motivation but also on fostering high levels of satisfaction, effectively managing stress, creating a trusting climate, and committing to employee learning. Failing at any of those things might hinder the effectiveness of the other concepts in the model. Of course, that systemic nature reveals another reality of organizational behaviour: It is often difficult to "fix" companies that struggle with OB issues. Such companies often struggle in a number of different areas and on a number of different levels. In each chapter we attempt use our ***OB on Screen*** feature to demonstrate OB concepts (and issues) drawn from well-known movies.

OB ON SCREEN

This feature is designed to illustrate OB concepts in action on the silver screen. Once you've learned about OB topics, you'll see them playing out all around you, especially in movies.

Moneyball

> *You don't put a team together with a computer, Billy.... Baseball isn't just numbers; it's not science. If it was, then anybody could do what we're doing. But they can't because they don't know what we know. They don't have our experience and they don't have our intuition.*

With those words, Grady Fuson (Ken Medlock) tries to show Billy Beane (Brad Pitt) the error of his ways in *Moneyball* (Dir. Bennett Miller, Columbia Pictures, 2011). Billy is the general manager of the Oakland Athletics (A's). After losing to the New York Yankees in the playoffs, Billy's been forced to trim a payroll that is already a third of what the Yankees pay. To the angst of his head scout Grady, Billy turns to Pete Brand, aka "Google boy," a recent hire with a degree in economics from Yale. Pete is well versed in "sabermetrics"—the scientific search for objective baseball knowledge begun by Bill James, with a nod to the Society for American Baseball Research (SABR).

© Columbia Pictures/Photofest

The film, based on the Michael Lewis bestseller,[25] shows how science can complement experience and intuition. For example, Pete's advanced analytics showed that "on-base percentage"—a statistic dependent not just on hits but also on walks—was a more valid indicator of a player's value than the home runs emphasized by traditional scouts. Ironically, the success of *Moneyball* caused a number of baseball teams to hire "sabermetricians," erasing some of the advantages that Billy's approach had given Oakland.[26] Indeed, the use of advanced analytics has taken hold in other professional sports, most notably the National Basketball Association.[27] Hopefully evidence-based management will allow organizational managers to do what sports managers are doing—test their theories of success with data.

HOW DO WE "KNOW" WHAT WE KNOW ABOUT ORGANIZATIONAL BEHAVIOUR?

Now that we've described what OB is and why it's an important topic of study, we turn to how we "know" what we know about the topic. In other words, where does the knowledge in this textbook come from? To answer this question, we must first explore how people "know" about anything. Philosophers have argued that there are several different ways of knowing things:[28]

- *Method of experience.* People hold firmly to some belief because it is consistent with their own experience and observations.
- *Method of intuition.* People hold firmly to some belief because it "just stands to reason"—it seems obvious or self-evident.
- *Method of authority.* People hold firmly to some belief because some respected official, agency, or source has said it is so.
- *Method of science.* People accept some belief because scientific studies have tended to replicate that result using a series of samples, settings, and methods.

1.5 What is the role of theory in the scientific method?

Consider the following prediction: "By providing social recognition, in the form of public displays of praise and appreciation for good behaviours, you will increase the performance and commitment of work units." Perhaps you feel that you "know" this to be true because you yourself have always responded well to praise and recognition. Or perhaps you feel that you "know" it to be true because it seems like common sense—who wouldn't work harder after a few public pats on the back? Maybe you feel that you "know" it to be true because a respected boss from your past has always hailed the value of public praise and recognition.

However, the methods of experience, intuition, and authority might also have led you to the opposite belief—that providing social recognition has no impact on the performance and commitment of work units. It may be that public praise has always made you uncomfortable or embarrassed, to the point that you've tried to hide especially effective behaviours to avoid being singled out by your boss. Or it may seem logical that social recognition will be viewed as "cheap talk," with employees longing for financial incentives rather than verbal compliments. Or perhaps the best boss you ever worked for never offered a single piece of social recognition in her life, yet her employees always worked their hardest on her behalf. From a scientist's point of view, it doesn't really matter what a person's experience, intuition, or authority suggests; the prediction must be tested with data. In other words, scientists don't simply assume that their beliefs are accurate; they acknowledge that their beliefs must be tested scientifically.

Scientific studies are based on the scientific method, originated by Sir Francis Bacon in the 1600s and adapted in Figure 1-3.[29] The method begins with **theory**, defined as a collection of assertions—both verbal and symbolic—that specify how and why variables are related, and the conditions in which they should (and should not) be related.[30] More simply, a theory tells a story and supplies the familiar who, what, where, when, and why elements found in any newspaper or magazine article.[31] Theories are often summarized with diagrams, the "boxes and arrows" that depict relationships between variables. Our integrative model of OB in Figure 1-1 represents one such diagram, and there will be many more to come in the remaining chapters of this textbook.

theory

A collection of verbal and symbolic assertions that specify how and why variables are related, as well as the conditions in which they should (and should not) be related

FIGURE 1-3

The Scientific Method

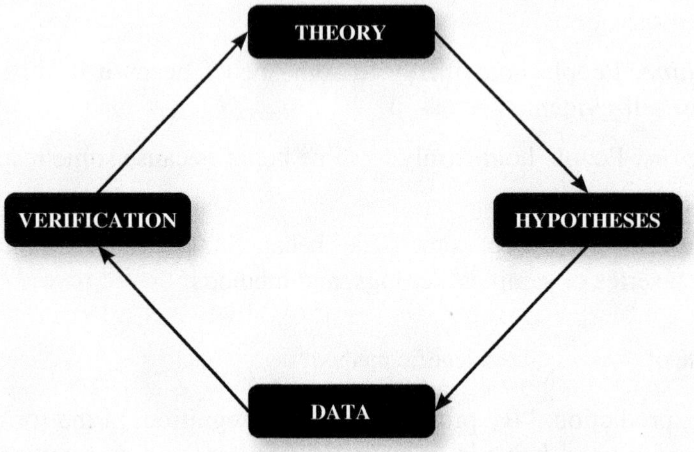

Source: Adapted from F. Bacon, M. Silverthorne, and L. Jardine, *The New Organon* (Cambridge: Cambridge University Press, 2000).

A scientist could build a theory explaining why social recognition might influence the performance and commitment of work units. From what sources would that theory be built? Well, because social scientists "are what they study," one source of theory building is introspection. However, theories may also be built from interviews with employees or from observations in which scientists take notes, keep diaries, and pore over company documents.[32] Alternatively, theories may be built from research reviews, which examine findings of previous studies to look for patterns or themes.[33]

Although many theories are interesting, logical, or thought-provoking, many also wind up being completely wrong. After all, scientific theories once predicted that the earth was flat and the sun revolved around it. Closer to home, OB theories once argued that money was not an effective motivator and that the best way to structure jobs was to make them as simple and mundane as possible.[34] Theories must therefore be tested to verify that their predictions are accurate. As is shown in Figure 1-3, the scientific method requires that theories be used to inspire **hypotheses**. Hypotheses are written predictions that specify relationships between variables. For example, a theory of social recognition might be used to inspire this hypothesis: "Social recognition behaviours on the part of managers will be positively related to the job performance and organizational commitment of their units." This hypothesis states, in black and white, the expected relationship between social recognition and unit performance.

hypotheses

Written predictions that specify relationships between variables

Assume a family member owned a chain of 21 fast-food restaurants and allowed you to test this hypothesis using the restaurants. Specifically, you decided to train the managers in a subset of the restaurants about how to use social recognition as a tool to reinforce behaviours. Meanwhile, you left another subset of restaurants unchanged as a control group. You then tracked the total number of social recognition behaviours exhibited by managers over the next nine months by observing the managers at specific time intervals. You measured job performance by tracking drive-through times for the next nine months and used those times to reflect the minutes it takes for a customer to approach the restaurant, order food, pay, and leave. You also measured the commitment of the work unit by tracking employee retention rates over the next nine months.

1.6 How are correlations interpreted?

So how can you tell whether your hypothesis was supported? You could analyze the data by examining the **correlation** between social recognition behaviours and drive-through times, as well as the correlation between social recognition behaviours and employee turnover. A correlation, abbreviated *r*, describes the statistical relationship between two variables. Correlations can be positive or negative and range from 0 (no statistical relationship) to 1 (a perfect statistical relationship). Picture a spreadsheet with two columns, one of which contains the total numbers of social recognition behaviours for all 21 restaurants and the other the average drive-through times for those same restaurants. The best way to get a feel for the correlation is to look at a *scatterplot*—a graph drawn using those two columns of numbers.

correlation

The statistical relationship between two variables, abbreviated *r*; it can be positive or negative and range from 0 (no statistical relationship) to ±1 (a perfect statistical relationship)

Figure 1-4 presents three scatterplots, each depicting a different-sized correlation. The strength of the correlation can be inferred from the "compactness" of its scatterplot. Panel (a) shows a perfect 1.0 correlation; knowing the score for social recognition allows you to predict the score for drive-through times perfectly. Panel (b) shows a correlation of .50, so the trend in the data is less obvious than in panel (a) but still easy to see with the naked eye. Finally, Panel (c) shows a correlation of .00—no statistical relationship. Understanding the correlation is important because OB questions are not "yes or no" in nature. That is, the question is not "*Does* social recognition lead to higher job performance?" but rather "*How often* does social recognition lead to higher job performance?" The correlation provides a number that expresses an answer to the "how often" question.

So what *is* the correlation between social recognition and job performance (and between social recognition and organizational commitment)? It turns out that a study very similar to the one described has actually been conducted, using a sample of 21 Burger King restaurants with 525 total employees.[35] The correlation found was .28. The restaurants that received training in social recognition averaged 44 seconds of drive-through time nine months later as against 62 seconds for the control-group locations. The correlation between social recognition and retention rates was .20. The restaurants that received training in social recognition had a 16 percent better retention rate than the control group locations nine months later. The study also instituted a financial "pay for performance" system in a subset of the locations and found that the social recognition effects were just as strong as the financial effects.

FIGURE 1-4

Three Different Correlation Sizes

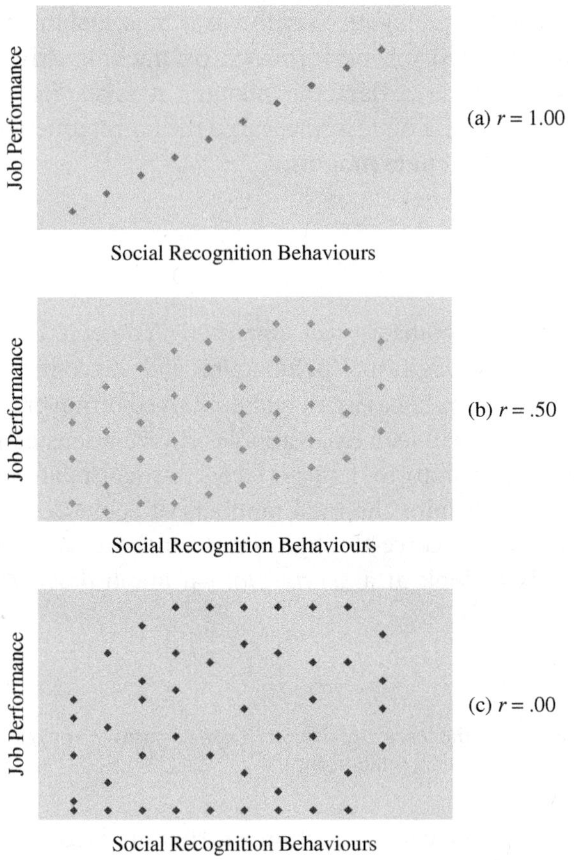

TABLE 1-4

Some Notable Correlations

Correlation Between:	r	Sample Size
Height and weight	.44	16,948
Viagra and sexual functioning	.38	779
Ibuprofen and pain reduction	.14	8,488
Antihistamines and reduced sneezing	.11	1,023
Smoking and lung cancer within 25 years	.08	3,956
Coronary bypass surgery and 5-year survival	.08	2,649

Source: From Robert Hogan, "In Defense of Personality Measurement: New Wine for Old Whiners," *Human Performance*, Vol. 18, 2005, pp. 331–41. Reprinted by permission of the publisher, Taylor & Frances Group, www.informaworld.com.

Of course, you might wonder whether correlations of .28 or .20 are impressive. To understand those numbers, let's consider some context for them. Table 1-4 provides notable correlations from other areas of science. If the correlation between height and weight is only .44, then a correlation of .28 between social recognition and job performance doesn't sound too bad! In fact, in organizational behaviour research a correlation of .50 is considered "strong," given the sheer number of things that can affect how employees feel and act.[36] A .30 correlation is considered "moderate," and many studies discussed in this book will have results in this range. Finally, a .10 correlation is considered "weak." It should be noted, however, that even "weak" correlations can be important if they predict costly behaviours such as theft or ethical violations. The .08 correlation between smoking and lung cancer within 25 years is a good example of how important small correlations can be.

A study of Burger King restaurants revealed a correlation between social recognition—praise and appreciation by managers—and employees' performance and commitment. Such studies contribute to the growing body of organizational behaviour knowledge.

Does this one study settle the debate about the value of social recognition for job performance and organizational commitment? Not really, for a variety of reasons. First, it included only 21 restaurants with 525 employees—maybe the results would have turned out differently if the study had included more locations. Second, it focused only on restaurant employees—maybe there's something unique about such employees that makes them particularly responsive to social recognition. Third, it may be that the trained locations differed from the control locations on something *other than* social recognition, and it was that "something" that was responsible for the performance differences. You may have heard the phrase, "Correlation does not imply causation." It turns out that making a **causal inference**—establishing that one variable really does cause another—requires establishing three things:[37] first, that the two variables are correlated; second, that the presumed cause precedes the presumed effect in time; third, that no alternative explanation exists for the correlation. The third criterion is often fulfilled in experiments, in which researchers have more control over the setting of the study.

causal inference

Concluding that one variable really does cause another

The important point is that little can be learned from a single study. The best way to test a theory is to conduct many studies, each of which is as different as possible from the ones that preceded it.[38] So if you really wanted to study the effects of social recognition, you would conduct several studies using different kinds of samples and different measures. After completing all of those studies, you could look back on the results and create some sort of average correlation across all of the studies. This process is what a technique called **meta-analysis** does. It takes all of the correlations found in studies of a particular relationship and calculates a weighted average (such that correlations based on studies with large samples are weighted more than correlations based on studies with small samples). It turns out that a meta-analysis has been conducted on the effects of social recognition and job performance and indicates an average correlation of .21 across studies conducted in 96 different organizations in the service industry.[39] That analysis offers more compelling support for the potential benefits of social recognition than the methods of experience, intuition, or authority could have provided.

meta-analysis
A method that combines the results of multiple scientific studies by essentially calculating a weighted-average correlation across studies (with larger studies receiving more weight)

Moving Forward in This Book

The chapters that follow will work through the integrative model of OB in Figure 1-1. Each chapter begins with a case scenario for context and discussion. Theories and research relevant to the chapter's topic are highlighted and discussed. The concepts in those theories are demonstrated in the ***OB on Screen*** features to show how OB phenomena have come to life in film. You also get to see how those concepts can be applied to student life in the ***OB for Students*** feature. In addition, the ***OB Internationally*** feature describes how those concepts operate differently in different cultures and nations. The ***OB Assessments*** feature at the end of each chapter allows you to gain valuable insight and knowledge about your own personality, abilities, job attitudes, and leadership styles. Finally, it is important to recognize that the knowledge contained in this text represents the collective efforts of a global community of researchers who carefully apply the scientific method to specific questions within the field of organizational behaviour. The ***OB Research in Canada*** feature in each chapter showcases a prominent (or promising) Canadian-based OB researcher.

Each chapter ends with three pedagogical sections. The first consists of a summarizing theory diagram that explains why some employees exhibit higher levels of a given concept than others. For example, the diagram for the chapter on job satisfaction explains why some employees are happier with their work than others.

The next end-of-chapter section describes the results of meta-analyses of the relationships between that chapter's topic and both job performance and organizational commitment. Over time, you'll get a feel for which of the topics in Figure 1-1 have strong, moderate, or weak relationships with these outcomes. This knowledge will help you recognize how everything in OB fits together and what the most valuable tools are for improving performance and commitment in the workplace. As you will discover, some of the topics in OB have a greater impact on how well employees perform their jobs, whereas others have a greater impact on how long employees remain with their organizations.

The final end-of-chapter section describes how the content of the chapter can be applied at a specific level in an actual organization. For example, the motivation chapter concludes with a section describing how compensation practices can be used to maximize employee effort. If you're currently working, we hope these concluding sections help you see how the concepts you're reading about might actually be used to improve your own organization. If you're not working, these sections give you a glimpse into how you will experience OB concepts once you begin your working life.

In closing, we are confident you will come to believe OB is an interesting subject, because almost everyone can relate to the concepts it deals with. Almost everyone has encountered a bad boss, instructor, or other authority figure, grappled with issues of trust, or had to find a way to cope with stress. You will read how noteworthy companies have dealt with these issues, but you can also ask yourself how you would react in the same situation. Happy reading!

TAKEAWAYS

1.1 Organizational behaviour is a field of study devoted to understanding and explaining the attitudes and behaviours of individuals and groups in organizations. More simply, it focuses on *why* individuals and groups in organizations act the way they do.

1.2 The two primary outcomes in organizational behaviour are job performance and organizational commitment.

1.3 A number of factors affect performance and commitment, including individual characteristics and mechanisms (personality, cultural values, and ability; job satisfaction; stress; motivation; trust, justice, and ethics; learning and decision making), relational mechanisms (communication; team characteristics and processes; power, influence, and negotiation; leadership styles and behaviours), and organizational mechanisms (organizational structure; organizational culture and change).

1.4 The effective management of organizational behaviour can help a company become more profitable because good people are a valuable resource. Not only are good people rare, but they are also hard to imitate. They create a history that cannot be bought or copied, they make numerous small decisions that cannot be observed by competitors, and they create socially complex resources such as culture, teamwork, trust, and reputation.

1.5 A theory is a collection of assertions, both verbal and symbolic, that specifies how and why variables are related, and the conditions in which they should (and should not) be related. Theories about organizational behaviour are built from a combination of interviews, observation, research reviews, and reflection. Theories form the beginning point for the scientific method and inspire hypotheses that can be tested with data.

1.6 A correlation is a statistic that expresses the strength of a relationship between two variables (ranging from 0 to ±1). In OB research, a .50 correlation is considered "strong," a .30 correlation is considered "moderate," and a .10 correlation is considered "weak."

KEY TERMS

bureaucracy
causal inference
correlation
history
human relations movement
human resources management
hypotheses
inimitable
meta-analysis
numerous small decisions
organizational behaviour (OB)
rare
resource-based view
rule of one-eighth
scientific management
socially complex resources
strategic management
theory

DISCUSSION QUESTIONS

1.1 Can you think of other service businesses that, like those listed in Table 1-3, seem to do an effective job with customer service? Which organizational behaviour topics would be most important to maintaining that high service level?

1.2 Think again of the worst co-worker you've ever had—one who did some of the things listed in Table 1-1. Think of what that co-worker's boss did (or didn't do) to try to improve his or her behaviour. What did the boss do well or poorly? What would you have done differently, and which organizational behaviour topics would have been most relevant?

1.3 Which of the individual characteristics and mechanisms in Figure 1-1 seem to drive your performance and commitment the most? Do you think you're unique in that regard, or do you think most people would answer that way?

1.4 Think of something you "know" to be true based on the method of experience, the method of intuition, or the method of authority. Could you test your knowledge using the method of science? How would you do it?

CASE: LEADING THE WAY

RBC is Canada's largest bank as measured by assets and market capitalization, and among the largest banks in the world in terms of market capitalization. It is a leading financial services company providing personal and commercial banking, wealth management services, insurance, corporate and investment banking, and transaction processing. In total, RBC employs approximately 79,000 full- and part-time employees who serve close to 16 million personal, business, public-sector, and institutional clients through offices in Canada, the United States, and 42 other countries.

The employees at RBC are very different on the surface. For instance, within Canada, the workforce demographics break down as follows: approximately 69 percent are women, 1.6 percent are Aboriginal, 3.7 percent are persons with disabilities, and 27.3 percent are visible minorities. According to Zabeen Hirji, Chief Human Resources Officer, differences in people and their talents are seen as valuable and as potential assets, and also a source of sustainable competitive advantage. It is not surprising to learn, therefore, that diversity for growth and innovation is one of RBC's core values and an integral part of their business strategy. What does this mean? Well, for RBC, this means understanding and drawing on the strength of diversity to meet the needs of clients around the world, building strong relationships in the many communities they serve, and fully engaging the talents of their people. Hirji goes on to say that "only by fully leveraging the talents and potential of a diverse workforce, can companies ensure economic prosperity in the face of changing conditions and challenging economic times."

But how does RBC implement its diversity strategy? Several key activities include hiring people who have the technical, behavioural, and diversity requirements for the position being filled, investing heavily in training throughout the company, and promoting internal mentoring relationships. One example is its Diversity Dialogues program, a reciprocal mentoring program in which mid-level women or visible minority employees are matched with senior leaders and executives. Says Cheryl Tjok-A-Tam, "it was one of the best experiences of my career. It gave me a remarkable insight not just into ways to promote diversity and inclusion but also into what it takes to advance to senior positions within the bank." According to Naim Kazmi, it was through the reciprocal mentoring program that "I got to tell my story to someone who was listening and wanted to help me bring my unique experiences and perspectives to the organization."

1.1 Most of you would agree that it is easy to get along and work with people who are similar to us. Yet diversity programs like the one described at RBC are intentionally designed to bring together people who are different in some way. Isn't this a recipe for conflict? What do you think might have to happen for these programs to be really successful? Explain.

1.2 In this case, we heard reactions from two participants in RBC's reciprocal mentoring program. Why do you think they call it reciprocal? What effects, if any, do you think participation might have on mentors? Explain.

1.3 According to Statistics Canada, approximately 51 percent of Canadians are women, 3.8 percent are Aboriginal, and 16.2 percent are visible minorities. According to Statistics Canada, we also know that more and more people will be leaving the labour force as the baby boomers decide to retire. What are the implications of these external realities for RBC and its approach to diversity management? Explain.

Sources: RBC website, www.rbc.com, accessed August 2014; Royal Bank of Canada, 2010 annual report; RBC, *2010 Diversity Progress Report*; RBC, *2009 RBC Employment Equity Report*; Statistics Canada website, www80.statcan.gc.ca/wes-esw/page1-eng.htm, accessed May 2011.

EXERCISE • IS OB COMMON SENSE?

The purpose of this exercise is to take some of the topics covered in this textbook and examine whether improving them is "just common sense." It uses groups of six participants, so your instructor will either assign you to a group of six or ask you to create your own such group. The exercise has the following steps:

1. Consider the theory diagram shown here. It explains why two "independent variables" (the quality of a movie's script and the fame of its stars) affect a "dependent variable" (how much the movie makes at the box office).

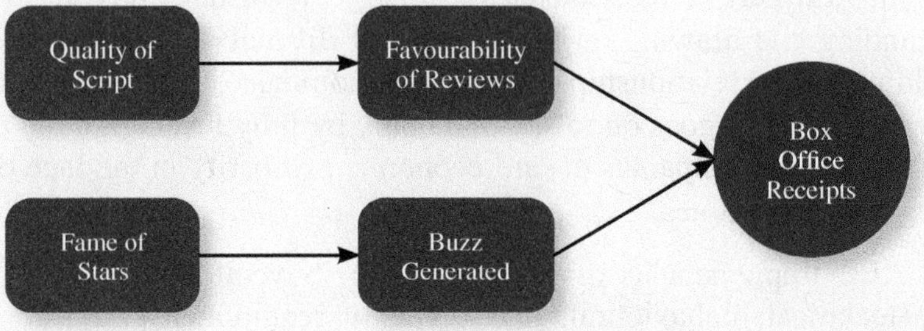

2. Now build your own theory diagram about organizational behaviour. In groups of four to six students, choose one of the following four topics to use as your dependent variable:

   - *Job satisfaction.* The pleasurable emotions felt when performing job tasks
   - *Strain.* The headaches, fatigue, or burnout resulting from workplace stress
   - *Motivation.* The intensity and persistence of job-related effort
   - *Trust in supervisor.* The willingness to allow a supervisor to have significant influence over key job issues

   Using a transparency or laptop, build a diagram that summarizes the factors that affect your chosen dependent variable. To be as comprehensive as possible, try to include at least four independent variables. Keep your books closed! You should build your diagrams using only your own experience and intuition.

3. Each group should present its diagram to the class. Do the predicted relationships make sense? Should anything be dropped? Should anything be added?

4. Now compare the theory diagram you created with those in the textbook (Figure 5-7 for job satisfaction, Figure 6-3 for stress, Figure 7-7 for motivation, and Figure 8-7 for trust in supervisor). How does your diagram compare with those in this textbook (search the boldfaced key terms for any jargon you don't understand)? Did you leave out some important independent variables or suggest some variables not supported by the academic research summarized in the chapters? If so, it shows that OB is more than just common sense.

OB ASSESSMENTS

The ***OB Assessments*** feature, which you will see in each chapter, is designed to illustrate how OB concepts actually get measured in practice. In many cases, these assessments will provide you with valuable insights into your own attitudes, skills, and personality.

The feature consists of survey questions. Two concepts are critical when evaluating how good the OB assessments are: *reliability* and *validity*. Reliability is defined as the degree to which the survey questions are free from random error; if survey questions are reliable, similar questions will yield similar answers. Validity is defined as the degree to which the survey questions seem to assess what they are meant to assess; if survey questions are valid, experts on the subject will agree that the questions seem appropriate.

Private Self-Consciousness

How reflective or introspective are you? This assessment is designed to measure private self-consciousness—the tendency to direct attention inward to better understand your attitudes and behaviours. Answer each question using the response scale provided. Then subtract your answers to the boldfaced questions from 4, with the difference being your new answers for those questions. For example, if your original answer for question 5 was 3, your new answer is 1 (= 4 – 3). Then sum your answers for the six questions.

0 Extremely Uncharacteristic of Me	1 Somewhat Uncharacteristic of Me	2 Neutral	3 Somewhat Characteristic of Me	4 Extremely Characteristic of Me	
1. I'm always trying to figure myself out.					____
2. Generally, I'm not very aware of myself.					____
3. I reflect about myself a lot.					____
4. I'm often the subject of my own daydreams.					____
5. I never scrutinize myself.					____
6. I'm generally attentive to my inner feelings.					____
7. I'm constantly examining my motives.					____
8. I sometimes have the feeling that I'm off somewhere watching myself.					____
9. I'm alert to changes in my mood.					____
10. I'm aware of the way my mind works when I work through a problem.					____

Scoring

If your scores sum up to 26 or above, you do a lot of self-reflection and are highly self-aware. You may find that many of the theories discussed in this textbook will help you better understand your attitudes and feelings about working life.

Source: From A. Fenigstein, M.F. Scheier, and A.H. Buss, "Public and Private Self-Consciousness: Assessment and Theory," *Journal of Consulting and Clinical Psychology*, Vol. 43, August 1975, pp. 522–27.

Job Performance

CHAPTER 2

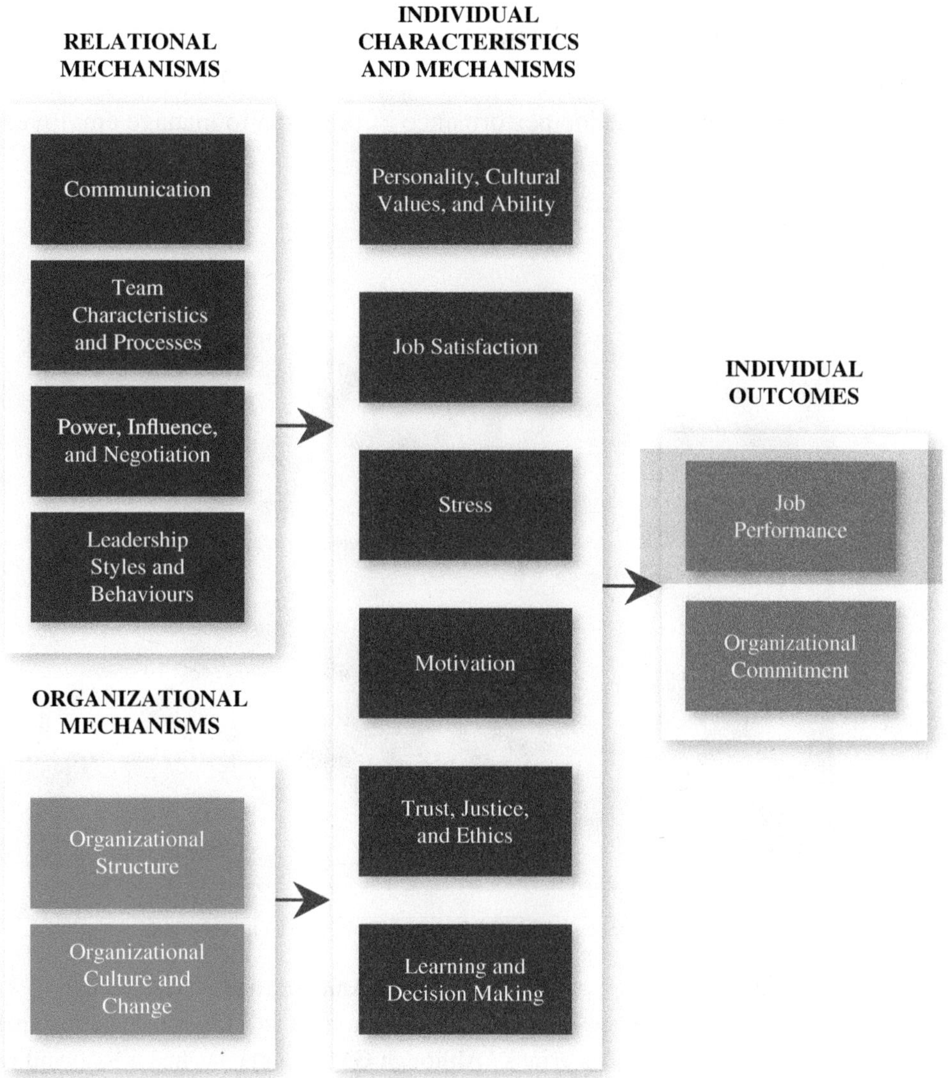
RELATIONAL MECHANISMS
Communication
Team Characteristics and Processes
Power, Influence, and Negotiation
Leadership Styles and Behaviours
ORGANIZATIONAL MECHANISMS
Organizational Structure
Organizational Culture and Change
INDIVIDUAL CHARACTERISTICS AND MECHANISMS
Personality, Cultural Values, and Ability
Job Satisfaction
Stress
Motivation
Trust, Justice, and Ethics
Learning and Decision Making
INDIVIDUAL OUTCOMES
Job Performance
Organizational Commitment

LEARNING OUTCOMES

After reading this chapter, you should be able to answer the following questions:

2.1 What is job performance?

2.2 What is task performance?

2.3 How do organizations identify the behaviours that underlie task performance?

2.4 What is citizenship behaviour?

2.5 What is counterproductive behaviour?

2.6 How can organizations use job performance information to manage employee performance?

GM Canada

© The Globe and Mail—Deborah Baic/The Canadian Press

General Motors Company is the largest automaker in North America, and a close second to Toyota in global sales of cars and trucks.[1] Its GM Canada division, headquartered in Oshawa, Ontario, operates assembly plants in Oshawa, Ingersoll, and St. Catharines.[2] Although GM Canada has had a long and rich history, the company, along with its parent, slid into financial trouble during the last recession. To assist GM Canada, in June 2009 the federal and Ontario governments provided a loan of $10.8 billion.[3] The company's management and other stakeholders knew that if GM Canada was to have a chance of becoming viable and paying back its debt to taxpayers, significant changes were in order.

The first steps were to cut costs and streamline operations. Among the most publicized actions was a significant reduction in the size of the company's salaried and hourly workforce.[4] As you might imagine, this had significant implications for the 23,000 employees who remained in Canadian operations.[5] Most obviously, with fewer employees left to do all the production, administrative, and managerial tasks required to design, manufacture, and sell cars and trucks, the number and scope of the activities employees needed to perform in their jobs increased. In short, what it took for GM's employees to be considered effective or ineffective in their jobs evolved as a consequence of the downsizing.

A second step involved a renewed vision of designing, building, and selling the world's best vehicles,[6] and this also had implications to employee job performance. Consider the five core principles that were instituted to accomplish this new vision: (1) put safety and quality first, (2) create lifelong customers, (3) innovate, (4) deliver longterm investment value to shareholders, and (5) make a positive difference in the workplace and world.[7] These principles mean that job performance at GM Canada involves activities such as promoting safety in facilities and products, listening to customers and striving to meet their needs, thinking of new ideas and implementing them to improve production processes and to delight customers, investing with the highest level of integrity, being a good team player, and volunteering in the community. Although some of these might seem indirectly related to the core task of building and selling cars and trucks, GM Canada believes these employee contributions are key to its chance of thriving in this millennium.

JOB PERFORMANCE

We begin our journey through the integrative model of organizational behaviour with job performance. Why begin with performance? Because understanding one's own performance is a critical concern for any employee, and understanding the performance of one's unit is a critical concern for any manager. Consider for a moment the job performance of your university's football coach. If you were the university's athletic director, you might gauge the coach's performance by paying attention to various behaviours. How effective are the coach's practices? Are his offensive and defensive systems well designed, and is his play-calling during games appropriate? Does he win? You might also gauge some other behaviour that falls outside the strict domain of football. Does the coach run a clean program? Do his players graduate on time? Does he represent the university well in media interviews?

This example illustrates one dilemma when examining job performance. Is performance a set of behaviours that a person does (or does not) perform, or is it the end result of those behaviours? You might be tempted to believe that it is more appropriate to define performance in terms of results rather than behaviours, because results seem more "objective" and are more connected to the central concern of managers or football coaches—the bottom line! For example, the job performance of salespeople is often measured by sales revenue generated over some time span (e.g., a month, a quarter, a year). For the most part, this makes perfect sense: Salespeople are hired by organizations to generate sales, and therefore those who meet or exceed sales goals are worth more to the organization and should be considered higher performers. It is very easy to appreciate how the sales revenue from each salesperson might be added up and used as an indicator of a business's financial performance.

However, sensible as this seems, using results to indicate job performance can create problems. First, employees contribute to their organization in ways that go beyond bottom-line results, and so evaluating an employee's performance on the basis of results alone might give you an inaccurate picture of which employees are worth more to the organization. Second, there is evidence that managers' focus on bottom-line results can create a bottom-line mentality in employees, which in turn results in *social undermining*—sabotaging co-workers' reputations or trying to make them look bad.[8]

Third, results are often influenced by factors beyond the employees' control—product quality, competition, equipment, technology, budget constraints, co-workers, and supervisors, to name a few. Fourth, even if these uncontrollable factors are less relevant in a given situation, there is another problem with a results-based view: results don't tell you how to reverse a "bad year." That is, performance feedback based on results does not provide people with the information they need to improve. As our opening example illustrates, GM Canada believes the key to its revitalization lies in practices and policies that encourage employee behaviours that support a new set of core principles. Similarly, other companies, such as Walgreens, use knowledge of the performance behaviours to create comprehensive training and development programs so that employees can be effective at various jobs they may have throughout their careers with the company.[9]

In sum, since the field of OB aims to understand, predict, and improve behaviour, we will think of job performance as *behaviour*, and use the term "results" or "job performance results" to describe the outcomes associated with those behaviours.

2.1 What is job performance?

So what types of employee behaviours constitute job performance? To understand this question, consider that **job performance** is formally defined as the value of the set of employee behaviours that contribute, either positively or negatively, to organizational goal accomplishment.[10] This definition includes behaviours within the control of employees, but it puts a boundary on which behaviours are (and are not) relevant to job performance. For example, consider the behaviour of a server in a restaurant that prides itself on world-class customer service. Texting a friend during a work break would not usually be relevant (in either a positive or a negative sense) to the accomplishment of organizational goals. That behaviour is therefore not relevant to the server's job performance. However, texting in the middle of taking a customer's order would be relevant (in a negative sense) to organizational goal accomplishment. That behaviour is therefore relevant.

job performance
Employee behaviours that contribute either positively or negatively to the accomplishment of organizational goals.

WHAT DOES IT MEAN TO BE A "GOOD PERFORMER"?

Our definition of job performance raises a number of important questions. Specifically, you might be wondering which employee behaviours fall under the umbrella of "job performance." In other words, what exactly do you have to do to be a "good performer"? We could probably spend an entire chapter just listing various behaviours relevant to job performance. However, those behaviours generally fit into three broad categories:[11] *task performance* and *citizenship behaviour*, both of which contribute positively to the organization, and *counterproductive behaviour*, which contributes negatively. The sections that follow describe these broad categories of job performance in greater detail.

2.2 What is task performance?

Task Performance

Task performance includes employee behaviours that are directly involved in the transformation of organizational resources into the goods or services that the organization produces.[12] If you read a description of a job in an employment ad online, that description will focus on task performance behaviours—the tasks, duties, and responsibilities that are a core part of the job. Put differently, task performance is the set of explicit obligations that an employee must fulfill to receive compensation and continued employment. For a flight attendant, task performance includes explaining and demonstrating safety procedures and checking the general condition of the aircraft cabin. For a firefighter, task performance includes controlling and extinguishing fires using manual and power equipment and rescuing victims from burning buildings and accident sites. For an accountant, task performance involves planning, setting up, and administering accounting systems, and preparing financial statements and reports.[13]

task performance

Employee behaviours that are directly involved in the transformation of organizational resources into the goods or services that the organization produces

Although the specific activities that constitute task performance differ widely from one job to another, task performance can also be understood in terms of more general categories. One way of categorizing task performance is to consider the extent to which the context of the job is routine or changing. **Routine task performance** involves well-known responses to demands that occur in a normal, routine, or otherwise predictable way. In these cases, employees tend to act in more or less habitual or programmed ways that vary little from one instance to another.[14] As an example of a routine task activity, you might recall watching an expressionless flight attendant robotically demonstrate how to insert the seatbelt tongue into the buckle before your flight takes off. Seatbelts haven't really changed since ... oh ... 1920, so the instructions to passengers tend to be conveyed the same way, over and over again.

routine task performance

Well-known or habitual responses by employees to predictable task demands

In contrast, **adaptive task performance**, or, more commonly, *adaptability*, involves employee responses to task demands that are novel, unusual, or at the very least, unpredictable.[15] For example, on August 2, 2005, Air France Flight 358, carrying 297 passengers and 12 crew members from Paris, France, to Toronto, Canada, skidded off the runway while landing and plunged into a ravine. Amid smoke and flames, the flight attendants quickly responded and assisted three-quarters of the 297 passengers safely off the plane within 52 seconds, before the emergency response team arrived! One minute later, the remaining passengers and 12 crew members were out safely. [16] From this example, you can see that flight attendants' task performance shifted from activities such as providing safety demonstrations and handing out beverages to performing emergency procedures to save passengers' lives. Although the attendants are trained handle situations like this, executing these behaviours effectively in the context of an actual emergency differs fundamentally from anything experienced previously.

adaptive task performance

Thoughtful responses by an employee to unique or unusual task demands

Adaptive behaviours are becoming increasingly important as globalization, technological advances, and knowledge-based work increase the pace of change in the workplace.[17] In fact, adaptive task performance has become crucial in today's global economy, in which companies have been faced with the challenge of becoming more productive with fewer employees on staff. For example, Sheboygan Falls, Wisconsin–based Johnsonville Sausage feels that adaptability is important for employees at all levels of the organization, and has invested significant resources in training to ensure that employees develop competency in this aspect of job performance. [18] As another example, at the German chemical and pharmaceutical company Bayer, the hiring of plant directors involves the search for candidates who possess not only a wide range of skills and abilities for adapting to job demands, but also competence in helping other employees adapt to workplace changes.[19] Table 2-1 provides a number of examples of adaptability relevant to many jobs in today's economy.[20]

TABLE 2-1

Behaviours Involved in Adaptability

Behaviour Title	Examples of Activities
Handling emergencies or crisis situations	Quickly analyzing options for dealing with danger or crises and their implications; making split-second decisions based on clear and focused thinking
Handling work stress	Remaining composed and cool when faced with difficult circumstances or a highly demanding workload or schedule; acting as a calming and settling influence to whom others can look for guidance
Solving problems creatively	Turning problems upside-down and inside-out to find fresh new approaches; integrating seemingly unrelated information and developing creative solutions
Dealing with uncertain and unpredictable work situations	Readily and easily changing gears in response to unpredictable or unexpected events and circumstances; effectively adjusting plans, goals, actions, or priorities to deal with changing situations
Learning work tasks, technologies, and work situations	Quickly and proficiently learning new methods or how to perform previously unlearned tasks; anticipating change in the work demands and searching for and participating in assignments or training to prepare for these changes
Demonstrating interpersonal adaptability	Being flexible and open-minded when dealing with others; listening to and considering others' viewpoints and opinions and altering own opinion when it is appropriate to do so
Demonstrating cultural adaptability	Willingly adjusting behaviour or appearance as necessary to comply with or show respect for others' values and customs; understanding the implications of one's actions and adjusting approach to maintain positive relationships with other groups, organizations, or cultures

Source: E.E. Pulakos, S. Arad, M.A. Donovan, and K.E. Plamondon, "Adaptability in the Workplace: Development of a Taxonomy of Adaptive Performance," *Journal of Applied Psychology* 85 (2000), pp. 612–24.

Finally, **creative task performance** is the degree to which individuals develop ideas or physical outcomes that are both novel and useful.[21] The necessity of including both novelty and usefulness in the definition of creativity can be illustrated with the following example of what effective performance for a swimsuit designer involves. Consider first the case of a designer who suggests in a meeting that next season's line of swimsuits be made entirely out of chromeplated steel. Although this idea might be very novel, for many reasons it is not likely to be useful. Indeed, someone who offered an idea like this would likely be considered silly rather than creative. Someone else suggests in the meeting that swimsuits for next season be made out of materials that are attractive and comfortable. Although under some circumstances such an idea might be useful, the idea is not novel because attractiveness and comfort are generally accepted design elements for swimsuits. Someone who offered an idea like this might be appreciated for offering input, but no one would consider him or her particularly creative. Finally, a third designer suggests that perhaps a two-piece design would be preferred by women, rather than a more traditional one-piece design. Although such an idea would not be considered creative today, it certainly was in 1946 when, in separate but nearly simultaneous efforts, Jacques Heim and Louis Reard introduced the bikini. [22]

creative task performance

Ideals or physical outcomes that are both novel and useful

Although you might be tempted to believe creative task performance is only relevant to jobs such as artist and inventor, its emphasis has been increasing across a wide variety of jobs. Indeed, more than half the total wages and salary in the Canada and the United States are paid to employees who need to be creative as part of their jobs, and consequently some have argued we are at the "dawn of the creative age."[23] This increase can be explained by the rapid technological change and intense competition that mark today's business landscape.[24] In this context, employee creativity is necessary to spark the types of innovations that enable organizations to stay ahead of their competition. Creative ideas do not always get implemented, making it important to recognize creative performance behaviours, and the creative outcomes that result from these behaviours.[25]

2.3 How do organizations identify the behaviours that underlie task performance?

Now that we've given you a general understanding of task performance behaviours, you might be wondering how organizations identify the sets of behaviours that represent "task performance" for different jobs. Many organizations do this by conducting a **job analysis**. There are many different ways to conduct a job analysis, but most boil down to three steps. First, a list of all the activities involved in the job is generated. This list generally draws on data from several sources, including observations, surveys, and interviews of employees. Second, each activity on this list is rated by "subject-matter experts" according to things like the importance and frequency of the activity. These persons generally have experience at the job in question or have managed people who perform it, and therefore are in a position to judge the degree to which specific activities contribute to the organization. Third, the activities rated highly in terms of their importance and frequency are retained and used to define task performance. Those retained behaviours then find their way into training programs as learning objectives and into performance appraisal systems as measures to evaluate task performance.

job analysis

A process by which an organization determines requirements of specific jobs

Consider the job of customer service representative (CSR) at your local bank. Apart from the technical activities routinely performed (e.g., processing customer cash deposits and withdrawals, obtaining and processing client information, balancing daily transactions using computer programs), many CSRs are expected to sell a variety of banking services and products and perform a wide range of face-to-face customer service behaviours.[26] Examples of the behaviours in these performance areas are listed in Table 2-2. After the behavioural information is collected for each CSR (from supervisors, co-workers, or clients), the bank manager is in a position to provide feedback and coaching to the employee about which types of behaviours need to change or improve. Put yourself in the place of a CSR for a moment. Wouldn't you rather have your task performance evaluated on the basis of the behaviours in Table 2-2 than on some overall index of results (e.g., errors committed, shortages, products sold)? After all, those behaviours are completely within your control, and the feedback from your boss will be more informative and helpful than the simple directive "Sell more next year."

TABLE 2-2

Performance Review Form for a Customer Service Representative at the Bank

Important Task Behaviours
Smiles when interacting with customers
Is attentive and considerate when communicating with customers
Demonstrates some flexibility with banking procedures to accommodate customers
Reads all available literature pertaining to new products/services
Follows the planned weekly selling "script"
Suggests potential bank services during normal counter interactions
Checks to see whether all pertinent information has been included on paperwork
Follows normal banking procedures regarding financial transactions
Processes client transactions quickly
Shares information that is relevant for others to carry out their assignments
Helps other CSRs who are experiencing difficulties
Develops and maintains effective working relationships with others in the bank

When organizations find it impractical to use job analysis to identify the set of behaviours needed to define task performance, they can turn to a database the government has created to help describe a wide variety of jobs. The **National Occupational Classification** (NOC), the nationally accepted reference on occupations in Canada, organizes over 40,000 job titles into 500 occupational group descriptions.[27] It is used daily by thousands of people to compile, analyze, and communicate information about occupations, and to understand the jobs found throughout Canada's labour market.

National Occupational Classification
A national database of occupations in Canada, organizing over 40,000 job titles into 500 occupational group descriptions

Of course, the NOC represents only a first step in figuring out the important tasks for a given job. Many organizations ask their employees to perform tasks that their competitors do not, so that their workforce performance is assessed in a unique and valuable way. The NOC cannot capture those sorts of unique task requirements, the "numerous small decisions" that distinguish the most effective organizations from their competitors.

Figure 2-1 shows the NOC output for a CSR. As you can see, it conveys that CSRs who work in financial service organizations perform routine banking transactions and respond to customers' needs. What it cannot do is convey the unique ways these activities are enacted in a particular corporate culture. For instance, a bank with a strong customer focus might encourage its CSRs to be flexible with policies and procedures to accommodate customer needs. Thus, though the NOC may be a good place to start, task information from its database should be supplemented with information regarding behaviours that support the organization's specific values and strategies.

FIGURE 2-1

National Occupational Classification Results for CSRs in Financial Institutions (Code 6551)

Customer service representatives in this unit group process customers' financial transactions and provide information on related banking products and services. They are employed by banks, trust companies, credit unions and similar financial institutions.

Main Duties

Customer service representatives in this unit group perform some or all of the following duties:

- Process customer cash deposits and withdrawals, cheques, transfers, bills and credit card payments, money orders, certified cheques, and other, related banking transactions
- Obtain and process information required for the provision of services, such as opening accounts and savings plans and purchasing bonds
- Sell travellers' cheques, foreign currency and money orders
- Answer enquiries and resolve problems or discrepancies concerning customers' accounts
- Inform customers of available banking products and services to address their needs

Source: Adapted from Human Resources and Skills Development Canada, 2011, *National Occupation Classification 2011*, ISBN 971-1-100-20020-0, p. 444.

Before concluding our section on task performance, it is important to note that task performance behaviours are not simply performed or not performed. Although poor performers often fail to complete required behaviours, it is just as true that the best performers often exceed all expectations for those behaviours. In fact, you can probably think of employees who have exhibited truly extraordinary performance.

Consider Chesley B. Sullenberger, the pilot of US Airways Flight 1549, which lost power after hitting a flock of birds shortly after taking off from New York's LaGuardia Airport on January 15, 2009.[28] Sullenberger calmly discussed the problem with air traffic control and decided that the only reasonable course of action was to land in the Hudson River. Three minutes after the bird strike, he executed a textbook landing on the water, saving the lives of all 150 passengers and crew. Experts agree that Sullenberger's performance that day was remarkable. Not only did he accurately assess the situation and make the right decision about where to ditch the aircraft, he also piloted the landing perfectly. If the plane had approached the water too slowly, it would have lost lift and crashed into the water nose first; if the plane had been going too fast, it would have flipped, cartwheeled, and disintegrated.[29]

The pilot of Flight 1549 displayed exceptional performance and saved the lives of his passengers and crew.

© AP Photo/Steven Day

2.4 What is citizenship behaviour?

Citizenship Behaviour

Sometimes employees go the extra mile by actually engaging in behaviours that are not within their job description, and so do not fall under the broad heading of task performance. This brings us to the second category of job performance, **citizenship behaviour**, defined as voluntary employee activities that may or may not be rewarded but that contribute to the organization by improving the overall quality of the setting in which work takes place.[30] Have you ever had a co-worker or fellow student who was especially willing to help someone who was struggling? Who typically attended optional meetings or social functions to support his or her colleagues? Who maintained a good attitude, even in trying times? We tend to call those people "good citizens" or "good soldiers."[31] High levels of citizenship behaviour earn them such titles. Although many different types of behaviours might seem to fit the definition of citizenship behaviour, research suggests two main categories that differ according to who benefits, co-workers or the organization (see Figure 2-2).[32]

FIGURE 2-2

Types of Citizenship Behaviours

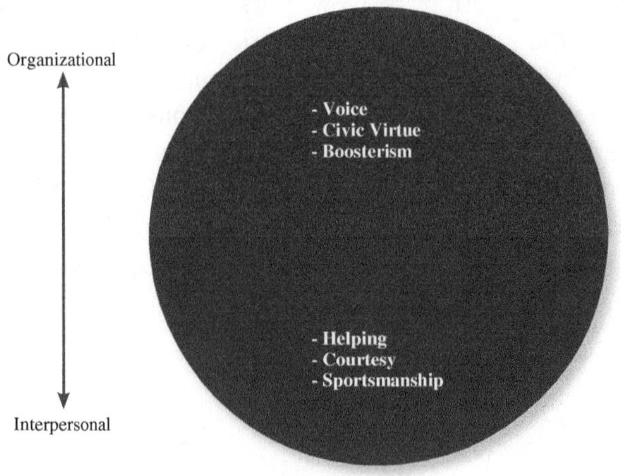

citizenship behaviour
Voluntary employee behaviours that contribute to organizational goals by improving the context in which work takes place

The first category of citizenship behaviour is the one with which you're most likely to be familiar: **interpersonal citizenship behaviour**. Such behaviour benefits co-workers and colleagues and involves assisting, supporting, and developing other organization members in a way that goes beyond normal job expectations.[33] For example, **helping** involves assisting co-workers who have heavy workloads, aiding them with personal matters, and showing new employees the ropes. (Do you consider yourself a helpful person? Check the ***OB Assessments*** feature at the end of this chapter to see how helpful you really are.) **Courtesy** refers to keeping co-workers informed about matters that are relevant to them. Some employees have a tendency to keep relevant facts and events secret. Good citizens do the opposite; they keep others in the loop because they never know what information might be useful to someone else. **Sportsmanship** involves maintaining a good attitude with co-workers, even when they've done something annoying or the unit is going through tough times. Whining and complaining are contagious; good citizens avoid being one who is always making mountains out of molehills.

interpersonal citizenship behaviour
Going beyond normal job expectations to assist, support, and develop co-workers and colleagues

helping
Assisting co-workers who have heavy workloads, aiding them with personal matters, and showing new employees the ropes

courtesy
Sharing important information with co-workers

sportsmanship
Maintaining a positive attitude with co-workers through good and bad times

Although interpersonal citizenship behaviour is important in many different job contexts, it may be especially important in small groups or teams. A team with members who tend to be helpful, respectful, and courteous is also likely to have a positive team atmosphere in which members trust one another. This type of situation is essential to foster the willingness of team members to work toward a common team goal rather than goals that may be more self-serving.[34] In fact, if you think about the behaviours that commonly fall under the "teamwork" heading, you'll probably agree that most are examples of interpersonal citizenship behaviour (see Chapter 11 for more discussion of such issues).[35]

The second category of citizenship behaviour is **organizational citizenship behaviour**, which means supporting and defending the company, working to improve its operations, and being especially loyal to it.[36] For example, **voice** involves speaking up and offering constructive suggestions for change. Good citizens react to bad rules or policies by constructively trying to change them as opposed to passively complaining about them (see Chapter 3 on organizational commitment for more discussion of such issues).[37] **Civic virtue** refers to participating in the company's operations at a deeper-than-normal level by attending voluntary meetings and functions, reading and keeping up with organizational announcements, and keeping abreast of business news that affects the company. **Boosterism** means representing the organization in a positive way when out in public, away from the office, and away from work. Think of friends you have had who worked for a restaurant. Did they always say good things about the restaurant when talking to you and keep any "kitchen horror stories" to themselves? If so, they were showing high levels of boosterism.

organizational citizenship behaviour
Going beyond normal expectations to improve operations of the organization, defend it, and be loyal to it

voice
Speaking up to offer constructive suggestions for change, often in reaction to a negative work event

civic virtue
Participating in company operations at a deeper-than-normal level through voluntary meetings, readings, and keeping up with news that affects the company

boosterism
Positively representing the organization when in public

Three important points should be emphasized about citizenship behaviours. First, as you have probably realized, citizenship behaviours are relevant in virtually any job, regardless of the particular nature of its tasks,[38] and research suggests that these behaviours can boost organizational effectiveness.[39] As examples, research conducted in a paper mill found that the quantity and quality of crew output was higher in crews that included more workers who engaged in citizenship behaviour.[40] Research in 30 restaurants also showed that higher levels of citizenship behaviour promoted higher revenue, better operating efficiency, higher customer satisfaction, higher performance quality, less food waste, and fewer customer complaints.[41] Thus, it seems clear that citizenship behaviours have a significant influence on the bottom line.

Second, because citizenship behaviours are relatively discretionary and influenced by the specific situation the employee is working in, they can vary significantly over time.[42] In other words, an employee who engages in citizenship behaviour at one time might not engage in citizenship behaviour at another. Perhaps you yourself have had a very positive experience working with another student or colleague on a project and been willing to make an extra effort to be helpful, but at some point the person did something that made you much less positive about the collaboration and you decided to focus your energies elsewhere.

Third, from an employee's perspective, it may be tempting to discount the importance of citizenship behaviours—to just focus on your own job tasks and leave aside any "extra" stuff. After all, citizenship behaviours appear to be voluntary and optional, whereas task performance requirements are not. However, discounting citizenship behaviours is a bad idea because supervisors don't always view such actions as optional. In fact, research on computer salespeople, insurance agents, petrochemical salespeople, pharmaceutical sales managers, office furniture makers, and sewing machine operators has shown that citizenship behaviours relate strongly to supervisor evaluations of job performance, even when differences in task performance are also considered.[43] As we discuss in our ***OB Internationally*** feature, the tendency of supervisors to consider citizenship behaviours in evaluating overall job performance appears to hold even across countries with vastly different cultures.[44] Of course, this issue has a lot of relevance to you, given that in most organizations, evaluations of employee job performance play a significant role in determining employee pay and promotions. Indeed, employee citizenship behaviour has been found to influence the salary and promotion recommendations people receive, over and above their task performance.[45] Put simply, it pays to be a good citizen!

2.5 What is counterproductive behaviour?

Counterproductive Behaviour

Now we move from the "good soldiers" to the "bad apples." Whereas task performance and citizenship behaviour refer to employee activities that help the organization achieve its goals and objectives, other activities in which employees engage do just the opposite. This third broad category of job performance is **counterproductive behaviour**, defined as employee behaviours that intentionally hinder organizational goal accomplishment. "Intentionally" is a key aspect of this definition; these are things that employees mean to do, not things they accidentally do. Although there are many different kinds of counterproductive behaviours, research suggests that—like task performance and citizenship behaviour—they can be grouped into more specific categories (see Figure 2-3).[46]

counterproductive behaviour
Employee behaviours that intentionally hinder organizational goal accomplishment

FIGURE 2-3

Types of Counterproductive Behaviours

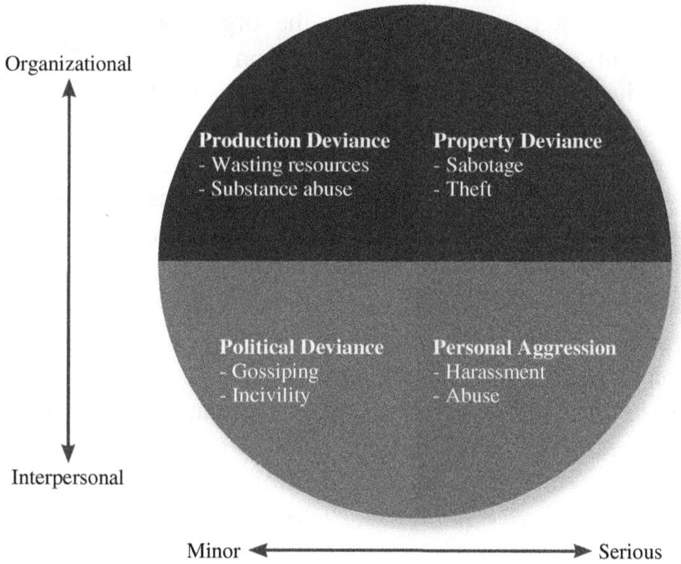

Source: Adapted from S.L. Robinson and R.J. Bennett, "A Typology of Deviant Workplace Behaviours: A Multidimensional Scaling Study," *Academy of Management Journal* 38 (1995), pp. 555–72.

OB INTERNATIONALLY

As we've already explained, citizenship behaviour tends to be viewed as relatively voluntary because it's not often explicitly outlined in job descriptions or directly rewarded. However, people in organizations vary in their beliefs regarding the degree to which citizenship behaviour is truly voluntary, and these differences have important implications.[47] As an example, consider a situation in which an employee engages in citizenship behaviours because of his or her belief that the behaviours are part of the job. However, this employee works for a supervisor who believes that citizenship behaviours are unnecessary. Assuming that the supervisor would not consider the citizenship behaviours on a performance evaluation, the employee would likely react negatively because he or she has not been recognized for putting effort into activities that help other members of the organization.

So what types of factors cause differences in beliefs regarding whether citizenship behaviour is discretionary? One that seems important is national culture. It is widely believed that the culture in countries like the United States, Canada, and the Netherlands encourages behaviours that support competition and individual achievement, whereas the culture in countries like China, Colombia, and Portugal encourages behaviours that promote cooperation and group interests over self-interest.[48] On the basis of these cultural differences, it seems logical to expect that people from the former set of countries would consider citizenship behaviour relatively unimportant compared with people from the latter set of countries. In reality, however, the findings from one recent study comparing Canadian and Chinese managers found that this cultural stereotype was simply not true.[49] Managers in both countries not only took citizenship behaviour into account when evaluating overall job performance, but gave the same weight to citizenship behaviour in their overall evaluation. One explanation for this is that the realities of running effective business organizations in a global economy have a significantly stronger impact on managerial practices than do cultural norms. It is important to note that the results of this study do not mean we can ignore culture when trying to understand employee job performance. In fact, there is reason to believe cultural differences are important considerations when designing and implementing systems to manage employee performance.[50]

Property deviance refers to behaviours that harm the organization's assets and possessions. For example, **sabotage** represents the intentional destruction of physical equipment, organizational processes, or company products. Do you know what a laser disc is? Probably not—and the reason you don't is because of sabotage. A company called DiscoVision (a subsidiary of MCA) manufactured laser discs in the late 1970s, with popular movie titles like *Smokey and the Bandit* and *Jaws* retailing for $15.95. Although this level matches the price of DVDs today, it was far less than the $50–$100 needed to buy videocassettes (which were of inferior quality) at the time. Unfortunately, laser discs had to be manufactured in "clean rooms," because specs of dust or debris could cause the image on the television to freeze, repeat, skip, or drop out. When MCA merged with IBM in 1979, the morale of the employees fell, and counterproductive behaviours began to occur. Employees sabotaged the devices that measured the cleanliness of the rooms. They also began eating in the rooms—even "popping" potato chip bags to send food particles into the air. This sabotage eventually created a 90 percent disc failure rate that completely alienated customers. As a result, despite its much lower production costs and higher-quality picture, the laser disc disappeared, and the organizations that supported the technology suffered incredible losses.[51]

property deviance
Behaviours that harm the organization's assets and possessions

sabotage
Intentional destruction of equipment, organizational processes, or company products

If you've never heard of the laser disc, you've certainly eaten in a restaurant. The cost of counterproductive behaviours in the restaurant industry is estimated to be 2–3 percent of revenues per year, but what may be more disturbing is the nature of those counterproductive behaviours.[52] Thirty-one percent of employees who responded to a survey knowingly served improperly prepared food, 13 percent intentionally sabotaged the work of other employees, and 12 percent admitted to intentionally contaminating food they prepared or served to a customer (yuck!). At minimum, such sabotage can lead to a bad meal and a customer's resolve never to return. It can also lead to food poisoning, health code violations, and a damaging lawsuit. Employees who sabotage customers may do so, under certain circumstances, as a response to perceived mistreatment by customers. It's important to note, however, that retaliation in this manner is not justified, and so it is still considered a form of counterproductive behaviour.[53]

Counterproductive behaviour by employees can be destructive to the organization's goals. In some settings, such as a restaurant, it can even be a problem for customers.

© Frank Wartenberg/Getty Images

Theft, another form of property deviance, can be just as expensive as sabotage (if not more). Research has shown that up to three-quarters of all employees have engaged in this type of behaviour, and the cost is staggering.[54] For example, one study estimated that 47 percent of store inventory shrinkage was due to employee theft and that this type of theft costs organizations approximately $14.6 billion per year.[55] Maybe you've enjoyed discounted (or even free) food and drinks at a restaurant or bar because you had friends who worked there; but, though beneficial to you, it's clearly quite counterproductive from the perspective of the organization.

theft

Stealing company products or equipment from the organization

Production deviance is also directed against the organization but focuses specifically on reducing the efficiency of work output. **Wasting resources** is the most common form of production deviance, when employees use too many materials or too much time to do too little work. Manufacturing employees who use too much wood or metal are wasting resources, as are restaurant employees who use too many ingredients when preparing the food. Workers who work too slowly or take too many breaks are also wasting resources because "time is money" (see Chapter 3 on organizational commitment for more discussion of such issues). **Substance abuse** represents another form of production deviance. If employees abuse drugs or alcohol while on the job or shortly before coming to work, the efficiency of their production will be compromised because their work will be done more slowly and less accurately.

production deviance
Intentionally reducing organizational efficiency of work output

wasting resources
Using too many materials or too much time to do too little work

substance abuse
The abuse of drugs or alcohol before coming to work or while on the job

In contrast to property and production deviance, **political deviance** refers to behaviours that intentionally disadvantage other individuals rather than the larger organization. **Gossiping**—casual conversations about other people in which the facts are not confirmed as true—is one form of political deviance. Everyone has experienced gossip at some point in time and knows the emotions people feel when they discover that other people have been talking about them. Such behaviours undermine the morale of both friendship groups and work groups. **Incivility** represents communication that is rude, impolite, discourteous, and lacking in good manners.[56] The erosion of manners seems like a society-wide phenomenon, and the workplace is no exception. Taken one by one, these political forms of counterproductive behaviour might not seem particularly serious to most organizations. However, in the aggregate, acts of political deviance can create an organizational climate characterized by distrust and unhealthy competitiveness. Beyond the productivity losses that result from a lack of cooperation among employees, organizations with this type of climate likely cannot retain good employees. Moreover, there's some evidence that gossip and incivility can "spiral"—get worse and worse until some tipping point, after which more serious forms of interpersonal actions can occur.[57]

political deviance
Behaviours that intentionally disadvantage other individuals

gossiping
Casual conversations about other people in which the facts are not confirmed as true

incivility
Communication that is rude, impolite, discourteous, and lacking in good manners

Those more serious interpersonal actions may involve **personal aggression**, defined as hostile verbal and physical actions directed toward other employees. **Harassment** falls under this heading and occurs when employees are subjected to unwanted physical contact or verbal remarks from a colleague. **Abuse** also falls under this heading; it occurs when an employee is assaulted or endangered in such a way that physical and psychological injuries may occur. You might be surprised to know that even the most extreme forms of personal aggression are actually quite prevalent in organizations. For example, on average in the United States about one employee each week is killed by a current or previous co-worker[58] (thankfully we live in Canada!). Sadly, millions of people are bullied at work each year.[59] Bullying involves psychological harassment and abuse directed toward an individual or group of individuals.[60] Examples of bullying include humiliation, social isolation, and systematic maltreatment, all of which results in the target of these behaviours feeling helpless.[61] It might surprise you to learn that the source of the bullying is often a boss. We don't believe that bosses are inherently evil, but some undoubtedly lose sight of the line between being tough and being a bully, and that what matters isn't the intent of the behaviour, but rather the perception of the person to whom the behaviour is targeted.[62] Actual or alleged acts of personal aggression can also be quite costly to organizations in terms of reputation. In recent years, for instance, the Royal Canadian Mounted Police has been forced to defend itself from allegations that some of its male members mistreated and harassed female staff simply because they were female.[63]

personal aggression
Hostile verbal and physical actions directed toward other employees

harassment
Unwanted physical contact or verbal remarks from a colleague

abuse
Employee assault or endangerment from which physical and psychological injuries may occur

OB RESEARCH IN CANADA

Dr. Michelle Inness, at the University of Alberta School of Business, is an expert on both the darker and the more affirmative forms of organizational behaviour. For example, her research has explored different forms of counterproductive behaviour, such as workplace aggression and substance abuse, and what managers can do to mitigate these negative behaviours. In stark contrast, Dr. Inness also has looked also at why some employees feel love for their work, and the factors that influence this feeling. In her words, "most people will spend a significant portion of their lives in the workplace. It is so fascinating how our day-to-day work experiences play such a major role in our overall life happiness."

Dr. Inness's publications have appeared in leading journals such as the Journal of Applied Psychology. She frequently gives talks on topics such as leadership, employee motivation, and fostering organizational citizenship behaviour. For more information, please visit her website at business.ualberta.ca/MichelleInness.

Three points should be noted about counterproductive behaviour. First, there is evidence that people who engage in one form of counterproductive behaviour also engage in others.[64] In other words, such behaviours tend to represent a pattern rather than isolated incidents. Second, like citizenship behaviour, counterproductive behaviour is relevant to any job. It doesn't matter what the job entails; there are going to be things to steal, resources to waste, and people to be uncivil toward. Third, it is often surprising which employees engage in counterproductive behaviour. You might suppose that it would be poor performers who mostly engage in it, and that highly effective performers do not. In fact, however, there is only a weak negative correlation between task performance and counterproductive behaviour.[65] If you think about it for a moment, you can probably come up with a few examples of people who are very effective in their jobs but also engage in high levels of counterproductive behaviour. Sometimes the best task performers are those who can best get away with it, because they are less likely to be suspected or blamed. Moreover, counterproductive behaviours might even be tolerated for a while when the individual is able to effectively accomplish very challenging tasks. Our ***OB on Screen*** feature illustrates an example of this apparent contradiction in behaviour.

OB ON SCREEN

FLIGHT

The FAA and the NTSB took 10 pilots, placed them in simulators, re-created the events that led to this plane falling out of the sky. Do you know how many of them were able to safely land the planes? Not one. Every pilot crashed the aircraft, killed everybody on board. You were the only one who could do it!

With those words, South Jet Air attorney Hugh Lang (Don Cheadle) tells Captain Whip Whitaker (Denzel Washington) that his performance as a pilot is extraordinary in the movie *Flight* (Dir. Robert Zemeckis, Paramount Pictures, 2012). On a trip from Orlando to Atlanta, the aircraft Whip was flying malfunctioned, and to get the plane out of an uncontrollable dive, Whip managed to invert it and fly it this way, eventually rolling it upright just before crash-landing in a field. Normally, a pilot who performs such a feat, and who saves the lives of most of his passengers and crew, would be considered a hero. But there's a hitch. You see, Whip not only consumed copious amounts of alcohol and drugs before flying, but he actually mixed himself a strong cocktail *while* flying. Although Whip had nothing to do with the equipment malfunction, and in spite of his heroics, responsibility for the crash and for the six deaths that resulted would likely rest with him and his employer if investigators found out about his condition.

The movie centres on a dichotomy in Whip's job performance. On the one hand, he's remarkably competent in the activities involved in flying a jet. In fact, to the extent that the equipment malfunction was totally unforeseen and required altogether new responses to cope with the situation, Whip is particularly strong in the adaptive performance aspect of task performance. On the other hand, substance abuse is considered a form of counterproductive behaviour. This contrast in positive and negative job performance behaviours should serve as a reminder that it is a mistake to presume that employees are effective or ineffective in their jobs on the basis of how well they do in one aspect of job performance, however visible this aspect may be.

Summary: What Does It Mean to Be a "Good Performer"?

So what does it mean to be a "good performer"? As is shown in Figure 2-4, being a good performer means a lot of different things. It means employees are good at the particular job tasks that fall within their job description, whether those tasks are routine or require adaptability or creativity. But it also means that employees engage in citizenship behaviours directed at both co-workers and the larger organization, and that they refrain from engaging in the counterproductive behaviours that can badly damage the climate of an organization. The goal for any manager is therefore to have employees who fulfill all three conditions of this description.

FIGURE 2-4

What Does It Mean to Be a "Good Performer"?

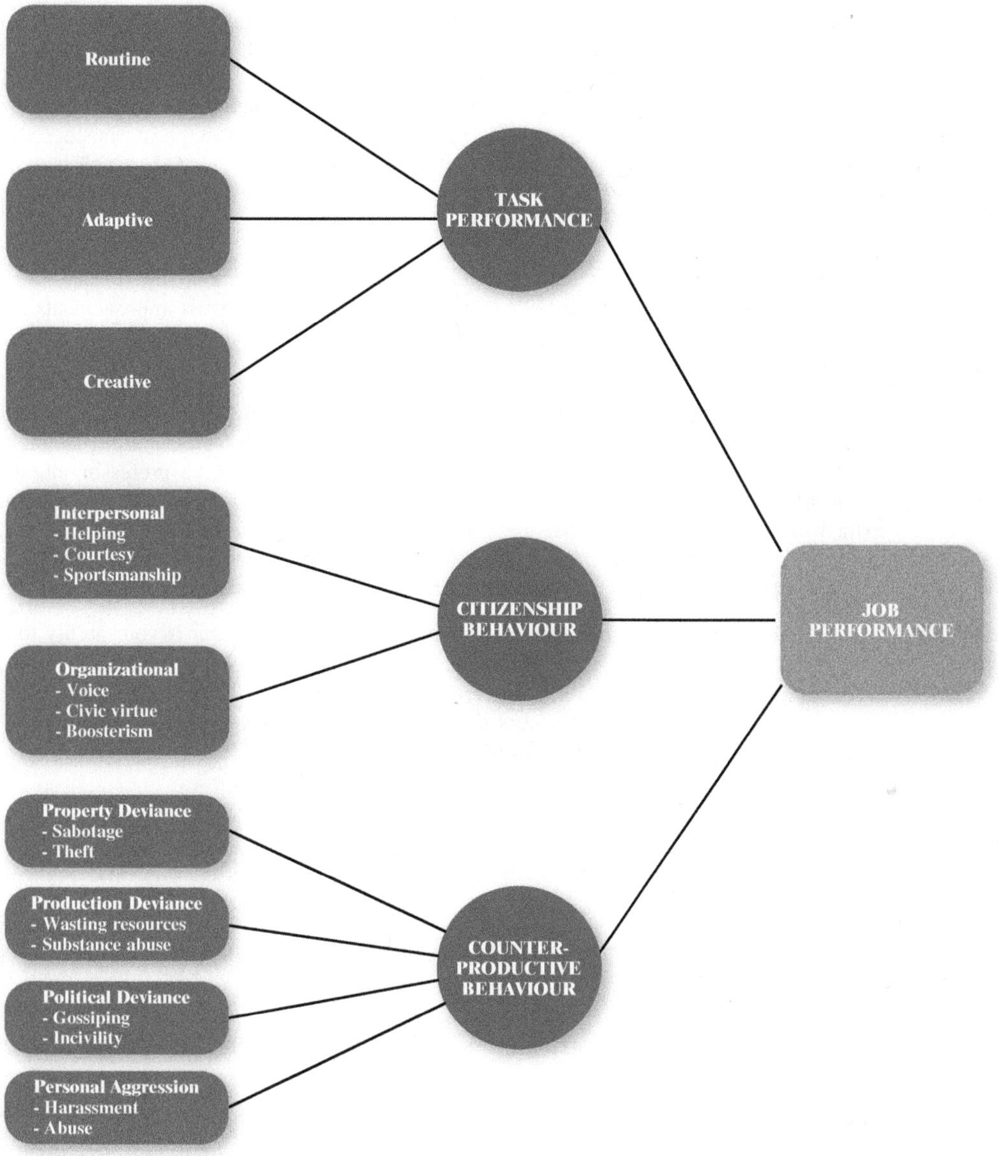

As you move forward in this book, you'll notice that almost every chapter includes a description of how that chapter's topic relates to job performance. For example, Chapter 5 on job satisfaction describes how employees' feelings about their jobs affect their job performance. You'll find that some chapter topics seem more strongly correlated with task performance, whereas others are more strongly correlated with citizenship behaviour or counterproductive behaviour. Such differences will help you understand exactly how and why a given topic, be it satisfaction, stress, motivation, or something else, influences job performance. By the end of the book, you'll have developed a good sense of the most powerful drivers of job performance. That knowledge will come in handy in your working life and, as described in our ***OB for Students*** feature, in your academic life as well.

OB FOR STUDENTS

What does performance mean to you as a student? For many of you, performance is likely to boil down to exam grades, course grades, and ultimately, grade point average. Although grades are certainly an important indicator of your effectiveness as a student, they are actually the results of your performance. So instead, think for a moment about the important types of performance behaviours that contribute to your effectiveness as a student. It is likely that most of you think about activities such as attending class, paying attention to lectures, completing assigned readings and other assignments, and studying for exams. Note that these activities might all be considered task performance. Each activity is focused on transforming information from readings, lectures, and experiences into knowledge, which is assessed using quizzes, exams, and other assignments. But did you ever consider how citizenship behaviour and counterproductive behaviour might contribute to your effectiveness as a student?

- First, in classes that require teamwork, your team will likely perform at a much higher level if you and your teammates are helpful to one another, actively participate in team meetings, and suggest improvements to the team's routine. Similarly, your team will likely perform at a lower level if you and your teammates gossip about one another, refuse to share information, or blame one another for errors.
- Second, many courses devote points to participation. It may be that displays of citizenship and counterproductive behaviours can influence professors' assessments of participation points. Although we are not advocating using these behaviours as "impression management" tactics, you can probably understand why a professor might give more participation points to a student who had high attendance, participated above the norm, attended voluntary office hours, and did extra work to improve his or her class standing. Similarly, you can probably understand why a professor might give fewer participation points to a student who routinely showed up late for class, chatted with neighbours and read newspapers during lectures, and was confrontational or argumentative.
- Third, it might be argued that the ultimate indicator of your effectiveness as a student is your ability to apply what you've learned to the real world. As we have noted elsewhere, citizenship and counterproductive behaviour will likely be considered by your employer when evaluating your overall performance. In essence, your career may depend on whether you routinely engage in the right behaviours on the job, even if they are not formally part of the job description (e.g., maintaining a good attitude with co-workers).

2.6 How can organizations use job performance information to manage employee performance?

APPLICATION: PERFORMANCE MANAGEMENT

Now that we have described what job performance is, it is time to discuss how organizations use job performance information. Good companies understand the linkage between employee job performance and organizational performance, and as a consequence they invest resources collecting information about employee performance so that it can be managed in a way that helps the organization achieve its mission. In this section, we describe general ways in which job performance information is used to manage employee performance. We spotlight four of the most representative practices: management by objectives, behaviourally anchored rating scales, 360-degree feedback, and forced ranking. We also discuss how social networking software is being used for performance management purposes in organizations.

Management by Objectives

Management by objectives (MBO) is a management philosophy that bases an employee's evaluations on whether the employee achieves specific performance goals.[66] How does MBO work? Typically, an employee meets with his or her manager to develop a set of mutually agreed-upon objectives that are measurable and specific (see Chapter 7 on motivation for more discussion of such issues). In addition, the employee and the manager agree on the time period for achieving those objectives and the methods used to do so. An example of a performance objective for a line manager in a factory might be something like: "Reducing production waste by 35 percent within three months by developing and implementing new production procedures." Employee performance can then be gauged by referring to the degree to which the employee achieves results consistent with the objectives. If the line manager cuts production waste by 37 percent within three months, his or her performance would be deemed effective, whereas if the manager only cuts production waste by 2 percent, his or her performance would be deemed ineffective. MBO is best suited for managing the performance of employees who work in contexts in which objective measures of performance can be quantified.

management by objectives (MBO)
A management philosophy that bases employee evaluations on whether specific performance goals have been met

Behaviourally Anchored Rating Scales

You may have noticed that MBO emphasizes the results of job performance as much as it does the performance behaviours themselves. In contrast, **behaviourally anchored rating scales (BARS)** measure performance by directly assessing job performance behaviours. The BARS approach uses "critical incidents"—short descriptions of effective and ineffective behaviours—to create a measure that can be used to evaluate employee performance.

Consider the measure of task performance shown in Table 2-3, which focuses on the "planning, organizing, and scheduling" dimension of task performance for a manager.[67] The rater reads the behaviours on the far left column of the measure and matches actual observations of the behaviour of the manager being rated to the corresponding level on the measure by putting a check in the blank.[68]

behaviourally anchored rating scales
Use of examples of critical incidents to evaluate an employee's job performance behaviours directly

Typically, supervisors rate several performance dimensions using BARS and score an employee's overall job performance by taking the average value across all the dimensions. Because the critical incidents convey the precise kinds of behaviours that are effective and ineffective, feedback from BARS can help an employee develop and improve over time. That is, employees can develop an appreciation of the types of behaviours that would make them effective. Such information provides a nice complement to MBO, which is less capable of providing specific feedback about why an objective might have been missed.

360-Degree Feedback

The **360-degree feedback** approach involves collecting performance information not just from the supervisor but from anyone else who might have first-hand knowledge about the employee's performance behaviours. These other sources are typically co-workers, subordinates, customers, and the employee him- or herself. With the exception of the supervisor's ratings, the ratings are combined so that the raters can remain anonymous to the employee. Most 360-degree feedback systems also ask the employee to provide ratings of his or her own performance. The hope is that this 360-degree perspective will provide a more balanced and comprehensive examination of performance. By explicitly comparing self-provided ratings with the ratings obtained from others, employees can develop a better sense of how their performance may be deficient in the eyes of others and exactly where they need to focus their energies to improve.

TABLE 2-3

BARS Example for "Planning, Organizing, and Scheduling"

Rating	Rating	Behavioural Anchors
[7]	Excellent	• Develops a comprehensive project plan, documents it well, obtains required approval, and distributes the plan to all concerned.
[6]	Very Good	• Plans, communicates, and observes milestones; states week by week where the project stands relative to plans. Maintains up-to-date charts of project accomplishment and backlogs and uses these to optimize any schedule modifications required. • Experiences occasional minor operational problems but communicates effectively.
[5]	Good	• Lays out all the parts of a job and schedules each part to beat schedule; will allow for slack. • Satisfies customer's time constraints; time and cost overruns occur infrequently.
[4]	Average	• Makes a list of due dates and revises them as the project progresses, usually adding unforeseen events; investigates frequent customer complaints. • May have a sound plan but does not keep track of milestones; does not report slippages in schedule or other problems as they occur.
[3]	Below Average	• Plans are poorly defined; unrealistic time schedules are common. • Cannot plan more than a day or two ahead; has no concept of a realistic project due date.
[2]	Very Poor	• Has no plan or schedule of work segments to be performed. • Does little or no planning for project assignments.
[1]	Unacceptable	• Seldom, if ever, completes project because of lack of planning and does not seem to care. • Fails consistently due to lack of planning and does not inquire about how to improve.

Source: D.G. Shaw, C.E. Schneier, and R.W. Beatty, "Managing Performance with a Behaviorally Based Appraisal System," in *Applying Psychology in Business: The Handbook for Managers and Human Resource Professionals*, ed. J.W. Jones, B.D. Steffy, and D.W. Bray (Lexington, MA: Lexington Books, 2001), pp. 314–25. Reprinted with permission of Lexington Books.

360-degree feedback

A performance evaluation system that uses ratings provided by supervisors, co-workers, subordinates, customers, and the employees themselves

Although the information from a 360-degree feedback system can be used to evaluate employees for administrative purposes such as raises or promotions, there are problems with that sort of application. First, because ratings vary across sources, there is the question of which source is most "correct." Even if multiple sources are taken into account in generating an overall performance score, it is often unclear how the information from each source should be weighted. Second, raters may give biased evaluations if they believe the information will be used for compensation, as opposed to just skill development. Peers in particular may be unwilling to provide negative information if they believe it will harm the person being rated. As a result, 360-degree feedback is best suited to improving or developing employee talent, especially if the feedback is accompanied by coaching in areas identified as points of concern.

Forced Ranking

One of the most notable strategies that Jack Welch, *Fortune*'s Manager of the 20th Century,[69] used to build a great workforce at General Electric involved evaluations that make clear distinctions among employees in terms of their job performance. Although Welch considered several systems that might differentiate employees, the most effective relied on the "vitality curve," depicted in Figure 2-5, which forces managers to rank each of their people into one of three categories: the top 20 percent (A players), the vital middle 70 percent (B players), or the bottom 10 percent (C players). The A players are thought to possess "the four Es of GE leadership: very high *energy* levels, the ability to *energize* others around common goals, the *edge* to make tough yes-and-no decisions, and finally the ability to consistently *execute* and deliver on their promises."[70] The B players are developed. According to Welch, B players are the backbone of the company but lack the passion of A's. The C players are those who cannot get the job done and are let go. The system was taken so seriously at GE that managers who couldn't differentiate their people tended to find themselves in the C category.[71]

Today, approximately 20 percent of Fortune 500 companies use some variant of Welch's **forced ranking** system, which is popularly known as "rank and yank" or the "dead man's curve."[72] However, there are important controversies to consider. For example, some believe the system is inherently unfair because it forces managers to give bad evaluations to employees who may be good performers, just to reach a preestablished percentage. Also, employees may become hypercompetitive with one another to avoid finding themselves in a lower category. This type of competitiveness is the opposite of what may be needed in today's team-based organizations.

forced ranking

A performance management system that forces managers to rank each of their people into one of three categories: the top 20 percent, the vital middle 70 percent, or the bottom 10 percent.

FIGURE 2-5

Vitality Curve

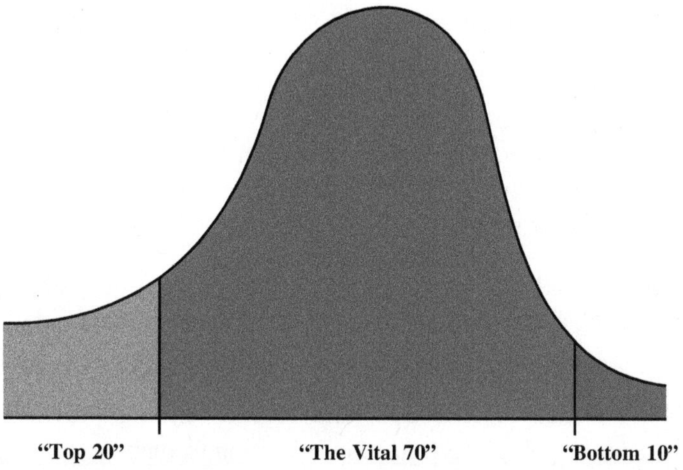

Source: From *Jack* by Jack Welch with John A. Byrne. Copyright © 2001 by the John F. Welch Jr. Foundation. By permission of Grand Central Publishing.

Social Networking Systems

Most of you reading this book are familiar with social networking services such as Facebook and Twitter. Well, this technology has recently been applied in organizational contexts to develop and evaluate employee job performance.[73] For example, Accenture uses a Facebook-style program called Performance Multiplier, which requires that employees post and update weekly and quarterly goals. Managers then monitor the information and provide feedback.[74] Another example is given by Rypple, a Toronto-based software company, which uses a Twitter-like program to enable employees to post questions about their own performance so that other employees can give them anonymous feedback.[75]

Although the effectiveness of social networking applications for performance evaluation and employee development purposes has not been studied scientifically, there are advantages that indicate they will grow in popularity. For example, these types of systems provide performance information that is much more timely relative to traditional practices that measure performance quarterly or even yearly. It might be unpleasant to learn from your peers that a presentation you gave was boring, but this is much better than giving 50 boring presentations and then getting the news from your boss a year later. The topic of social networking systems is covered again in Chapter 10 when our focus shifts to communication processes within work settings.

TAKEAWAYS

2.1 Job performance is the set of employee behaviours that contribute to organizational goal accomplishment. It has three dimensions: task performance, citizenship behaviour, and counterproductive behaviour.

2.2 Task performance includes employee behaviours that are directly involved in the transformation of organizational resources into the goods or services that the organization produces. Examples are routine task performance, adaptive task performance, and creative task performance.

2.3 Organizations gather information about relevant task behaviours using job analysis.

2.4 Citizenship behaviours are voluntary employee activities that may or may not be rewarded but that contribute to the organization by improving the overall quality of the setting in which work takes place. Examples are helping, courtesy, sportsmanship, voice, civic virtue, and boosterism.

2.5 Counterproductive behaviours are employee behaviours that intentionally hinder organizational goal accomplishment. Examples are sabotage, theft, wasting resources, substance abuse, gossiping, incivility, harassment, and abuse.

2.6 MBO, BARS, 360-degree feedback, and forced ranking practices are four ways that organizations can use job performance information to manage employee performance.

KEY TERMS

abuse
adaptive task performance
behaviourally anchored rating scales
boosterism
citizenship behaviour
civic virtue
counterproductive behaviour
courtesy
creative task performance
forced ranking
gossiping
harassment
helping
incivility
interpersonal citizenship behaviour
job analysis
job performance
management by objectives (MBO)
National Occupational Classification
organizational citizenship behaviour
personal aggression
political deviance
production deviance
property deviance
routine task performance
sabotage
sportsmanship
substance abuse
task performance
theft
360-degree feedback
voice
wasting resources

DISCUSSION QUESTIONS

2.1 Describe your "job" as a student in terms of the job performance dimensions discussed in this chapter. What would be the benefit of approaching student performance from a behaviour perspective rather than from an outcome (grades) perspective? What would the downsides of this approach be? How would grading policies in your classes have to change to accommodate a behaviour approach to student performance?

2.2 Describe the job you currently hold or hope to hold after graduation. Now look that job up in the National Occupational Classification (NOC) database, www5.hrsdc.gc.ca/NOC (also try looking up the job on the Occupational Information Network, www.onetonline.org). Does the profile of the job fit your expectations? Are any task behaviours missing from the online descriptions?

2.3 Describe a job in which citizenship behaviours would be especially critical to an organization's functioning, and one in which citizenship behaviours would be less critical. What is it about certain jobs that makes citizenship more important?

2.4 Figure 2-3 classifies production deviance and political deviance as more minor in nature than property deviance and personal aggression. When might those "minor" types of counterproductive behaviour prove especially costly?

2.5 Consider how you would react to 360-degree feedback. If you were the one receiving the feedback, whose views would you value most: your manager's or your peer's? If you were asked to assess a peer, would you want your opinion to affect his or her raises or promotions?

CASE: GM CANADA

To enable General Motors and its divisions, such as GM Canada, to compete effectively on a global basis with the likes of Toyota and Volkswagen, there has been a necessary shift in the nature of what constitutes effective job performance within the company. Hints of this change can be seen on the company's website, where its new guiding principles are highly visible and clearly stated.[76] These principles let employees know that their job performance involves not only carrying out the core tasks they were hired to do—designing, assembling, and selling vehicles—but also carrying them out in ways that promote safety, customer satisfaction, innovation, shareholder value, and social responsibility.

Of course, true change in an organization takes more than just revising a website. What else might indicate GM's commitment to the company's turnaround?

One sign that the company is serious about change is CEO Dan Akerson's regularly held "town hall meetings" with his employees. Not only has he been pressing them to embrace change, focus on customers, and behave with integrity—he has also been warning them that, if they can't play by these rules, they should look for work elsewhere.[77] Akerson has also indicated a sharp break from GM's long-standing tradition of strong centralized corporate control and micromanagement. How has he done this? He now praises plant employees who demonstrate proactivity in their job performance in order to make changes and fix problems. He has promised to cut red tape and streamline management to encourage this type of proactive performance, and he has urged employees to fix problems when they see something wrong and not to worry about asking for permission first.[78]

Other signs that the revitalization at General Motors is genuine involve changes to the company's management practices. For example, consider the steps the company has taken to develop creativity and urgency of engineers who need to introduce fresh new vehicles into the marketplace at an improved pace. Traditionally, engineers worked long-term product development cycles involving high levels of structure, control, and routine.[79] Engineers are now rotated through GM's racing teams for a season so that they can learn how to perform in a context where problem solving is quicker and more fluid. In racing, there's less information and time available, and as a consequence, engineers learn to become more comfortable making decisions based on their gut feelings and experience, rather than on an exhaustive analysis of data and consideration of benefits and costs from every conceivable vantage point, so that the best compromise can be reached. General Motors is willing to accept that some decisions will be wrong, however; decisions will be made quicker, and perhaps more importantly, knowledge gained from bad decisions can be used to inform better future decisions. How well will this practice work? Although it is difficult to predict, the 20 new vehicles that General Motors introduced in 2012 compare favourably to the 19 that its chief rival Toyota introduced in 2011.[80]

2.1 Which dimensions of job performance do you think General Motors emphasized prior to its revitalization effort? What are the advantages and disadvantages of this emphasis? How did this emphasis likely contribute to the company's problems?

2.2 Which dimensions of job performance do you think General Motors is emphasizing now? How might the change in emphasis improve the likelihood that GM can compete effectively?

2.3 Describe the potential advantages and disadvantages associated with rotating engineers through the racing teams. Explain how the experience on the racing teams could be used to develop GM employees who have other types of jobs.

EXERCISE • PERFORMANCE OF A SERVER

The purpose of this exercise is to explore what job performance means for a server in a restaurant. This exercise uses groups of six participants, so your instructor will either assign you to a group of six or ask you to create your own group of six. The exercise has the following steps:

2.1 Conduct a job analysis for a restaurant server. Begin by drawing a circle like the one shown here. Use that circle to summarize the major job dimensions of a restaurant server. For example, one dimension might be "Taking Meal Orders." Divide the circle up with four additional job dimensions. Now get more specific by listing two behaviours per dimension. For example, two behaviours within "Taking Meal Orders" might be "Describing the Menu" and "Making Recommendations." At the end of step 1, you should have a list of eight specific behaviours that summarize the tasks involved in being a restaurant server. Write your group's behaviours down on a transparency, laptop, or chalkboard, leaving space for additional behaviours down the line.

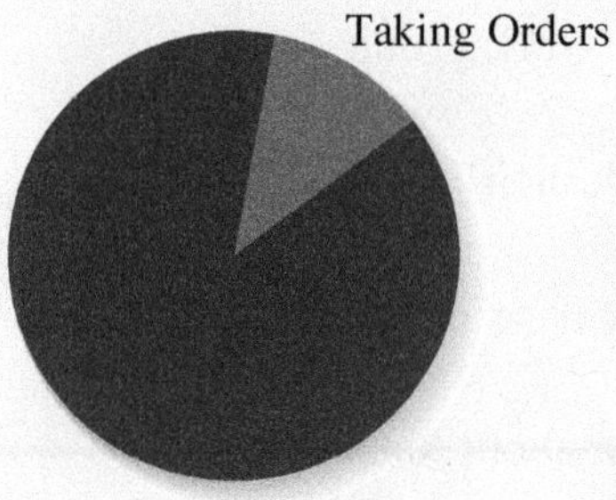

2.2 Take a look at the resulting list. Did you come up with any behaviours that might be described as "citizenship behaviours"? If you didn't include any in your list, does that mean citizenship behaviour isn't important in a restaurant setting? If your group includes someone who has worked as a server, ask him or her to describe the importance of citizenship behaviour. Come up with two especially important citizenship behaviours and add those to your list.

2.3 Take another look at your list. Did you come up with any behaviours that might be described as counterproductive? If you didn't include any in your list, does that mean counterproductive behaviour isn't an important concern in a restaurant setting? If your group includes someone who has worked as a server, ask him or her to describe the potential costs of counterproductive behaviour. Come up with two especially costly such behaviours and add those to your list.

2.4 Class discussion (whether in groups or as a class) should centre on how a restaurant owner or manager might use the resulting list to evaluate the performance of restaurant servers. How might this list be used to assess server performance? Would such an approach be valuable? Why or why not?

OB ASSESSMENTS • HELPING

How helpful are you? This assessment is designed to measure helping, an interpersonal form of citizenship behaviour. Think of the people you work with most frequently, either at school or at work. The questions below refer to these people as your "work group." Answer each question using the scale below, then add up your answers.

1 Strongly Disagree	**2 Moderately Disagree**	**3 Slightly Disagree**	**4 Neither Disagree nor Agree**	**5 Slightly Agree**	**6 Moderately Agree**	**7 Strongly Agree**	
1. I volunteer to do things for my work group.							____
2. I help orient new members of my work group.							____
3. I attend functions that help my work group.							____
4. I assist others in my group with their work for the benefit of the group.							____
5. I get involved to benefit my work group.							____
6. I help others in this group learn about the work							____
7. I help others in this group with their work responsibilities.							____

Scoring

If your scores add up to 40 or higher, you perform a high level of helping behaviour, which means you frequently engage in citizenship behaviours directed at your colleagues. This is good, as long as it doesn't distract you from fulfilling your own job duties and responsibilities. If your scores add up to less than 40, you perform a low level of helping behaviours. You might consider paying more attention to whether your colleagues need assistance while working on their task duties and pitching in when appropriate. Keep in mind, however, that when evaluating your scores on these assessments we need to consider the *reliability* and *validity* of these tools (see Chapter 1).

Source: L.V. Van Dyne and J.A. LePine, "Helping and Voice Extra-Role Behaviors: Evidence of Construct and Predictive Validity," *Academy of Management Journal* 41 (1998), pp. 108–19.

Organizational Commitment

CHAPTER 3

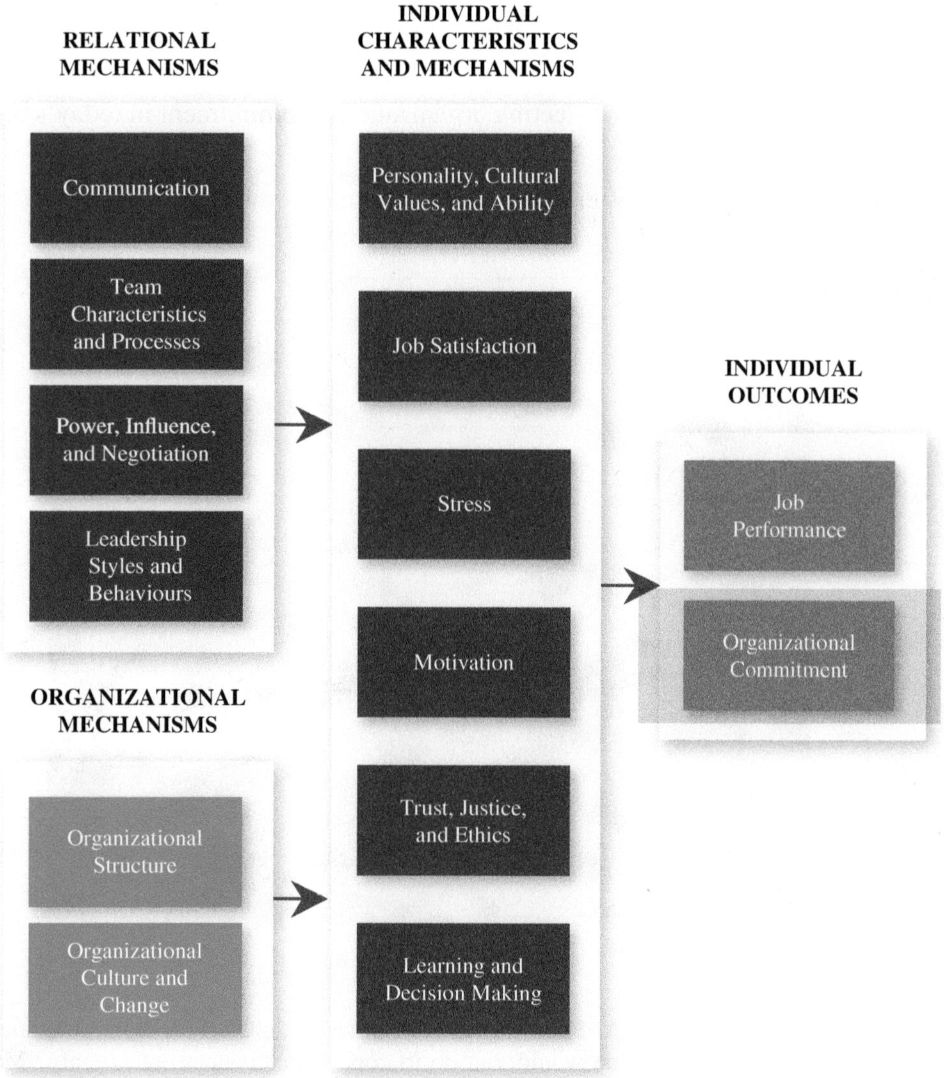

LEARNING OUTCOMES

After reading this chapter, you should be able to answer the following questions:

3.1 What is organizational commitment? What is withdrawal behaviour? How are the two connected?

3.2 What are the three forms of organizational commitment, and how do they differ?

3.3 What are the four primary responses to negative events at work?

3.4 What are some examples of psychological withdrawal? Of physical withdrawal? How do the different forms of withdrawal relate to each other?

3.5 What workplace trends are affecting organizational commitment in today's organizations?

3.6 How can organizations foster a sense of commitment among employees?

Costco

© Bloomberg via Getty Images

Picture this scenario. You're the CEO of one of the largest retailers in Canada, trying to guide your company through the economic downturn. What would you do to cope with financial uncertainty? Maybe you'd cut wages or staff, as Walmart, Best Buy, Home Depot, and Office Depot have done.[1] After all, that's a straightforward way to reduce costs. Jim Sinegal, co-founder and recently retired CEO of Costco, did the opposite—giving all hourly employees a wage increase.[2] The business model used at Costco is different from that of most of its competitors. It prices all of its groceries, home electronics, and office supplies at just 15 percent above cost, making it the price leader on virtually everything it sells. Costco's profits come from its $55 annual membership fee.

So why the wage increase? Because Costco understands that its profitability relies on customers renewing those memberships year after year. And that it needs customers to actually buy stuff when they visit, rather than simply "showrooming" products (i.e., visiting a retailer to view and research a product, then purchasing it for less online). And—when the downturn comes to an end—Costco needs those customers to keep it as part of their routine rather than viewing it as someplace they're embarrassed to visit. All of that requires committed and loyal employees who are knowledgeable and invested enough to make the Costco shopping experience fun and convenient.

Joe Carcello is one of those employees.[3] The 59-year-old has worked for Costco for 26 years, noting, "I'm just grateful to come here to work every day." Indeed, Costco pays its hourly workers an average of $20.89 an hour, three times the $7.25 minimum wage. Explains new CEO Jim Jelinek, "We know it's a lot more profitable in the long term to minimize employee turnover and maximize employee productivity, commitment, and loyalty.... If you treat consumers with respect and treat employees with respect, good things are going to happen to you." Good things do indeed seem to be happening at Costco, as its industry-leading turnover rate (5 percent) is matched only by its stock price (which has doubled since 2009).

ORGANIZATIONAL COMMITMENT

Organizational commitment sits side by side with job performance in our integrative model of organizational behaviour, reflecting one of the starting points for our journey through the concepts covered in this text. Why begin with a discussion of organizational commitment? Well, as illustrated in the Costco example, it is not enough simply to have talented employees who perform their jobs well. You also need to be able to retain those employees for long periods of time so that the organization can benefit from their efforts. In this chapter we go beyond job performance and start to consider another important work outcome—*retention*! The big question managers often struggle with is: Why do people stay or leave their jobs, teams, or organizations? Put yourself in the shoes of a business owner. Let's say you spent a great deal of time recruiting a graduate from the local university, selling her on your business, and making sure that she was as qualified as you initially believed her to be. Now assume that, she was once hired, you took a personal interest, showing her the ropes and acting as mentor and instructor. Then, she leaves to work for a competitor. As an employer, can you think of many things more distressing than that scenario?

One thing we will learn in this chapter is that withdrawal can come in many different forms than just quitting. How does this relate to organizational commitment? Well, it turns out that the most immediate cause of all forms of withdrawal behaviour is the level of overall commitment felt by an individual. For this reason, organizational commitment is considered a primary outcome in our integrative model.

Unfortunately, a growing number of Canadians plan to change their current jobs in the not-too-distant future.[4] Of course, just because employees want to leave doesn't mean they can. During the recession of 2008–2010, fewer Canadian workers voluntarily left their jobs, as suitable alternative employment opportunities were few and far between (especially in the private sector). However, as employment opportunities become more plentiful, the risk is that employees who want to leave might just do so.[5] This is especially worrisome with regard to high-performing or high-potential employees who are in high demand.[6] According to the Conference Board of Canada, job skills in the highest demand included accounting/finance, skilled trades, engineering (all types), information technology specialists, sales and marketing, management, professionals (e.g., lawyers), physical scientists, and healthcare professionals.[7] What this all means, frankly, is that talented employees in many fields are becoming increasingly scarce, and that the risk of turnover, among a firm's most valued employees, is getting higher all the time. Managers should be alarmed about these findings, because the cost of turnover can be substantial. Estimates suggest that it costs about .5 times the annual salary plus benefits to replace an hourly worker, 1.5 times the annual salary plus benefits to replace a salaried employee, and as much as 5 times the annual salary plus benefits to replace an executive.[8] Why so expensive? Those estimates include various costs, including the administrative costs involved in the separation, recruitment expenses, screening costs, and training and orientation expenses for the new hire.[9] They also include "hidden costs" due to decreased morale, lost organizational knowledge, and lost productivity.

3.1 What is organizational commitment? What is withdrawal behaviour? How are the two connected?

Organizational commitment is defined as the desire on the part of an employee to remain a member of the organization.[10] Organizational commitment influences whether an employee stays a member of the organization (is retained) or leaves to pursue another job (turns over). Our attention in this chapter is focused primarily on reducing voluntary turnover by keeping the employees whom the organization wants to keep, though we will touch on involuntary turnover in a discussion of layoffs and downsizing. Employees who are not committed to their organizations engage in **withdrawal behaviour**, defined as a set of actions that employees perform to avoid the work situation—behaviours that may eventually culminate in quitting the organization.[11] The relationship between commitment and withdrawal is illustrated in Figure 3-1. Some employees may exhibit much more commitment than withdrawal, finding themselves on the green end of the continuum. Other employees exhibit much more withdrawal than commitment, finding themselves on the red end of the continuum. The sections that follow review both commitment and withdrawal in more detail.

FIGURE 3-1

Organizational Commitment and Employee Withdrawal

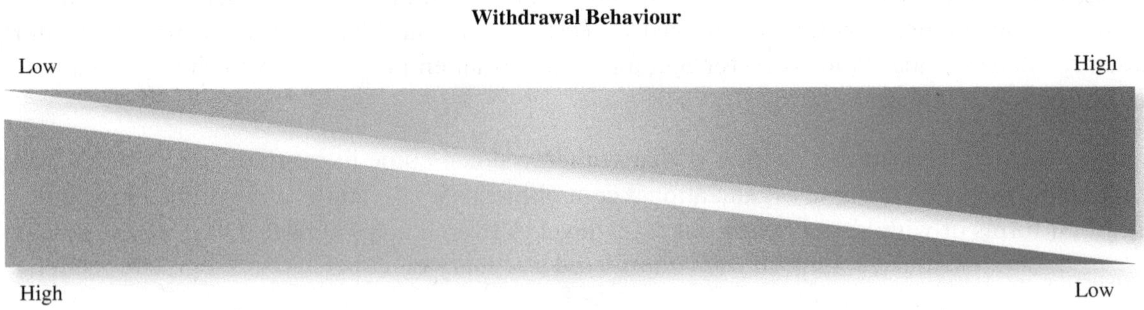

organizational commitment
An employee's desire to remain a member of an organization

withdrawal behaviour
Employee actions that are intended to avoid work situations

WHAT DOES IT MEAN TO BE "COMMITTED"?

One key to understanding organizational commitment is to understand where it comes from. In other words, what creates a desire to remain a member of an organization? To explore this question, consider the following scenario: You've been working full-time for your employer for around five years. The company gave you your start in the business, and you've enjoyed your time there. Your salary is competitive enough that you were able to purchase a new home in a family-oriented community, which is important because you have one young child and another on the way. Now assume that a competing firm contacted you while you were attending a conference and offered you a similar position in its company. What kinds of things might you think about? If you created a list to organize your thoughts, what kinds of issues would appear on that list?

3.2 What are the three forms of organizational commitment, and how do they differ?

Forms of Commitment

One potential list is shown in Table 3-1. The left-hand column reflects some emotional reasons for staying with the current organization, including feelings about friendships, the atmosphere or culture of the company, and a sense of enjoyment when completing job duties. These sorts of emotional reasons create **affective commitment**, defined as a desire to remain a member of an organization due to an emotional attachment to, and involvement with, that organization.[12] Put simply, you stay because you want to. The middle column reflects some cost-based reasons for staying, including issues of salary, benefits, and promotions, as well as concerns about uprooting a family. These sorts of reasons create **continuance commitment**, defined as a desire to remain a member of an organization because of an awareness of the costs associated with leaving it.[13] In other words, you stay because you have to. The right-hand column reflects some obligation-based reasons for staying with the current organization, including a sense that a debt is owed to a boss, a colleague, or the larger company. These sorts of reasons create **normative commitment**, defined as a desire to remain a member of an organization due to a feeling of obligation.[14] In this case, you stay because you ought to.

affective commitment
An employee's desire to remain a member of an organization due to a feeling of emotional attachment

continuance commitment
An employee's desire to remain a member of an organization due to an awareness of the costs of leaving

normative commitment
An employee's desire to remain a member of an organization due to a feeling of obligation

As is shown in Figure 3-2, the three forms of organizational commitment combine to create an overall sense of psychological attachment to the company. Of course, people may weight these three components of commitment differently. One person may be very rational and cautious by nature, focusing primarily on continuance commitment when evaluating his or her overall desire to stay. Another person may be more emotional and intuitive by nature, going more on "feel" than a calculated assessment of costs and benefits. The importance of the three components also may vary over the course of a career. For example, you might prioritize affective reasons early in your work life before shifting your attention to continuance reasons as you start a family or become more established in a community. Regardless of how the three forms are prioritized, however, they offer an important insight into why someone might be committed and what an organization can do to make employees feel more committed.

TABLE 3-1

The Three Forms of Organizational Commitment

What Makes Someone Stay with Their Current Organization?		
Affective Commitment (Emotion-Based)	**Continuance Commitment (Cost-Based)**	**Normative Commitment (Obligation-Based)**
Some of my best friends work in my office. I'd miss them if I left.	I'm due for a promotion soon. Will I advance as quickly at the new company?	My boss has invested so much time in me, mentoring me, training me, showing me the ropes.
I really like the atmosphere at my current job. It's fun and relaxed.	My salary and benefits get us a nice house in our town. The cost of living is higher in this new area.	My organization gave me my start. They hired me when others thought I wasn't qualified.
My current job duties are very rewarding. I enjoy coming to work each morning.	The school system is good here, my spouse has a good job. We've really put down roots where we are.	My employer has helped me out of a jam on a number of occasions. How could I leave now?
Staying because you *want* to.	**Staying because you *need* to.**	**Staying because you *ought* to.**

Committed employees often have strong positive feelings about one particular aspect of their job, such as their colleagues, their manager, or the particular work they do.

Figure 3-2 also shows that organizational commitment depends on more than just "the organization." That is, people aren't always committed to companies; they're also committed to the top management that leads the firm at a given time, the department in which they work, the manager who directly supervises them, or the specific team or co-workers with whom they work most closely.[15] We use the term **focus of commitment** to refer to the various people, places, and things that can inspire a desire to remain a member of an organization. For example, you might choose to stay with your current employer because you are emotionally attached to your work team, worry about the costs associated with losing your company's salary and benefits package, and feel a sense of obligation to your current manager. If so, your desire to remain cuts across multiple types of commitment (affective, continuance, and normative) and multiple foci (or focuses) of commitment (work team, company, manager). Now that you're familiar with the drivers of commitment in a general sense, let's go into more depth about each form.

FIGURE 3-2

Drivers of Overall Organizational Commitment

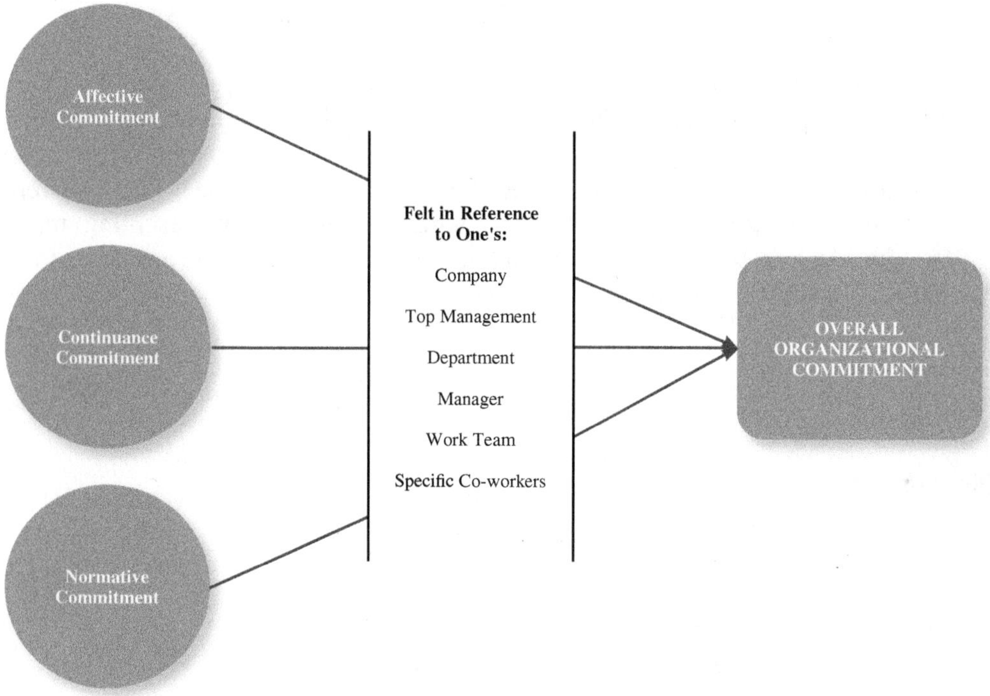

focus of commitment
The people, places, and things that inspire a desire to remain a member of an organization

Affective Commitment One way to understand the differences among the three forms of commitment is to ask yourself what you would feel if you left the organization. Consider the reasons listed in the left-hand column of Table 3-1. What would you feel if, even after taking all those reasons into account, you decided to leave your organization to join another one? Answer: You'd feel a sense of *sadness*. Employees who feel a sense of affective commitment identify with the organization, accept that organization's goals and values, and are more willing to exert extra effort on behalf of the organization.[16] By identifying with the organization, they come to view organizational membership as important to their sense of self.[17] Is affective commitment something that you feel for your current employer or have felt for a past employer? Check the ***OB Assessments*** feature at the end of the chapter to find out.

It's safe to say that if managers could choose which type of commitment they'd like to instill in their employees, they would choose affective commitment. Moreover, when a manager looks at an employee and says "She's committed" or "He's loyal," that manager usually is referring to a behavioural expression of affective commitment.[18] For example, employees who are affectively committed to their employer tend to engage in more interpersonal and organizational citizenship behaviours, such as helping, sportsmanship, and boosterism. One meta-analysis of 22 studies with more than 6,000 participants revealed a moderately strong correlation between affective commitment and citizenship behaviour.[19] (Recall that a meta-analysis averages out the results from multiple studies investigating the same relationship.) Such results suggest that emotionally committed employees express that commitment by going the extra mile whenever they can.

Because affective commitment reflects an emotional bond to the organization, it's only natural that the emotional bonds among co-workers influence it.[20] We can therefore gain a better understanding of affective commitment if we take a closer look at the bonds that tie employees together. Assume you were given a sheet with the names of all the employees in your department or members of your class. Then assume you were asked to rate the frequency with which you communicated with each of those people, as well as the emotional depth of those communications. Those ratings could be used to create a "social network" diagram that summarizes the bonds among employees. Figure 3-3 shows an example of such a diagram. The lines connecting the ten members of the work unit represent the communication bonds that connect each of them, with thicker lines representing more frequent communication with more emotional depth. The diagram illustrates that some employees are "nodes," with several direct connections to other employees, whereas others remain at the fringes of the network.

FIGURE 3-3

A Social Network Diagram

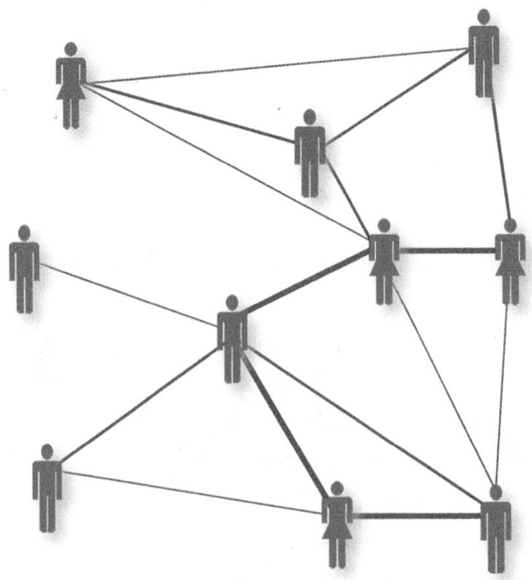

The **erosion model** suggests that employees with fewer bonds will be most likely to quit the organization.[21] If you look at Figure 3-3, who's most at risk for turning over? That's right—the employee who has only one bond with someone else (and a relatively weak bond at that). From an affective commitment perspective, that employee is likely to feel less emotional attachment to work colleagues, which makes it easier to decide to leave the organization. Social network diagrams can also help us understand another explanation for turnover. The **social influence model** suggests that employees who have direct linkages with "leavers" will themselves be more likely to leave.[22] In this way, reductions in affective commitment become contagious, spreading like a disease across the work unit. Think about the damage that would be caused if the central figure in the network (the one who has linkages to five other people) became unhappy with the organization.

erosion model

A model that suggests that employees with fewer bonds with co-workers are more likely to quit the organization

social influence model

A model that suggests that employees with direct linkages to co-workers who leave the organization will themselves be more likely to leave

More and more Canadian companies seem to understand the importance of affective commitment, and the need to promote emotional bonding among employees and between employees and the organization.[23] To support its "work hard, play hard" culture, The Keg involves staff in numerous restaurant (e.g., Bar Oscars and Kitchen Emmy nights) and corporate events (e.g., two-day ski challenges, softball tournaments). Clark Builders, an Edmonton-based construction and engineering firm, strengthens bonds with its employees by creating a corporate culture in which every team member is treated with respect and trust. Island Savings Credit Union, based in Duncan, B.C., is focused on fostering a highly personal employment experience for employees where they feel like "family." Other companies increase affective commitment in their employees by promoting opportunities for growth, achievement, and personal development. Earls, another restaurant chain, offers its employees an opportunity to climb the ladder from dish washer to manager. Amex Canada Inc., based in Markham, Ontario, helps its employees build their careers through training and education programs, and by celebrating their personal accomplishments and successes. These sorts of activities are examples of what companies can do to reinforce affective commitment.

Continuance Commitment Now consider the reasons for staying listed in the middle column of Table 3-1. What would you feel if, even after taking all those reasons into account, you decided to leave your organization to join another one? Answer: You'd feel a sense of *anxiety*. Continuance commitment exists when there's a profit associated with staying and a cost associated with leaving,[24] with high continuance commitment making it difficult to change organizations because of the steep penalties associated with the switch.[25] One factor that increases continuance commitment is the total amount of investment (in terms of time, effort, energy, etc.) employees have made in mastering their work roles or fulfilling their organizational duties.[26] Picture a scenario in which you've worked extremely hard for a number of years to finally master the ins and outs of working at a particular organization, and now you're beginning to enjoy the fruits of that labour in terms of financial rewards and better work assignments. That effort might be wasted if you moved to another organization (and had to start over on the learning curve).

Another factor that increases continuance commitment is a lack of employment alternatives.[27] If an employee has nowhere else to go, the need to stay will be higher. Employment alternatives themselves depend on several factors, including economic conditions, the unemployment rate, and the marketability of a person's skills and abilities.[28] Of course, no one likes to feel stuck in a situation, so it may not be surprising that the behavioural benefits associated with affective commitment don't really occur with continuance commitment. There is no statistical relationship between continuance commitment and citizenship behaviour, for example, or any other aspects of job performance.[29] Continuance commitment therefore tends to create more of a passive form of loyalty.

It is important to note that some of the reasons in the middle column of Table 3-1 centre on personal or family issues. Continuance commitment focuses on personal and family issues more than the other two commitment forms, because employees often need to stay for both work and non-work reasons. One concept that demonstrates the work and non-work forces that can bind us to our current employer is **embeddedness**, which summarizes employees' links to their organization and community, their sense of fit with their organization and community, and what they would have to sacrifice for a job change.[30] As is demonstrated in Table 3-2, embeddedness strengthens continuance commitment by providing more reasons employees need to stay in their current positions (and more sources of anxiety if they were to leave).[31] Research suggests that embeddedness helps employees weather negative events that occur,[32] and that it matters across cultures.[33]

embeddedness
An employee's connection to and sense of fit in the organization and community

TABLE 3-2

Embeddedness and Continuance Commitment

	"Embedded" People Feel:	
Facet	**For the Organization**	**For the Community**
Links	• I've worked here for such a long time. • I'm serving on so many teams and committees.	• Several close friends and family live nearby. • My family's roots are in this community.
Fit	• My job utilizes my skills and talents well. • I like the authority and responsibility I have at this company.	• The weather where I live is suitable for me. • I think of the community where I live as home.
Sacrifice	• The retirement benefits provided by the organization are excellent. • I would sacrifice a lot if I left this job.	• People respect me a lot in my community. • Leaving this community would be very hard.

Source: Adapted from T.R. Mitchell, B.C. Holtom, T.W. Lee, C.J. Sablynski, and M. Erez, "Why People Stay: Using Job Embeddedness to Predict Voluntary Turnover," *Academy of Management Journal* 44 (2001), pp. 1102–21.

Think about your current situation. If you're a college student who is working part-time, you likely don't feel very embedded. Your links to your job are probably only short-term, and you may feel that the job is more routine than you'd like from a fit perspective. You probably also wouldn't feel you were sacrificing much if you left the job. From a community perspective, you may be going to school in a different city or province than where you grew up, again resulting in few links, low perceived fit, or a lack of felt sacrifice. However, if you're a full-time employee who is relatively established in your job and community, you may feel quite embedded in your current situation.[34] See our ***OB on Screen*** feature for one employee's defence of low embeddedness.

We see many examples of Canadian organizations offering generous financial compensation combined with, in many cases, innovative benefit packages that make it hard for employees to leave.[35] For instance, if you work at KPMG, a large professional services firm specializing in audit, tax, and corporate finance, you might think twice about leaving an organization that offers parental leave top-up payments for new mothers and fathers (including adoptive parents) and financial support (to $20,000) to help cover adoption-related expenses.[36] In this era of ever-increasing gasoline prices, Shell Canada Ltd. of Calgary is confident that many of its members will find it hard to give up the discounts it offers employees on their personal fuel purchases.[37] People with cats or dogs will find it hard to replace the pet insurance program offered by Ceridian Canada Ltd., a Winnipeg-based company that provides HR and payroll solutions for businesses across the country.[38] Clearly there will be employees in all of these companies who will feel a bit anxious at the prospect of having to sacrifice these outcomes if a competitor came calling.

Normative Commitment Now consider the reasons for staying listed in the right-hand column of Table 3-1. What would you feel if, even after taking all those reasons into account, you decided to leave your organization to join another one? Answer: You'd feel a sense of *guilt*. Normative commitment exists when there is a sense that staying is the "right" or "moral" thing to do.[39] The sense that people *should* stay with their current employers may result from personal work philosophies or more general codes of right and wrong developed over the course of their lives. They may also be dictated by early experiences within the company, if employees are socialized to believe that long-term loyalty is the norm rather than the exception.[40]

Aside from personal work philosophies or organizational socialization, there seem to be two ways to build a sense of obligation-based commitment among employees. One way is to create a feeling that employees are in the organization's debt—that they owe something to the organization. For example, an organization may spend a great deal of money training and developing an employee. In recognition of that investment, the employee may feel obligated to "repay" the organization with several more years of loyal service.[41] Think about how you'd feel if your employer paid your tuition, allowing you to further your education, while also providing you with training and developmental job assignments that increased your skills. Wouldn't you feel a bit guilty if you took the first job opportunity that came your way?

Another possible way to build an obligation-based sense of commitment is by becoming a particularly charitable organization. Did you ever wonder why organizations spend time and money on charitable things—for example, building playgrounds in the local community? Don't those kinds of projects take away from research and development, product improvements, or profits for shareholders? Well, charitable efforts have several potential advantages. First, they can provide good public relations for the organization, potentially generating goodwill for its products and services and helping attract new recruits.[42] Second, they can help existing employees feel better about the organization, creating a deeper sense of normative commitment. Those benefits may be particularly relevant with younger employees. Some evidence indicates that members of Generation Y (those born between 1977 and 1994) are somewhat more charitably minded than other generations. In support of that view, a growing number of MBA graduates are joining socially conscious online networks, such as Netimpact.org (see Chapter 8 on trust, justice, and ethics for more discussion of such issues).[43]

OB ON SCREEN

Up in the Air

How much does your life weigh?

With those words, Ryan Bingham (George Clooney) begins his speech at a Hampton Inn in Columbus. In his spare time, Bingham hones a motivational speech extolling the virtues of being unencumbered. "Imagine for a second that you're carrying a back-pack," he continues. "I want you to pack it with all the stuff that you have in your life ... the shelves, the drawers, the knickknacks, then you start adding the larger stuff.... The backpack should be getting pretty heavy now.... Now I want you to fill it with people.... You get them into that backpack, feel the weight of that bag. Make no mistake, your relationships are the heaviest component in your life."

© Paramount Pictures/Photofest

Bingham's working life represents a paradox of sorts. On the one hand, he practises what he preaches. He travels 322 days a year, spending only 43 days in a spartan studio apartment in Omaha. He has no wife, few friends, and only the shallowest relationship with his family. On the other hand, his job revolves around understanding and appreciating how embedded people feel and react. You see, Bingham works for Career Transition Corporation (CTC). When a company wants to fire someone but doesn't want to do it directly, it hires CTC and Bingham delivers the news. It sounds like a horrible job, but Bingham believes in it, and he's good at it.

When a "transitionee" named Bob wonders what he'll tell his children, Bingham notes that Bob once minored in French culinary arts. "How much did they first pay you to give up on your dreams," Bingham asks. "And when were you gonna stop, and come back and do what makes you happy? I see guys who work at the same company their entire lives.... They clock in, they clock out, and they never have a moment of happiness. You have an opportunity here, Bob ... this is a rebirth." Ironically, when videoconferencing advancements threaten the way he does his job, it's Bingham's turn to grapple with that feeling of uncertainty. So he fights to stay on the road. Why? Because, "The slower we move the faster we die.... Make no mistake, moving is living."

Wardrop Engineering Ltd., based in Winnipeg, is in the business of providing engineering, environmental, and information technology solutions to companies around the world, and it is a company that clearly recognizes the value of normative commitment. As you might imagine, Wardrop is one of those organizations that finds itself competing globally for highly skilled employees. For some time, Wardrop has been recognized as one of the best employers for new Canadians.[44] Apart from providing a variety of programs aimed at promoting inclusiveness and workplace integration (e.g., providing cross-cultural and language training to new recruits and existing employees; providing in-house prayer facilities if requested), the company helps these new Canadians obtain their Canadian professional designations through an extensive technical mentoring and development program. In exchange for the support provided by organization, many of these new Canadians will, in all likelihood, feel an obligation to reciprocate this goodwill.[45] It is this sense of "wanting to give something back" or "feeling like you owe the organization" that is the essence of normative commitment. Employees stay because they feel it is the right thing to do—for Wardrop Engineering, this represents another effective business solution.

OB RESEARCH IN CANADA

Drs. John P. Meyer and Natalie J. Allen, professors in industrial and organizational psychology at the University of Western Ontario, are credited with the development of the three-component model of organizational commitment discussed above. Over the past 30 years, their research has demonstrated that employee commitment to an organization can take at least three different forms (emotion-based, cost-based, and obligation-based; see Table 3-1). These three forms of commitment, in addition to predicting who stays and who leaves their job, have been shown to make a difference in terms of citizenship and counterproductive behaviours as well (see Chapter 2).

Courtesy of Dr. John Meyer

Courtesy of Dr. Natalie Allen

In addition to their common interest and published works in organizational commitment, Drs. Meyer and Allen have separate interests and research expertise. Dr. Meyer studies work motivation (Chapter 7), organizational justice (Chapter 8), leadership (Chapter 13), and organizational change (Chapter 15). Dr. Allen investigates various psychological issues with work teams (Chapter 11). Their collaborative and independent works have been published in leading scientific journals in the field of organizational behaviour and management. For more information, you might wish to look up Drs. Meyer and Allen at www.uwo.ca.

Withdrawal Behaviour

As noted earlier, the risk of turnover tends to increase as our economy improves. Organizational commitment is therefore a vital concern, given that organizations will need to be fully staffed when business picks back up and industries become even more competitive. Indeed, organizational commitment is most important when employees are needed the most. To paraphrase the old saying, "When the going gets tough, the organization doesn't want you to get going." In tough times, organizations need their employees to demonstrate loyalty, not "get going" right out the door. Of course, it's those same tough times that put an employee's loyalty and allegiance to the test.

Consider the following scenario: You've been working at your company for three years and served on a key product development team for the past several months. Unfortunately, the team has been struggling of late. In an effort to enhance the team's performance, the organization has added a new member to the group. This member has a solid history of product development but is, by all accounts, a horrible person to work with. You can easily see the employee's talent but find yourself hating every moment spent in the employee's presence. This situation is particularly distressing because the team won't finish its work for another nine months, at the earliest. What would you do in this situation?

3.3 What are the four primary responses to negative events at work?

Research on reactions to negative work events suggests that you might respond in one of four general ways.[46] First, you might attempt to remove yourself from the situation, either by being absent from work more frequently or by voluntarily leaving the organization. This removal is termed **exit**, defined as an active, destructive response by which an individual either ends or restricts organizational membership.[47] Second, you might attempt to change the circumstances by meeting with the new team member to attempt to work out the situation. This action is termed *voice*, defined as an active, constructive response in which individuals attempt to improve the situation (see Chapter 2 on job performance for more discussion of such issues).[48] Third, you might just grin and bear it, maintaining your effort level despite your unhappiness. This response is termed **loyalty**, defined as a passive, constructive response that maintains public support for the situation while the individual privately hopes for improvement.[49] Fourth, you might just go through the motions, allowing your performance to deteriorate slowly as you mentally "check out." This reaction is termed **neglect**, defined as a passive, destructive response in which interest and effort in the job declines.[50] Sometimes neglect can be even more costly than exit, because it's not as readily noticed. Employees may neglect their duties for months (or even years) before their bosses catch on to their poor behaviours.

exit

An active response to a negative work event in which one ends or restricts organizational membership

loyalty

A passive response to a negative work event in which one publicly supports the situation but privately hopes for improvement

neglect

A passive, destructive response to a negative work event in which one's interest and effort in the job declines

Taken together, the exit–voice–loyalty–neglect framework captures most of the possible responses to a negative work event. Where does organizational commitment fit in? Organizational commitment should decrease the likelihood that an individual will respond to a negative work event with exit or neglect (the two destructive responses). At the same time, organizational commitment should increase the likelihood that the negative work event will prompt voice or loyalty (the two constructive responses). Consistent with that logic, research indeed suggests that organizational commitment increases the likelihood of voice and loyalty while decreasing the likelihood of exit and neglect.[51]

It's clear from this discussion that exit and neglect represent the flip side of organizational commitment: withdrawal behaviour. How common is withdrawal behaviour within organizations? Quite common, it turns out. One study clocked employees' on-the-job behaviours over a two-year period and found that only about 51 percent of their time was actually spent working! The other 49 percent was lost to late starts, early departures, long coffee breaks, personal matters, and other forms of withdrawal.[52] As a manager, wouldn't you like to feel like there was more than a coin-flip's chance that your employees were actually working during the course of a given day?

3.4 What are some examples of psychological withdrawal? Of physical withdrawal? How do the different forms of withdrawal relate to each other?

As is shown in Figure 3-4, withdrawal comes in two forms: psychological (or neglect) and physical (or exit). **Psychological withdrawal** consists in actions that provide a mental escape from the work environment.[53] Some business articles refer to psychological withdrawal as "warm-chair attrition," meaning that employees have essentially been lost even though their chairs remain occupied.[54] This withdrawal form comes in a number of shapes and sizes.[55] The least serious is **daydreaming**, when employees appear to be working but are actually distracted by random thoughts or concerns. **Socializing** refers to the verbal chatting about non-work topics that goes on in cubicles and offices or at the mailbox or vending machines. **Looking busy** indicates an intentional desire on the part of employees to look like they're working, even when they're not. Sometimes employees decide to reorganize their desks or go for a stroll around the building, even though they have nowhere to go. (Those who are very good at managing impressions do such things very briskly and with a focused look on their faces!) When employees engage in **moonlighting**, they use work time and resources to complete something other than their job duties, such as assignments for another job.

psychological withdrawal
Actions that provide a mental escape from the work environment

daydreaming
A form of psychological withdrawal in which one's work is interrupted by random thoughts or concerns

socializing
A form of psychological withdrawal in which one verbally chats with co-workers about non-work topics

looking busy

A form of psychological withdrawal in which one attempts to appear consumed with work when not performing actual work tasks

moonlighting

A form of psychological withdrawal in which employees use work time and resources to do non-work-related activities

FIGURE 3-4

Psychological and Physical Withdrawal

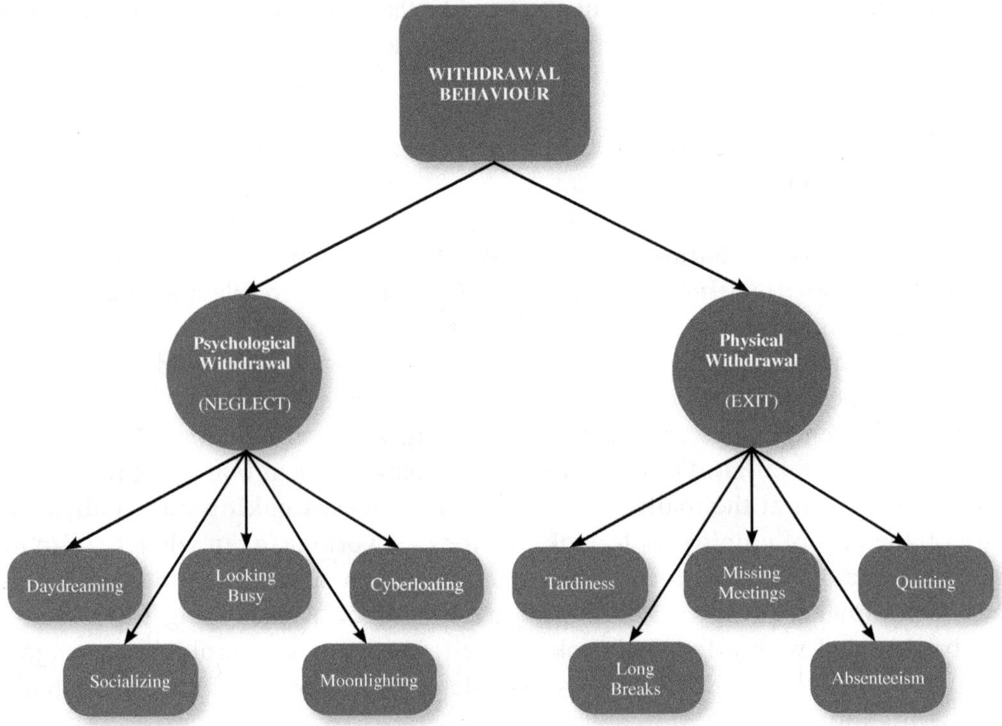

Perhaps the most widespread form of psychological withdrawal among white-collar employees is **cyberloafing**—using Internet, e-mail, and instant messaging access for their personal enjoyment rather than work duties.[56] Some estimates suggest that typical cubicle dwellers stop what they're doing about once every three minutes to send e-mail, check Facebook or Twitter, surf over to YouTube, and so forth.[57] Such distractions consume as much as 28 percent of employees' workdays, representing billions of dollars a year in lost productivity in Canada. Some employees view cyberloafing as a way of "balancing the scales" when it comes to personal versus work time. For example, one participant in a cyberloafing study noted, "It is alright for me to use the Internet for personal reasons at work. After all, I do work overtime without receiving extra pay from my employer."[58] Although such views may seem quite reasonable, other employees view cyberloafing as a means to retaliate for negative work events. One participant in the same study noted, "My boss is not the appreciative kind; I take what I can whenever I can. Surfing the net is my way of hitting back."

cyberloafing

A form of psychological withdrawal in which employees use Internet, e-mail, and instant messaging access for their personal enjoyment rather than work duties

Physical withdrawal consists of actions that provide a physical escape, whether short-term or long-term, from the work environment.[59] Physical withdrawal also comes in a number of shapes and sizes. **Tardiness** reflects the tendency to arrive at work late (or leave work early).[60] Of course, tardiness can sometimes be unavoidable, as when employees have car trouble or must fight through bad weather, but it often represents a calculated desire to spend less time at work.[61] **Long breaks** involve longer-than-normal lunches, coffee breaks, and so forth that provide a physical escape from work. Sometimes long breaks stretch into **missing meetings**, which means employees neglect important work functions while away from the office. As a manager, you'd like to be sure that employees who leave for lunch are actually going to come back, but sometimes that's not a safe bet!

physical withdrawal

A physical escape from the work environment

tardiness

A form of physical withdrawal in which employees arrive late to work or leave work early

long breaks

A form of physical withdrawal in which employees take longer-than-normal lunches or breaks to spend less time at work

missing meetings

A form of physical withdrawal in which employees neglect important work functions while away from the office

Absenteeism occurs when employees miss an entire day of work.[62] Of course, people stay home from work for a variety of reasons, including illness and family emergencies. There's also a rhythm to absenteeism. For example, employees are more likely to be absent on Mondays or Fridays. Moreover, streaks of good attendance create a sort of pressure to be absent, as personal responsibilities build until a day at home becomes irresistible.[63] That type of absence can sometimes be functional, because people may return to work with their "batteries recharged."[64] Group and departmental norms also affect absenteeism by signalling whether an employee can get away with missing a day here or there without being noticed.[65] These issues aside, a consistent pattern of absenteeism, month in and month out, is a symptom of the kind of low commitment that concerns most managers. Should absenteeism (in the form of missed classes) concern instructors as well? See our ***OB for Students*** feature to find out.

absenteeism

A form of physical withdrawal in which employees do not show up for an entire day of work

Finally, the most serious form of physical withdrawal is **quitting**—voluntarily leaving the organization. As with the other forms of withdrawal, employees can choose to "turn over" for a variety of reasons. The most frequent reasons include leaving for more money or a better career opportunity; dissatisfaction with supervision, working conditions, or working schedule; family factors; and health.[66]

Note that many of those reasons reflect avoidable turnover, meaning that the organization could have done something to keep the employee, perhaps by offering more money, more frequent promotions, or a better work situation. Family factors and health, in contrast, usually reflect unavoidable turnover that doesn't necessarily signal a lack of commitment on the part of employees.

OB FOR STUDENTS

What does withdrawal mean for you as a student? The most obvious form of withdrawal for students is missed classes—the academic version of absenteeism. Why do students choose to stay home from class on a given day? One study identified the top six reasons for missing class, ranked as follows:[67]

1. Needing to complete work for another class
2. The class is boring
3. Severe illness (e.g., flu)
4. Minor illness (e.g., cold, sore throat)
5. Tired from social activities
6. Oversleeping

These reasons illustrate that there are a number of factors that cause people to be absent. Some are avoidable, some unavoidable; some are related to the class, some unrelated. Of the factors listed, "The class is boring," most clearly captures absenteeism as a response to a negative class-related event. Students don't like the class, so they engage in exit behaviours. There's also a rhythm and seasonality to absenteeism, as students are most likely to miss Friday classes or classes near the end of the semester (when project deadlines become most pressing).

Here's the million-dollar question for any student: Does absenteeism affect your grades? The answer is clearly yes. One study examined the correlation between class attendance and course grades across 17 different class sections and identified correlations ranging from .29 to .73.[68] Another study found that students who attend all classes average a .45-point higher GPA in the course than students who only attend half the classes.[69] This result appears even when taking into account a student's prior cumulative GPA and his or her motivation levels.

These sorts of results explain why some instructors build an attendance requirement into their classes, causing students to sign in each day to reduce absences. The benefits of this policy were tested in two sections of a psychology course.[70] One section required students to sign in to record attendance; the other section didn't. Absenteeism was one-third lower in the section that required sign-ins, and the students in that section performed significantly better on seven of the eight quizzes in the class.

The bottom line is clear for you as a student—come to class and you'll get a better grade. Of course, showing up may be only half the battle, particularly if students are tempted to engage in neglect during lectures (e.g., reading the newspaper, surfing the web, falling asleep). If you are tempted to engage in those forms of psychological withdrawal, consider this: Students who participate during class increase their course GPAs by an average of .23 points.[71] So there's a reason to pay attention!

quitting
A form of physical withdrawal in which employees voluntarily leave the organization

Regardless of their reasons, some employees choose to quit after engaging in a very thorough, careful, and reasoned analysis. Typically some sort of "shock," whether it be a critical job change, a negative work experience, or an unsolicited job offer, jars employees enough that it triggers the thought of quitting.[72] Once the idea has entered their mind, employees begin searching for other places to work, compare those alternatives to their current job, and, if the comparisons seem favourable, quit.[73] This process may take days, weeks, or even months as employees grapple with the decision. In other cases, though, a shock may result in an impulsive, knee-jerk decision, with little or no thought given to alternative jobs (or how those jobs compare to the current one).[74] Of course, sometimes a shock never occurs. Instead, an employee decides to quit as a result of a slow but steady decrease in happiness until a "straw breaks the camel's back" and voluntary turnover results.

Figure 3-4 shows ten different behaviours that employees can perform to psychologically or physically escape from a negative work environment. A key question remains, though: "How do all those behaviours relate to one another?" Consider the following testimonials from uncommitted (admittedly fictional) employees:

- "I can't stand my job, so I do what I can to get by. Sometimes I'm absent, sometimes I socialize, sometimes I come in late. There's no real rhyme or reason to it; I just do whatever seems practical at the time."
- "I can't handle being around my boss. I hate to miss work, so I do what's needed to avoid being absent. I figure if I socialize a bit and spend some time surfing the web, I don't need to ever be absent. But if I couldn't do those things, I'd definitely have to stay home ... a lot."
- "I just don't have any respect for my employer anymore. In the beginning, I'd daydream a bit during work or socialize with my colleagues. As time went on, I began coming in late or taking a long lunch. Lately I've been staying home altogether, and I'm starting to think I should just quit my job and go somewhere else."

Each of these statements sounds like something that an uncommitted employee might say. However, each makes a different prediction about the relationships among the withdrawal behaviours in Figure 3-4. The first statement summarizes the **independent forms model** of withdrawal, which argues that the various withdrawal behaviours are uncorrelated with one another, occur for different reasons, and fulfill different needs on the part of employees.[75] From this perspective, knowing that an employee cyberloafs tells you nothing about whether that employee is likely to be absent. The second statement summarizes the **compensatory forms model** of withdrawal, which argues that the various withdrawal behaviours negatively correlate with one another—that doing one means you're less likely to do another. The idea is that any form of withdrawal can compensate for, or neutralize, a sense of dissatisfaction, which makes the other forms unnecessary. From this perspective, knowing that an employee cyberloafs tells you that the same employee probably isn't going to be absent. The third statement summarizes the **progression model** of withdrawal, which argues that the various withdrawal behaviours are positively correlated; the tendency to daydream or socialize leads to the tendency to come in late or take long breaks, which leads to the tendency to be absent or quit. From this perspective, knowing that an employee cyberloafs tells you that the same employee is probably going to be absent in the near future.

independent forms model

A model that predicts that the various withdrawal behaviours are uncorrelated, so that engaging in one type of withdrawal has little bearing on engaging in other types

compensatory forms model

A model indicating that the various withdrawal behaviours are negatively correlated, so that engaging in one type of withdrawal makes one less likely to engage in other types

progression model
A model indicating that the various withdrawal behaviours are positively correlated, so that engaging in one type of withdrawal makes one more likely to engage in other types

Which of the three models seems most logical to you? Although all three make some sense, the progression model has received the most scientific support.[76] Studies tend to show that the withdrawal behaviours in Figure 3-4 are positively correlated with one another.[77] Moreover, if you view the behaviours as a causal sequence moving from left (daydreaming) to right (quitting), the behaviours that are closest to each other in the sequence tend to be more highly correlated.[78] For example, quitting is more closely related to absenteeism than to tardiness, because absenteeism is right next to it in the withdrawal progression. These results illustrate that withdrawal behaviours may begin with very minor actions but eventually can escalate to more serious actions that may harm the organization.

Summary: What Does It Mean to Be "Committed"?

So what does it mean to be a "committed" employee? As is shown in Figure 3-5, it means a lot of different things. It means that employees have a strong desire to remain a member of the organization, maybe because they want to stay, need to stay, or feel they ought to stay. Regardless of the reasons for their attachment, retaining these employees means stopping the progression of withdrawal that begins with psychological forms and then escalates to behavioural forms. Note that the minus sign in Figure 3-5 illustrates that high levels of overall organizational commitment reduce the frequency of psychological and physical withdrawal. Note also that psychological withdrawal goes on to affect physical withdrawal, which represents the progressive nature of such behaviours.

FIGURE 3-5

What Does It Mean to Be "Committed"?

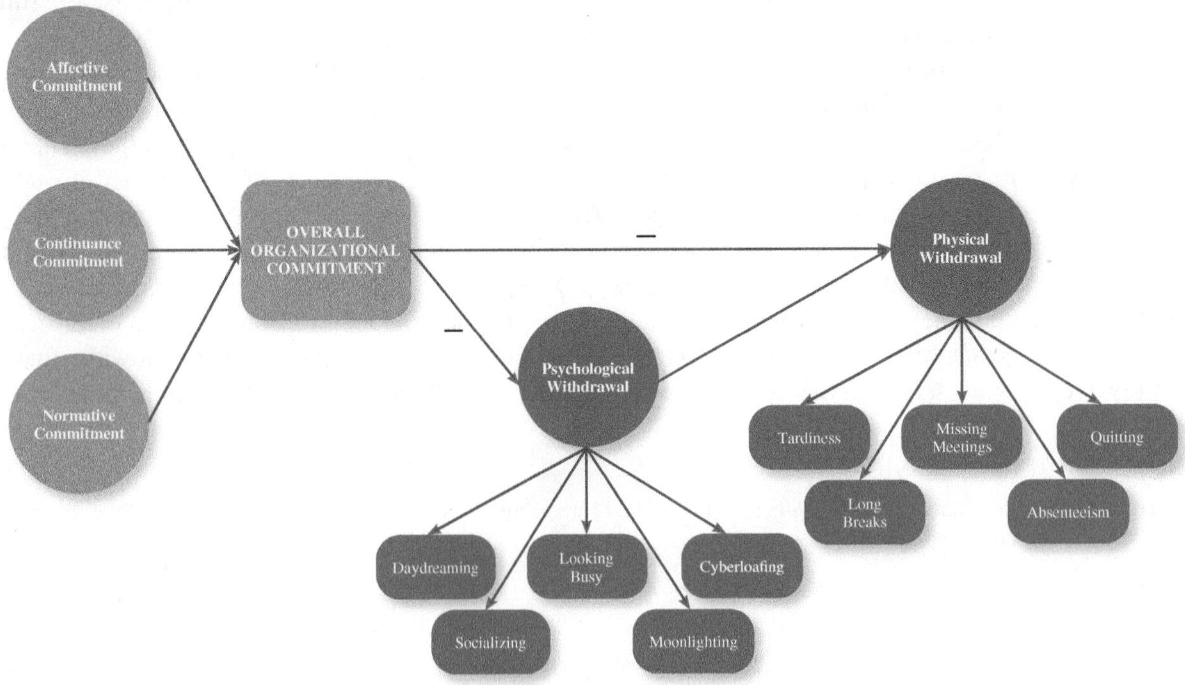

As you move forward in this book, you'll notice that every chapter includes a description of how that chapter's topic relates to organizational commitment. For example, Chapter 5 on job satisfaction describes how employees' satisfaction levels influence their organizational commitment. Chapter 8 on trust, justice, and ethics explains how employees' trust in management influences their organizational commitment. Sometimes you'll notice that a given chapter's topic relates more strongly to organizational commitment than to job performance. Other times, however, the topic may relate similarly to commitment and performance, or even relate more strongly to performance. Nevertheless, such differences will help you see exactly why the various topics in this book are so important to managers.

3.5 What workplace trends are affecting organizational commitment in today's organizations?

TRENDS THAT AFFECT COMMITMENT

Now that we've described exactly what organizational commitment represents, it's time to describe some of the trends that affect it in the contemporary workplace. Put simply, the composition of the workforce is changing, as is the traditional relationship between employees and employers. These trends put pressure on some types of commitment and alter the kinds of withdrawal seen in the workplace.

Diversity of the Workforce

One of the most visible trends affecting the workplace is the increasing diversity of the Canadian labour force. Demographically speaking, the participation rate of women continues to increase and now makes up approximately 47 percent of the overall labour force (53 percent for men).[79] These statistics show that the "white, male-dominated" workforce might slowly becoming a thing of the past. Another trend is the increased participation of visible minorities, expected to account for one-third of the Canadian labour force over the next 20 years, with this proportion even higher within urban settings.[80] Currently, visible minorities make up around 16 percent of the total workforce [81] Another diversity trend is the aging of the Canadian labour force. Back in 2011, the oldest baby boomers started to turn 65. From this point forward, the workplaces will experience a steady wave of retiring boomers, effectively reducing the overall supply of talent and changing the age structure within organizations.[82] Although large numbers of experienced employees will be eligible to retire over the next decade or so, the important question is when they will actually leave? Research suggests that remaining a member of the workforce is actually beneficial to older people's health, keeping them more mentally and physically fit. Moreover, medical advances are helping older employees stay vital longer, just as the physical labour component of most jobs keeps shrinking. The baby boomers are also one of the most educated generations, and research suggests that their continued participation in the workforce could add substantially to the country's economic output. Finally, as the economy continues to become more global, Canadian businesses face another important form of diversity: More and more employees are foreign-born. Over the next 20 years, roughly a quarter of all Canadian workers will be born outside the country.[83] See our ***OB Internationally*** feature for more discussion of organizational commitment in multinational corporations.

These forms of diversity make it more challenging to retain valued employees. Consider the social network diagram in Figure 3-3. As work groups become more diverse (e.g., gender, racial or ethnic origin, age), there's a danger that minorities or older employees will find themselves on the fringe of such networks, which potentially reduces their affective commitment. At the same time, foreign-born employees are likely to feel less embedded in their current jobs and perceive fewer links to their community and less fit with their geographic area. This feeling may reduce their sense of continuance commitment.

OB INTERNATIONALLY

Fostering organizational commitment can be more complex in multinational corporations, for two primary reasons. First, multinational corporations provide two distinct foci of commitment: Employees can be committed to the local subsidiary in which they work, or they can be committed to the global organization. Research on commitment in multinational corporations suggests that employees draw a distinction between those two foci when judging their commitment.[84] Specifically, employees distinguish between the prestige of their local subsidiary and the reputation of the larger organization. They also distinguish between the support provided by their local supervisor and the support provided by the global organization's top management. Such results reveal that it's possible to be committed to the local office but not the overall organization, or vice versa.

Second, multinational corporations require many employees to serve as expatriates for significant periods of time. Research suggests that the organizational commitment of expatriates depends, in part, on how well they adjust to their foreign assignments.[85] Research further suggests that expatriates' adjustment comes in three distinct forms:[86]

- *Work adjustment.* The degree of comfort with specific job responsibilities and performance expectations
- *Cultural adjustment.* The degree of comfort with the general living conditions, climate, cost of living, transportation, and housing offered by the host culture
- *Interaction adjustment.* The degree of comfort when socializing and interacting with members of the host culture

A study of multinational corporations in the transportation, service, manufacturing, chemical, and pharmaceutical industries showed that all three forms of adjustment relate significantly to affective commitment.[87] If expatriates cannot feel comfortable in their assignment, it's difficult for them to develop an emotional bond to their organization. Instead, they're likely to withdraw from the assignment, both psychologically and physically.

What factors contribute to an expatriate's adjustment levels? It turns out that work adjustment depends on many of the same things that drive domestic employees' job satisfaction and motivation.[88] Cultural adjustment and interaction adjustment, in con-trast, are very dependent on spousal and family comfort. If an expatriate's spouse or children are unhappy in their new environment, it becomes very difficult for the expatriate to remain committed. Fortunately, research suggests that cultural and interaction adjustment can increase with time, as experiences in the host nation gradually increase expatriates' sense of comfort, and ultimately their commitment to the work assignment.

The Changing Employee–Employer Relationship

A few generations ago, many employees assumed that they would work for a single organization for their entire career. The assumption was that they would exchange a lifetime of loyalty and good work for a lifetime of job security. That perception changed in the 1980s and 1990s as downsizing became a more common part of working life. Downsizing represents a form of involuntary turnover, when employees are forced to leave the organization regardless of their previous levels of commitment. The increase in downsizing has gone hand in hand with increases in temporary workers and outsourcing, fundamentally altering the way employees view their relationships with their employers.

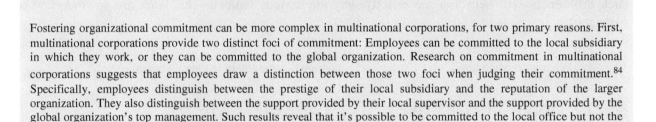

Companies usually downsize to cut costs, particularly during a recession or economic downturn. Does downsizing work? Does it make the company more profitable? One study suggests that the answer is "not usually." This study examined 3,628 companies between 1980 and 1994, of which 59 percent downsized 5 percent or more of their workforce at least once and 33 percent fired 15 percent or more of their workforce at least once.[89] The most important result was that downsizing actually harmed company profitability and stock price. In fact, it typically took firms two years to return to the performance levels that prompted the downsizing in the first place. The exception to this rule was companies that downsized in the context of some larger change in assets (e.g., the sale of a line of business, a merger, an acquisition). However, such firms were relatively rare; only one-eighth of the downsizers were involved in some sort of asset change at the time the layoffs occurred.

Why doesn't downsizing tend to work? One reason revolves around the organizational commitment levels of the so-called "survivors." The employees who remain in the organization after a downsizing are often stricken with "survivor syndrome," characterized by anger, depression, fear, distrust, and guilt.[90] One study found that downsizing survivors actually experienced more work-related stress than did the downsizing victims who went on to find new employment.[91] Survivor syndrome tends to reduce organizational commitment levels at the worst possible time, as downsizing survivors are often asked to work extra hard to compensate for their lost colleagues.

The change in employee–employer relationships brought about by a generation of downsizing makes it more challenging to retain valued employees. The most obvious challenge is finding a way to maintain affective commitment. The negative emotions aroused by survivor syndrome likely reduce emotional attachment to the organization. Moreover, if the downsizing has caused the loss of key figures in employees' social networks, their desire to stay will be harmed. However, a second challenge is to find some way to maintain normative commitment. The sense that people should stay with their employer may have been eroded by downsizing, with personal work philosophies now focusing on maximizing marketability for the next opportunity that comes along. Even if employees felt obligated to remain at a firm in the past, seeing colleagues get dismissed in a downsizing effort might change that belief rather quickly.

One way of quantifying the change in employee–employer relationships is to assess how employees view those relationships psychologically. Research suggests that employees tend to view their employment relationships in quasi-contractual terms. Specifically, **psychological contracts** reflect employees' beliefs about what they owe the organization and what the organization owes them.[92] These contracts are shaped by the recruitment and socialization activities that employees experience, which often convey promises and expectations that shape beliefs about reciprocal obligations. Some employees develop **transactional contracts** that are based on a narrow set of specific monetary obligations (e.g., the employee owes attendance and protection of proprietary information; the organization owes pay and advancement opportunities).[93] Other employees develop **relational contracts** that are based on a broader set of open-ended and subjective obligations (e.g., the employee owes loyalty and the willingness to go above and beyond; the organization owes job security, development, and support).[94] Seeing one's co-workers downsized can constitute a "breach" of an employee's psychological contract, and research suggests that psychological contract breach leads to psychological and physical withdrawal.[95] However, trends such as downsizing, use of temporary workers, and outsourcing may also cause employees to define their contracts in more transactional (as opposed to relational) terms.

psychological contracts

Employee beliefs about what employees owe the organization and what the organization owes them

transactional contracts

Psychological contracts that focus on a narrow set of specific monetary obligations

relational contracts

Psychological contracts that focus on a broad set of open-ended and subjective obligations

3.6 How can organizations foster a sense of commitment among employees?

APPLICATION: COMMITMENT INITIATIVES

Now that you've gained a good understanding of organizational commitment, and some of the workforce trends that affect it, let's close with a discussion of strategies and initiatives that can be used to maximize commitment. As the Costco example illustrates, almost every company could benefit from improving its commitment levels. What can they do to increase loyalty? At a general level, organizations can be supportive. **Perceived organizational support** reflects the degree to which employees believe that the organization values their contributions and cares about their well-being.[96] Organizations can do a number of things to be supportive, including providing adequate rewards, protecting job security, improving work conditions, and minimizing the impact of politics.[97] In a sense, such support represents the organization's commitment to its employees. A meta-analysis of 42 research studies with almost 12,000 participants revealed that perceptions of support are strongly related to organizational commitment.[98] That same review showed that perceptions of support are associated with lower levels of psychological and physical withdrawal.

perceived organizational support

The degree to which employees believe that the organization values their contributions and cares about their well-being

Beyond being supportive, organizations can engage in specific practices that target the three forms of commitment. From an affective commitment perspective, employer strategies could centre on increasing the bonds that link employees together. Several examples of these initiatives were presented earlier in this chapter (e.g., allowing employees time to play, social events that encourage employees to interact and develop friendships). Such opportunities promote tight bonding among employees and help to embed them within the social fabric of the organization—which may help to reduce voluntary turnover (or at least make leaving difficult). Other commitment-enhancing initiatives centre on the nature of the work performed (e.g., offering opportunities for personal growth and achievement). Learning about ways to design the work in such a way to "engage" workers is a topic that will be covered in Chapter 5.

From a continuance commitment perspective, the priority should be to create a salary and benefits package that creates a financial need to stay. One study compared the impact of a variety of human resources management practices on voluntary turnover and found that two of the most significant predictors were average pay level and quality of the benefits package.[99] Using compensation and benefits to lock people into jobs, however, should be carefully considered. Although high levels of continuance commitment have been shown to lower turnover, there seems to be very little payoff in terms of job performance or citizenship behaviour.[100] One factor that goes hand in hand with salaries and benefits is advancements and promotions, because salaries cannot remain competitive if employees get stuck in neutral when climbing the career ladder.[101] Paying attention to career paths is especially important for star employees and foreign-born employees, both of whom have many options for employment elsewhere.[102]

From a normative commitment perspective, the employer can provide various training and development opportunities for employees, which means investing in them to create the sense that they owe further service to the organization. As the nature of the employee–employer relationship has changed, opportunities for development have overtaken secure employment on the list of employee priorities.[103] IBM is one company with a reputation for prioritizing development. Its "workforce management initiative" keeps a database of 33,000 résumés to develop a snapshot of employee skills. IBM uses that snapshot to plan its future training and development activities, with $400 million of the company's $750 million training budget devoted to giving employees the skills they may need in the future. If employees find developmental activities beneficial and rewarding, they might be tempted to repay those efforts with further years of service.

A final practical suggestion centres on what to do if withdrawal begins to occur. Managers are usually tempted to look the other way when employees engage in minor forms of withdrawal. After all, sometimes such behaviours simply represent a break in an otherwise busy day. However, the progression model of withdrawal shows that even minor forms of psychological withdrawal often escalate, eventually to the point of absenteeism and turnover. The implication is therefore to stop the progression in its early stages by trying to root out the source of the reduced commitment. Many of the most effective companies take great strides to investigate the causes of low commitment, whether at the psychological withdrawal stage or during exit interviews. As one senior oil executive acknowledged, the loss of a talented employee warrants the same sort of investigation as a technical malfunction that causes significant downtime on an oil rig.[104]

TAKEAWAYS

3.1 Organizational commitment is the desire on the part of an employee to remain a member of the organization. Withdrawal behaviour is a set of actions that employees perform to avoid the work situation. Commitment and withdrawal are negatively related to each other—the more committed employees are, the less likely they are to engage in withdrawal.

3.2 There are three forms of organizational commitment. Affective commitment occurs when employees want to stay and is influenced by the emotional bonds between employees. Continuance commitment occurs when employees need to stay and is influenced by salary and benefits and the degree to which they are embedded in the community. Normative commitment occurs when employees feel that they ought to stay and is influenced by an organization investing in its employees or engaging in charitable efforts.

3.3 Employees can respond to negative work events in four ways: exit, voice, loyalty, and neglect. Exit is a form of physical withdrawal in which the employee either ends or restricts organizational membership. Voice is an active and constructive response by which employees attempt to improve the situation. Loyalty is passive and constructive; employees remain supportive while hoping the situation improves on its own. Neglect is a form of psychological withdrawal in which interest and effort in the job decrease.

3.4 Examples of psychological withdrawal include daydreaming, socializing, looking busy, moonlighting, and cyberloafing. Examples of physical withdrawal include tardiness, long breaks, missing meetings, absenteeism, and quitting. Consistently with the progression model, withdrawal behaviours tend to start with minor psychological forms before escalating to more major physical varieties.

3.5 The increased diversity of the workforce can reduce commitment if employees feel lower levels of affective commitment or become less embedded in their current jobs. The employee–employer relationship, which has changed due to decades of downsizing, can reduce affective and normative commitment, making it more of a challenge to retain talented employees.

3.6 Organizations can foster commitment among employees by fostering perceived organizational support, which reflects the degree to which the organization cares about employees' well-being. Commitment can also be fostered by specific initiatives directed at the three commitment types.

KEY TERMS

absenteeism
affective commitment
compensatory forms model
continuance commitment
cyberloafing
daydreaming
embeddedness
erosion model
exit
focus of commitment
independent forms model
long breaks
looking busy
loyalty
missing meetings
moonlighting
neglect
normative commitment
organizational commitment
perceived organizational support
physical withdrawal
progression model
psychological contracts

psychological withdrawal
quitting
relational contracts
social influence model
socializing
tardiness
transactional contracts
withdrawal behaviour

DISCUSSION QUESTIONS

3.1 Which form of organizational commitment (affective, continuance, or normative) do you think is most important to the majority of employees? Which do you think is most important to you?

3.2 Describe other ways that organizations can improve affective, continuance, and normative commitment, other than the strategies suggested in this chapter. How expensive are those strategies?

3.3 Consider times when you've reacted to a negative event with exit, voice, loyalty, or neglect. What was it about the situation that caused you to respond the way you did? Do you usually respond to negative events in the same way, or does your response vary across the four options?

3.4 Can organizations use a combination of monitoring and punishment procedures to reduce psychological and physical withdrawal? How might such programs work from a practical perspective? Do you think they would be effective?

3.5 Can you think of reasons the increased diversity of the workforce might actually increase organizational commitment? Why? Which of the three types of commitment might explain that sort of result?

3.6 Studies suggest that decades of downsizing have lowered organizational commitment levels. Can you think of a way that an organization can conduct layoffs without harming the commitment of the survivors? How?

CASE • COSTCO

As it tries to build on its success, Costco faces competition from two different flanks. The first, of course, is from Walmart—the only major retailer bigger than Costco. Although they compete for many of the same customers, Costco and Walmart are very different in a number of respects. Costco's employees make $20.89 per hour; Walmart's make $12.67.[105] "I just think people need to make a living wage," explains CEO Craig Jelinek. "It also puts more money back into the economy and creates a healthier country. It's really that simple." In contrast, Walmart has drawn criticism for cutting staff within its stores over the past five years.[106] Those cuts have resulted in longer lines, less help for customers, disorganized aisles, and unstocked shelves.

Costco's second competitor—Amazon—has no shelves to stock. Indeed, Amazon's business model relies, in part, on in-store shopping being so annoying that ordering online becomes the more relaxing alternative. Although the rise of Amazon has signalled a decline for a number of retailers, Costco has been able to hold its own, for three reasons.[107] First, the bulk discounts it receives from suppliers allow Costco to have lower prices than Amazon. Second, much of Costco's business revolves around groceries—a market Amazon has yet to crack. Third, Costco does have at least some online presence, its own website being the 17th most popular retail site in the United States. Will these advantages hold with online retail growing at roughly three times the rate of retail overall? Costco chair Jeff Brotman summarizes the sobering nature of such trends: "I used to get up every morning worried about Walmart.... Now I worry about them, and I worry whether we are up to the challenge of the shift in retail buying habits."[108]

The different threats represented by Walmart and Amazon pose something of an organizational commitment dilemma for Costco. On the one hand, Costco's 5 percent turnover rate gives it a cost and stability advantage that helps it beat traditional competitors. On the other hand, that retention limits the fresh ideas that outsiders can bring to a company. Indeed, Costco's executive turnover rate is only 1 percent, and it refuses to hire business school graduates (instead opting to send rank-and-file employees to school to earn degrees).[109] Indeed, even recently retired CEO Jim Sinegal, who is 77, has maintained an advising role. That potential for stagnation does not seem to be lost on Costco, however. John Matthews, vice-president of human resources, acknowledges that the company has become "awfully inbred." And Rotman admits, succinctly: "We're all old."

3.1 How exactly does Costco's low turnover rate help it in its battle against Walmart? Will any of those factors also help against Amazon?

3.2 What would a "perfect turnover rate" be for a company like Costco? Describe the consequences of a turnover rate that's *too* low.

3.3 If you were in charge of human resources at Costco, would you retain the philosophy of sending rank-and-file employees to school rather than hiring business school graduates? Why or why not?

EXERCISE • REACTING TO NEGATIVE EVENTS

The purpose of this exercise is to explore how individuals react to three all-too-common scenarios that represent negative workplace events. This exercise uses groups of six participants, so your instructor will either assign you to a group of six or ask you to create your own group of six. The exercise has the following steps:

3.1 Individually read the following three scenarios: the annoying boss, the boring job, and pay and seniority. For each scenario, write down two specific behaviours in which you would likely engage in response to that scenario. Write down what you would actually do, as opposed to what you wish you would do. For example, you may wish that you would march into your boss's office and demand a change, but if you would actually do nothing, write down "nothing."

Annoying Boss	You've been working at your current company for about a year. Over time, your boss has become more and more annoying to you. It's not that your boss is a bad person, or even necessarily a bad boss. It's more a personality conflict—the way your boss talks, the way your boss manages every little thing, even the facial expressions your boss uses. The more time passes, the more you just can't stand to be around your boss.	**Two Likely Behaviours** _____ _____
Boring Job	You've been working at your current company for about a year. You've come to realize that your job is pretty boring. It's the first real job you've ever had, and at first it was nice to have some money and something to do every day. But the "new job" excitement has worn off, and things are actually quite monotonous. Same thing every day. It's gotten to the point that you check your watch every hour, and Wednesdays feel like they should be Fridays.	**Two Likely Behaviours** _____ _____
Pay and Seniority	You've been working at your current company for about a year. The consensus is that you're doing a great job—you've gotten excellent performance evaluations and have emerged as a leader on many projects. As you've achieved this high status, however, you've come to feel that you are underpaid. Your company's pay procedures emphasize seniority much more than job performance. As a result, you look at other members of your project teams and see poor performers making much more than you, just because they've been with the company longer.	**Two Likely Behaviours** _____ _____

3.2 In groups, compare and contrast your likely responses to the three scenarios. Come to a consensus on the two most likely responses for the group as a whole. Elect one group member to write the two likely responses to each of the three scenarios on the board.

3.3 Class discussion (whether in groups or as a class) should centre on where the likely responses fit into the exit–voice–loyalty–neglect framework. What personal and situational factors would lead someone to one category of responses over another? Do any responses not fit into the framework?

OB ASSESSMENTS • AFFECTIVE COMMITMENT

How emotionally attached are you to your employer? This assessment is designed to measure affective commitment—the feeling that you want to stay with your current organization. Think of your current job or the last job that you held (even if it was a part-time or summer job). Answer each question using the response scale provided. Then subtract your answers to the boldfaced questions from 6, with the difference being your new answers for those questions. For example, if your original answer for question 3 was "4," your new answer is "2" (6 – 4). Then add up your answers for the six questions.

1 Strongly Disagree	2 Disagree	3 Neutral	4 Agree	5 Strongly Agree	
1. I would be very happy to spend the rest of my career in this organization.					____
2. I really feel as if this organization's problems are my own.					____
3. I do not feel like "part of the family" at my organization.					____
4. I do not feel "emotionally attached" to this organization.					____
5. This organization has a great deal of personal meaning for me.					____
6. I do not feel a strong sense of belonging to my organization.					____

Scoring and Interpretation

If your scores add up to 20 or more, you feel a strong sense of affective commitment to your current or past employer, which means that you feel an emotional attachment to the company, or the people within it, that lessens the likelihood that you would leave voluntarily. If your scores add up to less than 20, you have a weaker sense of affective commitment to your current or past employer. This result is especially likely if you responded to the questions in reference to a part-time or summer job, for which there is rarely enough time to develop a deep emotional bond. When interpreting your scores on these assessments remember to consider the *reliability* and *validity* of these tools (see Chapter 1, ***OB Assessments***).

Source: J.P. Meyer and N.J. Allen, 1997, *Commitment in the Workplace: Theory, Research, and Application.* Reproduced with permission of Sage Publications, Inc. via Copyright Clearance Center.

PART 2

Individual Characteristics and Mechanisms

Personality, Cultural Values, and Ability

CHAPTER 4

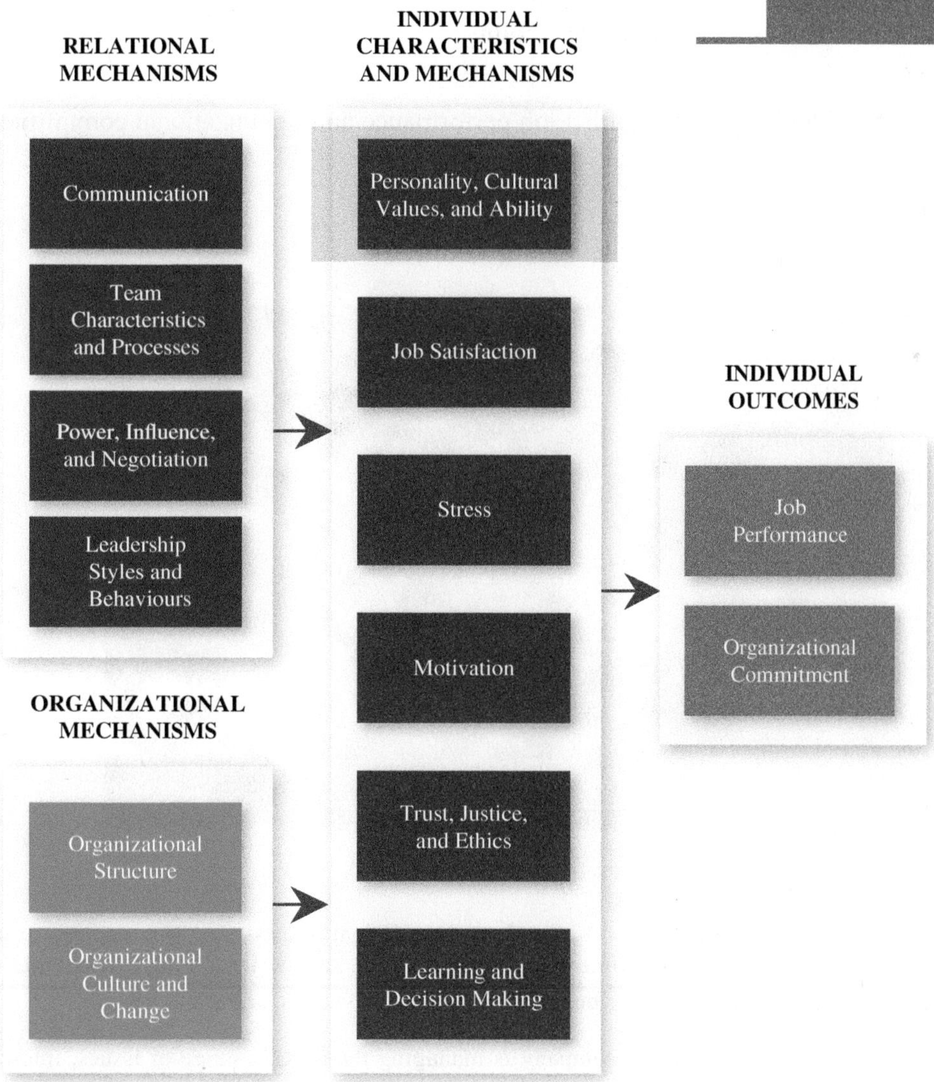

LEARNING OUTCOMES

After reading this chapter, you should be able to answer the following questions:

4.1 What is personality? What are cultural values? What is ability?

4.2 What are the "Big Five" factors of personality?

4.3 What taxonomies can be used to describe cultural values?

4.4 What are the various types of cognitive ability?

4.5 What are the various types of emotional ability?

4.6 What are the various types of physical ability?

4.7 How do individual differences affect job performance and organizational commitment?

Nexen

Photo Courtesy of Nexen

Nexen, a wholly owned subsidiary of CNOOC Limited, is a Calgary-based energy company responsibly developing energy resources in the U.K. North Sea, offshore West Africa, the United States, and western Canada. It has three principal businesses: conventional oil and gas, oil sands, and shale gas/oil.[1]

One of the challenges facing a truly global company is managing the diverse range of issues, interests, and backgrounds of employees and contractors in a way that promotes a strong, unified workplace culture. Closer to home, another challenge is maintaining a North American workforce at a time when chronic skill shortages exist in many key technical areas, which include legions of retiring baby boomers. These challenges have changed the playing field for many North American oil and gas companies.

Winning the "war for talent" requires attracting the attention of a shrinking pool of qualified job seekers who have many options. Why are people attracted to Nexen? For starters, the company has earned a reputation within the industry of finding the best and brightest talent. It aggressively seeks out individuals with the technical skills, knowledge, and abilities needed to be successful in their work roles. To be hired, individuals have to show they have personal qualities that fit a workplace culture that puts high value on safety, collaboration, innovation, and striving to exceed expectations.[2]

One of Nexen's signature human resources initiatives is its New Graduate Rotation Program, a development opportunity offered to new and recent graduates across a range of disciplines, including engineering, geology, geophysics, human resources, finance, and accounting. These young professionals spend their first three years learning on the job by rotating through different areas of the business and working on high-profile projects. A mentor is assigned each graduate to provide coaching and feedback. The program is just one part of Nexen's commitment to providing every employee with a rewarding career. The company also offers internships and summer student positions for young talent. Once hired, employees take an active role in mapping out a plan for their own career growth and development, supported by top-quality tools and resources. In addition, Nexen provides generous tuition subsidies for employment-related courses and subsidies for professional accreditations. For managers at every level, opportunities are targeted at enhancing leadership capabilities through intensive training programs.

As important as the traditional recruiting sources are for the company (e.g., colleges and universities), Nexen has been able to meet its staffing goals by attracting job seekers from locations around the world and from non-traditional sources. A growing and underutilized source of talent is the Aboriginal communities in which Nexen operates. Several strategic initiatives are under way to attract qualified Aboriginal applicants. Information sessions are offered at Aboriginal career centres, and in career and recruitment fairs at postsecondary institutions.

What have initiatives like these accomplished? In addition to being an employer of choice, Nexen is now recognized as one of the best employers in the country![3]

PERSONALITY, CULTURAL VALUES, AND ABILITY

4.1 What is personality? What are cultural values? What is ability?

It seems clear from the chapter-opening profile that Nexen focuses a great deal on the personal qualities of the people it hires. **Personality** refers to the structures and propensities inside people that explain their characteristic patterns of thought, emotion, and behaviour.[4] Personality creates people's social reputations—the way they are perceived by friends, family, co-workers, and supervisors.[5] In this way, personality captures *what people are like.* Although we sometimes describe people as having "a good personality," personality is actually a collection of multiple traits. **Traits** are defined as recurring regularities or trends in people's responses to their environment.[6] Adjectives such as responsible, easygoing, polite, and reserved are examples of traits that can be used to summarize someone's personality. **Cultural values** are defined as shared beliefs about desirable end states or modes of conduct in a given culture.[7] You can think of cultural values as capturing what cultures are like. Adjectives such as traditional, informal, risk-averse, or assertive are all examples of values that can be used to summarize a nation's culture. Cultural values can influence the development of people's personality traits, as well as how those traits are expressed in daily life. **Ability** refers to the relatively stable capabilities people have to perform a particular range of different but related activities.[8] In contrast to skills, which can be improved over time with training and experience, ability is relatively stable. Although abilities can change slowly over time with repeated practice and repetition, the level of a given ability generally limits how much a person can improve, even with the best training in the world. In contrast to personality and values, ability captures *what people can do*.

personality
The structures and propensities inside a person that explain his or her characteristic patterns of thought, emotion, and behaviour; personality reflects what people are like and creates their social reputation

traits
Recurring trends in people's responses to their environment

cultural values
Shared beliefs about desirable end states or modes of conduct in a given culture that influence the expression of traits

ability
Relatively stable capabilities of people for performing a particular range of related activities

HOW CAN WE DESCRIBE WHAT EMPLOYEES ARE LIKE?

We can use personality traits and cultural values to describe what employees are like. For example, how would you describe your first university roommate to one of your classmates? You'd start off using certain adjectives—maybe the roommate was funny and outgoing, or maybe polite and organized. Of course, it would take more than a few adjectives to describe your roommate fully. You could probably go on listing traits for several minutes, maybe even coming up with 100 traits or more. This might sound like a lot, but personality researchers note that the third edition of *Webster's Unabridged Dictionary* contains 1,710 adjectives that can be used to describe someone's traits![9] Was your roommate abrasive, adulterous, agitable, alarmable, antisocial, arbitrative, arrogant, asocial, audacious, aweless, and awkward? We hope not!

4.2 What are the "Big Five" factors of personality?

The Big Five Taxonomy

With 1,710 adjectives, you might be worrying about the length of this chapter (or the difficulty of your next exam!). Fortunately, it turns out that most adjectives are variations on five broad "factors" or "dimensions" that can be used to summarize our personalities:[10] **conscientiousness, agreeableness, neuroticism, openness to experience**, and **extraversion**—collectively dubbed the **Big Five**.[11] Figure 4-1 lists the traits that can be found within each of the Big Five dimensions. Would you like to see what your Big Five profile looks like? Our *OB Assessments* feature at the end of the chapter will show you where you stand on each of the five dimensions.

FIGURE 4-1

Trait Adjectives Associated with the Big Five

C	A	N	O	E
Conscientiousness	Agreeableness	Neuroticism	Openness	Extraversion
• Dependable • Organized • Reliable • Ambitious • Hardworking • Persevering	• Kind • Cooperative • Sympathetic • Helpful • Courteous • Warm	• Nervous • Moody • Emotional • Insecure • Jealous • Unstable	• Curious • Imaginative • Creative • Complex • Refined • Sophisticated	• Talkative • Sociable • Passionate • Assertive • Bold • Dominant
NOT	NOT	NOT	NOT	NOT
• Careless • Sloppy • Inefficient • Negligent • Lazy • Irresponsible	• Critical • Antagonistic • Callous • Selfish • Rude • Cold	• Calm • Steady • Relaxed • At ease • Secure • Contented	• Uninquisitive • Conventional • Conforming • Simple • Unartistic • Traditional	• Quiet • Shy • Inhibited • Bashful • Reserved • Submissive

Sources: G. Saucier, "Mini-Markers: A Brief Version of Goldberg's Unipolar Big-Five Markers," *Journal of Personality Assessment* 63 (1994), pp. 506–16; L.R. Goldberg, "The Development of Markers for the Big-Five Factor Structure," *Psychological Assessment* 4 (1992), pp. 26–42; R.R. McCrae and P.T. Costa Jr., "Validation of the Five-Factor Model of Personality Across Instruments and Observers," *Journal of Personality and Social Psychology* 52 (1987), pp. 81–90; and C.M. Gill and G.P. Hodgkinson, "Development and Validation of the Five-Factor Model Questionnaire (FFMQ): An Adjectival-Based Personality Inventory for Use in Occupational Settings," *Personnel Psychology* 60 (2007), pp. 731–66.

conscientiousness

Dimension of personality-reflecting traits like being dependable, organized, reliable, ambitious, hard-working, and persevering

agreeableness

Dimension of personality-reflecting traits like being kind, cooperative, sympathetic, helpful, courteous, and warm

neuroticism

Dimension of personality-reflecting traits like being nervous, moody, emotional, insecure, jealous, and unstable

openness to experience

Dimension of personality-reflecting traits like being curious, imaginative, creative, complex, refined, and sophisticated

extraversion

Dimension of personality-reflecting traits like being talkative, sociable, passionate, assertive, bold, and dominant

Big Five

The five major dimensions of personality: conscientiousness, agreeableness, neuroticism, openness to experience, and extraversion

Conscientiousness As shown in Figure 4-1, conscientious people are dependable, organized, reliable, ambitious, hard-working, and persevering.[12] It's difficult, if not impossible, to envision a job in which those traits will not be beneficial.[13] That's not a claim we make about all of the Big Five, because some jobs require high levels of agreeableness, extraversion, or openness, while others demand low levels of those same traits. We don't want to spoil the discussion "How Important Are These Individual Differences?" that concludes this chapter; suffice it to say that conscientiousness has the biggest influence on job performance of any of the Big Five. Of course, the key question therefore becomes: Why is conscientiousness so valuable?

One reason can be found in the general goals that people prioritize in their working life. Conscientious employees prioritize **accomplishment striving**, which reflects a strong desire to accomplish task-related goals as a means of expressing personality.[14] People who are "accomplishment strivers" have a built-in desire to finish work tasks, channel a high proportion of their efforts toward those tasks, and work harder and longer on task assignments. As evidence of their accomplishment-striving nature, one research study showed that conscientious salespeople set higher sales goals for themselves than unconscientious sales-people and were more committed to meeting those goals.[15] Another study of salespeople showed that conscientious salespeople's organizational skills were particularly valuable during their first year of employment, and their ambitious nature became more critical as they gained tenure and experience.[16]

accomplishment striving

A strong desire to accomplish task-related goals as a means of expressing one's personality

Research suggests that conscientious individuals actually live longer. A possible reason is that conscientiousness is associated with less risky driving behaviour.

© Ingram Publishing

A third research study provides particularly compelling evidence regarding the benefits of conscientiousness.[17] The study used data from the University of California, Berkeley's Intergenerational Studies, which collected data about a set of children in the late 1920s and early 1930s. Those researchers gathered personality data using interviews and assessments of the children by trained psychologists. Follow-up studies collected data on the same sample as they reached early adulthood, middle age, and late adulthood. This last time period included assessments of career success, which included ratings of annual income and occupational prestige. The results of the study showed that childhood conscientiousness was strongly correlated with ratings of career success five decades later! In fact, those conscientiousness effects were roughly twice as strong as the effects of the other Big Five dimensions.

Such findings show that it pays to be conscientious; other research even suggests that conscientiousness is good for your health. For example, one study gathered data about the conscientiousness of 1,528 children in the early 1920s.[18] Data on health-relevant behaviours were then gathered in 1950 for 1,215 of the original participants. By 1986, 419 of the participants had died and 796 were still living. The results of the study revealed that childhood conscientiousness was negatively related to mortality, including death from injuries, death from cardiovascular disease, and death from cancer. Why did conscientious participants live longer? The study also showed that conscientiousness was negatively related to alcohol consumption and smoking during adulthood. Other research has shown that conscientious people are less likely to abuse drugs, more likely to take preventive steps to remain healthy, and less likely to engage in risky behaviours as a driver or pedestrian.[19]

Agreeableness Agreeable people are warm, kind, cooperative, sympathetic, helpful, and courteous. Agreeable people prioritize **communion striving**, which reflects a strong desire to obtain acceptance in personal relationships as a means of expressing personality. Put differently, agreeable people focus on "getting along," not necessarily "getting ahead."[20] Unlike conscientiousness, agreeableness is not related to performance across all jobs or occupations.[21] Why not? The biggest reason is that communion striving is beneficial in some positions but detrimental in others. For example, managers often need to prioritize the effectiveness of the unit over a desire to gain acceptance. In such cases, effective job performance may demand being disagreeable in the face of unreasonable requests or demands.

communion striving
A strong desire to obtain acceptance in personal relationships as a means of expressing one's personality

Of course, in some jobs agreeableness can be beneficial. The most obvious example is service jobs, in which the employee has direct, face-to-face, or verbal contact with a customer. How many times have you encountered a customer service person who was cold, rude, or antagonistic? Did you tend to buy the company's product after such experiences? Research suggests that agreeable employees have stronger customer service skills.[22] One reason for their effectiveness in customer service environments is that they are reluctant to react to conflict with criticism, threats, or manipulation.[23] Instead, they tend to react to conflict by walking away, adopting a wait-and-see attitude, or giving in to the other person.

One study provides unique insights into the effects of agreeableness. It used a variation of "lived day analysis," in which a portion of a participant's daily routine is recorded and analyzed.[24] Ninety-six undergraduates completed assessments of the Big Five personality dimensions before being fitted with a digital recorder and an electronic microphone that could be clipped to their shirt collar. The microphone recorded 30 seconds of footage at 12-minute intervals over the course of two weekdays, with participants unable to track when footage was actually being recorded. Trained coders then rated the sounds and conversations recorded on the microphone. The results of the study revealed a number of interesting expressions of agreeableness. Agreeable participants were significantly less likely to be at home in their apartment during recordings; instead, they spent more time in public places. They were also less likely to use swear words and more likely to use words that conveyed personal rapport during conversations.

Extraversion Extraverted people are talkative, sociable, passionate, assertive, bold, and dominant (in contrast to introverts, who are quiet, shy, and reserved). Of the Big Five, extraversion is the easiest to judge in **zero acquaintance situations**—situations in which two people have only just met. Consider times when you've been around a stranger in a doctor's office, in line at a grocery store, or in an airport terminal. It only takes about five minutes to figure out whether that stranger is extraverted or introverted.[25] Extraversion is also the Big Five dimension that you knew your standing on, even before taking our self-assessment. People rarely consider how open they are to new experiences or how agreeable they are, but almost everyone already self-identifies as an "extravert" or "introvert."

zero acquaintance situations
Situations in which two people have just met

Like agreeableness, extraversion is not necessarily related to performance across all jobs or occupations. However, extraverted people prioritize **status striving**, which reflects a strong desire to obtain power and influence within a social structure as a means of expressing personality.[26] Extraverts care a lot about being successful and influential and direct their work efforts toward "moving up" and developing a strong reputation. Indeed, research suggests that extraverts are more likely to emerge as leaders in social and task-related groups.[27] They also tend to be rated as more effective in a leadership role by the people who are following them.[28] One possible reason for these findings is that people tend to view extraverts, who are more energetic and outgoing, as more "leader-like" than introverts.

status striving
A strong desire to obtain power and influence within a social structure as a means of expressing one's personality

In addition to being related to leadership emergence and effectiveness, research suggests that extraverts tend to be happier with their jobs. As we will see in this chapter, people's day-to-day moods can be categorized along two dimensions: pleasantness and activation. As is illustrated in Figure 4-2, extraverted employees tend to be high in what is called **positive affectivity**—a dispositional tendency to experience pleasant, engaging moods such as enthusiasm, excitement, and elation.[29] That tendency to experience positive moods across situations explains why extraverts tend to be more satisfied with their jobs.[30] Research now acknowledges that employees' genes have a significant impact on their job satisfaction and that much of that genetic influence is due to extraversion (and neuroticism, as discussed next). For example, one study of identical twins reared apart showed that twins' job satisfaction levels were significantly correlated, even when the twins held jobs that were quite different in terms of their duties, their complexity, and their working conditions.[31] In fact, this study suggested that around 30 percent of the variation in job satisfaction is due to genetic factors such as personality.

positive affectivity
A dispositional tendency to experience pleasant, engaging moods such as enthusiasm, excitement, and elation

FIGURE 4-2

Extraversion, Neuroticism, and Typical Moods

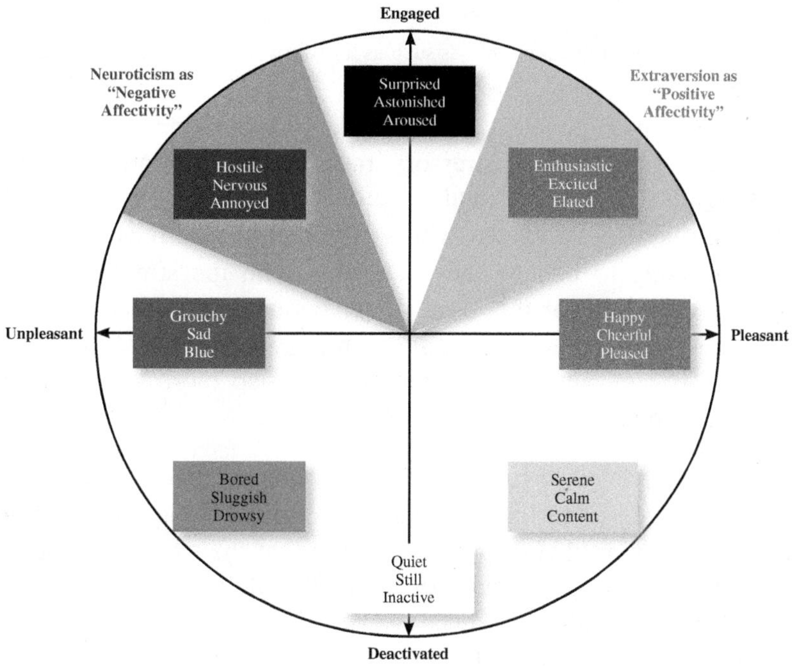

Other research suggests that extraverts have more to be happy about than just their jobs. Specifically, research suggests that extraversion is positively related to more general life satisfaction.[32] To shed light on that finding, one study asked students to complete a "life event checklist" by indicating whether various events had happened to them in the preceding four years.[33] The results showed that extraversion was associated with more positive events, such as joining a club or athletic team, going on vacation with friends, getting a raise at work, receiving an award for non-academic reasons, and getting married or engaged. Other studies have linked extraversion to number of same-sex peers, number of dating partners, frequency of alcohol consumption, and frequency of attendance at parties.[34] However, extraverts spend so much time doing those things that they wind up having less frequent interactions with their family.[35] Even parents of extraverts enjoy a phone call home now and again!

Neuroticism Neurotic people are nervous, moody, emotional, insecure, and jealous. Occasionally you may see this Big Five dimension called by its flip side: "emotional stability" or "emotional adjustment." If conscientiousness is the most important of the Big Five from the perspective of job performance, neuroticism is the second-most-important.[36] There are few jobs for which the traits associated with neuroticism are beneficial to on-the-job behaviours. Instead, most jobs benefit from employees who are calm, steady, and secure.

Whereas extraversion is synonymous with positive affectivity, neuroticism is synonymous with **negative affectivity**—a dispositional tendency to experience unpleasant moods such as hostility, nervousness, and annoyance (see Figure 4-2).[37] That tendency to experience negative moods explains why neurotic employees often experience lower levels of job satisfaction than their less neurotic counterparts.[38] Along with extraversion, neuroticism explains much of the impact of genetic factors on job satisfaction. Research suggests that the negative affectivity associated with neuroticism even influences more general life satisfaction, such that neurotic people tend to be less happy with their lives in general.[39]

negative affectivity
A dispositional tendency to experience unpleasant moods such as hostility, nervousness, and annoyance

Neuroticism also influences how people deal with stressful situations. Specifically, neuroticism is associated with a differential exposure to stressors, meaning that neurotic people are more likely to appraise day-to-day situations as stressful (and therefore feel like they are exposed to stressors more frequently).[40] Neuroticism is also associated with a differential reactivity to stressors, meaning that neurotic people are less likely to believe they can cope with the stressors that they experience.[41] Neuroticism is largely responsible for the Type A behaviour pattern that has been shown to affect employees' health and ability to manage stressful environments.[42] That is, they are much more likely to be "Type A's," whereas less neurotic individuals are much more likely to be "Type B's" (see Chapter 6 on stress for more discussion of these issues).

Neuroticism is also strongly related to **locus of control**, which reflects whether people attribute the causes of events to themselves or to the external environment.[43] Neurotic people tend to hold an external locus of control, meaning that they often believe that the events that occur around them are driven by luck, chance, or fate. Less neurotic people tend to hold an internal locus of control, meaning that they believe that their own behaviour dictates events. Table 4-1 provides more detail about the external-versus-internal distinction. It includes a number of beliefs representative of an external or an internal viewpoint, including beliefs about life in general, work, school, politics, and relationships. If you tend to agree more strongly with the beliefs in the left column, you have a more external locus of control; if you tend to agree more with the right column, your locus is more internal.

TABLE 4-1

External and Internal Locus of Control

People with an External Locus of Control Tend to Believe:	People with an Internal Locus of Control Tend to Believe:
Many of the unhappy things in people's lives are partly due to bad luck.	People's misfortunes result from the mistakes they make.
Getting a good job depends mainly on being in the right place at the right time.	Becoming a success is a matter of hard work; luck has little or nothing to do with it.
Many times exam questions tend to be so unrelated to course work that studying is really useless.	In the case of the well-prepared student, there is rarely if ever such a thing as an unfair test.
This world is run by the few people in power, and there is not much the little guy can do about it.	The average citizen can have an influence in government decisions.
There's not much use in trying too hard to please people; if they like you, they like you.	People are lonely because they don't try to be friendly.

Source: Adapted from J.B. Rotter, "Generalized Expectancies for Internal Versus External Control of Reinforcement," *Psychological Monographs* 80 (1966), pp. 1–28.

locus of control
One's tendency to view the cause of events and personal outcomes as internally or externally controlled

How important is locus of control? One meta-analysis of 135 different research studies showed that an internal locus of control was associated with higher levels of job satisfaction and job performance.[44] A second meta-analysis of 222 different research studies showed that people with an internal locus of control enjoyed better health, including higher self-reported mental well-being, fewer self-reported physical symptoms, lower blood pressure, and lower stress hormone secretion.[45] Internals also enjoyed more social support at work than externals and sensed that they had a stronger relationship with their supervisors. They viewed their jobs as having more beneficial characteristics, such as autonomy and significance, and fewer negative characteristics, such as conflict and ambiguity. In addition, those with an internal locus of control earned a higher salary than those with an external locus.

Openness to Experience The final dimension of the Big Five is openness to experience. Open people are curious, imaginative, creative, complex, refined, and sophisticated. Of all five, openness to experience has the most alternative labels; sometimes it's called "inquisitiveness" or "intellectualness" or even "culture" (not in the national culture sense—rather, in the "high culture" sense of knowing fine wine, art, and classical music). Much like agreeableness and extraversion, the traits associated with openness are beneficial in some jobs but not others. As a result, openness is not related to job performance across all occupations.

What jobs benefit from high levels of openness? Generally speaking, jobs that are very fluid and dynamic, with rapid changes in job demands. Research shows that open employees excel in learning and training environments, because their curiosity gives them a built-in desire to learn new things.[46] They also tend to be more adaptable and quick to identify when the "old way of doing things" is no longer effective, excelling at the search for a new and better approach.[47] In fact, conscientious employees are sometimes less effective than open employees in such environments, because their persevering nature sometimes prevents them from abandoning "tried and true" task strategies.

Openness to experience is also more likely to be valuable in jobs that require high levels of creative performance, where job holders need to be able to generate novel and useful ideas and solutions.[48] The relationship between openness and creative performance can be seen in Figure 4-3. Together with cognitive ability, openness to experience is a key driver of creative thought, as smart and open people excel at the style of thinking demanded by creativity. Creative thought results in creative performance when people come up with new ideas, create fresh approaches to problems, or suggest innovations that can improve the workplace.[49] The creativity benefits of openness likely explain why highly open individuals are more likely to migrate into artistic and scientific fields, in which novel and original products are so critical.[50]

BMW, the German automaker, seems to understand the importance of openness to experience, along with several of the other Big Five dimensions. BMW has worked hard to create a culture of innovation in which there is never a penalty for proposing new and outlandish ways of improving its cars.[51] Those proposed improvements include a "smart card" that can be taken out of your own BMW car and plugged into a rented one, passing along your music, podcast, and comfort settings to the new vehicle. Openness is needed to foster such creative thought, but agreeableness is also key to BMW's culture. Stefan Krause, BMW's chief financial officer, summarizes how to push a creative idea successfully:

"You can go into fighting mode or you can ask permission and get everyone to support you. If you do it without building ties, you will be blocked."

FIGURE 4-3

Openness to Experience and Creativity

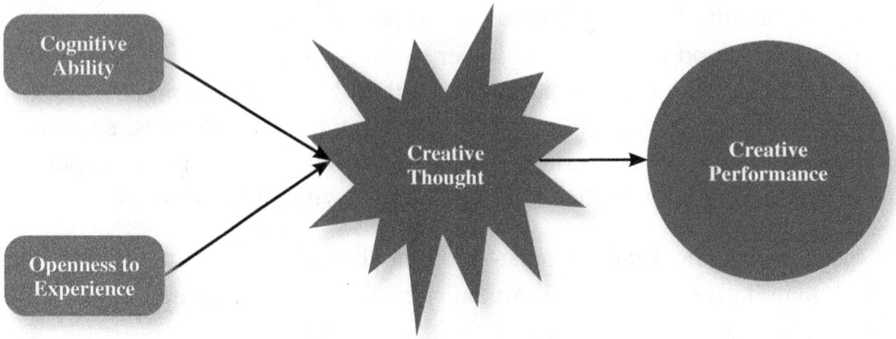

People who are open to new experiences tend to do well in situations that offer frequent opportunities to learn new things, such as teaching.

© Royalty-free/Corbis

BMW employees also draw on their conscientiousness when a new technology is introduced or production volume is expanded. In those critical time periods, employees from other factories may move into temporary housing far from home to put in extra hours on another plant's line. Why are employees so devoted? For one thing, no one at BMW can remember a layoff—which is quite unique in the auto industry. That's part of the reason BMW's human resources group receives more than 200,000 job applications annually. Those fortunate enough to make it to the interview stage participate in elaborate, day-long drills in teams to make sure their personalities are a good match for the company.

BMW's Leipzig facility, where the assembly line moves above work spaces to give employees a feel for the rhythm of the plant.

© AP Photo/Battle Creek Enquirer, John Grap

4.3 What taxonomies can be used to describe cultural values?

Cultural Values

Now that we've described a number of personality traits, we turn our attention to the cultural values. It turns out that the societies in which we were raised exerts a strong influence on the development of our personalities and the way our traits are expressed.[52] Societies can be described in a number of ways, including their climate and habitat, their sovereignty and political system, their language and religion, their education and technology levels, and their economic development.[53] However, one of the most important aspects of societies is culture. **Culture** is defined as the shared values, beliefs, motives, identities, and interpretations that result from common experiences of members of a society and are transmitted across generations.[54] It has been described as patterns resulting from societal traditions and as the collective programming of the mind that separates one society from another.[55] The shared values, societal traditions, and collective programming underlying culture influences the development of our personalities while also shaping how our traits are expressed. In this way, explaining "what we're like" requires an awareness of "where we're from."

culture

The shared values, beliefs, motives, identities, and interpretations that result from common experiences of members of a society and are transmitted across generations

To some extent, cultures provide societies with their own distinct personalities.[56] One study on the Big Five profiles of 51 different cultures showed that some societies tend to value certain personality traits more than other societies.[57] For example, people from India tend to be more conscientious than people from Belgium. People from the Czech Republic tend to be more agreeable than people from Hong Kong. People from Brazil tend to be more neurotic than people from China. People from Australia tend to be more extraverted than people from Russia. People from Denmark tend to be more open than people from Argentina. For their part, people in the Canada and the United States trend toward the high end of extraversion and openness, staying near the middle for the other Big Five dimensions. Of course, that doesn't mean that all of the members of these societies have exactly the same personality; the results merely convey that certain cultures tend to put a higher value on certain traits.

Although it's possible to contrast nations using the Big Five, as we just did, cross-cultural research focuses more attention on the shared values aspect of culture. The values salient in a given culture influence how people select and justify courses of action and how they evaluate themselves and other people.[58] To some extent, cultural values come to reflect the way things should be done in a given society.[59] Acting consistently with those values helps people to fit in, and going against them causes people to stand out. Just as there are a number of traits that can be used to describe personality, so there are a number of values that can be used to describe cultures. Given the sheer complexity of culture, it's not surprising that different studies have arrived at different taxonomies that can be used to summarize cultural values.

The most well-known taxonomy of cultural values is derived from a landmark study in the late 1960s and early 1970s by Geert Hofstede, who analyzed data from 88,000 IBM employees from 72 countries in 20 languages.[60] His research showed that employees working in different countries tended to prioritize different values, and those values clustered into several distinct dimensions, summarized in Table 4-2: **individualism–collectivism**, **power distance**, **uncertainty avoidance**, and **masculinity–femininity**. A subsequent study added a fifth dimension: **short-term vs. long-term orientation**.[61] Hofstede's research introduced scores on each of the dimensions for various cultures, providing researchers with a quantitative tool to summarize and to compare and contrast the cultures of different societies. Table 4-2 includes some of the countries that have high or low scores on Hofstede's dimensions.

individualism–collectivism

The degree to which a culture has a loosely knit social framework (individualism) or a tight social framework (collectivism)

power distance

The degree to which a culture prefers equal power distribution (low power distance) or an unequal power distribution (high power distance)

uncertainty avoidance

The degree to which a culture tolerates ambiguous situations (low uncertainty avoidance) or feels threatened by them (high uncertainty avoidance)

masculinity–femininity

The degree to which a culture values stereotypically male traits (masculinity) or stereotypically female traits (femininity)

short-term vs. long-term orientation

The degree to which a culture stresses values that are past- and present-oriented (short-term orientation) or future-oriented (long-term orientation)

TABLE 4-2

Hofstede's Dimensions of Cultural Values

Individualism–Collectivism	
Individualistic	**Collectivistic**
The culture is a loosely knit social framework in which people take care of themselves and their immediate family.	The culture is a tight social framework in which people take care of the members of a broader in-group and act loyally to it.
Canada, the Netherlands, France	*Indonesia, China, West Africa*
Power Distance	
Low	**High**
The culture prefers that power be distributed uniformly where possible, in a more egalitarian fashion.	The culture accepts the fact that power is usually distributed unequally within organizations.
Canada, Germany, the Netherlands	*Russia, China, Indonesia*
Uncertainty Avoidance	
Low	**High**
The culture tolerates uncertain and ambiguous situations and values unusual ideas and behaviours.	The culture feels threatened by uncertain and ambiguous situations and relies on formal rules to create stability.
Canada, Indonesia, the Netherlands	*Japan, Russia, France*
Masculinity–Femininity	
Masculine	**Feminine**
The culture values stereotypically male traits such as assertiveness and the acquisition of money and things.	The culture values stereotypically female traits such as caring for others and caring about quality of life.
Canada, Japan, Germany	*The Netherlands, Russia, France*
Short-Term vs. Long-Term Orientation	
Short-Term-Oriented	**Long-Term-Oriented**
The culture stresses values that are more past- and present-oriented, such as respect for tradition and fulfilling obligations.	The culture stresses values that are more future-oriented, such as persistence, prudence, and thrift.
Canada, Russia, West Africa	*China, Japan, the Netherlands*

Sources: G. Hofstede, *Culture's Consequences: Comparing Values, Behaviors, Institutions, and Organizations Across Nations* (Thousand Oaks, CA: Sage, 2001); G. Hofstede, "Cultural Constraints in Management Theories," *Academy of Management Executive* 7 (1993), pp. 81–94; and G. Hofstede and M.H. Bond, "The Confucius Connection: From Cultural Roots to Economic Growth," *Organizational Dynamics* 16 (1988), pp. 5–21.

Although Hofstede's dimensions have formed the foundation for much of the research on cross-cultural management, more recent studies have painted a more nuanced picture of cultural values. Project GLOBE (Global Leadership and Organizational Behavior Effectiveness) brings together 170 researchers from 62 cultures who have studied 17,300 managers in 951 organizations since 1991.[62] The main purpose of GLOBE is to examine the impact of culture on the effectiveness of various leader attributes, behaviours, and practices. In pursuing that goal, project researchers asked managers to rate the values held within their organizations and within their societies. That research identified nine different dimensions used to summarize cultures within GLOBE. Some of those dimensions can be viewed as replications of Hofstede's work. For example, GLOBE identified both power distance and uncertainty avoidance as key dimensions of cultural values. It also identified collectivism, though that dimension was differentiated into institutional collectivism (in which formalized practices encourage collective action and collective distribution of resources) and in-group collectivism (in which individuals express pride and loyalty to specific in-groups).

Other dimensions bear some similarity to Hofstede's work but are conceptually distinct. Those dimensions are listed below, along with some information on the cultures that score at the higher and lower ends on a given value. Note that GLOBE groups cultures into "country clusters." Those clusters include Anglo (United States, Canada, Australia, England), Latin America (Mexico, Brazil, Colombia, Venezuela), Latin Europe (France, Spain, Italy, Israel), Germanic Europe (Germany, Austria, the Netherlands, Switzerland), Nordic Europe (Denmark, Finland, Sweden), Eastern Europe (Poland, Hungary, Russia, Greece), the Middle East (Turkey, Egypt, Kuwait, Morocco), Southern Asia (India, Thailand, Indonesia, Malaysia), Confucian Asia (China, South Korea, Japan, Singapore), and Sub-Sahara Africa (Zimbabwe, Namibia, Nigeria). The following descriptions note some of the country clusters that earn high and low scores on a given cultural value. Note that the Anglo group, which includes Canada, scores in the middle on most of the cultural values.

- *Gender egalitarianism.* The culture promotes gender equality and minimizes role differences between men and women. High: Nordic Europe, Eastern Europe. Low: Middle East.
- *Assertiveness.* The culture values assertiveness, confrontation, and aggressiveness in social relationships. High: Germanic Europe, Eastern Europe. Low: Nordic Europe.
- *Future orientation.* The culture engages in planning and investment in the future while delaying individual or collective gratification. High: Germanic Europe, Nordic Europe. Low: Middle East, Latin America, Eastern Europe.
- *Performance orientation.* The culture encourages and rewards members for excellence and performance improvements. High: Anglo, Confucian Asia, Germanic Europe. Low: Latin America, Eastern Europe.
- *Humane orientation.* The culture encourages and rewards members for being generous, caring, kind, fair, and altruistic. High: Southern Asia, Sub-Saharan Africa. Low: Latin Europe, Germanic Europe.

Taken together, Hofstede's work and the GLOBE studies have identified between five and nine cultural value dimensions. However, the lion's share of cross-cultural research focuses on individualism–collectivism, perhaps the most fundamental means of differentiating cultures.[63] The individualism–collectivism distinction is relevant to various topics within organizational behaviour.[64] For example, collectivists exhibit higher levels of task performance and citizenship behaviours in work team settings, and also exhibit lower levels of counterproductive and withdrawal behaviours.[65] They are also more likely to feel affectively and normatively committed to their employers than individualists.[66] Research also suggests that collectivists tend to prefer rewards that are allocated equally on a group-wide basis as opposed to rewards tied solely to individual achievement.[67]

Regardless of the particular value of focus, research on cultural values illustrates the potential differences between the attitudes and beliefs of Canadian employees and the attitudes and beliefs of employees in other societies. Awareness of such variations is critical, given that those differences can influence reactions to change, conflict management styles, negotiation approaches, and reward preferences, to name just a few.[68] Failing to understand those differences can compromise the effectiveness of multinational groups and organizations. Such problems are particularly likely if employees are high in **ethnocentrism**, defined as a propensity to view one's own cultural values as "right" and those of other cultures as "wrong."[69] For more discussion of this issue, see our ***OB Internationally*** feature.

ethnocentrism

A propensity to view one's own cultural values as "right" and those of other cultures as "wrong"

OB INTERNATIONALLY

Research suggests that ethnocentrism hinders the effectiveness of expatriates, who are employees working full-time in other countries. Ethnocentrism makes expatriates less likely to adjust to a new culture, less likely to fulfill the duties required of their international assignment, and more likely to withdraw from that assignment. So how can organizations identify employees with the right personalities to serve as expatriates? One potentially useful tool is the *multicultural personality questionnaire*, which assesses five personality dimensions that can maximize the satisfaction, commitment, and performance of expatriates.[70] Those dimensions are listed below, along with some sample items for each:

- *Cultural empathy.* A tendency to empathize with the feelings, thoughts, and behaviours of individuals with different cultural values.
  - I understand other people's feelings.
  - I take other people's habits into consideration.
- *Open-mindedness.* A tendency to have an open and unprejudiced attitude toward other cultural values and norms.
  - I get involved in other cultures.
  - I find other religions interesting.
- *Emotional stability.* A tendency to remain calm in the kinds of stressful situations that can be encountered in foreign environments.
  - I can put setbacks in perspective.
  - I take it for granted that things will turn out right.
- *Social initiative.* A tendency to be proactive when approaching social situations, which aids in building connections.
  - I easily approach other people.
  - I am often the driving force behind things.
- *Flexibility.* A tendency to regard new situations as a challenge and to adjust behaviours to meet that challenge.
  - I could start a new life easily.
  - I feel comfortable in different cultures.

Research has linked these five personality traits to a number of expatriate success factors. For example, individuals with a "multicultural personality" are more likely to aspire to international positions, more likely to gain international experience, more likely to adjust to new assignments, and more likely to be happy with their lives during those assignments.[71] In fact, research even suggests that expatriates who fit this profile are actually healthier, both physically and mentally.

OB FOR STUDENTS

Are you psychologically collective (or are some of your fellow group members)? Past research suggests that people who hold collective values are more self-confident in group settings, are more cooperative by nature, and prefer to be evaluated and rewarded on a group-wide basis (as when student group members all receive the same grade on a class project).[72] Collective group members also perform their group duties at a higher level, engage in more citizenship behaviour, and refrain from counterproductive behaviours that might harm the group.[73] To assess your psychological collectivism, think about work groups to which you belong or have belonged. The items below ask about your relationship with, and thoughts about, those groups. Respond as honestly as possible using the scale provided. Then sum up your scores.

1 **Strongly Disagree**	2 **Disagree**	3 **Neutral**	4 **Agree**	5 **Strongly Agree**	
1. I preferred to work in those groups rather than working alone.					——
2. Working in those groups was better than working alone.					——
3. I wanted to work with those groups as opposed to working alone.					——
4. I felt comfortable counting on group members to do their part.					——
5. I was not bothered by the need to rely on group members.					——
6. I felt comfortable trusting group members to handle their tasks.					——
7. The health of those groups was important to me.					——
8. I cared about the well-being of those groups.					——
9. I was concerned about the needs of those groups.					——
10. I followed the norms of those groups.					——
11. I followed the procedures used by those groups.					——
12. I accepted the rules of those groups.					——
13. I cared more about the goals of those groups than my own goals.					——
14. I emphasized the goals of those groups more than my individual goals.					——
15. Group goals were more important to me than my personal goals.					——

Scoring and Interpretation

If you scored a 53 or above, you hold collectivistic work values, which means that you prioritize the needs and well-being of the groups to which you belong, and you adhere to the norms and goals of those groups.

Source: Copyright © 2006 by the American Psychological Association. Adapted with permission. The official citation that should be used in referencing this material is Psychological collectivism: A measurement validation and linkage to group member performance. Jackson, Christine L.; Colquitt, Jason A.; Wesson, Michael J.; Zapata-Phelan, Cindy P. *Journal of Applied Psychology*, Vol. 91(4), July 2006, 884–899. http://dx.doi.org/10.1037/0021-9010.91.4.884. No further reproduction or distribution is permitted without written permission from the American Psychological Association.

Summary: How Can We Describe What Employees Are Like?

So how can we explain what employees are like? As is shown in Figure 4-4, many of the thousands of adjectives we use to describe people boil down to the Big Five dimensions. Conscientiousness reflects the reliability, perseverance, and ambition of employees. Agreeableness captures their tendency to cooperate with others in a warm and sympathetic fashion. Neuroticism reflects the tendency to experience negative moods and emotions frequently on a day-to-day basis. Individuals high on openness to experience are creative, imaginative, and curious. Finally, extraverts are talkative, sociable, and assertive and typically experience positive moods and emotions. Beyond personality, however, what employees are like also depends on the culture in which they were raised. Cultural values like individualism–collectivism, power distance, and so forth also influence employees' thoughts, emotions, and behaviours.

FIGURE 4-4

How Can We Describe What Employees Are Like?

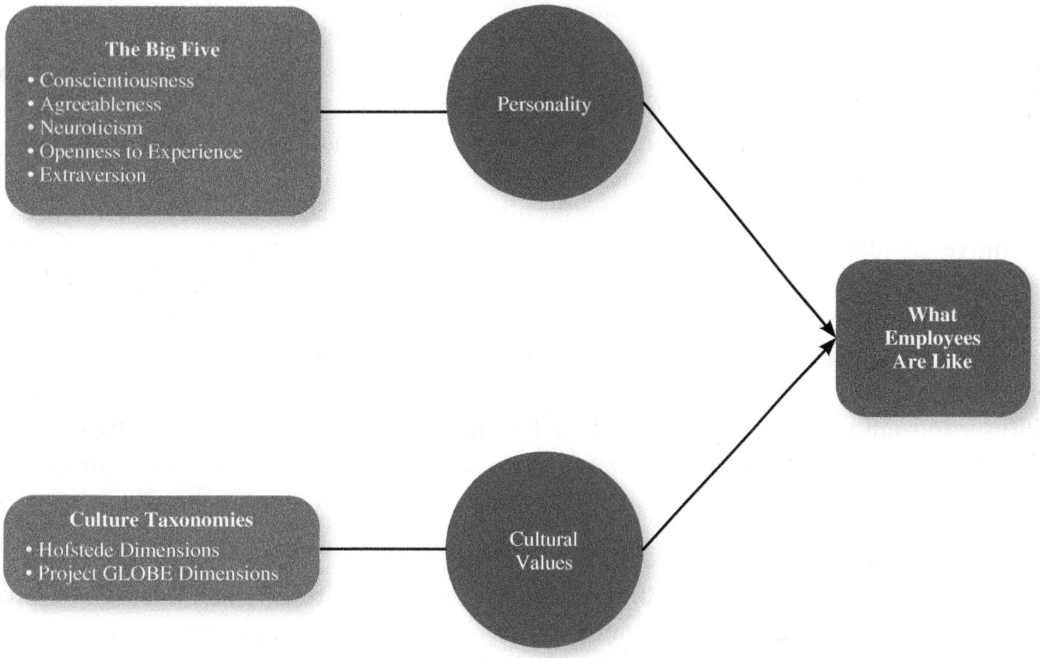

WHAT DOES IT MEAN FOR AN EMPLOYEE TO BE "ABLE"?

The topic of ability is probably already familiar to you, as "ability" is an everyday word in our language, and we've all developed a pretty good understanding of our own abilities. All of us have experience doing things that require different abilities, and we received feedback, in one form or another, as to how well we did. So knowing that you're already familiar with the topic of ability, why would we devote half of a chapter to it? Well, for one thing, there are many different abilities, some of which are important but might not be as familiar to you. Another reason is that although it might seem obvious that abilities are highly related to effectiveness in jobs, this relationship is truer in some circumstances than in others. Finally, it may be useful to understand how organizations use information about abilities to make good managerial decisions.

As was stated earlier, *ability* refers to the relatively stable capabilities people have to perform a particular range of different but related activities.[74] In contrast to skills, which can be improved over time with training and experience, ability is relatively stable. Although abilities can change slowly over time with instruction, repeated practice, and repetition, the level of a given ability generally limits how much a person can improve, even with the best training in the world. Are abilities a function of our genes, or are they something we develop as a function of our experiences and surroundings?

As it turns out, abilities are a function of both genes and the environment, and the amount attributable to each source depends somewhat on the nature of the ability. Consider for a moment abilities that are physical in nature. Although training that involves weightlifting, dancing, and swimming can improve a person's strength, equilibrium, and endurance, there are limits to how much improvement is possible with such training. As an example, millions of people take golf lessons and practise their swing for countless hours on a driving range, yet the vast majority of these could never compete in a professional golf tournament because they just can't manage to consistently hit that little white ball straight or far enough. As an example of abilities that are cognitive in nature, you likely know people who, even if they went to the best schools on Earth, would have great difficulty doing well in jobs such as theoretical astrophysics that require a lot of brainpower.

For cognitive abilities, it appears that genes and the environment play roughly equal roles.[75] However, differences due to the environment become less apparent as people get older, and this may be especially true for the effect of the family environment.[76] As an example, though neglect, abuse, and deprivation may have a negative impact on how children fare on standardized intelligence tests, the impact does not tend to carry over into adulthood. Beyond the family situation, what other factors in the environment affect cognitive abilities? First, the quantity of schooling may be important, because it provides opportunities for people to develop knowledge and critical thinking skills.[77] Second, there is evidence that our choice of occupations may have an influence. It appears that complex work develops and exercises our minds, which promotes higher performance on intelligence tests.[78] Third, certain biological factors are known to affect cognitive abilities negatively during childhood, such as malnutrition, exposure to toxins such as lead, and prenatal exposure to alcohol. In fact, over the past century, average scores on standardized intelligence tests have risen significantly in industrialized countries as the quality and availability of education and health factors have improved and the complexity of life has increased.[79]

As is detailed in the sections to follow, abilities can be grouped into three general categories: cognitive, emotional, and physical. Taken together, these abilities capture what people can do. That is in contrast to personality and cultural values, which captures what people are like. As we saw in the opening profile, successful organizations like Nexen focus on findings applicants whose abilities fit the demands of the work role.

4.4 What are the various types of cognitive ability?

Cognitive Ability

Cognitive ability refers to capabilities related to the acquisition and application of knowledge in problem solving.[80] Cognitive abilities are very relevant in the jobs most of you will be involved with: work involving the use of information to make decisions and solve problems. Chances are your cognitive abilities will be tested if you apply to pursue graduate-level study, for instance in law (LSAT, the Law School Admission Test), medicine (MCAT, the Medical College Admission Test), business administration (GMAT, the Graduate Management Admissions Test), or the social sciences (GRE, the Graduate Record Examinations). Tests like these present people with a variety of different questions. Some test your ability to do math problems; others assess your ability to complete sentences, solve logical problems, or make analogies. The different types of questions reflect the fact that several specific types of cognitive ability contribute to effectiveness on intellectual tasks. Table 4-3 lists many of these cognitive types, along with their specific facets and some jobs in which they are thought to be important.

cognitive ability
Capabilities related to the use of knowledge to make decisions and solve problems

TABLE 4-3

Types and Facets of Cognitive Ability

Type	More Specific Facet	Jobs Where Relevant
Verbal	*Oral and written comprehension.* Understanding written and spoken words and sentences *Oral and written expression.* Communicating ideas by speaking or writing so that others can understand	Business executives; police, fire, and ambulance dispatchers; clinical psychologists
Quantitative	*Number facility.* Performing basic math operations quickly and correctly *Mathematical reasoning.* Selecting the right method or formula to solve a problem	Treasurers; financial managers; mathematical technicians; statisticians
Reasoning	*Problem sensitivity.* Understanding when there is a problem or when something may go wrong *Deductive reasoning.* Applying general rules to specific problems *Inductive reasoning.* Combining specific information to form general conclusions *Originality.* Developing new ideas	Anesthesiologists; surgeons; business executives; fire inspectors; judges; police detectives; forensic scientists; cartoonists; designers
Spatial	*Spatial orientation.* Knowing where one is relative to objects in the environment *Visualization.* Imagining how something will look after it has been rearranged	Pilots; drivers; boat captains; photographers; set designers; sketch artists
Perceptual	*Speed and flexibility of closure.* Making sense of information and finding patterns *Perceptual speed.* Comparing information or objects with remembered information or objects	Musicians; firefighters; police officers; pilots; mail clerks; inspectors

Sources: Adapted from E.A. Fleishman, D.P. Costanza, and J. Marshall-Mies, "Abilities," in *An Occupational Information System for the 21st Century: The Development of O*NET*, eds. N.G. Peterson, M.D. Mumford, W.C. Borman, P.R. Jeanneret, and E.A. Fleishman (Washington DC: American Psychological Association, 1999), pp. 175–95; and *The O*NET Content Model: Detailed Outline with Descriptions*, www.onetcenter.org/content.html/1.a?d=1#cm_1.a, retrieved May 20, 2009.

Verbal Ability **Verbal ability** refers to various capabilities associated with understanding and expressing oral and written communication. *Oral comprehension* is the ability to understand spoken words and sentences, and *written comprehension* is the ability to understand written words and sentences. Although these two aspects of verbal ability would seem highly related—that is, people who have high oral comprehension would tend to have high written comprehensive, and vice versa—it is not difficult to think of people who might be high on one ability but low on the other. As an example, it has been reported that as a result of his dyslexia, Tom Cruise has poor written comprehension and can only learn his lines after listening to them on tape.[81]

verbal ability
Various capabilities associated with understanding and expressing oral and written communication

Tom Cruise has dyslexia, and so he struggles with written comprehension. He learns the lines for his movies by listening to them on tape.

Two other verbal abilities are *oral expression*, which refers to the ability to communicate ideas by speaking, and *written expression*, which refers to the ability to communicate ideas in writing. Again, though it might seem that these abilities should be highly correlated, they are not necessarily. You may have taken a class with a professor who has published several well-regarded books and articles but had a very difficult time expressing concepts and theories to students effectively. Although there could be many reasons, one possible explanation is that the professor had high ability in terms of written expression but low ability in terms of oral expression.

Generally speaking, verbal abilities are most important in jobs in which effectiveness depends on understanding and communicating ideas and information to others. The effectiveness of business executives depends on their ability to consider information from reports and other executives and staff, as well as their ability to articulate a vision and strategy that promotes employee understanding. As another example, consider how important the verbal abilities of a 911 dispatcher might be if a loved one suddenly became ill and stopped breathing one evening.

Quantitative Ability **Quantitative ability** refers to two types of mathematical capabilities. The first is *number facility*, which is the capability to do simple math operations (adding, subtracting, multiplying, and dividing). The second is *mathematical reasoning*, which refers to the ability to choose and apply formulas to solve problems that involve numbers. An example of a typical problem would be as follows: "Two trains 800 kilometres apart were travelling toward each other on the same track. The first began travelling at noon and averaged 70 kilometres per hour. The second started two hours later. What speed did the second train average if the two trains smashed into each other at

10 p.m. the same day?"Although number facility may be necessary to solve this problem, mathematical reasoning is crucial, because the test-taker needs to know which formulas to apply. Although most of us wish problems like this would be limited to test-taking contexts (especially this particular problem), quantitative abilities are important in countless situations. For example, consider the importance of quantitative ability in jobs involving statistics, accounting, and engineering. Quantitative abilities might be important in less complex, lower-level jobs as well. Have you ever been at a fast-food restaurant or convenience store and the clerk couldn't manage to count out change correctly or quickly? If so, you have witnessed a very good example of low quantitative ability (and perhaps some very annoyed customers!).

quantitative ability

Capabilities associated with doing basic mathematical operations and selecting and applying formulas to solve mathematical problems

Reasoning Ability **Reasoning ability** is actually a diverse set of abilities associated with sensing and solving problems using insight, rules, and logic. The first reasoning ability, *problem sensitivity*, is the ability to sense that there's a problem right now or likely to be one in the near future. Anesthesiology is a great example of a job for which problem sensitivity is crucial. Before surgeries, anesthesiologists give drugs to patients so that surgical procedures can take place painlessly. However, patients can have negative, even fatal reactions to the drugs. So the ability of the anesthesiologist to sense when something is wrong even before the problem is fully apparent can be a life-or-death matter.

reasoning ability

A diverse set of abilities associated with sensing and solving problems using insight, rules, and logic

The second type of reasoning ability is called *deductive reasoning*. This ability, which refers to the use of general rules to solve problems, is important in any job in which people are presented with a set of facts that need to be applied to make effective decisions. The job of a judge requires deductive reasoning, because it centres on making decisions by applying the rules of law to arrive at verdicts. In contrast, *inductive reasoning* refers to the ability to consider several specific pieces of information and then reach a more general conclusion regarding how those pieces are related. Inductive reasoning is required of police detectives and crime-scene investigators who much consider things like tire tracks, blood splatter, fibres, and fingerprints to reach conclusions about perpetrators of crimes and causes of death.

Finally, *originality* refers to the ability to develop clever and novel ways to solve problems. Larry Page and Sergey Brin, the two founders of Google, provide good examples of originality. They not only developed the search software that gave Google a competitive advantage but also created the first completely new advertising medium in nearly half a century. They also refuse to follow conventional wisdom when it comes to managerial practices and business decisions.[82] Clearly, originality is important in a wide variety of occupations, but in some jobs, originality is the most critical ability. For example, a cartoonist, designer, writer, or advertising executive without originality would find it difficult to be successful.

Spatial Ability There are two main types of **spatial ability**. The first is *spatial orientation*, which refers to having a good understanding of where one is relative to other things in the environment. A tourist with high spatial orientation would have no trouble finding her way back to her hotel on foot after a long day of sightseeing, even without a map or help from anyone on the street. The second spatial ability is called *visualization*, the ability to imagine how separate things will look if they were put together in a particular way. If you're good at imagining how a room would look if it were rearranged, or if your friends are impressed that you can buy things that go together well, chances are you would score high on visualization.

spatial ability
Capabilities associated with visual and mental representation and manipulation of objects in space

Perceptual Ability **Perceptual ability** refers to being able to perceive, understand, and recall patterns of information. More specifically, *speed and flexibility of closure* refers to being able to pick out a pattern of information quickly in the presence of distracting information, even without all the information present. People who work for the Canadian Security Intelligence Service likely need speed and flexibility of closure to break secret codes. Related to this ability is *perceptual speed*, which refers to being able to examine and compare numbers, letters, and objects quickly. If you can go into the produce section of a supermarket and choose the best tomatoes faster than the people around you, chances are you have high perceptual speed. Effectiveness in jobs in which people need to proofread documents, sort things, or categorize objects depends a lot on perceptual speed.

perceptual ability
The capacity to perceive, understand, and recall patterns of information

Pilots flying in conditions where there's poor visibility have to rely on various instruments and their spatial ability to visualize their absolute position, and just as important, their position relative to other objects, some of which are also moving.

© A.P. Sang Tan/The Canadian Press

General Mental Ability If you've read the preceding sections thoughtfully, you've probably thought about where you stand on the different types of cognitive abilities. In doing so, you may have also reached the conclusion that you are higher on some of these abilities and lower on others. Maybe you think of yourself as being smart in verbal abilities but not as smart in quantitative abilities. In fact, most people score more similarly across their cognitive abilities than they realize. People who are high on verbal abilities also tend to be high on reasoning, quantitative, spatial, and perceptual abilities, and people who are low on verbal abilities tend to be low on the other abilities. Although this consistency might not apply to everyone, it applies often enough that researchers have been trying to understand why this occurs for well over 100 years.[83]

The most popular explanation for the similarity in the levels of different cognitive abilities within people is that there is a **general cognitive ability**—sometimes called "g" or "the g factor"—that underlies or causes all of the more specific cognitive abilities we have discussed so far.[84] To understand what this ability means more clearly, consider the diagram in Figure 4-5, which depicts general mental ability as the area in common across the more specific cognitive abilities that we have discussed. This overlap exists because each of the specific abilities depends somewhat on the brain's ability to process information effectively. So, because some brains are capable of processing information more effectively than others, some people tend to score higher across the specific abilities, whereas others tend to score lower.

general cognitive ability
The general level of cognitive ability that plays an important role in determining the more narrow cognitive abilities

FIGURE 4-5

The g Factor

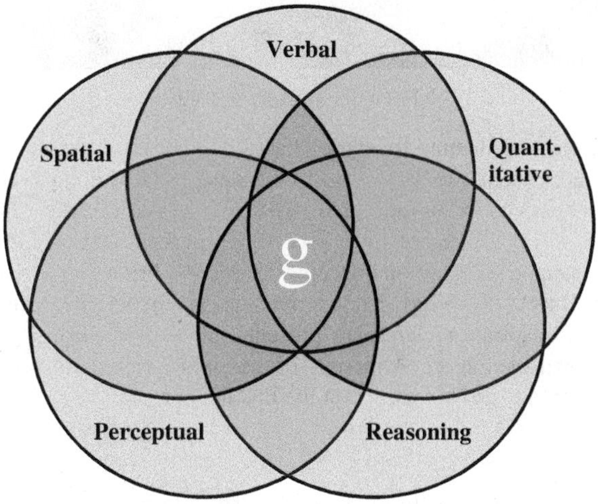

Source: Adapted from J.J. Johnson and J.B. Cullen, "Trust in Cross-Cultural Relationships," in *Blackwell Handbook of Cross-Cultural Management*, eds. M.J. Gannon and K.L. Newman (Malden, MA: Blackwell, 2002), pp. 335–60.

OB ON SCREEN

Admission

I'm not your typical student; my brain sort of goes on a little walkabout, you know?

With those words, Jeremiah (Nat Wolff) explains to a Princeton admissions officer named Portia (Tina Fey) why he should be admitted despite a high school grade point average well below what would normally be considered. *Admission* (Dir. Paul Weitz, Depth of Field, 2013) centres on the predicament of Jeremiah, who at the age of eight concluded that he couldn't learn much from his teachers, so he became an "autodidact" (someone self-taught). Although he learned a great deal, the knowledge he acquired isn't reflected in his high school grades, which are mostly D's and F's. He also came from a very modest background, and as a consequence he doesn't have the repertoire of experiences and references that others list on their applications. What makes Jeremiah's case interesting is that he earned extraordinary scores on standardized tests, which Princeton also considers in its admissions process. He received top scores in several advanced placement tests without ever taking any preparation courses—although some on the admissions committee feel this is impossible—and his SAT score is nearly perfect.

Jeremiah's situation represents a classic dilemma for those charged with considering college applicants. On the one hand, grade point averages and experiences seem highly relevant to the actual task of doing well in school, and they may appear to get at things like aspiration, which cannot be measured easily. On the other hand, standardized test scores, which tap intellect, are valid and reliable predictors of success in school, they're less susceptible to coaching, and they're fair to the extent that all applicants take the same test (albeit on different occasions). Princeton receives applications from individuals with excellent credentials on each facet considered. These applicants get favourable decisions because they're seen as safe bets in terms of their intellect and aspiration. Jeremiah presents greater risk insofar as his application indicates truly extraordinary intellect but unknown aspiration. Although Princeton's admissions process favours the former path, a number of factors align to cause Portia to put her career on the line to champion Jeremiah's case.

4.5 What are the various types of emotional ability?

Emotional Ability

Dwight Schrute, as played by Rainn Wilson on NBC's *The Office*, believes he's a great asset to his employer, Dunder Mifflin, and that he's multitalented, intelligent, and funny. He also believes that he really understands his co-workers and that he can control them to get his way. Unbeknownst to him, however, he actually comes across as pathetically insensitive and incompetent. Although this is entertaining to TV viewers, it isn't hard to imagine how such lack of self-awareness and inability to read emotions might result in significant problems for bosses and employees. In this section of the chapter, we describe the concept of emotional abilities—precisely the type of ability Dwight Schrute seems to lack.

Dwight Schrute has an inflated view of himself, and absolutely no understanding of or regard for how his antics affect the emotions of his co-workers.

So how is emotional ability different from cognitive ability? Most of us know someone who, while very smart from a "cognitive ability" or IQ standpoint, just can't manage to be effective in real-world situations that involve other people. As an example, you might have played Trivial Pursuit with friends and found someone at the table who could answer the majority of the questions correctly, but yet also managed to say odd or inappropriate things throughout the game. You might also know someone who doesn't seem very "book smart" but always seems able to get things done and says the right things at the right time. In the context of the same Trivial Pursuit game, such a person might have answered most of the game questions incorrectly, but sensing how uncomfortable and angry people were becoming with the annoying player, made jokes to lighten things up.

In fact, for several decades now, researchers have been investigating whether there is a type of ability that influences the degree to which people tend to be effective in social situations, regardless of their level of cognitive abilities.[85] Although there has been some debate among these researchers,[86] many believe that there is a human ability that affects social functioning called **emotional intelligence**[87] defined in terms of a set of distinct but related abilities, which we describe next.[88]

emotional intelligence
A set of abilities related to the understanding and use of emotions that affect social functioning

Self-Awareness The first type of emotional intelligence is **self-awareness**, or the appraisal and expression of emotions in oneself. This facet refers to the ability of an individual to understand the types of emotions he or she is experiencing, the willingness to acknowledge them, and the capability to express them naturally.[89] As an example, someone who is low in this aspect of emotional intelligence might not admit to himself or show anyone else that he is feeling somewhat anxious during the first few days of a new job. These types of emotions are perfectly natural in this job context, and ignoring them might increase the stress of the situation. Ignoring those emotions might also send the wrong signal to new colleagues, who might wonder, "Why isn't the new hire more excited about his new job?"

self-awareness
The ability to recognize and understand the emotions in oneself

Other Awareness The second facet of emotional intelligence is called **other awareness**, or the appraisal and recognition of emotion in others.[90] As the name implies, other awareness refers to a person's ability to recognize and understand the emotions others are feeling. People high in this aspect of emotional intelligence not only are sensitive to the feelings of others but also can anticipate the emotions people will experience in different situations. In contrast, people low in this aspect do not effectively sense the emotions others are experiencing, and if the emotions are negative, this inability might result in the person doing something that worsens the situation. Have you ever had a professor who could not sense that the students he was lecturing did not understand the material being presented? When that professor pressed on with the overheads, oblivious to the fact that the students were becoming even more confused, it was poor other awareness in action.

other awareness
The ability to recognize and understand the emotions that other people are feeling

Emotion Regulation The third facet of emotional intelligence, **emotion regulation**, refers to being able to recover quickly from emotional experiences.[91] Consider the possible responses of a man listening to the radio while driving to work who is cut off by an aggressive driver who, as she passes by, throws a beer can and shouts an obscenity. If this man is able to regulate his emotions effectively, he is able to recover quickly from his initial anger and shock. He can go back to listening, and by the time he gets to work the incident is likely all but forgotten. However, if the man is not able to regulate his emotions effectively, he might lose his temper, tailgate the aggressive driver, and ram her vehicle at the next stoplight. We hope it is obvious to you that the former response is much more appropriate than the latter, which might prove quite costly.

emotion regulation
The ability to recover quickly from emotional experiences

Other awareness is one aspect of emotional intelligence that allows us to empathize with others and understand their feelings.

© Digital Vision

Although this example highlights the importance of regulating negative emotions, we should also point out that this aspect of emotional intelligence applies to positive emotions. Consider the response of someone who is told that she is about to receive a significant pay raise. If this person is unable to regulate her own emotions effectively, she might feel excessively giddy and not be able to accomplish anything the rest of the day.

Use of Emotions The fourth aspect of emotional intelligence is the **use of emotions**.[92] This capability reflects the degree to which people can harness emotions and employ them to improve their chances of being successful in whatever they are seeking to do. To understand this facet of emotional intelligence, consider a writer struggling to finish a book, under a serious time crunch because of the contract with the publisher. If she is high in this aspect of emotional intelligence, she will likely psych herself up for the challenge and encourage herself to work hard through any bouts of writer's block. In contrast, if the writer is low in this aspect of emotional intelligence, she might begin to doubt her competence as a writer and think about different things she could do with her life. Because these behaviours will slow progress on the book even further, the number and intensity of self-defeating thoughts might increase, and ultimately, the writer might withdraw from the task entirely.

use of emotions

The degree to which people can harness emotions and employ them to improve their chances of being successful in whatever they are seeking to do

4.6 What are the various types of physical ability?

Physical Ability

Physical abilities are likely very familiar to you, because many of you took physical education classes early in your school career. Maybe you were evaluated on whether you could climb a rope to the ceiling of a gymnasium, run around a track several times, or kick a ball to a teammate who was running full stride. Or maybe you've applied for a job and had to take a test that assessed your ability to manipulate and assemble small mechanical parts. As a final example, and the one likely to be most familiar, you've probably been subjected to tests that measure the quality of your vision and hearing. Although these examples may not seem to be related, each refers to a different type of physical ability. In this section, we review a few important types of physical abilities, which are illustrated in Table 4-4.[93]

Strength Although **strength** generally refers to the degree to which the body is capable of exerting force, there are actually several different types of strength that are important, depending on the job. *Static strength* refers to the ability to lift, push, or pull very heavy objects using the hands, arms, legs, shoulder, or back. Static strength is involved in jobs in which people need to lift objects like boxes, equipment, machine parts, and heavy tools. With *explosive strength*, the person exerts short bursts of energy to move himself or an object. Employees who are required to run, jump, or throw things at work depend on their explosive strength to be effective. The final type of strength, *dynamic strength*, refers to the ability to exert force for a prolonged period of time without becoming overly fatigued and giving out. Dynamic strength is involved in jobs in which the person has to climb ropes or ladders or pull up onto platforms. Although jobs requiring physical strength may vary as to which category is important, there are also many jobs—such as firefighters—that require all three.[94]

strength
The degree to which the body is capable of exerting force

TABLE 4-4

Physical Abilities

Type	More Specific Facet	Jobs Where Relevant
Strength	*Static.* Lifting, pushing, pulling heavy objects *Explosive.* Exerting a short burst of muscular force to move oneself or objects *Dynamic.* Exerting muscular force repeatedly or continuously	Structural iron and steel workers; tractor trailer and heavy truck drivers; farm workers; firefighters
Stamina	*Exerting oneself over a period of time without circulatory system giving out.*	Athletes; dancers; commercial divers; firefighters
Flexibility and coordination	*Extent flexibility.* Degree of bending, stretching, twisting of body, arms, legs *Dynamic flexibility.* Speed of bending, stretching, twisting of body, arms, legs *Gross body coordination.* Coordinating movement of body, arms, and legs in activities that involve all three together *Gross body equilibrium.* Ability to regain balance in contexts where balance is upset	Athletes; dancers; riggers; industrial machinery mechanics; choreographers; commercial divers; structural iron and steel workers
Psychomotor	*Fine manipulative abilities.* Keeping hand and arm steady while grasping manipulating, and assembling small objects *Control movement abilities.* Making quick, precise adjustments to a machine while operating it *Response orientation.* Quickly choosing among appropriate alternative movements *Response time.* Quickly responding to signals with body movements	Fabric menders; potters; timing device assemblers; jewellers; construction drillers; agricultural equipment operators; photographers; highway patrol pilots; athletes
Sensory	*Near and far vision.* Seeing details of an object up close or at a distance *Night vision.* Seeing well in low light *Visual colour discrimination.* Detecting differences in colours and shades *Depth perception.* Judging relative distances *Hearing sensitivity.* Hearing differences in sounds that vary in terms of pitch and loudness *Auditory attention.* Focusing on a source of sound in the presence of other sources *Speech recognition.* Identifying and understanding the speech of others	Electronic testers and inspectors; highway patrol pilots; tractor trailer, truck, and bus drivers; airline pilots; photographers; musicians and composers; industrial machine mechanics; speech pathologists

Sources: Adapted from E.A. Fleishman, D.P. Costanza, and J. Marshall-Mies, "Abilities," in *An Occupational Information System for the 21st Century: The Development of O*NET*, eds. N.G. Peterson, M.D. Mumford, W.C. Borman, P.R. Jeanneret, and E.A. Fleishman (Washington DC: American Psychological Association, 1999), pp. 175–95; and O*NET website, *The O*NET Content Model: Detailed Outline with Descriptions*, www.onetcenter.org/content.html/1.A?D=1#Cm_1.A, retrieved May 20, 2009.

Stamina **Stamina** refers to the ability of a person's lungs and circulatory system to work efficiently while he or she is engaging in prolonged physical activity. Stamina may be important in jobs that require running, swimming, and climbing. In fact, stamina is involved whenever the nature of the physical activity causes the heart rate to climb and the depth and rate of breathing to increase for prolonged periods of time. As you might imagine, jobs with heavy physical demands will require stamina as well as strength.

stamina
The ability of a person's lungs and circulatory system to work efficiently while he or she is engaging in prolonged physical activity

Flexibility and Coordination Generally speaking, **flexibility** refers to the ability to bend, stretch, twist, or reach. When a job requires extreme ranges of motion—for example, when people need to work in a cramped compartment or an awkward position—the type of flexibility involved is called *extent flexibility*. If you've ever watched a person working inside the trunk of a car installing speakers, you've seen extent flexibility. When a job requires repeated and somewhat quick bends, stretches, twists, or reaches, the type of flexibility involved is called *dynamic flexibility*. To understand what dynamic flexibility involves, picture a house painter on a ladder trying to paint some trim just barely within reach.

flexibility
The ability to bend, stretch, twist, or reach

In addition to flexibility, **coordination**, or the quality of physical movement, may be important in some jobs. *Gross body coordination* refers to the ability to synchronize the movements of the body, arms, and legs to do something while the whole body is in motion. In contrast, *gross body equilibrium* involves the ability to maintain the balance of the body in unstable contexts or when the person has to change directions. Jumping rope effectively requires gross body coordination; walking on a balance beam requires gross body equilibrium. Both types of coordination are important in contexts that involve quick movements. However, gross body equilibrium is more important when the work environment is artificially elevated and inherently unstable.

coordination
The quality of physical movement in terms of synchronization of movements and balance

Psychomotor Ability There are several different examples of **psychomotor ability**, which generally refer to the capacity to manipulate and control objects. *Fine manipulative abilities* refer to the ability to keep the arms and hands steady while using the hands to do precise work, generally on small or delicate objects such as arteries, nerves, gems, and watches. *Control movement abilities* are important in tasks for which people have to make different precise adjustments using machinery to complete the work effectively. Anyone who drills things for a living, whether it be wood, concrete, or teeth, needs this type of ability. The ability to choose the right action quickly in response to several different signals is called *response orientation*. It shouldn't be too difficult to imagine the importance of response orientation for an airline pilot who responds to the flashing lights, buzzers, and verbal information triggered during an in-flight emergency. The final psychomotor ability we describe is called *response time*. This ability reflects how quickly an individual responds to signalling information after it occurs. Returning to an example given in Chapter 2, imagine how grateful the 155 passengers and crew aboard US Airways Flight 1549 must have felt for the fast response orientation and quick response time of the pilots who were able to successfully land in the Hudson River after striking a large flock of geese that took out both engines!

psychomotor ability
Capabilities associated with manipulating and controlling objects

Sensory Ability **Sensory ability** refers to capabilities associated with vision and hearing. Examples of important visual abilities include the ability to see things up close and at a distance (*near and far vision*) or in low-light contexts (*night vision*), and the ability to perceive colours and judge relative distances between things accurately (*visual colour discrimination* and *depth perception*). Many different jobs emphasize only one or two of these visual abilities. For example, whereas effectiveness as a watch repairer depends on good near vision, effectiveness as an interior designer depends on visual colour discrimination. However, in other jobs effectiveness might depend on almost all categories of visual abilities. A fighter pilot needs near vision to read instruments and checklists, far vision and depth perception to see enemy targets and landmarks, night vision to conduct operations in low light, and visual colour discrimination to interpret information from warning lights and computer readouts correctly.

sensory ability
Capabilities associated with vision and hearing

Abilities related to hearing, also referred to as *auditory abilities*, include the capability to hear and discriminate sounds that vary in terms of loudness and pitch (*hearing sensitivity*), being able to focus on a single sound in the presence of many other sounds (*auditory attention*), and the ability to identify and understand the speech of another person (*speech recognition*). Perhaps the most obvious jobs for which auditory abilities would be important are musicians and composers (yes, we are going to ignore exceptions like Beethoven, who was deaf at the time he wrote his Ninth Symphony). However, with these jobs, the emphasis would likely be on hearing sensitivity and auditory attention rather than speech recognition (who listens to lyrics these days?). Another job for which auditory abilities might be crucially important is bartending, especially if the bar is crowded and noisy. In this context, a bartender needs auditory attention and speech recognition to be able to isolate and understand the words of a single patron against the backdrop of the loud chatter.

Summary: What Does It Mean for an Employee to Be "Able"?

In this part of the chapter we have presented you with a fairly detailed description of the domain of human abilities, which are summarized in Figure 4-6. The list of abilities included in the figure might seem somewhat daunting, but we hope you appreciate that this set of abilities describes each and every one of us. Moreover, these abilities play an important role in determining how effective we can be at different tasks and jobs.

FIGURE 4-6

What Does It Mean for an Employee to Be "Able"?

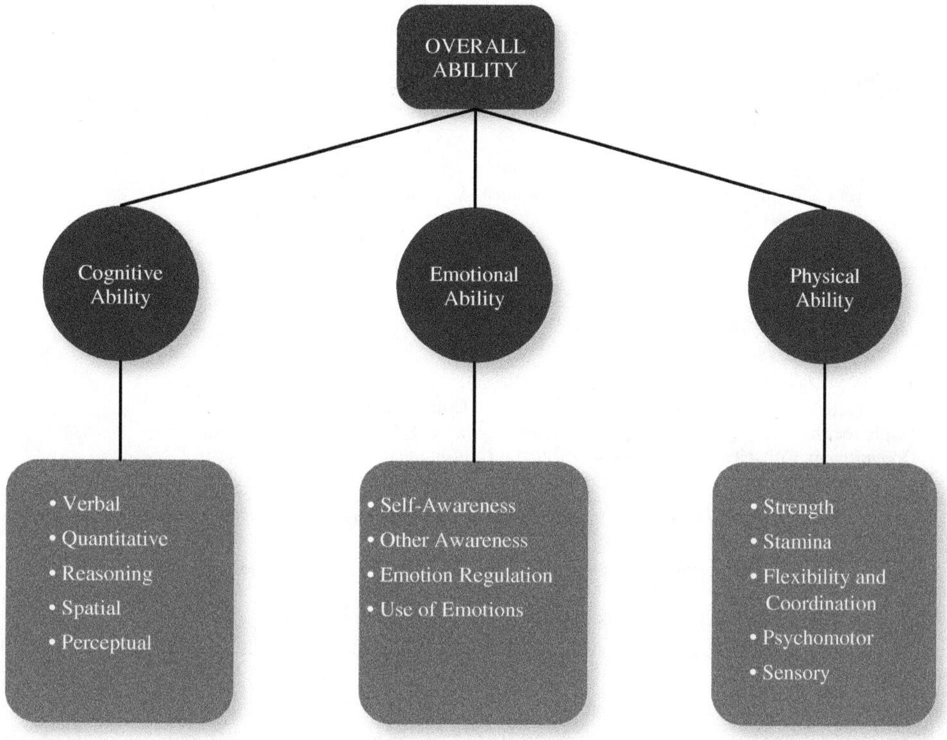

Source: Adapted from J.J. Johnson and J.B. Cullen, "Trust in Cross-Cultural Relationships," in *Blackwell Handbook of Cross-Cultural Management*, eds. M.J. Gannon and K.L. Newman (Malden, MA: Blackwell, 2002), pp. 335–60.

4.7 How do individual differences affect job performance and organizational commitment?

HOW IMPORTANT ARE THESE INDIVIDUAL DIFFERENCES?

We've already described a number of reasons why the Big Five should be important considerations, particularly in the case of conscientiousness. What if we focus specifically on the two outcomes in our integrative model of OB, performance and commitment? Figure 4-7 summarizes the research evidence linking conscientiousness to those two outcomes. The figure reveals that conscientiousness affects job performance. Of the Big Five, conscientiousness has the strongest effect on task performance,[95] partly because conscientious employees have higher levels of motivation than other employees.[96] They are more self-confident, perceive a clearer linkage between their effort and their performance, and are more likely to set goals and commit to them. For these reasons, conscientiousness is a key driver of what's referred to as **typical performance**, which reflects performance in the routine conditions that surround daily job tasks.[97] An employee's ability, in contrast, is a key driver of **maximum performance**, which reflects performance in brief, special circumstances that demand a person's best effort.

FIGURE 4-7

Effects of Personality on Performance and Commitment

Conscientiousness has a moderate positive effect on Performance. Conscientious employees have higher levels of *Task Performance*. They are also more likely to engage in *Citizenship Behaviour* and less likely to engage in *Counterproductive Behaviour*.

Conscientiousness has a moderate positive effect on Commitment. Conscientious employees have higher levels of *Affective Commitment* and higher levels of *Normative Commitment*. Conscientiousness has no effect on *Continuance Commitment*.

Represents a strong correlation (around .50 in magnitude).

Represents a moderate correlation (around .30 in magnitude).

Represents a weak correlation (around .10 in magnitude).

Sources: M.R. Barrick, M.K. Mount, and T.A. Judge, "Personality and Performance at the Beginning of the New Millennium: What Do We Know and Where Do We Go Next?," *International Journal of Selection and Assessment* 9 (2001), pp. 9–30; C.M. Berry, D.S. Ones, and P.R. Sackett, "Interpersonal Deviance, Organizational Deviance, and Their Common Correlates: A Review and Meta-analysis," *Journal of Applied Psychology* 92 (2007), pp. 410–24; A. Cooper-Hakim and C. Viswesvaran, "The Construct of Work Commitment: Testing an Integrative Framework," *Psychology Bulletin* 131 (2005), pp. 241–59; L.M. Hough and A. Furnham, "Use of Personality Variables in Work Settings," in *Handbook of Psychology*, Vol. 12, eds. W.C. Borman, D.R. Ilgen, and R.J. Klimoski (Hoboken, NJ: Wiley, 2003), pp. 131–69; J.E. Mathieu and D.M. Zajac, "A Review and Meta-analysis of the Antecedents, Correlates, and Consequences of Organizational Commitment," *Psychological Bulletin* 108 (1990), pp. 171–94; and J.F. Salgado, "The Big Five Personality Dimensions and Counterproductive Behaviors," *International Journal of Selection and Assessment* 10 (2002), pp. 117–25.

typical performance

Performance in the routine conditions that surround daily job tasks

maximum performance

Performance in brief, special circumstances that demand a person's best effort

Conscientious employees are also more likely to engage in citizenship behaviours.[98] Why? One reason is that conscientious employees are so punctual and have such good work attendance that they are simply more available to offer "extra mile" sorts of contributions. Another reason is that they engage in so much more work-related effort that they have more energy to devote to citizenship behaviours.[99] A third reason is that they tend to have higher levels of job satisfaction,[100] and positive feelings tend to foster spontaneous instances of citizenship. Finally, conscientious employees are less likely to engage in counterproductive behaviours,[101] for two major reasons. First, their higher job satisfaction levels make it less likely that they'll feel a need to retaliate against their organization. Second, even if they do

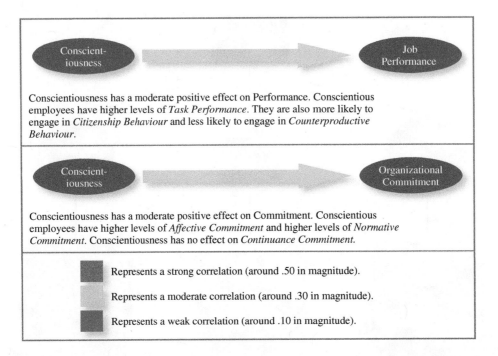

perceive some slight or injustice, their dependable and reliable nature should prevent them from violating organizational norms by engaging in negative actions.[102]

Figure 4-7 also reveals that conscientious employees tend to be more committed to their organization.[103] They're less likely to engage in day-to-day psychological and physical withdrawal behaviours because such actions go against their work habits. They're also significantly less likely to voluntarily leave the organization.[104] Why? One reason is that the persevering nature of conscientious employees prompts them to persist in a given course of action for long periods of time. That persistence can be seen in their daily work effort, but it extends to a sense of commitment to the organization as well.[105] Another reason is that conscientious employees are better at managing stress, perceiving lower levels of key stressors, and being less affected by them at work.[106] In some respects, Figure 4-7 understates the importance of conscientiousness (and personality, more generally). Why? Because personality becomes more important in some contexts than in others. The principle of **situational strength** suggests that "strong situations" have clear behavioural expectations, incentives, or instructions that make differences between individuals less important, whereas "weak situations" lack those cues.[107] Personality variables tend to be more significant drivers of behaviour in weak situations than in strong situations.[108] Similarly, the principle of **trait activation** suggests that some situations provide cues that trigger the expression of a given trait.[109] For example, a cry for help provides a cue that can trigger the expression of empathy. Personality variables tend to be more significant drivers of behaviours in situations that provide relevant cues than in situations in which those cues are lacking.

situational strength

The degree to which situations have clear behavioural expectations, incentives, or instructions that make differences between individuals less important

trait activation

The degree to which situations provide cues that trigger the expression of a given personality trait

Let's move on, and consider if ability really matters. Does ability have a significant impact on job performance and organizational commitment? The answer to this question depends on what type of ability you are referring to—cognitive, emotional, or physical. We focus our discussion on general cognitive ability because it's the most relevant form of ability across all jobs and is likely to be important in the kinds of positions that students in an OB course will be pursuing. As it turns out, there is a huge body of research linking general cognitive ability to job performance; see Figure 4-8.[110]

The figure reveals that general cognitive ability is a strong predictor of job performance—in particular, the task performance aspect. Across all jobs, smarter employees fulfill the requirements of their job descriptions more effectively than do less smart employees.[111] In fact, of all the variables discussed in this book, none has a stronger correlation with task performance than general cognitive ability. Thousands of organizations, and many that are quite well known, assess cognitive ability in an effort to select the best candidates available for specific jobs.[112] The use of cognitive ability tests for this purpose appears to be quite reasonable, given that scores on such tests have a strong positive correlation with measures of performance across different types of jobs.[113] So what explains why general cognitive ability relates to task performance? People who have higher general cognitive ability tend to be better at learning and decision making (which we will covered later in Chapter 9). They're able to gain more knowledge from their experiences at a faster rate, and as a result, they develop a bigger pool of knowledge regarding how to do their jobs effectively.[114] There are, however, three important caveats that we should mention. First, cognitive ability tends to be more strongly correlated with task performance than citizenship behaviour or counterproductive behaviour.[115] An increased amount of job knowledge helps an employee complete job tasks, but it doesn't necessarily affect the choice to help a co-worker or refrain from breaking an important rule. Second, the positive correlation between cognitive ability and performance is even stronger in jobs that are complex or situations that demand adaptability.[116] Third, people may do poorly on a test of general cognitive ability for reasons other than a lack of cognitive ability. As an example, people who come from economically disadvantaged backgrounds may do poorly on such tests, not because they lack the underlying cognitive ability but because they may not have had the learning opportunities needed to provide the appropriate responses.

FIGURE 4-8

Effects of General Cognitive Ability on Performance and Commitment

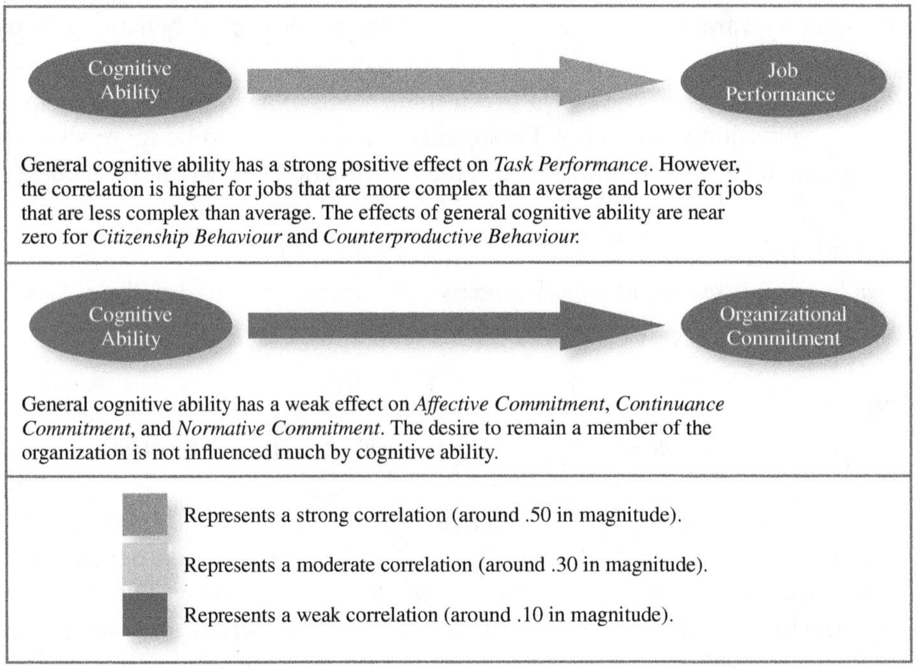

Cognitive Ability
Job Performance
General cognitive ability has a strong positive effect on *Task Performance*. However, the correlation is higher for jobs that are more complex than average and lower for jobs that are less complex than average. The effects of general cognitive ability are near zero for *Citizenship Behaviour* and *Counterproductive Behaviour.*
Cognitive Ability
Organizational Commitment
General cognitive ability has a weak effect on *Affective Commitment*, *Continuance Commitment*, and *Normative Commitment*. The desire to remain a member of the organization is not influenced much by cognitive ability.
Represents a strong correlation (around .50 in magnitude).
Represents a moderate correlation (around .30 in magnitude).
Represents a weak correlation (around .10 in magnitude).

Sources: J.W. Boudreau, W.R. Boswell, T.A. Judge, and R.D. Bretz, "Personality and Cognitive Ability as Predictors of Job Search Among Employed Managers," *Personnel Psychology* 54 (2001), pp. 25–50; S.M. Colarelli, R.A. Dean, and C. Konstans, "Comparative Effects of Personal and Situational Influences on Job Outcomes of New Professionals," *Journal of Applied Psychology* 72 (1987), pp. 558–66; D.N. Dickter, M. Roznowski, and D.A. Harrison, "Temporal Tempering: An Event History Analysis of the Process of Voluntary Turnover," *Journal of Applied Psychology* 81 (1996), pp. 705–16; F.L. Schmidt and J. Hunter, "General Mental Ability in the World of Work: Occupational Attainment and Job Performance," *Journal of Personality and Social Psychology* 86 (2004), pp. 162–73.

In contrast to relationships with job performance, research has not supported a significant linkage between cognitive ability and organizational commitment.[117] On the one hand, we might expect a positive relationship with commitment because people with higher cognitive ability tend to perform more effectively, and therefore, they might feel they fit well with their job. On the other hand, we might expect to see a negative relationship with commitment because people with higher cognitive ability possess more job knowledge, which increases their value on the job market, and in turn the likelihood that they would leave for another job.[118] In the end, knowing how smart an employee is tells us very little about the likelihood that he or she will remain a member of the organization.

OB RESEARCH IN CANADA

Dr. Kibeom Lee, at the University of Calgary, not only is an expert in human abilities and personality but also demonstrates in real life what can happen when you combine high cognitive ability with conscientiousness (especially accomplishment striving). Dr. Lee received his doctorate degree in industrial and organizational psychology from the University of Western Ontario. Over the next decade, from 2000 to 2011, Dr. Lee and his colleagues published well over 65 articles in scientific journals (four of these were published in Korean) and a number of book chapters—an extraordinary accomplishment for a relatively young scholar! To put this achievement in context, Dr. Lee's average annual output is roughly double the output of comparable faculty at other schools. It is only fitting that Dr. Lee's research looks at the link between individual differences (e.g., personality, ability) and work outcomes, such as job performance. You can look him up at www.ucalgary.ca.

Courtesy of Dr. Kibeom Lee

APPLICATION: PERSONALITY AND COGNITIVE ABILITY TESTS

Given how important personality and abilities can be to job performance and organizational commitment, it's not surprising that many organizations attempt to assess job applicants on these characteristics. But what's the best way to do that? Beginning with personality, it seems that many organizations try to assess an individual's traits through interviews by looking for cues that an applicant is conscientious or agreeable or has high levels of some other relevant personality dimension. Can you see a possible problem with this approach? Here's a hint: When was the last time you went into an interview and acted careless, sloppy, moody, or insecure? It's probably been a while. In fact, most interview preparation courses and books train applicants to exhibit the very personality traits that many employers are looking for!

To examine whether interviewers can gauge the Big Five, one study asked 26 interviewers, all of whom were human resources practitioners with more than 12 years of hiring experience, to assess the personalities of undergraduate business students who were on the job market.[119] The interviewers met with an average of three students for 30 minutes and were instructed to follow the interview protocols used in their own organizations. Once the interviews had concluded, the study gathered multiple ratings of the Big Five, including ratings from the interviewer, the student, and a close friend of the student. The results of the study showed that the interviewers' ratings of extraversion, agreeableness, and openness were fairly consistent with the students' own ratings, as well as their friends' ratings. In contrast, interviewers' ratings of conscientiousness and neuroticism were only weakly related to the students' and friends' ratings. This study therefore shows that interviewers are unable to gauge the two Big Five dimensions that are most highly related to job performance.

Rather than using interviews to assess personality, more and more companies are relying on paper-and-pencil "personality tests" like the kind shown in our ***OB Assessments*** at the end of this chapter. Table 4-5 provides a list of some of the most well-validated measures of the Big Five personality dimensions. The vendors that own these measures typically offer software and services for scoring the instruments, interpreting the data against relevant population norms, and creating feedback sheets.

TABLE 4-5

A Sampling of Well-Validated Measures of the Big Five

Name of Instrument	Vendor	Time Required
NEO Five-Factor Inventory (NEO-FFI)	Sigma Assessment Systems	15 minutes
Personal Characteristics Inventory (PCI)	Wonderlic	20 minutes
Personality Research Form (PRF)	Sigma Assessment Systems	45 minutes
Hogan Personality Inventory (HPI)	Hogan Assessment Systems	15 minutes
Big Five Inventory (BFI)	TestMaster	10 minutes

Given the strong relationship between general cognitive ability and job performance, it isn't surprising that many organizations apply the content of this chapter by using ability tests to hire new employees. One of the most widely used tests is the **Wonderlic Personnel Test**, a 12-minute test of general cognitive ability that consists of 50 questions. It has been in use for several decades now and given to more than 120 million people by thousands of organizations.[120] People who take the test receive one point for each correct response, and those points are summed to give a total score that can be used as a basis for selecting people for different jobs. The Wonderlic user's manual offers recommendations for minimum passing scores for different job families, some of which are included in Table 4-6. For example, a score of 17 is the minimum suggested score for unskilled labourer, a score of 21—which is the average for high school graduates, and which corresponds to an IQ of approximately 100—is the minimum suggested score for a firefighter. A score of 28 is the minimum suggested score for upper-level managerial and executive work and is around the average for all university graduates.

Wonderlic Personnel Test

A 12-minute test of general cognitive ability used to hire job applicants

TABLE 4-6

Suggested Minimum Wonderlic Scores for Various Jobs

Job	Minimum Score
Mechanical engineer	30
Attorney	29
Executive	28
Teacher	27
Nurse	26
Office manager	25
Advertising sales	24
Manager/supervisor	23
Police officer	22
Firefighter	21
Cashier	20
Hospital orderly	19
Machine operator	18
Unskilled labourer	17
Maid-matron	16

Source: *Wonderlic Cognitive Ability Test and Scholastic Level Exam: User's Manual* (Vernon Hills, IL: Wonderlic Cognitive Ability Test, Inc., 1992), pp. 28–29. Reprinted with permission.

Takeaways

4.1 Personality refers to the structures and propensities inside a person that explain his or her characteristic patterns of thought, emotion, and behaviour. It also refers to a person's social reputation—how he or she is perceived by others. Cultural values are shared beliefs about desirable end states or modes of conduct in a given culture that influence the expression of traits. Ability refers to the relatively stable capabilities of people to perform a particular range of different but related activities. Personality and values capture what people are like (unlike ability, which reflects what people can do).

4.2 The "Big Five" factors of personality include conscientiousness (e.g., dependable, organized, reliable), agreeableness (e.g., warm, kind, cooperative), neuroticism (e.g., nervous, moody, emotional), openness to experience (e.g., curious, imaginative, creative), and extraversion (e.g., talkative, sociable, passionate).

4.3 Hofstede's taxonomy of cultural values includes individualism–collectivism, power distance, uncertainty avoidance, masculinity–femininity, and short-term vs. long-term orientation. More recent research by Project GLOBE has replicated many of those dimensions and added five other means to distinguish among cultures: gender egalitarianism, assertiveness, future orientation, performance orientation, and humane orientation.

4.4 Cognitive abilities include verbal ability, quantitative ability, reasoning ability, spatial ability, and perceptual ability. General cognitive ability, or "g," underlies all of these more specific cognitive abilities.

4.5 Emotional intelligence includes four specific kinds of emotional skills: self-awareness, other awareness, emotion regulation, and use of emotions.

4.6 Physical abilities include strength, stamina, flexibility and coordination, psychomotor abilities, and sensory abilities.

4.7 Conscientiousness has a moderate positive relationship with job performance and a moderate positive relationship with organizational commitment. It has stronger effects on these outcomes than the rest of the Big Five. General cognitive ability has a strong positive relationship with job performance, due primarily to its effects on task performance. In contrast, general cognitive ability is not related to organizational commitment.

KEY TERMS

ability
accomplishment striving
agreeableness
Big Five
cognitive ability
communion striving
conscientiousness
coordination
cultural values
culture
emotion regulation
emotional intelligence
ethnocentrism
extraversion
flexibility
general cognitive ability
individualism–collectivism
locus of control
masculinity–femininity
maximum performance
negative affectivity
neuroticism
openness to experience

other awareness
perceptual ability
personality
positive affectivity
power distance
psychomotor ability
quantitative ability
reasoning ability
self-awareness
sensory ability
short-term vs. long-term orientation
situational strength
spatial ability
stamina
status striving
strength
trait activation
traits
typical performance
uncertainty avoidance
use of emotions
verbal ability
Wonderlic Personnel Test
zero acquaintance situations

DISCUSSION QUESTIONS

4.1 Based on your personal observation of others, perhaps focusing on people that you have known for a few years, do you think that personality is genetically determined or developed over time through life experiences? What life experiences could make someone more conscientious? More agreeable? More neurotic? More extraverted? More open to new experiences?

4.2 Consider the profile of Canada on Hofstede's cultural values, as shown in Table 4-2. Do you personally feel you fit the Canadian profile, or do your values differ in some respects? If you served as an expatriate, meaning you were working in another country, which cultural value differences would be most difficult for you to deal with?

4.3 What roles do learning, education, and other experiences play in determining a person's abilities? For which type of ability—cognitive, emotional, or physical—do these factors play the largest role?

4.4 Think of experiences you've had with people who demonstrated unusually high or low levels of emotional intelligence. Then consider how you would rate them in terms of their cognitive abilities. Do you think that emotional intelligence "bleeds over" to affect people's perceptions of cognitive ability?

4.5 What combination of personality and abilities is appropriate for the job of your dreams? Do you possess those characteristics? If you fall short on any of these attributes, what could you do to improve?

CASE • NEXEN

Nexen realizes that a diverse workforce, in terms of demographic (e.g., age, gender, ethnic origin) and individual characteristics (e.g., personality, cultural values, abilities), offers great opportunity for creativity, innovation, higher-quality problem solving, and relationship building within a global community. Harnessing the talents of a diverse workforce is much harder than it sounds. Consider the following. If it is easy to get along with people who are similar to you, imagine what it would be like to work closely with people who view the world differently from you? Everyday activities, such as communicating, coordinating with team members, and resolving conflicts, can all become more challenging within diverse workforces.

Earlier in the chapter-opening profile we learned that Nexen is a very successful company, in part because it has been able to harness the talents of many different kinds of people. We learned that the company puts particular emphasis on the notion of fit to the work role and with the organization's culture. We learned that the company works hard to ensure that new hires from different backgrounds experience welcoming and engaging work environments. An example of this is the cultural-awareness training that the company puts on to foster tolerance and appreciation of its Aboriginal employees.

4.1 Let's consider what "fitting in" means when you are different from others in the organization. Does it matter if those differences are demographic in nature (e.g., age, gender, ethnic origin) or if the differences are based on the individual characteristics discussed in this chapter (personality, cultural values, abilities)? Explain.

4.2 In addition to having the ability to perform their specific technical duties at Nexen, what personality characteristics and cultural values do you think a person would need to have to function effectively within a culturally diverse, team-based work environment?

4.3 Of the individual qualities covered in the chapter, which ones are more amenable to change through training and development experiences? Which ones tend to be "hard wired" and stable fixtures of a person's character?

4.4 If you had to design an optimal five-member student group, what mix of personality, cultural values, and abilities would you want members of the group to possess? Would you want members to be similar or dissimilar on these characteristics? Why? If your group consisted of members who were dissimilar, how would you handle any communication and coordination issues that may arise? Are there any risks associated with being too similar?

Sources: Nexen website, www.nexencnoocltd.com/en, retrieved December 27, 2014; J.R.W. Joplin and C.S. Daus, "Challenges of Leading a Diverse Workforce," *Academy of Management Executive* 11(3) (1997), pp. 32–47; G. Robinson and K. Dechant, "Building a Business Case for Diversity," *Academy of Management Executive* 11(3) (1997), pp. 21–31.

EXERCISE • GUESSING PERSONALITY PROFILES

The purpose of this exercise is to explore how noticeable the Big Five personality dimensions are among classmates. This exercise uses groups, so your instructor will either assign you to a group or ask you to create your own group. The exercise has the following steps:

4.1 Individually, complete the Big Five measure found in the ***OB Assessments*** box of this chapter.

4.2 Write your scores on a small white piece of paper, in the following format: C = _____, A = _____, N = _____, O = _____, E = _____. Try to disguise your handwriting to make it as plain and generic as possible. Fold your piece of paper so that others cannot see your "CANOE" scores.

4.3 In your group, mix up the pieces of paper. Begin by having one group member choose a piece of paper, reading the CANOE scores aloud. The group should then try to come to consensus on which member the scores belong to, given the norms for the various dimensions (C = 14, A = 16, N = 10, O = 15, E = 13). Keep in mind that group members may wind up reading their own pieces of paper aloud in some cases. Once the group guesses which member the paper belongs to, they should place the paper in front of that member.

4.4 Moving clockwise, the next group member should choose one of the remaining pieces of paper, continuing as before. The process repeats until all the pieces of paper have been assigned to a member. Members can be assigned only one piece of paper, and no switching is permitted once an assignment has been made.

4.5 Group members should then announce whether the piece of paper assigned to them was in fact their set of scores. If the assignment was incorrect, they should find their actual piece of paper and describe the differences in the scores.

4.6 Class discussion (whether in groups or as a class) should centre on the following topics: How accurate were the guesses? Were the guesses more accurate in groups that knew one another well than in groups with less familiarity? Which personality dimensions were relied upon most heavily when making assignment decisions? What is it that makes those dimensions more immediately observable?

OB ASSESSMENTS • THE BIG FIVE

What does your personality profile look like? This assessment is designed to measure the five major dimensions of personality: conscientiousness (C), agreeableness (A), neuroticism (N), openness to experience (O), and extraversion (E). Listed below are phrases describing people's behaviours. Write a number next to each statement that indicates the extent to which it accurately describes you. Answer each question using the response scale provided. Then subtract from 6 the sum of your answers to the boldfaced questions, with the difference being your new answer for those questions. For example, if your original answer for question 6 was "2," your new answer is "4" (6 – 2).

1 Very Inaccurate	2 Moderately Inaccurate	3 Neither Inaccurate nor Accurate	4 Moderately Accurate	5 Very Accurate	
1. I am the life of the party.					_____
2. I sympathize with others' feelings.					_____
3. I get chores done right away.					_____
4. I have frequent mood swings.					_____
5. I have a vivid imagination.					_____
6. I don't talk a lot.					_____
7. I am not interested in other people's problems.					_____
8. I often forget to put things back in their proper place.					_____
9. I am relaxed most of the time.					_____
10. I am not interested in abstract ideas.					_____
11. I talk to a lot of different people at parties.					_____
12. I feel others' emotions.					_____
13. I like order.					_____
14. I get upset easily.					_____
15. I have difficulty understanding abstract ideas.					_____
16. I keep in the background.					_____
17. I am not really interested in others.					_____
18. I make a mess of things.					_____
19. I seldom feel blue.					_____
20. I do not have a good imagination.					_____

Scoring and Interpretation

Conscientiousness. Add up items 3, 8, 13, and 18.

Agreeableness. Add up items 2, 7, 12, and 17.

Neuroticism. Add up items 4, 9, 14, and 19.

Openness to experience. Add up items 5, 10, 15, and 20.

Extraversion. Add up items 1, 6, 11, and 16.

Now chart your scores in the figure below to see whether you are above or below the norm for each dimension. Remember, when interpreting your scores on these assessments it is important to consider the *reliability* and *validity* of these tools (see Chapter 1, ***OB Assessments***).

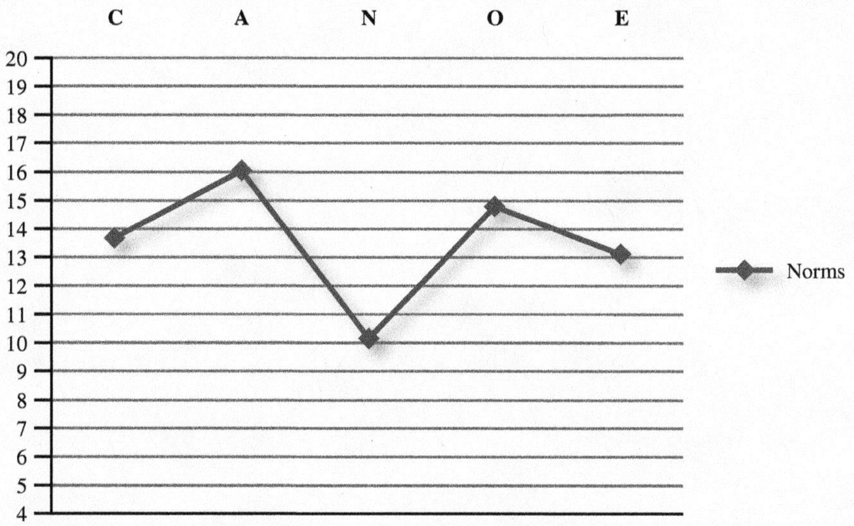

Source: Copyright © 2006 by the American Psychological Association. Reproduced with permission from M.B. Donnellan, F.L. Oswald, B.M. Baird, and R.E. Lucas, "The Mini-IPIP Scales: Tiny-Yet-Effective Measures of the Big Five Factors of Personality," *Psychological Assessment* 18 (2006), pp. 192–203. No further reproduction or distribution is permitted without written permission from the American Psychological Association.

Job Satisfaction

CHAPTER 5

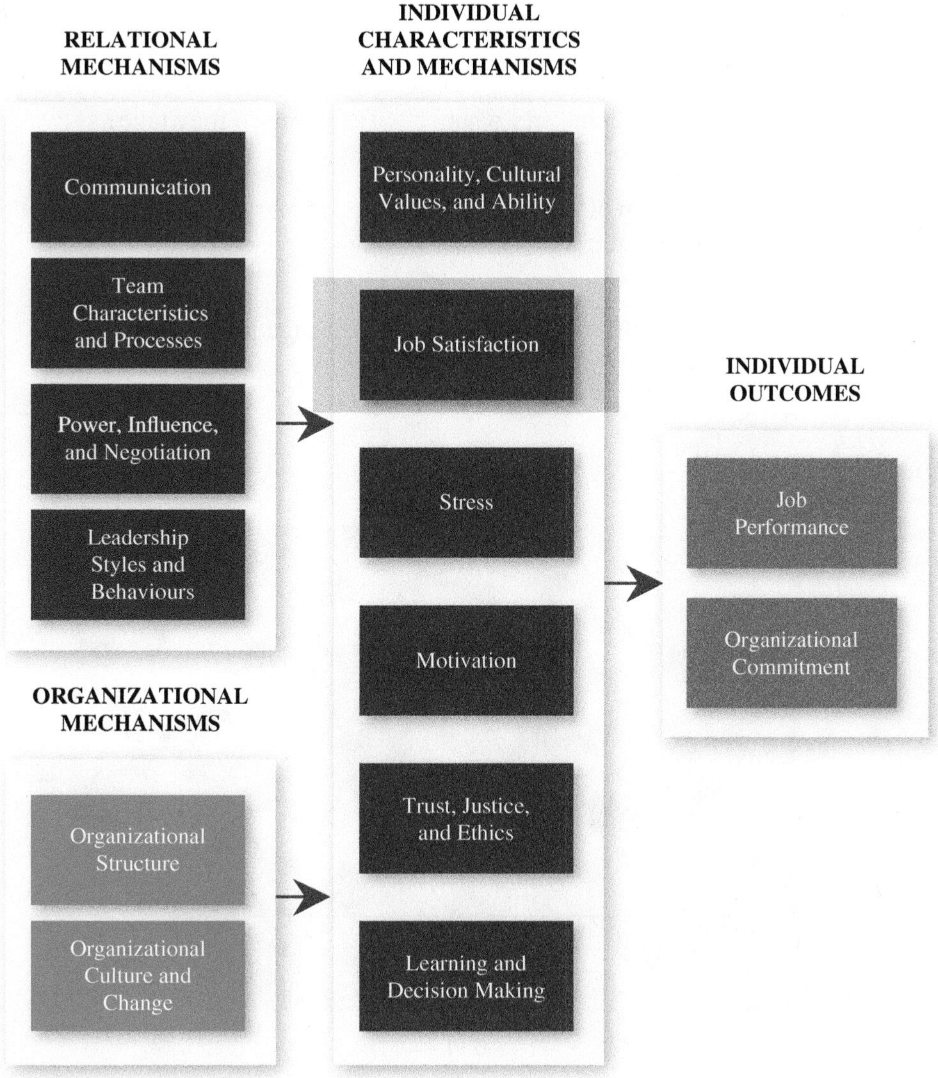

LEARNING OUTCOMES

After reading this chapter, you should be able to answer the following questions:

5.1 What is job satisfaction?

5.2 What are values, and how do they affect job satisfaction?

5.3 What specific facets do employees consider when evaluating their job satisfaction?

5.4 Which job characteristics can create a sense of satisfaction with the work itself?

5.5 How is job satisfaction affected by day-to-day events?

5.6 What are moods and emotions, and what specific forms do they take?

5.7 How does job satisfaction affect job performance and organizational commitment? How does it affect life satisfaction?

5.8 What steps can organizations take to assess and manage job satisfaction?

Zappos (Amazon)

Courtesy of Zappos

"Create fun and a little weirdness." That's one of the ten core values of Zappos.com, a highly successful member of the Amazon.com family of online retailers.[1] It is fitting to feature the Zappos story in a chapter on job satisfaction, given that management practices at this company are just so strange, if not a little controversial and counterintuitive.

What's weird at Zappos? For starters, senior managers there are referred to as "monkeys" because they all like bananas and work in a jungle.[2] The top monkey, Tony Hsieh, CEO, hosts company pajama parties and obsessively blogs about a variety of subjects,[3] from how Twitter can make you a happier person to whether eggnog tastes good on mashed potatoes.[4] The company also employs a full-time life coach.[5] Employees can talk about personal issues, chat off the record about their work group, or get advice on advancing at the company. The one requirement is that they sit on a red velvet throne during their session. Even the hiring process is a little weird, including some non-traditional interview questions such as "What's your theme song?," "If you could be a superhero, which one would you be?," and "How weird are you?"[6] Those who get through that process don't just read about fireable offences in some employment manual; instead, they watch human resources employees act out the "no-no's" in *Saturday Night Live*–style skits.[7]

Zappos currently showcases millions of products from over 1,000 clothing and shoe brands. So, in one sense, the employees at Zappos perform the kind of dreary work that you might see in a typical call centre, such as taking orders and communicating with customers over the phone and Internet. But there is nothing typical about Zappos. The company lives up to the "fun" part of its core values by taking steps to keep employees satisfied with their jobs. Employees understand that their job is to delight customers, and they're encouraged to use their imaginations—rather than some predetermined script—during calls. They might encourage customers to order two sizes of shoes, because Zappos offers free shipping for both purchases and returns, or will recommend a competitor for items that are out of stock. Zappos employees have even been known to send handwritten notes or flowers in cases in which customers complained about a tough workday. Such gestures can have a significant impact, because three-quarters of the company's purchases are made by repeat customers.

In addition to being able to use their discretion, employees at Zappos get free lunches and access to a nap room and concierge service.[8] Zappos also covers 100 percent of employees' health insurance premiums.[9] Employees can even give another employee a $50 bonus for a job well done.[10] Zappos also creates family feeling by encouraging managers to spend 10 to 20 percent of their time with employees outside the office. These sorts of practices help explain why Zappos.com has been recognized in 2009, 2010, 2011, 2012, 2013, and 2014 as one Fortune's "100 Best Companies to Work For."[11] Zappos takes great pride in the weird culture it's cultivated, and currently offers a 3-Day Culture Camp for other companies who are interested in transforming their own cultures into something a little more fun and weird.[12]

5.1 What is job satisfaction?

JOB SATISFACTION

Job satisfaction is one of several individual mechanisms within our integrative model that directly affect job performance and organizational commitment. As is shown in the Zappos example, if employees are very satisfied with their jobs and experience positive emotions while working, they may perform their jobs better and choose to remain with the company for a longer period. Think of the worst job that you've held in your life, even if it was just a summer job or a short-term work assignment. What did you feel during the course of the day? How did those feelings influence the way you behaved, in terms of your time spent on task and citizenship behaviours rather than counterproductive or withdrawal behaviours?

Job satisfaction is defined as a pleasurable emotional state resulting from the appraisal of one's job or job experiences.[13] In other words, it represents how you feel about your job and what you think about your job. Employees with high job satisfaction experience positive feelings when they think about their duties or take part in task activities. Employees with low job satisfaction experience negative feelings when they think about their duties or take part in their task activities. In spite of some bumpy economic periods, the majority of Canadians are generally happy and satisfied with their jobs (81 percent) and like the people they work with (88 percent).[14] It would appear that money isn't always the determining factor in job satisfaction. Canadians identified corporate culture, the opportunity to use skills, the opportunity to learn, and the ability to be creative as the top drivers of job satisfaction.[15] Interestingly, financial rewards and benefits, flexible work hours, and stress were among the least-cited reasons for job satisfaction.[16] Unravelling this puzzle and understanding why some employees are more satisfied than others, and what exactly drives job satisfaction levels, are issues explored in this chapter

job satisfaction

A pleasurable emotional state resulting from the appraisal of one's job or job experiences; represents how a person feels and thinks about his or her job

5.2 What are values, and how do they affect job satisfaction?

WHY ARE SOME EMPLOYEES MORE SATISFIED THAN OTHERS?

So what explains why some employees are more satisfied than others? At a general level, employees are satisfied when their job provides the things they value. **Values** are those things people consciously or subconsciously want to seek or attain.[17] Think about this question for a few moments: What do you want to attain from your job—that is, what things do you want your job to give you? A good wage? A sense of achievement? Colleagues who are fun to be around? If you had to make a list of the things you value with respect to your job, most or all of them would likely be among those shown in Table 5-1. This table summarizes the values assessed in the five most popular surveys of work values, broken down into more general categories.[18] Many of those values deal with the things that your work can give you, such as good pay or the chance for frequent promotions. Other values pertain to the context that surrounds your work, including whether you have a good boss or good co-workers. Still other values deal with the work itself, like whether your job tasks provide you with freedom or a sense of achievement.

values

Things that people consciously or unconsciously want to seek or attain

Consider the list of values in Table 5-1. Which would make your top five in terms of importance right now, at this stage of your life? Maybe you have a part-time job in which you value enjoyable co-workers or a comfortable work environment above everything else. Or maybe you're getting established in your career and starting a family, which makes a high salary and frequent promotions especially critical. Or perhaps you're at a point in your career that you feel a need to help others or find an outlet for your creative expression. Regardless of your top five, you can see that different people value different things and that your values may change during the course of your working life.

TABLE 5-1

Commonly Assessed Work Values

Category	Specific Values
Pay	High salary Secure salary
Promotions	Frequent promotions Promotions based on ability
Supervision	Good supervisory relations Praise for good work
Co-workers	Enjoyable co-workers Responsible co-workers
The work itself	Utilization of ability Freedom and independence Intellectual stimulation Creative expression Sense of achievement
Altruism	Helping others Moral causes
Status	Prestige Power over others Fame
Environment	Comfort Safety
Key Question: *Which of these things are most important to you?*	

Sources: Adapted from R.V. Dawis, "Vocational Interests, Values, and Preferences," in *Handbook of Industrial and Organizational Psychology*, Vol. 2, eds. M.D. Dunnette and L.M. Hough (Palo Alto, CA: Consulting Psychologists Press, 1991), pp. 834–71; D.M. Cable and J.R. Edwards, "Complementary and Supplementary Fit: A Theoretical and Empirical Investigation," *Journal of Applied Psychology* 89 (2004), pp. 822–34.

Value Fulfillment

Values play a key role in explaining job satisfaction. **Value-percept theory** argues that job satisfaction depends on whether you *perceive* that your job supplies the things that you *value*.[19] This theory can be summarized with the following equation:

$$\text{Dissatisfaction} = (V_{\text{want}} - V_{\text{have}}) \times (V_{\text{importance}})$$

In this equation, V_{want} reflects how much of a value an employee wants, V_{have} indicates how much of that value the job supplies, and $V_{importance}$ reflects how important the value is to the employee. Big differences between wants and haves create a sense of dissatisfaction, especially when the value in question is important. Note that the difference between V_{want} and V_{have} gets multiplied by importance, so existing discrepancies get magnified for important values and minimized for trivial values. As an example, say you're evaluating your pay satisfaction. You want to be earning around $70,000 a year but are currently earning $50,000, so there's a $20,000 discrepancy. Does that mean you feel a great deal of pay dissatisfaction? Only if pay is one of the most important values to you from Table 5-1. If pay isn't that important, you probably don't feel much dissatisfaction.

value-percept theory

A theory that argues that job satisfaction depends on whether the employee perceives that his or her job supplies those things that he or she values

5.3 What specific facets do employees consider when evaluating their job satisfaction?

Value-percept theory also suggests that people evaluate job satisfaction according to specific facets of the job.[20] After all, a job isn't one thing—it's a collection of tasks, relationships, and rewards.[21] The most common facets that employees consider in judging their job satisfaction appear in Figure 5-1. The figure includes the "want vs. have" calculations that drive satisfaction with pay, promotions, supervision, co-workers, and the work itself. The figure also shows how satisfaction with those five facets adds together to create "overall job satisfaction." Figure 5-1 shows that employees might be satisfied for all kinds of reasons. One might be satisfied because she's in a high-paying job and working for a good boss. Another might be satisfied because he has good co-workers and enjoyable work tasks. You may have noticed that a few of the values in Table 5-1, such as working for moral causes and gaining fame and prestige, are not represented in Figure 5-1. This is because those values are not relevant in all jobs, unlike pay, promotions, and so forth.

The first facet in Figure 5-1, **pay satisfaction**, refers to employees' feelings about their pay, including whether it's as much as they deserve, secure, and adequate for both normal expenses and luxury items.[22] Similarly to the other facets, pay satisfaction is based on a comparison of the pay that employees want and the pay they receive.[23] Although more money is almost always better, most employees base their desired pay on a careful examination of their job duties and the pay given to comparable colleagues.[24] As a result, even non-millionaires can be quite satisfied with their pay (thankfully for most of us!). At NuStar Energy, the company pays employees pays more than the industry average, with merit pay and equity grants for non-executives. And either everyone gets a bonus or no one does. Those sorts of pay policies make it more bearable to stand next to hot asphalt in a flame-retardant suit, hard hat, shatterproof glasses, and steel-toed boots!

pay satisfaction

Employees' feelings about the compensation for their jobs

The next facet in Figure 5-1, **promotion satisfaction**, refers to employees' feelings about the company's promotion policies and their execution, including whether promotions are frequent, fair, and based on ability.[25] In contrast to their feelings about pay, some employees may not want frequent promotions, because promotions bring more responsibility and increased work hours.[26] However, many do value promotions, because they provide opportunities for more personal growth, a better wage, and more prestige. Nordstrom, a high-end retailer new to Canada, does a good job fostering promotion satisfaction on the part of its employees. New sales clerks are often promoted within a year, with potential leaders put on the fast track with a six-month training program.[27] Indeed, five of the nine members of Nordstrom's executive committee started off on the sales floor. "Leadership is grounded in experience," notes one executive. "We want to make sure people get enough experiences to grow their career."

FIGURE 5-1

The Value-Percept Theory of Job Satisfaction

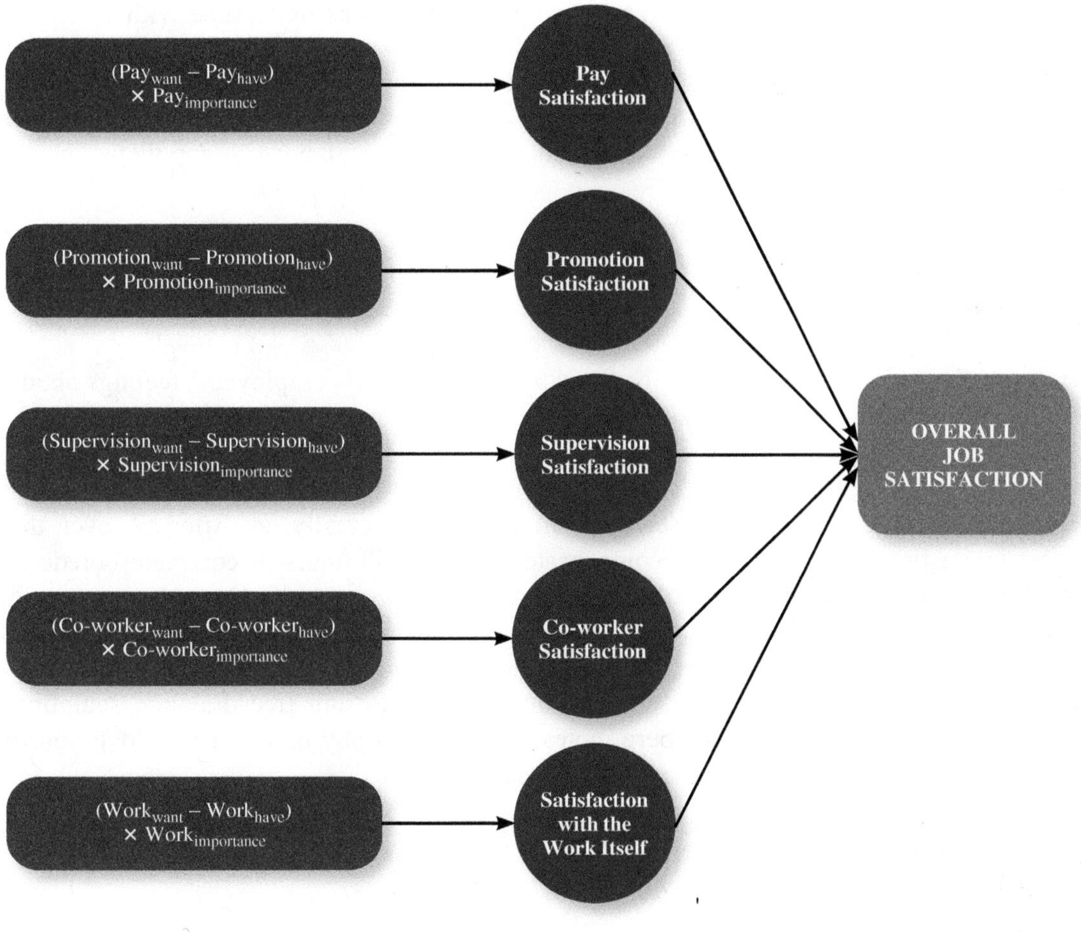

promotion satisfaction
Employees' feelings about how the company handles promotions

Supervision satisfaction reflects employees' feelings about their boss, including whether the boss is competent, polite, and a good communicator (rather than lazy, annoying, and too distant).[28] Most employees ask two questions about their supervisors: (1) "Can they help me attain the things that I value?" and (2) "Are they generally likable?"[29] The first question depends on whether supervisors provide rewards for good performance, help employees obtain necessary resources, and protect employees from unnecessary distractions. The second question depends on whether supervisors have good personalities, and values and beliefs similar to the employees' philosophies. In the chapter-opening profile, we see that, to facilitate affirmative answers to these questions, Zappos requires its managers to spend 10 to 12 percent of their time with employees outside the office.

supervision satisfaction

Employees' feelings about their boss, including his or her competency, communication, and personality

Co-worker satisfaction refers to employees' feelings about their fellow employees, including whether they are smart, responsible, helpful, fun, and interesting as opposed to lazy, gossipy, unpleasant, and boring.[30] Employees ask the same kinds of questions about their co-workers that they do about their supervisors: (1) "Can they help me do my job?" and (2) "Do I enjoy being around them?" The first question is critical, because most of us rely, to some extent, on our co-workers when performing job tasks. The second question is also important because we spend just as much time with co-workers as we do with members of our own family. Co-workers who are pleasant and fun can make the workweek go much faster, whereas ones who are disrespectful and annoying can make even a day seem like an eternity. In addition to encouraging frequent social interactions with managers, Zappos allows its employees to recognize their co-workers' achievements with a $50 bonus—a policy that focuses attention on the positive qualities of others.

co-worker satisfaction

Employees' feelings about their co-workers, including their abilities and personalities

The last facet in Figure 5-1, **satisfaction with the work itself**, reflects employees' feelings about their actual work tasks, including whether those tasks are challenging, interesting, respected, and make use of key skills rather than being dull, repetitive, and uncomfortable.[31] Whereas the previous four facets described the outcomes that result from work (pay, promotions) and the people who surround work (supervisors, co-workers), this facet focuses on what employees actually *do*. After all, even the best boss or most interesting co-workers can't compensate for 40 or 50 hours of complete boredom each week! How can employers instill a sense of satisfaction with the work itself? One way is to emphasize the most challenging and interesting parts of the job. At DreamWorks Animation, employees are encouraged to attend "Life's a Pitch" workshops that allow them to hone their presentation skills.[32] The company also helps employees flex their creative muscles by offering free drawing, sculpting, and improv classes. The CEO, Jeffrey Katzenberg, notes, "Our philosophy is that if you love your work, and you love coming to work, then the work will be exceptional."

satisfaction with the work itself

Employees' feelings about their actual work tasks

Employees at DreamWorks Animation can express their creativity at work in a number of ways, including free drawing, sculpting, and improv classes, and courses on honing their pitching and presentation skills.

© AP Photo/Paul Sakuma

In summary, value-percept theory suggests that employees will be satisfied when they perceive that their job offers the pay, promotions, supervision, co-workers, and work tasks that they value. Of course, this theory raises the question: Which of those ingredients is most important? In other words, which of the five facets in Figure 5-1 has the strongest influence on overall job satisfaction? Several research studies have examined these issues and come up with the results shown in Figure 5-2. The figure depicts the correlation between each of the five satisfaction facets and an overall index of job satisfaction. (Recall that correlations of .10, .30, and .50 indicate weak, moderate, and strong relationships, respectively.)

Figure 5-2 suggests that satisfaction with the work itself is the single strongest driver of overall job satisfaction.[33] Supervision and co-worker satisfaction are also strong drivers, and promotion and pay satisfaction have moderately strong effects. Why is satisfaction with the work itself so critical? Well, consider that a typical workweek contains around 2,400 minutes. How much of that time is spent thinking about how much money you make? 10 minutes? Maybe 20? The same is true for promotions—we may want them, but we don't necessarily spend hours a day thinking about them. We do spend a significant chunk of that time with other people though. Between lunches, meetings, hallway chats, and other conversations, we might easily spend 600 minutes a week with supervisors and co-workers. That leaves almost 1,800 minutes for just us and our work. As a result, it's hard to be satisfied with your job if you don't like what you actually do. To see how firefighters feel about their jobs, see our ***OB on Screen*** feature.

FIGURE 5-2

Correlations Between Satisfaction Facets and Overall Job Satisfaction

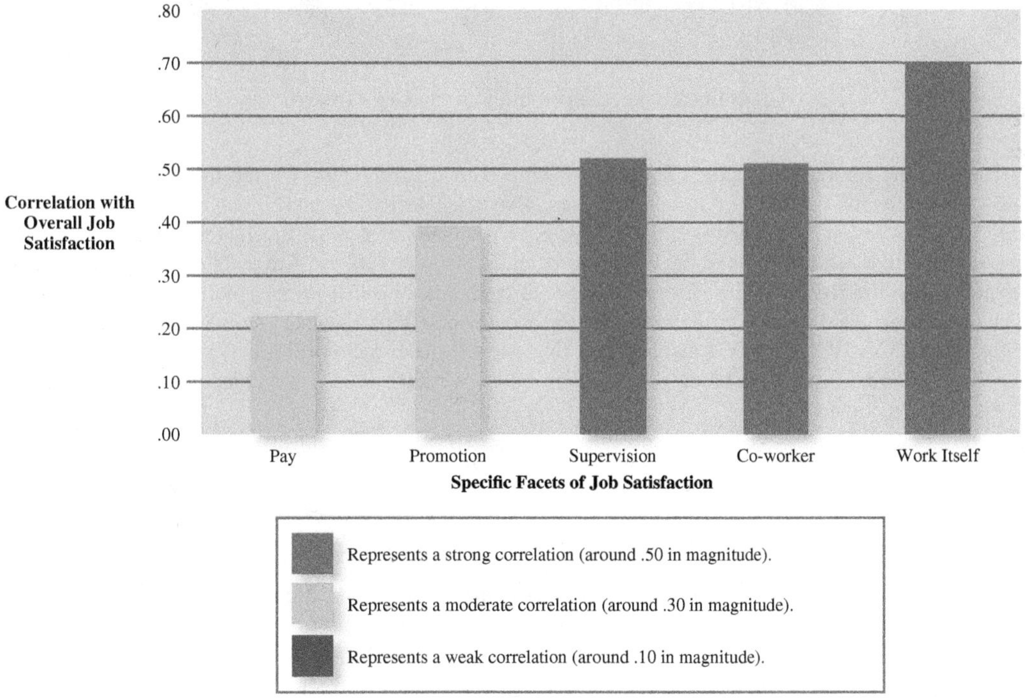

Sources: G.H. Ironson, P.C. Smith, M.T. Brannick, W.M. Gibson, and K.B. Paul, "Construction of a Job in General Scale: A Comparison of Global, Composite, and Specific Measures," *Journal of Applied Psychology* 74 (1989), pp. 193–200; S.S. Russell, C. Spitzmuller, L.F. Lin, J.M. Stanton, P.C. Smith, and G.H. Ironson, "Shorter Can Also Be Better: The Abridged Job in General Scale," *Educational and Psychological Measurement* 64 (2004), pp. 878–93.

OB ON SCREEN

Burn

I like coming to work, I look forward to it. I think you'll hear that from most of the guys. Ask anyone in the private sector and you'll probably hear differently.

With those words, Dave Miller—a firefighter for Engine Co. 50 on the east side of Detroit—summarizes his job satisfaction in *Burn* (Dir. Tom Putnam and Brenna Sanchez, Apostle and TBVE, 2012). The film is a documentary from executive producer Denis Leary (star of *Rescue Me*) that follows the Detroit Fire Department (DFD) for one year. Why Detroit? Well, it turns out that Detroit has more fires than any city in the United States, with 30,000 fire calls per year. Many of those fires are a direct result of the abandoned buildings that dot Detroit in the wake of the economic downturn. The city's population has fallen from 1.8 million to just over 700,000, with many citizens leaving behind their houses and furniture when they move to a new city. As one firefighter says, it's "Katrina without the hurricane."

© Lucas Oleniuk/Toronto Star via Getty Images

The film captures the paradoxical nature of job satisfaction among firefighters. On the one hand, the job is incredibly dangerous—especially for the DFD. "Out of 17 years, I've been in the hospital 15 of those years," volunteers one firefighter. The job also pays so poorly—$30,000 a year, on average—that most firefighters have a second job to make ends meet. On the other hand, life in the firehouse can be quite pleasant between fire calls. "We actually live together 24 hours," explains one fire-fighter. "Most firemen are social creatures. We like to hang out, we like to enjoy life." Then there's the significance of the work to their community and to society as a whole. Asks Dave Parnell, the field engine operator for Engine Co. 50, "What is a man's worth that doesn't make the world a better place?" Finally, at DFD, the firefighters feel enormous pride from being good at their craft. "We have people that come from cross country, round the world, to just watch us fight fire."

5.4 Which job characteristics can create a sense of satisfaction with the work itself?

Satisfaction with the Work Itself

Given how critical enjoyable work tasks are to overall job satisfaction, it's worth spending more time describing the kinds of tasks that most people find enjoyable. Researchers began focusing on this question in the 1950s and 1960s, partly in reaction to practices based in the "scientific management" perspective. As alluded to earlier (Chapter 1), scientific management focused on increasing the efficiency of job tasks by making them more simplified and specialized and using time and motion studies to plan task movements and sequences carefully.[34] The hope was that such steps would increase worker productivity and reduce the breadth of skills required to complete a job, ultimately improving organizational profitability. Instead, the simplified and routine jobs tended to lower job satisfaction while increasing absenteeism and turnover.[35] Put simply: Boring jobs may be easier, but they're not necessarily better.

So what kinds of work tasks are especially satisfying? Research suggests that three "critical psychological states" make work satisfying. The first is believing in the **meaningfulness of work**, the degree to which work tasks are viewed as something that "counts" in the employee's system of philosophies and beliefs (see Chapter 7 on motivation for more discussion of such issues).[36] Trivial tasks tend to be less satisfying than tasks that make employees feel like they're aiding the organization or society in some meaningful way. The second psychological state is perceiving **responsibility for outcomes**, the degree to which employees feel that they're key drivers of the quality of the unit's work.[37] Sometimes employees feel like their efforts don't really matter, because outcomes are dictated by effective procedures, efficient technologies, or more influential colleagues. Finally, the third psychological state is **knowledge of results**, the extent to which employees know how well (or how poorly) they're doing.[38] Many work in jobs in which they never find out about their mistakes or notice when they did particularly well.

meaningfulness of work

A psychological state indicating the degree to which work tasks are viewed as something that counts in the employee's system of philosophies and beliefs

responsibility for outcomes

A psychological state indicating the degree to which employees feel they are key drivers of the quality of work output

knowledge of results

A psychological state indicating the extent to which employees are aware of how well or how poorly they are doing

Think about times when you felt especially proud of a job well done. At that moment, you were probably experiencing all three psychological states. You were aware of the result (after all, some job had been done well). You felt you were somehow responsible for that result (otherwise, why would you feel proud?). Finally, you felt that the result of the work was somehow meaningful (otherwise, why would you have remembered it just now?). The next obvious question then becomes, "What kinds of tasks create these psychological states?" **Job characteristics theory**, which describes the central characteristics of intrinsically satisfying jobs, attempts to answer this question. As is shown in Figure 5-3, job characteristics theory argues that five core job characteristics (variety, identity, significance, autonomy, and feedback, which you can remember with the acronym "VISAF") result in high levels of the three psychological states, making work tasks more satisfying.[39]

job characteristics theory

A theory that argues that five core characteristics (variety, identity, significance, autonomy, and feedback) combine to result in high levels of satisfaction with the work itself

FIGURE 5-3

Job Characteristics Theory

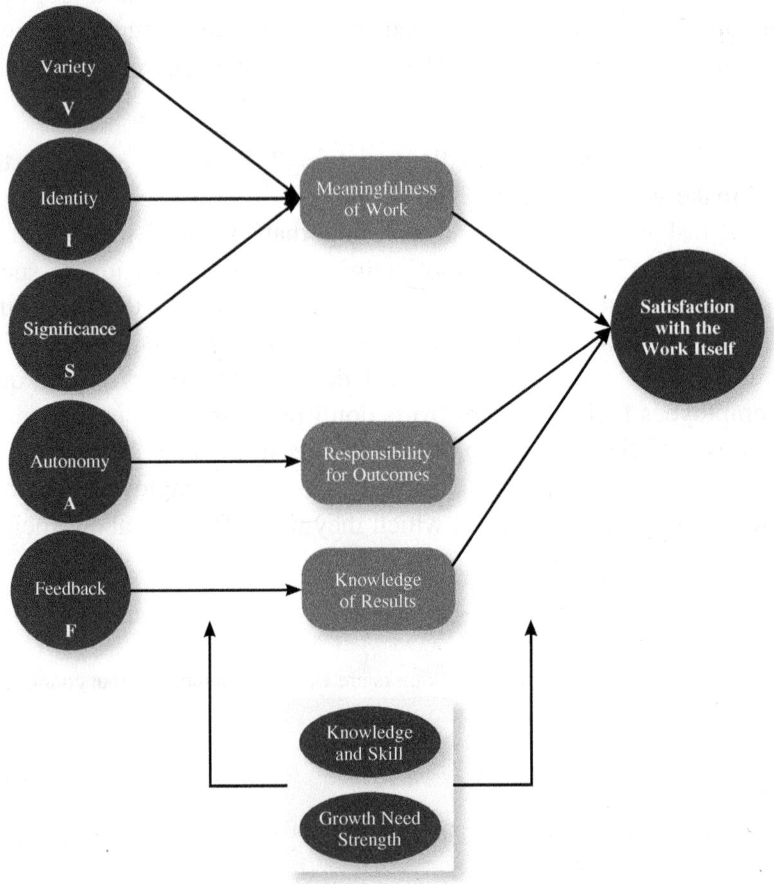

The first core job characteristic in Figure 5-3, **variety**, is the degree to which the job requires a number of different activities that involve a number of different skills and talents.[40] When variety is high, almost every workday is different in some way, and job holders rarely feel a sense of monotony or repetition.[41] Of course, we could picture jobs that have a variety of boring tasks, such as screwing differently sized nuts onto differently coloured bolts, but such jobs do not involve a number of different skills and talents.[42] To provide some examples of low and high job variety, we offer excerpts from Studs Terkel's classic book *Working: People Talk About What They Do All Day and How They Feel About What They Do.*

variety
The degree to which a job requires different activities and skills

▼ Low Variety: Phil Stallings, Spot Welder

I stand in one spot, about two- or three-feet area, all night. The only time a person stops is when the line stops. We do about thirty-two jobs per car, per unit. Forty-eight units an hour, eight hours a day. Thirty-two times forty-eight times eight. Figure it out. That's how many times I push that button.... It don't stop. It just goes and goes and goes. I bet there's men who have lived and died out there, never seen the end of that line. And they never will—because it's endless. It's like the serpent. It's just all body, no tail. It can do things to you.... (Laughs.)[43]

▲ High Variety: Eugene Russell, Piano Tuner

Every day is different. I work Saturdays and Sundays sometimes. Monday I'm tuning a piano for a record company that had to be done before nine o'clock. When I finish that, I go to another company and do at least four pianos. During that day there's a couple of harpsichords mixed in.... I get a big kick out of it, because there are so many facets. Other people go through a routine. At a certain time they punch a clock.... Then they're through with it and then their life begins. With us the piano business is an integral part of our life. I had a discussion with another tuner, who is a great guitar man. He said "Why are we tuners?" I said, "Because we want to hear good sounds."[44]

Evidence indicates that our preference for variety is hardwired into our brains. Research in psychiatry and neuroscience shows that the brain releases a chemical called dopamine whenever a novel stimulus (a new painting, a new meal, a new work challenge) is experienced, and we tend to find this dopamine release quite pleasurable. Unfortunately, the amount of dopamine present in our brains declines over our life spans. One neuroscientist therefore suggests that the best way to protect our dopamine system is through novel, challenging experiences, writing, "The sense of satisfaction after you've successfully handled unexpected tasks or sought out unfamiliar, physically and emotionally demanding activities is your brain's signal that you're doing what nature designed you to do."[45] Something to think about next time you plan to order the same old thing at your favourite restaurant!

The second core job characteristic in Figure 5-3, **identity**, is the degree to which the job requires completing a whole, identifiable, piece of work from beginning to end with a visible outcome.[46] When a job has high identity, employees can point to something and say, "There, I did that." The transformation from inputs to finished product is very visible, and the employee feels a distinct sense of beginning and closure.[47] Think of how you feel when you work for a while on some project but don't quite get it finished—does that lack of closure bug you? If so, identity is an important concern for you. Consider these further excerpts from *Working*:

identity
The degree to which a job offers completion of a whole, identifiable piece of work

▼ Low Identity: Mike Lefevre, Steelworker

It's not just the work. Somebody built the pyramids. Somebody's going to build something. Pyramids, Empire State Building—these things don't just happen. There's hard work behind it. I would like to see a building, say the Empire State, I would like to see on one side of it a foot-wide strip from top to bottom with the name of every bricklayer, the name of every electrician, with all the names. So when a guy walked by, he could take his son and say, "See, that's me over there on the forty-fifth floor. I put the steel beam in." Picasso can point to a painting. What can I point to? A writer can point to a book. Everybody should have something to point to.[48]

▲ High Identity: Frank Decker, Truck Driver

Every load is a challenge and when you finally off-load it, you have a feeling of having completed a job—which I don't think you get in.... a production line. I pick up a load at the mill, going to... Hotpoint ...in Milwaukee. I take a job and I go through all the process.... You feel like your day's work is well done when you're coming back. I used to have problems in the morning, a lot of heartburn, I couldn't eat. But once I off-loaded, the pressure was off. Then I could eat anything.[49]

Significance is the degree to which the job has a substantial impact on the lives of other people, particularly people in the world at large.[50] Virtually any job can be important if it helps put food on the table for a family, helps send kids to university, or makes employees feel like they're doing their part for the working world. That said, significance as a core job characteristic captures something beyond that—the belief that this job really matters. When employees feel that their jobs are significant, they can see that others value what they do and they're aware that their job has a positive impact on the people around them.[51] There's the sense that, if their job was taken away, society would be the worse for it.

significance
The degree to which a job really matters and impacts society as a whole

▼ Low Significance: Louis Hayward, Washroom Attendant

They come in. They wash their hands after using the service—you hope. (A soft chuckle.) I go through the old brush routine, stand back, expecting a tip. A quarter is what you expect when you hand the guy a towel and a couple of licks of the broom.... I'm not particularly proud of what I'm doing. The shine man and I discuss it quite freely. In my own habitat I don't go around saying I'm a washroom attendant at the Palmer House. Outside of my immediate family, very few people know what I do. They do know I work at the Palmer House and let that suffice. You say Palmer House, they automatically assume you're a ... waiter.... The whole thing is obsolete. It's on its way out. This work isn't necessary in the first place. It's so superfluous. It was *never* necessary. (Laughs.)[52]

▲ High Significance: Tom Patrick, Fireman

Last month there was a second alarm. I was off duty. I ran over there. I'm a bystander. I see these firemen on the roof, with the smoke pouring out around them, and the flames, and they go in.... You could see the pride that they were seein'. The f***** world's so f**** up, the country's f**** up. But the firemen, you actually see them produce. You see them put out a fire. You see them come out with babies in their hands. You see them give mouth-to-mouth when a guy's dying. You can't get around that s***. That's real. To me, that's what I want to be.[53]

Autonomy is the degree to which the job provides freedom, independence, and discretion to the individual performing the work.[54] When your job provides autonomy, you view the outcomes of it as the product of your efforts rather than the result of careful instructions from your boss or a well-written manual of procedures.[55] Autonomy comes in multiple forms, including the freedom to control the timing, scheduling, and sequencing of work activities, as well as the procedures and methods used to complete work tasks.[56] To many of us, high levels of autonomy are the difference between "having a long leash" and being "micromanaged."

autonomy
The degree to which a job provides freedom, independence, and discretion to perform the work

Despite the need for discipline and practice, the job of a jazz musician is one with a high degree of autonomy.

Toronto Star/GetStock.com

▼ Low Autonomy: Beryl Simpson, Airline Reservationist

They brought in a computer called Sabre.... It has a memory drum and you can retrieve that information forever.... With Sabre being so valuable, you were allowed no more than three minutes on the telephone. You had twenty seconds, busy-out time it was called, to put the information into Sabre. Then you had to be available for another phone call. It was almost like a production line. We adjusted to the machine. The casualness, the informality that had been there previously was no longer there.... You took thirty minutes for lunch, not thirty-one. If you got a break, you took ten minutes, not eleven.... With the airline I had no free will. I was just part of that stupid computer.[57]

▲ High Autonomy: Bud Freeman, Jazz Musician

I live in absolute freedom. I do what I do because I want to do it. What's wrong with making a living doing something interesting ... ? The jazz man is expressing freedom in every note he plays. We can only please the audience doing what *we* do. We have to please ourselves first. I want to play for the rest of my life. I don't see any sense in stopping. Were I to live another thirty years—that would make me ninety-five—why not try to play? I can just hear the critics: "Did you hear that wonderful note old man Freeman played last night?" (Laughs.) As Ben Webster says, "I'm going to play this g****** saxophone until they put it on top of me."[58]

The last core job characteristic in Figure 5-3, **feedback**, is the degree to which carrying out the activities required by the job provides the worker with clear information about how well he or she is performing.[59] A critical distinction must be noted: This core characteristic reflects feedback obtained directly from the job as opposed to feedback from co-workers or supervisors. Most employees receive formal performance appraisals from their bosses, but that feedback occurs once or maybe twice a year. When the job provides its own feedback, that feedback can be experienced almost every day.

feedback
In job characteristics theory, the degree to which the job itself provides information about how well the job holder is doing

▼ Low Feedback: Lilith Reynolds, Government Project Coordinator

I'm very discouraged about my job right now.... I'm to come up with some kind of paper on economic development. It won't be very hard because there's little that can be done. At the end of sixty days I'll present the paper. But because of the reorganization that's come up I'll probably never be asked about the paper.[60]

▲ High Feedback: Dolores Dante, Waitress

When somebody says to me, "You're great, how come you're *just* a waitress?" *Just* a waitress. I'd say, "Why, don't you think you deserve to be served by me?" ... Tips? I feel like Carmen. It's like a gypsy holding out a tambourine and they throw the coin. (Laughs.) ... People would ask for me.... I would like to say to the customer, "Go to so-and-so." But you can't do that, because you feel a sense of loyalty. So you would rush, get to your customers quickly. Some don't care to drink and still they wait for you. That's a compliment.[61]

The passages in this section illustrate the potential importance of each of the five core characteristics. But how important are the core characteristics to satisfaction with the work itself? Meta-analyses of around 200 different research studies employing around 90,000 total participants showed that the five core job characteristics are moderately to strongly related to work satisfaction.[62] However, those results don't mean that *every* employee wants more variety, more autonomy, and so forth. The bottom of Figure 5-3 includes two other variables: **knowledge and skill** and **growth need strength** (which captures whether employees have strong needs for personal accomplishment or developing themselves beyond where they currently are).[63] In the jargon of theory diagrams, these variables are called "moderators." Rather than directly affecting other variables in the diagram, moderators influence the strength of the relationships between variables. If employees lack the required knowledge and skill or lack a desire for growth and development, more variety and autonomy should *not* increase their satisfaction very much.[64] However, when employees are very talented and feel a strong need for growth, the core job characteristics become even more powerful. A graphical depiction of this moderator effect appears in Figure 5-4, where you can see that the relationship between the core job characteristics and satisfaction becomes stronger when growth need strength increases.

knowledge and skill
The degree to which employees have the aptitude and competence needed to succeed on their job

growth need strength
The degree to which employees desire to develop themselves further

Given how critical the five core job characteristics are to job satisfaction, many organizations have employed job characteristics theory to help improve satisfaction among their employees. The first step in this process is assessing the current level of the characteristics to arrive at a "satisfaction potential score." See our ***OB Assessments*** feature at the end of the chapter for more about that step. The organization, together with job design consultants, then attempts to redesign aspects of the job to increase the core job characteristic levels. Often this step results in **job enrichment**, such that the duties and responsibilities associated with a job are expanded to provide more variety, identity, autonomy, and so forth. Research suggests that such enrichment efforts can indeed boost job satisfaction levels.[65] Moreover, enrichment efforts can heighten work accuracy and customer satisfaction, though training and labour costs tend to rise as a result of such changes.[66] However, employees needn't necessarily wait for enrichment efforts to improve levels of the core job characteristics. Many employees can engage in **job crafting**, where they shape, mould, and redefine their jobs in a proactive way.[67] For example, they might alter the boundaries of their jobs by switching certain tasks, they might change specific collaborative relationships, or they might re-envison how they view their work, relative to the broader context of the organization's mission.

FIGURE 5-4

Growth Need Strength as a Moderator of Job Characteristic Effects

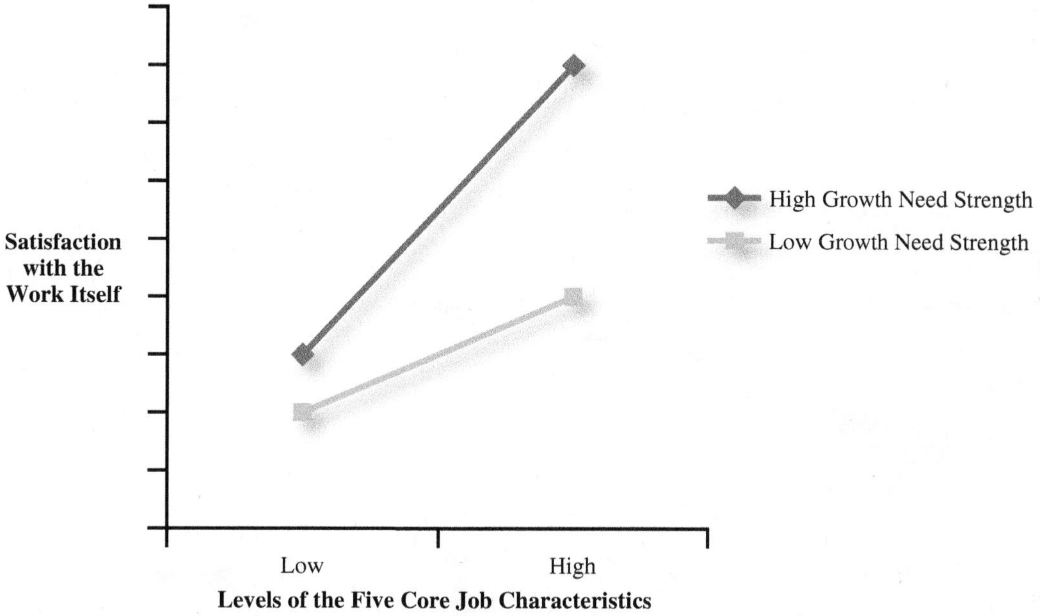

Source: Adapted from B.T. Loher, R.A. Noe, N.L. Moeller, and M.P. Fitzgerald, "A Meta-analysis of the Relation of Job Characteristics to Job Satisfaction," *Journal of Applied Psychology* 70 (1985), pp. 280–89.

job enrichment

When job duties and responsibilities are expanded to provide increased levels of core job characteristics

job crafting

When employees shape, mold, and redefine their job in a proactive way

5.5 How is job satisfaction affected by day-to-day events?

Mood and Emotions

Let's say you're a satisfied employee, maybe because you get paid well and work for a good boss or because your work tasks provide you with variety and autonomy. Does this mean you'll definitely be satisfied at 11:00 a.m. next Tuesday? Or 2:30 p.m. the following Thursday? Obviously it doesn't. Each employee's satisfaction levels fluctuate over time, rising and falling like some sort of emotional stock market. This fluctuation might seem strange, given that people's pay, supervisors, co-workers, and work tasks don't change from one hour to the next. The key lies in remembering that job satisfaction reflects what you think and feel about your job. So part of it is rational, based on a careful appraisal of the job and the things it supplies. But another part of it is emotional, based on what you feel "in your gut" while you're at work or thinking about work. So satisfied employees feel good about their job *on average,* but things happen during the course of the day to make them feel better at some times (and worse at others).

OB FOR STUDENTS

What does satisfaction mean for you as a student? After all, pay, promotions, and supervision are less relevant for full-time students than for full-time employees. One recent study examined the facets of satisfaction for students,[68] including:

- *University satisfaction.* Do students feel good about their university choice and experience, and would they recommend their university to others?
- *Housing satisfaction.* Do students feel good about where they live and the surrounding neighbourhood?
- *Leisure satisfaction.* Do students feel good about their social life, their leisure activities, and their friendships?

The results of the study showed that all three facets had moderately strong positive correlations with an index of overall student satisfaction. So students were more satisfied when they liked the university, liked where they lived, and felt that they were having a good time. In addition, the more satisfied the students were, the better they performed in terms of their grade point average (GPA). In other words, happy students tended to be better students.

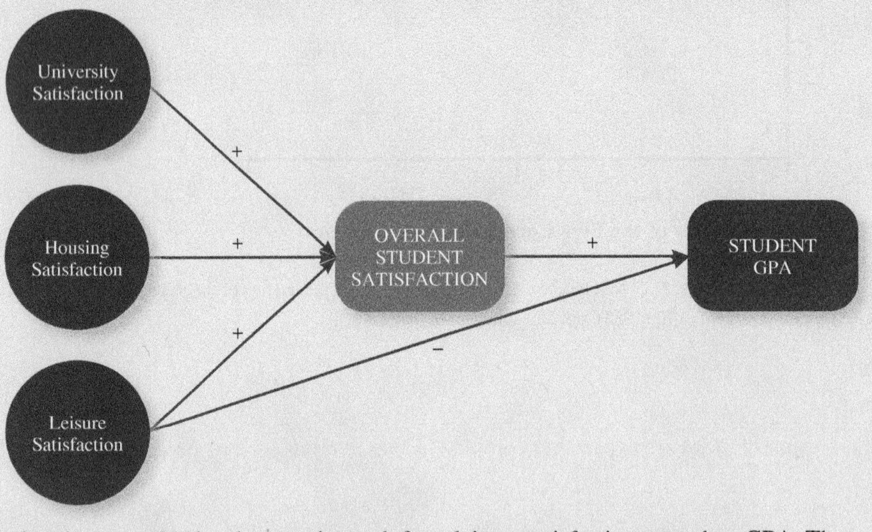

One word of caution, however. Notice the negative path from leisure satisfaction to student GPA. That path indicates that those two variables actually correlate negatively. In other words, having a lot of fun made students more satisfied, but it also made them perform less well in their classes. Moral of the story: You can have too much of a good thing!

Source: Republished with permission of Academy of Management, from "Life Satisfaction and Student Performance," *Academy of Management Learning and Education,* J.C. Rode, M.L. Arthaud-Day, C.H. Mooney, J.P. Near, T.T. Baldwin, W.H. Bommer, and R.S. Rubin, Vol. 4, No. 4, 2005; permission conveyed through Copyright Clearance Center, Inc.

Figure 5-5 illustrates the satisfaction levels for one employee during the course of a workday, from around 9:00 a.m. to 5:00 p.m. You can see that this employee did a number of different things during the day, from answering e-mails to eating lunch with friends to participating in a brainstorming meeting regarding a new project. You can also see that the employee came into the day feeling relatively satisfied, though satisfaction levels had several ebbs and flows during the next eight hours. What's responsible for those ebbs and flows in satisfaction levels? Two related concepts: mood and emotions.

FIGURE 5-5

Hour-by-Hour Fluctuations in Job Satisfaction During the Workday

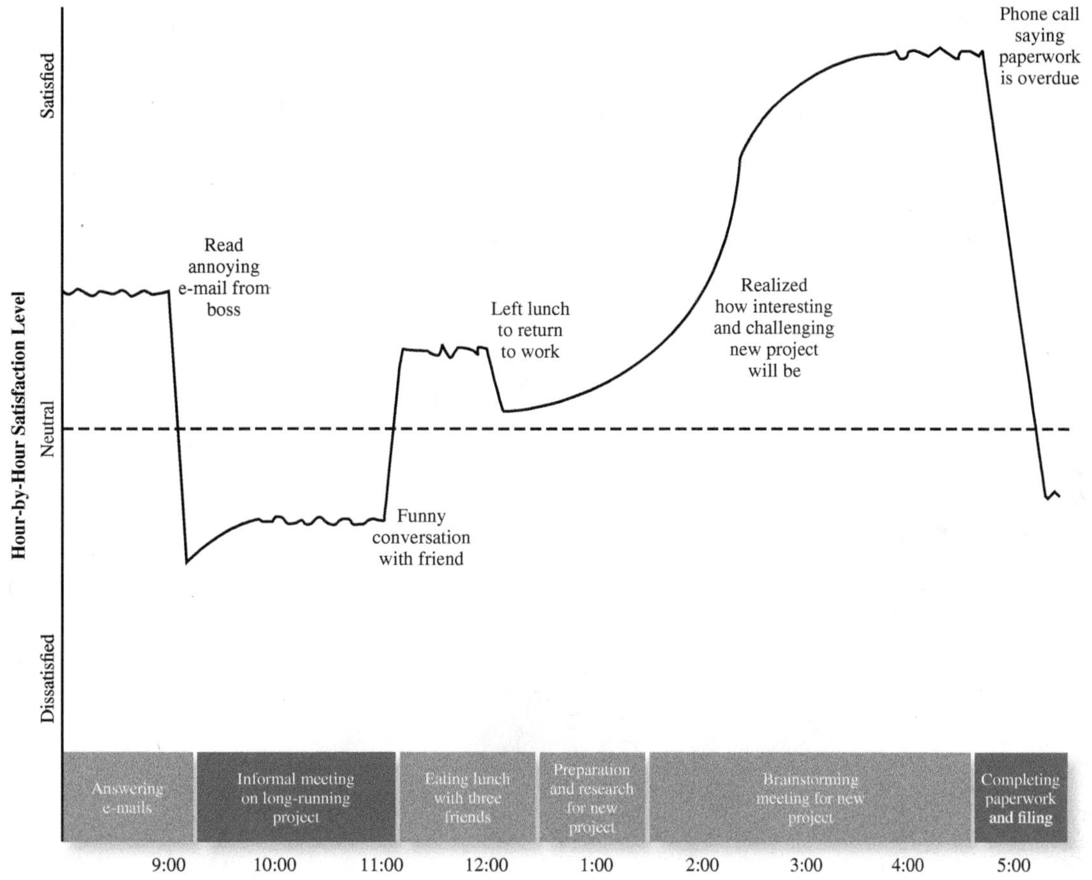

5.6 What are moods and emotions, and what specific forms do they take?

What kind of mood are you in right now? Good? Bad? Somewhere in between? Why are you in that kind of mood? Do you really even know? (If it's a bad mood, we hope it has nothing to do with this book!) **Moods** are states of feeling that are often mild in intensity, last for an extended period of time, and are not explicitly directed at or caused by anything.[69] When people are in a good or bad mood, they don't always know who (or what) deserves the credit or blame; they just happen to be feeling that way for a stretch of their day. Of course, it would be oversimplifying things to call all moods either good or bad. Sometimes we're in a serene mood; sometimes we're in an enthusiastic mood. Both are "good" but obviously feel quite different. Similarly, sometimes we're in a bored mood; sometimes we're in a hostile mood. Both are "bad" but, again, feel quite different.

moods
States of feeling that are mild in intensity, last for an extended period of time, and are not directed at anything

It turns out that there are a number of different moods that we might experience during the workday. Figure 5-6 summarizes the different moods in which people sometimes find themselves. The figure illustrates that moods can be categorized in two ways: **pleasantness** and **activation**. First, the horizontal axis of the figure reflects whether you feel pleasant (in a "good mood") or unpleasant (in a "bad mood").[70] The figure uses green to illustrate pleasant moods and red to illustrate unpleasant moods. Second, the vertical axis of the figure reflects whether you feel activated and aroused or deactivated and unaroused.[71] The figure uses darker colours to convey higher levels of activation and lighter colours to convey lower levels. Note that some moods are neither good nor bad. For example, being surprised or astonished (high activation) and quiet or still (low activation) are neither pleasant nor unpleasant. Accordingly, those latter moods are left colourless in Figure 5-6.

pleasantness
The degree to which an employee is in a good mood versus bad mood

activation
The degree to which moods are aroused and active, as opposed to unaroused and inactive

FIGURE 5-6

Different Kinds of Mood

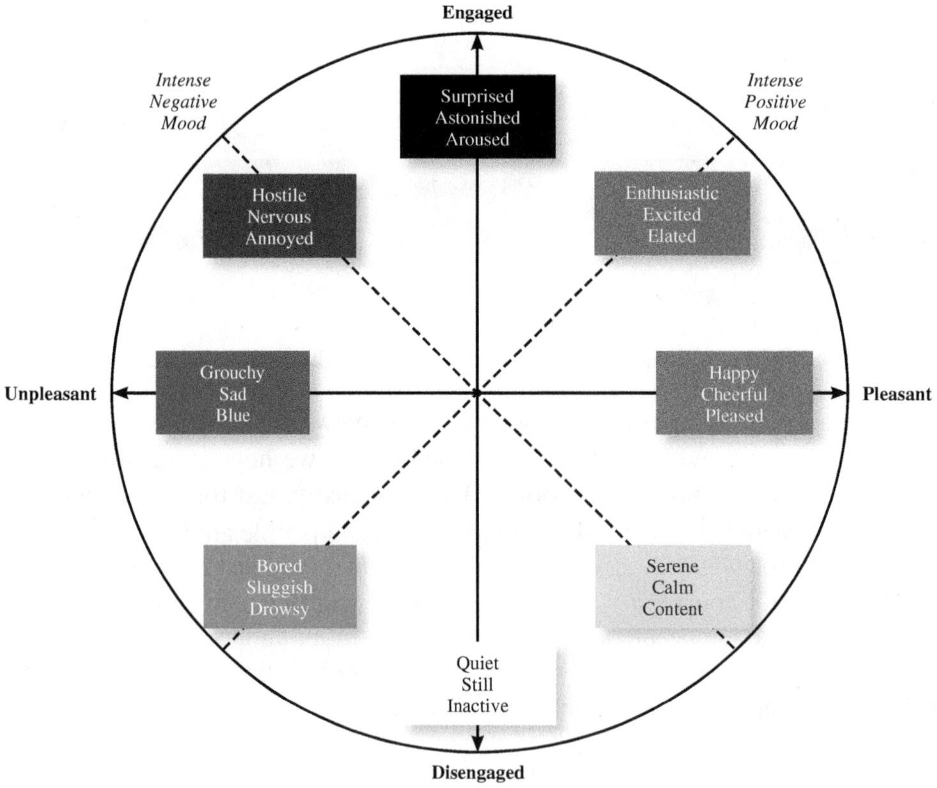

Sources: Adapted from D. Watson and A. Tellegen, "Toward a Consensual Structure of Mood," *Psychological Bulletin* 98 (1985), pp. 219–35; J.A. Russell, "A Circumplex Model of Affect," *Journal of Personality and Social Psychology* 39 (1980), pp. 1161–78; R.J. Larsen and E. Diener, "Promises and Problems with the Circumplex Model of Emotion," in *Review of Personality and Social Psychology: Emotion,* Vol. 13, ed. M.S. Clark (Newbury Park, CA: Sage, 1992), pp. 25–59.

Figure 5-6 illustrates that the most intense positive mood is characterized by feeling enthusiastic, excited, and elated. When employees feel this way, co-workers are likely to remark, "Wow, you're sure in a good mood!" In contrast, the most intense negative mood is characterized by feeling hostile, nervous, and annoyed. This kind of mood often triggers the question, "Wow, what's gotten you in such a bad mood?" If we return to our chart of hour-by-hour job satisfaction in Figure 5-5, what kind of mood do you think the employee was in while answering e-mails? Probably happy, cheerful, and pleased. What kind of mood was the employee in during the informal meeting on the long-running project? Probably grouchy, sad, and blue. Finally, what kind of mood do you think the employee was in during the brainstorming meeting for the new project? Clearly, enthusiastic, excited, and elated. This employee would report especially high levels of job satisfaction at this point in time.

OB RESEARCH IN CANADA

Dr. Catherine Connelly

Dr. Catherine Connelly is an expert on the attitudes (e.g., job satisfaction) and behaviours of workers who have employment arrangements that differ from what we might consider to be normal, full-time positions (e.g., "9 to 5"; 40-hour workweek; single employer). Examples of these unique roles are temporary workers, contractors, part-time workers, board members, volunteers, and mobile workers. Asked why she was drawn to studying people in these roles, Dr. Connelly replied, "I find it interesting to think about how our established OB theories might need to be revised in order to keep pace with our changing workforce. For example, what does the concept of 'organizational commitment' mean to someone who is self-employed or who works for several organizations at once?" In some of her other work, Dr. Connelly and her colleagues have studied the causes of aggression among teenage, part-time employees. Thus, it is fitting to feature Dr. Connelly in a chapter discussing how job satisfaction and emotional states affect job performance and organizational commitment—and the conditions for these relations.

Presently, Dr. Connelly is a Canada Research Chair and associate professor of organizational behaviour at the DeGroote School of Business at McMaster University, where she teaches courses on organizational behaviour and multivariate statistics. Her work is published in variety of books and leading scientific journal articles. According to Dr. Connelly, it is crucial for students to take at least one course in organizational behaviour, because there are so many popular misconceptions about how people and organizations should be managed. By looking at up-to-date evidence about what is actually effective, managers are able to make much better decisions and will be able to improve the performance of their employees and their organizations. You can look Dr. Connelly up at www.degroote.mcmaster.ca.

It seems that the most intense forms of positive mood often come directly from work activities, like the brainstorming project in Figure 5-5. Research suggests that two conditions are critical to triggering intense positive mood. First, the activity in question has to be challenging. Second, the employee must possess the unique skills needed to meet that challenge. That high challenge–high skill combination can result in **flow**—a state in which employees feel a total immersion in the task at hand, sometimes losing track of how much time has passed.[72] People often describe flow as being "in the zone" and report heightened states of clarity, control, and concentration, along with a sense of enjoyment, interest, and loss of self-consciousness.[73] Although you may have experienced flow during leisure activities, such as playing sports or making music, research suggests that we experience flow more often in our working lives. Much of our leisure time is spent in passive recreation, such as watching TV or chatting with friends, that lacks the challenge needed to trigger flow states. Work tasks, in contrast, may supply the sorts of challenges that require concentration and immersion—particularly when those tasks contain high levels of variety, significance, autonomy, and so forth (see Chapter 7 on motivation for more discussion of such issues).

flow

A state in which employees feel a total immersion in the task at hand, sometimes losing track of how much time has passed

Returning to Figure 5-5, it's clear that specific events triggered variations in satisfaction levels. According to **affective events theory**, workplace events can generate affective reactions—reactions that then can go on to influence work attitudes and behaviours.[74] Workplace events include happenings, like an annoying e-mail from a boss or a funny conversation with a friend, that are relevant to an employee's general desires and concerns. These events can trigger **emotions**, which are states of feeling that are often intense, last for only a few minutes, and are clearly directed at (and caused by) someone or some circumstance. The difference between moods and emotions becomes clear in the way we describe them to others. We describe moods by saying, "I'm feeling grouchy," but we describe emotions by saying, "I'm feeling angry *at my boss*."[75] According to affective events theory, these emotions can create the ebb and flow in satisfaction levels in Figure 5-5 and can also trigger spontaneous behaviours.[76] For example, positive emotions may trigger spontaneous instances of citizenship behaviour, whereas negative emotions may trigger spontaneous instances of counterproductive behaviour.

affective events theory

A theory that describes how workplace events can generate emotional reactions that impact work behaviours

emotions

Intense feelings, often lasting for a short duration, that are clearly directed at someone or some circumstance

As with mood, it's possible to differentiate between specific examples of positive and negative emotions. Table 5-2 provides a summary of many of the most important.[77] **Positive emotions** include joy, pride, relief, hope, love, and compassion. **Negative emotions** include anger, anxiety, fear, guilt, shame, sadness, envy, and disgust. What emotion do you think the employee experienced in Figure 5-5 when reading a disrespectful e-mail from the boss? Probably anger. What emotion do you think that same employee enjoyed during a funny conversation with a friend? Possibly joy, or maybe relief that lunch had arrived and a somewhat bad day was halfway over. Leaving lunch to return to work might have triggered either anxiety (because the bad day might resume) or sadness (because the fun time with friends had ended). Luckily, the employee's sense of joy at taking on a new project that was interesting and challenging was right around the corner. The day did end on a down note, however, as the phone call signalling overdue paperwork was likely met with some mix of anger, fear, guilt, or even disgust (no one likes paperwork!).

positive emotions

Employees' feelings of joy, pride, relief, hope, love and compassion

negative emotions

Employees' feelings of fear, guilt, shame, sadness, envy, and disgust

TABLE 5-2

Different Kinds of Emotions

Emotion	Description
Positive	
Joy	A feeling of great pleasure
Pride	Enhancement of identity by taking credit for achievement
Relief	A distressing condition has changed for the better
Hope	Fearing the worst but wanting better
Love	Desiring or participating in affection
Compassion	Being moved by another's situation
Negative	
Anger	A demeaning offence against me and mine
Anxiety	Facing an uncertain or vague threat
Fear	Facing an immediate and concrete danger
Guilt	Having broken a moral code
Shame	Failing to live up to your ideal self
Sadness	Having experienced an irreversible loss
Envy	Wanting what someone else has
Disgust	Revulsion aroused by something offensive

Source: Adapted from R.S. Lazarus, *Emotion and Adaptation* (New York: Oxford University, 1991).

Of course, just because employees feel many of the emotions in Table 5-2 during the workday doesn't mean they're allowed to display them. Some jobs demand that employees live up to the adage "Never let 'em see you sweat." In particular, service jobs in which employees make direct contact with customers often require those employees to hide any anger, anxiety, sadness, or disgust they might feel, suppressing the urge to spontaneously engage in some negative behaviour. Such jobs are high in what's called **emotional labour**—the need to manage emotions to complete job duties successfully.[78] Flight attendants are trained to "put on a happy face" in front of passengers, retail salespeople are trained to suppress any annoyance with customers, and restaurant servers are trained to act like they're having fun on their job even when they're not.

emotional labour

The management of their emotions that employees must do to complete their job duties successfully

Is it a good idea to require emotional labour on the part of employees? Research on **emotional contagion** shows that one person can "catch" or "be infected by" the emotions of another person.[79] If a customer service representative is angry or sad, those negative emotions can be transferred to a customer (like a cold or disease). If that transfer occurs, it becomes less likely that customers will view the experience favourably and spend money, which might affect the bottom line. From this perspective, emotional labour seems like a vital part of good customer service. Unfortunately, other evidence suggests that emotional labour puts great strain on employees and that their bottled-up emotions may end up bubbling over, sometimes resulting in angry outbursts against customers or emotional exhaustion and burnout on the part of employees (see Chapter 6, on stress, for more discussion of such issues).[80] A related concept, emotional intelligence, is discussed in Chapter 4.

emotional contagion

The idea that emotions can be transferred from one person to another

FIGURE 5-7

Why Are Some Employees More Satisfied Than Others?

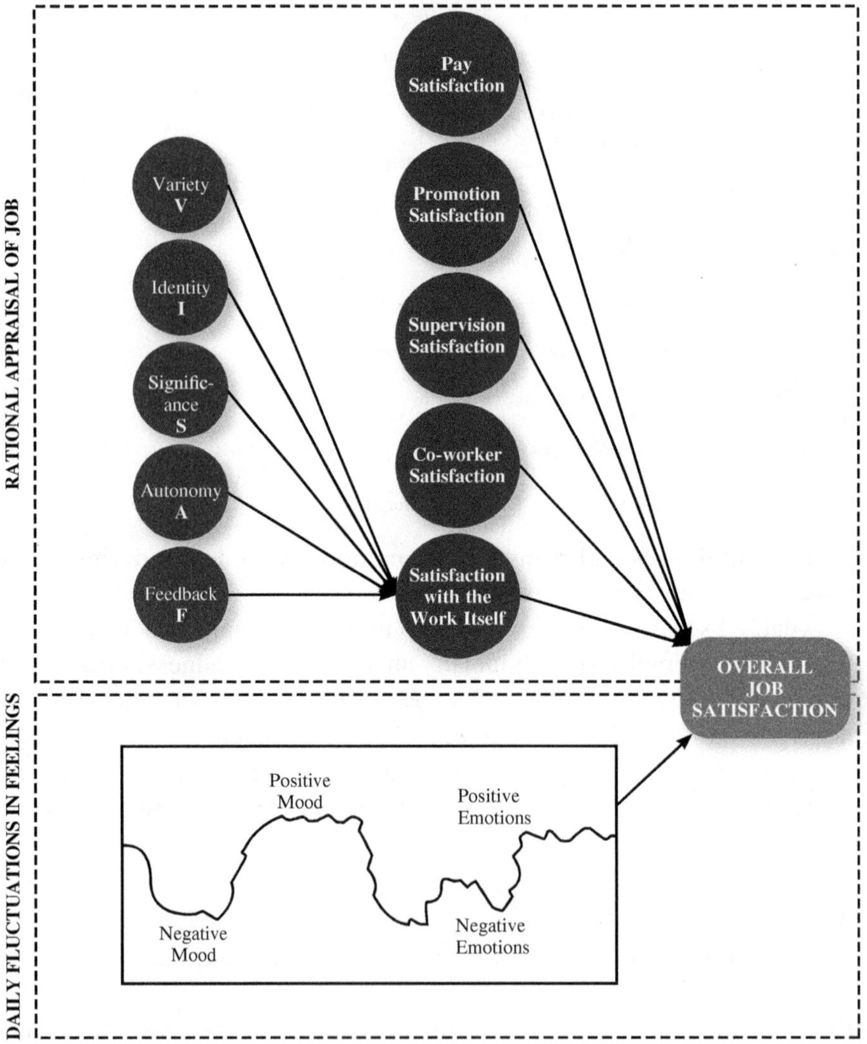

Summary: Why Are Some Employees More Satisfied Than Others?

So what explains why some employees are more satisfied than others? As we show in Figure 5-7, answering that question requires paying attention to the more rational appraisals people make about their job and the things it supplies for them, such as pay, promotions, supervision, co-workers, and the work itself. Satisfaction with the work itself, in turn, is affected by the five core job characteristics: variety, identity, significance, autonomy, and feedback. However, answering that question also requires paying attention to daily fluctuations in how people feel, in terms of their positive and negative moods and positive and negative emotions. In this way, a generally satisfied employee may act unhappy at a given moment, just as a generally dissatisfied employee may act happy at a given moment. Understanding those sorts of fluctuations can help managers separate long-term problems (boring tasks, incompetent co-workers) from more short-lived issues (a bad meeting, an annoying interaction).

5.7 How does job satisfaction affect job performance and organizational commitment? How does it affect life satisfaction?

HOW IMPORTANT IS JOB SATISFACTION?

Several factors influence an employee's job satisfaction, from pay to co-workers to job tasks to day-to-day moods and emotions. Of course, the most obvious remaining question is, "Does job satisfaction really matter?" More precisely, does job satisfaction have a significant impact on job performance and organizational commitment—the two primary outcomes in our integrative model of OB? Figure 5-8 summarizes the research evidence linking job satisfaction to job performance and organizational commitment. It reveals that job satisfaction does predict job performance. Why? One reason is that job satisfaction is moderately correlated with task performance. Satisfied employees do a better job of fulfilling the duties described in their job descriptions,[81] and evidence suggests that positive feelings foster creativity,[82] improve problem solving and decision making,[83] and enhance memory and recall of certain kinds of information.[84] Positive feelings also improve task persistence and attract more help and support from colleagues.[85] Apart from these sorts of findings, the benefits of job satisfaction for task performance might best be explained on an hour-by-hour basis. At any given moment, employees wage a war between paying attention to a given work task and attending to "off-task" things, such as stray thoughts, distractions, interruptions, and so forth. Positive feelings when working on job tasks can pull attention away from those distractions and channel people's attention to task accomplishment.[86] When such concentration occurs, an employee is more focused on work at a given point in time. Of course, the relationship between satisfaction and task performance can work in reverse to some extent, such that people tend to enjoy jobs that they can perform more successfully.[87] Meta-analyses tend to be less supportive of this causal direction, however.[88]

Job satisfaction also is correlated moderately with citizenship behaviour. Satisfied employees engage in more frequent "extra mile" behaviours to help their co-workers and their organization.[89] Positive feelings increase their desire to interact with others and often result in spontaneous acts of helping and other instances of good citizenship.[90] In addition, job satisfaction has a moderate negative correlation with counterproductive behaviour. Satisfied employees engage in fewer intentionally destructive actions that could harm their workplace.[91] Events that trigger negative emotions can prompt employees to lash out against the organization by engaging in rule-breaking, theft, sabotage, or other retaliatory behaviours.[92] The more satisfied employees are, the less likely they'll feel those sorts of temptations.

FIGURE 5-8

Effects of Job Satisfaction on Performance and Commitment

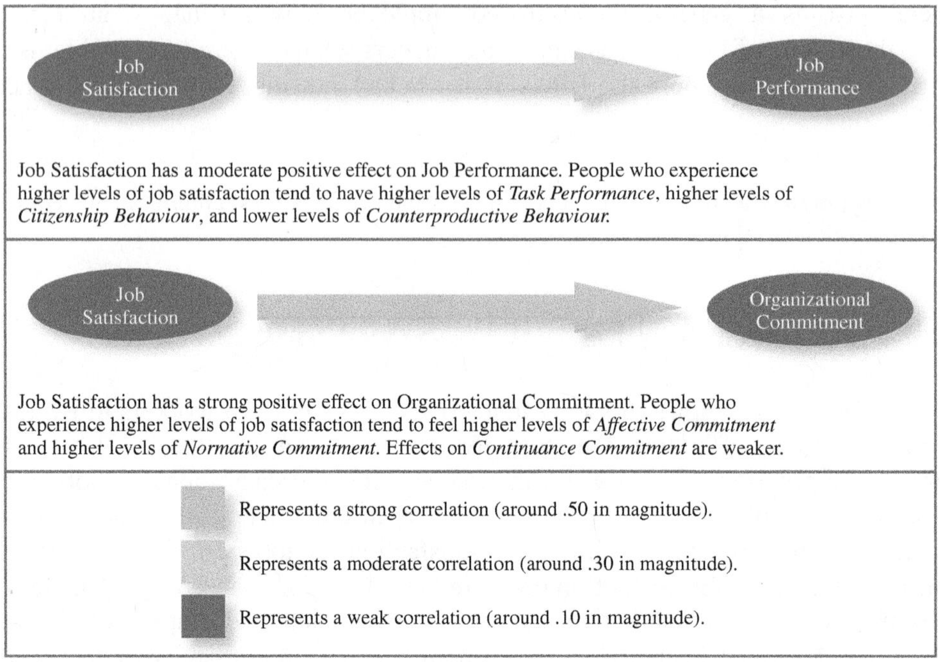

Job Satisfaction
Job Performance
Job Satisfaction has a moderate positive effect on Job Performance. People who experience higher levels of job satisfaction tend to have higher levels of *Task Performance*, higher levels of *Citizenship Behaviour*, and lower levels of *Counterproductive Behaviour.*
Job Satisfaction
Organizational Commitment
Job Satisfaction has a strong positive effect on Organizational Commitment. People who experience higher levels of job satisfaction tend to feel higher levels of *Affective Commitment* and higher levels of *Normative Commitment.* Effects on *Continuance Commitment* are weaker.
Represents a strong correlation (around .50 in magnitude).
Represents a moderate correlation (around .30 in magnitude).
Represents a weak correlation (around .10 in magnitude).

Sources: A. Cooper-Hakim and C. Viswesvaran, "The Construct of Work Commitment: Testing an Integrative Framework," *Psychological Bulletin* 131 (2005), pp. 241–59; R.S. Dalal, "A Meta-analysis of the Relationship Between Organizational Citizenship Behaviour and Counterproductive Work Behaviour," *Journal of Applied Psychology* 90 (2005), pp. 1241–55; D.A. Harrison, D.A. Newman, and P.L. Roth, "How Important are Job Attitudes? Meta-analytic Comparisons of Integrative Behavioural Outcomes and Time Sequences," *Academy of Management Journal* 49 (2006), pp. 305–25; T.A. Judge, C.J. Thoreson, J.E. Bono, and G.K. Patton, "The Job Satisfaction–Job Performance Relationship: A Qualitative and Quantitative Review," *Psychological Bulletin* 127 (2001), pp. 376–407; J.A. LePine, A. Erez, and D.E. Johnson, "The Nature and Dimensionality of Organizational Citizenship Behaviour: A Critical Review and Meta-analysis," *Journal of Applied Psychology* 87 (2002), pp. 52–65; J.P. Meyer, D.J. Stanley, L. Herscovitch, and L. Topolnytsky, "Affective, Continuance, and Normative Commitment to the Organization: A Meta-analysis of Antecedents, Correlates, and Consequences," *Journal of Vocational Behaviour* 61 (2002), pp. 20–52.

Figure 5-8 also indicates that job satisfaction influences organizational commitment. Why? It is strongly correlated with affective commitment, so satisfied employees are more likely to want to stay with the organization.[93] After all, why would employees want to leave a place where they're happy? Another reason is that job satisfaction is strongly correlated with normative commitment. Satisfied employees are more likely to feel an obligation to remain with their firm[94] and a need to "repay" the organization for whatever it is that makes them so satisfied, be it good pay, interesting job tasks, or effective supervision. However, job satisfaction is uncorrelated with continuance commitment, because it does not create a cost-based need to remain with the organization. Taken together, these commitment effects become more apparent when you consider the kinds of employees who withdraw from the organization. In many cases, dissatisfied employees are the ones who sit daydreaming at their desks, come in late, are frequently absent, and eventually decide to quit.

Life Satisfaction

Of course, job satisfaction is important for other reasons as well—reasons that have little to do with job performance or organizational commitment. For example, job satisfaction is strongly related to **life**

satisfaction, defined as the degree to which employees feel a sense of happiness with their lives in general. Research shows that job satisfaction is one of the strongest predictors of life satisfaction. Put simply, people feel better about their lives when they feel better about their jobs.[95] This link makes sense when you realize how much of our identity is wrapped up in our jobs. What's the first question that people ask one another after being introduced? That's right—"What do you do?" If you feel bad about your answer to that question, it's hard to feel good about your life.

life satisfaction
The degree to which employees feel a sense of happiness with their lives in general

The connection between job satisfaction and life satisfaction also makes sense given how much of our lives are spent at work. Table 5-3 presents the results of one study that examines time spent on daily activities, along with reported levels of positive and negative feelings during the course of those activities.[96] The participants in the study spent most of their day at work. Unfortunately, that time resulted in the highest levels of negative feelings and the second-lowest levels of positive feelings (behind only commuting). Home and leisure activities (e.g., socializing, relaxing, exercising, intimate relations) were deemed much more satisfying but took up a much smaller portion of the day. The implication is clear: If we want to feel better about our days, we need to find a way to be more satisfied with our jobs.

TABLE 5-3

How We Spend Our Days

Activity	Average Hours per Day	Positive Feelings	Negative Feelings
Working	6.9	3.62	.97
On the phone	2.5	3.92	.85
Socializing	2.3	4.59	.57
Eating	2.2	4.34	.59
Relaxing	2.2	4.42	.51
Watching TV	2.2	4.19	.58
Computer/e-mail/Internet	1.9	3.81	.80
Commuting	1.6	3.45	.89
Housework	1.1	3.73	.77
Interacting with kids	1.1	3.86	.91
Napping	.9	3.87	.60
Praying/meditating	.4	4.35	.59
Exercising	.2	4.31	.50
Intimate relations	.2	5.10	.36

Notes: Positive and negative feelings measured using a scale of 0 (not at all) to 6 (very much).

Source: From D. Kahneman, A.B. Krueger, D.A. Schkade, N. Schwarz, and A.A. Stone, "A Survey Method for Characterizing Daily Life Experience: The Day Reconstruction Method," *Science* 306 (2004), pp. 1776–80. Reprinted with permission from AAAS.

Indeed, increases in job satisfaction have a stronger impact on life satisfaction than do increases in salary or income. It turns out that the adage "Money can't buy happiness" is partially true. Research suggests that life satisfaction increases with one's salary up to a level of around $75,000 per year. After that, more money doesn't seem to bring more happiness.[97] Such findings may seem surprising, given that pay satisfaction is one facet of overall job satisfaction (see Figure 5-1). However, you might recall that pay satisfaction is a weaker driver of overall job satisfaction than other facets, such as the work itself, supervision, or co-workers (see Figure 5-2). For more on the relationship between money and happiness, see our ***OB Internationally*** feature.

OB INTERNATIONALLY

The "Money can't buy happiness" adage can even be supported using nation-level data. For example, survey data in the United States, Britain, and Japan show that people are no happier today than they were 50 years ago, even though average incomes have more than doubled during that span.[98] Another way of examining this issue explores the connection between national wealth and average happiness: Do wealthier nations have citizens with higher levels of life satisfaction? The figure below provides a representation of the relationship between average income per citizen for a nation and the percentage of respondents who describe themselves as happy, according to population surveys.[99]

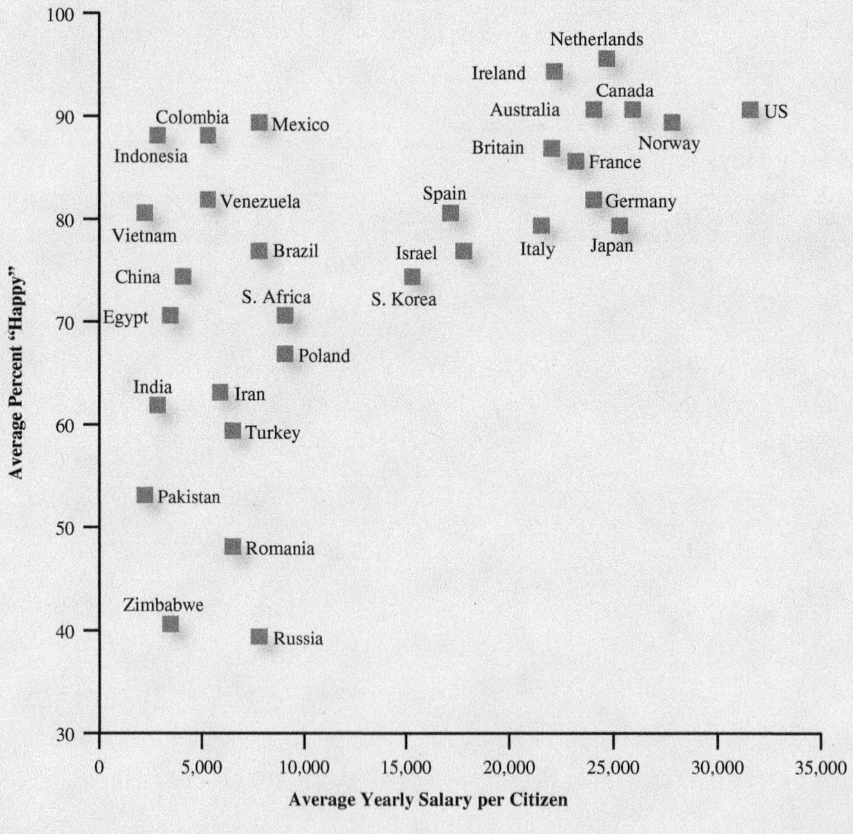

Comparing countries reveals that nations above the poverty line are indeed happier than nations below the poverty line. However, once that poverty threshold gets crossed, additional income is not associated with higher levels of life satisfaction.[100] For example, Canada, one of the richest countries on earth trails nations like the Netherlands and Ireland in life satisfaction. Understanding differences in life satisfaction across nations is important to organizations for two reasons. First, such differences may influence how receptive a given nation is to the company's products. Second, such differences may affect the kinds of policies and practices an organization needs to use when employing individuals in that nation.

5.8 What steps can organizations take to assess and manage job satisfaction?

APPLICATION: TRACKING SATISFACTION

Because job satisfaction seems to be a key driver of job performance, organizational commitment, and life satisfaction, it's important for managers to understand just how satisfied their employees are. Gauging satisfaction is vital for organizations like Zappos, whose employees have direct customer contact, but it can be important in other organizations as well. Several methods assess the job satisfaction of rank-and-file employees, including focus groups, interviews, and attitude surveys. Of those three choices, attitude surveys are often the most accurate and most effective.[101] Attitude surveys can provide a snapshot of how satisfied the workforce is and, if repeated over time, reveal trends in satisfaction levels. They also can explore the effectiveness of major job changes by comparing attitude survey results before and after a change.

Although organizations are often tempted to design their own attitude surveys, there are benefits to using existing surveys that are already in wide use. One of the most widely administered job satisfaction surveys is the **Job Descriptive Index (JDI)**. The JDI assesses all five satisfaction facets in Figure 5-1: pay satisfaction, promotion satisfaction, supervisor satisfaction, co-worker satisfaction, and satisfaction with the work itself. The JDI has also been subjected to a great deal of research attention that, by and large, supports its accuracy.[102] Furthermore, the JDI includes a companion survey—the Job in General (JIG) scale—that assesses overall job satisfaction.[103] Excerpts from the JDI and the JIG appear in Table 5-4.[104] One strength of the JDI is that the questions are written in a very simple and straightforward fashion so that they can be easily understood by most employees.

Job Descriptive Index (JDI)
A facet measure of job satisfaction that assesses an individual's satisfaction with pay, promotion opportunities, supervision, co-workers, and the work itself

The developers of the JDI offer several suggestions regarding its administration.[105] For example, they recommend surveying as much of the company as possible because any unsurveyed employees might feel that their feelings are less important. They also recommend that surveys be anonymous so that employees can be as honest as possible without worrying about being punished for any critical comments about the organization. Therefore, companies must be careful in collecting demographic information on the surveys. Some demographic information is vital for comparing satisfaction levels across relevant groups, but too much information will make employees feel like they could be identified. Finally, the developers suggest that the survey should be administered by the firm's human resources group or an outside consulting agency. This structure will help employees feel that their anonymity is more protected.

Once JDI data have been collected, a number of interesting questions can be explored.[106] First, the data can indicate whether the organization is satisfied or dissatisfied by comparing average scores for each facet with the JDI's "neutral levels" for those facets (the "neutral levels" are available in the JDI manual). Second, it becomes possible to compare the organization's scores with national norms to provide some context for the firm's satisfaction levels. The JDI manual also provides national norms for all facets and breaks down those norms according to relevant demographic groups (e.g., managers vs. nonmanagers, new vs. senior employees, gender, education). Third, the JDI allows for within-organization comparisons to determine which departments have the highest satisfaction levels and which have the lowest.

TABLE 5-4

Excerpts from the Job Descriptive Index and the Job in General Scale

Think of the work you do at present. How well does each of the following words or phrases describe your work? In the blank beside each word or phrase below, write

Y for "Yes" if it describes your work

N for "No" if it does *not* describe it

? for "?" if you cannot decide

Pay Satisfaction[a]		**Co-worker Satisfaction**[a]	
___	Well paid	___	Stimulating
___	Bad	___	Smart
___	Barely live on income	___	Unpleasant
Promotion Satisfaction[a]		**Satisfaction with Work Itself**[a]	
___	Regular promotions	___	Fascinating
___	Promotion on ability	___	Pleasant
___	Opportunities somewhat limited	___	Can see my results
Supervision Satisfaction[a]		**Overall Job Satisfaction**[b]	
___	Knows job well	___	Better than most
___	Around when needed	___	Worthwhile
___	Doesn't supervise enough	___	Worse than most

[a] The Job Descriptive Index, © Bowling Green State University (1975, 1985, 1997).

[b] The Job in General Scale, © Bowling Green State University (1982, 1985).

Source: W.K. Balzer, J.A. Kihn, P.C. Smith, J.L. Irwin, P.D. Bachiochi, C. Robie, E.F. Sinar, and L.F. Parra, 2000, "Users' Manual for the Job Descriptive Index (JDI; 1997 version) and the Job in General Scales." In J.N. Stanton and C.D. Crossley (eds.), *Electronic Resources for the JDI and JIG*. Bowling Green, OH, Bowling Green State University. Reprinted with permission.

The results of attitude survey efforts should then be fed back to employees so that they feel involved in the process. Of course, attitude surveys ideally should be a catalyst for some kind of improvement effort.[107] Surveys that never lead to any kind of on-the-job change eventually may be viewed as a waste of time. As a result, the organization should be prepared to react to the survey results with specific goals and action steps. For example, an organization with low pay satisfaction may react by conducting additional benchmarking to see whether compensation levels are trailing those of competitors. An organization with low promotion satisfaction might react by revising its system for assessing performance. Finally, an organization that struggles with satisfaction with the work itself could attempt to redesign key job tasks or, if that proves too costly, train supervisors in strategies for increasing the five core job characteristics on a more informal basis.

TAKEAWAYS

5.1 Job satisfaction is a pleasurable emotional state resulting from the appraisal of one's job or job experiences. It represents how you feel about your job and what you think about your job.

5.2 Values are things that people consciously or subconsciously want to seek or attain. According to value-percept theory, job satisfaction depends on whether you perceive that your job supplies those things that you value.

5.3 Employees consider a number of specific facets when evaluating their job satisfaction. These facets include pay satisfaction, promotion satisfaction, supervision satisfaction, co-worker satisfaction, and satisfaction with the work itself.

5.4 Job characteristics theory suggests that five "core characteristics"—variety, identity, significance, autonomy, and feedback—combine to result in particularly high levels of satisfaction with the work itself.

5.5 Apart from the influence of supervision, co-workers, pay, and the work itself, job satisfaction levels fluctuate during the course of the day. Rises and falls in job satisfaction are triggered by positive and negative events that are experienced. Those events trigger changes in emotions that eventually give way to changes in mood.

5.6 Moods are states of feeling that are often mild in intensity, last for an extended period of time, and are not explicitly directed at anything. Intense positive moods include being enthusiastic, excited, and elated. Intense negative moods include being hostile, nervous, and annoyed. Emotions are states of feeling that are often intense, last only for a few minutes, and are clearly directed at someone or some circumstance. Positive emotions include joy, pride, relief, hope, love, and compassion. Negative emotions include anger, anxiety, fear, guilt, shame, sadness, envy, and disgust.

5.7 Job satisfaction has a moderately positive relationship with job performance and a strong positive relationship with organizational commitment. It also has a strong positive relationship with life satisfaction.

5.8 Organizations can assess and manage job satisfaction using attitude surveys such as the Job Descriptive Index (JDI), which assesses pay satisfaction, promotion satisfaction, supervisor satisfaction, co-worker satisfaction, and satisfaction with the work itself. It can be used to assess the levels of job satisfaction experienced by employees, and its specific facet scores can identify interventions that could be helpful.

KEY TERMS

activation
affective events theory
autonomy
co-worker satisfaction

emotional contagion
emotional labour
emotions
feedback
flow
growth need strength
identity
job characteristics theory
job crafting
Job Descriptive Index (JDI)
job enrichment
job satisfaction
knowledge and skill
knowledge of results
life satisfaction
meaningfulness of work
moods
negative emotions
pay satisfaction
pleasantness
positive emotions
promotion satisfaction
responsibility for outcomes
satisfaction with the work itself
significance
supervision satisfaction
value-percept theory
values
variety

DISCUSSION QUESTIONS

5.1 Which of the values in Table 5-1 do you think are the most important to employees in general? Are there times when the values in the last three categories (altruism, status, and environment) become more important than the values in the first five categories (pay, promotions, supervision, co-workers, the work itself)?

5.2 What steps can organizations take to improve promotion satisfaction, supervision satisfaction, and co-worker satisfaction?

5.3 Consider the five core job characteristics (variety, identity, significance, autonomy, and feedback). Do you think that any one of those characteristics is more important than the other four? Is it possible to have too much of some job characteristics?

5.4 We sometimes describe colleagues or friends as moody. What do you think it means to be moody from the perspective of Figure 5-6?

5.5 Consider the list of positive and negative emotions in Table 5-2. Which of these emotions are most frequently experienced at work? What causes them?

5.6 If you were asked to fill out a satisfaction survey, such as the Job Descriptive Index, at your workplace would you participate? Why or why not?

CASE • ZAPPOS (AMAZON)

When a company actively promotes "a little weirdness," it becomes important to hire people who will be satisfied in that sort of environment. Zappos does so by carefully assessing fit during its hiring process. But what happens if new hires realize that they're not satisfied with their job, their co-workers, or the organization? After all, the craziness at Zappos is not for everyone! That's where "The Offer" comes in: New hires begin their Zappos employment with a four-week training period that acquaints them with the company's strategy and its approach to customer service, receiving their full salary along the way. One week in, the new hires are offered a bonus ... to quit. That's right—new hires can walk away with one week's salary and an extra $2,000 in their pocket. Zappos uses "The Offer" to give employees who may not enjoy working at Zappos an easy out.

The idea of "paying people to quit" has recently been picked up by Jeff Bezos, founder and CEO of Amazon.com (Zappos's parent company). Amazon recently shocked the corporate world by announcing a new policy: "If an employee isn't happy working at the online retail giant, they can earn up to $5,000 just for quitting." Bezos describes the program as being fairly simple: "Once a year we offer to pay our associates to quit. The first year the offer is made for $2,000. Then it goes up one thousand dollars a year until it reaches $5,000." "The goal is to encourage folks to take a moment and think about what they really want," Bezos explains. "In the long run, an employee staying somewhere they don't want to be isn't healthy for the employee or the company."

In addition to its "Pay to Quit" program, Amazon has adopted a couple of other employee empowerment initiatives. Career Choice is a program in which Amazon pre-pays 95 percent of tuition for its employees to take courses for in-demand fields, such as nursing or mechanics, even if the skills have nothing to do with a career at Amazon. Bezos explains, "The goal is to enable choice. We know that for some of our fulfillment center employees, Amazon will be a career. For others, Amazon might be a stepping stone on the way to a job somewhere else—a job that may require new skills. If the right training can make the difference, we want to help." A third initiative is called the Virtual Contact Center. Under this program, Amazon employees are able to provide customer service support while working at home. "This flexibility is ideal for many employees who, perhaps because they have young children or for another reason, either cannot or prefer not to work outside the home," explains Bezos.

5.1 What do you think of Amazon's approach to employee empowerment? Explain how this strategy might work at a strategy for maximizing job satisfaction within the organization?

5.2 Should the "pay to quit" programs used at Zappos and Amazon be used at other organizations? Are you concerned that programs like this might undermine the company's attempt to strengthen organizational commitment? Explain

5.3 When you consider your personal values (Table 5-1), would you experience job satisfaction or dissatisfaction within a company that prides itself on being "a little weird?" Would you fit in at Zappos or organizations like this? Why or why not?

Sources: Martha C. White, "Amazon Will Pay You $5,000 to Quit Your Job," *Time*, April 11th, 2014, www.time.com/58305/amazon-will-pay-you-5000-to-quit-your-job, retrieved December 30, 2014; Jeff Bezos, annual letter to shareholders, April 11, 2014, Exhibit 99.1, www.sec.gov/Archives/edgar/data/1018724/0001; K. McFarland, "Why Zappos Offers New Hires $2000 to Quit," *BusinessWeek*, September 16, 2008, www.businessweek.com/smallbiz/content/sep2008/sb20080916_288698.htm, retrieved May 19, 2011; J.M. O'Brien, "Zappos Knows How to Kick It," *Fortune*, February 2, 2009, pp. 55–60; B. Taylor, "Why Zappos Pays New Employees to Quit—and You Should Too," *Harvard Business Review*, May 19, 2008.

EXERCISE • JOB SATISFACTION ACROSS JOBS

The purpose of this exercise is to examine satisfaction with the work itself across jobs. This exercise uses groups of six participants, so your instructor will either assign you to a group of six or ask you to create your own group of six.

The exercise has the following steps:

5.1 Use the OB Assessment for this chapter to calculate the Satisfaction Potential Score (SPS) for the following four jobs:

a. A lobster fisherman who runs his own boat with his son
b. A standup comedian
c. A computer programmer whose assignment is to replace "98" with "1998" in thousands of lines of computer code
d. A leader of a political party in Canada

5.2 Which job has the highest SPS? Which core job characteristics best explain why some jobs have high scores and other jobs have low scores? Record the scores for the four jobs.

5.3 Class discussion (whether in groups or as a class) should centre on two questions. First, is the job that scored the highest really the one that would be the most enjoyable on a day-in, day-out basis? Second, does that mean it would be the job that you would pick if you could snap your fingers and magically attain one of the jobs on the list? Why or why not? What other job satisfaction theory might be relevant to this issue?

OB ASSESSMENTS • CORE JOB CHARACTERISTICS

How satisfying are your work tasks? This assessment is designed to measure the five core job characteristics derived from job characteristics theory. Think of your current job or the last job that you held (even if it was a part-time or summer job). Answer each question using the response scale provided. Then subtract your answers to the boldfaced question from 8, with the difference being your new answer for that question. For example, if your original answer for question 2 was "5," your new answer is "3" (8 – 5). Then use the formula at the bottom to compute a satisfaction potential score (SPS).

1	2	3	4	5	6	7	
Very Inaccurate	**Mostly Inaccurate**	**Slightly Inaccurate**	**Uncertain**	**Slightly Accurate**	**Mostly Accurate**	**Very Accurate**	

V1. The job requires me to use a number of complex or high-level skills. ____

V2. The job is quite simple and repetitive. ____

I1. The job is arranged so that I can do an entire piece of work from beginning to end. ____

I2. The job provides me the chance to completely finish the pieces of work I begin. ____

S1. This job is one where a lot of other people can be affected by how well the work gets done. ____

S2. The job itself is very significant and important in the broader scheme of things. ____

A1. The job gives me a chance to use my personal initiative and judgment in carrying out the work. ____

A2. The job gives me considerable opportunity for independence and freedom in how I do the work. ____

F1. Just doing the work required by the job provides many chances for me to figure out how well I am doing. ____

F2. After I finish a job, I know whether I performed well. ____

$$SPS = \left|\frac{V1+V2+I1+I2+S1+S2}{6}\right| \times \left|\frac{A1+A2}{2}\right| \times \left|\frac{F1+F2}{2}\right|$$ ____

$$SPS = \left|\frac{\qquad}{6}\right| \times \left|\frac{\qquad}{2}\right| \times \left|\frac{\qquad}{2}\right|$$

$$SPS = \boxed{\qquad} \times \boxed{\qquad} \times \boxed{\qquad} = \boxed{\qquad}$$

Scoring and Interpretation

If your score is 150 or above, your work tasks tend to be satisfying and enjoyable. If your score is less than 150, you might benefit from trying to "enrich" your job by asking your supervisor for more challenging assignments. When interpreting your scores on these assessments remember to consider the *reliability* and *validity* of these tools (see Chapter 1, ***OB Assessments***).

Sources: J.R. Hackman and G.R. Oldham, *The Job Diagnostic Survey: An Instrument for the Diagnosis of Jobs and the Evaluation of Job Redesign Projects* (New Haven, CT: Yale University, 1974); J.R. Idaszak and F. Drasgow, "A Revision of the Job Diagnostic Survey: Elimination of a Measurement Artifact," *Journal of Applied Psychology* 72 (1987), pp. 69–74.

Stress

CHAPTER

6

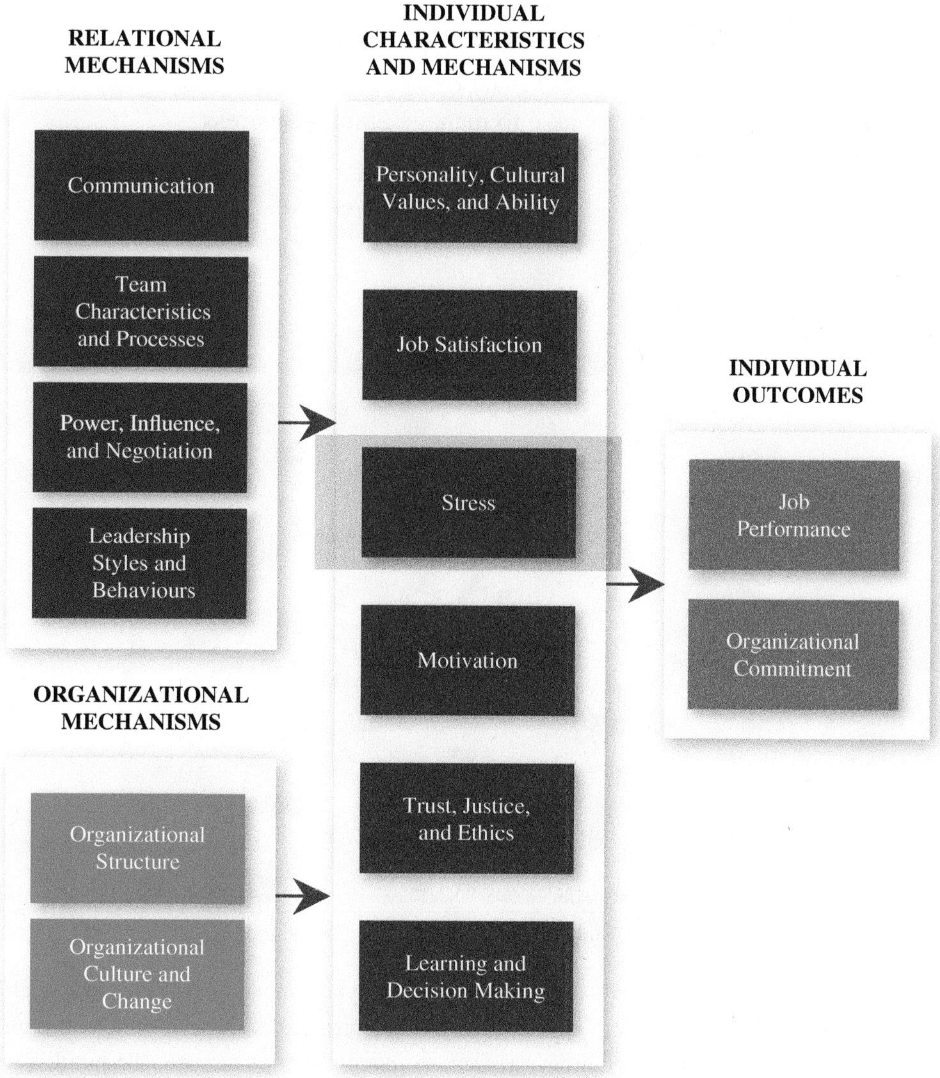

LEARNING OUTCOMES

After reading this chapter, you should be able to answer the following questions:

6.1 What is stress, and how is it different from stressors and strains?

6.2 What are the four main types of stressors?

6.3 How do individuals cope with stress?

6.4 How does the Type A Behaviour Pattern influence the stress process?

6.5 How does stress affect job performance and organizational commitment?

6.6 What steps can organizations take to manage employee stress?

Crew

Training initiatives such as CREW reduce stress by improving the quality of work relationships.

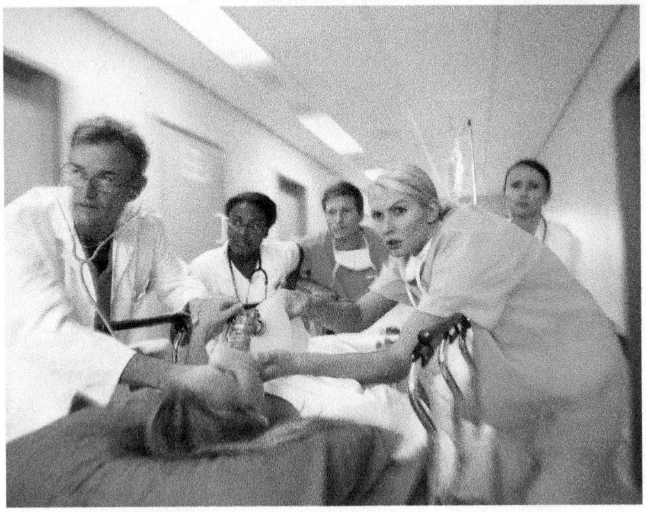

© OJO Images/Rex Features/The Canadian Press

According to Statistics Canada, nearly one in three employed Canadians report being either "quite" or "extremely" stressed.[1] More alarming is the fact those entrusted to provide health care (e.g., nurses, physicians), are themselves some of the most stressed-out people in the country![2] To put this in some context, only 31 percent of Canadians who do not work in health care report the same degree of stress.[3] And this may be only the tip of the iceberg. It seems that these stressed-out healthcare providers report lower levels of life satisfaction and general health than those who do not experience work stress on a daily basis.[4] All this invites the question: Why? What is it about working as a healthcare provider that is so stressful?

Of course, many factors are in play. More and more, studies are showing the importance of having healthy and positive relationships at work—not least, simply being civil to one another.[5] Civility involves behaving in a respectful and courteous manner. It involves simple things like remembering to say "please" when asking a colleague for a favour or refraining from making sarcastic comments. What's surprising is how something so seemingly trivial as being rude and disrespectful can have big effects. We know, for instance, that employees who experience incivility tend to be more stressed, spend less time at work, and have lower satisfaction and productivity levels than those treated with respect and courtesy.[6]

If incivility is alive and well within healthcare facilities, what can these organizations do? According to such experts as Dr. Michael Leiter at Acadia University in Nova Scotia, one of the first things they can do is simply to pay attention to the problem.[7] Instead of labelling it as relatively minor and innocuous, involving "personal issues that will sort themselves out," it is important to acknowledge that incivility is a problem that affects people, groups, and the overall organization.[8] The second thing they can do is address the problem head on. This is where CREW, a training program developed for Canadian healthcare facilities, comes in.

CREW stands for Civility, Respect, and Engagement at Work.[9] CREW Canada staff train on-site facilitators to lead groups within their organization and to provide ongoing support for them during the six-month process.[10] The results of this training are determined by means of staff surveys and anecdotal information gathered within healthcare groups (e.g., nursing units).

The upshot is: CREW works! The overall level of civility within units that received the training improved, and particularly the level of civility expressed by supervisors. Nurses experienced less stress and burnout, were more committed to their organization, and missed work less often.[11] Thus, not only does the CREW program reduce stress by fostering healthy work relationships, but it seems to contribute positively to organizational outcomes.

6.1 What is stress, and how is it different from stressors and strains?

STRESS

Stress is an OB topic that is probably quite familiar to you. Even if you don't have a lot of work experience, consider how you feel toward the end of a semester when you have to cram for several final exams and finish a couple of term projects. At the same time, you might have also been looking for a job or planning a trip with friends or family. Although some people might be able to deal with all of these demands without becoming too frazzled, most people would say that this type of scenario causes them to feel "stressed out." This feeling might even be accompanied by headaches, stomach upsets, backaches, or sleeping difficulties. Although you might believe your stress will diminish once you graduate and settle down, high stress on the job is more prevalent than ever. In fact, Statistics Canada estimates that a third of Canadian workers feel their jobs are "quite" or "extremely" stressful.[12] Unfortunately, high stress is even more prevalent in the types of jobs that most of you are likely to have after you graduate. In fact, managers are approximately 21 percent more likely than the average worker to describe their jobs as stressful.[13] Table 6-1 provides a list of jobs and their rank in terms of how stressful they are. As noted in the chapter-opening profile, Table 6-1 confirms that healthcare jobs, such as registered nurse and surgeon, are among the most stressful.

Stress is defined as a psychological response to demands that possess certain stakes for the person and that tax or exceed the person's capacity or resources.[14] The demands that cause people to experience stress are called **stressors**. The negative consequences that occur when demands tax or exceed a person's capacity or resources are called **strains**. This definition of stress illustrates that it depends on both the nature of the demand and the person who confronts it. People differ in terms of how they perceive and evaluate stressors and the way they cope with them. As a result, different people may experience different levels of stress even when confronted with the exact same situation.

stress
The psychological response to demands when there is something at stake for the individual, and when coping with these demands would tax or exceed the individual's capacity or resources

stressors
Demands that cause the stress response

strains
Negative consequences of the stress response

TABLE 6-1

Jobs Rated from Least Stressful to Most Stressful

Least Stressful Jobs	Stress Level	Most Stressful Jobs	Stress Level
1. Musical instrument repairer	18.77	212. Registered nurse	62.14
2. Florist	18.80	220. Lawyer	64.33
4. Actuary	20.18	223. Newspaper reporter	65.26
6. Appliance repairer	21.12	226. Architect	66.92
8. Librarian	21.40	228. Lumberjack	67.60
10. File clerk	21.71	229. Fisherman	69.82
11. Piano tuner	22.29	230. Stockbroker	71.65
16. Vending machine repairer	23.47	233. Real estate agent	73.06
18. Barber	23.62	234. Advertising account exec	74.55
24. Mathematician	24.67	238. Public relations exec	78.52
29. Cashier	25.11	240. Air traffic controller	83.13
30. Dishwasher	25.32	241. Airline pilot	85.35
32. Pharmacist	25.87	243. Police officer	93.89
40. Biologist	26.94	244. Astronaut	99.34
44. Computer programmer	27.00	245. Surgeon	99.46
50. Astronomer	28.06	246. Taxi driver	100.49
56. Historian	28.41	248. Senior corporate exec	108.62
67. Bank teller	30.12	249. Firefighter	110.93

Source: Adapted from L. Krantz, *Jobs Rated Almanac*, 6th ed. (Fort Lee, NJ: Barricade Books, Inc., 2002). The stress level score is calculated by summing points in 21 categories, including deadlines, competitiveness, environmental conditions, speed required, precision required, initiative required, physical demands, and hazards encountered.

WHY ARE SOME EMPLOYEES MORE "STRESSED" THAN OTHERS?

To fully understand what it means to feel "stressed," it's helpful to consider the **transactional theory of stress**. This theory explains how stressors are perceived and appraised, as well as how people respond to those perceptions and appraisals.[15] When people first encounter stressors, the process of **primary appraisal** is triggered.[16] As shown in Figure 6-1, primary appraisal occurs as people evaluate the significance and the meaning of the stressor they're confronting. Here, people first consider whether a demand causes them to feel stressed, and if it does, they consider the implications of the stressor in terms of their personal goals and overall well-being.

transactional theory of stress
A theory that explains how stressful demands are perceived and appraised, as well as how people respond to the perceptions of appraisals

primary appraisal
Evaluation of whether a demand is stressful and, if it is, the implications of the stressor in terms of personal goals and well-being

FIGURE 6-1

Transactional Theory of Stress

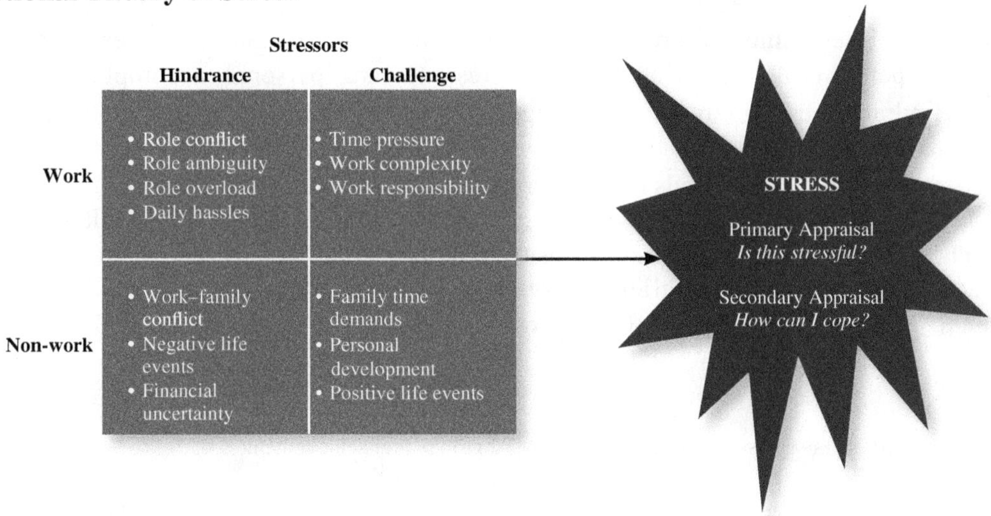

As an example of a primary appraisal, consider the job of a cashier at a well-run convenience store. In this store, cashiers engage in routine sales transactions with customers. Customers walk in the store and select merchandise, and the cashiers on duty ring up the sale and collect the money. Under normal day-to-day circumstances at this store, well-trained cashiers would not likely feel that these transactions are overly taxing or exceed their capacity, so those cashiers would not likely appraise these job demands as stressful. Job demands that tend not to be appraised as stressful are called **benign job demands**.

benign job demands
Job demands that are not appraised as being stressful

However, consider how convenience store cashiers would react in a different store in which the cash register and credit card machine break down often and without warning. The cashiers who work at this store would likely view their job as being more stressful. This is because they would have to diagnose and fix problems with equipment while dealing with customers who are growing more and more impatient. Furthermore, the cashiers in this store might appraise the stressful situation as one that unnecessarily prevents them from achieving their goal of being viewed as an effective employee in the eyes of the customers and the store manager.

Finally, consider a third convenience store in which the cashiers' workload is higher due to additional responsibilities that include receiving merchandise from vendors, taking physical inventory, and training new employees. In this store, the cashiers may appraise their jobs as stressful because of the higher workload and the need to balance different priorities. However, in contrast to the cashiers in the previous example, cashiers in this store might appraise these demands as providing an opportunity to learn and demonstrate the type of competence that often is rewarded with satisfying promotions and pay raises.

6.2 What are the four main types of stressors?

Types of Stressors

In the previous two examples, the cashiers were confronted with demands that a primary appraisal would label as "stressful." However, the specific demands in the two examples have an important difference. Having to deal with equipment breakdowns or unhappy customers is not likely to be perceived by most employees as having implications that are personally beneficial; in fact, the opposite is likely to be true. These kinds of stressors are called **hindrance stressors**, or stressful demands that people tend to perceive as hindering their progress toward personal accomplishments or goal attainment.[17] Hindrance stressors most often trigger negative emotions such as anxiety and anger.[18] In contrast, having to deal with additional responsibilities is likely to be perceived by most employees as having long-term benefits. These kinds of stressors are called **challenge stressors**, or stressful demands that people tend to perceive as opportunities for learning, growth, and achievement. Although challenge stressors can be exhausting, they often trigger positive emotions such as pride and enthusiasm. Figure 6-1 lists a number of hindrance and challenge stressors, some of which are experienced at work and some of which are experienced outside of work.[19]

hindrance stressors
Stressors that tend to be appraised as thwarting progress toward growth and achievement

challenge stressors
Stressors that tend to be appraised as opportunities for growth and achievement

Work Hindrance Stressors The various roles we fill at work are the source of different types of work-related hindrance stressors.[20] One type of work-related hindrance stressor is **role conflict**, which refers to conflicting expectations that other people may have of us.[21] As an example of role conflict that occurs from incompatible demands within a single role that a person may hold, consider the job of an emergency dispatch operator. Those holding these jobs are expected to communicate with and be responsive to people who are distressed and experiencing problems. Effectiveness in this requires the operator to spend time with callers. The expectation is also that operators spend as little time as possible with the people on the other end of the line. In short, emergency dispatch operators are put in a position in which they simply cannot meet both types of expectations.

role conflict

Others' having differing expectations of what an individual needs to do in a role

Emergency dispatch operators experience role conflict. On the one hand, they need to be polite and responsive to the people which whom they're speaking. On the other hand, they need to spend as little time as possible on each call.

© Peter Casolino/Alamy

Role ambiguity refers to a lack of information about what needs to be done in a role, as well as unpredictability regarding the consequences of performance in that role.[22] Employees are sometimes asked to work on projects for which they're given very few instructions or guidelines about how things are supposed to be done. In these cases, employees may not know how much money they can spend on the project, how long it's supposed to take, or what exactly the finished product is supposed to look like. Role ambiguity is often experienced among new employees who haven't been around long enough to receive instructions from supervisors or observe and model the role behaviours of more senior colleagues. Students sometimes experience role ambiguity when professors remain vague about particular course requirements or how grading is going to be performed. In such cases, the class becomes stressful, because it's not quite clear what it takes to get a good grade.

role ambiguity

A lack of direction and information about what needs to be done in a role

Role overload occurs when the number of demanding roles a person holds is so high that the person simply cannot perform some or all of the roles effectively.[23] Role overload as a source of stress is becoming very prevalent for employees in many different industries, and in fact, studies have shown that this source of stress is more prevalent than both role conflict and role ambiguity.[24] For example, the workload for executives and managers who work in investment banking, consulting, and law is so high that 80-hour workweeks are becoming the norm.[25] Although this trend may not be surprising to some of you, people holding these jobs also indicate that they would not be able to effectively complete most of the work that's required of them, even if they worked twice as many hours.

role overload
An excess of demands on an employee preventing him or her from working effectively

One final type of work-related hindrance stressor, **daily hassles**, refers to the relatively minor day-to-day demands that get in the way of accomplishing the things that we really want to accomplish.[26] Examples of hassles include having to deal with unnecessary paperwork, office equipment malfunctions, annoying interactions with abrasive co-workers, and useless communications. Although these examples of daily hassles may seem relatively minor, taken together, they can be extremely time-consuming and stressful. Indeed, according to one survey, 40 percent of executives spend somewhere between a half-day and a full day every week on communications that are not useful or necessary.[27]

daily hassles
Minor day-to-day demands that interfere with work accomplishment

OB INTERNATIONALLY

Although organizational researchers have studied job-related stress for many years, most of this work has been conducted in single countries, mainly in North America and the United Kingdom. An assumption in this work has been that work-related stressors, such as role ambiguity or role conflict, must lead to feelings of stress. But is this true? What about other countries and cultures?

A recent study by Sharon Glazer and Terry Beehr, two respected stress researchers, was designed to address this basic question.[28] In short, the researchers wanted to know if national context matters when it comes to employees' perception of and reaction to work-related stressors.

Four countries were studied: the United States, the United Kingdom, Italy, and Hungary. Data were provided by 1,396 nurses in four hospitals in Budapest, Hungary; three hospitals each in London, England, and in northern Italy; and five hospitals in the area of Baltimore, Maryland, in the United States. The choice to focus on healthcare providers, and nursing in particular, has particular relevance for Canada. Of all types of healthcare providers, registered nurses have been found to be among the *most* stressed![29]

The cross-cultural findings were quite interesting. Overall, the measures of role stressors (overload, conflict, and ambiguity) and job strain (job stress/anxiety) were in the low-to-moderate range, with nurses based in Hungary reporting the lowest scores when compared with nurses in the other three countries. Nurses based in the U.S. reported the highest level of job strain (confirming the Canadian data). Also, the patterns of correlations among the study variables were consistent across all four countries.

So do the same basic stress-related concepts discussed in this chapter exist in different countries? The answer is yes.[30] For insights into some of the causes of stress for these nurses, see our chapter-opening profile and chapter-ending case.

Work Challenge Stressors One type of work-related challenge stressor is **time pressure**—a strong sense that the amount of time you have to do a task is just not quite enough.[31] Although most people appraise situations with high time pressure as rather stressful, they also tend to appraise these situations as more challenging than hindering. Time pressure demands tend to be viewed as something worth striving for because success in meeting such demands can be intrinsically satisfying. As an example of this positive effect of high time pressure, consider Michael Jones, an architect at a top New

York firm. His job involves overseeing multiple projects with tight deadlines, and as a result, he has to work at a hectic pace. Although Jones readily acknowledges that his job is stressful, he also believes that the outcome of having all the stress is satisfying. Jones is able to see the product of his labour over the Manhattan skyline, which makes him feel like he's a part of something.[32]

time pressure
The sense that the amount of time allotted to do a job is not quite enough

Work complexity refers to the degree to which the requirements of the work, in terms of knowledge, skills, and abilities, tax or exceed the capabilities of the person who is responsible for performing the work.[33] Consider how organizations train future executives and leaders. In many cases, these employee development practices involve giving people jobs that require skills and knowledge the people do not yet possess. A successful marketing manager being groomed for an executive-level position may, for example, be asked to manage a poorly performing production facility with poor labour relations in a country halfway around the world. Although such learning experiences tend to be quite stressful, managers report that being stretched beyond their capacity is well worth the associated discomfort.[34]

work complexity
The degree to which job requirements tax or just exceed employee capabilities

The job of an air traffic controller is stressful because of the challenging demands. In particular, air traffic controllers know that during each shift they work, they'll be responsible for ensuring that thousands of people arrive at their destinations safely and on time.

© Monty Rakusen/Cultura/Getty Images

Work responsibility refers to the nature of the obligations a person has toward others.[35] Generally speaking, the level of responsibility in a job is higher when the number, scope, and importance of the obligations in that job are higher. As an example, the level of work responsibility for an air traffic controller, who may be accountable for the lives of tens of thousands of people every day, is very high.[36] Controllers understand that if they make an error while directing an aircraft—for example, saying "turn left" instead of "turn right"—hundreds of people can die in an instant. Although controller errors that result in midair collisions and crashes are extremely rare, the possibility weighs heavily on the minds of controllers, especially after they lose "the picture" (controller jargon for the mental representation of an assigned airspace and all the aircraft within it) due to extreme workloads, a loss of concentration, or equipment malfunctions. Like time pressure and work complexity, high responsibility makes demands on people that they evaluate as both stressful and potentially positive. For an example of a job filled with challenge stressors, see our ***OB on Screen*** feature.

work responsibility

The number and importance of the obligations an employee has to others

OB ON SCREEN

Argo

Okay, you got 6 people hiding out in a town of what, 4 million people, all of whom chant "death to America" all the livelong day. You want to set up a movie in a week. You want to lie to Hollywood, a town where everybody lies for a living. Then you're gonna sneak 007 over here into a country that wants CIA blood on their breakfast cereal, and you're gonna walk the Brady Bunch out of the most watched city in the world.

With those words, movie producer Lester Segal (Alan Arkin) lets makeup artist John Chambers (John Goodman) and CIA agent Tony Mendez (Ben Affleck) know what he thinks of their plan to rescue six American diplomats from Iran in 1980, in *Argo* (Dir. Ben Affleck, Warner Bros., 2012). You see, Tony's job is to "exfiltrate" the six fugitives who have been hiding out. His plan involves a cover story that the Americans are filmmakers who are scouting locations for a science fiction movie. Tony provides fake passports and identities to the Americans and has two days to prepare them so they can make it through Iranian security at the airport. Of course, Tony will be with them the whole time, pretending to be the film's executive producer.

© AP Photo/Warner Bros., Claire Folger

Although it might seem obvious to point out that Tony's job is stressful, it's useful to consider why this is the case to understand why Tony does it. After all, he puts himself in a situation where it's very unclear whether he can be successful, and the consequences of failure are quite dire. In short, Tony likely persists in his job because it's filled with challenge stressors. First, there's time pressure. The Iranians have started to figure out where the Americans are hiding, and Tony has only two days to rescue them. Second, there's work complexity. The opening quote makes it clear that many pieces have to come together for the plan to work. Third, there's responsibility. The lives of six Americans are in Tony's hands, and if he fails, they all die. So how does it turn out? If you're a history buff, you already know.

Non-work Hindrance Stressors Although the majority of people spend more time at the office than anywhere else,[37] there are a number of stressful demands outside of work that have implications for managing behaviour in organizations.[38] In essence, stressors experienced outside of work may have effects that "spill over" to affect the employee at work.[39] One example of non-work hindrance stressors is **work–family conflict**, a special form of role conflict in which the demands of a work role hinder the fulfillment of the demands of a family role (or vice versa).[40] We most often think of cases in which work demands hinder effectiveness in the family context, termed "work to family conflict." For example, employees who have to deal with lots of hindrances at work may have trouble switching off their frustration after they get home, and as a consequence, they may become irritable and impatient with family and friends. However, work–family conflict can occur in the other direction as well. For example, "family to work conflict" would occur if a salesperson experiencing the stress of marital conflict comes to work harbouring emotional pain and negative feelings, which makes it difficult to interact with customers effectively. Although there are many benefits to having an active and well-rounded life, it's important to recognize that both work to family conflict and family to work conflict tend to be higher for employees who are strongly embedded in their work organizations and their communities.[41]

work–family conflict

A form of role conflict in which the demands of a work role hinder the fulfillment of the demands in a family role (or vice versa)

Non-work hindrance stressors also come in the form of **negative life events**.[42] Research has revealed that a number of life events are perceived as quite stressful, particularly when they result in significant changes to a person's life.[43] Table 6-2 provides a listing of some commonly experienced life events, along with a score that estimates how stressful each event is perceived to be. As the table reveals, many of the most stressful life events do not occur at work. Rather, they include family events such as the death of a spouse or close family member, a divorce or marital separation, a jail term, or a personal illness. These events would be classified as hindrance stressors because they hinder the ability to achieve life goals and are associated with negative emotions.

negative life events

Events such as a divorce or death of a family member that tend to be appraised as a hindrance

A third type of non-work hindrance stressor is **financial uncertainty**—uncertainty with regard to the loss of livelihood, savings, or the ability to pay expenses. This type of stressor is highly relevant during recessions or economic downturns. When people have concerns about losing their jobs, homes, and life savings because of economic factors that are beyond their control, it's understandable why nearly half of the respondents to a recent survey indicated that stress was making it hard for them to do their jobs.[44]

financial uncertainty

Uncertainty with regard to the potential for loss of livelihood, savings, or the ability to pay expenses

TABLE 6-2

Stressful Life Events

Life Event	Stress Score	Life Event	Stress Score
Death of a spouse	100	Trouble with in-laws	29
Divorce	73	Outstanding achievement	28
Marital separation	65	Begin or end school	26
Jail term	63	Change in living conditions	25
Death of close family member	63	Trouble with boss	23
Personal illness	53	Change in work hours	20
Marriage	50	Change in residence	20
Fired at work	47	Change in schools	20
Marital reconciliation	45	Change in social activities	18
Retirement	45	Change in sleeping habits	16
Pregnancy	40	Change in family get-togethers	15
Gain of new family member	39	Change in eating habits	15
Death of close friend	37	Vacations	13
Change in occupation	36	The holiday season	12
Child leaving home	29	Minor violations of the law	11

Source: Adapted from T.H. Holmes and R.H. Rahe, "The Social Re-adjustment Rating Scale," *Journal of Psychosomatic Research* 11 (1967), pp. 213–18.

Non-work Challenge Stressors Of course, the non-work domain can be a source of challenge stressors as well.[45] **Family time demands** refer to the time a person must devote to an array of family activities and responsibilities, such as travelling, attending social events and organized activities, hosting parties, and planning and making home improvements. Examples of **personal development** activities are participation in formal education programs, music lessons, sports-related training, hobby-related self-education, participation in local government, and volunteer work. Finally, **positive life events**, such as the addition of a new family member and graduating from school, are stressful in their own way, even though associated with positive rather than negative emotions.

family time demands
The amount of time committed to fulfilling family responsibilities

personal development
Participation in activities outside of work that foster growth and learning

positive life events
Events such as marriage or the birth of a child that tend to be appraised as a challenge

6.3 How do individuals cope with stress?

How Do People Cope with Stressors?

According to the transactional theory of stress, after people appraise a stressful demand, they ask themselves, "What *should* I do?" and "What *can* I do?" to deal with this situation. These questions, which refer to the **secondary appraisal** shown in Figure 6-1, centre on the issue of how people cope with the various stressors they face.[46] **Coping** refers to the behaviours and thoughts that people use to manage both the stressful demands they face and the emotions associated with those stressful demands.[47] As Table 6-3 illustrates, coping can involve many different types of activities, and these activities can be grouped into four broad categories based on two dimensions.[48] The first dimension refers to the method of coping (behavioural versus cognitive), and the second dimension refers to the focus of coping (problem solving versus regulation of emotions).

secondary appraisal
When people determine how to cope with the various stressors they face

coping
Behaviours and thoughts used to manage stressful demands and the emotions associated with the stressful demands

TABLE 6-3

Examples of Coping Strategies

	Problem-Focused	Emotion-Focused
Behavioural methods	Working harder	Engaging in alternative activities
	Seeking assistance	Seeking support
	Acquiring additional resources	Venting anger
Cognitive methods	Strategizing	Avoiding, distancing, and ignoring
	Self-motivation	Looking for the positive in the negative
	Changing priorities	Reappraising

Source: Adapted from J.C. Latack and S.J. Havlovic, "Coping with Job Stress: A Conceptual Evaluation Framework for Coping Measures," *Journal of Organizational Behavior* 13 (1992), pp. 479–508.

The first part of our coping definition highlights the idea that methods of coping can be categorized on the basis of whether they involve behaviours or thoughts. **Behavioural coping** involves the set of physical activities that are used to deal with a stressful situation.[49] In one example of behavioural coping, a person who is confronted with a lot of time pressure at work might choose to cope by working faster. In another example, an employee who has several daily hassles might cope by avoiding work—coming in late, leaving early, or even staying home. As a final example, employees often cope with the stress of an international assignment by returning home from the assignment prematurely.

behavioural coping
Physical activities used to deal with a stressful situation

In contrast to behavioural coping, **cognitive coping** refers to the thoughts that are involved in trying to deal with a stressful situation.[50] For example, the person who is confronted with an increase in time pressure might cope by thinking about different ways of accomplishing the work more efficiently. As another example of cognitive coping, employees who are confronted with daily hassles might try to convince themselves that the hassles are not that bad after all, perhaps by dwelling on less annoying aspects of the daily events.

cognitive coping
Thoughts used to deal with a stressful situation

Whereas the first part of our coping definition refers to the method of coping, the second part refers to the focus of coping—that is, does the coping attempt to address the stressful demand or the emotions triggered by the demand?[51] **Problem-focused coping** refers to behaviours and cognitions intended to manage the stressful situation itself.[52] To understand problem-focused coping, consider how the people in the previous paragraphs coped with time pressure. In the first example, the person attempted to address the time pressure by working harder, whereas in the second example, the person thought about a strategy for accomplishing the work more efficiently. Although the specific coping methods differed, both of these people reacted to the time pressure similarly, in that they focused their effort on meeting the demand rather than trying to avoid it.

problem-focused coping
Behaviours and cognitions of an individual intended to manage the stressful situation itself

In contrast to problem-focused coping, **emotion-focused coping** refers to the various ways in which people manage their own emotional reactions to stressful demands.[53] The reactions to the daily hassles that we described previously illustrate two types of emotion-focused coping. In the first example, the employee used avoidance and distancing behaviours to reduce the emotional distress caused by the stressful situation. In the second example, the employee reappraised the demand to make it seem less stressful and threatening. Although people may be successful at changing the way different situations are construed to avoid feeling unpleasant emotions, the demand or problem that initially triggered the appraisal process remains.

emotion-focused coping
Behaviours and cognitions of an individual intended to help manage emotional reactions to the stressful demands

Of course, the coping strategy that's ultimately used has important implications for how effectively people can meet or adapt to the different stressors that they face. In the work context, for example, a manager would most likely want subordinates to cope with the stress of a heavy workload by using a problem-focused strategy—working harder—rather than an emotion-focused strategy—leaving work several hours early to create distance from the stressor. Of course, there are some situations in which emotion-focused coping may be functional for the person. As an example, consider someone who repeatedly fails to make it through the auditions for *The Voice*, despite years of voice lessons and countless hours of practice. At some point, if he did not have the capability to cope emotionally—perhaps by lowering his aspirations—his self-esteem could be damaged, which could translate into reduced effectiveness in other roles that they fill.

Although avoidance and distancing behaviours may reduce the emotional distress one feels, these strategies do not help manage the demand that's causing the stress.

© Manchan/Getty Images

How do people choose a particular coping strategy? One factor that influences this choice is the set of beliefs that people have about how well different coping strategies can address different demands. In essence, people are likely to choose the coping strategy they believe has the highest likelihood of meeting the demand they face. For example, successful students may come to understand that the likelihood of effectively coping with demanding final exams is higher if they study hard rather than trying to escape from the situation by going out until 3:00 a.m. The choice also depends on the degree to which people believe that they have what it takes to execute the coping strategy effectively. Returning to the previous example, if students have already failed the first two exams in the course, despite trying hard, they may come to believe that a problem-focused coping strategy won't work. In this situation, because students may feel helpless to address the demand directly, an emotion-focused coping strategy would be more likely.

Another critical factor that determines coping strategy choice is the degree to which people believe that a particular strategy gives them some degree of control over the stressor. If people believe that a demand can be addressed with a problem-focused coping strategy and have confidence that they can use that problem-focused strategy effectively, then they will feel some control over the situation and will likely use a problem-focused strategy. If people believe that a demand cannot be addressed with a problem-focused strategy or do not believe they can effectively execute that strategy, they'll feel a lack of control over the situation and will tend to use an emotion-focused coping strategy.

So what determines how people develop a sense of control? One important factor seems to be the nature of the stressful demand itself. In particular, people are likely to feel less control over a stressor when they appraise it as a hindrance rather than a challenge. Consider one of the life events in Table 6-2: "Trouble with boss." This event would most likely be appraised as a hindrance stressor because it serves to thwart goal achievement and triggers negative emotions. If you're like most people, you would want to change the behaviour of your boss so that the trouble would stop and you could get on with your work. However, it's also likely that you would feel like you have little control over this situation because bosses are in a position of power, and complaining to your boss's boss might not be an option for you. The anxiety and hopelessness triggered by the situation would further erode any sense of control over the situation, likely leading to emotion-focused coping.[54]

The Experience of Strain

Earlier in this chapter, we defined strain as the negative consequences associated with stress. But how exactly does stress cause strain? Consider the case of Naomi Henderson, the CEO of RIVA, a Rockville, Maryland–based market research firm. The job of CEO is quite demanding, and Henderson found herself working 120 hours a week to cope with the heavy workload. One night she woke up to go to the bathroom and found that she literally could not move—she was paralyzed. After she was rushed to the emergency room, the doctor told Henderson and her husband that her diagnosis was stress. The doctor recommended rest in bed for 14 hours a day for six weeks.[55] Although this example may seem extreme to you, the demands of many managerial and executive-level jobs are often excessive,[56] and the negative health consequences that result are fairly predictable. In fact, if you've ever been in a situation in which you've experienced heavy stress for more than a couple of days, you can probably appreciate the toll that stress can take on you. Although people react to stress differently, you may have felt unusually exhausted, irritable, and achy. What might be surprising to you is that the mechanism within your body that gives you the ability to function effectively in the face of stressful demands is the same one that ends up causing you these problems. So what is this mechanism?

Essentially, the body has a set of responses that allow it to adapt and function effectively in the face of stressful demands, but if the stressful demands do not ramp down or the demands occur too frequently, the body's adaptive responses become toxic.[57] More specifically, when people are confronted with a stressor, their bodies secrete chemical compounds that increase their heart rate and blood pressure, as blood is redirected away from vital organs, such as the spleen, to the brain and skeletal muscles.[58] Unfortunately, if the chemicals in the blood remain elevated because of prolonged or repeated exposure to the stressor, the body begins to break down, and several negative consequences are set into motion. As shown in Figure 6-2, those negative consequences come in three varieties: physiological strains, psychological strains, and behavioural strains.[59]

Physiological strains that result from stressors occur in at least four systems of the human body. First, stressors can reduce the effectiveness of the body's immune system, which makes it more difficult for the body to ward off illness and infection. Have you ever noticed that you're more likely to catch a cold during or immediately after final exam week? Second, stressors can harm the body's cardiovascular system, cause the heart to race, increase blood pressure, and create coronary artery disease. Third, stressors can cause problems in the body's musculoskeletal system. Tension headaches, tight shoulders, and back pain have all been linked to a variety of stressors. Fourth, stressors cause gastrointestinal system problems. Symptoms of this type of strain include stomachaches, indigestion, diarrhea, and constipation.[60]

physiological strains
Reactions from stressors that harm the human body

Although you might be tempted to dismiss the importance of physiological strains because the likelihood of serious illness and disease is low for people in their 20s and 30s, research shows that dismissal may be a mistake. For example, high-pressure work deadlines increase the chance of heart attack within the next 24 hours by a factor of six.[61] So even though your likelihood of suffering a heart attack may be low, who would want to increase their risk by 600 percent? Furthermore, the negative physiological effects of stress persist over time and may not show up until far into the future. One study showed that eye problems, allergic complaints, and chronic diseases could be attributed to stress measured eight years earlier.[62]

Psychological strains that result from stressors include depression, anxiety, anger, hostility, reduced self-confidence, irritability, inability to think clearly, forgetfulness, lack of creativity, memory loss, and (not surprisingly, given the rest of this list) a loss of sense of humour.[63] You might be tempted to think of these problems as isolated incidents; however, they may reflect a more general psychological condition known as **burnout**, which can be defined as the emotional, mental, and physical exhaustion

FIGURE 6-2

Examples of Strain

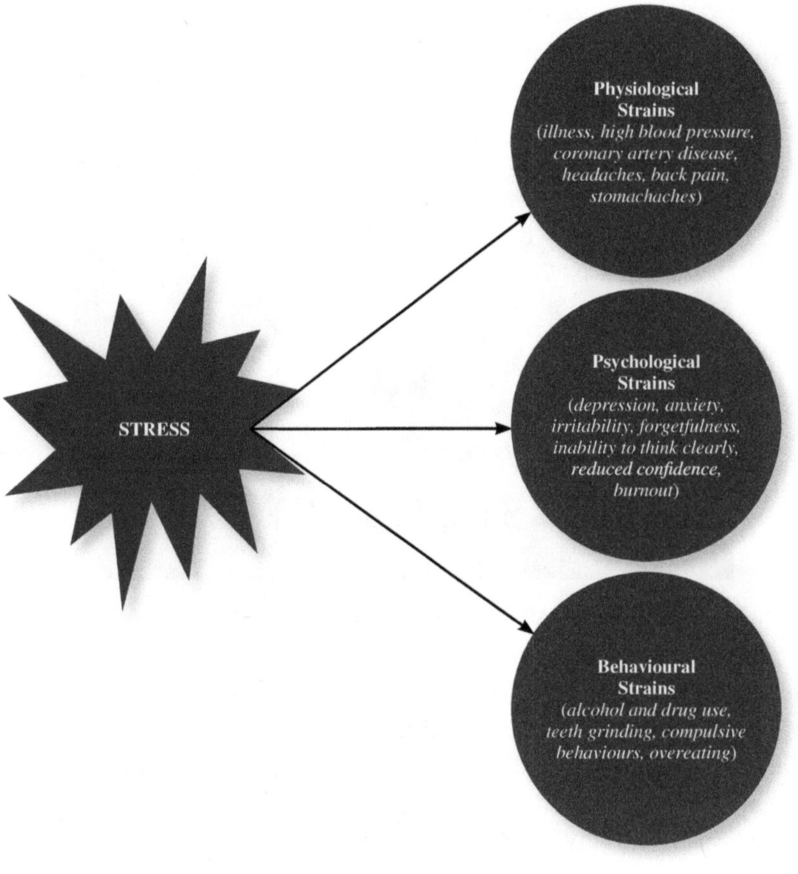

Source: M.E. Burke, *2005 Benefits Survey Report*, Society of Human Resource Management.

psychological strains
Negative psychological reactions from stressors such as depression, anxiety, and anger

that results from having to cope with stressful demands on an ongoing basis.[64] There are many familiar examples of people who have experienced burnout, and the majority of them illustrate how burnout can lead to a decision to quit a job or even change careers. As an example, after playing for 17 seasons for the Green Bay Packers, Brett Favre decided to retire from professional football after leading his team to the NFC championship game in 2008.[65] Favre explained to reporters that he was just tired of all the stress.[66] The pressure of the challenge of winning compelled him to spend an ever-increasing amount of time preparing for the next game, and over time, this pressure built up and resulted in exhaustion and reduced commitment. Of course, Favre would un-retire to play for the New York Jets in 2008, only to re-retire after the season. Favre again un-retired in 2009 and joined the Minnesota Vikings. He re-retired, for the final time, after the 2010 season. Such changes of heart are not unusual after someone retires from an exciting job due to burnout. A break from stressors associated with the work not only gives the person a chance to rest and recharge, but also provides a lot of free time to think about the excitement and challenge of performing again.

burnout

The emotional, mental, and physical exhaustion from coping with stressful demands on a continuing basis

Having started over 300 games straight, Brett Favre is well known among sports fans for his durability as an NFL quarterback. However, his durability did not mean that he was immune to the effects of stress. He retired from football three times in the span of three years, and burnout played an important role in these decisions.

© AP Photo/G. Newman Lowrance

Finally, in addition to physiological and psychological strains, the stress process can result in **behavioural strains**, which are patterns of negative behaviours associated with other strains—grinding one's teeth at night, being overly critical and bossy, excessive smoking, compulsive gum-chewing, overuse of alcohol, and compulsive eating.[67] Although it's unknown why exposure to stressors has these results, it's easy to see why they are undesirable from both personal and organizational standpoints.

behavioural strains

Patterns of negative behaviours associated with other strains

6.4 How does the Type A Behaviour Pattern influence the stress process?

Accounting for Individuals in the Stress Process

So far in this chapter, we've discussed how the typical or average person reacts to different sorts of stressors. However, we've yet to discuss how people differ in terms of how they react to demands. One way people differ in their reaction to stress depends on whether they exhibit the **Type A Behaviour Pattern**. "Type A" people have a strong sense of time urgency and tend to be impatient, hard-driving, competitive, controlling, aggressive, and even hostile.[68] If you walk, talk, and eat at a quick pace, and if you find yourself constantly annoyed with people who do things too slowly, chances are that you're a Type A person. That said, one way to tell for sure is to fill out the Type A questionnaire in the ***OB Assessments*** feature at the end of this chapter. Some individuals, however, exhibit what has been described as a "Type B" pattern, which is perfectly contrasted with the pattern exhibited by Type A's (e.g., generally patient, relaxed, easygoing, and at times lacking an overriding sense of urgency). Given that Type B is defined, essentially, as the opposite of Type A, it would be helpful to know more about why "Type A" patterns are important.

Type A Behaviour Pattern
A type of behaviour exhibited by people who tend to experience more stressors, to appraise more demands as stressful, and to be prone to experiencing more strains than most others

In the context of this chapter, the Type A Behaviour Pattern is important because it can influence stressors, stress, and strains. First, it may have a direct influence on the level of stressors a person confronts. To understand why this might be true, consider that Type A persons tend to be hard-driving and have a strong desire to achieve. Because the behaviours that reflect these tendencies are valued by the organization, Type A individuals receive "rewards" in the form of increases in the amount and level of work required. In addition, because Type A people tend to be aggressive and competitive, they may be more prone to interpersonal conflict. You would most likely agree that conflict with peers and co-workers is an important stressor.

Second, in addition to the effect on stressors, the Type A Behaviour Pattern is important because it influences the stress process itself.[69] This effect of the Type A Behaviour Pattern is easy to understand if you consider that hard-driving competitiveness makes people hypersensitive to demands that could potentially affect their progress toward their goal attainment. In essence, Type A individuals are simply more likely to appraise demands as being stressful rather than being benign.

Third, and perhaps most importantly, the Type A Behaviour Pattern has been directly linked to coronary heart disease[70] and other physiological, psychological, and behavioural strains.[71] The size of the relationship between the Type A Behaviour Pattern and these strains is not so strong as to suggest that if you're a Type A person, you should immediately call 911. However, the linkage is strong enough to suggest that the risk of these problems is significantly higher for people who typically engage in Type A behaviours.

Social support from friends, co-workers, and family can be a big help in managing stress, even though it often occurs outside the stress-causing environment.

© Ingram Publishing

Another individual factor that affects the way people manage stress is the degree of **social support** they receive. Social support refers to the help that people receive when they're confronted with stressful demands, and there are at least two major types.[72] One is **instrumental support**, the help people receive that can be used to address the stressful demand directly. For example, if a person is overloaded with work, a co-worker might provide instrumental support by taking over some of the work or offering suggestions about how to do the work more efficiently. A second type of social support is **emotional support**, the help people receive in addressing the emotional distress that accompanies stressful demands. The supervisor of someone overloaded with work might provide emotional support by showing interest in the employee's situation and being understanding and sympathetic. As shown in these examples, social support may come from co-workers and supervisors; but it may also come from family members and friends outside the context of the stressful demand.[73]

social support

The help people receive from others when confronted with stressful demands

instrumental support

The help people receive from others that can be used to address a stressful demand directly

emotional support

The empathy and understanding people receive from others that can be used to alleviate emotional distress from stressful demands

Like the Type A Behaviour Pattern, social support can influence the stress process in several different ways. However, most research on social support focuses on how social support buffers the relationship between stressors and strains.[74] According to this research, high levels of social support provide a person with instrumental or emotional resources useful for coping with the stressor, which tends to reduce the harmful consequences of the stressor to that individual. With low levels of social support, the person does not have extra coping resources available, so the stressor tends to have effects that are more harmful. In essence, this perspective casts social support as a "moderator" of the relationship between stressors and strains (recall that moderators are variables that affect the strength of the relationship between two other variables). In this particular case, the relationship between stressors and strain tends to be weaker at higher levels of social support and stronger at lower levels of social support. Although not every research study has found support for the buffering effect of social support,[75] the majority of research evidence has been supportive.[76]

Summary: Why Are Some Employees More "Stressed" Than Others?

So what explains why some employees are more stressed than others? As is shown in Figure 6-3, answering that question requires paying attention to the particular stressors the employee is experiencing, including hindrance and challenge stressors originating in both the work and non-work domains. However, it also depends on how those stressors are appraised and coped with, which determines whether physiological, psychological, and behavioural strains are experienced. Finally, answering the question depends on whether the employee is "Type A" and whether the employee has a high or low amount of social support. Understanding all of these factors can help explain why some people can shoulder stressful circumstances for weeks at a time, whereas others seem to be at the end of their rope when faced with even relatively minor job demands.

FIGURE 6-3

Why Are Some Employees More "Stressed" Than Others?

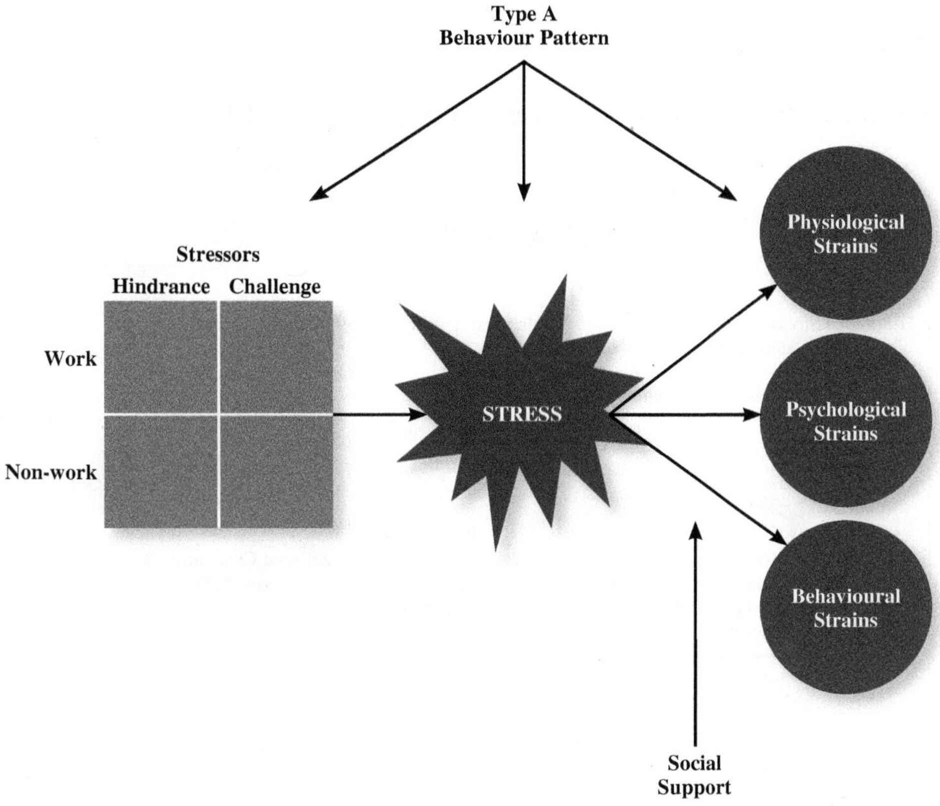

6.5 How does stress affect job performance and organizational commitment?

HOW IMPORTANT IS STRESS?

In the previous sections, we described how stressors and the stress process influence strains and, ultimately, people's health and well-being. Although these relationships are important to understand, you're probably more curious about the impact that stressors have on job performance and organizational commitment, the two outcomes in our integrative model of OB. Figure 6-4 summarizes the research evidence linking hindrance stressors to performance and commitment, and Figure 6-5 summarizes the research evidence linking challenge stressors to performance and commitment. We limit our discussion to relationships with work stressors rather than non-work stressors, because this is where researchers have focused the most attention.

Figure 6-4 reveals that hindrance stressors have a weak negative relationship with job performance.[77] A general explanation for this negative relationship is that hindrance stressors result in strains and negative emotions that reduce the overall level of physical, cognitive, and emotional energy that people could otherwise bring to their job duties.[78] The detrimental effect that strains have on job performance becomes quite easy to understand when you consider the nature of the individual strains that we mentioned in the previous section. Certainly, you would agree that physiological, psychological, and behavioural strains in the form of illnesses, exhaustion, and drunkenness would detract from employee effectiveness in almost any job context.

FIGURE 6-4

Effects of Hindrance Stressors on Performance and Commitment

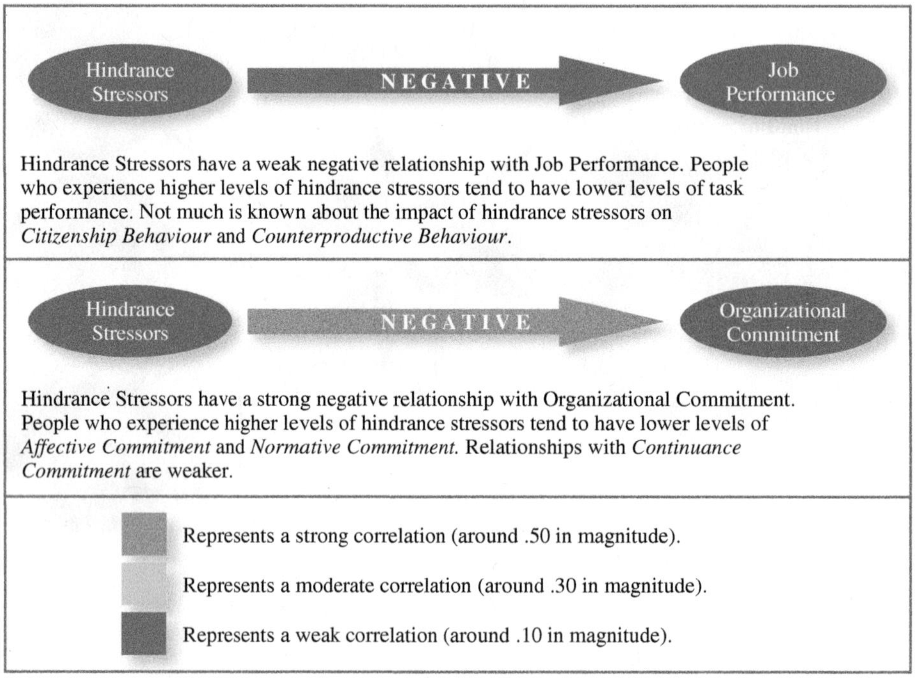

Sources: J.A. LePine, N.P. Podsakoff, and M.A. LePine, "A Meta-analytic Test of the Challenge Stressor–Hindrance Stressor Framework: An Explanation for Inconsistent Relationships Among Stressors and Performance," *Academy of Management Journal* 48 (2005), pp. 764–75; N.P. Podsakoff, J.A. LePine, and M.A. LePine, "Differential Challenge Stressor–Hindrance Stressor Relationships with Job Attitudes, Turnover Intentions, Turnover, and Withdrawal Behavior: A Meta-analysis," *Journal of Applied Psychology* 92 (2007), pp. 438–54.

Figure 6-4 also reveals that hindrance stressors have a strong negative relationship with organizational commitment.[79] Why might this be? Well, hindrance stressors evoke strains, which are generally dissatisfying to people, and as we discussed in the previous chapter, satisfaction has a strong impact on the degree to which people feel committed to their organization.[80] People who work at jobs that they know are causing them to feel constantly sick and exhausted will likely be dissatisfied with their jobs and feel less desire to stay with the organization and more desire to consider alternatives.

Turning now to challenge stressors, the story becomes somewhat different. As shown in Figure 6-5, challenge stressors have a weak relationship with job performance and a moderate relationship with organizational commitment. However, in contrast to the results for hindrance stressors, the relationships are positive rather than negative.[81] In other words, employees who experience higher levels of challenge stressors also tend to have higher levels of job performance and organizational commitment. These relationships stand in sharp contrast with the lower levels of job performance and organizational commitment that result when employees confront higher levels of hindrance stressors.

So what explains this difference? Although challenge stressors result in strains, which detract from performance and commitment, they also tend to trigger the type of positive emotions and problem-focused coping strategies characteristic of employees who are highly engaged in their jobs.[82] The net benefits of these positive emotions, problem-focused coping strategies, and engagement outweigh the costs of the added strain, meaning that challenge stressors tend to be beneficial to employee performance and commitment when both the positives and the negatives are considered.[83] These positive effects of challenge stressors have been demonstrated for executives,[84] employees in lower-level jobs,[85] and even students.[86] It's important to point out, however, that high levels of challenge stressors may have negative consequences that only become apparent over the long term. People whose jobs are filled with challenge stressors experience strains that can result in illness, but because they tend to be more satisfied, committed, and engaged with their jobs, they come to work anyway. This phenomenon, which is referred to as *presenteeism*, can result in prolonged illness, as well as the spread of illness, and ultimately a downward spiral of impaired performance and employee health.[87] In fact, it might surprise you to learn that the reductions in productivity that result from presenteeism are even larger than reductions in productivity that result from absenteeism.[88]

FIGURE 6-5

Effects of Challenge Stressors on Performance and Commitment

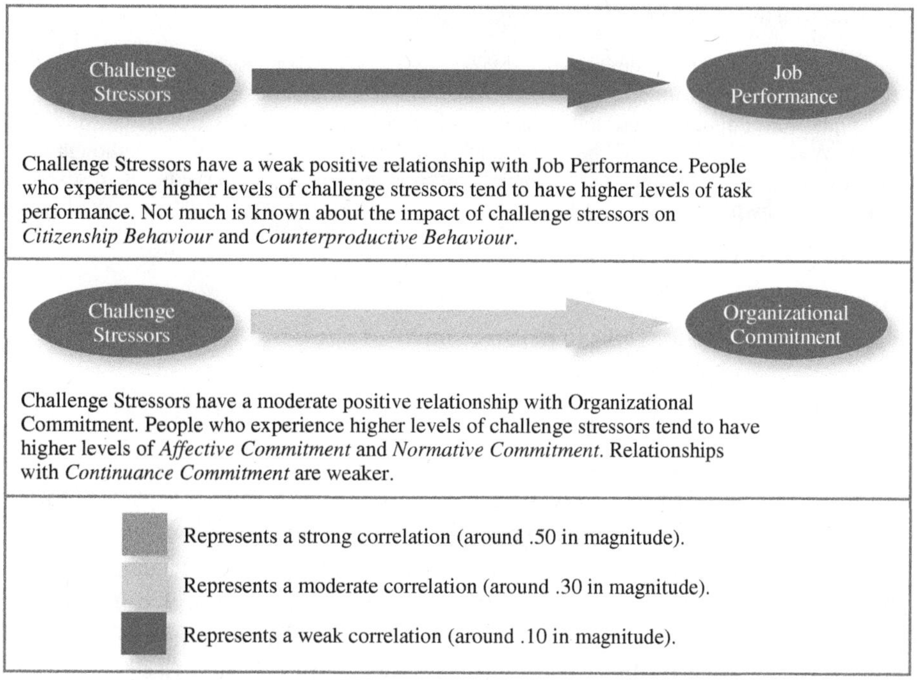

Sources: J.A. LePine, N.P. Podsakoff, and M.A. LePine, "A Meta-analytic Test of the Challenge Stressor–Hindrance Stressor Framework: An Explanation for Inconsistent Relationships Among Stressors and Performance," *Academy of Management Journal* 48 (2005), pp. 764–75; N.P. Podsakoff, J.A. LePine, and M.A. LePine, "Differential Challenge Stressor–Hindrance Stressor Relationships with Job Attitudes, Turnover Intentions, Turnover, and Withdrawal Behavior: A Meta-analysis," *Journal of Applied Psychology* 92 (2007), pp. 438–54.

OB FOR STUDENTS

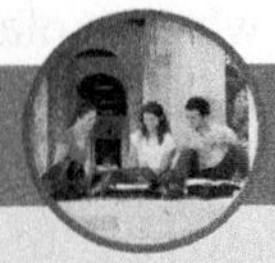

You might be wondering how the concepts and theories of stress apply in the context of your role as a student. Well, one recent study found that students face a number of hindrance stressors and challenge stressors in an academic context. Although the presence of different sorts of stressors might not surprise you, these researchers also found that these two types of stressors significantly affected the grades of the students but in different directions.[89]

Hindrance stressors included demands such as the amount of time spent on busywork for your classes, the degree to which favouritism affects final grades in your classes, and the amount of hassles you need to go through to get projects and assignments done. Challenge stressors included demands such as the difficulty of the work required in your classes, the volume of coursework that must be completed in your classes, and the time pressures experienced for completing work required in your classes. So how did these two types of stressors affect students' grades?

On the one hand, students who experienced higher levels of hindrance stressors tended to have lower grades. One reason is that coping with hindrance stressors was exhausting, and feeling this way made it more difficult to put forth the energy to study. A second reason is that hindrance stressors decreased students' motivation to learn. Students who faced a lot of hindrance stressors apparently did not believe that studying hard would result in good grades, and accordingly, they did not put forth the necessary effort.

On the other hand, students who experienced higher levels of challenge stressors tended to have higher grades. The authors' explanation for this effect was that challenge stressors motivated students to invest more effort in their learning. Although students felt that coping with challenge stressors was exhausting, the positive force of motivation was significantly more powerful. In essence, challenge stressors motivated students to work hard in spite of feeling extremely tired. What can you do with this information?

One option might be to try and change the situation by taking action to decrease the level of hindrance stressors you experience. Although this approach might be possible with some hindrances—asking professors to provide clarifying instruction for example—the approach may be more difficult with others—such as asking the professor to reduce the amount of busywork. A second option would be to try to think of hindrances as challenges. Although it might be difficult to convince yourself that coping with hindrances is beneficial to your growth and learning, the research findings suggest that the effort might be worthwhile.

6.6 What steps can organizations take to manage employee stress?

APPLICATION: STRESS MANAGEMENT

Previously, we described how employee stress results in strains that cost organizations in terms of reduced employee performance and commitment. However, there are other important costs to consider that relate to employee health. Most organizations provide some form of healthcare benefits for their employees. This is especially true for organizations trying to attract and retain hard-to-find skilled workers. To provide a sense of the financial cost of these benefits to employers, a national poll was conducted. Asked if they would trade their company-provided health benefits for an annual payment of $8,000, almost three-quarters of Canadians said they would keep their plan.[90] So what role does stress play in these costs?

Well, it turns out that these health-related costs are driven to a great extent by employee stress. Estimates are that between 60 percent and 90 percent of all doctor visits can be attributed to stress-related causes,[91] and the cost of providing health care to people who experience high levels of stress appears to be approximately 50 percent higher than that for those who experience lower levels of stress.[92]

What do all these costs mean to you as a student of organizational behaviour or as a manager? For one thing, the relationship between stress and healthcare costs means that there may be huge dividends for organizations that learn how to manage stress more effectively. Next, we describe some approaches organizations can use to manage employee stress.

Assessment

The first step in managing stress is to assess the level and sources of stress in the workplace. Although there are many ways to accomplish this type of evaluation, often referred to as a **stress audit**, managers can begin by asking themselves questions about the nature of the jobs in their organization to estimate whether high stress levels may be a problem.[93] The first category of questions might involve the degree to which the organization is going through change that would likely increase uncertainty among employees. As an example, a merger between two companies might increase employees' uncertainty about their job security and possible career paths. As another example, employees in an organization that has transitioned to team-based work might be concerned about how their individual performance contributions will be recognized and rewarded. A second category of questions might centre on the work itself. These questions typically focus on the level and types of stressors experienced by the employees. The third category of questions could involve the quality of relationships not only among employees but also between employees and the organization. Here, an important question to consider is whether organizational politics play a large role in administrative decisions.

stress audit
An assessment of the sources of stress in the workplace

The use of "napping pods" is just one example of how far some companies go to help manage employee stress and strains.

© National Geographic Image Collection/Alamy

Reducing Stressors

Once a stress audit reveals that stress may be a problem, the next step is to consider alternative courses of action. One general course of action involves managing stressors, which may be accomplished in one of two ways. First, organizations could try to eliminate or significantly reduce stressful demands. As an example of this approach, 19 percent of organizations in one recent survey used **job sharing** to reduce role overload and foster work–life balance.[94] Job sharing does not mean splitting one job into two, but rather that two people share a single job as though they were a single performing unit. The assumption underlying job sharing is that "although businesses are becoming 24/7, people don't."[95] You might be tempted to believe that job sharing would be most appropriate in lower-level jobs, where responsibilities and tasks are limited in number and relatively easy to divide. In actuality, job sharing is being used at all levels throughout the organization. Such arrangements can enable an organization to attract or retain valued employees who want more time to attend school or to care for family members. Of course, for this arrangement to work effectively it would be important that job-sharing partners be able to communicate well and coordinate their activities.[96]

job sharing
Two people sharing the responsibilities of a single job

Another example of how companies reduce stressors is employee sabbaticals, which are time off from work to engage in an alternative activity. It is estimated that 11 percent of large companies offer paid sabbaticals, and almost one-third offer unpaid sabbaticals.[97] PricewaterhouseCoopers, for instance, offers paid sabbaticals for up to six months for personal growth reasons or for work in social services; this program is available to employees with as little as two years' experience.[98] Relative to job sharing, sabbaticals allow for a cleaner break from the stressful routine for a fairly lengthy period of time, so, for the period of the sabbatical, the employee's stress may be quite low. However, because the level of stressors never changes in the job itself, the employee is likely to experience the same level of stress upon returning from the sabbatical.

Providing Resources

Although reducing stressors may reduce the overall level of stress that a person experiences, this approach is likely to be most beneficial when the focus of the effort is on hindrance stressors rather than challenge stressors.[99] Hindrance stressors such as role ambiguity, conflict, and politics not only cause strains but also decrease commitment and job performance. In contrast, though challenge stressors such as time pressure and responsibility cause strains, they also tend to be motivating and satisfying, and as a consequence they are generally positively related to commitment and performance.

So as a supplement to reducing stressors, organizations can provide resources that help employees cope with stressful demands.[100] One way organizations provide resources to employees is through **training interventions** aimed at increasing job-related competencies and skills. Employees who possess more competencies and skills can handle more demands, rather than appraising the demands as overly taxing or exceeding their capacity. Training that increases employee competencies and skills is also beneficial to the extent that it promotes a sense that the demands are more controllable, and, as we discussed in a previous section, a sense of control promotes problem-focused coping strategies. CREW training provided to healthcare providers (see chapter-opening profile) is an excellent example of providing resources—in this case teaching co-workers to manage their relationships by being civil and respectful to one another.

training interventions

Practices that increase employees' competencies and skills

OB RESEARCH IN CANADA

Dr. Arla Day is a professor in the Department of Psychology at Saint Mary's University in Nova Scotia. Over the years, Dr. Day has played an important role in several large-scale, funded research projects that have examined the ability of organizational programs and interventions to improve the health of both employees and organizations. Along with her colleagues, she has developed the ABLE program (Achieving Balance in Life & Employment)—a phone-based coaching program to help employees manage work and non-work demands. Readers will be interested to learn that Dr. Day is one of the core researchers associated with CREW (Civility, Respect, and Engagement at Work) featured in our chapter-opening profile. CREW has demonstrated the effectiveness of a group-based intervention to reduce incivility and burnout and improve civility and health. In addition to her teaching and research, Dr. Day consults with a number of private and public organizations on a variety of organizational health issues, and she regularly gives workshops and talks on issues related to her expertise.

Courtesy of Dr. Arla Day

Currently, Dr. Day holds a prestigious Canada Research Chair in Industrial and Organizational Psychology, and is a Fellow of the Canadian Psychology Association. She has authored many articles and book chapters pertaining to healthy workplaces, occupational stress, employee well-being, emotional intelligence (Chapter 4), and work–life balance. Dr. Day puts her research and consulting into action by trying to balance her work with her non-work life—with her very entertaining family and friends, her two overly exuberant dogs, and her one relatively well-behaved horse. You can look her up at www.arladay.com.

A second way organizations provide resources to employees so they can cope more effectively is through **supportive practices** that help employees manage and balance the demands of their different roles. At Vancity, Canada's largest credit union, robberies are major causes of stress among branch employees. The organization helps employees cope in many ways. For instance, in addition to thorough training regarding robbery procedure, and added security-guard presence (if requested), if an event should occur, the company is quick to dispatch a professional trauma team for affected staff members, and a personal follow-up visit by an executive or senior management team member.[101] Table 6-4 lists a few examples of the steps employers can take to reduce stress and promote a healthy work–life balance.

supportive practices

Ways in which organizations help employees manage and balance their demands

TABLE 6-4

Examples of Supportive Practices Used by Organizations

• Offer flexible hours.
• Allow workers to work from home where possible and appropriate.
• Encourage staff to stay home with sick children or elderly relatives when needed.
• Permit those returning from a leave to gradually build up to a full-time schedule.
• Train managers on how to support work–life balance.
• Eliminate unnecessary meetings.
• Communicate expectations clearly to staff.
• Allow staff to control their own priorities as much as possible.

Source: Re-printed with permission, © 2008, Canadian Mental Health Association, http://www.cmha.ca.

Organizations that use flextime give employees some degree of latitude in terms of which hours they need to be present at the workplace. Flexible working hours give employees the ability to cope with demands away from work so that they don't have to worry about these demands while they're at work. Another example is allowing workers to work at home or telecommute on a part-time basis. By providing the opportunity to work at home or some other location with computer access, employees are put in a better position to cope with demands that might be impossible to cope with otherwise (e.g., caring for a sick child or elderly parent). Making an effort to accommodate and support employees who are returning to work after a disabling injury or illness, or after a lengthy leave, not only facilitates successful reintegration but also conveys a message, generally, that the organization cares about and values its members.[102] In addition to employee training mentioned earlier, managers can be trained to understand how their behaviours help or hinder their employees' efforts to cope with job stressors and balance competing work and non-work demands. For instance, to minimize role stressors (e.g., overload, ambiguity, conflict), managers can reduce the number of face-to-face meetings, clarify expectations, and allow employees more personal latitude and personal control (increased autonomy) over their day-to-day work activities.

People can learn how to reduce strain using biofeedback technology.

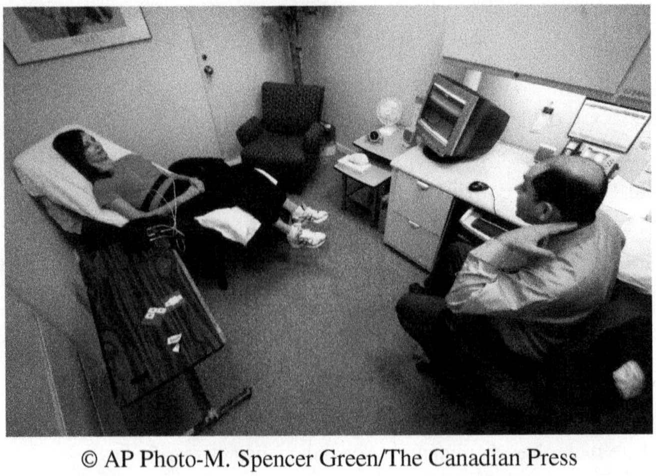

© AP Photo-M. Spencer Green/The Canadian Press

Reducing Strains

As an alternative to managing stressors, many organizations use practices that reduce strains.[103] One type of strain-reducing practice involves **relaxation techniques**, such as progressive muscle relaxation, meditation, and miscellaneous calming activities like taking walks, writing in a journal, and deep breathing.[104] Although these techniques differ, the basic idea is the same—they teach people how to counteract the effects of stressors by engaging in activities that slow the heart rate, breathing rate, and blood pressure.[105] As an example of a relatively simple relaxation technique, consider the recommendation of Herbert Benson, a physician and president of the Mind/Body Medical Institute in Boston. He suggests that people under stress should repeat a word, sound, prayer, phrase, or motion for 10 to 20 minutes once or twice a day and, during that time, try to completely ignore other thoughts that may come to mind.[106] As another example, recall the case of Naomi Henderson, the market research firm CEO who literally became paralyzed by all the stress in her job. Happily, Henderson got better, but only after being treated by a physician who taught her to reduce her own strains with "mental aerobics." This involved breaks every hour to stretch and do deep breathing, short naps to replenish energy, and learning to say no politely to unreasonable demands.[107]

relaxation techniques
Calming activities to reduce stress

A second general category of strain-reducing practices involves **cognitive–behavioural techniques**. In general, these techniques attempt to help people appraise and cope with stressors in a rational manner.[108] To understand what they involve, think of someone you know who not only exaggerates the level and importance of stressful demands but also predicts doom and disaster after quickly concluding that the demands simply cannot be met. If you know someone like this, you might recommend cognitive–behavioural training that involves "self-talk," a technique in which people learn to say things about stressful demands that reflect rationality and optimism. So, when confronted with a stressful demand, this person might be trained to say, "This demand isn't so tough; if I work hard I can accomplish it." In addition, cognitive–behavioural training typically involves instruction about tools that foster effective coping. So, in addition to the self-talk, the person might be trained to prioritize demands, manage time, communicate needs, and seek support.[109]

cognitive–behavioural techniques
Various practices that help workers cope with life's stressors in a rational manner

A third category of strain-reducing practices involves **health and wellness programs**. Canadian organizations have begun to embrace the concept of workplace health promotion. The most recent estimate is that approximately 64 percent of employers offer their employees at least one wellness initiative.[110] Examples of workplace wellness programs that try to improve employee health and foster, in employees, a sense of well-being are smoking cessation, stress management, weight control, physical fitness, nutrition awareness, cardiovascular health/hypertension/diabetes awareness, and back care.[111]

health and wellness programs
Employee assistance programs that help workers with personal problems such as alcoholism and other addictions

TAKEAWAYS

6.1 Stress refers to the psychological response to demands when there's something at stake for the individual and coping with these demands would tax or exceed the individual's capacity or resources. Stressors are the demands that cause the stress response, and strains are the negative consequences of the stress response.

6.2 Stressors come in two general forms: challenge stressors, which are perceived as opportunities for growth and achievement, and hindrance stressors, which are perceived as hurdles to goal achievement. These two stressors can be found in both work and non-work domains.

6.3 Coping with stress involves thoughts and behaviours that address one of two goals: addressing the stressful demand or decreasing the emotional discomfort associated with the demand.

6.4 Individual differences in the Type A Behaviour Pattern affect how people experience stress in three ways. Type A people tend to experience more stressors, appraise more demands as stressful, and are prone to experiencing more strains.

6.5 The effects of stress depend on the type of stressor. Hindrance stressors have a weak negative relationship with job performance and a strong negative relationship with organizational commitment. In contrast, challenge stressors have a weak positive relationship with job performance and a moderate positive relationship with organizational commitment.

6.6 Because of the high costs associated with employee stress, organizations assess and manage stress using a number of different practices. In general, these practices focus on reducing or eliminating stressors, providing resources that employees can use to cope with stressors, or trying to reduce the strains.

KEY TERMS

behavioural coping
behavioural strains
benign job demands
burnout
challenge stressors
cognitive–behavioural techniques
cognitive coping
coping
daily hassles
emotional support
emotion-focused coping
family time demands
financial uncertainty

health and wellness programs
hindrance stressors
instrumental support
job sharing
negative life events
personal development
physiological strains
positive life events
primary appraisal
problem-focused coping
psychological strains
relaxation techniques
role ambiguity
role conflict
role overload
secondary appraisal
social support
strains
stress
stress audit
stressors
supportive practices
time pressure
training interventions
transactional theory of stress
Type A Behaviour Pattern
work complexity
work–family conflict
work responsibility

DISCUSSION QUESTIONS

6.1 Prior to reading this chapter, how did you define stress? Did your definition of stress reflect stressors, the stress process, strains, or some combination?

6.2 Describe your dream job and then provide a list of the types of stressors that you would expect to be present. How much of your salary, if any at all, would you give up to eliminate the most important hindrance stressors? Why?

6.3 If you had several job offers after graduating, to what degree would the level of challenge stressors in the different jobs influence your choice of which job to take? Why?

6.4 How would you assess your ability to handle stress? Given the information provided in this chapter, what could you do to improve your effectiveness in this area?

6.5 If you managed people in an organization in which there were lots of hindrance stressors, what actions would you take to help ensure that your employees coped with the stressors using a problem-focused (as opposed to emotion-focused) strategy?

CASE • DO NURSES "EAT THEIR YOUNG?"

In the chapter-opening profile, we introduced CREW, an innovative program aimed at restoring healthy and positive relationships within healthcare organizations. If you think the issue of nurse-to-nurse incivility is puzzling, consider that most of this hostility tends to be directed at new nurses! In fact, a recent study has estimated that one-third of new nurses are bullied and verbally abused by seasoned nurses, and that new nurses experience a disproportionate degree of stress, burnout (emotional exhaustion), cynicism, and lower self-confidence than nurses in general. So is it true? Do seasoned nurses actually "eat their young?" For Kathleen Bartholomew, the issue is a complex one. To hear Kathleen Bartholomew discuss this issue, go to www.youtube.com/watch?v=1IGPE9IbRFY.

Further insights are attained if we consider that this issue of nurse-to-nurse or "horizontal" hostility can be understood from different perspectives. We might view it from the perspective of new graduates or student nurses. For them, the level of incivility and hostility directed toward them is very real. It is not uncommon for young nurses to say that it's a struggle to survive, every day, and that the workplace often feels more like a "battlefield" than a nursing unit! Young nurses often report incidents of overt bullying, belittlement, and humiliation by seasoned nurses. It is common to hear stories in which young nurses are made to feel unappreciated and that what they learned in school is not relevant. Most frustrating is the fact that all this hostility seems to occur at precisely the time when these beginners are looking to their experienced peers for support and approval. For a sampling of comments from young nurses with respect to nurse-to-nurse hostility, go to www.realityrn.com/more-articles/nurse-relationships/why-nurses-eat-their-young%E2%80%A6/542.

Through the eyes and experiences of the seasoned or experienced nurse, things look quite different. Nursing is a tough job that comes with a lot of responsibility. The problem for many is that the student nurses or new graduates come on to the units thinking they know a lot more than they really do. These "young nurses" have no experience with the difficult, often daunting day-to-day challenges that more experienced nurses face every day—and worse still, they don't respect the fact that much of nursing can't be learned from a textbook or in a lecture. More seasoned nurses believe that experience matters; that a day in the trenches is worth a year in the classroom. As one experienced nurse said, "behavior that might seem hostile to them is just us passionately protecting the safety of our patients." For a sampling of how seasoned nurses view nurse-to-nurse hostility, go to www.realityrn.com/more-articles/nurse-relationships/why-nurses-eat-their-young%E2%80%A6/542.

6.1 Adopt the perspective of a new nurse. What stressors (and types of stressors) are you most likely to encounter? What role issues might you have to deal with (e.g., conflict, ambiguity, and overload)?

6.2 Adopt the perspective of a seasoned nurse. What stressors (and types of stressors) might you have to deal with? What kind of stressor(s) do the new nurses represent, and why?

6.3 What coping strategy (or strategies) would you recommend to new nurses? Seasoned nurses?

6.4 What does the model in Figure 6-3 tell us about what is likely to happen in this situation? What are the likely effects for new and seasoned nurses? Do you think CREW training would work? Explain how this type of intervention might reduce stress on the nursing units.

6.5 Do you think that the concept of nurses "eating their young" applies to other occupations? Explain with some examples.

Sources: K. Bartholomew, *Ending Nurse-to-Nurse Hostility: Why Nurses Eat Their Young and Each Other* (Marblehead, MA: HCPro, 2006); H.K.S. Laschinger, A.L. Grau, J. Finegan, and P. Wilk, "New Graduate Nurses' Expectations of Bullying and Burnout in Hospital Settings," *Journal of Advanced Nursing*, 2010, pp. 2732–2742; "New Nurses, Real Conversations: Why Nurses Eat Their Young," interview with Kathleen Bartholomew, www.realityrn.com/more-articles/nurse-relationships/why-nurses-eat-their-young%E2%80%A6/542, retrieved April 1, 2015.

EXERCISE • MANAGING STRESS

The purpose of this exercise is to explore ways of managing stress to reduce strain. This exercise uses groups of six participants, so your instructor will either assign you to a group of six or ask you to create your own group of six.

The exercise has the following steps:

6.1 One method of managing stress is finding a way to reduce the hindrance stressors encountered on the job. In groups of four to six students, describe the hindrance stressors you are currently experiencing. Each student should describe the two to three most important stressors. Other students should then offer strategies for reducing or alleviating the stressors.

Hindrance Stressors Experienced	**Strategies for Managing Stressors**
Role conflict	________________ ________________
Role ambiguity	________________ ________________
Role overload	________________ ________________
Daily hassles	________________ ________________

6.2 Another method of managing stress is to improve work–life balance. The circle below represents how "waking hours" are divided among five types of activities: school, work, personal relaxation, time with friends, and time with family. Draw two versions of your own circle: your waking hours as they currently are and your waking hours as you wish them to be. Other students should then offer strategies for making the necessary life changes.

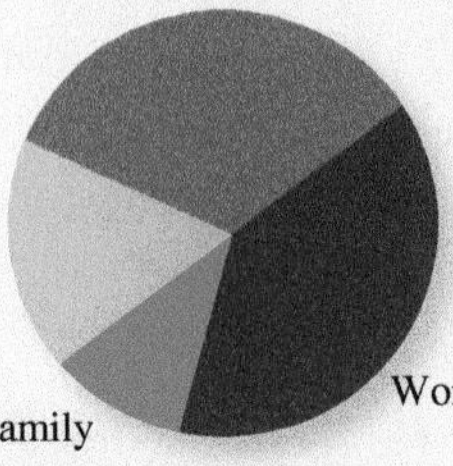

6.3 A third method of managing stress is improving hardiness—a sort of mental and physical health that can act as a buffer, preventing stress from resulting in strain. The following table lists a number of questions that can help diagnose your hardiness. Discuss your answers for each question, and then with the help of other students, brainstorm ways to increase that hardiness factor.

Hardiness Factor	Strategies for Improving Factor
Relaxation. Do you spend enough time reading, listening to music, meditating, or pursuing your hobbies?	______________________ ______________________
Exercise. Do you spend enough time doing cardiovascular, strength, and flexibility sorts of exercises?	______________________ ______________________
Diet. Do you manage your diet adequately by eating healthily and avoiding foods high in fat?	______________________ ______________________

6.4 Class discussion (whether in groups or as a class) should centre on two issues. First, many of the stress-managing factors, especially in steps 2 and 3, take up precious time. Does this make them an ineffective strategy for managing stress? Why or why not? Second, consider your Type A score in the ***OB Assessments*** below. If you are high on Type A, does that make these strategies more or less important?

Source: Adapted from D. Marcic, J. Seltzer, and P. Vail, *Organizational Behavior: Experiences and Cases* (Cincinnati: South-Western, 2001).

OB ASSESSMENTS • TYPE A BEHAVIOUR PATTERN

Do you think that you are especially sensitive to stress? This assessment is designed to measure the extent to which you're a Type A person—someone who typically engages in hard-driving, competitive, and aggressive behaviour. Answer each question using the response scale provided. Then subtract your answers to the boldfaced questions from 8, with the difference being your new answers for those questions. For example, if your original answer for question 3 was "2," your new answer is "6" (8 – 2). Then add up your answers for the 12 questions.

1 **Strongly Disagree**	2 **Disagree**	3 **Slightly Disagree**	4 **Neutral**	5 **Slightly Agree**	6 **Agree**	7 **Strongly Agree**	
1. Having work to complete "stirs me into action" more than other people.							____
2. When a person is talking and takes too long to come to the point, I frequently feel like hurrying the person along.							____
3. Nowadays, I consider myself to be relaxed and easygoing.							____
4. Typically, I get irritated extremely easily.							____
5. My best friends would rate my general activity level as very high.							____
6. I definitely tend to do most things in a hurry.							____
7. I take my work much more seriously than most.							____
8. I seldom get angry.							____
9. I often set deadlines for myself work-wise.							____
10. I feel very impatient when I have to wait in line.							____
11. I put much more effort into my work than other people do.							____
12. Compared with others, I approach life much less seriously.							____

Scoring and Interpretation

If your scores add up to 53 or above, you would be considered a Type A person, which means that you may perceive higher stress levels in your life and be more sensitive to that stress. If your scores add up to 52 or below, you would be considered a Type B person. This means that you sense less stress in your life and are less sensitive to the stress that is experienced. Remember, when interpreting your scores on these assessments it is important to consider the *reliability* and *validity* of these tools (see Chapter 1, ***OB Assessments***).

Source: C.D. Jenkins, S.J. Zyzanski, and R.H. Rosenman, "Progress Toward Validation of a Computer Scored Test for the Type A Coronary Prone Behavior Pattern," *Psychosomatic Medicine* Vol. 22, 193, 202 (1971). Reprinted with permission of Lippincott, Williams & Wilkins.

Motivation

CHAPTER 7

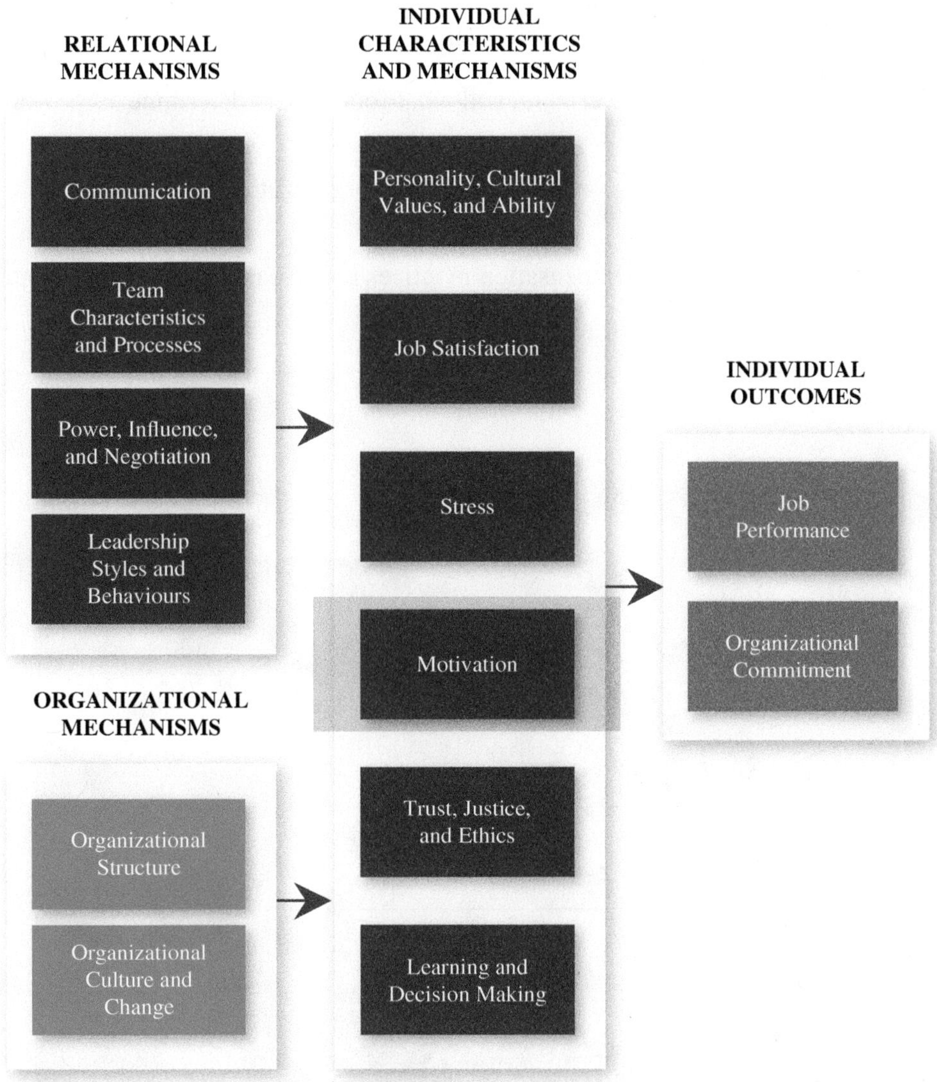

LEARNING OUTCOMES

After reading this chapter, you should be able to answer the following questions:

7.1 What is motivation?

7.2 What three beliefs help determine work effort, according to expectancy theory?

7.3 What two qualities make goals strong predictors of task performance, according to goal setting theory?

7.4 What does it mean to be equitably treated according to equity theory, and how do employees respond to inequity?

7.5 What is psychological empowerment, and what four beliefs determine empowerment levels?

7.6 How does motivation affect job performance and organizational commitment?

7.7 How do organizations use compensation practices to increase employee motivation?

Netflix

At Netflix, employees are motivated using a "freedom and responsibility" approach.

Consider this pop quiz: What accounts for a third of all Internet traffic in North America on a typical weeknight?[1] If you hadn't seen the heading above, you probably would've guessed YouTube, Hulu, or iTunes. But the answer is Netflix, with millions of customers tuning in to watch movies or television shows between dinnertime and bedtime. Netflix has come a long way from its original incarnation as a distributor of DVDs. These days its subscribers tend to rely on streaming video rather than physical DVDs, with all of Netflix's catalogue stored in the cloud.

Much of Netflix's success can be credited to its founder and CEO, Reed Hastings.[2] Hastings built Netflix around a "freedom and responsibility" philosophy.[3] The freedom component of the philosophy comes in the form of very few rules, as Netflix employees are free to structure their work the way they want. Netflix employees can also structure their compensation by choosing how much of their pay comes in salary versus stock. The ultimate freedom, however, comes in the form of unlimited vacations. Employees are free to choose how long they take off, and how frequently.

Now for the responsibility component. Hastings expects exceptional performance from his employees, believing that they should do the work of three or four people.[4] Heather McIlhany, a marketing manager, describes the company as a tough, fulfilling, fully formed adult culture, noting, "There's no place to hide at Netflix." Employees who perform at only an average level are shown the door. In fact, Netflix offers an exceptionally generous severance package to make managers feel less guilty about firing average employees. Employees who live up to expectations are handsomely rewarded, however. Whereas most companies go to great lengths to pay just enough to attract and retain talent, Netflix pays significantly more than the typical Silicon Valley rate. As Hastings deadpans, "We're unafraid to pay high." Pay increases are also tied to the job market, rather than to performance evaluations. Moreover, the company is constantly gathering market compensation data—boosting salaries when needed to stay "ahead of the curve" on pay.

7.1 What is motivation?

MOTIVATION

Few OB topics matter more to employees and managers than motivation. How many times have you wondered to yourself, "Why can't I get myself going today?" Or how many times have you looked at a friend or co-worker and wondered, "Why are they working so slowly right now?" Both of these questions are asking about "motivation," which is a derivation of the Latin word for movement, *movere*.[5] Those Latin roots nicely capture the meaning of motivation, as motivated employees simply move faster and longer than unmotivated employees. More formally, **motivation** is defined as a set of energetic forces that originates both within and outside an employee, initiates work-related effort, and determines its direction, intensity, and persistence.[6] Motivation is a critical consideration because effective job performance often requires high levels of both ability and motivation (see Chapter 4 on personality, cultural values, and ability for more discussion of such issues).[7]

motivation
A set of energetic forces that determine the direction, intensity, and persistence of an employee's work effort

The first part of our motivation definition illustrates that motivation is not one thing but rather a set of distinct forces. Some of those forces are internal to the employee, such as a sense of purpose or confidence, whereas others are external to the employee, such as the goals or incentives an employee is given. The next part of that definition illustrates that motivation determines a number of facets of an employee's work effort. These facets are summarized in Figure 7-1, which depicts a scenario in which your boss has given you an assignment to work on. Motivation determines *what* employees do at a given moment—the direction in which their effort is channelled. Every moment of the workday offers choices between task and citizenship sorts of actions or withdrawal and counterproductive sorts of actions. When it's 3:00 p.m. on a Thursday, do you keep working on the assignment your boss gave you, or do you send e-mails or surf the web for a while? Once the direction of effort has been decided, motivation goes on to determine *how hard* an employee works—the intensity of effort—and *for how long*—the persistence of effort. We all have friends or co-workers who work extremely hard for, say, 5 minutes. We also have friends or co-workers who work extremely long hours but always seem to be functioning at half-speed. Neither of those groups of people would be described as extremely motivated.

FIGURE 7-1

Motivation and Effort

MOTIVATION DETERMINES THE . . .

DIRECTION of Effort	INTENSITY of Effort	PERSISTENCE of Effort
What are you going to do right now?	***How hard are you going to work on it?***	***How long are you going to work on it?***
☑ The assignment your boss gave you yesterday	As hard as you can, or only at half-speed?	For five hours or five minutes?
☐ Send e-mails to your friends		
☐ Surf the web for a while		

As the chapter-opening example illustrates, organizations are always on the lookout for new and better ways to motivate their employees. These days, however, those discussions are more likely to focus on a concept called **engagement**. You can think of engagement as a contemporary synonym, more or less, for high levels of intensity and persistence in work effort. Employees who are "engaged" completely invest themselves and their energies into their jobs.[8] Outwardly, engaged employees devote a lot of energy to their jobs, striving as hard as they can to take initiative and get the job done.[9] Inwardly, engaged employees focus a great deal of attention and concentration on their work, sometimes becoming so absorbed, involved, and interested in their tasks that they lose track of time (see Chapter 5 on job satisfaction for more discussion of such issues).[10] Many companies attempt to measure engagement on their annual employee surveys, often by assessing factors believed to foster intense and persistent work effort.[11] One recent survey suggests that only 30 percent of employees are engaged—a percentage that has held fairly steady for a decade.[12] Given those numbers, it's not surprising that a recent survey of human resources executives indicated an increased emphasis on improving engagement levels.[13] That emphasis is critical, as research suggests that low levels of engagement can be contagious, crossing over from one employee to another.[14] To get a glimpse of a disengaged hero, see our ***OB on Screen*** feature.

engagement
A widely used term in contemporary workplaces that has different meanings depending on the context; most often refers to motivation, but can refer to affective commitment

OB ON SCREEN

The Dark Knight Rises

Bruce Wayne: *The Batman wasn't needed anymore. We won.*

Jim Gordon: *The Batman has to come back.*

Bruce Wayne: *What if he doesn't exist anymore?*

With those words, Bruce Wayne (Christian Bale) reveals a crisis of motivation in *The Dark Knight Rises* (Dir. Christopher Nolan, Warner Bros., 2012). It's been eight long years since the Batman defeated the Joker during the events of *The Dark Knight*. In that time, the streets of Gotham have been cleaned up—the war on crime has been won. No longer needed by those he'd sworn to protect, the Batman has faded from view, taking his alter ego with him. As a frail and reclusive Bruce explains to his loyal butler, Alfred (Michael Caine), "There's nothing out there for me." "But you're not living, you're just waiting," Alfred shoots back. "Hoping for things to go bad again."

© Warner Bros./Photofest

This being Gotham, things were indeed starting to go bad again. A mercenary named Bane was planning something deep within the sewers of the city, shooting Police Commissioner Jim Gordon when he got too close. Would Bane's plot give Bruce a sense of purpose again—would it motivate him to reclaim his cape and cowl? As Bruce wrestles with that possibility and decides to visit Gordon in the hospital, he detours for his own checkup. "There is no cartilage in your knee, and not much of any use in your elbows or your shoulders," notes the doctor, a few floors from where Gordon is recovering. Could Bruce even still *be* Batman in his condition?

If the eventual battle with Bane didn't ease all of Bruce's doubts about his strength, it did convince him that he was needed once again. Defeating Bane would take every ounce of his motivation but he was willing to try. Even as his new ally, Selina Kyle (Anne Hathaway) pleads, "Come with me.... Save yourself.... You don't owe these people any more.... You've given them everything," a now reengaged Batman responds simply, "Not everything. Not yet."

WHY ARE SOME EMPLOYEES MORE MOTIVATED THAN OTHERS?

There are a number of theories and concepts that attempt to explain why some employees are more motivated (or engaged) than others. The sections that follow review those theories and concepts in some detail. Most of them are relevant to each of the effort facets described in Figure 7-1. However, some are uniquely suited to explaining the direction of effort, whereas others do a better job of explaining the intensity and persistence of effort.

Expectancy Theory

What makes you decide to direct your effort to work assignments rather than taking a break or wasting time? Or what makes you decide to be a "good citizen" by helping out a colleague or attending some optional company function? **Expectancy theory** describes the cognitive process that employees go through to make choices among different voluntary responses.[15] Drawing on earlier models from psychology, expectancy theory argues that employee behaviour is directed toward pleasure and away from pain or, more generally, toward certain outcomes and away from others.[16] How do employees make the choices that take them in the "right direction"? The theory suggests that our choices depend on three specific beliefs based in our past learning and experience: expectancy, instrumentality, and valence. These are summarized in Figure 7-2. Let's review each of them in turn.

FIGURE 7-2

Expectancy Theory

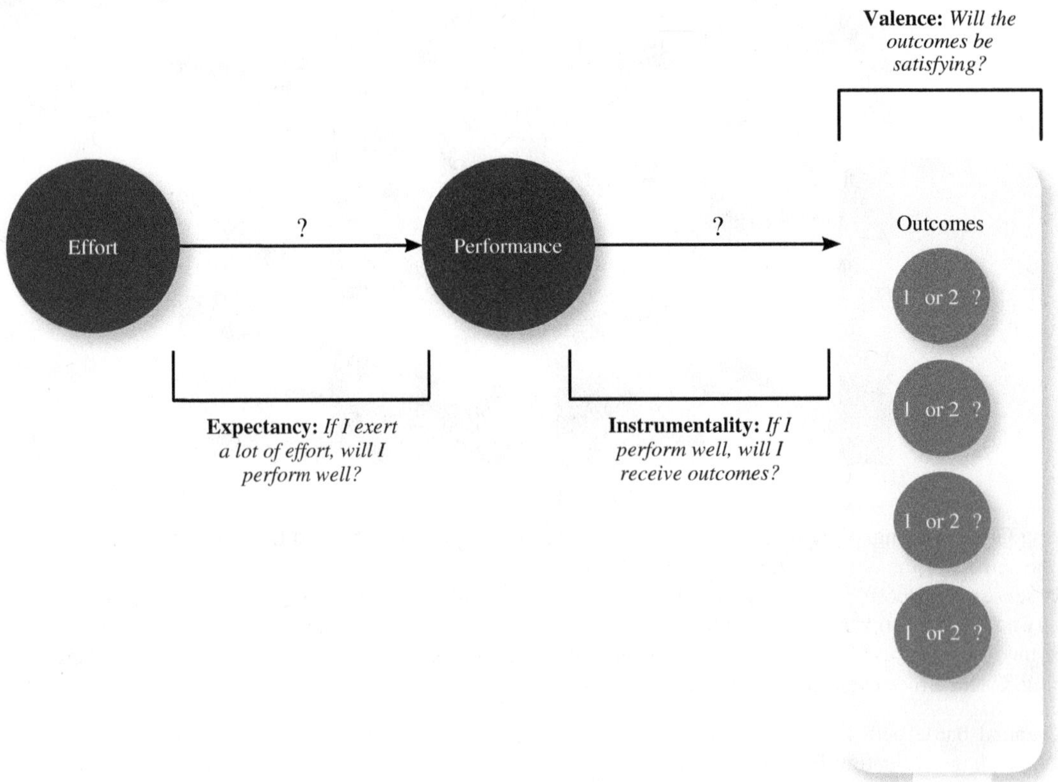

Source: Adapted from V.H. Vroom, *Work and Motivation* (New York: Wiley, 1964).

expectancy theory
A theory that describes the cognitive process employees go through to make choices among different voluntary responses

7.2 What three beliefs help determine work effort, according to expectancy theory?

Expectancy **Expectancy** represents the belief that exerting a high level of effort will result in the successful performance of some task. More technically, expectancy is a subjective probability, ranging from 0 (no chance!) to 1 (a mortal lock!) that a specific amount of effort will result in a specific level of performance (abbreviated $E \rightarrow P$). Think of a task at which you're not particularly good, such as writing romantic poetry. You may not be very motivated at that task because you don't believe that your effort, no matter how hard you try, will result in a poem that "moves" your significant other. As another example, you'll be more motivated to work on the assignment described in Figure 7-1 if you're confident that trying hard will allow you to complete it successfully.

expectancy
The belief that exerting a high level of effort will result in successful performance on some task

What factors shape our expectancy for a particular task? One of the most critical is **self-efficacy**, defined as the belief that a person has the capabilities needed to execute the behaviours required for success.[17] Think of self-efficacy as a kind of self-confidence or a task-specific version of self-esteem.[18] Employees who feel more "efficacious" (i.e., self-confident) with regard to a particular task will tend to perceive higher levels of expectancy—and therefore be more likely to choose to exert high levels of effort. Why do some employees have higher self-efficacy for a given task than other employees? Figure 7-3 can help explain such differences.

self-efficacy
The belief that a person has the capabilities needed to perform the behaviours required on some task

When employees consider efficacy levels for a given task, they first consider their *past accomplishments*—the degree to which they have succeeded or failed in similar sorts of tasks in the past.[19] They also consider *vicarious experiences* by taking into account their observations and discussions with others who have performed such tasks.[20] Self-efficacy is also dictated by *verbal persuasion*, because friends, co-workers, and leaders can persuade employees that they can "get the job done." Finally, efficacy is dictated by *emotional cues*, in that feelings of fear or anxiety can create doubts about task accomplishment, whereas pride and enthusiasm can bolster confidence levels.[21] Taken together, these efficacy sources shape analyses of how difficult the task requirements are and how adequate an employee's personal and situational resources will prove to be.[22] They also explain the content of most pre-game speeches offered by coaches before the big game; such speeches commonly include references to past victories (past accomplishments), pep talks about how good the team can be (verbal persuasion), and cheers to rally the troops (emotional cues).

FIGURE 7-3

Sources of Self-Efficacy

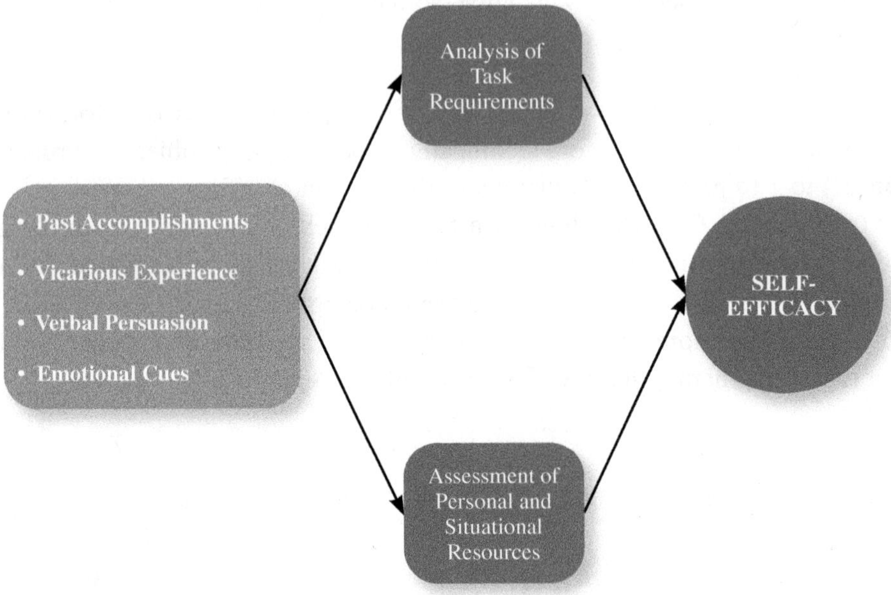

Sources: Adapted from A. Bandura, "Self-Efficacy: Toward a Unifying Theory of Behavioral Change," *Psychological Review* 84 (1977), pp. 191–215; and M.E. Gist and T.R. Mitchell, "Self-Efficacy: A Theoretical Analysis of Its Determinants and Malleability," *Academy of Management Review* 17 (1992), pp. 183–211.

Instrumentality **Instrumentality** represents the belief that successful performance will result in some outcome(s).[23] More technically, instrumentality is a set of subjective probabilities, each ranging from 0 (no chance!) to 1 (a mortal lock!) that successful performance will bring a set of outcomes (abbreviated $P \rightarrow O$). The term "instrumentality" makes sense when you consider the meaning of the adjective "instrumental." We say something is "instrumental" when it helps attain something else—for example, reading this chapter will be instrumental in your getting a good grade in an OB class (at least, we hope so!).[24] Unfortunately, evidence indicates that many employees don't perceive high levels of instrumentality in their workplace. One survey of more than 10,000 employees revealed that only 35 percent viewed performance as the key driver of their pay.[25] By comparison, 60 percent viewed seniority as the key driver.

instrumentality
The belief that successful performance will result in some outcome or outcomes

Although organizations often struggle to foster instrumentality in the best of times, linking performance to outcomes is even more difficult during an economic downturn. One human resources consulting firm estimated that 31 percent of organizations froze pay in 2009, with that estimate falling to 13 percent in 2010, and 2 percent in 2011.[26] 3M, the maker of Post-it notes and Scotch tape, is one example of a firm that is only now unfreezing its pay. Executives at 3M indicated that pay increases would return after being frozen since 2009. Summarizes one human resources consultant, "There really is a mindset that you can only do that for so long."[27] As the economy improves, good performers will begin to expect rewards, and may look elsewhere if their company does not provide them.

Valence **Valence** reflects the anticipated value of the outcomes associated with performance (abbreviated V).[28] Valences can be positive ("I would prefer *having* outcome X to not having it"), negative ("I would prefer *not having* outcome X to having it"), or zero ("I'm bored ... are we still talking about outcome X?"). Salary increases, bonuses, and more informal rewards are typical examples of "positively valenced" outcomes, whereas disciplinary actions, demotions, and terminations are typical examples of "negatively valenced" outcomes.[29] In this way, employees are more motivated when successful performance helps them attain attractive outcomes, such as bonuses, while helping them avoid unattractive outcomes, such as disciplinary actions. What exactly makes some outcomes more "positively valenced" than others? In general, outcomes are deemed more attractive when they help satisfy needs. **Needs** can be defined as cognitive groupings or clusters of outcomes that are viewed as having critical psychological or physiological consequences.[30]

valence
The anticipated value of the outcomes(s) associated with successful performance

needs
Groupings or clusters of outcomes viewed as having critical psychological or physiological consequences

Scholars such as Abraham Maslow have long recognized that human needs are important for understanding why people are drawn to different outcomes.[31] Maslow proposed that human needs arrange themselves in a hierarchy of relative prepotency, meaning that when one need level has been satisfied, outcomes associated with the next-highest-level need will become attractive. Let's consider how this might work to affect the valence. Maslow proposed that the most fundamental human needs are physiological in nature, such as our desire for food, water, and sex. When our psychological needs go unsatisfied, little else matters, and the outcomes associated with satisfaction of these basic needs will be viewed as most attractive of all.[32] Once powerful physiological needs have been satiated, Maslow proposed that our need to be safe from real or imagined dangers will move to the fore, effectively making outcomes associated with safety the most attractive.[33] If both the physiological and the safety needs are fairly well gratified, Maslow proposed that our need for love and belongingness will take precedence, and the outcomes associated with satisfaction of these needs will be viewed as most attractive.[34] Once love and belongingness needs have been gratified, the desire for a stable and positive evaluation of oneself becomes important. Such *esteem needs* include things like the desire for achievement, personal growth, independence, reputation (prestige), and personal importance (status). When esteem needs are dominant, outcomes that provide satisfaction of them will be viewed as "positively valenced."[35] Finally, even if esteem needs are satisfied, we may still experience discontent. The need for self-actualization reflects our innate desire for self-fulfillment—that is, to become more and more of what one is, to become everything one is capable of becoming.[36] When this need state is present, outcomes that help people experience a sense of self-actualization will be most attractive. [37]

Over the years, our view of needs has changed. Clayton Alderfer proposed, for instance, that Maslow's five need levels might be effectively reduced to three basic needs: for existence (physiological and safety), for relatedness (love and belongingness), and for growth (esteem and self-actualization).[38] One increasingly popular need framework suggests that people are drawn to goals and outcomes that lead to the satisfaction of three innate psychological needs: for competence, for autonomy, and for relatedness.[39] The implications for valence, and what we find attractive at any given time, should be evident. For example, an employee with a strong need to feel competent and to experience growth likely will find an opportunity to take challenging training more attractive than one to socialize with co-workers. Note that the higher positive valence associated with a "growth opportunity" outcome, in comparison to a "social opportunity" outcome, would likely be reversed if the employee's need for relatedness were stronger than her need for growth.

Table 7-1 describes many of the needs commonly studied in OB.[40] The terms and labels assigned to those needs often vary, so the table includes those we have used here alternative ones that might sometimes be encountered.

TABLE 7-1

Commonly Studied Needs in OB

Need Label	Alternative Labels	Description
Existence	Physiological, safety	The need for the food, shelter, safety, and protection required for human existence
Relatedness	Love, belongingness	The need to create and maintain lasting, positive interpersonal relationships
Control	Autonomy, responsibility	The need to be able to predict and control one's future
Esteem	Self-regard, growth	The need to hold a high evaluation of oneself and to feel effective and respected by others
Meaning	Self-actualization	The need to perform tasks that one cares about and that appeal to one's ideals and sense of purpose

Sources: Adapted from E.L. Deci and R.M Ryan, "The 'What' and 'Why' of Goal Pursuits: Human Needs and the Self-Determination of Behavior," *Psychological Inquiry* 11 (2000), pp. 227–68; R. Cropanzano, Z.S. Byrne, D.R. Bobocel, and D.R. Rupp, "Moral Virtues, Fairness Heuristics, Social Entities, and Other Denizens of Organizational Justice," *Journal of Vocational Behavior* 58 (2001), pp. 164–209; A.H. Maslow, "A Theory of Human Motivation," *Psychological Review* 50 (1943), pp. 370–96; and C.P. Alderfer, "An Empirical Test of a New Theory of Human Needs," *Organizational Behavior and Human Performance* 4 (1969), pp. 142–75.

Table 7-2 lists some of the most commonly considered outcomes in studies of motivation. Outcomes deemed particularly attractive are likely to satisfy a number of different needs. For example, praise can signal that interpersonal bonds are strong (satisfying relatedness needs) while also signalling competence (satisfying esteem needs). Note also that some of the outcomes in the table, such as bonuses, promotions, and praise, result from other people acknowledging successful performance. These outcomes foster **extrinsic motivation**—motivation controlled by some contingency that depends on task performance.[41] Other outcomes in the table, such as enjoyment, interestingness, and personal expression, are self-generated, originating in the mere act of performing the task. These outcomes foster **intrinsic motivation**—motivation felt when task performance serves as its own reward.[42] Taken together, extrinsic and intrinsic motivation represent an employee's "total motivation" level.

extrinsic motivation

Desire to put forth work effort due to some contingency that depends on task performance

intrinsic motivation

Desire to put forth work effort due to the sense that task performance serves as its own reward

TABLE 7-2

Extrinsic and Intrinsic Outcomes

Extrinsic Outcomes	Intrinsic Outcomes
Pay	Enjoyment
Bonuses	Interestingness
Promotions	Accomplishment
Benefits and perks	Knowledge gain
Spot awards	Skill development
Praise	Personal expression
Job security	(Lack of) Boredom
Support	(Lack of) Anxiety
Free time	(Lack of) Frustration
(Lack of) Disciplinary actions	
(Lack of) Demotions	
(Lack of) Terminations	

Sources: Adapted from E.E. Lawler III and J.L. Suttle, "Expectancy Theory and Job Behavior," *Organizational Behavior and Human Performance* 9 (1973), pp. 482–503; J. Galbraith and L.L. Cummings, "An Empirical Investigation of the Motivational Determinants of Task Performance: Interactive Effects Between Instrumentality–Valence and Motivation–Ability," *Organizational Behavior and Human Performance* 2 (1967), pp. 237–57; E. McAuley, S. Wraith, and T.E. Duncan, "Self-Efficacy, Perceptions of Success, and Intrinsic Motivation for Exercise," *Journal of Applied Social Psychology* 21 (1991), pp. 139–55; A.S. Waterman, S.J. Schwartz, E. Goldbacher, H. Green, C. Miller, and S. Philip, "Predicting the Subjective Experience of Intrinsic Motivation: The Roles of Self-Determination, the Balance of Challenges and Skills, and Self-Realization Values," *Personality and Social Psychology Bulletin* 29 (2003), pp. 1447–58.

You might wonder which of the outcomes in the table are most attractive to employees. That's a difficult question to answer, given that different employees emphasize different needs. However, two things are clear. First, the attractiveness of many rewards varies across cultures. One expert on cross-cultural recognition programs notes, "Different cultures have different motivators. In fact, giving a gift card could be extremely insulting because it could be saying that you are bribing them to do what they already do."[43] Good performance on a project in a Canadian company might earn a trip to Las Vegas. However, trips to alcohol and gambling-intensive areas are taboo in parts of Asia or the Middle East.[44] A better award in India would be tickets to a newly released movie or a moped for navigating congested areas.[45]

Second, research suggests that employees underestimate how powerful a motivator pay is to them.[46] When employees rank the importance of extrinsic and intrinsic outcomes, they often put pay in fifth or sixth place. However, research studies show that financial incentives often have a stronger impact on motivation than other sorts of outcomes.[47] One reason is that money is relevant to many of the needs in Table 7-1. For example, money can help satisfy existence needs by helping employees buy food, afford a house, and save for retirement. However, money also conveys a sense of esteem, as it signals that employees are competent and well regarded.[48] In fact, research suggests that people differ in how they view the **meaning of money**—the degree to which they view money as having symbolic, not just economic, value.[49] The symbolic value of money can be summarized in at least three dimensions: achievement (i.e., money symbolizes success), respect (i.e., money brings respect in one's community), and freedom (i.e., money provides opportunity).[50]

meaning of money
The idea that money can have symbolic value (e.g., achievement, respect, freedom) in addition to economic value

Who's more likely to view money from these more symbolic perspectives? Some research suggests that men are more likely to view money as representing achievement, respect, and freedom than are women.[51] Research also suggests that employees with higher salaries are more likely to view money in achievement-related terms.[52] Younger employees are less likely to view money in a positive light, relative to older employees.[53] Differences in education do not appear to impact the meaning of money, however.[54]

How do you view the meaning of money? See our ***OB Assessments*** feature at the end of the chapter to find out.

Motivational Force According to expectancy theory, the direction of effort is dictated by three beliefs: expectancy ($E \rightarrow P$), instrumentality ($P \rightarrow O$), and valence (V). More specifically, the theory suggests that the total "motivational force" to perform a given action can be described using the following formula:[55]

- Motivational Force $= E \rightarrow P \times \Sigma[(P \rightarrow O) \times V]$

The Σ symbol in the equation signifies that instrumentalities and valences are judged with various outcomes in mind, and motivation increases as successful performance is linked to more and more attractive outcomes. Note the significance of the multiplication signs in the formula: Motivational force equals zero if any one of the three beliefs is zero. In other words, it doesn't matter how confident you are if performance doesn't result in any outcomes. Similarly, it doesn't matter how well performance is evaluated and rewarded if you don't believe you can perform well.

Goal Setting Theory

So, returning to the choice shown in Figure 7-1, let's say that you feel confident you can perform well on the assignment your boss gave you and that you also believe successful performance will bring valued outcomes. Now that you've chosen to direct your effort to that assignment, two critical questions remain: How hard will you work, and for how long? To shed some more light on these questions, you stop by your boss's office and ask her, "So, when exactly do you need this done?" After thinking about it for a while, she concludes, "Just do your best." After returning to your desk, you realize that you're still not sure how much to focus on the assignment, or how long you should work on it before turning to something else.

7.3 What two qualities make goals strong predictors of task performance, according to goal setting theory?

Goal setting theory views goals as the primary drivers of the intensity and persistence of effort.[56] Goals are defined as the objective or aim of an action and typically refer to attaining a specific standard of proficiency, often within a specified time limit.[57] More specifically, the theory argues that assigning employees **specific and difficult goals** will result in higher levels of performance than assigning no goals, easy goals, or "do your best" goals.[58] Why are specific and difficult goals more effective than do-your-best ones? After all, doesn't "your best" imply the highest possible levels of effort? The reason is that few people know what their "best" is (and even fewer managers can tell whether employees are truly doing their "best"). Assigning specific and difficult goals gives people a number to shoot for—a "measuring stick" that can be used to tell them how hard they need to work and for how long. So if your boss had said, "Have the assignment on my desk by 10:30 a.m. on Tuesday, with no more than two mistakes," you would have known exactly how hard to work and for how long.

goal setting theory

A theory that views goals as the primary drivers of the intensity and persistence of effort

specific and difficult goals

Goals that stretch an employee to perform at his or her maximum level while still staying within the boundaries of his or her ability

Of course, a key question then becomes "What's a difficult goal?" Figure 7-4 illustrates the predicted relationship between goal difficulty and task performance. When goals are easy, there's no reason to work your hardest or your longest, so task effort is lower. As goals move from moderate to difficult, the intensity and persistence of effort become maximized. At some point, however, the limits of a person's ability get reached, and self-efficacy begins to diminish. Also at that point, goals move from difficult to impossible, and employees feel somewhat helpless when attempting to achieve them. In turn, effort and performance inevitably decline. So a difficult goal is one that stretches employees to perform at their maximum level while staying within the boundaries of their ability.

FIGURE 7-4

Goal Difficulty and Task Performance

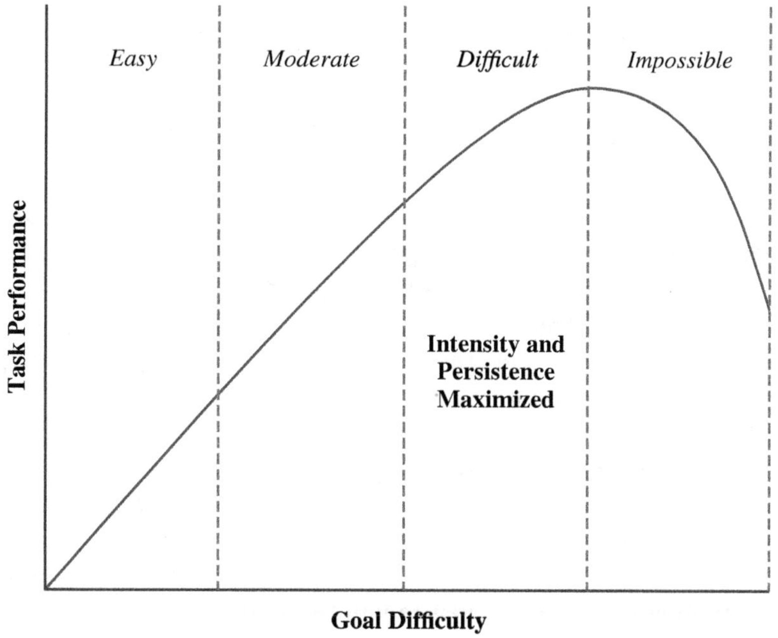

Source: Adapted from E.A. Locke and G.P. Latham, *A Theory of Goal Setting and Task Performance* (Englewood Cliffs, NJ: Prentice Hall, 1990).

The effects of specific and difficult goals on task performance have been tested in several hundred studies using many kinds of settings and tasks. A sampling of those settings and tasks is shown in Table 7-3.[59] Overall, around 90 percent of the goal setting studies support the beneficial effects of specific and difficult goals on task performance.[60] Although some of the settings and tasks shown in the table are unlikely to be major parts of your career (archery, handball, LEGO construction), others should be very relevant to the readers (and authors!) of this book (managing and supervision, studying, faculty research). Then again, who wouldn't want a career in LEGO construction?

TABLE 7-3

Settings and Tasks Used in Goal Setting Research

Settings and Tasks	
Air traffic control	Management training
Archery	Marine recruit performance
Arithmetic	Maze learning
Beverage consumption	Mining
Chess	Proofreading
Computer games	Production and manufacturing
Course work	Puzzles
Energy conservation	Safety behaviours
Exercise	Sales
Faculty research	Scientific and R&D work
Juggling	Sit-ups
LEGO construction	Studying
Logging	Weight lifting
Managing and supervision	Weight loss

Source: Adapted from E.A. Locke and G.P. Latham, *A Theory of Goal Setting and Task Performance* (Englewood Cliffs, NJ: Prentice Hall, 1990).

Why exactly do specific and difficult assigned goals have such positive effects? Figure 7-5 presents goal setting theory in more detail to understand that question better.[61] We know that the effects of an assigned goal on an individual's effort level, persistence (i.e., effort over time), and task strategizing will only happen if the assigned goal is internalized as a personal goal. The motivational logic follows the old proverb "You can lead a horse to water but you can't make it drink." What exactly does this mean? Well, according to the proverb, the critical motivational factor is what the horse *intends* to do; and the same is true for people. Thus, to motivate someone using this approach, what needs to change are the goals people set for themselves. It is these **self-set goals**—which people use to monitor their own task progress—that have been shown to drive motivation and behaviour.[62] Goal setting works well when the assigned goal alters the level of the self-set (or personal) goal. If assigned goals are unable to change internal goals, motivation and performance will be unaffected.

self-set goals
The internalized goals that people use to monitor their own progress

FIGURE 7-5

Goal Setting Theory

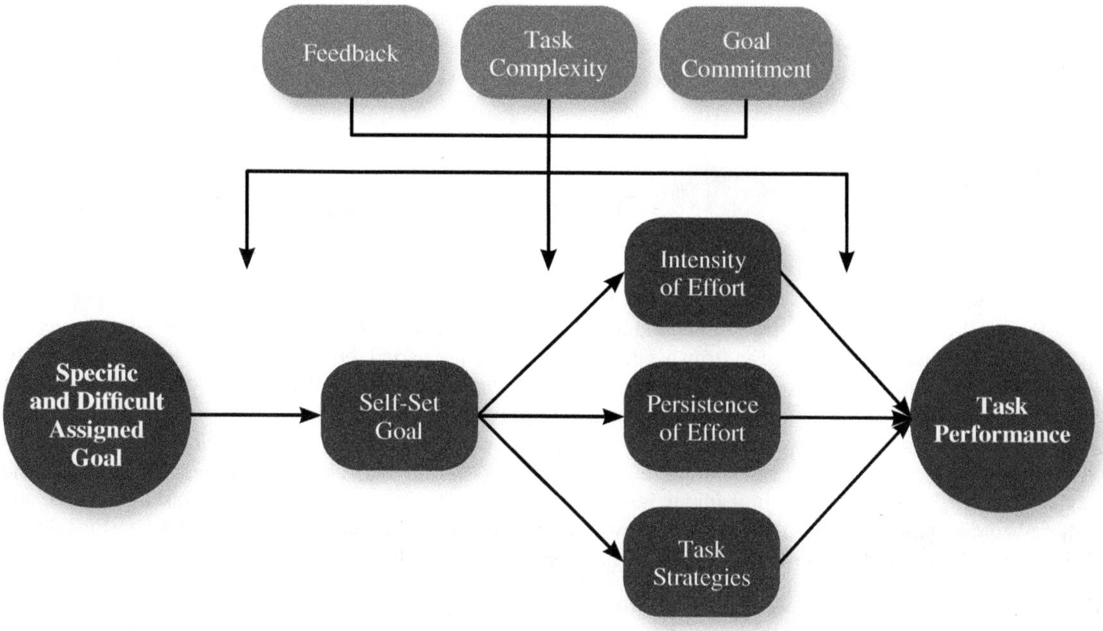

Sources: Adapted from E.A. Locke and G.P. Latham, *A Theory of Goal Setting and Task Performance* (Englewood Cliffs, NJ: Prentice Hall, 1990); E.A. Locke and G.P. Latham, "Building a Practically Useful Theory of Goal Setting and Task Motivation: A 35-Year Odyssey," *American Psychologist* 57 (2002), pp. 705–17; and G.P. Latham, "Motivate Employee Performance Through Goal-Setting," in *Blackwell Handbook of Principles of Organizational Behavior*, ed. E.A. Locke (Malden, MA: Blackwell, 2000), pp. 107–19.

Okay, assuming an individual has internalized a specific and difficult assigned goal as her self-set goal, then what? From Figure 7-5, we know that internal goals mobilize energy and effort levels. When goals are easy, not much effort is required to be successful. However, as self-set goals become more difficult, the intensity of effort has to increase to reach the desired performance level. In addition to affecting effort intensity, we know that wanting to reach a specific and difficult goal causes people to persist at tasks even when they experience difficulties or setbacks. Finally, we know that having a specific and difficult self-set goal triggers people to think about and consider different ways of reaching it—especially as goals get harder. What we know is that people who have hard, self-set goals tend to spend more time developing task strategies than those who have easy goals. Put differently, assigned goals can motivate employees to work both harder and smarter.

Figure 7-5 also includes three variables that specify when assigned goals will have stronger or weaker effects on task performance. In the jargon of theory diagrams, these variables are "moderators." Rather than directly affecting other variables in the diagram, moderators affect the strength of the relationships between variables. One moderator is **feedback**, which consists of updates on employee progress toward goal attainment.[63] Imagine being challenged to beat a friend's score on a video game but having your own score hidden as you played. How would you know how hard to try? Another moderator is **task complexity**, which reflects how complicated the information and actions involved in a task are, and how much the task changes.[64] In general, the effects of specific and difficult goals are almost twice as strong on simple tasks as on complex tasks, though the effects of goals remain beneficial even in complex cases.[65]

feedback
In goal setting theory, progress updates on work goals

task complexity
The degree to which the information and actions needed to complete a task are complicated

OB RESEARCH IN CANADA

Dr. Travor Brown is professor of labour relations and human resources management in the Faculty of Business Administration at Memorial University of Newfoundland. Before moving to St. John's, Newfoundland, Dr. Brown earned his Ph.D. at the University of Toronto. Dr. Brown's research interests are varied, but he has done a lot of work to advance knowledge of goal setting theory and how this motivational technique can be used to improve training effectiveness. Specifically, his work has looked at how best to set goals to improve learning processes (Chapter 9), teamwork behaviour (Chapter 11), and leadership development (Chapter 13). Asked how he got interested in the field, Dr. Brown replied, "I was a former competitive swimmer and a swim coach. The sports world's focus on coaching, development, and the inherent role of goal setting sparked my initial interest in organizational behaviour and remains today as I am just finishing my role as past president of Swimming Newfoundland & Labrador. As I often joke with my students, I have never left the coaching world—just moved from the aquatic environment to the workplace!"

Dr. Brown has published numerous articles in prestigious scientific journals, and has presented his work at Canadian, U.S., and international conferences. His academic background is coupled with extensive industry experience. He worked in the telecommunications and manufacturing sectors prior to completing his Ph.D. at the University of Toronto and remains active in the practitioner community. You can look him up at www.business.mun.ca/why-us/meet-our-people/faculty-instructor-profiles/travor-brown.php.

Courtesy of Dr. Travor Brown

The final moderator shown in Figure 7-5 is **goal commitment**, defined as the degree to which a person accepts a goal and is determined to try to reach it.[66] When goal commitment is high, assigning specific and difficult goals will have significant benefits for task performance; when it is low, those effects will be much weaker.[67] The importance of commitment raises the question of how best to foster it when assigning goals to employees. Table 7-4 summarizes some of the most powerful strategies for fostering goal commitment, which range from rewards to supervisory support to employee participation.[68]

goal commitment
The degree to which a person is determined to reach the goal

TABLE 7-4

Strategies for Fostering Goal Commitment

Strategy	Description
Rewards	Tie goal achievement to the receipt of monetary or non-monetary rewards.
Publicity	Publicize the goal to significant others and co-workers to create some social pressure to attain it.
Support	Provide supportive supervision to aid employees if they struggle to attain the goal.
Participation	Collaborate on setting the specific proficiency level and due date for a goal so that the employee feels a sense of ownership of the goal.
Resources	Provide the resources needed to attain the goal and remove any constraints that might hold back task efforts.

Sources: Adapted from J.R. Hollenbeck and H.J. Klein, "Goal Commitment and the Goal-Setting Process: Problems, Prospects, and Proposals for Future Research," *Journal of Applied Psychology* 72 (1987), pp. 212–20; H.J. Klein, M.J. Wesson, J.R. Hollenbeck, and B.J. Alge, "Goal Commitment and the Goal-Setting Process: Conceptual Clarification and Empirical Synthesis," *Journal of Applied Psychology* 84 (1999), pp. 885–96; E.A. Locke, G.P. Latham, and M. Erez, "The Determinants of Goal Commitment," *Academy of Management Review* 13 (1988), pp. 23–29; G.P. Latham, "The Motivational Benefits of Goal-Setting," *Academy of Management Executive* 18 (2004), pp. 126–29.

Microsoft recently revised its use of goal setting principles in an effort to boost goal commitment and task performance.[69] The company had become concerned that employees viewed their goals as objectives they *hoped* to meet rather than objectives they were *committed* to meeting. Moreover, approximately 25–40 percent of employees were working under goals that were either not specific enough or not measurable enough to offer feedback. To combat these trends, managers are now trained to identify five to seven **S.M.A.R.T. goals** for each employee and to link rewards directly to goal achievement. The acronym, standing for Specific, Measurable, Achievable, Results-based, and Time-sensitive, summarizes many beneficial goal characteristics. (Although the acronym is a useful reminder, note that it omits the all-important characteristic "difficult.") Managers and employees at Microsoft participate jointly in the goal setting process, and managers offer support by suggesting task strategies that employees can use to achieve the goals. In this way, managers and employees come to understand the "how" of achievement, not just the "what."[70] For insights into how goal setting operates across cultures, see our ***OB Internationally*** feature.

S.M.A.R.T. goals

Specific, Measurable, Achievable, Results-based, Time-sensitive goals, which Microsoft managers are trained to encourage in employees

OB INTERNATIONALLY

Research in cross-cultural OB suggests that there are some "universals" when it comes to motivation. For example, interesting work, pay, achievement, and growth are billed as motivating forces whose importance does not vary across cultures. Of course, some motivation principles do vary in their effectiveness across cultures, including some of the strategies for fostering goal commitment.

Types of goals. Should goals be given on an individual or a group-wide basis? North American employees usually prefer to be given individual goals. In contrast, employees in other countries, including China and Japan, prefer to receive team goals.[71] This difference likely reflects the stronger emphasis on collective responsibility and cooperation in those cultures.

Rewards. Rewards tend to increase goal commitment across cultures, but cultures vary in the types of rewards that they value. North American employees prefer to have rewards allocated according to merit. In contrast, employees in other countries, including China, Japan, and Sweden, prefer that rewards be allocated equally across members of the work unit.[72] Employees in India prefer a third allocation strategy—doling out rewards according to need. These cultural differences show that nations differ in how they prioritize individual achievement, collective solidarity, and the welfare of others.

Participation. National culture also affects the importance of participation in setting goals. Research suggests that employees in North America are likely to accept assigned goals because the culture emphasizes hierarchical authority. In contrast, employees in Israel, which lacks a cultural emphasis on hierarchy, do not respond so well to assigned goals.[73] Instead, employees in Israel put a premium on participation in goal setting.

Feedback. Culture also influences how individuals respond when they receive feedback regarding goal progress. As with participation, research suggests that employees in North America are more likely to accept feedback, because they are comfortable with hierarchical authority relationships and have a strong desire to reduce uncertainty.[74] Other cultures, such as England, put less value on reducing uncertainty, making feedback less critical to them.

7.4 What does it mean to be equitably treated according to equity theory, and how do employees respond to inequity?

Equity Theory

Returning to our running example in Figure 7-1, imagine that at this point, you've decided to work on the assignment your boss gave you, and you've been told that it's due by Tuesday at 10:30 a.m. and can't have more than two mistakes in it. That's a specific and difficult goal, so your browser hasn't been launched in a while, and you haven't even thought about checking your e-mail. In short, you've been working very hard for a few hours, until the guy from across the hall pops his head in. You tell him what you're working on, and he nods sympathetically, saying, "Yeah, the boss gave me a similar assignment that sounds just as tough. I think she realized how tough it was, though, because she said I could use the company's playoff tickets if I finish it on time." Playoff tickets? Playoff tickets?? Looks like it's time to check that e-mail after all....

Unlike the first two theories, **equity theory** acknowledges that motivation doesn't just depend on your own beliefs and circumstances but also on what happens to *other people*.[75] More specifically, equity theory suggests that employees create a "mental ledger" of the outcomes (or rewards) they get from their job duties.[76] What outcomes might be part of your mental ledger? That's completely up to you and depends on what you find valuable, though Table 7-5 provides a listing of some commonly considered outcomes. Equity theory further suggests that employees create a mental ledger of the inputs (or contributions and investments) they bring to their job duties.[77] Again, the composition of your mental ledger is completely specific to you, but Table 7-5 provides a listing of some inputs that seem to matter to most employees.

equity theory

A theory that suggests that employees create a mental ledger of the outcomes they receive for their job inputs, relative to some comparison other

TABLE 7-5

Some Outcomes and Inputs Considered by Equity Theory

Outcomes	Inputs
Pay	Effort
Seniority benefits	Performance
Fringe benefits	Skills and abilities
Status symbols	Education
Satisfying supervision	Experience
Workplace perks	Training
Intrinsic rewards	Seniority

Source: Adapted from J.S. Adams, "Inequity in Social Exchange," in *Advances in Experimental Social Psychology*, Vol. 2, ed. L. Berkowitz (New York: Academic Press, 1965), pp. 267–99.

So what exactly do you do with these mental tallies of outcomes and inputs? Equity theory argues that you compare your ratio of outcomes and inputs to the ratio of some **comparison other**—some person who seems to provide an intuitive frame of reference for judging equity.[78] There are three general possibilities that can result from this "cognitive calculus," as shown in Figure 7-6. The first is that the ratio of outcomes to inputs is balanced between you and your comparison other. In this case, you feel a sense of equity, and are likely to maintain the intensity and persistence of your effort. In the example given above, this would have occurred if you had been offered playoff tickets like your colleague.

comparison other

Another person who provides a frame of reference for judging equity

The second possibility is that your ratio of outcomes to inputs is less than your comparison other's ratio. According to equity theory, any imbalance in ratios triggers **equity distress**—an internal tension that can only be alleviated by restoring balance to the ratios.[79] In an underreward case, the equity distress likely takes the form of negative emotions such as anger or envy. One way to stop feeling those emotions is to try to restore the balance in some way, and Figure 7-6 reveals two methods of doing so. You might be constructive and proactive by talking to your boss and explaining why you deserve better outcomes. Such actions would result in the growth of your outcomes, restoring balance to the ratio. Of course, anger often results in actions that are destructive rather than constructive, and research shows that feelings of underreward inequity are among the strongest predictors of counterproductive behaviours, such as employee theft (see Chapter 8 on trust, justice, and ethics for more on such issues).[80] Another means of restoring balance, more relevant to this chapter, is to shrink your inputs by lowering the intensity and persistence of effort. Remember, it's not the total outcomes or inputs that matter in equity theory—only the ratio.

equity distress
An internal tension that results from being overrewarded or underrewarded relative to some comparison other

FIGURE 7-6

Three Possible Outcomes of Equity Theory Comparisons

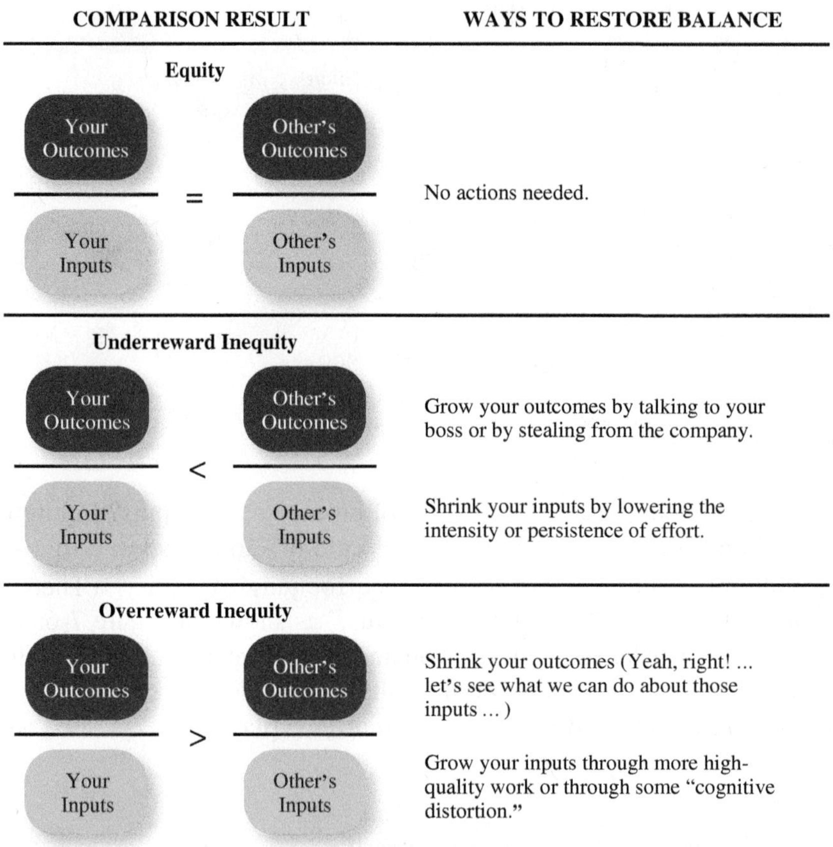

Source: Adapted from J.S. Adams, "Inequity in Social Exchange," in *Advances in Experimental Social Psychology*, Vol. 2, ed. L. Berkowitz (New York: Academic Press, 1965), pp. 267–99.

The third possibility is that your ratio of outcomes to inputs is greater than your comparison other's ratio. Equity distress again gets experienced, and the tension likely creates negative emotions such as guilt or anxiety. Balance could be restored by shrinking your outcomes (taking less money, giving something back to the comparison other), but the theory acknowledges that such actions are unlikely in most cases.[81] Instead, the more likely solution is to increase your inputs in some way. You could increase the intensity and persistence of your task effort or decide to engage in more "extra mile" citizenship behaviours. At some point though, there may not be enough hours in the day to increase your inputs any further. An alternative (and less labour-intensive) means of increasing your inputs is to simply rethink them—to reexamine your mental ledger to see if you may have "undersold" your true contributions. On second thought, you might tell yourself, maybe your education or seniority is more critical than you realized, or maybe your skills and abilities are more vital to the organization. This **cognitive distortion** allows you to restore balance mentally, without altering your behaviour in any way.

cognitive distortion

A reevaluation of the inputs an employee brings to a job, often occurring in response to equity distress

One other way of restoring balance, regardless of underreward or overreward circumstances, is not depicted in Figure 7-6: changing your comparison other. After all, we compare our "lots in life" to a variety of other individuals. Table 7-6 summarizes the different kinds of comparison others that can be used.[82] Some of those comparisons are **internal comparisons**, meaning that they refer to someone in the same company.[83] Others are **external comparisons**, meaning that they refer to someone in a different company. If any given comparison results in high levels of anger and envy or high levels of guilt and anxiety, the frame of reference may be shifted. In fact, research suggests that employees don't just compare themselves to one other person; instead, they make multiple comparisons to a variety of different others.[84] Although it may be possible to create a sort of "overall equity" judgment, research shows that people draw distinctions between the various equity comparisons shown in the table. For example, one study showed that job equity was the most powerful driver of citizenship behaviours, whereas occupational equity was the most powerful driver of employee withdrawal.[85]

internal comparisons

Comparing oneself to someone in your same company

external comparisons

Comparing oneself to someone in a different company

These mechanisms make it clear that judging equity is a very subjective process. Recent data from a Salary.com report highlight that very subjectivity. A survey of 1,500 employees revealed that 65 percent of the respondents planned to look for a new job in the next three months, 57 percent doing so because they felt underpaid. However, Salary.com estimated that only 19 percent of those workers really were underpaid, taking into account their relevant inputs and the current market conditions. In fact, it was estimated that 17 percent were actually being overpaid by their companies! On the one hand, that subjectivity is likely to be frustrating to most managers in charge of compensation. On the other hand, it's important to realize that the intensity and persistence of employees' effort is driven by their own equity perceptions, not anyone else's.

Some organizations grapple with concerns about equity by emphasizing pay secrecy. One survey indicated that 36 percent of companies explicitly discourage employees from discussing pay with their colleagues, and surveys also indicate that most employees approve of pay secrecy.[86] Is pay secrecy a good idea? Although it has not been the subject of much research, there appear to be pluses and minuses associated with pay secrecy. On the plus side, such policies may reduce conflict between employees while appealing to concerns about personal privacy. On the minus side, employees may respond to a lack of accurate information by guessing at equity levels, possibly perceiving more underpayment inequity than truly exists. In addition, the insistence on secrecy might cause employees to view the company with a sense of distrust (see Chapter 8 on trust, justice, and ethics for more about this issue).[87] How might these sorts of secrecy policies affect you as a student? See our ***OB for Students*** feature for a discussion of grade secrecy.

TABLE 7-6

Judging Equity with Different Comparison Others

Comparison Type	Description and Sample Survey Item
Job equity	Compare with others doing the same job in the same organization. Sample survey item: *Compared with others doing the same job as me in my company with similar education, seniority, and effort, I earn about:* ________
Company equity	Compare with others in the same organization doing substantially different jobs. Sample survey item: *Compared with others in my company on other jobs doing work that is similar in responsibility, skill, effort, education, and working condition required, I earn about:* ________
Occupational equity	Compare with others doing essentially the same job in other organizations. Sample survey item: *Compared with others doing my job in other companies in the area with similar education, seniority, and effort, I earn about:* ________
Educational equity	Compare with others who have attained the same education level. Sample survey item: *Compared with people I know with similar education and responsibility as me, I earn about:* ________
Age equity	Compare with others of the same age. Sample survey item: *Compared with those of my age, I earn about:* ________

40% less	30% less	20% less	10% less	About the same	10% more	20% more	30% more	40% more

Source: R.W. Scholl, E.A. Cooper, and J.F. McKenna, "Referent Selection in Determining Equity Perceptions: Differential Effects on Behavioral and Attitudinal Outcomes," *Personnel Psychology* 40 (1987), pp. 113–24. Copyright © 1987, John Wiley & Sons. Reprinted with permission.

7.5 What is psychological empowerment, and what four beliefs determine empowerment levels?

Psychological Empowerment

Now we return, one last time, to our running example in Figure 7-1. When last we checked in, your motivation levels had suffered because you learned your co-worker was offered the company's playoff tickets for successfully completing a similar assignment. As you browse the web in total "time-wasting mode," you begin thinking about all the reasons you hate working on this assignment. Aside from the issue of goals and rewards, you keep coming back to this issue: you would never have taken on this project *by choice*. Specifically, the project itself doesn't seem very meaningful, and you doubt it will have any real impact on the functioning of the organization.

OB FOR STUDENTS

Grades are one of the primary motivators for students, as more effort is needed to earn A's than C's in most classes. Think about your own motivation levels as a student—how much of that motivation is due to trying for a higher grade?

Now here's the question we want you to consider: What would happen to your motivation to learn if your grades became secret, or more specifically, if your school adopted a policy that prohibited you or your university from disclosing grades to recruiters? The rationale for grade secrecy policies is twofold. First, grade secrecy is believed to reduce competitiveness between students, fostering a more cohesive atmosphere within student cohorts. Second, grade secrecy is meant to allow students to take tougher, more challenging electives without worrying about their GPA.

So what would happen to your motivation levels if grade secrecy was instituted at your school? The more salient norm of secrecy might discourage you from sharing grades with your classmates, making it more difficult to judge the equity of your grades relative to those received by other students. Grade secrecy might also reduce the valence of the grades themselves, with an A losing some of its anticipated value relative to a B or C. If those effects occurred, motivation to learn would decline under a grade secrecy system.

Which side would you take in this debate?

Those sentiments signal a low level of **psychological empowerment**, which reflects an energy rooted in the belief that work tasks contribute to some larger purpose.[88] Psychological empowerment represents a form of intrinsic motivation, in that merely performing the work tasks provides a way of satisfying our needs for mastery, for autonomy and for relatedness,[89] supplying many of the intrinsic outcomes shown in Table 7-2. The concept of psychological empowerment has much in common with our discussion of "satisfaction with the work itself" in Chapter 5 on job satisfaction. That discussion illustrated that jobs with high levels of variety, significance, and autonomy can be intrinsically satisfying.[90] Models of psychological empowerment argue that a similar set of concepts can make work tasks intrinsically motivating. Four concepts are particularly important: meaningfulness, self-determination, competence, and impact.

psychological empowerment
An energy rooted in the belief that tasks are contributing to some larger purpose

Meaningfulness captures the value of a work goal or purpose, relative to a person's own ideals and passions.[91] When a task is relevant to a meaningful purpose, it becomes easier to concentrate on the task and get excited about it. You might even find yourself cutting other tasks short so you can devote more time to the meaningful one or thinking about the task outside of work hours.[92] In contrast, working on tasks that are not meaningful brings a sense of emptiness and detachment. As a result, you might need to mentally force yourself to keep working on the task. Managers can instill a sense of meaningfulness by articulating an exciting vision or purpose and fostering a non-cynical climate in which employees are free to express idealism and passion without criticism.[93] For their part, employees can build their own sense of meaningfulness by identifying and clarifying their own passions. Employees fortunate enough to be passionate about their work sometimes describe it as "a calling"—something they were born to do.[94]

meaningfulness
A psychological state reflecting one's feelings about work tasks, goals, and purposes, and the degree to which they contribute to society and fulfill one's ideals and passions

Self-determination reflects a sense of choice in the initiation and continuation of work tasks. Employees with high levels of self-determination can choose what tasks to work on, how to structure those tasks, and how long to pursue those tasks. That sense of self-determination is a strong driver of intrinsic motivation, because it allows employees to pursue activities that they themselves find meaningful and interesting.[95] Managers can instill a sense of self-determination in their employees by delegating work tasks, rather than micromanaging them, and by trusting employees to come up with their own approach to certain tasks.[96] For their part, employees can gain more self-determination by earning the trust of their bosses and negotiating for the latitude that comes with that increased trust.

self-determination
A sense of choice in the initiation and continuation of work tasks

Competence captures a person's belief in his or her capability to perform work tasks successfully.[97] Competence is identical to the self-efficacy concept reviewed previously in this chapter; employees with a strong sense of competence (or self-efficacy) believe they can execute the particular behaviours needed to achieve success at work. Competence brings with it a sense of pride and mastery that is itself intrinsically motivating. Managers can instill a sense of competence in their employees by providing opportunities for training and knowledge gain, expressing positive feedback, and providing challenges that are an appropriate match for employees' skill levels.[98] Employees can build their own competence by engaging in self-directed learning, seeking out feedback from their managers, and managing their own workloads.

competence
The capability to perform work tasks successfully

Impact reflects the sense that a person's actions "make a difference"—that progress is being made toward fulfilling some important purpose.[99] Phrases such as "moving forward," "being on track," and "getting there" convey a sense of impact.[100] The polar opposite of impact is "learned helplessness"—the sense that it doesn't matter what a person does, nothing will make a difference. Here, phrases such as "stuck in a rut," "at a standstill," or "going nowhere" become more relevant. Managers can instill a sense of impact by celebrating milestones along the journey to task accomplishment, particularly for tasks that span a long time frame.[101] Employees can attain a deeper sense of impact by building the collaborative relationships needed to speed task progress and initiating their own celebrations of "small wins" along the way.

impact
The sense that a person's actions "make a difference"—that progress is being made toward fulfilling some important purpose

Studies of generational trends point to the increasing interest of psychological empowerment as a motivating force. For example, one survey of 3,332 teens worldwide revealed that 78 percent viewed personal fulfillment as a key motivator.[102] There is also a sense that younger employees enter the workplace with higher expectations for the importance of their roles, the autonomy they'll be given, and the progress they'll make in their organizational careers. That trend is especially apparent in India, where the younger generation is coming of age in a time of unprecedented job opportunities due to the tech-services boom. MindTree, an IT consulting firm headquartered in New Jersey and Bangalore,

India, takes steps to prevent young employees from feeling "lost in a sea of people."[103] The company places new hires into "houses" with their own assembly space and work areas, providing opportunities for more personal attention and mentoring. Infosys, another IT consulting firm based in Bangalore, established a "Voice of Youth Council" that puts a dozen under-30 employees on its executive management committee. The committee gives younger employees the chance to impact the company's operations. Bela Gupta, the council's youngest member at 24 years of age, describes the experience as "very empowering."

Young employees at MindTree, an information technology consulting firm, are given mentoring and personal attention to build a sense of empowerment.

© AP Photo/Nama Bhojani

Summary: Why Are Some Employees More Motivated Than Others?

So what explains why some employees are more motivated than others? As is shown in Figure 7-7, answering that question requires considering all the energetic forces that initiate work-related effort, including expectancy theory concepts (expectancy, instrumentality, valence), the existence (or absence) of specific and difficult goals, perceptions of equity, and feelings of psychological empowerment. Unmotivated employees may simply lack confidence due to a lack of expectancy or competence or the assignment of an unachievable goal. Alternatively, such employees may feel their performance is not properly rewarded due to a lack of instrumentality, a lack of valence, or feelings of inequity. Finally, it may be that their work simply isn't challenging or intrinsically rewarding due to the assignment of easy or abstract goals or the absence of meaningfulness, self-determination, and impact.

FIGURE 7-7

Why Are Some Employees More Motivated Than Others?

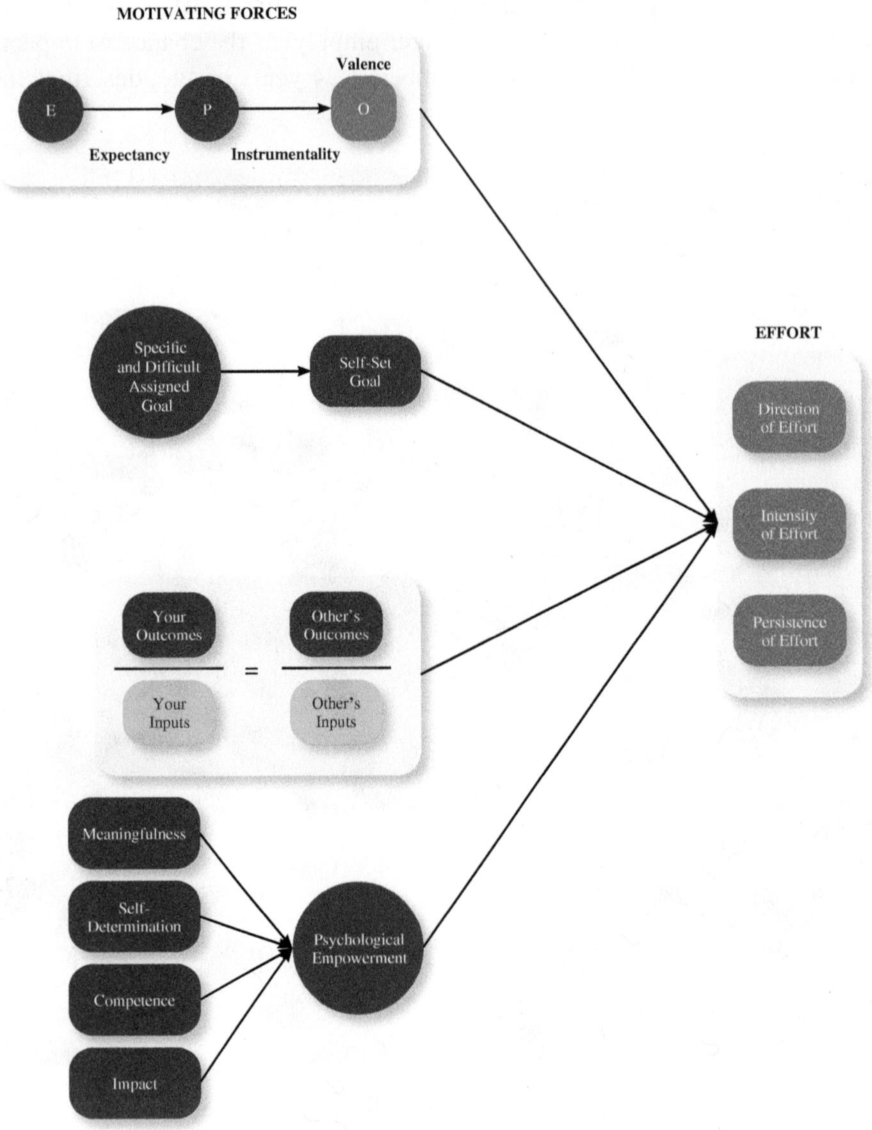

7.6 How does motivation affect job performance and organizational commitment?

HOW IMPORTANT IS MOTIVATION?

Does motivation have a significant impact on the two primary outcomes in our integrative model of OB—does it correlate with job performance and organizational commitment? Answering that question is somewhat complicated, because motivation is not just one thing but rather a set of energetic forces. Figure 7-8 summarizes the research evidence linking motivation to job performance and organizational commitment. The figure expresses the likely combined impact of those energetic forces on the two outcomes in our OB model.

FIGURE 7-8

Effects of Motivation on Performance and Commitment

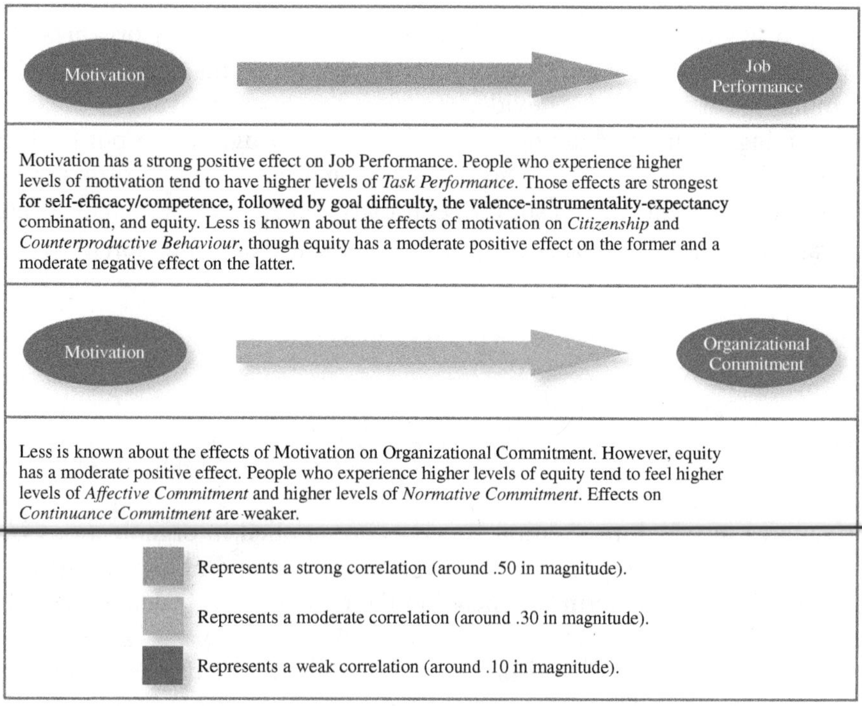

Motivation
Job Performance
Motivation has a strong positive effect on Job Performance. People who experience higher levels of motivation tend to have higher levels of *Task Performance*. Those effects are strongest for self-efficacy/competence, followed by goal difficulty, the valence-instrumentality-expectancy combination, and equity. Less is known about the effects of motivation on *Citizenship* and *Counterproductive Behaviour*, though equity has a moderate positive effect on the former and a moderate negative effect on the latter.
Motivation
Organizational Commitment
Less is known about the effects of Motivation on Organizational Commitment. However, equity has a moderate positive effect. People who experience higher levels of equity tend to feel higher levels of *Affective Commitment* and higher levels of *Normative Commitment*. Effects on *Continuance Commitment* are weaker.
Represents a strong correlation (around .50 in magnitude).
Represents a moderate correlation (around .30 in magnitude).
Represents a weak correlation (around .10 in magnitude).

Sources: Y. Cohen-Charash and P.E. Spector, "The Role of Justice in Organizations: A Meta-analysis," *Organizational Behavior and Human Decision Processes* 86 (2001), pp. 287–321; J.A. Colquitt, D.E. Conlon, M.J. Wesson, C.O.L.H. Porter, and K.Y. Ng, "Justice at the Millennium: A Meta-analytic Review of 25 Years of Organizational Justice Research," *Journal of Applied Psychology* 86 (2001), pp. 425–45; J.P. Meyer, D.J. Stanley, L. Herscovitch, and L. Topolnytsky, "Affective, Continuance, and Normative Commitment to the Organization: A Meta-analysis of Antecedents, Correlates, and Consequences," *Journal of Vocational Behavior* 61 (2002), pp. 20–52; A.D. Stajkovic and F. Luthans, "Self-Efficacy and Work-Related Performance: A Meta-analysis," *Psychological Bulletin* 124 (1998), pp. 240–61; W. Van Eerde and H. Thierry, "Vroom's Expectancy Models and Work-Related Criteria: A Meta-analysis," *Journal of Applied Psychology* 81 (1996), pp. 575–86; and R.E. Wood, A.J. Mento, and E.A. Locke, "Task Complexity as a Moderator of Goal Effects: A Meta-analysis," *Journal of Applied Psychology* 72 (1987), pp. 416–25.

Turning first to job performance, literally thousands of studies support the relationships between the various motivating forces and task performance. The motivating force with the strongest performance effect is self-efficacy/competence, because people who feel a sense of internal self-confidence tend to outperform those who doubt their capabilities.[104] Difficult goals are the second most powerful motivating force; people who receive such goals outperform the recipients of easy goals.[105] The motivational force created by high levels of valence, instrumentality, and expectancy is the next most powerful motivational variable for task performance.[106] Finally, perceptions of equity have a somewhat weaker effect on task performance.[107]

Less attention has been devoted to the linkages between motivation variables and citizenship and counterproductive behaviour. With respect to the former, employees who engage in more work-related effort would seem more likely to perform "extra mile" sorts of actions, because those actions themselves require extra effort. The best evidence in support of that claim comes from research on equity. Specifically, employees who feel a sense of equity on the job are more likely to engage in citizenship behaviours, particularly when those behaviours aid the organization.[108] The same employees are less likely to engage in counterproductive behaviours, because such behaviours often serve as a retaliation against perceived inequities.[109]

As with citizenship behaviours, the relationship between motivation and organizational commitment seems straightforward. After all, the psychological and physical forms of withdrawal that characterize less committed employees are themselves evidence of low levels of motivation. Clearly employees who are daydreaming, coming in late, and taking longer breaks are struggling to put forth consistently high levels of work effort. Research on equity and organizational commitment offers the clearest insights into the motivation–commitment relationship. Specifically, employees who feel a sense of equity are more emotionally attached to their firms and feel a stronger sense of obligation to remain.[110]

7.7 How do organizations use compensation practices to increase employee motivation?

APPLICATION: COMPENSATION SYSTEMS

The most important area in which motivation concepts are applied in organizations is in the design of compensation systems. Table 7-7 provides an overview of many of the elements used in typical compensation systems. We use the term "element" in the table to acknowledge that most organizations use a combination of multiple elements to compensate their employees. Two points must be noted about Table 7-7. First, the descriptions of the elements are simplified; the reality is that each of the elements can be implemented and executed in a variety of ways.[111] Second, the elements are designed to do more than just motivate. For example, plans that put pay "at risk" rather than creating increases in base salary are geared toward control of labour costs. As another example, elements that stress individual achievement are believed to alter the composition of a workforce over time, with high achievers drawn to the organization while less motivated employees are selected out. Finally, plans that reward unit or organizational performance are designed to reinforce collaboration, information sharing, and monitoring among employees, regardless of their impact on motivation levels.

One way of judging the motivational impact of compensation plan elements is to consider whether the elements provide difficult and specific goals for channelling work effort. Merit pay and profit sharing offer little in the way of difficult and specific goals, because both essentially challenge employees to make next year as good (or better) than this year. In contrast, lump-sum bonuses and gain sharing provide a forum for assigning difficult and specific goals; the former does so at the individual level and the latter at the unit level. Partly for this reason, both types of plans have been credited with improvements in employee productivity.[112]

Another way of judging the motivational impact of the compensation plan elements is to consider the correspondence between individual performance levels and individual monetary outcomes. After all, that correspondence influences perceptions of both instrumentality and equity. Profit sharing, for example, is unlikely to have strong motivational consequences because an individual employee can do little to improve the profitability of the company, regardless of his or her job performance.[113] Instrumentality and equity are more achievable with gain sharing, because the relevant unit is smaller and the relevant outcomes are more controllable. Still, the highest instrumentality and equity levels will typically be achieved through individual-focused compensation elements, such as piece-rate plans or merit pay plans.

TABLE 7-7

Compensation Plan Elements

Element	Description
Individual-Focused	
Piece-rate pay	A specified rate is paid for each unit produced, each unit sold, or each service provided.
Merit pay	An increase to base salary is made in accordance with performance evaluation ratings.
Lump-sum bonuses	A bonus is received for meeting individual goals but no change is made to base salary. The potential bonus represents "at risk" pay that must be re-earned each year. Base salary may be lower in cases in which potential bonuses may be large.
Recognition awards	Tangible awards (gift cards, merchandise, trips, special events, time off, plaques) or intangible awards (praise) are given on an impromptu basis to recognize achievement.
Unit-Focused	
Gain sharing	An approach in which employees actively participate with managers to develop strategies for increasing performance, usually by reducing costs (e.g., labour, materials). Any financial gains that result from the performance improvements are shared with employees in the form of a gain-sharing payout. No change is made to base salary. The potential payout represents "at risk" pay that must be re-earned each year.
Organization-Focused	
Profit sharing	A bonus is received when the publicly reported earnings of a company exceed some minimum level, with the magnitude of the bonus contingent on the magnitude of the profits. No change is made to base salary. The potential bonus represents "at risk" pay that must be re-earned each year. Base salary may be lower in cases in which potential bonuses may be large.

Of the two individual-focused elements, merit pay is by far the more common, given that it is difficult to apply piece-rate plans outside of manufacturing, sales, and service contexts. Indeed, one review estimated that merit pay is used by around 90 percent of organizations.[114] Criticisms of merit pay typically focus on a smaller than expected differentiation in pay across employees. One survey reported that pay increases for top performers (5.6 percent on average) are only modestly greater than the pay increases for average performers (3.3 percent on average).[115] Such differences seem incapable of creating a perceived linkage between performance and outcomes (though merit reviews can also have indirect effects on pay by triggering promotions).[116]

A number of factors constrain instrumentality and equity in most applications of merit pay. As was noted earlier, one such factor is budgetary constraints, as many organizations freeze or limit pay increases during an economic downturn. Another factor is the accuracy of the actual performance evaluation. Think of all the times you've been evaluated by someone else, whether in school or in the workplace. How many times have you reacted by thinking, "Where did that rating come from?" or "I think I'm being evaluated on the wrong things!" Performance evaluation experts suggest that employees should be evaluated on behaviours that are controllable by the employees (see Chapter 2 on job performance for more discussion of such issues), observable by managers, and critical to the implementation of the firm's strategy.[117] The managers who conduct evaluations also need to be trained in how to conduct them, which typically involves gaining knowledge of the relevant behaviours ahead of time and being taught to keep records of employee behaviour between evaluation sessions.[118]

Even if employees are evaluated on the right things by a boss who has a good handle on their performance, other factors can still undermine accuracy. Some managers might knowingly give inaccurate evaluations due to workplace politics or a desire not to make waves. One survey showed that 70 percent of managers have trouble giving poor ratings to underachieving employees.[119]

Unfortunately, such practices only serve to damage instrumentality and equity, because they fail to separate star employees from struggling employees. To ensure that such separation occurs, Yahoo instituted a "stacked ranking" system to determine compensation, in which managers rank all the employees within their unit from top to bottom.[120] Employees at the top end of those rankings then receive higher bonuses than employees at the bottom end. Although such practices raise concerns about employee morale and excessive competitiveness, research suggests that such forced distribution systems can boost the performance of a company's workforce, especially in the first few years after their implementation.[121]

TAKEAWAYS

7.1 Motivation is defined as a set of energetic forces that originates both within and outside an employee, initiates work-related effort, and determines its direction, intensity, and persistence.

7.2 According to expectancy theory, effort is directed toward behaviours when effort is believed to result in performance (expectancy), performance is believed to result in outcomes (instrumentality), and those outcomes are anticipated to be valuable (valence). Differences in need states help to explain why some outcomes are more attractive ("positively valenced") than others.

7.3 According to goal setting theory, goals become strong drivers of motivation and performance when they are difficult and specific. Specific and difficult goals affect performance by increasing self-set goals and task strategies. Those effects occur more frequently when employees are given feedback, tasks are not too complex, and goal commitment is high.

7.4 According to equity theory, rewards are equitable when a person's ratio of outcomes to inputs matches those of some relevant comparison other. A sense of inequity triggers equity distress. Underreward inequity typically results in lower levels of motivation or higher levels of counterproductive behaviour. Overreward inequity typically results in cognitive distortion, in which inputs are reevaluated in a more positive light.

7.5 Psychological empowerment reflects an energy rooted in the belief that tasks are contributing to some larger purpose. Psychological empowerment is fostered when work goals appeal to employees' passions (meaningfulness), employees have a sense of choice regarding work tasks (self-determination), employees feel capable of performing successfully (competence), and employees feel they are making progress toward fulfilling their purpose (impact).

7.6 Motivation has a strong positive relationship with job performance and a moderate positive relationship with organizational commitment. Of all the energetic forces subsumed by motivation, self-efficacy/competence has the strongest relationship with performance.

7.7 Organizations use compensation practices to increase motivation. Those practices may include individual-focused elements (piece-rate, merit pay, lump-sum bonuses, recognition awards), unit-focused elements (gain sharing), or organization-focused elements (profit sharing).

KEY TERMS

cognitive distortion
comparison other
competence
engagement
equity distress
equity theory
expectancy
expectancy theory
external comparisons
extrinsic motivation
feedback
goal commitment
goal setting theory
impact
instrumentality
internal comparisons
intrinsic motivation
meaningfulness
meaning of money
motivation
needs
psychological empowerment
S.M.A.R.T. goals
self-determination
self-efficacy
self-set goals
specific and difficult goals
task complexity
valence

DISCUSSION QUESTIONS

7.1 Which of the outcomes in Table 7-2 are most appealing to you? Are you more attracted to extrinsic outcomes or intrinsic outcomes? Do you think that your preferences will change as you get older?

7.2 Assume that you were working on a group project and that one of your teammates was nervous about speaking in front of the class during the presentation. Drawing on Figure 7-3, what exactly could you do to make your classmate feel more confident?

7.3 Consider the five strategies for fostering goal commitment (rewards, publicity, support, participation, and resources). Which of those strategies do you think is most effective? Can you picture any of them having potential drawbacks?

7.4 How do you tend to respond when you experience overreward and underreward inequity? Why do you respond that way rather than with some other combination in Figure 7-6?

7.5 Think about a job that you've held in which you felt very low levels of psychological empowerment. What could the organization have done to increase empowerment levels?

CASE: NETFLIX

Observers describe Reed Hastings as existing in one of two states: actively engaged or actively disengaged.[122] Interestingly, he's disengaged about a number of things that other CEOs obsess over. For example, he never even looked at the plans for Netflix's new corporate headquarters, preferring to discover it at the same time the other employees did. "It was the symbolism of not having me focus on the building," explains Hastings.[123] As another example, Hastings doesn't even have an office—he just roams around the building with his laptop, retreating to a glass cubed conference room on the roof of the building when he needs solitude. And Hastings is especially disengaged about micromanaging the motivation of his employees. "Hard work, like long hours at the office, doesn't matter as much to us," notes Hastings.[124] "We care about great work. This requires thoughtful, mature high-performance employees."

What does Hastings get engaged about? Understanding the motivations of his customers. Netflix is always striving to better understand the choices made by its 36 million subscribers.[125] That understanding helps Netflix in three ways. First, it informs decisions about what titles to add to its catalogue in the future. Second, it helps the company position files on its servers so that they're closer to the regions most likely to download them. Third, it impacts how titles are arrayed on subscribers' home screens when they log onto the site. Because much of Netflix's catalogue is old or niche-ish in its appeal, the company needs the home screen's choices to be as enticing as possible. Indeed, understanding customers' motivations became even more important when that home screen began to include Netflix-produced original content, like *House of Cards, Arrested Development, Hemlock Grove*, and *Orange Is the New Black*.

How does Netflix maintain and improve its understanding of customers' motivations? Data, data, data. Netflix employs teams of mathematicians, designers, and programmers to analyze why customers direct their viewing efforts toward some titles and away from others. "We think of the technology as a vehicle for creating a better, more modern experience for the content we have," explains Hastings.[126] "What we're really competing for quite broadly is people's time." To do that, Hastings knows that the company needs to continuously improve on its ability to exploit data. "We are trying to set this up as a continuously learning organization," he notes. "My role is creating that learning atmosphere." Hastings himself even got into the act a few years back, determined that he could come up with an algorithm that improved on his engineers' predictive abilities. He couldn't. But that failure motivated Hastings to create the Netflix Prize, a $1 million windfall that would go to the person or team who most improved the company's "prediction engine."

7.1 To what extent do employees look to their CEOs for motivational signals? Do you think Netflix employees grow to be motivated by the same things that engage Hastings?

7.2 Which theories seem relevant to customers' motivations (to pick certain titles), not just employees' motivations (to perform their tasks well)?

7.3 When it comes to complex work—like Netflix engineers analyzing data on customer viewing habits—will intrinsic or extrinsic motivators prove more effective? Why?

EXERCISE • EXPLAINING PAY DIFFERENCES

The purpose of this exercise is to demonstrate how compensation can be used to influence motivation. This exercise uses groups, so your instructor will either assign you to a group or ask you to create your own group. The exercise has the following steps:

7.1 Read the following scenario:

> Chris Clements and Pat Palmer are both computer programmers working for the same Fortune 500 company. One day they found out that Chris earns $60,820 per year, while Pat earns $72,890. Chris was surprised and said, "I can't think of any reason why we should be paid so differently." "I can think of at least 10 reasons," Pat responded.

Can you, like Pat, think of at least ten reasons that might cause this difference in salary between two people? The reasons can be legal or illegal, wise or unwise.

7.2 Going around the group from member to member, generate a list of ten conceivable reasons why Pat may be earning more than Chris. Remember, the reasons can be legal or illegal, wise or unwise.

7.3 Consider whether the theories discussed in the chapter—expectancy theory, goal setting theory, equity theory, and psychological empowerment—are relevant to the list of reasons you've generated. Maybe one of the theories supports the wisdom of a given reason. For example, maybe Pat's job is more difficult than Chris's job. Equity theory would support the wisdom of that reason because job difficulty is a relevant input. Maybe one of the theories questions the wisdom of a given reason. For example, maybe Chris's boss believes that salary increases are a poor use of limited financial resources. Expectancy theory would question the wisdom of that reason because that philosophy harms instrumentality.

7.4 Elect a group member to write the group's ten reasons on the board. Then indicate which theories are relevant to the various reasons by writing one or more of the following abbreviations next to a given reason: EX for expectancy theory, GS for goal setting theory, EQ for equity theory, and PE for psychological empowerment.

7.5 Class discussion (whether in groups or as a class) should centre on which theories seem most relevant to the potential reasons for the pay differences between Chris and Pat. Are there some potential reasons that don't seem relevant to any of the four theories? Do those reasons tend to be legal or illegal, wise or unwise?

Source: Adapted from M.K. Renard, "It's All About the Money: Chris and Pat Compare Salaries," *Journal of Management Education* 32 (2008), pp. 248–61.

OB ASSESSMENTS • THE MEANING OF MONEY

How do you view money—what meaning do you attach to it? This assessment will tell you where you stand on the three facets of the meaning of money—money as achievement, money as respect, and money as freedom. Answer each question using the response scale provided. Then follow the instructions below to score yourself.

1 **Strongly Disagree**	2 **Disagree**	3 **Slightly Disagree**	4 **Neutral**	5 **Slightly Agree**	6 **Agree**	7 **Strongly Agree**	

1. Money represents one's achievement. _____
2. Money is a symbol of success. _____
3. Money is the most important goal in my life. _____
4. Money can buy everything. _____
5. Money makes people respect you in the community. _____
6. Money will help you express your competence and abilities. _____
7. Money can bring you many friends. _____
8. Money is honourable. _____
9. Money gives you autonomy and freedom. _____
10. Money can give you the opportunity to be what you want to be. _____
11. Money in the bank is a sign of security. _____
12. Money means power. _____

Scoring

Money as achievement. Add up items 1–4. _____

Money as respect. Add up items 5–8. _____

Money as freedom. Add up items 9–12. _____

Interpretation

Money as achievement. High = 13 or above. Low = 12 or below.

Money as respect. High = 15 or above. Low = 14 or below.

Money as freedom. High = 20 or above. Low = 19 or below.

If you scored high on all three dimensions, you view money as having multiple, non-economic meanings. This result means that money is likely a powerful motivator for you. Remember, when interpreting your scores on these assessments it is important to consider the *reliability* and *validity* of these tools (see Chapter 1, ***OB Assessments***).

Source: Adapted from T.L. Tang, "The Meaning of Money Revisited," *Journal of Organizational Behaviour* 13 (1992), pp. 197–202.

Trust, Justice, and Ethics

CHAPTER 8

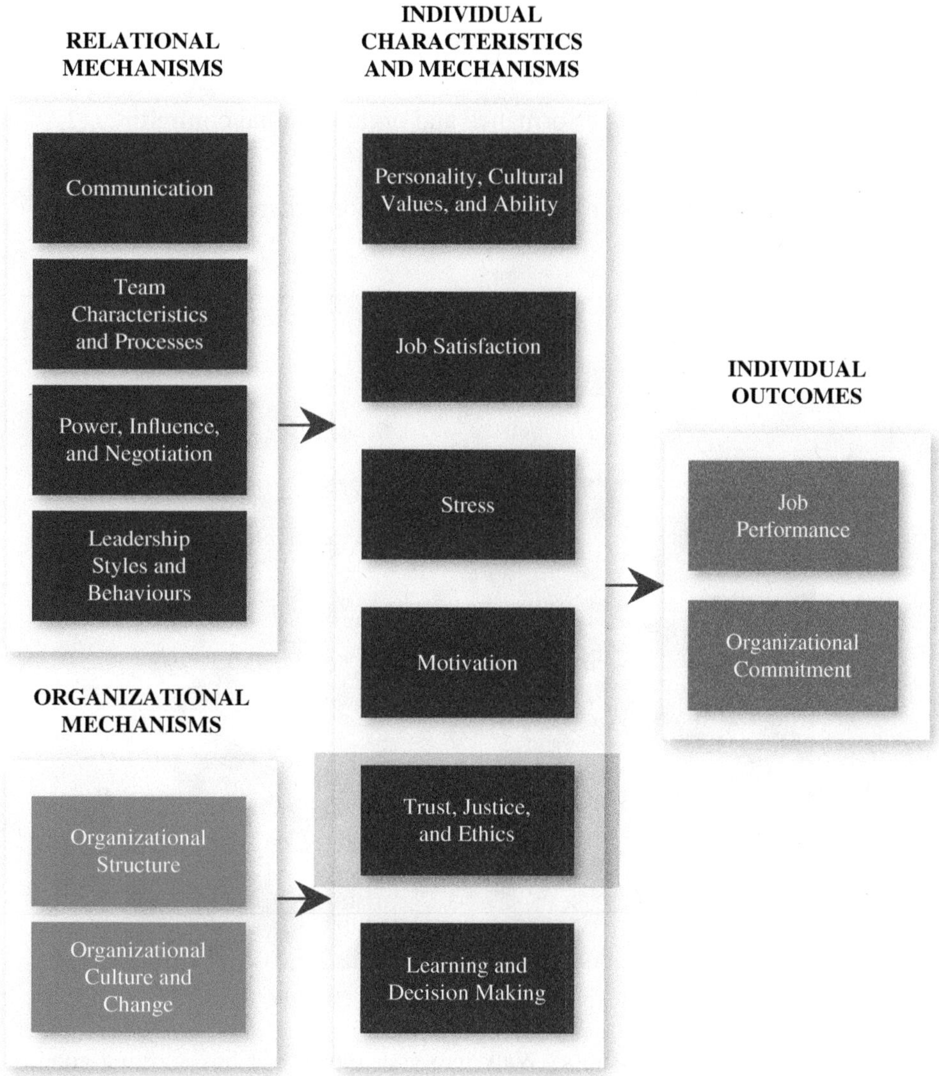

LEARNING OUTCOMES

After reading this chapter, you should be able to answer the following questions:

8.1 What is trust, and how does it relate to justice and ethics?

8.2 In what three sources can trust be rooted?

8.3 What dimensions can be used to describe the trustworthiness of an authority?

8.4 What dimensions can be used to describe the fairness of an authority's decision making?

8.5 What is the four-component model of ethical decision making?

8.6 How does trust affect job performance and organizational commitment?

8.7 What steps can organizations take to become more trustworthy?

Nike

Nike has worked hard to rebuild its reputation as an organization worthy of trust.

© AP Photo-Richard Vogel/The Canadian Press

Shopping for a new pair of running shoes? Walk into your typical big-box sporting-goods store and you're very likely to see an entire wall displaying hundreds of potential choices. How do you decide which pair of running shoes to try on? Price? Colour? Nike hopes you narrow down your choices by focusing on brand. The shoe giant has been a dominant force in the shoe and athletic apparel markets for decades. Scores of weekend warriors have looked to the Nike Air—that lightweight air pocket in the heels of many Nike shoes—to give them that extra step or that added bit of comfort.[1] In the 1990s, however, many of those same weekend warriors were confronted with the reality of how those shoes were made. That's when disclosures of sweatshop conditions and labour abuses sparked protests outside Nike stores and boycotts on many college campuses. In 1998, founder and then-CEO Phil Knight was forced to admit that the "Nike product has become synonymous with slave wages, forced overtime, and arbitrary abuse."[2]

Nike has worked hard to rebuild trust in its brand over the past decade. Nike became the first company in the industry to post the names and locations of its 700 factories—most located in China, Vietnam, Indonesia, and Thailand—on the web (see www.nikeresponsibility.com/how/value/plan).[3] It created a code of conduct that sets standards for wages, the number of hours in a standard workweek, and the rules for overtime pay. It also paid a network of auditors to perform inspections of factories, giving each a grade between A and D. Unfortunately, it's not clear that those efforts are paying off. A recent analysis of the inspection data by a professor at MIT noted that despite "significant efforts and investments by Nike ... workplace conditions in almost 80% of its suppliers have either remained the same or worsened over time."[4] Almost one-third of the factories in one audit earned D grades because of multiple violations, including failing to pay the minimum wage and forcing employees to work more than 14 days in a row.

Why has it been so difficult for Nike to improve the working conditions in its factories? One reason is that government regulations are weak in emerging economies, putting more pressure on companies to police their factories.[5] And many of the facilities compete for Nike's business, with higher employee salaries making their pricing less competitive.[6] Those factories often find themselves working under tight deadlines, with power outages or design adjustments triggering work shift abuses. Other factories have learned to fool the audits by keeping fake records, distributing scripts for employees to read if they're questioned, or shifting work to secret subcontractors that violate standards. And dropping a troubled facility can raise its own ethical issues for Nike, as it results in the loss of jobs that may be vital to that local economy. For its part, Nike has reacted to the limitations of its auditing strategy by helping convert factories to more modern manufacturing techniques and seeking to limit its own last-minute design adjustments.[7] Those sorts of steps will reduce the pressures on the facilities, eliminating some of the need for overtime and excessively long work schedules. Nike's current CEO, Mark Parker, summarizes this state of affairs by noting, "I'm proud of what we've accomplished, but we're still not where we need to be. This is a never-ending challenge."[8]

8.1 What is trust, and how does it relate to justice and ethics?

TRUST, JUSTICE, AND ETHICS

One reason why companies such as Nike care about ethical issues is that a firm's **reputation** is one of its most prized possessions, since it reflects the prominence of its brand in the minds of the public and the perceived quality of its goods and services.[9] Reputation is an intangible asset that can take a long time to build, and it can be damaged easily. That's especially the case today, when one bad experience with any company can be tweeted, shared on Facebook, posted on a blog, or videotaped and uploaded to YouTube. Although we typically think about a company's reputation in reference to potential consumers, it matters to employees as well. Recruitment experts maintain that top performers want to work at organizations with clean reputations, in part because they want to protect their own personal image. Indeed, one survey found that 78 percent of adults would rather work at a company with an excellent reputation and an average salary than at a company with a high salary and a poor reputation.[10] Who are some companies with excellent reputations? It is common these days to see companies ranked in terms of their public reputations, such as on the annual "Canada's 50 Best Employers" list.[11]

reputation
The prominence of an organization's brand in the minds of the public and the perceived quality of its goods and services

Reputations depend on many things, but one of the most important factors is trust. **Trust** is defined as the willingness to be vulnerable to a trustee based on positive expectations about the trustee's actions and intentions.[12] Although different views of trust exist, all are rooted in a fundamental belief that a trustee (e.g., a manager, the organization) is trustworthy and will act in a way that benefits the trustor (e.g., an employee, a customer) and protect him or her from exploitation and harm.[13] A key part of this definition hinges on the notion of dependency; that is, trust only becomes an issue when an individual is dependent on and vulnerable to the actions of another party.[14] If a customer in a shoe store trusts the quality of Nike's products, that customer is willing to accept the consequences of paying money for Nike shoes. If a potential recruit trusts the words of Nike management, that individual is willing to accept the consequences of becoming a member of the organization. Both examples illustrate that trusting reflects a willingness to put yourself out there, even though doing so might be result in disappointment. The examples also highlight the difference between "trust" and "risk." Actually making yourself vulnerable—by buying shoes or accepting a job—constitutes risk. Trust reflects the willingness to take that risk. Unfortunately, trust in many companies has declined sharply due to corporate scandals and changing economic times.[15]

trust
The willingness to be vulnerable to an authority because of positive expectations about the authority's actions and intentions

This chapter focuses on trust in organizational authorities, a group that could include the CEO of an organization, its top management team, or supervisors and managers within the firm. These authorities put a face on a company, giving employees and customers a means of judging a company's reputation. They can also have a significant influence on the performance and commitment of employees. As you'll see in the chapter, trust in these authorities depends on two related concepts. **Justice** reflects the perceived fairness of an authority's decision making.[16] When employees perceive high levels of justice, they believe that decision outcomes are fair and that decision-making processes are designed and implemented in a fair manner. Justice concepts can be used to explain why employees judge some authorities to be more trustworthy than others.[17] **Ethics** reflects the degree to which the behaviours of an authority are in accordance with generally accepted moral norms.[18] When employees perceive high levels of ethics, they believe that things are being done the way they "should be" or "ought to be" done. Ethics concepts can be used to explain why authorities decide to act in a trustworthy or untrustworthy manner.

justice
The perceived fairness of an authority's decision making

ethics
The degree to which the behaviours of an authority are in accordance with generally accepted moral norms

WHY ARE SOME AUTHORITIES MORE TRUSTED THAN OTHERS?

Why are firefighters, nurses, farmers, doctors, and teachers consistently among the most trusted Canadians, whereas real estate agents, publicists, car salespeople, and politicians are among the least trusted?[19] Think about a particular boss or instructor—one with whom you've spent a significant amount of time. Do you trust that person? Would you be willing to let that person have significant influence over your professional or educational future? For example, would you be willing to let that person serve as a reference for you or write you a letter of recommendation, even though you'd have no way of monitoring what he or she says? When you think about the level of trust you feel for that particular authority, what exactly makes you feel that way? This question speaks to the factors that drive trust—the factors that help inspire a willingness to be vulnerable.

8.2 In what three sources can trust be rooted?

Trust

As is shown in Figure 8-1, trust is rooted in three different kinds of factors. **Disposition-based trust** means your personality traits include a general propensity to trust others; **cognition-based trust** means your trust is rooted in a rational assessment of the authority's trustworthiness[20]; and **affect-based trust** means your trust depends on feelings toward the authority that go beyond any rational assessment.[21] The sections that follow describe each of these trust forms in more detail.

disposition-based trust
Trust rooted in one's own personality, as opposed to a careful assessment of the trustee's trustworthiness

cognition-based trust
Trust rooted in a rational assessment of the authority's trustworthiness

affect-based trust
Trust dependent on feelings toward the authority that go beyond any rational assessment of trustworthiness

Disposition-Based Trust Disposition-based trust has less to do with a particular authority and more to do with the trustor. Some trustors are high in **trust propensity**—a general expectation that the words, promises, and statements of individuals and groups can be relied upon.[22] Some researchers have argued that trust propensity represents a sort of "faith in human nature," in that trusting people view others in more favourable terms than suspicious people do.[23] The importance of trust propensity is most obvious in interactions with strangers, in which any acceptance of vulnerability would amount to "blind trust."[24] On the one hand, people high in trust propensity may be fooled into trusting others who are not worthy of it.[25] On the other hand, people low in trust propensity may be penalized by not trusting someone who is actually deserving of it. Both situations can be damaging; as one scholar noted, "We are doomed if we trust all and equally doomed if we trust none."[26] Where do you stack up on trust propensity? See our ***OB Assessments*** feature at the end of the chapter to find out.

trust propensity
A general expectation that the words, promises, and statements of individuals can be relied upon

FIGURE 8-1

Factors That Influence Trust Levels

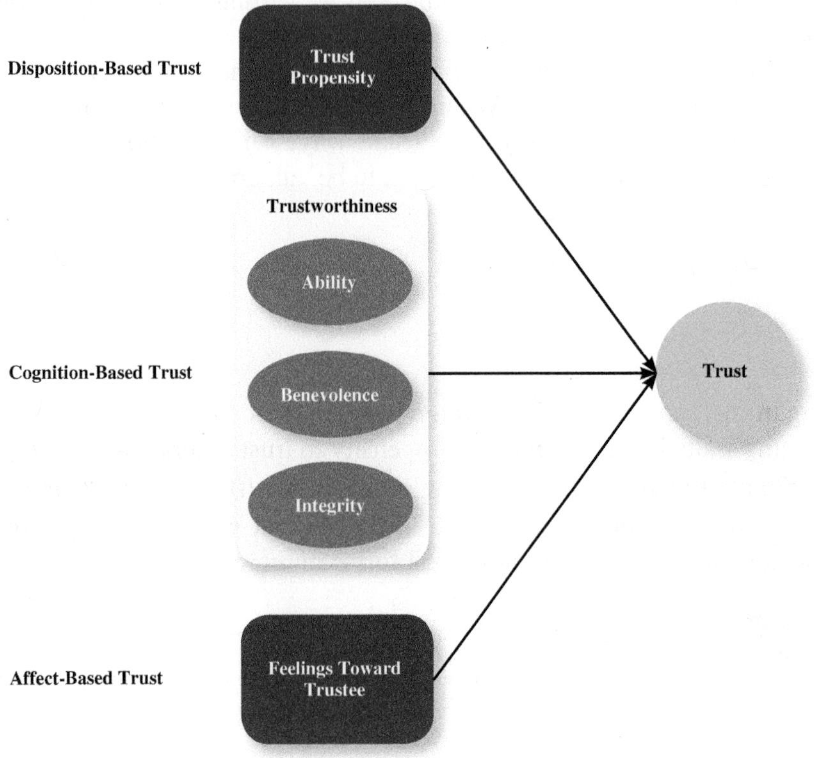

Sources: Adapted from R.C. Mayer, J.H. Davis, and F.D. Schoorman, "An Integrative Model of Organizational Trust," *Academy of Management Review* 20 (1995), pp. 709–34; and D.J. McAllister, "Affect- and Cognition-Based Trust as Foundations for Interpersonal Cooperation in Organizations," *Academy of Management Journal* 38 (1995), pp. 24–59.

Where does our trust propensity come from? As with all traits, trust propensity is a product of both nature and nurture (see Chapter 4 on personality and cultural values for more discussion of such issues). If our parents are dispositionally suspicious, we may either inherit that tendency genetically or model it as we watch them exhibit distrust in their day-to-day lives. Research also suggests that trust propensity is shaped by early childhood experiences.[27] In fact, trust propensity may be one of the first personality traits to develop, because infants must immediately learn to trust their parents to meet their needs. The more our needs are met as children, the more trusting we become; the more we are disappointed as children, the less trusting we become. Our propensities continue to be shaped later in life as we gain experiences with friends, schools, churches, local government authorities, and other relevant groups.[28]

The nation in which we live also affects our trust propensity. Research by the World Values Study Group examines differences between nations on various attitudes and perceptions. The study group collects interview data from 45 different societies with a total sample size of more than 90,000 participants. One of the questions asked by the study group measures trust propensity. Specifically, participants are asked, "Generally speaking, would you say that most people can be trusted or that you can't be too careful in dealing with people?" Figure 8-2 shows the percentage of participants who answered "Most people can be trusted" for this question, as opposed to "Can't be too careful," for several of the nations included in the study. The results reveal that trust propensity levels are actually relatively high in Canada, especially in relation to countries in Europe and South America.

FIGURE 8-2

Trust Propensities by Nation

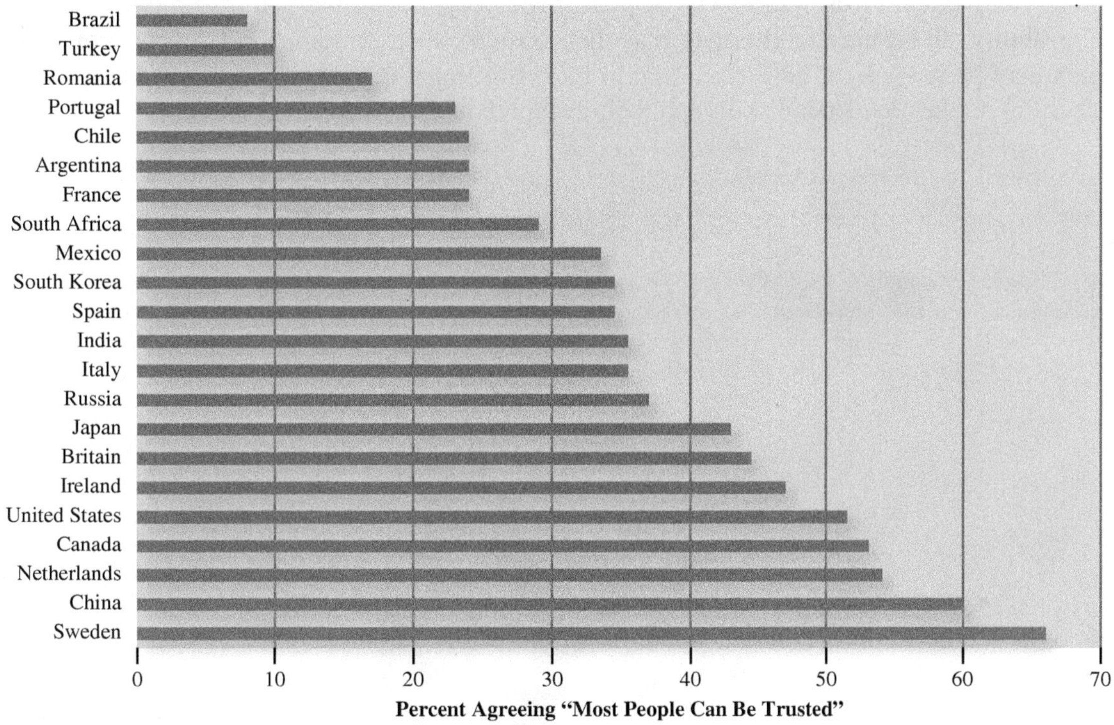

Source: Adapted from J.J. Johnson and J.B. Cullen, "Trust in Cross-Cultural Relationships," in *Blackwell Handbook of Cross-Cultural Management*, ed. M.J. Gannon and K.L. Newman (Malden, MA: Blackwell, 2002), pp. 335–60.

8.3 What dimensions can be used to describe the trustworthiness of an authority?

Cognition-Based Trust Disposition-based trust guides us in cases in which we don't yet have data about a particular authority. However, eventually we gain enough knowledge to gauge the authority's **trustworthiness**, defined as the characteristics or attributes of a trustee that inspire trust.[29] At that point, our trust begins to be based on cognitions we've developed about the authority, as opposed to our own personality or disposition. In this way, cognition-based trust is driven by the authority's "track record."[30] If that track record has shown the authority to be trustworthy, vulnerability to the authority can be accepted. If that track record is spotty however, trust may not be warranted. Research suggests that we gauge the track record of an authority along three dimensions: ability, benevolence, and integrity.[31]

trustworthiness
Characteristics or attributes of a person that inspire trust, including perceptions of ability, benevolence, and integrity

The first dimension of trustworthiness is **ability**, defined as the skills, competencies, and areas of expertise that enable an authority to be successful in some specific area (see Chapter 4 on ability for more discussion of such issues).[32] Think about the decision-making process that you go through when choosing a doctor, lawyer, or mechanic. Clearly one of the first things you consider is ability, because you're not going to trust them if they don't know a scalpel from a retractor, a tort from a writ, or a camshaft from a crankshaft. Of course, listing a specific area is a key component of the ability definition; you wouldn't trust a mechanic to perform surgery, nor would you trust a doctor to fix your car! The ability of business authorities may be considered on a number of levels. For example, managers may be judged not only according to their functional expertise in a particular vocation but also according to their leadership skills and their general business sense.

ability (dimension of trustworthiness)
The skills, competencies, and areas of expertise that enable an authority to be successful in some specific area

Children whose needs are generally met tend to grow into trusting adults.

© Brand X Pictures/PunchStock

The second dimension of trustworthiness is **benevolence**, defined as the belief that the authority wants to do good for the trustor, apart from any selfish or profit-centred motives.[33] When authorities are perceived as benevolent, it means that they care for employees, are concerned about their well-being, and feel a sense of loyalty to them. The mentor–protégé relationship provides a good example of benevolence at work, in that the best mentors go out of their way to be helpful apart from concerns about financial rewards.[34] The management at Meijer, a supermarket chain, seems to understand the importance of benevolence.[35] Meijer recently added a five-day course on "positive organizational scholarship" to its leadership training program. The training stresses the importance of positive communication and a culture of kindness in the organization. The chain, which operates 180 stores with 60,000 employees, is attempting to compete with the likes of Walmart by maximizing the commitment of its workforce. David Beach, the company's vice-president of workforce planning and development, noted, "We realized that we need our company to be a place where people want to work."[36]

benevolence (dimension of trustworthiness)
The belief that an authority wants to do good for a trustor, apart from any selfish or profit-centred motives

The third dimension of trustworthiness is **integrity**, defined as the perception that the authority adheres to a set of values and principles that the trustor finds acceptable.[37] When authorities have integrity, they are of sound character—they have good intentions and strong moral discipline.[38] Integrity also conveys an alignment between words and deeds—a sense that authorities keep their promises, "walk the talk," and "do what they say they will do."[39] Unfortunately, one survey indicated that only around 20 percent of American workers view senior managers as acting in accordance with their words.[40] Domino's Pizza recently showed an unusual amount of integrity in its advertising and business operations. Despite the fact that its market share was holding steady, the company admitted that customers didn't think its pizza was all that great.[41] Domino's president vowed to put 40 percent more herbs in its sauce, use better cheese, and add a special glaze to its crust. The end result is a better-tasting pizza, an increase in sales,[42] and the sense that Domino's management "tells it like it is."

integrity (dimension of trustworthiness)
The perception that an authority adheres to a set of values and principles that the trustor finds acceptable

After admitting that the company needed to change its pizza recipe and ingredients, Domino's set out to get people to try the new and improved version.

© Press Association via AP Photo

Questions about integrity extend beyond senior management, however. For example, studies suggest that rank-and-file employees lie more frequently when communicating by e-mail because there are no "shifty eyes" or nervous ticks to give them away. Indeed, one study showed that people were more likely to lie via e-mail than when writing letters using pen and paper.[43] Why would those contexts differ, when neither is face to face? Perhaps e-mail feels more fleeting than paper, and the ability to delete what you write—even if you ultimately don't—makes you choose words more casually. In any case, the lies can begin even before employees are hired: one survey of managers by CareerBuilder.com revealed that 49 percent had caught an applicant lying on a résumé.[44]

Affect-Based Trust Although ability, benevolence, and integrity provide three good reasons to trust authority, the third form of trust isn't actually rooted in reason. Affect-based trust is more emotional than rational. With affect-based trust, we trust because we have feelings for the person in question; we really like them and have a fondness for them. Those feelings are what prompt us to accept vulnerability to another person. Put simply, we trust them because we like them. Some of that trust can even be chemical, as research shows that something as common as a hug can stimulate a hormone called oxytocin—sometimes called the "cuddle chemical"—that causes your brain to be more trusting.[45]

Affect-based trust acts as a supplement to the types of trust discussed previously.[46] Figure 8-3 describes how the various forms of trust can build on one another over time. In new relationships, trust depends solely on our own trust propensity. In most relationships, that propensity eventually gets supplemented by knowledge about ability, benevolence, or integrity, at which point cognition-based trust develops. In a select few of those relationships, an emotional bond develops, and our feelings for the trustee further increase our willingness to accept vulnerability. These relationships are characterized by a mutual investment of time and energy, a sense of deep attachment, and the realization that both parties would feel a sense of loss if the relationship were dissolved.[47] For more discussion of the drivers of trust, see our ***OB on Screen*** feature.

FIGURE 8-3

Types of Trust over Time

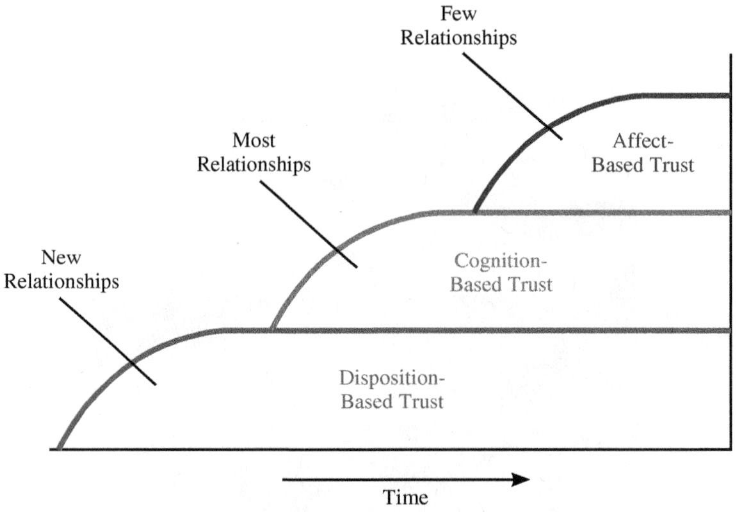

Sources: Adapted from R.J. Lewicki and B.B. Bunker, "Developing and Maintaining Trust in Work Relationships," in *Trust in Organizations: Frontiers of Theory and Research*, ed. R.M. Kramer and T.R. Tyler (Thousand Oaks, CA: Sage, 1996), pp. 114–39; and R.C. Mayer, J.H. Davis, and F.D. Schoorman, "An Integrative Model of Organizational Trust," *Academy of Management Review* 20 (1995), pp. 709–34.

Summary Taken together, disposition-based trust, cognition-based trust, and affect-based trust provide three completely different sources of trust in a particular authority. In the case of disposition-based trust, our willingness to be vulnerable has little to do with the authority and more to do with our genes and our early life experiences. In the case of affect-based trust, our willingness to be vulnerable has little to do with a rational assessment of the authority's merits and more to do with our emotional fondness for the authority. Only in the case of cognition-based trust do we rationally evaluate the pluses and minuses of an authority, in terms of its ability, benevolence, and integrity. But how exactly do we gauge those trustworthiness forms? One way is to consider whether authorities adhere to rules of justice.

OB ON SCREEN

Man of Steel

Clark Kent: *That ship that appeared last night, I'm the one they're looking for.*

Father Leone: *Do you know ... why they want you?*

Clark Kent: *No, but this General Zod ... even if I surrender, there's no guarantee he'll keep his word. But if there's a chance I can save Earth by turning myself in, shouldn't I take it?*

Father Leone: *What does your gut tell you?*

Clark Kent: *That Zod can't be trusted. The problem is, I'm not sure the people of Earth can be either.*

With that exchange, Clark Kent (Henry Cavill) summarizes the trust dynamics at play in *Man of Steel* (Dir. Zack Snyder, Warner Bros., 2013). Transported to Earth as an infant when Krypton exploded, Clark was raised in Smallville, Kansas, by Jonathan and Martha Kent. Jonathan was protective of his adopted son—suspicious of what the world would do if it discovered an alien with superpowers. As Clark explains to Lois Lane (Amy Adams), "My father believed that if the world found out who I really was, they'd reject me ... out of fear." Jonathan worried that the people of Earth wouldn't be benevolent toward Clark because they couldn't be sure Clark would be benevolent toward them. Those mutual doubts would sow anxiety on both sides, further undermining trust.

© Warner Bros./Photofest

Clark's concerns become moot when General Zod (Michael Shannon)—a Kryptonian criminal—arrives on Earth, demanding that Clark be turned over to him. If Clark's been uncertain about the trustworthiness of the people of Earth, he at least knows that Zod can't be trusted. Zod demonstrated a lack of benevolence and integrity back on Krypton when he murdered members of the ruling council. So, as an initial step toward confronting Zod, Clark turns himself in to the U.S. military. Even after his deeds help inspire the hope that he—as Superman—can make the world a better place, hints of the distrust that Jonathan feared persist. When a general asks, "How do we know you won't one day act against America's interests?" Clark responds by appealing to patriotic emotions: "I grew up in Kansas, General. I'm about as American as it gets."

Justice

It's often difficult to assess the ability, benevolence, and integrity of authorities accurately, particularly early in a working relationship. What employees need in such circumstances is some sort of observable behavioural evidence that an authority might be trustworthy. Justice provides that sort of behavioural evidence, because authorities who treat employees more fairly are usually judged to be more trustworthy.[48] As is shown in Table 8-1, employees can judge the fairness of an authority's decision making along four dimensions: distributive justice, procedural justice, interpersonal justice, and informational justice.

TABLE 8-1

The Four Dimensions of Justice

Fairness Rules	Description (of Evidence)
Distributive Justice Rules	
Equity vs. equality vs. need	Are rewards allocated according to the proper norm?
Procedural Justice Rules	
Voice	Do employees get to provide input into procedures?
Correctability	Do procedures build in mechanisms for appeals?
Consistency	Are procedures consistent across people and time?
Bias Suppression	Are procedures neutral and unbiased?
Representativeness	Do procedures consider the needs of all groups?
Accuracy	Are procedures based on accurate information?
Interpersonal Justice Rules	
Respect	Do authorities treat employees with sincerity?
Propriety	Do authorities refrain from improper remarks?
Informational Justice Rules	
Justification	Do authorities explain procedures thoroughly?
Truthfulness	Are those explanations honest?

Sources: J.S. Adams, "Inequity in Social Exchange," in *Advances in Experimental Social Psychology*, Vol. 2, ed. L. Berkowitz (New York: Academic Press, 1965), pp. 267–99; R.J. Bies and J.F. Moag, "Interactional Justice: Communication Criteria of Fairness," in *Research on Negotiations in Organizations*, Vol. 1, ed. R.J. Lewicki, B.H. Sheppard, and M.H. Bazerman (Greenwich, CT: JAI Press, 1986), pp. 43–55; G.S. Leventhal, "The Distribution of Rewards and Resources in Groups and Organizations," in *Advances in Experimental Social Psychology*, Vol. 9, ed. L. Berkowitz and W. Walster (New York: Academic Press, 1976), pp. 91–131; G.S. Leventhal, "What Should Be Done with Equity Theory? New Approaches to the Study of Fairness in Social Relationships," in *Social Exchange: Advances in Theory and Research*, ed. K. Gergen, M. Greenberg, and R. Willis (New York: Plenum Press, 1980), pp. 27–55; and J. Thibaut and L. Walker, *Procedural Justice: A Psychological Analysis* (Hillsdale, NJ: Erlbaum, 1975).

Distributive Justice **Distributive justice** reflects the perceived fairness of decision-making outcomes.[49] Employees gauge distributive justice by asking whether decision outcomes, such as pay, rewards, evaluations, promotions, and work assignments, are allocated using proper norms. In most business situations, the proper norm is equity, with more outcomes allocated to those who contribute more inputs (see Chapter 7 on motivation for more discussion of such issues). The equity norm is typically judged to be the fairest choice in situations in which the goal is to maximize the productivity of individual employees.[50]

distributive justice
The perceived fairness of decision-making outcomes

8.4 What dimensions can be used to describe the fairness of an authority's decision making?

However, other allocation norms become appropriate in situations in which other goals are critical. In team-based work, building harmony and solidarity in work groups can become just as important as individual productivity. In such cases, an equality norm may be judged fairer, such that all team members receive the same amount of relevant rewards.[51] The equality norm is typically used in student project groups, in which all group members receive exactly the same grade on a project, regardless of their individual productivity levels. In cases in which the welfare of a particular employee is the critical concern, a need norm may be judged fairer. For example, some organizations protect new employees from committee assignments and other extra activities, so that they can get their careers off to a productive start.

Procedural Justice In addition to judging the fairness of a decision outcome, employees may consider the process that led to that outcome. **Procedural justice** reflects the perceived fairness of decision-making processes.[52] Procedural justice is fostered when authorities adhere to rules of fair process. One of those rules is *voice*, or giving employees a chance to express their opinions and views during the course of decision making.[53] A related rule is *correctability*, which provides employees with a chance to request an appeal when a procedure seems to have worked ineffectively. Research suggests that these rules improve employees' reactions to decisions,[54] largely because they give employees a sense of ownership over them. Employees tend to value voice and correctability even when they don't result in the desired outcome,[55] because they like to be heard. That is, the expression of opinions is a valued end, in and of itself, when employees believe that their opinions have been truly considered.

procedural justice
The perceived fairness of decision-making processes

Aside from voice and correctability, procedural justice is fostered when authorities adhere to four rules that serve to create equal employment opportunity.[56] The *consistency, bias suppression, representativeness*, and *accuracy* rules help ensure that procedures are neutral and objective, as opposed to biased and discriminatory. These sorts of procedural rules are relevant in many areas of working life. For example, the rules can be used to make hiring practices more fair by ensuring that interview questions are unbiased and asked in the same manner across applications, and to make compensation practices fairer by ensuring that accurate measures of job performance are used to provide input for merit raises.

These sorts of procedural justice rules are critical to ensure that non-relevant demographic characteristics, such as an individual's gender or ethnic or racial origin, do not bias organizational decision making. In Canada we have federal and provincial human rights acts that lay down the rules to achieve fair-treatment outcomes.[57] But even if not formally required by law to adopt an inclusive hiring strategy, many organizations have discovered that these strategies produce larger talent pools from which to select employees (i.e., with more choice, the likelihood of finding a successful match increases). Another persistent fairness issue concerns the wage gap that continues to exist between women and men who perform work of equal value.[58] Such pay differences are likely due to procedural injustice in some form, with pay-determining procedures functioning in an inconsistent, biased, and inaccurate manner across male- and female-dominated jobs. Although the wage gap has narrowed over the years, today, in Canada, full-time working women still earn less, on average, than full-time working men in comparable jobs. Of course, some companies do a better job than others at achieving pay equity, promoting workplace diversity, and implementing inclusiveness decision making. Table 8-2 provides the list of employers who have been recognized for their exceptional fair treatment of women; members of visible minority groups; persons with disabilities; Aboriginal people; and lesbian, gay, bisexual, and transgendered peoples.[59]

TABLE 8-2

Some of Canada's Best Diversity Employers

Aboriginal Peoples Television Network	Nexen Energy ULC
BC Public Service	Procter & Gamble Inc.
Business Development Bank of Canada (BDC)	Royal Bank of Canada (RBC)
Canadian Security Intelligence Service (CSIS)	SaskTel
Corus Entertainment Inc.	Shell Canada Limited
Deloitte LLP	Simon Fraser University
Enbridge Inc.	Sunnybrook Health Sciences Centre
KPMG LLP	TELUS Corporation
Labatt Breweries of Canada	University of Toronto
Loblaw Companies Limited	Vancouver, City of
Manitoba Hydro	Yukon, Government of

Source: Canada's Best Diversity Employers is an annual competition organized by the editors at Mediacorp Canada Inc., publishers of the annual Canada's Top 100 Employers project.

You might be wondering, "Does procedural justice really matter—don't people just care about the outcomes that they receive?" To answer this question, one has only to look at the annual ranking of Canadian universities by *Maclean's* magazine. For many years, concerns have been expressed about the procedures (methodology) used to compile data and determine overall rankings—so much so that a number of institutions decided to withdraw their participation from the process altogether. The issue for these universities was not the outcome (ranking), per se, but rather the procedures used to determine their ranks.[60] Research suggests that distributive justice and procedural justice combine to influence employee reactions; see Figure 8-4.[61] It's true that when outcomes are good, people don't spend as much time worrying about how fair the process was, as is illustrated by the green line in the figure, which shows that procedural justice has little impact on reactions when outcome favourability is high. However, when outcomes are bad, procedural justice becomes enormously important, as shown by the red line. Research shows that negative or unexpected events trigger a thorough examination of process issues, making adherence to rules like consistency, bias suppression, and accuracy much more vital.[62]

In fact, research shows that procedural justice tends to be a stronger driver of reactions to authorities than distributive justice. For example, a meta-analysis of 183 studies showed that procedural justice was a stronger predictor of satisfaction with supervision, overall job satisfaction, and organizational commitment than distributive justice.[63] Why does the decision-making process sometimes matter more than the outcome? Likely because employees understand that outcomes come and go—some may be in your favour while others may be a bit disappointing. Procedures, however, are longer-lasting and stay in place until the organization redesigns them or a new authority arrives to revise them.

FIGURE 8-4

Combined Effects of Distributive and Procedural Justice

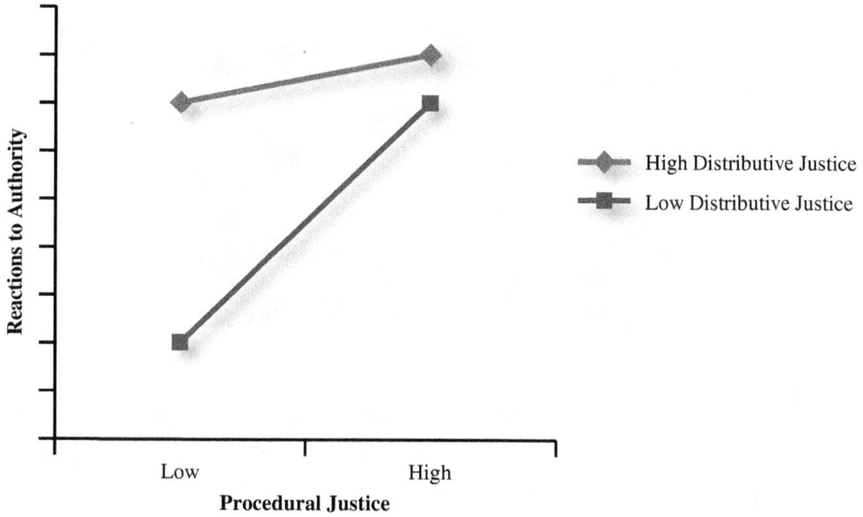

Source: Adapted from J. Brockner and B.M. Wiesenfeld, "An Integrative Framework for Explaining Reactions to Decisions: Interactive Effects of Outcomes and Procedures," *Psychological Bulletin* 120 (1996), pp. 189–208.

Interpersonal Justice In addition to judging the fairness of decision outcomes and processes, employees might consider how authorities treat them as the procedures are implemented. **Interpersonal justice** reflects the perceived fairness of the treatment received by employees from authorities.[64] Interpersonal justice is fostered when authorities adhere to two particular rules. The *respect* rule pertains to whether authorities treat employees in a dignified and sincere manner, and the *propriety* rule reflects whether authorities refrain from making improper or offensive remarks. From this perspective, interpersonal *injustice* occurs when authorities are rude or disrespectful to employees, or when they refer to them with inappropriate labels.[65]

interpersonal justice
The perceived fairness of the interpersonal treatment received by employees from authorities

Taken to the extremes, interpersonally unjust actions create **abusive supervision**, defined as the sustained display of hostile verbal and nonverbal behaviours, excluding physical contact.[66] A national study suggests that approximately 15 percent of employees are victims of abusive behaviours, ranging from angry outbursts to public ridiculing to being used as scapegoats for negative events.[67] In addition to exhibiting more absenteeism and lower productivity,[68] employees who are abused by their supervisors report more anxiety, burnout, and strain, as well as less satisfaction with their lives in general.[69] They are also more likely to strike back at their supervisors with counterproductive behaviours—a response that may even spill over to their co-workers and the larger organization.[70]

abusive supervision

The sustained display of hostile verbal and nonverbal behaviours, excluding physical contact, by a supervisor

When interpersonal injustice gets taken to the extreme, it can turn into abusive supervision. Estimates suggest that 15 percent of employees are victims of abusive behaviours at work.

© Dynamic Graphics/PictureQuest

Why are interpersonally unjust actions so damaging? One reason may be that people remember unfair acts more vividly than fair ones. A recent study asked 41 employees to complete a survey on interactions with authorities and co-workers four times a day for two to three weeks.[71] Two kinds of interactions were coded—positive experiences and negative experiences—and participants also reported on their current mood (e.g., happy, pleased, sad, blue, unhappy). The results showed that positive interactions were more common than negative interactions, but the effects of negative interactions on mood were five times stronger than the effects of positive interactions. Such findings suggest that a violation of the respect and propriety rules looms much larger than adherence to those rules.[72] For these reasons, some companies have taken advantage of a growing number of "civility training" programs offered by consulting firms.[73] One such program, CREW (Civility, Respect, and Engagement at Work), was featured in Chapter 6.

Informational Justice Finally, employees may consider the kind of information that authorities provide during the course of organizational decision making. **Informational justice** reflects the perceived fairness of the communications provided to employees from authorities.[74] Informational justice is fostered when authorities adhere to two particular rules. The *justification* rule mandates that authorities explain decision-making procedures and outcomes in a comprehensive and reasonable manner, and the *truthfulness* rule requires that those communications be honest and candid. Although it seems like common sense that organizations would explain decisions in a comprehensive and adequate manner, that's often not the case. A particularly striking example comes from south of the border. RadioShack, the Texas-based home electronics retailer (in Canada, this company has evolved into The Source), was criticized for firing 400 employees via e-mail.[75] Employees at its Fort Worth headquarters received messages on a Tuesday morning saying: "The work force reduction notification is currently in progress. Unfortunately your position is one that has been eliminated." After receiving the 18-word message, employees had 30 minutes to make phone calls and say goodbye to fellow employees, before packing up their belongings in boxes and plastic bags.

informational justice

The perceived fairness of the communications provided to employees from authorities

These sorts of informational injustices are all too common, for a variety of reasons. One factor is that sharing bad news is the worst part of the job for most managers, leading them to distance themselves when it's time to play messenger.[76] A survey of 372 human resources professionals revealed that almost 75 percent felt stress, anxiety, and depression when they had to conduct layoffs during the economic downturn.[77] Another factor may be that managers worry about triggering a lawsuit if they comprehensively and honestly explain the reasons for a layoff, a poor evaluation, or a missed promotion. Ironically, that defence mechanism is typically counterproductive, because research suggests that honest and adequate explanations are actually a powerful strategy for reducing retaliation responses against the organization.[78] In fact, low levels of informational justice can come back to haunt the organization if a wrongful termination claim is actually filed. How? Because the organization typically needs to provide performance evaluations for the terminated employee over the past few years, to show that the employee was fired for poor performance.[79] If managers refrained from offering candid and honest explanations on those evaluations, the organization can't offer anything to justify the termination.

One study provides a particularly effective demonstration of the power of informational justice (and interpersonal justice). The study occurred in three plants of a manufacturing company that specialized in small mechanical parts for the aerospace and automotive industries.[80] The company had recently lost two of its largest contracts and was forced to cut wages by 15 percent in two of the three plants. The company was planning to offer a short, impersonal explanation for the pay cut to both of the affected plants. However, as part of a research study, the company was convinced to offer a longer, more sincere explanation at one of the plants. Theft levels were then tracked before, during, and after the 10-week pay cut using the company's standard accounting formulas for inventory "shrinkage."

The results of the study are shown in Figure 8-5. In the plant without the pay cut, no change in theft levels occurred over the ten-week period. In the plant with the short, impersonal explanation, theft rose dramatically during the pay cut, likely as a means of retaliating for perceived inequity, before falling to previous levels once the cut had passed. Importantly, in the plant with the long, sincere explanation, the rise in theft was much less significant during the pay cut, with theft levels again falling back to normal levels once the cut had ended. Clearly, the higher levels of informational and interpersonal justice were worth it from a cost-savings perspective. The difference in theft across the two plants is remarkable, given that the long, sincere explanation was only a few minutes longer than the short, impersonal explanation. What's a few extra minutes if it can save a few thousand dollars?

Summary Taken together, distributive, procedural, interpersonal, and informational justice can be used to describe how fairly employees are treated by authorities. When an authority adheres to the justice rules in Table 8-1, those actions provide behavioural data that the authority might be trustworthy. Indeed, studies show that all four justice forms have strong correlations with employee trust levels.[81] All else being equal, employees trust authorities who allocate outcomes fairly; make decisions in a consistent, unbiased, and accurate way; and communicate decision-making details in a respectful, comprehensive, and honest manner. Which authorities are most likely to adhere to these sorts of rules? Research on ethics can provide some answers.

Ethics

Research on ethics seeks to explain why people behave in a manner consistent with generally accepted norms of morality, and why they sometimes violate those norms.[82] The study of business ethics has two primary threads to it. One thread is *prescriptive* in nature, with scholars in philosophy debating how people *ought* to act using various codes and principles.[83] The prescriptive model is the dominant lens in discussions of legal ethics, medical ethics, and much of economics. The second thread is *descriptive* in nature, with scholars relying on scientific studies to observe how people *tend* to act based on certain individual and situational characteristics. The descriptive model is the dominant lens in psychology. Although the differences between these two threads give the study of business ethics a certain complexity, the philosophical and empirical approaches can be integrated to develop a more complete understanding of ethical behaviour.

FIGURE 8-5

The Effects of Justice on Theft During a Pay Cut

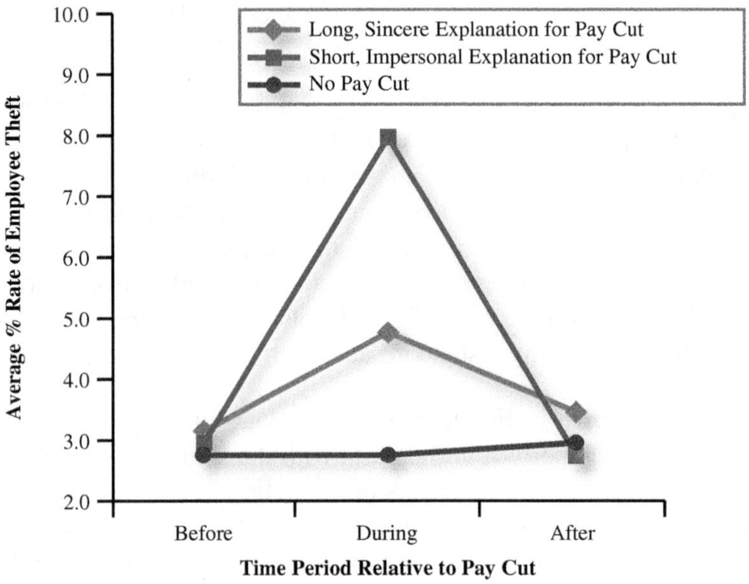

Source: Adapted from J. Greenberg, "Employee Theft as a Reaction to Underpayment Inequity: The Hidden Cost of Paycuts," *Journal of Applied Psychology* 75 (1990), pp. 561–68.

Some studies of business ethics focus on unethical behaviour—behaviour that clearly violates accepted norms of morality.[84] Unethical behaviours in organizations can be directed at employees (e.g., discrimination, harassment, health and safety violations, ignoring labor laws), customers (e.g., invading privacy, violating contract terms, using false advertising, fabricating test results), financiers (e.g., falsifying financial information, misusing confidential information, trading securities based on inside information), or society as a whole (e.g., violating environmental regulations, exposing the public to safety risks, doing business with third parties who are themselves unethical).[85] How prevalent are such behaviours? Recent surveys suggest that 76 percent of employees have observed illegal or unethical conduct in their organizations within the past 12 months.[86] Those base rates may be even higher in some countries, as described in our ***OB Internationally*** feature.

Other studies focus on what might be termed "merely ethical" behaviour—behaviour that adheres to some minimally accepted standard of morality.[87] Merely ethical behaviours might include obeying labour laws and complying with formal rules and contracts. Still other studies focus on what might be called "especially ethical" behaviours—ones that exceed some minimally accepted standard of

OB INTERNATIONALLY

If unethical actions are defined as behaviours that fall below minimum standards of morality, the key question becomes "Whose standards of morality?" Research on business ethics across cultures reveals that different countries have different baseline levels of unethical actions. Transparency International is an organization that monitors unethical practices in countries around the world. Using data from businesspeople, risk analysts, investigative journalists, country experts, and public citizens, the organization rates countries on a scale of 1 (unethical) to 10 (ethical).[88] Here are some of the scores from the 1999 version of the rankings:

Score	Country	Score	Country
10.0	Denmark	3.8	South Korea
9.8	Finland	3.6	Turkey
9.4	Sweden	3.4	China
9.2	Canada	3.4	Mexico
8.7	Australia	3.2	Thailand
8.6	Germany	3.0	Argentina
7.7	Hong Kong	2.9	Colombia
7.7	Ireland	2.9	India
7.5	United States	2.6	Ukraine
6.8	Israel	2.6	Venezuela
6.6	France	2.6	Vietnam
6.0	Japan	2.4	Russia
4.9	Greece	1.6	Nigeria
4.7	Italy	1.5	Cameroon

These rankings reveal the challenges involved for any multinational corporation that does business in areas at the top and bottom of the rankings. Should the company have the same ethical expectations for employees in all countries, regardless of ethical norms? For now, that seems to be the most common position. For example, the Coca-Cola Company's Code of Business Conduct "applies to all the Company's business worldwide and to all Company employees."[89] The code is given to all employees and covers topics such as conflicts of interest, dealing with government officials, customer and supplier interactions, and political contributions. The code also describes the disciplinary actions associated with any violations of the code.

morality. Especially ethical behaviours might include charitable giving or **whistle-blowing**, which occurs when former or current employees expose illegal or immoral actions by their organization.[90] Whistle-blowing can be viewed as especially ethical, because whistle-blowers risk potential retaliation by other members of the organization, especially when whistle-blowers lack status and power.[91] Ironically, the company often winds up benefitting from that risk taking, as whistle-blowing can bring significant improvements to the ethical culture in an organization over the long term.[92]

whistle-blowing
Employees' exposing illegal or immoral actions by their employer

8.5 What is the four-component model of ethical decision making?

Why do some authorities behave unethically while others do not? One set of answers can be derived from research in social psychology. The **four-component model** of ethical decision making argues that ethical behaviours result from a multistage sequence beginning with *moral awareness*, continuing on to *moral judgment*, then to *moral intent*, and ultimately to *ethical behaviour*.[93] Figure 8-6 presents an adaptation of this model. In addition to depicting the four components, the figure illustrates that unethical behaviour can be triggered by characteristics of a person or the situation.[94] Put differently, and drawing on the adage "One bad apple spoils the barrel," ethical behaviour can be driven by both good versus bad apples and good versus bad barrels.[95] The sections that follow review the components of this model in detail.

four-component model
A model that argues that ethical behaviours result from the multistage sequence of moral awareness, moral judgment, moral intent, and ethical behaviour

FIGURE 8-6

The Four-Component Model of Ethical Decision Making

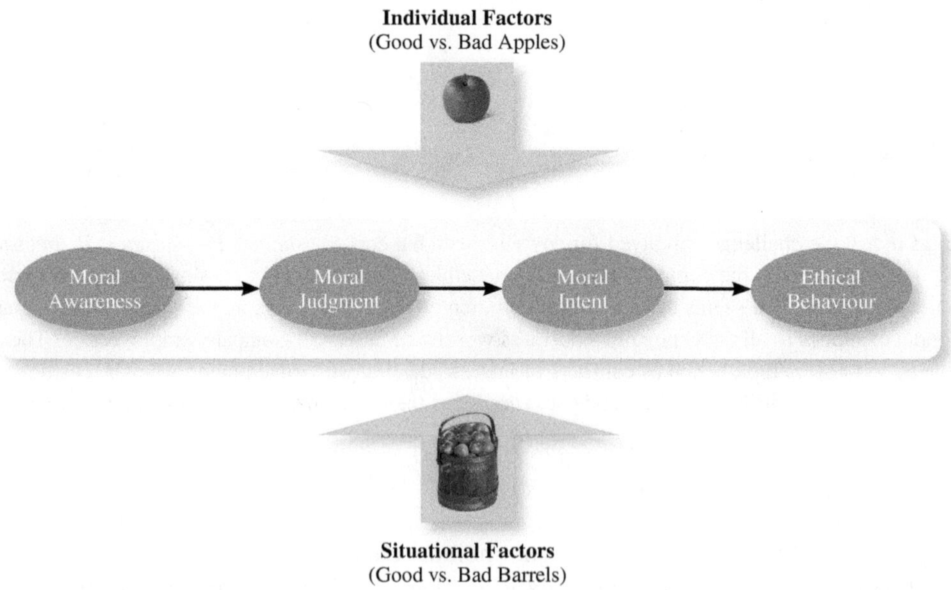

Source: Adapted from J.R. Rest, *Moral Development: Advances in Research and Theory* (New York: Praeger, 1986).

Moral Awareness The first step needed to explain why an authority acts ethically is **moral awareness**, which occurs when an authority recognizes that a moral issue exists in a situation or that an ethical code or principle is relevant to the circumstance.[96] Ethical issues rarely come equipped with red flags that mark them as morally sensitive.[97] Sometimes authorities act unethically simply because they don't perceive that moral issues are relevant in a given situation, so the ethical merits of certain actions are never debated. Let's say you own a clothing retailer that specializes in fashion-forward styles at low prices. You know that Diane von Furstenberg's styles are hot this year, and your buying team has just discovered a vendor that makes cheap knockoffs of those styles. Do you buy clothes from that vendor and hang them on your racks? On the one hand, you might be tempted to say that imitation is how fashion trends spread—that the gurus of style *expect* their products to be copied. Besides, a skirt is a skirt, and knockoffs are part of the game in a lot of businesses. On the other hand, Diane von Furstenberg's styles are her intellectual property, and the people that work for her label put a great deal of time, effort, and talent into their clothes.

moral awareness
Recognition by an authority that a moral issue exists in a situation

Moral awareness depends in part on characteristics of the issue itself, as some issues have more built-in ethical salience than others. A concept called **moral intensity** captures the degree to which an issue has ethical urgency.[98] As is described in Table 8-3, moral intensity is driven by two general concerns, both of which have more specific facets.[99] First and foremost, a particular issue is high in moral intensity if the potential for harm is perceived to be high. An act that might injure 1,000 people is more morally intense than an act that might injure 10 people, and an act that might result in death is more morally intense than an act that might result in illness.[100] Second, a particular issue is high in moral intensity if there is social pressure surrounding it. An act that violates a clear social norm is more morally intense than an act that seems similar to what everyone else is doing.

moral intensity
The degree to which an issue has ethical urgency

TABLE 8-3

The Dimensions of Moral Intensity

General Dimension	Specific Facet	Description
Potential for harm	Magnitude of consequences	How much harm would be done to other people?
	Probability of effect	How likely is it that the act will actually occur and that the assumed consequences will match predictions?
	Temporal immediacy	How much time will pass between the act and the onset of its consequences?
	Concentration of effect	Will the consequences be concentrated on a limited set of people, or will they be more far reaching?
Social pressure	Social consensus	How much agreement is there that the proposed act would be unethical?
	Proximity	How near (in a psychological or physical sense) is the authority to those who will be affected?

Sources: Adapted from T.M. Jones, "Ethical Decision Making by Individuals in Organizations: An Issue-Contingent Model," *Academy of Management Review* 16 (1991), pp. 366–95; and A. Singhapakdi, S.J. Vitell, and K.L. Kraft, "Moral Intensity and Ethical Decision-Making of Marketing Professionals," *Journal of Business Research* 36 (1996), pp. 245–55.

Moral awareness also depends on the way authorities observe and perceive the events that happen around them. A concept called **moral attentiveness** captures the degree to which people chronically perceive and consider issues of morality during their experiences.[101] Research in cognitive psychology shows that people pay more attention to stimuli that are significant, vivid, and recognizable. Authorities who are morally attentive tend to view the world through a lens of morality, giving ethical issues a particular significance, vividness, and recognizability. That lens colours the way they identify and interpret information and also shapes the way they analyze and reflect on it. Morally attentive people are likely to report that they face several ethical dilemmas in a typical day, that many of the decisions they face have ethical consequences, that they regularly think about issues of morality, and that they enjoy pondering moral issues.

moral attentiveness

The degree to which people chronically perceive and consider issues of morality during their experiences

Moral Judgment Some authorities may recognize that a moral issue exists in a given situation but then be unable to determine whether a given course of action is right or wrong. The second step needed to explain why an authority acts ethically is therefore **moral judgment**, which reflects the process people use to determine whether a particular course of action is ethical or unethical.[102] One of the most important factors influencing moral judgment is described in Kohlberg's theory of **cognitive moral development**.[103] This theory argues that as people age and mature, they move through various stages of moral development—each more mature and sophisticated than the prior one. All else equal, authorities who operate at more mature stages of moral development should demonstrate better moral judgment. You might wonder how the moral development of a person can be measured. One approach is to give people a series of ethical dilemmas like the one in Table 8-4, then ask questions to gain insights into their decision-making process.[104]

moral judgment

The process people use to determine whether a particular course of action is ethical or unethical

cognitive moral development

People's movement through several states of moral development, each more mature and sophisticated than the prior one

According to Kohlberg, people begin their moral development at the *preconventional* stage.[105] At this stage, right versus wrong is viewed in terms of the consequences of various actions for the individual. For example, children seek to avoid punishment for its own sake, regardless of any concern about moral order. Similarly, children obey adults for its own sake, regardless of the respect or wisdom shown by those adults. Over time, the desire to obtain pleasure and avoid pain expands to the formation of "you scratch my back, I'll scratch yours" sort of exchanges. Such relationships remain self-interested however, with little concern for loyalty, gratitude, or fairness. In the case of the ethical dilemma in Table 8-4, viewing question 1 as one of the most important issues would signal preconventional thinking.

As people mature, their moral judgment reaches the *conventional* stage.[106] At this stage, right versus wrong is referenced to the expectations of one's family and one's society. At first, people seek the approval of friends and family members, conforming to stereotypes about what's right. Question 2 in

Table 8-4 reflects this sort of priority. Over time, people come to emphasize the laws, rules, and orders that govern society. Concepts such as doing one's duty and maintaining the social order come to be valued for their own sake. Question 3 reflects this level of moral sophistication. Research suggests that most adults find themselves at the conventional stage.[107] That positioning is relevant to organizations, because it shows that moral judgment can be influenced by organizational policies, practices, and norms.

TABLE 8-4

Ethical Dilemma Used to Assess Moral Development

Pat is responsible for providing expenditure estimates for his/her unit to the controller in his/her company who then determines the budget for all units in the company. Upper management has always emphasized the importance of providing timely and accurate financial estimates, and they have backed up this policy by disciplining managers for inaccurate or late estimates. Pat recently realized that the figures that he/she supplied contained a mistake. The mistake was that an expense was projected to be larger than it should have been. It will not affect the ability of the company to stay within the budget. However, the money could be used to cover other company expenditures. Up to this point, no one else has identified the mistake and it is unlikely that they will. Should Pat report the mistake?
On a scale from 1 = *No Importance* to 5 = *Great Importance*, rate how important each of the following questions is to your decision:
1. Could Pat receive a more harsh punishment if the company finds the mistake without his/her help?
2. Whether Pat's subordinates and peers would lose faith in Pat if he/she is caught instead of reporting the mistake him-/herself.
3. Whether company policy ought to be respected by all employees.
4. Would reporting the mistake do any good for Pat or society?
5. What values Pat has set for him-/herself in his/her personal code of behaviour?

Source: From Greg Lovisckу, *Journal of Business Ethics*, "Assessing Managers' Ethical Decision-Making: An Objective Measure of Managerial Moral Judgment," Vol. 73. Copyright © 2007, Springer Netherlands. Reprinted with permission.

TABLE 8-5

Moral Principles Used in the Principled Stage

Type of Principle	Specific Principle	Description (and Contributors)
Consequentialist	Utilitarianism	An act is morally right if it results in the greatest amount of good for the greatest number of people—sometimes termed the "greatest happiness principle" (Jeremy Bentham, John Stuart Mill).
	Egoism	An act is morally right if the decision maker freely decides to pursue either short-term or long-term interests. Markets are purported to limit the degree to which one egoist's interests harm the interests of another (Adam Smith).
Nonconsequentialist	Ethics of duties	An act is morally right if it fulfills the "categorical imperative"—an unambiguously explicit set of three crucial maxims: (a) the act should be performable by everyone with no harm to society; (b) the act should respect human dignity; (c) the act should be endorsable by others (Immanuel Kant).
	Ethics of rights	An act is morally right if it respects the natural rights of others, such as the right to life, liberty, justice, expression, association, consent, privacy, and education (John Locke, John Rawls).
	Virtue ethics	An act is morally right if it allows the decision maker to lead a "good life" by adhering to virtues like wisdom, honesty, courage, friendship, mercy, loyalty, modesty, and patience (Aristotle).

Source: Adapted from A. Crane and D. Matten, *Business Ethics* (New York: Oxford University Press, 2007).

The most sophisticated moral thinkers reach the *principled* (or *postconventional*) stage.[108] At this stage, right versus wrong is referenced to a set of defined, established moral principles. Research suggests that fewer than 20 percent of people reach this principled stage.[109] Philosophers have identified a number of **moral principles** that serve as prescriptive guides for making moral judgments; some of the most influential are shown in Table 8-5. Rather than viewing a given principle as the single, best lens for making decisions, it's better to view the principles as a prism for shedding light on a given situation from a number of different angles.[110] The consequentialist principles in Table 8-5 judge the morality of an action according to its goals, aims, or outcomes (these principles are sometimes termed "teleological," after the Greek word for "goal").[111] Question 4 in Table 8-4 reflects these sorts of concerns. The nonconsequentialist principles judge the morality of an action solely on its intrinsic desirability (these principles are sometimes termed *deontological*, after the Greek word for "duty," or "formalist," due to their emphasis on formalized codes and standards). Viewing question 5 as one of the most important issues in the dilemma would signal nonconsequentialist thinking.

moral principles
Prescriptive guides for making moral judgments

Moral Intent Assuming that an authority recognizes that a moral issue exists in a situation and possesses the cognitive moral development to choose the right course of action, one step remains: The authority has to *want* to act ethically. **Moral intent** reflects an authority's degree of commitment to the moral course of action.[112] The distinction between awareness or judgment on the one hand and intent on the other is important, because many unethical people know and understand that what they're doing is wrong—they just choose to do it anyway. Why? Sometimes situational factors encourage people to go against their moral convictions. For example, organizations may possess unethical cultures, where violations of moral codes become the rule rather than the exception (see Chapter 15 on organizational culture for more discussion of such issues).[113] As another example, economic pressures from assigned goals or specific incentives can encourage people to set aside their moral judgment, at least for a time.[114]

moral intent
An authority's degree of commitment to the moral course of action

What explains the ability of some people to resist situational pressures and stay true to their moral judgment? One factor is **moral identity**—the degree to which a person self-identifies as a moral person.[115] Our self-concepts have a number of components to them: We may define ourselves by what we do, where we come from, what our family status is, or what cultural or ethnic groups we belong to. People with strong moral identities define themselves as compassionate, generous, honest, kind, fair, and hard-working. Their emotional well-being and sense of self is wrapped up in living up to those virtues. Moreover, the actions they take in their daily life, from the things they buy to the hobbies they have to the groups they join, are viewed as symbols of those virtues. Research suggests that people with strong moral identities volunteer more for charitable work and donate more to charity drives.[116] Research also suggests that moral identity "moderates" the effects of moral judgment on ethical behaviour. Recall that, in the language of theory diagrams, moderators affect the strength of the relationship between two variables. For example, one study shows that managers who emphasize specific ethics principles are less likely to engage in unethical behaviours (e.g., calling in sick to take a day off, ignoring others' unethical actions), but only when they define themselves as a moral person.[117] When morality is not an important piece of their identity, their moral principles have no relationship with their actual behaviour.

moral identity
The degree to which a person views himself or herself as a moral person

Summary Taken together, the stages of the four-component model can be used to explain why authorities act in an ethical or unethical manner. When authorities are morally aware, when they have sophisticated moral judgment, and when they possess strong moral intent, chances are their actions will tend to be ethical. By extension, those authorities should attend more to the rules of distributive, procedural, interpersonal, and informational justice, because treating employees fairly is itself an ethical act.[118] Those authorities should also be viewed as trustworthy, in that moral awareness, judgment, and intent should result in higher levels of both benevolence and integrity.

OB RESEARCH IN CANADA

Courtesy of Dr. Karl Aquino

Dr. Karl Aquino is a professor within the Sauder School of Business at the University of British Columbia, and is an expert on some of the topics covered in this chapter, including organizational justice and moral cognition and behaviour. Back in 2009, Dr. Aquino established the *Immorality Lab* on the UBC Campus (immoralitylab.webs.com). According to Dr. Aquino, the purpose of this lab is "to study the many ways people mistreat one another and contribute to the sum total of misery and unhappiness in the world." In addition to studying immorality and why humans routinely commit acts of aggression, cruelty, and mayhem, Dr. Aquino also studies the capacity for humans to forgive and reconcile with those who have mistreated them. Evidently studying some of the "dark" topics in organizational behaviour has not put a dent in his productivity: Dr. Aquino is credited with over 80 journal publications and book chapters on these and other topics. On top of that, he is an avid basketball player. For more information about Dr. Aquino's fascinating research, look him up at www.sauder.ubc.ca.

Summary: Why Are Some Authorities More Trusted Than Others?

So what explains why some authorities are more trusted than others? As is illustrated in Figure 8-7, answering that question requires understanding the different sources in which trust can be rooted, including dispositions, cognitions, and affect. Disposition-based trust is rooted in an individual's trust propensity, whereas affect-based trust is rooted in a fondness for the authority. Cognition-based trust is driven by perceptions of trustworthiness, as employees attempt to assess the ability, benevolence, and integrity of authorities. Unfortunately, it's often difficult to gauge trustworthiness accurately, so employees instead look to more observable behaviours that can be used as indirect evidence of trustworthiness. Those behaviours may centre on the justice of authorities, with employees considering the distributive, procedural, interpersonal, and informational justice they have experienced at work. The justice and general trustworthiness of authorities in turn can be explained by authorities' own moral awareness, moral judgment, and moral intent.

FIGURE 8-7

Why Are Some Authorities More Trusted Than Others?

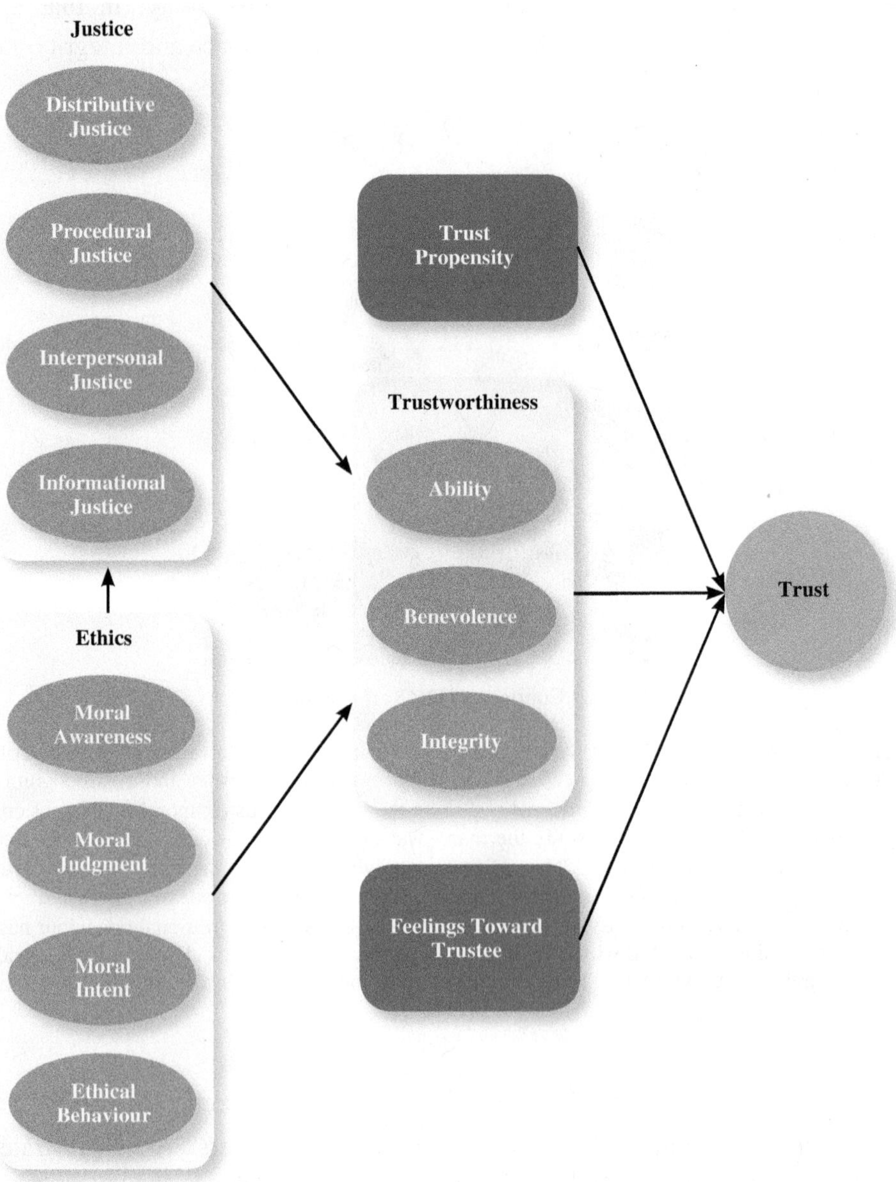

8.6 How does trust affect job performance and organizational commitment?

HOW IMPORTANT IS TRUST?

Does trust have a significant impact on the two primary outcomes in our integrative model of OB—does it correlate with job performance and organizational commitment? Figure 8-8 summarizes the research evidence linking trust to job performance and organizational commitment. The figure reveals that trust does affect job performance. Why? One reason is that trust is moderately correlated with task performance. A study of employees in eight plants of a tool manufacturing company sheds light on why trust benefits task performance.[119] The study gave employees survey measures of their trust in two different authorities: their plant's manager and the company's top management team. Both trust measures were significant predictors of employees' **ability to focus**, which reflects the degree to which employees can devote their attention to work, as opposed to "covering their backside," "playing politics," and "keeping an eye on the boss." The ability to focus is clearly vital to task performance in many jobs, particularly when job duties become more complex.

ability to focus
The degree to which employees can devote their attention to work

FIGURE 8-8

Effects of Trust on Performance and Commitment

Trust has a moderate positive effect on Job Performance. Employees who are willing to be vulnerable to authorities tend to have higher levels of *Task Performance*. They are also more likely to engage in *Citizenship Behaviour* and less likely to engage in *Counterproductive Behaviour*.

Trust has a strong positive effect on Organizational Commitment. Employees who are willing to be vulnerable to authorities tend to have higher levels of *Affective Commitment* and higher levels of *Normative Commitment*. Trust has no effect on *Continuance Commitment*.

Represents a strong correlation (around .50 in magnitude).

Represents a moderate correlation (around .30 in magnitude).

Represents a weak correlation (around .10 in magnitude).

Sources: K.T. Dirks and D.L. Ferrin, "Trust in Leadership: Meta-analytic Findings and Implications for Research and Practice," *Journal of Applied Psychology* 87 (2002), pp. 611–28; and J.A. Colquitt, B.A. Scott, and J.A. LePine, "Trust, Trustworthiness, and Trust Propensity: A Meta-analytic Test of Their Unique Relationships with Risk Taking and Job Performance," *Journal of Applied Psychology* 92 (2007), pp. 909–27.

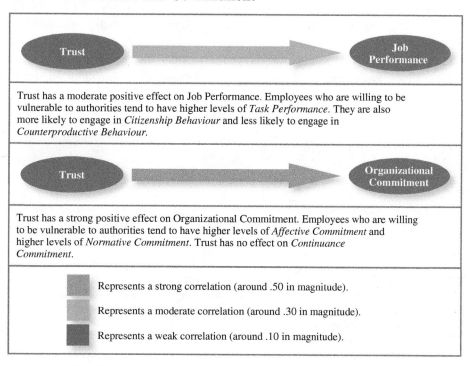

Trust also influences citizenship behaviour and counterproductive behaviour. Why? One reason is that the willingness to accept vulnerability changes the nature of the employee–employer relationship. Employees who don't trust their authorities have **economic exchange** relationships that are based on narrowly defined, quid pro quo obligations that are specified in advance and have an explicit repayment schedule.[120] Economic exchanges are impersonal, and resemble contractual agreements in that employees agree to fulfill the duties in their job description in exchange for financial compensation. As trust increases, **social exchange** relationships develop based on vaguely defined obligations that are open-ended and long-term in their repayment schedule.[121] Social exchanges are characterized by mutual investment; employees agree to go above and beyond their duties in exchange for fair and proper treatment by authorities. In social exchange contexts, employees are willing to engage in beneficial behaviours because they trust that those efforts will eventually be rewarded (see Chapter 3 on organizational commitment for more discussion of such issues).

economic exchange

Work relationships that resemble a contractual agreement by which employees fulfill job duties in exchange for financial compensation

social exchange

Work relationships characterized by mutual investment, with employees willing to engage in "extra mile" sorts of behaviours because they trust that their efforts will eventually be rewarded

Figure 8-8 also reveals that trust affects organizational commitment. Why? One reason is that trusting an authority increases the likelihood that an emotional bond will develop,[122] particularly if that trust is rooted in positive feelings for the authority. Trusting an authority also makes it more likely that a sense of obligation will develop, because employees feel more confident that the authority deserves that obligation. When negative events occur, employees who trust the authority are willing to accept the vulnerability that comes with continued employment,[123] remaining confident in their belief that the situation will eventually improve.

OB FOR STUDENTS

The most relevant form of unethical behaviour for students is cheating on exams and assignments. How common is cheating? One survey of almost 50,000 students at 69 schools found that 26 percent of undergraduate business majors admitted to serious cheating on exams, with 54 percent admitting to cheating on written assignments (including plagiarism or using a friend's homework).[124]

Why do students cheat? One likely reason is that grade pressures reduce moral intent: Even when students recognize that cheating is a moral issue and that the right decision is not to cheat, they do it anyway. Some support for this notion comes from a recent study of cheating among 5,331 students at 54 colleges and universities.[125] The students filled out anonymous surveys measuring 13 different cheating behaviours, along with four potential predictors of cheating: (1) understanding of academic integrity policies, (2) likelihood of being reported by a peer if caught cheating, (3) perceived severity of cheating penalties, and (4) how often they had observed another student cheating. Of those four potential predictors, which do you think had the strongest effect? That's right—observing another student cheating. In fact, none of the other three factors had any statistical relationship with cheating behaviours.

(Continued)

It may be that seeing others cheat creates a sort of peer pressure to keep up with one's classmates, particularly when classes are graded on a curve. What are some other reasons? Is it possible that students' moral judgments about the act have changed? Consider this example: A first-year computer-science student at Ryerson University was accused of cheating after it was discovered that he helped to run a Facebook study group used by 146 of his fellow students.[126] The student claimed that the study group was simply a forum for other students to ask questions and help each other with their homework assignments. Do you think this student was cheating? Do you think his behaviour or the behaviours of the other 146 students were unethical? Answers to these questions help schools gain a much deeper understanding of why students cheat if such behaviours are to be curbed.

8.7 What steps can organizations take to become more trustworthy?

APPLICATION: SOCIAL RESPONSIBILITY

Now that you understand the factors that drive trust in authorities and the importance of trust levels to performance and commitment, we turn our attention to a very practical question: "How can organizations become more trustworthy?" Certainly that's a big question with no single answer. However, one strategy is to focus the organization's attention on **corporate social responsibility**, a perspective that acknowledges that the responsibilities of a business encompass the economic, legal, ethical, and citizenship expectations of society.[127] This perspective maintains the belief that the foundation of any business is profitability, because organizations must fulfill their economic responsibilities to their employees and their shareholders. However, the social responsibility lens supplements that belief by arguing that the company's obligations do not end with profit maximization.

corporate social responsibility

A perspective that acknowledges that the responsibility of a business encompasses the economic, legal, ethical, and citizenship expectations of society

The legal component of corporate social responsibility argues that the law represents society's codification of right and wrong and must therefore be followed.[128] Fulfilling this component speaks to the integrity of the organization and suggests that it has reached the conventional level of moral development. Further violations of labour laws on Nike's part would signal a breach of this component, so protecting its reputation will likely require a continuing emphasis on monitoring and inspections. What steps can organizations take to promote legal compliance? In Canada, for instance, occupational health and safety laws are in place across the country to protect people. To raise awareness and promote healthy and safe workplaces, and ensure legal compliance, many organizations form internal committees made up of company and employee (or union) representatives.[129] The roles of these committees are varied, but generally include being aware of relevant safety issues and hazards, monitoring the effectiveness of ongoing programs, investigating complaints, and providing annual reports for external agencies.[130] These committees often represent a tangible sign, both internally and externally, that the organization "walks the walk" with respect to caring for the well-being of its employees.

The ethical component of corporate social responsibility argues that organizations have an obligation to do what is right, just, and fair and to avoid harm.[131] Fulfilling this component is relevant to the benevolence and integrity of the organization and suggests that it has reached the principled level of moral development.[132] Regardless of its legal implications, the way Nike manages the employees who work in its factories speaks to the ethical makeup of its culture. What can organizations do to improve that culture? An example of an organization committed to the ethical component of corporate social responsibility is TELUS, one of the largest telecommunications companies in Canada. At TELUS, the corporate ethics policy provides guidelines for the standards of ethical conduct by all managers and employees.[133] The policy spells out, and illustrates with case examples, a set of core values that people can use to navigate day-to-day moral dilemmas.[134] In fact, to promote awareness of the corporate ethics policy all organizational members have to, every year, complete an online course as a term of employment.[135]

The citizenship component of corporate social responsibility argues that organizations should contribute resources to improve the quality of life in the communities in which they work.[136] A great example is Canadian Tire's JumpStart program, which helps kids in financial need participate in organized sport and recreation such as hockey, soccer, and swimming. Since its launch in 2005, JumpStart has already helped thousands of kids.[137] However, the citizenship component may also involve efforts geared toward environmental sustainability. The citizenship component may also involve efforts geared toward environmental sustainability. On that front, Nike has joined a number of notable companies, including TELUS, in adopting "green" processes. TELUS, for instance, has taken steps to reduce its energy consumption and carbon emissions as part of its role as a responsible corporate citizen.[138]

TAKEAWAYS

8.1 Trust is the willingness to be vulnerable to an authority on the basis of positive expectations about the authority's actions and intentions. Justice reflects the perceived fairness of an authority's decision making and can be used to explain why employees judge some authorities as more trustworthy than others. Ethics reflects the degree to which the behaviours of an authority are in accordance with generally accepted moral norms and can be used to explain why authorities choose to act in a trustworthy manner.

8.2 Trust can be disposition-based, meaning that one's personality includes a general propensity to trust others. Trust can also be cognition-based, meaning that it's rooted in a rational assessment of the authority's trustworthiness. Finally, trust can be affect-based, meaning that it's rooted in feelings toward the authority that go beyond any rational assessment of trustworthiness.

8.3 Trustworthiness is judged along three dimensions. Ability reflects the skills, competencies, and areas of expertise that an authority possesses. Benevolence is the degree to which an authority wants to do good for the trustor, apart from any selfish or profit-centred motives. Integrity is the degree to which an authority adheres to a set of values and principles that the trustor finds acceptable.

8.4 The fairness of an authority's decision making can be judged along four dimensions. Distributive justice reflects the perceived fairness of decision-making outcomes. Procedural justice reflects the perceived fairness of decision-making processes. Interpersonal justice reflects the perceived fairness of the treatment received by employees from authorities. Informational justice reflects the perceived fairness of the communications provided to employees from authorities.

8.5 The four-component model of ethical decision making argues that ethical behaviour depends on three concepts. Moral awareness reflects whether an authority recognizes that a moral issue exists in a situation. Moral judgment reflects whether the authority can accurately identify the "right" course of action. Moral intent reflects an authority's degree of commitment to the moral course of action.

8.6 Trust has a moderate positive relationship with job performance and a strong positive relationship with organizational commitment.

8.7 Organizations can become more trustworthy by emphasizing corporate social responsibility, a perspective that acknowledges that the responsibilities of a business encompass the economic, legal, ethical, and citizenship expectations of society.

KEY TERMS

ability (dimension of trustworthiness)
ability to focus
abusive supervision
affect-based trust
benevolence (dimension of trustworthiness)
cognition-based trust
cognitive moral development
corporate social responsibility
disposition-based trust
distributive justice
economic exchange
ethics
four-component model
informational justice
integrity (dimension of trustworthiness)
interpersonal justice
justice
moral attentiveness
moral awareness
moral identity
moral intensity
moral intent
moral judgment
moral principles
procedural justice
reputation
social exchange
trust
trust propensity
trustworthiness
whistle-blowing

DISCUSSION QUESTIONS

8.1 Which would be more damaging in organizational life—being too trusting or not being trusting enough? Why do you feel that way?

8.2 Consider the three dimensions of trustworthiness (ability, benevolence, and integrity). Which of those dimensions would be most important when deciding whether to trust your boss? What about when deciding whether to trust a friend? If your two answers differ, why do they?

8.3 Putting yourself in the shoes of a manager, which of the four justice dimensions (distributive, procedural, interpersonal, informational) would you find it most difficult to maximize? Which would be the easiest to maximize and why?

8.4 Which component of ethical decision making do you believe best explains student cheating: moral awareness, moral judgment, or moral intent? Why do you feel that way?

8.5 Assume you were applying for a job at a company known for its corporate social responsibility. How important would that be to you when deciding whether to accept a job offer?

CASE • NIKE

Hannah Jones serves as Nike's vice-president of corporate social responsibility, overseeing a 135-person team and reporting directly to CEO Mark Parker. Jones's team is charged with weaving issues of corporate social responsibility throughout Nike's operations. That mission includes auditing and managing Nike's factories around the world. However, it also includes issues of environmental sustainability. In 1992, a German magazine pointed out that the signature Nike Air pocket included more than just air—it also contained sulfur hexafluoride, or SF_6, a potent greenhouse gas more commonly linked to older refrigerators and air conditioners. SF_6 breaks down slowly in the atmosphere, which means that even very small amounts have a significant environmental impact. Estimates suggest that at the peak of SF_6 production in 1997, Nike Air footwear carried a greenhouse effect equivalent to the tailpipes of one million automobiles.

It took Nike almost 14 years to devise a new air pocket that was as light, durable, and shock-absorbing as the SF_6 version. The breakthrough wound up utilizing nitrogen, held in by a redesigned sole that includes 65 wafer-thin layers of plastic film. The new approach, which debuted with Nike's Air Max 360, allows the air pocket to stretch throughout the sole, giving even more comfort at even less weight. The company has also devised a program that calculates an environmental impact rating for each shoe, based on use of toxic adhesives, curbing of waste, and use of recycled materials. Even the Air Jordan—arguably Nike's flagship shoe—was designed with environmental impact in mind, such that the shoe's sole consists of ground-up bits of old Nike sneakers. You won't see these issues discussed in television or print ads for Nike shoes, however. Unlike other major corporations which aggressively trumpet their "green" initiatives, Nike prefers to deemphasize sustainability in its marketing efforts. One independent branding consultant explains that strategy by noting, "Nike has always been about winning. How is sustainability relevant to its brand?"

8.1 Do you agree with Nike's decision to downplay "green" issues when marketing its shoes? Why or why not?

8.2 Assuming price and quality are both acceptable, to what degree do you consider the ethical reputation of a company when buying a or service?

8.3 Does it seem like Nike is doing enough to build and maintain the trust in its brand? If not, what else would you like to see the company pursue?

Sources: S. Holmes, "Nike Goes for the Green," *BusinessWeek*, September 25, 2006, pp. 106–108; R. Jana, "Nike Goes Green. Very Quietly," *BusinessWeek*, June 22, 2009; E. Levenson, "Citizen Nike," *Fortune*, November 24, 2008, pp. 165–70.

EXERCISE • UNETHICAL BEHAVIOUR

The purpose of this exercise is to explore how authorities can prevent unethical behaviours on the part of their employees. This exercise uses groups, so your instructor will either assign you to a group or ask you to create your own group. The exercise has the following steps:

8.1 Read the following scenario:

> Alex Grant recently graduated from university and is excited to be starting his first job as a store manager for The Grocery Cart, a large supermarket chain. The company has a very good management training program, and it is one of the fastest-growing chains in the nation. If Alex does well managing his first store, there are a number of promising advancement opportunities in the company. After completing the store management training program, Alex met with Regina Hill, his area supervisor. She informed him that he would be taking charge of a medium-volume store ($250,000 in sales/week) in an upper-class neighbourhood. This store had been operating without a manager for the past six months. The store had also not made a profit in any of the monthly financial reports for the last year.
>
> Hill also shared the following information with Alex: Because the store has been without a store manager for the past six months, the assistant manager (Drew Smith) has been in charge. Drew is known for being highly competent and a solid performer. However, there have been complaints that he is frequently rude to employees and insults and ridicules them whenever they make mistakes. Turnover among sales clerks and cashiers at this store has been somewhat higher than in other stores in the area. The average pay of clerks and cashiers is $6.44/hour. The last two semiannual inventories at this store showed significant losses. There has been a large amount of theft from the stockroom (an area where only employees are allowed). Given that the store has generally done well in sales (compared with others in the area) and that most expenses seem well under control, Hill believes that the profitability problem for this store is primarily due to theft. Therefore, she suggested that Alex's plans for the store should focus on this.

8.2 As a manager, what steps should Alex take to reduce employee theft? Come up with three ideas. Elect a group member to write these ideas on the board or on a transparency.

8.3 Now read the following scenario:

When Alex arrived for his first day of work in his new store, he saw that Drew was in the process of terminating an employee (Rudy Johnson) who had been caught stealing. Alex immediately went to the break room where the termination interview was being conducted to learn more. Drew informed Alex that Rudy had been a grocery clerk for the past six weeks and that he had apparently figured out how to tell if the alarms to the stockroom doors were off. Rudy would then open the back doors and stack cases of beer outside to pick up after his shift. After Drew had caught Rudy doing this, Drew had had a conversation with one of his friends who works as a restaurant manager down the street. Drew's friend noted that he had hired Rudy a few months ago and that he'd been caught stealing there too.

Turning to Rudy, Drew asked, "So, Rudy, what do you have to say for yourself?" Rudy quickly replied: "Look here, [expletive], you don't pay me enough to work here and put up with this garbage. In fact, you're always riding everyone like they're your personal servant or something. So I was trying to get some beer. I've seen you let stockers take home damaged merchandise a dozen times. So just because they cut open a box of cookies, which we all know they do on purpose, they get to take stuff home for free. For that matter, we've all seen you do the same thing! I've never seen you make a big deal about this stuff before. Why can't I get a few cases of beer? What's the big deal?"

8.4 Do these events give you any additional insights into how to decrease employee theft in this store? If so, elect a group member to write an additional one or two reasons in your spot on the board or on your transparency.

8.5 Class discussion (whether in groups or as a class) should centre on whether the theft that's occurring at The Grocery Cart reveals a problem of moral awareness, moral judgment, or moral intent. In addition, does the theft point to a problem with "bad apples," a "bad barrel," or both?

Source: Adapted from E.C. Tomlinson, "Teaching the Interactionist Model of Ethics," *Journal of Management Education* 33 (2009), pp. 142–65.

OB ASSESSMENTS • TRUST PROPENSITY

Are you by nature trusting or suspicious? This assessment is designed to measure trust propensity—a dispositional willingness to trust other people. Answer each question using the response scale provided. Then subtract your answers to the boldfaced questions from 6, with the difference being your new answers for those questions. For example, if your original answer for question 4 was "4," your new answer is "2" (6 – 4). Then add up your answers for the eight questions.

1 Strongly Disagree	2 Disagree	3 Neutral	4 Agree	5 Strongly Agree	
1. One should be very cautious with strangers.					______
2. Most experts tell the truth about the limits of their knowledge.					______
3. Most people can be counted on to do what they say they will do.					______
4. These days, you must be alert or someone is likely to take advantage of you.					______
5. Most salespeople are honest in describing their products.					______
6. Most repair people will not overcharge people who are ignorant of their specialty.					______
7. Most people answer public opinion polls honestly.					______
8. Most adults are competent at their jobs.					______

Scoring and Interpretation

If your scores add up to 21 or more, you tend to be trusting of other people, which means you are often willing to accept some vulnerability to others under conditions of risk. If your scores add up to 20 or less, you tend to be suspicious of other people, which means you are rarely willing to accept some vulnerability to others under conditions of risk. Remember, when interpreting your scores on these assessments it is important to consider the *reliability* and *validity* of these tools (see Chapter 1, ***OB Assessments***).

Sources: R.C. Mayer and J.H. Davis, "The Effect of the Performance Appraisal System on Trust for Management: A Field Quasi-Experiment," *Journal of Applied Psychology* 84 (1999), pp. 123–36. See also F.D. Schoorman, R.C. Mayer, C. Roger, and J.H. Davis, "Empowerment in Veterinary Clinics: The Role of Trust in Delegation," presented in a symposium on trust at the 11th Annual Conference, Society for Industrial and Organizational Psychology (SIOP), April 1996, San Diego.

Learning and Decision Making

CHAPTER 9

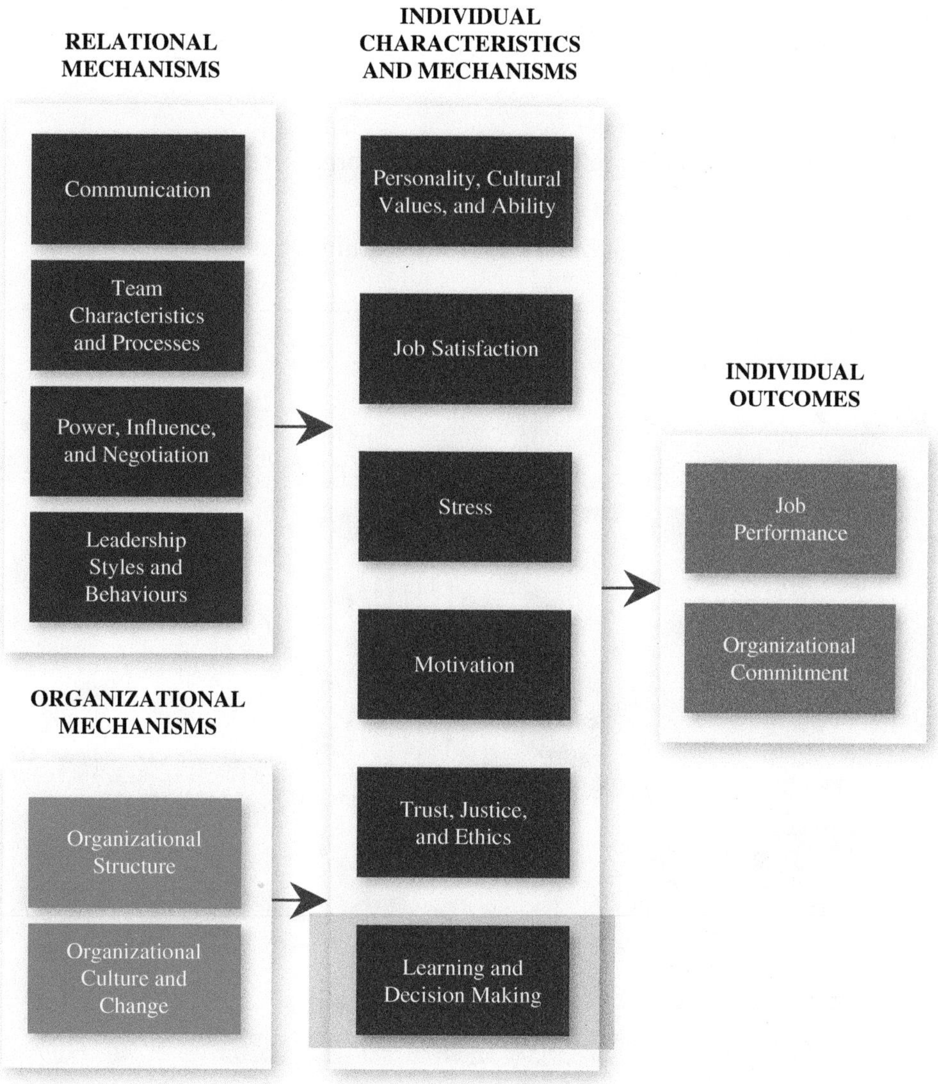

Learning Outcomes

After reading this chapter, you should be able to answer the following questions:

9.1 What is learning, and how does it affect decision making?

9.2 What types of knowledge can employees gain as they learn and build expertise?

9.3 What are the methods by which employees learn in organizations?

9.4 What two methods can employees use to make decisions?

9.5 What decision-making problems can prevent employees from translating their learning into accurate decisions?

9.6 How does learning affect job performance and organizational commitment?

9.7 What steps can organizations take to foster learning?

KPMG Canada

Learning how to be a professional accountant requires the mastery of many behavioural competencies that can only be acquired through on-the-job experience.

Getty/Yellow Dog Productions RF

KPMG Canada is affiliated with KPMG International, a global network of professional firms that provide audit, tax, and advisory (consulting) services to public and private business, not-for-profit, and public-sector organizations.[1] With 700 partners and more than 6,000 employees spread across the country in 34 locations,

KPMG Canada generated roughly $1.3 billion of revenue in 2014.[2] One of the major challenges facing KPMG Canada is to sustain a labour-intensive business at a time when many of its seasoned professional staff are approaching retirement age.

An example of a large office facing this challenge is KPMG Vancouver. Every year, this office tries to hire between 40 and 60 Chartered Accountant (CA) students. Some of these may have worked for the firm in co-op positions, but many come to the firm directly from university-based accounting programs. Becoming or replacing a CA is not an easy process. In addition to an appropriate university degree, CA students need several years of practical experience with a public practice accounting firm, and need to pass the Uniform Final Evaluation (UFE),[3] which is the CA exam. Once this exam is passed, employees start to be moved around to different areas of the firm, such as Canadian tax. By the employee's fifth year, the firm usually promotes the employee to manager, or signals that it is time to move on to other career paths.

Sandi,* 25, was one of the top accounting students in her hiring year. Growing up outside of the city, she had always wondered what it would be like to work in a downtown office. So when she was presented with an opportunity to work as a CA student at KPMG's Vancouver office, it was like a dream come true.

During new-staff orientation, Sandi quickly realized that she couldn't just rely on the technical competence she had mastered in her university courses. She had always impressed her professors and performed well on class assignments and exams; but this was different. Not only did KPMG expect incoming CA students to have a good working knowledge of accounting and applicable audit standards, it was also evident that new competencies would have to be acquired and mastered on the job.[4]

How would she survive in such a highly competitive and driven culture? Could she work with clients (some difficult) and identify improvement opportunities for them? How would she be able to manage time and stress? Who could she trust? Would she be able to form allies and networks to help her get things done? Could she portray the right attitude that commands respect from people in the firm who were much more experienced? All these questions ran through her mind. With no textbooks, no lectures, and certainly no professors to provide answers, how was she ever going to learn what she needed to know in order to be successful?

*Fictional character; any resemblance to anyone living or dead is purely coincidental.

9.1 What is learning, and how does it affect decision making?

LEARNING AND DECISION MAKING

Sandi in the chapter-opening vignette is clearly concerned about learning the ropes quickly. What she may not realize is that KPMG also shares her concern, because learning and decision making are so important to the organization. **Learning** reflects relatively permanent changes in an employee's knowledge or skill that result from experience.[5] The more employees learn, the more they bring to the table when they come to work. Why is learning so important? Because it has a significant impact on **decision making**, which refers to the process of generating and choosing from a set of alternatives to solve a problem. The more knowledge and skills employees possess, the more likely they are to make accurate and sound decisions. The risk, at KPMG and other organizations, is that less experienced employees will lack the knowledge base needed to make the right decisions when stepping into new roles.

learning

A relatively permanent change in an employee's knowledge or skill that results from experience

decision making
The process of generating and choosing from a set of alternatives to solve a problem

One reason inexperience can be so problematic is that learning is not necessarily easy. Have you ever watched "experts" perform their jobs? How does one become an expert? How does an accountant gain the trust of her client after several brief meetings? It takes a significant amount of time to become proficient at most complex jobs. It takes most employees anywhere from three months to a year to perform at a satisfactory level.[6] To develop high levels of expertise takes significantly longer.[7] This difficulty makes it even more important for companies to find a way to improve learning and decision making by their employees.

WHY DO SOME EMPLOYEES LEARN TO MAKE DECISIONS BETTER THAN OTHERS?

After a few days at her new job, Sandi felt overwhelmed with the pace of the work within the KPMG office. Quietly she wondered whether she would be able to fit in and keep up with other, more experienced CA students. In this situation, Sandi realized that her co-workers had more **expertise**—that is, knowledge and skills that distinguish experts from novices and less experienced people.[8] Research shows that the differences between experts and novices are almost always a function of learning, contrary to the more popular view that intelligence or other innate differences make the difference.[9] Although learning cannot be directly seen or observed, we can tell when people have learned by observing their behaviours, and it is changes in those behaviours that can be used to show that learners are gaining knowledge. It might be possible to mimic a behaviour once or twice, or get lucky with a few key decisions, but true learning only occurs when changes in behaviour become relatively permanent and are repeated over time. Understanding why some employees prove better at this than others requires understanding what exactly employees learn and how they do it.

expertise
The knowledge and skills that distinguish experts from novices

9.2 What types of knowledge can employees gain as they learn and build expertise?

Types of Knowledge

Employees learn two basic types of knowledge, both of which have important implications for organizations. **Explicit knowledge** is the kind of information you're likely to think about when you picture someone sitting down at a desk to learn. It's information that's relatively easily communicated and a large part of what companies teach during training sessions. Think of it this way: If you can put the information or knowledge in a manual or write it down for someone else, chances are good you're talking about explicit knowledge. As you read this textbook, we're doing our best to communicate explicit knowledge to you that will be useful to you in your future job. Although such information is necessary to perform well, it winds up being a relatively minor portion of what you need to know.

explicit knowledge
Knowledge that is easily communicated and available to everyone

Expertise is the accumulation of superior knowledge and skills in a field that separates experts from everyone else.

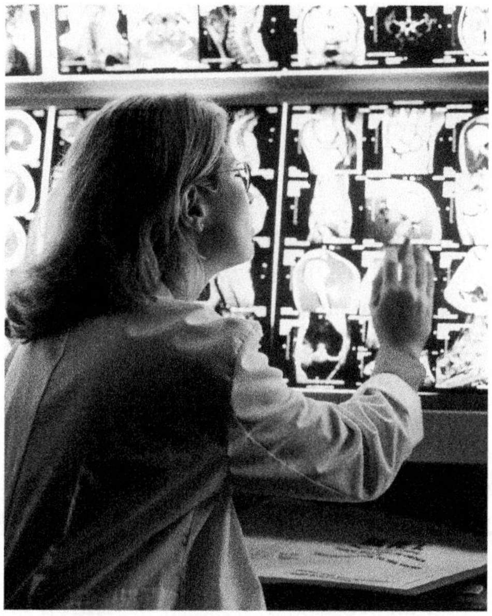

© Dynamic Graphics/Jupiterimages

Tacit knowledge, in contrast, is what employees can typically learn only through experience.[10] It's not easily communicated but could very well be the most important aspect of what we learn in organizations.[11] In fact, it's been argued that up to 90 percent of the knowledge contained in organizations occurs in tacit form.[12] Did you ever get to be so good at something that you had the ability to do it but couldn't really explain it to someone else? That's a common way to explain tacit knowledge. It's been described as the "know-how," "know-what," and "know-who" acquired solely through experience.[13] Others have used terms such as intuition, skills, insight, beliefs, mental models, and practical intelligence.[14]

TABLE 9-1

Characteristics of Explicit and Tacit Knowledge

Explicit Knowledge	Tacit Knowledge
Easily transferred through written or verbal communication	Very difficult, if not impossible, to articulate to others
Readily available to most	Highly personal in nature
Can be learned through books	Based on experience
Always conscious and accessible information	Sometimes holders don't even recognize that they possess it
General information	Typically job- or situation-specific

Source: Adapted from R. McAdam, B. Mason, and J. McCrory, "Exploring the Dichotomies Within the Tacit Knowledge Literature: Towards a Process of Tacit Knowing in Organizations," *Journal of Knowledge Management* 11 (2007), pp. 43–59.

tacit knowledge
Knowledge that employees can only learn through experience

Table 9-1 lists the qualities that help explain the differences between explicit and tacit knowledge. Some would say that explicit knowledge is what everyone can find and use, but tacit knowledge is what separates experts from common people.[15]

9.3 What are the methods by which employees learn in organizations?

Methods of Learning

Tacit and explicit knowledge are extremely important to employees and organizations. As an employee, it's hard to build a high level of tacit knowledge without some level of explicit knowledge to build from. From an organization's perspective, the tacit knowledge its employees accumulate may be the single most important strategic asset a company possesses.[16] The question then becomes: How do employees learn these types of knowledge? The short answer is that we learn through reinforcement (i.e., rewards and punishment), observation, and experience.

Reinforcement We've long known that managers use various methods of reinforcement to induce desirable or reduce undesirable behaviours by their employees. B.F. Skinner was the first to pioneer the notion, originally known as *operant conditioning*, that we learn by observing the link between our voluntary behaviour and the consequences that follow it. Research has continually demonstrated that people will exhibit specific behaviours if they're rewarded for doing so. Not surprisingly, we have a tendency to repeat behaviours that result in consequences that we like and to reduce behaviours that result in consequences we don't like. Figure 9-1 depicts this operant conditioning process.

FIGURE 9-1

Operant Conditioning Components

In the model in Figure 9-1, you can see that there are antecedents or events that precede or signal certain behaviours, which are then followed by consequences. Antecedents in organizations are typically goals, rules, instructions, or other types of information that help show employees what is expected of them. Although antecedents are useful for motivational reasons, it's primarily the consequences of actions that drive behaviour. This entire process of reinforcement is a continuous cycle, and the repetition of behaviours is strengthened to the degree that reinforcement continues to occur. There are four specific consequences typically used by organizations to modify employee behaviour, known as the **contingencies of reinforcement**.[17] Figure 9-2 summarizes these contingencies. It's important to separate them according to what they're designed to do, namely, increase desired behaviours or decrease unwanted behaviours.

contingencies of reinforcement
Four specific consequences used by organizations to modify employee behaviour

FIGURE 9-2

Contingencies of Reinforcement

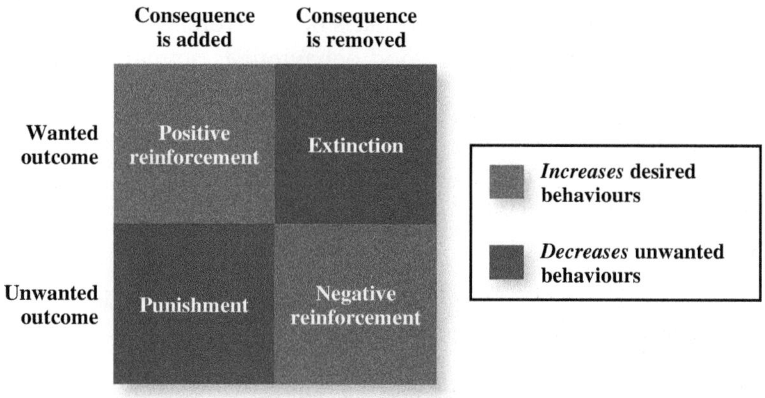

Two contingencies of reinforcement are used to increase desired behaviours. **Positive reinforcement** occurs when a positive outcome follows a desired behaviour. It's perhaps the most common type of reinforcement and the type we think of when an employee receives some type of "reward." Increased pay, promotions, praise from a manager or co-workers, and public recognition would all be considered positive reinforcement when given as a result of an employee exhibiting desired behaviours. For positive reinforcement to be successful, employees need to see a direct link between their behaviours and desired outcomes (see Chapter 7 on motivation for more discussion of such issues). If the consequences aren't realized until long after the specific behaviours, the odds that employees will link the two are minimized. **Negative reinforcement** occurs when an unwanted outcome is removed following a desired behaviour. Have you ever performed a task for the specific reason of not getting yelled at? If so, you learned to perform certain behaviours through the use of negative reinforcement. Perhaps there are some tasks your job requires that you don't enjoy. If your manager removes these responsibilities specifically because you perform well at another aspect of your job, this could also be seen as negative reinforcement. It's important to remember that even though the word "negative" has a sour connotation to it, it's designed to *increase* desired behaviours.

positive reinforcement
A reinforcement contingency in which a positive outcome follows a desired behaviour

negative reinforcement
A reinforcement contingency in which an unwanted outcome is removed following a desired behaviour

The next two contingencies of reinforcement are designed to decrease undesired behaviours. **Punishment** occurs when an unwanted outcome follows an unwanted behaviour. Punishment is exactly what it sounds like. In other words, employees are given something they don't like as a result of performing behaviours that the organization doesn't like. Suspending an employee for showing up to work late, assigning job tasks generally seen as demeaning for not following safety procedures, or even firing an employee for gross misconduct are all examples of punishment. **Extinction** occurs when there is the removal of a consequence following an unwanted behaviour. The use of extinction to reinforce behaviour can be purposeful or accidental. Perhaps employees receive attention from co-workers when they act in ways that are somewhat childish at work. Finding a way to remove the attention would be a purposeful act of extinction. Similarly though, perhaps employees work late every now and then to finish up job tasks when work gets busy, but their manager stops acknowledging that hard work. Desired behaviour that's not reinforced will diminish over time. In this way, a manager who does nothing to reinforce good behaviour is actually decreasing the odds that it will be repeated!

punishment
An unwanted outcome that follows an unwanted behaviour

extinction
The removal of a positive outcome following an unwanted behaviour

In general, positive reinforcement and extinction should be the most common forms of reinforcement used by managers to create learning among their employees. Positive reinforcement doesn't have to be in the form of material rewards to be effective. There are many ways for managers to encourage wanted behaviours. Offering praise, providing feedback, public recognition, and small celebrations are all ways to encourage employees and increase the chances they will continue to exhibit desired behaviours. At the same time, extinction is an effective way to stop unwanted behaviours. Both of these contingencies deliver their intended results; but, perhaps more importantly, they do so without creating feelings of animosity and conflict. Although punishment and negative reinforcement will work, they tend to bring other, detrimental consequences along with them.

Positive reinforcement, like public recognition, both encourages employees and helps ensure that desirable behaviours will be imitated and repeated.

© Digital Vision

Whereas the type of reinforcement used to modify behaviour is important, research also shows that the timing of reinforcement is equally important.[18] Therefore, it's important to examine the timing of when the contingencies are applied, referred to as **schedules of reinforcement**. Table 9-2 provides a summary of the five schedules of reinforcement. **Continuous reinforcement** is the simplest schedule and happens when a specific consequence follows each and every occurrence of a desired behaviour. New learning is acquired most rapidly under a continuous schedule.[19] For most jobs, continuous reinforcement is impractical. As a manager, can you imagine providing positive reinforcement every time someone exhibits a desired behaviour? It's a good thing that research also shows that under many circumstances, continuous reinforcement might be considered the least long lasting, because as soon as the consequence stops, the desired behaviour stops along with it.[20] Once a behaviour has been acquired, some form of intermittent scheduling is more effective.[21]

schedules of reinforcement

The timing of when contingencies are applied or removed

continuous reinforcement

A schedule of reinforcement in which a specific consequence follows each and every occurrence of a certain behaviour

TABLE 9-2

Schedules of Reinforcement

Reinforcement Schedule	Reward Given Following:	Potential Level of Performance	Example
Continuous	Every desired behaviour	High, but difficult to maintain	Praise
Fixed interval	Fixed time periods	Average	Paycheque
Variable interval	Variable time periods	Moderately high	Supervisor walk-by
Fixed ratio	Fixed number of desired behaviours	High	Piece-rate pay
Variable ratio	Variable number of desired behaviours	Very high	Commission pay

The other four schedules differ in terms of their variability and the basis of the consequences. Two schedules are interval-based; that is, they distribute reinforcement on the basis of the amount of time that passes. A **fixed-interval schedule** is probably the single most common form of reinforcement schedule. With this schedule, workers are rewarded after a certain amount of time, and the length of time between reinforcement periods stays the same. Every time employees get a paycheque after a predetermined period of time, they're being reinforced on a fixed interval schedule. A **variable-interval schedule** is designed to reinforce behaviour at more random points in time. A supervisor walking around at different points of time every day is a good example of a variable-interval schedule. If that supervisor walked around at the same exact time every day, do you think workers would be more or less prone to exhibit good behaviours throughout the day?

fixed-interval schedule

A schedule whereby reinforcement occurs at fixed time periods

variable-interval schedule

A schedule whereby reinforcement occurs at random periods of time

The other two reinforcement schedules are based on actual behaviours. A **fixed-ratio schedule** reinforces behaviours after a certain number of them have been exhibited. Some manufacturing plants have created piece-rate pay systems in which workers are paid according to the number of items they produce. Employees know ahead of time how many items they have to produce to be reinforced. A **variable-ratio schedule** rewards people after a varying number of exhibited behaviours. Salespeople, for example, are often compensated based on commission because they receive extra pay every time they sell an item. However, a car salesperson doesn't make a sale every time someone walks in the door of the dealership. Sometimes it takes exhibiting good sales behaviours to eight or nine customers to make a sale. Think of a slot machine: it doesn't reward you for every lever pull or even every ten—you never know when or if the winning pull will be. Do slot machines do a good job of reinforcing behaviour the casinos would like you to have? You bet!

fixed-ratio schedule
A schedule whereby reinforcement occurs following a fixed number of desired behaviours

variable-ratio schedule
A schedule whereby behaviours are reinforced after a varying number of them have been exhibited

On the whole, research has consistently shown that variable schedules lead to higher levels of performance than fixed schedules.[22] Think about it this way: Do you study more consistently in a class that gives pop quizzes or one that simply tests you three set times a semester? Research also shows that desired behaviours tend to disappear much more quickly when reinforcement is discontinued under fixed plans. However, variable schedules are not always appropriate for some types of reinforcement. How would you like it if your employer decided to give you your paycheques on a variable schedule? Sorry, you're not getting paid this week—maybe next week! Moreover, studies suggest that continuous or fixed schedules can be better for reinforcing new behaviours or behaviours that don't occur on a frequent basis.

Observation **Social learning theory** argues that in addition to learning through reinforcement, people in organizations have the ability to learn through the observation of others.[23] In fact, many would argue that social learning is the primary way employees gain knowledge in organizations.[24] Think about where you're most likely to get your cues while working in an organization. When possible, chances are good you'll look around at other employees to figure out the appropriate behaviours on your job. Not only do employees have the ability to see the link between their own behaviours and their consequences, they can also observe the behaviours and consequences of others.[25] When employees observe the actions of others, learn from what they observe, and then repeat the observed behaviour, they're engaging in **behavioural modelling**.

social learning theory
Theory that argues that people in organizations learn by observing others

behavioural modelling
Employees' observing the actions of others, learning from what they observe, and then repeating the observed behaviour

For behaviour modelling to occur successfully, a number of processes have to take place. See Figure 9-3. First, the learner must focus attention on an appropriate model and accurately perceive the critical behaviour the model exhibits. That model might be a supervisor, a co-worker, or even a subordinate.

Some organizations go out of their way to supply role models for newcomers or inexperienced workers to watch and learn from. In our opening vignette, KPMG Vancouver routinely assigned its new CA students to teams that consisted of at least one manager, and sometimes one of the firm's partners, in hopes of capturing the tacit knowledge they had acquired. Sandi discovered that she learned the most simply by watching her manager interact with clients—observing what he said to clients and how he responded to their questions, and what he wrote down at meetings. In fact, because tacit knowledge is so difficult to communicate, modelling might be the single best way to acquire it. For that reason, modelling is a continual process that is used at all levels of many organizations.

FIGURE 9-3

The Modelling Process

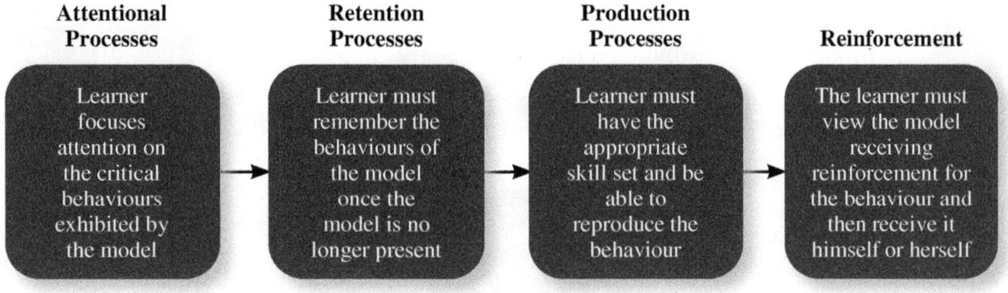
Attentional Processes
Retention Processes
Production Processes
Reinforcement
Learner focuses attention on the critical behaviours exhibited by the model
Learner must remember the behaviours of the model once the model is no longer present
Learner must have the appropriate skill set and be able to reproduce the behaviour
The learner must view the model receiving reinforcement for the behaviour and then receive it himself or herself

Source: Adapted from H.M. Weiss, "Learning Theory and Industrial and Organizational Psychology," in *Handbook of Industrial and Organizational Psychology*, eds. M.D. Dunnette and L.M. Hough (Palo Alto, CA: Consulting Psychologists Press, 1990), pp. 75–169.

Needless to say, choosing a good model is important, and not all models are good ones. For instance, if managers and leaders demonstrate unethical behaviours, employees who look up to them are likely to imitate what they see.[26] Salomon Brothers, the New York–based investment bank, learned this the hard way when employees began to model the unethical behaviours of their managers and leaders.[27] In addition to unethical behaviour, there is substantial evidence that employees will behaviour-model counterproductive work behaviours such as aggression and absenteeism when they see others in the organization exhibit those behaviours.[28]

Second, the learner needs to remember exactly what the model's behaviour was and how they did it. This step is very difficult when watching experts perform their job, because so much of what they do remains unspoken and can occur at a rapid pace. Third, the learner must undertake production processes, or actually be able to reproduce what the model did. Not only must the learner have the requisite knowledge and physical skills to be able to perform the task; now he or she must translate what's been observed into action. Do you remember the first time you drove a car? Chances are you'd been watching other drivers for many years, picking up bits and pieces of how to do it through observation. However, things became different when you were behind the wheel for the first time. Suddenly, there was a lot of information to process, and years and years of observation had to be put into action.

Fourth, the last step of behavioural modelling is reinforcement. This reinforcement can come from observation, direct experience, or both. The learner can observe the consequences of the model having exhibited the behaviour (positive reinforcement or punishment), which in itself will help engrain the desirability of performing the behaviour. In addition, it's important for the learner to receive reinforcement after replicating the behaviour. If the newly acquired behaviours are positively reinforced, the likelihood of continued behaviour increases.

Goal Orientation Before we leave this section, it's important to recognize that people learn somewhat differently according to their predispositions or attitudes toward learning and performance. These differences are reflected in different "goal orientations" that capture the kinds of activities and goals that people prioritize. Some people have what's known as a **learning orientation**, in which building competence is deemed more important than demonstrating competence. "Learning-oriented" persons enjoy working on new kinds of tasks, even if they fail during their early experiences. Such people view failure in positive terms—as a means of increasing knowledge and skills in the long run.[29]

learning orientation

A predisposition or attitude according to which building competence is deemed more important by an employee than demonstrating competence

Ursula Burns was provided an unusual opportunity to learn by observation and behavioural modelling before becoming CEO of Xerox. She essentially co-led with her predecessor for two years to gain insider experience before taking the helm.

© Ramin Talaie/Bloomberg via Getty Images

For others, the demonstration of competence is deemed a more important goal than the building of competence. That demonstration of competence can be motivated by two different thought processes. Those with a **performance–prove orientation** focus on demonstrating their competence so that others think favourably of them. Those with a **performance–avoid orientation** focus on demonstrating their competence so that others will not think poorly of them. In either case, "performance-oriented" people tend to work mainly on tasks at which they're already good, preventing them from failing in front of others. Such individuals view failure in negative terms—as an indictment of their ability and competence.

performance–prove orientation

A predisposition or attitude by which employees focus on demonstrating their competence so that others think favourably of them

performance–avoid orientation

A predisposition or attitude by which employees focus on demonstrating their competence so that others will not think poorly of them

Research has shown that a learning goal orientation improves self-confidence, feedback-seeking behaviour, learning strategy development, and learning performance.[30] Research on the two performance orientations is more mixed. Although it would seem that focusing on performance should improve performance-based outcomes, research shows that isn't necessarily the case. On the whole, a performance–prove orientation tends to be a mixed bag, producing varying levels of performance and outcomes. What's more clear are the detrimental effects of having a performance–avoid orientation. Employees who enter learning situations with a fear of looking bad in front of others tend to learn less and have substantially higher levels of anxiety.[31] What kind of orientation do you tend to exhibit? See our ***OB Assessments*** feature at the end of the chapter to find out. Regardless of an individual's general tendency though, it has been found that managers or trainers can set training-specific orientations toward learning.[32] In other words, they can instruct you to have a specific goal orientation before you start a training session. Under such conditions, setting learning-oriented goals for those in training is likely to foster more skill development than setting performance-oriented goals.[33]

9.4 What two methods can employees use to make decisions?

Methods of Decision Making

How do employees take explicit and tacit knowledge, however it's gained, and turn that knowledge into effective decision making? Sometimes that process is very straightforward. **Programmed decisions** are decisions that become somewhat automatic because people's knowledge allows them to recognize and identify a situation and the course of action that needs to be taken. As is illustrated in Figure 9-4, experts often respond to an identified problem by realizing that they've dealt with it before. That realization triggers a programmed decision that's implemented and then evaluated according to its ability to deliver the expected outcome. For experts who possess high levels of explicit and tacit knowledge, many decisions they face are of this programmed variety. That's not to say that the decisions are necessarily easy. It simply means that their experience and knowledge allows them to see the problems more easily and recognize and implement solutions more quickly.

programmed decisions
Decisions that are somewhat automatic because the decision maker's knowledge allows him or her to recognize the situation and the course of action to be taken

To experts, programmed decisions sometimes comes across as intuition or a gut feeling. **Intuition** can be described as emotionally charged judgments that arise through quick, nonconscious, and holistic associations.[34] There is almost unanimous consent among researchers that intuition is largely a function of learning—tacit knowledge gained through reinforcement, observation, and experience allow a decision maker to decide more quickly and confidently.[35] Because of their tacit knowledge, experts sometimes cannot put into words why they know that a problem exists, why a solution will work, or how they accomplished a task. They "just know." Of course, the difficulty arises in knowing when to trust that gut instinct and when not to.[36] As a rule of thumb, you should probably ask yourself how much expertise you have about the subject of the judgment. Research is clear that intuition can be a very effective way to make decisions, but only when those making the decisions have a high level of domain expertise.[37] In other words, don't go laying down your life savings on a spin of the roulette wheel in Vegas because your intuition tells you "red"!

intuition
An emotional judgment based on quick, unconscious gut feelings

FIGURE 9-4

Programmed and Nonprogrammed Decisions

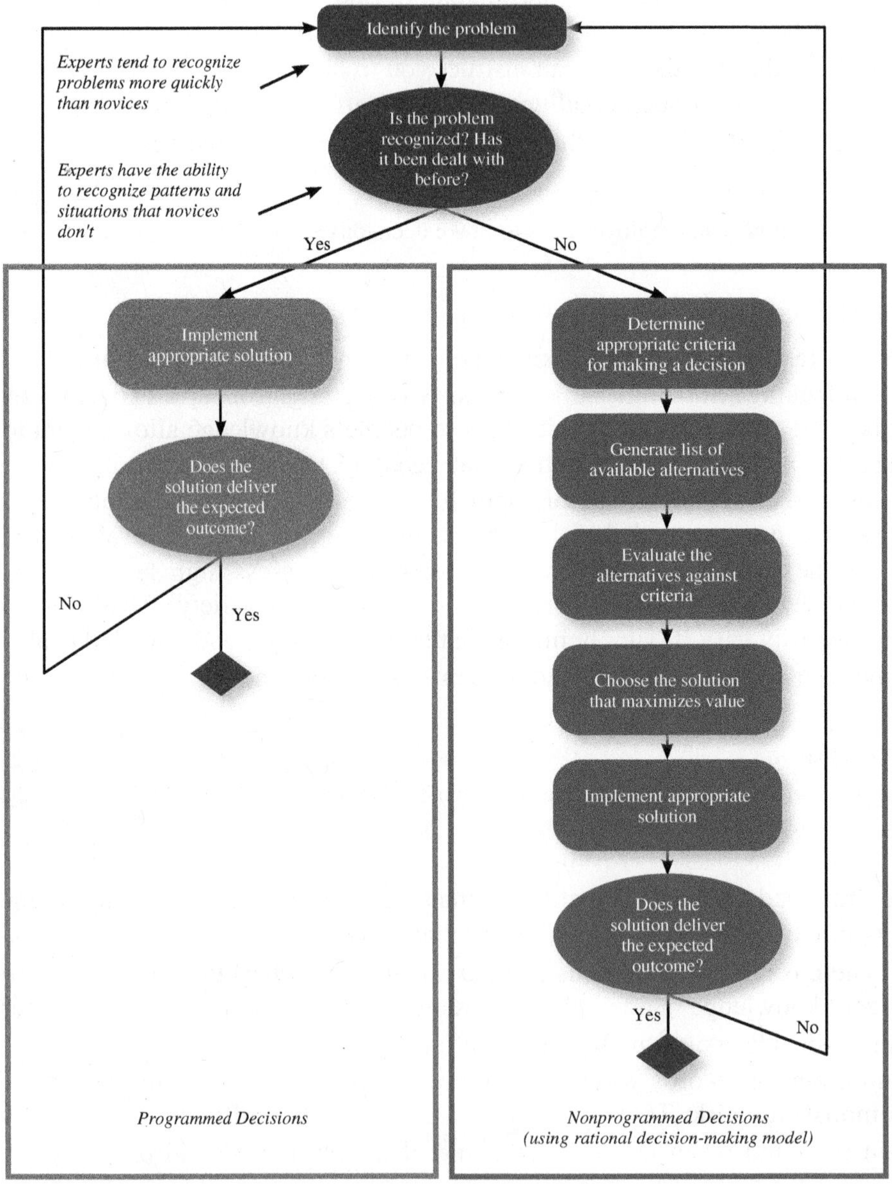

Intuitive decision making is perhaps never more important than during a crisis. A **crisis situation** is a change—whether sudden or evolving—that results in an urgent problem that must be addressed immediately. For businesses, a crisis is anything with the potential to cause sudden and serious damage to its employees, reputation, or bottom line. One of the key factors in almost all crises is that decisions must be made quickly.[38] Unless there has been some form of specific preplanning for that crisis, managers (who should have the most tacit knowledge to support their decisions) must use their intuition rather than take a lengthy period of time to think through all of their options.[39] When a manager uses intuition to make a decision in a crisis situation, followers often misinterpret the manager's intent, because the managers can't put the reasons for their decisions into words (or don't have the time to do so).[40] In turn, the implementation of their plan often suffers. Therefore, managers who make decisions face two major questions: How can they ensure that others follow their lead when the path is unclear, and how can they confirm that their intuition is not faulty? Karl Weick, a preeminent scholar on crisis management, suggests five steps for communicating intent to others when using intuition:

1. *Here's what I think we face.* (How does the manager perceive the situation?)
2. *Here's what I think we should do.* (Make a task-focused statement of what the manager wants to happen.)
3. *Here's why.* (Give the reasoning behind the decision.)
4. *Here's what we should keep our eye on.* (What things should the staff look for to ensure the intuition is correct or that the situation hasn't changed?)
5. *Now, talk to me.* (Confirm that everyone understands their roles and that there is no other information to consider.)[41]

crisis situation
A change—sudden or evolving—that results in an urgent problem that must be addressed immediately

These communications steps are important for a manager making intuitive decisions because they help others follow directives more easily, while also providing a check on the manager to ensure he or she observes the crisis environment correctly.

When a situation arises that is new, complex, and not recognized, it calls for a **nonprogrammed decision** on the part of the employee. Organizations are complex and changing environments, and many workers face uncertainty on a daily basis. In these instances, employees have to make sense of their environment, understand the problems they're faced with, and come up with solutions to overcome them. Generally, as employees move up the corporate ladder, a larger percentage of their decisions become less and less programmed. How should decision making proceed in such contexts? The **rational decision-making model** offers a step-by-step approach to making decisions that maximize outcomes by examining all available alternatives. As is illustrated in Figure 9-4, this model becomes relevant when people don't recognize a problem as one they've dealt with before.

nonprogrammed decision
One made by employees when a problem is new, complex, or not recognized

rational decision-making model
A step-by-step approach to making decisions that is designed to maximize outcomes by examining all available alternatives

The first step in the rational decision-making model is to identify the criteria that are important in making the decision, taking into account all involved parties. The second step is to generate a list of all available alternatives that might be potential solutions to the problem. At this point, evaluating the alternatives is not necessary. The responsibility simply lies in coming up with as many potential solutions as possible. The third step in the model is the evaluation of those alternatives against the criteria laid out in the first step. Does it matter how much the alternative costs? What exactly will happen as a result of various choices? What will the side effects of the alternative be? The fourth step is to select the alternative that results in the best outcome. That is, given the costs and benefits of each alternative, which alternative provides us with the most value? The fifth step is to implement the alternative.

The rational decision-making model assumes that people are, of course, perfectly rational. However, problems immediately arise when we start to examine some of the assumptions the model makes about human decision makers.[42] The model assumes there is a clear and definite problem to solve and that people have the ability to identify what that exact problem is. It also assumes that decision makers have perfect information—that they know and are able to identify the available alternatives and the outcomes that would be associated with those alternatives. The model further assumes that time and money are generally not issues when it comes to making a decision, that decision makers always choose the solution that maximizes value, and that they will act in the best interests of the organization. Given all these assumptions, perhaps we shouldn't label the model "rational" after all! See our ***OB on Screen*** feature for different decision-making methods in action.

OB ON SCREEN

Star Trek into Darkness

What I am about to do, it doesn't make any sense. It is not logical. It is a gut feeling. I have no idea what I'm supposed to do, I only know what I can do.

© AP Photo/Paramount Pictures/Zade Rosenthal

With those words, Captain James T. Kirk (Chris Pine) of the U.S.S. *Enterprise* tries to explain his decision-making method to Commander Spock (Zachary Quinto) in *Star Trek into Darkness* (Dir. J.J. Abrams, Paramount, 2013). Many of us may be familiar with these two characters from the many *Star Trek* television episodes and movies that have come before this one. Captain Kirk is the brash, emotional, quick decision maker who relies on action, instinct, and intuition to guide his decisions. Commander Spock, on the other hand, is half Vulcan and half human. Vulcans are known for their

(Continued)

ability to suppress their emotions and make decisions using pure deductive reasoning and logic. Many of the major moments in the series rely on the interplay between Kirk and Spock and their desire to move in opposite directions on the basis of their decision-making methods when facing a major problem.

In the scene highlighted above, the crew of the *Enterprise* faces a crisis in which there is limited, ambiguous information and few apparent options. Kirk wants to try to solve the problem by using the first thing that comes to his mind. Spock counters with: "I cannot allow you to do this. It is my function aboard this ship to advise you in making the wisest decisions possible, something I firmly believe you are incapable of doing in this moment." The order of the captain wins out and Kirk rushes off to meet the situation head-on. While doing this, though, Spock continues the rational process by seeking out every available piece of information to make the best decision. In the end, it is a combination of the two's approaches that eventually allows them to be successful. Kirk is saved by Spock's rationality (end of movie) and Spock is saved by Kirk's instinct and willingness to act outside rationality (beginning of movie).

9.5 What decision-making problems can prevent employees from translating their learning into accurate decisions?

Decision-Making Problems

Because employees don't always make rational decisions, it's easy to second-guess decisions after the fact. Many decisions made inside organizations look good at the time and were made with perfectly good justifications to support them but turn out to have what are perceived as "bad results." The reality, however, is that it's a lot easier to question decisions in hindsight. As Warren Buffett, CEO of Berkshire Hathaway, is often quoted as saying, "In the business world, the rearview mirror is always clearer than the windshield."[43] Our responsibility here is not to rehash all the poor decisions employees and managers have made (and there are many!) but rather to detail some of the most common reasons for bad decision making. When are people most likely to falter in terms of the rational decision-making model and why?

Limited Information Although most employees perceive themselves as rational decision makers, the reality is that they are all subject to **bounded rationality**. Bounded rationality is the notion that decision makers simply do not have the ability or resources to process all available information and alternatives to make an optimal decision.[44] A comparison of bounded rationality and rational decision making is presented in Table 9-3. This limit results in two major problems for making decisions. First, people have to filter and simplify information to make sense of their complex environment and the myriad potential choices they face.[45] This simplification leads them to miss information when perceiving problems, generating and evaluating alternatives, or judging the results. Second, because people cannot possibly consider every single alternative when making a decision, they satisfice. **Satisficing** results when decision makers select the first acceptable alternative considered.[46]

bounded rationality

The notion that people do not have the ability or resources to process all available information and alternatives when making a decision

satisficing

What a decision maker is doing who chooses the first acceptable alternative considered

TABLE 9-3

Rational Decision Making vs. Bounded Rationality

To Be Rational Decision Makers, We SHOULD:	Bounded Rationality Says We ARE LIKELY TO:
Identify the problem by thoroughly examining the situation and considering all interested parties.	Boil down the problem to something that is easily understood.
Develop an exhaustive list of alternatives to consider as solutions.	Come up with a few solutions that tend to be straightforward, familiar, and similar to what is currently being done.
Evaluate all the alternatives simultaneously.	Evaluate each alternative as soon as we think of it.
Use accurate information to evaluate alternatives.	Use distorted and inaccurate information during the evaluation process.
Pick the alternative that maximizes value.	Pick the first acceptable alternative (satisfice).

Sources: Adapted from H.A. Simon, "Rational Decision Making in Organizations," *American Economic Review* 69 (1979), pp. 493–513; D. Kahneman, "Maps of Bounded Rationality: Psychology for Behavioral Economics," *The American Economic Review* 93 (2003), pp. 1449–75; and S.W. Williams, *Making Better Business Decisions* (Thousand Oaks, CA: Sage, 2002).

In addition to choosing the first acceptable alternative, decision makers tend to come up with alternatives that are straightforward and not that different from what they're already doing. When you and another person are deciding where to go out for dinner tonight, will you sit down and list every restaurant available to you within a certain distance? Of course not. You'll start listing alternatives, generally starting with the closest and most familiar, until you hit on a restaurant acceptable to both of you. Making decisions this way is no big deal when it comes to deciding where to go for dinner, because the consequences of a poor decision are minimal. However, many managers make decisions that have critical consequences for their employees and their customers. In those cases, making a decision without thoroughly looking into the alternatives becomes a problem!

Faulty Perceptions As decision makers, employees are forced to rely on their perceptions to make decisions. Perception is the process of selecting, organizing, storing, and retrieving information about the environment. Although perceptions can be very useful, because they help us to make sense of the environment around us, they can often become distorted versions of reality. Perceptions can be dangerous in decision making, because we tend to make assumptions or evaluations on the basis of them. **Selective perception** is the tendency for people to see their environment only as it affects them and as it is consistent with their expectations. Has someone ever told you, "You only see what you want to see"? If a relative, spouse, or significant other said that to you, chances are it probably wasn't the best experience. He or she was likely upset that you didn't perceive the environment (or what was important to them) the same way he or she did. Selective perception affects our ability to identify problems, generate and evaluate alternatives, and judge outcomes. In other words, we take shortcuts when we process information. Let's discuss some of the ways we do this when dealing with people and situations.

selective perception
The tendency for people to see their environment only as it affects them and as it is consistent with their expectations

One false assumption people tend to make when it comes to other people is the belief that others think, feel, and act the same way they do. This assumption is known as a **projection bias**. That is, people project their own thoughts, attitudes, and motives onto other people. "I would never do that—that's unethical" equates to "They would never do that—that's unethical." Projection bias causes problems in decision making because it limits our ability to develop appropriate criteria for a decision and evaluate decisions carefully. The bias causes people to assume that everyone's criteria will be just like theirs and that everyone will react to a decision just as they would.

projection bias
The faulty perception by decision makers that others think, feel, and act as they do

Another example of faulty perceptions is caused by the way we cognitively organize people into groups. **Social identity theory** holds that people identify themselves by the groups to which they belong and perceive and judge others by their group memberships.[47] There is a substantial amount of research that shows that we like to categorize people on the basis of the groups to which they belong.[48] These groups might be based on demographic information (gender, race, religion, hair colour), occupational information (scientists, engineers, accountants), where they work (TELUS, Air Canada, TD Bank), what country they're from (Canadians, French, Chinese), or any other criterion that makes sense to the perceiver. You might categorize students on campus by whether they're a member of a fraternity or sorority, as those inside the Greek system do. And people within a certain fraternity might group their own members on the basis of whom they hang out with the most. There is practically no end of subgroups that people can come up with.

social identity theory
A theory that people identify themselves according to the various groups to which they belong and judge others according to the groups they associate with

A **stereotype** occurs when assumptions are made about others on the basis of their membership in a social group.[49] Although not all stereotypes are bad per se, our decision-making process becomes faulty when we make inaccurate generalizations. Many companies work hard to help their employees avoid stereotyping, because doing so can lead to illegal discrimination in the workplace. Increasingly, Canadian companies, such as RBC (see Chapter 1), have developed extensive diversity training programs to help their employees overcome specific cultural, racial, and gender stereotypes in the workplace.

stereotype
Assumptions made about others based on their social group membership

When confronted with situations of uncertainty that require a decision on our part, we often use **heuristics**—simple, efficient, rules of thumb that allow us to make decisions more easily. In general, heuristics are not bad. In fact, they lead to correct decisions more often than not.[50] However, they can also bias us toward inaccurate decisions. One of the earliest studies on decision-making heuristics says, "Consider the letter R. Is R more likely to appear in the first position of a word or the third position of a word?"[51] If your answer was the first position of a word, you answered incorrectly and fell victim to one of the most frequently mentioned heuristics. The **availability bias** is the tendency for people to base their judgments on information that is easier to recall. It's significantly easier for almost everyone to remember words in which *R* is the first letter as opposed to the third. The availability bias is why more people are afraid to fly than statistics would support. Every single plane crash is plastered all over the news, making plane crashes more available in memory than successful plane landings.

heuristics
Simple and efficient rules of thumb that allow one to make decisions more easily

availability bias
The tendency for people to base their judgments on information that is easier to recall

TABLE 9-4

Decision-Making Biases

Name of Bias	Description
Anchoring	The tendency to rely too heavily, or "anchor," on one trait or piece of information when making decisions even when the anchor might be unreliable or irrelevant. *Example.* One recent study showed that initial bids for a bottle of wine in an auction could be heavily influenced by simply having subjects write down the last two digits of their Social Security number prior to putting a value on the bottle. Those with higher two-digit numbers tended to bid 60–120 percent more for a bottle of wine than those with low numbers.
Framing	The tendency to make different decisions on the basis of how a question or situation is phrased. *Example.* Why do gas stations (or any retailer) give out discounts for paying cash as opposed to adding a surcharge for using a credit card? The discount is seen as a gain while the surcharge is seen as a loss. Because humans are loss-averse, we're more likely to give up the discount (the gain) than accept the surcharge (the loss).
Representativeness	The tendency to assess the likelihood of an event by comparing it to a similar event and assuming it will be similar. *Example.* Assuming because a flipped coin has come up heads ten times in a row, the likelihood that it will come up tails is greater than 50–50. Sometimes referred to as the "gambler's fallacy."
Contrast	The tendency to judge things erroneously based on a reference that is near to them. *Example.* If you were to take your hand out of a bowl of hot water and place it in a bowl of lukewarm water, you would describe that water as "cold." If someone else were to take their hand out of a bowl of extremely cold water and place it in the same bowl of lukewarm water, they would describe that water as "hot."
Recency	The tendency to weigh recent events more than earlier events. *Example.* A manager's tendency to weight ratings in performance evaluations based on an employee's behaviour during the prior month as opposed to his or her behaviour over the entire evaluation period.
Ratio effect	The tendency to judge the same probability of an unlikely event as lower when the probability is presented in the form of a ratio of smaller rather than of larger numbers. *Example.* When offered an opportunity to win $1 if they drew a red jellybean, people frequently elected to draw from a bowl that contained a greater number but a smaller proportion of red beans (e.g., 7 in 100 vs. 1 in 10). Participants knew the probabilities were against them, but they "felt" they had a better chance when there were more beans.

Sources: J. Baron, *Thinking and Deciding*, 3rd ed. (Cambridge, UK: Cambridge University Press, 2000); V. Denes-Raj and S. Epstein "Conflict Between Intuitive and Rational Processing: When People Behave Against Their Better Judgment," *Journal of Personality and Social Psychology* 66 (1994), pp. 819–29; R.E. Nisbett and L. Ross, *Human Inference: Strategies and Shortcomings of Social Judgment* (Englewood Cliffs, NJ: Prentice Hall, 1980); D.G. Meyers, *Social Psychology* (Boston, MA: McGraw-Hill, 2005); G. Gigerenzer, P.M. Todd, and ABC Research Group, *Simple Heuristics That Make Us Smart* (New York: Oxford University Press, 1999); D. Kahneman, A. Tversky, and P. Slovic, *Judgment Under Uncertainty: Heuristics & Biases* (Cambridge, UK: Cambridge University Press, 1982); and D. Kahneman and A. Tversky, "Choices, Values and Frames," *American Psychologist* 39 (1984), pp. 341–50.

Aside from the availability bias, there are many other biases that affect the way we make decisions. Table 9-4 describes six more of the most well-researched decision-making biases. After reading them, you might wonder how we ever make accurate decisions at all! The answer is that we do our best to think rationally through our most important decisions prior to making them, and tend to use heuristics for decisions that are less important or that need to be made more quickly. Regardless of how often we fall victim to the biases, being aware of potential decision errors can help us make them less frequently. Interestingly enough, Lowe's, the home improvement retailer, and several other companies are actually trying to take advantage of these types of biases and behavioural economics in order to get employees to make better decisions about their health benefits.[52]

OB RESEARCH IN CANADA

Dr. Silvia Bonaccio is an associate professor in the Telfer School of Management at the University of Ottawa, where she teaches courses in organizational behaviour and human resources management. Dr. Bonaccio is also the director of the Ph.D. in Management program. One important theme of her research has been to increase our understanding of the psychological principles that underlie decision making. For instance, how people use information during decision making, and how such information influences the decision-making processes and outcomes we have been reading about in this chapter. Another research theme has been to study how non-cognitive individual differences (e.g., personality, emotional states) influence the assessment of cognitive abilities during employee selection (for more on these topics see Chapters 4 and 5).

Telfer School of Management, University of Ottawa

In addition to being an expert in decision making, Dr. Bonaccio is often called on by the print and radio media to discuss how to best give advice, and when and why advice-giving backfires or just goes terribly wrong. Even more impressive is the fact that Dr. Bonaccio can do all this in English, French, Italian, and Spanish. (Watch out, Dr. Phil!) Look her up at www.telfer.uottawa.ca/en/directory/professors/bonaccio-silvia.

Faulty Attributions Another category of decision-making problems centres on how we explain the actions and events around us. Research on attributions suggests that when people witness a behaviour or outcome, they make a judgment about whether it was internally or externally caused. For example, when a co-worker of yours named Joe shows up late to work and misses an important group presentation, you'll almost certainly make a judgment about why that happened. You might attribute Joe's outcome to internal factors—for example, suggesting that he is lazy or has a poor work ethic. Or you might attribute Joe's outcome to external factors—for example, suggesting that there was unusually bad traffic that day or that other factors prevented him from arriving on time.

The **fundamental attribution error** argues that people have a tendency to judge others' behaviours as due to internal factors.[53] This error suggests that you would likely judge Joe as having low motivation, poor organizational skills, or some other negative internal attribute. What if you yourself had showed up late? It turns out that we're less harsh when judging ourselves. The **self-serving bias** occurs when we attribute our own failures to external factors and our own successes to internal factors. Interestingly, evidence suggests that attributions across cultures don't always work the same way; see our ***OB Internationally*** feature for more discussion of this issue.

fundamental attribution error

The tendency for people to judge others' behaviours as being due to internal factors such as ability, motivation, or attitudes

self-serving bias

When one attributes one's own failures to external factors and success to internal factors

One model of attribution processes suggests that when people have a level of familiarity with the person being judged, they'll use a more detailed decision framework. This model is illustrated in Figure 9-5.[54] To return to our previous example, if we want to explore why Joe arrived late to work, we can ask three kinds of questions:

FIGURE 9-5

Consensus, Distinctiveness, and Consistency

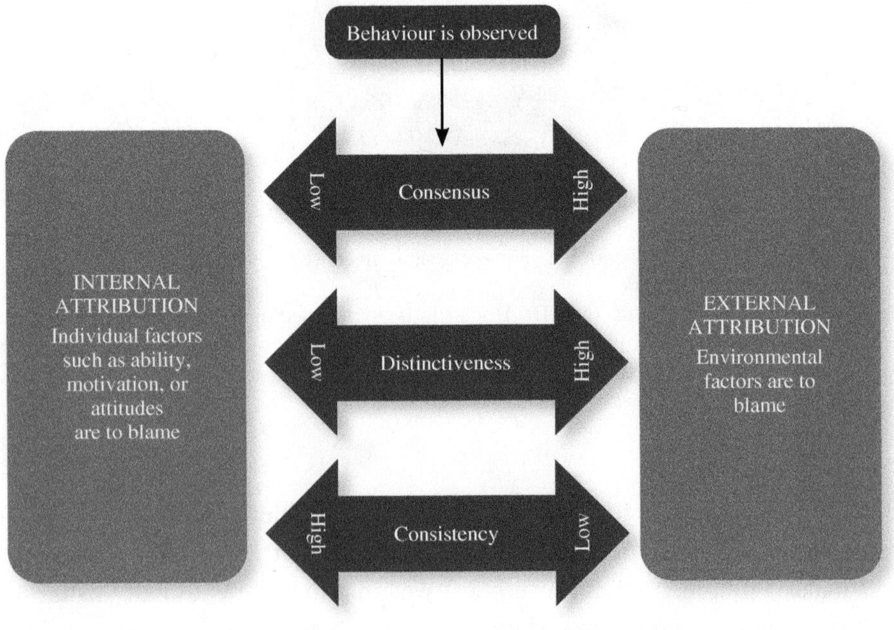

- **Consensus**—Did others act the same way under similar situations? In other words, did others arrive late on the same day?

- **Distinctiveness**—Does this person tend to act differently in other circumstances? In other words, is Joe responsible when it comes to personal appointments, not just work appointments?
- **Consistency**—Does this person always do this when performing this task? In other words, has Joe arrived late for work before?

consensus

Used by decision makers to attribute cause; whether other individuals behave the same way under similar circumstances

distinctiveness

Used by decision makers to attribute cause; whether the person being judged acts in a similar fashion under different circumstances

consistency

Used by decision makers to attribute cause; whether this individual has behaved this way before under similar circumstances

OB INTERNATIONALLY

Anytime a major accident occurs in a company, or anytime a significant breach of ethics occurs, a company is expected to respond accordingly. One of the natural reactions of employees, customers, and other observers is to attribute the cause of the negative event to someone. Whom this blame gets placed on might be very different, depending on the part of the world in which the company is operating. Cultures such as Canada or United States tend to blame the particular individuals most responsible for the event, whereas East Asian (China, Korea, Japan) cultures tend to blame the organization itself.[55] For example, when scandals within organizations occur (e.g., excessive executive compensation), newspapers in Canada often publish the name of the employee and discuss the individual worker involved, whereas East Asian newspapers refer to the organization itself.[56]

Interestingly, these biases put different responsibilities on the leaders of organizations in these countries. In East Asian cultures, it's typical for the leader of an organization to take the blame for accidents, regardless of whether he or she had direct responsibility for them.[57] For example, the director of a hospital in Tokyo was forced to resign when the cover-up of a medical accident was discovered, even though he hadn't started in his job until after the cover-up! Similar events are common, such as the resignation of the CEO of Japan Airlines after a jet crashed, killing 500 people. In Canada and the United States, in contrast, CEOs rarely take the same level of blame. When Exxon CEO Joseph Hazelwood crashed the *Exxon Valdez* into the Alaskan coastline, there were no calls him to resign; it was simply assumed by the public that he had had nothing to do with the accident.

Much of the reasoning for such differences has to do with the way the cultures view individuals and groups. East Asian cultures tend to treat groups as entities and not as individuals, whereas North American culture tends to see individuals acting of their own accord.[58] This difference means that organizational leaders should be very cognizant of how to handle crises, depending on the country in which the negative event occurs. An apology offered by a senior leader is likely to be seen by East Asians as the company taking responsibility, whereas in our country it's more likely to be taken as an admission of personal guilt.[59]

How these questions are answered will determine if an internal or external attribution is made. An internal attribution, such as laziness or low motivation for Joe, will occur if there is low consensus (others arrived on time), low distinctiveness (Joe is irresponsible with other commitments as well), and high consistency (Joe has arrived late before). An external attribution, such as bad traffic or a power outage, will occur if there is high consensus (others arrived late), high distinctiveness (Joe is responsible with other commitments), and low consistency (Joe has never come late to work before).

Escalation of Commitment Our last category of decision-making problems centres on what happens as a decision begins to go wrong. **Escalation of commitment** refers to the decision to continue to follow a failing course of action.[60] The expression "throwing good money after bad" captures this common decision-making error. An enormous amount of research shows that people have a tendency, when presented with a series of decisions, to escalate their commitment to previous decisions, even in the face of obvious failures.[61] Why? Perhaps they wish to avoid looking incompetent, or admitting they made a mistake. Those escalation tendencies become particularly strong when decision makers have invested a lot of money in the decision and when the project in question seems quite close to completion.[62]

escalation of commitment
A common decision-making error, in which the decision maker continues to follow a failing course of action

One prominent example of escalation of commitment is United Airlines' slow abandonment of the automated baggage handling system at the Denver International Airport. When it initially opened (after a two-year delay), the system, with roughly 42 kilometres of track designed to haul across three terminals, was supposed to be the single most advanced baggage handling system in the world. However, a series of delays and technological problems caused the cost of the system, originally scheduled at $186 million, to skyrocket by $1 million per day. And the system never really worked very well. In fact, United was the only airline in the airport willing to use it. It took ten years and many mangled and lost suitcases before the company finally cut its losses, saving itself $1 million a month in maintenance fees.[63] If you ever find yourself in this predicament, recent research suggests that by focusing on what you have to gain by moving on, rather than what you have to lose by quitting, will reduce your chances of committing escalation of commitment.[64]

United Airlines took ten years to finally abandon an expensive, faulty baggage handling system at Denver International Airport, demonstrating the error known as escalation of commitment.

© Kevin Moloney/The New York Times/Redux

Summary: Why Do Some Employees Learn to Make Decisions Better Than Others?

So what explains why some employees learn to make better decisions than others? As shown in Figure 9-6, answering that question requires understanding how employees learn, what kind of knowledge they gain, and how they use that knowledge to make decisions. Employees learn from a combination of reinforcement and observation, and that learning depends in part on whether they are learning-oriented or performance-oriented. Some of that learning results in increases in explicit knowledge, and some results in increases in tacit knowledge. Those two forms of knowledge, which combine to form an employee's expertise, are then used in decision making. If a given problem has been encountered before, decision making occurs in a more automatic, programmed fashion. If the problem is new or unfamiliar, nonprogrammed decision making occurs and, in the best-case scenario, follows the rational decision-making model. Unfortunately, a number of decision-making problems can hinder the effectiveness of such decisions, including limited information, faulty perceptions, faulty attributions, and escalation of commitment.

FIGURE 9-6

Why Do Some Employees Learn to Make Decisions Better Than Others?

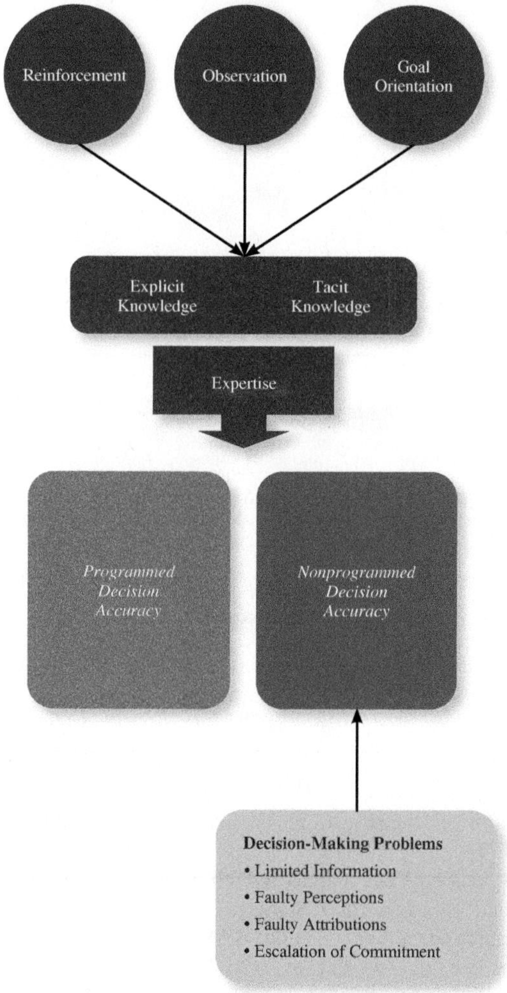

9.6 How does learning affect job performance and organizational commitment?

HOW IMPORTANT IS LEARNING?

Does learning have a significant impact on the two primary outcomes in our integrative model of OB—does it correlate with job performance and organizational commitment? Figure 9-7 summarizes the research evidence linking learning to job performance and organizational commitment. The figure reveals that learning does influence job performance. Why? The primary reason is that learning is moderately correlated with task performance. It's difficult to fulfill one's job duties if the employee doesn't possess adequate levels of job knowledge. In fact, there are reasons to suggest that the moderate correlation depicted in the figure is actually an underestimate of learning's importance. That's because most of the research linking learning to task performance focuses on explicit knowledge, which is more practical to measure. It's difficult to measure tacit knowledge because of its unspoken nature, but clearly such knowledge is relevant to task performance. Learning seems less relevant to citizenship behaviour and counterproductive behaviour however, given that those behaviours are often less dependent on knowledge and expertise.

FIGURE 9-7

Effects of Learning on Performance and Commitment

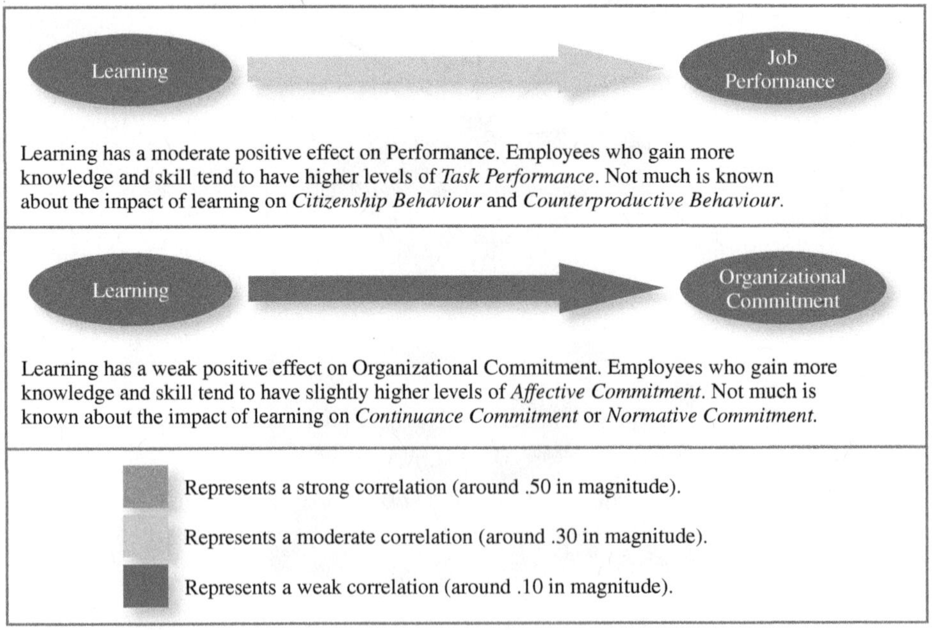

Sources: G.M. Alliger, S.I. Tannenbaum, W. Bennett Jr., H. Traver, and A. Shotland, "A Meta-analysis of the Relations Among Training Criteria," *Personnel Psychology* 50 (1997), pp. 341–58; J.A. Colquitt, J.A. LePine, and R.A. Noe, "Toward an Integrative Theory of Training Motivation: A Meta-analytic Path Analysis of 20 Years of Research," *Journal of Applied Psychology* 85 (2000), pp. 678–707; and J.P. Meyer, D.J. Stanley, L. Herscovitch, and L. Topolnytsky, "Affective, Continuance, and Normative Commitment to the Organization: A Meta-analysis of Antecedents, Correlates, and Consequences," *Journal of Vocational Behavior* 61 (2002), pp. 20–52.

Figure 9-7 also reveals that learning is only weakly related to organizational commitment.[65] In general, having higher levels of job knowledge is associated with slight increases in emotional attachment to the firm. It's true that companies that have a reputation as organizations that value learning tend to receive higher-quality applicants for jobs.[66] However, there's an important distinction between organizations that offer learning opportunities and employees who take advantage of those opportunities to actually gain knowledge. Moreover, it may be that employees with higher levels of expertise become more highly valued commodities on the job market, thereby reducing their levels of continuance commitment.

9.7 What steps can organizations take to foster learning?

APPLICATION: TRAINING

How can organizations improve learning in an effort to boost employee expertise and, ultimately, improve decision making? One approach is to rely on **training**, which represents a systematic effort by organizations to facilitate the learning of job-related knowledge and behaviour. Organizations across North America spend billions of dollars annually on employee learning and development (estimated at roughly $1,300 per employee).[67] A full discussion of all the types of training companies offer is beyond the scope of this section, but suffice it to say that companies are using many different methods to help their employees acquire explicit and tacit knowledge. Technological changes are altering the way those methods are delivered, as instructor-led classroom training has declined while online self-study programs have increased.[68] As described in our ***OB for Students*** section, these technological changes are now common on university and college campuses. Indeed, some of you may be working in a virtual classroom right now!

OB FOR STUDENTS

What do learning and training have to do with you as a student? We hope this is a reasonably clear question for you already! However, changes are on the way in how you might get taught in the future by both companies and universities. Technology and the changing marketplace (that includes you!) are forcing universities to incorporate online education as part of their ongoing strategies.[69] Online courses are growing by leaps and bounds across campuses all over the country and internationally. If you're not already experiencing virtual content in some form, chances are many of you will have the opportunity to receive it in the not-too-distant future. Overall, higher education enrollment in North America is relatively stable, but enrollment in online courses is increasing exponentially.[70]

One of the reasons universities have been slow to incorporate online education is the belief by many faculty members that the same level of knowledge cannot be transmitted online. However, a recent meta-analysis suggests that this belief is unfounded! Research shows no difference between online and regular classroom instruction in terms of the measured learning of explicit knowledge. Interestingly enough though, the study found that the highest levels of learning occurred when the two methods were mixed (part of the class online, part in the classroom).[71] It may be that two different learning strategies are used under such scenarios, which allows different kinds of learners to take advantage of what suits them best.[72] At the moment, companies are well ahead of the curve at delivering effective online classes. Edmonton-based Intuit, the maker of personal and small business software including Quicken and TurboTax, has been using the mixed method of training for quite a while. It employs face-to-face training to establish relationships prior to moving into a virtual classroom.[73] Such corporate efforts will likely help establish a blueprint for universities to follow as they expand their online offerings.

training

A systematic effort by organizations to facilitate the learning of job-related knowledge and behaviour

In addition to traditional training experiences, companies are also heavily focused on **knowledge transfer** from their older, experienced workers to their younger employees. Some companies are using variations of **behaviour modelling training** to ensure that employees have the ability to observe and learn from those in the company with significant amounts of tacit knowledge. For example, Raytheon, the defence and aerospace supplier, has created a training program called Leave-a-Legacy that pairs employees holding vital knowledge with high-potential subordinates. The program is not one of those "have lunch once a month" affairs; it's a relatively regimented program in which younger workers follow older workers around for extended periods of time, ensuring adequate opportunities for observation. Each pair of employees is also assigned a third-party coach who helps the knowledge transfer take place.[74] Such sharing of information between workers is not always easy, especially in competitive or political environments. One recent study suggests that one key to helping the passing of tacit information between co-workers is trust.[75] (See Chapter 8 for a more detailed description of how to foster trust.) One of the most difficult but most necessary periods of learning for employees is when they are sent outside their home country to work (when they are referred to as *expatriates*). Ernst & Young has around 2,600 employees placed in international locations at any given time. The company uses "mobility experts," partners who have been overseas, to help expatriates learn how to operate and live in these new cultures. The cost of that training is far less than the cost associated with an unsuccessful employee. Director Troy Dickerson says, "We want to ensure a strong return on investment for both the individual and Ernst & Young."[76]

knowledge transfer

The exchange of knowledge between employees

behaviour modelling training

When employees observe the actions of others, learn from what they observe, and then repeat the observed behaviour

Another form of knowledge transfer that's being used by companies more frequently is social networking (see Chapter 10 for more discussion on this topic). An example of this type of networking is **communities of practice**, which are groups of employees who learn from one another by collaborating over an extended period of time.[77] Many companies such as John Deere, Shell, and Verizon are adopting this newer form of informal social learning.[78] Cadbury, the Birmingham, England, confectionary manufacturer, has developed a global knowledge community to distribute knowledge throughout the company. Due to the fact that Cadbury has grown mainly by acquiring other companies all around the world, the company feels that these communities break down some of the walls created by having 64 worksites in 36 countries.[79] Communities of practice are not without their own complications, but their potential for transferring knowledge through employees is significant.[80]

communities of practice

Groups of employees who learn from one another through collaboration over an extended period of time

The success of these programs, as well as more traditional types of training, hinges on transfer of training. **Transfer of training** occurs when the knowledge, skills, and behaviours used on the job are maintained by the learner once training ends and generalized to the workplace once the learner returns to the job.[81] Transfer of training can be fostered if organizations create a **climate for transfer**—an environment that can support the use of new skills. There are a variety of factors that can help organizations foster such a climate. The degree to which the trainee's manager supports the importance of the newly acquired knowledge and skills and stresses their application to the job is perhaps the most important factor. Peer support is helpful, because having multiple trainees learning the same material reduces anxiety and allows the trainees to share concerns and work through problems. Opportunities to use the learned knowledge are also crucial, because practice and repetition are key components of learning. Because companies have a huge stake in increasing and transferring knowledge within their employee base, creating a climate for the transfer of that knowledge is imperative to the success of formal learning systems.

transfer of training

Occurs when employees retain and demonstrate the knowledge, skills, and behaviours required for their job after training ends

climate for transfer

An organizational environment that supports the use of new skills

TAKEAWAYS

9.1 Learning is a relatively permanent change in an employee's knowledge or skill that results from experience. Decision making refers to the process of generating and choosing from a set of alternatives to solve a problem. Learning allows employees to make better decisions by making those decisions more quickly and by being able to generate a better set of alternatives.

9.2 Employees gain both explicit and tacit knowledge as they build expertise. Explicit knowledge is easily communicated and available to everyone. Tacit knowledge, however, is something employees can learn only through experience.

9.3 Employees learn new knowledge through reinforcement and observation of others. That learning also depends on whether the employees are learning-oriented or performance-oriented.

9.4 Programmed decisions are decisions that become somewhat automatic because a person's knowledge allows him or her to recognize and identify a situation and the course of action that needs to be taken. Many task-related decisions made by experts are programmed decisions. Nonprogrammed decisions are made when a problem is new, complex, or not recognized. Ideally, such decisions are made by following the steps in the rational decision-making model.

9.5 Employees are less able to translate their learning into accurate decisions when they struggle with limited information, faulty perceptions, faulty attributions, and escalation of commitment.

9.6 Learning has a moderate positive relationship with job performance and a weak positive relationship with organizational commitment.

9.7 Through various forms of training, companies can give employees more knowledge and a wider array of experiences that they can use to make decisions.

KEY TERMS

availability bias
behaviour modelling training
behavioural modelling
bounded rationality
climate for transfer
communities of practice
consensus
consistency
contingencies of reinforcement
continuous reinforcement
crisis situation
decision making
distinctiveness
escalation of commitment
expertise
explicit knowledge
extinction
fixed-interval schedule
fixed-ratio schedule
fundamental attribution error
heuristics
intuition
knowledge transfer
learning
learning orientation
negative reinforcement
nonprogrammed decision
performance–avoid orientation
performance–prove orientation
positive reinforcement
programmed decisions
projection bias
punishment
rational decision-making model
satisficing

schedules of reinforcement
selective perception
self-serving bias
social identity theory
social learning theory
stereotype
tacit knowledge
training
transfer of training
variable-interval schedule
variable-ratio schedule

DISCUSSION QUESTIONS

9.1 In your current or past workplaces, what types of tacit knowledge did experienced workers possess? What did this knowledge allow them to do?

9.2 Companies rely on employees with substantial amounts of tacit knowledge. Why do companies struggle when these employees leave the organization unexpectedly? What can companies do to help ensure that they retain tacit knowledge?

9.3 What does the term "expert" mean to you? What exactly do experts do that novices don't?

9.4 Do you consider yourself to be a "rational" decision maker? For what types of decisions are you determined to be the most rational? What types of decisions are likely to cause you to behave irrationally?

9.5 Given your background, which of the decision-making biases listed in the chapter do you most struggle with? What could you do to overcome those biases to make more accurate decisions?

CASE • SANDI

Without classrooms, textbooks, lectures, or professors, how was Sandi going to survive her challenging new job at KPMG? Well, as it turned out … very well! In fact, after the first year, Sandi found herself working closely with people she liked and with high-profile clients on complex and interesting projects. It wasn't long before Sandi was working 60 to 70 hours per week. As her reputation increased, she noticed that it was much easier to get her manager to approve training opportunities, and that key people within the firm were seeking her out. Some of her peers, however, were not as fortunate. Many were put on easy jobs that were not big money-makers or were assigned jobs that others did not want to do. This was the worst kind of punishment—not to get training opportunities or to be ignored by the movers and shakers within the firm! After passing the CA exam, Sandi was quickly promoted to a management position. It would appear that her dream had indeed come true!

If her dream had really come true, then why did she feel so conflicted? The long working days combined with the high pressure were starting to take their toll. Is this the life she really wanted? But after investing so many years preparing for a career in a prestigious accounting firm like

KPMG, could she leave? She was aware that an alternative career in the profession would be to work as an auditor or controller in government or industry. Although the work would be more routine, potentially boring, and would require a more focused set of technical skills, it would be a lot more predictable and structured in terms of hours—she could have a life! And another thought occurred to her. Because she had always performed so well in university, perhaps she should pursue graduate study and work toward a doctorate degree and become a professor. One of her professors had strongly encouraged her to look at that option. Going back to school would require Sandi leave the accounting profession altogether.

9.1 How does the organization facilitate learning of tacit knowledge?

9.2 What kind of decision is Sandi currently faced with? What kind of information should she consider? What are the risks that may lead to a poor choice? What do you think she will do?

Sources: KPMG International, www.kpmg.com/GLOBAL/EN/ABOUT/OVERVIEW/Pages/default.aspx; KPMG Canada, www.kpmg.com/ca/en/about/performance/pages/default.aspx, retrieved January 27, 2015; CPA Canada, "CA UFE Guide and Report," www.cpacanada.ca/en/become-a-cpa/cpa-certification-program-evaluation/ca-ufe-guide, retrieved April 14, 2015; CPA Canada, www.becomeacaincanada.ca/item47117.html, retrieved April 14, 2015.

EXERCISE • DECISION-MAKING BIAS

The purpose of this exercise is to illustrate how decision making can be influenced by decision heuristics, availability bias, and escalation of commitment. This exercise uses groups of six participants, so your instructor will either assign you to a group of six or ask you to create your own group of six. The exercise has the following steps:

9.1 In your groups, come to consensus on an answer to each of the problems below.

A. A certain town is served by two hospitals. In the larger hospital about 45 babies are born every day, and in the smaller hospital about 15 babies are born every day. Although the overall proportion of boys is about 50 percent, the actual proportion at either hospital may be greater or less than 50 percent on any given day. At the end of a year, which hospital will have the greater number of days on which more than 60 percent of the babies born were boys?
   a. The large hospital
   b. The small hospital
   c. Neither; the number of days will be about the same (within 5 percent of each other)

B. Linda is 31, single, outspoken, and very bright. She majored in philosophy in university. As a student, she was deeply concerned with discrimination and other social issues and participated in antinuclear demonstrations. Which of the statements below is more likely?
   a. Linda is a bank teller.
   b. Linda is a bank teller and active in the feminist movement.

C. A cab was involved in a hit-and-run accident. Two cab companies serve the city: the Green, which operates 85 percent of the cabs, and the Blue, which operates the remaining 15 percent. A witness identifies the hit-and-run cab as Blue. When the court tests the reliability of the witness under circumstances similar to those on the night of the accident, he correctly identifies the colour of the cab 80 percent of the time and misidentifies it the other 20 percent. What's the probability that the cab involved in the accident was Blue, as the witness stated?

D. Imagine that you face this pair of concurrent decisions. Examine these decisions, then indicate which choices you prefer.

Decision I. Choose between

a. A sure gain of $240
b. A 25 percent chance of winning $1,000 and a 75 percent chance of winning nothing

Decision II. Choose between

a. A sure loss of $750
b. A 75 percent chance of losing $1,000 and a 25 percent chance of losing nothing

Decision III. Choose between

a. A sure loss of $3,000
b. An 80 percent chance of losing $4,000 and a 20 percent chance of losing nothing

E. a. You've decided to see a play and have bought a $40 ticket. As you enter the theatre, you realize you've lost your ticket. You can't remember the seat number, so you can't prove to the management that you bought a ticket. Would you spend $40 for a new ticket?

b. You've reserved a seat for a play, for which the ticket price is $40. As you enter the theatre to buy your ticket, you discover you've lost $40 from your pocket. Would you still buy the ticket? (Assume you have enough cash left to do so.)

F. Imagine you have operable lung cancer and have to choose between two treatments: surgery and radiation. Of 100 people having surgery, 10 die during the operation, 32 (including those original 10) are dead after 1 year, and 66 are dead after 5 years. Of 100 people having radiation therapy, none dies during treatment, 23 are dead after one year, and 78 after 5 years. Which treatment would you prefer?

9.2 Your instructor will give you the correct answer to each problem.

9.3 Class discussion, whether in groups or as a class, should focus on the following questions: How accurate were the descriptions you reached? What decision-making problems were evident in the decisions you reached? Consider especially where decision heuristics, availability, and escalation of commitment may have influenced your decisions. How might you improve your decision making to make it more accurate?

Sources: John M. Ivancevich, Robert Konopaske, and Michael T. Matteson, *Organizational Behavior and Management*, 7th ed. (New York: McGraw-Hill, 2005); reprinted with permission of The McGraw-Hill Companies. Original exercises based on: A. Tversky and D. Kahneman, "Rational Choice and the Framing of Decisions," *Journal of Business* 59 (1986), pp. 251–78; A. Tversky and D. Kahneman, "The Framing of Decisions and the Psychology of Choice," *Science* 211 (1981), pp. 453–58; A. Tversky and D. Kahneman, "Extensional vs. Intuitive Reasoning: The Conjunction Fallacy in Probability Judgment," *Psychological Review* 90 (1983), pp. 293–315; and K. McKean, "Decisions, Decisions," *Discovery Magazine*, June 1985.

OB ASSESSMENTS • GOAL ORIENTATION

What does your goal orientation look like? This assessment is designed to measure all three dimensions of goal orientation. Please write a number next to each statement that indicates the extent to which it accurately describes your attitude toward work while you are on the job. Answer each question using the response scale provided. Then add up your answers for each of the three dimensions.

1	2	3	4	5
Strongly Disagree	**Disagree**	**Neutral**	**Agree**	**Strongly Agree**

1. I am willing to select challenging assignments that I can learn a lot from.	_____
2. I often look for opportunities to develop new skills and knowledge.	_____
3. I enjoy challenging and difficult tasks where I'll learn new skills.	_____
4. For me, development of my ability is important enough to take risks.	_____
5. I prefer to work in situations that require a high level of ability and talent.	_____
6. I like to show that I can perform better than my co-workers.	_____
7. I try to figure out what it takes to prove my ability to others at work.	_____
8. I enjoy it when others at work are aware of how well I am doing.	_____
9. I prefer to work on projects where I can prove my ability to others.	_____
10. I would avoid taking on a new task if there was a chance that I would appear incompetent to others.	_____
11. Avoiding a show of low ability is more important to me than learning a new skill.	_____
12. I'm concerned about taking on a task at work if my performance would reveal that I had low ability.	_____
13. I prefer to avoid situations at work where I might perform poorly.	_____

Scoring and Interpretation

Learning orientation. Add up items 1–5.

Performance–prove orientation. Add up items 6–9.

Performance–avoid orientation. Add up items 10–13.

For learning orientation, scores of 20 or more are above average, and scores of 19 or less are below average. For the two performance orientations, scores of 15 or more are above average, and scores of 14 or less are below average. Remember, when interpreting your scores on these assessments it is important to consider the *reliability* and *validity* of these tools (see Chapter 1, ***OB Assessments***).

Source: Adapted from J.F. Brett and D. VandeWalle, "Goal Orientation and Goal Content as Predictors of Performance in a Training Program," *Journal of Applied Psychology* 84 (1999), pp. 863–73.

PART 3

Relational Mechanisms

CHAPTER 10

Communication

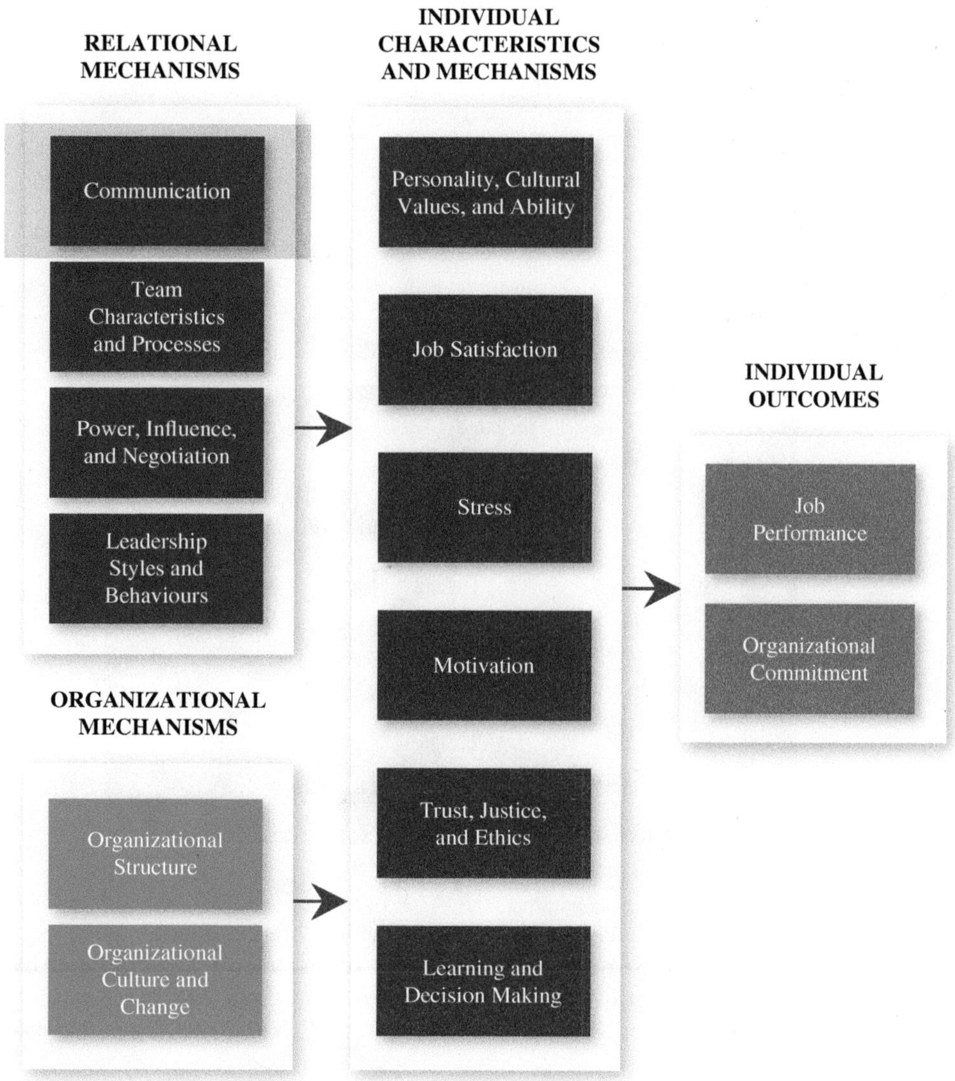

LEARNING OUTCOMES

After reading this chapter, you should be able to answer the following questions:

10.1 What is communication, and how does this relate to organizational behaviour?

10.2 How does the communication process work?

10.3 What do face-to-face and computer-mediated communication offer?

10.4 What are some of the more important issues that can affect the communication process?

10.5 How does information flow within organizations?

10.6 How does communication affect job performance and organizational commitment?

10.7 What can people do to facilitate effective communication during the job interview?

TD Canada Trust

By harnessing the power of social networking applications, TD Canada Trust has transformed the way individuals communicate and interact with each other.

© The Canadian Press/Tibor Kolley

TD Bank Group is a world-class company that understands the importance of communication. The company, headquartered in Toronto, represents a number of financial subsidiaries, including retail banking in both Canada and the United States.[1] With over a trillion dollars in assets and 22 million customers, TB Bank Group has now emerged as one the top 10 banks in North America.[2] It also ranks among the world's leading online financial services firms, with approximately 8 million online and mobile users.[3] Not surprisingly, it has also emerged as a leader in customer service. In Canada, the company has been consistently ranked by J.D. Power as having the highest customer satisfaction among the Big Five domestic retail banks.[4]

TD Canada Trust's reputation as a high-performing, customer-service organization has evolved over time. The retail bank we see today has its roots in a critical merger that occurred back in 2000 between Toronto-Dominion Bank and Canada Trust.[5] Tim Hockey, a senior manager during that period, recalled, "the complementary element was that TD had a strong commercial banking presence and sales culture but its service culture wasn't as strong. Canada Trust had a very strong service culture, but it had no business banking presence to speak of, and its sales culture (as is usual with service organizations) was probably a little less strong."[6]

Today, the challenge for the bank has been to develop and sustain its strong sales and service culture among a large, increasingly diverse, technology-savvy, and geographically dispersed workforce. To facilitate the bank's ability to connect its various stakeholders, since 2010, TD Canada Trust had been focused on becoming a social organization.[7] To actively engage and communicate with its customers, the company has established an active presence on major social media and networking sites such as Facebook, Twitter, and YouTube.[8] One of the best illustrations of this innovation has been WOW Moments, an internal social networking program that gives employees the opportunity to post stories about the things they have observed others doing, or done themselves, to build and support the bank's service and sales culture.[9]

WOW Moments was developed for TD Canada Trust by TemboSocial, a Toronto-based provider of interactive engagement and community-building software.[10] The actual program is based on The Hive, a social networking system that allows anyone within the bank to post a story related to customer experience; then, other employees, managers, and even top executives are able and encouraged to comment on that story.[11] "Sharing stories with one another is a fantastic way to communicate clearly what we all need to be focused on," says Karey Stanley, a senior manager at the bank. Since the onset of this program, TD Canada Trust employees have sent more than 300,000 WOW-Moments messages to each other.[12] Once the stories have been checked for relevance and appropriateness, they are tagged with a corporate value and stored in a searchable database that allows users to browse and search stories by value, keyword, region, or person.[13] "One of the great things about the stories that we've seen thus far is that very often they're not just by one person about one other person, they're about two or three other people," Stanley says. "For every *WOW Moment* created in the system, there are 1.4 recipients. So it really touches many people within the organization"[14]

10.1 What is communication, and how does this relate to organizational behaviour?

COMMUNICATION

In this chapter we focus attention on **communication**, defined as the process by which information and meaning is transferred from a sender to a receiver.[15] When you think about it, many of the activities and interactions that occur within work settings rest on the assumption that people are able to communicate effectively. How could groups of people coordinate themselves—for even simple activities—if communication were not possible? Even a relatively straightforward non-work event, like hosting a dinner party for a few friends, would be nearly impossible without at least some form of communication. And the very same is true in organizational settings, especially when highly interdependent activities are performed by two or more people.

communication

The process by which information and meaning is transferred from a sender to a receiver

Let's consider briefly the importance of communication for the two primary individual outcomes presented back in Chapter 1 (see Figure 1-1) Whether employees are performing routine tasks, adapting to novel situations, or trying to formulate innovate ideas, virtually all jobs require us to process and act upon information provided by others. Even the performance of solitary tasks, such as a those of home-based designer, will at some point have to communicate with clients and suppliers so that coordination can occur. Communicating helpful information to a struggling teammate may be viewed as a form of interpersonal citizenship behaviour. And if you look at the types of counterproductive behaviour (see Figure 2-3), communication processes are implied, albeit negative and harmful in focus. The whole concept of performance management rests largely on measurement, feedback, and management—three processes that could not occur without communication. The other primary employee outcome was employee commitment. In Chapter 3 we learned that the bases for the different forms of commitment rest on our understanding and interpretation of our relationship with the organization and its members. The social influence model of affective commitment, for instance, proposes that employees who interact and communicate more frequently are more likely to be influenced by those employees, and vice versa. These connections or links between people define paths by which communication occurs.

As we move beyond the two fundamental individual outcomes and consider the topics covered thus far, one would be hard pressed to come up with examples how the models of job satisfaction, stress, motivation, and trust could work in the absence of communication. The processes that underlie learning and decision making are highly integrated with the ideas of information processing and exchange. In Chapter 4 we learned about individual differences (e.g., personality, emotional intelligence, sensory abilities) that might help or hinder communication with others. How could task work and teamwork processes occur or team states exist without communication? Acquisition of power, enacting influence, successful negation, and leadership are all deeply rooted in one's ability to effectively communicate with others.

It would seem, then, that communication plays a central role in virtually all of the topics covered thus far. In this chapter we will examine the communication process and the different forms communication can take. Evidently, some forms we describe in this chapter are observable by the naked eye. An outside observer would be able to see a crew of astronauts communicating with each other about the status of the systems in their capsule. Others are less visible. An observer wouldn't necessarily be able to see the nonverbal messages exchanged among a surgical team, as members perform their technical roles yet quickly adjust and adapt to changing circumstances.

We will also review some of the more important issues or concerns that need to be managed for effective communication to occur, and examine several different communication structures. Finally, we will describe how communication might relate to our job performance and organizational commitment, and discuss communication within an interview context—an application many students can relate to.

10.2 How does the communication process work?

The Communication Process

One way to understand communication is to consider the model depicted in Figure 10-1.[16] On the side left is the source or sender of information. In a team that manufactures steel engine parts, for example, the sender might be one team member who wants to share information with another. More specifically, the sender might want to let the other person know that the team has to work more quickly to reach a difficult performance goal. To accomplish this goal, the sender will need to translate (encode) an idea into a verbal, written, or nonverbal message. Continuing with our example, the sender may choose to use arm and hand movements to convey the idea that the team needs to work faster. This encoded message is transmitted to a receiver, who needs to interpret or decode the message to form an understanding of the information it contains. In our example, the message is transmitted visually because the members are working face to face, but messages can be transmitted in written form, electronically, or even indirectly through other individuals. With this basic model of communication in mind, we can begin to understand the various factors that influence this process, and, in doing so, determine what it means to be a good communicator.

FIGURE 10-1

The Communication Process

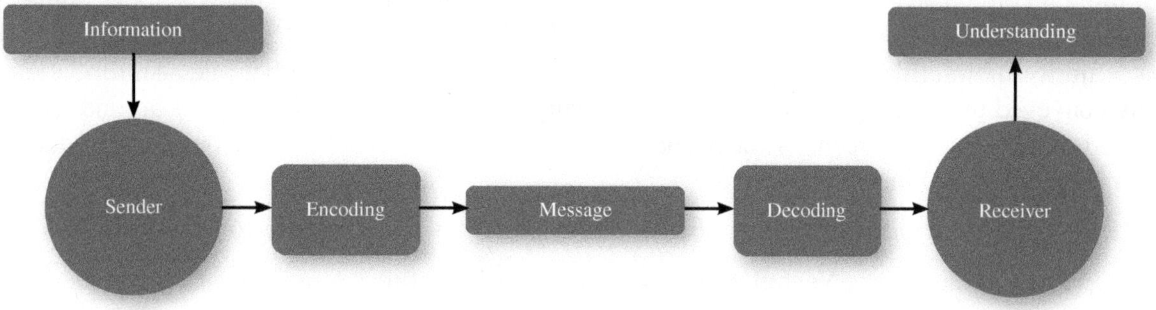

WHAT DOES IT MEAN TO BE A "GOOD COMMUNICATOR"?

Our description of the communication process (Figure 10-1) raises important questions. With so many different ways that people communicate with each other, you might be wondering what it means be a "good communicator." What issues do we all need to be aware of and carefully manage in our day-to-day work lives? In this section we explore these questions from the perspective of two broad categories of interpersonal communication within work settings. The first is face-to-face communication, and the important distinction between verbal and nonverbal forms. The second consists of related yet distinct forms of computer-mediated communication, including e-mail, videoconferencing, corporate wikis. We will look at how social networking applications have been used to facilitate communication within workplaces. In addition, we highlight possible issues "good communicators" need to be aware of when sending and receiving messages.

10.3 What do face-to-face and computer-mediated communication offer?

Face-to-Face Communication

As the term implies, **face-to-face communication** refers to the exchange of information and meaning that occurs when one or more individuals are physically present, and where communication occurs without the aid of any mediating technology. Face-to-face exchanges are natural, immediate, and embody a type of comprehensive interdependence (Chapter 11) in the sense that we "act and react" in real time to the content and tone of the messages being exchanged. The nature of communication in face-to-face encounters often has both verbal (spoken and written language) and nonverbal qualities (voice inflections, hand gestures, facial expressions) that together provide an extremely rich information source. No wonder face-to-face communication is considered the "gold standard of communication"; it tends to engage more human senses than mediated communication.[17]

face-to-face communication

The exchange of information and meaning when one or more individuals are physically present, and where communication occurs without the aid of any mediating technology

Today, e-mail and other forms of mediated communication are gradually reducing the frequency of face-to-face communication in work settings. Associated with this new reality are some unintended consequences for the communication process outlined in Figure 10-1. It has been estimated that the vast majority of information we process face to face is based on nonverbal cues—information not easily conveyed using computer technology.[18] Not surprisingly, a survey of managers around the world revealed that almost 70 percent of them said their organizations would actually be more productive if leaders communicated in person more often.[19]

Now let's look at two forms of communication that typically characterize face-to-face exchanges.

Verbal Communication **Verbal communication** can be defined as a form of communication in which messages are sent and received using written and spoken language. The sentence you are currently reading is an example (i.e., words are being used to convey information). When two or more people are communicating verbally they will engage in one or more of the following activities: reading, writing, speaking, and/or listening.

verbal communication

A form of communication in which messages are sent and received using written and spoken language

Regardless of its form, verbal communication is the primary way organizational members communicate with each other, and with individuals and groups outside the organization. Through oral and written language, leaders coordinate and control the activities of employees. For instance, a department manager might specify, in a formally written attendance policy, exactly how much unexcused absence will be allowed before a medical certificate is required. In a unionized setting the collective agreement represents a large archive of written rules that clearly explain the roles and responsibilities of union members and management in such areas as safety, employee discipline, and the procedures for resolving conflicts. More than just written policies and rules, verbal communication is the vehicle for obtaining, transferring, and storing information and knowledge within the organization.[20]

Written messages, such as text-based documents and e-mail, are ubiquitous within organizations and serve many different purposes. Examples of written communication that conveys what is important are a company's mission statement, its corporate goals and values, its annual report, and shorter-term and longer-term plans. Examples of written communication that convey how and why things are done are written job descriptions, explicit and standardized work procedures, training and operational manuals, contracts, performance appraisals, and meeting agendas and minutes.[21]

Oral communication is probably more prevalent than written communication in organizational settings, in large part because managers and supervisors generally prefer speaking to writing.[22] To be sure, face-to-face communication can be either written or oral, but it is more uniquely associated with the latter. Speaking, listening, and responding, supported and supplemented with written materials, are often expected during face-to-face encounters. Oral communication within work settings can be formal and structured, such as you might hear in job interviews, team meetings, performance appraisals, formal presentations, and of course when the boss is assigning work. But it can also be informal and spontaneous, including the normal, relationship-building chitchat that takes place among co-workers (e.g., "How was your weekend?") or the casual information exchange that takes place between two or more people performing interdependent tasks.[23]

Nonverbal Communication At its simplest level, **nonverbal communication** refers to any form of information exchange that doesn't involve spoken or written words. It is common to think of it as one's deliberate or unconscious use of body language to convey information. People might express themselves through the inflection, tone, and volume of their voice; hand gestures and facial expression; body posture and stance; eye contact and movements; smell; and dress and appearance. Famous management guru Peter F. Drucker once said "The most important thing in communication is hearing what isn't said." And don't forget the old saying that actions speak louder than words. What do these sayings have in common? Both imply that effective communication involves more than what is said or read. Researchers have estimated that 70 to 90 percent of a message's meaning is conveyed, not by words, but rather by body language.[24] Moreover, nonverbal body language seems to have universal relevance for virtually all types of face-to-face interactions—a lesson Alex "Hitch" Hitchens tried to explain to the nerdy Albert Brenneman in the hit movie *Hitch*: "60% of all human communication is nonverbal body language; 30% is your tone, so that means 90% of what you're saying ain't coming out of your mouth."

nonverbal communication

Any form of information exchange that doesn't involve spoken or written words

The main reason face-to-face exchanges are so rich from a communication perspective is that this medium involves and integrates both verbal and nonverbal information.[25] Teasing apart the effects of body language from the verbal cues in face-to-face interactions can be challenging. Still, such research has reached interesting findings. It appears that we tend to evaluate and judge the quality of our relationships on the basis of nonverbal instead of verbal cues.[26] For example, although handshakes are fairly standard practice in business settings, we know that how they are delivered conveys information about the relationship between the individuals. How might you interpret a weak, almost timid handshake? Or the message conveyed by someone who squeezes your hand too hard while maintaining an intense stare? Or by someone who, after shaking hands, reaches out and offers a warm hug? Dating couples will sometimes use kisses to assess the quality of their relationship: Is the kiss spine-tingling, is it sending shivers from your neck to your toes, or does it feel like you've just licked a wet fish?[27] (Not a recommended work practice, by the way.)

Another interesting finding is that during face-to-face exchanges, receivers tend to see nonverbal messages as more credible, believable, and trustworthy sources of information. This is especially true when there is a discrepancy between the verbal and nonverbal messages. For instance, an interviewee is saying he is interested in the job and motivated to do well, yet his body language is saying just the opposite.[28] How would you interpret these mixed signals? If you're like most people, you would probably trust the body language and not hire the person. Yet another interesting observation is that our interpretations of nonverbal cues—much more than verbal communication—have important contexts that need to be considered. We discuss the role of context later in the chapter; for now, consider how one's interpretation of eye contact depends on cultural context. In Canada, degree of eye contact is often used as a sign of the other person's interest and engagement. If a female employee of Japanese heritage avoids looking her supervisor in the eyes, she is not showing lack of interest, nor is she demonstrating a lack of self-confidence; she is being polite, respectful, and appropriate according to her culture.[29] The lesson here is that better communicators need to not only pay attention to nonverbal cues (i.e., what isn't being said) but the contexts in which this information is shared. See the ***OB Internationally*** feature here for more information on cultural differences with respect to communication.

OB INTERNATIONALLY

Today, as business becomes more global in scope, people who have been raised in different national cultures are interacting, communicating, and working together. If you think the communication process is challenging in the typical Canadian company, imagine the obstacles when you have senders and receivers who have different language capabilities.

Language challenges are obvious. Less obvious are the culturally based interpretations of body gestures. Gayle Cotton, a communications expert and author, recommends that, when it comes to hand gestures, it might be best to *keep your fingers to yourself!* Consider a few examples.

In Brazil, Germany, Russia, and many other countries around the world, forming a circle with thumb and index finger and the other fingers extended is a gesture that refers to a private bodily orifice and offensive to most people. However, in Canada, it is the OK sign, a nonverbal cue that signals approval. In Japan, our OK gesture refers to money, and in France it is used to convey the concept "zero" or "worthless."

Another example is the common V sign (palm outward), originally used to convey the concept of victory or peace. If you make that gesture to someone in Australia, the United Kingdom, or South Africa with your palm facing inward, you will have insulted him or her.

The "thumbs up" is commonly used in Canada and many other cultures to signify a job well done. However, if it is used in Australia, Greece, or the Middle East, especially if done like a typical hitchhiking gesture, the message would be "Up yours!" The gesture can also create real problems for those who count on their fingers. In Germany and Hungary, the upright thumb is used to represent the number "1." But an upright thumb in Japan means "5."

When it comes to body language in the communication process, the important thing to keep in mind is that what we say is said with words and body movements. When it comes to hand gestures, one "rule of thumb" is clear. Almost every gesture involving fingers is sure to offend someone, somewhere, sometime. Unless you are absolutely sure that the gesture won't be misinterpreted, *keep your fingers to yourself.*

Source: Parts of this article reprinted courtesy of communications expert and author Gayle Cotton, "Gestures to Avoid in Cross-Cultural Business: In Other Words, Keep Your Fingers to Yourself!," *Huffington Post*, June 13, 2013, www.huffingtonpost.com/gayle-cotton/cross-cultural-gestures_b_3437653.html, accessed June 26, 2014.

Nonverbal communication occurs when people express themselves through inflection, tone, and volume of voice; hand gestures and facial expression; body posture and stance; eye contact and movement; smell; and dress and appearance.

© Juice Images/Alamy

Computer-Mediated Communication

Computer-mediated communication—the exchange of information and meaning using an electronic, digital medium—is both an omnipresent and unavoidable reality in virtually all organizations.[30] To be sure, computer-mediated technology has greatly enhanced the flow of communication within workplaces, and increasingly this form of communication is being used to connect and coordinate intra-organizational activities. In this section we review some of the more popular digital mediums, including e-mail, videoconferencing, corporate wikis, and social networking tools.

computer-mediated communication
The exchange of information and meaning using an electronic, digital medium

The latter two channels are examples of a trend toward an environment known as **Web 2.0**—the term used to describe the world of websites and applications that allow users to actively interact, create, collaborate, and communicate (e.g., YouTube, Facebook, Wikipedia).

Web 2.0
Describes websites and applications through which users actively interact, create, collaborate, and communicate

In spite of the intrinsic appeal of computer-mediated communication, in this section we consider some important challenges associated with these tools.

E-Mail **E-mail** (electronic mail) is a popular method of exchanging written digital messages from an author to one or more recipients, and is now the preferred way to communicate with co-workers, customers, and other colleagues.[31] In spite of its popularity, e-mail communication has introduced unique challenges.

e-mail

A popular method of exchanging written digital messages from an author to one or more recipients

A concern you often hear is that e-mail lacks the same richness as a face-to-face conversation or even a telephone call. The immediacy and informal nature of e-mail messages (e.g., they often begin "Hi") encourages many senders to construct cryptic, idiosyncratic messages that can be hard to interpret. Another concern arises when text-based verbal e-mail messages are used to communicate messages with emotional content, because e-mail lacks the nonverbal cues such as facial expressions and tone of voice needed to convey feelings.[32] Consider a manager, for instance, who notices that one of her team is having difficulty meeting timelines and so sends an e-mail offering the assistance of another team member. The intended tone might have been empathy and caring, but the one inferred by the employee might easily be frustration and disappointment.

In fact, the likelihood of conflicts and misunderstandings increases substantially among those who are limited to e-mail communication, such as members of virtual teams.[33] Furthermore, extensive reliance on e-mail can been shown to adversely impact personal relationships. One study of faculty and staff within a university setting found that as the level of e-mail use increased *all other forms of communication decreased*. Apparently e-mail conversations had eliminated the need for casual face-to-face interactions, which, in turn, had left employees feeling less connected to each other.[34]

Yet another concern is the sheer volume of e-mails (and spam messages) being transmitted every day, contributing to information overload.[35]

There are a few ways people can manage work e-mail more efficiently.[36] The first is to use the labelling and filing capabilities of your e-mail program to sort and organize incoming mail into different folders (e.g., collect all e-mails from your boss into one folder). Second, don't forget where your delete button is. Third, to reduce the ever-increasing amount of junk e-mail, unsubscribe to websites that send regular promotional materials, and be mindful of copying too many people on your outgoing messages. Finally, experts recommend limiting your time on e-mail. You might want to set aside one or more times of the day to process your e-mail (preferably times that don't conflict with other work). We may never fully get a comfortable handle on the flood of e-mail, but modest attempts to organize and prioritize should help to reduce feelings of being overwhelmed.

Videoconferencing **Videoconferencing** is a communication medium that permits real-time, live interaction and discussion between remote individuals and individuals or groups via satellite or Internet. Videoconferencing has provided an option for those who are unable to travel due to time, cost, or fatigue but need to interact in real time using both verbal and nonverbal-plus-verbal communication. Take, for example, Microsoft's popular videoconferencing application Skype.[37] Students may find it interesting that name "skype" was intended to represent the concepts of "sky" and "peer-to-peer." Tools like this are easy to use. Once accounts have been established and connections made, two or more people communicate over the Internet by voice using a microphone, by video using a webcam, and by instant messaging, and can exchange information using file transfer applications.

videoconferencing

A communication medium that permits real-time, live interaction and discussion between remote individuals or groups via satellite or Internet

Like all electronic mediums, this one holds promise and presents challenges. Videoconferencing tools tend to be cost-efficient and more task-oriented than typical face-to-face interactions.[38] Videoconferencing works rather well for tasks that require simple information exchanges, cooperative problem solving, or making routine decisions.[39] Unfortunately, the level of interaction afforded by videoconferencing prevents users from making eye contact with other participants, which, in turn, reduces general awareness of the social dynamics within the group.[40] Expressed another way, videoconferencing, like other forms of computer-mediated communication, limits some of the natural, informal nonverbal messaging that facilitates the communication process described in Figure 10-1.[41] For these reasons, it tends to be less effective for tasks that require more "communication bandwidth," such as bargaining, conflict resolution, negotiation, or getting to know people.[42]

Wikis A **wiki** is a highly flexible Web 2.0 application that allows people to quickly exchange verbal information, and collaboratively solve problems, learn, manage projects, and create knowledge.[43] (The term *wiki* is derived from the Hawaiian word for "fast.") In terms of structure and logic, wikis are similar to blogs (weblogs, or discussion/information sites consisting of discrete, usually short articles). Wikis, however, allow anyone (or anyone in a designated community), to edit or delete written content, including the work of previous authors, using a web browser interface.[44]

wiki

A highly flexible Web 2.0 application that allows people to quickly exchange verbal information, and collaboratively solve problems, learn, manage projects, and create knowledge

You are probably familiar with Wikipedia, the popular Internet encyclopedia. What you might not realize is that it is a "living and growing information repository" (at last count 30 million articles in almost 300 languages) written and maintained collaboratively by volunteers all around the world.[45]

Our interest here, however, is in how wikis are applied to facilitate verbal communication and knowledge management within corporate settings.[46] There, they tend to be explicitly controlled by one or more "owners." Owners can be assigned by the company or they can informally emerge around a topic of interest within a community of users (e.g., an individual steps forward and sets up a wiki to coordinate volunteer opportunities). Owners' role is to define the purpose of the wiki and establish access privileges.[47] The design features that characterize corporate wikis (open access, transparency in terms of who contributes what, peer-based management) allow owners to track the relative contributions of users.[48]

You might be wondering how increased accountability and transparency affects the communication process. A recent study at IBM revealed that wiki owners and users experienced two competing motives when deciding how to participate in wiki-related activity.[49] On the one hand, the engineers in this study reported that the opportunity to collaborate and communicate with others was an exciting and engaging way to work with others, and active participation in the wiki was seen as way to achieve personal and organizational goals. On the other hand, the same group also seemed aware of the risks (e.g., exposing incompetence, looking foolish in front of one's peers), which called for a more cautious approach. The study revealed enthusiastic yet somewhat restrained participation.[50] A similar response pattern was noted by Wendy Arnott, Vice-President, Social Media and Digital Communications, at TD Canada Trust. Within their internal suite of social-media applications, which included wikis, Arnott states that "individuals tend to think carefully before sending messages or participating" knowing that their peers, managers, and other organizational members might see their contributions.[51]

OB RESEARCH IN CANADA

Dr. Ofer Arazy is a professor of information systems in the Alberta School of Business, University of Alberta, who has a keen interest in communication. In particular, Dr. Arazy studies how computer-mediated (Web 2.0-based) communication and collaboration tools, such as wikis, affect the motivation (Chapter 7) and behaviour of its users. When asked why he finds this topic interesting, Dr. Arazy replied, "coming from the high-tech industry before academia, I was very aware of the challenges of coordinating collaborative, knowledge-based work (e.g., software development), and how the features and affordances of Web 2.0 tools helped *and* hindered the behavior of individual contributors. Years ago, I saw the success of Wikipedia as a self-governing collaborative process and wondered whether a peer-production model like this would work in a corporate setting. To answer this question, my work has been devoted to understanding how the characteristics of individual users, task/organization, and information technology all come together."

Courtesy of Dr. Ofer Arazy

It turns out that others share Dr. Arazy's passion for this topic, and today he works with colleagues and organizations all around the world (some of this work was cited earlier in the chapter under "Wikis"). His published articles appear in some of his field's most prestigious journals, such as *MIS Quarterly*, *Journal of Management and Information Systems*, and *Journal of the Association for Information Systems*. For more information, look up Dr. Arazy at professor.business.ualberta.ca/oferarazy or oferarazy.com.

Social Network Applications As previously mentioned, a growing trend has been to adapt interactive Web 2.0 technology for applications in the workplace. The appeal of these social applications is that they are highly interactive and conversational, and greatly enhance the exchange of verbal information between senders and receivers.[52] As mentioned in our discussion of wikis, initiatives such as these bring people together around a goal or purpose in a context of accountability, allowing for natural communities to emerge. By connecting people and ideas, the promise is that internal social networks can be leveraged to increase individual and team performance by providing information that facilitates how people perform their technical roles. Social network applications help to align the human resources function with strategic goals (e.g., peer-based reward and recognition programs focused on building core competencies), and support the psychological environment in which technical activities occur by strengthening emotional links between people and increasing feelings of empowerment. In spite of their intuitive appeal, social network applications in workplace settings are still developing. In this section we draw attention to three examples widely used in organizations: LinkedIn, Achievers, and Connections.

LinkedIn is a business-oriented social networking service used by over 300 million people around the world for professional networking.[53] This network is leveraged to help users find jobs, find people who have similar educational backgrounds or career interests, follow companies where they might want to work, and find business opportunities.[54] Users create a profile that includes a wide variety of information, including formal education, work experiences, contact information, and a professional photo.[55] Then, they can invite others to be part of their personal network (or the program will suggest connections with users that they might know). Strictly speaking, LinkedIn is not an *internal* social network application. However, we have included it in this section because it has rapidly become one of the most important and powerful recruiting sources used by Canadian companies. Some of the challenges and responsibilities LinkedIn presents are well known, such as maintaining your personal security to minimize the threat of unauthorized data-scraping activities or to limit risks to your personal identity by changing passwords often, limiting what information you reveal about yourself, and reviewing privacy settings. Because the content on the site is managed by the users themselves, some of your connections' credentials are likely embellished or fabricated. In short, be careful! Learning how to manage privacy and reputation is an issue we examine later in the chapter.

Achievers is an example of how social network technology has been used within workplaces.[56] Razor Suleman founded the Toronto-based company that operates this platform back in 2002.[57] Today, the tool is used by companies all around the world, including some of Canada's leading ones such as 3M Canada.[58] At the core of this software is a powerful tool that facilitates top-down, bottom-up, and peer-to-peer communication. Of particular interest here is how the Achievers system uses the logic of social networking to communicate, throughout the organization, the values, behaviours, and achievements that are really important. Employees are encouraged to watch each other to see who best reflects important company's core values, be it innovation or customer service. Each week, every employee votes on who among them best exemplifies those core values. That individual then receives company-wide recognition.[59] As one manager put it, "I can't be everywhere. I can't see everything. But 200 people have a vote each week."[60] In addition to social employee recognition, the Achievers software can be expanded to include a variety of other interfaces to promote verbal communication, such as quickly collecting and processing feedback from employees regarding their issues and concerns, and sending this message up the communication network to senior managers. However, as we saw with wikis, Web 2.0 applications within corporate environments are not anonymous. To help employees remember this, the Achievers software includes a pop-up message that reminds them that what they're sharing will be seen by everyone—and why they should use discretion and common sense when using these communication tools.[61]

Connections, by IBM, is another example of an integrated software tool offers an innovate way for people interact, communicate, coordinate, and collaborate.[62] In fact, the Wow Moments program described in the chapter-opening profile is integrated with the Connections platform.[63] Not only is open and direct communication valued by TD Canada Trust, but also it has proven invaluable in times of organizational change—when employees want straight talk from managers and the freedom to openly share and discuss issues.[64] Teams, for instance, can use Connections to share files, organize their task work (Chapter 11), tap expertise within the team, set up online communities, and work together on projects.[65] As with most social network applications, all employees will create a personal profile (skills, knowledge, certifications) available to for viewing by all other members in the organization, and have a home page where they can see what is happening across the network. Various applications within Connections can be tailored to the job and the organizational context.[66] For instance, the activities module enables groups of people to easily view, manage, collaborate, and organize work tasks. Team members are able to track their work items, mark them complete, and monitor upcoming deadlines. Other applications allow individuals, team leaders, or managers to share files, create and maintain blogs, use wiki collaboration tools, set up forums to start discussion about a specific topic or shared problem, collect data (e.g., take internal polls), and define communities based on common interests, roles, and expertise.[67]

To summarize, computer-mediated communication is not only intrinsically appealing but offers an excellent way for large numbers of employees to collaborate, exchange information, and coordinate themselves. One could easily argue that these tools can greatly enhance a sense of "community" within the organization and foster strong versus weak culture (Chapter 15). Clearly, a major strength of computer-mediated communication is that it greatly enhances engagement and verbal exchanges. However, regardless of whether we're considering e-mail communication, videoconference technologies, wikis, or social networking applications, the verbal advantage may come at the cost of reduced nonverbal communication (see Figure 10-2). Even videoconferencing, which permits, to some degree, a channel for nonverbal cues, has proved superior for only some kinds of tasks. The unavoidable fact is that when individuals have to perform interdependent tasks that require greater communication bandwidth (permitting verbal and nonverbal messaging), face-to-face communication is better, because senders and receivers simply have more information to work with.

FIGURE 10-2

Forms of Communication and Verbal and Nonverbal Messages

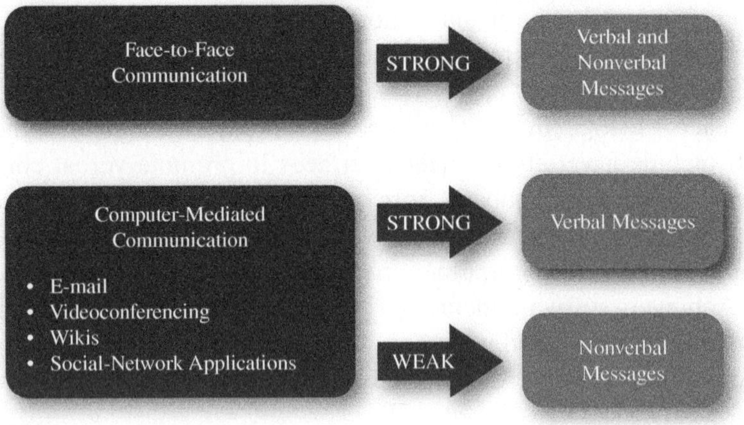

10.4 What are some of the more important issues that can affect the communication process?

The Communication Process: Potential Issues

Regardless of whether individuals are using face-to-face or computer-mediated communication channels, there are various issues that might facilitate or forestall the fundamental communication process described in Figure 10-1. We now turn to a discussion of these potential issues.

Communicator Competence One important factor that influences the communication process is the communicators themselves. Whether interacting face-to-face or electronically, the communication process assumes **communicator competence**, defined as the ability of communicators to encode and interpret messages. Ability differences with respect to these activities have been shown to be a major source of communication problems.[68] Earlier in the chapter we alluded to the employee who was working in loud manufacturing environment and used hand and arm gestures to tell his co-worker to speed up. Cues like this can be ambiguous, because frantic gestures can also signal danger or that something has gone wrong. A skilled communicator should be able to process the nonverbal information, and extract the intended meaning. The point here is that some are better than others at using and processing verbal and nonverbal messages. More importantly, the communication process will suffer if the participants lack communication competence.[69] In fact, it may already have occurred to you that perhaps the sender in our example should have chosen an alternative way to communicate the message. Along the same lines, a receiver who isn't skilled in listening carefully to a sender's message may misinterpret a message or miss it altogether.

communicator competence
The ability of communicators to encode and interpret messages

An additional issue relevant to the communication process in teams relates to the emotions and emotional intelligence of the individuals involved,[70] issues we discussed in Chapter 5 on job satisfaction and Chapter 4 on personality, cultural values, and ability. Emotions can impact how people express themselves and cloud their interpretation of information they receive from others.[71] Therefore, communicators' ability to regulate their emotions and understand the emotions of others can result in clearer communications that are less prone to misunderstanding. You might think emotions are mostly relevant to communications involving face-to-face interactions, but they can also interfere with computer-mediated communications, and so they are relevant to virtual teams as well.[72]

Noise A second factor that influences the communication process is the presence of **noise**, defined as disturbing or distracting stimuli (e.g., sounds, environmental events, technical issues) that block or interfere with the transmission of a message.[73] Face-to-face communication is particularly sensitive to the presence or absence of noise.

noise
Disturbing or distracting stimuli that block or interfere with the transmission of a message

Depending on how the message is being transmitted, noise can take several different forms. In the context of our manufacturing example, the sender and receiver may be working several metres from one another, and steam from the manufacturing process may make it difficult to see and appreciate the meaning of the hand and arm gestures being exchanged. As another example, you've probably had difficulty trying to hold a conversation with someone in a restaurant or at a party because of blaring music or the bustle of a crowd. If so, you understand how noise increases the effort communicators need to exert to make the communication process work. The sender has to talk louder and more clearly and perhaps increase the use of alternative means of communicating, such as hand gestures. In addition, the receiver has to listen more carefully and think harder to fill in the spaces left by spoken words that are impossible to hear. If one of the two parties isn't willing to put in the extra effort to send and receive messages when there is noise, the conversation likely will not last very long.

Information Richness A third issue that influences the communication process is **information richness**, defined as the amount and depth of the information transmitted in a message.[74] Messages transmitted through face-to-face channels have the highest level of richness,[75] because senders can convey meaning through not only words but also body language, facial expressions, and tone of voice. Face-to-face communication also provides the opportunity for senders and receivers to get feedback, which allows them to verify and ensure their messages are received and interpreted correctly.

information richness

The amount and depth of the information transmitted in a message

At the opposite end of the information richness spectrum are computer-generated reports that consist largely of numbers.[76] Although these types of reports might include a lot of information, they're limited to information that's quantifiable, and there's an absence of additional cues that might provide context and meaning.

A good example of a message with a moderate level of information richness is a personal written note.[77] Although a note is limited to the words on the page, the choice of words and punctuation can add meaning beyond the words themselves. Although recipients of e-mail messages do try to interpret the emotions of the sender from the content, they unfortunately often perceive the emotion as negative when it's not.[78]

From our description, it may sound as though higher levels of information richness are preferable to lower levels. This is true when the situation or task at hand is complex and difficult to understand.[79] In that case, the more cues available to the receiver, the more likely the message will be understood the way the sender intended it to be. Information richness may overcomplicate the communication process when the task at hand is relatively simple and straightforward.[80] The additional information that needs to be interpreted by the receiver increases the chance that some of the cues will seem contradictory; when this happens, receivers may feel they're being given mixed messages.

In summary, the appropriate level of information richness depends on the purpose of the communication and the complexity of the task at hand: the greater the complexity of the work, the more likely the benefits of information richness will outweigh its costs.

Gender Differences Another issue that can influence the communication process is our gender. **Gender differences** refer to the different ways men and women tend to process and interpret information and communicate with others. Men tend to use a style of communication that helps them achieve and maintain status, power, and independence, whereas women tend to send messages and use a style that builds and strengthens their relationships.[81] Examples of ways that men use communication to establish status would be showing off their ability or knowledge within a team meeting, telling stories or jokes (to be the centre of attention), being direct when asking someone else to do something, or taking credit for something good they have done. When did you last see a man asking for directions? However, it is very different for women. The natural communication style of women tends to be oriented toward building rapport. For instance, showing concern and support (e.g., saying "I'm sorry" when a co-worker shares bad news), asking questions, asking for help or feedback, buffering criticism with praise (e.g., saying something constructive and positive to a team member before saying something critical), using compliments to build relationships (e.g., telling a team member she did a good job, assuming a compliment will be returned), being indirect and subtle when sending messages to others.

gender differences

Different ways men and women tend to process and interpret information and communicate with others

Gender differences in communication style can be serious, because they can lead to misunderstandings between male and female team members, and often to faulty inferences about each other's confidence and competence, especially for women.[82] To be effective communicators, people need to aware of these differences, and be ready to adapt their natural communication style to fit the demands of the situation.[83]

Men tend to use a communication style that helps them achieve and maintain status, whereas women tend to use a style that builds and strengthens relationships.

© Tetra Images/Alamy

Privacy The final issue that affects the broader context for the communication process is **privacy**. Given that more and more of our daily communication activities are channelled through e-mail, text messages, or social networking applications, it is reasonable to wonder, "How much of this is private? Are there conditions or limits on privacy?" To address these concerns, the federal and provincial governments have revised, or are in the process of revising, laws and commissions to regulate how personal information is collected, used, and disclosed.[84] Ultimately the aim of government legislation and corporate privacy policies is to protect privacy rights while allowing us to benefit from these new communication channels.

privacy

A state in which individuals can express themselves freely without being observed, recorded, or disturbed by other, unauthorized individuals or groups

The question of privacy becomes more complex when we consider communication within a work setting—and especially computer-mediated communication. Can employers or prospective employers access your personal social networking sites, and use this information to make decisions that affect you? The short answer is yes. To lay down ground rules for these activities, it is very typical for companies to have a clear privacy policy that defines how employee information is handled.[85]

For example, Calgary-based Agrium Inc., a global supplier of agricultural projects, has its own Employee Privacy Policy. The policy has several objectives: to ensure that the company and its members comply with privacy legislation in the jurisdictions in which it operates; clarify expectations of privacy; to define what information is personal; and to explain why information is collected and how it is to be used. The policy also describes employee monitoring activities and understandings with respect to notification and consent.

How might these concerns about privacy and reputation affect the communication process? To answer this question, consider that the Internet has always been a place where anonymity reigns supreme. It is commonplace for individuals to join websites and post comments (e.g., blogs and online newspapers) under opaque usernames and fictitious profiles. That anonymity encourages users to say virtually anything and in any way (even if rude, impolite, and uncivil). Do you think those same users would communicate the same way if they had to use their real names and provide valid contact information? The answer should be obvious. In a context of increased accountability and control, messages sent via computer-mediated communication channels may be more guarded than those sent face to face. But the downside is that this mindset may undermine creative expression and innovation, as communicators seek to reduce personal risk.

For more information and discussion on the importance of privacy, and what you can do to protect yourself, look at the ***OB for Students*** feature here.

OB FOR STUDENTS

Over the past decade, social networking sites have rapidly become a cultural phenomenon. Recent polling tells us that at least 75 percent of young Canadian adults (18-to-29-year-olds) are heavy users of social networking technology (e.g., Facebook, Twitter). It would seem a safe bet that well over 90 percent of postsecondary students routinely use computer-mediated communication, especially since many courses now have a "social" component.

As we discuss throughout the chapter, interactive (Web 2.0) social applications are now commonplace in Canadian work settings. We will continue to debate the virtues of computer-mediated communication, and wonder if this technology has helped or hindered interpersonal relationships. We likely all agree that social media are here to stay. We use this technology to share our lives with others. But we also assume our personal information on these sites is private ("What happens in Vegas stays in Vegas"), when in reality it is often available to friends, university officials, and even parents. At work, the information we share is often available to co-workers, managers, and in some cases customers and clients.

More importantly, our personal information is able to be seen and used by people we don't even know, and many years after the event! In a year or two, most of you will graduate. Consider how a prospective employer might react to that embarrassing photo taken several years ago?

(Continued)

© Wavebreak Media Ltd./Alamy

What can you do to protect yourself and to avoid embarrassment? Various information and privacy commissioners across the country (look up the Federal Privacy Commissioner's office or your provincial counterpart's website) recommend the following:

- Never expect absolute privacy. Know what you're getting into by reading the privacy statement and policies. Many sites allow all registered users to view all the information you post on your site with no exceptions.
- Before you join a site and post your profile, find out if you can join a closed network, where only those with an e-mail address from your school can register, for example. Find out if the site allows others to see your profile without your consent.
- Choose the highest and most restrictive security setting available and do not give out information like your birthday, full name, phone number, social insurance number, or address.
- Take a second to think about what you're posting about yourself and your friends. Is it something you would post if your professor, boss, kid sister, or arch-rival were standing right behind you? Even though we tend to think of our personal sites as private, in reality many can be seen by just about anyone. Is there information about you that is embarrassing or that fraudsters could use? Also, remember that what you post may be online forever.
- Keep in mind that even sites with extensive privacy options may be required to make your personal information available to certain authorized persons, including law enforcement agencies.

Sources: Perverseff, T. (2014). "The Social Media Revolution: It's Here, Are We Ready?" Presentation delivered at the *Work and Workplaces of the Future: Implications for Western Canada* conference. The Conference Board of Canada, Calgary, May 5, 2014; Denham, E. (2010). "Work and Play in the Age of Social Networking." Presentation delivered at the IAPP Knowledgenet Conference, Calgary, Alberta. https://www.priv.gc.ca/media/spd/2010/spd_20100512_ed_e.asp (accessed June 19, 2014); Office of the Information and Privacy Commissioner of Alberta, http://www.oipc.ab.ca/pages/FOIP/QAs.aspx?id=1534 (accessed June 19, 2014); Office of the Information and Privacy Commissioner of Canada, http://www.priv.gc.ca/index_e.asp (accessed June 19, 2014).

Summary: What Does It Mean to Be a "Good Communicator"?

So what does it mean to be a "good communicator"? As is illustrated in Figure 10-3, it means attending to the fundamental elements of the communication process, and managing issues that might undermine it. Better communicators have mastered both the sending and receiving sides of the equation. This begins by knowing themselves and others. It is important to be able to craft and deliver meaning using channels that your intended target will be able to process and understand. The above discussion of gender differences reminds us that men and women tend to use different communication styles, and attend to different kinds of information. Good communicators are also effective listeners. Skilled receivers often have to process and integrate different sources of information, and confirm with senders that interpretations are accurate. This is especially true because so much communication is conveyed via body language that can be confusing, and at times inconsistent with verbal messages. Better communicators are able to use their skills to discern and resolve these difficulties.

FIGURE 10-3

What Does It Mean to Be a "Good Communicator"?

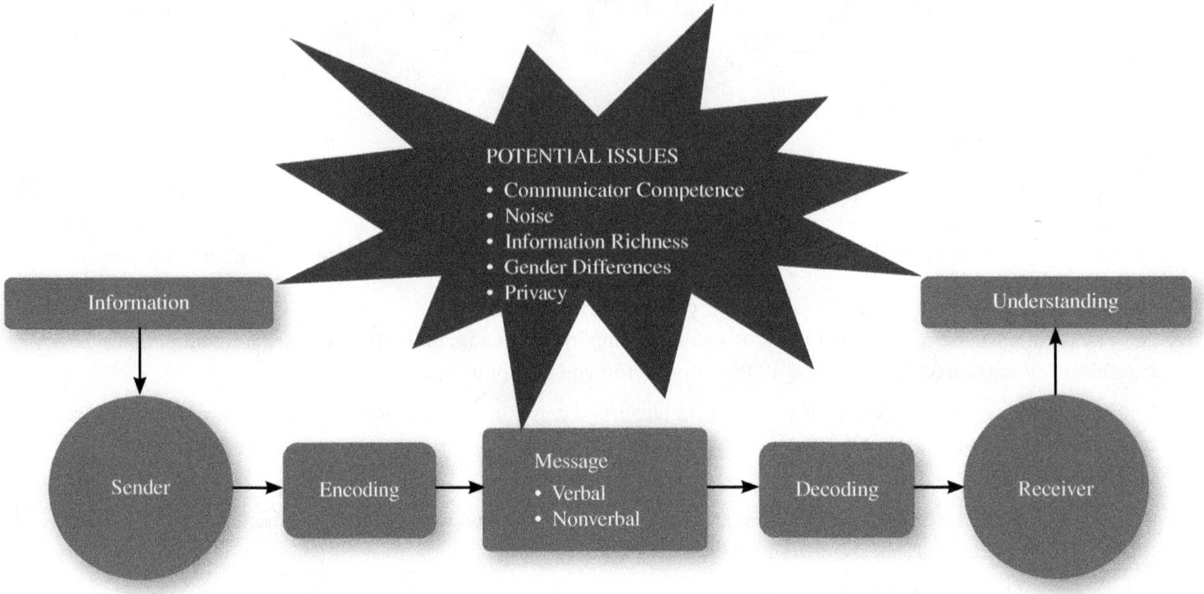

A point worth repeating is that use of technology does not necessarily improve the communication process. Some individuals may lack the competence or confidence to use these newer means of communication, resulting in their reluctance or inability to participate fully in collaborative efforts that take place using these technologies. As another example, social media reduce an individual's perceived cost of expressing their ideas and opinions. This could result in an overabundance of information, and the spread of misinformation and rumours that add "noise" to communication. The use of Twitter during the Haiti earthquake, for example, led to rumours that contributed to anxiety and uncertainty of those directly and indirectly involved in the disaster.[86]

Finally, beyond their ability to send and receive messages, better communicators appreciate the context in which communication is occurring, such as the intended purpose of the communication, the nature of the task, and the implications of the messages for yourself and others. Watch how better communicators on television, such as charismatic politicians, manage the communication process. They clearly understand what message they want to send, who they are targeting, and the best way to communicate the message so that the intended meaning and intensity is transmitted.

For example, after reading the ***OB on Screen*** feature you may ask yourself: Would Jordan Belfort's message have been so effective if he had sent out e-mail memos to his salespeople? The answer is no. Jordan demonstrates an exceptionally high level of communication skill, weaving poignant verbal and emotion-evoking nonverbal elements into a rich informational fabric. Pay attention to how Jordan uses noise and chaos to enhance the intensity and urgency within the room. In another context, this shouting and use of profanity would completely undermine the communication process.

OB ON SCREEN

The Wolf of Wall Street

I'm going to let you in on a secret about those telephones. They're not going to dial themselves, okay? Without you, they're just worthless hunks of plastic. Like a loaded M16 without a trained marine to pull the trigger. And in the case of the telephone, it's up to each and every one you, my highly trained Strattonites! My killers! My killers, who will not take "no" for an answer! My warriors, who will not hang up the phone ... until their client either buys or dies!

With these words and a powerful delivery, Jordan Belfort (Leonardo DiCaprio) whips his salespeople into a frenzy and orders them into "battle" armed with telephones. The movie *The Wolf of Wall Street* (Dir. Martin Scorsese, Red Granite Pictures, 2013) tells of the rise and fall of Jordon Belfort, a stock broker. In this particular quote, Jordan uses communication techniques to transform a fairly routine sales speech ("Get out there and sell, sell, sell") into a life-or-death struggle. Specifically, he skillfully uses the spoken word to evoke images of trained soldiers using loaded M16s, military assault rifles well suited for jungle warfare. In one breath, these warlike concepts are compared to, and used to define, his salespeople (trained killers) and their telephones (lethal weapons). Use of analogy shifts the mindset from "cold-calling clients" to a military operation, in which the clients are cast as the "enemy" who must be made to comply ("buy or die"). Not only do the words convey the urgency and imperative of the mission, but Jordan effectively signals that failure will not be accepted (i.e., salespeople who are not successful will also "die").

© Moviestore collection Ltd/Alamy

To ensure that the verbal message motivates rather than creates feelings of anxiety, Jordon skillfully uses nonverbal communication techniques to manage the emotions of the sales team. When you watch this clip, note how Jordan's nonverbal cues are perfectly aligned with the aggressive verbal content, reinforcing the verbal messages and generating an excited emotional response within individuals and the group as a whole. To create strong feelings of confidence and invincibility, Jordon skillfully uses his voice and delivery (e.g., changes tone, raises the volume of his voice, speaks quickly but in short machine-gun-like bursts punctuated by profanity [omitted from the quote]). Observe how his body movements (e.g., moving back and forth quickly like a caged predator ready to attack, hitting his head with the microphone) match the aggressive verbal messages. With the crowd mesmerized and frenzied, Jordon runs through it and jumps onto the stage. He turns to the crowd with a distorted facial expression (extending his jaw, exposing his canine teeth), conveying a visceral, almost "wolf-like," stance that signals an impending fight (a universally recognized sign of aggression in the animal kingdom). Responding to this cue, the crowd starts primal chanting and stomping—"*The pack is ready for the kill.*"

COMMUNICATION NETWORKS

So far in our discussion of communication, we've kept things simple by focusing on the flow of information between two people—a sender and a receiver. Of course, communication processes within work settings typically involve more than just two people, so it's important to consider the implications of this additional complexity. Adding to the complexity is whether communication occurs within one level in the organization or across levels as when a supervisor provides feedback to her direct reports. It shouldn't surprise too many students to learn that not all communication within organizations is formal or officially sanctioned by management—as we shall see there is large informal and unofficial communication system that operates in parallel and sometimes conflicts with the formal system.

We start this discussion with the concept of network structure, defined as the pattern of communication that typically occurs among members of a formal work unit.[87] To provide context for our discussion of network structures, let's review different types of formal communication within organizational settings. We'll then shift our attention from formal to informal communication networks.

10.5 How does information flow within organizations?

Formal Communication

Some formal communication occurs through *vertical* channels, with information flowing along lines of authority and reporting relationships. Often we can "see" these pathways by looking at an organizational chart. For instance, the plant manager has authority over a production supervisor who, in turn, has authority over a production employee. Such a chart also tells us about reporting relationships (e.g., the production employee reports to the production supervisor, who in turn reports to the plant manager). Other formal communication occurs through *horizontal* channels, with information flowing between people who work at the same level within the organization but in different functional areas (e.g., marketing, production).

Official vertical and horizontal communication channels are necessary for coordination as an organization grows and its tasks become more complex and interdependent.[88] The topic of vertical and horizontal organizational structure and the implications for communication processes is explored in more depth in Chapter 14. Before describing different formal communication networks, let's briefly review three forms of formal communication: downward, upward, and horizontal.

Downward Communication As the term implies, **downward communication** is communication that flows from the top to the bottom of the vertical channel, reinforcing the hierarchical nature of the organization. Downward communication has several important purposes.[89] First, managers often use a top-down approach to relay directives, decisions, plans, goals, and instructions to their subordinates in the hierarchy. Second, downward communication via written policies, procedures, and rules are often used to increase the level of consistency within the organization (e.g., attendance control policies are implemented to control the level of employee absenteeism within the organization). Third, managers often use a top-down approach when evaluating their subordinates' job performance. It is true that sometimes the performance-appraisal process involves a two-way discussion, but ultimately it is the manager's responsibility to manage the performance of her subordinates. There are concerns associated with downward communication that can undermine its effectiveness.[90] First, the sheer volume of information flowing from the top of the organization to the bottom requires managers at each level to process and filter the information they pass down. Passing along too much information might cause subordinates to feel overwhelmed and lead them to prioritize the messages. Too many e-mail memos from "administration" might encourage people to ignore or discount the messages altogether. Of course, excessive filtering might lead to misunderstandings and information gaps. Second, downward communication is notoriously slow—in part because of the filtering decisions at each level.

downward communication

Communication that flows from the top to the bottom of the vertical channel

Upward Communication **Upward communication** is communication that flows from the bottom to the top of the vertical channel—as happens when, for example, managers at higher levels are informed about relevant activities and outcomes at lower levels, unsolved work problems, suggestions for improvements, and how subordinates feel about their jobs.[91] As with downward communication, there are concerns associated with it that can undermine the effectiveness of this approach. For an individual within the organization, there is often some risk associated with sending messages to a superior. What if the manager doesn't like what I say? Or feels personally threatened by the feedback? Is it a good idea for employees to admit that they are having difficulty with a task—will this make them vulnerable? Only when people feel they can trust their superior with open and honest feedback will this approach be effective (see Chapter 8).[92] Another concern is that upward communication can be politically motivated and used as an influence tactic (see Chapter 12). Ironically, maybe the best way to improve the willingness of employees to communicate upward is to enhance the quality of downward communication—creating conditions for effective two-way communication to occur.[93]

upward communication

Communication that flows from the bottom to the top of the vertical channel

Horizontal Communication **Horizontal communication** occurs when information flows among members of work groups, teams, or functional units who reside at the same level in the organization. In this context, communication is used to coordinate effort, solve problems, share information, resolve conflicts, and build rapport.[94] The effectiveness of horizontal communication will be closely linked to how well the members are able to work together as a team. For an expanded discussion of team structures and processes, see Chapter 11.

horizontal communication

Communication that flows among members of work groups, teams, or functional units who reside at the same level in the organization

Formal Networks

Communication networks refer to the ways members of a team or work unit typically interact and exchange messages. As you will see, these networks often involve elements of downward, upward, and/or horizontal communication. In a universe of possible configurations, what is the best way characterize these networks? One approach is to focus on the extent to information within the network flows freely among members or whether communication is controlled or restricted by a single member such as a leader. In Figure 10-4 we present several different network examples organized in terms of their centralization, or degree to which the communication flows through some members rather than others.[95] The more communication flowing through fewer members of the team, the higher the degree of centralization. Think of the circles in the figure as team members, and the lines between the circles as the flow of communication back and forth.

FIGURE 10-4

Communication Network Structures

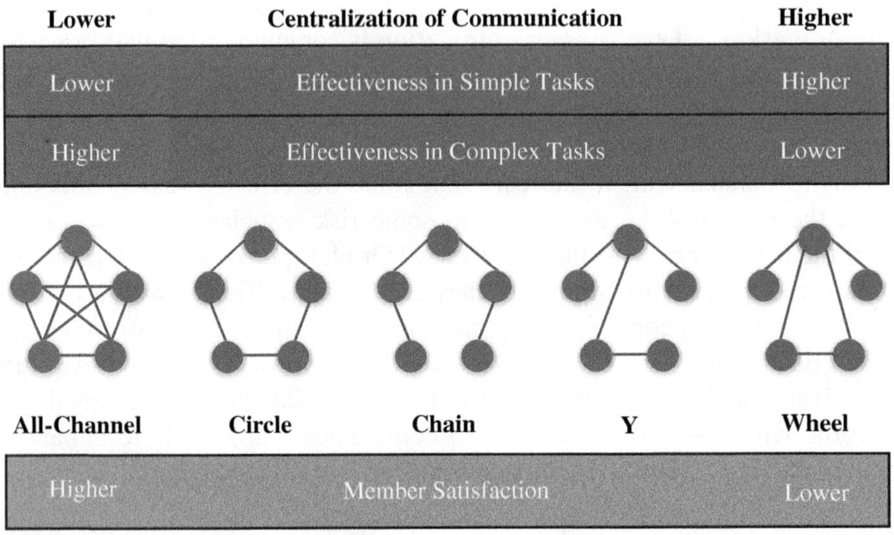

On the far left side of the figure we depict decentralized structures. The **all-channel network structure** is one in which any member can send and receive messages from any other. Not only is all information shared equally, but this configuration allows members to verify the accuracy of messages received. Student teams typically communicate using this type of structure. Within the **circle network structure** members send and receive messages from individuals who are immediately adjacent to them. It is similar to the all-channel configuration in the sense that all information is shared within the group. As the name implies, information with the circle configuration flows in a serial manner, from one member to another. A concern might be that if, at any point, the message becomes distorted or embellished, these misunderstandings are passed along. Unfortunately, the nature of the circle does not permit members to check or verify the content of the messages received with non-adjacent members in the network—the only check would be when the message you originally sent eventually makes it back to you. What might make for a fun party game (people arrange themselves in a circle; you whisper a message to the person on your immediate right, who in turn whispers the message to the person on his or her right, and so on until it comes back to you—then you compare the message you initially sent with the one your received) might not be much fun in a work setting if critical information is altered or omitted during the communication process.

all-channel network structure
A communication network in which any member can send and receive messages from any other

circle network structure

A communication network in which members send and receive messages from individuals who are immediately adjacent to them

We define the **chain network structure** as a communication network in which information is passed from member to member, from one end of the chain to the other. This type of communication network is fairly typical in hierarchical organizational structures, and epitomizes downward communication. Upward communication, when it occurs, is usually facilitated by a chain structure. Regardless of the direction of information flow, communication within a chain structure relies on each intervening member to faithfully pass along the message. As with the circle configuration, a possible weakness (or strength) is that the receiver is completely dependent on the adjacent person for information. As we will see, whether a "strict chain of (communication) control" is a problem or a strength very much depends on the nature of the task being performed by the team or work unit.

chain network structure

A communication network in which information is passed from member to member, from one end of the chain to the other

On the right side of Figure 10-4 we see two highly centralized networks. Note that in the **Y network structure** and the **wheel network structure** information tends to flow through a single member. In the Y configuration one member controls the flow of information between one set of members (who might interact) and another. In the wheel configuration there is little or no direct formal communication between the "spokes." The person occupying the central position (e.g., leader) within the wheel controls all information flow and communication, and decides who receives information and who doesn't. The Y has many centralized characteristics of the wheel, but communication is allowed between certain members (in this example the Y represents a blend of the wheel and chain structures). Teams or work units that use centralized networks often consist of a formal leader who makes final decisions on the basis of recommendations from members who have special expertise.

Y network structure

A communication network in which one member controls the flow of information between one set of members and another

wheel network structure

A communication network in which all communication between members is controlled by a single member

So why are communication network structures important to learn about? Quite a bit of research on this topic suggests that the patterns have important implications for how well the team or work group is able to coordinate its activities. We also know that whether a network structure is appropriate depends on the nature of the team's work.[96] When the work is simple and straightforward, a centralized structure tends to result in faster solutions with fewer mistakes. When the work is complex and difficult to understand, a decentralized structure tends to be more efficient—apparently because members can communicate with anyone to get assistance, innovate, or resolve problems. When the work is simple and easy to understand, the additional communication channels afforded by a decentralized structure become unnecessary and divert members' attention from the task.

Overall, communication among team members in organizations has become more decentralized over the past decade or so. One reason is that social network media have become inexpensive and easy to use. Earlier in the chapter we reviewed examples of user-centred Web 2.0 tools and communication software, such as IBM's Connections, that allow individuals to share information and collaborate in real time. It's important to mention, however, that employees generally prefer decentralized network structures. They tend to be more satisfied with the team when they are "in the loop," even though their position in the loop might not help the team perform more effectively.

Informal Communication Networks

Unlike formal communication, which reflects the exchange of officially sanctioned messages, **informal communication networks** refer to spontaneous and emergent patterns of communication that result from the choices individuals make on their own.[97] Rather than being designated by managers, these networks tend to be rooted in personal friendships, physical proximity, and shared interests. They can be quite small, involving relatively few people; or they can be very large and ubiquitous (e.g., "the grapevine"—see below).

informal communication networks
Spontaneous and emergent patterns of communication that result from the choices individuals make on their own

As we will discuss momentarily, information travels very fast in these informal networks, the content of the messages often confirming, contradicting, and elaborating upon information that travels through more formal channels. For instance, say the chief executive officer sends out formal reports to all employees congratulating everyone for a terrific year, and stating that the company will be expanding soon. Later that day, you might overhear a conversation in the coffee room about the loss of a major client, and the resulting closure of the company's Mississauga facility. Which information source would you find more credible—the CEO or a casual conversation between two sales representatives? So, in addition to filling in the gaps within the formal system, information gleaned from informal sources can sometimes be viewed as more trustworthy.

Grapevine The term **grapevine** refers to *the* primary informal communication network within an organization, used by people to circulate information about their work or other people. Think of it as an invisible highway (channel) on which informal and unofficial messages travel freely. In comparison to one of the organized networks portrayed in Figure 10-4, the grapevine's configuration would seem to be very random, unsystematic, and arbitrary. And, like an actual grapevine, the source can be extremely difficult to locate, often crossing hierarchical levels, functional roles, and professional affiliations within the organization.[98]

grapevine
The primary informal communication network within an organization

Other interesting characteristics of the channel are the speed with which information (especially bad news) travels, and its relative accuracy (roughly 75 percent).[99] In some ways it mimics social media technology like Twitter (e.g., there is rapid dissemination); however, in the grapevine information is passed verbally by means of "word of mouth" technology. Unlike in social media applications, in which logs are kept and identities of sources easily traced, messages transmitted through the grapevine tend to come without a "paper trail"—a record of who said what and when.

Given the grapevine's vital role for overall communication effectiveness, you would think that cultivating and carefully managing these informal contacts would be an imperative for all managers.[100] Sadly, the research suggests the opposite. In fact, it seems far more likely that organizations have no formal policy to deal with the grapevine, and most managers don't take an active role in managing or controlling informal communication networks.[101] That said, sometimes senior managers will use the grapevine to spread information that can't be shared officially or if they want a subtle way to test employee reactions to new policies before announcing anything.

The grapevine is the primary informal communication network within an organization. Using the grapevine can be an excellent way to communicate unfiltered "sensitive" messages and to facilitate upward communication and lateral (peer-to-peer) communication.

Comstock/PunchStock

Rumours and Gossip If the grapevine represents communication infrastructure, then we can think of **rumours** as one kind of message that travels along this network. What are rumours? Perhaps the best answer is that they represent sets of messages that lack evidence as to their truth or validity, yet explain confusing events and flourish in an atmosphere of secrecy and competition.[102] In short, rumours are unverified statements currently being circulated. This information might be informational in nature (e.g., the president of the company is considering retirement; a merger with a competitor seems imminent), or it can be personal. When rumours are about other people, we call this **gossip**. The concept of gossip is rarely viewed in a positive light, and is often associated with idle chatter or chitchat. Gossip is defined as informal and evaluative talk in an organization, usually among not more than a few individuals, about another member of that organization who is not present.[103] Students will recall that in Chapter 2 gossip was identified as an example of an interpersonal-focused counterproductive behaviour. Unfortunately, when gossip is spread through the grapevine, people's reputations, careers, and lives can be destroyed very rapidly.[104]

rumours

Messages that travel along the grapevine that lack evidence as to their truth or validity

gossip
Rumours about other people

Summary The informal communication network within the organization plays a very important role. It helps to clarify and supplement the formal communication networks, especially during turbulent times or when changes are occurring and people feel the need for more information than what is being provided. Using the grapevine can be an excellent way to communicate unfiltered "sensitive" messages and to facilitate upward communication and lateral (peer-to-peer) communication.

In spite of its virtues, the very open and unregulated nature of the informal system leaves it susceptible to misuse. Human nature being what it is means that at some point the grapevine will be used to spread false, misleading, or distorted information.[105] Attempts to shut down the grapevine will likely also remove an important channel through which employees can vent work-related stress and anxiety, translate and interpret organizational directives and policies, and nurture a sense of unity and group cohesiveness within the organization.[106]

Perhaps the best advice to managers is to pay attention to the grapevine (i.e., listen to what people are saying) and to do a much better job communicating messages through the formal system. After all, the more restrictive and limited the formal communication networks become, the more people will be motivated to participate in the exchange of information through informal channels.[107] Thus, simply improving the quality and integrity of the formal messaging should help to reduce the need for employees to rely on unverified, possibly false information.

10.6 How does communication affect job performance and organizational commitment?

HOW IMPORTANT IS COMMUNICATION?

Does communication have a significant impact on the two primary outcomes in our integrative model of OB? Figure 10-5 summarizes the research evidence linking one form of downward communication, **supervisor feedback** (regarding how well the subordinate performs his or her job), to future job performance and organizational commitment. The figure reveals that supervisor feedback—*on its own*—has a relatively weak correlation with job performance.[108] Why? For communication regarding one's performance to produce changes a number of things must be considered. For instance, is the feedback positive or negative? Studies show that extremely negative feedback from a manager can actually demoralize and discourage a subordinate employee, resulting in lower rather than higher performance.[109] Also important is whether the feedback is acceptable to the subordinate. Do the subordinates see the feedback as relevant to their job and something that they can act on, and do they find the source of the feedback credible?[110] If the feedback is rejected, motivation to change won't increase. We also know that ability (Can they perform?) and personality play a role, conscientious employees tending to respond more favourably to feedback.[111] If a manager's feedback is accepted and the subordinate wants to change, performance improvements can be expected, providing the subordinate has the necessary knowledge, skills, abilities, and personality traits (and necessary tools and equipment) needed for higher performance.[112] The point here is that the relationship between the supervisor's message and performance is complex, hinging on an intervening process and on conditions.

FIGURE 10-5

Effects of Communication on Performance and Commitment

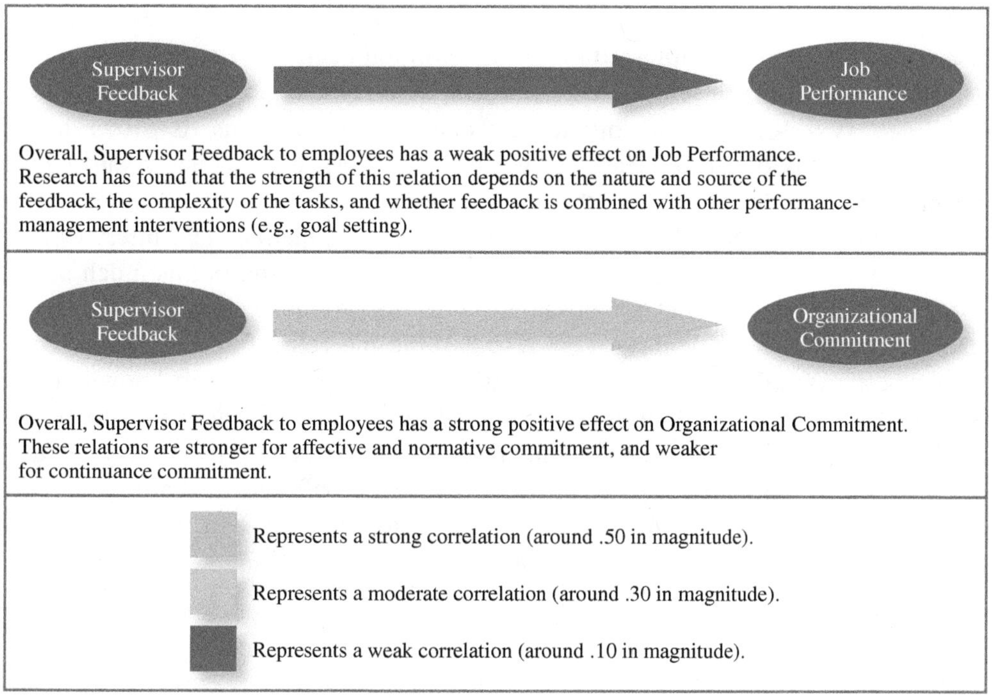

Supervisor Feedback
Job Performance
Overall, Supervisor Feedback to employees has a weak positive effect on Job Performance. Research has found that the strength of this relation depends on the nature and source of the feedback, the complexity of the tasks, and whether feedback is combined with other performance-management interventions (e.g., goal setting).
Supervisor Feedback
Organizational Commitment
Overall, Supervisor Feedback to employees has a strong positive effect on Organizational Commitment. These relations are stronger for affective and normative commitment, and weaker for continuance commitment.
Represents a strong correlation (around .50 in magnitude).
Represents a moderate correlation (around .30 in magnitude).
Represents a weak correlation (around .10 in magnitude).

Sources: Allen, N.J., & Meyer, J.P. (1990). The measurement and antecedents of affective, continuance, and normative commitment to the organization. *Journal of Occupational Psychology*, 63, 1–18; Harris, M.J., & Rosenthal, R. (1985). Mediation of interpersonal expectancies effects: 31 meta-analyses. *Psychological Bulletin*, 97, 363–386; Kluger, A.N., & DeNisi, A. (1996). The effects of feedback interventions on performance: A historical review, a meta-analysis, and a preliminary intervention theory. *Psychological Bulletin*, 119, 256–284; Mathieu, J.E., & Zajac, D. (1990). A review and meta-analysis of the antecedents, correlates, and consequences of organizational commitment. *Psychological Bulletin*, 108, 171–194; Smither, J.W., London, M., & Reilly, R.R. (2005). Does performance improve following multisource feedback? A theoretical model, meta-analysis, and review of the empirical findings. *Personnel Psychology*, 58, 33–66.

supervisor feedback
A form of downward communication in which the supervisor provides information to a subordinate about his or her job performance

Figure 10-5 also shows that the link between supervisor feedback and organizational commitment is generally strong, but that this relation might depend on the form of commitment.[113] Why? Accurate and timely (helpful) downward communication by a supervisor, manager, or leader should enhance the work environment, and convey messages of genuine support and confidence—perhaps encouraging subordinates to share information, offer suggestions to solve problems, and participate in decision making.[114] In turn, this should make it easier for employees to understand their role, feel valued and appreciated, and feel emotionally connected with the work, the leader, and the organization. It isn't surprising to see strong positive correlations between positive supervisor feedback and affective commitment, and to a lesser extent normative commitment.[115] Interestingly, positive leader communications (such as feedback) have been shown to lower feelings of continuance commitment.[116] It would seem, then, that one way a manager can reduce feelings of continuance commitment (see Chapter 3 for a full explanation of this concept) is to use communication skills.

10.7 What can people do to facilitate effective communication during the job interview?

APPLICATION: INTERVIEWING

In this section we examine an application of the communication process in a context that has tremendous implications for both senders and receivers. That context is none other than the dreaded **job interview**, defined as a conversation initiated by one or more persons to gather information and evaluate the qualifications of an applicant for a job.[117] In short, job interviews are decision-making tools. Applicants (interviewees) assume the roles of senders and receivers in the communication process, as they listen, decode, and respond to requests for information (i.e., interview questions), as well as ask their own questions. The aim of the job applicant is to find out as much as he or she can about the job, the organization, and career possibilities in order to make an informed decision should an offer be made. Across the table, interviewers also assume the role of senders and receivers as they explicitly probe, for example, the interviewee's prior work experience, job knowledge, behavioural patterns, and interpersonal skills. Information extracted during the interview and the inferences based on it provide evidence of a candidate's suitability. Misunderstandings at any point during the communication process potentially impacts the impressions and inferences of all parties. Learning how to manage this process is important, because the job interview (of one variety or another) is the selection procedure most frequently used by Canadian organizations.[118]

job interview

A conversation initiated by one or more person to gather information and evaluate the qualifications of the applicant for a job

Given the importance of the job interview for hiring decisions, it is everyone's best interest to increase the degree of **reliability** and **predictive validity** of this popular selection procedure. In this context, reliability refers to the extent to which the job interview (as a measure) is free from random error, and predictive validity refers to the degree to which job-interview ratings predict future on-the-job performance. Research with these procedures clearly shows that both reliability and predictive validity improve when these conversations are structured rather than unstructured.[119] In contrast to interviews using unstructured, free-wheeling, conversational styles, structured interviews often involve a standardized set of questions with established scoring keys, and questions that are job-relevant (i.e., based on careful analysis of job demands and skill requirements).[120]

reliability

The extent to which the selection procedure (e.g., job interview) is free from random error

predictive validity

The extent to which the selection procedure (e.g., job interview) predicts future job performance

Two types of interviews, *behavioural description* and *situational*, have been shown to effectively incorporate structure and job relevance. In behavioural description interviewing, applicants are told about important job attributes of the role they are applying for (e.g., effective teamwork, sharing leadership, dealing effectively with customer complaints), and then asked to reflect upon their past work experience and describe behaviours that demonstrate the attribute in question (e.g., effective teamwork, sharing leadership, dealing effectively with customer complaints). Applicants are asked to structure their answers in the following way: (1) describe the circumstances that led up to the behaviours, (2) describe what was done (i.e., the behaviour), (3) describe the consequences of the behaviour for the team and organization, and (4) provide the name of someone who can verify the information. Rather than probe past behaviours, situational interviews look to the future. Interviewers who opt for a situational approach present several realistic job scenarios that each involve a dilemma that needs to be resolved (e.g., the scenario description reveals tension between the need to maintain production with the need to maintain safety). Applicants are asked to reflect upon the problem and express their true intentions in this situation (i.e., "What would you do?"). These responses are then evaluated according to a scoring guide previously developed for the particular job context. Both interview formats have been shown to be reliable and to be valid predictors of job success, and both have been found superior to unstructured interviews.[121]

Of course, the messages conveyed by applicants during face-to-face job interviews involve more than just their verbal responses to structured questions. The nonverbal behaviours exhibited during the job interview also play a role. As we have discussed earlier in the chapter, the essential question is whether the "body-language answers" (e.g., eye contact, head movement, smiling, hand movements, body posture) support or undermine the verbal responses? Research shows that interviewers will often use nonverbal cues to make inferences about a candidate's assertiveness, motivation, self-confidence, enthusiasm, and sociability.[122] What this means is that students (and applicants) need to be ask concerned about their nonverbal performance during job interviews.

Interview expert Dr. Ronald Riggio has suggested that three categories of nonverbal cues need attention (and practice).[123] The first is *poise*. When going for an interview, it is important for the applicant to appear confident, comfortable, and "in charge." This means making an effort to control nervous behaviour, and to try and appear attentive and "ready to take on the world." Of course, conveying confidence and comfort nonverbally comes with repeated practice.[124] Second, your body language needs to convey *interest*, such as no yawning, looking bored, or looking away. It will be important to make eye contact (not too much), be attentive, and lean forward slightly.[125] Finally, your body language must demonstrate *expressiveness*. When communicating their responses, applicants need to try and exhibit positive energy (not too much) and emotion by smiling occasionally (not too much) and at the appropriate time.[126]

TAKEAWAYS

10.1 Communication refers to the process by which information and meaning is transferred from a sender to a receiver. Communication also represents a very tangible way in which we connect to others, and is a primary means by which the organization coordinates the efforts of its members. The cognitive and emotional processes that underlie models of job satisfaction, stress, motivation, trust, justice, moral development, learning and decision making assume the capability to process, interpret, and respond to verbal and nonverbal messages provided by others. Teams simply won't function if the members are unable to communicate effectively. An individual's and team's ability to use power effectively or to exhibit leadership is rooted in strong communication skills, and the ability to leverage communication networks. Structure and culture reflect both formal and informal information flows with the organization.

10.2 The communication process involves the steps needed to convey a message from one entity to another. It begins with a sender having an idea or concept that needs to be communicated. Senders must translate (encode) their ideas into a message, which in turn is expressed through an appropriate channel. Receivers begin with the sender's expressed message that then has to be processed and interpreted (decoded) so that the true meaning is known. The communication is successful when senders and receivers are able to accurately exchange information and meaning.

10.3 Face-to-face communication offers a natural and immediate way for individuals to exchange verbal (spoken and written language) and nonverbal (e.g., voice inflections, hand gestures, facial expressions) messages. Face-to-face communication is considered the "gold standard" of communication, because it tends to engage more human senses than mediated communication. Computer-mediated communication offers a very powerful way to enhance the flow and exchange of information within the workplace. Social networking tools (based on Web 2.0 technology) have found their way into many workplaces, allowing large numbers of users (across organizational levels and geographically dispersed units) to actively interact, create, collaborate, and communicate.

10.4 Regardless of the channel used, various issues might interfere with the communication process. The first concerns the competence of the communicators. Do senders and receivers have the ability to effectively encode and decode messages, and do they have the emotional intelligence to respond appropriately? The second factor is noise. Is the communication processes occurring in a context where disturbing or distracting stimuli are present, effectively blocking or interfering with the transmission of a message? A third concern refers to the amount and depth of information transmitted. When messages are deficient in their information quality the likelihood that the intended meaning will be received is reduced. A fourth issue concerns gender differences. Males and females process information differently and tend to use very different communication styles, which can interfere with the communication process. Finally, the issue of communication privacy is becoming more and more important, as are the effects privacy concerns have on the communication process.

10.5 Within organizations information flows both formally and informally. Formally, information flows downward, upward, and horizontally. We can identify a number of formal communication network structures, including the all-channel, circle, chain, Y, and wheel. Information flow within organizations flows informally too, primarily through the grapevine. Information flowing through the grapevine is unregulated and often unverified. Rumours and gossip will travel through an organization's informal communication network.

10.6 The relationship between communication and job performance is complex. Performance feedback from a supervisor can have a positive effect on performance, providing the feedback is accepted by the subordinate as relevant and credible, providing feedback is combined with other performance-enhancing inducements (e.g., goal setting), and providing the subordinate has the level of knowledge, skills, abilities, and personality traits necessary for higher job performance. In comparison, the relationship between communication and organizational commitment is stronger and more direct. Accurate and timely (helpful) downward communication by a supervisor, manager, or leader should enhance the work environment, and convey messages of genuine support and confidence—perhaps encouraging subordinates to share information, offer suggestions to solve problems, and participate in decision making. In turn, this should make it easier for employees to understand their role and to feel valued, appreciated, and emotionally connected with the work, the leader, and the organization.

10.7 Face-to-face employment interviews are rife with verbal and nonverbal cues that signal to interviewers whether candidates are suitable and interested in the position, and the extent to which they will fit with the culture. Perhaps most telling are the body-language answers to the interviewers' questions. At the same time, interviewees are using their exchange with interviewers to learn about the company and assess the fit. Given all of the issues that can interfere with effective communication, both interviewers and interviewees should be wary of inferences drawn from these brief exchanges. Ways to increase the validity and reliability of interviews include keeping the focus job relevant and structured. Two popular interview methods are behaviour description interviews and situational interviews.

KEY TERMS

all-channel network structure
chain network structure
circle network structure
communication
communicator competence
computer-mediated communication
downward communication
e-mail
face-to-face communication
gender differences
gossip
grapevine
horizontal communication
informal communication networks
information richness
job interview
noise
nonverbal communication
predictive validity
privacy
reliability
rumours
supervisor feedback
upward communication

verbal communication
videoconferencing
Web 2.0
wheel network structure
wiki
Y network structure

DISCUSSION QUESTIONS

10.1 Due to the complex nature of the communication process, it is relatively easy to misinterpret verbal and nonverbal messages. Has this ever happened to you? Describe what took place and your reactions to the incident (i.e., briefly share the circumstances leading up to the event, the messages sent, your interpretation, and what happened next).

10.2 Do you trust body language? Why or why not? In your own life and interactions do you pay more attention to verbal or nonverbal communication?

10.3 In spite of the fact that computer-mediated communication has been shown to be inferior to face-to-face communication, why is the former becoming the preferred mode of communication in today's workplaces? Are these preferences driven by the values of the people involved, the nature of the work performed, or something else? Explain.

10.4 Describe the communication process in a student team of which you've been a member. Were there examples of "noise" that detracted from the team members' ability to communicate with one another? What was the primary mode of communication among members? Did this mode of communication possess an appropriate level of information richness? Which network structure comes closest to describing the one that the team used to communicate? Was the level of centralization appropriate?

10.5 Should the informal communication network of an organization (e.g., rumour mill, grapevine) be monitored and managed, and why might managers want to do this? How might information gleaned from the grapevine help or hinder some of the other topics we've covered in the course? Why do you think information travels so fast through the grapevine, and what drives this?

CASE • TD CANADA TRUST

To build and sustain a consistent service and sales culture across 1,150 branches and support offices, TD Canada Trust faced the challenge of aligning the behaviours of over 45,000 employees with a set of corporate values (e.g., "legendary customer experiences," "operate with excellence"). To accomplish this goal, the bank has had to develop a sophisticated communication network capable of handling the exchange of technical and social information within the organization, and capable of connecting meaningfully with customers.

The WOW Moments program featured in the chapter-opening profile is an example of how the bank has harnessed the power of computer-mediated communication to support its strategic goals. By collecting and maintaining a searchable archive of WOW Moments (i.e., history of personal anecdotes and stories), the company has a homegrown knowledge base tailored to its corporate values. Not only does this resource promote learning within the organization (e.g., training materials can be developed around the client interactions; new employees can look up how others handled similar situations; featured WOW moments communicate to new employees how they need to perform their day-to-day activities), but the intrinsic appeal of Web 2.0 technology provides a powerful source of feedback and rewards for those employees who are recognized by their peers and managers.

In addition to facilitating communication processes within the bank, these tools have important management implications. The Hive—the program that hosts the social media applications and on which Wow Moments is based—is fully integrated with the firm's human resources database, so that basic details about the individuals being recognized are automatically incorporated, and so that stories can be linked to employees' personnel files. It also provides some very powerful metrics, so that, among other things, management can see how many employees are posting stories, how many have stories posted about them, and how many are just reading the stories. High performers and those who epitomize the company's core values are easily spotted, and will likely, over time, be groomed and prepared for new roles and increased responsibilities within the bank.

However, for most employees, the virtues of social-media applications might be offset to some degree by the reality that this technology allows one's messages and posts to potentially reach everyone (bottom to top) within the organization. Poorly crafted messages or messages that might (accidently or inadvertently) reflect negatively on one's competence, loyalty, or reputation are as easily distributed and archived as Wow Moments. A senior manager at the bank said it best: "Knowing that one's peers, managers, and other organizational members might see their contributions does predispose people to think carefully before sending messages or participating in social applications."

10.1 Might there be a problem if employees thought and acted with elevated concerns about the personal consequences and risks before sending messages? Explain.

10.2 Is full, open, and candid communication desirable from the bank's perspective? Why or why not? Should the bank control what and how messages are sent within the organization (and externally to customers)? Explain. Is there a darker side to this issue?

10.3 Do you like how social-media applications such as Wow Moments are integrated with the human resources information system? Do you have any concerns? Explain.

10.4 Is there any value in incorporating nonverbal content into these computer-mediated communication processes? Explain.

Sources: TD Bank Corporate website, www.td.com/about-tdbfg/corporate-information/tds-guiding-principles/guidingprinciples.jsp, accessed June 18, 2014; William Keenan Jr., "'Wow Moments' Helps TD Canada Trust Nurture Employee Engagement, Grow," *Engagement Strategies Magazine*, Winter 2010, www.engagementstrategiesonline.com/Wow-Moments-Helps-TD-Canada-Trust-Nurture-Employee-Engagement-Growth, accessed May 22, 2014; W. Arnott, "Becoming a Social Organization: TD Group (2010 to 2014)," presentation delivered at conference *Work and Workplaces of the Future: Implications for Western Canada,* The Conference Board of Canada, Calgary, May 5, 2014.

EXERCISE • COMMUNICATING WITHOUT WORDS

When you're learning to communicate effectively, there's more to it than writing and speaking. Good communicators must learn how to send messages without using words. Sometimes groups have to coordinate themselves without words. We have to be aware of what messages our facial expressions and body are communicating to others, as well as being able to read other people's nonverbal cues.

In this exercise we adapt a classic party game to help us understand the power of nonverbal communication. This will help you practise your nonverbal skills, and will require communication and coordination with others. The challenge, of course, is doing it without using words.

For this exercise, the instructor will need a regular pack of playing cards.

Procedure

1. Prior to the class, the instructor writes well-known names, words, or phrases on playing cards (try to have an equal number of hearts, clubs, diamonds, and spades; divide the class size by four to come up with the approximate number). The selected items may be famous people, songs, books, movies, television shows, etc.—even OB concepts we have covered here.
2. Before the exercise starts, the instructor shuffles the deck well and walks around the room giving each student a card.
3. The students keep what's on their cards a secret, and no one may see the type or colour of another's card.
4. It is made clear to students that they will not be able to talk during this exercise.
5. Students are instructed to assemble into four groups according to suit (hearts, clubs, diamonds, spades) using nonverbal communication.
6. Once students get into those groups, they must determine who goes first—again, not using any words, just nonverbal communication.
7. The selected player then pantomimes the word or phrase on his or her playing card for the others.
   a. *Book.* Unfold your hands as if they were a book.
   b. *Movie.* Pretend to crank an old-fashioned movie camera.
   c. *Play.* Pretend to pull the rope that opens a theater curtain.
   d. *Song.* Pretend to sing. (But don't make any noise!)
   e. *TV.* Draw a rectangle to outline the TV screen.
   f. *Quote or phrase.* Make quotation marks in the air with your fingers.
8. Each group is given 20 minutes to solve as many "charades" as possible. Once the word or phrase has been correctly guessed, a point is awarded to the group. The person who came up with the correct answer goes next. The process continues until all members have had a chance to act out their word or phrase, or until the instructor calls the time.
9. The group with the most points wins.
10. The instructor then opens up the class for discussion to assess what nonverbal strategies worked best, what part of this was the most difficult, and why. Students are asked (a) how it felt to do the exercise, (b) what they liked about it, (c) what they didn't like, and (d) if they have any questions about the exercise.

Note: The exercise can be modified (if classes are large), extended to other topic areas, and varied if it seems to be effective for some of your students.

OB ASSESSMENTS • ARE YOU AN ACTIVE LISTENER?

Purpose This self-assessment is designed to help you estimate your strengths and weaknesses on various dimensions of active listening.

Instructions Think back to face-to-face conversations you have had with a co-worker or client in the office, hallway, factory floor, or other setting. Indicate the extent that each item below describes your behaviour during those conversations. Answer each item as truthfully as possible so that you get an accurate estimate of where your active listening skills need improvement. Then use the scoring key provided in the Instructor's Manual for this book to calculate your results for each scale. This exercise should be completed alone so you can assess yourself honestly without concerns of social comparison. However, class discussion will focus on the important elements of active listening.

Active Listening Skills Inventory

When listening to others in face-to-face, telephone, or similar conversations, how often do you do the following?	Never or Rarely	Seldom	Sometimes	Often	Almost Always
1. I keep an open mind when others describe their ideas.	○	○	○	○	○
2. I organize the speaker's ideas while s/he is talking to me.	○	○	○	○	○
3. I ask questions to show I understand and am focused on the speaker's message.	○	○	○	○	○
4. I interrupt before the speaker sufficiently presents his/her views.	○	○	○	○	○
5. While listening, I mentally sort out the speaker's ideas so s/he makes sense to me.	○	○	○	○	○
6. I use gestures and words (nodding, agreeing) to show I am listening.	○	○	○	○	○
7. I let my mind wander when listening to people.	○	○	○	○	○
8. I try to visualize and feel the speaker's experience while s/he is describing those events.	○	○	○	○	○
9. I summarize the speaker's ideas to confirm that I understand him/her correctly.	○	○	○	○	○
10. I focus on what the speaker is saying to me even when it doesn't sound interesting.	○	○	○	○	○
11. I see the topic from my perspective rather than from the speaker's perspective.	○	○	○	○	○
12. I show interest while listening to others.	○	○	○	○	○

Team Characteristics and Processes

CHAPTER 11

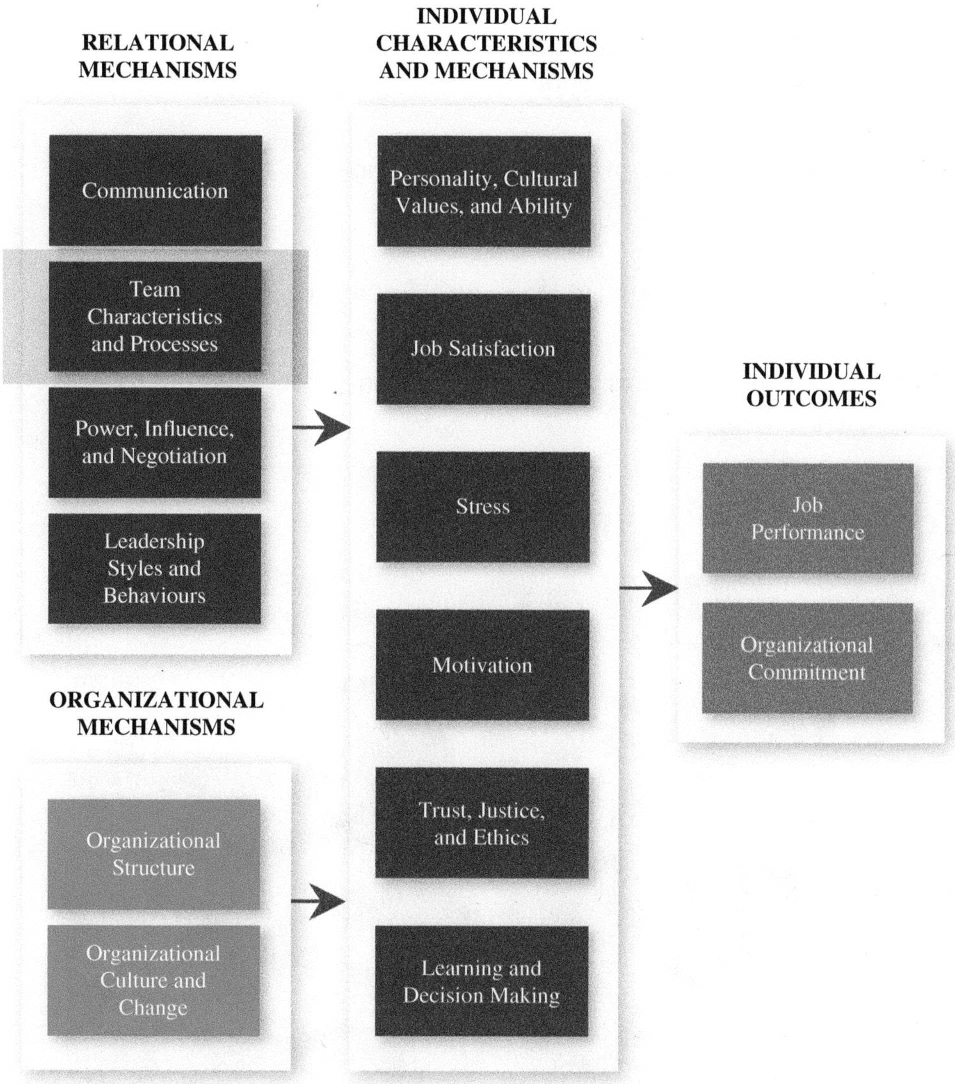

LEARNING OUTCOMES

After reading this chapter, you should be able to answer the following questions:

11.1 What are the five general team types and their defining competencies?

11.2 What are the three general types of team interdependence?

11.3 What factors are involved in team composition?

11.4 What are the types of team diversity and how do they influence team functioning?

11.5 What are task work and teamwork processes, and what are some examples of team activities that fall into these process categories?

11.6 What are team states, and what are some examples of the states that fall into this process category?

11.7 How do team characteristics and processes affect team performance and team commitment?

11.8 What steps can organizations take to improve team processes?

Rocket Men (and Women)

Canadian Space Agency astronaut Julie Payette (bottom, middle) is shown with her team members on the International Space Station in July 2009.

In the 1970s hit "Rocket Man," Elton John sings about an astronaut who's all by himself on a long flight to an assignment on Mars.[1] The image of this solitary astronaut who feels "lonely out in space on such a timeless flight," however, stands in contrast to the reality an astronaut often faces. That is, although astronauts sometimes work and live in isolated and extreme environments for extended periods, they often do so with others, as part of a small team, more often referred to as a *crew*, in quarters that are quite cramped.[2]

Supporting these small teams in space are very impressive and large teams working on Earth, such as the Canadian Space Agency (CSA). Over the past 25 years, the CSA has worked closely and collaboratively with the National Aeronautics and Space Administration (NASA) and its international partners on a range of space programs. The CSA has about 670 employees, approximately 90 percent of them employed at the John H. Chapman Space Centre, the Agency's headquarters located in Longueuil, Quebec.[3] Its mission, simply, is to develop and apply space knowledge for the benefit of Canadians and humanity.

Since the early 1980s, in cooperation with NASA, Canada has developed its own astronauts with eight participating on 16 space missions.[4] Some of them have become household names: Roberta Lynn Bondar, Marc Garneau, and Chris Hadfield.[5] Together, these brave people have flown missions, conducting scientific research and helping to advance and develop technology.[6]

A great example of space technology was the famous robotic arm, the Canadarm, which debuted on the Space Shuttle *Columbia* in November 1981. The design and building of the Canadarm marked the beginning of Canada's close collaboration with the NASA in human space flight and represented a sterling example of successful international cooperation in space.[7]

This history of collaboration continues to this day. Currently the CSA, in conjunction with over 40 Canadian companies and universities, is working hard to design and build a fleet of terrestrial rovers—the grandparents of the robots that may one day explore the surface of new worlds, acting as eyes and ears for scientists, or even working hand in hand with astronauts as robotic helpers.[8]

As you might imagine, working in space is not for everyone. Astronauts not only have to cope with the discomfort of travelling, working, and living in artificial environments, but also have to learn to function with other astronauts as a cohesive unit to accomplish complex and dangerous tasks. Obviously, the crews need to carry out activities involved in safely flying or orbiting their vessels; they also have to carry out all the tasks of their missions—exploration and experiments intended to better understand the Earth and other bodies in space. What might be less obvious is that they need to plan and coordinate their activities, monitor resources, and help each other. Crews that fail to effectively carry out any of these activities put not only the mission in jeopardy but their lives as well.

Currently, the international space community continues to recruit and train astronauts for duty on the International Space Station and for planned missions to asteroids and Mars.[9] Recruits are quite diverse with regard to demographic characteristics and areas of expertise.[10] On the one hand, this type of diversity allows organizations like NASA to compose crews for a wide variety of missions. On the other hand, it increases opportunities for misunderstandings during missions that could undermine crew cohesion and effectiveness. Although training for astronaut candidates emphasizes the development of knowledge and skills related to operating equipment and systems, the ultimate effectiveness of astronaut crews is likely to depend on knowledge and skills related to teamwork as well.[11]

TEAM CHARACTERISTICS

The topic of teams is likely familiar to almost anyone who might be reading this book. In fact, you've probably had first-hand experience with several different types of teams at different points in your life. As an example, most of you have played a team sport or two (yes, playing soccer in gym class counts). Most of you have also worked in student teams to complete projects or assignments for courses you've taken. Or perhaps you've worked closely with a small group of people to accomplish a task that was important to you—planning an event, raising money for a charity, or starting and running a small cash business. Finally, some of you have been members of organizational teams responsible for making a product, providing a service, or generating recommendations for solving company problems.

But what exactly is a team, and what is it that makes a team more than a "group"? A **team** consists of two or more people who work *interdependently* over some time period to accomplish *common goals* related to some *task-oriented purpose.*[12] Think of teams as a special type of group, and a group as just a collection of two or more people. Teams are special for two reasons. First, the interactions among members revolve around a deeper dependence on one another than the interactions within groups. Second, the interactions within teams occur with a specific task-related purpose in mind. Although the members of a friendship group might frequently engage in small talk or in-depth conversations, the members of a team depend on one another for critical information, materials, and actions needed to accomplish goals related to their purpose for being together. National surveys of large and small Canadian organizations have shown that almost half use some form of teamwork to accomplish work activities.[13]

team

Two or more people who work interdependently over some time period to accomplish common goals related to some task-oriented purpose

Why have teams become so widespread? The most obvious reason is that the nature of today's work requires them. As work has become more complex, interactions among multiple team members have become more vital. This is because interactions allow the team to pool complementary knowledge and skills. As an example, surgical teams consist of individuals who receive specialized training in the activities needed to conduct surgical procedures. The team consists of a surgeon who received training for the procedure in question, an anesthesiologist who received training necessary to manage patient pain, and an operating room nurse who was trained to provide overall care for the patient. Teams may also be useful to organizations in ways beyond just accomplishing the work itself. For example, one study revealed that problem-solving teams composed primarily of rank-and-file workers could boost productivity in steel mills by devising ways to increase the efficiency of production lines and quality control processes.[14] Although implementing teams often makes sense in settings such as these, for which the nature of the work and work-related problems are complex, teams vary a great deal from one another in terms of their effectiveness. The goal of this chapter is to help you understand factors that influence team effectiveness.

A surgical team consists of specialized members who depend on one another to accomplish tasks that are both complex and important.

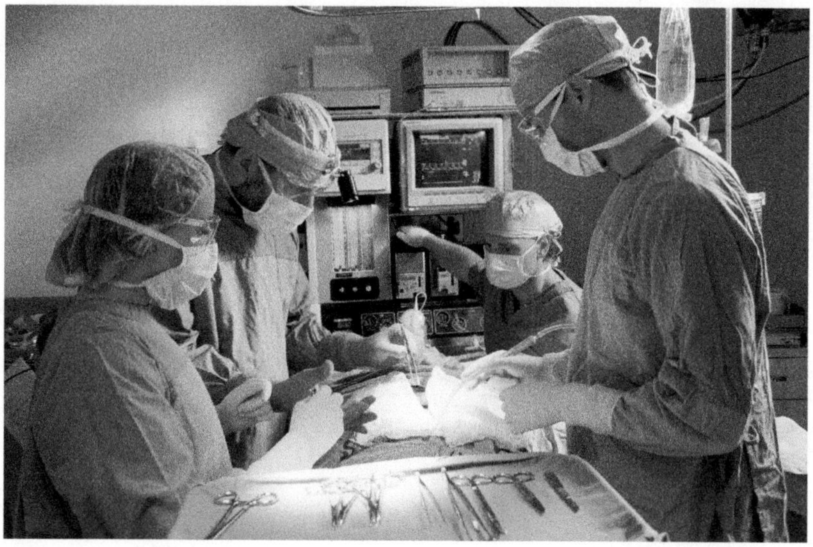

© Stockbyte/Getty Images

WHAT CHARACTERISTICS CAN BE USED TO DESCRIBE TEAMS?

We begin with a description of characteristics, that is, the task, unit, and member qualities, that can be used to describe teams. Team characteristics provide a means of categorizing and examining teams, which is important because teams come in so many shapes and sizes. They play an important role in determining what a team is capable of achieving, and may influence the strategies and processes the team uses to reach its goals. As you will see, however, there's more to understanding team characteristics than meets the eye. Diversity, for example, can have many meanings, and its effect on team functioning and effectiveness depends on what type you're concerned with and several other complicating factors. Later in the chapter we focus on team processes—the specific actions and behaviours that teams can engage in to achieve synergy. The concepts in this chapter will help explain why some teams are more or less effective than their characteristics would suggest they should be. For now, however, we turn our attention to this question: "What characteristics can be used to describe teams?"

11.1 What are the five general team types and their defining competencies?

Types of Teams

One way to describe teams is to take advantage of existing taxonomies that place teams into various types. One such taxonomy is illustrated in Table 11-1. The table illustrates that there are five general types of teams and that each is associated with a number of defining characteristics,[15] the most notable of which are the team's purpose, the length of its existence, and the amount of time involvement it requires of its individual members. The sections to follow review these types of teams in turn.

TABLE 11-1

Types of Teams

Type of Team	Purpose and Activities	Life Span	Member Involvement	Specific Examples
Work team	Produce goods or provide services	Long	High	Self-managed work team Production team Maintenance team Sales team
Management team	Integrate activities of subunits across business functions	Long	Moderate	Top management team
Parallel team	Provide recommendations and resolve issues	Varies	Low	Quality circle Advisory council Committee
Project team	Produce a one-time output (product, service, plan, design, etc.)	Varies	Varies	Product design team Research group Planning team
Action team	Perform complex tasks that vary in duration and take place in highly visible or challenging circumstances	Varies	Varies	Surgical team Musical group Expedition team Sports team

Sources: S.G. Cohen and D.E. Bailey, "What Makes Teams Work: Group Effectiveness Research from the Shop Floor to the Executive Suite," *Journal of Management* 27 (1997), pp. 239–90; and E. Sundstrom, K.P. De Meuse, and D. Futrell, "Work Teams: Applications and Effectiveness," *American Psychologist* 45 (1990), pp. 120–33.

Work Teams **Work teams** are designed to be relatively permanent. Their purpose is to produce goods or provide services, and they generally require members' full-time commitment. Consider how cars and trucks are manufactured at Toyota.[16] Teams are composed of four to eight members who do the physical work, and a leader who supports the team and coordinates with other teams. Although the teams are responsible for the work involved in the assembly of the vehicles, they are also responsible for quality control and developing ideas for improvements in the production process. Team members inspect each other's work, and when they see a problem, they stop the line until they are able to resolve the problem.

work teams

Relatively permanent teams in which members work together to produce goods and/or provide services

Management Teams **Management teams** are similar to work teams in that they are designed to be relatively permanent; however, they are also distinct in a number of important ways. Whereas work teams focus on the accomplishment of core operational-level production and service tasks, management teams participate in managerial-level tasks that affect the entire organization. Specifically, they are responsible for coordinating the activities of organizational subunits—typically departments or functional areas—to help the organization achieve its long-term goals. Top management teams, for example, consist of senior-level executives who meet to make decisions about the strategic direction of the organization. It might also be worth mentioning that, because members of management teams are typically heads of departments, their commitment to the management team is offset somewhat by the responsibilities they have in leading their unit.

management teams

Relatively permanent team that participates in managerial-level tasks that affect the entire organization

A Toyota work team is responsible for vehicle assembly and quality control.

© Toru Yamanaka/AFP/Getty Images

Parallel Teams **Parallel teams** are composed of members from various jobs who provide recommendations to managers about important issues that run "parallel" to the organization's production process.[17] Parallel teams require only part-time commitment from members, and they can be permanent or temporary, depending on their aim. Quality circles, for example, consist of individuals who normally perform core production tasks, but who also meet regularly with individuals from other work groups to identify production-related problems and opportunities for improvement. As an example of a more temporary parallel team, committees often form to deal with unique issues or issues that arise only periodically. Examples of issues that can spur the creation of committees include changes to work procedures, purchases of new equipment or services, and non-routine hiring.

parallel teams

Teams composed of members from various jobs within the organization that meet to provide recommendations about important issues

Project Teams **Project teams** are formed to take on one-time tasks that are generally complex and require a lot of input from members with different types of training and expertise.[18] Although project teams exist only as long as it takes to finish a project, some projects are quite complex and can take years. Members of some project teams work full-time, whereas other teams demand only a part-time commitment. A planning team comprising engineers, architects, designers, and builders, charged with designing a suburban town centre, might work together full-time for a year or more. In contrast, the engineers and artists who constitute a design team responsible for creating an electric toothbrush might work together for a month on the project while also serving on other project teams.

project teams

Teams formed to take on one-time tasks, most of which tend to be complex and require input from members from different functional areas

The Australian Band AC/DC, formed in 1973, is an example of an action team that has stayed together for a long time.

© Robert Vos/Corbis

Action Teams **Action teams** perform tasks that are normally limited in duration. However, those tasks are quite complex and take place in contexts that are either highly visible to an audience or of a highly challenging nature.[19] Some types of action teams work together for an extended period. For example, sports teams remain intact for at least one season, and musical groups like AC/DC may stick together for decades. Other types of action teams stay together only as long as the task takes to complete. Surgical teams and aircraft flight crews may only work together as a unit for a single two-hour surgery or flight.

action teams

Teams of limited duration that performs complex tasks in contexts that tend to be highly visible and challenging

Summary So how easy is it to classify teams into one of the types summarized in Figure 11-1? Well, it turns out that teams often fit into more than one category. As an example, consider the teams at Pixar, the company that has produced many computer-animated hit films, such as *Toy Story*, *Monsters Inc.*, *Finding Nemo*, *Cars*, *Wall-E*, *Up*, *Brave*, and *Monsters University*. On the one hand, because the key members of Pixar teams have stuck together for each film the company has produced, it might seem like Pixar uses work teams.[20] On the other hand, because the creation of each film can be viewed as a project, and because members are likely involved in multiple ongoing projects, it might seem reasonable to say that Pixar uses project teams. It's probably most appropriate to say that at Pixar, teams have characteristics of both work teams and project teams.

Variations Within Team Types

Even knowing whether a team is a project team, an action team, or some other type doesn't tell you the whole story. In fact, there are important variations within those categories that are needed to understand a team's functioning.[21] As one example, teams can vary with respect to the degree to which they have autonomy and are self-managed.[22] If you've ever been on a team where members have a great deal of freedom to work together to establish their own goals, procedures, roles, and

FIGURE 11-1

Types of Teams

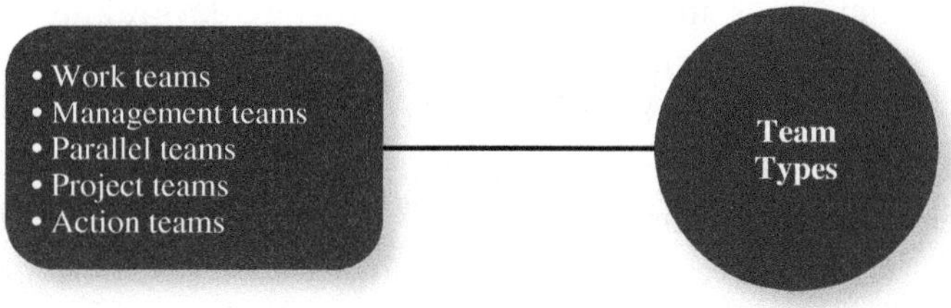

membership, you've worked on a team where the level of autonomy and self-management is high. You may also have worked on a team where the level of autonomy and self-management is low. In these teams, there are strict rules regarding goals, procedures, and roles, and team leaders or managers make most of the decisions regarding management of the team with respect to membership. Research has shown that although people generally prefer working in teams where the level of autonomy and self-management is high, the appropriate level of self-management with regard to overall team effectiveness may depend on a variety of factors.[23] For example, research has shown that high levels of self-management may be most advantageous for teams where team members' have high levels of team-relevant knowledge obtained from outside experts and others in their social networks.[24]

The Pixar team, shown here at the Cannes Film Festival, has characteristics of both work teams and project teams. Trying to characterize this team is even more complicated when you consider that key members are involved in the management of the company, and their involvement in the films runs parallel to these other responsibilities.

© Daniele Venturelli/WireImage/Getty Images

Another way teams can vary relates to how the members typically communicate with each other. **Virtual teams** are teams in which the members are geographically dispersed, and interdependent activity occurs through electronic communications—primarily e-mail, instant messaging, and web conferencing. Although communications and group networking software is far from perfect, it has advanced to the point that it's possible for teams doing all sorts of work to function virtually. In fact, there has been an 800 percent increase in the number of virtual employees over the last decade or so, and likely tens of millions of virtual teams are operating today.[25] At IBM at least 40 percent of the employees work virtually.[26] At TRW, one of the world's largest automotive suppliers, virtual teams provide an efficient way to accomplish work on projects when members are geographically separated.[27] In fact, many companies in high-tech industries are leveraging virtual teams to make continuous progress on work tasks without members having to work 24/7. For example, Logitech, the Swiss company that makes such things as computer mice and keyboards, universal remotes for home entertainment systems, and gaming controllers, attributes its success to teams of designers and engineers located in different places around the world.[28] Although you might be inclined to believe that time-zone differences would be a hindrance to this sort of team, Logitech turned it into a competitive advantage by letting the work *follow the sun.*[29] Specifically, work at Logitech is accomplished continuously because members of a team who have finished their workday in one country electronically hand off the work to team members in another country who have just arrived at the office. Because these electronic hand-offs occur continuously, product development and other work needed to bring innovative products to the market can be completed much more quickly.

virtual teams

Team in which the members are geographically dispersed, and interdependent activity occurs through e-mail, web conferencing, and instant messaging

In addition to varying in their "virtuality," teams of any type can differ in the amount of experience they have working together. One way to understand this point is to consider what occurs in teams at different stages of their development as they progress from a newly formed team to one that's well established. According to the most well-known theory, teams go through a progression of five stages shown in the top panel of Figure 11-2.[30]

In the first stage, called *forming*, members orient themselves by trying to understand their boundaries in the team. Members try to get a feel for what is expected of them, what types of behaviours are out of bounds, and who's in charge. In the next stage, called *storming*, members remain committed to ideas they bring with them to the team. This initial unwillingness to accommodate others' ideas triggers conflict that negatively affects some interpersonal relationships and harms the team's progress. During the next stage, *norming*, members realize that they need to work together to accomplish team goals, and consequently, they begin to cooperate with one another. Feelings of solidarity develop as members work toward team goals. Over time, norms and expectations develop regarding what different members are responsible for doing. In the fourth stage of team development, which is called *performing*, members are comfortable working within their roles, and the team makes progress toward goals. Finally, because the lifespan of many teams is limited, there's a stage called *adjourning*. In this stage, members experience anxiety and other emotions as they disengage and ultimately separate from the team.

But does this sequence of forming, storming, norming, performing, and adjourning apply to the development of all types of teams? Chances are you've had experiences with teams that would lead you to answer no. In fact, although this theory of group development is intuitively appealing and identifies things that may occur as teams gain experience working together, there are factors in work organizations that can significantly alter what occurs over a team's life.[31] One situation in which this developmental sequence is less applicable is when teams are formed with clear expectations regarding what's expected from the team and its members. With many action teams, for example, there are established rules and standard operating procedures that guide team members' behaviours and their

FIGURE 11-2

Two Models of Team Development

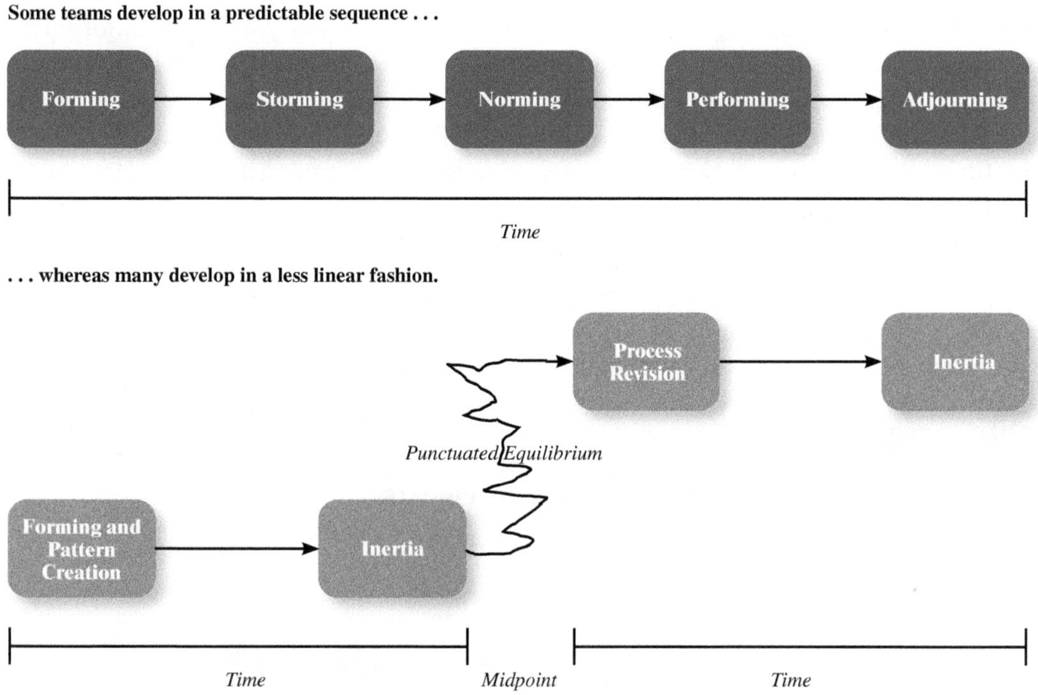

interactions. For example, an aircraft flight crew doesn't have to go through the forming, storming, norming, and performing stages to figure out that the pilot flies the plane and the flight attendant serves the beverages. As another example, though the adjourning stage only happens once for each type of team, the implications are likely to be more significant for team types with longer lifespans that require high member involvement. Dissolving a work team that's been together for four years is likely to trigger greater anxiety and stronger emotions among members than a situation in which a committee that meets briefly once a month for a year is disbanded.

Another situation in which the development sequence is less applicable may be in certain types of project teams that follow a pattern of development called **punctuated equilibrium**.[32] This sequence appears in the bottom panel of Figure 11-2. At the initial team meeting, members make assumptions and establish a pattern of behaviour that lasts for the first half of its life. That pattern continues to dominate the team's behaviour as it settles into a sort of inertia. At the midway point of the project—and this is true regardless of the length of the project—something remarkable happens: Members realize that they have to change their task paradigm fundamentally to complete it on time. Teams that take this opportunity to plan a new approach during this transition tend to do well, and the new framework dominates their behaviour until task completion. However, teams that don't take the opportunity to change their approach tend to persist with their original pattern and may "go down with a sinking ship."

punctuated equilibrium

A sequence of team development during which not much gets done until the halfway point of a project, after which teams make necessary changes to complete the project on time

11.2 What are the three general types of team interdependence?

Team Interdependence

In addition to taxonomies of team types, we can describe teams by talking about the interdependence that governs connections among team members. In a general sense, you can think of interdependence as the way in which the members of a team are linked to one another. That linkage between members is most often thought of in terms of the interactions that take place as the team accomplishes its work. However, linkages among team members also exist with respect to their goals and rewards. In fact, you can find out where your student project team stands on different aspects of interdependence using our ***OB Assessments*** feature at the end of the chapter.

Task Interdependence **Task interdependence** refers to the degree to which team members interact with and rely on other team members for the information, materials, and resources needed to accomplish work for the team.[33] As Figure 11-3 illustrates, there are four primary types of task interdependence, and each requires a different degree of interaction and coordination.[34]

FIGURE 11-3

Task Interdependence and Coordination Requirements

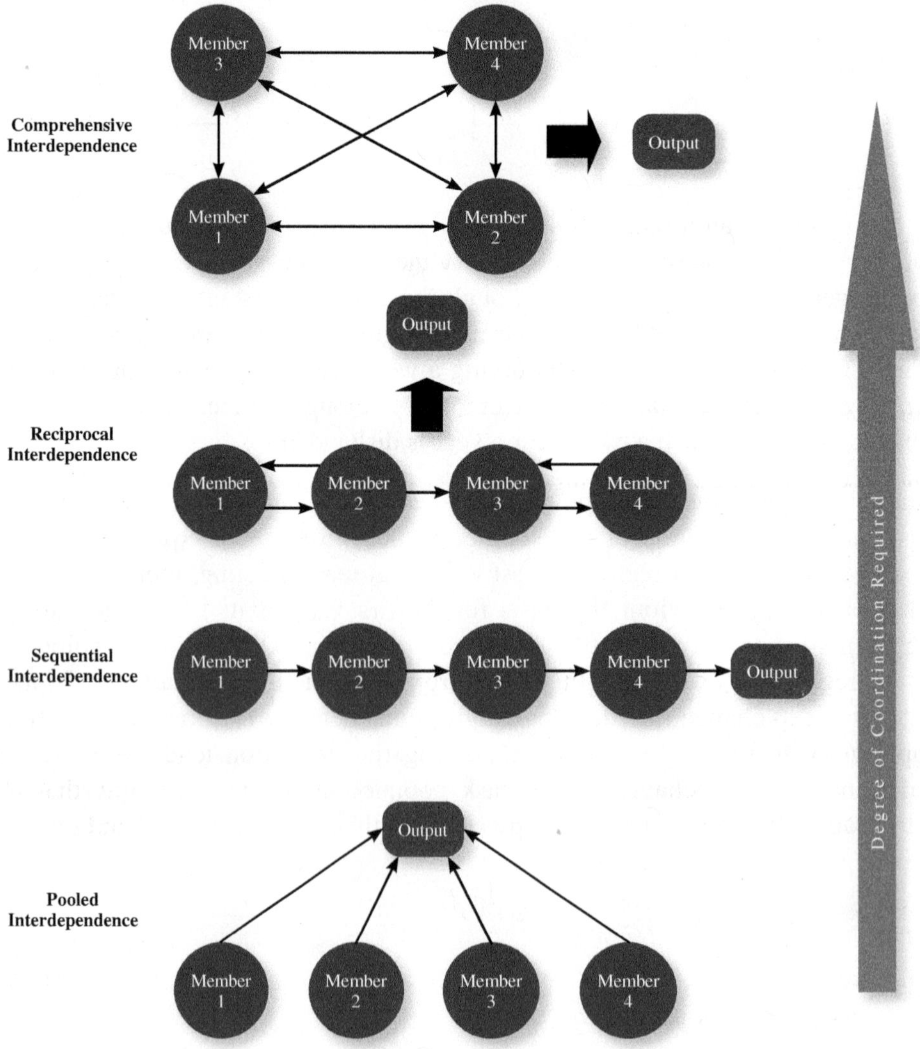

task interdependence

The degree to which team members interact with and rely on other team members for information, materials, and resources needed to accomplish work for the team

The type of task interdependence with the lowest degree of required coordination is *pooled interdependence*.[35] With this type of interdependence, group members complete their work assignments independently, and then this work is simply "piled up" to represent the group's output. Consider what pooled interdependence would be like on a fishing boat. Each person would bait a pole, drop the baited line into the water, reel the fish in, remove the fish from the hook, and, finally, throw the fish into a tank filled with ice and other fish. At the end of the day, the boat's production would be the total weight of the fish caught.

The next type of task interdependence is called *sequential interdependence*.[36] With this type of interdependence, different tasks are done in a prescribed order, and the group is structured such that the members specialize in these tasks. Although members in groups with sequential interdependence interact to carry out their work, the interaction occurs only between members who perform tasks that are next to each other in the sequence. Moreover, the member performing the task in the latter part of the sequence depends on the member performing the task in the earlier part of the sequence, but not the other way around. The classic assembly line in manufacturing contexts provides an excellent example of this type of interdependence. In this context, an employee attaches a part to the unit being built, and once this is accomplished, the unit moves on to another employee who adds another part. The process typically ends with the unit being inspected and then packaged for shipping.

Reciprocal interdependence is the next type of task interdependence.[37] Similarly to sequential interdependence, members are specialized to perform specific tasks. However, instead of a strict sequence of activities, members interact with a subset of other members to complete the team's work. To understand reciprocal interdependence, consider a team of people involved in a business that designs custom homes for wealthy clients. After meeting with a client, the salesperson would provide general criteria, structural and aesthetic details, and some rough sketches to an architect who would work up initial plans and elevations. The architect then would submit the initial plans to the salesperson, who would review the plans with the customer. Typically, the plans need to be revised by the architect several times, and during this process customers have questions and requests that require the architect to consult with other members of the team. For example, the architect and structural engineer may have to meet to decide where to locate support beams and load-bearing walls. The architect and construction supervisor might also have to meet to discuss revisions to a design feature that turns out to be too costly. As a final example, the salesperson might have to meet with the designers to assist the customer in the selection of additional features, materials, and colours, which would then need to be included in a revision of the plan by the architect.

Finally, *comprehensive interdependence* requires the highest level of interaction and coordination among members as they try to accomplish work.[38] In groups with comprehensive interdependence, each member has a great deal of discretion in terms of what they do and with whom they interact in the course of the collaboration involved in accomplishing the team's work. Teams at IDEO, arguably the world's most successful product design firm, function with comprehensive interdependence. These teams are composed of individuals from very diverse backgrounds, and they meet as a team quite often to share knowledge and ideas to solve problems related to their design projects.[39]

It's important to note that there's no one right way to design teams with respect to task interdependence. However, it's also important to recognize the trade-offs associated with the different types. On the one hand, as the level of task interdependence increases, members must spend increasing amounts of time communicating and coordinating with other members to complete tasks. This type of coordination can result in decreases in productivity, which is the ratio of work completed per the amount of time worked. On the other hand, increases in task interdependence increase the ability of the team to adapt to new situations. The more members interact and communicate with other members, the more likely the team will be able to devise solutions to novel problems it may face.

Face-to-face team meetings that involve comprehensive interdependence can consume a lot of time, yet these meetings are an important part of accomplishing work that requires collaboration.

© Digital Vision/Getty Images

Goal Interdependence In addition to being linked to one another by task activities, members may be linked by their goals.[40] A high degree of **goal interdependence** exists when team members have a shared vision of the team's goal and align their individual goals with that vision as a result.[41] To understand the power of goal interdependence, visualize a small boat with several people on board, each with a paddle.[42] If each person on the boat wants to go to the exact same place on the other side of a lake, they will all row in the same direction, and the boat will arrive at the desired location. If, however, each person believes the boat should go someplace different, everyone will row in a different direction, and the boat will have major problems getting anywhere.

goal interdependence

The degree to which team members have a shared goal and align their individual goals with that vision

So how do you create high levels of goal interdependence? One thing to do would be to ensure that the team has a formalized mission statement that members buy in to. Mission statements can take a variety of forms, but good ones clearly describe what the team is trying to accomplish in a way that creates a sense of commitment and urgency among team members.[43] Mission statements can come directly from the organization or team leaders, but in many circumstances, it makes more sense for teams to go through the process of developing their own mission statements. This process not only helps members identify important team goals and the actions the team needs to take to achieve these goals, but it also increases feelings of ownership toward the mission statement itself.

Although you might believe that the mission for some team tasks is very obvious, all too often this isn't the case. In student teams, for example, you might expect that the obvious goal in the minds of the team members would be to learn the course material. However, it's typically the case that students come to a team like this with individual goals that are surprisingly different. Some students might be more interested in just getting by with a passing grade because they already have a job and only need their degree. Other students might want to do well in the course, but are more concerned with maintaining balance with the demands of their lives outside of school. Finally, other students might be focused solely on their grades, perhaps because they want to get into a prestigious graduate school in an unrelated discipline. Of course, the problem here is that each of these goals is associated with a different approach to working in the team. Students who want to learn the course material will work hard on the team assignments and will want to spend extra time discussing assignment-related issues with teammates; students who just want to get by will do the minimum; students who want to maintain their work–life balance will look for the most efficient way to do things; and students who are focused on their grades will be willing to take shortcuts that might limit their learning. Although trying to reach a consensus on a team mission may not be easy in a situation in which the members have goals that vary along these lines, research has shown that teams of students experience significantly greater effectiveness if they invest time and effort into doing so soon after the team first forms.[44]

Outcome Interdependence The final type of interdependence relates to how members are linked to one another in terms of the feedback and outcomes they receive as a consequence of working in the team.[45] A high degree of **outcome interdependence** exists when team members share in the rewards that the team earns, with reward examples including pay, bonuses, formal feedback and recognition, pats on the back, extra time off, and continued team survival. Of course, because team achievement depends on the performance of each team member, high outcome interdependence also implies that team members depend on the performance of other team members for the rewards that they receive. In contrast, low outcome interdependence exists in teams in which individual members receive rewards and punishments on the basis of their own performance, without regard to the performance of the team. Research into project teams involved in consulting, financial planning, and research and development shows that in teams in which members reflect on their performance, higher levels of outcome interdependence increase the amount of information shared among members, which promotes learning, and ultimately team performance.[46]

outcome interdependence

The degree to which team members share equally in the feedback and rewards that result from the team achieving its goals

11.3 What factors are involved in team composition?

Team Composition

You probably already have a sense that team effectiveness hinges on **team composition**—or the mix of people who make up the team. If you've been a member of a particularly effective team, you may have noticed that the team seemed to have the right mix of knowledge, skills, abilities, and personalities. Not only were team members capable of performing their role responsibilities effectively, but they also cooperated and got along fairly well together. In this section, we identify the most important characteristics to consider in team composition, and describe how these elements combine to influence team functioning and effectiveness. As is shown in Figure 11-4, five aspects of team composition are crucial: roles, ability, personality, diversity, and team size.

FIGURE 11-4

Five Aspects of Team Composition

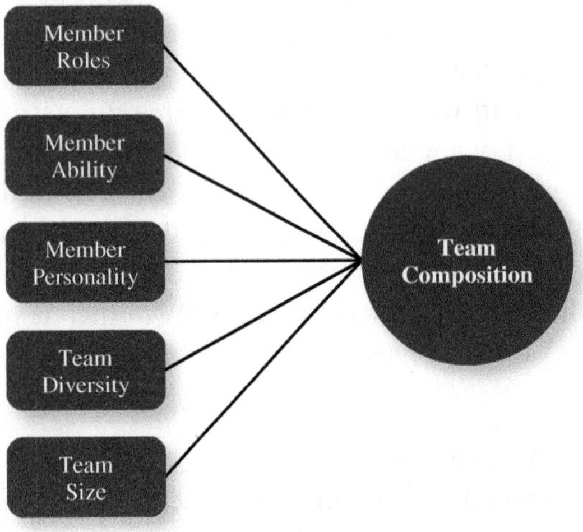

team composition

The mix of the various characteristics that describe the individuals who work in the team

Member Roles A **role** is defined as a pattern of behaviour a person is generally expected to display in a given context.[47] In a team setting, there are a variety of roles that members can take or develop in the course of interacting with one another, and depending on the specific situation the presence or absence of members who possess these roles may have a strong impact on team effectiveness.[48] One obvious way roles can be distinguished is by considering the specific sets of task-focused activities that define what the individual members are expected to do for their team.

role

A pattern of behaviour a person is generally expected to display in a given context

Another way to distinguish roles is to consider what leaders and members do. In *leader–staff teams*, the leader makes decisions for the team and provides direction and control over members who perform assigned tasks, so this distinction makes sense in that the responsibilities of the leader and the rest of the team are distinct.[49] Typically, however, team members have some latitude with respect to the behaviours they exhibit. In these situations, team roles can be described in terms of categories that are more general than the task-focused roles described above. By "general" we mean that these roles can apply to many different types of teams. As is shown in Table 11-2, these general roles include team task roles, team-building roles, and individualistic roles.[50]

TABLE 11-2

Team and Individualistic Roles

Team Task Roles	Description
Initiator-contributor	Proposes new ideas
Coordinator	Tries to coordinate activities among team members
Orienter	Determines the direction of the team's discussion
Devil's advocate	Offers challenges to the team's status quo
Energizer	Motivates the team to strive to do better
Procedural-technician	Performs routine tasks needed to keep progress moving
Team-Building Roles	**Description**
Encourager	Praises the contributions of other team members
Harmonizer	Mediates differences between group members
Compromiser	Attempts to find the halfway point to end conflict
Gatekeeper-expediter	Encourages participation from teammates
Standard setter	Expresses goals for the team to achieve
Follower	Accepts the ideas of teammates
Individualistic Roles	**Description**
Aggressor	Deflates teammates, expresses disapproval with hostility
Blocker	Acts stubbornly resistant and disagrees beyond reason
Recognition seeker	Brags and calls attention to himself or herself
Self-confessor	Discloses personal opinions inappropriately
Slacker	Acts cynically, or nonchalantly, or goofs off
Dominator	Manipulates team members for personal control

Source: Adapted from K. Benne and P. Sheats, "Functional Roles of Group Members," *Journal of Social Issues* 4 (1948), pp. 41–49.

Team task roles refer to behaviours that directly facilitate the accomplishment of team tasks. Examples are the *orienter* who establishes the direction for the team, the *devil's advocate* who offers constructive challenges to the team's status quo, and the *energizer* who motivates team members to work harder toward team goals. As you may have realized, the importance of specific task-oriented roles depends on the nature of the work in which the team is involved. The orienter role may be particularly important in teams that have autonomy over how to accomplish their work. The devil's advocate role may be particularly important in team contexts in which decisions are "high stakes" in nature. Finally, the energizer role may be most important in team contexts in which the work is important but not intrinsically motivating.

team task roles

Behaviours that directly facilitate the accomplishment of team tasks

In contrast to task-oriented roles, **team-building roles** refer to behaviours that influence the quality of the team's social climate. Examples of team-building roles are the *harmonizer* who steps in to resolve differences among teammates, the *encourager* who praises the work of teammates, and the *compromiser* who helps the team see alternative solutions that teammates can accept. As you might have gathered as you read these examples, the presence of members who take on social roles helps teams manage conflicts that might hinder team effectiveness.

team-building roles
Behaviours that influence the quality of the team's social climate

Finally, whereas task roles and team-building roles focus on activities that benefit the team, **individualistic roles** reflect behaviours that benefit the individual at the expense of the team. For example, the *aggressor* "puts down" or deflates fellow teammates. The *recognition seeker* takes credit for team successes. The *dominator* manipulates teammates to acquire control and power. If you've ever had an experience in a team in which members took on individualistic roles, you probably realize just how damaging they can be to the team. Individualistic role behaviours foster negative feelings among team members, which serve to hinder a team's ability to function and perform effectively.[51]

individualistic roles
Behaviours that benefit the individual at the expense of the team

Member Ability Team members possess a wide variety of abilities (see Chapter 4 for more discussion of such issues). Depending on the nature of the tasks involved in the team's work, some of these may be important to consider in team design. For example, for teams involved in physical work, relevant physical abilities will be important to take into account. Consider the types of abilities required of pit crew members in stock car racing, in which margins of victory can be one-tenth of a second. When a car pulls into pit row, pit crew members need to leap over the pit wall and lift heavy tires, jacks, and other equipment to get the race car back on the track—ideally in about 14 seconds. In this setting, flexibility, cardiovascular endurance, and explosive strength are required, and in fact, racing teams have hired professional trainers and even built gyms to improve these abilities of their pit crew members.[52]

It's also important to take cognitive abilities into account when designing teams. General cognitive ability is important to many different types of teams. In general, smarter teams perform better because teamwork tends to be quite complex.[53] Team members not only have to be involved in several different aspects of the team's task, but they also have to learn how best to combine their individual efforts to accomplish team goals.[54] In fact, the more this type of learning is required, the more important member cognitive ability becomes. For example, research has shown that cognitive ability is more important to teams when team members have to learn from one another to adapt to unexpected changes, compared with contexts in which team members perform their assigned tasks in a routine fashion.[55]

Of course, not every member needs high levels of these physical or cognitive abilities. If you've ever played Trivial Pursuit using teams, you might recall playing against another team in which only one of the team members was smart enough to answer any of the questions correctly. In fact, in tasks with an objectively verifiable best solution, the member who possesses the highest level of the ability relevant to the task will have the most influence on the effectiveness of the team. These types of tasks are called *disjunctive tasks*.[56] You may also recall situations in which it was crucial that everyone on the team possessed the relevant abilities. Returning to the pit crew example, stock cars cannot leave the pit area until all the tires are mounted, and so the length of the pit stop is determined by the physical abilities of the slowest crew member. Tasks like this, for which the team's performance depends on the abilities of the "weakest link," are called *conjunctive tasks*. Finally, there are *additive tasks*, for which the contributions resulting from the abilities of every member add up to determine team performance. The amount of money a peewee hockey team earns from selling frozen pizzas is the sum of what each member of the team is able to sell on his own.

A task that can go only as quickly as the slowest team member, like a pit stop in a car race, is a conjunctive task.

© George Tiedmann/Corbis

Member Personality Team members also possess a wide variety of personality traits (see Chapter 4 for more discussion of such issues). These personality traits affect the roles that team members take on,[57] and how teams function and perform as units.[58] For example, the agreeableness of team members has an important influence on team effectiveness.[59] Why? Because agreeable people tend to be more cooperative and trusting, and these tendencies promote positive attitudes about the team and smooth interpersonal interactions. Moreover, because agreeable people may be more concerned about their team's interests than their own, they should work hard on behalf of the team.[60] There's a caveat regarding agreeableness in teams, however. Because agreeable people tend to prefer harmony and cooperation rather than conflict and competition, they may be less apt to speak up and offer constructive criticisms that might help the team improve.[61] Thus, if a team has too many highly agreeable members, there's a chance the members will behave in a way that enhances harmony of the team at the expense of task accomplishment.[62]

As another example, team composition in terms of members' conscientiousness is important to teams.[63] After all, almost any team would benefit from having members who tend to be dependable and work hard to achieve team goals. What might be less obvious to you is the strong negative effect on the team of having even one member who is particularly low on conscientiousness.[64] To understand why this is true, consider how you would react to a team member who was not dependable and did not appear to be motivated to work hard toward team goals. If you're like most people, you would find the situation dissatisfying, and you would consider different ways of dealing with it. Some people might try to motivate the person to be more responsible and work harder; others might try to get the person ejected from the team.[65] The problem is that these natural reactions to a low conscientiousness team member not only divert attention away from accomplishing work responsibilities, but they also can result in some very uncomfortable and time-consuming interpersonal conflicts. Moreover, even if you and the other members of the team work harder to compensate for this person, it would be difficult for your team to perform as effectively as other teams in which all members are more interpersonally responsible and engaged in the team's work.

Finally, the personality characteristic of extraversion is relevant to team composition.[66] People who are extraverted tend to perform more effectively in interpersonal contexts and are more positive and optimistic in general.[67] Therefore, it shouldn't surprise you to hear that having extraverted team members is generally beneficial to the social climate of the group, as well as to team effectiveness in the eyes of supervisors.[68] At the same time, however, research has shown that having too many members who are very high on extraversion can hurt the team. The reason for this can be attributed to extraverts' tendency to be assertive and dominant. As you would expect when there are too many members with these types of tendencies, power struggles and unproductive conflict occur with greater frequency.[69]

11.4 What are the types of team diversity and how do they influence team functioning?

Team Diversity Another aspect of team composition refers to the degree to which members are different from one another in terms of any attribute that might be used by someone as a basis of categorizing people. We refer to those differences as **team diversity**.[70] Trying to understand the effects of team diversity is somewhat difficult because there are so many different characteristics that may be used to categorize people. Beyond obvious differences among people in their physical appearance, there can be separation among members in terms of their values and beliefs, variety among members in their knowledge and expertise, and disparity among members in their social status and power.[71] Moreover, diversity of team member characteristics may matter more or less depending on the nature of the team and organizational context.[72] For example, you might imagine how the dynamics in a team consisting of both men and women could vary depending on whether the team is in an organization dominated by men (or women) or whether it's balanced in terms of the employees' sex. There are also several reasons diversity might influence team functioning and effectiveness, and some of these reasons seem contradictory.

team diversity
The degree to which team members are different from one another

One predominant theory that has been used to explain why diversity has positive effects is called the **value in diversity problem-solving approach**.[73] According to this perspective, diversity in teams is beneficial because it provides for a larger pool of knowledge and perspectives from which a team can draw as it carries out its work.[74] Having greater diversity in knowledge perspectives stimulates the exchange of information, which in turn fosters learning among team members.[75] The knowledge that results from this learning is then shared and integrated with the knowledge of other members, ultimately helping the team perform more effectively.[76] Research has shown that these benefits of diversity are more likely to occur when the team includes members who are able and willing to put in the effort necessary to understand and integrate different perspectives.[77] Teams that engage in work that's relatively complex and requires creativity tend to benefit most from diversity, and research on teams that are diverse in terms of many different characteristics related to knowledge and perspectives—ethnicity, expertise, personality, attitudes—supports this idea.[78]

value in diversity problem-solving approach

A theory that supports team diversity because it provides a larger pool of knowledge and perspectives

A theory that's been used widely to explain why diversity may have detrimental effects on teams is called the **similarity-attraction approach**.[79] According to this perspective, people tend to be more attracted to others who are perceived as more similar. People also tend to avoid interacting with those who are perceived to be dissimilar, to reduce the likelihood of having uncomfortable disagreements. Consistent with this perspective, research has shown that diversity on attributes such as cultural background, race, and attitudes are associated with communication problems and ultimately poor team effectiveness.[80]

similarity-attraction approach

A theory explaining that team diversity can be counterproductive because people tend to avoid interacting with others who are unlike them

So it appears that there are two different theories about diversity effects that are relevant to teams, and each has been supported in research. Which perspective is correct? As it turns out, a key to understanding the impact of team diversity requires that you consider both the general type of diversity and the length of time the team has been in existence.[81] **Surface-level diversity** refers to diversity regarding observable attributes such as race, ethnicity, sex, and age.[82] Although this type of diversity may have a negative impact on teams early in their existence because of similarity-attraction issues, those negative effects tend to disappear as members become more knowledgeable about one another. In essence, the stereotypes that members have about one another based on surface differences are replaced with knowledge regarding underlying characteristics that are more relevant to social and task interactions.[83]

surface-level diversity

Diversity of observable attributes such as race, gender, ethnicity, and age

Surface-level diversity can sometimes create issues for teams as they begin their tasks, but such problems usually disappear over time.

© Bethean/Corbis

One complication here is that *fault lines* often occur in diverse groups, whereby informal subgroups develop based on similarity in surface-level attributes such as gender or other characteristics.[84] The problem with fault lines is that knowledge and information possessed by one subgroup may not be communicated to other subgroups in a manner that might help the entire team perform more effectively. In a study of boards of directors, for example, the presence of strong fault lines decreased the amount of discussion that board members had with each other in regards to entrepreneurial issues that could affect their companies.[85] Research has shown, however, that the detrimental effects of having subgroups can be offset with training that reinforces the idea that teams may benefit from their diversity.[86] Leadership or reward practices that reinforce the value of sharing information and promote a strong sense of team identity also help diverse teams perform more effectively.[87]

Deep-level diversity, in contrast, refers to diversity with respect to attributes that are less easy to observe initially but that can be inferred after more direct experience. Differences in attitudes, values, and personality are good examples of deep-level diversity.[88] In contrast to the effects of surface-level diversity, time appears to increase the negative effects of deep-level diversity on team functioning and effectiveness.[89] Over time, as team members learn more about one another, differences that relate to underlying values and goals become increasingly apparent. Those differences can therefore create problems among team members that ultimately result in reduced effectiveness.

deep-level diversity
Diversity of attributes that are inferred through observation or experience, such as one's values or personality

Fortunately, it appears that the negative effects of deep-level diversity can be managed.[90] As an example, diversity in members' approach to pursing goals has been shown to hinder team functioning and effectiveness, but this effect can be reduced if teams are instructed to take the time to reflect on their progress toward goals and their strategies.[91] Deep-level diversity has also been shown to have positive effects on team creativity when members are instructed to take the perspective of their teammates.[92] As another example, negative effects of deep-level diversity with respect to members' values have been found to be reduced when team leaders emphasize the teams' task and provide explicit direction regarding team procedures, standards, roles, and expectations.[93] We should also point out, however, that team leaders can also exacerbate problems associated with deep-level diversity. Conflict that results from diversity in members' values appears to increase in teams with leaders who emphasize things like freedom of expression and participation.[94] See our ***OB Internationally*** feature for a discussion of the challenges of managing deep-level diversity in teams that include members from different cultures.

We should also mention an important caveat here. Although personality is normally considered a deep-level diversity variable,[95] some specific personality types do not function this way.[96] In the previous section on personality, for example, we pointed out that though having team members who are extraverted and agreeable is generally a good thing, problems arise if a team has too many members with these attributes. So whereas diversity on most deep-level characteristics is problematic for teams, this claim does not apply to extraversion and agreeableness, because for these two personality characteristics, teams are likely to benefit from having a mix of members.

OB INTERNATIONALLY

Businesses are increasingly using teams composed of members from different cultures, and so teams today often possess members who differ from one another in terms of their attitudes, values, ideas, goals, and behaviours.[97] These types of teams, called *multicultural teams*, can approach problems from several different perspectives, which opens the door to highly innovative solutions.[98] Cultural diversity also allows teams to serve a diverse customer base that may differ in terms of culture and nationality.[99]

Unfortunately, the attributes that give multicultural teams these advantages also give them disadvantages. As an example, people from different cultures communicate differently, which can lead to misunderstandings. For example, to people in Canada and the United States, the phrase "to table something" means to put it off until later, whereas to people in some European countries, it means discuss it right now.[100] Imagine your reaction if you didn't know this difference, and you told a team you were leading that you wanted to table something, and then one of your team members started to discuss options and recommendations about the issue. There are differences in the directness of communications as well. Westerners tend to be very direct and to the point, but to people in other countries, such as Japan, this directness may cause embarrassment and a sense of disrespect.[101] There are also cultural differences in decision-making processes.[102] In some cultures, decisions can be made only after careful consideration and reconsideration of all relevant issues, which is much different from the style in other cultures, such as Canada, where decisions are made rather quickly and with less analysis.[103] Although these differences might seem trivial, they often lead to misunderstandings that reduce the willingness of team members to cooperate. So how can multicultural teams be managed to ensure the advantages outweigh the disadvantages? Although there's no one best way to manage multicultural teams, one proven approach is to encourage team members to take the time to communicate openly with each other about cultural differences and to proactively develop strategies the team can use to accommodate them.[104]

Team Size Two adages are relevant to team size: "The more the merrier" and "Too many cooks spoil the broth." Which one do you believe is true with regard to how many members to include on a team? The answer, according to the results of one meta-analysis, is that having a greater number of members is beneficial for management and project teams but not for teams engaged in production tasks.[105] Management and project teams engage in work that's complex and knowledge intensive, and these teams therefore benefit from the additional resources and expertise contributed by additional members.[106] In contrast, production teams tend to engage in routine tasks that are less complex. Having additional members beyond what's necessary to accomplish the work tends to result in unnecessary coordination and communication problems. Additional members therefore may be less productive because there's more socializing, and they feel less accountable for team outcomes.[107] Although making a claim about the absolute best team size is impossible, research with undergraduate students concluded that team members tend to be most satisfied with their team when the number of members is between four and five.[108] Of course, there are other rules of thumb you can use to keep team size optimal. Jeff Bezos, the CEO of Amazon.com, uses the two-pizza rule: "If a team can't be fed by two pizzas, it's too large."[109]

Summary: What Characteristics Can Be Used to Describe Teams?

The preceding sections illustrate that there are a variety of characteristics that can be used to describe teams. As Figure 11-5 illustrates, teams can be described using taxonomies of team types. For example, teams can be described by categorizing them as a work team, a management team, a parallel team, a project team, or an action team. Teams can also be described using the nature of the team's interdependence with regard to its task, goals, and outcomes. Finally, teams can be described in terms of their composition. Relevant member characteristics include member roles, member ability, member personality, team diversity, and team size.

FIGURE 11-5

What Characteristics Can Be Used to Describe Teams?

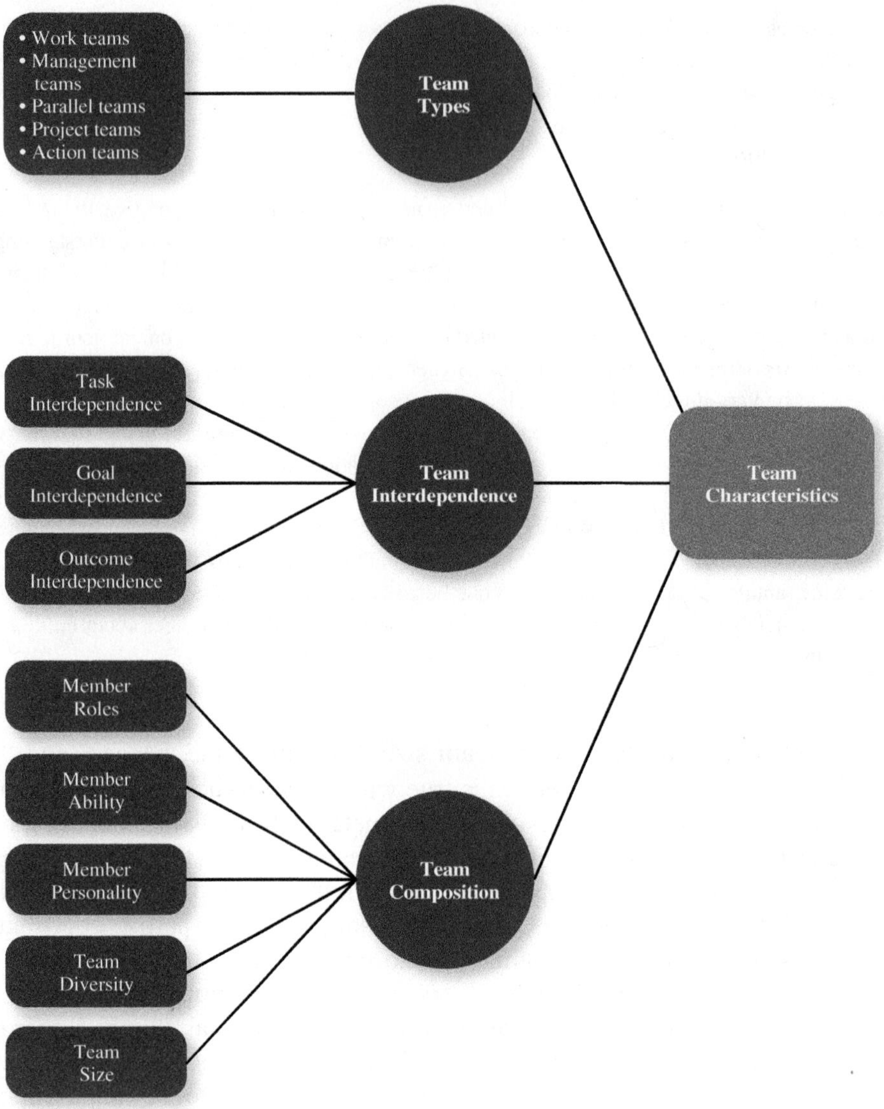

TEAM PROCESSES

In the first half of this chapter we discussed team types and characteristics, the linkages between members, and issues relating to team composition. In the second half of the chapter we shift our attention to how teams work. **Team process** is a term that reflects the different types of interactions that occur within teams that contribute to their ultimate end goals.[110] Team characteristics, like member diversity, task interdependence, team size, and so forth, affect team processes. Those processes, in turn, have a strong impact on team effectiveness.

team process

The different types of activities and interactions that occur within a team as the team works toward its goals

Some of the team processes we describe are observable by the naked eye. An outside observer would be able to see a crew of astronauts performing an interdependent task. Other processes are less visible. An outside observer wouldn't be able to see the sense of cohesion felt by the members of this crew or the shared mental models that cause them to work together so efficiently. Thus, team processes include interactions among members that occur behaviourally, as well as the hard-to-see feelings and thoughts that coalesce as a consequence of member interactions.

WHY ARE SOME TEAMS MORE THAN THE SUM OF THEIR PARTS?

Take a second and try to think of a few teams that have been successful. It's likely that the success of some of these teams was expected because the team had members who are very talented and skilled. The success of other teams may be more difficult to understand just by looking at the rosters of their members. These teams might have members who appear to be less talented and skilled, but as they work together, they somehow became more than the sum of their parts. Getting more from the team than you would expect according to the capabilities of its individual members is called **process gain**. This capability, which is synonymous with "synergy," is most critical in situations in which the complexity of the work is high or tasks require members to combine their knowledge, skills, and efforts to solve problems. In essence, process gain is important because it results in useful resources and capabilities that did not exist before the team created them.[111]

process gain
Achievement of team outcomes greater than those one would expect on the basis of the capabilities of the individual members

Now consider the polar opposite, **process loss**, that is, getting less from the team than you would expect on the basis of the capabilities of its individual members. What factors conspire to create process loss? One is that in teams, members have to work to not only accomplish their own tasks but also coordinate their activities with the activities of their teammates.[112] Although this extra effort focused on integrating work is a necessary aspect of the team experience, it's called *coordination loss* because it consumes time and energy that might otherwise be devoted to task activity.[113] Such coordination losses are often driven by *production blocking*, which occurs when members have to wait on one another before they can do their part of the team task.[114] If you've ever worked in a team in which you felt like you couldn't get any of your own work done because of all the time spent in meetings, following up on requests for information from other team members, and waiting on team members to do their part, you already understand how frustrating production blocking (and coordination loss) can be.

process loss
Achievement of team outcomes less than those one would expect on the basis of the capabilities of the individual members

Another factor is *motivational loss*, or the loss in team productivity that occurs when team members don't work as hard as they could.[115] Why does motivation loss occur in team contexts? One explanation is that it's often quite difficult to gauge exactly how much each team member contributes to the team. Members of teams can work together on projects over an extended period of time, and as a consequence, it's difficult to keep an accurate accounting of who does what. Similarly, members contribute to their team in many different ways, and contributions of some members may be less obvious than others. Finally, members of teams don't always work together at the same time as a unit. Regardless of the reasons for it, uncertainty regarding "who contributes what" results in team members feeling less accountable for team outcomes. Those feelings of reduced accountability, in turn, cause members to exert less effort when working on team tasks than they would if they worked alone on those same tasks. This phenomenon is called *social loafing*,[116] and it can significantly hinder a team's effectiveness.[117] For example, motivational loss and social loafing may result if players on a hockey team come to depend on a star player to win games for the team. For another example of process loss, see our ***OB on Screen*** feature.

OB ON SCREEN

The Avengers

The Avengers. It's what we call ourselves, sort of like a team. "Earth's Mightiest Heroes" type thing.

With those words, Iron Man Tony Stark (Robert Downey Jr.) lets Loki (Tom Hiddleston) know what he's up against, in the movie *The Avengers* (Dir.: Joss Whedon, Marvel Studies and Paramount Pictures, 2012). Loki is an exiled god who has his sights set on subjugating Earth. He stole a mysterious source of unlimited power called the Tesseract and agrees to give it to the Chitauri, a race of aliens bent on taking over the galaxy, in exchange for their help in achieving his goal. Loki is not very worried about the Avengers, however. Although the Avengers are a superhero dream team with regard to their powers, they're a pretty dysfunctional group, and consequently Loki feels they'll have difficulty achieving the type of synergy necessary to overcome him and his incredibly powerful Chitauri allies.

© Walt Disney Studios Motion Pictures/Photofest

Among the most important causes of the Avengers' process problems are personal issues that prevent them from being fully motivated by the team's mission and coordinating effectively. Tony Stark has a huge ego, Bruce Banner (Mark Ruffalo) wants to be left alone so that he can avoid turning into the Incredible Hulk, and the god Thor (Chris Hemsworth) is interested in bringing Loki back with him to his home planet (Loki is Thor's brother). These issues result in bickering, arguments, and even physical confrontations, all of which hinder the team's ability to function effectively and achieve a common goal. In one scene, for example, Thor tries to free Loki and ends up fighting with Iron Man and Captain America (Chris Evans). Ultimately, however, the Avengers begin to realize that Loki's strategy of defeating them is to leverage their differences in a way that keeps them from coalescing into a true team. He understands that if the Avengers combine their powers in a synergistic way, they would become a much more compelling adversary. Unfortunately for Loki, it's the Avengers' realization that they'd been played this way that inspires them to work together.

11.5 What are taskwork and teamwork processes, and what are some examples of team activities that fall into these process categories?

Taskwork Processes

Having described process gains and process losses, it's time to describe the particular team processes that can help teams increase their synergy while reducing their inefficiency. One relevant category of team processes is **taskwork processes**, which are the activities of team members that relate directly to the accomplishment of team tasks. In a general sense, taskwork occurs any time that team members interact with the tools or technologies that are used to complete their work. In this regard, taskwork is similar to the concept of task performance described in Chapter 2 on job performance. However, in the context of teams, especially those that engage in knowledge work, three types of taskwork processes are crucially important: creative behaviour, decision making, and boundary spanning. These three taskwork processes are shown in Figure 11-6.

taskwork processes

The activities of team members that relate directly to the accomplishment of team tasks

FIGURE 11-6

Taskwork Processes

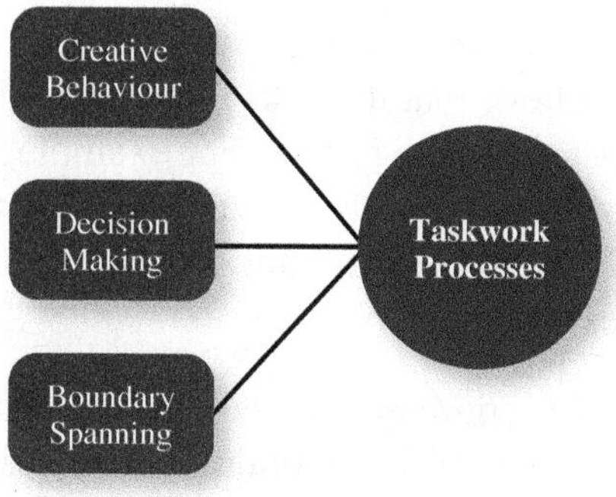

Creative Behaviour When teams engage in creative behaviour, their activities are focused on generating novel and useful ideas and solutions.[118] In Chapter 4 we noted that creative behaviour is driven in part by the creativity of individual employees, because some employees are simply more original and imaginative than others. Researchers have also found that creativity in teams may be affected by characteristics such as conformity and attention to detail.[119] However, the team environment is also uniquely suited to fostering creative behaviour.[120] As a consequence, organizations IDEO, mentioned above, rely on teams to come together and combine their members' unique sets of knowledge and skill in a manner that results in novel and useful ideas.[121] However, achieving such outcomes depends on much more than just putting a diverse mix of people together and letting them go at it. In fact, creative behaviour in teams can be fostered when members participate in a specific set of activities.

Perhaps the best-known activity that teams use to foster creative behaviour is *brainstorming*. Generally speaking, brainstorming involves a face-to-face meeting of team members in which each offers as many ideas as possible about some focal problem or issue.[122] Most brainstorming sessions centre around the following rules:

1. Express all ideas that come to mind (no matter how strange).
2. Go for quantity of ideas rather than quality.
3. Don't criticize or evaluate the ideas of others.
4. Build on the ideas of others.

The theory is that if a team follows these rules, it will develop a large pool of ideas that it can use to address the issue at hand.[123] This concept sounds good in theory, and almost all of us have been in some sort of brainstorming meeting at some point. It may surprise you to learn then that such brainstorming sessions rarely work as well as intended. In fact, research suggests that team members would be better off coming up with ideas on their own, as individuals, before pooling those ideas and evaluating them to arrive at a solution.[124]

Why doesn't brainstorming work as well as individual idea generation? There appear to be at least three reasons.[125] First, there may be a tendency for people to social loaf in brainstorming sessions. That is, members may not work as hard thinking up ideas as they would if they had to turn in an individually generated list with their name on it. Second, though the brainstorming rules explicitly forbid criticizing others' ideas, members may be hesitant to express ideas that seem silly or not well thought out. Third, brainstorming results in production blocking because members have to wait their turn to express their ideas. This waiting around consumes time that could otherwise be used by individuals to generate new ideas. Given the problems associated with brainstorming, why do organizations continue to use it? One reason is that the general idea of brainstorming is well known, and common sense leads people to believe that it works as advertised. Another reason is that there are benefits of brainstorming beyond just generating ideas. For example, brainstorming builds morale and results in the sharing of knowledge that might otherwise be locked inside the minds of the individual team members.[126] Although this knowledge may not be useful for the particular problem being debated, it might be useful for issues that arise in the future.

One offshoot of brainstorming that addresses some of its limitations is the *nominal group technique*.[127] This process, similar to a traditional brainstorming session, starts off by bringing the team together and outlining the purpose of the meeting. The next step takes place on an individual level, however, as members have a set period of time to write down their own ideas on a piece of paper. The subsequent step goes back into the team setting, as members share their ideas with the team in round-robin fashion. After the ideas are recorded, members have a discussion intended to clarify the ideas and build on the ideas of others. After this, it's back to an individual environment; members rank-order ideas on a card that they submit to a facilitator. A facilitator then tabulates the scores to determine the winning idea. From this description, you can probably guess how the nominal group technique addresses the problems with brainstorming. By making people write down ideas on their own, it decreases social loafing and production blocking. Although team members might still be hesitant about expressing wild ideas to the group, doing so might be less threatening than having nothing to contribute to the group. In addition, ranking items as individuals makes people less apprehensive about going "against the grain" by voicing support for an unpopular idea.

Decision Making In Chapter 9 on learning and decision making, we described how people use information and intuition to make specific decisions. In team contexts, however, decisions result from the interaction among team members. In some team contexts, for example, members share information regarding a problem or task, and they work together to reach a *consensus*, or general agreement among members in regards to the final solution. Juries provide a good example of how this type of decision making works. Members of a jury listen to information provided by lawyers and witnesses, and after they're given instructions by a judge, they meet privately to discuss the information with the goal being to reach a consensus regarding the verdict. In many other team contexts, decision making involves multiple members gathering and considering information that's relevant to their area of specialization, and then making recommendations to a team leader who is ultimately responsible for the final decision.[128] Although the degree of member specialization and hierarchical structure of teams vary a great deal,[129] you can understand this type of decision-making process if you consider what happens on the TV show *Celebrity Apprentice*. The show typically begins with Donald Trump assigning two teams a fairly complex task. A celebrity member from each team then volunteers to be project leader, and this person assigns roles such as marketing, logistics, and sales to the other team members. Throughout the project, members make suggestions and recommendations to the leader, who's ultimately responsible for making the decisions that determine the success of the project. Of course, project success is important, because someone from the losing team—most often the project leader—will have to endure hearing Trump say those famous words: "You're fired."

Like many teams in the real world, those on *Celebrity Apprentice* often struggle to make good decisions.

© PRNewsFoto/LG Electronics USA, Inc.

What factors account for a team's ability to make effective decisions? At least three factors appear to be involved.[130] The first factor is *decision informity*, which reflects whether members possess adequate information about their own task responsibilities. Project teams on *Celebrity Apprentice* often fail, for example, because the team member in charge of marketing doesn't gather information necessary to help the team understand the desires and needs of the client. The second factor is *staff validity*, which refers to the degree to which members make good recommendations to the leader. Team members can possess all the information needed to make a good recommendation but then fail to do so because of a lack of ability, insight, or good judgment. The third factor is *hierarchical sensitivity*, which reflects the degree to which the leader effectively weighs the recommendations of the members. Whom does the leader listen to, and whom does the leader ignore? Teams that make good decisions tend to have leaders that do a good job giving recommendations the weight they deserve. Together, these three variables play a large role in how effective teams are in terms of their decision making.[131]

The decision informity, staff validity, and hierarchical sensitivity concepts can be used to make specific recommendations for improving team decision making. For example, research shows that more experienced teams tend to make better decisions because they develop an understanding of the information that's needed and how to use it, and have leaders that develop an understanding of which members provide the best recommendations.[132] As another example, team decision making may be improved by giving members feedback about the three variables involved in the decision-making process.[133] For instance, a team can improve its decision making if the members are told that they have to share and consider additional pieces of information before making recommendations to the leader. Although this recommendation may seem obvious, all too often teams receive feedback only about their final decision. In addition, there may be a benefit to separating the process of sharing information from the process of making recommendations and final decisions, at least in terms of how information is communicated among members.[134] Whereas teams tend to share more information when they meet face-to-face, leaders do a better job considering recommendations and making final decisions when they're away from the members. Leaders who are separated don't have to deal with pressure from members who may be more assertive or better at articulating and defending their positions.

Boundary Spanning The third type of taskwork process is *boundary spanning*, which involves three types of activities with individuals and groups other than those who are considered part of the team.[135] *Ambassador activities* refer to communications that are intended to protect the team, persuade others to support the team, or obtain important resources for the team. As you might have guessed from this description, members who engage in ambassador activities typically communicate with people who are higher up in the organization. For example, a member of a marketing team might meet with senior management to request an increase in the budget for an expanded television ad campaign. *Task coordinator activities* involve communications that are intended to coordinate task-related issues with people or groups in other functional areas. Continuing with the marketing team example, a member of the team might meet with someone from manufacturing to work out how a coupon might be integrated into the product packaging materials. Finally, *scout activities* refer to things team members do to obtain information about technology, competitors, or the broader marketplace. The marketing team member who meets with an engineer to seek information about new materials is engaging in scout activities. Taken together, research suggests that these boundary-spanning activities may be as important to determining team success as the processes that occur entirely within the team.[136]

Teamwork Processes

Another category of team process that helps teams increase their process gain while minimizing their process loss is **teamwork processes**—the interpersonal activities that facilitate the accomplishment of the team's work but do not directly involve task accomplishment itself.[137] Think of teamwork processes as the behaviours that create the setting or context in which taskwork can be carried out.

teamwork processes
The interpersonal activities that promote the accomplishment of team tasks but do not involve task accomplishment itself

So what types of behaviours do teamwork processes involve? Figure 11-7 summarizes the set of teamwork processes discussed in this chapter.[138]

FIGURE 11-7

Teamwork Processes

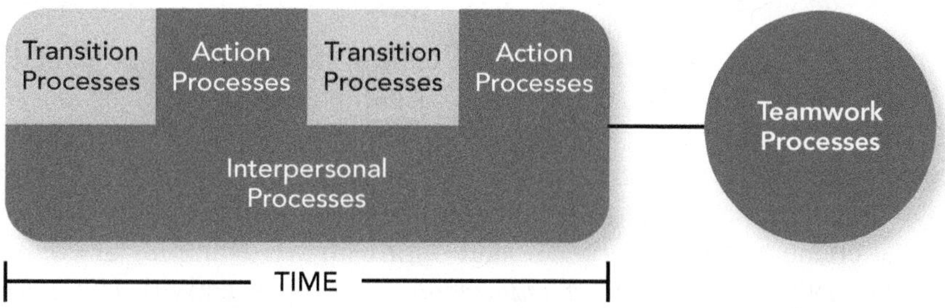

Transition Processes Teamwork processes become important as soon as teams first begin their work. **Transition processes** are teamwork activities that focus on preparation for future work. For example, *mission analysis* involves an analysis of the team's task, the challenges that face the team, and the resources available for completing the team's work. *Strategy formulation* refers to the development of courses of action and contingency plans, and then adapting those plans in light of changes that occur in the team's environment. Finally, *goal specification* involves the development and prioritization of goals related to the team's mission and strategy. Each of these transition processes is relevant before the team actually begins to conduct the core aspects of its work. However, these transition processes also may be important between periods of work activity. For example, think about the halftime adjustments made by a basketball team that's losing a game badly. The team could consider the strengths of its opponent and develop a new strategy intended to neutralize them. In this way, teams may switch from transition processes to taskwork, then back to transition processes. As another example, after-action reviews, which refer to systematic discussions and reviews of performance episodes, have been used by the military for decades. However, because they work so well in improving the effectiveness of teams, their use is spreading to non-military organizations as well.[139]

transition processes

Teamwork processes, such as mission analysis and planning, that focus on preparation for future work in the team

Action Processes Whereas transition processes are important before and between periods of taskwork, **action processes** are important as the taskwork is being accomplished. One type of action process involves *monitoring progress toward goals.* Teams that pay attention to goal-related information—perhaps by charting the team's performance relative to team goals—are typically in a good position to realize when they are "off track" and need to make changes. *Systems monitoring* involves keeping track of things that the team needs to accomplish its work. A team that does not engage in systems monitoring may fail because it runs out of inventory, time, or other necessary resources. *Helping behaviour* involves members going out of their way to help or back up other team members. Team members can provide indirect help to their teammates in the form of feedback or coaching, and direct help in the form of assistance with members' tasks and responsibilities. Helping behaviour may be most beneficial when workload is distributed unequally among team members.[140] *Coordination* refers to synchronizing team members' activities in a way that makes them mesh effectively and seamlessly. Poor coordination results in team members constantly having to wait on others for information or other resources necessary to do their part of the team's work.[141]

action processes

Teamwork processes, such as helping and coordination, that aid in the accomplishment of teamwork as the work is actually taking place

Interpersonal Processes The third category of teamwork processes is called **interpersonal processes**. The processes in this category are important before, during, or between periods of taskwork, and each relates to the manner in which team members manage their relationships. The first type of interpersonal process is *motivating and confidence building*, which refers to things team members do or say that affect the degree to which members are motivated to work hard on the team's task. Expressions that create a sense of urgency and optimism are examples of communications that would fit in this category. Similarly, *affect management* involves activities that foster a sense of emotional balance and unity. If you've ever worked in a team in which members got short-tempered when facing pressure or blamed one another when there were problems, you have first-hand experience with poor affect management.

interpersonal processes

Teamwork processes, such as motivating and confidence building, that focus on the management of relationships among team members

Another important interpersonal process is *conflict management*, which involves the activities that the team uses to manage conflicts that arise in the course of its work. Conflict tends to have a negative impact on a team, but the nature of this effect depends on the focus of the conflict as well as the manner in which the conflict is managed.[142] *Relationship conflict* refers to disagreements among team members in terms of interpersonal relationships or incompatibilities with respect to personal values or preferences. This type of conflict centres on issues that are not directly connected to the team's task. Not only is relationship conflict dissatisfying to most people, but also it tends to result in reduced team performance. *Task conflict*, in contrast, refers to disagreements among members about the team's task. Logically speaking, this type of conflict can be beneficial to teams if it stimulates conversations that result in the development and expression of new ideas.[143] Research findings, however, indicate that task conflict tends to result in reduced team effectiveness unless several conditions are present.[144] First, members need to trust one another and be confident that they can express their opinions openly without fear of reprisals. Second, team members need to engage in effective conflict management practices. In fact, because task conflict tends to be most beneficial to teams when relationship conflict is low, there are reasons to focus efforts on trying to reduce this aspect of conflict.[145] Third, there's some evidence that task conflict may benefit teams as long as they're composed in certain ways. For example, task conflict has been shown to be most beneficial to teams composed with members who are either emotionally stable or open to new experiences.[146] (For more discussion of conflict management issues, see Chapter 12 on power, influence, and negotiation.)

What does effective conflict management involve? First, when trying to manage conflict, it's important for members to stay focused on the team's mission. If members do this, they can rationally evaluate the relative merits of each position.[147] Second, any benefits of task conflict disappear if the level of the conflict gets too heated, if parties appear to be acting in self-interest rather than in the best interest of the team, or if there's high relationship conflict.[148] Third, to effectively manage task conflict, members need to discuss their positions openly and be willing to exchange information in a way that fosters collaborative problem solving.[149] If you've ever had an experience in an ongoing relationship in which you tried to avoid uncomfortable conflict by ignoring it, you probably already understand that this strategy tends to only make things worse in the end.

For task conflict to be productive, team members must feel free to express their opinions and know how to manage conflict effectively.

© Lisette Le Bon/SuperStock

OB FOR STUDENTS

Conflict among team members about the team's task can result in improved team performance, for several reasons. Primarily, task conflict can foster the sharing of information that results in superior solutions to the problems that arise in the team's work. However, if you have experience working in student teams in your courses, you know that this type of conflict can have some really negative consequences—not the least of which is the discomfort it provokes and the huge waste of time that can ensue. To avoid this dissatisfying experience, many students try to avoid conflict in their team. One strategy that may be familiar to you involves splitting up parts of the assignment, performing the work independently, and finally slapping the parts together to produce the team outcome. Although a team might be able to complete assignments using this strategy, the end product tends not to be as good as it might be.

Might there be a better way for student teams to manage task conflict? One study of teams of undergraduate business students investigated the role that task conflict had on two important team outcomes—the grade on a semester-long team project and members' satisfaction with the team experience.[150] The results indicated that the effects of task conflict on these two outcomes depended a lot on the way the team managed its conflict.

First, higher levels of task conflict tended to result in higher scores on team projects, but only for teams that approached the conflict proactively. Members of these teams openly discussed points of disagreement and tried to resolve their disagreements collaboratively. In contrast, teams tended to perform less well on team projects when the members managed high levels of task conflict in a more passive way. These teams tended to avoid openly expressing disagreements or ended potential disagreement prematurely by being overly accommodating of other members' positions.

Second, higher levels of task conflict resulted in higher levels of satisfaction with the team experience, but only for teams that managed conflict in an agreeable manner. Individuals in these teams expressed opposing positions in a relaxed and nonconfrontational way. When members expressed their positions harshly or in a more emotional way, higher levels of task conflict tended to reduce member satisfaction.

11.6 What are team states, and what are some examples of the states that fall into this process category?

Team States

A third category of team processes that helps teams increase their process gain while minimizing their process loss is less visible to the naked eye. **Team states** are specific types of feelings and thoughts that coalesce in the minds of team members as a consequence of their experience working together. For example, as a consequence of supportive leadership and member interactions, team members may develop feelings of *psychological safety*, or the sense that it is okay to do things that are interpersonally risky, or that by expressing opinions and making suggestions that challenge the status quo you won't meet with embarrassment and rejection by teammates.[151] Ostracism in a team context can be painful and lead to disengagement and other negative consequences to the individual and to the team.[152] Although there are many types of team states that we might review in this chapter, Figure 11-8 summarizes those we discuss here.

FIGURE 11-8

Team States

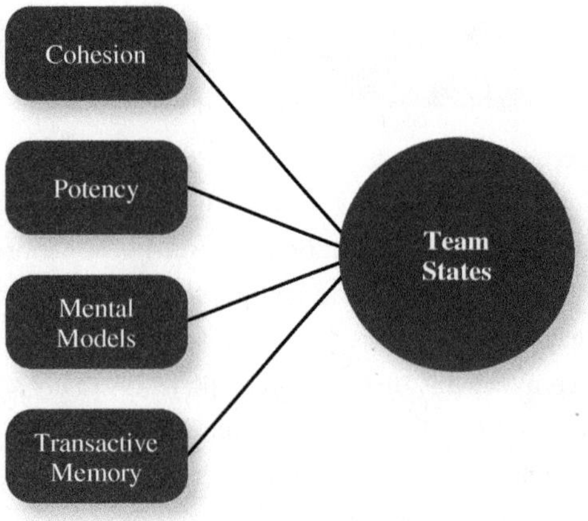

team states

Specific types of feelings and thoughts that coalesce in the minds of team members as a consequence of their experience working together

Cohesion For a number of reasons, such as having trusting relationships, members of teams can develop strong emotional bonds to other members of their team and to the team itself.[153] This emotional attachment, which is called **cohesion,**[154] tends to foster high levels of motivation and commitment to the team, and as a consequence, cohesiveness tends to promote higher levels of team performance.[155] But is a cohesive team *necessarily* a good team? According to researchers, the answer to this question is no. In highly cohesive teams, members may try to maintain harmony by striving toward consensus on issues without ever offering, seeking, or seriously considering alternative viewpoints and perspectives. Sometimes this drive toward conformity, at the expense of other team priorities, is called **groupthink** and is thought to be associated with feelings of overconfidence about the team's capabilities.[156] Groupthink has been blamed for decision-making fiascos in politics as well as in business. Famous examples include NASA's decision to launch the space shuttle *Challenger* in unusually cold weather,[157] and Enron's board of directors' decisions to ignore illegal accounting practices.[158]

cohesion

A team state that occurs when members of the team develop strong emotional bonds to other members of the team and to the team itself

groupthink

Behaviours that support conformity and team harmony at the expense of other team priorities

Potency The second team state, **potency**, refers to the degree to which members believe that the team can be effective across a variety of situations and tasks.[159] When a team has high potency, members are confident that their team can perform well, and as a consequence they focus more of their energy on team tasks and teamwork in hopes of achieving team goals.[160] When a team has low potency, members are not as confident about their team, and so they begin to question the team's goals and one another. Ultimately, this reaction can result in members focusing their energies on activities that don't benefit the team. In the end, research has shown that potency has a strong positive impact on team performance.[161] The one caveat here is that a strong sense of confidence too early in a team's existence can decrease the amount of beneficial discussions centered on different positions that are relevant to a team.[162]

potency

A team state reflecting the degree of confidence among team members that the team can be effective across situations and tasks

So how does high potency develop in teams? Team members' confidence in their own capabilities, their trust in other members' capabilities, and feedback about past performance are all likely to play a role.[163] Specifically, team potency is promoted in teams in which members are confident in themselves and their teammates and when the team has experienced success in the past.

Mental Models **Mental models** refer to the level of common understanding among team members with regard to important aspects of the team and its task.[164] A team may have shared mental models with respect to the capabilities that members bring to the team as well as the processes the team needs to use to be effective.[165] How can these two types of mental models foster team effectiveness? When team members share in their understanding of one another's capabilities, they're more likely to know where to go for the help they might need to complete their work. In addition, they should be able to anticipate when another member needs help to do his or her work. When members have a shared understanding of which processes are necessary to help the team be effective, they can carry out these processes efficiently and smoothly. To help you understand why this is true, consider what would happen in a team of students who had different understandings about how the team should manage conflict. Few disagreements would get resolved if some of the members believed that direct confrontation was best, whereas others believed that avoidance was best.

mental models

The degree to which team members have a shared understanding of important aspects of the team and its task

Transactive Memory Whereas mental models refer to the degree to which the knowledge is shared among members, **transactive memory** refers to how specialized knowledge is distributed among members in a manner that results in an effective system of memory for the team.[166] This concept takes into account the idea that not everyone on a team has to possess the same knowledge. Instead, team effectiveness requires that members understand when their own specialized knowledge is relevant to the team and how their knowledge should be combined with the specialized knowledge of other members to accomplish team goals. If you've ever worked on a team that had effective transactive memory, you may have noticed that work got done very efficiently.[167] Everyone focused on his or her specialty and what he or she did best, members knew exactly where to go to get information when there were gaps in their knowledge, and the team produced synergistic results. Of course, transactive memory can also be fragile because the memory system depends on each and every member.[168] If someone is slow to respond to another member's request for information or forgets something important, the team's system of memory fails. Alternatively, if a member of the team leaves, you lose an important node in the memory system.

transactive memory
The degree to which team members' specialized knowledge is integrated into an effective system of memory for the team

Summary: Why Are Some Teams More Than the Sum of Their Parts?

So what explains why some teams become more than the sum of their parts (whereas other teams become less)? As is shown in Figure 11-9, teams become more than the sum of their parts if their team process achieves process gain rather than process loss. Teams can accomplish that goal by engaging in activities involved in effective taskwork processes, teamwork processes, and team states. Important taskwork processes include creative behaviour, decision making, and boundary spanning. Important teamwork processes include transition processes, action processes, and interpersonal processes. Team states refer to variables such as cohesion, potency, mental models, and transactive memory. In contrast to the taskwork processes, teamwork processes, and team states offer less visible and observable reasons for why some teams possess an effective synergy whereas others seem quite inefficient.

11.7 How do team characteristics and processes affect team performance and team commitment?

HOW IMPORTANT ARE TEAM CHARACTERISTICS AND PROCESSES?

In previous chapters, we have described individual characteristics and mechanisms and discussed how these variables affect individual performance and commitment. In this chapter, we're concerned with team characteristics and processes, and so naturally we're interested in how they influence team effectiveness. One aspect of team effectiveness is *team performance*, which may include metrics such as the quantity and quality of goods or services produced, customer satisfaction, the effectiveness or accuracy of decisions, victories, completed reports, and successful investigations. A second aspect of team effectiveness is team commitment, which is sometimes called *team viability*. Team viability refers to the likelihood that the team can work together effectively into the future.[169] If the team experience is not satisfying, members may become disillusioned and focus their energy on activities away from the team. Although a team with low viability might be able to work together on short-term projects, over the long run a team such as this is bound to have significant problems.[170] Thus, our question becomes: Do team characteristics and processes affect the performance of teams and the degree to which teams are capable of remaining together as ongoing entities?

FIGURE 11-9

Why Are Some Teams More Than the Sum of Their Parts?

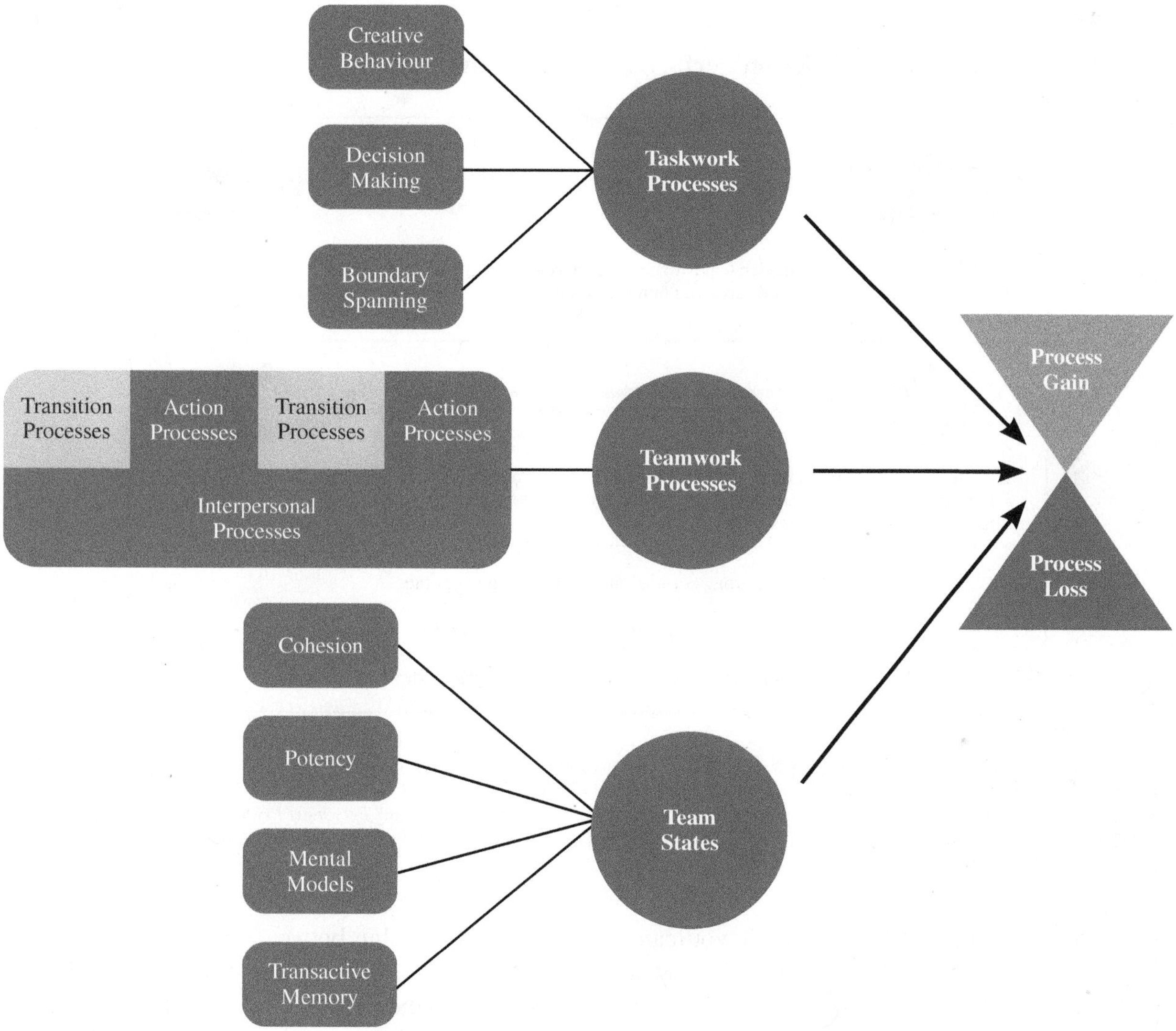

We first turn our attention to team characteristics. Of course, it's difficult to summarize the relationship between team characteristics and team performance and commitment when so many characteristics can be used to describe teams. Here we focus our discussion on the impact of task interdependence, because high task interdependence is one of the things that distinguishes true teams from mere groups of individuals. As Figure 11-10 shows, it turns out that the relationship between task interdependence and team performance is moderately positive.[171] That is, task performance tends to be higher in teams in which members depend on one another and have to coordinate their activities rather than when members work more or less independently. It's important to mention that the relationship between task interdependence and team performance is significantly stronger in teams that are responsible for completing complex knowledge work rather than simple tasks. When work is more complex, interdependence is necessary, because there is a need for members to interact and share resources and information. When work is simple, sharing information and resources is less necessary, because members can do the work by themselves.

FIGURE 11-10

Effects of Team Characteristics on Performance and Commitment

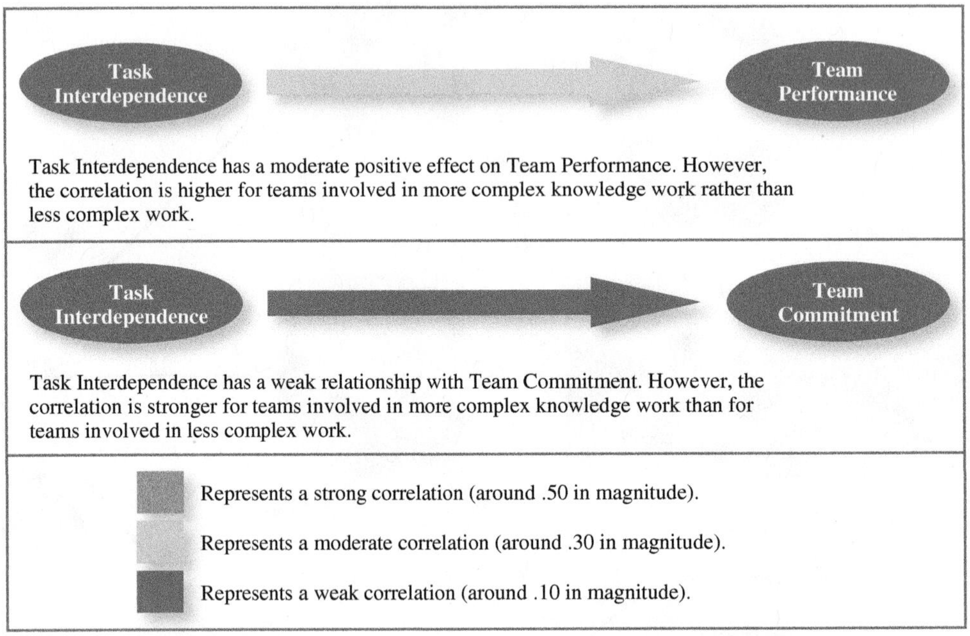
Task Interdependence
Team Performance
Task Interdependence has a moderate positive effect on Team Performance. However, the correlation is higher for teams involved in more complex knowledge work rather than less complex work.
Task Interdependence
Team Commitment
Task Interdependence has a weak relationship with Team Commitment. However, the correlation is stronger for teams involved in more complex knowledge work than for teams involved in less complex work.
Represents a strong correlation (around .50 in magnitude).
Represents a moderate correlation (around .30 in magnitude).
Represents a weak correlation (around .10 in magnitude).

Sources: M.A. Campion, G.J. Medsker, and A.C. Higgs, "Relations Between Work Group Characteristics and Effectiveness: Implications for Designing Effective Work Groups," *Personnel Psychology* 46 (1993), pp. 823–49; M.A. Campion, E.M. Papper, and G.J. Medsker, "Relations Between Work Team Characteristics and Effectiveness: A Replication and Extension," *Personnel Psychology* 49 (1996), pp. 429–52; and G.L. Stewart, "A Meta-analytic Review of Relationships Between Team Design Features and Team Performance," *Journal of Management* 32 (2006), pp. 29–54.

In the lower portion of Figure 11-10, you can see that the relationship between task interdependence and team commitment is weaker.[172] Teams with higher task interdependence have only a slightly higher probability of including members who are committed to their team's continued existence. As with the relationship with team performance, task interdependence has a stronger effect on viability for teams doing complex knowledge work. Apparently, sharing resources and information in a context in which it's unnecessary is dissatisfying to members and results in a team with reduced prospects of continued existence.

Do team processes affect performance and commitment? Again, answering this question is somewhat complicated, because there are several different types of team processes that we could consider. In Figure 11-11, we characterize the relationship among team processes, performance, and commitment by focusing specifically on research involving teamwork processes. The figure therefore represents a summary of existing research on transition processes, action processes, and interpersonal processes.

FIGURE 11-11

Effects of Teamwork Processes Performance and Commitment

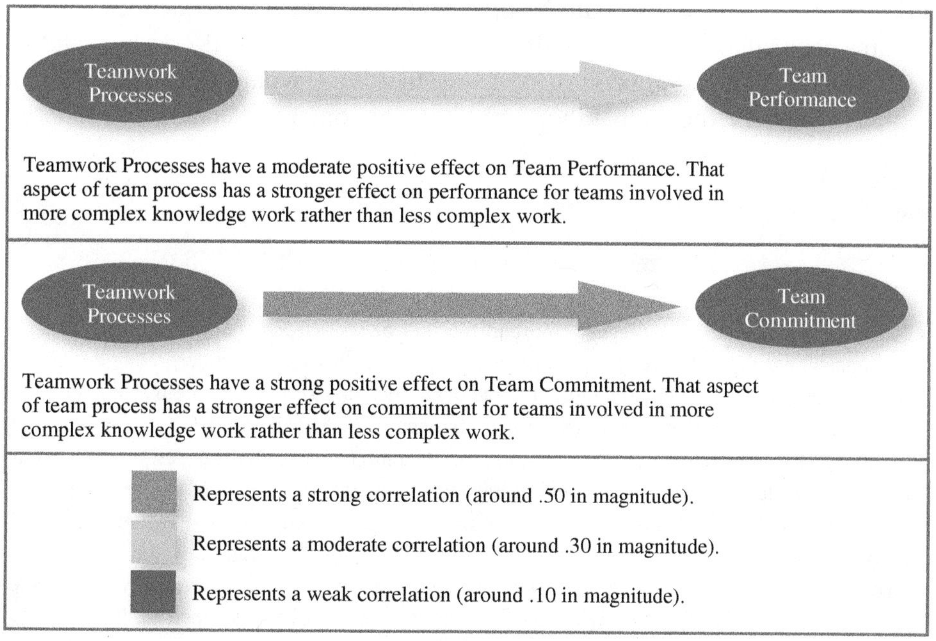
Teamwork Processes
Team Performance
Teamwork Processes have a moderate positive effect on Team Performance. That aspect of team process has a stronger effect on performance for teams involved in more complex knowledge work rather than less complex work.
Teamwork Processes
Team Commitment
Teamwork Processes have a strong positive effect on Team Commitment. That aspect of team process has a stronger effect on commitment for teams involved in more complex knowledge work rather than less complex work.
Represents a strong correlation (around .50 in magnitude).
Represents a moderate correlation (around .30 in magnitude).
Represents a weak correlation (around .10 in magnitude).

Source: J.A. LePine, R.F. Piccolo, C.L. Jackson, J.E. Mathieu, and J.R. Saul, "A Meta-analysis of Team Process: Towards a Better Understanding of the Dimensional Structure and Relationships with Team Effectiveness Criteria," *Personnel Psychology* 61 (2008), pp. 356–76.

Research conducted in a wide variety of team settings has shown that teamwork processes have a moderate positive relationship with team performance.[173] This same moderate positive relationship appears to hold true, regardless of whether the research examines transition processes, action processes, or interpersonal processes. Why might the relationships between these different types of processes and team performance be so similarly positive? Apparently, effectiveness with respect to a wide variety of interactions is needed to help teams achieve process gain and, in turn, perform effectively. The interpersonal activities that prepare teams for future work appear to be just as important as those that help members integrate their taskwork and those that build team confidence and a positive team climate. Researchers have also found that the importance of team processes to team performance may be more strongly positive in teams in which there are higher levels of interdependence.[174] This relationship can be explained quite easily: Activities that are meant to improve the integration of team members' work are simply more important in team contexts in which the work of team members needs to be integrated.

Research also indicates that teamwork processes have a strong positive relationship with team commitment.[175] In other words, teams that engage in effective teamwork processes tend to continue to exist together into the future. Why should teamwork and team commitment be so strongly related? One reason is that people tend to be satisfied in teams in which there are effective interpersonal interactions, and as a consequence, they go out of their way to do things that they believe will help the team stick together. Think about a team situation that you've been in when everyone shared the same goals for the team, work was coordinated smoothly, and everyone was positive, pleasant to be around, and willing to do their fair share of the work. If you've ever actually been in a situation like this—and we hope that you have—chances are that you did your best to make sure the team could continue on together. It's likely that you worked extra hard to make sure that the team achieved its goals. It's also likely that you expressed positive sentiments about the team and your desire for the team to remain together. Of course, just the opposite would be true in a team context in which members had different goals for the team, coordination was difficult and filled with emotional conflict, and everyone was pessimistic and disagreeable. Members of a team like this would not only find the situation dissatisfying but, also make it known that they would be very open to a change of scenery.

OB RESEARCH IN CANADA

Dr. François Chiocchio is an associate professor of organizational behaviour and human resources management at the Telfer School of Management at the University of Ottawa where he teaches various undergraduate and graduate classes. His primary research interests, however, are more in line with the topics covered in this chapter. Specifically, Dr. Chiocchio's work focuses on teams and teamwork, project management, and the factors that enhance and detract from collaboration. In 2006, Dr. Chiocchio received a prestigious teaching award for the design of a collaborative web platform that helped student teams communicate and successfully manage their projects. He recently edited two books: *Advancing Human Resource Project Management* (2014, Wiley) and *The Psychology and Management of Project Teams* (2015, Oxford University Press). Asked why people should care about team characteristics and processes, Dr. Chiocchio was quick to reply, "Teamwork is a crucial skill everyone needs to master." Anyone who has worked in teams, and has depended on the efforts and skills of others, will no doubt agree that teamwork is much easier to read about than to actually practise on a daily basis.

Telfer School of Management, University of Ottawa

Dr. Chiocchio's views on team characteristics, diversity, processes, and communication stem in part from his experiences working in the Canadian federal public service as a project manager, from managing many international research projects, and from running his own consulting company. You can look up Dr. Chiocchio and his work at www.telfer.uottawa.ca/en/directory/professors/chiocchio-francois.

11.8 What steps can organizations take to improve team processes?

APPLICATION: TRAINING TEAMS

Team-based organizations invest a significant amount of resources into training that's intended to improve team processes. These types of investments seem to be a smart thing to do, given that team processes have a positive impact on both team performance and team commitment. In this section, we review several different approaches that organizations use to train team processes.

Transportable Teamwork Competencies

One approach to training teams is to help individual team members develop general competencies related to teamwork activities. Table 11-3 shows that this type of training could involve many different forms of knowledge, skills, and abilities.[176] Taken together, such knowledge, skills, and abilities are referred to as **transportable teamwork competencies.**[177] This label reflects the fact that trainees can transport what they learn about teamwork from one team context and apply it in another. As a specific example of how this type of training might work, consider a recent study of teamwork training for naval aviators in an advanced pilot training program.[178] In this study, one group of pilots went through two days of training, during which they received instruction on preferred communication practices, communicating suggestions and asking questions, and communicating about potential problems. The pilots who went through the training believed that in addition to building teamwork knowledge and skills, the training would increase their mission effectiveness and flight safety. Most importantly, teams that were composed of pilots who went through the training were significantly more effective than teams composed of pilots who did not go through the training. Effectiveness was judged by performance in dangerous scenarios, such as ice buildup on the aircraft wings and instructions from the air traffic control tower that were conflicting or ambiguous.

TABLE 11-3

Teamwork Knowledge, Skills, and Abilities

Competency	Description
Conflict resolution	• Can distinguish between desirable and undesirable conflict. • Encourages desirable conflict and discourages undesirable conflict. • Uses win–win strategies to manage conflict.
Collaborative problem solving	• Can identify situations requiring participative problem solving. • Uses the appropriate degree of participation. • Recognizes and manages obstacles to collaborative problem solving.
Communications	• Understands communication networks. • Communicates openly and supportively. • Listens without making premature evaluations. • Uses active listening techniques. • Can interpret nonverbal messages of others. • Engages in ritual greetings and small talk.
Goal setting and performance management	• Helps establish specific and difficult goals for the team. • Monitors, evaluates, and provides performance-related feedback.
Planning and task coordination	• Coordinates and synchronizes activities among team members. • Establishes expectations to ensure proper balance of workload within the team.

Source: Adapted from M.J. Stevens and M.A. Campion, "The Knowledge, Skill, and Ability Requirements for Teamwork: Implications for Human Resource Management," *Journal of Management* 20 (1994), pp. 503–30.

transportable teamwork competencies

Team training that involves helping people develop general teamwork competencies that they can transport from one team context to another

Cross-Training

A second type of team training involves training members in the duties and responsibilities of their teammates. The idea behind this type of training, which is called **cross-training,**[179] is that team members can develop shared mental models of what's involved in each of the roles in the team and how the roles fit together to form a system.[180] What exactly does cross-training involve? Researchers have found that cross-training may involve instruction at three different levels of depth.[181] At the shallowest level, there is *personal clarification*. With this type of training, members simply receive information regarding the roles of the other team members. As an example, the highly specialized members of surgical teams—surgeons, anesthesiologists, operating room nurses—might meet so that they can learn about others' roles and how each contributes to the team's goal of achieving overall patient well-being.

cross-training

Training team members in the duties and responsibilities of their teammates

At the next level of cross-training, there is *positional modelling*, which involves team members observing how other members perform their roles. In the case of the surgical teams, the surgeons might spend a day shadowing operating room nurses as they perform their duties. The shadowing not only helps the surgeons gain a better understanding of what the job of a nurse entails but also may provide insight into how the activities involved in their respective jobs could be integrated more effectively. Finally, the deepest level of cross-training involves *positional rotation*. This type of training gives members actual experience carrying out the responsibilities of their teammates. Although this type of hands-on experience could expand skills of members so that they might actually perform the duties of their teammates if they had to, the level of training required to achieve proficiency or certification in many situations may be prohibitive. For example, because it takes years of specialized training to become a surgeon, it would be impractical to train an operating room nurse to perform this job by means of positional rotation.

Team Process Training

Cross-training and training in transportable teamwork competencies focus on individual experiences that promote individual learning. **Team process training**, in contrast, occurs in the context of a team experience that facilitates the team being able to function and perform more effectively as an intact unit. One type of team process training is called *action learning*. With this type of training, which has been used successfully at companies such as Motorola and General Electric, a team is given a real problem that's relevant to the organization and then held accountable for analyzing the problem, developing an action plan, and finally carrying out the action plan.[182]

team process training

The use of team experiences that facilitates the team's ability to function and perform more effectively as an intact unit

How does this type of experience develop effective team processes? First, the team receives coaching to help facilitate more effective processes during different phases of the project. Second, there are meetings during which team members are encouraged to reflect on the team processes they've used as they worked on the project. In these meetings, the members discuss not only what they observed and learned from their experiences but also what they would do differently in the future.

A second type of team process training involves experience in a team context when there are task demands that highlight the importance of effective teamwork processes. As an example, United Airlines uses pit crew training for its ramp crews.[183] Although teams of ramp workers at an airline like United must work with luggage, belt loaders, and baggage carts, there are parallels with the work of NASCAR pit crews who work with tires, jacks, and air guns. Primarily, effective performance in both contexts means performing work safely within tight time constraints. Moreover, in both of these contexts, achieving goals requires teamwork, communication, and strict adherence to standardized team procedures. The real value of the pit crew training to the ramp crews is that it conveys the lessons of teamwork in a very vivid way. If a team fails to follow procedures and work together when trying to change tires, tools will be misplaced, parts will be dropped, and members will get in one another's way. As a consequence, a pit stop may take minutes rather than seconds.

Team Building

The fourth general type of team process training is called **team building**. This type of training normally is conducted by a consultant and intended to facilitate the development of team processes related to goal setting, interpersonal relations, problem solving, and role clarification.[184] The "ropes course" is a very popular task used in team building. It requires team members to work together to traverse wooden beams, ropes, and zip lines while dangling in a harness 20–50 feet in the air. Other examples include laser tag and paintball,[185] WhirlyBall (think lacrosse played in bumper cars with a whiffle ball and plastic scoops),[186] whitewater rafting, scavenger hunts, and beating drums in a drum circle.[187] Team-building activities such as these are hugely popular with organizations of all sizes, and they do seem like an awful lot of fun.

team building
Fun activities that facilitate team problem solving, trust, relationship building, and the clarification of role responsibilities

Ropes courses are enjoyable to participants and provide a unique opportunity for team members to get to know each other. But can they really build effective teams?

© AP Photo/La Cruces Sun-News, Shari Vialpando

But can you really build effective teams by having them participate in enjoyable activities that seem so unrelated to their jobs? Although it's somewhat difficult to gauge the effectiveness of team-building interventions because so many different types of exercises have been used, research has been conducted that provides mixed support. The findings of one meta-analysis found that team building did not have a significant effect on team performance when performance was defined in terms of productivity.[188] However, the research found that it is most likely to have positive effects for smaller teams and when the exercise emphasizes the importance of clarifying role responsibilities. The facilitator of the team-building session also needs to be competent in helping members see the connections between the exercise and their work, and also to ensure inclusion and participation of all members.[189]

TAKEAWAYS

11.1 There are several different types of teams—work teams, management teams, parallel teams, project teams, and action teams—but many teams in organizations have characteristics that fit in multiple categories and differ from one another in other ways.

11.2 Teams can be interdependent in terms of team tasks, goals, and outcomes. Each type of interdependence has important implications for team functioning and effectiveness.

11.3 Team composition refers to the characteristics of the members who work in the team. These characteristics include roles, ability, personality, member diversity, and number of team members.

11.4 The effect of diversity on the team depends on time and whether the diversity is surface-level or deep-level. The effects of surface-level diversity tend to diminish with time, whereas the effects of deep-level diversity tend to increase over time.

11.5 Taskwork processes are the activities of team members that relate directly to the accomplishment of team tasks. Taskwork processes include creative behaviour, decision making, and boundary spanning. Teamwork processes refer to the interpersonal activities that facilitate the accomplishment of the team's work but do not directly involve task accomplishment itself. Teamwork processes include transition processes, action processes, and interpersonal processes.

11.6 Team states refer to specific types of feelings and thoughts that coalesce in the minds of team members as a consequence of their experience working together. Team states include cohesion, potency, mental models, and transactive memory.

11.7 Task interdependence has a moderate positive relationship with team performance and a weak relationship with team commitment. Teamwork processes have a moderate positive relationship with team performance and a strong positive relationship with team commitment.

11.8 Organizations can use training interventions to improve team processes. Such interventions may include training in transportable teamwork competencies, cross-training, team process training, and team building.

KEY TERMS

action processes
action teams
cohesion
cross-training

deep-level diversity
goal interdependence
groupthink
individualistic roles
interpersonal processes
management teams
mental models
outcome interdependence
parallel teams
potency
process gain
process loss
project teams
punctuated equilibrium
role
similarity-attraction approach
surface-level diversity
task interdependence
taskwork processes
team
team building
team-building roles
team composition
team diversity
team process
team process training
team states
team task roles
teamwork processes
transactive memory
transition processes
transportable teamwork competencies
value in diversity problem-solving approach
virtual teams
work teams

DISCUSSION QUESTIONS

11.1 In which types of teams have you worked? Were these teams consistent with the team types discussed in this chapter, or were they a combination of types?

11.2 Think about your student teams. Which aspects of both models of team development apply the most and least to teams in this context? Do you think these teams function best in an additive, disjunctive, or conjunctive manner? What are the advantages and disadvantages of each structure?

11.3 How would you describe your student team in terms of its diversity? In what ways would there be advantages and disadvantages to increasing its diversity? How might you be able to manage some of the disadvantages so that your team is able to capitalize on the potential advantages?

11.4 Think about a highly successful team with which you are familiar. What types of task, goal, and outcome interdependence does this team have? Describe how changes in task, goal, and outcome interdependence might have a negative impact on this team.

11.5 Think of a team you worked in that performed poorly. Were any of the causes of the poor performance related to the forces that tend to create process loss? If so, which force was most particularly problematic? What steps, if any, did your team take to deal with the problem?

11.6 Think of a team you worked in that performed exceptionally well. What type of taskwork process did the team engage in? Which teamwork processes did the team seem to depend on most to produce the exceptional results?

11.7 Think about the team states described in this chapter. If you joined a new team, how long do you think it would take you to get a feel for those team states? Which states would you be able to gauge first? Which would take longer?

11.8 Which types of teamwork training would your student team benefit most from? What exactly would this training cover? What specific benefits would you expect? What would prevent a team from training itself on this material?

CASE • ROCKET MEN (AND WOMEN)

NASA, in collaboration with the international space community, is planning a mission to send a crew of astronauts to Mars. Among other objectives, scientists are interested in the possibility of growing food in space, and there are now reasons to believe that Mars may be a good place to farm.[190] Although this mission isn't scheduled until the year 2030 or so, NASA has already begun to explore how aspects of the mission are likely to impact the crew's ability to function effectively.[191] You see, the assigned crew of six to eight will be living and working together in a noisy capsule about the size of an average kitchen for three years—it takes 6 months to get there, they'll stay for 18 months, and then there's the 6-month journey home.[192] Given the constraints of their environment, and the fact that the crew will be working long hours under very demanding conditions, it's inevitable that they'll get on one another's nerves on occasion. There's literally no place to go to escape minor annoyances, and as frustration builds, the probability of emotional outbursts and interpersonal conflict increases.[193]

Of course, it goes without saying that conflict among astronauts in a small space capsule millions of miles away from Earth is not a good thing. Astronauts who fail to fulfill a responsibility because they're preoccupied with conflict could put the mission, and the lives of the entire crew, in jeopardy, and this is true whether the conflict is bubbling under or has risen to the surface. Hard feelings might hinder teamwork as well, and the failure to communicate an important piece of information or to provide help to a member of the crew in need of assistance, for example, might also lead to disaster. Unfortunately, however, the duration and demands of the mission are almost without precedent, and therefore the specific practices that need to be implemented to facilitate crew functioning in this context are unknown.

To address this issue, NASA has awarded grants to psychologists to study teams that have to live and work together in isolated, confined, and extreme environments for extended periods.[194] To help increase understanding of conflict and teamwork and how it can be better managed, the psychologists are working on technology that tracks the whereabouts of each crew member, and his or her vocal intensity and vital functions such as heart rate.[195] This information would be used to pinpoint where and when conflict occurs and to understand how conflict influences subsequent crew interactions. The crew will be given feedback so they can learn how conflict hurts teamwork and cohesion. This feedback could also motivate crews to take the time to discuss teamwork issues and to devise ways to manage conflict and other process problems.

Although it's impossible to anticipate all the issues that might arise on the mission to Mars, NASA believes that research on team process is necessary to enhance the viability and performance of the crew that is ultimately charged with the task.

11.1 Which team processes do you believe are most important to the crew of astronauts travelling to Mars? Why? Are there specific team processes you feel are relatively unimportant? Explain.

11.2 Describe additional types of information that could be collected by the psychologists to help crews better understand their interactions and how they influence crew effectiveness.

11.3 Discuss how team training could be used to build effective processes for the crew travelling to Mars.

EXERCISE • PAPER PLANE CORPORATION

The purpose of this exercise is to analyze the advantages and disadvantages of sequential versus pooled interdependence on a team production project. This exercise uses groups of six participants, so your instructor will either assign you to a group of six or ask you to create your own group of six. The exercise has the following steps.

11.1 Your professor will supply you with the materials you need to create your final product: as many paper airplanes as you can fold to quality standards in three five-minute rounds. Instructions for folding the planes and judging their quality are provided below. Before you start work, do the following:

a. As a group, select a team manager (who will supervise operations and get additional resources as needed) and a team inspector (who will judge the quality of the work on airplanes).

b. Familiarize yourself with how to make a paper airplane by folding one according to the instructions below.

c. Be sure you are in a space where all of the team members can work comfortably.

d. To the extent possible, move away from other groups.

e. Familiarize yourself with the information about the Paper Plane Corporation.

Plane Folding Instructions

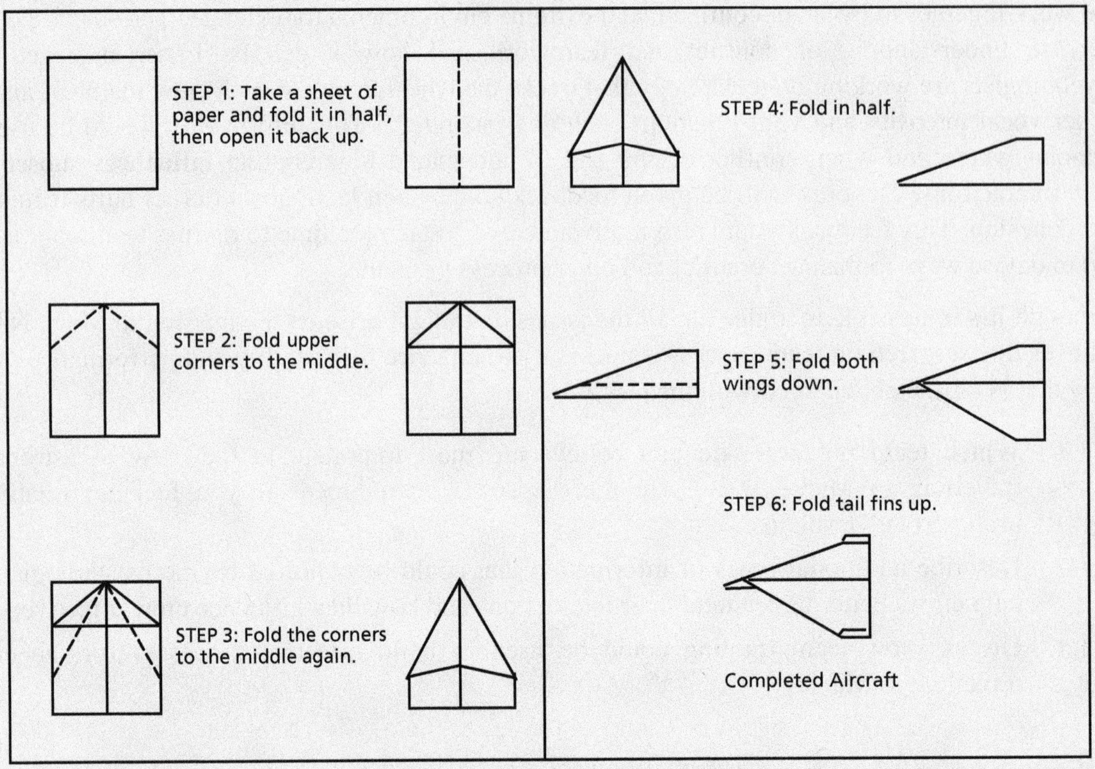

STEP 1: Take a sheet of paper and fold it in half, then open it back up.
STEP 2: Fold upper corners to the middle.
STEP 3: Fold the corners to the middle again.
STEP 4: Fold in half.
STEP 5: Fold both wings down.
STEP 6: Fold tail fins up.
Completed Aircraft

11.2 Your group is the complete workforce for the Paper Plane Corporation. The company, established in 1943, has led the market in paper plane production. Presently under new management, the company is contracting to make aircraft for the Canadian Forces. You must determine the most efficient method for producing these aircraft. You must make your contract with the Air Force under the following conditions:

a. The Canadian Forces will pay $200,000 per airplane.
b. The aircraft must pass a strict inspection by a quality control manager.
c. A penalty of $250,000 per airplane will be subtracted for failure to meet the production requirements.
d. Labour and other overhead will be computed at $3,000,000.
e. Cost of materials will be $30,000 per bid plane. If you bid for 10 but only make 8, you must pay the cost of materials for those you failed to make or those that did not pass inspection.

11.3 In the first round of airplane manufacturing process, you have been asked to focus on individuality. Each Paper Plane worker should manufacture his or her own planes from start to finish. When each plane is finished, it should be put in a central location for quality inspection. When time is called, you will record your team profit on the Summary Sheet.

11.4 In the second round of manufacturing, you have been asked to give each worker a specific job. In other words, the manufacturing process will take place in an assembly-line fashion. When planes come off the assembly line, they will be given directly to the quality control manager for inspection. When time is called, you will record your team profit on the Summary Sheet.

11.5 In the final round of manufacturing, your team has been asked to devise a manufacturing process that will maximize both efficiency and effectiveness. You may do whatever you like in terms of creating paper airplanes. You will have the same amount of time that you did in the two previous rounds. When time is called, you will record your team profit on the Summary Sheet shown below.

11.6 Class discussion (whether in groups or as a class) should centre on the following questions:

a. Did pooled interdependence (round 1) or sequential interdependence (round 2) work better for your group in terms of the number of planes made correctly? Why do you think you got the result you did?

b. How did you change your work structure in round 3? Did the changes you implemented help you achieve better productivity? Why or why not?

c. From your perspective, what are the advantages and disadvantages of pooled and/or sequential interdependence?

Summary Sheet

Round 1

Bid: _______ Aircraft @ $200,000 per aircraft = ____________________

Results: _______ Aircraft @ $200,000 per aircraft = ____________________

Subtract: $3,000,000 overhead + _______ × $30,000 cost of raw materials +
_______ × $250,000 penalty for not completing a bid plane = ____________________

Profit: ____________________

Round 2

Bid: _______ Aircraft @ $200,000 per aircraft = ____________________

Results: _______ Aircraft @ $200,000 per aircraft = ____________________

Subtract: $3,000,000 overhead + _______ × $30,000 cost of raw materials +
_______ × $250,000 penalty for not completing a bid plane = ____________________

Profit: ____________________

Round 3

Bid: _______ Aircraft @ $200,000 per aircraft = ____________________

Results: _______ Aircraft @ $200,000 per aircraft = ____________________

Subtract: $3,000,000 overhead + _______ × $30,000 cost of raw materials +
_______ × $250,000 penalty for not completing a bid plane = ____________________

Profit: ____________________

Sources: Adapted from J.M. Ivancevich, R. Konopaske, and M. Matteson, *Organizational Behavior and Management*, 7th ed. (New York: McGraw-Hill/Irwin, 2005). Original exercise by Louis Potheni in F. Luthans, *Organizational Behavior* (New York: McGraw-Hill, 1985), p. 555.

OB ASSESSMENTS • INTERDEPENDENCE

How interdependent is your student project team? This assessment is designed to measure three types of interdependence: task interdependence, goal interdependence, and outcome interdependence. Read each of the following questions with a relevant student team in mind. Answer each question using the response scale provided. Then follow the instructions below to score yourself.

1 Totally Disagree	2 Disagree	3 Somewhat Disagree	4 Neutral	5 Somewhat Agree	6 Agree	7 Totally Agree	
1. I cannot accomplish my tasks without information or materials from other members of my team.							____
2. Other members of my team depend on me for information or materials needed to perform their tasks.							____
3. Within my team, jobs performed by team members are related to one another.							____
4. My work goals come directly from the goals of my team.							____
5. My work activities on any given day are determined by my team's goals for that day.							____
6. I do very few activities on my job that are not related to the goals of my team.							____
7. Feedback about how well I am doing my job comes primarily from information about how well the entire team is doing.							____
8. Evaluations of my performance are strongly influenced by how well my team performs.							____
9. Many rewards from my work (e.g., pay, grades) are determined in large part by my contributions as a team member.							____

Scoring and Interpretation

- *Task interdependence.* Sum up items 1–3. _____
- *Goal interdependence.* Sum up items 4–6. _____
- *Outcome interdependence.* Sum up items 7–9. _____

If you scored 14 or above, then your team may be above average on a particular dimension. If you scored 13 or below, your team may be below average on a particular dimension. Remember, when interpreting your scores on these assessments it is important to consider the *reliability* and *validity* of these tools (see Chapter 1, ***OB Assessments***).

Source: From M.A. Campion, E.M. Papper, and G.J. Medsker, "Relations Between Work Team Characteristics and Effectiveness: A Replication and Extension," *Personnel Psychology* 49 (1996), pp. 429–52. Reprinted with permission of John Wiley & Sons, Inc.

Power, Influence, and Negotiation

CHAPTER 12

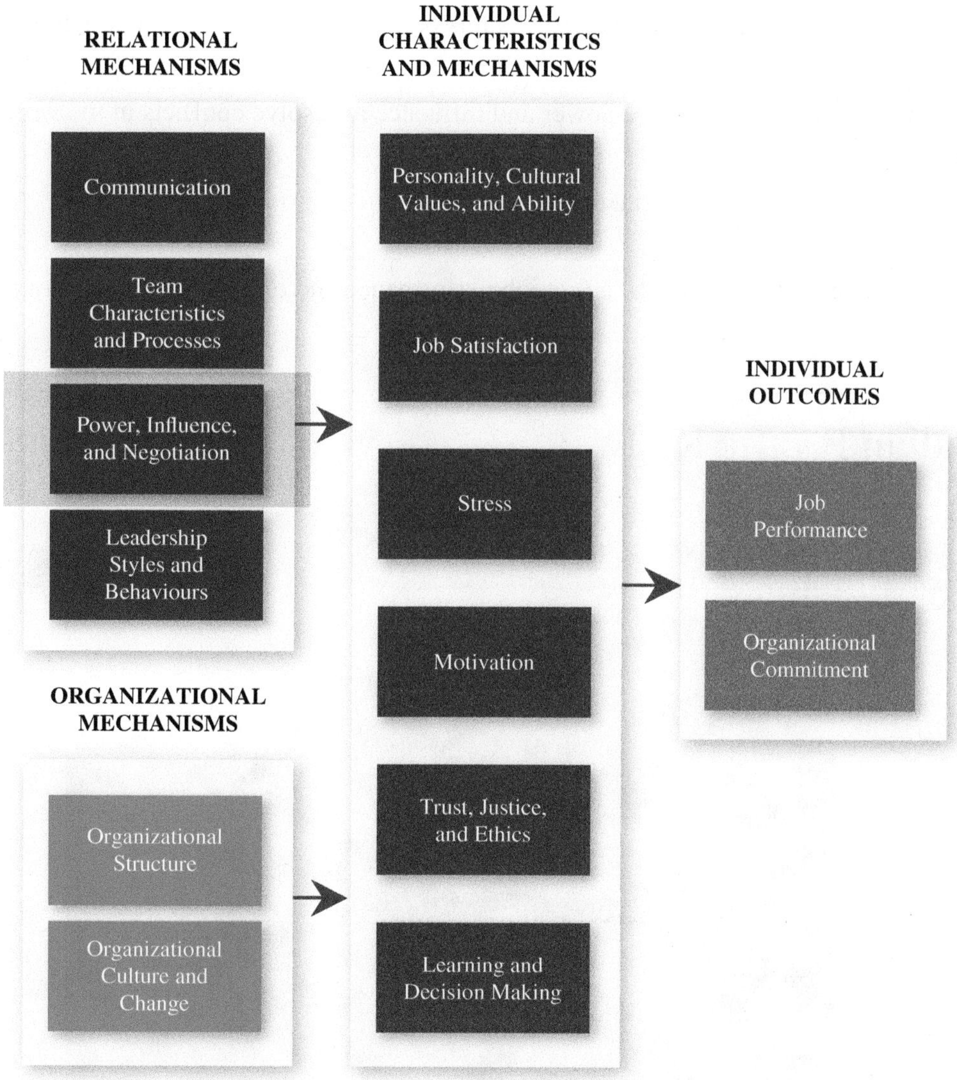

LEARNING OUTCOMES

After reading this chapter, you should be able to answer the following questions:

12.1 What is power?

12.2 What are the different types of power that people can have, and when can they use those types most effectively?

12.3 What behaviours do people exhibit when trying to influence others, and which of these are most effective?

12.4 What is organizational politics, and when is political behaviour most likely to occur?

12.5 How do individuals use their power and influence to resolve conflicts in the workplace?

12.6 What are the ways in which leaders negotiate in the workplace?

12.7 How do power and influence affect job performance and organizational commitment?

Canadian Pacific Railway

Since his arrival at Canadian Pacific Railway Ltd. in mid-2012, few would argue with Hunter Harrison's ability to influence how things are done within the company.

Canadian Pacific Rail

The history of Canada is closely tied to railway. Not long after Confederation, July 1, 1867, the Canadian Pacific Railway Limited (CP) was founded to connect Canada's emerging population centres in Ontario and Quebec with the vast potential of its relatively unpopulated West.[1] In spite of great political obstacles and the enormous engineering challenges associated with traversing the Canadian Rockies, the "last spike" was finally driven in on November 7, 1885 at Craigellachie, British Columbia.[2] Although the cost of construction nearly ruined the fledgling company, within three years of the first transcontinental train leaving Montreal and Toronto for Port Moody, B.C., on June 28, 1886, CP's financial house was once again in order.[3] Over the years, as CP grew so did the company's interest in non-railway ventures, such as manufacturing, shipping, hotels, airlines, natural oil and gas extraction, bus transportation, trucking, pulp and paper, and waste management.[4] Today, CP has divested itself of non-core businesses and is primarily a freight railway company, headquartered in Calgary. The company owns roughly 22,500 kilometres of track all across Canada and into the United States, stretching from Montreal to Vancouver, and as far north as Edmonton.[5]

Recently, as in the beginning, the company has found itself facing great challenges. Throughout the 2000s, the company had been battling strong headwinds, and by 2012 CP was in very rough shape, sporting the worst operating performance among all the major North American railroads.[6] For instance, the company's operating ratio—a productivity index that represents operating costs as a percentage of revenue—was a dismal 80 percent, making it one of the least profitable railroads in North America.[7] Once again, the company was flirting with financial ruin.

Hunter Harrison, a seasoned railway executive and proven turnaround expert, was brought out of retirement to serve as the company's CEO in mid-2012. Harrison's vision for CP included longer, faster trains and better customer service at lower cost.[8] To achieve these goals, it would be imperative for him to introduce and implement radical changes quickly within an established bureaucracy so that CP could once again become efficient and flexible. Some of these changes would involve the elimination of surplus positions (mainly through attrition and/or voluntary turnover; reducing the workforce from 19,500 to 14,700 employees), the shedding of 400 older locomotives and 11,000 cars, dropping some terminals, and initiating disciplinary actions against employees who failed to comply with safety and working rules.[9] At the end the 2013, the company's operating ratio had dropped to 65.99 percent—*on a par with industry leaders* and a full three years ahead of schedule. As Harrison was recently quoted saying, "We're doing things that people didn't think were imaginable."[10]

POWER, INFLUENCE, AND NEGOTIATION

As evidenced by CP, powerful people within organizations can make a huge difference to the success of an organization or group. It would be easy after reading the opening example to anoint Hunter Harrison as a great leader and try to simply adopt his behavioural examples to follow in his footsteps. However, things aren't quite that simple. Many other leaders who exhibited similar behaviours have not been nearly as successful. We'll soon see that there are many different types of leaders, many of whom can excel, given the right circumstances. This chapter focuses on how people *get* the power and influence they use to influence others, and the ways power and influence are utilized in organizations, including through negotiation.

12.1 What is power?

WHY ARE SOME PEOPLE MORE POWERFUL THAN OTHERS?

What exactly comes to mind when you hear the term "power"? Does it convey a positive or a negative image? Certainly it's easy to think of leaders who have used power for what we would consider good purposes, but it's just as easy to think of leaders who have used it for unethical or immoral purposes. For now, try not to focus on how leaders use power but instead on how they acquire it. **Power** can be defined as the ability to influence the behaviour of others and resist unwanted influence in return.[11] Note that this definition gives us a couple of key points to think about. First, just because a person has the ability to influence others does not mean they will actually choose to do so. In many organizations, the most powerful employees don't even realize how influential they could be! Second, in addition to influencing others, power can be seen as the ability to resist the influence attempts of others.[12] This resistance might come in the form of the simple voicing of a dissenting opinion, the refusal to perform a specific behaviour, or the organization of an opposing group of co-workers.[13] Sometimes leaders need to resist the influence of other leaders or higher-ups to do what's best for their own unit. Other times they need to avoid being a pushover and resist the influence of employees who try to go their own way.

power
The ability to influence the behaviour of others and resist unwanted influence in return

Acquiring Power

Think of the people you work with or have worked with, or think of students involved in many of the same activities you are. Do any of these people seem to have especially high levels of power, meaning that they have the ability to influence your behaviour? What is it that gives them that power? In some cases, their power may come from some formal position (e.g., supervisor, team leader, teaching assistant, resident advisor). However, sometimes the most powerful people we know lack any sort of formal authority. It turns out that power in organizations can come from a number of different sources. Specifically, there are five major types, which can be grouped along two dimensions: organizational and personal.[14] These types of power are illustrated in Figure 12-1.

12.2 What are the different types of power that people can have, and when can they use those types most effectively?

Organizational Power The three types of organizational power derive primarily from a person's position within the organization. They are considered more formal in nature.[15] **Legitimate power** derives from a position of authority inside the organization and is sometimes referred to as *formal authority*. People with legitimate power have some title—some term on an organizational chart or on their door that says, "Look, I'm supposed to have influence over you." Those with legitimate power have the understood right to ask others to do things that are considered within the scope of their authority. When managers ask an employee to stay late to work on a project, work on one task instead of another, or work faster, they are exercising legitimate power. Generally speaking, the higher up in an organization a person is, the more legitimate power he or she possesses.

FIGURE 12-1

Types of Power

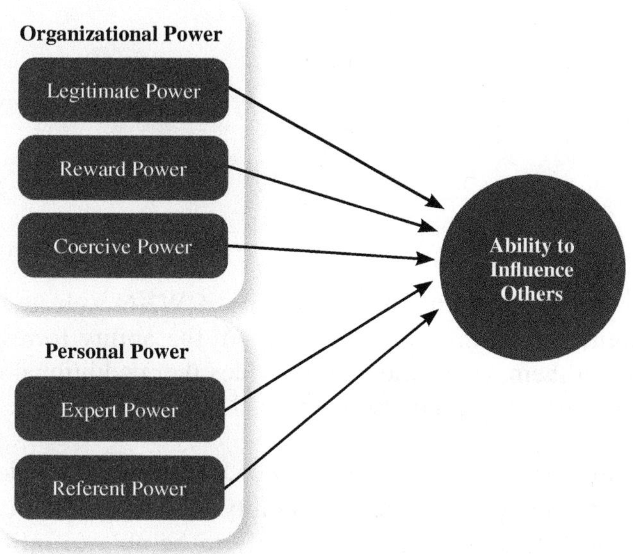

Since 1997, the *Women's Executive Network* (WXN), a Toronto-based networking and advocacy group, has identified the most powerful women in Canada. In any given year, the women listed on the WXN website have legitimate power, in that the position they hold affords them the ability to influence others.

However, legitimate power does have its limits. It doesn't generally give a person the right to ask employees to do something outside the scope of their jobs or roles within the organization. For example, if a manager asked an employee to wash his or her car or mow the lawn, it would likely be seen as an inappropriate request. Also, as we'll see later in this chapter, there's a big difference between having legitimate power and using it effectively. Used ineffectively, legitimate power can be a very weak form of it. In our opening example, Harrison doesn't simply go bossing everyone in the organization around; he manages his legitimate power effectively to earn respect and get people to commit to their endeavours.

legitimate power
A form of organizational power based on authority or position

The next two forms of organizational power are somewhat intertwined with legitimate power. **Reward power** exists when someone has control over the resources or rewards another person wants. For example, managers generally have control over raises, performance evaluations, awards, more desirable job assignments, and the resources an employee might require to perform a job effectively. Those with reward power have the ability to influence others if those being influenced believe they will get the rewards by behaving in a certain way. **Coercive power** exists when a person has control over punishments in an organization. Coercive power operates primarily on the principle of fear. It exists when one person believes that another has the ability to punish him or her and is willing to use that power. For example, a manager might have the right to fire, demote, suspend, or lower the pay of an employee. Sometimes the limitations of a manager to impose punishments are formally spelled out in an organization. However, in many instances, managers have considerable leeway in this regard. Coercive power is generally regarded as a poor form of power to use regularly, because it tends to result in negative feelings toward those who wield it.

reward power
A form of organizational power based on the control of resources or benefits

coercive power
A form of organizational power based on the ability to hand out punishment

Personal Power Of course, the women who appear on the WXN website don't appear on that list just because they have some formal title that affords them the ability to reward and punish others. There's something else about them, as people, that provides them additional capabilities to influence others. Personal forms of power capture that "something else."

Expert power derives from a person's expertise, skill, or knowledge on which others depend. When people have a track record of high performance, the ability to solve problems, or specific knowledge that's necessary to accomplish tasks, they're more likely to be able to influence other people who need that expertise. Consider a lone programmer who knows how to operate a piece of antiquated software, a machinist who was recently trained to operate a new piece of equipment, or the only engineer who has experience working on a specific type of project. All of these persons will have a degree of expert power because of what they individually bring to the organization. There is perhaps no place where expert power comes into play more than in Silicon Valley, where it's widely perceived that the best leaders are those with significant technological experience and expertise. At Intel, senior advisor and former CEO Andy Grove "fostered a culture in which 'knowledge power' would trump 'position power.' Anyone could challenge anyone else's idea, so long as it was about the idea and not the person—and so long as you were ready for the demand 'Prove it.'"[16]

expert power
A form of organizational power based on expertise or knowledge

Referent power exists when others have a desire to identify and be associated with a person. This desire is generally derived from affection, admiration, or loyalty toward a specific individual.[17] Although our focus is on individuals within organizations, there are many examples of political leaders, celebrities, and sports figures who seem to possess high levels of referent power. Justin Trudeau, Drake, and Sidney Crosby all possess referent power to some degree because others want to emulate them. The same might be said of leaders in organizations who possess a good reputation, attractive personal qualities, or a certain level of charisma. Hunter Harrison, as detailed in our opening chapter case, clearly wields great referent power. Members of the business and investment community who have been watching and admiring the transformation at CP (as well as the increased stock prices) not only attribute this turnaround to Harrison but would like to copy his approach in other organizations.

referent power
A form of organizational power based on the attractiveness and charisma of the leader

Of course, it's possible for a person to possess all the forms of power at the same time. In fact, the most powerful leaders have bases of power that include all five dimensions. From an employee's perspective, it's sometimes difficult to gauge what form of power is most important. Why, exactly, do you do what your boss asks you to do? Is it because the boss has the formal right to provide direction, because the boss controls your evaluations, or because you admire and like the boss? Many times, we don't know exactly what type of power leaders possess until they attempt to use it.

Generally speaking, the personal forms of power are more strongly related to organizational commitment and job performance than the organizational forms. Those authorities for whom you worked the hardest probably possessed some form of expertise and charisma rather than just an ability to reward and punish. That's not to say, though, that organizational forms of power cannot successfully achieve objectives at times. Some useful guidelines for wielding each of the forms of power can be found in Table 12-1.

TABLE 12-1

Guidelines for Using Power

Type of Power	Guidelines for Use
Legitimate	• Make polite, clear requests. • Explain the reason for the request. • Don't exceed your scope of authority. • Follow up to verify compliance. • Insist on compliance if appropriate.
Reward	• Offer the types of rewards people desire. • Offer rewards that are fair and ethical. • Don't promise more than you can deliver. • Explain the criteria for giving rewards and keep it simple. • Provide rewards as promised if requirements are met. • Don't use rewards in a manipulative fashion.
Coercive	• Explain rules and requirements and ensure people understand the serious consequences of violations. • Respond to infractions promptly and without favouritism. • Investigate to get facts before following through. • Provide ample warnings. • Use punishments that are legitimate, fair, and commensurate with the seriousness of the noncompliance.
Expert	• Explain the reasons for a request and why it's important. • Provide evidence that a proposal will be successful. • Don't make rash, careless, or inconsistent statements. • Don't exaggerate or misrepresent the facts. • Listen seriously to the person's concerns and suggestions. • Act confidently and decisively in a crisis.
Referent	• Show acceptance and positive regard. • Act supportive and helpful. • Use sincere forms of ingratiation. • Defend and back up people when appropriate. • Do unsolicited favours. • Make self-sacrifices to show concern. • Keep promises.

Source: From Gary A. Yukl, *Leadership in Organizations*, 7th edition © 2010. Reproduced by permission of Pearson Education, Inc., Upper Saddle River, New Jersey.

Contingency Factors Certain situations in organizations are likely to increase or decrease the degree to which leaders can use their power to influence others. Most of these situations revolve around the idea that the more other employees depend on a person, the more powerful that person becomes. A person can have high levels of expert and referent power, but if he or she works alone and performs tasks that nobody sees, the ability to influence others is greatly reduced. That said, there are four factors that can affect the strength of a person's ability to use power to influence others,[18] summarized in Table 12-2.

TABLE 12-2

The Contingencies of Power

Contingency	Leader's Ability to Influence Others Increases When ...
Substitutability	There are no substitutes for the rewards or resources the leader controls.
Centrality	The leader's role is important and interdependent with others in the organization.
Discretion	The leader has the freedom to make his or her own decisions without being restrained by organizational rules.
Visibility	Others know about the leader and the resources he or she can provide.

Substitutability is the degree to which people have alternatives in accessing resources. Leaders that control resources to which no one else has access can use their power to gain greater influence. **Discretion** is the degree to which managers have the right to make decisions on their own. If managers are forced to follow organizational policies and rules, their ability to influence others is reduced. **Centrality** represents how important a person's job is and how many people depend on that person to accomplish their tasks. Leaders who perform critical tasks and interact with others regularly have a greater ability to use their power to influence others. **Visibility** is how aware others are of a leader's power and position. If everyone knows that a leader has a certain level of power, the ability to use that power to influence others is likely to be high.

substitutability
The degree to which people have alternatives in accessing the resources that a leader controls

discretion
The degree to which managers have the right to make decisions on their own

centrality
How important a person's job is and how many people depend on that person to accomplish their tasks

visibility
How aware others are of a leader and the resources that leader can provide

Using Influence

Up to now, we've discussed the types of power leaders possess and when their opportunities to use that power will grow or diminish. Now we turn to the specific strategies that leaders use to translate that power into actual influence.

Recall that having power increases our *ability* to influence behaviour. It doesn't mean that we will use or exert that power. **Influence** is the use of an actual behaviour that causes behavioural or attitudinal changes in others.[19] There are two important aspects of influence to keep in mind. First, influence can be seen as directional. It most frequently occurs downward (managers influencing employees), but it can also be lateral (peers influencing peers) or upward (employees influencing managers). Second, influence is all relative. The absolute power of the influencer and "influencee" isn't as important as the disparity between them.[20]

influence

The use of behaviours to cause behavioural or attitudinal changes in others

12.3 What behaviours do people exhibit when trying to influence others, and which of these are most effective?

Influence Tactics Leaders depend on a number of tactics to cause behavioural or attitudinal changes in others. In fact, there are at least ten types of tactics leaders can use.[21] These and their general levels of effectiveness are illustrated in Figure 12-2. The four most effective tactics have been shown to be rational persuasion, inspirational appeals, consultation, and collaboration.

FIGURE 12-2

Influence Tactics and Their Effectiveness

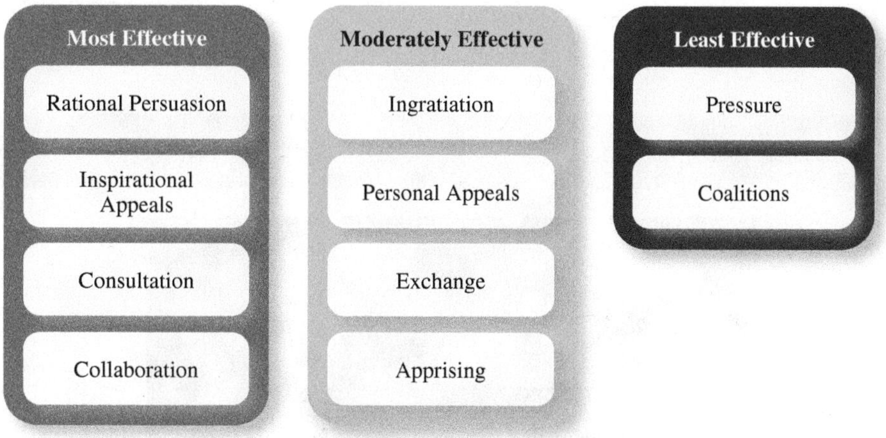

Source: Adapted from J.J. Johnson and J.B. Cullen, "Trust in Cross-Cultural Relationships," in *Blackwell Handbook of Cross-Cultural Management*, ed. M.J. Gannon and K.L. Newman (Malden, MA: Blackwell, 2002), pp. 335–60.

Rational persuasion is the use of logical arguments and hard facts to show the target that the request is a worthwhile one. Research shows that rational persuasion is most effective when it helps show that the proposal is important and feasible.[22] Rational persuasion is particularly important because it's the only tactic consistently successful in the case of upward influence.[23] At Google, for example, data is all-important. CEO Larry Page has been willing to change his mind in the face of conflicting information. Douglas Merrill, a former Google CIO, said, "Larry would wander around the engineers and he would see a product being developed, and sometimes he would say, 'Oh I don't like that,' but the engineers would get some data to back up their idea, and the amazing thing was that Larry was fine to be wrong. As long as the data supported them, he was okay with it. And that was such an incredibly morale-boosting interaction for engineers."[24] An **inspirational appeal** is a tactic designed to appeal to the target's values and ideals, thereby creating an emotional or attitudinal reaction. To use this tactic effectively, leaders must have insight into what kinds of things are important to the target. **Consultation** occurs when the target is allowed to participate in deciding how to carry out or implement a request. This tactic increases commitment from the target, who now has a stake in seeing that his or her opinions are valued. A leader uses **collaboration (as influence method)** by attempting to make it easier for the target to complete the request. Collaboration could involve the leader helping complete the task, providing required resources, or removing obstacles.[25]

rational persuasion

The use of logical arguments and hard facts to show someone that a request is worthwhile

inspirational appeal

An influence tactic designed to appeal to one's values and ideals, thereby creating an emotional or attitudinal reaction

consultation

An influence tactic whereby the target is allowed to participate in deciding how to carry out or implement a request

collaboration (as influence method)

An influence tactic whereby the leader makes it easier for the target to complete a request by offering to work with and help the target

Larry Page (left), CEO of Google, is known for his willingness to allow employees to use rational persuasion (data) to change his mind on an issue.

© AP Photo/Paul Sakuma

Four other influence tactics are effective only sometimes. **Ingratiation** is the use of favours, compliments, or friendly behaviour to make the target feel better about the influencer. You might more commonly hear this referred to as "sucking up," especially when used in an upward influence sense. Ingratiation has been shown to be more effective as a long-term strategy and not nearly as effective when used immediately prior to making an influence attempt.[26] **Personal appeals** occur when the requestor asks for something on the basis of personal friendship or loyalty. The stronger the friendship, the more successful the attempt is likely to be. (The ***OB Internationally*** feature following shows that, as with other influence attempts, there are cultural differences when it comes to this kind of an appeal.) An **exchange tactic** is used when the requestor offers a reward or resource to the target in return for performing a request. This type of request requires that the requestor have something of value to offer.[27] Finally, **apprising** occurs when the requestor clearly explains why performing the request will benefit the target personally. It differs from rational persuasion in that it focuses solely on the benefit to the target as opposed to simple logic or benefits to the group or organization. It differs from exchange in that the benefit is not necessarily something the requestor gives to the target but rather something that results from the action.[28]

ingratiation

The use of favours, compliments, or friendly behaviour to make the target feel better about the influencer

personal appeals

An influence tactic in which the requestor asks for something based on personal friendship or loyalty

exchange tactic

An influence tactic in which the requestor offers a reward in return for performing a request

apprising

An influence tactic in which the requestor clearly explains why performing the request will benefit the target personally

The two tactics that have been shown to be least effective and might result in resistance from the target are pressure and coalitions; of course, this doesn't mean they aren't used or can't be effective. **Pressure** is the use of coercive power through threats and demands. As we've discussed previously, it is a poor way to influence others and may bring benefits only over the short term. **Coalitions** occur when the influencer enlists other people to help influence the target—peers, subordinates, or one of the target's superiors. Coalitions are generally used in combination with one of the other tactics. For instance, if rational persuasion is not strong enough, the influencer might bring in another person to show that that person agrees with the logic of the argument.

pressure

An influence tactic in which the requestor attempts to use coercive power through threats and demands

coalitions

An influence tactic in which the influencer enlists other people to help influence the target

Two points should be noted about the use of influence tactics. First, they tend to be most successful in combination.[29] Many tactics have limitations or weaknesses that can be overcome using other tactics. Second, the influence tactics that tend to be most successful are those that are "softer" in nature, such as rational persuasion, inspirational appeals, consultation, and collaboration, which take advantage of personal rather than organizational forms of power. Leaders that are the most effective at influencing others will generally rely on such tactics, make appropriate requests, and ensure the tactics they use match the types of power they have.

OB INTERNATIONALLY

When Google hired Kai-Fu Lee as vice-president of engineering and president of Google Greater China, with a more than $10 million compensation package, the company was counting on his continued ability to use the same skills that allowed him to be a huge success at Microsoft.[30] What was it that Lee possessed that made him so worthwhile? Lee argues that it was his understanding of *guanxi* (pronounced "gwan-she"; literally, "relationships").[31] In the Chinese culture, guanxi is the ability to influence decisions by creating obligations between parties based on personal relationships.

Guanxi represents a relationship between two people that involves both sentiment and obligation.[32] Individuals with high levels of guanxi tend to be tied together on the basis of shared institutions such as kinship, places of birth, schools attended, and past working relationships.[33] Although such shared institutions might get someone's foot in the door in the United States, in China they become a higher form of obligation. Influence through guanxi just happens—it's an unspoken obligation that must be addressed.[34] It is, in a sense, a blend of formal and personal relationships that exists at a different level than in the United States. There is no such thing as a "business only" relationship, and the expectation is simply that if you take, you must also give back.[35] Lee (who left Google) and his guanxi were so great that Google's Chinese product managers insisted that their business cards read "Special Assistant to Kai-Fu Lee" and that their desks be placed within 100 feet of his so that they could effectively do business outside the company.[36]

Evidence suggests that companies like Microsoft and Google that possess guanxi have higher levels of performance.[37] American managers who go to work overseas must be conscious of these different types of relationships and expectations. In addition to understanding the power of guanxi, evidence suggests that Chinese managers from different areas (e.g., Hong Kong, Taiwan, Mainland China) have different beliefs when it comes to which influence tactics are the most effective.[38] There is also recent evidence that the norms around guanxi in China are changing with time.[39] If anything, it goes to show that managers need to be acutely aware of both general and more specific cultural differences when trying to influence others in China.

Responses to Influence Tactics As is illustrated in Figure 12-3, there are three possible responses people have to influence tactics.[40] **Internalization** occurs when the target of influence agrees with and becomes committed to the influence request.[41] For a leader, this is the best outcome, because it results in employees putting forth the greatest level of effort in accomplishing what they are asked to do. Internalization reflects a shift in both the behaviours and the attitudes of employees. **Compliance** occurs when targets of influence are willing to do what the leader asks, but they do it with a degree of ambivalence. Compliance reflects a shift in the behaviours of employees but not their attitudes. This behaviour is the most common response to influence attempts in organizations, because anyone with some degree of power who makes a reasonable request is likely to achieve compliance. That response allows leaders to accomplish their purpose, but it doesn't bring about the highest levels of employee effort and dedication. Still, it's clearly preferable to **resistance (to influence tactics)**, which occurs when the target refuses to perform the influence request and puts forth an effort to avoid having to do it. Employee resistance might come in the form of making excuses, trying to influence the requestor in return, or simply refusing to carry out the request. The response is most likely when the influencer's power is low relative to the target or when the request itself is inappropriate or unreasonable.[42]

internalization

A response to influence tactics in which the target agrees with and becomes committed to the request

compliance

A response to influence tactics in which the target is willing to do what the leader asks but does it with a degree of ambivalence

resistance (to influence tactics)

A response to influence tactics in which the target refuses to perform a request and puts forth an effort to avoid having to do it

FIGURE 12-3

Responses to Influence Attempts

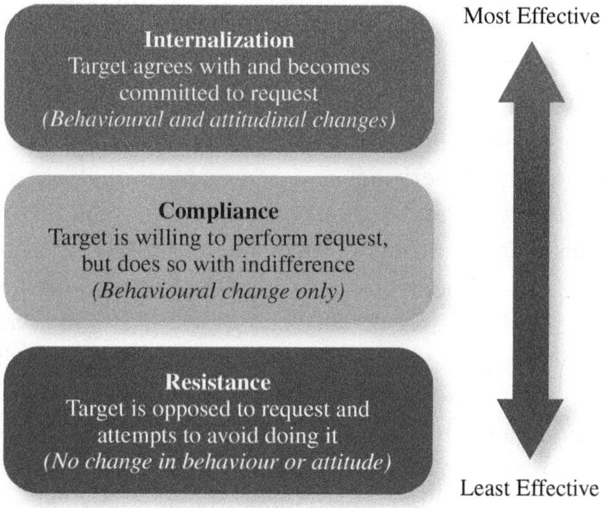

Power and Influence in Action

In this section, we look at two major ways leaders can use power to influence others: through navigating the environment of organizational politics within the organization and through using power and influence to help solve conflicts within the organization. As it turns out, it's easy for these two areas to coincide.

Organizational Politics If any term has more negative connotations than *power*, it might be *politics*. You've probably had people give you career advice such as "Stay away from office politics" or "Avoid being seen as political." The truth is, you can't escape it; politics is a fact of life in organizations![43] Although you might hear company executives, such as former Vodafone CEO Sir Christopher Gent, make statements such as "[When I was CEO] we were mercifully free of company politics and blame culture,"[44] you can be pretty sure that wasn't actually the case—especially given that England's Vodafone is one of the world's largest mobile phone operators. Most leaders, such as Allison Young, vice-president of Blue Cross and Blue Shield, will tell you, "You have to assess the political situation early on and make decisions on forward-looking strategy not only on the facts, but also the political landscape."[45] Whether we like it or not, organizations are filled with independent, goal-driven individuals who must take into account the possible actions and desires of others to get what they want.[46]

12.4 What is organizational politics, and when is political behaviour most likely to occur?

Organizational politics can be seen as actions by individuals that are directed toward the goal of furthering their own interests.[47] Although there's generally a negative perception of politics, it's important to note that this definition doesn't imply that furthering one's interests is necessarily in opposition to the company's interests. A leader needs to be able to push his or her ideas and influence others through the use of organizational politics. Research has recently supported the notion that, to be effective, leaders must have a certain degree of political skill.[48] In fact, universities and some organizations such as Becton, Dickinson and Company—a leading global medical technology company—are training their future leaders to be attuned to their political environment and develop their political skill.[49]

organizational politics
Individual actions directed toward the goal

Political skill is the ability to effectively understand others at work and use that knowledge to influence others in ways that enhance personal and/or organizational objectives.[50] Two aspects of political skill are *networking ability*, or an adeptness at identifying and developing diverse contacts, and *social astuteness*, or the tendency to observe others and accurately interpret their behaviour.[51] (To see where you stand on these two dimensions, see our ***OB Assessments*** feature at the end of the chapter.) Political skill also involves two other capabilities: *interpersonal influence*, having an unassuming and convincing personal style that's flexible enough to adapt to different situations,[52] and *apparent sincerity*, appearing to others to have high levels of honesty and genuineness.[53] Taken together, these four skills provide a distinct advantage when navigating the political environments in organizations. Individuals who exhibit these types of skills have higher ratings of both task performance and organizational citizenship behaviours from others, especially when the social requirements of the job are high.[54]

political skill
The ability to understand others and the use of that knowledge to influence them to further personal or organizational objectives

Although organizational politics can lead to positive outcomes, people's perceptions of politics are generally negative. This is certainly understandable, as anytime someone acts in a self-serving manner it's potentially to the detriment of others.[55] In a highly charged political environment in which people are trying to capture resources and influence one another toward potentially opposing goals, it's only natural that some will feel stress about the uncertainty they face at work. Environments perceived as extremely political have been shown to cause lower job satisfaction, increased strain, lower job performance (both task- and extra-role-related), higher turnover intentions, and lower organizational commitment among employees.[56] In fact, high levels of organizational politics have even been shown to be detrimental to company performance as a whole.[57]

As a result, organizations (and leaders) do their best to minimize the perceptions of self-serving behaviours associated with organizational politics. This goal requires identifying the organizational circumstances that cause politics to thrive. As is illustrated in Figure 12-4, organizational politics is driven by both personal characteristics and organizational characteristics.[58] Some employees have a strong need for power that provides them with an incentive to engage in political behaviours. Still others have "Machiavellian" tendencies, meaning they're willing to manipulate and deceive others to acquire power.[59]

FIGURE 12-4

The Causes and Consequences of Organizational Politics

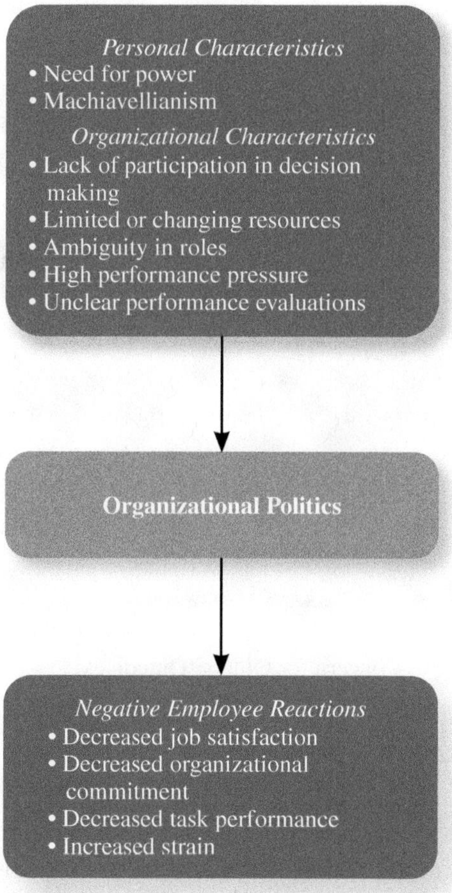

The organizational factors most likely to increase politics are those that raise the level of uncertainty in the environment. When people are uncertain about an outcome or event, they'll generally act in ways that help reduce that uncertainty. A number of events can trigger uncertainty, including limited or changing resources, ambiguity in role requirements, high performance pressures, or unclear performance evaluation measures.[60] A lack of employee participation in decision making has also been found to increase perceptions of organizational politics.[61] These sorts of organizational factors generally have a much stronger effect on political behaviour than personal factors. That's actually a good thing for organizations, because it may be easier to clarify performance measures and roles than it is to change the personal characteristics of a workforce.

Conflict Resolution In addition to using their power to shape office politics, leaders can use their influence in the context of conflict resolution. Conflict arises when two or more individuals perceive that their goals are in opposition. Conflict and politics are clearly intertwined, because the pursuit of one's own interests often breeds conflict in others. When conflict arises in organizations, leaders have the ability to use their power and influence to resolve it. Figure 12-5 illustrates five different styles a leader can use when handling conflict, each of which is appropriate in different circumstances.[62] The five styles can be viewed as combinations of two separate factors: how *assertive* leaders want to be in pursuing their own goals and how *cooperative* they are with regard to the concerns of others.

FIGURE 12-5

Styles of Conflict Resolution

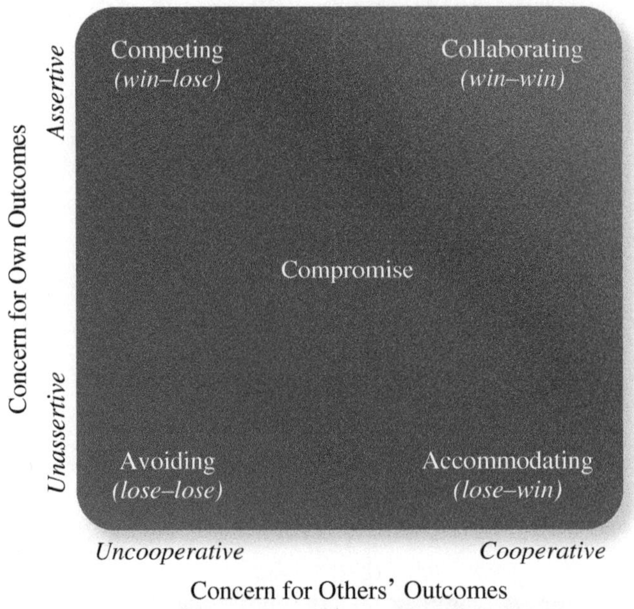

12.5 How do individuals use their power and influence to resolve conflicts in the workplace?

Competing (high assertiveness, low cooperation) occurs when one party attempts to get his or her own goals met without concern for the other party's results. It could be considered a win–lose approach to conflict management. Competing occurs most often when one party has high levels of organizational power and can use legitimate or coercive power to settle the conflict. It also generally involves the hard forms of influence, such as pressure or coalitions. Although this strategy for resolving conflict might get the result initially, it won't win a leader many friends, given the negative reactions that tend to accompany such tactics. It's best used in situations in which the leader knows he or she is right and a quick decision needs to be made.

competing

A conflict resolution style by which one party attempts to get his or her own goals met without concern for the other party's results

Avoiding (low assertiveness, low cooperation) occurs when one party wants to remain neutral, stay away from conflict, or postpone the conflict to gather information or let things cool down. Avoiding usually results in an unfavourable result for everyone, including the organization, and may result in negative feelings toward the leader. Most importantly, avoiding never really resolves the conflict. **Accommodating** (low assertiveness, high cooperation) occurs when one party gives in to the other and acts in a completely unselfish way. Leaders will typically use an accommodating strategy when the issue is really not that important to them but is very important to the other party. It's also an important strategy to think about when the leader has less power than the other party. If leaders know they are going to lose the conflict due to their lack of power anyway, it might be a better long-term strategy to give in to the demands from the other party.

avoiding

A conflict resolution style by which one party wants to remain neutral, stay away from conflict, or postpone the conflict to gather information or let things cool down

accommodating

A conflict resolution style by which one party gives in to the other and acts in a completely unselfish way

Collaboration (as conflict resolution method) (high assertiveness, high cooperation) occurs when both parties work together to maximize outcomes. Collaboration is seen as a win–win form of conflict resolution. Collaboration is generally regarded as the most effective form of conflict resolution, especially in reference to task-oriented rather than personal conflicts.[63] However, it's also the most difficult to come by because it requires full sharing of information by both parties, a full discussion of concerns, relatively equal power between parties, and a lot of time investment to arrive at a resolution. But this style also results in the best outcomes and reactions from both parties. **Compromise** (moderate assertiveness, moderate cooperation) occurs when conflict is resolved through give-and-take concessions. Compromise is perhaps the most common form of conflict resolution, whereby each party's losses are offset by gains and vice versa. It is seen as an easy form of resolution, maintains relations between parties, and generally results in favourable evaluations for the leader.[64] Women are also more likely to use compromise as a tactic in comparison to men, whereas men are more likely than women to use competing as a tactic.[65] Recent research shows that individuals with higher levels of emotional intelligence (see Chapter 4) are more likely to adopt constructive forms of conflict management (the green areas of Figure 12-5).[66] Like most things when it comes to power and influence, it's not so much a function of which style you use, but rather of when you use it, that determines success. It is a mistake to think one specific style is superior to another—research has shown that whether a certain style is effective is dependent on lots of situational issues.[67] For instance, trust (see Chapter 8) is extremely important when using the more cooperative forms of conflict resolution, especially when there is a larger degree of conflict.[68]

collaboration (as conflict resolution method)

A conflict resolution style whereby both parties work together to maximize outcomes

compromise

A conflict resolution style by which conflict is resolved through give-and-take concessions

For more detail on when to use the various conflict resolution strategies, see Table 12-3.

TABLE 12-3

When to Use the Various Conflict Resolution Styles

Resolution Style	Use During the Following Situations:
Competing	• When quick decisive action is vital (i.e., emergencies). • On important issues for which unpopular actions need implementation. • On issues vital to company welfare when you know you're right. • Against people who take advantage of noncompetitive people.
Avoiding	• When an issue is trivial or more important issues are pressing. • When you perceive no chance of satisfying your concerns. • When potential disruption outweighs the benefits of resolution. • To let people cool down and regain perspective. • When gathering information supersedes an immediate decision. • When others can resolve the conflict more effectively. • When issues seem tangential or symptomatic of other issues.
Collaborating	• To find an integrative solution when both sets of concerns are too important to be compromised. • When your objective is to learn. • To merge insights from people with different perspectives. • To gain commitment by incorporating concerns into a consensus. • To work through feelings that have interfered with a relationship.
Accommodating	• When you find you are wrong, to allow a better position to be heard, to learn, and to show your reasonableness. • When issues are more important to others than yourself, to satisfy others and maintain cooperation. • To build social credits for later issues. • To minimize loss when you are outmatched and losing. • When harmony and stability are especially important. • To allow subordinates to develop by learning from mistakes.
Compromising	• When goals are important but not worth the effort of potential disruption of more assertive modes. • When opponents with equal power are committed to mutually exclusive goals. • To achieve temporary settlements to complex issues. • To arrive at expedient solutions under time pressure. • As a backup when collaboration or competition is unsuccessful.

Source: From K.W. Thomas, "Toward Multi-dimensional Values in Teaching: The Example of Conflict Behaviors," *Academy of Management Review* 1, pp. 484–90. Copyright © 1997. Reproduced with permission of Academy of Management via Copyright Clearance Center.

One example of conflict resolution is the One Laptop per Child project. Nicholas Negroponte is the founder and chairperson of this nonprofit organization, whose mission is to give millions of laptops to undereducated children in the world's poorest nations. Five hundred thousand laptops—one for each primary schoolchild—have already been distributed in Uruguay; 1 million have gone out in Peru.[69] In total, over 2.4 million laptops have been given out to students and teachers worldwide.[70] Needless to say, manufacturing a cheap laptop (named the XO and generally costing around $200 to produce) is no small feat. During the founding, Negroponte had to lead a network of vastly different individuals, all working on their own time or on loan from other organizations, through a painstaking collaboration process of design and manufacturing. The process wasn't always easy. Negroponte had to adopt a competing style of conflict resolution to make a custom wireless system for the laptop function. This competitive response upset a faction of volunteers who subsequently quit the project. However, Negroponte has also facilitated collaboration among very disparate groups. As a leader with varying degrees of power, he constantly has to balance the needs of the project with the needs of individuals and attempt to resolve conflict effectively.[71] Surprisingly, conflict arises most frequently with regard to the countries to which the project wants to give the laptops![72] For an example of how to select the proper conflict management style, see this chapter's ***OB on Screen*** feature.

The One Laptop per Child project intends to provide millions of laptops for the world's poorest children. Founder and chair Nicholas Negroponte put together a large team of volunteers, "borrowed" workers from many different organizations, and worked to establish an effective collaboration among them by adopting a wide variety of conflict resolution strategies.

Courtesy of One Laptop per Child

12.6 What are the ways in which leaders negotiate in the workplace?

Negotiations

There is perhaps no better place for leaders to use their power, influence, political, and conflict resolution skills than when conducting negotiations. **Negotiation** is a process in which two or more interdependent individuals discuss and attempt to come to an agreement about their different preferences. Negotiations can take place inside the organization or when dealing with organizational outsiders. Negotiations can involve settling a contract dispute between labour and management, determining a purchasing price for products, haggling over a performance review rating, or determining the starting salary for a new employee. Clearly, negotiations are a critical part of organizational life, for both leaders and employees. Successful leaders are good at negotiating outcomes of all types, and doing it well requires knowledge of power structures, how best to influence the other party, and awareness of their own biases in decision making.[73]

negotiation
A process in which two or more interdependent individuals discuss and attempt to reach agreement about their differences

OB ON SCREEN

Skyfall

As long as I am head of this department, I choose my own operatives.

With those words, M (Judi Dench) takes a decidedly competitive style of conflict resolution toward Gareth Mallory (Ralph Fiennes) in *Skyfall* (Dir. Sam Mendes, MGM, 2012). Leading up to this scene, James Bond (Daniel Craig) had been injured and presumed dead. He returns after the headquarters of MI6 (Britain's Secret Intelligence Service) is destroyed in a terrorist attack. Bond has just been put through a series of physical and psychological tests by the agency and is sitting in the office ready to learn the results of these tests when Mallory, chair of the British Parliament's Intelligence and Security Committee, enters the room. It is clear that Mallory's preference (in spite of M's revelation that Bond has passed his tests) is that Bond not be cleared to return to active duty. He questions M's decision making and tells her that she's making a sentimental decision and not a rational one.

M, the director of MI6, is put in a tough position. Although Mallory's committee doesn't have formal authority over MI6, he reports directly to Britain's prime minister who does. M has to make a decision quickly given the events that are happening and knows that Bond's reinstatement would be unpopular given his prior actions and current state. However, she also believes strongly that MI6 is better with Bond on the case and through prior experience knows that Mallory can be a bit of a bully and is unlikely to bend on the issue.

Given all this, look through Table 12-3 and try to figure out which style of conflict resolution would be best. M takes a competitive (win–lose) style and tells Mallory that the decision is hers to make. She clearly uses the legitimate power based on her position, but Mallory also knows that M's expert and referent power will likely win the day with the prime minister given the situation. Mallory therefore minimizes his losses (perhaps building some credits for later in the process) by taking an accommodating style.

Negotiation Strategies There are two general strategies leaders must choose between when it comes to negotiations: distributive bargaining and integrative bargaining.[74] **Distributive bargaining** involves win–lose negotiating over a "fixed pie" of resources.[75] That is, when one person gains, the other person loses (also known as a *zero-sum* condition). The classic example of a negotiation with distributive bargaining is the purchase of a car. When you walk into a car dealership, there's a stated price on the side of the car that's known to be negotiable. In these circumstances though, every dollar you save is a dollar the dealership loses. Similarly, every dollar the salesperson negotiates for, you lose. Distributive bargaining is similar in nature to a competing approach to conflict resolution. Some of the most visible negotiations that have traditionally been approached with a distributive bargaining tactic are union–management labour negotiations. Whether it be automobile manufacturers, airlines, or nurses at hospitals, the negotiations for these sessions are typically viewed through a win–lose lens.

distributive bargaining

A negotiation strategy in which one person gains and the other person loses

Many negotiations within organizations, including labour–management sessions, are beginning to occur with a more integrative bargaining strategy. **Integrative bargaining** is aimed at accomplishing a win–win scenario.[76] It involves the use of problem solving and mutual respect to achieve an outcome that's satisfying for both parties. Leaders who thoroughly understand the conflict resolution style of collaboration are likely to thrive in these types of negotiations. In general, integrative bargaining is a preferable strategy whenever possible, because it allows a long-term relationship to form between the parties (because neither side feels like the loser). In addition, integrative bargaining has a tendency to produce a higher level of outcome favourability when both parties' views are considered, compared with distributive bargaining.[77]

As an example, picture a married couple negotiating where to go on vacation.[78] The husband wants to stay in a log cabin in the mountains while the wife wants to stay at a luxury resort on the beach. This would seem to be a case of distributive bargaining—one party will win and the other will lose! After much discussion, though, the couple finds that location (in the mountains) is more important to the husband and style of accommodations (luxury hotel) more important to the wife. The two can come to a solution that provides mutually beneficial outcomes to both parties—a luxury hotel in the mountains.

However, not all situations are appropriate for integrative bargaining. Integrative bargaining is most appropriate in situations in which multiple outcomes are possible, there is an adequate level of trust, and parties are willing to be flexible.[79] Please don't approach your next used-car purchase with an integrative bargaining strategy!

integrative bargaining

A negotiation strategy that achieves an outcome that is satisfying for both parties

Negotiation Stages Regardless of the strategy used, the actual negotiating process typically goes through a series of stages:[80]

- *Preparation.* Arguably the single most important stage of the negotiating process. During preparation, each party determines what its goals are for the negotiation and whether the other party has anything to offer. Each party also should determine its *best alternative to a negotiated agreement*, or **BATNA**. A BATNA describes each negotiator's bottom line. In other words, at what point are you willing to walk away? At the BATNA point, a negotiator is actually better off not negotiating at all. In their seminal book *Getting to Yes: Negotiating Without Giving In*, Roger Fisher and William Ury state that people's BATNA is the standard by which all proposed agreements should be measured.[81]

BATNA
Acronym for a negotiator's *best alternative to a negotiated agreement*

- *Exchanging information.* In this nonconfrontational process, each party makes a case for its position and attempts to put all favourable information on the table. Each party also informs the other how it has arrived at its conclusions and which issues it believes are important. When the other party is unfamiliar, this stage likely contains active listening and lots of questions. Studies show that successful negotiators ask many questions and gather much information during this stage.[82]
- *Bargaining.* This stage is the one most people imagine when think of "negotiation." Success at this stage depends mightily on how well the previous two stages have proceeded. The goal is for each party to walk away feeling like it has gained something of value (regardless of the actual bargaining strategy). During this stage, both parties likely must make concessions and give up something to get something in return. To the degree that each party keeps the other party's concerns and motives in mind, this stage should go smoothly.
- *Closing and commitment.* This stage entails the process of formalizing an agreement reached during the previous stage. For large, complex negotiations such as labour contracts established between an organization and a union, it can be a very long stage. For others, such as a negotiation between two co-workers about how they might handle their future relationship, no formal documents or contracts are required, and a simple handshake might suffice. Ideally, there will be no issues or misconceptions about the agreement arrived at during the bargaining stage. If they do exist, the negotiation process can regress to the bargaining stage, and start all over again.

  The closing and commitment stage might also be simply a recognition that the parties reached an impasse with no agreement! In this case, several options are still available, as we discuss in the Application section at the end of this chapter.

Negotiator Biases It is important for negotiators to be aware of their biases when approaching a negotiation. While there are numerous biases to be aware of, the perceived power relationship between the parties and negotiator emotions are two of the most important. Research has shown that when negotiators perceive themselves as being in a position of power in comparison to the other party, they are more likely to demand more, concede less, and behave more aggressively during negotiations—in other words, they are likely to take a more distributive approach to negotiations.[83] Similarly, when two parties perceive themselves as relatively equal in power, they take a more integrative approach to negotiations.[84] As we all know, negotiations are generally a very emotion-laden affair, and negotiator emotions can also play a large role in the ability of two parties to reach successful conclusions during bargaining.[85] (See Chapter 4 for a discussion of the ability of individuals to control their emotions during stressful times such as negotiations.) As it turns out, both positive and negative emotions can influence negotiation success in a negative way.[86] Positive emotions, while they generally lead to a more integrative bargaining approach, can also cause negotiators to be overconfident and make decisions too quickly. Negative emotions tend to lead toward a more distributive bargaining approach and lower judgment accuracy.[87]

OB FOR STUDENTS

Nine out of ten recruiters say that their initial compensation offer to a job candidate is lower than they are prepared to pay.[88] Many of you are in the midst of or starting to consider a job search as you graduate. Research has plenty to say about your ability to negotiate and secure an acceptable salary. One major issue is that the majority of us never attempt to negotiate the offered salary.[89] A second major issue is that those who do negotiate do a pretty poor job of it. Although the conventional wisdom that men negotiate more often than women is false, a study of MBA students showed that men do perhaps negotiate more effectively than their female counterparts and that these differences could account for a lot of money over time.[90] Regardless, here are some suggestions for negotiating your salary:[91]

1. Know your worth going in. You should know the approximate salaries for others within your major or functional area. You can ask your career centre for this information in many cases.
2. You need to know your "BATNA"—your best alternative to a negotiated agreement. What is the lowest possible offer that you would be willing to accept? At what point would you be willing to walk away? Negotiators with a clear BATNA generally walk away with higher results.
3. What is your goal for a salary? Do not be afraid to put this number on the table. Avoid vague responses like "I want more money," which does nothing to further the negotiation process.
4. You need to be prepared to sell yourself. What value do you bring to the table that they might not know about? If you want to convince the company that raising your offer is a win–win result, you need to be able to convince the company that your value is more significant than it thought it was.
5. Last but not least: Don't threaten to leave the table unless you are really prepared to do it. Do you indeed have a worthwhile backup plan?

Summary: Why Are Some People More Powerful Than Others?

So what explains why some people more powerful and influential than others? As shown in Figure 12-6, answering that question requires an understanding of the types of power people acquire, what kinds of influence tactics they have available to them, and how they can use that influence to alter the attitudes and behaviours of their employees. Leaders acquire both organizational (legitimate, reward, coercive) and personal (expert, referent) forms of power, which gives them the ability to influence others. They can then use that power to influence others through influence tactics. Those tactics can help achieve organizational goals or may be applied more specifically to dealing with organizational politics, conflict resolution, or negotiation situations. In the end, there are three possible responses to influence attempts: internalization, compliance, and resistance. The effectiveness of those attempts will depend on an individual's skill at performing them and how well they match the forms of power they have with the appropriate types of influence.

FIGURE 12-6

Why Are Some People More Powerful Than Others?

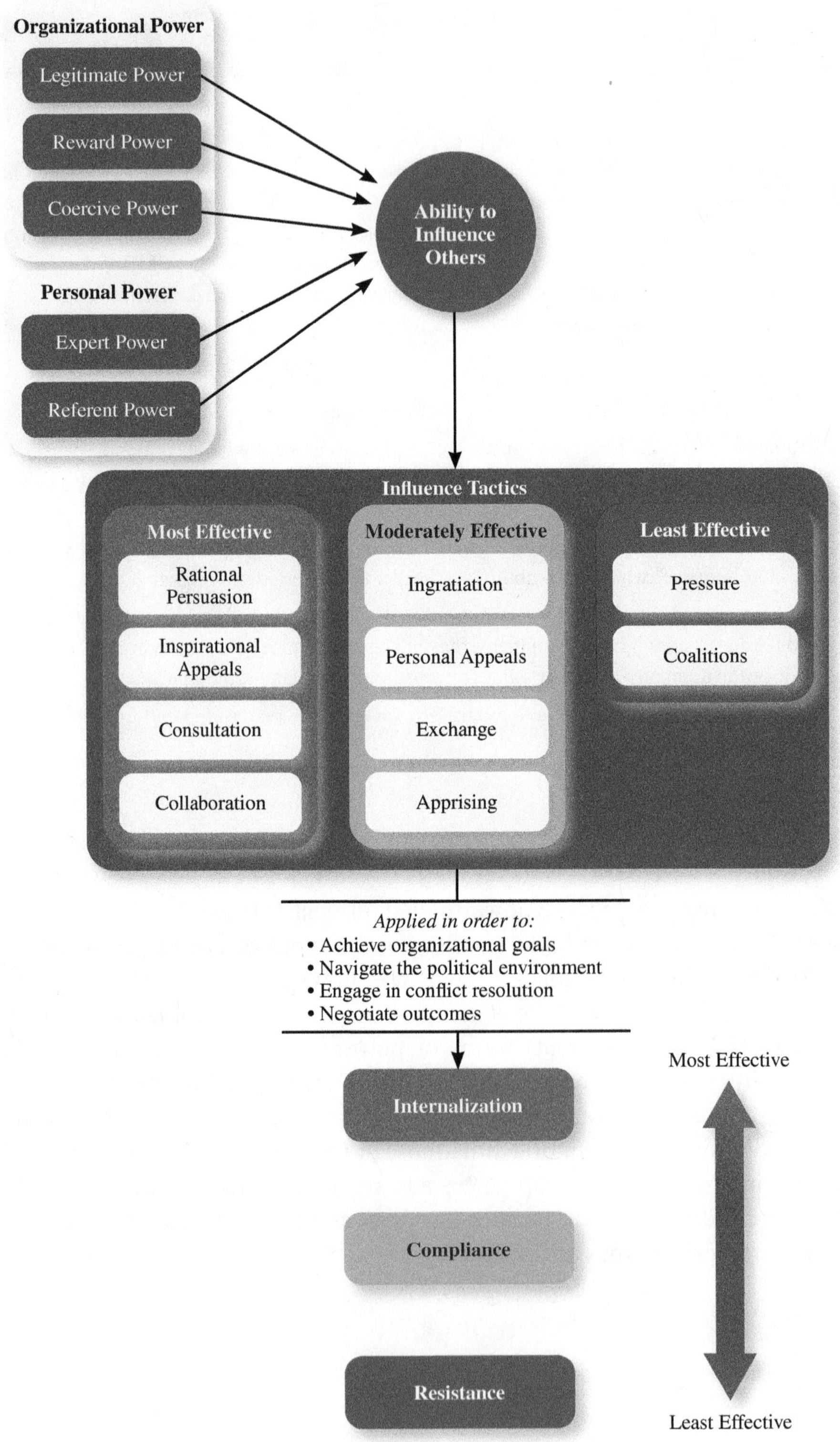

HOW IMPORTANT ARE POWER AND INFLUENCE?

How important is an individual's ability to use power and influence? In other words, does a leader's power and influence correlate with job performance and organizational commitment? Figure 12-7 summarizes the research evidence linking power and influence to job performance and organizational commitment. The figure reveals that power and influence are moderately correlated with job performance. When used correctly and focused on task-related outcomes, power and influence can create internalization in workers, such that they are both behaviourally and attitudinally focused on high levels of task performance. That internalization also helps increase citizenship behaviour, whereas the compliance associated with power and influence can decrease counterproductive behaviour. These job performance benefits make sense given that the effective use of power and influence can increase the *motivation* levels of employees, whereas the ineffective use of power and influence can increase the *stress* levels of employees.

FIGURE 12-7

Effects of Power and Influence on Performance and Commitment

Power and Influence have a moderate positive effect on Job Performance. When used effectively, they can increase internalization and compliance, which facilitates *Task Performance*. The internalization and compliance facilitated by power and influence can also increase *Citizenship Behaviour* and decrease *Counterproductive Behaviour*.

Power and Influence can have a moderate positive effect on Organizational Commitment. The use of personal forms of power, such as expert and referent, is associated with increased *Affective Commitment*. It should be noted, however, that more organizational forms of power, or hard influence tactics, can decrease that form of commitment. Not much is known about the impact of power and influence on *Continuance Commitment* or *Normative Commitment*.

Represents a strong correlation (around .50 in magnitude).

Represents a moderate correlation (around .30 in magnitude).

Represents a weak correlation (around .10 in magnitude).

Sources: R.T. Sparrowe, B.W. Soetjipto, and M.L. Kraimer, "Do Leaders' Influence Tactics Relate to Members' Helping Behavior? It Depends on the Quality of the Relationship," *Academy of Management Journal* 49 (2006), pp. 1194–1208; G. Yukl, H. Kim, and C.M. Falbe, "Antecedents of Influence Outcomes," *Journal of Applied Psychology* 81 (1996), pp. 309–17; and P.P. Carson, K.D. Carson, and C.W. Rowe, "Social Power Bases: A Meta-analytic Examination of Interrelationships and Outcomes," *Journal of Applied Social Psychology* 23 (1993), pp. 1150–69.

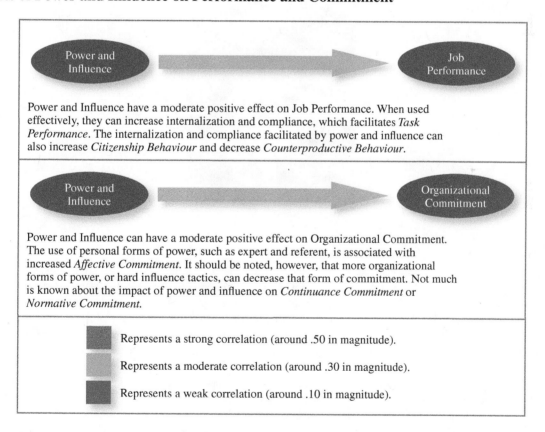

12.7 How do power and influence affect job performance and organizational commitment?

Figure 12-7 also reveals that power and influence are moderately related to organizational commitment. When a leader draws on personal sources of power, such as expert power and referent power, a stronger emotional bond can be created with the employee, boosting affective commitment. The effective use of such power should increase *job satisfaction* and a sense of *trust* in the leader, all of which are associated with increased commitment levels. As with job performance, however, it's important to note that an ineffective use of power can also decrease commitment levels. In particular, repeated uses of coercive power or repeated reliance on hard influence tactics such as pressure or coalitions could actually decrease organizational commitment levels.

OB RESEARCH IN CANADA

Courtesy of Dr. Kevin Tasa

Dr. Kevin Tasa teaches and conducts research in organizational behaviour at the Schulich School of Business at York University. It is fitting to feature Dr. Tasa in this chapter, given that his expertise is in decision making and motivational processes within team and negotiation contexts. Some of the questions that Dr. Tasa's work attempts to answer are: (1) How do the type of goals negotiators set influence their ability to create value and avoid negotiation impasses? (2) Does a person's level of confidence regarding his or her negotiation skills positively or negatively influence his or her negotiation performance? and (3) What factors determine the level of confidence in a team? According to Dr. Tasa, these questions are important because "people negotiate every day. Whether we are talking about settling a strike or deciding who is going to do the dishes, negotiation skills can help us get deals that leave everyone better off. And understanding the factors that contribute to successful outcomes in negotiation is critically important in today's business environment." For more information, look up Dr. Tasa at schulich.yorku.ca.

APPLICATION: ALTERNATIVE DISPUTE RESOLUTION

There is always the possibility that, despite a leader's best efforts, negotiations and/or conflict management will result in an impasse. In many organizations, disputes that might escalate into actual legal battles are settled through alternative dispute resolution.[92] **Alternative dispute resolution** is a process by which two parties resolve conflicts through the use of a specially trained, neutral third party. There are various types of alternative dispute resolution that offer each party more or less control over the outcomes in question.[93] Which types of resolution are chosen are generally a function of time pressures, dispute intensity, and the type of conflict involved.[94] Two of the most common forms are mediation and arbitration.

alternative dispute resolution

A process by which two parties resolve conflicts through the use of a specially trained, neutral third party

Mediation requires a third party to facilitate the dispute resolution process, though this third party has no formal authority to dictate a solution. In essence, a mediator plays the role of a neutral, objective party who listens to the arguments of each side and attempts to help two parties come to an agreement. In serious, potentially litigious situations, trained mediators offer a relatively easy and quick way out of difficult disputes. A more definite form of alternative resolution is **arbitration**, which occurs when a third party determines a binding settlement to a dispute. The arbitrator can be an individual or a group (board) whose job is to listen to the various arguments and then make a decision about the solution to the conflict. In some ways, arbitration is much riskier for both parties, because the outcome of the dispute rests solely in the arbitrator's hands. The arbitrator's role isn't to make everyone happy but rather to arrive at the most equitable solution in his or her opinion. In conventional arbitrations, arbitrators can create a solution of their choosing, mixing and matching available alternatives. In contrast, in final-offer arbitration, each party presents its fairest offer, and the arbitrator chooses the one identified as most reasonable.

mediation

A process by which a third party facilitates a dispute resolution process but with no formal authority to dictate a solution

arbitration

A process by which a third party determines a binding settlement to a dispute between two parties

The two forms of alternative dispute resolution can be voluntary or mandatory, with many companies starting to create policies that make alternative dispute resolution mandatory for employees. However, there is evidence that taking away the "voluntariness" of the process lowers employees' feelings of procedural justice (see Chapter 8).[95]

Of course, the goal of dispute resolution is always to have the two parties come to a voluntary agreement. Traditionally, mediation is the first step in alternative dispute resolution; if the mediator cannot help the two parties come to an agreement, the process continues to arbitration. Research suggests though that an opposite approach might lead to better results. That is, the two parties undergo the arbitration process, and the arbitrator makes a decision, which is placed in a sealed envelope. The two parties then go through the process of mediation; if they still can't come to an agreement, they turn to the arbiter's decision. Flipping the order resulted in significantly higher voluntary agreement rates between the two parties.[96]

TAKEAWAYS

12.1 Power is the ability to influence the behaviour of others and resist unwanted influence in return. Power is necessary, in that it gives individuals the ability to influence others.

12.2 There are potentially five types of power available to individuals within organizations. There are three organizational forms of power: Legitimate power is based on authority or position; reward power is based on the distribution of resources or benefits; and coercive power is based on the handing out of punishments. There are two personal forms of power: Expert power is derived from expertise and knowledge, whereas referent power is based on the attractiveness and charisma of the individual. These types of power can be used most effectively when the individuals are central to the work process, highly visible, have discretion, and are the sole controllers of resources and information.

12.3 Ten different influence tactics are commonly used in organizational settings. The most effective are rational persuasion, inspirational appeals, consultation, and collaboration. The least effective are pressure and the forming of coalitions. Tactics with moderate levels of effectiveness are ingratiation, personal appeals, exchange, and apprising.

12.4 Organizational politics are individual actions that are directed toward the goal of furthering a person's self-interest. Political behaviour is most likely to occur in organizational situations in which individual outcomes are uncertain.

12.5 Power and influence can be used to resolve conflicts in five distinct ways: avoidance, competing, accommodating, collaborating, and compromising. The most effective and also most difficult tactic is collaboration.

12.6 Leaders use both distributive and integrative bargaining strategies to negotiate outcomes. The process of negotiating effectively includes four steps: preparation, exchanging information, bargaining, and closing and commitment.

12.7 Power and influence have moderate positive relationships with job performance and organizational commitment. However, for these beneficial effects to be realized, leaders must wield their power effectively and rely on effective influence tactics in negotiating outcomes.

KEY TERMS

accommodating
alternative dispute resolution
apprising
arbitration
avoiding

BATNA
centrality
coalitions
coercive power
collaboration (as conflict resolution method)
collaboration (as influence method)
competing
compliance
compromise
consultation
discretion
distributive bargaining
exchange tactic
expert power
influence
ingratiation
inspirational appeal
integrative bargaining
internalization
legitimate power
mediation
negotiation
organizational politics
personal appeals
political skill
power
pressure
rational persuasion
referent power
resistance (to influence tactics)
reward power
substitutability
visibility

DISCUSSION QUESTIONS

12.1 Which forms of power do you consider to be the strongest? Which types of power do you currently have? How could you go about obtaining higher levels of the forms that you're lacking?

12.2 Who is the most influential leader you have come in contact with personally? What forms of power did they have, and which types of influence did they use to accomplish objectives?

12.3 What would it take to have a "politically free" environment? Is that possible?

12.4 Think about the last serious conflict you had with a co-worker or group member. How was that conflict resolved? Which approach did you take to resolve it?

12.5 Think of a situation in which you negotiated an agreement. Which approach did you take? Was it the appropriate one? How might the negotiation process have gone more smoothly?

CASE • CANADIAN PACIFIC RAILWAY

As was said in the chapter-opening profile, few would argue with Hunter Harrison's ability to influence how things are done within the company. In addition to restructuring the organization, Harrison has worked hard to instill a new culture built on the core values of good service, safe operations, asset optimization, cost control, and developing people (for related discussion on culture change, see Chapter 15). According to Harrison it all boils down to more personal accountability and responsibility, "it is a matter of here's your job … do it … if you don't, you aren't going to stay. That looks to me a pretty simple contract." Doug Finnson, a Teamsters vice-president who represents the running trades (e.g., locomotive engineers and conductors), noted that the number of arbitrated discipline and dismissal cases had skyrocketed in his area of the company. Brian Stevens, an official within the Unifor union, acknowledged that "Harrison has gone further, harder, and been more aggressive in disciplining and terminating employees than he did in making over CN. The Board has given him the power—he did not have that power at CN."

To communicate the new vision and to drive his message of personal accountability and responsibility home, Harrison instituted whiteboard sessions in which managers could "blue-sky" ideas. He also revived his Hunter Camps, first introduced during his time at CN Rail, as three-day retreats that brought people at all levels together, including the occasional union leader, to learn the principles straight from Harrison's mouth. The camps have provided Harrison a forum to communicate directly, thus "cutting through the mud." Harrison's new vision for the company has also affected employees in the management ranks. Traditional roles and the scope of work activities, particularly among the non-unionized management ranks (roughly 2,000), have been blurred. For example, all management employees—in addition to their administrative roles—are now required to take training and get certified to work on freight trains.

Rapid change has not been easy for the company's unionized employees. In response to CP's move toward greater efficiency and flexibility, union leaders have raised concerns about their pensions, benefits (e.g., health spending accounts) and new work rules. The unions have expressed concerns about the safety of having "office workers" being cross-trained to operate large, heavy equipment, potentially replacing conductors and locomotive engineers. Moreover, the unions allege that Harrison's changes have contributed to "dysfunctional working conditions" within the company, and have raised concerns over work schedules, fatigue management (e.g., work breaks, mandatory rest periods), and the installation of crew-recording devices in train cabs. Complicating matters for the unions has been the fact the current federal government will not tolerate a lengthy rail strike, and is ready to pass back-to-work legislation should a work stoppage threaten economic recovery within Canada.

12.1 Analyze the different influence tactics available to Hunter, and discuss how these options relate to his power source(s). Which of his available tactics have been used thus far to bring about change at the company? Do you think his approach will lead to internalization, compliance, or resistance? Explain why.

12.2 Analyze the different influence tactics available to the unions, and discuss how these options relate to their power source(s). If the threat of a strike is muted due to potential intervention by the federal government, then what other influence tactics are likely to be used? Explain.

12.3 When negotiating, what approach do you feel would be most effective for the company? For the unions involved? Is it possible to achieve a win–win solution? Explain.

12.4 What are the risks in this situation? Consider this question from the perspective of the company, of the unions, and of the federal government. Consider topics covered in other chapters

Sources: Canadian Pacific Railway Ltd. website, www.cpr.ca/en/about-cp/our-history, retrieved February 12, 2015; en.wikipedia.org/wiki/Canadian_Pacific_Railway, retrieved February 12, 2015; Gordon Pitts, "Turnaround Ace: Inside the Hunter Harrison Era at CP Railway," *The Globe and Mail*, April 25, 2014, www.theglobeandmail.com/report-on-business/rob-magazine/hunter-harrison-cp-report-on-business-magazine/article18190120, retrieved February 15, 2015); Kristine Owram, "CP Rail's Hunter Harrison: 'We're Doing Things That People Didn't Think Were Imaginable,'" *Financial Post*, October 4, 2014, business.financialpost.com/2014/10/04/cp-rails-hunter-harrison-were-doing-things-that-people-didnt-think-were-imaginable, retrieved February 15, 2015; "Federal Government Orders End to CP Rail Strike," *CTV News*, June 11, 2012, www.ctvnews.ca/federal-government-orders-end-to-cp-rail-strike-1.832408, retrieved February 15, 2015; Alison Bailey, "Union Sees CP Rail Training Program as a Safety Problem," *Vancouver News 1130*, July 22, 2014, www.news1130.com/2014/07/22/union-sees-cp-rail-training-program-as-safety-problem/comment-page-1, retrieved February 12, 2015; Kyle Bakx, "CP Rail Encourages Office Workers to Learn How to Drive Trains: Safety Concerns Arise over Training, Qualifications, and Experience Level, as Possible Strike Looms," *CBC News*, February 2, 2015, www.cbc.ca/news/business/cp-rail-encourages-office-workers-to-learn-how-to-drive-trains-1.2935065, retrieved February 15, 2015; Kristine Owram, *Financial Post*, February 11, 2015, business.financialpost.com/2015/02/11/canadian-pacific-railway-ltd-prepares-for-weekend-strike-amid-ongoing-talks, retrieved February 15, 2015; Eric Atkins, "'Difficult' CP Labour Dispute Nears Strike Deadline," *The Globe and Mail*, February 13, 2015, www.theglobeandmail.com/report-on-business/difficult-cp-labour-dispute-nears-strike-deadline/article22992898, retrieved February 15, 2015.

EXERCISE • LOBBYING FOR INFLUENCE

The purpose of this exercise is to give you experience in using influence tactics to modify the behaviour of others. Follow these steps:

12.1 During this exercise, your objective is to get other people in the class to give you their points. If you get more than 50 percent of the total number of points distributed to the whole class, you'll win. Each person in the class has a different number of points, as shown in the class list. You can keep or give away your points in whatever manner you choose, as long as you follow the rules for each round of the process. There are five rounds, described next.

Round 1. In this round, you will write memos to your classmates. You can say whatever you want in your memos, and write them to whomever you choose, but for the 10-minute writing period, there will be no talking, only writing. You will deliver all your messages at one time, at the end of the 10 minutes.

Round 2. In this round, you will respond in writing to the messages you received in the first round. You can also write new memos as you see fit. Again, there is to be no talking! At the end of 15 minutes, you can distribute your memos.

Round 3. In round 3, you can talk as much as you like. You will have 15 minutes to talk with anyone about anything.

Round 4. In this round, you will create ballots to distribute your points any way you see fit. To distribute your points, put a person's name on an index card, along with the number of points you want that person to have. If you choose to keep any of your points, put your own name on the card, along with the number of points you want to keep. Do not hand in your cards until asked to do so by your instructor.

Round 5. If there is no clear winner, round 5 will be used to repeat steps 3 and 4.

12.2 Class discussion (whether in groups or as a class) should focus on the following questions:

- What kinds of social influence attempts did you make during this exercise?
- How successful were you at influencing others to go along with you?
- What kinds of influence did others use on you?
- What was the most successful way you saw someone else use influence during the memo-writing and discussion sections?
- What other factors determined how you voted?

Source: Adapted from "Voting for Dollars" in the Instructor's Manual for D.A. Whetten and K.S. Cameron, *Developing Management Skills*, 7th ed. (Englewood Cliffs, NJ: Prentice Hall, 2007).

OB ASSESSMENTS • POLITICAL SKILL

How much political skill do you have? This assessment is designed to measure two dimensions of political skill. Please write a number next to each statement that indicates the extent to which it accurately describes your attitude toward work while you were on the job. Alternatively, consider the statements in reference to school rather than work. Answer each question using the response scale provided. Then add up your answers for each of the dimensions.

1 Strongly Disagree	2 Disagree	3 Neutral	4 Agree	5 Strongly Agree	
1. I spend a lot of time and effort networking with others.					_____
2. I know a lot of important people and am well connected.					_____
3. I am good at using my connections and networks to make things happen.					_____
4. I have developed a large network of colleagues and associates whom I can call on for support when I really need to get things done.					_____

(*Continued*)

5. I spend a lot of time making connections.	_____
6. I always seem to instinctively know the right thing to say or do to influence others.	_____
7. I have a good intuition or savvy about how to present myself to others.	_____
8. I am particularly good at sensing the motivations and hidden agendas of others.	_____
9. I pay close attention to people's facial expressions.	_____
10. I understand people very well.	_____

Scoring and Interpretation

Networking ability. Add up items 1–5. _________

Social astuteness. Add up items 6–10. _________

For networking ability, scores of 18 or more are above average and scores of 17 or less are below average. For social astuteness, scores of 19 or more are above average and scores of 18 or less are below average. Remember, when interpreting your scores on these assessments it is important to consider the *reliability* and *validity* of these tools (see Chapter 1, ***OB Assessments***).

Source: Adapted from G.R. Ferris, D.C. Treadway, R.W. Kolodinsky, W.A. Hochwarter, C.J. Kacmar, C. Douglas, and D.D. Frink, "Development and Validation of the Political Skill Inventory," *Journal of Management* 31 (2005), pp. 126–52. Reproduced with permission of Sage Publications, Inc. via Copyright Clearance Center.

Leadership Styles and Behaviours

CHAPTER 13

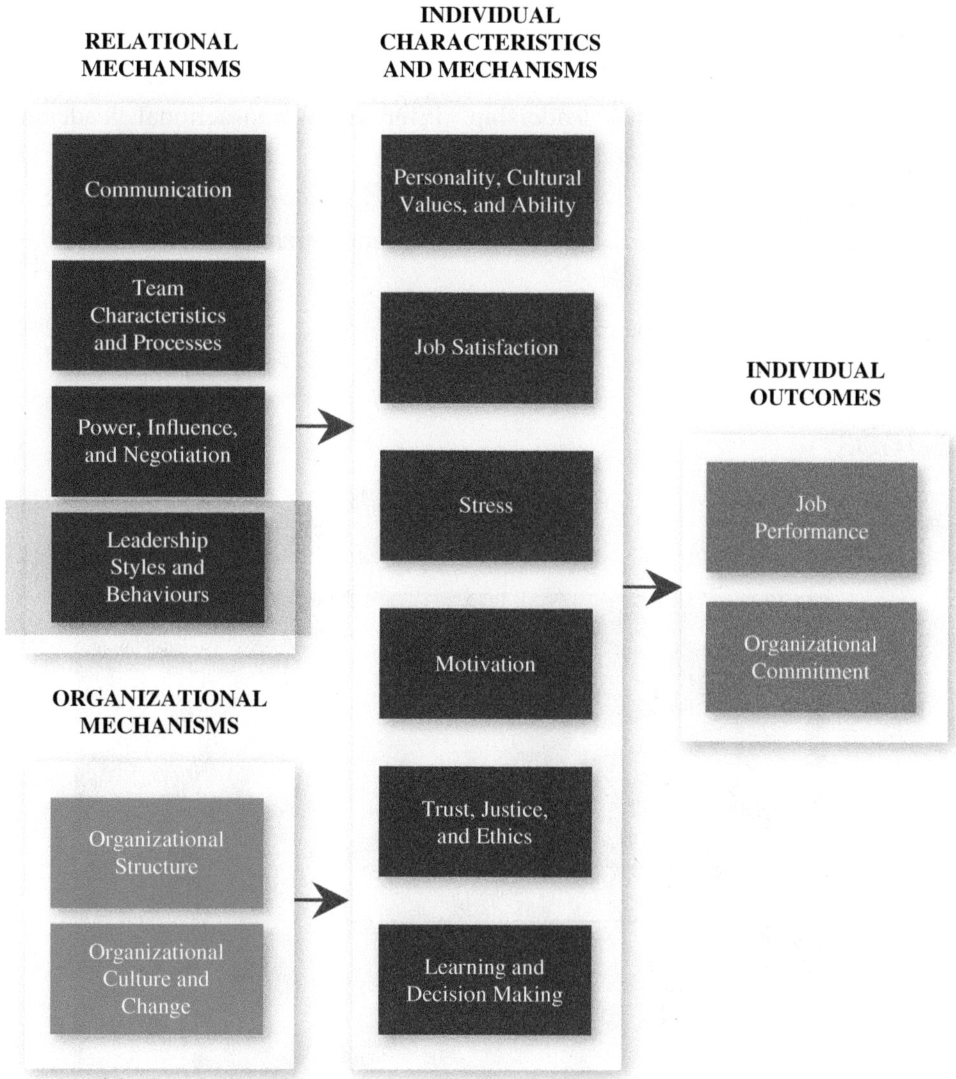

LEARNING OUTCOMES

After reading this chapter, you should be able to answer the following questions:

13.1 What is leadership and what does it mean for a leader to be "effective"?

13.2 What traits and characteristics are related to leader emergence and leader effectiveness?

13.3 What four styles can leaders use to make decisions, and what factors combine to make these styles more effective in a given situation?

13.4 What two dimensions capture most of the day-to-day leadership behaviours in which leaders engage?

13.5 How does transformational leadership differ from transactional leadership, and which behaviours set it apart?

13.6 How does leadership affect job performance and organizational commitment?

13.7 Can leaders be trained to be more effective?

Steve Jobs

Steve Jobs will be remembered for his extraordinary vision and leadership, forever changing the way we interact with technology.

© AP-Jeff Chiu/The Canadian Press

Whether Steve Jobs will be remembered as an inventor, an entrepreneur, or an "evil genius,"[1] most will agree that this was a leader who had great vision. Not only was Jobs a co-founder and CEO of Apple, one of the most innovative and successful companies in the world, but his influence changed the way we experience and interact with technology.

In 1975, at age 20, Jobs along with Steve Wozniak started Apple. Over the next decade, Apple grew from "two guys in a garage" into a major corporation of 4,000 employees, producing one of the first successful lines of personal computers.[2] In 1984, Jobs, who personally led the project team, unveiled the "Mac," the Macintosh personal computer.[3] The Mac's unique appeal was in its mouse-driven, graphical user interface (the first computer to do this, predating Microsoft's Windows environment) that engaged users and transformed how they related to the computer.[4]

Then, at the pinnacle of his success, Jobs lost a power struggle with Apple's board of directors and was fired![5] Years later, he reflected on that time, saying, "What had been the focus of my entire adult life was gone, and it was devastating. But something slowly began to dawn on me. I still loved what I did. The turn of events at Apple had not changed that one bit. I'd been rejected but I was still in love. And so I decided to start over."[6]

For Steve Jobs "starting over" meant spending the next 12 years involved in some very creative technical endeavours. During this period, he founded another computer company, NeXT Computer.[7] Also during that period, Jobs bought Lucasfilm's computer graphics division, which he later renamed Pixar Studios. With the help of Disney, in 1995 Pixar released its first computer-animated feature film, *Toy Story*. This turned out to be a box-office hit and instantly brought fame and critical acclaim to Pixar. In the years that followed, a number of films were produced, including *Finding Nemo*, *The Incredibles*, *Ratatouille*, *WALL-E*, *Up*, and *Toy Story 3*.[8] Eventually Disney ended up buying Pixar in an all-stock purchase, effectively making Jobs the largest single shareholder of Disney stock and giving him a seat on the board of directors.[9]

Jobs's "walk in the wilderness" ended with a triumphant return to Apple. In 1997, after more than a decade of declining fortunes and on the brink of bankruptcy, Apple agreed to buy NeXT and restore Steve Jobs's role with the company, initially as a technical advisor and then as CEO in 2000.[10] With the purchase of NeXT, much of the company's technology found its way into Apple products, most notably NeXTSTEP, which evolved into Mac OS X (and, in turn, iOS).[11]

It was during this renewal that Jobs's extraordinary vision and leadership engineered one of the most dramatic corporate turnarounds in history.[12] Exciting new product lines, such as the iMac computer, characterized the new Apple. But the transformed Apple was much more than computers. With the introduction of the iPod portable music player, iTunes digital music software, and the iTunes Store, the company made forays into consumer electronics and music distribution. Apple entered the cellular phone business with the introduction of the iPhone, which also included the features of the iPod and, with its own mobile browser, revolutionized the mobile browsing scene.[13] More recently, iPad, combining features of a laptop with those of a portable media player, has been a runaway success.

The Apple Store has exposed the company and its products to millions of new users, and fortified one of the world's more venerable brands. On August 10, 2011, for the very first time, Apple surpassed Exxon Mobil Corp. to seize the title of world's most valuable company.[14] Two weeks later, Steve Jobs officially resigned as CEO of Apple for health reasons.[15] He passed away October 5, 2011. Even today, his leadership continues to affect employees at Apple in profound ways.[16]

13.1 What is leadership and what does it mean for a leader to be "effective"?

LEADERSHIP: STYLES AND BEHAVIOURS

In business circles perhaps no subject is more written about than that of leadership. A quick search on Amazon.com of the topic will generate a list of more than 130,000 books! That number doesn't even count the myriad videos, podcasts, CDs, and other items designed to help people become better leaders. Given all the interest, a natural question arises: "What exactly is a leader?"

We define **leadership** as the use of power and influence to direct the activities of followers toward goal achievement.[17] That direction can affect followers' interpretation of events, the organization of their work activities, their commitment to key goals, their relationships with other followers, or their access to cooperation and support from other work units.[18] In this chapter we will discover that there are many different types of leaders, many of whom can excel given the right circumstances. In the case of Steve Jobs, his power was derived from his history with Apple, his technical and design expertise, and his remarkable charisma. Over his career, Jobs clearly used his power and influence effectively, and this was why Apple had its dramatic turnaround between 1997 and 2011, and why his legacy continues.

leadership
The use of power and influence to direct the activities of followers toward goal achievement

Of course, most leaders can't judge their performance by pointing to the number of companies they have created. Fortunately, leader effectiveness can be gauged in a number of ways. Leaders might be judged by objective evaluations of unit performance, such as profit margins, market share, sales, returns on investment, productivity, quality, costs in relation to budgeted expenditures, and so forth.[19] If those sorts of indices are unavailable, the leader's superiors may judge the performance of the unit on a more subjective basis. Other approaches to judging leader effectiveness centre more on followers, including indices such as absenteeism, retention of talented employees, grievances filed, requests for transfer, and so forth.[20] Those sorts of indices can be complemented by employee surveys that assess the perceived performance of the leader, the perceived respect and legitimacy of the leader, and employee commitment, satisfaction, and psychological well-being. The top panel of Table 13-1 provides one example of these sorts of measures.

One source of complexity when judging leader effectiveness, particularly with more subjective, employee-centred approaches, is "Whom do you ask?" The members of a given unit often disagree about how effective their leader is. **Leader–member exchange theory**, which describes how leader–member relationships develop over time on a dyadic basis, can explain why those differences exist.[21] The theory argues that new leader–member relationships are typically marked by a **role taking** phase, during which a manager describes role expectations to an employee and the employee attempts to fulfill those expectations with his or her job behaviours.[22] In this period of sampling and experimentation, the leader tries to get a feel for the talent and motivation levels of the employee. For some employees, that initial role taking phase may eventually be supplemented by **role making**, during which the employee's own expectations for the dyad get mixed in with those of the leader.[23] The role making process is marked by a free-flowing exchange in which the leader offers more opportunities and resources and the employee contributes more activities and effort.

TABLE 13-1

Employee-Centred Measures of Leader Effectiveness

Unit-Focused Approach
Ask all members of the unit to fill out the following survey items, then average the responses across the group to get a measure of leader effectiveness.
1. My supervisor is effective in meeting our job-related needs.
2. My supervisor uses methods of leadership that are satisfying.
3. My supervisor gets us to do more than we expected to do.
4. My supervisor is effective in representing us to higher authority.
5. My supervisor works with us in a satisfactory way.
6. My supervisor heightens our desire to succeed.
7. My supervisor is effective in meeting organizational requirements.
8. My supervisor increases our willingness to try harder.
9. My supervisor leads a group that is effective.
Dyad-Focused Approach
Ask members of the unit to fill out the following survey items in reference to their particular relationship with the leader. The responses are not averaged across the group; rather, differences across people indicate differentiation into "ingroups" and "outgroups" within the unit.
1. I always know how satisfied my supervisor is with what I do.
2. My supervisor understands my problems and needs well enough.
3. My supervisor recognizes my potential.
4. My supervisor would use his/her power to help me solve work problems.
5. I can count on my supervisor to "bail me out" at his/her expense if I need it.
6. My working relationship with my supervisor is extremely effective.
7. I have enough confidence in my supervisor to defend and justify his/her decisions when he/she is not present to do so.

Sources: Adapted from B. Bass and B. Avolio, *MLQ Manual* (Menlo Park, CA: Mind Garden, Inc., 2004); and G.B. Graen and M. Uhl-Bien, "Relationship-Based Approach to Leadership: Development of Leader–Member Exchange (LMX) Theory of Leadership over 25 Years: Applying a Multi-level Multi-domain Perspective," *Leadership Quarterly* 6 (1995), pp. 219–47.

leader–member exchange theory
A theory describing how leader–member relationships develop over time on a dyadic basis

role taking
The phase in a leader–follower relationship when a leader provides an employee with job expectations and the follower tries to meet those expectations

role making

The phase in a leader–follower relationship when a follower voices his or her own expectations for the relationship, resulting in a free-flowing exchange of opportunities and resources for activities and effort

Over time, the role taking and role making processes result in two general types of leader–member dyads, as shown in Figure 13-1. One type is the "high-quality exchange" dyad, marked by the frequent exchange of information, influence, latitude, support, and attention. Those dyads form the leader's "ingroup" and are characterized by higher levels of communication, mutual trust, respect, and obligation.[24] The other type is the "low-quality exchange" dyad, marked by a more limited exchange of information, influence, latitude, support, and attention. Those dyads form the leader's "outgroup" and are characterized by lower levels of communication, trust, respect, and obligation.[25] Tests of the theory suggest that employees who are competent, likeable, and similar to the leader in personality will be more likely to end up in the leader's ingroup; those factors have even greater impact than age, gender, or racial similarity.[26] These ingroup relationships can be very powerful attachments for some workers. Research suggests that employees are less likely to leave an organization when they have a high LMX relationship with a specific leader, but they are more likely to leave following a leadership succession.[27] Leader–member exchange theory also suggests that judgments of leader effectiveness should gauge how effective the most critical leader–member dyads appear to be. The bottom panel of Table 13-1 provides one example of this sort of measure, with more agreement indicating a higher-quality exchange relationship and thus higher levels of leader effectiveness on a dyadic basis.[28] Two recent meta-analyses have found that employees with higher-quality exchange relationships have higher levels of job performance and exhibit more organizational citizenship behaviours on average.[29] It should be noted, though, that the development of high-LMX relationships has proven more effective in individualistic (Western) cultures than in collectivistic (Asian) cultures.[30]

FIGURE 13-1

Leader–Member Exchange Theory

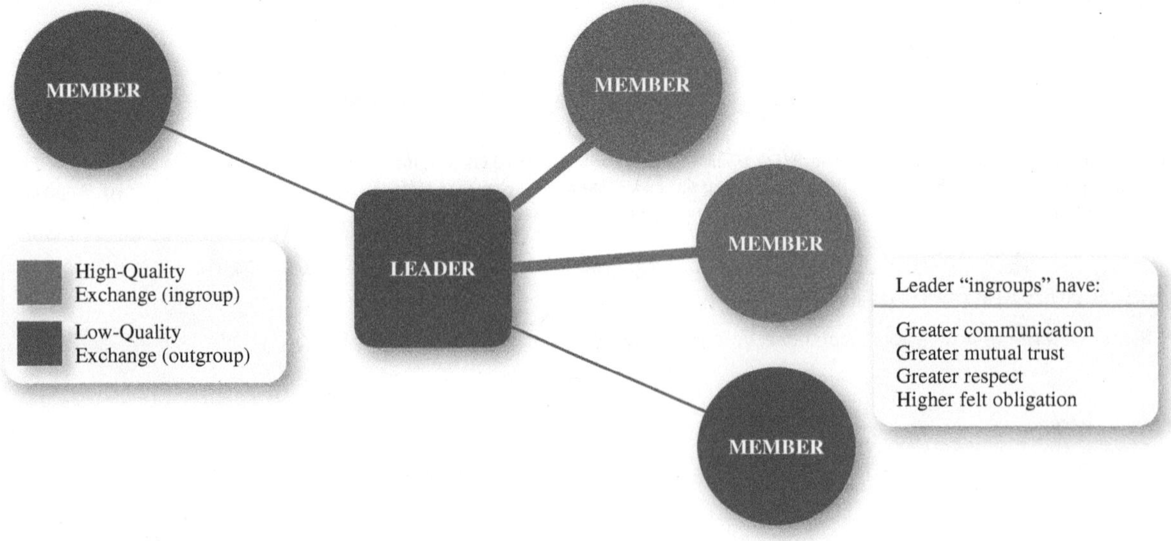

13.2 What traits and characteristics are related to leader emergence and leader effectiveness?

WHY ARE SOME LEADERS MORE EFFECTIVE THAN OTHERS?

For our purposes, **leader effectiveness** will be defined as the degree to which the leader's actions result in the achievement of the unit's goals, the continued commitment of the unit's employees, and the development of mutual trust, respect, and obligation in leader–member dyads. Now that we've described what it means for a leader to be effective, we turn to the critical question in this chapter: "Why are some leaders more effective than others?" That is, why exactly are some leaders viewed as more effective on a unit-wide basis, and why exactly are some leaders better at fostering high-quality exchange relationships? As far back as 1904, research on leadership has attempted to answer such questions by looking for particular traits or characteristics of effective leaders.[31] The search for traits and characteristics is consistent with "great person" theories of leadership that suggest that "leaders are born, not made."[32] Early research in this area frequently focused on physical features (e.g., gender, height, physical attractiveness, energy level), whereas subsequent research focused more on personality and ability (see Chapter 4 for more discussion of such issues).

leader effectiveness

The degree to which the leader's actions result in the achievement of the unit's goals, the continued commitment of the unit's employees, and the development of mutual trust, respect, and obligation in leader–member dyads

After a century of research, leadership scholars now acknowledge that there is no generalizable profile of effective leaders from a trait perspective.[33] In fact, most studies have concluded that traits are more predictive of **leader emergence** (i.e., who becomes a leader in the first place) than they are of leader effectiveness (i.e., how well people actually do in a leadership role).

leader emergence

The process of becoming a leader in the first place

Table 13-2 reviews some of the traits and characteristics found to be correlated with leader emergence and leader effectiveness. Although a number of traits and characteristics are relevant to leadership, two limitations of this work have caused leadership research to move in a different direction. First, many of the trait–leadership correlations are weak, particularly when leader effectiveness serves as the outcome. Second, the focus on leader traits has less practical relevance than a focus on leader actions. Although research shows that traits can seemingly have an effect on leader effectiveness, these effects are generally explained much more strongly by leader behaviour.[34] What exactly can leaders *do* that can make them more effective? This chapter reviews three types of leader actions: decision-making styles, day-to-day behaviours, and behaviours that fall outside of a leader's typical duties.

TABLE 13-2

Traits/Characteristics Related to Leader Emergence and Effectiveness

Description of Trait/Characteristic	Linked to Emergence?	Linked to Effectiveness?
High conscientiousness	√	
Low agreeableness	√	
Low neuroticism		
High openness to experience	√	√
High extraversion	√	√
High general cognitive ability	√	√
High energy level	√	√
High stress tolerance	√	√
High self-confidence	√	√

Sources: Adapted from T.A. Judge, J.E. Bono, R. Ilies, and M.W. Gerhardt, "Personality and Leadership: A Qualitative and Quantitative Review," *Journal of Applied Psychology* 87 (2002), pp. 765–80; T.A. Judge, A.E. Colbert, and R. Ilies, "Intelligence and Leadership: A Quantitative Review and Test of Theoretical Propositions," *Journal of Applied Psychology* 89 (2004), pp. 542–52; G. Yukl, *Leadership in Organizations*, 4th ed. (Englewood Cliffs, NJ: Prentice Hall, 1998).

13.3 What four styles can leaders use to make decisions, and what factors combine to make these styles more effective in a given situation?

Leader Decision-Making Styles

Of course, one of the most important things leaders do is make decisions. Think of the job you currently hold or the last job you had. Now picture your boss. How many decisions did he or she have to make in a given week? How did he or she go about making those decisions? A leader's decision-making style reflects the process the leader uses to generate and choose from a set of alternatives to solve a problem (see Chapter 9 on learning and decision making for more discussion of such issues). Decision-making styles capture *how* a leader decides as opposed to *what* a leader decides.

The most important element of a leader's decision-making style is this: Does the leader decide most things for him- or herself, or does the leader involve others in the process? We've probably all had bosses (or professors, or even parents) who made virtually all decisions by themselves, stopping by to announce what had happened once the call had been made. We've probably also had other bosses (or professors, or parents) who tended to do the opposite—involving us, asking our opinion, or seeking our vote even when we didn't care about what was being discussed. It turns out that this issue of leader versus follower control can be used to define some specific decision-making styles. Figure 13-2 shows those styles, arranged on a continuum from high follower control to high leader control.

FIGURE 13-2

Leader Decision-Making Styles

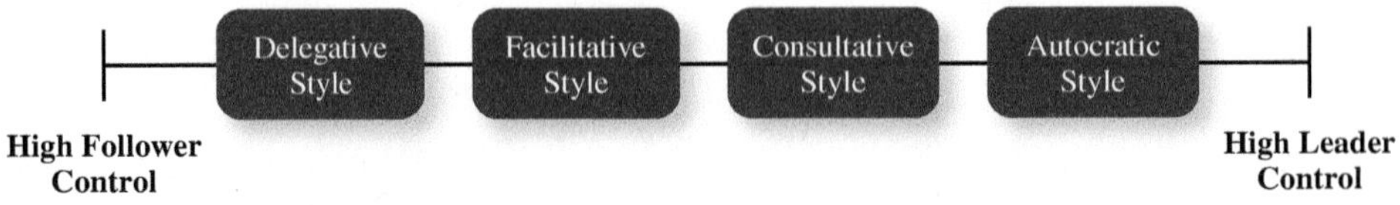

Defining the Styles With an **autocratic style**, the leader makes the decision alone without asking for the opinions or suggestions of the employees in the work unit.[35] The employees may provide information that the leader needs but are not asked to generate or evaluate potential solutions. In fact, they may not even be told about the decision that needs to be made, knowing only that the leader wants information for some reason. This decision-making style seems to be a favourite of Fiat-Chrysler CEO Sergio Marchionne, who is doing his best to make sure decisions are made extraordinarily quickly at Chrysler—and he's doing that by making them himself. Marchionne has flattened Chrysler's organizational chart with him at the top and has 25 direct reports (not counting 21 at Fiat). One might think this would cause a major bottleneck with regard to decisions, but Marchionne swears that speed is the only thing that will save Chrysler at this point and he is always within reach through the use of one of his six BlackBerrys. Marchionne says, "BlackBerrys are divine instruments. They [his direct reports] have access to me 24/7." The CEO is known for making decisions within minutes or even seconds.[36]

autocratic style

A leadership style in which the leader makes the decision alone without asking for opinions or suggestions of the employees in the work unit

Sergio Marchionne, CEO of Fiat-Chrysler, is known for his autocratic and speedy decision-making style.

© Andrew Harrer/Bloomberg via Getty Images

The next two styles in Figure 13-2 offer more employee involvement. With a **consultative style**, the leader presents the problem to individual employees or a group of employees, asking for their opinions and suggestions before ultimately making the decision him- or herself.[37] With this style, employees do "have a say" in the process, but the ultimate authority still rests with the leader. That ultimate authority changes with a **facilitative style**, in which the leader presents the problem to a group of employees and seeks consensus on a solution, making sure that his or her own opinion receives no more weight than anyone else's.[38] With this style, the leader is more facilitator than decision maker. Robert W. Selander, executive vice-chair of MasterCard, said he had learned over time to encourage discussion in a group. "From sort of a style standpoint, I prefer to do what I call more of a consensus style of decision-making," he said. "So when I'm around the table with our executive committee, the senior leadership of the company, I could easily make a bilateral decision. You're knowledgeable about your area. I may have the best knowledge about your area or second best around the table. You and I agree. Let's get on with it. What we haven't done is we haven't benefited from the wisdom, the insight, and the experience of the others around the table. And while they may not have as much insight or knowledge about your area as you do, there's a chance that we missed something. So I try to get more engagement and discussion around topics and avoid what I would call bilateralism. I think what happens is sometimes you get an insight that's startling and important and affects the decision, but you also get participative involvement so that there is buy-in and a recognition of how we got to that decision. It's not as if the boss went off in a corner and waved a magic wand and, bang, out came the decision."[39]

consultative style

A leadership style in which the leader presents the problem to employees asking for their opinions and suggestions before ultimately making the decision him- or herself

facilitative style

A leadership style in which the leader presents the problem to a group of employees and seeks consensus on a solution, making sure his or her own opinion receives no more weight than anyone else's

With a **delegative style**, the leader gives an individual employee or a group of employees the responsibility for making the decision within some set of specified boundary conditions.[40] The leader plays no role in the deliberations unless asked, though he or she may offer encouragement and provide necessary resources behind the scenes. "I think the most difficult transition for anybody from being a worker bee to a manager is this issue of delegation," says Tachi Yamada, president of the Bill and Melinda Gates Foundation's Global Health Program. "What do you give up? How can you have the team do what you would do yourself without your doing it? If you're a true micromanager and you basically stand over everybody and guide their hands to do everything, you don't have enough hours in the day to do what the whole team needs to do."[41] Daniel Amos, CEO and chair of Aflac, also believes strongly in a delegative style. He says, "My theory is that when you start telling people what to do, they no longer are responsible; you are. I'll give them my opinion and say; 'Look, this is my opinion, but if you choose that and you fail, you're not blaming it on me. It is your fault.' I think it makes them stronger."[42]

delegative style

A leadership style in which the leader gives the employee the responsibility for making decisions within some set of specified boundary conditions

When Are the Styles Most Effective? Which decision-making style is best? As you may have guessed, there is no one decision-making style that's effective across all situations, and all styles have their pluses and minuses. There are many factors to consider when leaders choose a decision-making style.[43] The most obvious is the quality of the resulting decision, because making the correct decision is the ultimate means of judging the leader. However, leaders also have to consider whether employees will accept and commit to their decision. Research studies have repeatedly shown that allowing employees to participate in decision making increases their job satisfaction.[44] Such participation also helps develop employees' own decision-making skills.[45]

Of course, such participation has a downside for employees, because it takes up time. Many employees view meetings as an interruption of their work. One recent study found that employees spend, on average, six hours a week in scheduled meetings, and that time spent in meetings relates negatively to job satisfaction when employees don't depend on others in their jobs, focus on their own task accomplishment, and believe meetings are run ineffectively.[46] Diane Bryant, CIO at Intel, argues that "You need people who are critical to making the decisions on the agenda, not people who are there only because they'll be impacted. At Intel, if we see someone who doesn't need to be there, people will say, 'Bob, I don't think we need you here. Thanks for coming.'"[47] Similarly, executives at GM are trying to change the slow bureaucratic culture that has hampered the automaker for decades—the company is known for decisions having to be made by committee. Once, they even appointed a committee to take a look at how many committee meetings should be held![48]

How can leaders effectively manage their choice of decision-making styles? The **time-driven model of leadership** offers one potential guide.[49] It suggests that the focus should shift away from autocratic, consultative, facilitative, and delegative *leaders* to autocratic, consultative, facilitative, and delegative *situations*. More specifically, the model suggests that seven factors combine to make some decision-making styles more effective in a given situation and other styles less effective. Those seven factors include:

- *Decision significance.* Is the decision significant to the success of the project or the organization?
- *Importance of commitment.* Is it important that employees "buy in" to the decision?
- *Leader expertise.* Does the leader have significant knowledge or expertise regarding the problem?
- *Likelihood of commitment.* How likely is it that employees will trust the leader's decision and commit to it?
- *Shared objectives.* Do employees share and support the same objectives, or do they have an agenda of their own?
- *Employee expertise.* Do the employees have significant knowledge or expertise regarding the problem?
- *Teamwork skills.* Do the employees have the ability to work together to solve the problem, or will they struggle with conflicts or inefficiencies?

time-driven model of leadership

A leadership model in which the focus shifts away from autocratic, consultative, facilitative, and delegative *leaders* to autocratic, consultative, facilitative, and delegative *situations*, and in which several factors combine to make some decision-making styles more effective in a given situation and others less effective

Figure 13-3 illustrates how these seven factors can be used to determine the most effective decision-making style in a given situation. The figure asks whether the levels of each of the seven factors are high (H) or low (L). The figure functions like a funnel, moving from left to right, each answer taking you closer to the recommended style (dashes mean that a given factor can be skipped for that combination). Although the model seems complex at first glance, the principles within it are straightforward. Autocratic styles are reserved for decisions that are insignificant or for which employee commitment is unimportant. The only exception is when the leader's expertise is high and the leader is trusted. An autocratic style in these situations should result in an accurate decision that makes the most efficient use of employees' time. Delegative styles should be reserved for circumstances in which employees have strong teamwork skills and are not likely to commit blindly to whatever decision the leader provides. Deciding between the remaining two styles—consultative and facilitative—is more nuanced and requires a more complete consideration of all seven factors.

FIGURE 13-3

The Time-Driven Model of Leadership

START HERE

Decision Significance	Importance of Commitment	Leader Expertise	Likelihood of Commitment	Shared Objectives	Employee Expertise	Teamwork Skills	
H	H	H	H	-	-	-	Autocratic
			L	H	H	H	Delegative
						L	Consultative
					L	-	
				L	-	-	
		L	H	H	H	H	Facilitative
						L	Consultative
					L	-	
				L	-	-	
			L	H	H	H	Facilitative
						L	Consultative
					L	-	
				L	-	-	
	L	H	-	-	-	-	Autocratic
		L	-	H	H	H	Facilitative
						L	Consultative
					L	-	
				L	-	-	
L	H	-	H	-	-	-	Autocratic
			L	-	-	H	Delegative
						L	Facilitative
	L	-	-	-	-	-	Autocratic

END HERE

Source: Adapted from V.H. Vroom, "Leadership and the Decision-Making Process," *Organizational Dynamics* 28 (2000), pp. 82–94.

For our earlier example of Sergio Marchionne, decision significance is high, importance of commitment is low, and leader expertise is high, so he adopts an autocratic decision style. However, for Jack Griffin, CEO of Time Inc., autocratic decision making didn't seem to go over too well. Griffin became known within the company for his "imperious" decision-making behaviour. For example, he insisted that every magazine include a masthead with his name at the top (an extra page that cost the company about $5 million a year) almost right after hundreds of employees were laid off—a decision that used to be left up to individual editors. A source within the company was quoted as saying, "Time Inc. has long operated on the collegial consensus approach and I don't think that was Jack's strength."[50] With magazine publishing operating during such a precarious time, we would label decision significance as high, importance of commitment as high, and the leader not appearing to have expertise in the subject matter of the decisions. As a result, his autocratic style led to a rebellion by those working for him and his termination only six months after his appointment. A key point about Figure 13-3 is that unless a leader is an expert with regard to the focus of the decision, autocratic decisions are not the right style to choose.

Research tends to support many of the time-driven model's propositions, particularly when it uses practising managers as participants.[51] For example, one study asked managers to recall past decisions, the context surrounding those decisions, and the eventual successes (or failures) of their decisions.[52] When managers used the decision-making styles recommended by the model, those decisions were rated as successful 68 percent of the time. When managers went against the model's prescriptions, their decisions were rated as successful only 22 percent of the time. It's also interesting to note that studies suggest that managers tend to choose the style recommended by the model only around 40 percent of the time and exhibit less variation in styles than the model suggests they should.[53] In particular, managers seem to overuse the consultative style and underutilize autocratic and facilitative styles. Sheila Lirio Marcelo, the CEO of Care.com, takes a unique approach, actually letting her staff know what type of decisions will be made prior to each meeting. "We do Type 1, Type 2, Type 3 decisions," she said. "Type 1 decisions are the decision-maker's sole decision—dictatorial [autocratic]. Type 2: people can provide input, and then the person can still make the decision [consultative]. Type 3, it's consensus [facilitative]. It's a great way to efficiently solve a problem."[54]

13.4 What two dimensions capture most of the day-to-day leadership behaviours in which leaders engage?

Day-to-Day Leadership Behaviours

Leaving aside how they go about making decisions, what do leaders *do* on a day-to-day basis? When you think of bosses you've had, what behaviours did they tend to perform as part of their daily leadership responsibilities?

A series of studies at Ohio State in the 1950s attempted to answer that question. Working under grants from the Office of Naval Research and the International Harvester Company, the studies began by generating a list of all the behaviours leaders engage in—around 1,800 in all.[55] Those were trimmed down to 150 specific examples, then grouped into several categories, as shown in Table 13-3.[56] The table reveals that many leaders spend their time engaging in a mix of initiating, organizing, producing, socializing, integrating, communicating, recognizing, and representing behaviours. Although 8 categories are easier to remember than 1,800, further analysis suggested that the categories in Table 13-3 really boil down to just two dimensions: initiating structure and consideration.[57]

Initiating structure reflects the extent to which the leader defines and structures the roles of employees in pursuit of goal attainment.[58] Leaders who are high on initiating structure play a more active role in directing group activities and prioritize planning, scheduling, and trying out new ideas. They might emphasize the importance of meeting deadlines, describe explicit standards of performance, ask employees to follow formalized procedures, and criticize poor work when necessary.[59] **Consideration** reflects the extent to which leaders create job relationships characterized by mutual trust, respect for employee ideas, and consideration of employee feelings.[60] Leaders who are high on consideration create a climate of good rapport and strong, two-way communication and exhibit a deep concern for the welfare of employees. They might do personal favours for employees, take time to listen to their problems, go to bat for them when needed, and treat them as equals.[61]

initiating structure
A pattern of behaviour in which the leader defines and structures the roles of employees in pursuit of goal attainment

consideration

A pattern of behaviour in which the leader creates job relationships characterized by mutual trust, respect for employee ideas, and consideration of employee feelings

TABLE 13-3

Day-to-Day Behaviours Performed by Leaders

Behaviour	Description
Initiating Structure	
Initiation	Originating, facilitating, and sometimes resisting new ideas and practices
Organization	Defining and structuring work, clarifying leader versus member roles, and coordinating employee tasks
Production	Setting goals and providing incentives for the effort and productivity of employees
Consideration	
Membership	Mixing with employees, stressing informal interactions, and exchanging personal services
Integration	Encouraging a pleasant atmosphere, reducing conflict, and promoting individual adjustment to the group
Communication	Providing information to employees, seeking information from them, and showing an awareness of matters that affect them
Recognition	Expressing approval or disapproval of the behaviours of employees
Representation	Acting on behalf of the group, defending the group, and advancing the interests of the group

Source: R.M. Stogdill, *Manual for the Leader Behavior Description Questionnaire-Form XII, Bureau of Business Research*, The Ohio State University, 1963.

The Ohio State studies argued that initiating structure and consideration were (more or less) independent concepts, meaning that leaders could be high on both, low on both, or high on one and low on the other. That view differed from that of a series of studies conducted at the University of Michigan during the same period, which identified concepts similar to initiating structure and consideration, calling them production-centred (or task-oriented) and employee-centred (or relations-oriented) behaviours.[62] However, the Michigan studies framed their task-oriented and relations-oriented concepts as two ends of one continuum, implying that leaders couldn't be high on both dimensions.[63] In fact, a recent meta-analysis of 78 studies showed that initiating structure and consideration are only weakly related—knowing whether a leader engages in one brand of behaviour says little about whether he or she engages in the other brand.[64] To see how much initiating structure and consideration you engage in during leadership roles, see our ***OB Assessments*** feature.

After an initial wave of research on initiating structure and consideration, leadership experts began to doubt the usefulness of the two dimensions for predicting leadership effectiveness.[65] More recent research has painted a more encouraging picture, however. A meta-analysis of 103 studies showed that initiating structure and consideration both had beneficial relationships with a number of outcomes.[66] For example, consideration had a strong positive relationship with perceived leader effectiveness, employee motivation, and employee job satisfaction. It also had a moderate positive relationship with overall unit performance. For its part, initiating structure had a strong positive relationship with employee motivation and moderate positive relationships with perceived leader effectiveness, employee job satisfaction, and overall unit performance. One of the most amusing and upbeat CEOs in the country, Panda Express's Andrew Cherng, agrees that both are important to a leader's success. Cherng states, "Before, we used to be more task-based, but now, if you want to be a manager at Panda, you have to be committed to being positive, to continuous learning."[67]

Although initiating structure and consideration tend to be beneficial across situations, there may be circumstances in which they become more or less important. The **life cycle theory of leadership** (sometimes also called the *situational model of leadership*) argues that the optimal combination of initiating structure and consideration depends on the readiness of the employees in the work unit.[68] **Readiness** is broadly defined as the degree to which employees have the ability and the willingness to accomplish their specific tasks.[69] As is shown in Figure 13-4, the theory suggests that readiness varies across employees and can be expressed in terms of four important snapshots: R1–R4. To find the optimal combination of leader behaviours for a particular readiness snapshot, put your finger on the relevant R, then move it straight down to the recommended combination of behaviours.

FIGURE 13-4

The Life Cycle Theory of Leadership

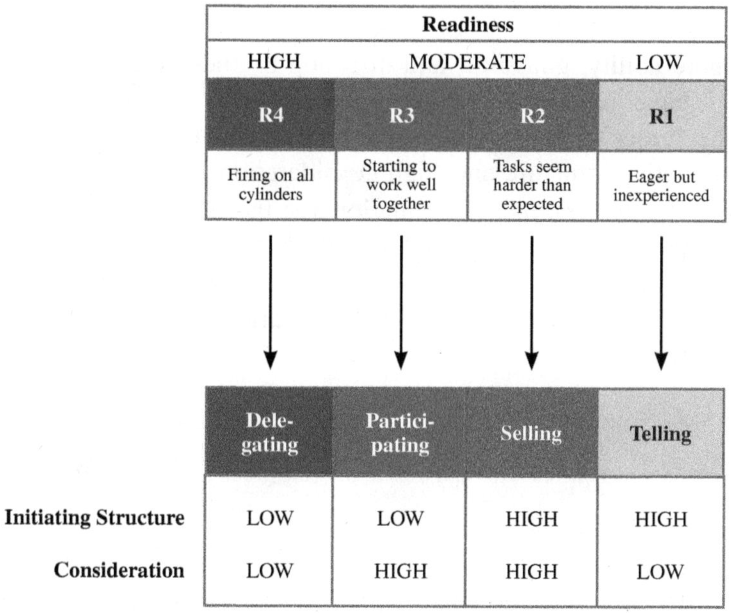

Source: Adapted from P. Hersey and K. Blanchard, "Revisiting the Life-Cycle Theory of Leadership," *Training and Development*, January 1996, pp. 42–47.

life cycle theory of leadership

A theory stating that the optimal combination of initiating structure and consideration depends on the readiness of the employees in the work unit

readiness

The degree to which employees have the ability and the willingness to accomplish their specific tasks

The description of the first two R's has varied over time and across different formulations of the theory. One formulation described the R's as similar to stages of group development.[70] R1 refers to a group of employees who are working together for the first time and are eager to begin, but they lack the experience and confidence needed to perform their roles. Here the optimal combination of leader behaviours is **telling**—high initiating structure and low consideration—in which case the leader provides specific instructions and closely supervises performance. The lion's share of the leader's attention must be devoted to directing followers in this situation, because their goals and roles need to be clearly defined. In the R2 stage, the members have begun working together and, as typically happens, are finding that their work is more difficult than they had anticipated. As eagerness turns to dissatisfaction, the optimal combination of leader behaviours is **selling**—high initiating structure and high consideration—in which the leader supplements his or her directing with support and encouragement to protect the confidence levels of the employees.

telling

When the leader provides specific instructions and closely supervises performance

selling

When the leader explains key issues and provides opportunities for clarification

As employees gain more ability, guidance, and direction by the leader become less necessary. At the R3 stage, employees have learned to work together well, though they still need support and collaboration from the leader to help them adjust to their more self-managed state of affairs. Here **participating**—low initiating structure and high consideration—becomes the optimal combination of leader behaviours. Finally, the optimal combination for the R4 readiness level is **delegating**—low initiating structure and low consideration—such that the leader turns responsibility for key behaviours over to the employees. Here the leader gives them the proverbial ball and lets them run with it. All that's needed from the leader is some degree of observation and monitoring to make sure that the group's efforts stay on track.

participating

Leader behaviour in which the leader shares ideas and tries to help the group conduct its affairs

delegating

Leader behaviour in which the leader turns responsibility for key behaviours over to employees

Estimates suggest that the life cycle theory has been incorporated into leadership training programs at around 400 of the firms in the *Fortune* 500, with more than one million managers exposed to it annually.[71] Unfortunately, the application of the theory has outpaced scientific testing of its propositions, and the shifting nature of its terminology and predictions has made scientific testing somewhat difficult.[72] The research that has been conducted supports the theory's predictions only for low readiness situations, suggesting that telling and selling sorts of behaviours may be more effective when ability, motivation, or confidence are lacking.[73] When readiness is higher, these tests suggest that leader behaviours simply matter less, regardless of their particular combinations. Tests also suggest that leaders only use the recommended combinations of behaviours between 14 and 37 percent of the time,[74] likely because many leaders adhere to the same leadership philosophy regardless of the situation. It should also be noted that tests of the theory have been somewhat more supportive when conducted on an across-job, rather than within-job, basis. For example, research suggests that the performance of lower-ranking university employees (e.g., maintenance workers, custodians, landscapers) depends more on initiating structure and less on consideration than the performance of higher-ranking university employees (e.g., professors, instructors).[75]

OB FOR STUDENTS

Even if you aren't currently working and haven't worked in the past, the life cycle theory of leadership has some relevance to you. After all, you've experienced at least two kinds of leaders already: parents and teachers.

The originators of the life cycle theory suggest that it offers predictions for how parenting behaviours should vary over the course of a child's time at home.[76] Telling should be effective early in life, because initiating structure is needed as children learn to navigate their daily lives. As the child enters school and begins to demonstrate his or her own responsibility and work ethic, telling should give way to selling to build trust and mutual respect. As the child moves into high school and college or university, the responsibility for key decisions becomes his or her own, with the parent offering mostly support in accordance with a participating style. Finally, as the now young adult makes his or her own living and starts a family, a delegating style seems most appropriate.

Although those predictions have never been formally tested, research has supported the importance of parenting behaviours to academic success in university. One study of 236 undergraduates asked the students to rate their parents on three types of behaviours: consideration, demandingness (one aspect of initiating structure), and autonomy granting (reflecting the use of a more participating and delegating style).[77] The students were asked to rate those behaviours in reference to two time periods: now and during their childhood (around eight years old). As would be expected based on the life cycle theory, current levels of autonomy granting were significantly related to student GPA, but childhood levels were not. However, autonomy granting at both time periods was related to students' confidence, persistence, involvement, and rapport with instructors. Its importance did not vary, as would be expected by the theory. Similarly, the study showed that consideration was related to students' confidence and persistence in the classroom and their rapport with their instructors, again regardless of whether the behaviours occurred currently or in childhood. For its part, demandingness had little impact on student outcomes, regardless of the relevant time period.

13.5 How does transformational leadership differ from transactional leadership, and which behaviours set it apart?

Transformational Leadership Behaviours

By describing decision-making styles and day-to-day leader behaviours, we've covered a broad spectrum of what it is that leaders do. Still, something is missing. Take a small piece of scrap paper and jot down five people who are famous for their effective leadership. They can come from inside or outside the business world and can be either living people or historical figures. All that's important is that their name be practically synonymous with great leadership. Once you've compiled your list, take a look at the names. Do they appear on your list because they tend to use the right decision-making styles in the right situations and engage in effective levels of consideration and initiating structure?

The missing piece of this leadership puzzle is what leaders do to motivate their employees to perform beyond expectations. **Transformational leadership** involves inspiring followers to commit to a shared vision that provides meaning to their work while also serving as a role model who helps followers develop their own potential and view problems from new perspectives.[78] Transformational leaders heighten followers' awareness of the importance of certain outcomes while increasing their confidence that those outcomes can be achieved.[79] What gets "transformed" is the way followers view their work, causing them to focus on the collective good more than just their own short-term self-interests and to perform beyond expectations as a result.[80]

transformational leadership

A pattern of behaviour in which the leader inspires followers to commit to a shared vision that provides meaning to their work while also serving as a role model who helps followers develop their own potential and view problems from new perspectives

Mother Teresa's inspiring humanitarian work with India's sick and poor, and her founding of the influential Missionaries of Charity, became known around the world and suggest that she was a transformational leader. She was awarded the Nobel Peace Prize in 1979.

© Tim Graham/Getty Images

Transformational leadership is viewed as a more motivational approach to leadership than other managerial approaches. Figure 13-5 contrasts various approaches to leadership according to how active or passive they are and, ultimately, how effective they prove to be. The coloured cubes in the figure represent five distinct approaches to motivating employees, and the depth of the cubes represent how much a leader prioritizes each of the approaches. The figure therefore represents an optimal leadership approach that prioritizes more effective and more active behaviours. That optimal approach includes low levels of **laissez-faire** (i.e., hands-off) **leadership**, represented by the red cube, which is the avoidance of leadership altogether.[81] Important actions are delayed, responsibility is ignored, and power and influence go unutilized. One common measure of leadership reflects laissez-faire styles with this statement: "The leader avoids getting involved when important issues arise."[82]

laissez-faire leadership
A type of leadership in which the leader avoids leadership duties altogether

FIGURE 13-5

Laissez-Faire, Transactional, and Transformational Leadership

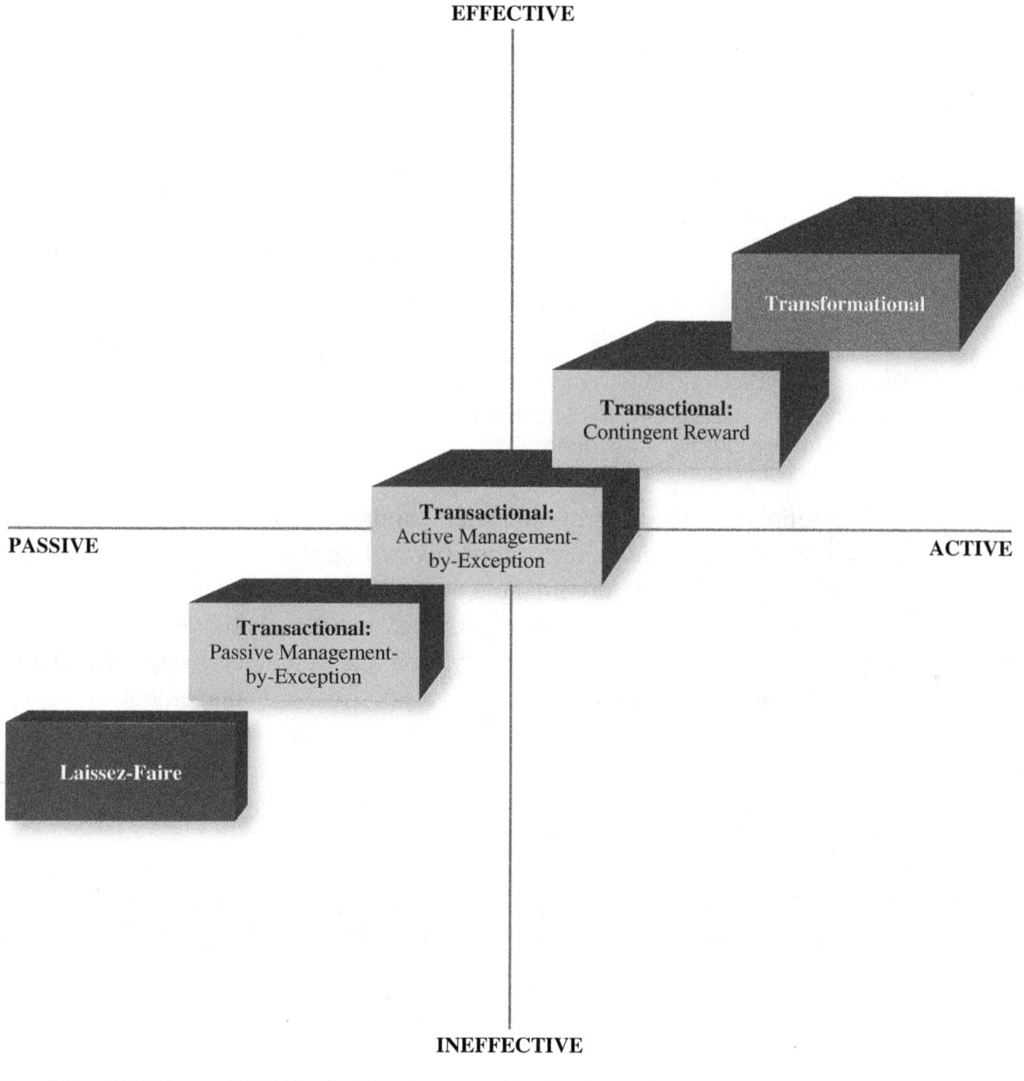

Source: Adapted from B.M. Bass and R.E. Riggio, *Transformational Leadership*, 2nd ed. (Mahwah, NJ: Erlbaum, 2006).

The three yellow cubes represent **transactional leadership**, which occurs when the leader rewards or disciplines the follower depending on the adequacy of the follower's performance.[83] With **passive management-by-exception**, the leader waits around for mistakes and errors, then takes corrective action as necessary.[84] After all, "If it ain't broke, don't fix it!"[85] This approach is represented by statements like: "The leader takes no action until complaints are received."[86] With **active management-by-exception**, the leader arranges to monitor mistakes and errors actively and again takes corrective action when required.[87] This approach is represented by statements like: "The leader directs attention toward failures to meet standards."[88] **Contingent reward** represents a more active and effective brand of transactional leadership, in which the leader attains follower agreement on what needs to be done using promised or actual rewards in exchange for adequate performance.[89] Statements like "The leader makes clear what one can expect to receive when performance goals are achieved" exemplify contingent reward leadership.[90]

transactional leadership

A pattern of behaviour in which the leader rewards or disciplines the follower on the basis of performance

passive management-by-exception

A type of transactional leadership in which the leader waits around for mistakes and errors, then takes corrective action as necessary

active management-by-exception

A type of transactional leadership in which the leader arranges to monitor mistakes and errors actively, and takes corrective action when required

contingent reward

A more active and effective type of transactional leadership, in which the leader attains follower agreement on what needs to be done using rewards in exchange for adequate performance

Transactional leadership represents the "carrot-and-stick" approach to leadership, with management-by-exception providing the "sticks" and contingent reward supplying the "carrots." Of course, transactional leadership represents the dominant approach to motivating employees in most organizations, and research suggests that it can be effective. A meta-analysis of 87 studies showed that contingent reward was strongly related to follower motivation and perceived leader effectiveness[91] (see Chapter 7 on motivation for more discussion of such issues). Active management-by-exception was only weakly related to follower motivation and perceived leader effectiveness, however, and passive management-by-exception seemed actually to harm those outcomes.[92] Such results support the progression shown in Figure 13-5, with contingent reward standing as the most effective approach under the transactional leadership umbrella.

Finally, the green cube represents transformational leadership—the most active and effective approach in Figure 13-5. How effective is transformational leadership? Well, we'll save that discussion for the "How Important Is Leadership?" section that concludes this chapter, but suffice it to say that transformational leadership has the strongest and most beneficial effects of any of the leadership variables described in this chapter. It's also the leadership approach most universally endorsed across cultures, as described in our ***OB Internationally*** feature. In addition, it probably captures the key qualities of the famous leaders we asked you to list a few paragraphs back. To understand why it's so powerful, we need to dig deeper into the specific kinds of actions and behaviours that leaders can utilize to become more transformational. It turns out that the full spectrum of transformational leadership can be summarized using four dimensions: idealized influence, inspirational motivation, intellectual stimulation, and individualized consideration. Collectively, these dimensions are often called "The Four I's."[93] For our discussion of transformational leadership, we'll return to the chapter-opening profile and use Steve Jobs as a running example.[94]

OB INTERNATIONALLY

Does the effectiveness of leader styles and behaviours vary across cultures? Answering that question is one of the objectives of Project GLOBE's test of *culturally endorsed implicit leadership theory*, which argues that effective leadership is "in the eye of the beholder."[95] To test the theory, researchers asked participants across cultures to rate a number of leader styles and behaviours using a scale of 1 (very ineffective) to 7 (very effective). The figure below shows how three of the styles and behaviours described in this chapter were rated across ten different regions (note that the term "Anglo" represents people of English ethnicity, including the United States, Great Britain, and Australia).

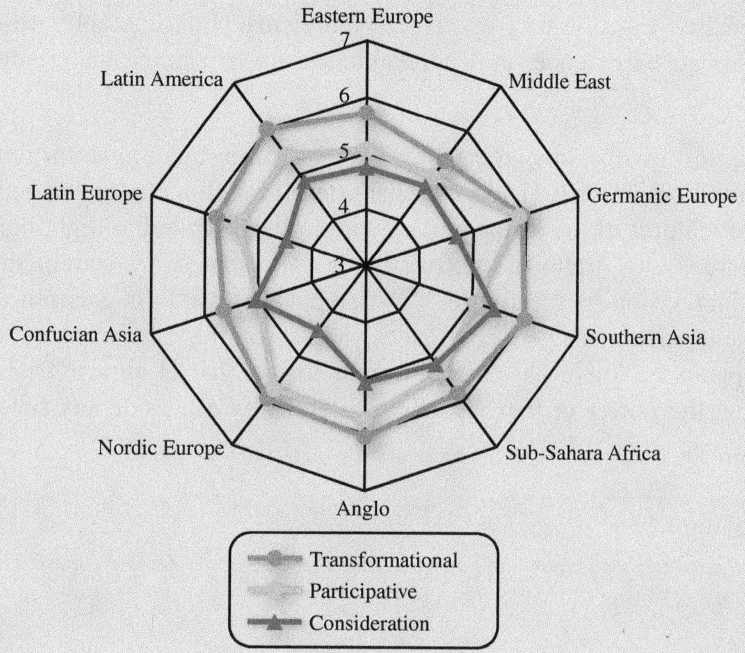

It turns out that transformational leadership is the most universally accepted approach to leadership of any of the concepts studied by Project GLOBE,[96] receiving an average rating near 6 in every region except the Middle East. That appeal is likely explained by the fact that transformational leaders emphasize values like idealism and virtue that are endorsed in almost all countries.[97] The figure also shows that a participative style is favourably viewed in most countries, though more variation is evident. Even more variation is seen with consideration behaviours, which are endorsed a bit less across the board but especially in Europe. Understanding these kinds of results can help organizations select and train managers who will fit the profile of an effective leader in a given region.

Idealized influence involves behaving in ways that earn the admiration, trust, and respect of followers, causing followers to want to identify with and emulate the leader.[98] Idealized influence is represented by statements like: "The leader instills pride in me for being associated with him/her."[99] Idealized influence is synonymous with *charisma*—a Greek word that means "divinely inspired gift"—which reflects a sense among followers that the leader possesses extraordinary qualities.[100] "Charisma" is a word that was often associated with Steve Jobs. One observer noted that even though Jobs could be very difficult to work with, his remarkable charisma created a mysterious attraction that drew people to him, keeping them loyal to his collective sense of mission.[101] Interestingly, it is during times of uncertainty, stress, and turbulence when people seem to long for charismatic leaders, and when their encouraging, confident, and idealistic visions resonate more deeply. See this chapter's ***OB on Screen*** feature for a great example.

idealized influence

The power held by a leader who behaves in ways that earn the admiration, trust, and respect of followers, causing followers to want to identify with and emulate the leader

To some extent, discussions of charisma serve as echoes of the "great person" view of leadership that spawned the trait research described in Table 13-2. In fact, research suggests that there is a genetic component to charisma specifically and to transformational leadership more broadly. Studies on identical twins reared apart show that such twins have very similar charismatic profiles, despite their differing environments.[102] Indeed, such research suggests that almost 60 percent of the variation in charismatic behaviour can be explained by genes. One explanation for such findings is that genes influence the personality traits that give rise to charisma. For example, research suggests that extraversion, openness to experience, and agreeableness have significant effects on perceptions of leader charisma.[103]

Inspirational motivation involves behaving in ways that foster an enthusiasm for and commitment to a shared vision of the future.[104] That vision is transmitted through a sort of "meaning-making" process in which the negative features of the status quo are emphasized while highlighting the positive features of the potential future.[105] Inspirational motivation is represented by statements like: "The leader articulates a compelling vision of the future."[106] At Apple, Steve Jobs was renowned for spinning a "reality distortion field" that reshaped employees' views of the current work environment.[107] One Apple employee explained, "Steve has this power of vision that is almost frightening. When Steve believes in something, the power of that vision can literally sweep aside any objections, problems, or whatever. They just cease to exist."[108]

inspirational motivation

A type of influence in which the leader behaves in ways that foster an enthusiasm for and commitment to a shared vision of the future

Intellectual stimulation involves behaving in ways that challenge followers to be innovative and creative by questioning assumptions and reframing old situations in new ways.[109] Intellectual stimulation is represented by statements like: "The leader gets others to look at problems from many different angles."[110] Intellectual stimulation was a staple of Jobs's tenure at Apple. He pushed for a different power supply on the Apple II so that the fan could be removed, preventing it from humming and churning like other computers of the time. Years later, he insisted on removing the floppy drive from the iMac because it seemed silly to transfer data one megabyte at a time, a decision that drew merciless criticism when the iMac debuted. One employee talking about Jobs stated, "There would be times when we'd rack our brains on a user interface problem, and think we'd considered every option, and he would go 'Did you think of this?' He'd redefine the problem or approach, and our little problem would go away."[111]

intellectual stimulation

A type of influence in which the leader behaves in ways that challenge followers to be innovative and creative by questioning assumptions and reframing old situations in new ways

Individualized consideration involves behaving in ways that help followers achieve their potential through coaching, development, and mentoring.[112] Not to be confused with the consideration behaviour derived from the Ohio State studies, individualized consideration represents treating employees as unique individuals with specific needs, abilities, and aspirations that need to be tied into the unit's mission. Individualized consideration is represented by statements like: "The leader spends time teaching and coaching."[113] Of the four facets of transformational leadership, Steve Jobs seemed lowest on individualized consideration. Employees who were not regarded as his equals were given a relatively short leash and sometimes faced an uncertain future in the company. In fact, some Apple employees resisted riding the elevator for fear of ending up trapped with Jobs for the ride between floors. As one observer describes it, by the time the doors open, you might have had your confidence undermined for weeks.[114]

individualized consideration

A type of influence in which the leader behaves in ways that help followers achieve their potential through coaching, development, and mentoring

OB ON SCREEN

Lincoln

We are stepped out upon the world stage now. Now! With the fate of human dignity in our hands. Blood's been spilt to afford us this moment. Now! Now! Now!

With those words, Abraham Lincoln (Daniel Day Lewis) exhibits a transformational leadership approach toward a group of political allies and advisors in *Lincoln* (Dir. Steven Spielberg, Disney, 2012). The film, covering the last four months of Lincoln's life, is based in January 1865. Lincoln is trying desperately to acquire enough votes in the United States House of Representatives to pass the Thirteenth Amendment to the United States Constitution (the abolishment of slavery). With the Civil War starting to wind down (but not over), Lincoln is beset on all sides by individuals who have varying opinions about how to go about doing things and what the priorities for Lincoln and the country should be. There are many great examples of Lincoln using transformational leadership throughout the movie.

© AP Photo/DreamWorks, Twentieth Century Fox, David James

In one scene Lincoln provides a great example of *individualized consideration* as he sits down with an outgoing congressman and convinces him of the difference he can still make with his vote. He exhibits *intellectual stimulation* in having those around him change what seem to be insurmountable problems by reframing the questions they are asking. In the dramatic scene in question, Lincoln sits and listens to the constant bickering of his allies and confidants until he can't

(*Continued*)

take it anymore. The quote above illustrates his use of *idealized influence* and it's easy to see the charisma that Lincoln exudes. He also uses *inspirational motivation* to refocus the men on what the stakes are and what the vision for the future needs to be as he reiterates that the amendment "settles the fate for all coming time. Not only of the millions now in bondage, but of unborn millions to come." When Congressman James Ashley (David Costabile) and Secretary of State William Seward (David Strathairn) continue to question, Lincoln exerts his power and attempts to give his followers a sense that they can carry that power into the political battle with them.

Summary: Why Are Some Leaders More Effective Than Others?

So what explains why some leaders are more effective than others? As is shown in Figure 13-6, answering that question requires an understanding of the particular styles that leaders use to make decisions and the behaviours they perform in their leadership role. Regarding decision-making styles, do they choose the most effective combination of leader and follower control in terms of the autocratic, consultative, facilitative, and delegative styles, particularly considering the importance of the decision and the expertise in the unit? Regarding day-to-day behaviours, do they engage in adequate levels of initiating structure and consideration? Finally, do they use an effective combination of transactional leadership behaviours, such as contingent reward, and transformational leadership behaviours, such as idealized influence, inspirational motivation, intellectual stimulation, and individualized consideration?

FIGURE 13-6

Why Are Some Leaders More Effective Than Others?

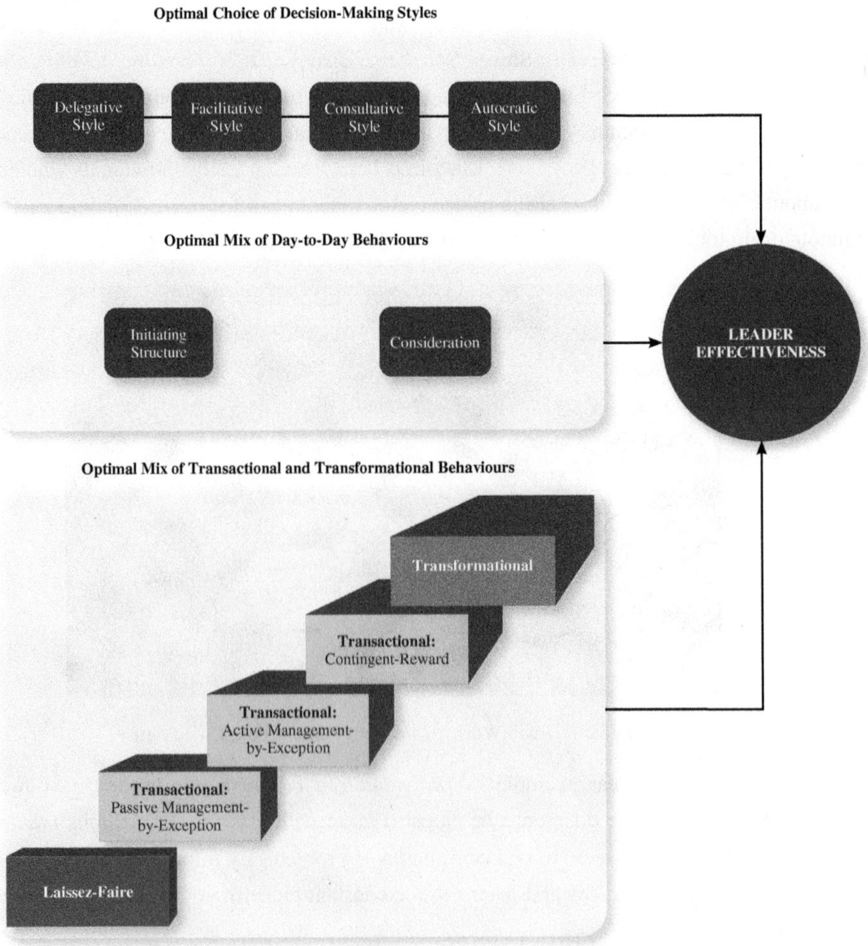

13.6 How does leadership affect job performance and organizational commitment?

HOW IMPORTANT IS LEADERSHIP?

How important is leadership? As with some other topics in organizational behaviour, that's a complicated question, because "leadership" isn't just one thing. Instead, all of the styles and behaviours summarized in Figure 13-6 have their own unique importance. However, transformational leadership stands apart from the rest to some extent, with particularly strong effects in organizations. For example, transformational leadership is more strongly related to unit-focused measures of leadership effectiveness, like the kind shown in the top panel of Table 13-1.[115] Units led by a transformational leader tend to be more financially successful and bring higher-quality products and services to market at a faster rate.[116] Transformational leadership is also more strongly related to dyad-focused measures of leader effectiveness, like the kind shown in the bottom panel of Table 13-1. Transformational leaders tend to foster leader–member exchange relationships that are of higher quality, marked by especially strong levels of mutual respect and obligation.[117]

What if we focus specifically on the two outcomes in our integrative model of OB, performance and commitment? Figure 13-7 summarizes the research evidence linking transformational leadership to those outcomes. The figure reveals that transformational leadership indeed affects the job performance of the employees who report to the leader. Employees with transformational leaders tend to have higher levels of task performance and engage in higher levels of citizenship behaviours.[118] Why? One reason is that employees with transformational leaders have higher levels of *motivation* than other employees.[119] They feel a stronger sense of psychological empowerment, feel more self-confident, and set more demanding work goals for themselves.[120] They also *trust* the leader more, making them willing to exert extra effort even when that effort might not be immediately rewarded.[121]

Figure 13-7 also reveals that employees with transformational leaders tend to be more committed to their organization.[122] They feel a stronger emotional bond with their organization and a stronger sense of obligation to remain present and engaged in their work.[123] Why? One reason is that employees with transformational leaders have higher levels of *job satisfaction* than other employees.[124] One study showed that transformational leaders can make employees feel that their jobs have more variety and significance, enhancing intrinsic satisfaction with the work itself.[125] Other studies have shown that charismatic leaders express positive emotions more frequently and that those emotions are "caught" by employees through a sort of "emotional contagion" process.[126] For example, followers of transformational leaders tend to feel more optimism and less frustration during their workday, which makes it a bit easier to stay committed to work.[127]

Although leadership is very important to unit effectiveness and the performance and commitment of employees, there are contexts in which the importance of the leader can be reduced. The **substitutes for leadership model** suggests that certain characteristics of the situation can constrain the influence of the leader, making it more difficult for the leader to influence employee performance.[128] Those situational characteristics come in two varieties, as shown in Table 13-4. **Substitutes** reduce the importance of the leader while simultaneously providing a direct benefit to employee performance. For example, a cohesive work group can provide its own sort of governing behaviours, making the leader less relevant, while providing its own source of motivation and job satisfaction. **Neutralizers**, in contrast, only reduce the importance of the leader; they themselves have no beneficial impact on performance.[129] For example, spatial distance lessens the impact of a leader's behaviours and styles, but distance itself has no direct benefit for employee job performance.

substitutes for leadership model

A model that suggests that characteristics of the situations can constrain the influence of the leader, which makes it more difficult for the leader to influence employee performance

substitutes

Situational characteristics that reduce the importance of the leader while simultaneously providing a direct benefit to employee performance

neutralizers

Situational characteristics that reduce the importance of the leader and do not improve employee performance in any way

FIGURE 13-7

Effects of Transformational Leadership on Performance and Commitment

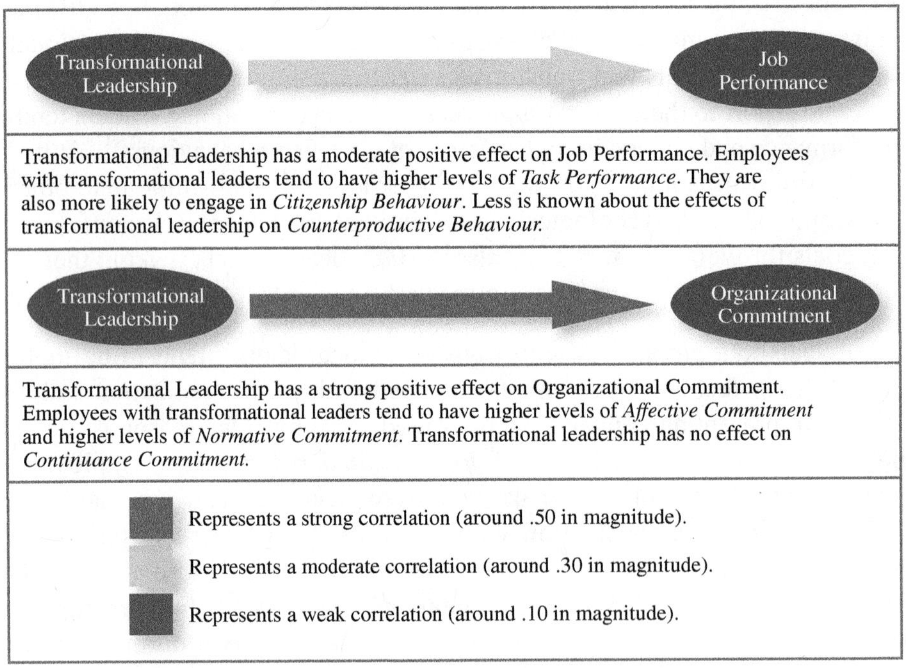

Sources: T.A. Judge and R.F. Piccolo, "Transformational and Transactional Leadership: A Meta-analytic Test of Their Relative Validity," *Journal of Applied Psychology* 89 (2004), pp. 755–68; J.P. Meyer, D.J. Stanley, L. Herscovitch, and L. Topolnytsky, "Affective, Continuance, and Normative Commitment to the Organization: A Meta-analysis of Antecedents, Correlates, and Consequences," *Journal of Vocational Behavior* 61 (2002), pp. 20–52; and P.M. Podsakoff, S.B. MacKenzie, J.B. Paine, and D.G. Bachrach, "Organizational Citizenship Behaviors: A Critical Review of the Theoretical and Empirical Literature and Suggestions for Future Research," *Journal of Management* 26 (2000), pp. 513–63.

The substitutes for leadership model offers a number of prescriptions for a better understanding of leadership in organizations. First, it can be used to explain why a leader who seemingly does the right things doesn't seem to be making any difference.[130] It may be that the leader's work context possesses high levels of neutralizers and substitutes. Second, it can be used to explain what to do if an ineffective person is in a leadership role with no immediate replacement waiting in the wings.[131] If the leader can't be removed, perhaps the organization can do things to make that leader more irrelevant. Studies of the substitutes for leadership model have been inconsistent in showing that substitutes and neutralizers actually make leaders less influential in the predicted manner.[132] What is clearer is that the substitutes in Table 13-4 have beneficial effects on the job performance and organizational commitment of employees. In fact, the beneficial effects of the substitutes is sometimes even greater than the beneficial effects of the leader's own behaviours and styles. Some leadership experts even recommend that leaders set out to create high levels of the substitutes in their work units wherever possible, even if the units might ultimately wind up "running themselves."[133]

TABLE 13-4

Leader Substitutes and Neutralizers

Substitutes	Description
Task feedback	Receiving feedback on performance from the task itself
Training and experience	Gaining the knowledge to act independently of the leader
Professionalism	Having a professional specialty that offers guidance
Staff support	Receiving information and assistance from outside staff
Group cohesion	Working in a close-knit and interdependent work group
Intrinsic satisfaction	Deriving personal satisfaction from one's work
Neutralizers	**Description**
Task stability	Having tasks with a clear, unchanging sequence of steps
Formalization	Having written policies and procedures that govern one's job
Inflexibility	Working in an organization that prioritizes rule adherence
Spatial distance	Being separated from one's leader by physical space

Source: Adapted from S. Kerr and J.M. Jermier, "Substitutes for Leadership: Their Meaning and Measurement," *Organizational Behavior and Human Performance* 22 (1978), pp. 375–403.

OB RESEARCH IN CANADA

Dr. Christian Vandenberghe

(*Continued*)

Dr. Christian Vandenberghe is a professor of organizational behaviour at HEC Montreal (Quebec). It is fitting to feature Dr. Vandenberghe's work in a chapter devoted to leadership. Some of his recent research has examined how employees' organizational commitment is affected by the actions of their leaders, and how individuals' relationships with their superiors affects their motivation (Chapter 7), withdrawal behaviours (Chapter 3), and job performance (Chapter 2). He has also looked at how mutual commitments develop in the context of supervisor–employee dyads: Have a look at the leader–member exchange theory (Figure 13-1). Asked why he studies these issues, Dr. Vandenberghe replied that leaders "represent the lens through which most employees discover and get in touch with the organization's realm, its values and goals. For many employees, their relationship with the organization depends on how they see and respond to their superior." For more information, look up Dr. Vandenberghe at www.hec.ca.

13.7 Can leaders be trained to be more effective?

APPLICATION: LEADERSHIP TRAINING

Given the importance of leadership, what can organizations do to maximize the effectiveness of their leaders? One training analyst explains the increasing emphasis on leadership training this way: "The biggest problem that companies face today is an acute shortage of midlevel managers. They look around and just don't have enough qualified people."[134] This is exactly the determination that Walmart's president and CEO Bill Simon made when he instituted a 16-week military-style leadership training program. Walmart's senior vice-president of talent development Celia Swanson says, "Our analysis showed we were capable of building new stores faster than we could prepare new store managers."[135]

Leadership training programs often focus on very specific issues, like conducting more accurate performance evaluations, being a more effective mentor, structuring creative problem solving, or gaining more cultural awareness and sensitivity.[136] However, training programs can also focus on much of the content covered in this chapter. For example, content could focus on contextual considerations that alter the effectiveness of decision-making styles or particular leader behaviours, such as initiating structure and consideration. This is exactly what Campbell Soup Company is doing through its "CEO Institute"—a two-year program focused on personal leadership development.[137] Farmers Insurance puts all its upper-level executives through a program that gives them direct feedback from their peers on their leadership behaviours. The executives use this information to create individual leadership development plans.[138] What about transformational leadership? Given how dependent charisma is on personality and genetic factors, could it be that transformational leaders are born, not made?

It turns out that many training programs focus on transformational leadership content, and research suggests that those programs can be effective.[139] One study of transformational leadership training occurred in one of the largest bank chains in Canada.[140] Managers at all of the branches in one region were randomly assigned to either a transformational training group or a control group. The managers in the training group took part in a one-day training session that began by asking them to describe the best and worst leaders they had ever encountered. Where applicable, the behaviours mentioned as belonging to the best leaders were framed around transformational leadership. The transformational dimensions were then described in a lecture-style format. Participants set goals for how they could behave more transformationally and engaged in role-playing exercises to practise those behaviours. The managers then created specific action plans, with progress on those plans monitored during four "booster sessions" over the next month. The results of the study showed that managers who participated in the training were rated as more transformational afterward. More importantly, their employees reported higher levels of organizational commitment, and their branches enjoyed better performance in terms of personal loan sales and credit card sales.

TAKEAWAYS

13.1 Leadership is defined as the use of power and influence to direct the activities of followers toward goal achievement. An "effective leader" improves the performance and well-being of his or her overall unit, as judged by profit margins, productivity, costs, absenteeism, retention, employee surveys, and so forth. An "effective leader" also cultivates high-quality leader–member exchange relationships on a dyadic basis through role-taking and role-making processes.

13.2 Leader emergence has been linked to a number of traits, including conscientiousness, disagreeableness, openness, extraversion, general cognitive ability, energy level, stress tolerance, and self-confidence. Of that set, the last six traits also predict leader effectiveness.

13.3 Leaders can use a number of styles to make decisions. Beginning with high leader control and moving to high follower control, they include autocratic, consultative, facilitative, and delegative styles. According to the time-driven model of leadership, the appropriateness of these styles depends on decision significance, the importance of commitment, leader expertise, the likelihood of commitment, shared objectives, employee expertise, and teamwork skills.

13.4 Most of the day-to-day leadership behaviours that leaders engage in are examples of either initiating structure or consideration. Initiating structure behaviours include initiation, organization, and production sorts of duties. Consideration behaviours include membership, integration, communication, recognition, and representation sorts of duties.

13.5 Transactional leadership emphasizes "carrot-and-stick" approaches to motivating employees, whereas transformational leadership fundamentally changes the way employees view their work. More specifically, transformational leadership inspires employees to commit to a shared vision or goal that provides meaning and challenge to their work. The specific behaviours that underlie transformational leadership include the Four I's: idealized influence, inspirational motivation, intellectual stimulation, and individualized consideration.

13.6 Transformational leadership has a moderate positive relationship with job performance and a strong positive relationship with organizational commitment. It has stronger effects on these outcomes than other leadership behaviours.

13.7 Leaders can be trained to be effective. In fact, such training can be used to increase transformational leadership behaviours, despite the fact that charisma is somewhat dependent on personality and genetic factors.

KEY TERMS

active management-by-exception
autocratic style
consideration
consultative style
contingent reward
delegating
delegative style
facilitative style
idealized influence
individualized consideration
initiating structure
inspirational motivation
intellectual stimulation
laissez-faire leadership
leader effectiveness
leader emergence
leader–member exchange theory
leadership
life cycle theory of leadership
neutralizers
participating
passive management-by-exception
readiness
role making
role taking
selling
substitutes
substitutes for leadership model
telling
time-driven model of leadership
transactional leadership
transformational leadership

DISCUSSION QUESTIONS

13.1 Before reading this chapter, which statement did you feel was more accurate: "Leaders are born" or "Leaders are made"? How do you feel now, and why do you feel that way?

13.2 The time-sensitive model of leadership argues that leaders aren't just concerned about the accuracy of their decisions when deciding among autocratic, consultative, facilitative, and delegative styles; they're also concerned about the efficient use of time. What other considerations could influence a leader's use of the four decision-making styles?

13.3 The time-sensitive and life cycle models of leadership both potentially suggest that leaders should use different styles and behaviours for different followers. Can you think of any negative consequences of that advice? How could those negative consequences be managed?

13.4 Consider the four dimensions of transformational leadership: idealized influence, inspirational motivation, intellectual stimulation, and individualized consideration. Which of those dimensions would you respond to most favourably? Why?

13.5 Can you think of any "dark sides" to transformational leadership? What might they be?

CASE • STEVE JOBS

Steve Jobs will be remembered for his ability to single-handedly change the world with his vision and innovative products. As a leader, however, Jobs was always an enigma. Much has been made of Jobs's aggressive and demanding personality. He was the consummate perfectionist who insisted on having his hand in every aspect of a project, from start to finish. Stories of his erratic and legendary temper were also well documented. It was said that Jobs tended to see the world in binary terms. Products, in his view, were "insanely great" or "shit." Subordinates were geniuses or "bozos," indispensable or no longer relevant. People in his orbit regularly flipped, at a second's notice, from one category to another, in what early Apple colleagues came to call his "hero–shithead roller coaster." Other personal abuses were also legend. It was reported that he periodically reduced subordinates to tears, and fired employees in angry tantrums.

Yet Jobs's employees remain devoted, because his negative tendencies were balanced by his famous charisma. Andy Hertzfeld, lead designer of the original "Mac team," says Jobs imbued him and his co-workers with "messianic zeal"—"He can make the task of designing a power supply feel like a mission from God!" And because Jobs's approval was so hard to win, Apple staffers laboured tirelessly to please him. "He has the ability to pull the best out of people," says Ratzlaff, who worked closely with Jobs on OS X for 18 months. "I learned a tremendous amount from him." A former Apple executive who had been involved with the launch of the original Macintosh computer in 1984 had similar things to say about Steve Jobs: "[He] was the most difficult human being I've ever worked for—but he was also the most technologically brilliant. No one knew technology better than he did, and no one had a clearer sense of where it was going." In a similar vein, a former Pixar employee said of his time working under Steve Jobs, "You just dreaded letting him down. He believed in you so strongly that the thought of disappointing him just killed you."

When asked to comment on his demanding reputation, Jobs responded by saying "My job is not to be easy on people. My job is to make them better. My job is to pull things together from different parts of the company and clear the ways and get the resources for the key projects. And to take these great people we have and to push them and make them even better, coming up with more aggressive versions of how it could be."

13.1 Do you think Steve Jobs epitomizes an effective leader? Why? Why not? Explain your answer by making reference to Figure 13-6.

13.2 Explore Jobs's leadership style from the perspective of the leader-member exchange theory? Explain.

13.3 Are there risks associated with the extreme detail-oriented, micromanaging style Steve Jobs is famous for? Explain. Reconcile your answer with the life cycle theory of leadership (see Figure 13-4).

13.4 How would you survive a leader like Steve Jobs?

Sources: B. Morris, "Steve Jobs Speaks Out," interview, *Fortune*, February 2008, money.cnn.com/galleries/2008/fortune/0803/gallery.jobsqna.fortune/index.html; R.M. Kramer, "The Great Intimidators," *Harvard Business Review*, February 2006, pp. 88–96; Leander Kahney, "How Apple Got Everything Right by Doing Everything Wrong," *Wired Magazine*, March 18, 2008, www.wired.com/print/techbiz/it/magazine/16-04/bz_apple; P. Elkind, "The Trouble with Steve Jobs," *Fortune*, March 5, 2008, money.cnn.com/2008/03/02/news/companies/elkind_jobs.fortune/index.htm.

EXERCISE · TAKE ME TO YOUR LEADER

The purpose of this exercise is to explore the commonalities in effective leadership across different types of leaders. This exercise uses groups, so your instructor will either assign you to a group or ask you to create your own group. The exercise has the following steps:

13.1 Imagine that a space alien has descended to Earth and actually uttered the famous line "Take me to your leader!" Having read a bit about leadership, your group knows that leaders come in a number of shapes and sizes. Instead of showing the alien just one leader, your group decides it might be beneficial to show the alien a whole variety of leaders. Each member should choose one type of leader from the table to focus on (each must choose a different type). Try to choose examples that are personally interesting but that also maximize the diversity within the group.

Orchestra conductor	Fashion designer	Drummer in rock band
Coach	Personal tax accountant	Point guard in basketball
Film director	Night club DJ	Bartender
College professor	Fitness trainer	Sheriff
Talk show host	Prison guard	Millionaire philanthropist
Stock broker	Real estate broker	Agent
Psychotherapist	MBA program director	Auditor
Campaign manager	Construction project supervisor	CEO
Diplomat	Sports colour commentator	Vice-president of marketing

13.2 Individually, jot down some thoughts that highlight for the alien what is truly distinctive about "leadership" for this type of leader. For example, if you were showing the alien a coach, you might call attention to how coaches cannot control the game itself very much but instead must make their influence felt on the practice field by instilling skills while being anticipatory in their thinking. You might also call attention to how coaches need to be creative and adapt quickly during the game itself.

13.3 Share the thoughts you've jotted down in your groups, going from member to member, with each person describing what "leadership" means for the given types of leaders.

13.4 Once all these thoughts about the various types of leaders have been shared, think about whether certain traits, styles, or behaviours are universal across all the types. For example, maybe all of the types have some kind of organizing quality to them (e.g., leaders need to be organized, leaders need to do things to help others be organized). Create a list of four "leadership universals."

13.5 Now consider the situational challenges faced by the types of leaders you discussed, including challenges rooted in the task, their followers, or the surrounding work context. For example, the fact that the coach has little direct impact on the game is a situational challenge. Do other leader types also grapple with lack of direct control? Create a list of four "situational challenges" faced by multiple types of leaders.

13.6 Elect a group member to write the group's four universals and four challenges on the board.

13.7 Class discussion (in groups or as a class) should centre on whether the theories described in the chapter discuss some of the leadership universals identified by the groups. Are there theories that also include some of the situational challenges uncovered? Which leadership theory seems best equipped for explaining effective leadership across a wide variety of leader types?

Source: From D. Marcic, J. Seltzer, and P. Vail, *Organizational Behavior: Experiences and Cases* (Cincinnati, OH: South-Western, 2001).

OB ASSESSMENTS • INITIATING STRUCTURE AND CONSIDERATION

How do you act when you're in a leadership role? This assessment is designed to measure the two dimensions of leaders' day-to-day behaviours: initiating structure and consideration. Write a number next to each statement that reflects how frequently you engage in the behaviour described. Answer each question using the response scale provided. Then subtract your answers to the boldfaced questions from 6, the difference being your new answer for that question. For example, if your original answer for question 16 was "4," your new answer is "2" (6 – 4). Then add up your answers for each of the dimensions.

1 Never	2 Seldom	3 Occasionally	4 Often	5 Always

1. I let group members know what is expected of them. ______
2. I encourage the use of uniform procedures. ______
3. I try out my ideas in the group. ______
4. I make my attitudes clear to the group. ______
5. I decide what shall be done and how it shall be done. ______
6. I assign group members to particular tasks. ______
7. I make sure that my part in the group is understood by the group members. ______
8. I schedule the work to be done. ______
9. I maintain definite standards of performance. ______
10. I ask group members to follow standard rules and regulations. ______
11. I am friendly and approachable. ______
12. I do little things to make it pleasant to be a member of the group. ______
13. I put suggestions made by the group into operation. ______
14. I treat all group members as equals. ______
15. I give advance notice of changes. ______
16. **I keep to myself.** ______
17. I look out for the personal welfare of group members. ______
18. I am willing to make changes. ______
19. **I refuse to explain my actions.** ______
20. **I act without consulting the group.** ______

Scoring and Interpretation

Initiating structure. Add up items 1–10.
Consideration. Add up items 11–20.

For initiating structure, scores of 38 or more are high. For consideration, scores of 40 or more are high. Remember, when interpreting your scores on these assessments it is important to consider the *reliability* and *validity* of these tools (see Chapter 1, ***OB Assessments***).

Source: R.M. Stogdill, *Manual for the Leader Behavior Description Questionnaire—Form XII* (Columbus, OH: Bureau of Business Research, The Ohio State University, 1963).

PART 4

Organizational Mechanisms

Organizational Structure

CHAPTER 14

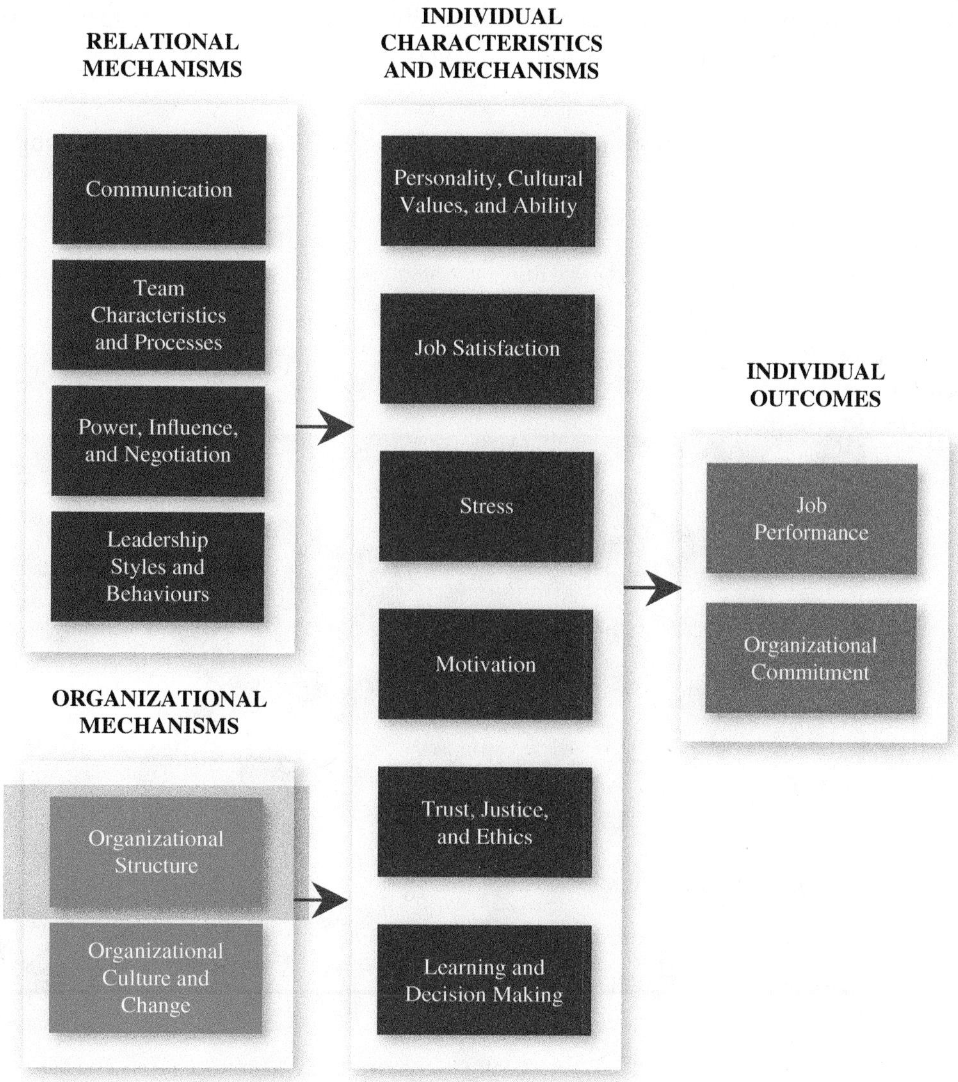

LEARNING OUTCOMES

After reading this chapter, you should be able to answer the following questions:

14.1 What is an organization's structure, and what does it consist of?

14.2 What are the major elements of an organizational structure?

14.3 What is organizational design, and what factors does the organizational design process depend on?

14.4 What are some of the more common organizational forms that an organization might adopt for its structure?

14.5 When an organization makes changes to its structure, how does that restructuring affect job performance and organizational commitment?

14.6 What steps can organizations take to reduce the negative effects of restructuring efforts?

Cheesecake Factory

In order to be successful the Cheesecake Factory has learned to carefully manage its organizational structure.

© Jeff Greenberg/Alamy

For many Canadians lucky enough to live within driving distance of the United States border, a stop at one of 175 Cheesecake Factory restaurants is a definite "must do." Mike, from Toronto, on a return trip from Buffalo, New York, had this this to say about the Cheesecake Factory: "Wow, was I amazed! The place looks like a cruise ship inside and there seems to always be a line up."[1] Lambert, also from Toronto, added: "If you've never been to the Cheesecake Factory I think you need to believe the hype. Their menu is a book ... the thing is pretty much a 20+ page listing of craziness."[2]

Comments like those are not unusual; the Cheesecake Factory (not to be confused with the Cheesecake Café) is famous for its extremely generous portions and has one of the most massive and varied menus in the industry. The over 300 dinner items and 20 choices of beverages on offer will take you a while to get through. That sounds impressive enough, but then you find out that everything is made from scratch! Except for one thing, that is: the cheesecake, which is actually made at headquarters in Calabasas, California.

The Cheesecake Factory serves more than 80 million people every year, has over 33,000 total staff, and is listed as one of *Fortune*'s 100 Most Admired Companies.[3] How can the restaurant manage all these items, people, and customers so effectively? Part of the answer lies in the how the company is structured.

One reason the restaurant is so popular is its consistency. Chuck Wensing, a vice-president of performance development, says, "We want someone to eat at a Cheesecake Factory in Las Vegas and another in Buffalo and be able to have the same experience. On a periodic basis, each restaurant is evaluated by 'mystery guests' who are trained to evaluate service, food, and experience based on a standardized scorecard."[4] The Cheesecake Factory has an efficient, hierarchical structure designed to focus on its products and services. Everything you see as a customer has likely been double- and triple-checked before it ever reaches your table.[5] Kitchen and restaurant managers are constantly giving feedback to cooks and servers anytime something doesn't seem exactly right.

You might think employees would need to be robots to thrive in such a system. But Cheesecake Factory employees don't feel that way, judging from the company's turnover rate, which is 15 percent below the competition.[6] In addition to efficiency, one thing a hierarchical organizational structure can also provide is a clear career path. Something you don't see as a diner is that many of the restaurant's managers have moved up through the ranks. This not only provides motivation for workers at lower levels (in addition to good salaries, the company gives every manager a new BMW every three years), but also encourages managers to respect those underneath them.[7]

14.1 What is an organization's structure, and what does it consist of?

ORGANIZATIONAL STRUCTURE

An organization's structure dictates more than you might think. As the Cheesecake Factory example illustrates, it can have a significant impact on its financial performance and ability to manage its employees. The decisions senior managers have made regarding the restaurant's organizational structure affect how employees communicate and cooperate with one another (Chapters 10 and 11), how power is distributed (Chapter 12), and how individuals view their work environment. We've spent a great deal of time in this book talking about how employee attitudes and behaviours are shaped by individual characteristics, such as personality and ability, and group mechanisms, such as teams and leaders. In this and the following chapter, we will discuss how the organization as a whole affects employee attitudes and behaviour.

Think of some jobs you've held in the past (or perhaps the one you hope to hold after graduation). What types of employees did you interact with daily? Did they perform the same tasks as you? If not, did they serve the same customer? How many employees did your manager supervise? Was every decision you made scrutinized by your supervisor, or were you given a long leash? The answers to all these questions are influenced by organizational structure. An **organizational structure** formally dictates how jobs and tasks are divided and coordinated between individuals and groups within the company. It can be relatively simple when a company has only 5–20 employees, but can grow incredibly complex, as in the case of the Cheesecake Factory's 33,000 employees.

organizational structure
Formally dictates how jobs and tasks are divided and coordinated between individuals and groups within the company

WHY DO SOME ORGANIZATIONS HAVE DIFFERENT STRUCTURES THAN OTHERS?

One way of getting a feel for an organization's structure is by looking at an organizational chart. An **organizational chart** is a drawing that represents every job in the organization and the formal reporting relationships between those jobs. It helps organizational members and outsiders understand and comprehend how work is structured within the company. Figure 14-1 illustrates two sample organizational charts. In a real chart, the boxes would contain actual names and job titles.

organizational chart
A drawing that represents every job in the organization and the formal reporting relationships between those jobs

FIGURE 14-1

Two Sample Organizational Structures

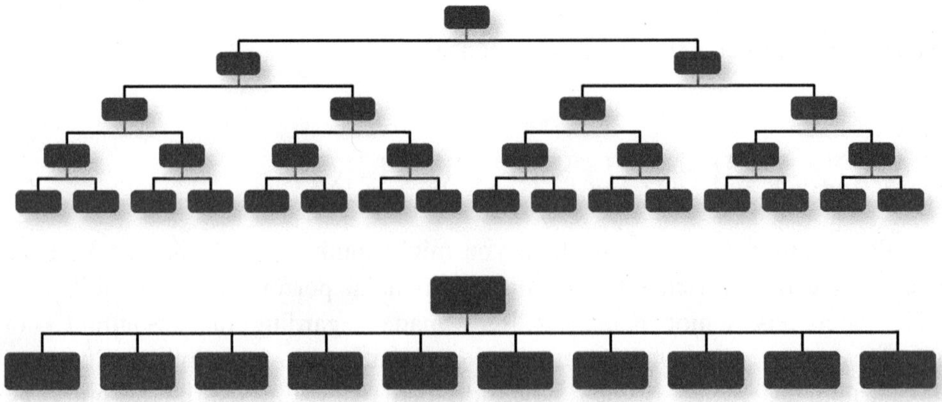

As might be expected, companies' organizational charts get more complex as they grow larger. Imagine drawing an organizational chart that included every one of the Cheesecake Factory's 33,000 employees! Not only would it require a lot of boxes and a lot of paper, but it would probably take a couple of months (plus, as soon as someone left the organization, you would have to update it!).

14.2 What are the major elements of an organizational structure?

Elements of Organizational Structure

The organizational charts described in this chapter are relatively simple and designed to illustrate specific points (if you want to see how complex some of these charts can get, do a search on the Internet for "organizational chart," and you'll begin to see how varied organizations can be in the way they design their company). For example, the charts in Figure 14-1 illustrate the five key elements of an organization's structure. Those elements, summarized in Table 14-1, describe how work tasks, authority relationships, and decision-making responsibilities are organized within the company. These elements will be discussed in the next several sections.

TABLE 14-1

Elements of Organizational Structure

Organizational Structure Dimension	Definition
Work specialization	Represents the degree to which tasks in an organization are divided into separate jobs.
Chain of command	Answers the question of who reports to whom and signifies formal authority relationships.
Span of control	Represents how many employees each manager in the organization has responsibility for.
Centralization	Refers to where decisions are formally made in organizations.
Formalization	Represents the degree to which rules and procedures are used to standardize behaviours and decisions in an organization.

Work Specialization **Work specialization** is the way tasks in an organization are divided into separate jobs. In some organizations, this categorization is referred to as a company's division of labour. How many tasks does any one employee perform? To some degree, work specialization is a never-ending trade-off among productivity, flexibility, and worker motivation. Take an assembly-line worker at Ford. Henry Ford was perhaps the earliest (and clearly most well-known) believer in extreme work specialization. He divided manufacturing to such a degree that each employee might perform only a single task, over and over again, all day long. Having only one task allowed workers to be extremely good at it. It also meant that the training of replacement workers was much easier.

work specialization
The degree to which tasks in an organization are divided into separate jobs

However, there are trade-offs. Highly specialized jobs can undermine employees' flexibility. Spending all their time performing specialized tasks well, they fail to update or practise other skills. Accounting majors, for example, might specialize in taxes or auditing, and some larger companies might hire them for their ability in one of these areas, but not both. Other companies might be looking for an accountant who can do both types of work well, depending on how they divide up accounting duties within their organization. Still other companies might want to hire "general managers" who understand accounting, finance, management, marketing, and operations as part of their job. Thus, although a high level of specialization might be acceptable in larger firms, it can be problematic in smaller firms in which employees have to be more versatile.

Organizations may also struggle with employee job satisfaction when they make jobs highly specialized. Recall the Chapter 5 discussion of five core characteristics of jobs that significantly affect satisfaction. One was variety, or the degree to which the job requires different activities involving different skills and talents.[8] You might be very efficient and productive performing a job involving only one task, but how happy would you be doing that job every day? One of the most famous films in early motion picture history was *Modern Times*, in which Charlie Chaplin was relegated to performing the same task over and over, very quickly. The movie ridiculed work specialization and the trend of treating employees as machines.

Modern Times (1932), starring Charlie Chaplin, ridiculed work specialization and the treating of employees as machines. Have things changed since then?

© Sunset Boulevard/Corbis

Chain of Command The **chain of command** within an organization essentially answers the question "Who reports to whom?" Every employee in a traditional organizational structure has one person to whom they report. That person then reports to someone else, and on and on, until the buck stops with the CEO (though in a public company, even the CEO is responsible to the board of directors). The chain of command can be seen as the specific flow of authority down through the levels of an organization's structure. At some companies, such as Valve Corporation, the videogame maker, 300 employees work with no managers or assigned projects. (Valve's website lets you know the company has been "boss free" since its founding in 1996.)[9] However, such organizations are the exception. Most depend on a chain of command's flow of authority to attain order, control, and predictable performance.[10] Some newer organizational structures make this chain a bit more complex. It has become common to have positions that report to two or more different managers. For example, Intel placed two people apiece in charge of the two largest divisions—although questions have arisen as to how their duties will be split up and whether employees will know whom it is they report to.[11]

chain of command

Specifies who reports to whom; signifies formal authority relationships

Span of Control A manager's **span of control** represents how many employees he or she is responsible for. The organizational charts in Figure 14-1 provide an illustration of the differences in span of control. In the top chart, each manager is responsible for leading two subordinates; in most instances, this would be considered a narrow span of control. In the bottom chart, the manager is responsible for ten employees; typically, this would be considered a wide span of control. Of course, the key question is often how many employees one manager can supervise effectively. Answering this requires a better understanding of the benefits of narrow and wide spans of control.

span of control

Represents how many employees each manager in the organization has responsibility for

Narrow spans of control allow managers to be much more hands-on with employees, using directive leadership styles while developing close mentoring relationships. A narrow span of control is especially important if the manager has substantially more skill or expertise than the subordinates. Early writings on management assumed that the narrower the span of control, the more productive employees would become.[12] However, a narrow span of control requires organizations to hire many managers, which can significantly increase labour costs. Moreover, if the span of control becomes too narrow, employees can become resentful of their close supervision and long for more latitude in their day-to-day decision making. In fact, current research suggests that a moderate span of control is best for an organization's productivity.[13]

This relationship is illustrated in Figure 14-2. Note that organizational performance increases as span of control increases, but only up to the point that managers no longer have the ability to coordinate and supervise the large numbers of employees underneath them. Most organizations work hard to try to find the right balance, and this balance differs for every organization, depending on its unique circumstances. However, there is no question that spans of control in organizations have increased significantly in recent years.[14] Organizations such as Coca-Cola have vice-presidents with up to 90 employees reporting to them![15]

FIGURE 14-2

Span of Control and Organizational Performance

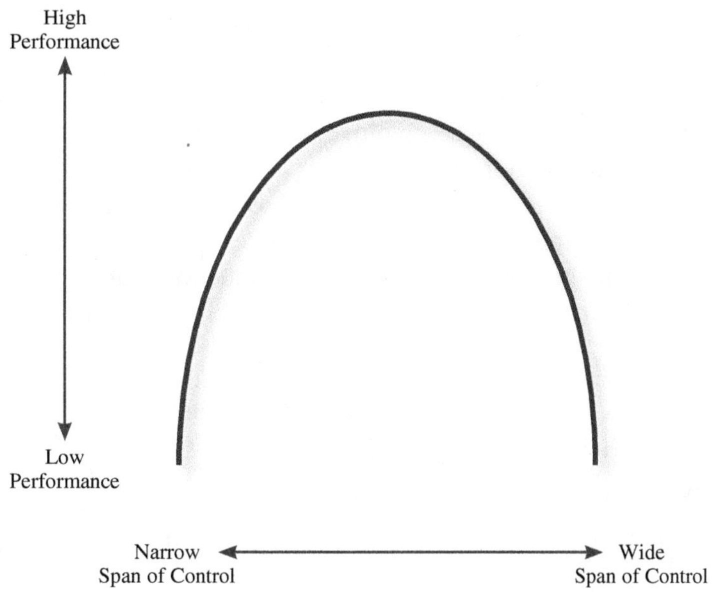

Source: Adapted from N.A. Theobald and S. Nicholson-Crotty, "The Many Faces of Span of Control: Organizational Structure Across Multiple Goals," *Administration and Society* 36 (2005), pp. 648–60.

An organization's span of control affects how "tall" or "flat" its organizational chart becomes. For example, the top panel of Figure 14-1 depicts a tall structure with many hierarchical levels and a narrow span of control, whereas the bottom panel depicts a flat organization with few levels and a wide span of control. Think about what happens when an organization becomes "taller." First, more layers of management means having to pay more management salaries. Second, communication in the organization becomes more complex as each new layer becomes one more point through which information must pass when travelling upward or downward. Third, the organization's ability to make decisions becomes slower, because decisions have to be approved at every step.

Throughout the 1990s and the 2000s, organizations worked to become flatter to reduce the costs associated with multiple layers of management and increase their ability to adapt to their environment. Intel, for example, announced a reduction in its managerial ranks of 1,000 positions (or 1 percent of its 100,000 employees). A spokesperson from Intel announced that "This [layoff] is designed to improve costs and improve decision making and communications across the company."[16] Putnam Investment Company also went through a flattening of its organization, reducing the workforce by 11 percent—including 25 of its 50 highest-paid executives. Putnam CEO Ed Haldeman noted: "To attract and retain the best people, it's necessary to provide them with the autonomy and independence to make decisions."[17]

Centralization **Centralization** refers to where decisions are formally made in organizations. If only the top managers within a company have the authority to make final decisions, we would say the organization has a highly "centralized" structure. In contrast, if lower-level employees are given authority to make decisions, an organization has a "decentralized" structure. Decentralization becomes necessary as a company grows larger. Sooner or later, the top management of an organization will not be able to make every single decision within the company. Centralized organizational structures tend to concentrate power in a relatively tight group of individuals in the firm, because they're the ones who have formal authority over important decisions.

centralization
Aspect of structure that dictates where decisions are formally made in organizations

Many organizations are moving toward a more decentralized structure. A manager can't have 20 employees reporting to him or her if those employees aren't allowed to make some decisions on their own. Airbus, the French manufacturer of airplanes, is doing its best to decentralize decision making. CEO Fabrice Brégier believes it's taking the company way too long to make decisions. "We make some of the world's most complex products, but that doesn't mean we have to be overly complex about how we do things." His goal is to give Airbus's production managers more independence to set priorities and move more quickly. Brégier states, "We need to funnel this down to just the people required to make decisions."[18]

Have the organizations where you've worked been largely centralized or decentralized? See our ***OB Assessments*** feature at the end of the chapter to find out.

Formalization A company is high in **formalization** when there are many specific rules and procedures used to standardize behaviours and decisions. Although it is not something you can necessarily see on an organizational chart, the impact of formalization is felt throughout the organization. Rules and procedures are a necessary mechanism for control in every organization. Although the word *formalization* has a somewhat negative connotation, imagine your reaction if the

Cheesecake Factory made its most popular menu items in different ways at each location. Or think about this: Would it bother you if every time you called Rogers for technical support, you got an operator who treated you differently and gave you conflicting answers? Formalization is a necessary coordination mechanism that organizations rely on to get a standardized product or deliver a standardized service.

formalization

The degree to which rules and procedures are used to standardize behaviours and decisions in an organization

Elements in Combination You may have noticed that some elements of an organization's structure seem to go hand-in-hand with others. For example, wide spans of control tend to be associated with decentralization in decision making. A high level of work specialization tends to bring about a high level of formalization. Moreover, if you take a closer look at the elements, you might notice that many of the elements capture the struggle between efficiency and flexibility. **Mechanistic organizations** are efficient, rigid, predictable, and standardized organizations that thrive in stable environments. They are typified by a structure that relies on high levels of formalization, a rigid and hierarchical chain of command, high degrees of work specialization, centralization of decision making, and narrow spans of control. In contrast, **organic organizations** are flexible, adaptive, outward-focused organizations that thrive in dynamic environments. Organic organizations are typified by a structure that relies on low levels of formalization, weak or multiple chains of command, low levels of work specialization, and wide spans of control. Table 14-2 sums up the differences between the two types of organizations.

mechanistic organizations

Efficient, rigid, predictable, and standardized organizations that thrive in stable environments

organic organizations

Flexible, adaptive, outward-focused organizations that thrive in dynamic environments

TABLE 14-2

Characteristics of Mechanistic vs. Organic Structures

Mechanistic Organizations	Organic Organizations
High degree of work specialization; employees are given a very narrow view of the tasks they are to perform.	Low degree of work specialization; employees are encouraged to take a broad view of the tasks they are to perform.
Very clear lines of authority; employees know exactly whom they report to.	Although there might be a specified chain of command, employees think more broadly in terms of where their responsibilities lie.
High levels of hierarchical control; employees are not encouraged to make decisions without their manager's consent.	Knowledge and expertise are decentralized; employees are encouraged to make their own decisions when appropriate.
Information is passed through vertical communication between an employee and his or her supervisor.	Lateral communication is encouraged, focusing on information and advice as opposed to orders.
Employees are encouraged to develop firm-specific knowledge and expertise within their area of specialization.	Employees are encouraged to develop knowledge and expertise outside of their specialization.

Source: Adapted from T. Burns and G.M. Stalker, *The Management of Innovation* (London: Tavistock, 1961).

If you think about the differences between the two types, it probably wouldn't be too difficult to come up with a few companies that fall more toward one end of the continuum or the other. Where would you place the Cheesecake Factory? Evidence indicates that a mechanistic or organic culture can have a significant effect on the types of employee practices a company adopts, such as selection, training, recruitment, compensation, and performance systems.[19] In addition, organic structures are more likely to allow for transformational leadership to have a positive effect on employees.[20] However, it's important to remember that few organizations are perfect examples of either extreme. Most fall somewhere near the middle, with certain areas within the organization having mechanistic qualities and others being more organic in nature. Microsoft is a good example. It has many organic qualities, but it has had teams that worked completely apart from each other while developing a major software platform who, when they finally came together, found that what they had done was incompatible—a mistake they tried to rectify during the creation of later versions of Windows.[21]

Although it's tempting to label mechanistic as "bad" and organic as "good," being mechanistic is the only way for many organizations to survive, and it can be a highly appropriate and fruitful way to structure work functions. To find out why that's the case, we need to explore why organizations develop the kinds of structures they do.

14.3 What is organizational design, and what factors does the organizational design process depend on?

Organizational Design

Organizational design is the process of creating, selecting, or changing the structure of an organization. Ideally, organizations don't just let a structure develop on its own; they proactively design it to match their circumstances and needs. Research shows that this is indeed how it works in most cases.[22] However, some organizations aren't so proactive and find themselves with a structure that has developed on its own, without any careful planning; they may then be forced to change their structure to become more effective.

organizational design

The process of creating, selecting, or changing the structure of an organization

A number of factors should influence the process of organizational design, including the environment in which the organization does business, its corporate strategy and technology, and the size of the firm. However, for some firms in dire straits, changing the structure becomes a strategy in and of itself, often leading to very poor results.[23]

Business Environment An organization's **business environment** consists of its customers, competitors, suppliers, distributors, and other factors external to the firm, all of which influence organizational design. One of the biggest factors is whether the outside environment is stable or dynamic. Stable environments don't change frequently or quickly, so they they allow organizations to focus on efficiency. In contrast, dynamic environments change on a frequent basis and require organizations to have structures that are more adaptive.[24] Sony made a famous mistake when it failed to meet the needs of its changing business environment to match Apple's iPod.[25] Because it took it so long to recognize and adapt to this shift, Sony has struggled to be profitable. Some would argue the world is changing so fast that the majority of companies can no longer keep up.

business environment

The outside environment, including customers, competitors, suppliers, distributors, and other factors external to the firm, which all affect organizational design

Company Strategy A **company strategy** describes an organization's objectives and goals and how it tries to capitalize on its assets. The whole variety of organizational strategies is too involved to discuss here; but suffice it to say that two common strategies revolve around being either a low-cost producer or a differentiator.[26] Companies that focus on a low-cost producer strategy rely on selling products at the lowest possible cost. To do this well, they have to focus on being as efficient as possible. Such companies are more likely to take a mechanistic approach to organizational design. Other companies might follow a differentiation strategy. Rather than focusing on supplying a product or service at the lowest cost, they believe people will pay more for a product that's unique in some way. Perhaps their product has a higher level of quality or offers features a low-cost product doesn't. A differentiation strategy often hinges on adjusting to changing environments quickly, tends to make an organic structure more appropriate.

company strategy

An organization's objectives and goals and how it tries to capitalize on its assets to make money

Technology An organization's **technology** is the method by which it transforms inputs into outputs. Very early on in the study of organizations, it was assumed that technology was the major determinant of an organization's structure.[27] Since then, the picture has become less clear regarding the appropriate relationship between technology and structure.[28] Although not completely conclusive, research suggests that the more routine a technology is, the more mechanistic a structure should be. In many ways, this suggestion makes perfect sense: If a company makes the exact same thing over and over, it should focus on creating that one thing as efficiently as possible by having high levels of specialization, formalization, and centralization. However, if technologies need to be changed or altered to suit the needs of various consumers, it follows that decisions would be more decentralized and the rules and procedures the organization relies on would need to be more flexible.

technology

The method by which an organization transforms inputs to outputs

Partly due to its organizational structure, Sony was unable to adjust to its changing business environment, allowing Apple to dominate the portable music player market with its innovative line of iPods.

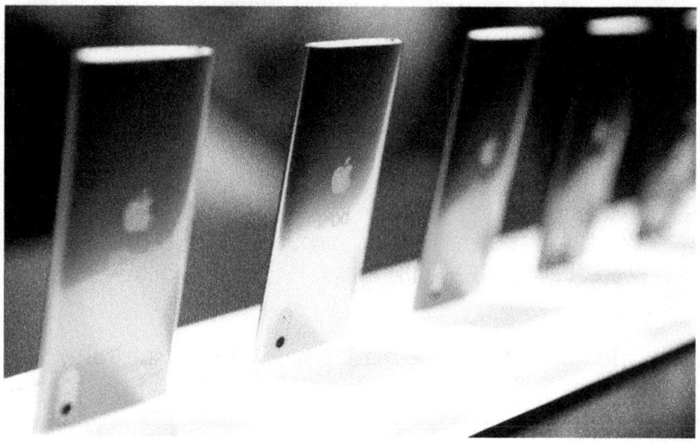

© AP-Jeff Chiu/The Canadian Press

Company Size There is no question that there is a significant relationship between **company size,** or the total number of employees, and structure.[29] As organizations become larger, they need to rely on some combination of specialization, formalization, and centralization to control their activities, thereby becoming more mechanistic in nature. When it comes to organizational performance, however, there is no definite answer as to when an organization's structure should be revised, or "how big is too big."[30] As many organizations get bigger, they attempt to create smaller units within the firm to create a "feeling of smallness." W.L. Gore did just that by attempting to prevent any one location in the company from having more than 150 employees. Top management was convinced that a size of 150 would still allow all the employees to talk to one another in the hallways. However, even Gore hasn't been able to maintain that goal; the company has grown to encompass 7,300 employees in 45 locations.[31] Even if they can't technically create smaller groups due to their overwhelming size, some companies such as PepsiCo and snack food company Mondelēz International (110,000 employees) are going so far as to send their employees to spend time in some technology and media start-up firms so that they can come back with a sense of "smallness" that they hope will create an entrepreneurial spirit within their larger organizations.[32]

company size

The number of employees in a company

14.4 What are some of the more common organizational forms that an organization might adopt for its structure?

COMMON ORGANIZATIONAL FORMS

Our discussion of organizational design described how an organization's business environment, strategy, technology, and size conspire to make some organizational structures more effective than others. Now we turn our attention to a logical next question: What structures do most organizations utilize? The sections that follow describe some of the most common organizational forms. As you read their descriptions, think about whether these forms would fall on the mechanistic or the organic side of the structure continuum. You might also consider what kinds of design factors would lead an organization to choose that particular form.

Simple Structures A **simple structure** is perhaps the most common form of organizational design, primarily because there are more small organizations than large ones. In fact, more than 80 percent of employing organizations have fewer than 19 employees.[33] Small accounting and law firms, family-owned grocery stores, individual-owned retail outlets, independent churches, and landscaping services are all likely to use a simple structure.

simple structure

An organizational form that features one person as the central decision-making figure

Figure 14-3 shows a simple structure for a manager-owned restaurant. The figure reveals that simple structures are just that. They are generally used by extremely small organizations in which the manager, president, and owner are all the same person. A simple structure is a flat organization with one person as the central decision-making figure; it is not large enough to have a high degree of formalization and will have only very basic differences in work specialization.

FIGURE 14-3

An Organizational Structure for a Small Restaurant

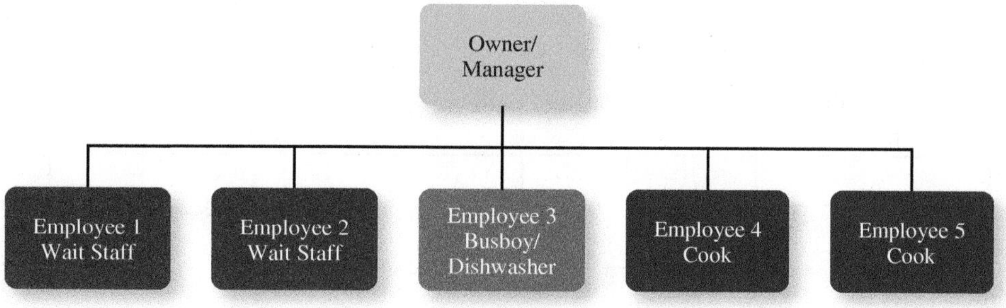

A simple structure makes perfect sense for a small organization, because employees can come and go with no major ripple effects. However, as the business grows, the coordinating efforts on the part of the owner/manager become increasingly more complex. Let's assume that the growth of a restaurant requires the owner to spend time doing lots of little things to manage the employees. Now the manager has lost the ability to spend time focusing on the actual business at hand. He or she then decides to add a supervisor to handle the day-to-day activities. This arrangement works well until the owner decides to open a second restaurant needing its own supervisor. Now let's assume that this second restaurant is much larger, leading the owner to decide to have separate supervisors directly in charge of the wait staff and the kitchen. All of a sudden, our little restaurant has three layers of management!

Bureaucratic Structures When you think of bureaucracy, what ideas come to mind? Most likely, things like "stuffy," "boring," "restrictive," "formal," "hard to change," "needlessly complex," etc. Even so, chances are very good that you either currently work in a bureaucracy or will after you graduate. A **bureaucratic structure** is an organizational form that exhibits many of the facets of the mechanistic organization. Bureaucracies are designed for efficiency and rely on high levels of work specialization, formalization, centralization of authority, rigid and well-defined chains of command, and relatively narrow spans of control. As mentioned previously, when an organization grows it almost has to develop some form of bureaucracy.

bureaucratic structure
An organizational form that exhibits many of the facets of a mechanistic organization

Of the numerous types of bureaucratic structures on which we might focus, the most basic is the **functional structure**. As is shown in Figure 14-4, a functional structure groups employees by the roles they fulfill in the organization. For example, employees with marketing expertise are grouped together, those with finance duties are grouped together, and so on. The success of the functional structure is based on the efficiency advantages that come with having a high degree of work specialization that's centrally coordinated.[34] Managers have expertise in an area and interact with others with the same type of expertise to create the most efficient solutions for the company. As illustrated in our previous example of the fast-growing restaurant, many small companies naturally evolve into functionally based structures as they grow larger.

functional structure
An organizational form in which employees are grouped by the functions they perform for the organization

FIGURE 14-4

Functional and Multi-divisional Structures

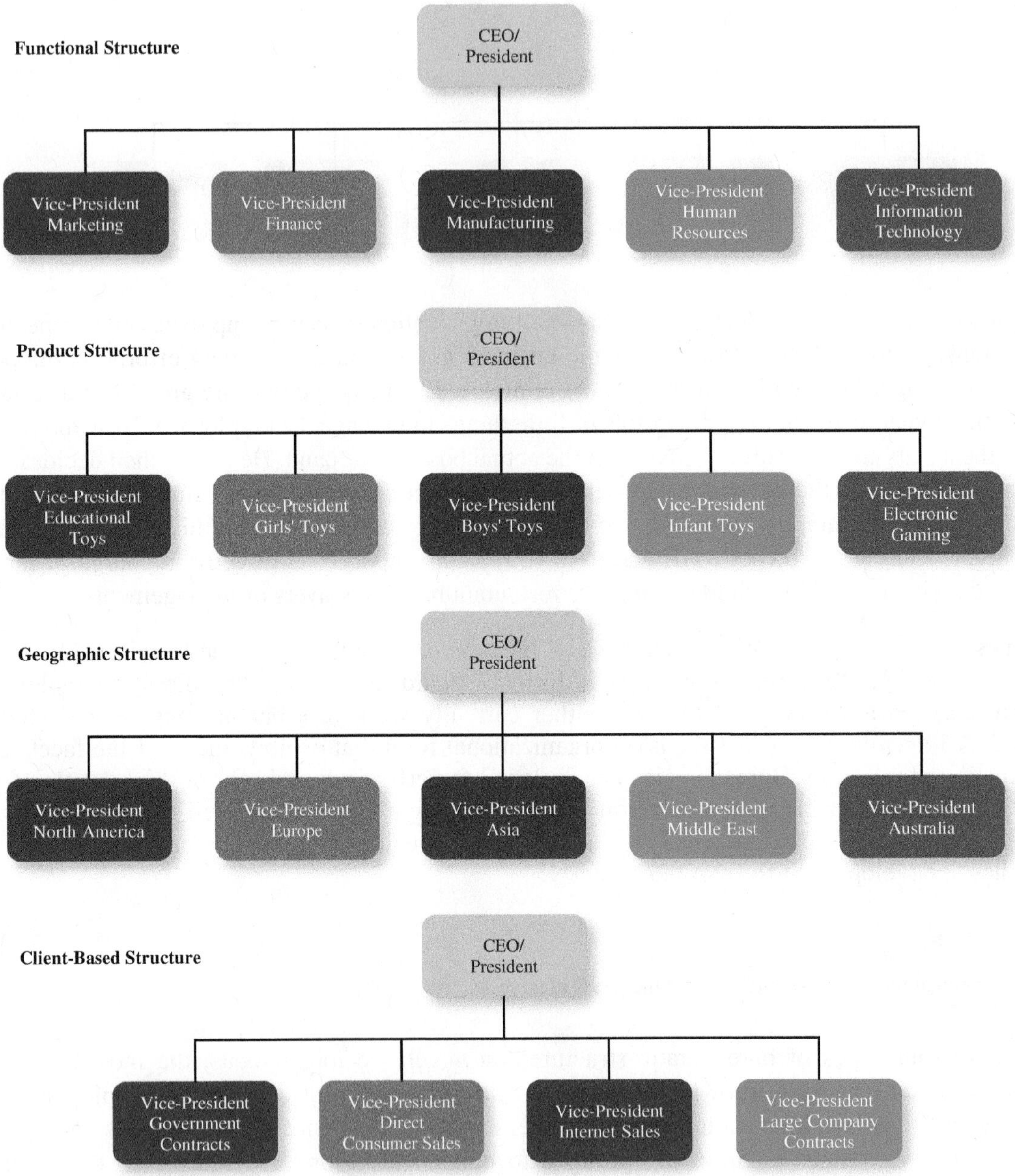

Functional structures are extremely efficient when the organization as a whole has a relatively narrow focus, fewer product lines or services, and a stable environment. The biggest weaknesses of a functional structure tend to revolve around the fact that individuals within each function get so wrapped up in their own goals and viewpoints that they lose sight of the bigger organizational picture. In other words, employees don't communicate as well across functions as they do within functions. The Sony example also highlights this danger: hardware engineers failed to communicate with software developers, which prevented the hardware and software people from seeing all the pieces of the puzzle.[35]

OB FOR STUDENTS

Whether it's obvious to you or not, structure has a significant effect on you as a student. What organizations are you a part of? Fraternities, sororities, professional associations, student government, and other campus organizations all have structures that influence how decisions are made, where the power lies, and how involved members are in the day-to-day goings-on. Indeed, even your university as a whole affects you by the way it is structured.

As you begin to search for jobs, there is evidence you will be attracted to certain organizations on the basis of their structure. On the whole, university-level job seekers tend to find centralization an unattractive characteristic in organizations. It's not hard to see why. Most job seekers like the idea of being able to make decisions on their own without someone else's approval.

Does anyone find centralization attractive? Not usually, but there is evidence that some job seekers are less affected by centralization than others. For example, research has shown that job seekers with high self-esteem are less bothered by centralization.[36] That is, the negative effect of centralization on organizational attractiveness is weaker for them. Perhaps they feel confident they can "fight the system" if they need to!

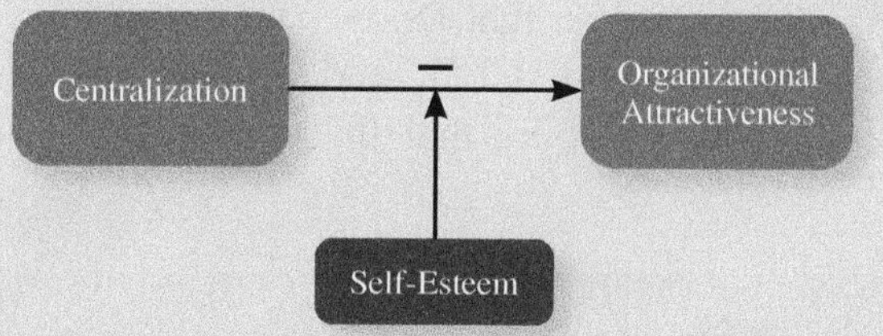

Regardless, when you begin your search for a job, some good questions to ask in an interview might revolve around the structure of the company. How many people will be working for your immediate supervisor? How does the group you are looking to work with fit in with the rest of the organization? Will you be working for one direct supervisor or will you have reporting responsibilities to a number of managers? Questions like these are likely to impress an interviewer. Understanding these aspects of organizational structure might also help you decide between multiple job offers.

In contrast to a functional structure, a **multi-divisional structure** is a bureaucratic organizational form in which employees are grouped into divisions around products, geographic regions, or clients (see Figure 14-4). Each of these divisions operates relatively autonomously from the others and has its own functional groups. Multi-divisional structures generally develop from companies with functional structures whose interests and goals become too diverse for that structure to handle. For example, if a company with a functional structure begins to add customers that require localized versions of its product, the company might adopt a geographic structure to handle the product variations. Which form a company chooses will likely depend on where the diversity in its business lies.

multi-divisional structure

An organizational form in which employees are grouped by product, geography, or client

A **product structure** groups business units around different products that the company produces. Each of those divisions becomes responsible for manufacturing, marketing, and doing research and development for the products in its own division. Boeing, Procter & Gamble, and Sony are companies that have developed product structures. Product structures make sense when firms diversify to the point that the products they sell are so different that managing them becomes overwhelming.

product structure

An organizational form in which employees are grouped around different products that the company produces

Hewlett-Packard's organizational structure recently changed to become more product-based. The company did this because its sales force (in a centralized functional structure) simply had way too many products to sell (from the largest servers to the smallest printers). Organizing into three product divisions allowed salespeople to concentrate on a core set of products, which had a reinvigorating effect on their work.[37]

However, there are downsides to a product structure. Sometimes the divisions don't communicate and they don't have the ability to learn from one another. Darden Restaurants (perhaps the largest competitor of the Cheesecake Factory, this chapter's opening example) is, for the first time, bringing the headquarters for all of its restaurants under one roof in Orlando, Florida. Their hope is that it will allow managers from Olive Garden, Red Lobster, and Longhorn Steakhouse to learn from each other and focus on best practices.[38]

Not all companies want their divisions to share, though—they want them to compete. Fiat-Chrysler CEO Sergio Marchionne has reorganized so that Dodge, Jeep, and Chrysler are essentially operating as separate companies, each with its own CEO, and are forced to compete for marketing and development resources. Marchionne is hoping that the competition will help turn all three brands around.[39]

Clarence Otis, CEO of Darden Restaurants, is bringing all of the company's restaurants together in order to have them share information with one another.

A **geographic structure** is generally based on the different locations where the company does business. The functions required to serve a business are placed under a manager who is in charge of a specific location. Reasons for developing a geographic structure revolve around the different tastes of customers in different regions, the size of the locations that need to be covered by different salespeople, or the fact that the manufacturing and distribution of a product are better served by a geographic breakdown.

geographic structure
An organizational form in which employees are grouped around the different locations where the company does business

Before the Regus Group (a U.K. company) and HQ Global Workplaces (a U.S. company) merged, they had had different structures. Now, the new Regus Group, with 750 office suite facilities in 350 cities across 60 countries, is the world's largest supplier of meeting spaces and office suites; and because of the necessarily geographically based nature of their business (i.e., the distances between facilities and the range of customers), it is structured by geographic region.[40]

Many other global companies are organized by geographic location. IBM was one of the first, but that might be changing, as is discussed in our ***OB Internationally*** feature.

OB INTERNATIONALLY

Traditionally, IBM has structured its 200,000-employee organization along geographic lines. Some might argue that IBM was the company that pioneered the first multinational geographic structure by setting up mini-IBMs in countries around the globe. Each country in which IBM operated had its own workforce and management team that reacted to the clients for whom it provided services in that country. The structure made perfect sense in a world in which consultants needed to be on location with their clients when those customers were having software or computer issues. However, IBM's environmental factors are changing rapidly. Competitors, especially those coming out of India, are providing many of the same services for significantly less money.

To change along with its competitors and respond to the "flattening world," IBM is reorganizing its workforce by creating and utilizing what it calls "competency centres," which will group employees from around the world on the basis of the skill sets they have to offer clients. Some will be grouped into one location that can service clients all over the world through the use of technology. For instance, IBM recently announced that it will invest $300 million over ten years in its new Costa Rica service centre, which serves as the newest strategic services hub for the company and intends to employ up to 1,000 people by 2014. The facility will support clients mainly as a cloud computing centre of competency.[41] In Boulder, Colorado, IBM employs 6,200 professionals as part of a call centre that monitors clients' computing functions worldwide. If something goes wrong in one of IBM's 426 data centres, employees in Boulder will more than likely be the ones to handle it or send it to someone who can. Other IBM workers will be grouped by broader geographic locations so that they can still be in relatively close proximity to their customers. When these employees are needed by a client, IBM has a computer database that allows it to put together teams of highly specialized consultants by examining the skill sets listed on 70,000 IBM résumés.

Does this change in structure sound familiar to you? It should—though IBM is maintaining some of its geographic structure, its organization is becoming more functional. As the world becomes flatter through technology, clients expect the best talent from around the world, not just the best talent that happens to be sitting in their city. These structural changes will allow IBM to give clients just that. For IBM, these are the necessary changes that come with being a global company.[42] In fact, IBM has recently been called "the world's most complex organization."[43] It's not just about structure though, according to IBM Senior Vice-President Robert W. Moffat Jr.: "Globalization is more than that. Our customers need us to put the right skills in the right place at the right time."[44]

One last form of multi-divisional structure is the **client structure**. When organizations have a number of very large customers or groups of customers that all act similarly, they might organize their businesses around those customers. For example, small banks traditionally organize themselves into divisions such as personal banking, small business banking, personal lending, and commercial lending. Similarly, consulting firms often organize themselves into divisions that are responsible for small business clients, large business clients, and federal clients. After spending its entire existence organized around a product structure (as are most technology companies), Dell recently adopted a client structure in order to give its top managers more responsibility and flexibility. The company is now structured around four customer groupings: consumers, corporations, small and midsized businesses, and government and educational buyers.[45]

client structure
An organizational form in which employees are organized around serving customers

A **matrix structure** is a more complex design that tries to take advantage of two types of structures at the same time. Companies such as Xerox, General Electric, and Dow Corning were among the first to adopt this type of structure.[46] Figure 14-5 provides an example of a matrix structure in which employees are distributed into teams or projects within the organization on the basis of both their functional expertise and the product they happen to be working on. Thus, the matrix represents a combination of a functional and a product structure. There are two important points to understand about such a structure. First, the matrix allows an organization to put together very flexible teams on the basis of experiences and skills;[47] this enables it to adjust much more quickly to the environment than a traditional bureaucratic structure would. Second, the matrix gives each employee two chains of command, two groups with which to interact, and two sources of information to consider. This doubling of traditional structural elements can create high stress levels for employees if the demands of their functional grouping are at odds with the demands of their product- or client-based grouping.[48] The situation can become particularly stressful if one of the two groupings has more power than the other. For example, perhaps the functional manager assigns employees to teams, conducts performance evaluations, and decides raises—making that manager more powerful than the product- or client-based manager.[49]

matrix structure
A complex form of organizational structure that combines a functional and multi-divisional grouping

Although matrix structures have been around since the 1960s, the number of organizations using them is growing as teams become a more common form of organizing work. They have also become more common in global companies, with the functional grouping balanced by a geographic grouping. In fact, numerous companies now have matrix structures with enough layers to be considered four- or five-dimensional.[50] Bristol-Myers Squibb, the biopharmaceutical company, is heavily matrixed throughout. Jane Luciano, vice-president of global learning and organizational development, explains: "We have the matrix every way it can be organized, including geographically, functionally, and on a product basis. Based on our size and in a highly regulated industry, the matrix helps us to gain control of issues as they travel around the globe and to aleverage economies of scale."[51]

FIGURE 14-5

Matrix Structure

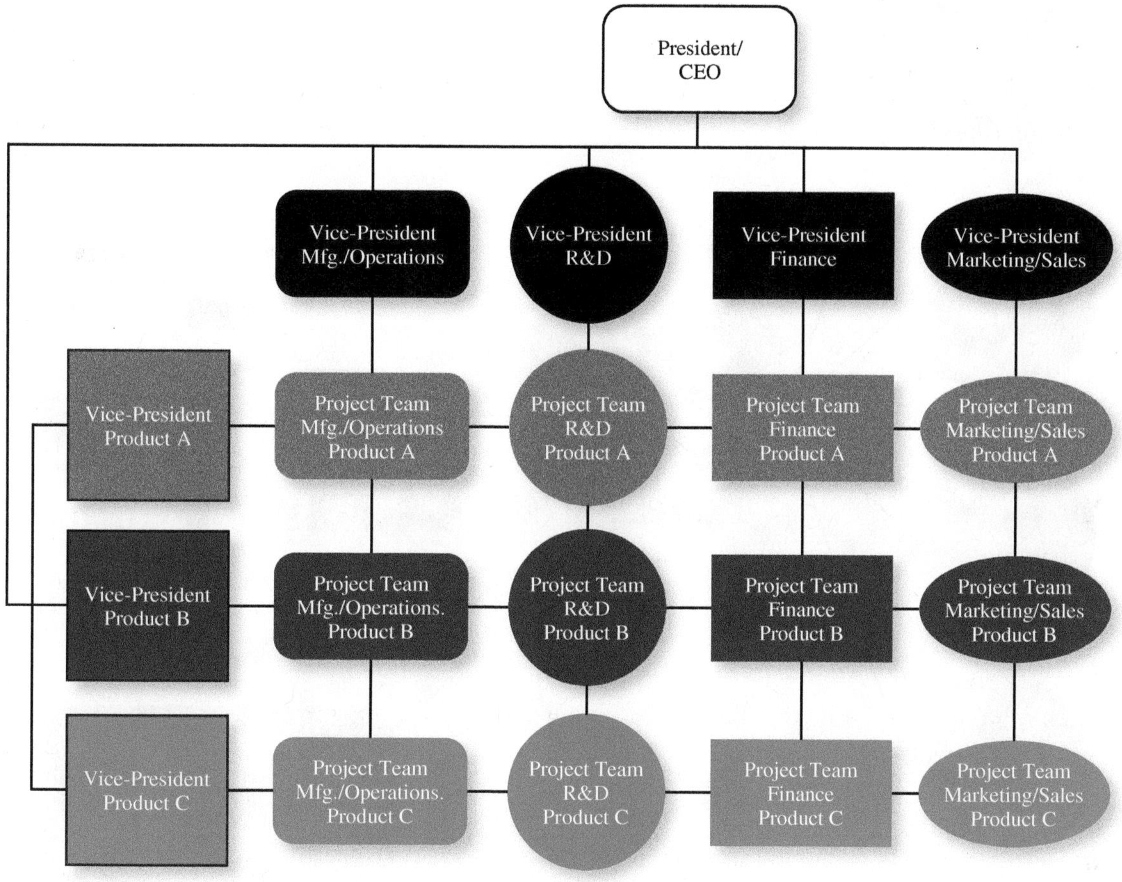

Summary: Why Do Some Organizations Have Different Structures Than Others?

So why do some organizations have different structures? Figure 14-6 shows how differences in the business environment, company strategy, technology, and firm size cause some organizations to be designed differently than others. The differences create variations in the five elements of organizational structure: work specialization, chain of command, span of control, centralization, and formalization. These elements then combine to form one of a number of common organizational forms, including (1) a simple structure; (2) a bureaucratic structure, which may come in functional, product, geographic, or client forms; or (3) a matrix structure. Some of these forms are more mechanistic, whereas others are more organic. Taken together, these structures explain how work is organized within a given company.

FIGURE 14-6

Why Do Some Organizations Have Different Structures Than Others?

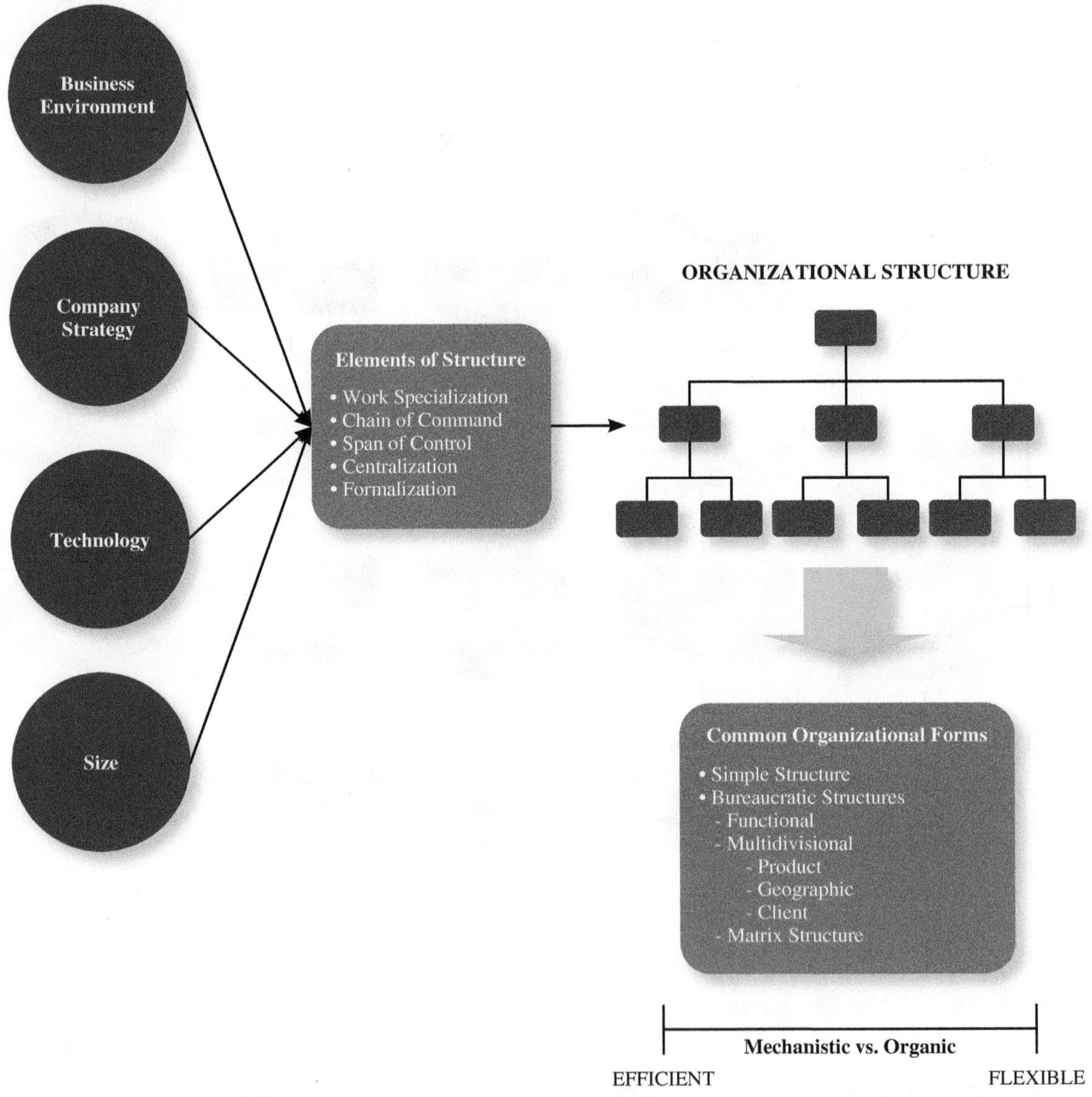

14.5 When an organization makes changes to its structure, how does that restructuring affect job performance and organizational commitment?

HOW IMPORTANT IS STRUCTURE?

To some degree, an organization's structure provides the foundation for almost everything in organizational behaviour. Think of all the things it affects: communication patterns between employees, the tasks an employee performs, the types of groups an organization uses, the freedom employees have to innovate and try new things, how power and influence are divided up in the company ... we could go on and on.

For example, the occupants of a house can decorate or personalize the structure as best they can; they can make it more attractive according to their preferences by adding and taking away furniture. But at the end of the day they're stuck with that structure. They have to work within the confines of what the builder envisioned (unless they're willing to tear down walls or build new ones at the expense of considerable time, effort, and money!). Organizational structures are much the same. A manager can do many things to try to motivate, inspire, and set up an effective work environment so that employees have high levels of performance and commitment. At the end of the day, however, that manager must work within the structure created by the organization.

Given how many organizational forms there are, it's almost impossible to accurately represent the impact of organizational structure on job performance. We might even say that an organization's structure determines what job performance is supposed to look like! In addition, specific elements of structure are not necessarily good or bad for performance. For example, a narrow span of control is not necessarily better than a broad one; rather, the organization must find the optimal solution based on its environment and culture. One thing we can say, as illustrated in Figure 14-7, is that changes to an organization's structure can have negative effects on the employees who work for the company, at least in the short term.

FIGURE 14-7

Effects of Organizational Structure on Performance and Commitment

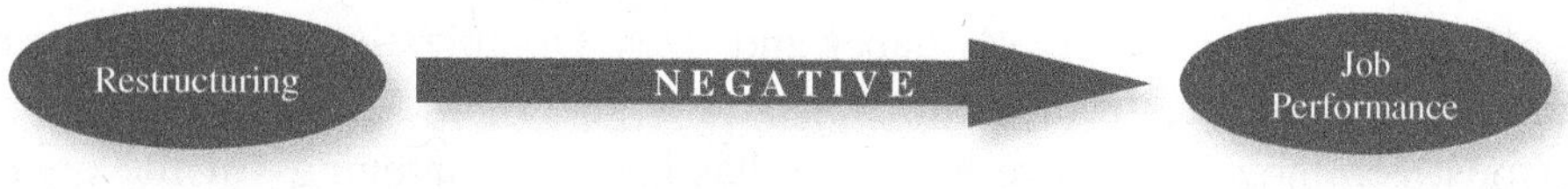

Restructuring has a weak negative effect on Job Performance. *Task Performance* tends to be somewhat lower in organizations that restructure. Not much is known about the impact of restructuring on *Citizenship Behaviour* or *Counterproductive Behaviour*.

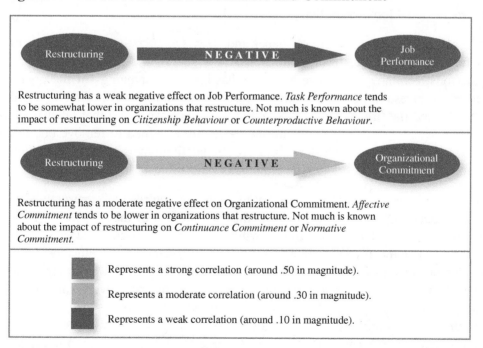

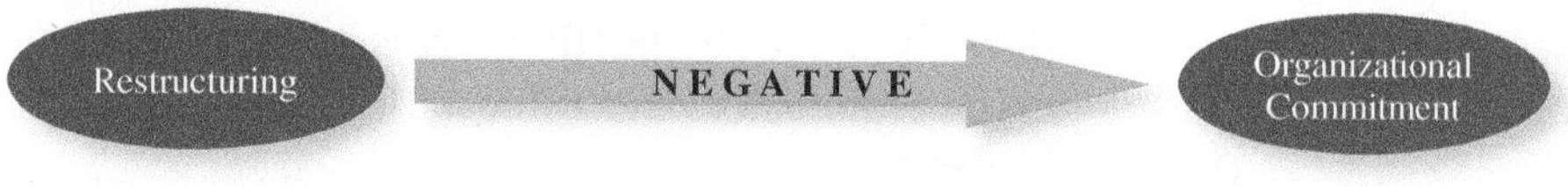

Restructuring has a moderate negative effect on Organizational Commitment. *Affective Commitment* tends to be lower in organizations that restructure. Not much is known about the impact of restructuring on *Continuance Commitment* or *Normative Commitment*.

Represents a strong correlation (around .50 in magnitude).

Represents a moderate correlation (around .30 in magnitude).

Represents a weak correlation (around .10 in magnitude).

Sources: K.P. DeMeuse, M.L. Marks, and G. Dai, "Organizational Downsizing, Mergers and Acquisitions, and Strategic Alliances: Using Theory and Research to Enhance Practice." In *APA Handbook of Industrial and Organizational Psychology*, Vol. 3, ed. S. Zedeck. Washington: APA (2011), pp. 729–68; C. Gopinath and T.E. Becker, "Communication, Procedural Justice, and Employee Attitudes: Relationships under Conditions of Divestiture," *Journal of Management* 26 (2000), pp. 63–83; and J. Brockner, G. Spreitzer, A. Mishra, W. Hockwarter, L. Pepper, and J. Weinberg, "Perceived Control as an Antidote to the Negative Effects of Layoffs on Survivors' Organizational Commitment and Job Performance," *Administrative Science Quarterly* 49 (2004), pp. 76–100.

The process of changing an organization's structure is called **restructuring**. Research suggests that restructuring has a small negative effect on task performance, likely because changes in specialization, centralization, or formalization may lead to confusion about how exactly employees are supposed to do their jobs, which hinders *learning* and *decision making*. Restructuring has a more significant negative effect on organizational commitment, however. Restructuring efforts can increase *stress* and jeopardize employees' *trust* in the organization.[52] There is some evidence that the end result is a lower level of affective commitment on the part of employees, because they feel less emotionally attached to the firm.

restructuring
The process of changing an organization's structure

14.6 What steps can organizations take to reduce the negative effects of restructuring efforts?

APPLICATION: RESTRUCTURING

Reading through our discussion of organizational structure, you may have noticed how important it is for organizations to adapt to their environment. The first step in adapting is recognizing the need to change. The second (and sometimes much more problematic) step is actually adapting through restructuring. Organizations attempt to restructure all the time—in fact, it's difficult to pick up a copy of *Bloomberg Businessweek* or *Fortune* without reading about some organization's restructuring initiatives. General Motors has undertaken a massive restructuring effort no less than eight times over the past 25 years![53] (And look where that got them ...!)

Restructuring efforts come in a variety of shapes and sizes. Organizations may change from a product-based to a functional structure, from a functional to a geographic-based structure, and on and on. However, the most common form in recent years has been a "flattening" of the organization. Why? Primarily to show investors they are reducing costs to become more profitable. Think back to our discussion of tall and flat organizational hierarchies, in which we noted that taller organizations have more layers of management. Many restructuring efforts are designed to remove one or more of those layers to reduce costs. Of course, this doesn't just mean deleting boxes on an organizational chart; there are actual people in those boxes! Flattening requires organizations to lay off managers.

When employees get a sense that their company might be getting ready to restructure, it causes a great deal of stress because they become worried that they will be one of those to lose their jobs. When ex-CEO Carly Fiorina decided to restructure Hewlett-Packard, it caused widespread fear, even panic, among employees. For the 60 days prior to the actual restructuring announcement, work came to a standstill—tales of high stress, low motivation, political battles, and power struggles abounded.[54] It's estimated that Hewlett-Packard as a company lost an entire quarter's worth of productivity.[55] Since Fiorina's actions, two subsequent CEOs have restructured the company when they took over. Mark Hurd essentially undid everything Fiorina had done by unmerging units she had merged. Now, Meg Whitman, HP's newest CEO, has just come in and reorganized it all again by re-merging HP's PC and printer units (of course, accompanied by an announcement of further layoffs).[56] For one example of how restructuring and layoffs can affect employees, see this chapter's ***OB on Screen***.

OB ON SCREEN

The Company Men

What do you want me to do? Parrot back everything you say? I've always told you what I think, right or wrong, and this ... is wrong.

With those words, Gene McClary (Tommy Lee Jones) makes a last-ditch plea to CEO James Sallinger (Craig T. Nelson) to avoid another round of layoffs in *The Company Men* (Dir. John Wells, Weinstein Company, 2010). McClary (along with Sallinger) is one of the co-founders of Boston company GTX, currently second in command, and is in charge of the last vestige of heavy manufacturing (ship-building) in the company. Although the layoffs will likely raise the stock price and make him considerably wealthier, having his company release thousands of people from their jobs tears at him emotionally—eventually ruining a lifetime friendship and getting him fired as well. One scene depicts the process of deciding whom to lay off and McClary questioning the ethics of the company's choices even if they're legally defensible.

The movie's main story line gives us a glimpse into the trials and tribulations of some of those laid off, namely Bobby Walker (Ben Affleck) and Phil Woodward (Chris Cooper), and details the struggle of trying to find a new job through outplacement services (Bobby ends up working for his home-renovating brother-in-law [Kevin Costner] for a period). However, it also shows us employees who are left behind and the feelings they typically have during the restructuring process. We see high levels of anxiety and stress due to employees' not knowing if they will have a job the next day or not. The first interactions Bobby Walker has with fellow employees after his exit interview are not statements of sympathy, but rather "Have you heard anything about me?" questions. Following the restructuring, layoff survivors grapple with how they're going to get all the work done with fewer people around to do it. One employee asks McClary, "I'm already traveling two out of every four weeks, what am I supposed to tell my kids?" McClary's quick response is, "Tell them you're lucky enough to have a job."

One of the ways managers can assist a restructuring effort succeed is to help manage the layoff survivors (i.e., employees who remain with the company following a layoff). Many of them are known to experience a great deal of guilt and remorse following an organization's decision to remove some employees.[57] Researchers and practitioners have recently been trying to understand layoff survivors better and learn how to help them adjust.

One of the major problems for survivors is the increased job demands put on them. After all, that co-worker or boss the employee had was doing *something*. Layoff survivors are generally burdened with having to pick up the leftover tasks that used to be done by somebody else.[58] This burden creates a sense of uncertainty and stress.[59]

Research suggests that one of the best ways to help layoff survivors adjust is to do things that give them a stronger sense of control,[60] such as giving them a voice in how to move forward or help them set the plans about how to accomplish future goals. In addition, honest and frequent communication with them greatly helps reduce feelings of uncertainty and stress.[61] Communication is especially necessary when the organization is hiring at the same time it's firing. For instance, Boeing planned to cut 9,000 jobs in 2009, but in the same year it had more than 1,500 current and anticipated job openings.[62] Many other employers, such as Microsoft, AT&T, and Time Warner, have experienced something similar.[63] This sends mixed messages both to those being laid off and the survivors. One sobering fact is that the survivors never know whether the restructuring will lead to success, or if it's simply a process of grasping at straws to avoid the ultimate demise of the company. For a restructuring to be truly successful, it requires more than simply changing lines on an organizational chart; it demands a different way of working for employees.[64]

OB RESEARCH IN CANADA

Dr. Kai Lamertz teaches and conducts research in the areas of organizational behaviour and organizational theory at the John Molson School of business at Concordia University. It is fitting to feature Dr. Lamertz's research in this chapter, because he studies, among other things, how the behaviour (e.g., citizenship) and beliefs (e.g., social identity) of individuals and groups are influenced by their social and organizational contexts.

Anna J. Gunaratnam

Students might be interested to learn that Dr. Lamertz has conducted extensive studies in the beer brewing industry. Asked how social networks affect individual behaviour and attitudes, Dr. Lamertz replied, "It's the relationships that connect us to other people serve as pipelines for information about opportunities to perform vital tasks or support others and those relationships create a web of expectations by others about what we should do, say, or think." He went on to say that we are "social creatures, involved in relationships, groups, and societies, which affect our personal thoughts, choices, and actions. The beer brewing industry is a case in point: today's craft breweries are part of an industry subculture in which business is not just about money and self-interest but also pleasure and community." To learn more about Dr. Lamertz and his work, look him up at www.concordia.ca.

TAKEAWAYS

14.1 An organization's structure formally dictates how jobs and tasks are divided and coordinated between individuals and groups within the organization. This structure, partially illustrated through the use of organizational charts, provides the foundation for organizing jobs, controlling employee behaviour, shaping communication channels, and providing a lens through which employees view their work environment.

14.2 There are five major elements to an organization's structure: work specialization, chain of command, span of control, centralization of decision making, and formalization. These elements can be organized in such a way as to make an organization more mechanistic in nature, which allows it to be highly efficient in stable environments, or more organic in nature, which allows it to be flexible and adaptive in changing environments.

14.3 Organizational design is the process of creating, selecting, or changing the structure of an organization. Factors to be considered in organizational design include a company's business environment, its strategy, its technology, and its size.

14.4 There are literally thousands of organizational forms. The most common is the simple structure, which is used by most small companies. Larger companies adopt a more bureaucratic structure. This structure may be functional in nature, so that employees are grouped by job tasks, or multi-divisional, so that employees are grouped by product, geography, or client. Organizations may also adopt a matrix structure that combines functional and multi-divisional grouping.

14.5 Organizational restructuring efforts have a weak negative effect on job performance. They have a more significant negative effect on organizational commitment, because employees tend to feel less emotional attachment to organizations that are restructuring.

14.6 To reduce the negative effects of restructuring, organizations should focus on managing the stress levels of the employees who remain after the restructuring. Providing employees with a sense of control can help them learn to navigate their new work environment.

KEY TERMS

bureaucratic structure
business environment
centralization
chain of command
client structure
company size
company strategy
formalization
functional structure
geographic structure
matrix structure
mechanistic organizations

multi-divisional structure
organic organizations
organizational chart
organizational design
organizational structure
product structure
restructuring
simple structure
span of control
technology
work specialization

DISCUSSION QUESTIONS

14.1 Is it possible to be a great leader of employees in a highly mechanistic organization? What special talents or abilities might be required?

14.2 Why do the elements of structure, such as work specialization, formalization, span of control, chain of command, and centralization, have a tendency to change together? Which of the five do you feel is the most important?

14.3 Which is more important for an organization: the ability to be efficient or the ability to adapt to its environment? What does this say about how an organization's structure should be set up?

14.4 Which of the organizational forms described in this chapter do you think leads to the highest levels of motivation among workers? Why?

14.5 If you worked in a matrix organization, what career development challenges might you face? Does the idea of working in a matrix structure appeal to you? Why or why not?

CASE • CHEESECAKE FACTORY

The Cheesecake Factory is one of the fastest-growing restaurants in the world. Over the past ten years, the company has more than tripled its sales to over $2 billion and quadrupled its restaurant locations from 41 to 175, which includes a number of international locations such as Dubai.[65] As it grows so fast, a number of core issues rise to the top—such as how does it maintain the level of service guests have come to appreciate, but still control costs? Chuck Wensing, VP of performance development, says, "One of our biggest challenges is the notion of how to get big, but remain small." The restaurant wants to be able to take advantage of all the efficiencies of scale that come with size, but it doesn't want you to sit down and feel like you are at a McDonald's.

The Cheesecake Factory has two big costs to control and manage—groceries and labour. The grocery issue is addressed partly through what it calls call "guest forecasting." Dan Gordon, the COO, says, "We have forecasting models based on historical data—the trend of the past six weeks and also the trend of the previous year."[66] The company can predict food needs ahead of time with staggering accuracy based on a number of factors including things like weather and sporting events.

This allows the restaurant to have an average efficiency rating of 97.5 percent. What does that mean exactly? It means that its managers aim to throw away no more than 2.5 percent of the groceries they purchase without running out of the food that customers will want at any given point in time.[67]

The labour issue is not that different. The Cheesecake Factory has worked out a staff-to-customer ratio that keeps everyone working efficiently, but still leaves room for unexpected large groups of customers.[68] Although it is 15 percent below its competition when it comes to turnover, it still runs at about a 90 percent annual rate.[69] Needless to say, this makes training new employees a huge concern. As in everything else, the restaurant tries to be as efficient as possible and is using what it considers to be the cutting edge of efficiency—creating computer games for training purposes. For instance, the restaurant has built an iPhone app that teaches employees how to make "glamburgers."[70] To compound the new employee problem, the Cheesecake Factory changes its menu every six months.[71] One recent menu shift resulted in the addition of 13 items. That doesn't sound like a huge amount until you think how many people have to be trained to cook those items to perfection every time. The restaurant wants the new menu rollout to take no more than seven weeks, start to finish.[72] The company starts by bringing in regional managers and kitchen managers for training. These managers not only learn to make the new items, they also learn how to *teach others* to make the new items. The information is passed down with surprising efficiency.

14.1 What aspects of the Cheesecake Factory's business do you think are helped by becoming larger? What aspects might be hurt?

14.2 Would you like to work for a company with the hierarchical structure and standardization that the Cheesecake Factory has? How might the company overcome some of these issues when it comes to its employees?

14.3 Based on what you've read, would you say the Cheesecake Factory has a centralized or decentralized structure? Does this help or hurt the company in your opinion?

EXERCISE • CREATIVE CARDS, INC.

The purpose of this exercise is to demonstrate the effects of structure on organizational efficiency. This exercise uses groups, so your instructor will either assign you to a group or ask you to create your own group. The exercise has the following steps:

14.1 Creative Cards, Inc., is a small but growing company, started ten years ago by Angela Naom, a graphic designer. The company has added many employees over the years but without a master plan. Now Angela wants to reorganize the company. The current structure of Creative Cards is shown in the figure. Review the organizational chart given here, and identify at least ten problems with the design of Creative Cards, Inc. Be sure to consider work specialization, chain of command, span of control, centralization, and formalization in developing your answer.

14.2 Create a new organizational design that you think would help the company operate more efficiently and effectively.

14.3 Class discussion, whether in groups or as a class, should centre on how Creative Cards might best manage such a significant restructuring.

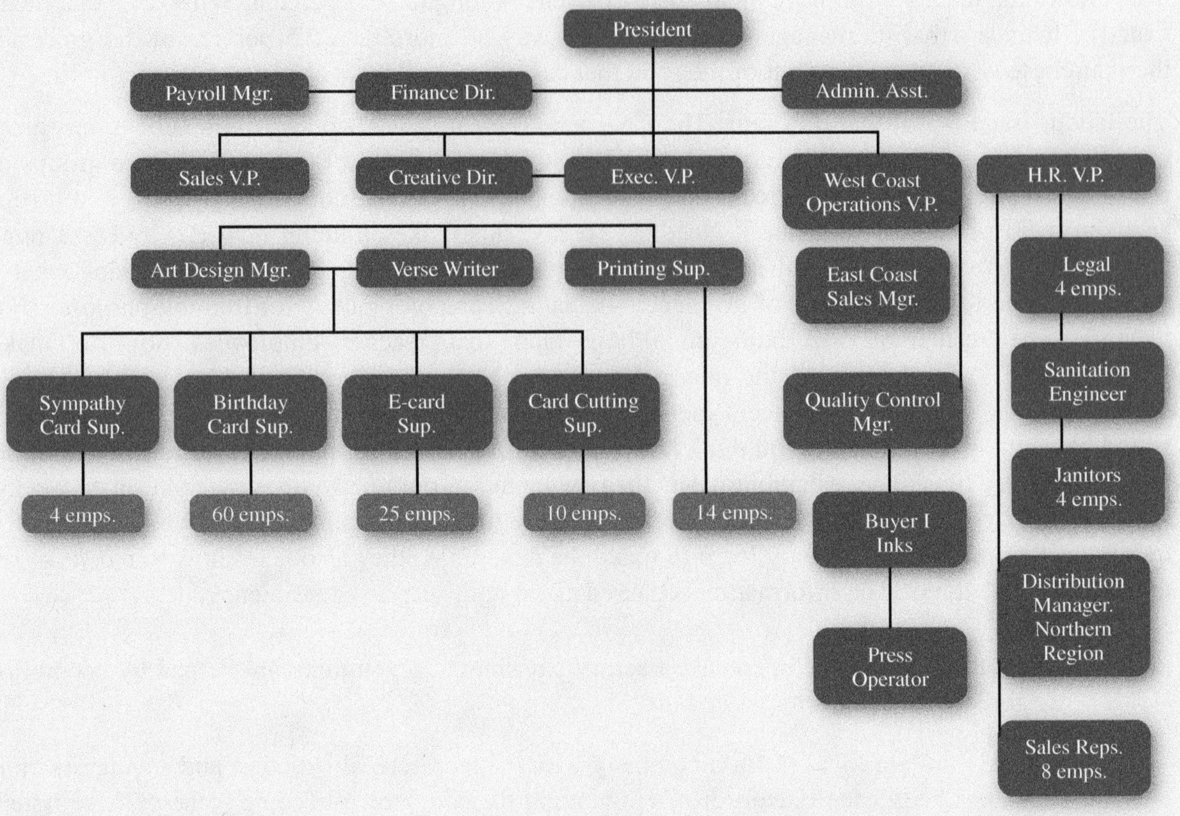

OB ASSESSMENTS • CENTRALIZATION

Have you experienced life inside an organization with a highly centralized structure? This assessment is designed to measure two facets of what would be considered a centralized organizational structure. Those two facets are *hierarchy of authority*, which reflects the degree to which managers are needed to approve decisions, and *participation in decision making*, which reflects how involved rank-and-file employees are in day-to-day deliberations. Think of the last job you held (even if it was a part-time or summer job). Alternatively, think of a student group of yours that seems to have a definite "leader." Then answer each question using the response scale provided.

1 **Strongly Disagree**	2 **Disagree**	3 **Neutral**	4 **Agree**	5 **Strongly Agree**	
1. There can be little action here until a supervisor approves a decision.					______
2. A person who wants to make his own decisions would be quickly discouraged.					______
3. Even small matters have to be referred to someone higher up for a final answer.					______

(*Continued*)

4. I have to ask my boss before I do almost anything.	______
5. Any decision I make has to have my boss' approval.	______
6. I participate frequently in the decision to adopt new programs.	______
7. I participate frequently in the decision to adopt new policies and rules.	______
8. I usually participate in the decision to hire or adopt new group members.	______
9. I often participate in decisions that affect my working environment.	______

Scoring and Interpretation

Hierarchy of authority. Add up items 1–5.

Participation in decision making. Add up items 6–9.

A centralized structure would be one in which hierarchy of authority is high and participation in decision making is low. If your score is above 20 for hierarchy of authority and below 8 for participation in decision making, your organization (or student group) has a highly centralized structure. Remember, when interpreting your scores on these assessments it is important to consider the *reliability* and *validity* of these tools (see Chapter 1, ***OB Assessments***).

Source: Adapted from M. Schminke, R. Cropanzano, and D.E. Rupp, "Organization Structure and Fairness Perceptions: The Moderating Effects of Organizational Level," *Organizational Behavior and Human Decision Processes* 89 (2002), pp. 881–905.

Organizational Culture and Change

CHAPTER 15

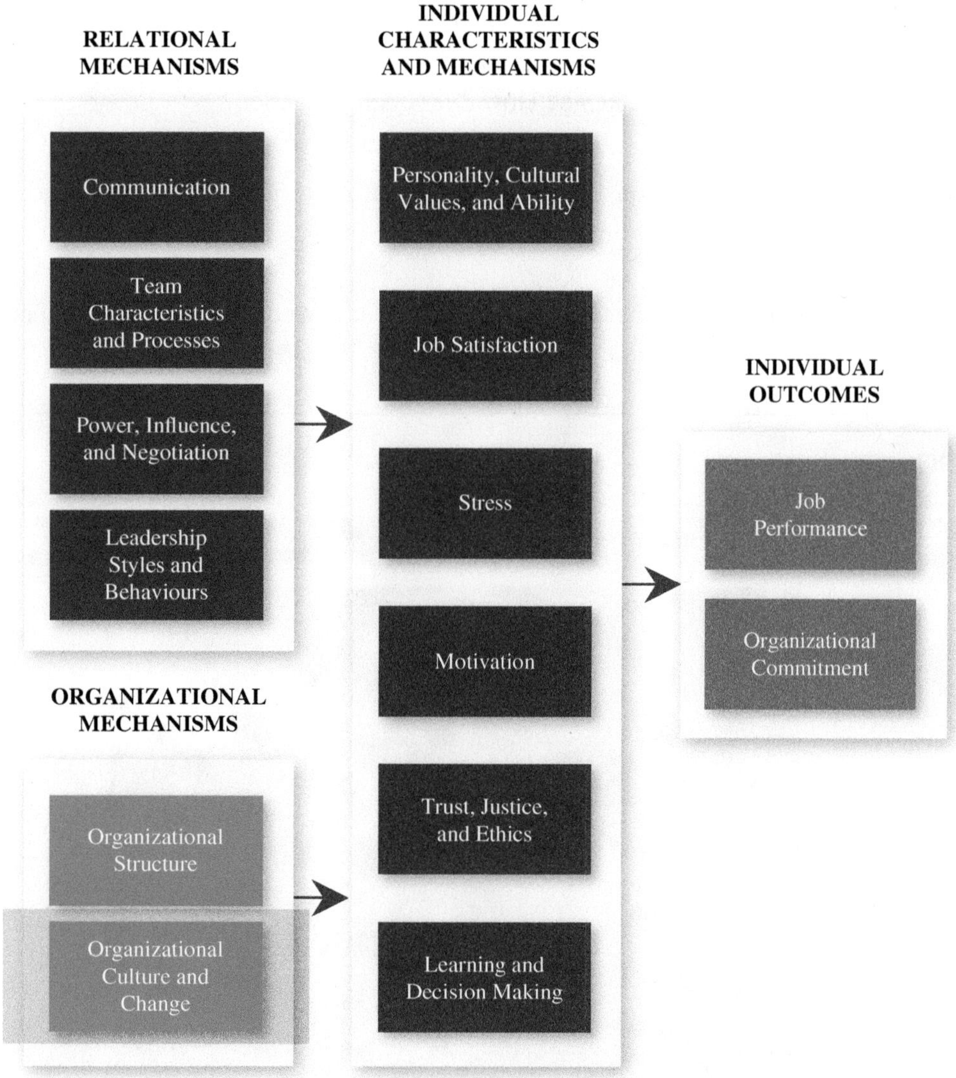

LEARNING OUTCOMES

After reading this chapter, you should be able to answer the following questions:

15.1 What is organizational culture, and what are its components?

15.2 What general and specific types can be used to describe an organization's culture?

15.3 What makes a culture strong, and is it always good for an organization to have a strong culture?

15.4 How do organizations maintain their culture?

15.5 Can organizational culture change? How does change happen?

15.6 What is person–organization fit and how does it affect job performance and organizational commitment?

15.7 What steps can organizations take to make sure that newcomers will fit with their culture?

Yahoo

Leaders at Yahoo understand the importance of changing its overall culture to align with organizational goals.

© AP Photo/Paul Sakuma

When multinational Internet corporation Yahoo hired Marissa Mayer away from Google to be its new CEO, it was supposed to help Yahoo rejuvenate its culture. When it was founded in the 1990s, Yahoo was the place to be in Silicon Valley. That changed when Yahoo's top talent started leaving for other companies.[1] Its board of directors felt that Mayer—a computer programmer well versed in Google's enviable hacker-centric culture—could breathe new life into Yahoo's Sunnyvale, California, headquarters and make it the place to work again.[2] During her first interview as CEO, Mayer stated, "I believe that really strong companies have strong cultures. Each has their unique and individual flavor. I want to find Yahoo's and amplify it."[3]

One of the things Mayer is trying to focus on is changing the culture to one that acts more quickly simply by being willing to work harder—something she exemplified at Google where she pulled 250 all-nighters during her first five years on the job.[4] To help in that regard, two of Mayer's first actions as CEO were to buy everyone in the company a new iPhone (and pay their phone bill), and to make the food in Yahoo's cafeterias free to full-time employees.[5] She evidently plans for everyone to be around more. One story has Mayer meeting with a product development team early after arriving and liking what she saw so much that she moved the product's planned shipping date up by a substantial margin. She told the team that they had a week to figure out how to make it happen, or she would find another team that could.[6]

While Yahoo wrestles with revamping its own culture, it also has to deal with other firms' cultures as well, since the company has gone on a massive buying spree including the $1 billion acquisition of Tumblr (a popular blogging and social networking website). That purchase pits the 14,000-employee behemoth against the 200-employee start-up. Mayer is pretty clear about the fact that Tumblr will be allowed to stay independent of Yahoo's culture. She states, "Tumblr has a really good thing going. I'm cognizant of the fact that we don't want to mess that up. Especially when you have a hyper-growth company, you want them to operate independently so they can run as fast as they can."[7] How acquisitions like Tumblr will affect Yahoo and how Yahoo will affect Tumblr remains to be seen.

15.1 What is organizational culture, and what are its components?

ORGANIZATIONAL CULTURE

In almost every chapter so far, we have simply given you definitions of important topics. However, in this case, it's important for you to understand that there are just about as many definitions of organizational culture as there are people who study it. In fact, research on organizational culture has produced well over 50 different definitions![8] It seems that the term "culture" means a great many things to a great many people. Definitions have ranged from as broad as "The way we do things around here"[9] to as specific as ... well, suffice it to say they can get complicated.

Not surprisingly, the various definitions of organizational culture stem from how people have studied it. Sociologists use a broad lens and anthropological research methods like those applied to tribes and civilizations. Psychologists tend to use survey methods. In fact, many actually prefer the term "climate," but for our purposes we'll use the two terms interchangeably.

In this chapter, we define **organizational culture** as the shared social knowledge within an organization regarding the rules, norms, and values that shape the attitudes and behaviours of its employees.[10]

organizational culture

The shared social knowledge within an organization regarding the rules, norms, and values that shape the attitudes and behaviours of its employees

This definition highlights a number of facets of organizational culture. First, culture is social knowledge among members of the organization. Employees learn about most important aspects of culture through other employees. This transfer of knowledge might be through explicit communication, simple observation, or other, less obvious methods. In addition, culture is shared knowledge, which means that members of the organization understand and have a degree of consensus regarding what the culture is. Second, culture tells employees what the rules, norms, and values are within the organization. What are the most important work outcomes to focus on? What behaviours are appropriate or inappropriate at work? How should a person act or dress while at work? Indeed, some cultures go so far as to say how employees should act when they aren't at work. Third, organizational culture shapes and reinforces certain employee attitudes and behaviours by creating a system of control over employees.[11] There is evidence that your individual goals and values will grow over time to match those of the organization for which you work.[12] This development really isn't that hard to imagine, given how much time employees spend working inside an organization.

WHY DO SOME ORGANIZATIONS HAVE DIFFERENT CULTURES THAN OTHERS?

One of the most common questions people ask when you tell them where you are employed is, "So tell me … what's it like there?" The description you use in your response is likely to have a lot to do with what the organization's culture is all about. In calculating your response to the question, you might consider describing the kinds of people who work at your company. More than likely, you'll do your best to describe the work atmosphere on a regular day. Perhaps you'll painstakingly describe the facilities you work in or how you feel the employees are treated. You might even go so far as to describe what it is that defines "success" at your company. All of those answers give clues that help organizational outsiders understand what a company is actually like. To give you a feel for the full range of potential answers to the "what's it like there?" question, it's necessary to review the facets of culture in more detail.

Culture Components

There are three major components to any organization's culture: observable artifacts, espoused values, and basic underlying assumptions. You can understand the differences among these three components if you view culture as an onion, as in Figure 15-1. Some components are readily apparent and observable, like the skin of an onion. However, others are less observable to outsiders or newcomers. To them, the organizational culture remains a mystery until they can peel back the outside layers to gauge the values and assumptions that lie beneath. The sections that follow review the culture components in more detail.

Observable Artifacts **Observable artifacts** are the manifestations of an organization's culture that employees can easily see or talk about. They supply the signals that employees interpret to gauge how they should act during the workday. Artifacts supply the primary means of transmitting an organization's culture to its workforce. It's difficult to overestimate the importance of artifacts, because they help show not only current employees but also potential employees, customers, shareholders, and investors what the organization is all about. There are six major types of artifacts: symbols, physical structures, language, stories, rituals, and ceremonies.[13]

observable artifacts
Aspects of an organization's culture that employees and outsiders can easily see or talk about

FIGURE 15-1

The Three Components of Organizational Culture

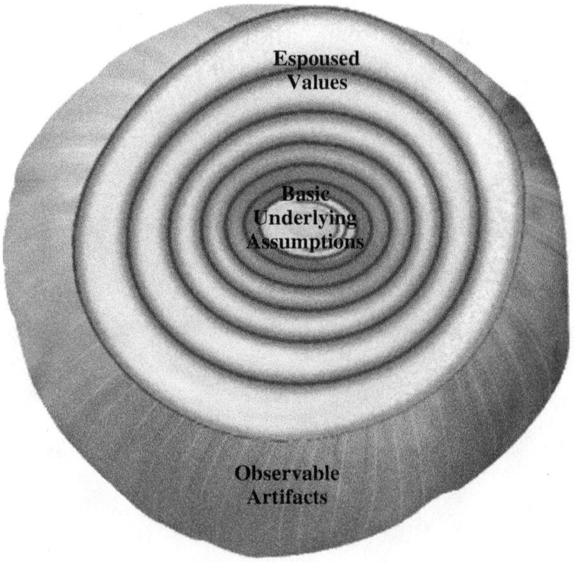

Symbols can be found throughout an organization, from its corporate logo to the images it puts on its website to the uniforms its employees wear. Think about what Nike's "swoosh" represents: speed, movement, velocity. What might that symbol convey about Nike's culture? Or consider Apple Computer's "apple" logo. That symbol refers to Newton's discovery of gravity under the apple tree, conveying the importance of innovation within Apple's culture.

symbols
The images an organization uses, which generally convey messages

Physical structures also say a lot about a culture. Is the workplace open? Does top management work in a separate section of the building? Is the setting devoid of anything unique, or can employees express their personalities?

Takanobu Ito, CEO of Honda Motor, sends a message about the company's culture in his office. Ito works at a plain wooden desk in a room with a dozen other executives.[14] John Childress, founding partner of The Principia Group, tells the story of a Ford executive he worked with whose entire office had burned down: "He'd been having terrible problems between departments. There were barriers that meant information wasn't flowing. He had to quickly rent new premises and all he could find was an open-plan building. The culture changed overnight because of the different ways of working."[15] IDEO, a creative design firm, also has an open-office environment, though IDEO lets employees set up their offices however they like. When you walk around their work areas, you'll be walking underneath bicycles hanging over your head and crazy objects and toys in every direction.[16] Reed Hastings, CEO of Netflix, doesn't even have an office! Hastings simply walks around meeting with people. When he needs a quiet space to think he heads to his "watchtower"—a room-sized glass square on the top of Netflix's main building.[17]

The next time you meet with your professor, have a look at how the office furniture is configured. You might see a large desk dividing the office so that students have to sit across from the professor. Or the desk might be positioned against a side wall, allowing students to sit beside him or her. Which of these configurations conveys a collaborative, informal orientation toward students? What would it say about the culture of a university if faculty and staff were allowed to have beach-themed office furniture?

physical structures

The organization's buildings and internal office designs

The ability to set up your own work space, as at the design firm IDEO, is a hallmark of an open corporate culture. Would this environment suit your working style?

Language reflects the jargon, slang, and slogans used within the walls of an organization. Do you know what a CTR, CPC, or Crawler is? Chances are you don't. If you worked for Yahoo (our opening chapter example), however, those terms would be second nature to you: CTR stands for click-through rate, CPC stands for cost-per-click, and a Crawler is a computer program that gathers information from other websites. If you worked at Microsoft and got an e-mail from a software developer telling you that they were "licking the cookie," what would you think? For Microsoft employees, this means a person or group is announcing that they are working on a feature or product and it is now off limits for others to work on.[18] Home Depot has the slogan "Stack it high and watch it fly," which reflects its approach to sales. Yum Brands Inc., which owns Pizza Hut, Taco Bell, KFC, and other fast-food restaurants, expects employees to be "customer maniacs"[19] —language that conveys its culture for customer interaction.

language

The jargon, slang, and slogans used within an organization

Stories consist of anecdotes, accounts, legends, and myths that are passed down from cohort to cohort within an organization. Telling stories can be a major mechanism through which leaders and employees describe what the company values or finds important. You've probably heard how Apple Computers was started by two 20-something boy wonders in a garage. Or that the initial WestJet concept was roughed out on a napkin by a small group of entrepreneurs in a Calgary steakhouse. Regardless of the whether these stories are embellished over time, the point is that they provide an accepted (and celebrated) account of something the organization values, such as innovation or entrepreneurial spirit. Howard Schultz, CEO of Starbucks, tells the story of how (to improve quality) he forbade the common practice of re-steaming milk. What this rule inadvertently created was the loss of millions of dollars of milk, as thousands of gallons of lukewarm liquid poured down the drain. One of his store managers came up with a simple, brilliant suggestion: Put etched lines inside the steaming pitchers so baristas would know how much milk to pour for the drink size they were making, instead of just guessing.[20] Paul Wiles, president/CEO of a large healthcare organization, believes strongly in the power of storytelling to foster culture; he claims, "Talk about numbers, and people's eyes glaze over; talk about one child who died unnecessarily, and no one can walk away from that."[21]

stories
Anecdotes, accounts, legends, and myths passed down from cohort to cohort within an organization

Rituals are the daily or weekly planned routines that occur in an organization. A popular ritual many white-collar organizations have adopted is "casual Fridays." One day a week, employees are permitted to leave the suit at home and come to work dressed in jeans or other casual attire. The ritual reinforces the idea that work can be relaxed and fun. A variation on this theme would be to permit employees to bring their pets to work on a designated day each month. At UPS, every driver and package handler attends a mandatory "three-minute meeting" with their manager to help with communication. The strict time limit sends a message about the importance of punctuality in the UPS culture. An annual ritual for TELUS Corporation is that every employee must take and pass a course on ethics.[22]

rituals
The daily or weekly planned routines that occur in an organization

Consider some of the rituals you or your family regularly perform—what messages do they convey about what is valued?

Ceremonies are formal events, generally performed in front of an audience of organizational members. Graduates and their families experience a public celebration of hard work, achievement, and accomplishment during their convocation ceremony. Organizations frequently use public reward ceremonies to recognize individuals and teams who best exemplify what the culture values (e.g., safety, high performance, cost-saving suggestions). Ceremonies can also be used to convey important cultural changes.

ceremonies
Formal events, generally performed in front of an audience of organizational members

At Care.com, all workers are forced to move desks every year at the same time. CEO Sheila Marcelo assigns the seats. She says, "People don't have a choice where they sit. Part of the reason was to embrace change, to remove turfiness so that you're not just chatting with your friends and sitting with your friends. You sit with somebody else from a different team so you get to know their job. What are they doing? What are they saying on the phone? How do they tick? And it's getting to know different people so that we build a really big team. And we do that every year. And it's now actually become an exciting thing that people embrace."[23]

In the process of turning around the company, Continental Airlines held a ceremony to burn an employee-despised 800-page policy manual. Gordon Bethune, then CEO, put together a task force that came up with a new, 80-page manual.[24]

Espoused Values **Espoused values** are the beliefs, philosophies, and norms that a company explicitly states. Espoused values can range from published documents, such as a company's vision or mission statement on its website or annual report, to verbal statements made to employees by executives and managers.

espoused values

The beliefs, philosophies, and norms that a company explicitly states

A great example comes from Calgary-based Enbridge Corporation. Explicit company statements clearly spell out to its managers, employees, customers, and community stakeholders what is valued within the organization on a day-by-day basis. Paramount for this company is the value put on integrity, safety, and respect. Every day, Enbridge employees are expected to take responsibility for their actions, follow through on commitments, and ensure the safety of their communities, their customers, and each other. They are also expected to take the time to understand the perspective of others and treat others with dignity.[25]

It's certainly important distinguish between espoused and enacted values. It's one thing for a company to outwardly say something is important; it's another for employees to consistently act in ways that support those values. When a company holds to its espoused values over time and regardless of the situations it operates in, the values become more believable both to employees and outsiders. However, in times of economic downturn, staying true to espoused values isn't always easy. Marriott International has been struggling in the most recent economic downturn, like many of its competitors in the lodging/travel business. It has been very tempting for the company to do everything it can to slash expenses, but its espoused value of always treating its people right prevents cuts that would harm employee benefits. The company's chairperson and CEO states, "If the employees are well taken care of, they'll take care of the customer and the customer will come back. That's basically the core value of the company."[26]

Basic Underlying Assumptions **Basic underlying assumptions** are taken-for-granted beliefs and philosophies that are so engrained that employees simply act on them rather than questioning the validity of their behaviour in a given situation.[27] These assumptions, representing the deepest and least observable part of a culture, may not be consciously apparent even to organizational veterans.

basic underlying assumptions

The engrained beliefs and philosophies of employees

Edgar Schein, one of the preeminent scholars on the topic of organizational culture, uses the example of safety in an engineering firm. He states, "In an occupation such as engineering, it would be inconceivable to deliberately design something that is unsafe; it is a taken-for-granted assumption that things should be safe."[28] Whatever a company's underlying assumptions, it is its hidden beliefs that are most likely to dictate employee behaviour and affect employee attitudes. They are also the aspects of an organizational culture that are the most long-lasting and difficult to change.[29]

15.2 What general and specific types can be used to describe an organization's culture?

General Culture Types

Once we see organizational culture as the combination of an organization's observable artifacts, espoused values, and underlying assumptions, we can begin to classify it along various dimensions. Of course, there are many types, just as there are many types of personalities. Some researchers have tried to create typologies.

One popular typology divides organizational culture along two dimensions: solidarity and sociability. *Solidarity* is the degree to which group members think and act alike, and *sociability* represents how friendly employees are to one another.[30] Figure 15-2 shows how we might describe organizations that are either high or low on these dimensions. Organizations low on both dimensions have a **fragmented culture**, in which employees are distant and disconnected from one another. An organization in which employees think alike but aren't friendly to one another can be considered a **mercenary culture**. These types of organizations are likely to be very political, "What's in it for me?" environments. If all employees are friendly to one another, but everyone thinks differently and does his or her own thing, we have a **networked culture**; many highly creative organizations have such a culture. An organization with friendly employees who all think alike represents a **communal culture**.

FIGURE 15-2

A Typology of Organizational Culture

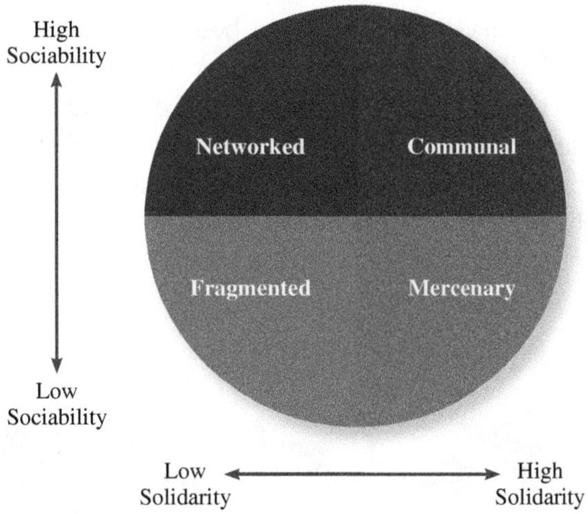

Source: Adapted from R. Goffee and G. Jones, *The Character of a Corporation* (New York: Harper Business, 1998).

fragmented culture

An organizational culture type in which employees are distant and disconnected from one another

mercenary culture

An organizational culture type in which employees think alike but are not friendly to one another

networked culture

An organizational culture type in which employees are friendly to one another, but everyone thinks differently and does his or her own thing

communal culture

An organizational culture type in which employees are friendly to one another and all think

There is evidence that organizations have a tendency to move through the culture types as they get larger. Small ones generally start out as communal cultures oriented around the owner and founder. As companies grow, they might move toward a networked culture, because solidarity is harder to foster when groups get really large.[31] Although we like to think of culture as being stable, it can change, as we discuss later in this chapter.

Specific Culture Types

The typology shown in Figure 15-2 is general enough to be applied to almost any organization. However, there are obviously other ways to classify an organization's culture, as we describe a little later in the chapter. In fact, many organizations attempt to manipulate observable artifacts and espoused values to create specific cultures that help them achieve their organizational goals. Some of these specific cultures are more relevant in certain industries than in others. Although the number of specific cultures that an organization might strive for are virtually endless, we will focus on four examples: customer service cultures, safety cultures, diversity cultures, and creativity cultures.

Many organizations try to create a **customer service culture** focused on service quality. Organizations that have successfully created a service culture have been shown to change employee attitudes and behaviours toward customers.[32] These changes manifest themselves in higher levels of customer satisfaction and sales.[33] Figure 15-3 illustrates the process of creating a service culture and the effects it has on company results. Earlier in the book, we introduced WestJet as an organization widely recognized for having a strong customer service culture—one that fosters a common set of values among its members, such as being friendly, passionate, and showing appreciation for their "guests."[34]

FIGURE 15-3

The Service Culture Process

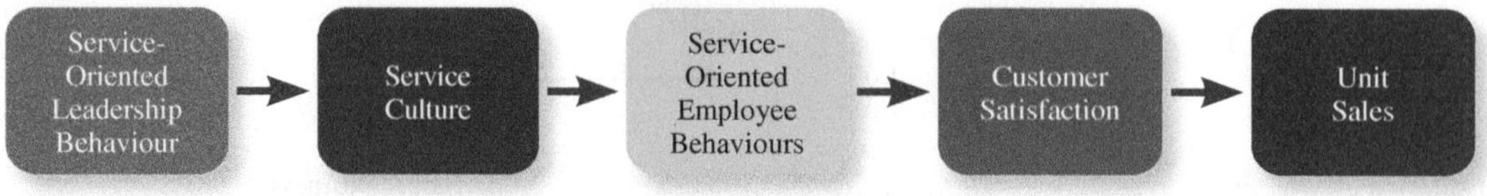

Source: Adapted from B. Schneider, M.G. Ehrhart, D.M. Mayer, J.L. Saltz, and K. Niles-Jolly, "Understanding Organization–Customer Links in Service Settings," *Academy of Management Journal* 48 (2005), pp. 1017–32.

customer service culture
A specific culture type focused on service quality

Some companies require that their employees work in environments where the risk of accidents or injuries is very high. For these organizations, creating a **safety culture** is of paramount importance.[35] The payoff for these organizations is often an increased level of safety-related awareness and behaviours, and lower accidents.[36] Syncrude Canada Ltd. is one of several major organizations that process the vast oil sands deposit in northeastern Alberta. For this company, safety is critical, given that each stage of the processing (i.e., mining, extraction, and upgrading/refining) is so dangerous—as one engineer put it, "We can launch things here." The question is how you instill core safety values in several thousand employees, who are performing hundreds of different technical jobs. For Syncrude, the answer includes strong management commitment to protecting and promoting safety, careful selection and training of its new employees, extensive and mandatory safety rules and procedures, required safety-knowledge training and testing, and opportunities for members to participate in world-class emergency response teams. How has this culture affected the company? Well, Syncrude consistently reports among the lowest time-lost records in the industry! [37] Sadly, we have also witnessed the effects of companies who promote weak safety cultures. On July 6, 2013, many of us woke to hear about the worst rail accident in Canadian history. During the night a freight train loaded with crude oil had derailed and exploded in the centre of the town of Lac-Mégantic, Quebec, killing 47 people and destroying dozens of buildings.[38] A report by the Transportation Safety Board of Canada the following year revealed that the company, Montreal, Maine & Atlantic, failed to comply with proper safety procedures and willingly cut corners on safety despite the fact that it was carrying increasing amounts of hazardous cargo.[39]

safety culture
A specific culture type focused on the safety of employees

In its report of the tragic Lac-Mégantic rail disaster on July 6, 2013, the Transportation Safety Board of Canada put a lot of the blame on a weak safety culture within the railroad company.

There are a number of reasons why an organization might want to foster a **diversity culture**. For Royal Bank of Canada (RBC), having a culture that values diversity has helped the bank to fully leverage the talents of women, aging baby boomers, Aboriginals, visible minorities, and newcomers to the country. According to Zabeen Hirji, executive vice-president and chief human resources officer at RBC, striving to foster an inclusive work environment that brings out the best in everyone contributes to the creation of innovative solutions for clients and communities—in short, "Differences in people are seen as valuable and potential assets."[40] Some activities RBC uses to implement its diversity strategy include hiring people who have the technical, behavioural, and diversity requirements for the position being filled, investing heavily in training throughout the company, and promoting internal mentoring relationships.[41] Diversity isn't just for big companies. Teshmont Engineering Consultants, a small (less than 100 employees) Canadian-based company, has a culture centred around diversity as well, with 31 different mother tongues being spoken at the firm.[42]

diversity culture

A specific culture type focused on fostering or taking advantage of a diverse group of employees

Given the importance of new ideas and innovation in many industries, it's understandable that some organizations focus on fostering a **creativity culture**. Creativity cultures affect both the quantity and quality of creative ideas within an organization.[43] 3M Canada believes that creativity comes from freedom and not control; workers in R&D are allowed to spend 15 percent of their time researching whatever they want.[44] At Dyson, the extremely innovative UK-based appliances manufacturing company, CEO and founder James Dyson forbids the wearing of suits or ties and the writing of memos. He feels that workers will be more creative if they talk to each other about their ideas. New engineers are required to disassemble and reassemble a Dyson vacuum cleaner on their first day.[45] In part to foster a culture of creativity, Pfizer Canada has banned all e-mails and voice mails on weekends and after 6 p.m. on weekdays to keep their employees fresh while on the job. It feels this 12-hour break has led to a higher-quality flow of ideas and provided a morale boost to go along with it.[46]

In order to foster a creativity culture, James Dyson (pictured) has engineers assemble and disassemble a Dyson vacuum cleaner their first day on the job.

© Bruno Vincent/Getty Images

creativity culture
A specific culture type focused on fostering a creative atmosphere

To see whether you've spent time working in a creativity culture, see our ***OB Assessments*** feature at the end of the chapter.

15.3 What makes a culture strong, and is it always good for an organization to have a strong culture?

Culture Strength

Although most organizations seem to strive for one, not all companies have a culture that creates a sense of definite norms and appropriate behaviours for their employees. If you've worked for a company and can't identify whether it has a strong culture, it probably doesn't. A high level of **culture strength** exists when employees definitively agree about the way things are supposed to happen within the organization (high consensus) and when their subsequent behaviours are consistent with those expectations (high intensity).[47] As is shown in Figure 15-4, a strong culture serves to unite and direct employees. Weak cultures exist when employees disagree about the way things are supposed to be or what is expected of them, meaning there is nothing to unite or direct their attitudes and actions.

culture strength
The degree to which employees agree about how things should happen within the organization and behave accordingly

FIGURE 15-4

Culture Strength and Subcultures

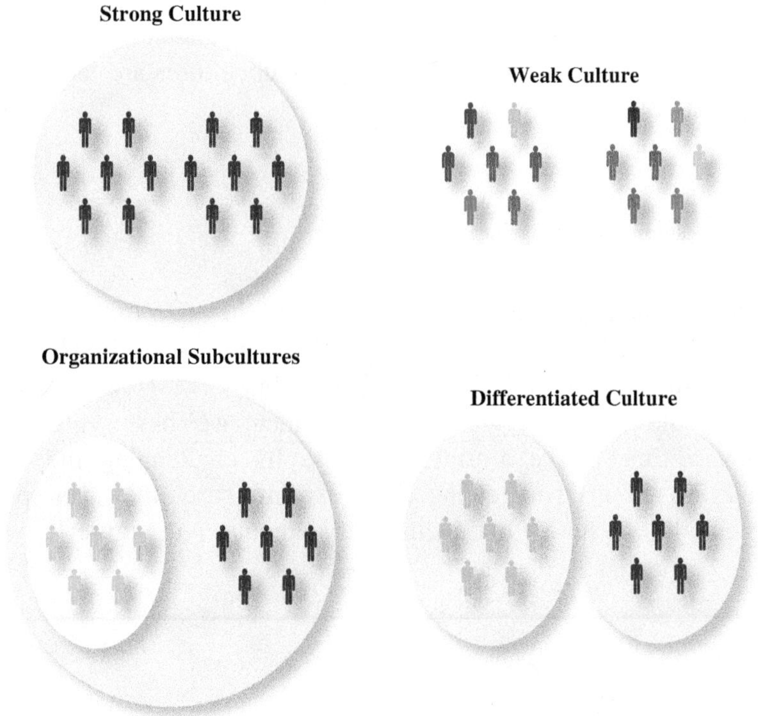

Strong cultures take a long time to develop and are very difficult to change. Individuals working within strong cultures are typically very aware of it. However, this discussion brings us to an important point: "Strong" cultures are not always "good" ones. They do guide employee attitudes and behaviours, but that doesn't always mean they guide them toward the most successful outcomes. Consequently, it's useful to recognize some of the positive and negative aspects of having a strong organizational culture. Table 15-1 lists some of the advantages and disadvantages.[48] You may have noticed that all the advantages in the left-hand column of Table 15-1 allow the organization to become more efficient at whatever aspect of culture is strong within the organization. The right-hand column's disadvantages all lead toward an organization's inability to adapt.

TABLE 15-1

Pros and Cons of a Strong Culture

Advantages of a Strong Culture	Disadvantages of a Strong Culture
Differentiates the organization from others	Makes merging with another organization more difficult
Allows employees to identify themselves with the organization	Attracts and retains similar kinds of employees, thereby limiting diversity of thought
Facilitates desired behaviours among employees	Can be "too much of a good thing" if it creates extreme behaviours among employees
Creates stability within the organization	Makes adapting to the environment more difficult

In some cases, the culture of an organization is not really strong or weak. Instead, there might be **subcultures** that unite a smaller subset of the organization's employees. These subgroups may be created because there is a strong leader in one area of the company that engenders different norms and values, or because different divisions in a company act independently and create their own cultures. As is shown in Figure 15-4, subcultures exist when the overall organizational culture is supplemented by another one governing a more specific set of employees. Subcultures are more likely to exist in large organizations than in small ones.[49]

subcultures

Cultures created within small subsets of the organization's employees

Most organizations don't mind having subcultures, as long as they don't interfere with the values of the overall culture. In fact, subcultures can be very useful for organizations if certain areas of the organization have different demands and needs for their employees.[50] However, sometimes their values don't match those of the larger organization, and then we have **countercultures**. Although countercultures can sometimes serve a useful purpose by challenging the values of the overall organization or signifying the need for change,[51] in extreme cases they can split the organization's culture right down the middle, resulting in the differentiated culture in Figure 15-4.

countercultures

Subcultures whose values do not match those of the organization

15.4 How do organizations maintain their culture?

Maintaining an Organizational Culture

No matter how we describe a culture—whether in terms of espoused values and basic underlying assumptions, general dimensions such as solidarity or sociability, or more specific types such as service cultures or safety cultures—it will be put to the test when an organization's founders and original employees begin to recruit and hire new members. If those newcomers do not fit in, the culture may be weakened or changed. However, two processes, known as attraction–selection–attrition and socialization, can work together to keep cultures strong.

Attraction–Selection–Attrition (ASA) The **ASA framework** holds that potential employees will be attracted to organizations whose cultures match their own personality, meaning that some potential job applicants won't apply due to a perceived lack of fit.[52] In addition, organizations will select candidates on the basis of whether their personalities fit the culture, further weeding out potential "misfits." Finally, those people who still don't fit will either be unhappy or ineffective when working in the organization, which leads to attrition (i.e., voluntary or involuntary turnover).

ASA framework

A theory (attraction–selection–attrition) that states that employees will be drawn to organizations with cultures that match their personality, organizations will select employees that match, and employees will leave or be forced out when they are not a good fit

Several companies can provide an example of ASA in action. FedEx has worked hard to create a culture of ethics. The executives at FedEx believe a strong ethical culture will attract ethical employees who will then strengthen moral behaviour at FedEx.[53] Headhunters and corporate recruiters are well aware of the fact that employees who have lots of experience in certain types of cultures (i.e., places they "fit") will have a hard time adapting to other types of cultures. One type of culture they look out for specifically is high levels of bureaucracy—recruiters point to British Airways, General Mills, and Occidental Petroleum as prime examples of non-risk-taking, bureaucratic cultures whose employees are rarely successful when they leave to go somewhere else.[54] Of course, attraction and selection processes don't always align employees' personalities with organizational culture—one reason voluntary and involuntary turnover occurs in every organization.

Socialization In addition to taking advantage of attraction–selection–attrition, organizations also maintain an organizational culture by shaping and moulding new employees. Starting a new job with a company is a stressful, complex, and challenging undertaking for both employees and organizations.[55] In reality, no outsider can fully grasp or understand the culture of an organization simply by looking at artifacts visible from outside the company. A complete understanding of organizational culture is a process that happens over time. **Socialization** is the primary process by which employees learn the social knowledge that enables them to understand and adapt to the organization's culture. It's one that begins before an employee starts work and doesn't end until an employee leaves the organization.[56]

socialization

The primary process by which employees learn the social knowledge that enables them to understand and adapt to the organization's culture

What is it that an employee needs to learn and adapt to in order to be socialized into his or her new role within an organization? Most of the important information can be grouped into six dimensions, highlighted in Figure 15-5.[57] Research shows that each of these dimensions is important in socialization; each has unique contributions to job performance, organizational commitment, and person–organization fit.[58]

FIGURE 15-5

Dimensions Addressed in Most Socialization Efforts

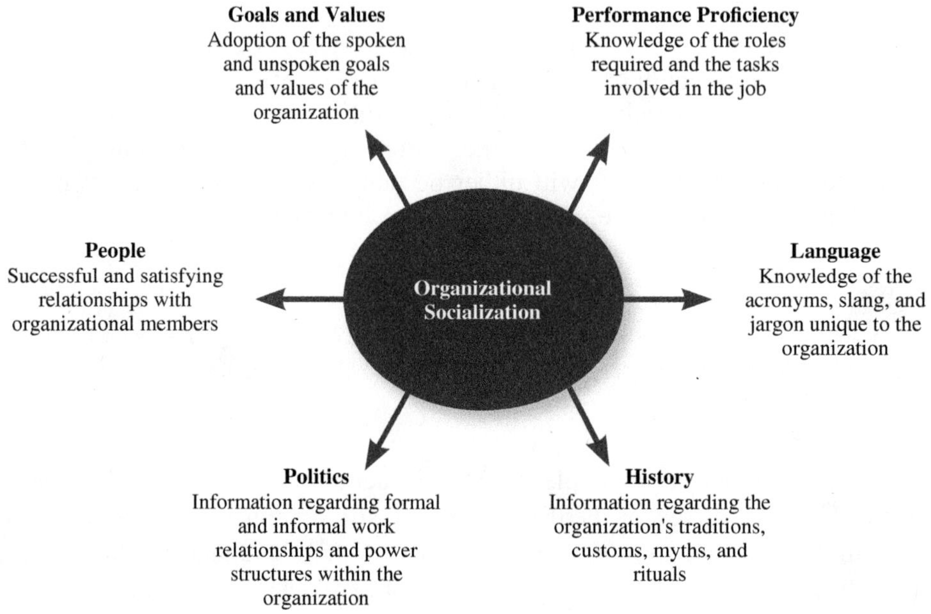

Source: G.T. Chao, A.M. O'Leary-Kelly, S. Wolf, H.J. Klein, and P.D. Gardner, "Organizational Socialization: Its Content and Consequences," *Journal of Applied Psychology*, Vol. 79, 1994, pp. 730–43. Copyright © 1994 by the American Psychological Association. Adapted with permission. No further reproduction or distribution is permitted without written permission from the American Psychological Association.

Socialization happens in three relatively distinct stages. The **anticipatory stage** happens prior to an employee spending even one second on the job. It starts the moment a potential employee hears the name of the organization. When you see the name Microsoft, what comes to mind? Anticipatory socialization begins as soon as a potential employee develops an image of what it must be like to work for a given company. The bulk of the information acquired during this stage occurs during the recruitment and selection processes new employees go through; it includes how employees are treated during recruitment, what insiders tell them about the organization, and other knowledge about what the organization is like and what working there entails.

anticipatory stage

A stage of socialization that begins as soon as a potential employee develops an image of what it would be like to work for a company

The **encounter stage** begins the day an employee starts work. There are some things about an organization and its culture that can only be learned once a person becomes an organizational insider. During this stage, new employees compare the information they acquired as outsiders during the anticipatory stage with what the organization is really like now that they're insiders. To the degree that the information in the two stages is similar, employees will have a smoother time adjusting to the organization. Problems occur when the two sets of information don't quite match, and we have **reality shock**. Reality shock is best exemplified by the employee who says something like "Working at this company is not nearly what I expected it to be." Surveys suggest that as many as one-third of new employees leave an organization within the first 90 days as a result of unmet expectations.[59] The goal of the organization's socialization efforts should be to minimize reality shock as much as possible. We'll describe some ways this can be done effectively in the Application section that concludes this chapter.

encounter stage

A stage of socialization beginning the day an employee starts work, during which the employee compares the information as an outsider to the information learned as an insider

reality shock

A mismatch of information that occurs when an employee finds that aspects of working at a company are not what the he or she expected them to be

The final stage of socialization is one of **understanding and adaptation**. During this stage, newcomers come to learn the content areas of socialization and internalize norms and expected behaviours. The important part of this stage is change on the part of the employee.

understanding and adaptation

The final stage of socialization, during which newcomers come to learn the content areas of socialization and internalize the norms and expected behaviours of the organization

Figure 15-5 indicates what a perfectly socialized employee might look like. He or she has adopted the goals and values of the organization, understands what the organization has been through, and can converse with others in the organization using technical language and specific terms only insiders would understand. In addition, he or she enjoys and gets along with other employees in the organization, knows who to go to in order to make things happen, and understands and can perform the key functions of the job. Talk about the perfect employee! Needless to say, that's quite a bit of information to gain—it's not a process that happens overnight. Some would say that this last stage of socialization never truly ends, as an organization's culture continues to evolve.[60] However, organizations also know that the more quickly and effectively an employee is socialized, the sooner he or she becomes a productive worker. It's important to note that the length of the socialization process varies with the characteristics of the employee and not just of the company. For example, some might progress more rapidly through the stages because of the knowledge they have, their ability to recognize cultural cues, or their adaptability to their environment. In fact, there is growing evidence that proactivity on the part of the employee being socialized has a significant effect on socialization outcomes.[61] Some organizations might help their employees socialize more quickly because they have stronger cultures or cultures that are more easily understandable. The biggest difference, though, is that some organizations simply work harder at it.

Summary: Why Do Some Organizations Have Different Cultures Than Others?

So why do some organizations have different cultures than others? As shown in Figure 15-6, attraction–selection–attrition processes and socialization processes shape the three components of organizational culture: basic underlying assumptions, espoused values, and observable artifacts. Specific combinations of those culture components then give rise to both general and specific culture types. For example, cultures can be categorized on the basis of solidarity and sociability into fragmented, mercenary, communal, and networked types. Cultures can also be categorized into more specific types, such as customer service, safety, diversity, and creativity. Finally, those general and specific types can be further classified according to the strength of the culture. Taken together, these processes explain "what it's like" within the hallways of a given organization.

FIGURE 15-6

Why Some Organizations Have Different Cultures Than Others

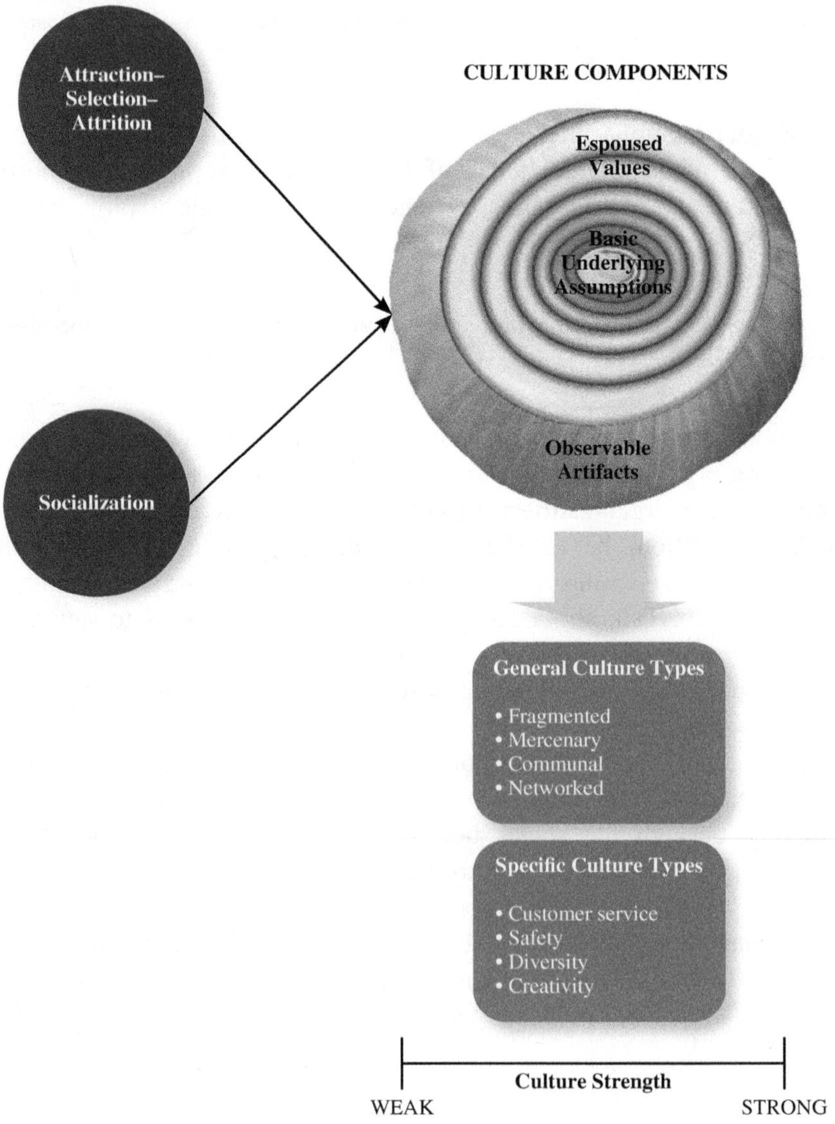

15.5 Can organizational culture change? How does change happen?

THE CULTURE CHANGE PROCESS

Once cultures are established and maintained, the good news is that they tend to persist. This, of course, is bad news if it turns out the culture no longer fits with or supports what the company is trying to achieve. How does one go about changing a history of shared understandings, common values, and well-established norms? For answers we now look at how scholars and managers have approached the topic of change.

One of the oldest and widely held perspectives on organizational change suggests a basic process for it in three steps, *unfreezing*, *change initiative*, and *refreezing*. Unfreezing occurs when the organization comes to some realization that the status quo is unacceptable. For instance, an increase in customer complaints about product quality may trigger an awareness that a company's culture is out of step with its mission to be a high-quality manufacturer. Or low employee morale, revealed on a company-wide survey, may trigger a realization that change is needed. Once this has been recognized, the second step is to plan and implement the change initiative. In the case of culture change, this may involve bringing in a new leader, introducing a new reward system, or implementing a new training program. The third step is to refreeze, meaning that the newly developed attitudes and behaviours (i.e., new ways of thinking, feeling, and acting) need to "harden up," becoming entrenched as new norms, values, and shared understandings.

At eBay, unfreezing occurred when its top executives, John Donahoe and Mark Carges, came to the realization that every little decision was a painful exercise in bureaucracy, with careful examination of all permutations of a possible outcome before acting. These perceptions triggered an awareness that all employees needed to adopt and accept new ways of thinking and acting. "Now we're actually going to put something out before we've got all the answers," claims Carges.[63] They wanted eBay's employees to think about technology differently—a major shift for the company and many of its analytically inclined employees. To induce culture change, one initiative required employees who traditionally would not have interacted, such as business staffers and software developers, to sit next to each other.[64]

While this overall three-stage view of the change process is a helpful starting point, a more recent approach has been to emphasize the day-to-day details.[65] Attention to the details of culture change requires an awareness of and answers to the following four broad sets of questions. The first of these question sets concerns whether change is needed and, if so, where change efforts should be directed. Increasingly, analytic and diagnostic tools are being used to provide answers. As we have discussed earlier in this chapter and in previous chapters, modern organizations often embody many complex and interdependent systems (e.g., structures, teams, communication, and leadership processes)—perhaps not everything has to change. Another important set of questions is whether change will be resisted and, more generally, what the conditions are that might help or hinder the change effort. People are creatures of habit, and once attitudes, values, and behaviours are established, it can be quite difficult for us to adopt new ways. A third set of questions attempts to shed light on the appropriateness of the change initiatives for the problem at hand. As we will see shortly, some interventions are more effective than others, some take longer to work than others, and some are more disruptive than others. All of these options need to be considered in light of the desired outcomes as well as the realities of the organization. A final set of questions help us understand whether the change effort was successful. Even if an organization is able to work through all of these day-to-day details, change is neither easy nor assured, and it will need to be evaluated; estimates put the rate of successful culture change at only around 30 percent.[66] Why is change so difficult? To help answer this question, let's briefly review each of these question sets in more detail.

Analysis and Diagnosis: Is There a Need to Change?

Perhaps the most obvious starting point is to determine whether culture change is needed or if the status quo is working. To address this question, leaders, consultants, and other change agents will consider both the current state of the culture and where the culture should be. During the initial analysis and diagnostic phase, the primary focus is on gathering and interpreting the information. Three popular methods of gathering information from the organization and its members are interviews, focus groups, and structured approaches.

Interviews and focus groups are generally conducted by third-party facilitators or consultants so that the anonymity and confidentiality of participating leaders, managers, and employees are protected. Interviews tend to be one on one, while focus groups tend to involve several individuals at the same time. A benefit of interviewing one on one is that the interviewee may be willing to share more information than would be shared in the presence of others. Focus groups also have their benefits. First, because they involve a representative group of organizational members they are more efficient to conduct from a time perspective than one-on-one interviews, and, second, the nature of focus groups allows for multiple perspectives, discussion, and creative brainstorming (Chapter 2). Generally, facilitators and change consultants believe that interviews and focus groups can be a rich source of information of where the problems lie and what can be done about it. A concern, however, is that the overall assessment is based only on the experiences and observations of a relatively few participants. Structured approaches offer an opportunity to gather information from a wider range of organizational members, and permit statistical analyses.

One structured diagnostic tool used successfully by consultants and change agents is the **OCAI** (organizational culture assessment instrument).[67] An attractive feature of the OCAI is its ability to categorize an organization's culture in relation to its core values.

> **OCAI**
>
> Organizational culture assessment instrument (OCAI), a structured diagnostic tool used to describe and categorize corporate cultures

The OCAI is based on a framework of competing values and organized around two primary dimensions that, together, help to define the nature of an organization's culture.[68] The first dimension distinguishes cultures that emphasize the values of flexibility, discretion, and dynamism from cultures that emphasize the values of stability, order, and control. The second dimension distinguishes cultures that are internally oriented, in which integration, coordination, and cohesion among members are valued, from cultures that are externally oriented, in which risk taking, entrepreneurship, and results are stressed above all. As can be seen in Figure 15-7, when these two dimensions are crossed, four culture clusters emerge.[69]

FIGURE 15-7

Competing Values Framework

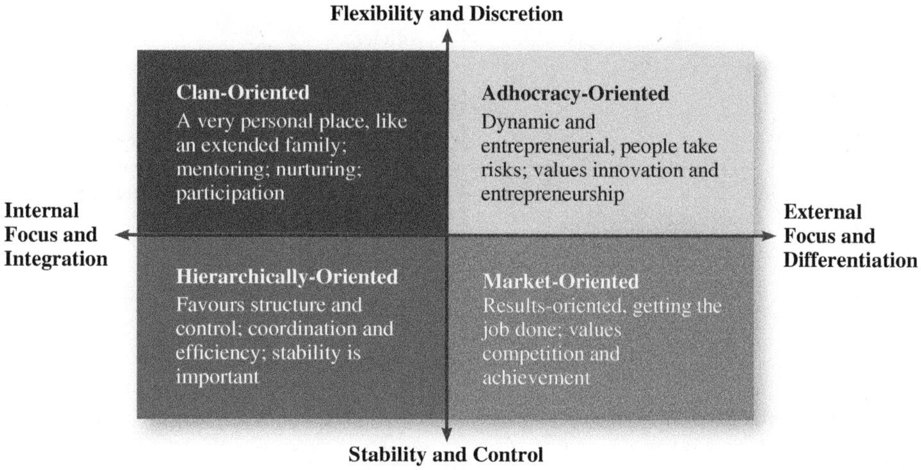

Source: Adapted from K.S. Cameron and R.E. Quinn, *Diagnosing and Changing Organizational Culture*, 3rd ed. (San Francisco: Jossey-Bass, 2011).

Hierarchically-oriented cultures are those whose members value stability and control, but which are inwardly focused with respect to coordination and efficiency. Perhaps the best examples would be those with bureaucratic structures (Chapter 14), such as government agencies and companies where standardized outputs and quality control are critical performance criteria (e.g., Ford Motor Company, Tim Hortons).[70] *Market-oriented cultures* are those that also value stability and control, but have a strong external orientation. Cultures that fall within this quadrant are primarily focused on transactions with suppliers, customers, contractors, unions and regulators; they define success by how well they manage external transactions in relation to their competitors.[71] *Clan-oriented cultures* are closest to what you might see in a family, characterized by teamwork, cohesiveness, commitment, collaboration, and permeated by a sense of "we-ness."[72] *Adhocracy-oriented cultures* are those that combine flexibility and discretion with a strong external focus. The clue here is the term "ad hoc" embedded in the name, which refers to something temporary, specialized, and dynamic. For organizations with adhocracy-oriented cultures, survival means the ability to innovate and adapt quickly to new or changing opportunities. An example of an organization with a strong adhocracy culture might be a small start-up company.[73]

The OCAI provides scores in each of the four quadrants. Figure 15-8 illustrates the organizational culture profile for a high-tech manufacturer.[74] The red lines in the figure connect the scores in each of the quadrants, providing a visual culture profile. From Figure 15-8, we can see this organization is dominated by values that are most consistent with adhocracy culture. This shouldn't be too surprising, as the organization's effectiveness, and likely survival, depends heavily on whether the company can continuously create new products and services in a highly volatile and uncertain environment. Note that the values in the other quadrants are represented in the overall profile, but those associated with a strong external focus, flexibility, and discretion are more pronounced.

FIGURE 15-8

Organizational Cultural Profile (High-Tech Manufacturer)

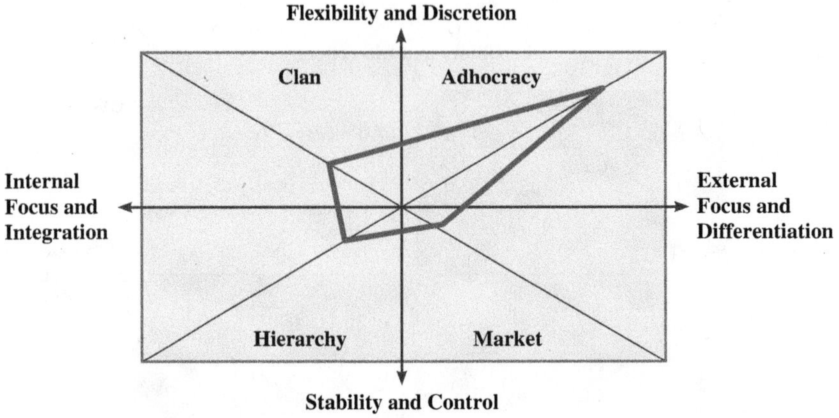

Source: Adapted from K.S. Cameron and R.E. Quinn, *Diagnosing and Changing Organizational Culture*, 3rd ed. (San Francisco: Jossey-Bass, 2011).

The profile depicted in Figure 15-9, however, tells a very different story.[75] As you see, the data systems firm has a score close to zero in the adhocracy culture. The most dominant values appear to straddle the hierarchy and market quadrants, suggesting that effectiveness for this firm depends on its ability to maintain control while still being able to respond well to customers' needs.

FIGURE 15-9

Organizational Cultural Profile (Data Systems Firm)

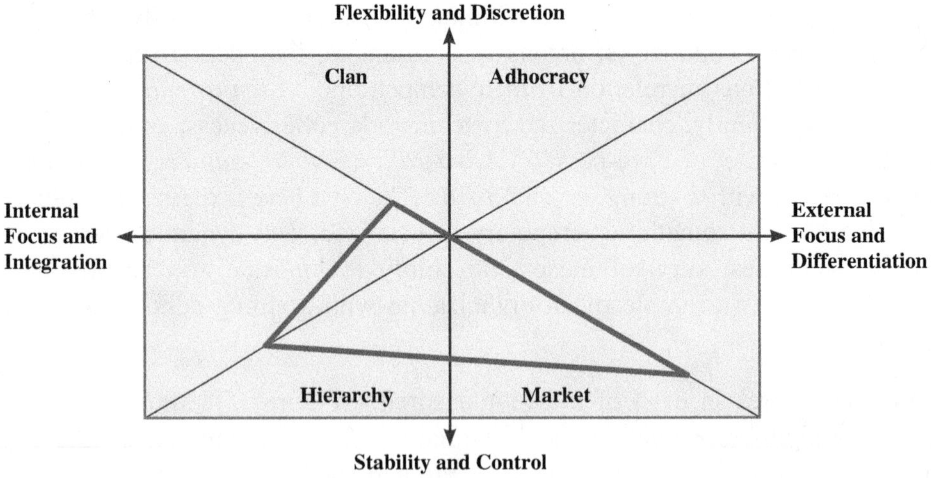

Source: Adapted from K.S. Cameron and R.E. Quinn, *Diagnosing and Changing Organizational Culture*, 3rd ed. (San Francisco: Jossey-Bass, 2011).

Structured approaches, such as the OCAI, help to assess whether an organization's culture profile is compatible with business and environmental realities or mismatched. To illustrate how the OCAI can be used to define and target change initiatives, consider the following scenario. Figure 15-10 depicts two possible culture profiles of an organization. The solid red line is where the CEO currently sees the company, and the dashed black line depicts the CEO's vision of where the culture should be. Currently, it would appear that the company's overall culture is inherently competitive, reflecting features of both market and adhocracy culture. A potential problem with highly competitive and entrepreneurial cultures is that the degree of communication, integration, and cooperation among members might suffer. This is exactly what the CEO observed, as far too many managers and division leads were running their own personal "kingdoms" and doing their own thing rather than thinking about how to achieve organizational goals together. The CEO saw a clear need for a new culture that retained its strong external focus but tempered these behaviours with greater collaboration, more teamwork, and customer service. From the figure, we see that the CEO desired culture change in the following areas: an increased presence in clan culture (e.g., more empowerment, more teamwork, more cooperation) and a reduced presence in hierarchy culture (e.g., fewer formal controls). The promise here is that if members exhibited more communication and cooperation, not only would innovation increase, but eventually social control would replace the need for formal control.

FIGURE 15-10

Using the OCAI for Diagnosis and Analysis

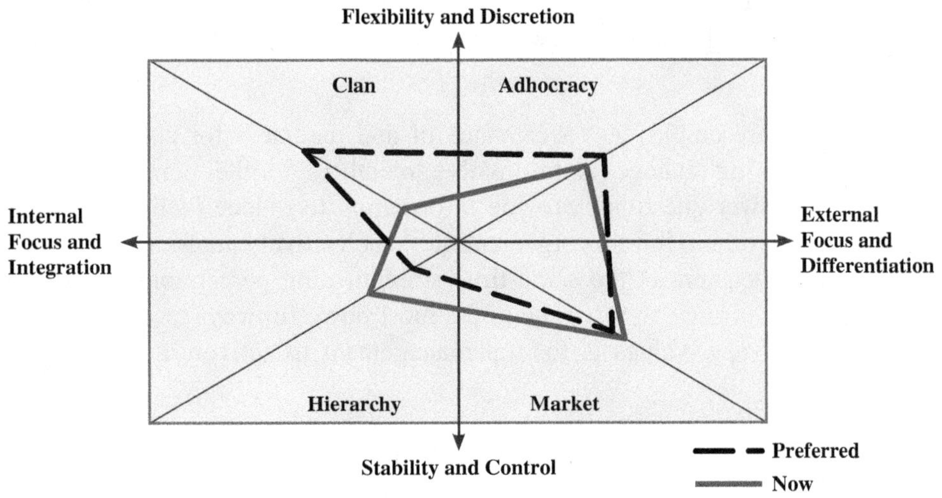

Source: Adapted from K.S. Cameron and R.E. Quinn, *Diagnosing and Changing Organizational Culture*, 3rd ed. (San Francisco: Jossey-Bass, 2011).

Understanding and Managing Resistance?

Assuming that our analysis and diagnosis confirms a need for change, what then? It might be tempting to jump right into a change initiative (e.g., implement a new reward system), but research and experience suggest a better idea is to consider whether conditions are favourable for change. As mentioned earlier, roughly 70 percent of change efforts fail to live up to expectations.[76] Some of these problems can be attributed to a poor appreciation for resistance.

We define **resistance** in this context as the deliberate act of opposing or withstanding change. Why does resistance occur? From an employee's point of view, change almost always introduces some level of uncertainty. Questions an employee might ask herself include: "Will this change impact my job?" "Will the proposed changes alter the kind and level of knowledge and skills I need to have in order to do my job?" "Will this change put my position at risk?" "Will my status within the organization change?" To the extent that answers these questions go unanswered, understanding and acceptance of the change initiative is likely to be low, and especially when the organization and its leaders are not trusted (Chapter 8).

resistance
The deliberate act of opposing or withstanding change

Research shows that employees express resistance in many different ways. For instance, resistance can be expressed through job performance (Chapter 2), such as reduced task performance, lower levels of organizational citizenship behaviour, elevated counterproductive behaviour (e.g., property and production deviance, aggression toward management) and withdrawal behaviour (Chapter 3).[77]

Another source of resistance stems from the properties of culture itself. Earlier in the chapter we defined organizational culture as shared social knowledge. People, especially in the presence of a strong culture (Figure 15-4), naturally feel pressure to conform to the rules, norms, and values that shape attitudes and behaviour.[78] Pressure to conform is strengthened by the fact that deviance from well-established social norms is often not tolerated well by other members, and can entail unwanted outcomes (e.g., deviants being ostracized). To the extent that change requires members to "deviate" from the status quo, resistance will likely be high until the new rules, norms, and values have become accepted social knowledge.

What can be done to increase employees' acceptance of and readiness for change? Perhaps the best advice for leaders considering change is to involve members in the planning process, actively encourage participation, answer questions, provide information to reduce feelings of uncertainty, and explain why change is important for the organization.[79] Collectively, these actions should help to minimize feelings of apprehension, at the same time strengthening perceptions of procedural justice and trust (Chapter 8). As we discuss shortly, one of the most powerful ways to sanction new rules, new norms, and the adoption of new values is for top management to actively and visually support the change effort.

Change Interventions?

Assuming that the goals and the conditions for change are understood, the next major decision is to select one or more change interventions. In this section we review some of the more popular ways that leaders have initiated organizational and culture change. In Table 15-2 we summarize the virtues and concerns associated with three related yet distinct management practices (selection, training, and performance management), changes in leadership, and mergers and acquisitions. As you will see, not all these are appropriate in all situations. For instance, changing the way new hires are selected might be a very painless and effective strategy over the longer term, whereas a change in leadership might be painful at first but able to produce results relatively quickly.

Selection Selection is the process of choosing one or more new employees from a pool of applicants on the basis of job-related criteria. Using selection as a mechanism to change culture requires that managers consider job skills and the extent to which applicants exhibit the values, attitudes, behaviours that fit the *target* culture. If it is true that culture is determined, fundamentally, by the people who are in the organization,[80] changing the composition of people in a deliberate way should, over time, bring about a new culture. Altering recruiting strategies and hiring criteria are fairly innocuous changes that should encounter low levels of resistance. A concern, however, might be the length of time needed for underlying assumptions, norms, and values to change.

TABLE 15-2

Comparing Different Change Interventions

Intervention	Examples	Resistance	Speed	Advantages	Disadvantages
Selection	Revised pre-employment testing	Low	Slow	Changes the mix of values, skills, and behaviours	Takes time for the new hires to impact change
Training	Teamwork training	Low	Slow	Expands the type and level of employee skills	Can be costly
				Increase explicit and tacit knowledge	Takes time to implement
					Gradual behavioural change
Performance management	Goal-setting combined with 360-degree feedback	Moderate	Moderate	Focuses attention on the things that matter most	Managers require training; takes time to organize
	Contingent rewards			Facilitates learning	Gradual behavioural change
				Can be very motivating for employees	If not managed well, can erode motivation
					Might create a culture of "winners and losers"
Changes in leadership	New CEO	High	Fast	Implemented quickly	Existing relationships disrupted
					Uncertainty within the organization
					Can be threatening for some members
Mergers and acquisitions	Two organizations form one	High	Fast	Implemented quickly	Can be difficult for the organization to adjust to
					May involve significant job losses
					May take time before benefits realized

One company that actively uses selection procedures to shape its culture is Google.[81] In addition to strong cognitive abilities (Chapter 4) and job fit, interviewers routinely look for signs of "Googliness"—how well an applicant is perceived to fit into its workplace culture. For instance, is the applicant innately curious? Can he think outside the box? Does she like working in teams and getting people to work together?"[82]

Training Training is an activity aimed at helping employees and managers acquire new knowledge, skills, and competencies needed to support a desired culture, and is often part of a company's overall socialization effort (Figure 15-5). In fact, training and development has a long history as a change intervention that can be directed at individuals, groups, or the organization as a whole.[83] Advantages of training interventions include their flexibility with respect to content (what is taught) and process (how learning occurs), and the fact that training initiatives tend to evoke relatively low levels of resistance. If there is a concern, it might be that training can be time-consuming and expensive, especially if the training occurs over time and involves external trainers and facilities.

One of the best examples of a company that uses training as a tool to build and fortify its culture is Zappos.com, Inc., an online retailer within Amazon.com, Inc.[84] As is described in Chapter 5, Zappos uses an intense training and development program to instill the company's values within all new employees. In addition to a four-week orientation, all new hires must successfully complete training in courses such as Zappos History and Culture, Science of Happiness 101, and Tribal Leadership.[85]

Performance Management Performance management is the deliberate process of measuring and motivating job behaviours (Chapters 2 and 7). As we have discussed earlier in this book, setting goals combined with feedback (Chapter 7) and managing reinforcement contingencies (Chapter 9) are potent ways of shaping, motivating, and strengthening not only job-specific behaviours (i.e., activities unique to a particular job) but also job-general behaviours that everyone—regardless of the specific job—needs to exhibit to support culture change.

As we also discussed earlier, the success of performance-management strategies often hinges on a few important conditions. For instance, it is important that new behavioural goals be accepted by employees and internalized as self-set goals (Chapter 7). It is important that behavioural measures and feedback be viewed as credible to employees and relevant (Chapter 2). Rewards, when used to fortify performance management initiatives, must be desired by employees and applied on an appropriate schedule (Chapter 9). In addition, team leaders and managers may require additional training to use these measurement and motivational techniques. Given that success will depend on how well employees respond and how well managers implement these procedures, overall we expect that resistance will be moderate, as will the speed of change (Table 15-2).

Changes in Leadership As evidenced by this chapter's opening case in Yahoo and CEO Marissa Mayer, there is perhaps no bigger driver of culture than the leaders and top executives. Just as the founders and originators set the tone and develop the culture of a new company, subsequent CEOs and presidents leave their mark on it. Many times, leaders are expected simply to sustain the culture already created.[86] At other times, they have to be a driving force for change as the environment shifts. This expectation is one of the biggest reasons organizations change their top leadership.

For example, Nortel Networks hired two former Cisco executives into the roles of chief operating officer and chief technology officer. Nortel hoped they would quickly bring some of Cisco's culture of aggressiveness to Nortel and thus allow the company to compete more effectively in the high-technology industry environment.[87] Not all such moves work out, though. Retailer JCPenney brought in former Apple retail executive Ron Johnson as CEO in 2012. One of Johnson's first moves was to rename the company and introduce an "Apple-like" culture. While senior managers welcomed the change, long-term employees did not. They felt they were being treated poorly, always being judged, and were sick of the constant Apple references. Less than a year later, after dismal results and low employee morale, Johnson was removed, and an ex-CEO familiar with the underlying JCPenney culture took over.[88]

So, although changes in leadership often bring about rapid change, resistance can also be high unless managed carefully (Table 15-2). See the ***OB on Screen*** feature here for an example of a new leader taking over and trying to create a new culture.

Mergers and Acquisitions Merging two companies with distinct cultures is a sure-fire way to change the culture in an organization. The problem is that there is just no way to know what the culture will look like afterwards; it will be a function of both the strength of the two cultures involved in the merger and how similar they are.[89] Ideally, a new culture would be created as a compromise in which the best of both companies is represented.

OB ON SCREEN

Price Check

I took this job to change that. We are going to change that. Starting here. Right now. In this room.

With those words, Susan Felders (Parker Posey) lets her new subordinates know that things are going to be changing in *Price Check* (Dir. Michael Walker, IFC Films). The film basically begins with the introduction of new boss Felders—a smart, ambitious, fast-talking, yet at times highly inappropriate woman who is transferred in to take over the pricing department of Wolsky's, a struggling Long Island–based supermarket chain. Felders doesn't waste time letting those around her know that she's in charge and that they had better be ready to outwork her if they want to stick around. If you've ever wondered what you would say as a brand-new leader to a group of established employees to change the culture to what you want, this probably isn't the example to go by. Felders manages to be confident, controlling, awkward, and scary all at the same time.

© IFC Films/Photofest

One of the first things Felders does is make the decision to get rid of one of the long-term employees to show a good-faith cost-cutting measure to corporate. Prior to doing this she meets with employee Pete Cozy (Eric Mabius) at his house to ask his opinion about whom to fire. Reluctantly, Pete gives up the name of a colleague who he thinks is lowest in terms of performance. The next day, he walks in to find that she's fired somebody completely different! When asked about it, Felders makes it clear that she's in charge, but lets Pete know that the employee she fired was low on culture fit. Felders is fantastic at times—giving praise to employees when they least expect it; inappropriate at times—getting gym memberships for everyone and staring at one woman in particular as she announces it; and conniving at times—clearly willing to undercut other employees. As a department, Felders's group is given a great many mixed messages about what is expected of them over the course of the film—certainly not a culture most of us would like to work in.

Many stories have arisen from the mergers of companies with very different cultures: AOL/Time Warner, Exxon/Mobil, HP/Compaq, and RJR/Nabisco, to name a few. Unfortunately, very few of these stories are good ones. Mergers rarely result in the strong culture managers hope for. One reason might be that the forces that drive resistance are poorly managed. Another might be that culture issues are sometimes considered only after a merger or acquisition decision has been made. In fact, most merged companies operate under a differentiated culture for an extended period of time. Some of them never really adopt a new identity, and when they do, many are seen as failures by the outside world. This perception is especially true in global mergers, in which each of the companies not only has a different organizational culture but is from a different country as well, as our ***OB Internationally*** box details.

Every now and then, though, a merger happens in which the leadership focuses on culture from the start. This was the case with the merger of Delta and Northwest Airlines. Rather than risk creating a fragmented culture, Delta CEO Richard Anderson went to the extreme of changing the ID numbers on every employee's security badge, so that employees could not tell whether a colleague had started with Delta or Northwest. According to Anderson, he wanted to avoid a situation in which "employees were constantly sizing up which side you were on."[90]

Much like changes in leadership, we see mergers and acquisitions as powerful ways to implement change quickly; however, there are significant hurdles to overcome, and resistance is likely to be high (Table 15-2).

OB INTERNATIONALLY

As mentioned previously, there is perhaps no more perilous journey for a company to take than merging with or acquiring another large firm. These problems are exacerbated when the two companies are from different countries. As few as 30 percent of international mergers and acquisitions create shareholder value.[91]

While global mergers and acquisitions have remained flat for several years, experts believe another upswing is coming.[92] Why? Hopefully, we've illustrated the inherent difficulties of trying to merge two different cultures even when the organizations are in the same country. These cultural differences can be magnified when international culture plays a role as well. Your college experiences have probably shown you that different countries have different cultures, just like organizations. People from different countries tend to view the world differently and have different sets of values as well.

For example, DaimlerChrysler bought a controlling stake in Mitsubishi Motors, thinking that a strong alliance between the two automotive companies would result in high levels of value for both. Unfortunately, the merger broke up, for reasons that have been attributed to the international culture differences between the two firms.[93] The Japanese managers tended to avoid "unpleasant truths" and stay away from major change efforts—a tendency that DaimlerChrysler never confronted but also could not accept.

There are many stories of failed international mergers, and one of the greatest reasons for such failure is that corporations don't recognize the impact of national culture differences (in addition to organizational culture differences). One such acquisition that doesn't intend to fall victim to this issue is the purchase of Volvo Car Corporation (Sweden) from Ford by China's Geely Holding Group. Although the relationship started out extremely rocky, with Geely executives storming out of an initial meeting in Sweden because they felt they were being treated like they were stupid, the two companies seem to have agreed to some compromises. Volvo, somewhat against their more safe and family-friendly culture, is now producing high-end luxury models to compete with Mercedes-Benz and BMW, which fit with Chinese desires. In addition, although Geely wanted to build three assembly plants in China to jump-start sales, the company is following a slower, quality approach at the behest of Volvo's CEO. For now, it seems that both CEOs are open to each company learning from the other.[94]

Evaluating the Change Process?

As with any intervention, the big question, of course, is: Did change occur? And if so, did the change happen in the desired direction? Are we better off? Fortunately or unfortunately, there are many different ways to detect if culture change occurred. If structured diagnostic tools were used during the planning phase, such as the OCAI, one idea would be to re-administer the assessment to see if desired culture change had occurred. Another idea might be to look at evidence of improved job performance, stronger (and the right kind of) commitment, reduced turnover, higher job satisfaction, less stress, increased motivation, greater trust, better decisions, less conflict within project teams, more effective communication processes, and more favourable reaction to leaders. In other words, we might assess the effectiveness of a change initiative on many, if not all, of the topics covered in our integrative model (Figure 1-1). We might also want to look at the organizational level for evidence of improved results (e.g., higher productivity, cost reduction, improved safety records), some of which might be directly attributable to culture change.

An example of a change intervention that has had a tremendous payoff in terms of organizational results is the recent turnaround at Calgary-based CP Railway (see Chapter 12).[95] In early 2012, CP was one of the worst-performing railroads in all North America.[96] Hunter Harrison was installed as the new CEO mid-2012. His challenge was to change a long-established culture that had become far too "sleepy" and entitled to one that valued customer service, greater efficiency, better use of the company's resources, and personal accountability, responsibility, and discipline among all members.[97] When Hunter took over, the operating ratio (i.e., a productivity index that reflects costs as a percentage of revenues), at 80 percent, was one of the worst in the industry. Within one short year, that critical ratio had dropped to 65 percent while maintaining the lowest frequency of accidents in the industry.[98] Evidently, these changes were noticed by others. Not only did Hunter's initiatives transform the culture at CP Railway, but over this time the company's stock price doubled.

Of course, it would be disingenuous to suggest all change initiatives have dramatic effects like at CP Railway. The truth is, culture change can be difficult to evaluate. Sometimes change initiatives have their desired effects, but the metrics used to detect change are poorly chosen. An example would be if a new training initiative improved the level of cooperation, civility, and morale within a call centre but the metric used to assess culture change was heavily focused on individual results. Change initiatives often have very specific behavioural effects (e.g., improved selection procedures within the administrative group might lower turnover for these individuals) that are not detected using more general measures of organizational productivity (e.g., overall turnover within the organization). Finally, culture change tends to occur slowly, and so might be missed using measures with shorter time frames.

We leave this section with a reminder that change is often a chaotic, messy process. It is rarely the neat, apolitical, linear process you might expect.[99] It would be convenient if change efforts fit nicely into the three steps of *unfreezing*, *change initiative*, and *refreezing*. Perhaps a more realistic approach is to view change as an ongoing, continual process involving regular diagnosis and analysis, design and implementation of appropriate interventions, and follow-up measures to provide feedback and to facilitate organizational learning. Given that culture is complex, nuanced, and constantly evolving, attempts to evaluate change initiatives will need to take this into consideration.

15.6 What is person–organization fit and how does it affect job performance and organizational commitment?

HOW IMPORTANT IS ORGANIZATIONAL CULTURE?

Normally, this is where we summarize the importance of organizational culture by describing how it affects job performance and organizational commitment—the two outcomes in our integrative model of OB. However (similarly to organizational structure in Chapter 14), it's difficult because there are so many different types and dimensions of the concept. Although there has been some support for distinct culture types having an effect on employee attitudes,[100] all have different effects on performance and commitment—effects that likely vary across different types of organizations and industries.

Regardless of the type of culture we're talking about, however, one concept remains important for any employee in any business: fit. Think for a moment about working for an organization whose culture doesn't match your own values. Maybe you work for an organization that produces a product that you don't believe in or that might be harmful to others, such as Rothmans, Benson & Hedges, or Labatt Breweries of Canada. Maybe your employer organization expects you to perform ethically questionable actions or produces a poor-quality product. **Person–organization fit** is the degree to which a person's personality and values match the culture of an organization. Employees judge fit by thinking about the values they prioritize the most, then judging whether the organization shares those values. Table 15-3 lists a set of values that many people have used to judge fit. Which of these would you say are most important to you?

person–organization fit
The degree to which a person's personality and values match the culture of an organization

TABLE 15-3

Values Used to Judge Fit with a Culture

Flexibility	Adaptability
Stability	Predictability
Being innovative	Taking advantage of opportunities
A willingness to experiment	Risk taking
Being careful	Autonomy
Being rule-oriented	Being analytical
Paying attention to detail	Being precise
Being team-oriented	Sharing information freely
Emphasizing a single culture	Being people-oriented
Fairness	Respect for the individual's rights
Tolerance	Informality
Being easygoing	Being calm
Being supportive	Being aggressive

Source: C.A. O'Reilly, J.A. Chatman, and D.F. Caldwell, "People and Organizational Culture: A Profile Comparison Approach to Assessing Person–Organization Fit," *Academy of Management Journal* Vol. 34, 1991, pp. 487–516. Copyright © 1991. Reproduced with permission via Copyright Clearance Center.

Two meta-analyses illustrate the importance of person–organization fit to employees.[101] When employees feel that their values and personality match those of the organization, they experience higher levels of *job satisfaction* and feel less *stress* about their day-to-day tasks. They also feel higher levels of *trust* toward their managers. Taken together, those results illustrate why person–organization fit is so highly correlated with organizational commitment, one of the two outcomes in our integrative model of OB (see Figure 15-11). When employees feel they fit with their organization's culture, they're much more likely to develop an emotional attachment to the company. The effects of fit on job performance are weaker, however. In general, person–organization fit is more related to citizenship behaviours than to task performance. Employees who sense a good fit are therefore more likely to help their colleagues and go the extra mile for the company.

FIGURE 15-11

Effects of Person–Organization Fit on Performance and Commitment

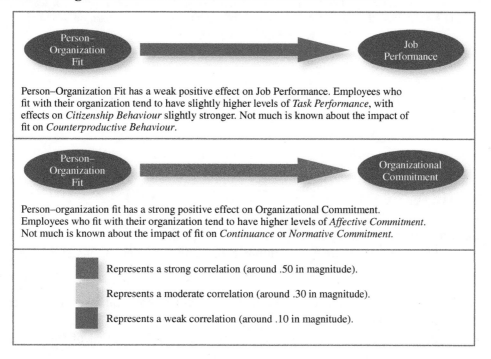

Person–Organization Fit has a weak positive effect on Job Performance. Employees who fit with their organization tend to have slightly higher levels of *Task Performance*, with effects on *Citizenship Behaviour* slightly stronger. Not much is known about the impact of fit on *Counterproductive Behaviour*.

Person–organization fit has a strong positive effect on Organizational Commitment. Employees who fit with their organization tend to have higher levels of *Affective Commitment*. Not much is known about the impact of fit on *Continuance* or *Normative Commitment*.

Represents a strong correlation (around .50 in magnitude).

Represents a moderate correlation (around .30 in magnitude).

Represents a weak correlation (around .10 in magnitude).

Sources: W. Arthur Jr., S.T. Bell, A.J. Villado, and D. Doverspike, "The Use of Person–Organization Fit in Employment-Related Decision Making: An Assessment of Its Criterion-Related Validity," *Journal of Applied Psychology* 91 (2007), pp. 786–801; and A.L. Kristof-Brown, R.D. Zimmerman, and E.C. Johnson, "Consequences of Individuals' Fit at Work: A Meta-analysis of Person–Job, Person–Organization, Person–Group, and Person–Supervisor Fit," *Personnel Psychology* 58 (2005), pp. 281–342.

OB RESEARCH IN CANADA

Jia Lin Xie is currently Magna Professor in Management in Rotman School of Management at the University of Toronto. Dr. Xie's areas of expertise include job design, job stress, cross-cultural organizational behaviour, and knowledge management. Her cross-cultural research focuses on the comparisons between Chinese and North Americans on job-related attitudes and behaviour. It is common to view the Chinese as holding collective and interdependent cultural values

Dr. Jia Lin Xie

(*Continued*)

(Chapter 4). By tracking a group of 486 Chinese employees, Dr. Xie found evidence of variation in these traditional values, and that these variations were linked to stress coping and health (Chapter 6). In other work, she was able to show how perceptions of organizational culture influence individual behaviours, such as absenteeism. It seems that employees in both China and Canada base their decisions to attend or be absent from work, in part, on what they believe to be a legitimate and acceptable (expected) level of absence within the group.

For more information about Dr. Xie's research, please look her up at www.utoronto.ca.

15.7 What steps can organizations take to make sure that newcomers will fit with their culture?

APPLICATION: MANAGING SOCIALIZATION

Most organizations recognize the importance of having employees adapt to the culture of their organization quickly. Luckily, there are a number of actions organizations can take to help their employees adapt from the first day they walk in the door.

Table 15-4 highlights some of the different tactics organizations can use when socializing their employees. Note that companies can take two very different approaches to the socialization process. The left-hand column represents a view of socialization in which the goal of the process is to have newcomers adapt to the organization's culture. This view assumes that the organization has a strong culture and definite norms and values that it wants employees to adopt, which is not always the case. Some organizations don't have a strong culture that they want employees to adapt to, or they might be trying to change their culture and want new employees to shake things up. The tactics listed in the right-hand column might be more appropriate in such circumstances.

TABLE 15-4

Tactics Organizations Use to Socialize New Employees

Tactics Designed to *Encourage* Adaptation to the Organization's Culture	Tactics Designed to *Discourage* Adaptation to the Organization's Culture
Orient new employees along with a group of other new employees	Orient new employees by themselves
Put newcomers through orientation apart from current organizational members	Allow newcomers to interact with current employees while they are being oriented
Provide hurdles that are required to be met prior to organizational membership	Allow organizational membership regardless of whether any specific requirements have been met
Provide role models for newcomers	Use no examples of what an employee is supposed to be like
Constantly remind newcomers that they are now part of a group and that this new group helps define who they are	Constantly affirm to newcomers that they are to be themselves and that they were chosen for the organization on the basis of who they are

Sources: Adapted from G.R. Jones, "Socialization Tactics, Self-Efficacy, and Newcomers' Adjustments to Organizations," *Academy of Management Journal* 29 (1986), pp. 262–79; J. Van Maanen and E.H. Schein, "Toward a Theory of Organizational Socialization," *Research in Organizational Behavior* 1 (1979), pp. 209–64.

In addition to the tactics listed in the table, there are three other major ways organizations routinely and effectively speed up the socialization process of newcomers: realistic job previews, orientation programs, and mentoring.

Realistic Job Previews One of the most inexpensive and effective ways of reducing early turnover among new employees is the use of **realistic job previews.**[102] Realistic job previews (RJPs) occur during the anticipatory stage of socialization during the recruitment process. They involve making sure a potential employee has an accurate picture of what working for an organization is going to be like by providing both the positive *and* the negative aspects of the job.[103] Kal Tire, a leading Canadian automotive retail outlet, arranges for job candidates to spend an entire day inside the company getting familiar with the organization and the job they are applying for. By thus allowing them to see what the organization's idea of customer service is and the job demands of road tire repairs, the company effectively reduces the likelihood of significant reality shock and shortens the encounter stage that generally accompanies initial employment.[104]

realistic job previews

The process of ensuring that a prospective employee understands both the positive and the negative aspects of the job

Orientation Programs One effective way to start the socialization process is by having new employees attend some form of **newcomer orientation** session. Apparently most organizations agree, given that 64–93 percent of all organizations use some form of orientation training process.[105] Not all orientation programs are alike, however, and different types of orientation training can be more effective than others.[106] Orientation programs have been shown to be effective transmitters of socialization content; employees who complete them have higher levels of satisfaction, commitment, and performance.[107] Jet Blue CEO Dave Barger believes strongly in such sessions, and has been to over 250 over the past decade. He tells his new hires, "The hard product—airplanes, leather seats, satellite TVs, bricks and mortar—as long as you have a checkbook, they can be replicated. It's the culture that can't be replicated. It's how we treat each other. Do we trust each other? Can we push back on each other? The human side of the equation is the most important part of what we're doing."[108]

newcomer orientation

A common form of training during which new hires learn more about the organization

Mentoring One of the most popular pieces of advice given to college students as they begin their careers is that they need to find a mentor or coach within their organization.[109] **Mentoring** is a process by which a junior-level employee (protégé) develops a deep and long-lasting relationship with a more senior-level employee (mentor) within the organization. The mentor can provide social knowledge, resources, and psychological support to the protégé both at the beginning of employment and as the protégé continues his or her career with the company. Mentoring has always existed in companies on an informal basis. However, as organizations continue to learn about the strong benefits of these relationships, they're more frequently instituting formal mentoring programs.[110] In fact, nearly 76 percent of companies use mentoring in order to develop skills.[111] Formal programs allow the company to provide consistent information, train mentors, and ensure that all newcomers have the opportunity to develop one of these fruitful relationships. If you may recall from our discussion in Chapter 1, one of the ways RBC promotes its diversity culture is through a formal mentoring program (Diversity

Dialogues) that pairs protégés with seasoned mentors. Mentoring does not just occur in business organizations, however. See our ***OB for Students*** feature for a discussion of mentoring for university students.

mentoring

The process by which a junior-level employee develops a deep and long-lasting relationship with a more senior-level employee within the organization

OB FOR STUDENTS

What does culture mean for you as a student? Think back on all the things you had to learn and all the ambiguity you faced during your first semester in university. Just as organizational newcomers experience reality shock when they enter an organization, so do first-year students when they initially enter the university culture. Just as organizations have a culture that affects employees, universities have a culture that affects students. One recent study at a university investigated whether it was worthwhile to help socialize students in much the same way that organizations socialize new employees. The university set up a mentoring program to help facilitate the transition toward being a successful student.

As is shown in the diagram here, whether a first-year student was provided a mentor and the quality of the relationship he or she had with that mentor positively affected both satisfaction with and commitment to the university. In turn, levels of satisfaction with and commitment to the university had positive effects on the student's intention to graduate.

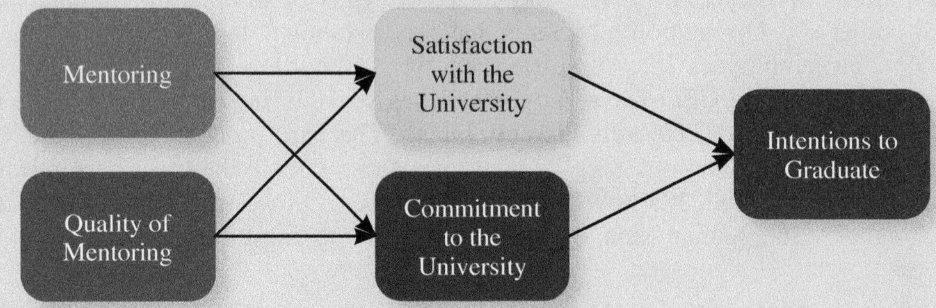

Of course, many of you may now be wondering why your university hasn't done this for you! You probably had some type of informal mentor to rely on to a degree. But if not, that disadvantage explains why formal mentoring programs can be important: Formal programs help ensure equal access for everyone. If your university doesn't have a formal mentoring program or orientation session, you might consider being an informal mentor yourself to an incoming first-year student.

Source: Republished with permission of Academy of Management, from "Peer-Mentoring Freshmen: Implications for Satisfaction, Commitment, and Retention to Graduation," *Academy of Management Learning and Education,* R.J. Sanchez, T.N. Bauer, and M.E. Paronto, Vol. 5, No. 1, 2006; permission conveyed through Copyright Clearance Center, Inc.

TAKEAWAYS

15.1 Organizational culture is the shared social knowledge within an organization regarding the rules, norms, and values that shape the attitudes and behaviors of its employees. There are three components of organizational culture: observable artifacts (symbols, physical structures, language, stories, rituals, ceremonies), espoused values, and basic underlying assumptions.

15.2 An organization's culture can be described on dimensions such as solidarity and sociability to create four general culture types: networked, communal, fragmented, and mercenary. Organizations often strive to create a more specific cultural emphasis, as in customer service cultures, safety cultures, diversity cultures, and creativity cultures.

15.3 Strong cultures have the ability to influence employee behaviours and attitudes. Strong cultures exist when employees agree on the way things are supposed to happen and their behaviours are consistent with those expectations. Strong cultures are not necessarily good or bad. Generally, a culture's effectiveness depends on how well it matches the company's outside environment. To this degree, adaptive cultures can be very useful.

15.4 Organizations maintain their cultures through attraction, selection, and attrition processes and socialization practices. Organizations change their cultures by changing their leadership or through mergers and acquisitions.

15.5 Changing an organization's culture is a complex process that involves careful diagnosis and analysis, understanding and managing resistance, careful choice of change interventions (selection, training, performance management, change in leaders, and mergers/acquisitions), and evaluation of the change effort to facilitate learning and adjustments. Culture change is often a slow, chaotic, and messy process. Perhaps a more realistic approach is to view culture change as an ongoing process.

15.6 Person–organization fit is the degree to which a person's values and personality match the culture of the organization. It has a weak positive effect on job performance and a strong positive effect on organizational commitment.

15.7 There are a number of practices organizations can utilize to improve the socialization of new employees, including realistic job previews, orientation programs, and mentoring.

KEY TERMS

anticipatory stage
ASA framework
basic underlying assumptions
ceremonies
communal culture
countercultures
creativity culture

culture strength
customer service culture
diversity culture
encounter stage
espoused values
fragmented culture
language
mentoring
mercenary culture
networked culture
newcomer orientation
observable artifacts
OCAI
organizational culture
person–organization fit
physical structures
realistic job previews
reality shock
resistance
rituals
safety culture
socialization
stories
subcultures
symbols
understanding and adaptation

DISCUSSION QUESTIONS

15.1 Have you or a family member ever worked for an organization with a strong culture? If so, what made it strong? Did you or they enjoy working there? What do you think led to that conclusion?

15.2 Is it possible for an employee to have personal values that are inconsistent with the values of the organization? If so, how is this inconsistency likely to affect the employee's behaviour and attitudes while at work?

15.3 How can two companies in the same industry with very different cultures both be successful? Shouldn't one company's culture automatically be a better fit for the environment?

15.4 Imagine what the Canada Revenue Agency's culture must be like. Where do these impressions come from? Do you think your impressions are accurate? What might make them inaccurate?

15.5 Think about the last job you started. What unique things might companies do to reduce the reality shock new employees encounter? Are these methods likely to be expensive?

CASE • YAHOO

Sometimes companies try to change their culture quietly and behind the scenes, whereas others are forced to react to their proposed changes in public. Yahoo's push to change its culture landed square in the latter category during the spring of 2013. Of course, when you are a $5 billion company whose main business is the Internet, changes are harder to hide.

New CEO Marissa Mayer introduced some bold and major changes partially on the basis of what she had learned about creating an effective culture at Google.[112] The hiring of Mayer got glowing reviews and Yahoo recorded a stock price increase of 35 percent.[113] But once the first, easy, and fun initiatives of providing free iPhones and meals in the cafeteria were in place, Mayer took two major controversial steps to stimulate an even faster culture shift. First, she banned employees from telecommuting. Second, she had to personally approve all new employees. Neither decision went over exceptionally well.

While many organizational experts believed the no-telecommuting policy was a good one given what Yahoo was trying to do, the general public and media reacted differently. "Epic fail," "hypocrite," and "idiotic" were some of the nicer criticisms flung in Mayer's direction following that edict.[114] Part of the problem was the way the new policy was delivered—in a poorly worded memo from an HR executive, which was then leaked to a tech blogger and released for the world to see online. The change in policy stood fast, though. Mayer said, "People are more productive when they are alone, but they're more innovative and collaborative when they're together."[115] She knew this directly from helping Google foster its culture using the same technique. The move wasn't because Yahoo believes its workers aren't working, but because being in the office increases human interaction.[116] Mayer believes that when workers run into each other in the office, they are more likely to share ideas and talk about work-related issues and solutions, and the goal is to create a collaborative culture.[117]

One of the other major ways companies can control culture is through hiring, and one of the low-key, unwritten policies at Google is that executives have the final say in the hiring process. Mayer's recent decision to take the same stance has ruffled some feathers. Those who don't like it say that needing Mayer's approval on every hire slows the hiring process too much in an environment such as Silicon Valley where quick hiring is an imperative. Dan Flinnigan, CEO of a job recruitment and applicant tracking firm, notes: "With a company the size of Yahoo's, it's a challenge to meet every hire—there's only so much time in a day, and she knows that. So clearly, she's decided that the downside risk is worth the upside benefit of changing the culture into something she thinks is more competitive and likely to win. No big decision is going to influence culture without risks."[118]

15.1 Is it possible for a company the size of Yahoo to change its culture dramatically without the push of a forceful leader? If yes, how could that happen?

15.2 What are the dangers for Yahoo in having Marissa Mayer trying to duplicate much of the culture at Google?

15.3 Do employees have to be present to have a strong culture? What are the advantages and disadvantages, for a tech company such as Yahoo, of a no-telecommuting policy?

EXERCISE • UNIVERSITY CULTURE

The purpose of this exercise is to explore how organizational culture is transmitted through observable artifacts. This exercise uses groups, so your instructor will either assign you to a group or ask you to create your own group. The exercise has the following steps:

15.1 Using the table below, consider the observable artifacts that transmit the organizational culture of your university.

Symbols	Think about the logo and images associated with your university. What message do they convey about the university's culture?
Physical structures	Think about the most visible physical structures on campus. What do those structures say about your university's culture?
Language	Think about the jargon, slang, slogans, and sayings associated with your university. What insights do they offer into the university's culture?
Stories	What anecdotes, accounts, legends, and myths are associated with your university? What messages do they convey about your university's culture?
Rituals	What are the daily or weekly routines that occur at your university, and what do they say about the culture?
Ceremonies	What formal events and celebrations occur at your university, and what cultural signals do they convey?

15.2 Consider the sorts of values listed in Table 15-3. If you consider the symbols, physical structures, language, stories, rituals, and ceremonies identified in step 15.1, what core values seem to summarize your university's culture? Using a transparency, laptop, or board, list the one value that seems most central to your university's culture. Then list the three cultural artifacts most responsible for transmitting that core value. Present your results to the class.

15.3 Class discussion (whether in groups or as a class) should centre on the following topics: Do you like how your university's culture is viewed, as represented in the group presentations? Why or why not? If you wanted to change the university's culture to represent other sorts of values, what process would you use?

OB ASSESSMENTS • CREATIVITY CULTURE

Have you experienced a creativity culture? This assessment is designed to measure two facets of that type of culture. Think of your current job, or the last job that you held (even if it was just a part-time or summer job). If you haven't worked, think of a current or former student group that developed strong norms for how tasks should be done. Answer each question using the response scale provided. Then subtract your answers to the boldfaced questions from 6, with the difference being your new answer for that question. For example, if your original answer for question 7 was "4," your new answer is "2" (6 – 4). Then add up your scores for the two facets.

1 **Strongly Disagree**	2 **Disagree**	3 **Uncertain**	4 **Agree**	5 **Strongly Agree**	
1. New ideas are readily accepted here.					_____
2. This company is quick to respond when changes need to be made.					_____
3. Management here is quick to spot the need to do things differently.					_____
4. This organization is very flexible; it can quickly change procedures to meet new conditions and solve problems as they arise.					_____
5. People in this organization are always searching for new ways of looking at problems.					_____
6. It is considered extremely important here to follow the rules.					_____
7. People can ignore formal procedures and rules if it helps to get the job done.					_____
8. Everything has to be done by the book.					_____
9. It is not necessary to follow procedures to the letter around here.					_____
10. Nobody gets too upset if people break the rules around here.					_____

Scoring and Interpretation

Innovation. Add up items 1–5. ______

Formalization. Add up items 6–10. ______

If your score is 22 or above for either facet, your organization or work group is high on that particular dimension. Creative cultures tend to be high on innovation and low on formalization. So if your score was 22 or above for innovation and 21 or below for formalization, chances are you've experienced a strong creativity culture.

Remember, when interpreting your scores on these assessments it is important to consider the *reliability* and *validity* of these tools (see Chapter 1, ***OB Assessments***).

Source: From Malcolm G. Patterson, Michael A. West, Viv J. Shackleton, Jeremy F. Dawson, Rebecca Lawthom, Sally Maitlis, David L. Robinson, and Alison M. Wallace, "Validating the Organizational Climate Measure: Links to Managerial Practices, Productivity and Innovation," *Journal of Organizational Behavior*, Vol. 26, 2005, pp. 379–408. Reprinted with permission of John Wiley & Sons, Inc.

Glossary

ability Relatively stable capabilities of people for performing a particular range of related activities

ability (dimension of trustworthiness) The skills, competencies, and areas of expertise that enable an authority to be successful in some specific area

ability to focus The degree to which employees can devote their attention to work

absenteeism A form of physical withdrawal in which employees do not show up for an entire day of work

abuse Employee assault or endangerment from which physical and psychological injuries may occur

abusive supervision The sustained display of hostile verbal and nonverbal behaviours, excluding physical contact, by a supervisor

accommodating A conflict resolution style by which one party gives in to the other and acts in a completely unselfish way

action processes Teamwork processes, such as helping and coordination, that aid in the accomplishment of teamwork as the work is actually taking place

action teams Teams of limited duration that performs complex tasks in contexts that tend to be highly visible and challenging

activation The degree to which moods are aroused and active, as opposed to unaroused and inactive

active management-by-exception A type of transactional leadership in which the leader arranges to monitor mistakes and errors actively, and takes corrective action when required

adaptive task performance Thoughtful responses by an employee to unique or unusual task demands

affect-based trust Trust dependent on feelings toward the authority that go beyond any rational assessment of trustworthiness

affective commitment An employee's desire to remain a member of an organization due to a feeling of emotional attachment

affective events theory A theory that describes how workplace events can generate emotional reactions that impact work behaviours

agreeableness Dimension of personality-reflecting traits like being kind, cooperative, sympathetic, helpful, courteous, and warm

all-channel network structure A communication network in which any member can send and receive messages from any other

alternative dispute resolution A process by which two parties resolve conflicts through the use of a specially trained, neutral third party

anticipatory stage A stage of socialization that begins as soon as a potential employee develops an image of what it would be like to work for a company

apprising An influence tactic in which the requestor clearly explains why performing the request will benefit the target personally

arbitration A process by which a third party determines a binding settlement to a dispute between two parties

ASA framework A theory (attraction–selection–attrition) that states that employees will be drawn to organizations with cultures that match their personality, organizations will select employees that match, and employees will leave or be forced out when they are not a good fit

autocratic style A leadership style in which the leader makes the decision alone without asking for opinions or suggestions of the employees in the work unit

autonomy The degree to which a job provides freedom, independence, and discretion to perform the work

availability bias The tendency for people to base their judgments on information that is easier to recall

avoiding A conflict resolution style by which one party wants to remain neutral, stay away from conflict, or postpone the conflict to gather information or let things cool down

basic underlying assumptions The engrained beliefs and philosophies of employees

BATNA Acronym for a negotiator's *best alternative to a negotiated agreement*

behaviour modelling training When employees observe the actions of others, learn from what they observe, and then repeat the observed behaviour

behavioural coping Physical activities used to deal with a stressful situation

behavioural modelling Employees' observing the actions of others, learning from what they observe, and then repeating the observed behaviour

behavioural strains Patterns of negative behaviours associated with other strains

behaviourally anchored rating scales Use of examples of critical incidents to evaluate an employee's job performance behaviours directly

benevolence (dimension of trustworthiness) The belief that an authority wants to do good for a trustor, apart from any selfish or profit-centred motives

benign job demands Job demands that are not appraised as being stressful

Big Five The five major dimensions of personality: conscientiousness, agreeableness, neuroticism, openness to experience, and extraversion

boosterism Positively representing the organization when in public

bounded rationality The notion that people do not have the ability or resources to process all available information and alternatives when making a decision

bureaucracy An organizational form that emphasizes the control and coordination of its members through a strict chain of command, formal rules and procedures, high specialization, and centralized decision making

bureaucratic structure An organizational form that exhibits many of the facets of a mechanistic organization

burnout The emotional, mental, and physical exhaustion from coping with stressful demands on a continuing basis

business environment The outside environment, including customers, competitors, suppliers, distributors, and other factors external to the firm, which all affect organizational design

causal inference Concluding that one variable really does cause another

centrality How important a person's job is and how many people depend on that person to accomplish their tasks

centralization Aspect of structure that dictates where decisions are formally made in organizations

ceremonies Formal events, generally performed in front of an audience of organizational members

chain network structure A communication network in which information is passed from member to member, from one end of the chain to the other

chain of command Specifies who reports to whom; signifies formal authority relationships

challenge stressors Stressors that tend to be appraised as opportunities for growth and achievement

circle network structure A communication network in which members send and receive messages from individuals who are immediately adjacent to them

citizenship behaviour Voluntary employee behaviours that contribute to organizational goals by improving the context in which work takes place

civic virtue Participating in company operations at a deeper-than-normal level through voluntary meetings, readings, and keeping up with news that affects the company

client structure An organizational form in which employees are organized around serving customers

climate for transfer An organizational environment that supports the use of new skills

coalitions An influence tactic in which the influencer enlists other people to help influence the target

coercive power A form of organizational power based on the ability to hand out punishment

cognition-based trust Trust rooted in a rational assessment of the authority's trustworthiness

cognitive ability Capabilities related to the use of knowledge to make decisions and solve problems

cognitive–behavioural techniques Various practices that help workers cope with life's stressors in a rational manner

cognitive coping Thoughts used to deal with a stressful situation

cognitive distortion A reevaluation of the inputs an employee brings to a job, often occurring in response to equity distress

cognitive moral development People's movement through several states of moral development, each more mature and sophisticated than the prior one

cohesion A team state that occurs when members of the team develop strong emotional bonds to other members of the team and to the team itself

collaboration (as conflict resolution method) A conflict resolution style whereby both parties work together to maximize outcomes

collaboration (as influence method) An influence tactic whereby the leader makes it easier for the target to complete a request by offering to work with and help the target

communal culture An organizational culture type in which employees are friendly to one another and all think

communication The process by which information and meaning is transferred from a sender to a receiver

communicator competence The ability of communicators to encode and interpret messages

communion striving A strong desire to obtain acceptance in personal relationships as a means of expressing one's personality

communities of practice Groups of employees who learn from one another through collaboration over an extended period of time

company size The number of employees in a company

company strategy An organization's objectives and goals and how it tries to capitalize on its assets to make money

comparison other Another person who provides a frame of reference for judging equity

compensatory forms model A model indicating that the various withdrawal behaviours are negatively correlated, so that engaging in one type of withdrawal makes one less likely to engage in other types

competence The capability to perform work tasks successfully

competing A conflict resolution style by which one party attempts to get his or her own goals met without concern for the other party's results

compliance A response to influence tactics in which the target is willing to do what the leader asks but does it with a degree of ambivalence

compromise A conflict resolution style by which conflict is resolved through give-and-take concessions

computer-mediated communication The exchange of information and meaning using an electronic, digital medium

conscientiousness Dimension of personality-reflecting traits like being dependable, organized, reliable, ambitious, hard-working, and persevering

consensus Used by decision makers to attribute cause; whether other individuals behave the same way under similar circumstances

consideration A pattern of behaviour in which the leader creates job relationships characterized by mutual trust, respect for employee ideas, and consideration of employee feelings

consistency Used by decision makers to attribute cause; whether this individual has behaved this way before under similar circumstances

consultation An influence tactic whereby the target is allowed to participate in deciding how to carry out or implement a request

consultative style A leadership style in which the leader presents the problem to employees asking for their opinions and suggestions before ultimately making the decision him- or herself

contingencies of reinforcement Four specific consequences used by organizations to modify employee behaviour

contingent reward A more active and effective type of transactional leadership, in which the leader attains follower agreement on what needs to be done using rewards in exchange for adequate performance

continuance commitment An employee's desire to remain a member of an organization due to an awareness of the costs of leaving

continuous reinforcement A schedule of reinforcement in which a specific consequence follows each and every occurrence of a certain behaviour

coordination The quality of physical movement in terms of synchronization of movements and balance

coping Behaviours and thoughts used to manage stressful demands and the emotions associated with the stressful demands

corporate social responsibility A perspective that acknowledges that the responsibility of a business encompasses the economic, legal, ethical, and citizenship expectations of society

correlation The statistical relationship between two variables, abbreviated *r*; it can be positive or negative and range from 0 (no statistical relationship) to ± 1 (a perfect statistical relationship)

countercultures Subcultures whose values do not match those of the organization

counterproductive behaviour Employee behaviours that intentionally hinder organizational goal accomplishment

courtesy Sharing important information with co-workers

co-worker satisfaction Employees' feelings about their co-workers, including their abilities and personalities

creative task performance Ideals or physical outcomes that are both novel and useful

creativity culture A specific culture type focused on fostering a creative atmosphere

crisis situation A change—sudden or evolving—that results in an urgent problem that must be addressed immediately

cross-training Training team members in the duties and responsibilities of their teammates

cultural values Shared beliefs about desirable end states or modes of conduct in a given culture that influence the expression of traits

culture The shared values, beliefs, motives, identities, and interpretations that result from common experiences of members of a society and are transmitted across generations

culture strength The degree to which employees agree about how things should happen within the organization and behave accordingly

customer service culture A specific culture type focused on service quality

cyberloafing A form of psychological withdrawal in which employees use Internet, e-mail, and instant messaging access for their personal enjoyment rather than work duties

daily hassles Minor day-to-day demands that interfere with work accomplishment

daydreaming A form of psychological withdrawal in which one's work is interrupted by random thoughts or concerns

decision making The process of generating and choosing from a set of alternatives to solve a problem

deep-level diversity Diversity of attributes that are inferred through observation or experience, such as one's values or personality

delegating Leader behaviour in which the leader turns responsibility for key behaviours over to employees

delegative style A leadership style in which the leader gives the employee the responsibility for making decisions within some set of specified boundary conditions

discretion The degree to which managers have the right to make decisions on their own

disposition-based trust Trust rooted in one's own personality, as opposed to a careful assessment of the trustee's trustworthiness

distinctiveness Used by decision makers to attribute cause; whether the person being judged acts in a similar fashion under different circumstances

distributive bargaining A negotiation strategy in which one person gains and the other person loses

distributive justice The perceived fairness of decision-making outcomes

diversity culture A specific culture type focused on fostering or taking advantage of a diverse group of employees

downward communication Communication that flows from the top to the bottom of the vertical channel

economic exchange Work relationships that resemble a contractual agreement by which employees fulfill job duties in exchange for financial compensation

e-mail A popular method of exchanging written digital messages from an author to one or more recipients

embeddedness An employee's connection to and sense of fit in the organization and community

emotion regulation The ability to recover quickly from emotional experiences

emotional contagion The idea that emotions can be transferred from one person to another

emotional intelligence A set of abilities related to the understanding and use of emotions that affect social functioning

emotional labour The management of their emotions that employees must do to complete their job duties successfully

emotional support The empathy and understanding people receive from others that can be used to alleviate emotional distress from stressful demands

emotion-focused coping Behaviours and cognitions of an individual intended to help manage emotional reactions to the stressful demands

emotions Intense feelings, often lasting for a short duration, that are clearly directed at someone or some circumstance

encounter stage A stage of socialization beginning the day an employee starts work, during which the employee compares the information as an outsider to the information learned as an insider

engagement A widely used term in contemporary workplaces that has different meanings depending on the context; most often refers to motivation, but can refer to affective commitment

equity distress An internal tension that results from being overrewarded or underrewarded relative to some comparison other

equity theory A theory that suggests that employees create a mental ledger of the outcomes they receive for their job inputs, relative to some comparison other

erosion model A model that suggests that employees with fewer bonds with co-workers are more likely to quit the organization

escalation of commitment A common decision-making error, in which the decision maker continues to follow a failing course of action

espoused values The beliefs, philosophies, and norms that a company explicitly states

ethics The degree to which the behaviours of an authority are in accordance with generally accepted moral norms

ethnocentrism A propensity to view one's own cultural values as "right" and those of other cultures as "wrong"

exchange tactic An influence tactic in which the requestor offers a reward in return for performing a request

exit An active response to a negative work event in which one ends or restricts organizational membership

expectancy The belief that exerting a high level of effort will result in successful performance on some task

expectancy theory A theory that describes the cognitive process employees go through to make choices among different voluntary responses

expert power A form of organizational power based on expertise or knowledge

expertise The knowledge and skills that distinguish experts from novices

explicit knowledge Knowledge that is easily communicated and available to everyone

external comparisons Comparing oneself to someone in a different company

extinction The removal of a positive outcome following an unwanted behaviour

extraversion Dimension of personality-reflecting traits like being talkative, sociable, passionate, assertive, bold, and dominant

extrinsic motivation Desire to put forth work effort due to some contingency that depends on task performance

face-to-face communication The exchange of information and meaning when one or more individuals are physically present, and where communication occurs without the aid of any mediating technology

facilitative style A leadership style in which the leader presents the problem to a group of employees and seeks consensus on a solution, making sure his or her own opinion receives no more weight than anyone else's

family time demands The amount of time committed to fulfilling family responsibilities

feedback In goal setting theory, progress updates on work goals; in job characteristics theory, the degree to which the job itself provides information about how well the job holder is doing

financial uncertainty Uncertainty with regard to the potential for loss of livelihood, savings, or the ability to pay expenses

fixed-interval schedule A schedule whereby reinforcement occurs at fixed time periods

fixed-ratio schedule A schedule whereby reinforcement occurs following a fixed number of desired behaviours

flexibility The ability to bend, stretch, twist, or reach

flow A state in which employees feel a total immersion in the task at hand, sometimes losing track of how much time has passed.

focus of commitment The people, places, and things that inspire a desire to remain a member of an organization

forced ranking A performance management system that forces managers to rank each of their people into one of three categories: the top 20 percent, the vital middle 70 percent, or the bottom 10 percent.

formalization The degree to which rules and procedures are used to standardize behaviours and decisions in an organization

four-component model A model that argues that ethical behaviours result from the multistage sequence of moral awareness, moral judgment, moral intent, and ethical behaviour

fragmented culture An organizational culture type in which employees are distant and disconnected from one another

functional structure An organizational form in which employees are grouped by the functions they perform for the organization

fundamental attribution error The tendency for people to judge others' behaviours as being due to internal factors such as ability, motivation, or attitudes

gender differences Different ways men and women tend to process and interpret information and communicate with others

general cognitive ability The general level of cognitive ability that plays an important role in determining the more narrow cognitive abilities

geographic structure An organizational form in which employees are grouped around the different locations where the company does business

goal commitment The degree to which a person is determined to reach the goal

goal interdependence The degree to which team members have a shared goal and align their individual goals with that vision

goal setting theory A theory that views goals as the primary drivers of the intensity and persistence of effort

gossip rumours about other people

gossiping Casual conversations about other people in which the facts are not confirmed as true

grapevine The primary informal communication network within an organization

groupthink Behaviours that support conformity and team harmony at the expense of other team priorities

growth need strength The degree to which employees desire to develop themselves further

harassment Unwanted physical contact or verbal remarks from a colleague

health and wellness programs Employee assistance programs that help workers with personal problems such as alcoholism and other addictions

helping Assisting co-workers who have heavy workloads, aiding them with personal matters, and showing new employees the ropes

heuristics Simple and efficient rules of thumb that allow one to make decisions more easily

hindrance stressors Stressors that tend to be appraised as thwarting progress toward growth and achievement

history A collective pool of experience, wisdom, and knowledge that benefits the organization

horizontal communication Communication that flows among members of work groups, teams, or functional units who reside at the same level in the organization

human relations movement Field of study that recognizes that the psychological attributes of individual workers and the social forces within work groups have important effects on work behaviours

human resources management Field of study that focuses on the applications of OB theories and principles in organizations

hypotheses Written predictions that specify relationships between variables

idealized influence The power held by a leader who behaves in ways that earn the admiration, trust, and respect of followers, causing followers to want to identify with and emulate the leader

identity The degree to which a job offers completion of a whole, identifiable piece of work

impact The sense that a person's actions "make a difference"—that progress is being made toward fulfilling some important purpose

incivility Communication that is rude, impolite, discourteous, and lacking in good manners

independent forms model A model that predicts that the various withdrawal behaviours are uncorrelated, so that engaging in one type of withdrawal has little bearing on engaging in other types

individualism–collectivism The degree to which a culture has a loosely knit social framework (individualism) or a tight social framework (collectivism)

individualistic roles Behaviours that benefit the individual at the expense of the team

individualized consideration A type of influence in which the leader behaves in ways that help followers achieve their potential through coaching, development, and mentoring

influence The use of behaviours to cause behavioural or attitudinal changes in others

informal communication networks Spontaneous and emergent patterns of communication that result from the choices individuals make on their own

information richness The amount and depth of the information transmitted in a message

informational justice The perceived fairness of the communications provided to employees from authorities

ingratiation The use of favours, compliments, or friendly behaviour to make the target feel better about the influencer

inimitable Incapable of being imitated or copied

initiating structure A pattern of behaviour in which the leader defines and structures the roles of employees in pursuit of goal attainment

inspirational appeal An influence tactic designed to appeal to one's values and ideals, thereby creating an emotional or attitudinal reaction

inspirational motivation A type of influence in which the leader behaves in ways that foster an enthusiasm for and commitment to a shared vision of the future

instrumental support The help people receive from others that can be used to address a stressful demand directly

instrumentality The belief that successful performance will result in some outcome or outcomes

integrative bargaining A negotiation strategy that achieves an outcome that is satisfying for both parties

integrity (dimension of trustworthiness) The perception that an authority adheres to a set of values and principles that the trustor finds acceptable

intellectual stimulation A type of influence in which the leader behaves in ways that challenge followers to be innovative and creative by questioning assumptions and reframing old situations in new ways

internal comparisons Comparing oneself to someone in your same company

internalization A response to influence tactics in which the target agrees with and becomes committed to the request

interpersonal citizenship behaviour Going beyond normal job expectations to assist, support, and develop co-workers and colleagues

interpersonal justice The perceived fairness of the interpersonal treatment received by employees from authorities

interpersonal processes Teamwork processes, such as motivating and confidence building, that focus on the management of relationships among team members

intrinsic motivation Desire to put forth work effort due to the sense that task performance serves as its own reward

intuition An emotional judgment based on quick, unconscious gut feelings

job analysis A process by which an organization determines requirements of specific jobs

job characteristics theory A theory that argues that five core characteristics (variety, identity, significance, autonomy, and feedback) combine to result in high levels of satisfaction with the work itself

job crafting When employees shape, mold, and redefine their job in a proactive way

Job Descriptive Index (JDI) A facet measure of job satisfaction that assesses an individual's satisfaction with pay, promotion opportunities, supervision, co-workers, and the work itself

job enrichment When job duties and responsibilities are expanded to provide increased levels of core job characteristics

job interview A conversation initiated by one or more person to gather information and evaluate the qualifications of the applicant for a job

job performance Employee behaviours that contribute either positively or negatively to the accomplishment of organizational goals.

job satisfaction A pleasurable emotional state resulting from the appraisal of one's job or job experiences; represents how a person feels and thinks about his or her job

job sharing Two people sharing the responsibilities of a single job

justice The perceived fairness of an authority's decision making

knowledge and skill The degree to which employees have the aptitude and competence needed to succeed on their job

knowledge of results A psychological state indicating the extent to which employees are aware of how well or how poorly they are doing

knowledge transfer The exchange of knowledge between employees

laissez-faire leadership A type of leadership in which the leader avoids leadership duties altogether

language The jargon, slang, and slogans used within an organization

leader effectiveness The degree to which the leader's actions result in the achievement of the unit's goals, the continued commitment of the unit's employees, and the development of mutual trust, respect, and obligation in leader–member dyads

leader emergence The process of becoming a leader in the first place

leader–member exchange theory A theory describing how leader–member relationships develop over time on a dyadic basis

leadership The use of power and influence to direct the activities of followers toward goal achievement

learning A relatively permanent change in an employee's knowledge or skill that results from experience

learning orientation A predisposition or attitude according to which building competence is deemed more important by an employee than demonstrating competence

legitimate power A form of organizational power based on authority or position

life cycle theory of leadership A theory stating that the optimal combination of initiating structure and consideration depends on the readiness of the employees in the work unit

life satisfaction The degree to which employees feel a sense of happiness with their lives in general

locus of control One's tendency to view the cause of events and personal outcomes as internally or externally controlled

long breaks A form of physical withdrawal in which employees take longer-than-normal lunches or breaks to spend less time at work

looking busy A form of psychological withdrawal in which one attempts to appear consumed with work when not performing actual work tasks

loyalty A passive response to a negative work event in which one publicly supports the situation but privately hopes for improvement

management by objectives (MBO) A management philosophy that bases employee evaluations on whether specific performance goals have been met

management teams Relatively permanent team that participates in managerial-level tasks that affect the entire organization

masculinity–femininity The degree to which a culture values stereotypically male traits (masculinity) or stereotypically female traits (femininity)

matrix structure A complex form of organizational structure that combines a functional and multi-divisional grouping

maximum performance Performance in brief, special circumstances that demand a person's best effort

meaningfulness A psychological state reflecting one's feelings about work tasks, goals, and purposes, and the degree to which they contribute to society and fulfill one's ideals and passions

meaningfulness of work A psychological state indicating the degree to which work tasks are viewed as something that counts in the employee's system of philosophies and beliefs

meaning of money The idea that money can have symbolic value (e.g., achievement, respect, freedom) in addition to economic value

mechanistic organizations Efficient, rigid, predictable, and standardized organizations that thrive in stable environments

mediation A process by which a third party facilitates a dispute resolution process but with no formal authority to dictate a solution

mental models The degree to which team members have a shared understanding of important aspects of the team and its task

mentoring The process by which a junior-level employee develops a deep and long-lasting relationship with a more senior-level employee within the organization

mercenary culture An organizational culture type in which employees think alike but are not friendly to one another

meta-analysis A method that combines the results of multiple scientific studies by essentially calculating a weighted-average correlation across studies (with larger studies receiving more weight)

missing meetings A form of physical withdrawal in which employees neglect important work functions while away from the office

moods States of feeling that are mild in intensity, last for an extended period of time, and are not directed at anything

moonlighting A form of psychological withdrawal in which employees use work time and resources to do non-work-related activities

moral attentiveness The degree to which people chronically perceive and consider issues of morality during their experiences

moral awareness Recognition by an authority that a moral issue exists in a situation

moral identity The degree to which a person views himself or herself as a moral person

moral intensity The degree to which an issue has ethical urgency

moral intent An authority's degree of commitment to the moral course of action

moral judgment The process people use to determine whether a particular course of action is ethical or unethical

moral principles Prescriptive guides for making moral judgments

motivation A set of energetic forces that determine the direction, intensity, and persistence of an employee's work effort

multi-divisional structure An organizational form in which employees are grouped by product, geography, or client

National Occupational Classification A national database of occupations in Canada, organizing over 40,000 job titles into 500 occupational group descriptions

needs Groupings or clusters of outcomes viewed as having critical psychological or physiological consequences

negative affectivity A dispositional tendency to experience unpleasant moods such as hostility, nervousness, and annoyance

negative emotions Employees' feelings of fear, guilt, shame, sadness, envy, and disgust

negative life events Events such as a divorce or death of a family member that tend to be appraised as a hindrance

negative reinforcement A reinforcement contingency in which an unwanted outcome is removed following a desired behaviour

neglect A passive, destructive response to a negative work event in which one's interest and effort in the job declines

negotiation A process in which two or more interdependent individuals discuss and attempt to reach agreement about their differences

networked culture An organizational culture type in which employees are friendly to one another, but everyone thinks differently and does his or her own thing

neuroticism Dimension of personality-reflecting traits like being nervous, moody, emotional, insecure, jealous, and unstable

neutralizers Situational characteristics that reduce the importance of the leader and do not improve employee performance in any way

newcomer orientation A common form of training during which new hires learn more about the organization

noise Disturbing or distracting stimuli that block or interfere with the transmission of a message

nonprogrammed decision One made by employees when a problem is new, complex, or not recognized

nonverbal communication Any form of information exchange that doesn't involve spoken or written words

normative commitment An employee's desire to remain a member of an organization due to a feeling of obligation

numerous small decisions Small decisions that people make every day

observable artifacts Aspects of an organization's culture that employees and outsiders can easily see or talk about

OCAI Organizational culture assessment instrument (OCAI), a structured diagnostic tool used to describe and categorize corporate cultures

openness to experience Dimension of personality-reflecting traits like being curious, imaginative, creative, complex, refined, and sophisticated

organic organizations Flexible, adaptive, outward-focused organizations that thrive in dynamic environments

organizational behaviour (OB) Field of study devoted to understanding, explaining, and ultimately improving the attitudes and behaviours of individuals and groups in organizations

organizational chart A drawing that represents every job in the organization and the formal reporting relationships between those jobs

organizational citizenship behaviour Going beyond normal expectations to improve operations of the organization, defend it, and be loyal to it

organizational commitment An employee's desire to remain a member of an organization

organizational culture The shared social knowledge within an organization regarding the rules, norms, and values that shape the attitudes and behaviours of its employees

organizational design The process of creating, selecting, or changing the structure of an organization

organizational politics Individual actions directed toward the goal

organizational structure Formally dictates how jobs and tasks are divided and coordinated between individuals and groups within the company

other awareness The ability to recognize and understand the emotions that other people are feeling

outcome interdependence The degree to which team members share equally in the feedback and rewards that result from the team achieving its goals

parallel teams Teams composed of members from various jobs within the organization that meet to provide recommendations about important issues

participating Leader behaviour in which the leader shares ideas and tries to help the group conduct its affairs

passive management-by-exception A type of transactional leadership in which the leader waits around for mistakes and errors, then takes corrective action as necessary

pay satisfaction Employees' feelings about the compensation for their jobs

perceived organizational support The degree to which employees believe that the organization values their contributions and cares about their well-being

perceptual ability The capacity to perceive, understand, and recall patterns of information

performance–avoid orientation A predisposition or attitude by which employees focus on demonstrating their competence so that others will not think poorly of them

performance–prove orientation A predisposition or attitude by which employees focus on demonstrating their competence so that others think favourably of them

personal aggression Hostile verbal and physical actions directed toward other employees

personal appeals An influence tactic in which the requestor asks for something based on personal friendship or loyalty

personal development Participation in activities outside of work that foster growth and learning

personality The structures and propensities inside a person that explain his or her characteristic patterns of thought, emotion, and behaviour; personality reflects what people are like and creates their social reputation

person–organization fit The degree to which a person's personality and values match the culture of an organization

physical structures The organization's buildings and internal office designs

physical withdrawal A physical escape from the work environment

physiological strains Reactions from stressors that harm the human body

pleasantness The degree to which an employee is in a good mood versus bad mood

political deviance Behaviours that intentionally disadvantage other individuals

political skill The ability to understand others and the use of that knowledge to influence them to further personal or organizational objectives

positive affectivity A dispositional tendency to experience pleasant, engaging moods such as enthusiasm, excitement, and elation

positive emotions Employees' feelings of joy, pride, relief, hope, love and compassion

positive life events Events such as marriage or the birth of a child that tend to be appraised as a challenge

positive reinforcement A reinforcement contingency in which a positive outcome follows a desired behaviour

potency A team state reflecting the degree of confidence among team members that the team can be effective across situations and tasks

power The ability to influence the behaviour of others and resist unwanted influence in return

power distance The degree to which a culture prefers equal power distribution (low power distance) or an unequal power distribution (high power distance)

predictive validity The extent to which the selection procedure (e.g., job interview) predicts future job performance

pressure An influence tactic in which the requestor attempts to use coercive power through threats and demands

primary appraisal Evaluation of whether a demand is stressful and, if it is, the implications of the stressor in terms of personal goals and well-being

privacy A state in which individuals can express themselves freely without being observed, recorded, or disturbed by other, unauthorized individuals or groups

problem-focused coping Behaviours and cognitions of an individual intended to manage the stressful situation itself

procedural justice The perceived fairness of decision-making processes

process gain Achievement of team outcomes greater than those one would expect on the basis of the capabilities of the individual members

process loss Achievement of team outcomes less than those one would expect on the basis of the capabilities of the individual members

product structure An organizational form in which employees are grouped around different products that the company produces

production deviance Intentionally reducing organizational efficiency of work output

programmed decisions Decisions that are somewhat automatic because the decision maker's knowledge allows him or her to recognize the situation and the course of action to be taken

progression model A model indicating that the various withdrawal behaviours are positively correlated, so that engaging in one type of withdrawal makes one more likely to engage in other types

project teams Teams formed to take on one-time tasks, most of which tend to be complex and require input from members from different functional areas

projection bias The faulty perception by decision makers that others think, feel, and act as they do

promotion satisfaction Employees' feelings about how the company handles promotions

property deviance Behaviours that harm the organization's assets and possessions

psychological contracts Employee beliefs about what employees owe the organization and what the organization owes them

psychological empowerment An energy rooted in the belief that tasks are contributing to some larger purpose

psychological strains Negative psychological reactions from stressors such as depression, anxiety, and anger

psychological withdrawal Actions that provide a mental escape from the work environment

psychomotor ability Capabilities associated with manipulating and controlling objects

punctuated equilibrium A sequence of team development during which not much gets done until the halfway point of a project, after which teams make necessary changes to complete the project on time

punishment An unwanted outcome that follows an unwanted behaviour

quantitative ability Capabilities associated with doing basic mathematical operations and selecting and applying formulas to solve mathematical problems

quitting A form of physical withdrawal in which employees voluntarily leave the organization

rare In short supply

rational decision-making model A step-by-step approach to making decisions that is designed to maximize outcomes by examining all available alternatives

rational persuasion The use of logical arguments and hard facts to show someone that a request is worthwhile

readiness The degree to which employees have the ability and the willingness to accomplish their specific tasks

realistic job previews The process of ensuring that a prospective employee understands both the positive and the negative aspects of the job

reality shock A mismatch of information that occurs when an employee finds that aspects of working at a company are not what the he or she expected them to be

reasoning ability A diverse set of abilities associated with sensing and solving problems using insight, rules, and logic

referent power A form of organizational power based on the attractiveness and charisma of the leader

relational contracts Psychological contracts that focus on a broad set of open-ended and subjective obligations

relaxation techniques Calming activities to reduce stress

reliability The extent to which the selection procedure (e.g., job interview) is free from random error

reputation The prominence of an organization's brand in the minds of the public and the perceived quality of its goods and services

resistance The deliberate act of opposing or withstanding change

resistance (to influence tactics) A response to influence tactics in which the target refuses to perform a request and puts forth an effort to avoid having to do it

resource-based view A model that argues that rare and inimitable resources help firms maintain competitive advantage

responsibility for outcomes A psychological state indicating the degree to which employees feel they are key drivers of the quality of work output

restructuring The process of changing an organization's structure

reward power A form of organizational power based on the control of resources or benefits

rituals The daily or weekly planned routines that occur in an organization

role A pattern of behaviour a person is generally expected to display in a given context

role ambiguity A lack of direction and information about what needs to be done in a role

role conflict Others' having differing expectations of what an individual needs to do in a role

role making The phase in a leader–follower relationship when a follower voices his or her own expectations for the relationship, resulting in a free-flowing exchange of opportunities and resources for activities and effort

role overload An excess of demands on an employee preventing him or her from working effectively

role taking The phase in a leader–follower relationship when a leader provides an employee with job expectations and the follower tries to meet those expectations

routine task performance Well-known or habitual responses by employees to predictable task demands

rule of one-eighth The belief that at best one-eighth, or 12 percent, of organizations will actually do what is required to build profits by putting people first

rumours Messages that travel along the grapevine that lack evidence as to their truth or validity

sabotage Intentional destruction of equipment, organizational processes, or company products

safety culture A specific culture type focused on the safety of employees

satisfaction with the work itself Employees' feelings about their actual work tasks

satisficing What a decision maker is doing who chooses the first acceptable alternative considered

schedules of reinforcement The timing of when contingencies are applied or removed

scientific management Using scientific methods to design optimal and efficient work processes and tasks

secondary appraisal When people determine how to cope with the various stressors they face

selective perception The tendency for people to see their environment only as it affects them and as it is consistent with their expectations

self-awareness The ability to recognize and understand the emotions in oneself

self-determination A sense of choice in the initiation and continuation of work tasks

self-efficacy The belief that a person has the capabilities needed to perform the behaviours required on some task

self-serving bias When one attributes one's own failures to external factors and success to internal factors

self-set goals The internalized goals that people use to monitor their own progress

selling When the leader explains key issues and provides opportunities for clarification

sensory ability Capabilities associated with vision and hearing

short-term vs. long-term orientation The degree to which a culture stresses values that are past- and present-oriented (short-term orientation) or future-oriented (long-term orientation)

significance The degree to which a job really matters and impacts society as a whole

similarity-attraction approach A theory explaining that team diversity can be counterproductive because people tend to avoid interacting with others who are unlike them

simple structure An organizational form that features one person as the central decision-making figure

situational strength The degree to which situations have clear behavioural expectations, incentives, or instructions that make differences between individuals less important

S.M.A.R.T. goals Specific, Measurable, Achievable, Results-based, Time-sensitive goals, which Microsoft managers are trained to encourage in employees

social exchange Work relationships characterized by mutual investment, with employees willing to engage in "extra mile" sorts of behaviours because they trust that their efforts will eventually be rewarded

social identity theory A theory that people identify themselves according to the various groups to which they belong and judge others according to the groups they associate with

social influence model A model that suggests that employees with direct linkages to co-workers who leave the organization will themselves be more likely to leave

social learning theory Theory that argues that people in organizations learn by observing others

social support The help people receive from others when confronted with stressful demands

socialization The primary process by which employees learn the social knowledge that enables them to understand and adapt to the organization's culture

socializing A form of psychological withdrawal in which one verbally chats with co-workers about non-work topics

socially complex resources Resources created by people, such as culture, teamwork, trust, and reputation

span of control Represents how many employees each manager in the organization has responsibility for

spatial ability Capabilities associated with visual and mental representation and manipulation of objects in space

specific and difficult goals Goals that stretch an employee to perform at his or her maximum level while still staying within the boundaries of his or her ability

sportsmanship Maintaining a positive attitude with co-workers through good and bad times

stamina The ability of a person's lungs and circulatory system to work efficiently while he or she is engaging in prolonged physical activity

status striving A strong desire to obtain power and influence within a social structure as a means of expressing one's personality

stereotype Assumptions made about others based on their social group membership

stories Anecdotes, accounts, legends, and myths passed down from cohort to cohort within an organization

strains Negative consequences of the stress response

strategic management Field of study devoted to exploring the product choices and industry characteristics that affect an organization's profitability

stress The psychological response to demands when there is something at stake for the individual, and when coping with these demands would tax or exceed the individual's capacity or resources

stress audit An assessment of the sources of stress in the workplace

stressors Demands that cause the stress response

subcultures Cultures created within small subsets of the organization's employees

substance abuse The abuse of drugs or alcohol before coming to work or while on the job

substitutability The degree to which people have alternatives in accessing the resources that a leader controls

substitutes Situational characteristics that reduce the importance of the leader while simultaneously providing a direct benefit to employee performance

substitutes for leadership model A model that suggests that characteristics of the situations can constrain the influence of the leader, which makes it more difficult for the leader to influence employee performance

supervision satisfaction Employees' feelings about their boss, including his or her competency, communication, and personality

supervisor feedback A form of downward communication in which the supervisor provides information to a subordinate about his or her job performance

supportive practices Ways in which organizations help employees manage and balance their demands

surface-level diversity Diversity of observable attributes such as race, gender, ethnicity, and age

symbols The images an organization uses, which generally convey messages

tacit knowledge Knowledge that employees can only learn through experience

tardiness A form of physical withdrawal in which employees arrive late to work or leave work early

task complexity The degree to which the information and actions needed to complete a task are complicated

task interdependence The degree to which team members interact with and rely on other team members for information, materials, and resources needed to accomplish work for the team

task performance Employee behaviours that are directly involved in the transformation of organizational resources into the goods or services that the organization produces

taskwork processes The activities of team members that relate directly to the accomplishment of team tasks

team Two or more people who work interdependently over some time period to accomplish common goals related to some task-oriented purpose

team building Fun activities that facilitate team problem solving, trust, relationship building, and the clarification of role responsibilities

team-building roles Behaviours that influence the quality of the team's social climate

team composition The mix of the various characteristics that describe the individuals who work in the team

team diversity The degree to which team members are different from one another

team process The different types of activities and interactions that occur within a team as the team works toward its goals

team process training The use of team experiences that facilitates the team's ability to function and perform more effectively as an intact unit

team states Specific types of feelings and thoughts that coalesce in the minds of team members as a consequence of their experience working together

team task roles Behaviours that directly facilitate the accomplishment of team tasks

teamwork processes The interpersonal activities that promote the accomplishment of team tasks but do not involve task accomplishment itself

technology The method by which an organization transforms inputs to outputs

telling The leader providing specific instructions and closely supervises performance

theft Stealing company products or equipment from the organization

theory A collection of verbal and symbolic assertions that specify how and why variables are related, as well as the conditions in which they should (and should not) be related

360-degree feedback A performance evaluation system that uses ratings provided by supervisors, co-workers, subordinates, customers, and the employees themselves

time-driven model of leadership A leadership model in which the focus shifts away from autocratic, consultative, facilitative, and delegative *leaders* to autocratic, consultative, facilitative, and delegative *situations*, and in which several factors combine to make some decision-making styles more effective in a given situation and others less effective

time pressure The sense that the amount of time allotted to do a job is not quite enough

training A systematic effort by organizations to facilitate the learning of job-related knowledge and behaviour

training interventions Practices that increase employees' competencies and skills

trait activation The degree to which situations provide cues that trigger the expression of a given personality trait

traits Recurring trends in people's responses to their environment

transactional contracts Psychological contracts that focus on a narrow set of specific monetary obligations

transactional leadership A pattern of behaviour in which the leader rewards or disciplines the follower on the basis of performance

transactional theory of stress A theory that explains how stressful demands are perceived and appraised, as well as how people respond to the perceptions of appraisals

transactive memory The degree to which team members' specialized knowledge is integrated into an effective system of memory for the team

transfer of training Occurs when employees retain and demonstrate the knowledge, skills, and behaviours required for their job after training ends

transformational leadership A pattern of behaviour in which the leader inspires followers to commit to a shared vision that provides meaning to their work while also serving as a role model who helps followers develop their own potential and view problems from new perspectives

transition processes Teamwork processes, such as mission analysis and planning, that focus on preparation for future work in the team

transportable teamwork competencies Team training that involves helping people develop general teamwork competencies that they can transport from one team context to another

trust The willingness to be vulnerable to an authority because of positive expectations about the authority's actions and intentions

trust propensity A general expectation that the words, promises, and statements of individuals can be relied upon

trustworthiness Characteristics or attributes of a person that inspire trust, including perceptions of ability, benevolence, and integrity

Type A Behaviour Pattern A type of behaviour exhibited by people who tend to experience more stressors, to appraise more demands as stressful, and to be prone to experiencing more strains than most others

typical performance Performance in the routine conditions that surround daily job tasks

uncertainty avoidance The degree to which a culture tolerates ambiguous situations (low uncertainty avoidance) or feels threatened by them (high uncertainty avoidance)

understanding and adaptation The final stage of socialization, during which newcomers come to learn the content areas of socialization and internalize the norms and expected behaviours of the organization

upward communication Communication that flows from the bottom to the top of the vertical channel

use of emotions The degree to which people can harness emotions and employ them to improve their chances of being successful in whatever they are seeking to do

valence The anticipated value of the outcomes(s) associated with successful performance

value in diversity problem-solving approach A theory that supports team diversity because it provides a larger pool of knowledge and perspectives

value-percept theory A theory that argues that job satisfaction depends on whether the employee perceives that his or her job supplies those things that he or she values

values Things that people consciously or unconsciously want to seek or attain

variable-interval schedule A schedule whereby reinforcement occurs at random periods of time

variable-ratio schedule A schedule whereby behaviours are reinforced after a varying number of them have been exhibited

variety The degree to which a job requires different activities and skills

verbal ability Various capabilities associated with understanding and expressing oral and written communication

verbal communication A form of communication in which messages are sent and received using written and spoken language

videoconferencing A communication medium that permits real-time, live interaction and discussion between remote individuals or groups via satellite or Internet

virtual teams Team in which the members are geographically dispersed, and interdependent activity occurs through e-mail, web conferencing, and instant messaging

visibility How aware others are of a leader and the resources that leader can provide

voice An active response, often in reaction to a negative work event, in which an employee attempts to improve the situation

wasting resources Using too many materials or too much time to do too little work

Web 2.0 Describes websites and applications through which users actively interact, create, collaborate, and communicate

wheel network structure A communication network in which all communication between members is controlled by a single member

whistle-blowing Employees' exposing illegal or immoral actions by their employer

wiki A highly flexible Web 2.0 application that allows people to quickly exchange verbal information, and collaboratively solve problems, learn, manage projects, and create knowledge

withdrawal behaviour Employee actions that are intended to avoid work situations

Wonderlic Personnel Test A 12-minute test of general cognitive ability used to hire job applicants

work complexity The degree to which job requirements tax or just exceed employee capabilities

work–family conflict A form of role conflict in which the demands of a work role hinder the fulfillment of the demands in a family role (or vice versa)

work responsibility The number and importance of the obligations an employee has to others

work specialization The degree to which tasks in an organization are divided into separate jobs

work teams Relatively permanent teams in which members work together to produce goods and/or provide services

Y network structure A communication network in which one member controls the flow of information between one set of members and another

zero acquaintance situations Situations in which two people have just met

Chapter Notes

Chapter 1

1. "Canada's 10 Most Admired Corporate Cultures Program," Waterstone Human Capital website, www.waterstonehc.com/cmac/canadas-10, retrieved August 5, 2014.
2. "Gregg Saretsky," WestJet website, www.westjet.com/guest/en/media-investors/gregg-saretsky.shtml, retrieved May 3, 2011.
3. "Ferio Pugliese," WestJet website, www.westjet.com/guest/en/media-investors/ferio-pugliese.shtml, retrieved May 3, 2011.
4. "Hall of Fame," Waterstone Human Capital website, www.waterstonehc.com/cmac/hall-fame, retrieved August 5, 2014.
5. "CEO Message," RBC website, www.rbc.com/diversity/ceo-message.html, retrieved May 3, 2011.
6. "Hall of Fame," Waterstone Human Capital website, www.waterstonehc.com/cmac/hall-fame, retrieved August 5, 2014.
7. F.W. Taylor, *The Principles of Scientific Management* (New York: Norton, 1974).
8. M. Weber, "Bureaucracy," in H.H. Gerth and C. Wright Mills, *From Max Weber: Essays in Sociology* (London: Routledge and Kegan Paul, 1922, 1948); M. Weber, *The Protestant Ethic and the Spirit of Capitalism*, trans. Talcott Parsons (New York: Scribners, 1958).
9. F.J. Roethlisberger and W.J. Dickson. *Management and the Worker* (Cambridge, MA: Harvard University, 1939); C.D. Wrege and R.G. Greenwood, "The Hawthorne Studies," in D.A. Wren and J.A. Pearce II, eds., *Papers Dedicated to the Development of Modern Management*. Academy of Management, 1986.
10. D. Kiley, "Hyundai Still Gets No Respect," *Businessweek*, May 21, 2007, pp. 68–70.
11. M. Ihlwan and C. Dawson, "Building a 'Camry Fighter': Can Hyundai Transform Itself into One of the World's Top Auto Makers?," *Businessweek*, September 6, 2004, www.businessweek.com/magazine/content/04_36/b3898072.htm, retrieved May 5, 2011.
12. M. Ihlwan, L. Armstrong, and M. Eldam, "Kissing Clunkers Goodbye," *Businessweek*, May 17, 2004, www.businessweek.com/magazine/content/04_20/b3883054.htm, retrieved May 5, 2011.
13. H. Aguinis and C.A. Henle, "The Search for Universals in Cross-cultural Organizational Behaviour," in J. Greenberg, ed., *Organizational Behaviour: The State of the Science* (Mahwah, NJ: Lawrence Erlbaum Associates, 2003, pp. 373–411).
14. J. Barney, "Firm Resources and Sustained Competitive Advantage," *Journal of Management* 17 (1991), pp. 99–120.
15. Francine Kopun, "Microsoft's First Canadian Retail Store to Open at Yorkdale: Sneak Peek," *Toronto Star*, November 15, 2012, retrieved August 5, 2014.
16. "Store List," Apple (Canada) website, www.apple.com/ca/retail/storelist, retrieved August 5, 2014.
17. D. Frommer, "Microsoft's New Retail Stores Look Just Like Apple Stores," *Business Insider*, November 1, 2009, www.businessinsider.com/microsofts-new-retail-stores-look-just-like-apple-stores-2009-11.
18. F. Hansen, "Admirable Qualities," *Workforce Management*, June 23, 2008, pp. 25–32.
19. G. Colvin, "The World's Most Admired Companies," *Fortune*, March 21, 2011, pp. 109–24.
20. M.A. Huselid, "The Impact of *Human Resource Management* Practice on Turnover, Productivity, and Corporate Financial Performance," *Academy of Management Journal* 38 (1995), pp. 635–72.
21. T.M., Welbourne and A.O. Andrews. "Predicting the Performance of Initial Public Offerings: Should *Human Resource Management* Be in the Equation?," *Academy of Management Journal* 39 (1996), pp. 891–919.
22. "Canada's 10 Most Admired Corporate Cultures Program," www.waterstonehc.com/cmac/canadas-10, retrieved August 5, 2014.
23. "Hall of Fame," www.waterstonehc.com/cmac/hall-fame, retrieved August 5, 2014.
24. J. Pfeffer and J.F. Veiga. "Putting People First for Organizational Success," *Academy of Management Executive* 13 (1999), pp. 37–48.
25. M. Lewis, *Moneyball* (New York: Norton, 2003).
26. J. Fox, "The Moneyball Myth," *Bloomberg Businessweek*, October 20, 2011, pp. 110–111.
27. J. Schwartz, "Net Loss," *Slate*, February 28, 2013, www.slate.com/articles/sports/sports_nut/2013/02/nba_stats_gurus_can_t_work_together_anymore_that_s_a_problem.html.
28. F.N. Kerlinger and H.B. Lee, *Foundations of Behavioral Research* (Fort Worth, TX: Harcourt, 2000).
29. F. Bacon, M. Silverthorne, and L. Jardine, *The New Organon* (Cambridge: Cambridge University Press, 2000).
30. J.P. Campbell, "The Role of Theory in Industrial and Organizational Psychology," in *Handbook of Industrial and Organizational Psychology* Vol. 1, eds. M.D. Dunnette and L.M. Hough (Palo Alto, CA: Consulting Psychologists Press, 1990), pp. 39–74.
31. D.A. Whetten, "What Constitutes a Theoretical Contribution?," *Academy of Management Review* 14 (1989), pp. 490–95.
32. K. Locke, "The Grounded Theory Approach to Qualitative Research," in *Measuring and Analyzing Behavior in Organizations*, eds. F. Drasgow and N. Schmitt (San Francisco: Jossey-Bass, 2002, pp. 17–43).
33. E.A. Locke and G.P. Latham, "What Should We Do About Motivation Theory? Six Recommendations for the Twenty-First Century," *Academy of Management Review* 29 (2004), pp. 388–403.
34. F. Herzberg, B. Mausner, and B.B. Snyderman, *The Motivation to Work* (New York: John Wiley, 1959); F.W. Taylor, *The Principles of Scientific Management* (New York: Harper & Row, 1911).
35. S.J. Peterson and F. Luthans, "The Impact of Financial and Nonfinancial Incentives on Business-Unit Outcomes over Time." *Journal of Applied Psychology* 91 (2006), pp. 156–65.
36. J. Cohen, P. Cohen, S.G. West, and L.S. Aiken, *Applied Multiple Regression/Correlation Analysis for the Behavioral Sciences* (Mahwah, NJ: Erlbaum, 2003).
37. W.R. Shadish, T.D. Cook, and D.T. Campbell, *Experimental and Quasi-Experimental Designs for Generalized Causal Inference* (Boston: Houghton-Mifflin, 2002).
38. Ibid.
39. A.D. Stajkovic and F. Luthans, "A Meta-analysis of the Effects of Organizational Behaviour Modification on Task Performance, 1975–1995," *Academy of Management Journal* 40 (1997), pp. 1122–49.

Chapter 2

1. T. Krisher, "Toyota Still World's No. 1 in Global Vehicle Sales for First Quarter, Outpacing GM, Volkswagen," *Washington Post*, April 24, 2013, articles.washingtonpost.com/2013-04-24/business/38772691_1_toyota-motor-corp-gm-and-volkswagen-volkswagen-ag.
2. "About GM Canada," GM Canada website, www.gm.ca/gm/english/corporate/about/ourcompany/overview, retrieved November 19, 2014.
3. Mark Milke, "Canada's Auto Bailout: Still Waiting for Payback," *Financial Post*, May 31, 2013, opinion.financialpost.com/2013/05/31/canadas-auto-bailout-still-waiting-for-payback, retrieved November 19, 2014.
4. S. Langlois and C. Hinton, "General Motors to Cut 12% of U.S. Workforce,"

MarketWatch, February 10, 2009, articles.marketwatch.com/2009-02-10/news/30714976_1_salaried-workforce-morgan-analyst-himanshu-patel-white-collar0workforce.
5. "About GM Canada," GM Canada Corporate website, www.gm.ca/gm/english/corporate/about/ourcompany/overview, retrieved November 19, 2014.
6. "About Our Company," General Motors website, 2013, www.gm.com/company/aboutGM/our_company.html, retrieved April 28, 2013.
7. Ibid.
8. M.K. Duffy, K.L. Scott, J.D. Shaw, B.J. Tepper, and K. Aquino, "A Social Context Model of Envy and Social Undermining." *Academy of Management Journal* 55 (2012), pp. 643–66; R.L. Greenbaum, M.B. Mawritz, and G. Eissa, "Bottom-Line Mentality as an Antecedent of Social Undermining and the Moderating Roles of Core Self-Evalutions and Conscientiousness," *Journal of Applied Psychology* 97 (2012), pp. 343–59.
9. T. Shawel, "Homegrown Career Development," *HR Magazine*, April 2011, pp. 36–38.
10. J.P. Campbell, "Modeling the Performance Prediction Problem in Industrial and Organizational Psychology," in *Handbook of Industrial and Organizational Psychology*, Vol. 1, 2nd ed., ed. M.D. Dunnette and L.M. Hough (Palo Alto, CA: Consulting Psychologists Press, 1990), pp. 687–732; S.J. Motowidlo, W.C. Borman, and M.J. Schmit, "A Theory of Individual Differences in Task and Contextual Performance," *Human Performance* 10 (1997), pp. 71–83.
11. W.C. Borman and S.J. Motowidlo, "Expanding the Criterion Domain to Include Elements of Contextual Performance," in N. Schmitt and W.C. Borman, eds., *Personnel Selection in Organizations* (San Francisco: Jossey-Bass, 1993), pp. 71–98.
12. Ibid.
13. Occupational Information Network (O*NET) OnLine, online.onetcenter.org.
14. H.M. Weiss and D.R. Ilgen, "Routinized Behavior in Organizations," *Journal of Behavioral Economics* 24 (1985), pp. 57–67.
15. J.A. LePine, J.A. Colquitt, and A. Erez, "Adaptability to Changing Task Contexts: Effects of General Cognitive Ability, Conscientiousness, and Openness to Experience," *Personnel Psychology* 53 (2000), pp. 563–93.
16. "Plane Fire at Pearson Airport: Flight 358," CBC News, August 8, 2005, www.cbc.ca/news/background/plane_fire.
17. D.R. Ilgen and E.D. Pulakos, "Employee Performance in Today's Organizations," in *The Changing Nature of Work Performance: Implications for Staffing, Motivation, and Development*, eds. D.R. Ilgen and E.D. Pulakos (San Francisco: Jossey-Bass, 1999), pp. 1–20.
18. L. Haneberg, "Training for Agility: Building the Skills Employees Need to Zig and Zag," *Training and Development*, September 2011, pp. 51–56.
19. Associated Press, "Unemployed Find Old Jobs Now Require More Skills," *Gainesville Sun*, October 11, 2010, p. 7A.
20. E.D. Pulakos, S. Arad, M.A. Donovan; K.E. Plamondon, "Adaptability in the Workplace: Development of a Taxonomy of Adaptive Performance," *Journal of Applied Psychology* 85 (2000), pp. 612–24.
21. T.M. Amabile, "How to Kill Creativity," *Harvard Business Review* 76 (1998), pp. 76–88.
22. "Bikini Trivia: History of the Bikini," Everything Bikini website, n.d., www.everythingbikini.com/bikini-history.html.
23. R. Florida, "America's Looming Creativity Crisis," *Harvard Business Review* 82 (2004), pp. 122–36.
24. A.M., Grant, and J.W. Berry, "The Necessity of Others Is the Mother of Invention: Intrinsic and Prosocial Motivations, Perspective Taking, and Creativity," *Academy of Management Journal* 54 (2011), pp. 73–96; J.M. George, "Creativity in Organizations," *Academy of Management Annals*, Vol. 1, eds. J.P. Walsh and A.P. Brief (New York: Erlbaum, 2007), pp. 439–77.
25. M. Baer, "Putting Creativity to Work: The Implementation of Creative Ideas in Organizations," *Academy of Management Journal* 55 (2012), pp. 1102–19.
26. National Occupational Classification (NOC) online, www5.hrsdc.gc.ca/NOC/English/NOC/2011/AboutNOC.aspx, retrieved November 20, 2014.
27. Ibid.
28. R.D. McFadden, "Pilot Is Hailed After Jetliner's Icy Plunge," NYTimes.com, January 16, 2009, www.nytimes.com/2009/01/16/nyregion/16crash.html?_r=1&hp.
29. R. Newman, "How Sullenberger Really Saved US Airways Flight 1549," USNews.com, April 13, 2009, www.usnews.com/blogs/flowchart/2009/2/3/how-sullenberger-really-saved-us-airways-flight-1549.html.
30. Borman and Motowidlo, "Expanding the Criterion Domain."
31. D.W. Organ, *Organizational Citizenship Behavior: The Good Soldier Syndrome* (Lexington, MA: Lexington Books, 1988).
32. V.I. Coleman and W.C. Borman, "Investigating the Underlying Structure of the Citizenship Performance Domain," *Human Resource Management Review* 10 (2000), pp. 25–44.
33. Ibid.
34. P. MacMillan, *The Performance Factor: Unlocking the Secrets of Teamwork* (Nashville, TN: Broadman & Holman, 2001).
35. J.A. LePine, R.F. Piccolo, C.L. Jackson, J.E. Mathieu, and J.R. Saul, "A Meta-analysis of Teamwork Process: Towards a Better Understanding of the Dimensional Structure and Relationships with Team Effectiveness Criteria," *Personnel Psychology* 61 (2008), pp. 273–307.
36. Coleman and Borman, "Investigating the Underlying Structure."
37. E.R. Burris, "The Risks and Rewards of Speaking Up: Managerial Responses to Employee Voice," *Academy of Management Journal* 55 (2012), pp. 851–75; L. Van Dyne and J.A. LePine, "Helping and Voice Extra-role Behavior: Evidence of Construct and Predictive Validity," *Academy of Management Journal* 41 (1998), pp. 108–19.
38. S.J. Motowidlo, "Some Basic Issues Related to Contextual Performance and Organizational Citizenship Behavior in *Human Resource Management*," *Human Resource Management Review* 10 (2000), pp. 115–26.
39. N.P. Podsakoff, S.W. Whiting, P.M. Podsakoff, and B.D. Blume, "Individual- and Organizational-Level Consequences of Organizational Citizenship Behaviors: A Meta-analysis," *Journal of Applied Psychology* 94 (2009), pp. 122–41; P.M. Podsakoff, S.B. MacKenzie, J.B. Paine, and D.G. Bachrach, "Organizational Citizenship Behaviors: A Critical Review of the Theoretical and Empirical Literature and Suggestions for Future Research," *Journal of Management* 26 (2000), pp. 513–63.
40. P.M. Podsakoff, M. Ahearne, and S.B. MacKenzie, "Organizational Citizenship Behavior and the Quantity and Quality of Work Group Performance," *Journal of Applied Psychology* 82 (1997), pp. 262–70.
41. S.M. Walz and B.P. Neihoff, "Organizational Citizenship Behaviors and Their Effect on Organizational Effectiveness in Limited-Menu Restaurants," in *Academy of Management Best Papers Proceedings*, eds. J.B. Keys and L.N. Dosier (Statesboro, GA: College of Business Administration at Georgia Southern University, 1996), pp. 307–11.
42. R.S. Dalal, H. Lam, H.M. Weiss, E.R. Welch, and C.L. Hulin, "A Within-Person Approach to Work Behavior and Performance: Concurrent and Lagged Citizenship-Counterproductivity Associations, and Dynamic Relationships with Affect and Overall Job Performance," *Academy of Management Journal* 52 (2009), pp. 1051–66.
43. T.D. Allen and M.C. Rush, "The Effects of Organizational Citizenship Behavior on Performance Judgments: A Field Study and a Laboratory Experiment," *Journal of Applied Psychology* 83 (1998), pp. 247–60; R.A. Avila, E.F. Fern, and O.K. Mann, "Unraveling Criteria for Assessing the Performance of Sales People: A Causal Analysis," *Journal of Personal Selling and Sales Management* 8 (1988), pp. 45–54; C.M. Lowery and T.J. Krilowicz, "Relationships Among Nontask Behaviors, Rated Performance, and Objective Performance Measures," *Psychological Reports* 74 (1994), pp. 571–78; S.B. MacKenzie, P.M. Podsakoff, and R. Fetter, "Organizational Citizenship Behavior and Objective Productivity as

Determinants of Managerial Evaluations of Salespersons' Performance," *Organizational Behavior and Human Decision Processes* 50 (1991), pp. 123–50; S.B. MacKenzie, P.M. Podsakoff, and R. Fetter, "The Impact of Organizational Citizenship Behavior on Evaluation of Sales Performance," *Journal of Marketing* 57 (1993), pp. 70–80; S.B. MacKenzie, P.M. Podsakoff, and J.B. Paine, "Effects of Organizational Citizenship Behaviors and Productivity on Evaluation of Performance at Different Hierarchical Levels in Sales Organizations," *Journal of the Academy of Marketing Science* 27 (1999), pp. 396–410; S.J. Motowidlo and J.R. Van Scotter, "Evidence That Task Performance Should Be Distinguished from Contextual Performance," *Journal of Applied Psychology* 79 (1994), pp. 475–80; P.M. Podsakoff and S.B. MacKenzie, "Organizational Citizenship Behaviors and Sales Unit Effectiveness," *Journal of Marketing Research* 3 (February 1994), pp. 351–63; J.R. Van Scotter and S.J. Motowidlo, "Interpersonal Facilitation and Job Dedication as Separate Facets of Contextual Performance," *Journal of Applied Psychology* 81 (1996), pp. 525–31.

44. M. Rotundo and P.R. Sackett, "The Relative Importance of Task, Citizenship, and Counterproductive Performance to Global Ratings of Job Performance: A Policy Capturing Approach," *Journal of Applied Psychology* 87 (2002), pp. 66–80.
45. Allen and Rush, "The Effects of Organizational Citizenship Behavior on Performance Judgments"; D.S. Kiker and S.J. Motowidlo, "Main and Interaction Effects of Task and Contextual Performance on Supervisory Reward Decisions," *Journal of Applied Psychology* 84 (1999), pp. 602–9; O.S. Park and H.P. Sims Jr., "Beyond Cognition in Leadership: Prosocial Behavior and Affect in Managerial Judgment," working paper, Seoul National University and Pennsylvania State University, 1989.
46. S.L. Robinson and R.J. Bennett, "A Typology of Deviant Workplace Behaviors: A Multidimensional Scaling Study," *Academy of Management Journal* 38 (1995), pp. 555–72.
47. E.W. Morrison, "Role Definitions and Organizational Citizenship Behavior: The Importance of the Employee's Perspective," *Academy of Management Journal* 37 (1994), pp. 1543–67.
48. G. Hofstede, *Cultures and Organizations: Software of the Mind* (New York: McGraw-Hill, 1991).
49. M. Rotundo and J.L. Xie, "Understanding the Domain of Counterproductive Work Behavior in China," working paper, University of Toronto, 2007.
50. F.F.T. Chiang and T.A. Birtch, "Appraising Performance Across Borders: An Empirical Examination of the Purposes and Practices of Performance Appraisal in a Multi-country Context," *Journal of Management Studies* 47 (2010), pp. 1365–92.
51. D.R. Cellitti, "MCA DiscoVision: The Record That Plays Pictures," June 25, 2002, www.oz.net/blam/DiscoVision/RecordPlaysPictures.htm.
52. L. Hollweg, "Inside the Four Walls of the Restaurant: The Reality and Risk of Counter-Productive Behaviors," 2003, www.batrushollweg.com/files/Website.Inside_the_Four_Walls_of_the_Restaurant1.Reprint_9.pdf.
53. M. Wang, H. Liao, Y. Zhan, and J. Shi, "Daily Customer Mistreatment and Employee Sabotage Against Customers: Examining Emotion and Resource Perspectives," *Academy of Management Journal* 54 (2011), pp. 31.
54. D. Harper, "Spotlight Abuse—Save Profits," *Industrial Distribution* 79 (1990), pp. 47–51.
55. R.C. Hollinger and L. Langton, *2004 National Retail Security Survey* (Gainesville: University of Florida, Security Research Project, Department of Criminology, Law and Society, 2005).
56. L.M. Andersson and C.M. Pearson, "Tit for Tat? The Spiraling Effect of Incivility in the Workplace," *Academy of Management Review* 24 (1999), pp. 452–71.
57. Ibid.
58. S. Armour, "Managers Not Prepared for Workplace Violence," *USA Today*, July 19, 2004, www.usatoday.com/money/workplace/2004-07-15-workplace-violence2_x.htm.
59. T.A. Daniel, "Tough Boss or Workplace Bully?," *HR Magazine*, June 2009, pp. 83–86.
60. E. Baillien, N. De Cuyper, and H. De Witte, "Job Autonomy and Workload as Antecedents of Workplace Bullying: A Two-Wave Test of Karasek's Job Demand Control Model for Targets and Perpetrators," *Journal of Occupational and Organizational Psychology* 84 (2010), pp. 191–208.
61. H. Cowie, P. Naylor, I. Rivers, P.K. Smith, and B. Pereira, "Measuring Workplace Bullying," *Aggression and Violent Behavior* 7 (2002), pp. 35–51; Baillien et al., "Job Autonomy and Workload as Antecedents of Workplace Bullying"; S.S. Einarsen, B. Matthisen, and L.J. Hauge, "Bullying and Harassment at Work," in *The Oxford Handbook of Personnel Psychology*, eds. S. Cartwright and C.L. Cooper (London: Sage, 2009), pp. 464–95.
62. Ibid.
63. "RCMP Lawsuit May Be Joined by Dozens of Women," December 20, 2011, CBC News, www.cbc.ca/news/canada/british-columbia/story/2011/12/20/bc-rcmp-harassment-class-action-grows.html, retrieved January 4, 2012; "More Women Join RCMP Class Action Lawsuit," *The Montreal Gazette*, December 21, 2011, www.montrealgazette.com/technology/More+women+join+RCMP+class+action+lawsuit/5892145/story.html#ixzz1iXxUxhl9, retrieved January 4, 2012.
64. P.R. Sackett, "The Structure of Counterproductive Work Behaviors: Dimensionality and Performance with Facets of Job Performance," *International Journal of Selection and Assessment* 10 (2002), pp. 5–11.
65. P.R. Sackett and C.J. DeVore, "Counterproductive Behaviors at Work," in *Handbook of Industrial, Work, and Organizational Psychology*, Vol. 1, eds. N. Anderson, D.S. Ones, H.K. Sinangil, and C. Viswesvaran (Thousand Oaks, CA: Sage, 2001), pp. 145–51.
66. P.F. Drucker, *The Practice of Management* (New York: Harper and Brothers, 1954).
67. D.G. Shaw, C.E. Schneier, and R.W. Beatty, "Managing Performance with a Behaviourally Based Appraisal System," in *Applying Psychology in Business: The Handbook for Managers and Human Resource Professionals*, eds. J.W. Jones, B.D. Steffy, and D.W. Bray (Lexington, MA: Lexington Books, 2001), pp. 314–25.
68. E.D. Pulakos, "Behavioral Performance Measures," in *Applying Psychology in Business: The Handbook for Managers and Human Resource Professionals*, eds. J.W. Jones, B.D. Steffy, and D.W. Bray (Lexington, MA: Lexington Books, 2001), pp. 307–13.
69. "Fortune Selects Henry Ford Businessman of the Century," November 1, 1999, www.timewarner.com/corp/print/0,20858,667526,00.html.
70. J.F. Welch Jr., *Jack: Straight from the Gut* (New York: Warner Books, 2001), p. 158.
71. Ibid.
72. G. Johnson, "Forced Ranking: The Good, the Bad, and the Alternative," *Training Magazine*, May 2004, pp. 24–34.
73. J. McGregor, "Job Review in 140 Keystrokes: Social Networking-Style Systems Lighten up the Dreaded Performance Evaluation," *Businessweek*, March 29, 2009, p. 58.
74. Ibid.
75. Ibid.
76. "About Our Company," General Motors website, 2013, www.gm.com/company/aboutGM/our_company.html, retrieved April 28, 2013.
77. J. Lichterman, "General Motors' CEO Dan Akerson Urges Employees to 'Behave with Integrity,'" *Workforce*, August 10, 2012, www.workforce.com/apps/pbcs.dll/article?AID=/20120810/NEWS01/120819996&template=printarticle.
78. Ibid.
79. T. Higgins, "Racing Helps GM Spur Urgency in Engineering," *Arizona Republic*, March 24, 2013, p. CL2.
80. Ibid.

Chapter 3

1. B. Stone, "Costco CEO Craig Jelinek Leads the Cheapest, Happiest Company in the World," *Bloomberg Businessweek*, June 6, 2013, www.businessweek.com/articles/2013-06-06/

costco-ceo-craig-jelinek-leads-the-cheapest-happiest-company-in-the-world#p1; R. Dudley, "Walmart Faces the Cost of Cost-Cutting: Empty Shelves," *Bloomberg Businessweek*, March 28, 2013, www.businessweek.com/articles/2013-03-28/walmart-faces-the-cost-of-costcutting-empty-shelves.
2. Stone, "Costco CEO Craig Jelinek Leads the Cheapest, Happiest Company in the World."
3. Ibid.
4. R. Maurino, "Employee Loyalty Wanes as Workers Question Their Value in Organizations," *The Globe and Mail*, August 18, 2014, www.theglobeandmail.com/report-on-business/careers/management/employee-loyalty-dropping-off-as-workers-question-their-value-in-organizations/article20095357; L. Nguyen, "More Canadians Leaving Their Jobs After Just 2 Years: Workopolis Poll," *The Canadian Press*, April 17, 2014, www.ctvnews.ca/business/more-canadians-leaving-their-jobs-after-just-2-years-workopolis-poll-1.1779950.
5. J. Kirby, "Quittin' Time," *Maclean's*, October 28, 2010, www.macleans.ca/economy/business/quittin-time, retrieved December 6, 2014.
6. Ibid.
7. "Talent Management—Engage," *Valuing Your Talent: Human Resources Trends and Metrics*, Conference Board of Canada Report 2010, www.conferenceboard.ca/e-library/abstract.aspx?did=3623, retrieved December 6, 2014.
8. N. Stewart and E. Lamontagne, "Compensation Planning Outlook 2014," *Conference Board of Canada*, www.conferenceboard.ca/e-library/abstract.aspx?did=5737.
9. "The High Cost of Turnover," www.canadahrcentre.com/solutions/calculating-cost/high-cost-of-turnover, retrieved December 6, 2014.
10. J.P. Meyer and N.J. Allen, *Commitment in the Workplace* (Thousand Oaks, CA: Sage, 1997); R.T. Mowday, R.M. Steers, and L.W. Porter, "The Measurement of Organizational Commitment," *Journal of Vocational Behavior* 14 (1979), pp. 224–47.
11. C.L. Hulin, "Adaptation, Persistence, and Commitment in Organizations," in *Handbook of Industrial and Organizational Psychology*, Vol. 2, eds. M.D. Dunnette and L.M. Hough (Palo Alto, CA: Consulting Psychologists Press, 1991), pp. 445–506.
12. N.J. Allen and J.P. Meyer, "The Measurement and Antecedents of Affective, Continuance and Normative Commitment to the Organization," *Journal of Occupational Psychology* 63 (1990), pp. 1–18; J.P. Meyer and N.J. Allen, "A Three-Component Conceptualization of Organizational Commitment," *Human Resource Management Review* 1 (1991), pp. 61–89; Meyer and Allen, *Commitment in the Workplace.*
13. Ibid.
14. Ibid.
15. Meyer and Allen, *Commitment in the Workplace*; J.P. Meyer and L. Herscovitch, "Commitment in the Workplace: Towards a General Model," *Human Resource Management Review* 11 (2001), pp. 299–326; J.P. Meyer, L.J. Stanley, and N.M. Parfyonova, "Employee Commitment in Context: The Nature and Implication of Commitment Profiles," *Journal of Vocational Behavior* 80 (2012), pp. 1–16.
16. Mowday et al., "The Measurement of Organizational Commitment."
17. B.E. Ashforth, S.H. Harrison, and K.G. Corley, "Identification in Organizations: An Examination of Four Fundamental Questions," *Journal of Management* 34 (2008), pp. 325–74.
18. Ibid.
19. J.P. Meyer, D.J. Stanley, L. Herscovitch, and L. Topolnytsky, "Affective, Continuance, and Normative Commitment to the Organization: A Meta-analysis of Antecedents, Correlates, and Consequences," *Journal of Vocational Behavior* 61 (2002), pp. 20–52.
20. J.E. Mathieu and D.M. Zajac, "A Review and Meta-analysis of the Antecedents, Correlates, and Consequences of Organizational Commitment," *Psychological Bulletin* 108 (1990), pp. 171–94.
21. G. Johns, "The Psychology of Lateness, Absenteeism, and Turnover," in *Handbook of Industrial, Work, and Organizational Psychology*, eds. N. Anderson, D.S. Ones, H.K. Sinangil, and C. Viswesvaran (Thousand Oaks, CA: Sage, 2001), pp. 232–52.
22. Ibid.
23. Canada's Best 50 Employers," *Maclean's*, October 28, 2010, www.2.macleans.ca/2010/10/28/canadas-best-50-employers-2011, retrieved May 14, 2011.
24. R.M. Kanter, "Commitment and Social Organization: A Study of Commitment Mechanisms in Utopian Communities," *American Sociological Review* 33 (1968), pp. 499–517.
25. R.A. Stebbins, *Commitment to Deviance: The Nonprofessional Criminal in the Community* (Westport, CT: Greenwood Press, 1970).
26. H.S. Becker, "Notes on the Concept of Commitment," *American Journal of Sociology* 66 (1960), pp. 32–42.
27. C.E. Rusbult and D. Farrell, "A Longitudinal Test of the Investment Model: The Impact of Job Satisfaction, Job Commitment, and Turnover of Variations in Rewards, Costs, Alternatives, and Investments," *Journal of Applied Psychology* 68 (1983), pp. 429–38.
28. Meyer and Allen, *Commitment in the Workplace.*
29. Meyer et al., "Affective, Continuance, and Normative Commitment."
30. T.R. Mitchell, B.C. Holtom, T.W. Lee, C.J. Sablynski, and M. Erez, "Why People Stay: Using Job Embeddedness to Predict Voluntary Turnover," *Academy of Management Journal* 44 (2001), pp. 1102–21.
31. W. Felps, T.R. Mitchell, D.R. Hekman, T.W. Lee, B.C. Holtom, and W.S. Harman. "Turnover Contagion: How Coworkers' Job Embeddedness and Job Search Behaviors Influence Quitting," *Academy of Management Journal* 52 (2009), pp. 545–61; P.W. Hom, A.S. Tsui, J.B. Wu, T.W. Lee, A.Y. Zhang, P.P. Fu, and L. Li, "Explaining Employment Relationships with Social Exchange and Job Embeddedness," *Journal of Applied Psychology* 94 (2009), pp. 277–97.
32. J.P. Burton, B.C. Holtom, C.J. Sablynski, T.R. Mitchell, and T.W. Lee, "The Buffering Effects of Job Embeddedness on Negative Shocks," *Journal of Vocational Behavior* 76 (2010), pp. 42–51.
33. A. Ramesh and M.J. Gelfand, "Will They Stay or Will They Go? The Role of Job Embeddedness in Predicting Turnover in Individualistic and Collectivistic Cultures," *Journal of Applied Psychology* 95 (2010), pp. 807–23.
34. T.W.H. Ng and D.C. Feldman, "Organizational Embeddedness and Occupational Embeddedness Across Career Stages," *Journal of Vocational Behavior* 70 (2007), pp. 336–51.
35. Canada's Best 50 Employers," *Maclean's*, October 28, 2010, www.2.macleans.ca/2010/10/28/canadas-best-50-employers-2011, retrieved May 14, 2011.
36. "Canada's Top 100 Employers 2011," www.canadastop100.com/toronto, retrieved May 14, 2011.
37. Ibid.
38. Ibid.
39. Allen and Meyer, "The Measurement and Antecedents of Affective, Continuance and Normative Commitment to the Organization"; Meyer and Allen, "A Three-Component Conceptualization"; Meyer and Allen, *Commitment in the Workplace.*
40. Y. Wiener, "Commitment in Organizations: A Normative View," *Academy of Management Review* 7 (1982), pp. 418–28.
41. Meyer and Allen, "A Three-Component Conceptualization."
42. B. Grow, "The Debate over Doing Good," *Businessweek*, August 15, 2005, pp. 76–78.
43. Ibid.
44. "Best Employers for New Canadians," www.canadastop100.com/immigrants, retrieved May 14, 2011.
45. R.S. Eisenberger, Armeli, B. Rexwinkle, P.D. Lynch, and L. Rhoades, "Reciprocation of Perceived Organizational Support," *Journal of Applied Psychology* 86 (2001), pp. 42–51; R. Eisenberger, R. Huntington, S. Hutchison, and D. Sowa, "Perceived Organizational Support," *Journal of Applied Psychology* 71 (1986), pp. 500–507; L. Rhoades and R. Eisenberger, "Perceived Organizational Support: A Review of the Literature," *Journal of Applied Psychology* 87 (2002), pp. 698–714.
46. A.O. Hirschman, *Exit, Voice, and Loyalty: Responses to Decline in Firms,*

Organizations, and States (Cambridge, MA: Harvard University Press, 1970); D. Farrell, "Exit, Voice, Loyalty, and Neglect as Responses to Job Dissatisfaction: A Multidimensional Scaling Study," *Academy of Management Journal* 26 (1983), pp. 596–607.

47. Hirschman, *Exit, Voice, and Loyalty*; Farrell, "Exit, Voice, Loyalty, and Neglect"; C.E. Rusbult, D. Farrell, C. Rogers, and A.G. Mainous III, "Impact of Exchange Variables on Exit, Voice, Loyalty, and Neglect: An Integrating Model of Responses to Declining Job Satisfaction," *Academy of Management Journal* 31 (1988), pp. 599–627.
48. Ibid.
49. Ibid.
50. Farrell, "Exit, Voice, Loyalty, and Neglect"; Rusbult et al., "Impact of Exchange Variables."
51. M.J. Withey and W.H. Cooper, "Predicting Exit, Voice, Loyalty, and Neglect," *Administrative Science Quarterly* 34 (1989), pp. 521–39; E.R. Burris, J.R. Detert, and D.S. Chiaburu, "Quitting Before Leaving: The Mediating Effects of Psychological Attachment and Detachment on Voice," *Journal of Applied Psychology* 93 (2008), pp. 912–22.
52. D. Cherrington, *The Work Ethic* (New York: AMACOM, 1980).
53. C.L. Hulin, M. Roznowski, and D. Hachiya, "Alternative Opportunities and Withdrawal Decisions: Empirical and Theoretical Discrepancies and an Integration," *Psychological Bulletin* 97 (1985), pp. 233–50.
54. A. Fisher, "Turning Clock-Watchers into Stars," *Fortune*, March 22, 2004, p. 60.
55. Hulin et al., "Alternative Opportunities and Withdrawal Decisions."
56. V.K.G. Lim, "The IT Way of Loafing on the Job: Cyberloafing, Neutralizing, and Organizational Justice," *Journal of Organizational Behavior* 23 (2002), pp. 675–94.
57. M. Jackson, "May We Have Your Attention, Please?," *Businessweek*, June 23, 2008, p. 55.
58. Lim, "The IT Way of Loafing on the Job."
59. Hulin et al., "Alternative Opportunities and Withdrawal Decisions."
60. M. Koslowsky, A. Sagie, M. Krausz, and A.D. Singer, "Correlates of Employee Lateness: Some Theoretical Considerations," *Journal of Applied Psychology* 82 (1997), pp. 79–88.
61. G. Blau, "Developing and Testing a Taxonomy of Lateness Behavior," *Journal of Applied Psychology* 79 (1994), pp. 959–70.
62. P.M. Muchinsky, "Employee Absenteeism: A Review of the Literature," *Journal of Vocational Behavior* 10 (1977), pp. 316–40; D.A. Harrison, "Time for Absenteeism: A 20-Year Review of Origins, Offshoots, and Outcomes," *Journal of Management* 24 (1998), pp. 305–50.
63. M. Fichman, "Motivational Consequences of Absence and Attendance: Proportional Hazard Estimation of a Dynamic Motivation Model," *Journal of Applied Psychology* 73 (1988), pp. 119–34.
64. J.J. Martocchio and D.I. Jimeno, "Employee Absenteeism as an Affective Event," *Human Resource Management Review* 13 (2003), pp. 227–41.
65. N. Nicholson and G. Johns, "The Absence Climate and the Psychological Contract: Who's in Control of Absence?," *Academy of Management Review* 10 (1985), pp. 397–407; P. Bamberger and M. Biron, "Group Norms and Excessive Absenteeism: The Role of Peer Referent Others," *Organizational Behavior and Human Decision Processes* 103 (2007), pp. 179–96; I.R. Gellatly, "Individual and Group Determinants of Employee Absenteeism: Test of a Causal Model," *Journal of Organizational Behavior* 16 (1995), pp. 469–86; D. Harrison, G. Johns, and J. Martocchio, "Changes in Technology, Teamwork and Diversity: New Directions for a New Century of Absenteeism Research," *Research in Personnel and Human Resource Management* 18 (2000), pp. 43–91; J.J. Martocchio, "The Effects of Absence Culture on Individual Absence," *Human Relations* 47 (1994), pp. 243–62; J.R. Rentsch and R.P. Steel, "What Does Unit-Level Absence Mean? Issues for Future Unit-Level Absence Research," *Human Resource Management Review* 13 (2003), pp. 185–202.
66. M.A. Campion, "Meaning and Measurement of Turnover: Comparison of Alternative Measures and Recommendations for Research," *Journal of Applied Psychology* 76 (1991), pp. 199–212.
67. M.L. Van Blerkom, "Class Attendance in Undergraduate Courses," *Journal of Psychology* 126 (1992), pp. 487–94.
68. Ibid.
69. S. Devadoss and J. Foltz, "Evaluation of Factors Influencing Student Class Attendance and Performance," *American Journal of Agricultural Economics* 78 (1996), pp. 499–507.
70. E. Shimoff and A. Catania, "Effects of Recording Attendance on Grades in Introductory Psychology," *Teaching of Psychology* 28 (2001), pp. 192–95.
71. Devadoss and Foltz, "Evaluation of Factors."
72. T.W. Lee and T.R. Mitchell, "An Alternative Approach: The Unfolding Model of Voluntary Employee Turnover," *Academy of Management Review* 19 (1994), pp. 51–89; T.W. Lee and T.R. Mitchell, "An Unfolding Model of Voluntary Employee Turnover," *Academy of Management Journal* 39 (1996), pp. 5–36; T.W. Lee, T.R. Mitchell, B.C. Holtom, L.S. McDaniel, and J.W. Hill, "The Unfolding Model of Voluntary Turnover: A Replication and Extension," *Academy of Management Journal* 42 (1999), pp. 450–62; T.H. Lee, B. Gerhart, I. Weller, and C.O. Trevor, "Understanding Voluntary Turnover: Path-Specific Job Satisfaction Effects and the Importance of Unsolicited Job Offers," *Academy of Management Journal* 51 (2008), pp. 651–71.
73. W. Mobley, "Intermediate Linkages in the Relationship Between Job Satisfaction and Employee Turnover," *Journal of Applied Psychology* 62 (1977), pp. 237–40; P.W. Hom, R. Griffeth, and C.L. Sellaro, "The Validity of Mobley's (1977) Model of Employee Turnover," *Organizational Behavior and Human Performance* 34 (1984), pp. 141–74.
74. Lee and Mitchell, "An Alternative Approach"; Lee and Mitchell, "An Unfolding Model of Voluntary Employee Turnover"; Lee and Mitchell, "The Unfolding Model of Voluntary Turnover"; L.W. Porter and R.M. Steers, "Organizational, Work, and Personal Factors in Employee Turnover and Absenteeism," *Psychological Bulletin* 80 (1973), pp. 151–76.
75. Johns, "The Psychology of Lateness, Absenteeism, and Turnover."
76. J.G. Rosse, "Relations Among Lateness, Absence, and Turnover: Is There a Progression of Withdrawal?," *Human Relations* 41 (1988), pp. 517–31.
77. A. Mitra, G.D. Jenkins Jr., and N. Gupta, "A Meta-analytic Review of the Relationship Between Absence and Turnover," *Journal of Applied Psychology* 77 (1992), p. 879–89; Koslowsky et al., "Correlates of Employee Lateness"; R.W. Griffeth, P.W. Hom, and S. Gaertner, "A Meta-analysis of Antecedents and Correlates of Employee Turnover: Update, Moderator Tests, and Research Implications for the Next Millennium," *Journal of Management* 26 (2000), pp. 463–88.
78. Koslowsky et al., "Correlates of Employee Lateness."
79. Statistics Canada, 2013, www.statcan.gc.ca/tables-tableaux/sum-som/l01/cst01/labor05-eng.htm, retrieved December 23, 2014.
80. Statistics Canada Report, www.statcan.gc.ca/daily-quotidien/100309/dq100309a-eng.htm, retrieved May 16, 2011.
81. "Labour Market Challenges and the Human Resources Planning Agenda," *Valuing Your Talent: Human Resources Trends and Metrics*, Conference Board of Canada, 2010, www.conferenceboard.ca/temp/f386df25-929a-4535-a46e-97dd25390b34/11-001_HR-TrendsAndMetricsRpt_WEB.pdf.
82. Ibid.
83. Statistics Canada Report, www.statcan.gc.ca/daily-quotidien/100309/dq100309a-eng.htm, retrieved May 16, 2011.
84. C. Reade, "Antecedents of Organizational Identification in Multinational Corporations: Fostering Psychological Attachment to the Local Subsidiary and the Global Organization," *International Journal of Human Resource Management* 12 (2001), pp. 1269–91.
85. M.A. Shaffer and D.A. Harrison, "Expatriates' Psychological Withdrawal

from International Assignments: Work, Nonwork, and Family Influences," *Personnel Psychology* 51 (1998), pp. 87–118; R. Hechanova, T.A. Beehr, and N.D. Christiansen, "Antecedents and Consequences of Employees' Adjustment to Overseas Assignment: A Meta-analytic Review," *Applied Psychology: An International Review* 52 (2003), pp. 213–36.

86. J.S. Black, M. Mendenhall, and G. Oddou, "Toward a Comprehensive Model of International Adjustment: An Integration of Multiple Theoretical Perspectives," *Academy of Management Review* 16 (1991), pp. 291–317.
87. Shaffer and Harrison, "Expatriates' Psychological Withdrawal."
88. Hechanova et al., "Antecedents and Consequences of Employees' Adjustment."
89. J.R. Morris, W.F. Cascio, and C.E. Young, "Downsizing After All These Years: Questions and Answers About Who Did It, How Many Did It, and Who Benefited from It," *Organizational Dynamics* 27 (1999), pp. 78–87.
90. K. Devine, T. Reay, L. Stainton, and R. Collins-Nakai, "Downsizing Outcomes: Better a Victim Than a Survivor?," *Human Resource Management* 42 (2003), pp. 109–24.
91. Ibid.
92. D.M. Rousseau, "Psychological and Implied Contracts in Organizations," *Employee Responsibilities and Rights Journal* 2 (1989), pp. 121–39.
93. D.M. Rousseau, "New Hire Perceptions of Their Own and Their Employer's Obligations: A Study of Psychological Contracts," *Journal of Organizational Behavior* 11 (1990), pp. 389–400; S.L. Robinson, M.S. Kraatz, and D.M. Rousseau, "Changing Obligations and the Psychological Contract: A Longitudinal Study," *Academy of Management Journal* 37 (1994), pp. 137–52; S.L. Robinson and E.W. Morrison, "Psychological Contracts and OCB: The Effect of Unfulfilled Obligations on Civic Virtue Behavior," *Journal of Organizational Behavior* 16 (1995), pp. 289–98.
94. Ibid.
95. S.L. Robinson, "Violating the Psychological Contract: Not the Exception but the Norm," *Journal of Organizational Behavior* 15 (1994), pp. 245–59; S.L. Robinson, "Trust and Breach of the Psychological Contract," *Administrative Science Quarterly* 41 (1996), pp. 574–99; H. Zhao, S.J. Wayne, B.C. Glibkowski, and J. Bravo, "The Impact of Psychological Contract Breach on Work-Related Outcomes: A Meta-analysis," *Personnel Psychology* 60 (2007), pp. 647–80.
96. R. Eisenberger, R. Huntington, S. Hutchison, and D. Sowa, "Perceived Organizational Support," *Journal of Applied Psychology* 71 (1986), pp. 500–507.
97. L. Rhoades and R. Eisenberger, "Perceived Organizational Support," *Journal of Applied Psychology* 87 (2002), pp. 698–714; D.G. Allen, L.M. Shore, and R.W. Griffeth, "The Role of Perceived Organizational Support and Supportive Human Resources Practices in the Turnover Process," *Journal of Management* 29 (2003), pp. 99–118.
98. Rhoades and Eisenberger, "Perceived Organizational Support."
99. G. Dessler, "How to Earn your Employees' Commitment," *Academy of Management Executive* 13 (1999), pp. 58–67.
100. Meyer and Allen, *Commitment in the Workplace.*
101. Robert Levering and Milton Moskowitz, "In Good Company: The Full List of Fortune's 100 Best Companies to Work for in 2007," *Fortune*, January 29, 2007, archive.fortune.com/magazines/fortune/fortune_archive/2007/01/22/8398125/index.htm, accessed July 6, 2015.
102. P. Cappelli, "Managing Without Commitment," *Organizational Dynamics* 28 (2000), pp. 11–24.
103. N. Byrnes and A. Barrett, "Star Search: How to Recruit, Train, and Hold on to Great People. What Works, What Doesn't," *Businessweek*, October 10, 2005, p. 68.
104. Ibid.
105. Stone, "Costco CEO Craig Jelinek Leads the Cheapest, Happiest Company in the World."
106. Dudley, "Walmart Faces the Cost of Cost-Cutting."
107. Stone, "Costco CEO Craig Jelinek Leads the Cheapest, Happiest Company in the World."
108. Ibid.
109. Ibid.

Chapter 4

1. "About Us," Nexen Inc. website, www.nexencnoocltd.com/en/AboutUs.aspx, retrieved December 27, 2014.
2. "Interview Tips," Nexen Inc. website, www.nexencnoocltd.com/en/Careers/HiringProcess/InterviewTips.aspx, retrieved December 27, 2014.
3. "Alberta's Top Employers," www.canadastop100.com/alberta, retrieved December 27, 2014.
4. D.C. Funder, "Personality," *Annual Review of Psychology* 52 (2001), pp. 197–221; R.T. Hogan, "Personality and Personality Measurement," in M.D. Dunnette and L.M. Hough, eds., *Handbook of Industrial and Organizational Psychology*, Vol. 2 (Palo Alto, CA: Consulting Psychologists Press, 1991), pp. 873–919.
5. Hogan, "Personality and Personality Measurement."
6. Ibid.
7. M. Rokeach, *The Nature of Human Values* (New York: The Free Press, 1973); R.M. Steers and C.J. Sanchez-Runde, "Culture, Motivation, and Work Behavior," in M.J. Gannon and K.L. Newman, eds., *Blackwell Handbook of Cross-Cultural Management* (Malden, MA: Blackwell, 2002, pp. 190–213).
8. E.A. Fleishman, D.P. Costanza, and J. Marshall-Mies, "Abilities," in N.G. Peterson, M.D. Mumford, W.C. Borman, P.R. Jeanneret, and E.A. Fleishman, eds., *An Occupational Information System for the 21st Century: The Development of O*NET* (Washington, DC: American Psychological Association, 1999), pp. 175–95.
9. L.R. Goldberg, "From Ace to Zombie: Some Explorations in the Language of Personality," in C.D. Spielberger and J.N. Butcher, eds., *Advances in Personality Assessment*, Vol. 1 (Hillsdale, NJ: Erlbaum, 1982), pp. 203–34; Allport, G.W., and H.S. Odbert. "Trait-Names: A Psycho-Lexical Study," *Psychological Monographs* 47(1) (1936), Whole No. 211; W.T. Norman, *2800 Personality Trait Descriptors: Normative Operating Characteristics for a University Population* (Ann Arbor, MI: University of Michigan Department of Psychology, 1967).
10. E.C. Tupes and R.E. Christal, "Recurrent Personality Factors Based on Trait Ratings," USAF ASD Technical Report No. 61–97 (Lackland Air Force Base, TX: United States Air Force, 1961), reprinted in *Journal of Personality* 60, pp. 225–51; W.T. Norman, "Toward an Adequate Taxonomy of Personality Attributes: Replicated Factor Structure in Peer Nomination Personality Ratings," *Journal of Abnormal and Social Psychology* 66 (1963), pp. 574–83; J.M. Digman and N.K. Takemoto-Chock, "Factors in the Natural Language of Personality: Re-analysis, Comparison, and Interpretation of Six Major Studies," *Multivariate Behavioral Research* 16 (1981), pp. 149–70; R.R. McCrae and P.T. Costa Jr., "Updating Norman's 'Adequate Taxonomy': Intelligence and Personality Dimensions in Natural Language and in Questionnaires," *Journal of Personality and Social Psychology* 49 (1985), pp. 710–21; L.R. Goldberg, "An Alternative 'Description of Personality': The Big-Five Factor Structure," *Journal of Personality and Social Psychology* 59 (1990), pp. 1216–29.
11. L.R. Goldberg, "Language and Individual Differences: The Search for Universals in Personality Lexicons," in L. Wheeler, ed., *Review of Personality and Social Psychology*, Vol. 2 (Beverly Hills, CA: Sage, 1981), pp. 141–65.
12. G. Saucier, "Mini-markers: A Brief Version of Goldberg's Unipolar Big-Five Markers," *Journal of Personality Assessment* 63 (1994), pp. 506–16; L.R. Goldberg, "The Development of Markers for the Big-Five Factor Structure," *Psychological Assessment* 4 (1992), pp. 26–42; R.R. McCrae and P.T. Costa Jr., "Validation of the Five-Factor Model of Personality Across Instruments and Observers," *Journal of Personality and Social Psychology* 52 (1987), pp. 81–90.
13. M.R. Barrick and M.K. Mount, "The Big Five Personality Dimensions and Job Performance: A Meta-analysis," *Personnel Psychology* 44 (1991), pp. 1–26.

14. M.R. Barrick, G.L. Stewart, and M. Piotrowski, "Personality and Job Performance: Test of the Mediating Effects of Motivation Among Sales Representatives," *Journal of Applied Psychology* 87 (2002), pp. 43–51.
15. M.R. Barrick, M.K. Mount, and J.P. Strauss, "Conscientiousness and Performance of Sales Representatives: Test of the Mediating Effects of Goal Setting," *Journal of Applied Psychology* 78 (1993), pp. 715–22.
16. G.L. Stewart, "Trait Bandwidth and Stages of Job Performance: Assessing Differential Effects for Conscientiousness and its Subtraits," *Journal of Applied Psychology* 84 (1999), pp. 959–68.
17. T.A. Judge, C.A. Higgins, C.J. Thoreson, and M.R. Barrick, "The Big Five Personality Traits, General Mental Ability, and Career Success Across the Life Span," *Personnel Psychology* 52 (1999), pp. 621–52.
18. H.S. Friedman, J.S. Tucker, J.E. Schwartz, L.R. Martin, C. Tomlinson-Keasey, D.L. Wingard, and M.H. Criqui, "Childhood Conscientiousness and Longevity: Health Behaviors and Cause of Death," *Journal of Personality and Social Psychology* 68 (1995), pp. 696–703.
19. B.W. Roberts, O.S. Chernyshenko, S. Stark, and L.R. Goldberg, "The Structure of Conscientiousness: An Empirical Investigation Based on Seven Major Personality Dimensions," *Personnel Psychology* 58 (2005), pp. 103–39.
20. J. Hogan and B. Holland, "Using Theory to Evaluate Personality and Job-Performance Relations: A Socioanalytic Perspective," *Journal of Applied Psychology* 88 (2003), pp. 100–12.
21. Barrick and Mount, "The Big Five Personality Dimensions."
22. R.L. Frei and M.A. McDaniel, "Validity of Customer Service Measures in Personnel Selection: A Review of Criterion and Construct Evidence," *Human Performance* 11 (1998), pp. 1–27.
23. W.G. Graziano, L.A. Jensen-Campbell, and E.C. Hair, "Perceiving Interpersonal Conflict and Reacting to It: The Case for Agreeableness," *Journal of Personality and Social Psychology* 70 (1996), pp. 820–35.
24. M.R. Mehl, S.D. Gosling, and J.W. Pennebaker, "Personality in Its Natural Habitat: Manifestations and Implicit Folk Theories of Personality in Daily Life," *Journal of Personality and Social Psychology* 90 (2006), pp. 862–77.
25. L. Albright, D.A. Kenny, and T.E. Malloy, "Consensus in Personality Judgments at Zero Acquaintance," *Journal of Personality and Social Psychology* 55 (1988), pp. 387–95; M.J. Levesque and D.A. Kenny, "Accuracy of Behavioral Predictions at Zero Acquaintance: A Social Relations Analysis," *Journal of Personality and Social Psychology* 65 (1993), pp. 1178–87.
26. M.R. Barrick, G.L. Stewart, and M. Piotrowski, "Personality and Job Performance: Test of the Mediating Effects of Motivation Among Sales Representatives," *Journal of Applied Psychology* 87 (2002), pp. 43–51.
27. T.A. Judge, J.E. Bono, R. Ilies, and M.W. Gerhardt, "Personality and Leadership: A Qualitative and Quantitative Review," *Journal of Applied Psychology* 87 (2002), pp. 765–80.
28. Ibid.
29. C.J. Thoreson, S.A. Kaplan, A.P. Barsky, C.R. Warren, and K. de Chermont, "The Affective Underpinnings of Job Perceptions and Attitudes: A Meta-analytic Review and Integration," *Psychological Bulletin* 129 (2003), pp. 914–45.
30. Ibid.; T.A. Judge, D. Heller, and M.K. Mount, "Five-Factor Model of Personality and Job Satisfaction: A Meta-analysis," *Journal of Applied Psychology* 87 (2003), pp. 530–41; S. Kaplan, J.C. Bradley, J.N. Luchman, and D. Haynes, "On the Role of Positive and Negative Affectivity in Job Performance: A Meta-analytic Investigation," *Journal of Applied Psychology* 94 (2009), pp. 162–76.
31. R.D. Arvey, T.J. Bouchard, N.L. Segal, and L.M. Abraham, "Job Satisfaction: Environmental and Genetic Components," *Journal of Applied Psychology* 74 (1989), pp. 187–92.
32. P. Steel, J. Schmidt, and J. Shultz, "Refining the Relationship Between Personality and Subjective Well-Being," *Psychological Bulletin* 134 (2008), pp. 138–161; P. Steel and D.S. Ones, "Personality and Happiness: A National-Level Analysis," *Journal of Personality and Social Psychology* 83 (2002), pp. 767–81.
33. K. Magnus, E. Diener, F. Fujita, and W. Pavot, "Extraversion and Neuroticism as Predictors of Objective Life Events: A Longitudinal Analysis," *Journal of Personality and Social Psychology* 65 (1992), pp. 1046–53.
34. S.V. Paunonen, "Big Five Predictors of Personality and Replicated Predictions of Behavior," *Journal of Personality and Social Psychology* 84 (2003), pp. 411–24; J.B. Asendorpf and S. Wilpers, "Personality Effects on Social Relationships," *Journal of Personality and Social Psychology* 74 (1998), pp. 1531–44.
35. Asendorpf and Wilpers, "Personality Effects on Social Relationships."
36. M.R. Barrick and M.K. Mount, "Select on Conscientiousness and Emotional Stability," in E.A. Locke, ed., *Blackwell Handbook of Principles of Organizational Behavior* (Malden, MA: Blackwell, 2000), pp. 15–28.
37. Thoreson et al., "The Affective Underpinnings."
38. Ibid.
39. K.M. DeNeve and H. Cooper, "The Happy Personality: A Meta-analysis of 137 Personality Traits and Subjective Well-Being," *Psychological Bulletin* 124 (1998), pp. 197–229.
40. N. Bolger and A. Zuckerman, "A Framework for Studying Personality in the Stress Process," *Journal of Personality and Social Psychology* 69 (1995), pp. 890–902.
41. Ibid.
42. M. Friedman and R.H. Rosenman, *Type A Behavior and Your Heart* (New York: Knopf, 1974).
43. J.B. Rotter, "Generalized Expectancies for Internal Versus External Control of Reinforcement," *Psychological Monographs* 80 (1966), pp. 1–28.
44. T.A. Judge and J.E. Bono, "Relationship of Core Self-Evaluations Traits—Self-Esteem, Generalized Self-Efficacy, Locus of Control, and Emotional Stability—with Job Satisfaction and Job Performance: A Meta-analysis," *Journal of Applied Psychology* 86 (2001), pp. 80–92.
45. T.W.H. Ng, K.L. Sorensen, and L.T. Eby, "Locus of Control at Work: A Meta-analysis," *Journal of Organizational Behavior* 27 (2006), pp. 1057–87.
46. Barrick and Mount, "The Big Five Personality Dimensions"; D.F. Cellar, M.L. Miller, D.D. Doverspike, and J.D. Klawsky, "Comparison of Factor Structures and Criterion-Related Validity Coefficients for Two Measures of Personality Based on the Five Factor Model," *Journal of Applied Psychology* 81 (1996), pp. 694–704.
47. J.A. LePine, J.A. Colquitt, and A. Erez, "Adaptability to Changing Task Contexts: Effects of General Cognitive Ability, Conscientiousness, and Openness to Experience," *Personnel Psychology* 53 (2000), pp. 563–93; C.J. Thoreson, J.C. Bradley, P.D. Bliese, and J.D. Thoreson, "The Big Five Personality Traits and Individual Job Performance Growth Trajectories in Maintenance and Transitional Job Stages," *Journal of Applied Psychology* 89 (2004), pp. 835–853.
48. C.E. Shalley, J. Zhou, and G.R. Oldham, "The Effects of Personal and Contextual Characteristics on Creativity: Where Should We Go from Here?," *Journal of Management* 30 (2004), pp. 933–58.
49. J. Zhou and J.M. George, "When Job Dissatisfaction Leads to Creativity: Encouraging the Expression of Voice," *Academy of Management Journal* 44 (2001), pp. 682–96.
50. G.J. Feist, "A Meta-analysis of Personality in Scientific and Artistic Creativity," *Personality and Social Psychology Review* 2 (1998), pp. 290–309.
51. G. Edmondson, "BMW's Dream Factory," *Businessweek*, October 16, 2006, pp. 70–80.
52. D.P. McAdams and J.L. Pals, "A New Big Five: Fundamental Principles for an Integrative Science of Personality," *American Psychologist* 61 (2006), pp. 204–17.
53. A.S. Tsui, S.S. Nifadkar, and A.Y. Ou, "Cross-national, Cross-cultural Organizational Behavior Research: Advances, Gaps, and Recommendations," *Journal of Management* 33 (2007), pp. 426–78.
54. R.J. House, P.J. Hanges, M. Javidan, P.W. Dorfman, and V. Gupta, *Culture,*

Leadership, and Organizations: The GLOBE Study of 62 Societies (Thousand Oaks, CA: Sage, 2004).

55. A.L. Kroeber and C. Kluckhohn, *Culture: A Critical Review of Concepts and Definitions* (Cambridge, MA: Harvard University Press, 1952); G. Hofstede, *Cultures and Organizations: Software of the Mind* (London: McGraw-Hill, 1991).
56. S.J. Heine and E.E. Buchtel, "Personality: The Universal and the Culturally Specific," *Annual Review of Psychology* 60 (2009), pp. 369–94.
57. R.R. McCrae, A. Terracciano, et al. "Personality Profiles of Cultures: Aggregate Personality Traits," *Journal of Personality and Social Psychology* 89 (2005), pp. 407–25.
58. S.H. Schwartz, "Universals in the Content and Structure of Values: Theoretical Advances and Empirical Tests in 20 Countries," in M.P. Zanna, ed., *Advances in Experimental Social Psychology*, Vol. 25 (San Diego, CA: Academic Press, 1992), pp. 1–65.
59. House et al., *Culture, Leadership, and Organizations.*
60. G. Hofstede, *Culture's Consequences: Comparing Values, Behaviors, Institutions, and Organizations Across Nations* (Thousand Oaks, CA: Sage, 2001); B.L. Kirkman, K.B. Lowe, and C.B. Gibson, "A Quarter Century of Culture's Consequences: A Review of Empirical Research Incorporating Hofstede's Cultural Values Framework," *Journal of International Business Studies* 37 (2006), pp. 285–320.
61. G. Hofstede and M.H. Bond, "The Confucius Connection: From Cultural Roots to Economic Growth," *Organizational Dynamics* 16 (1988), pp. 5–21.
62. House et al., *Culture, Leadership, and Organizations.*
63. Y. Chen, K. Leung, and C.C. Chen, "Bringing National Culture to the Table: Making a Difference with Cross-Cultural Differences and Perspectives," *Academy of Management Annals* 3 (2009), pp. 217–49.
64. D. Oyserman, H.M. Coon, and M. Kemmelmeier, "Rethinking Individualism and Collectivism: Evaluation of Theoretical Assumptions and Meta-analyses," *Psychological Bulletin* 128 (2002), pp. 3–72; P.C. Earley and C.B. Gibson, "Taking Stock in Our Progress on Individualism–Collectivism: 100 Years of Solidarity and Community," *Journal of Management* 24 (1998), pp. 265–304.
65. C.L. Jackson, J.A. Colquitt, M.J. Wesson, and C.P. Zapata-Phelan, "Psychological Collectivism: A Measurement Validation and Linkage to Group Member Performance," *Journal of Applied Psychology* 91 (2006), pp. 884–99.
66. S.A. Wasti and O. Can, "Affective and Normative Commitment to Organization, Supervisor, and Coworker: Do Collectivist Values Matter?," *Journal of Vocational Behavior* 73 (2008), pp. 404–13.
67. Earley and Gibson, "Taking Stock in Our Progress."
68. Kirkman et al., "A Quarter Century."
69. J.S. Black, "The Relationship of Personal Characteristics with the Adjustment of Japanese Expatriate Managers," *Management International Review* 30 (1990), pp. 119–34.
70. K.I. Van der Zee and J.P. Van Oudenhoven, "The Multicultural Personality Questionnaire: Reliability and Validity of Self- and Other Ratings of Multicultural Effectiveness," *Journal of Research in Personality* 35 (2001), pp. 278–88.
71. K.I. Van der Zee and U. Brinkmann, "Construct Validity Evidence for the Intercultural Readiness Check Against the Multicultural Personality Questionnaire," *International Journal of Selection and Assessment* 12 (2004), pp. 285–90; J.P. Van Oudenhoven and K.I. Van der Zee, "Predicting Multicultural Effectiveness of International Students: The Multicultural Personality Questionnaire," *International Journal of Intercultural Relations* 26 (2002), pp. 679–94; J.P. Van Oudenhoven, S. Mol, and K.I. Van der Zee, "Study of the Adjustment of Western Expatriates in Taiwan ROC with the Multicultural Personality Questionnaire," *Asian Journal of Social Psychology* 6 (2003), pp. 159–70.
72. T.H. Cox, S.A. Lobel, and P.L. McLeod, "Effects of Ethnic Group Cultural Differences on Cooperative and Competitive Behavior on a Group Task," *Academy of Management Journal* 34 (1991), pp. 827–47; L.T. Eby and G.H. Dobbins, "Collectivistic Orientation in Teams: An Individual and Group-Level Analysis," *Journal of Organizational Behavior* 18 (1997), pp. 275–95; N. Ramamoorthy and S.J. Carroll, "Individualism/Collectivism Orientations and Reactions Toward Alternative Human Resource Management Practices," *Human Relations* 51 (1998), pp. 571–88.
73. Jackson et al., "Psychological Collectivism."
74. E.A. Fleishman, D.P. Costanza, and J. Marshall-Mies, "Abilities," in *An Occupational Information System for the 21st Century: The Development of O*NET*, eds. N.G. Peterson, M.D. Mumford, W.C. Borman, P.R. Jeanneret, and E.A. Fleishman (Washington, DC: American Psychological Association, 1999), pp. 175–95.
75. U. Neisser, G. Boodoo, T.J. Bouchard, A.W. Boykin, N. Brody, S.J. Ceci, D.F. Halpern, J.C. Loehlin, R. Perloff, R.J. Sternberg, and S. Urbina, "Intelligence: Knowns and Unknowns," *American Psychologist* 51 (1996), pp. 77–101.
76. K. McCartney, M.J. Harris, and F. Bernieri, "Growing Up and Growing Apart: A Developmental Meta-analysis of Twin Studies," *Psychological Bulletin* 107 (1990), pp. 226–37.
77. S.J. Ceci, "How Much Does Schooling Influence General Intelligence and Its Cognitive Components? A Reassessment of the Evidence," *Developmental Psychology* 27 (1991), pp. 703–22.
78. M.L. Kohn and C. Schooler, "Occupational Experience and Psychological Functioning: An Assessment of Reciprocal Effects," *American Sociological Review* 38 (1973), pp. 97–118; M.L. Kohn and C. Schooler, *Work and Personality: An Inquiry into the Impact of Social Stratification* (Norwood, NJ: Ablex, 1983); Neisser et al., "Intelligence."
79. L. Winerman, "Smarter Than Ever?," *Monitor on Psychology*, March 2013, pp. 30–33.
80. O*NET OnLine, online.onetcenter.org/find/descriptor/browse/Abilities/#cur, retrieved June 5, 2006.
81. "Famous People with Disabilities," *Disability Fact Sheet Handbook* (Irvine: University of California, 2006), www.disability.uci.edu/disability_handbook/famous_people.htm, retrieved June 9, 2006.
82. F. Vogelstein, "Google @ $165: Are These Guys for Real?," *Fortune* 150(12) (December 13, 2004), p. 98. ProQuest database, retrieved May 14, 2007.
83. J.B. Carroll, *Human Cognitive Abilities: A Survey of Factor-Analytic Studies* (New York: Cambridge University Press, 1993); R.B. Cattell, "The Measurement of Adult Intelligence," *Psychological Bulletin* 40 (1943), pp. 153–93; F. Galton, *Inquiries into Human Faculty and Its Development* (London: Macmillan, 1883); C. Spearman, "General Intelligence, Objectively Determined and Measured," *American Journal of Psychology* 15 (1904), pp. 201–93; L.L. Thurstone, "Primary Mental Abilities," *Psychometric Monographs* (Whole No. 1, 1938); P.E. Vernon, *The Structure of Human Abilities* (London: Methuen, 1950).
84. Spearman, "General Intelligence"; C. Spearman, *The Abilities of Man: Their Nature and Measurement* (New York: MacMillan, 1927).
85. R. Bar-On, *Development of the Bar-On EQ-i: A Measure of Emotional Intelligence and Social Intelligence* (Toronto: Multi-Health Systems, 1997); H. Gardner, *The Shattered Mind* (New York: Knopf, 1975); D. Goleman, *Emotional Intelligence: Why It Can Matter More Than IQ* (New York: Bantam Books, 1995); R.K. Thorndike, "Intelligence and Its Uses," *Harper's Magazine* 140 (1920), pp. 227–335.
86. G. Matthews, A.K. Emo, R.D. Roberts, and M. Zeidner, "What Is This Thing Called Emotional Intelligence?," in K.R. Murphy, ed., *A Critique of Emotional Intelligence: What Are the Problems and How Can They Be Fixed?* (Mahwah, NJ: Lawrence Erlbaum Associates, 2006), pp. 3–36; J.D. Mayer, P. Salovey, and D.R. Caruso, "Emotional Intelligence: New Ability or Eclectic Traits?," *American Psychologist* 63 (2008), pp. 503–17.
87. P. Salovey and J.D. Mayer, "Emotional Intelligence," *Imagination, Cognition, and Personality* 9 (1990), pp. 185–211; J.D.

Mayer, R.D. Roberts, and S.G. Barside, "Human Abilities: Emotional Intelligence," *Annual Review of Psychology* 59 (2008), pp. 507–36.
88. M. Davies, L. Stankov, and R.D. Roberts, "Emotional Intelligence: In Search of an Elusive Construct," *Journal of Personality and Social Psychology* 75 (1998), pp. 989–1015.
89. Davies et al., "Emotional Intelligence"; K.S. Law, C.S. Wong, and L.J. Song, "The Construct and Criterion Validity of Emotional Intelligence and Its Potential Utility for Management Studies," *Journal of Applied Psychology* 89 (2004), pp. 483–96.
90. Ibid.
91. Ibid.
92. Ibid.
93. E.A. Fleishman, "Human Abilities and the Acquisition of Skill," in E.A. Bilodeau, ed., *Acquisition of Skill* (New York: Academic Press, 1966), pp. 147–67; Fleishman et al., "Abilities"; E.A. Fleishman and M.E. Reilly, *Handbook of Human Abilities: Definitions, Measurements, and Job Task Requirements* (Palo Alto, CA: Consulting Psychologists Press, Inc., 1992).
94. S. Kazmi, "Firefighters Put Through Paces in One-Stop Testing," *Knight Ridder Tribune Business News*, August 18, 2005, p. 1. ProQuest database, retrieved May 13, 2006.
95. M.R. Barrick, M.K. Mount, and T.A. Judge, "Personality and Performance at the Beginning of the New Millennium: What Do We Know and Where Do We Go Next?," *International Journal of Selection and Assessment* 9 (2001), pp. 9–30; L.M. Hough and A. Furnham, "Use of Personality Variables in Work Settings," in W.C. Borman, D.R. Ilgen, and R.J. Klimoski, eds., *Handbook of Psychology*, Vol. 12 (Hoboken, NJ: Wiley, 2003), pp. 131–69.
96. T.A. Judge and R. Ilies, "Relationship of Personality to Performance Motivation: A Meta-analysis," *Journal of Applied Psychology* 87 (2002), pp. 797–807.
97. P.R. Sackett, S. Zedeck, and L. Fogli, "Relations Between Measures of Typical and Maximum Job Performance," *Journal of Applied Psychology* 73 (1988), pp. 482–86.
98. Hough and Furnham, "Use of Personality Variables in Work Settings"; R. Ilies, I.S. Fulmer, M. Spitzmuller, and M.D. Johnson, "Personality and Citizenship Behavior: The Mediating Role of Job Satisfaction," *Journal of Applied Psychology* 94 (2009), pp. 945–59.
99. M.K. Mount and M.R. Barrick, "The Big Five Personality Dimensions: Implications for Research and Practice in Human Resources Management," in G.R. Ferris, ed., *Research in Personnel and Human Resource Management* (Greenwich, CT: JAI Press, 1995), pp. 153–200.
100. Ilies et al., "Personality and Citizenship Behavior"; Judge et al., "Five-Factor Model."
101. J.F. Salgado, "The Big Five Personality Dimensions and Counterproductive Behaviors," *International Journal of Selection and Assessment* 10 (2002), pp. 117–25.
102. M.J. Cullen and P. Sackett, "Personality and Counterproductive Work Behavior," in M.A. Barrick and A.M. Ryan, eds., *Personality and Work* (San Francisco: Jossey-Bass, 2003), pp. 150–82.
103. A. Cooper-Hakim and C. Viswesvaran, "The Construct of Work Commitment: Testing an Integrative Framework," *Psychological Bulletin* 131 (2005), pp. 241–59; Mathieu and Zajac, "A Review and Meta-analysis."
104. Salgado, "The Big Five Personality Dimensions"; R.D. Zimmerman, "Understanding the Impact of Personality Traits on Individuals' Turnover Decisions: A Meta-analytic Path Model," *Personnel Psychology* 61 (2008), pp. 309–48.
105. Cooper-Hakim and Viswesvaran, "The Construct of Work Commitment."
106. S. Grant and J. Langan-Fox, "Personality and Occupational Stressor–Strain Relationships: The Role of the Big Five," *Journal of Occupational Health Psychology* 12 (2007), pp. 20–33.
107. W. Mischel, "The Interaction of Person and Situation," in D. Magnusson and N.S. Endler, eds., *Personality at the Crossroads: Current Issues in Interactional Psychology* (Hillsdale, NJ: Erlbaum, 1977), pp. 333–52; H.M. Weiss and S. Adler, "Personality and Organizational Behavior," in B.M. Staw and L.L. Cummings, eds., *Research in Organizational Behavior*, Vol. 6 (Greenwich, CT: JAI Press, 1984), pp. 1–50; M.J. Withey, I.R. Gellatly, and M. Annett, "The Moderating Effect of Situational Strength on the Relationship Between Personality and Provision of Effort," *Journal of Applied Social Psychology* 35 (2005), pp. 1587–1608; W.H. Cooper and M.J. Withey, "The Strong Situation Hypothesis," *Personality and Social Psychology Review* 13 (2009), pp. 62–72; R.D. Meyer, R.S. Dalal, and R. Hermida, "A Review and Synthesis of Situational Strength in the Organizational Sciences," *Journal of Management* 36 (2010), pp. 121–140.
108. M.R. Barrick and M.K. Mount, "Autonomy as a Moderator of the Relationship Between the Big Five Personality Dimensions and Job Performance," *Journal of Applied Psychology* 78 (1993), pp. 111–18; I.R. Gellatly and P.G. Irving, "Personality, Autonomy, and Contextual Performance of Managers," *Human Performance* 14 (2001), pp. 229–243.
109. R.P. Tett and D.D. Burnett, "A Personality Trait–Based Interactionist Model of Job Performance," *Journal of Applied Psychology* 88 (2003), pp. 500–17.
110. D. Lubinski, "Introduction to the Special Section on Cognitive Abilities: 100 Years After Spearman's (1904) 'General Intelligence,' 'Objectively Determined and Measured,'" *Journal of Personality and Social Psychology* 86 (2004), pp. 96–111.
111. J.E. Hunter and F.L. Schmidt, "Intelligence and Job Performance: Economic and Social Implications," *Psychology, Public Policy, and Law* 2 (1996), pp. 447–72; Lubinski, "Introduction to the Special Section"; F.L. Schmidt and J. Hunter, "General Mental Ability in the World of Work: Occupational Attainment and Job Performance," *Journal of Personality and Social Psychology* 86 (2004), pp. 162–73.
112. D. Seligman, "Brains in the Office," *Fortune*, January 13, 1997, p. 38. ProQuest database, retrieved May 14, 2007.
113. F.L. Schmidt and J.E. Hunter, "Select on Intelligence," in E.A. Locke, ed., *Blackwell Handbook of Principles of Organizational Behavior* (Malden, MA: Blackwell Publishers, Inc., 2000), pp. 3–14.
114. Hunter and Schmidt, "Intelligence and Job Performance"; F.L. Schmidt, J.E. Hunter, A.N. Outerbridge, and S. Goff, "The Joint Relations of Experience and Ability with Job Performance: A Test of Three Hypotheses," *Journal of Applied Psychology* 73 (1988), pp. 46–57.
115. S.J. Motowidlo, W.S. Borman, and M.J. Schmit, "A Theory of Individual Differences in Task and Contextual Performance," *Human Performance* 10 (1997), pp. 71–83.
116. J.A. LePine, J.A. Colquitt, and A. Erez, "Adaptability to Changing Task Contexts: Effects of General Cognitive Ability, Conscientiousness, and Openness to Experience," *Personnel Psychology* 53 (2000), pp. 563–93; Schmidt and Hunter, "Select on Intelligence."
117. J.W. Boudreau, W.R. Boswell, T.A. Judge, and R.D. Bretz, "Personality and Cognitive Ability as Predictors of Job Search Among Employed Managers," *Personnel Psychology* 54 (2001), pp. 25–50; S.M. Colarelli, R.A. Dean, and C. Konstans, "Comparative Effects of Personal and Situational Influences on Job Outcomes of New Professionals," *Journal of Applied Psychology* 72 (1987), pp. 558–66; D.N. Dickter, M. Roznowski, and D.A. Harrison, "Temporal Tempering: An Event History Analysis of the Process of Voluntary Turnover," *Journal of Applied Psychology* 81 (1996), pp. 705–16.
118. Boudreau et al., "Personality and Cognitive Ability."
119. M.R. Barrick, G.K. Patton, and S.N. Haugland, "Accuracy of Interviewer Judgments of Job Applicant Personality Traits," *Personnel Psychology* 53 (2000), pp. 925–51.
120. Wonderlic website, www.wonderlic.com/Products/product.asp?prod_id4, retrieved July 12, 2006.

Chapter 5

1. "Zappos Family Core Values," about.zappos.com/our-unique-culture/zappos-core-values, retrieved December 30, 2014.
2. "Meet Our Monkeys," about.zappos.com/meet-our-monkeys/tony-hsieh-ceo,

retrieved December 31, 2014; "Zappos 2014 Media Kit," www.zapposinsights.com/about/zappos/press-kit, retrieved December 30, 2014.

3. J.M. O'Brien, "Zappos Knows How to Kick It," *Fortune*, February 2, 2009, pp. 55–60.
4. "Zappos Blogs: CEO and COO Blog," January 25, 2009. blogs.zappos.com/blogs/ceo-and-coo-blog, retrieved June 12, 2009.
5. O'Brien, "Zappos Knows How to Kick It."
6. J.M. O'Brien, "The 10 Commandments of Zappos," *Fortune*, January 22, 2009, money.cnn.com/2009/01/21/news/companies/obrien_zappos10.fortune/index.htm, retrieved May 17, 2011.
7. O'Brien, "The 10 Commandments of Zappos."
8. R. Levering, and M. Moskowitz, "And the Winners Are . . . ," *Fortune*, February 2, 2009, pp. 67–78; O'Brien, "Zappos Knows How to Kick It."
9. Ibid.
10. O'Brien, "Zappos Knows How to Kick It."
11. "Zappos 2014 Media Kit," www.zapposinsights.com/about/zappos/press-kit, retrieved December 30, 2014.
12. "3-Day Culture Camp," ww.zapposinsights.com/training/3-day-culture-camp#what, retrieved December 30, 2014.
13. E.A. Locke, "The Nature and Causes of Job Satisfaction," in *Handbook of Industrial and Organizational Psychology*, ed. M. Dunnette (Chicago: Rand McNally, 1976), pp. 1297–1350.
14. Canadian Education and Research Institute for Counselling (CERIC), "Despite Recent Tough Economic Times, Canadians Satisfied with Work, Optimistic About Career Goals," Canada NewsWire release, February 2, 2011, www.cnw.ca/en/releases/archive/February2011/02/c6366.html, retrieved May 17, 2011.
15. Debra Chapman, "A New Look at Job Satisfaction in Canada: Workopolis Study: The Top 20 Jobs in Canada," March 2007, sssubaiei.kau.edu.sa/Files/0005441/Subjects/Top20JobsWhitepaper.pdf, retrieved May 17, 2011.
16. Ibid.
17. Locke, "The Nature and Causes of Job Satisfaction"; M. Rokeach, *The Nature of Human Values* (New York: Free Press, 1973); S.H. Schwartz, "Universals in the Content and Structure of Values: Theoretical Advances and Empirical Tests in 20 Countries," in *Advances in Experimental Social Psychology*, Vol. 25, ed. M. Zanna (New York: Academic Press, 1992), pp. 1–65; J.R. Edwards and D.M. Cable, "The Value of Value Congruence," *Journal of Applied Psychology* 94 (2009), pp. 654–77.
18. R.V. Dawis, "Vocational Interests, Values, and Preferences," in *Handbook of Industrial and Organizational Psychology*, Vol. 2, eds. M.D. Dunnette and L.M. Hough (Palo Alto, CA: Consulting Psychologists Press, 1991), pp. 834–71; D.M. Cable and J.R. Edwards, "Complementary and Supplementary Fit: A Theoretical and Empirical Integration," *Journal of Applied Psychology* 89 (2004), pp. 822–34.
19. Locke, "The Nature and Causes of Job Satisfaction."
20. T.A. Judge and A.H. Church, "Job Satisfaction: Research and Practice," in *Industrial and Organizational Psychology: Linking Theory with Practice*, eds. C.L. Cooper and E.A. Locke Judge (Oxford, UK: Blackwell, 2000), pp. 166–98.
21. Locke, "The Nature and Causes of Job Satisfaction."
22. P.C. Smith, L.M. Kendall, and C.L. Hulin, *The Measurement of Satisfaction in Work and Retirement* (Chicago: Rand McNally), 1969.
23. E.E. Lawler, *Pay and Organizational Effectiveness: A Psychological View* (New York: McGraw-Hill, 1971).
24. Locke, "The Nature and Causes of Job Satisfaction."
25. Smith et al., *The Measurement of Satisfaction.*
26. Locke, "The Nature and Causes of Job Satisfaction."
27. Tkaczyk, C. "Nordstrom," *Fortune*, October 18, 2010, p. 37.
28. Smith et al., "The Measurement of Satisfaction."
29. Locke, "The Nature and Causes of Job Satisfaction."
30. Smith et al., "The Measurement of Satisfaction."
31. Ibid.
32. R.M. Murphy, "Happy Campers," *Fortune*, April 25, 2011.
33. G.H. Ironson, P.C. Smith, M.T. Brannick, W.M. Gibson, and K.B. Paul, "Construction of a Job in General Scale: A Comparison of Global, Composite, and Specific Measures," *Journal of Applied Psychology* 74 (1989), pp. 193–200; S.S. Russell, C. Spitzmuller, L.F. Lin, J.M. Stanton, P.C. Smith, and G.H. Ironson, "Shorter Can Also Be Better: The Abridged Job in General Scale," *Educational and Psychological Measurement* 64 (2004), pp. 878–93; N.A. Bowling and G.D. Hammond, "A Meta-analytic Examination of the Construct Validity of the Michigan Organizational Assessment Questionnaire Job Satisfaction Subscale," *Journal of Vocational Behavior* 73 (2008), pp. 63–77; T.A. Judge, R.F. Piccolo, N.P. Podsakoff, J.C. Shaw, and B.L. Rich, "The Relationship between Pay and Job Satisfaction: A Meta-analysis," *Journal of Vocational Behavior* 77 (2010), pp. 157–67.
34. F.W. Taylor, *The Principles of Scientific Management* (New York: Wiley, 1911); F.B. Gilbreth, *Motion Study: A Method for Increasing the Efficiency of the Workman* (New York: Van Nostrand, 1911).
35. J.R. Hackman and E.E. Lawler III, "Employee Reactions to Job Characteristics," *Journal of Applied Psychology* 55 (1971), pp. 259–86.
36. J.R. Hackman and G.R. Oldham, *Work Redesign* (Reading, MA: Addison-Wesley, 1980).
37. Ibid.
38. Ibid.
39. J.R. Hackman and G.R. Oldham, "Motivation Through the Design of Work: Test of a Theory," *Organizational Behavior and Human Decision Processes* 16 (1976), pp. 250–79.
40. Hackman and Oldham, *Work Redesign.*
41. A.N. Turner and P.R. Lawrence, *Industrial Jobs and the Worker* (Boston: Harvard University Graduate School of Business Administration, 1965).
42. Hackman and Lawler, "Employee Reactions."
43. S. Terkel, *Working People Talk About What They Do All Day and How They Feel About What They Do* (New York: Pantheon Books, 1974), pp. 159–60.
44. Ibid., pp. 318–21.
45. G. Berns, *Satisfaction: The Science of Finding True Fulfillment* (New York: Henry Holt and Company, 2005), p. xiv.
46. Hackman and Oldham, *Work Redesign.*
47. Turner and Lawrence, *Industrial Jobs.*
48. Terkel, *Working*, p. xxxii.
49. Ibid., pp. 213–14.
50. Hackman and Oldham, *Work Redesign.*
51. A.M. Grant, "The Significance of Task Significance: Job Performance Effects, Relational Mechanisms, and Boundary Conditions," *Journal of Applied Psychology* 93 (2008), pp. 108–24.
52. Terkel, *Working*, pp. 107–109.
53. Ibid., p. 589.
54. Hackman and Oldham, *Work Redesign.*
55. Turner and Lawrence, *Industrial Jobs.*
56. J.A. Breaugh, "The Measurement of Work Autonomy. *Human Relations* 38 (1985), pp. 551–70.
57. Terkel, *Working*, pp. 49–50.
58. Ibid., pp. 458–61.
59. Hackman and Oldham, *Work Redesign.*
60. Terkel, *Working*, p. 346.
61. Ibid., pp. 295–96.
62. S.E. Humphrey, J.D. Nahrgang, and F.P. Morgeson, "Integrating Motivational, Social, and Contextual Work Design Features: A Meta-analytic Summary and Theoretical Extension of the Work Design Literature," *Journal of Applied Psychology* 92 (2007), pp. 1332–56; Y. Fried and G.R. Ferris, "The Validity of the Job Characteristics Model: A Review and Meta-analysis," *Personnel Psychology* 40 (1987), pp. 287–322.
63. Hackman and Oldham, *Work Redesign.*
64. B.T. Loher, R.A. Noe, N.L. Moeller, and M.P. Fitzgerald, "A Meta-analysis of the Relation of Job Characteristics to Job Satisfaction," *Journal of Applied Psychology* 70 (1985), pp. 280–89.
65. M.A. Campion and C.L. McClelland, "Interdisciplinary Examination of the Costs and Benefits of Enlarged Jobs: A Job Design Quasi-experiment," *Journal of Applied Psychology* 76 (1991), pp. 186–98.
66. Ibid.
67. A. Wrzesniewski and J.E. Dutton, "Crafting a Job: Revisioning Employees as Active Crafters of Their Work," *Academy of Management Review* 26 (2001),

pp. 179–201; M. Tims, A.B. Bakker, and D. Derks, "Development and Validation of the Job Crafting Scale," *Journal of Vocational Behavior* 80 (2012), pp. 173–86.
68. J.C. Rode, M.L. Arthaud-Day, C.H. Mooney, J.P. Near, T.T. Baldwin, W.H. Bommer, and R.S. Rubin, "Life Satisfaction and Student Performance," *Academy of Management Learning and Education* 4 (2005), pp. 421–33.
69. W.N. Morris, *Mood: The Frame of Mind* (New York: Springer-Verlag, 1989).
70. D. Watson and A. Tellegen, "Toward a Consensual Structure of Mood," *Psychological Bulletin* 98 (1985), pp. 219–35; J.A. Russell, "A Circumplex Model of Affect," *Journal of Personality and Social Psychology* 39 (1980), pp. 1161–78; R.J. Larsen and E. Diener, "Promises and Problems with the Circumplex Model of Emotion," in *Review of Personality and Social Psychology*: Emotion, Vol. 13, ed. M.S. Clark (Newbury Park, CA: Sage, 1992), pp. 25–59.
71. Ibid.
72. M. Csikszentmihalyi, *Finding Flow: The Psychology of Engagement with Everyday Life* (New York: Basic Books, 1997); M. Csikszentmihalyi, *Flow: The Psychology of Optimal Experience* (New York: HarperPerennial, 1990); M. Csikszentmihalyi, *Beyond Boredom and Anxiety* (San Francisco: Jossey-Bass, 1975).
73. R.W. Quinn, "Flow in Knowledge Work: High Performance Experience in the Design of National Security Technology," *Administrative Science Quarterly* 50 (2005), pp. 610–41; S.A. Jackson and H.W. Marsh, "Development and Validation of a Scale to Measure Optimal Experience: The Flow State Scale," *Journal of Sport and Exercise Psychology* 18 (1996), pp. 17–35; A.B. Bakker, "The Work-Related Flow Inventory: Construction and Initial Validation of the WOLF," *Journal of Vocational Behavior* 72 (2008), pp. 400–14.
74. H.M. Weiss and R. Cropanzano, "Affective Events Theory: A Theoretical Discussion of the Structure, Causes, and Consequences of Affective Experiences at Work," in *Research in Organizational Behavior*, Vol. 18, eds. B.M. Staw and L.L. Cummings (Greenwich, CT: JAI Press, 1996), pp. 1–74.
75. H.M. Weiss and K.E. Kurek, "Dispositional Influences on Affective Experiences at Work," in *Personality and Work: Reconsidering the Role of Personality in Organizations*, eds. M.R. Barrick and A.M. Ryan (San Francisco: Jossey-Bass, 2003), pp. 121–49.
76. Weiss and Cropanzano, "Affective Events Theory."
77. R.S. Lazarus, *Emotion and Adaptation* (New York: Oxford University, 1991).
78. A.R. Hochschild, *The Managed Heart: Commercialization of Human Feeling* (Berkeley: University of California Press, 1983); A. Rafaeli and R.I. Sutton, "The Expression of Emotion in Organizational Life," *Research in Organizational Behavior* 11 (1989), pp. 1–42.
79. E. Hatfield, J.T. Cacioppo, and R.L. Rapson, *Emotional Contagion* (New York: Cambridge University Press, 1994).
80. N.M. Ashkanasy, C.E.J. Hartel, and C.S. Daus, "Diversity and Emotion: The New Frontiers in Organizational Behavior Research," *Journal of Management* 28 (2002), pp. 307–38.
81. T.A. Judge, C.J. Thoreson, J.E. Bono, and G.K. Patton, "The Job Satisfaction–Job Performance Relationship: A Qualitative and Quantitative Review," *Psychological Bulletin* 127 (2001), pp. 376–407.
82. M. Baas, C.K.W. De Dreu, and B.A. Nijstad, "A Meta-analysis of 25 Years of Mood—Creativity Research: Hedonic Tone, Activation, or Regulatory Focus," *Psychological Bulletin* 134 (2008), pp. 779–806; S. Lyubomirsky, L. King, and E. Diener, "The Benefits of Frequent Positive Affect: Does Happiness Lead to Success?," *Psychological Bulletin* 131 (2005), pp. 803–55.
83. A.P. Brief and H.M. Weiss, "Organizational Behavior: Affect in the Workplace," *Annual Review of Psychology* 53 (2002), pp. 279–307.
84. A.M. Isen and R.A. Baron, "Positive Affect as a Factor in Organizational Behavior," *Research in Organizational Behavior* 13 (1991), pp. 1–53.
85. W.C. Tsai, C.C. Chen, and H.L. Liu, "Test of a Model Linking Employee Positive Moods and Task Performance," *Journal of Applied Psychology* 92 (2007), pp. 1570–83.
86. D.J. Beal, H.M. Weiss, E. Barros, and S.M. MacDermid, "An Episodic Process Model of Affective Influences on Performance," *Journal of Applied Psychology* 90 (2005), pp. 1054–68; A.G. Miner and T.M. Glomb, "State Mood, Task Performance, and Behavior at Work: A Within-Persons Approach," *Organizational Behavior and Human Decision Processes* 112 (2010), pp. 43–57.
87. Locke, "The Nature and Causes of Job Satisfaction."
88. M. Riketta, "The Causal Relation Between Job Attitudes and Job Performance: A Meta-analysis of Panel Studies," *Journal of Applied Psychology* 93 (2008), pp. 472–81.
89. J.A. LePine, A. Erez, and D.E. Johnson, "The Nature and Dimensionality of Organizational Citizenship Behavior: A Critical Review and Meta-analysis," *Journal of Applied Psychology* 87 (2002), pp. 52–65.
90. Lyubomirsky et al., "The Benefits of Frequent Positive Affect"; R.S. Dalal, H. Lam, H.M. Weiss, E.R. Welch, and C.L. Hulin, "A Within-Person Approach to Work Behavior and Performance: Concurrent and Lagged Citizenship-Counterproductivity Associations, and Dynamic Relationships with Affect and Overall Job Performance," *Academy of Management Journal* 52 (2009), pp. 1051–66.
91. R.S. Dalal, "A Meta-analysis of the Relationship Between Organizational Citizenship Behavior and Counterproductive Work Behavior," *Journal of Applied Psychology* 90 (2005), pp. 1241–55.
92. J. Yang and J.M. Diefendorff, "The Relations of Daily Counterproductive Workplace Behavior with Emotions, Situational Antecedents, and Personality Moderators: A Diary Study in Hong Kong," *Personnel Psychology* 62 (2009), pp. 259–95; Dalal et al., "A Within-Person Approach to Work Behavior and Performance."
93. A. Cooper-Hakim and C. Viswesvaran, "The Construct of Work Commitment: Testing an Integrative Framework," *Psychological Bulletin* 131 (2005), pp. 241–59; D.A. Harrison, D. Newman, and P.L. Roth, "How Important Are Job Attitudes? Meta-analytic Comparisons of Integrative Behavioral Outcomes and Time Sequences," *Academy of Management Journal* 49 (2006), pp. 305–25; J.P. Meyer, D.J. Stanley, L. Herscovitch, and L. Topolnytsky, "Affective, Continuance, and Normative Commitment to the Organization: A Meta-analysis of Antecedents, Correlates, and Consequences," *Journal of Vocational Behavior* 61 (2002), pp. 20–52.
94. Ibid.
95. M. Tait, M.Y. Padgett, and T.T. Baldwin, "Job and Life Satisfaction: A Reexamination of the Strength of the Relationship and Gender Effects as a Function of the Date of the Study," *Journal of Applied Psychology* 74 (1989), pp. 502–507; T.A. Judge and S. Watanabe, "Another Look at the Job Satisfaction–Life Satisfaction Relationship," *Journal of Applied Psychology* 78 (1993), pp. 939–48; B. Erdogan, T.N. Bauer, D.M. Truxillo, and L.R. Mansfield, "Whistle While You Work: A Review of the Life Satisfaction Literature," *Journal of Management* 38 (2012), pp. 1038–83.
96. D. Kahneman, A.B. Krueger, D.A. Schkade, N. Schwarz, and A.A. Stone, "A Survey Method for Characterizing Daily Life Experience: The Day Reconstruction Method," *Science* 306 (2004), pp. 1776–80.
97. D. Kahneman and A. Deaton, "High Income Improves Evaluation of Life but Not Emotional Well-Being," *Proceedings of the National Academy of Sciences* 107 (2010). pp. 16489–93.
98. R. Layard, *Happiness* (New York: Penguin Press, 2005), p. 41.
99. R. Layard, quoted in E. Diener and E. Suh, "National Differences in Subjective Well-Being," in *Well-Being: The Foundations of Hedonic Psychology*, eds. D. Kahneman, E. Diener, and N. Schwarz (New York: Russell Sage Foundation, 1999), pp. 434–50.
100. Layard, *Happiness*.
101. L.M. Saari and T.A. Judge. "Employee Attitudes and Job Satisfaction," *Human Resource Management* 43 (2004), pp. 395–407.

102. A.J. Kinicki, F.M. McKee-Ryan, C.A. Schriesheim, and K.P. Carson, "Assessing the Construct Validity of the Job Descriptive Index: A Review and Meta-analysis," *Journal of Applied Psychology* 87 (2002), pp. 14–32; K.A. Hanisch, "The Job Descriptive Index Revisited: Questions About the Question Mark," *Journal of Applied Psychology* 77 (1992), pp. 377–82; K.G. Jung, A. Dalessio, and S.M. Johnson, "Stability of the Factor Structure of the Job Descriptive Index," *Academy of Management Journal* 29 (1986), pp. 609–16.
103. Ironson et al., "Construction"; Russell et al., "Shorter Can Also Be Better."
104. W.K. Balzer, J.A. Kihn, P.C. Smith, J.L. Irwin, P.D. Bachiochi, C. Robie, E.F. Sinar, and L.F. Parra, "Users' Manual for the Job Descriptive Index (JDI; 1997 version) and the Job in General Scales," in *Electronic Resources for the JDI and JIG*, eds. J.M. Stanton and C.D. Crossley (Bowling Green, OH: Bowling Green State University, 2000).
105. Ibid.
106. Ibid.
107. Saari and Judge, "Employee Attitudes."

Chapter 6

1. K. Wilkins, "Work Stress Among Health Care Providers," *Health Reports* (Statistics Canada, Catalogue 82-003) 18(4) (2007), pp. 33–36.
2. "Health-Care Providers Report High Stress Levels: Report," CBC News, November 14, 2007, www.cbc.ca/news/health/story/2007/11/13/stress-statscan.html, retrieved May 19, 2011.
3. Ibid.
4. Wilkins, "Work Stress Among Health Care Providers."
5. A. Day, M.P. Leiter, H.K.S. Laschinger, and D.G. Oore, "Developing Healthy Workplaces: What's Civility Got to Do with It?," *Good Company e-Newsletter* 4(2) (2010), www.phwa.org/resources/article/158 5/19/2011, retrieved May 19, 2011; CREW, Centre for Organizational Research and Development, Acadia University, Nova Scotia, cord.acadiau.ca/crew-interventions.html, retrieved May 22, 2011.
6. Ibid.
7. Ibid.
8. Ibid.
9. Ibid.
10. Ibid.
11. Ibid.
12. Wilkins, "Work Stress Among Health Care Providers."
13. S.R. Johnson and L.D. Eldridge, "Employee-Related Stress on the Job: Sources, Consequences, and What's Next," Technical Report #003 (Rochester, NY: Genesee Survey Services, Inc., 2004).
14. R.S. Lazarus and S. Folkman, *Stress, Appraisal, and Coping* (New York: Springer, 1984).
15. Ibid.
16. Ibid.
17. J.A. LePine, M.A. LePine, and C.L. Jackson, "Challenge and Hindrance Stress: Relationships with Exhaustion, Motivation to Learn, and Learning Performance," *Journal of Applied Psychology* 89 (2004), pp. 883–91; J.A. LePine, N.P. Podsakoff, and M.A. LePine, "A Meta-analytic Test of the Challenge Stressor–Hindrance Stressor Framework: An Explanation for Inconsistent Relationships Among Stressors and Performance," *Academy of Management Journal* 48 (2005), pp. 764–75; N.P. Podsakoff, J.A. LePine, and M.A. LePine, "Differential Challenge Stressor–Hindrance Stressor Relationships with Job Attitudes, Turnover Intentions, Turnover, and Withdrawal Behavior: A Meta-analysis," *Journal of Applied Psychology* 92 (2007), pp. 438–54.
18. J.B. Rodell and T.A. Judge, "Can 'Good' Stressors Spark 'Bad' Behaviors? The Mediating Role of Emotions in the Links of Challenge and Hindrance Stressors with Citizenship and Counterproductive Behaviors," *Journal of Applied Psychology* 94 (2009), pp. 1438–51.
19. J.A. LePine, M.A. LePine, and J.R. Saul, "Relationships Among Work and Non-work Challenge and Hindrance Stressors and Non-work and Work Criteria: A Theory of Cross-Domain Stressor Effects," in *Research in Occupational Stress and Well Being*, eds. P.L. Perrewé and D.C. Ganster (San Diego: JAI Press/Elsevier, 2006), pp. 35–72.
20. R. Kahn, D. Wolfe, R. Quinn, J. Snoek, and R.A. Rosenthal, *Organizational Stress: Studies in Role Conflict and Ambiguity* (New York: Wiley, 1964); J. Pearce, "Bringing Some Clarity to Role Ambiguity Research," *Academy of Management Review* 6 (1981), pp. 665–74.
21. Kahn et al., *Organizational Stress*; J.R. Rizzo, R.J. House, and S.I. Lirtzman, "Role Conflict and Ambiguity in Complex Organizations," *Administrative Science Quarterly* 15 (1970), pp. 150–63.
22. Ibid.
23. Kahn et al., *Organizational Stress*.
24. L. Narayanan, S. Menon, and P. Spector, "Stress in the Workplace: A Comparison of Gender and Occupations," *Journal of Organizational Behavior* 20 (1999), pp. 63–74.
25. J. Miller and M. Miller, "Get a Life!," *Fortune*, November 28, 2005, pp. 109–124.
26. K. Chamerlain and S. Zika, "The Minor Events Approach to Stress: Support for the Use of Daily Hassles," British *Journal of Psychology* 18 (1990), pp. 469–81.
27. M. Mandel, "The Real Reasons You're Working So Hard . . . and What You Can Do About It," *Businessweek*, October 3, 2005, pp. 60–67, www.proquest.com, retrieved March 27, 2007.
28. S. Glazer and T.A. Beehr, "Consistency of Implications of Three Role Stressors Across Four Countries," *Journal of Organizational Behavior* 26 (2005), pp. 467–87.
29. K. Wilkins, "Work Stress Among Health Care Providers," *Health Reports* (Statistics Canada, Catalogue 82-003) 2007, 18(4), pp. 33–36.
30. Glazer and Beehr, "Consistency of Implications."
31. Kahn et al., *Organizational Stress*.
32. A. O'Connor, "Cracking Under Pressure? It's Just the Opposite for Some; Sick of Work—Last of Three Articles: Thriving Under Stress," *The New York Times*, September 10, 2004, Section A, Column 5, p. 1, www.proquest.com, retrieved March 27, 2007.
33. J. Schaubroeck, D.C. Ganster, and B.E. Kemmerer, "Job Complexity, 'Type A' Behavior, and Cardiovascular Disorder: A Prospective Study," *Academy of Management Journal* 37 (1994), pp. 426–439.
34. M.W. McCall, M.M. Lombardo, and A.M. Morrison, *The Lessons of Experience: How Successful Executives Develop on the Job* (Lexington, MA: Lexington Books, 1988).
35. J.R. Edwards and R.V. Harrison, "Job Demands and Worker Health: Three-Dimensional Reexamination of the Relationships Between Person–Environment Fit and Strain," *Journal of Applied Psychology* 78 (1993), pp. 628–48; J.R.P. French Jr., R.D. Caplan, and R.V. Harrison, *The Mechanisms of Job Stress and Strain* (New York: Wiley, 1982).
36. S. Abrahm, "From Wall Street to Control Tower," *The New York Times*, March 20, 2010, www.nytimes.com/2010/03/21/jobs/21preoccupations.html.
37. S. Neufeld, "Work-Related Stress: What You Need to Know" (n.d.), healthyplace.healthology.com/focus_article.asp?f5mentalhealth&c5work_related_stress.
38. J.M. Hoobler, S.J. Wayne, and G. Lemmon, "Bosses' Perceptions of Family–Work Conflict and Women's Promotability: Glass Ceiling Effects," *Academy of Management Journal* 52 (2009), pp. 939–57.
39. A. Crouter, "Spillover from Family to Work: The Neglected Side of the Work–Family Interface," *Human Relations* 37 (1984), pp. 425–42; R.W. Rice, M.R. Frone, and D.B. McFarlin, "Work and Nonwork Conflict and the Perceived Quality of Life," *Journal of Organizational Behavior* 13 (1992), pp. 155–68.
40. R.G. Netemeyer, J.S. Boles, R. McMurrian, "Development and Validation of Work–Family Conflict and Family–Work Conflict Scales," *Journal of Applied Psychology* 81 (1996), pp. 400–410.
41. T.W.H. Ng and D.C. Feldman, "The Effects of Organizational and Community Embeddedness on Work-to-Family and Family-to-Work Conflict," *Journal of Applied Psychology* 97 (2012), pp. 1233–51.
42. S. Cohen, D.A. Tyrrell, and A.P. Smith, "Negative Life Events, Perceived Stress, Negative Affect, and Susceptibility to the Common Cold," *Journal of Personality and Social Psychology* 64 (1993), pp. 131–40.

43. T.H. Holmes and R.H. Rahe, "The Social Readjustment Rating Scale," *Journal of Psychosomatic Research* 11 (1967), pp. 213–18; U.S. Department of Health and Human Services, Office of the Surgeon General, "Mental Health: A Report of the Surgeon General" (n.d.), www.surgeongeneral.gov/library/mentalhealth/home.html.
44. E. Frauenheim and J. Marquez, "Reducing the Fear Factor," *Workforce Management*, November 18, 2008, pp. 17–22.
45. LePine et al., "Relationships Among Work and Non-work Challenge and Hindrance Stressors and Non-work and Work Criteria."
46. Lazarus and Folkman, *Stress, Appraisal, and Coping*.
47. S. Folkman, R.S. Lazarus, C. Dunkel-Schetter, A. Delongis, and R.J. Gruen, "Dynamics of a Stressful Encounter: Cognitive Appraisal, Coping, and Encounter Outcomes," *Journal of Personality and Social Psychology* 50 (1986), pp. 992–1003.
48. J.C. Latack and S.J. Havlovic, "Coping with Job Stress: A Conceptual Evaluation Framework for Coping Measures," *Journal of Organizational Behavior* 13 (1992), pp. 479–508.
49. Ibid.
50. *Global Relocation Trends, 2005 Survey Report* (Woodridge, IL: GMAC Global Relocation Services, 2006), www.gmacglobalrelocation.com/insight_support/global_relocation.asp.
51. J.S. Black, M. Mendenhall, and G. Oddou, "Toward a Comprehensive Model of International Adjustment: An Integration of Multiple Theoretical Perspectives," *Academy of Management Review* 16 (1991), pp. 291–317.
52. P. Bhaskar-Shrinivas, D.A. Harrison, M.A. Shaffer, and D.M. Luk, "Input-Based and Time-Based Models of International Adjustment: Meta-analytic Evidence and Theoretical Extensions," *Academy of Management Journal* 48 (2005), pp. 257–81.
53. M.E. Mendenhall, T.M. Kulmann, G.K. Stahl, and J.S. Osland, "Employee Development and Expatriate Assignments," in *Blackwell Handbook of Cross-cultural Management*, eds. M.J. Gannon and K.L. Newman (Malden, MA: Blackwell, 2002), pp. 155–84.
54. R.S. Lazarus, "Progress on a Cognitive–Motivational–Relational Theory of Emotion," *American Psychologist* 46 (1991), pp. 819–34.
55. C. Daniels, "The Last Taboo: It's Not Sex. It's Not Drinking. It's Stress—and It's Soaring," *Fortune*, October 28, 2002, pp. 136–44, www.proquest.com, retrieved March 27, 2007.
56. Miller and Miller, "Get a Life!"
57. H. Selye, *The Stress of Life* (New York: McGraw-Hill, 1976).
58. W.B. Cannon, "Stresses and Strains of Homeostasis," *American Journal of Medical Science* 189 (1935), pp. 1–14; D.L. Goldstein, *Stress, Catecholamines, & Cardiovascular Disease* (New York: Oxford University Press, 1995).
59. R.L. Kahn and P. Byosiere, "Stress in Organizations," in *Handbook of Industrial and Organizational Psychology*, Vol. 4, eds. M.D. Dunette, J.M.R. Hough, and H.C. Triandis (Palo Alto, CA: Consulting Psychologists Press, 1992), pp. 517–650.
60. R.S. Defrank and J.M. Ivancevich. "Stress on the Job: An Executive Update," *Academy of Management Executive* 12 (1998), pp. 55–66; C. Haran, "Do You Know Your Early Warning Stress Signals?," 2005, abcnews.go.com/Health/Healthology/story?id=421825.
61. M.C. Stöppler, "High Pressure Work Deadlines Raise Heart Attack Risk," stress.about.com/od/heartdissease/a/deadline.htm, retrieved October 1, 2005.
62. K. Leitner and M.G. Resch, "Do the Effects of Job Stressors on Health Persist over Time? A Longitudinal Study with Observational Stress Measures," *Journal of Occupational Health Psychology* 10 (2005), pp. 18–30.
63. Defrank and Ivancevich, "Stress on the Job"; Haran, "Do You Know?"
64. A. Pines and D. Kafry, "Occupational Tedium in the Social Services," *Social Work* 23 (1978), pp. 499–507.
65. "Mentally Tired Favre Tells Packers His Playing Career Is Over," ESPN.com, March 4, 2008, sports.espn.go.com/nfl/news/story?id=3276034.
66. "Brett Favre Retirement Press Conference Transcript—March 6," Packers.com, March 6, 2008, www.packers.com/news-and-events/article-1/Brett-Favre-Retirement-Press-Conference-Transcript---March-6/9e8481c7-5aa4-11df-a3b6-528cc843f916, retrieved June 8, 2015.
67. Defrank and Ivancevich, "Stress on the Job."
68. M. Friedman and R.H. Rosenman, *Type A Behavior and Your Heart* (New York: Knopf, 1974).
69. D.C. Ganster, "Type A Behavior and Occupational Stress. Job Stress: From Theory to Suggestion," *Journal of Organizational Behavior* Management 8 (1987), pp. 61–84.
70. Friedman and Rosenman, *Type A Behavior*; P.R. Yarnold and F.B. Bryant, "A Note on Measurement Issues in Type A Research: Let's Not Throw Out the Baby with the Bath Water," *Journal of Personality Assessment* 52 (1988), pp. 410–19.
71. R. Abush and E.J. Burkhead, "Job Stress in Midlife Working Women: Relationships Among Personality Type, Job Characteristics, and Job Tension," *Journal of Counseling Psychology* 31 (1984), pp. 36–44; M.J. Dearborn and J.E. Hastings, "Type A Personality as a Mediator of Stress and Strain in Employed Women," *Journal of Human Stress* 13 (1987), pp. 53–60; J.H. Howard, D.A. Cunningham, and P.A. Rechnitzer, "Role Ambiguity, Type A Behavior, and Job Satisfaction: Moderating Effects on Cardiovascular and Biochemical Responses Associated with Coronary Risk," *Journal of Applied Psychology* 71 (1986), pp. 95–101.
72. C.L. Cooper, P.J. Dewe, and M.P. O'Driscoll, *Organizational Stress* (Thousand Oaks, CA: Sage, 2001).
73. M.R. Fusilier, D.C. Ganster, and B.T. Mayes, "Effects of Social Support, Role Stress, and Locus of Control on Health," *Journal of Management* 13 (1987), pp. 517–28.
74. I. Nahum-Shani and P.A. Bamberger, "Explaining the Variable Effects of Social Support on Work-Based Stressor–Strain Relations: The Role of Perceived Pattern of Support Exchange," *Organizational Behavior and Human Decision Processes* 114 (2011), pp. 49–63.
75. S. Jayaratne, T. Tripodi, and W.A. Chess, "Perceptions of Emotional Support, Stress, and Strain by Male and Female Social Workers," *Social Work Research and Abstracts* 19 (1983), pp. 19–27; S. Kobasa, "Commitment and Coping in Stress Among Lawyers," *Journal of Personality and Social Psychology* 42 (1982), pp. 707–17; J.M. LaRocco and A.P. Jones, "Co-worker and Leader Support as Moderators of Stress–Strain Relationships in Work Situations," *Journal of Applied Psychology* 63 (1978), pp. 629–34.
76. Kahn and Byosiere, "Stress in Organizations."
77. LePine et al., "A Meta-analytic Test."
78. S. Cohen, "After Effects of Stress on Human Performance and Social Behavior: A Review of Research and Theory," *Psychological Bulletin* 88 (1980), pp. 82–108; E.R. Crawford, J.A. LePine, and B.L. Rich, "Linking Job Demands and Resources to Employee Engagement and Burnout: A Theoretical Extension and Meta-analytic Test," *Journal of Applied Psychology* 95 (2010), pp. 834–48.
79. Podsakoff et al., "Differential Challenge Stressor–Hindrance Stressor Relationships."
80. A.G. Bedeian and A. Armenakis, "A Path-analytic Study of the Consequences of Role Conflict and Ambiguity," *Academy of Management Journal* 24 (1981), pp. 417–24; J. Schaubroeck, J.L. Cotton, and K.R. Jennings, "Antecedents and Consequences of Role Stress: A Covariance Structure Analysis," *Journal of Organizational Behavior* 10 (1989), pp. 35–58.
81. LePine et al., "A Meta-analytic Test"; Podsakoff et al., "Differential Challenge Stressor–Hindrance Stressor Relationships."
82. Crawford, LePine, and Rich, "Linking Job Demands and Resources to Employee Engagement and Burnout."
83. Ibid.
84. M.A. Cavanaugh, W.R. Boswell, M.V. Roehling, and J.W. Boudreau, "An Empirical Examination of Self-Reported Work Stress Among U.S. Managers," *Journal of Applied Psychology* 85 (2000), pp. 65–74.

85. W.R. Boswell, J.B. Olson-Buchanan, and M.A. LePine, "The Relationship Between Work-Related Stress and Work Outcomes: The Role of Felt-Challenge and Psychological Strain," *Journal of Vocational Behavior* 64 (2004), pp. 165–81.
86. LePine et al., "Challenge and Hindrance Stress."
87. L. Myers, "Transforming Presenteeism into Productivity," *Workspan*, July 2009, pp. 40–43.
88. S. Miller, "Most Employees Underestimate Health Impact on Productivity," *HR Magazine*, June 2009, p. 20.
89. LePine et al., "Challenge and Hindrance Stress."
90. "Canadian Employers Rate Health Plans over Cash," *The Globe and Mail*, May 12, 2004.
91. A. Perkins, "Medical Costs: Saving Money by Reducing Stress," *Harvard Business Review* 72(6) (1994), p. 12.
92. S. Sauter, L. Murphy, M. Colligan, N. Swanson, J. Hurrell Jr., F. Scharf Jr., R. Sinclair, P. Grubb, L. Goldenhar, T. Alterman, J. Johnston, A. Hamilton, and J. Tisdale, "Is Your Boss Making You Sick?," abcnews.go.com/GMA/Careers/story?id=1251346&gma=true, retrieved October 27, 2005.
93. Defrank and Ivancevich, "Stress on the Job"; C.L. Cooper, "The Costs of Stress at Work," *The Safety & Health Practitioner* 19 (2001), pp. 24–26.
94. M.E. Burke, *2005 Benefits Survey Report* (Alexandria, VA: Society of *Human Resource Management* Research Department, 2005).
95. Miller and Miller, "Get a Life!"
96. R. Noe, J.R. Hollenbeck, B. Gerhart, P.M. Wright, and S. Steen, Fundamentals of *Human Resource Management*, 1st Canadian ed. (Toronto: McGraw-Hill Ryerson, 2006), p. 89.
97. J. Sahadi, "The World's Best Perk," CNNMoney.com, June 13, 2006, money.cnn.com/2006/06/13/commentary/everyday/sahadi/index.htm, retrieved May 8, 2009.
98. Ibid.
99. LePine et al., "A Meta-analytic Test"; Podsakoff et al., "Differential Challenge Stressor–Hindrance Stress Relationships."
100. S. Sonnentag and M. Frese, "Stress in Organizations," in W.C. Borman, D.R. Ilgen, and R.J. Klimoski, eds., *Comprehensive Handbook of Psychology*, Vol. 12: *Industrial and Organizational Psychology* (New York: Wiley, 2003), pp. 453–91.
101. "2002–03 Accountability Report," www.vancity.com/AboutUs/OurBusiness/OurReports/AnnualReports/0203AccountabilityReport/CommitmentFour/#six, retrieved January 9, 2012.
102. R. Eisenberger, R. Huntington, S. Hutchison, and D. Sowa, "Perceived Organizational Support," *Journal of Applied Psychology* 71 (1986), pp. 500–07; L. Rhoades, and R. Eisenberger, "Perceived Organizational Support: A Review of the Literature," *Journal of Applied Psychology* 87 (2002), pp. 698–714.
103. L.R. Murphy, "Stress Management in Work Settings: A Critical Review of Health Effects," *American Journal of Health Promotion* 11 (1996), pp. 112–35.
104. Neufeld, "Work-Related Stress."
105. Haran, "Do You Know?"
106. Ibid.
107. Daniels, "The Last Taboo."
108. Sonnentag and Frese, "Stress in Organizations."
109. Neufeld, "Work-Related Stress."
110. K. Bachmann, "Health Promotion Programs at Work: A Frivolous Cost or a Sound Investment?" (Conference Board of Canada, October 2002).
111. Ibid.

Chapter 7

1. Ashlee Vance, "The Man Who Ate the Internet," *Bloomberg Businessweek*, May 9, 2013, pp. 56–62.
2. M. Boyle, "Questions for . . . Reed Hastings," *Fortune*, May 23, 2007, money.cnn.com/magazines/fortune/fortune_archive/2007/05/28/100034248/index.htm, retrieved June 20, 2008.
3. M. Conlin, "Netflix: Flex to the Max," *Businessweek*, September 24, 2007, pp. 72–74.
4. Ibid.
5. R.M. Steers, R.T. Mowday, and D. Shapiro, "The Future of Work Motivation," *Academy of Management Review* 29 (2004), pp. 379–87; G.P. Latham, *Work Motivation: History, Theory, Research, and Practice* (Thousand Oaks, CA: Sage, 2006).
6. G.P. Latham and C.C. Pinder, "Work Motivation Theory and Research at the Dawn of the Twenty-First Century," *Annual Review of Psychology* 56 (2005), pp. 485–516.
7. N.R.F. Maier, *Psychology in Industry*, 2nd ed. (Boston: Houghton Mifflin, 1955).
8. W.A. Kahn, "Psychological Conditions of Personal Engagement and Disengagement at Work," *Academy of Management Journal* 33 (1990), pp. 692–724.
9. B.L. Rich, J.A. LePine, and E.R. Crawford, "Job Engagement: Antecedents and Effects on Job Performance," *Academy of Management Journal* 52 (2009), pp. 617–35; W.B. Schaufeli, M. Salanova, V. Gonzalez-Roma, and A.B. Bakker, "The Measurement of Engagement and Burnout: A Two Sample Confirmatory Factor Analytic Approach," *Journal of Happiness Studies* 3 (2002), pp. 71–92; W.H. Macy and B. Schneider, "The Meaning of Employee Engagement," *Industrial and Organizational Psychology* 1 (2008), pp. 3–30.
10. Ibid.; N.P. Rothbard, "Enriching or Depleting? The Dynamics of Engagement in Work and Family Roles," *Administrative Science Quarterly* 46 (2001), pp. 655–84.
11. J.K. Harter, F.L. Schmidt, and T.H. Hayes, "Business-Unit-Level Relationship Between Employee Satisfaction, Employee Engagement, and Business Outcomes: A Meta-analysis," *Journal of Applied Psychology* 87 (2002), pp. 268–79.
12. E. O'Boyle and J. Harter, "State of the American Workplace," Gallup.com, June 29, 2013, www.gallup.com/strategicconsulting/163007/state-american-workplace.aspx.
13. S. Woolley, "New Priorities for Employers," *Bloomberg Businessweek*, September 13–19, 2010, p. 54.
14. A.B. Bakker and D. Xanthopoulou, "The Crossover of Daily Work Engagement: Test of an Actor–Partner Interdependence Model," *Journal of Applied Psychology* 94 (2009), pp. 1562–71.
15. V.H. Vroom, *Work and Motivation* (New York: Wiley, 1964).
16. Ibid.; see also E.L. Thorndike, "The Law of Effect," *American Journal of Psychology* 39 (1964), pp. 212–22; C.L. Hull, *Essentials of Behavior* (New Haven: Yale University Press, 1951); L. Postman, "The History and Present Status of the Law of Effect," *Psychological Bulletin* 44 (1947), pp. 489–563.
17. A. Bandura, "Self-Efficacy: Toward a Unifying Theory of Behavioral Change," *Psychological Review* 84 (1977), pp. 191–215.
18. J. Brockner, *Self-Esteem at Work* (Lexington, MA: Lexington Books, 1988).
19. Bandura, "Self-Efficacy."
20. Ibid.
21. Ibid.
22. M.E. Gist and T.R. Mitchell, "Self-Efficacy: A Theoretical Analysis of Its Determinants and Malleability," *Academy of Management Review* 17 (1992), pp. 183–211.
23. Vroom, *Work and Motivation.*
24. C.C. Pinder, *Work Motivation* (Glenview, IL: Scott, Foresman, 1984).
25. J. Stillings and L. Snyder, "Up Front: The Stat," *Businessweek*, July 4, 2005, p. 12.
26. T. Henneman, "Cracks in the Ice," *Workforce Management*, November 2010, pp. 30–36.
27. Henneman, "Cracks in the Ice."
28. Vroom, *Work and Motivation.*
29. Pinder, *Work Motivation.*
30. F.J. Landy and W.S. Becker, "Motivation Theory Reconsidered," in *Research in Organizational Behavior*, Vol. 9, eds. B.M. Staw and L.L. Cummings (Greenwich, CT: JAI Press, 1987), pp. 1–38; J.C. Naylor, D.R. Pritchard, and D.R. Ilgen, *A Theory of Behavior in Organizations* (New York: Academic Press, 1980).
31. A.H. Maslow, "A Theory of Human Motivation," *Psychological Review* 50 (1943), pp. 370–96; C.P. Alderfer, "An Empirical Test of a New Theory of Human Needs," *Organizational Behavior and Human Performance* 4 (1969), pp. 142–75.
32. A.H. Maslow, "A Theory of Human Motivation."
33. Ibid.

34. Ibid.
35. Ibid.
36. Ibid.
37. Ibid.
38. C.P. Alderfer, "An Empirical Test of a New Theory of Human Needs," *Organizational Behavior and Human Performance* 4 (1969), pp. 142–75.
39. E.L. Deci and R.M. Ryan, "The 'What' and 'Why' of Goal Pursuits: Human Needs and the Self-Determination of Behavior," *Psychological Inquiry* 11(4) (2000), pp. 227–68; M. Gagné and E.L. Deci, "Self-Determination Theory and Work Motivation," *Journal of Organizational Behavior* 26(4) (2005), pp. 331–62; R.M. Ryan and E.L. Deci, "Self-Determination Theory and the Facilitation of Intrinsic Motivation, Social Development, and Well-Being," *American Psychologist* 55(1) (2000), pp. 68–78.
40. S.L. Rynes, B. Gerhart, and K.A. Minette, "The Importance of Pay in Employee Motivation: Discrepancies Between What People Say and What They Do," *Human Resource Management* 43 (2004), pp. 381–94.
41. T.R. Mitchell and A.E. Mickel, "The Meaning of Money: An Individual Differences Perspective," *Academy of Management Review* 24 (1999), pp. 568–78.
42. T.L. Tang, "The Meaning of Money Revisited," *Journal of Organizational Behavior* 13 (1992), pp. 197–202; A.E. Mickel and L.A. Barron, "Getting 'More Bang for the Buck,'" *Journal of Management Inquiry* 17 (2008), pp. 329–38.
43. T.L. Tang, "The Development of a Short Money Ethic Scale: Attitudes Toward Money and Pay Satisfaction Revisited," *Personality and Individual Differences* 19 (1995), pp. 809–16.
44. Tang, "The Meaning of Money Revisited."
45. Ibid.; Tang, "The Development of a Short Money Ethic Scale."
46. Tang, "The Development of a Short Money Ethic Scale."
47. Vroom, *Work and Motivation*; E.E. Lawler III and J.L. Suttle, "Expectancy Theory and Job Behavior," *Organizational Behavior and Human Performance* 9 (1973), pp. 482–503.
48. E.A. Locke, "Toward a Theory of Task Motivation and Incentives," *Organizational Behavior and Human Performance* 3 (1968), pp. 157–89.
49. E.A. Locke, K.N. Shaw, L.M. Saari, and G.P. Latham, "Goal Setting and Task Performance: 1969–1980," *Psychological Bulletin* 90 (1981), pp. 125–52.
50. E.A. Locke and G.P. Latham, *A Theory of Goal Setting and Task Performance* (Englewood Cliffs, NJ: Prentice Hall, 1990).
51. Ibid.
52. Ibid.
53. Ibid.; see also E.A. Locke and G.P. Latham, "Building a Practically Useful Theory of Goal Setting and Task Motivation: A 35-Year Odyssey," *American Psychologist* 57 (2002), pp. 705–17; G.P. Latham, "Motivate Employee Performance Through Goal-Setting," in *Blackwell Handbook of Principles of Organizational Behavior*, eds. E.A. Locke (Malden, MA: Blackwell, 2000), pp. 107–19.
54. Locke and Latham, *A Theory of Goal Setting.*
55. Locke et al., "Goal Setting and Task Performance."
56. Ibid.; Locke and Latham, *A Theory of Goal Setting;* Locke and Latham, "Building a Practically Useful Theory."
57. R.E. Wood, A.J. Mento, and E.A. Locke, "Task Complexity as a Moderator of Goal Effects: A Meta-analysis," *Journal of Applied Psychology* 72 (1987), pp. 416–25.
58. Ibid.
59. A. Barrett, "Cracking the Whip at Wyeth," *Businessweek*, February 6, 2006, pp. 70–71.
60. J.R. Hollenbeck and H.J. Klein, "Goal Commitment and the Goal-Setting Process: Problems, Prospects, and Proposal for Future Research," *Journal of Applied Psychology* 72 (1987), pp. 212–20; see also Locke et al., "Goal Setting and Task Performance."
61. Ibid.; see also E.A. Locke and G.P. Latham, "Building a Practically Useful Theory of Goal Setting and Task Motivation: A 35-Year Odyssey," *American Psychologist* 57 (2002), pp. 705–17; G.P. Latham, "Motivate Employee Performance Through Goal-Setting," in E.A. Locke, ed., *Blackwell Handbook of Principles of Organizational Behavior* (Malden, MA: Blackwell, 2000), pp. 107–19.
62. Locke and Latham, *A Theory of Goal Setting.*
63. Ibid.; Locke and Latham, *A Theory of Goal Setting*; Locke and Latham, "Building a Practically Useful Theory."
64. R.E. Wood, A.J. Mento, and E.A. Locke, "Task Complexity as a Moderator of Goal Effects: A Meta-analysis," *Journal of Applied Psychology* 72 (1987), pp. 416–25.
65. Ibid.
66. J.R. Hollenbeck and H.J. Klein, "Goal Commitment and the Goal-Setting Process: Problems, Prospects, and Proposal for Future Research," *Journal of Applied Psychology* 72 (1987), pp. 212–20; see also Locke et al., "Goal Setting and Task Performance."
67. H.J. Klein, M.J. Wesson, J.R. Hollenbeck, and B.J. Alge, "Goal Commitment and the Goal-Setting Process: Conceptual Clarification and Empirical Synthesis," *Journal of Applied Psychology* 84 (1999), pp. 885–96; J.J. Donovan and D.J. Radosevich, "The Moderating Role of Goal Commitment on the Goal Difficulty–Performance Relationship: A Meta-analytic Review and Critical Reanalysis," *Journal of Applied Psychology* 83 (1998), pp. 308–15.
68. Hollenbeck and Klein, "Goal Commitment and the Goal-Setting Process"; Klein et al., "Goal Commitment"; E.A. Locke, G.P. Latham, and M. Erez, "The Determinants of Goal Commitment," *Academy of Management Review* 13 (1988), pp. 23–29; G.P. Latham, "The Motivational Benefits of Goal-Setting," *Academy of Management Executive* 18 (2004), pp. 126–29.
69. K.N. Shaw, "Changing the Goal Setting Process at Microsoft," *Academy of Management Executive* 18 (2004), pp. 139–42.
70. Ibid.
71. M. Erez and P.C. Earley, "Comparative Analysis of Goal-Setting Strategies Across Cultures," *Journal of Applied Psychology* 72 (1987), pp. 658–65; P.G. Audia and S. Tams, "Goal Setting, Performance Appraisal, and Feedback Across Cultures," in M.J. Gannon and K.L. Newman, eds., *Blackwell Handbook of Cross-Cultural Management* (Malden, MA: Blackwell, 2002), pp. 142–54.
72. Ibid.
73. Ibid.
74. Ibid.
75. J.S. Adams and W.B. Rosenbaum, "The Relationship of Worker Productivity to Cognitive Dissonance About Wage Inequities," *Journal of Applied Psychology* 46 (1962), pp. 161–64.
76. J.S. Adams, "Inequity in Social Exchange," in *Advances in Experimental Social Psychology*, Vol. 2, ed. L. Berkowitz (New York: Academic Press, 1965), pp. 267–99; G.C. Homans, *Social Behaviour: Its Elementary Forms* (London: Routledge & Kegan Paul, 1961).
77. Ibid.
78. Adams, "Inequity in Social Exchange."
79. Ibid.
80. J. Greenberg, "Employee Theft as a Reaction to Underpayment Inequity: The Hidden Cost of Paycuts," *Journal of Applied Psychology* 75 (1990), pp. 561–68; J. Greenberg, "Stealing in the Name of Justice: Informational and Interpersonal Moderators of Theft Reactions to Underpayment Inequity," *Organizational Behavior and Human Decision Processes* 54 (1993), pp. 81–103.
81. Adams, "Inequity in Social Exchange."
82. R.W. Scholl, E.A. Cooper, and J.F. McKenna, "Referent Selection in Determining Equity Perceptions: Differential Effects on Behavioral and Attitudinal Outcomes," *Personnel Psychology* 40 (1987), pp. 113–24.
83. Ibid.
84. Ibid.; see also R.H. Finn and S.M. Lee, "Salary Equity: Its Determination, Analysis, and Correlates," *Journal of Applied Psychology* 56 (1972), pp. 283–92.
85. Scholl et al., "Referent Selection."
86. A. Colella, R.L. Paetzold, A. Zardkoohi, and M. Wesson, "Exposing Pay Secrecy," *Academy of Management Review* 32 (2007), pp. 55–71.
87. Ibid.
88. K.W. Thomas and B.A. Velthouse, "Cognitive Elements of Empowerment: An 'Interpretive' Model of Intrinsic Task

Motivation," *Academy of Management Review* 15 (1990), pp. 666–81.

89. E.L. Deci and R.M. Ryan, "The 'What' and 'Why' of Goal Pursuits: Human Needs and the Self-Determination of Behavior," *Psychological Inquiry* 11(4) (2000), pp. 227–68; M. Gagné and E.L. Deci, "Self-Determination Theory and Work Motivation," *Journal of Organizational Behavior* 26(4) (2005), pp. 331–62; R.M. Ryan and E.L. Deci, "Self-Determination Theory and the Facilitation of Intrinsic Motivation, Social Development, and Well-Being," *American Psychologist* 55(1) (2000), pp. 68–78.
90. J.R. Hackman and G.R. Oldham, *Work Redesign* (Reading, MA: Addison-Wesley, 1980).
91. Thomas and Velthouse, "Cognitive Elements of Empowerment"; G.M. Spreitzer, "Psychological Empowerment in the Workplace: Dimensions, Measurement, and Validation," *Academy of Management Journal* 38 (1995), pp. 1442–65; R.M. Ryan and E.L. Deci, *Intrinsic Motivation and Self-Determination in Human Behavior* (New York: Plenum, 1985); Hackman and Oldham, *Work Redesign.*
92. K.W. Thomas, *Intrinsic Motivation at Work: Building Energy and Commitment* (San Francisco: Berrett-Koehler, 2000).
93. Ibid.
94. J.S. Bunderson and J.A. Thompson, "The Call of the Wild: Zookeepers, Callings, and the Double-Edged Sword of Deeply Meaningful Work," *Administrative Science Quarterly* 54 (2009), pp. 32–57; R.D. Duffy and W.E. Sedlacek, "The Presence of and Search for a Calling: Connections to Career Development," *Journal of Vocational Behavior* 70 (2007), pp. 590–601; T. Hagmaier and A.E. Abele, "The Multidimensionality of Calling: Conceptualization, Measurement and a Bicultural Perspective," *Journal of Vocational Behavior* 81 (2012). pp. 39–51.
95. Thomas and Velthouse, "Cognitive Elements of Empowerment"; Spreitzer, "Psychological Empowerment."
96. Thomas, *Intrinsic Motivation at Work.*
97. Thomas and Velthouse, "Cognitive Elements of Empowerment"; Spreitzer, "Psychological Empowerment."
98. Thomas, *Intrinsic Motivation at Work.*
99. Thomas and Velthouse, "Cognitive Elements of Empowerment."
100. Thomas, *Intrinsic Motivation at Work.*
101. S. Glucksberg, "The Influence of Strength of Drive on Functional Fixedness and Perceptual Recognition," *Journal of Experimental Psychology* 63 (1962), pp. 36–41.
102. L. Gerdes, "Get Ready for a Pickier Workforce," *Businessweek*, September 18, 2006, p. 82.
103. S. Hamm, "Young and Impatient in India," *Businessweek*, January 28, 2008, pp. 45–48.
104. A.D. Stajkovic and F. Luthans, "Self-Efficacy and Work-Related Performance: A Meta-analysis," *Psychological Bulletin* 124 (1998), pp. 240–61.
105. Wood et al., "Task Complexity as a Moderator."
106. W. Van Eerde and H. Thierry, "Vroom's Expectancy Models and Work-Related Criteria: A Meta-analysis," *Journal of Applied Psychology* 81 (1996), pp. 575–86.
107. Y. Cohen-Charash and P.E. Spector, "The Role of Justice in Organizations: A Meta-analysis," *Organizational Behavior and Human Decision Processes* 86 (2001), pp. 287–321; J.A. Colquitt, D.E. Conlon, M.J. Wesson, C.O.L.H. Porter, and K.Y. Ng, "Justice at the Millennium: A Meta-analytic Review of 25 Years of Organizational Justice Research," *Journal of Applied Psychology* 86 (2001), pp. 425–45.
108. Ibid.
109. Ibid.
110. Ibid.
111. E.E. Lawler III, *Rewarding Excellence: Pay Strategies for the New Economy* (San Francisco: Jossey-Bass, 2000); B. Gerhart, S.L. Rynes, and I.S. Fulmer, "Pay and Performance: Individuals, Groups, and Executives," *Academy of Management Annals*, 3 (2009), pp. 251–315.
112. Ibid.; see also C.C. Durham and K.M. Bartol, "Pay for Performance," in *Handbook of Principles of Organizational Behavior*, ed. E.A. Locke (Malden, MA: Blackwell, 2000), pp. 150–65; B. Gerhart, H.B. Minkoff, and R.N. Olsen, "Employee Compensation: Theory, Practice, and Evidence," in *Handbook of Human Resource Management*, eds. G.R. Ferris, S.D. Rosen, and D.T. Barnum (Malden, MA: Blackwell, 1995), pp. 528–47.
113. Ibid.
114. Gerhart et al., "Pay and Performance"; K. Cohen, "The Pulse of the Profession: 2006–2007 Budget Survey," *Workspan*, September 2006, pp. 23–26.
115. F. Hansen, "Merit-Pay Payoff?," *Workforce Management*, November 3, 2008, pp. 33–39.
116. Ibid.
117. G. Latham and S. Latham, "Overlooking Theory and Research in Performance Appraisal at One's Peril: Much Done, More to Do," in *Industrial and Organizational Psychology: Linking Theory with Practice*, eds. C.L. Cooper and E.A. Locke (Oxford, UK: Blackwell, 2000), pp. 199–215.
118. Ibid.
119. K. Sulkowicz, "Straight Talk at Review Time," *Businessweek*, September 10, 2007, p. 16.
120. J. McGregor, "The Struggle to Measure Performance," *Businessweek*, January 9, 2006, pp. 26–28.
121. S.E. Scullen, P.K. Bergey, and L. Aiman-Smith, "Forced Distribution Rating Systems and the Improvement of Workforce Potential: A Baseline Simulation," *Personnel Psychology* 58 (2005), pp. 1–32.
122. Vance, "The Man Who Ate the Internet."
123. Ibid.
124. R. Hastings, "How to Set Your Employees Free," *Bloomberg Businessweek*, April 12, 2012, pp. 62.
125. Vance, "The Man Who Ate the Internet."
126. Ibid.

Chapter 8

1. S. Holmes, "Nike Goes for the Green," *Businessweek*, September 25, 2006, pp. 106–108.
2. E. Levenson, "Citizen Nike," *Fortune*, November 24, 2008, pp. 165–70.
3. Ibid.
4. Ibid.
5. Ibid.
6. D. Roberts and P. Engardio, "Secrets, Lies, and Sweatshops," *Businessweek*, November 27, 2006, pp. 50–58.
7. Ibid.; Levenson, "Citizen Nike."
8. Levenson, "Citizen Nike."
9. V.P. Rindova, I.O. Williamson, A.P. Petkova, and J.M. Sever, "Being Good or Being Known: An Empirical Examination of the Dimensions, Antecedents, and Consequences of Organizational Reputation," *Academy of Management Journal* 48 (2005), pp. 1033–49.
10. E. Frauenheim, "Does Reputation Matter?," *Workforce Management*, November 20, 2006, pp. 22–26.
11. "Canada's 50 Best Employers of 2014," *MacLean's*, November 7, 2014, retrieved January 23, 2015. www.macleans.ca/work/bestcompanies/canadas-50-best-employers-of-2014.
12. G. Dietz and D.N. Den Hartog, "Measuring Trust Inside Organizations," *Personnel Review* 35 (2006), pp. 557–88; R.M. Kramer, "Trust and Distrust in Organizations: Emerging Perspectives, Enduring Questions," *Annual Review of Psychology* 50 (1999), pp. 569–98; R.C. Mayer, J.H. Davis, and F.D. Schoorman, "An Integrative Model of Organizational Trust," *Academy of Management Review* 20 (1995), pp. 709–34; S.A. Robinson, "Trust and Breach of the Psychological Contract," *Administrative Science Quarterly* 41 (1996), pp. 574–99; D.M. Rousseau, S.B. Sitkin, R.S. Burt, and C. Camerer, "Not So Different After All: A Cross-discipline View of Trust," *Academy of Management Review* 23 (1998), pp. 393–404; R. Searle, A. Weibel, and D.N. Den Hartog, "Employee Trust in Organizational Contexts," in G.P. Hodgkinson and J.K. Ford, eds., *International Review of Industrial and Organizational Psychology*, Vol. 26 (2011), pp. 143–191; E.M. Whitener, "Do 'High Commitment' Human Resource Practices Affect Employee Commitment? A Cross-level Analysis Using Hierarchical Linear Modelling," *Journal of Management* 27 (2001), pp. 515–35; E.M. Whitener, S.E. Brodt, M.A. Korsgaard, and J.M. Werner, "Managers as Initiators of Trust: An Exchange Relationship Framework for Understanding Managerial Trustworthy Behaviour," *Academy of Management Review* 23 (1998), pp. 513–530.
13. Ibid.
14. Ibid.

15. G. Colvin, "The World's Most Admired Companies," *Fortune*, March 16, 2009, pp. 75–78.
16. J. Greenberg, "A Taxonomy of Organizational Justice Theories," *Academy of Management Review* 12 (1987), pp. 9–22.
17. E.A. Lind, "Fairness Heuristic Theory: Justice Judgments as Pivotal Cognitions in Organizational Relations," in J. Greenberg and R. Cropanzano, eds., *Advances in Organizational Justice* (Stanford, CA: Stanford University Press, 2001), pp. 56–88; K. Van den Bos, "Fairness Heuristic Theory: Assessing the Information to Which People Are Reacting Has a Pivotal Role in Understanding Organizational Justice," in S. Gilliland, D. Steiner, and D. Skarlicki, eds., *Theoretical and Cultural Perspectives on Organizational Justice* (Greenwich, CT: Information Age Publishing, 2001), pp. 63–84; K. Van den Bos, E.A. Lind, and H.A.M. Wilke, "The Psychology of Procedural and Distributive Justice Viewed from the Perspective of Fairness Heuristic Theory," in R. Cropanzano, ed., *Justice in the Workplace*, Vol. 2 (Mahwah, NJ: Erlbaum, 2001), pp. 49–66.
18. L.K., Treviño, G.R. Weaver, and S.J. Reynolds, "Behavioral Ethics in Organizations: A Review," *Journal of Management* 32 (2006), pp. 951–90.
19. M.J. Douglas, "What Are the Most-Trusted Occupations?," Monster.ca, March 27, 2006; "Canada's Most Trusted Occupations," *Reader's Digest Canada Magazine*, May 2012, www.readersdigest.ca/magazine/2013-trust-poll/canadas-most-trusted-professions-2012-trust-poll-results, retrieved January 23 2015.
20. D.J. McAllister, "Affect- and Cognition-Based Trust as Foundations for Interpersonal Cooperation in Organizations," *Academy of Management Journal* 38 (1995), pp. 24–59.
21. Ibid.
22. Mayer et al., "An Integrative Model"; J.B. Rotter, "A New Scale for the Measurement of Interpersonal Trust," *Journal of Personality* 35 (1967), pp. 651–65; J.B. Rotter, "Generalized Expectancies for Interpersonal Trust," *American Psychologist* 26 (1971), pp. 443–52; J.B. Rotter, "Interpersonal Trust, Trustworthiness, and Gullibility," *American Psychologist* 35 (1980), pp. 1–7.
23. M. Rosenberg, "Misanthropy and Political Ideology," *American Sociological Review* 21 (1956), pp. 690–95; L.S. Wrightsman Jr., "Measurement of Philosophies of Human Nature," *Psychological Reports* 14 (1964), pp. 743–51.
24. Mayer et al., "An Integrative Model."
25. W.H. Jones, L.L. Couch, and S. Scott, "Trust and Betrayal: The Psychology of Getting Along and Getting Ahead," in *Handbook of Personality Psychology*, eds. R. Hogan, J.S. Johnson, and S.R. Briggs (San Diego, CA: Academic Press, 1997), pp. 465–82.
26. L.C. Stack, "Trust," in *Dimensionality of Personality*, eds. H. London and J.E. Exner Jr. (New York: Wiley, 1978), pp. 561–99.
27. W.M. Webb and P. Worchel, "Trust and Distrust," in *Psychology of Intergroup Relations*, eds. S. Worchel and W.G. Austin (Chicago: Nelson-Hall, 1986), pp. 213–28; E.H. Erickson, *Childhood and Society*, 2nd ed. (New York: Norton, 1963).
28. Stack, "Trust."
29. Mayer et al., "An Integrative Model."
30. McAllister, "Affect- and Cognition-Based Trust as Foundations for Interpersonal Cooperation in Organizations"; R.J. Lewicki and B.B. Bunker, "Developing and Maintaining Trust in Work Relationships," in *Trust in Organizations: Frontiers of Theory and Research*, eds. R.M. Kramer and T.R. Tyler (Thousand Oaks, CA: Sage, 1996), pp. 114–39.
31. Mayer et al., "An Integrative Model."
32. Ibid.; J.J. Gabarro, "The Development of Trust, Influence, and Expectations," in *Interpersonal Behavior: Communication and Understanding in Relationships*, eds. G. Athos and J.J. Gabarro (Englewood Cliffs, NJ: Prentice Hall, 1978), pp. 290–303.
33. Mayer et al., "An Integrative Model."
34. Ibid.
35. J. Marquez, "Kindness Pays . . . Or Does It?," *Workforce Management*, June 25, 2007, pp. 41–49.
36. Ibid.
37. Mayer et al., "An Integrative Model."
38. T.A. Wright and J. Goodstein, "Character Is Not 'Dead' in Management Research: A Review of Individual Character and Organizational-Level Virtue," *Journal of Management* 33 (2007), pp. 928–58; Gabarro, "The Development of Trust, Influence, and Expectations."
39. Mayer et al., "An Integrative Model"; T. Simons, "Behavioral Integrity: The Perceived Alignment between Managers' Words and Deeds as a Research Focus," *Organization Science* 13 (2002), pp. 18–35; B.R. Dineen, R.J. Lewicki, and E.C. Tomlinson, "Supervisory Guidance and Behavioral Integrity: Relationships with Employee Citizenship and Deviant Behavior," *Journal of Applied Psychology* 91 (2006), pp. 622–35.
40. Dineen et al., "Supervisory Guidance"; S. Bates, "Poll: Employees Skeptical About Management Actions," *HR Magazine*, June 2002, p. 12.
41. P. Lencioni, "The Power of Saying 'We Blew It,'" *Bloomberg Businessweek*, February 22, 2010, p. 84.
42. A.L. Penenberg, "Doctor Love," *Fast Company*, July/August 2010, pp. 78–83, 113.
43. C.E. Naquin, T.R. Kurtzerg, and L.Y. Belkin, "The Finer Points of Lying Online: E-mail Versus Pen and Paper," *Journal of Applied Psychology* 95 (2010), pp. 387–94.
44. D. Stead, ". . . And I Invented Velcro," *Businessweek*, August 4, 2008, p. 15.
45. Penenberg, "Doctor Love."
46. McAllister, "Affect- and Cognition-Based Trust"; Lewicki and Bunker, "Developing and Maintaining Trust"; J.D. Lewis and A. Weigert, "Trust as a Social Reality," *Social Forces* 63 (1985), pp. 967–85.
47. McAllister, "Affect- and Cognition-Based Trust."
48. Lind, "Fairness Heuristic Theory: Assessing"; Van den Bos, "Fairness Heuristic Theory: Justice"; Van den Bos et al., "The Psychology of Procedural and Distributive Justice."
49. J.S. Adams, "Inequity in Social Exchange," in *Advances in Experimental Social Psychology*, Vol. 2, ed. L. Berkowitz (New York: Academic Press, 1965), pp. 267–99; G.S. Leventhal, "The Distribution of Rewards and Resources in Groups and Organizations," in *Advances in Experimental Social Psychology*, Vol. 9, eds. L. Berkowitz and W. Walster (New York: Academic Press, 1976), pp. 91–131.
50. Leventhal, "The Distribution of Rewards."
51. Ibid.
52. G.S. Leventhal, "What Should Be Done with Equity Theory? New Approaches to the Study of Fairness in Social Relationships," in *Social Exchange: Advances in Theory and Research*, eds. K. Gergen, M. Greenberg, and R. Willis (New York: Plenum Press, 1980), pp. 27–55; J. Thibaut and L. Walker, *Procedural Justice: A Psychological Analysis* (Hillsdale, NJ: Erlbaum, 1975).
53. R. Folger, "Distributive and Procedural Justice: Combined Impact of 'Voice' and Improvement on Experienced Inequity," *Journal of Personality and Social Psychology* 35 (1977), pp. 108–19.
54. J.A. Colquitt, D.E. Conlon, M.J. Wesson, C.O.L.H. Porter, and K.Y. Ng, "Justice at the Millennium: A Meta-analytic Review of 25 Years of Organizational Justice Research," *Journal of Applied Psychology* 86 (2001), pp. 425–45.
55. T.R. Tyler, K.A. Rasinski, and N. Spodick, "Influence of Voice on Satisfaction with Leaders: Exploring the Meaning of Process Control," *Journal of Personality and Social Psychology* 48 (1985), pp. 72–81; P.C., Earley and E.A. Lind, "Procedural Justice and Participation in Task Selection: The Role of Control in Mediating Justice Judgments," *Journal of Personality and Social Psychology* 52 (1987), pp. 1148–60; E.A. Lind, R. Kanfer, and P.C. Earley, "Voice, Control, and Procedural Justice: Instrumental and Noninstrumental Concerns in Fairness Judgments," *Journal of Personality and Social Psychology* 59 (1990), pp. 952–59; M.A. Korsgaard and L. Roberson. "Procedural Justice in Performance Evaluation: The Role of Instrumental and Non-instrumental Voice in Performance Appraisal Discussions," *Journal of Management* 21 (1995), pp. 657–69.
56. Leventhal, "What Should Be Done with Equity Theory?"
57. R.A. Noe, J.R. Hollenbeck, B. Gerhart, P.M. Wright, and S. Steen, Fundamentals of *Human Resource Management*, Canadian ed. (McGraw-Hill Ryerson: Toronto, 2006), pp. 42–46.

58. Ibid.
59. "Canada's Best Diversity Employers 2011," Mediacorp Canada Inc., www.canadastop100.com/diversity, retrieved June 13, 2011. Canada's Best Diversity Employers is a trademark of Mediacorp Canada Inc.
60. Signed letter to Mr. Tony Keller, Managing Editor, Special Projects, *Maclean's* magazine, August 14, 2006, from Dalhousie University, McMaster University, Simon Fraser University, University of Alberta, University of British Columbia, University of Calgary, University of Lethbridge, University of Manitoba, Université de Montréal, University of Ottawa, and University of Toronto.
61. J. Brockner and B.M. Wiesenfeld, "An Integrative Framework for Explaining Reactions to Decisions: Interactive Effects of Outcomes and Procedures," *Psychological Bulletin* 120 (1996), pp. 189–208.
62. Ibid.
63. Colquitt et al., "Justice at the Millennium"; Y. Cohen-Charash and P.E. Spector, "The Role of Justice in Organizations: A Meta-analysis," *Organizational Behavior and Human Decision Processes* 86 (2001), pp. 278–321.
64. R.J. Bies and J.F. Moag, "Interactional Justice: Communication Criteria of Fairness," in *Research on Negotiations in Organizations*, Vol. 1, eds. R.J. Lewicki, B.H. Sheppard, and M.H. Bazerman (Greenwich, CT: JAI Press, 1986), pp. 43–55; J. Greenberg, "The Social Side of Fairness: Interpersonal and Informational Classes of Organizational Justice," in *Justice in the Workplace: Approaching Fairness in Human Resource Management*, ed. R. Cropanzano (Hillsdale, NJ: Erlbaum, 1993), pp. 79–103.
65. R.J. Bies, "Interactional (In)justice: The Sacred and the Profane," in *Advances in Organizational Justice*, eds. J. Greenberg and R. Cropanzano (Stanford, CA: Stanford University Press, 2001), pp. 85–108.
66. B.J. Tepper, "Consequences of Abusive Supervision," *Academy of Management Journal* 43 (2000), pp. 178–90.
67. A.C.H. Schat, M.R. Frone, and E.K. Kelloway, "Prevalence of Workplace Aggression in the U.S. Workforce: Findings from a National Study," in *Handbook of Workplace Violence*, eds. E.K. Kelloway, J. Barling, and J.J. Hurrell (Thousand Oaks, CA: Sage, 2006), pp. 47–89.
68. B.J. Tepper, M.K. Duffy, C.A. Henle, and L.S. Lambert, "Procedural Injustice, Victim Precipitation, and Abusive Supervision," *Personnel Psychology* 28 (2006), pp. 101–23.
69. B.J. Tepper, "Abusive Supervision in Work Organizations: Review, Synthesis, and Research Agenda," *Journal of Management* 33 (2007), pp. 261–89.
70. M.S. Mitchell and M.L. Ambrose, "Abusive Supervision and Workplace Deviance and the Moderating Effects of Negative Reciprocity Beliefs," *Journal of Applied Psychology* 92 (2007), pp. 1159–68; B.J. Tepper, C.A. Henle, L.S. Lambert, R.A. Giacalone, and M.K. Duffy, "Abusive Supervision and Subordinates' Organizational Deviance," *Journal of Applied Psychology* 93 (2008), pp. 721–32; B.J. Tepper, J.C. Carr, D.M. Breaux, S. Geider, C. Hu, and W. Hua, "Abusive Supervision, Intentions to Quit, and Employees' Workplace Deviance: A Power/Dependence Analysis," *Organizational Behavior and Human Decision Processes* 109 (2009), pp. 156–67.
71. A.G. Miner, T.M. Glomb, and C. Hulin, "Experience Sampling Mode and Its Correlates at Work," *Journal of Occupational and Organizational Psychology* 78 (2005), pp. 171–93.
72. S.W. Gilliland, L. Benson, and D.H. Schepers, "A Rejection Threshold in Justice Evaluations: Effects on Judgment and Decision-Making," *Organizational Behavior and Human Decision Processes* 76 (1998), pp. 113–31.
73. S.G. Hauser, "The Degeneration," *Workforce Management*, January 2011, pp. 16–21.
74. R.J. Bies and J.F. Moag, "Interactional Justice: Communication Criteria of Fairness," in R.J. Lewicki, B.H. Sheppard, and M.H. Bazerman, eds., *Research on Negotiations in Organizations*, Vol. 1 (Greenwich, CT: JAI Press, 1986), pp. 43–55; J. Greenberg, "The Social Side of Fairness: Interpersonal and Informational Classes of Organizational Justice," in R. Cropanzano, ed., *Justice in the Workplace: Approaching Fairness in Human Resource Management* (Hillsdale, NJ: Erlbaum, 1993), pp. 79–103.
75. "RadioShack Fires 400 Employees by Email," www.ctv.ca/CTVNews/SciTech/20060831/radioshack_employees_060831, retrieved June 14, 2011.
76. R. Folger and D.P. Skarlicki, "Fairness as a Dependent Variable: Why Tough Times Can Lead to Bad Management," in *Justice in the Workplace: From Theory to Practice*, ed. R. Cropanzano (Mahwah, NJ: Erlbaum, 2001), pp. 97–118.
77. J. Marquez, E. Frauenheim, and M. Schoeff Jr., "Harsh Reality," *Workforce Management*, June 22, 2009, pp. 18–23.
78. J.C. Shaw, R.E. Wild, and J.A. Colquitt, "To Justify or Excuse?: A Meta-analysis of the Effects of Explanations," *Journal of Applied Psychology* 88 (2003), pp. 444–58.
79. M. Orey, "Fear of Firing," *Businessweek*, April 23, 2007, pp. 52–62.
80. J. Greenberg, "Employee Theft as a Reaction to Underpayment Inequity: The Hidden Cost of Paycuts," *Journal of Applied Psychology* 75 (1990), pp. 561–68.
81. Colquitt et al., "Justice at the Millennium"; Cohen-Charash and Spector, "The Role of Justice."
82. Treviño et al., "Behavioral Ethics," A.E. Tenbrunsel and K. Smith-Crowe, "Ethical Decision Making: Where We've Been and Where We're Going," *Academy of Management Annals* 2 (2008), pp. 545–607.
83. T. Donaldson and T.W. Dunfee, "Toward a Unified Conception of Business Ethics: Integrative Social Contracts Theory," *Academy of Management Review* 19 (1994), pp. 252–84.
84. Treviño et al., "Behavioral Ethics."
85. M. Kaptein, "Developing a Measure of Unethical Behavior in the Workplace: A Stakeholder Perspective," *Journal of Management* 34 (2008), pp. 978–1008.
86. S.M.R. Covey, *The Speed of Trust: The One Thing That Changes Everything* (New York: The Free Press, 2006).
87. Treviño et al., "Behavioral Ethics," A.E. Tenbrunsel and K. Smith-Crowe, "Ethical Decision Making: Where We've Been and Where We're Going," *Academy of Management Annals* 2 (2008), pp. 545–607.
88. D.C. Robertson, "Business Ethics Across Cultures," in *The Blackwell Handbook of Cross-Cultural Management*, eds. M.J. Gannon and K.L. Newman (Malden, MA: Blackwell, 2002), pp. 361–92.
89. Ibid.
90. J.P. Near and M.P. Miceli, "Organizational Dissidence: The Case of Whistle-Blowing," *Journal of Business Ethics* 4 (1985), pp. 1–16.
91. M.T. Rehg, M.P. Miceli, J.P. Near, and J.R. Van Scotter, "Antecedents and Outcomes of Retaliation Against Whistleblowers: Gender Differences and Power Relationships," *Organization Science* 19 (2008), pp. 221–40.
92. M.P. Miceli, J.P. Near, and T.M. Dworkin, "A Word to the Wise: How Managers and Policy-Makers Can Encourage Employees to Report Wrongdoing," *Journal of Business Ethics* 86 (2009), pp. 379–96.
93. J.R. Rest, *Moral Development: Advances in Research and Theory* (New York: Praeger, 2006).
94. L.K. Treviño, "Ethical Decision Making in Organizations: A Person–Situation Interactionist Model," *Academy of Management Review* 11 (1996), pp. 601–17; J.J. Kish-Gephart, D.A. Harrison, and L.K. Treviño, "Bad Apples, Bad Cases, and Bad Barrels: Meta-analytic Evidence About Sources of Unethical Decisions at Work," *Journal of Applied Psychology* 95 (2010), pp. 1–31.
95. E.C. Tomlinson, "Teaching the Interactionist Model of Ethics," *Journal of Management* Education 33 (2009), pp. 142–65; L.K. Treviño and M.E. Brown, "Managing to Be Ethical: Debunking Five Business Ethics Myths," *Academy of Management Executive* 18 (2004), pp. 69–83.
96. Rest, *Moral Development.*
97. K.D. Butterfield, L.K. Treviño, and G.R. Weaver, "Moral Awareness in Business Organizations: Influence of Issue-Related and Social Context Factors," *Human Relations* 53 (2000), pp. 981–1017.

98. T.M. Jones, "Ethical Decision Making by Individuals in Organizations: An Issue-Contingent Model," *Academy of Management Review* 16 (1991), pp. 366–95.
99. A. Singhapakdi, S.J. Vitell, and K.L. Kraft, "Moral Intensity and Ethical Decision-Making of Marketing Professionals," *Journal of Business Research* 36 (1996), pp. 245–55.
100. Jones, "Ethical Decision Making by Individuals in Organizations."
101. S.J. Reynolds, "Moral Attentiveness: Who Pays Attention to the Moral Aspects of Life?," *Journal of Applied Psychology* 93 (2008), pp. 1027–41.
102. Rest, *Moral Development.*
103. L. Kohlberg, "Stage and Sequence: The Cognitive Developmental Approach to Socialization," in *Handbook of Socialization Theory*, ed. D.A. Goslin (Chicago: Rand McNally, 1969), pp. 347–480; L. Kohlberg, "The Claim to Moral Adequacy of a Highest Stage of Moral Judgment," *Journal of Philosophy* 70 (1973), pp. 630–46.
104. J. Rest, *Manual for the Defining Issues Test* (Minneapolis, MN: Center for the Study of Ethical Development, 1986); G.E. Loviscky, L.K. Treviño, and R.R. Jacobs, "Assessing Managers' Ethical Decision-Making: An Objective Measure of Managerial Moral Judgment," *Journal of Business Ethics* 73 (2007), pp. 263–85.
105. Kohlberg, "Stage and Sequence"; Kohlberg, "The Claim to Moral Adequacy."
106. Ibid.
107. Treviño et al., "Behavioral Ethics."
108. Kohlberg, "Stage and Sequence"; Kohlberg, "The Claim to Moral Adequacy."
109. Treviño et al., "Behavioral Ethics"; J. Rest, D. Narvaez, M.J. Bebeau, and S.J. Thoma, *Postconventional Moral Thinking: A Neo-Kohlbergian Approach* (Mahwah, NJ: Erlbaum, 1999).
110. A. Crane and D. Matten, *Business Ethics* (New York: Oxford University Press, 2007).
111. Ibid.
112. Rest, *Moral Development.*
113. M. Kaptein, "Developing and Testing a Measure for the Ethical Culture of Organizations: The Corporate Ethics Virtues Model," *Journal of Organizational Behavior* 29 (2008), pp. 923–47; M. Schminke, M.L. Ambrose, and D.O. Neubaum, "The Effect of Leader Moral Development on Ethical Climate and Employee Attitudes," *Organizational Behavior and Human Decision Processes* 97 (2005), pp. 135–51; Treviño, "Ethical Decision Making in Organizations."
114. M.E. Schweitzer, L. Ordòñez, and B. Douma, "Goal Setting as a Motivator of Unethical Behavior," *Academy of Management Journal* 47 (2004), pp. 422–32.
115. K. Aquino and A. Reed II, "The Self-Importance of Moral Identity," *Journal of Personality and Social Psychology* 83 (2002), pp. 1423–40.
116. Ibid.
117. S.J. Reynolds and T.L. Ceranic, "The Effects of Moral Judgment and Moral Identity on Moral Behavior: An Empirical Examination of the Moral Individual," *Journal of Applied Psychology* 92 (2007), pp. 1610–24.
118. M. Schminke, M.L. Ambrose, and T.W. Noel, "The Effects of Ethical Frameworks on Perceptions of Organizational Justice," *Academy of Management Journal* 40 (1997), pp. 1190–1207; C.A. Wendorf, S. Alexander, and I.J. Firestone, "Social Justice and Moral Reasoning: An Empirical Integration of Two Paradigms in Psychological Research," *Social Justice Research* 15 (2002), pp. 19–39.
119. R.C. Mayer and M.B. Gavin, "Trust in Management and Performance: Who Minds the Shop While the Employees Watch the Boss?," *Academy of Management Journal* 48 (2005), pp. 874–88.
120. P. Blau, *Exchange and Power in Social Life* (New York: Wiley, 1964); L.M. Shore, L.E. Tetrick, P. Lynch, and K. Barksdale, "Social and Economic Exchange: Construct Development and Validation," *Journal of Applied Social Psychology* 36 (2006), pp. 837–67.
121. Ibid.
122. K.T. Dirks and D.L. Ferrin, "Trust in Leadership: Meta-analytic Findings and Implications for Research and Practice," *Journal of Applied Psychology* 87 (2002), pp. 611–28.
123. Ibid.
124. R.C. Mayer and M.B. Gavin, "Trust in Management and Performance: Who Minds the Shop While the Employees Watch the Boss?," *Academy of Management Journal* 48 (2005), pp. 874–88.
125. H. Oh, "Biz Majors Get an F for Honesty," *Businessweek*, February 6, 2006, p. 14.
126. D.L. McCabe, "Academic Dishonesty in Graduate Business Programs: Prevalence, Causes, and Proposed Action," *Academy of Management Learning and Education* 5 (2006), pp. 294–305.
127. A.B. Carroll, "A Three-Dimensional Model of Corporate Social Performance," *Academy of Management Review* 4 (1979), pp. 497–505; A.B. Carroll, "The Pyramid of Corporate Social Responsibility: Toward the Moral Management of Organizational Stakeholders," *Business Horizons* 34 (1991), pp. 39–48; A.B. Carroll, "The Four Faces of Corporate Citizenship," *Business and Society Review* 100 (1998), pp. 1–7; A.B. Carroll, "Corporate Social Responsibility—Evolution of a Definitional Construct," *Business and Society* 38 (1999), pp. 268–95.
128. Carroll, "The Pyramid."
129. Noe et al., Fundamentals of *Human Resource Management.*
130. Ibid.
131. Carroll, "The Pyramid."
132. M. Schoeff Jr., "J.M. Smuckers Co," *Workforce Management*, March 13, 2006, p. 19.
133. "2011 Ethics Policy," TELUS Corporation website, about.telus.com/docs/DOC-1648/version/1, retrieved June 15, 2015.
134. Ibid.
135. "2009 Corporate Social Responsibility Report," TELUS Corporation website, csr.telus.com/content/pdf/telus_csr_2009-en.pdf, retrieved June 15, 2015.
136. Carroll, "The Pyramid."
137. JumpStart website, www.canadiantire.ca/jumpstart/index.html, retrieved July 15, 2008.
138. "2009 Corporate Social Responsibility Report," TELUS Corporation website.

Chapter 9

1. KPMG International, www.kpmg.com/GLOBAL/EN/ABOUT/OVERVIEW/Pages/default.aspx; KPMG Canada, www.kpmg.com/ca/en/about/performance/pages/default.aspx, retrieved January 27 2015.
2. Ibid.
3. "2015 CA UFE Guide and Report," www.cpacanada.ca/en/become-a-cpa/cpa-certification-program-evaluation/ca-ufe-guide, retrieved March 20, 2015.
4. "Information for Internationally Trained Accountants," www.becomeacaincanada.ca/item47117.html, retrieved March 21, 2015.
5. H.M. Weiss, "Learning Theory and Industrial and Organizational Psychology," in *Handbook of Industrial and Organizational Psychology*, eds. M.D. Dunnette and L.M. Hough (Palo Alto, CA: Consulting Psychologists Press, 1990), pp. 75–169.
6. B. Tai and N.R. Lockwood, "Organizational Entry: Onboarding, Orientation, and Socialization," SHRM research paper, www.shrm.org, retrieved June 4, 2007.
7. Ibid.
8. K.A. Ericsson, "An Introduction to Cambridge Handbook of Expertise and Expert Performance: Its Development, Organization, and Content," in K.A. Ericsson, N. Charness, P.J. Feltovich, and R.R. Hoffman, eds., *The Cambridge Handbook of Expertise and Expert Performance* (New York: Cambridge University Press, 2006), pp. 3–19.
9. K.A. Ericsson and A.C. Lehmann, "Experts and Exceptional Performance: Evidence of Maximal Adaptation to Task Constraints," *Annual Review of Psychology* 47 (1996), pp. 273–305.
10. E.N. Brockmann and W.P. Anthony, "Tacit Knowledge and Strategic Decision Making," *Group & Organizational Management* 27, December 2002, pp. 436–55.
11. R.K. Wagner and R.J. Sternberg, "Practical Intelligence in Real-World Pursuits: The Role of Tacit Knowledge," *Journal of Personality and Social Psychology* 4 (1985), pp. 436–58.
12. L. Wah, "Making Knowledge Stick," *Management Review* 88 (1999), pp. 24–33.
13. T.R. Eucker, "Understanding the Impact of Tacit Knowledge Loss," *Knowledge*

Management Review, March 2007, pp. 10–13.
14. R. McAdam, B. Mason, and J. McCrory, "Exploring the Dichotomies Within the Tacit Knowledge Literature: Towards a Process of Tacit Knowing in Organizations," *Journal of Knowledge Management* 11 (2007), pp. 43–59.
15. C. Lawson and E. Lorenzi, "Collective Learning, Tacit Knowledge, and Regional Innovative Capacity," *Regional Studies* 21 (1999), pp. 487–513.
16. J.C. Bou-Llusar, and M. Segarra-Ciprés, "Strategic Knowledge Transfer and Its Implications for Competitive Advantage: An Integrative Conceptual Framework," *Journal of Knowledge Management* 10 (2006), pp. 100–12; I. Nonaka, "The Knowledge-Creating Company," *Harvard Business Review* 69 (1991), pp. 96–104; I. Nonaka, "A Dynamic Theory of Organizational Knowledge Creation," *Organizational Science* 5 (1994), pp. 14–37.
17. F. Luthans and R. Kreitner, *Organizational Behavior Modification and Beyond* (Glenview, IL: Scott, Foresman, 1985).
18. G.P. Latham and V.L. Huber, "Schedules of Reinforcement: Lessons from the Past and Issues for Future," *Journal of Organizational Behavior* Management 13 (1992), pp. 125–49.
19. C. Pinder, *Work Motivation in Organizational Behavior* (New York: Psychology Press, 2008).
20. Luthans and Kreitner, *Organizational Behavior Modification.*
21. Pinder, *Work Motivation.*
22. Ibid.
23. A. Bandura, *Social Foundations of Thought and Action: A Social Cognitive Theory* (Englewood Cliffs, NJ: Prentice Hall, 1986).
24. Weiss, "Learning Theory."
25. A. Pescuric and W.C. Byham, "The New Look of Behavior Modeling," *Training & Development*, July 1996, pp. 24–30.
26. R.R, Sims and J. Brinkmann, "Leaders as Moral Role Models: The Case of John Gutfreund at Salomon Brothers," *Journal of Business Ethics* 35 (2002), pp. 327–40.
27. Ibid.
28. M. Biron and P. Bamberger, "Aversive Workplace Conditions and Absenteeism: Taking Referent Group Norms and Supervisor Account into Account," *Journal of Applied Psychology* 97 (2012), pp. 901–12; M.S. Mitchell and M.L. Ambrose, "Employee's Behavioral Reactions to Supervisor Aggression: An Examination of Individual and Situational Factors," *Journal of Applied Psychology* 97 (2012), pp. 1148–70.
29. D. VandeWalle, "Development and Validation of a Work Domain Goal Orientation Instrument," *Educational and Psychological Measurement* 8 (1997), pp. 995–1015.
30. S.C. Payne, S. Youngcourt, and J.M. Beaubien, "A Meta-analytic Examination of the Goal Orientation Nomological Net," *Journal of Applied Psychology* 92 (2007), pp. 128–50.
31. Ibid.
32. J.A. Cannon-Bowers, L. Rhodenizer, E. Salas, and C. Bowers, "A Framework for Understanding Pre-practice Conditions and Their Impact on Learning," *Personnel Psychology* 51 (1998), pp. 291–320.
33. J. Mesmer-Magnus and C. Viswesvaran, "The Role of Pre-training Interventions in Learning: A Meta-analysis and Integrative Review," *Human Resource Management Review* 20 (2010), pp. 261–82.
34. E. Dane and M.G. Pratt, "Exploring Intuition and Its Role in Managerial Decision Making," *Academy of Management Review* 32 (2007), pp. 33–54; A.M. Hayashi, "When to Trust Your Gut," *Harvard Business Review*, February 2001, pp. 59–65.
35. Hogarth, R.M. "Intuition: A Challenge for Psychological Research on Decision Making," *Psychological Inquiry* 21 (2010), pp. 338–53.
36. J.G. March, *A Primer on Decision Making* (New York: The Free Press, 1994).
37. E. Dane, K.W. Rockmann, and M.G. Pratt, "When Should I Trust My Gut? Linking Domain Expertise to Intuitive Decision-Making Effectiveness," *Organizational Behavior and Human Decision Processes* 119 (2012), pp. 187–94.
38. M.W. Seeger, T.L. Sellnow, and R.R. Ulmer, "Communication, Organization and Crisis," *Communication Yearbook* 21 (1998), pp. 231–75.
39. K.E. Weick and K.M. Sutcliffe, *Managing the Unexpected: Resilient Performance in an Age of Uncertainty*, 2nd ed. (San Francisco: Jossey-Bass, 2007).
40. G. Klein, *Sources of Power* (Cambridge, MA: MIT Press, 1999).
41. K.E. Weick, "Managerial Thought in the Context of Action," in *The Executive Mind*, ed. S. Srivasta (San Francisco: Jossey-Bass, 1983), pp. 221–42; Weick and Sutcliffe, *Managing the Unexpected*; G. Klein, *The Power of Intuition* (New York: Currency Doubleday, 2003).
42. H.A. Simon, "A Behavioral Model of Rational Choice," *Quarterly Journal of Economics* 69 (1955), pp. 99–118.
43. "Quotation Details," www.quotationspage.com/quote/25953.html, retrieved April 2011.
44. H.A. Simon, "Rational Decision Making in Organizations," *American Economic Review* 69 (1979), pp. 493–513.
45. J.G. March and H.A. Simon, *Organizations* (New York: Wiley, 1958).
46. Ibid.
47. M.A. Hogg and D.J. Terry, "Social Identity and Self-Categorization Process in Organizational Contexts," *Academy of Management Review* 25, January 2000, pp. 121–40.
48. C.M. Judd and B. Park, "Definition and Assessment of Accuracy in Social Stereotypes," *Psychological Review* 100, January 1993, pp. 109–28.
49. B.E. Ashforth and F. Mael, "Social Identity Theory and the Organization," *Academy of Management Review* 14 (1989), pp. 20–39; J.A. Howard, "Social Psychology of Identities," *Annual Review of Sociology* 26 (2000), pp. 367–93.
50. D. Kahneman, P. Slovic, and A. Tversky, eds., *Judgment Under Uncertainty: Heuristics and Biases* (Cambridge, UK: Cambridge University Press, 1982).
51. D. Kahneman and A. Tversky, "On the Psychology of Prediction," *Psychological Review* 80 (1973), pp. 237–51.
52. J. Smerd, "In Workers' Heads," *Workforce Management*, June 22, 2009, pp. 34–39.
53. L. Ross, "The Intuitive Psychologist and His Shortcomings: Distortions in the Attribution Process," in *Advances in Experimental Social Psychology*, ed. L. Berkowitz (New York: Academic Press, 1977), pp. 173–220. See also E.E. Jones and V.A. Harris. "The Attribution of Attitudes," *Journal of Experimental Social Psychology* 3 (1967), pp. 1–24.
54. H.H. Kelley, "The Processes of Casual Attribution," *American Psychologist* 28 (1973), pp. 107–28; H.H. Kelley, "Attribution in Social Interaction," in *Attribution: Perceiving the Causes of Behavior*, ed. E. Jones (Morristown, NJ: General Learning Press, 1972).
55. Y. Zemba, M.I. Young, and M.W. Morris, "Blaming Leaders for Organizational Accidents: Proxy Logic in Collective Versus Individual-Agency Cultures," *Organizational Behavior and Human Decision Processes* 101 (2006), pp. 36–51.
56. T. Menon, M.W. Morris, C. Chiu, and Y. Hong, "Culture and the Construal of Agency: Attribution to Individual Versus Group Dispositions," *Journal of Personality and Social Psychology* 76 (1999), pp. 701–17.
57. Zemba et al., "Blaming Leaders."
58. C. Chiu, M.W. Morris, Y. Hong, and T. Menon, "Motivated Cultural Cognition: The Impact of Implicit Cultural Theories on Dispositional Attribution Varies as a Function of Need for Closure," *Journal of Personality and Social Psychology* 78 (2000), pp. 247–59.
59. Zemba et al., "Blaming Leaders."
60. B.M. Staw and J. Ross, "Behavior in Escalation Situations: Antecedents, Prototypes, and Solutions," in *Research in Organizational Behavior*, Vol. 9, eds. L.L. Cummings and B.M. Staw (Greenwich, CT: JAI Press, 1987), pp. 39–78; B.M. Staw, "Knee-Deep in the Big Muddy: A Study of Escalating Commitment to a Chosen Course of Action," *Organizational Behavior and Human Performance* 16 (1976), pp. 27–44.
61. J. Brockner, "The Escalation of Commitment to a Failing Course of Action: Toward Theoretical Progress," *Academy of Management Review* 17 (1992), pp. 39–61; B.M. Staw, "The Escalation of Commitment: An Update and Appraisal," in *Organizational Decision Making*, ed. Z. Shapira (New York: Cambridge University Press, 1997).

62. D.E. Conlon and H. Garland, "The Role of Project Completion Information in Resource Allocation Decisions," *Academy of Management Journal* 36 (1993), pp. 402–13; H. Moon, "Looking Forward and Looking Back: Integrating Completion and Sunk-Cost Effects within an Escalation of Commitment Progress Decision," *Journal of Applied Psychology* 86 (2001), pp. 104–13.
63. K. Johnson, "Denver Airport to Mangle Last Bag," *The New York Times*, August 27, 2005.
64. D.C. Molden and C.M. Hui, "Promoting De-escalation of Commitment: A Regulatory-Focus Perspective on Sunk Costs," *Psychological Science* 22 (2011), pp. 8–12.
65. G.M. Alliger, S.I. Tannenbaum, W. Bennett Jr., H. Traver, and A. Shotland, "A Meta-analysis of the Relations Among Training Criteria," *Personnel Psychology* 50 (1997), pp. 341–58; J.A. Colquitt, J.A. LePine, and R.A. Noe, "Toward an Integrative Theory of Training Motivation: A Meta-analytic Path Analysis of 20 Years of Research," *Journal of Applied Psychology* 85 (2000), pp. 678–707; J.P. Meyer, D.J. Stanley, L. Herscovitch, and L. Topolnytsky, "Affective, Continuance, and Normative Commitment to the Organization: A Meta-analysis of Antecedents, Correlates, and Consequences," *Journal of Vocational Behavior* 61 (2002), pp. 20–52.
66. J. Averbrook, "Connecting CLO's with the Recruiting Process," *Chief Learning Officer* 4 (2005), pp. 24–27.
67. A. Paradise, "Investment in Learning Remains Strong," *T+D*, November 2008, pp. 44–51.
68. D. Folkers, "Competing in the Marketspace: Incorporating Online Education into Higher Education—An Organizational Perspective," *Information Resources Management Journal* 18 (2005), pp. 61–77.
69. D. Golden, "Degrees@StateU: Online University Enrollment Soars as Quality Improves; Tuition Funds Other Projects," *The Wall Street Journal*, May 9, 2006, p. B1.
70. Ibid.
71. J.B. Arbaugh, "Is There an Optimal Design for On-line MBA Courses?," *Academy of Management Learning and Education* 4 (2005), pp. 135–49.
72. R.C. Clark, "Harnessing the Virtual Classroom," *T+D* 59 (2005), pp. 40–45.
73. K. Tyler, "Training Revs Up," *HR Magazine*, 50 (2005), pp. 58–63.
74. D. Stamps, "Communities of Practice," *Training*, February 1997, pp. 35–42.
75. J.S. Holste and D. Fields, "Trust and Tacit Knowledge Sharing and Use," *Journal of Knowledge Management* 14 (2010), pp. 128–40.
76. S. Ladika, "Shipping and Handling: Picking the Right People to Head Overseas Is Paramount," *Workforce Management*, March 1, 2013, www.workforce.com/article/20130301/NEWS02/130309992/shipping-and-handling-picking-the-right-people-to-head-overseas-is.
77. K.S. Retna and P.T. Ng, "Communities of Practice: Dynamics and Success Factors," *Leadership and Organization Development Journal* 32 (2011), pp. 41–59; E. Sauve, "Informal Knowledge Transfer," *T+D* 61 (2007), pp. 22–24.
78. N. Ligdas, "Using a Wiki Portal to Support Organizational Excellence at Shell," *Knowledge Management Review*, October 2009, p. 1; B. Allan and D. Lewis, "Virtual Learning Communities as a Vehicle for Workforce Development: A Case Study," *Journal of Workplace Learning* 18 (2006), pp. 367–83.
79. J. Twentyman, "Connecting People Is a Recipe for Innovation at Cadbury," *Knowledge Management Review*, December 2009, p. 1.
80. R.A. Noe, *Employee Training and Development* (New York: Irwin/McGraw-Hill, 1999).
81. J.B. Tracey, S.I. Tannenbaum, and M.J. Kavanaugh, "Applying Trained Skills on the Job: The Importance of the Work Environment," *Journal of Applied Psychology* 80 (1995), pp. 239–52.

Chapter 10

1. "Corporate Profile," TD Bank Group website, www.td.com/about-tdbfg/corporate-information/corporate-profile/profile.jsp, retrieved May 22, 2014.
2. Ibid., retrieved May 22, 2014.
3. TD Bank Group website, www.td.com/about-tdbfg/corporate-information/corporate-profile/profile.jsp, retrieved May 22, 2014.
4. "Awards," www.td.com/about-tdbfg/media-room/awards/awards.jsp, retrieved May 22, 2014.
5. D. Ovsey, "Behind the Scenes of TD Canada Trust's Cultural Evolution," *Financial Post*, November 20, 2012, business.financialpost.com/2012/11/20/behind-the-scenes-of-td-canada-trusts-cultural-evolution, retrieved May 23, 2014.
6. Ibid.
7. W. Arnott, "Becoming a Social Organization: TD Group (2010 to 2014)," presentation delivered at conference Work and Workplaces of the Future: Implications for Western Canada, Conference Board of Canada, Calgary, May 5, 2014.
8. "Social Media," TD Bank Group website, www.td.com/about-tdbfg/media-room/social-media/social-media.jsp, retrieved May 23, 2014.
9. William Keenan Jr., "'Wow Moments' Helps TD Canada Trust Nurture Employee Engagement, Growth," *Engagement Strategies Magazine*, Winter 2010, www.engagementstrategiesonline.com/Wow-Moments-Helps-TD-Canada-Trust-Nurture-Employee-Engagement-Growth, retrieved May 22, 2014.
10. Ibid.
11. Ibid.
12. Steven Green, "IBM Connections and the Social Enterprise: How Social Recognition Drives Legendary Customer Experiences," white paper, www.tembosocial.com/ibm-connections-and-the-social-enterprise, retrieved May 22, 2014; www.tembosocial.com, retrieved May 22, 2014.
13. Ibid.
14. Keenan, "'Wow Moments' Helps."
15. J. Langan-Fox, "Communication in Organizations: Speed, Diversity, Networks, and Influence on Organizational Effectiveness, Human Health, and Relationships," in *Handbook of Industrial, Work, and Organizational Psychology*, Vol. 2, eds. N. Anderson, D.S. Ones, and H.K. Sinangil (Thousand Oaks, CA: Sage, 2001), pp. 188–205.
16. K.J. Krone, F.M. Jablin, and L.L. Putman, "Communication Theory and Organizational Communication: Multiple Perspectives," in *Handbook of Organizational Communication*, eds. F.M. Jablin, K.L. Putman, KH. Roberts, and L.W. Porter (Newbury Park, CA: Sage, 1987); C.E. Shannon and W. Weaver, *The Mathematical Theory of Communication* (Urbana: University of Illinois Press, 1964).
17. Bonnie A. Nardi and Steve Whittaker, "The Place of Face-to-Face Communication in Distributed Work," in *Distributed Work*, eds. Pamela J. Hinds and Sara B. Kiesler (MIT Press, 2002), p. 83; Kevin B. Wright and Lynne M. Webb, *Computer-Mediated Communication in Personal Relationships* (New York: Peter Lang, 2011), p. 139.
18. John McFerran, "Face-to-Face Communication Still Best Way to Get Job Done," *Winnipeg Free Press*, December 11, 2010, www.winnipegfreepress.com/business/face-to-face-communication-still-best-way-to-get-job-done-111714554.html, retrieved June 9, 2014.
19. Ibid.
20. T.E. Harris, *Applied Organizational Communication: Principles and Pragmatics for Future Practice* (Mahwah, NJ: Lawrence Erlbaum Associates, 2002).
21. Ibid.
22. S. Armour, "E-mail 'A Blessing' for Business," *USA Today*, July 2–5, 1988), p. 1A.
23. Harris, *Applied Organizational Communication.*
24. R.A. Anderson, *Nonverbal Communication: Forms and Functioning* (Mountain View, CA: Mayfield, 1999).
25. Harris, *Applied Organizational Communication.*
26. Ibid.
27. "The Chemistry of Kissing," www.chemistry.com/datingadvice/ChemistryofKissing, retrieved June 10, 2014.
28. Harris, *Applied Organizational Communication*; "Nonverbal Communication," www.helpguide.org/mental/eq6_nonverbal_communication.htm, retrieved June 10, 2014.
29. Harris, *Applied Organizational Communication*; "Nonverbal

Communication," en.wikipedia.org/wiki/Nonverbal_communication, retrieved June 10, 2014.
30. D. McQuail, *McQuail's Mass Communication Theory*, 6th ed. (Thousand Oaks, CA: Sage Publications, 2010).
31. Harris, *Applied Organizational Communication*; Langan-Fox, "Communication in Organizations"; P. Palvia, P. Pinjani, S. Cannoy, and T. Jacks, "Contextual Constraints in Media Choice: Beyond Information Richness," *Decision Support Systems* 51(3) (2011), pp. 657–70; K. Byron, "Carrying Too Heavy a Load? The Communication and Miscommunication of Emotion by Email," *Academy of Management Review* 33 (2008), pp. 309–327; Jordie van Rijn, "The Ultimate Mobile Email Statistics Overview," 2014, www.emailmonday.com/mobile-email-usage-statistics, retrieved June 4, 2014; S. Armour, "You Have (Too Much) Email," *USA Today*, March 2, 1999, p. 38.
32. Langan-Fox, "Communication in Organizations"; Byron, Carrying Too Heavy a Load?"
33. R.A. Friedman and S.C. Currall, "Conflict Escalation: Dispute Exacerbation Elements of Email Communication," *Human Relations* 56 (2003), pp. 1325–47.
34. M. Sarbaugh-Thompson and M.S. Feldman, "Electronic Mail and Organizational Communication: Does Saying 'Hi' Really Matter?," *Organization Science* 9 (1998), pp. 685–698.
35. G.F. Thomas and C.L. King, "Reconceptualizing E-mail Overload," *Journal of Business and Technical Communication* 20(3) (2006), pp. 252–87; S.R. Barley, D.E. Meyerson, and S. Grodal, "E-mail as a Source and Symbol of Stress," *Organizational Science* 22(4) (2011), 887–906.
36. Lindsay Olson, "How to Use Your Work Email Efficiently: Four Tips for Keeping Your Inbox Organized," *US News and World Report*, June 21, 2012, money.usnews.com/money/blogs/outside-voices-careers/2012/06/21/how-to-use-your-work-email-efficiently, retrieved June 7, 2014.
37. "Skype," en.wikipedia.org/wiki/Skype, retrieved June 9, 2014.
38. Langan-Fox, "Communication in Organizations."
39. Ibid.
40. Ibid.
41. Ibid.
42. Ibid.
43. "Welcome to Wikipedia," en.wikipedia.org/wiki/Main_Page, retrieved May 19, 2014.
44. Ibid.
45. Ibid.
46. O. Arazy and I.R. Gellatly, "Corporate Wikis: The Effects of Owners' Motivation and Behavior on Group Members' Engagement," *Journal of Management Information Systems* 29(3) (2013), pp. 91–121; O. Arazy, I.R. Gellatly, S. Jang, and R. Patterson, "Wiki Deployment in Corporate Settings," *IEEE Technology and Society Magazine* 28(2) (2009), pp. 57–64; A. Majchrzak, C. Wagner, and D. Yates, *Corporate Wiki Users: Results of a Survey* (New York: ACM, 2006), pp. 99–104.
47. Arazy and Gellatly, "Corporate Wikis."
48. Ibid.; Arazy et al., "Wiki Deployment in Corporate Settings"; C. Wagner, "Wiki: A Technology for Conversational Knowledge Management and Group Collaboration," *Communications of the Association for Information Systems* 13 (2004), pp. 265–89; D. Yates, C. Wagner, and A. Majchrzak, "Factors Affecting Shapers of Organizational Wikis," *Journal of the American Society for Information Science and Technology* 61(3) (2010), pp. 543–554.
49. Arazy and Gellatly, "Corporate Wikis."
50. Ibid.
51. Arnott, "Becoming a Social Organization."
52. R.D. Waters et al., "Engaging Stakeholders Through Social Networking: How Nonprofit Organizations Are Using Facebook," *Public Relations Review* 35(2) (2009), pp. 102–06; J. Cunningham, "New Workers, New Workplace? Getting the Balance Right," *Strategic Direction* 26(1) (2010), p. 5; A.M. Kaplan and M. Haenlein, "Users of the World, Unite! The Challenges and Opportunities of Social Media," *Business Horizons* 53(1) (2010): pp. 59–68.
53. LinkedIn.ca, ca.linkedin.com, retrieved May 19, 2014.
54. Ibid.; "LinkedIn," en.wikipedia.org/wiki/LinkedIn, retrieved May 19, 2014.
55. LinkedIn.ca, ca.linkedin.com, retrieved May 19, 2014.; "LinkedIn," en.wikipedia.org/wiki/LinkedIn, retrieved May 19, 2014.
56. Achievers.com, www.achievers.com, retrieved May 20, 2014.
57. "Achievers: 10 Years and Counting," September 10, 2013, www.youtube.com/watch?v=prHD3vl_VZg, retrieved May 20, 2014.
58. "Partners in Employee Success: 3M + Achievers," November 7, 2013, www.youtube.com/watch?v=iT7nvJyuIfc, retrieved May 20, 2014; Aberdeen Group Inc., *Rewards and Recognition: Achievers Clients Achieving More*, September 2011, research brief, www.achievers.com/uploads/2011/10/Aberdeen-Customer-Performance-Report.pdf, retrieved May 19, 2014.
59. Becky Reuber, "How This Employer Stopped Worker Exodus," *Globe and Mail*, November 16, 2012, www.theglobeandmail.com/report-on-business/small-business/sb-managing/human-resources/how-this-employer-stopped-worker-exodus/article5271363/#dashboard/follows, retrieved May 20, 2014.
60. Ibid.
61. Dan Ovsey, "Is There Such a Thing as Too Much Transparency?," *Financial Post*, April 23, 2014. business.financialpost.com/2014/04/23/is-there-such-a-thing-as-too-much-transparency, retrieved May 20, 2014.
62. "IBM Connections," www-03.ibm.com/software/products/en/conn, retrieved May 20, 2014; "Why Use IBM Connections?," November 8, 2011, www.youtube.com/watch?v=YG-2J2cL9Y4, retrieved May 20, 2014; "IBM Connections 4.0 Overview," September 4, 2012, www.youtube.com/watch?v=JOynRkYWFSM, retrieved May 20, 2014.
63. Steven Green, "IBM Connections and the Social Enterprise: How Social Recognition Drives Legendary Customer Experiences," white paper, www.tembosocial.com/ibm-connections-and-the-social-enterprise, retrieved May 22, 2014.; TemboSocial website, www.tembosocial.com, retrieved May 22, 2014.
64. "Communication and Recognition," www.tdcanadatrust.com/easyweb5/crr-2011/workplace/communication_recognition/index.jsp, retrieved May 23, 2014.
65. "Why Use IBM Connections?," November 8, 2011, www.youtube.com/watch?v=YG-2J2cL9Y4, retrieved May 20, 2014.
66. "IBM Connections 4.0 Overview"; "Why Use IBM Connections?"; "What's New in IBM Connections 4.5," March 29, 2013, www.youtube.com/watch?v=jL8QKyVa4KI, retrieved May 20, 2014; "IBM Connections," www-03.ibm.com/software/products/en/conn, retrieved May 20, 2014.
67. "IBM Connections 4.0 Overview"; "Why Use IBM Connections?"; "What's New in IBM Connections 4.5"; "IBM Connections," www-03.ibm.com/software/products/en/conn, retrieved May 20, 2014.
68. K.J. Krone, F.M. Jablin, and L.L. Putman, "Communication Theory and Organizational Communication: Multiple Perspectives," in *Handbook of Organizational Communication*, eds. F.M. Jablin, K.L. Putman, KH. Roberts, and L.W. Porter (Newbury Park, CA: Sage, 1987); C.E. Shannon and W. Weaver, *The Mathematical Theory of Communication* (Urbana: University of Illinois Press, 1964).
69. F.M. Jablin and P.M. Sias, "Communication Competence," in *The New Handbook of Organizational Communication: Advances in Theory, Research, and Methods*, eds. F.M. Jablin and L.L. Putnam (Thousand Oaks, CA: Sage, 2001), pp. 819–64.
70. P.J. Jordan and A.C. Troth, "Managing Emotions During Team Problem Solving: Emotional Intelligence and Conflict Resolution, *Human Performance* 17 (2004), pp. 195–218.
71. A. Rafaeli and R.I. Sutton, "Expression of Emotion as Part of the Work Role," *Academy of Management Review* 12 (1987), pp. 23–37.
72. M. Warkentin and P.M. Beranek, "Training to Improve Virtual Team Communication," *Information Systems Journal* 9 (1999), pp. 271–89.
73. Krone et al., "Communication Theory and Organizational Communication"; Shannon and Weaver, *The Mathematical Theory of Communication*.
74. R.L. Daft and R.H. Lengel, "Information Richness: A New Approach to Managerial

Behavior and Organizational Design," in *Research in Organizational Behavior*, eds. B.M. Staw and L.L. Cummings (Greenwich, CT: JAI Press, 1984), pp. 191–233.

75. Ibid.
76. Ibid.
77. Ibid.
78. K. Byron, "Carrying Too Heavy a Load? The Communication and Miscommunication of Emotion by Email," *Academy of Management Review* 33 (2008), pp. 309–27.
79. Daft and Lengel, "Information Richness."
80. Ibid.
81. D. Tannen, "The Power of Talk: Who Gets Heard and Why," *Harvard Business Review*, September/October 1995, pp. 138–48.
82. Ibid.
83. Ibid.
84. Office of the Information and Privacy Commissioner of Canada, www.priv.gc.ca/index_e.asp, retrieved June 22, 2014; T. Perverseff, "The Social Media Revolution: It's Here, Are We Ready?," presentation delivered at conference Work and Workplaces of the Future: Implications for Western Canada, Conference Board of Canada, Calgary, May 5, 2014; E. Denham, *Work and Play in the Age of Social Networking*, presentation delivered at IAPP Knowledgenet Conference, Calgary, 2010, www.priv.gc.ca/media/sp-d/2010/sp-d_20100512_ed_e.asp, retrieved June 19, 2014.
85. Agrium Inc., "Privacy Policy," www.agrium.com/employee_privacy.jsp, retrieved June 22, 2014.
86. O. Oh, H.K. Kyounghee, and H.R. Rao, "An Exploration of Social Media in Extreme Events: Rumor Theory and Twitter During the Haiti Earthquake 2010," ICIS 2010 proceedings, aisel.aisnet.org/icis2010_submissions/231.
87. H.J. Leavitt, "Some Effects of Certain Communication Patterns on Group Performance," *Journal of Abnormal and Social Psychology* 436 (1951), pp. 38–50.
88. R.B. Adler and J.M. Elmhorst, *Communicating at Work: Principles and Practices for Business and the Professions*, 10th ed. (New York: McGraw-Hill, Inc., 2009).
89. Harris, *Applied Organizational Communication.*
90. Ibid.
91. Ibid.
92. Ibid.
93. Ibid.
94. Ibid.
95. M. Glanzer and R. Glaser, "Techniques for the Study of Group Structure and Behavior: II. Empirical Studies of the Effects of Structure in Small Groups," *Psychological Bulletin* 58 (1961), pp. 1–27.
96. R.V. Farace, P.R. Monge, and H.M. Russell, "Communication in Micro-networks," in *Organizational Communication*, 2nd ed., eds. F.D. Ferguson and S. Ferguson (New Brunswick, NJ: Transaction Books, 1988), pp. 365–69.
97. N.B. Kurland and L.H. Pelled, "Passing the Word: Toward a Model of Gossip and Power in the Workplace," *Academy of Management Review*, 25(2000), pp. 428–38.
98. Langan-Fox, "Communication in Organizations."
99. Ibid.
100. Adler and Elmhorst, *Communicating at Work.*
101. S.N. Crampton, J.W. Hodge, and J.M. Mishra, "The Informal Communication Network: Factors Influencing Grapevine Activity," *Public Personnel Management* 27(4) (1998), pp. 569–84.
102. Langan-Fox, "Communication in Organizations."
103. Kurland and Pelled, "Passing the Word."
104. "Grapevine Communication," www.people-communicating.com/grapevine-communication.html, retrieved July 11, 2014.
105. A.J. Kimmel, *Rumors and Rumor Control: A Manager's Guide to Understanding and Combatting Rumors* (Mahwah, NJ: Lawrence Erlbaum Associates, Publishers, 2004.
106. Ibid.
107. Ibid.
108. M.J. Harris and R. Rosenthal, "Mediation of Interpersonal Expectancies Effects: 31 Meta-analyses," *Psychological Bulletin* 97, pp. 363–86; A.N. Kluger and A. DeNisi, "The Effects of Feedback Interventions on Performance: A Historical Review, a Meta-analysis, and a Preliminary Intervention Theory," *Psychological Bulletin* 119 (1996), pp. 256–84; J.W. Smither, M. London, and R.R. Reilly, "Does Performance Improve Following Multisource Feedback? A Theoretical Model, Meta-analysis, and Review of the Empirical Findings," *Personnel Psychology* 58 (2005), pp. 33–66.
109. Kluger and DeNisi, "The Effects of Feedback Interventions on Performance."
110. D.R. Ilgen, C.D. Fisher, and M.S. Taylor, "Consequences of Individual Feedback on Behavior in Organizations," *Journal of Applied Psychology* 64 (1979), pp. 349–71.
111. Smither et al., "Does Performance Improve Following Multisource Feedback?"
112. Ilgen et al., "Consequences of Individual Feedback on Behavior in Organizations"; Smither et al., "Does Performance Improve Following Multisource Feedback?"
113. N.J. Allen and J.P. Meyer, "The Measurement and Antecedents of Affective, Continuance, and Normative Commitment to the Organization," *Journal of Occupational Psychology* 63 (1990), pp. 1–18; Mathieu and Zajac, "A Review and Meta-analysis."
114. Mathieu and Zajac, "A Review and Meta-analysis."
115. Allen and Meyer, "The Measurement and Antecedents of Affective, Continuance, and Normative Commitment to the Organization."
116. Ibid.
117. R.L. Dipboye, T. Macan, and C. Shahani-Denning, "The Selection Interview from the Interviewer and Applicant Perspectives: Can't Have One Without the Other," in N. Schmitt, ed., *The Oxford Handbook of Personnel Assessment and Selection* (pp. 323–52) (New York: Oxford University, 2012); R.A. Posthuma, F.R. Morgeson, and M.A. Campion, "Beyond Employment Interview Validity: A Comprehensive Narrative Review of Research and Trends over Time," *Personnel Psychology* 55 (2002), pp. 1–81.
118. R.A. Noe, J.R. Hollenbeck, B. Gerhart, P.M. Wright, and L.E. Eligh, *Strategic Human Resource Management: Gaining a Competitive Advantage*, 1st Canadian ed. (Toronto: McGraw-Hill Ryerson, 2012).
119. A.I. Huffcutt and W.A. Arthur, "Hunter and Hunter (1984) Revisited: Interview Validity for Entry-Level Jobs," *Journal of Applied Psychology* 79 (1994), pp. 184–190; M.A. McDaniel, D.L. Whetzel, F.L. Schmidt, and S.D. Maurer, "The Validity of Employment Interviews: A Comprehensive Review and Meta-analysis," *Journal of Applied Psychology* 79 (1994), pp. 599–616; W.H. Wiesner and S.F. Cronshaw, "A Meta-analytic Investigation of the Impact of Interview Format and Degree of Structure on the Validity of the Employment Interview," *Journal of Occupational Psychology* 61(4) (1988), pp. 275–90.
120. Wiesner and Cronshaw, "A Meta-analytic Investigation."
121. R.W. Eder and G.R. Ferris, *The Employment Interview: Theory, Research and Practice* (Newbury Park, CA: Sage, 1989).
122. R.D. Gatewood and H.S. Field, *Human Resource Selection*, 2nd ed. (Fort Worth, TX: The Dryden Press. (1990).
123. R.E. Riggio, "Using Effective Non-verbal Communication in Job Interviews: Using Subtle Body Language to Give You an Interviewing Edge," *Psychology Today*, January 5, 2011, www.psychologytoday.com/blog/cutting-edge-leadership/201101/using-effective-nonverbal-communication-in-job-interviews, retrieved July 24, 2014.
124. Ibid.
125. Ibid.
126. Ibid.

Chapter 11

1. E. John and B. Taupin, "Rocket Man" (Santa Monica, CA: Universal Music Publishing Group, 1972).
2. A. Novotney, "I/O Psychology Goes to Mars," *Monitor on Psychology*, March 2013, pp. 38–41.
3. "Organization," Canadian Space Agency website, www.asc-csa.gc.ca/eng/about/csa_organization.asp, retrieved February 2, 2015.
4. "Mission and Mandate," Canadian Space Agency website, www.asc-csa.gc.ca/eng/about/mission.asp, accessed February 2, 2015.

5. "Canadian Astronauts—Former," Canadian Space Agency website, www.asc-csa.gc.ca/eng/astronauts/former.asp, accessed February 2, 2015.
6. Ibid.
7. "Canadarm," Canadian Space Agency website, www.asc-csa.gc.ca/eng/canadarm/default.asp, accessed February 2, 2015.
8. "The Canadian Space Agency's Fleet of Rovers," Canadian Space Agency website, www.asc-csa.gc.ca/eng/rovers/default.asp, accessed February 2, 2015.
9. T. Halvorson, "8 Score Astronaut Spots out of 6,300 NASA Applicants," *USA Today*, June 18, 2013, www.usatoday.com/story/tech/2013/06/18/eight-score-astronaut-spots-nasa/2433565.
10. Ibid.
11. Novotney, "I/O Psychology Goes to Mars."
12. D.R. Ilgen, D.A. Major, J.R. Hollenbeck, and D.J. Sego, "Team Research in the 1990s," in *Leadership Theory and Research: Perspectives and Directions*, eds. M.M. Chemers and R. Ayman (New York: Academic Press, 1993), pp. 245–70.
13. R. Morissette and J.M. Rosa, "Alternative Work Practices and Quit Rates: Methodological Issues and Empirical Evidence for Canada," Statistics Canada Catalogue No. 11F0019MiE—No. 199, March 2003.
14. B. Boning, C. Ichniowski, and K. Shaw, "Opportunity Counts: Teams and the Effectiveness of Production Incentives," *Journal of Labor Economics* 25 (2007), pp. 613–50.
15. S.G. Cohen and D.E. Bailey, "What Makes Teams Work: Group Effectiveness Research from the Shop Floor to the Executive Suite," *Journal of Management* 23 (1997), pp. 239–90.
16. J.K. Liker, *The Toyota Way* (New York: McGraw-Hill, 2004).
17. Cohen and Bailey, "What Makes Teams Work."
18. Ibid.
19. E. Sundstrom, M. McIntyre, T. Halfhill, and H. Richards, "Work Groups: From the Hawthorne Studies to Work Teams of the 1990s and Beyond," *Group Dynamics, Theory, Research, and Practice* 4 (2000), pp. 44–67.
20. B. Schlender, "The Man Who Built Pixar's Incredible Innovation Machine," *Fortune*, November 15, 2004, p. 206. ProQuest database, retrieved May 28, 2007.
21. J.R. Hollenbeck, B. Beersma, and M.E. Schouten, "Beyond Team Types and Taxonomies: A Dimensional Scaling Conceptualization for Team Description," *Academy of Management Review* 37 (2012), pp. 82–106.
22. J.R. Hackman, "The Design of Work Teams," in *Handbook of Organizational Behavior*, ed. J. Lorsch (Englewood Cliffs, NJ: Prentice Hall, 1987), pp. 315–42.
23. S.G. Cohen and G.E. Ledford, "The Effectiveness of Self-Managing Teams: A Quasi-experiment," *Human Relations* 47 (1994), pp. 13–34; J.L. Cordery, W.S. Mueller, and L.M. Smith, "Attitudinal and Behavioral Effects of Autonomous Group Working: A Longitudinal Field Study," *Academy of Management Journal* 34 (1991), pp. 464–76; T.D. Wall, N.J. Kemp, P.R. Jackson, and C.W. Clegg, "Outcomes of Autonomous Work Groups: A Long-Term Field Experiment," *Academy of Management Journal* 29 (1986), pp. 280–304.
24. M.R. Hass, "The Double-Edged Swords of Autonomy and External Knowledge: Analyzing Team Effectiveness in a Multinational Organization," *Academy of Management Journal* 53 (2010), pp. 989–1008.
25. A. Fisher, "How to Build a (Strong) Virtual Team," *CNNMoney.com*, December 10, 2009, money.cnn.com/2009/11/19/news/companies/ibm_virtual_manager.fortune/index.htm.
26. Fisher, "How to Build a (Strong) Virtual Team."
27. H. Duckworth, "How TRW Automotive Helps Global Virtual Teams Perform at the Top of Their Game," *Development and Learning in Organizations* 23 (2008), pp. 6–16.
28. D. Schiff, "Global Teams Rock Around the Clock," *Electronic Engineering Times* 1435 (August 7, 2006), pp. 12, 20.
29. V. Godinez, "Sunshine 24/7: As EDS' Work Stops in One Time Zone, It Picks Up in Another," *Knight Ridder Tribune Business News*, January 2, 2007, ProQuest database, retrieved February 12, 2007; Schiff, "Global Teams Rock"; J.J. Treinen and S.L. Miller-Frost, "Following the Sun: Case Studies in Global Software Development," *IBM Systems Journal* 45 (2006), pp. 773–83.
30. B.W. Tuckman, "Developmental Sequence in Small Groups," *Psychological Bulletin* 63 (1965), pp. 384–99; B.W. Tuckman and M.A.C. Jensen, "Stages of Small-Group Development Revisited," *Group and Organization Management* 2 (1977), pp. 419–27.
31. R.A. Guzzo and G.P. Shea, "Group Performance and Intergroup Relations in Organizations," *Handbook of Industrial and Organizational Psychology*, Vol. 3, eds. M.D. Dunnette and L.M. Hough (Palo Alto, CA: Consulting Psychologists Press, 1992), pp. 269–313.
32. C.J.G. Gersick, "Time and Transition in Work Teams: Toward a New Model of Group Development," *Academy of Management Journal* 33 (1988), pp. 9–41; C.J.G. Gersick, "Marking Time: Predictable Transitions in Task Groups," *Academy of Management Journal* 32 (1989), pp. 274–309.
33. J.D. Thompson, *Organizations in Action* (New York: McGraw-Hill, 1967); A.H. Van de Ven, A.L. Delbecq, and R. Koenig, "Determinants of Coordination Modes within Organizations," *American Sociological Review* 41 (1976), pp. 322–38.
34. Ibid.
35. Thompson, *Organizations in Action.*
36. Ibid.
37. Ibid.
38. Van de Ven et al., "Determinants of Coordination Modes."
39. T. Kelley, *The Art of Innovation* (New York: Doubleday, 2001).
40. R. Saavedra, P.C. Earley, and L. Van Dyne, "Complex Interdependence in Task Performing Groups," *Journal of Applied Psychology* 78 (1993), pp. 61–72.
41. M. Deutsch, *The Resolution of Conflict* (New Haven, CT: Yale University Press, 1973); A. Wong, D. Tjosvold, and Zi-you Yu, "Organizational Partnerships in China: Self-Interest, Goal Interdependence, and Opportunism," *Journal of Applied Psychology* 90 (2005), pp. 782–91.
42. P.S. MacMillan, *The Performance Factor: Unlocking the Secrets of Teamwork* (Nashville, TN: Broadman & Holman, 2001).
43. Ibid.
44. J.E. Mathieu and T.L. Rapp, "The Foundation for Successful Team Performance Trajectories: The Roles of Team Charters and Performance Strategies," *Journal of Applied Psychology* 94 (2009), pp. 90–103.
45. G.P. Shea and R.A. Guzzo, "Groups as Human Resources," in *Research in Personnel and Human Resources Management*, Vol. 5, eds. K.M. Rowland and G.R. Ferris (Greenwich, CT: JAI Press, 1987), pp. 323–56.
46. C.K.W. De Dreu, "Outcome Interdependence, Task Reflexivity, and Team Effectiveness: Motivated Information Processing Perspective," *Journal of Applied Psychology* 92 (2007), pp. 628–38.
47. B.J. Biddle, *Role Theory: Expectations, Identities, and Behavior* (New York: Academic Press, 1979); D. Katz and R.L. Kahn, *The Social Psychology of Organizations*, 2nd ed. (New York: Wiley, 1978).
48. S.E. Humphrey, F.P. Morgeson, and M.J. Mannor, "Developing a Theory of the Strategic Core of Teams: A Role Composition Model of Team Performance," *Journal of Applied Psychology* 94 (2009), pp. 48–61.
49. B. Brehmer and R. Hagafors, "Use of Experts in Complex Decision Making: A Paradigm for the Study of Staff Work," *Organizational Behavior and Human Decision Processes* 38 (1986), pp. 181–95.
50. K. Benne and P. Sheats, "Functional Roles of Group Members," *Journal of Social Issues* 4 (1948), pp. 41–49.
51. M.S. Cole, F. Walter, and H. Bruch, "Affective Mechanisms Linking Dysfunctional Behavior to Performance in Work Teams: A Moderated Mediation Study," *Journal of Applied Psychology* 95 (2008), pp. 945–58.
52. L. Spencer, "Conditioning Has Become an Important Tool: Let's Get Physical," *Stock Car Racing* (n.d.), www.stockcarracing.com/howto/stock_car_pit_crew_-conditioning.
53. D.J. Devine and J.L. Philips, "Do Smarter Teams Do Better: A Meta-analysis of

Cognitive Ability and Team Performance," *Small Group Research* 32 (2001), pp. 507–32; G.L. Stewart, "A Meta-analytic Review of Relationships Between Team Design Features and Team Performance," *Journal of Management* 32 (2006), pp. 29–54.

54. J.A. LePine, J.R. Hollenbeck, D.R. Ilgen, and J. Hedlund, "Effects of Individual Differences on the Performance of Hierarchical Decision-Making Teams: Much More than *g*," *Journal of Applied Psychology* 82 (1997), pp. 803–11.
55. J.A. LePine, "Team Adaptation and Postchange Performance: Effects of Team Composition in Terms of Members' Cognitive Ability and Personality," *Journal of Applied Psychology* 88 (2003), pp. 27–39; J.A. LePine, "Adaptation of Teams in Response to Unforeseen Change: Effects of Goal Difficulty and Team Composition in Terms of Cognitive Ability and Goal Orientation," *Journal of Applied Psychology* 90 (2005), pp. 1153–67.
56. I.D. Steiner, *Group Process and Productivity* (New York: Academic Press, 1972).
57. G.L. Stewart, I.S. Fulmer, and M.R. Barrick, "An Exploration of Member Roles as a Multilevel Linking Mechanism for Individual Traits and Team Outcomes," *Personnel Psychology* 58 (2005), pp. 343–65.
58. S.T. Bell, "Deep Level Composition Variables as Predictors of Team Performance: A Meta-analysis," *Journal of Applied Psychology* 92 (2007), pp. 395–415; M.A.G. Peeters, H.F.J.M. Tuijl, C.G. van Rutte, and I.M.M.J. Reymen, "Personality and Team Performance: A Meta-analysis," *European Journal of Personality* 20 (2006), pp. 377–96.
59. Ibid.
60. D.R. Comer, "A Model of Social Loafing in Real Work Groups," *Human Relations* 48 (1995), pp. 647–67; J.A. Wagner, III, "Studies of Individualism–Collectivism: Effects on Cooperation in Groups," *Academy of Management Journal* 38 (1995), pp. 152–72.
61. J.A., LePine and L. Van Dyne, "Voice and Cooperative Behavior as Contrasting Forms of Contextual Performance: Evidence of Differential Relationships with Personality Characteristics and Cognitive Ability," *Journal of Applied Psychology* 86 (2001), pp. 326–36.
62. J.E. McGrath, "The Influence of Positive Interpersonal Relations on Adjustment and Interpersonal Relations in Rifle Teams," *Journal of Abnormal and Social Psychology* 65 (1962), pp. 365–75.
63. Bell, "Deep Level Composition Variables"; Peeters et al., "Personality and Team Performance."
64. M.R. Barrick, G.L. Stewart, M.J. Neubert, and M.K. Mount, "Relating Member Ability and Personality to Work-Team Processes and Team Effectiveness," *Journal of Applied Psychology* 83 (1998), pp. 377–91; LePine et al., "Effects of Individual Differences"; G.A. Neuman and J. Wright, "Team Effectiveness: Beyond Skills and Cognitive Ability," *Journal of Applied Psychology* 84 (1999), pp. 376–89.
65. J.A. LePine and L. Van Dyne, "Peer Responses to Low Performers: An Attributional Model of Helping in the Context of Work Groups," *Academy of Management Review* 26 (2001), pp. 67–84.
66. Bell, "Deep Level Composition Variables"; Peeters et al., "Personality and Team Performance."
67. M.R. Barrick and M.K. Mount, "The Big Five Personality Dimensions and Job Performance: A Meta-analysis," *Personnel Psychology* 44 (1991), pp. 1–26.
68. Barrick et al., "Relating Member Ability and Personality."
69. B. Barry and G.L. Stewart, "Composition, Process, and Performance in Self-Managed Groups: The Role of Personality," *Journal of Applied Psychology* 82 (1997), pp. 62–78.
70. K. Williams and C. O'Reilly, "The Complexity of Diversity: A Review of Forty Years of Research," in *Research in Organizational Behavior*, Vol. 21, eds. B. Staw and R. Sutton (Greenwich, CT: JAI Press, 1998), pp. 77–140.
71. D.A. Harrison and K.J. Klein, "What's the Difference? Diversity Constructs as Separation, Variety, or Disparity in Organizations," *Academy of Management Review* 32 (2007), pp. 1199–1228.
72. A. Joshi and H. Roh, "The Role of Context in Work Team Diversity Research: A Meta-analytic Review," *Academy of Management Journal* 52 (2009), pp. 599–627.
73. T. Cox, S. Lobel, and P. McLeod, "Effects of Ethnic Group Cultural Differences on Cooperative and Competitive Behavior on a Group Task," *Academy of Management Journal* 34 (1991), pp. 827–47; E. Mannix and M.A. Neal, "What Differences Make a Difference? The Promise and Reality of Diverse Teams in Organizations," *Psychological Science in the Public Interest* 6 (2005), pp. 31–55.
74. S.E. Page, "Making the Difference: Applying the Logic of Diversity," *Academy of Management Perspectives* 21 (2007), pp. 6–20.
75. D. van Knippenberg, C.K.W. DeDreu, and A.C. Homan, "Work Group Diversity and Group Performance: An Integrative Model and Research Agenda," *Journal of Applied Psychology* 89 (2004), pp. 1008–22.
76. Ibid.
77. E. Kearney, D. Gebert, and S.C. Voelpel, "When and How Diversity Benefits Teams: The Importance of Team Members' Need for Cognition," *Academy of Management Journal* 52 (2009), pp. 581–98.
78. A.A. Canella Jr., J.H. Park, and H.U. Lee, "Top Management Team Functional Background Diversity and Firm Performance: Examining the Roles of Team Member Colocation and Environmental Uncertainty," *Academy of Management Journal* 51 (2008), pp. 768–84; D.H. Gruenfeld, E.A. Mannix, K.Y. Williams, and M.A. Neale, "Group Composition and Decision Making: How Member Familiarity and Information Distribution Affect Processes and Performance," *Organizational Behavior and Human Decision Processes* 67 (1996), pp. 1–15; L. Hoffman, "Homogeneity and Member Personality and Its Effect on Group Problem Solving," *Journal of Abnormal and Social Psychology* 58 (1959), pp. 27–32; L. Hoffman and N. Maier, "Quality and Acceptance of Problem Solutions by Members of Homogeneous and Heterogeneous Groups," *Journal of Abnormal and Social Psychology* 62 (1961), pp. 401–7; C.J. Nemeth, "Differential Contributions of Majority and Minority Influence," *Psychological Review* 93 (1986), pp. 22–32; G. Stasster, D. Steward, and G. Wittenbaum, "Expert Roles and Information Exchange During Discussion: The Importance of Knowing Who Knows What," *Journal of Experimental Social Psychology* 57 (1995), pp. 244–65; H. Triandis, E. Hall, and R. Ewen, "Member Heterogeneity and Dyadic Creativity," *Human Relations* 18 (1965), pp. 33–55; W. Watson, K. Kuman, and I. Michaelsen, "Cultural Diversity's Impact on Interaction Process and Performance: Comparing Homogeneous and Diverse Task Groups," *Academy of Management Journal* 36 (1993), pp. 590–602.
79. D. Byrne, *The Attraction Paradigm* (New York: Academic Press, 1971); T.M. Newcomb, *The Acquaintance Process* (New York: Holt, Rinehart and Winston, 1961).
80. D. Byrne, G. Clore, and P. Worchel, "The Effect of Economic Similarity-Dissimilarity as Determinants of Attraction," *Journal of Personality and Social Psychology* 4 (1996), pp. 220–24; J. Lincoln and J. Miller, "Work and Friendship Ties in Organizations: A Comparative Analysis of Relational Networks," *Administrative Science Quarterly* 24 (1979), pp. 181–99; H. Triandis, "Cognitive Similarity and Interpersonal Communication in Industry," *Journal of Applied Psychology* 43 (1959), pp. 321–26; H. Triandis, "Cognitive Similarity and Communication in a Dyad," *Human Relations* 13 (1960), pp. 279–87.
81. S.E. Jackson, K.E. May, and K. Whitney, "Understanding the Dynamics of Diversity in Decision-Making Teams," in *Team Decision-Making Effectiveness in Organizations*, eds. R.A. Guzzo and E. Salas (San Francisco: Jossey-Bass, 1995), pp. 204–61; F.J. Milliken and L.L. Martins, "Searching for Common Threads: Understanding the Multiple Effects of Diversity in Organizational Groups," *Academy of Management Review* 21 (1996), pp. 402–33.
82. D.A. Harrison, K.H. Price, and M.P. Bell, "Beyond Relational Demography: Time and the Effects of Surface- and Deep-Level Diversity on Work Group Cohesion," *Academy of Management Journal* 41 (1998), pp. 96–107; D.A. Harrison, K.H. Price, J.H. Gavin, and A.T. Florey, "Time,

Teams, and Task Performance: Changing Effects of Surface- and Deep-Level Diversity on Group Functioning," *Academy of Management Journal* 45 (2002), pp. 1029–45.
83. Ibid.
84. D. Lau and J.K. Murnighan, "Demographic Diversity and Faultlines: The Compositional Dynamics of Organizational Groups," *Academy of Management Review* 23 (1998), pp. 325–40; D. Lau and J.K. Murnighan, "Interactions with Groups and Subgroups: The Effects of Demographic Faultlines," *Academy of Management Journal* 48 (2005), pp. 645–59.
85. C.S. Tuggle, J. Schnatterly, and R.A. Johnson, "Attention Patterns in the Boardroom: How Board Composition and Process Affect Discussion of Entrepreneurial Issues," *Academy of Management Journal* 53 (2010), pp. 550–71.
86. A.C. Homan, D. van Knippenberg, G.A. Van Kleef, and C.K.W. De Dreu, "Bridging Faultlines by Valuing Diversity: Diversity Beliefs, Information Elaboration, and Performance in Diverse Work Groups," *Journal of Applied Psychology* 92 (2007), pp. 1189–99.
87. A.C. Homan, J.R. Hollenbeck, S.E. Humphrey, D. van Knippenberg, D.R. Ilgen, and G.A. van Kleef, "Facing Differences with an Open Mind: Openness to Experience, Salience of Intragroup Differences, and Performance of Diverse Work Groups," *Academy of Management Journal* 51 (2008), pp. 1204–22; E. Kearney and D. Gebert, "Managing Diversity and Enhancing Team Outcomes: The Promise of Transformational Leadership," *Journal of Applied Psychology* 94 (2009), pp. 77–89.
88. Ibid.
89. Ibid.
90. S. Mohammed and S. Nadkarni, "Temporal Diversity and Team Performance: The Moderating Role of Team Temporal Leadership," *Academy of Management Journal* 54 (2011), pp. 489–508.
91. A.N. Pieterse, D. van Knippenberg, and W.P. van Ginkel, "Diversity in Goal Orientation, Team Reflexivity, and Team Performance," *Organizational Behavior and Human Decision Processes* 114 (2011), pp. 153–64.
92. I.J. Hoever, D. van Knippenberg, W.P. van Ginkel, and H.G. Barkema, "Fostering Team Creativity: Perspective Taking as Key to Unlocking Diversity's Potential," *Journal of Applied Psychology* 97 (2012), pp. 982–96.
93. K.J. Klein, A.P. Knight, J.C. Ziegert, B.C. Lim, and J.L. Salz, "When Team Members' Values Differ: The Moderating Role of Team Leadership," *Organizational Behavior and Human Decision Processes* 114 (2011), pp. 25–36.
94. Ibid.
95. M. Harris, *Cultural Anthropology*, 2nd ed. (New York: Harper and Row, 1987); H.C. Triandis, *Culture and Social Behavior* (New York: McGraw-Hill, 1994).
96. S. Gupta, "Mine the Potential of Multicultural Teams: Mesh Cultural Differences to Enhance Productivity," *HR Magazine* (October 2008), pp. 79–84.
97. Ibid.
98. Ibid.
99. J. Brett, K. Behfar, and M.C. Kern, "Managing Multicultural Teams," *Harvard Business Review* 84 (November 2006), pp. 84–91.
100. Ibid.
101. Ibid.
102. Ibid.
103. Bell, "Deep Level Composition Variables."
104. S.E. Humphrey, J.R. Hollenbeck, C.J. Meyer, and D.R. Ilgen, "Trait Configurations in Self-Managed Teams: A Conceptual Examination of Seeding for Maximizing and Minimizing Trait Variance in Teams," *Journal of Applied Psychology* 92 (2007), pp. 885–92.
105. Stewart, "A Meta-analytic Review."
106. S.W.J. Kozlowski and B.S. Bell, "Work Groups and Teams in Organization," in *Comprehensive Handbook of Psychology: Industrial and Organizational Psychology*, Vol. 12, eds. W.C. Borman, D.R. Ilgen, and R.J. Klimoski (New York: Wiley, 2003), pp. 333–75.
107. R.Z. Gooding and J.A. Wagner III, "A Meta-analytic Review of the Relationship Between Size and Performance: The Productivity and Efficiency of Organizations and Their Subunits," *Administrative Science Quarterly* 30 (1985), pp. 462–81; S.E. Markham, F. Dansereau, and J.A. Alutto, "Group Size and Absenteeism Rates: A Longitudinal Analysis," *Academy of Management Journal* 25 (1982), pp. 921–27.
108. J.R. Hackman and N.J. Vidmar, "Effects of Size and Task Type on Group Performance and Member Reactions," *Sociometry* 33 (1970), pp. 37–54.
109. J.L. Yank, "The Power of Number 4.6," *Fortune* 153(11) (June 12, 2006), p. 122. ProQuest database, retrieved May 28, 2007.
110. "Process," *Merriam-Webster Online Dictionary* (n.d.), www.merriam-webster.com/dictionary/process.
111. Hackman, "The Design of Work Teams."
112. I.D. Steiner, *Group Processes and Productivity* (New York: Academic Press, 1972).
113. Hackman, "The Design of Work Teams."
114. H. Lamm and G. Trommsdorff, "Group Versus Individual Performance on Tasks Requiring Ideational Proficiency (Brainstorming)," *European Journal of Social Psychology* 3 (1973), pp. 361–87.
115. Hackman, "The Design of Work Teams."
116. B. Latane, K. Williams, and S. Harkins, "Many Hands Make Light the Work: The Causes and Consequences of Social Loafing," *Journal of Personality and Social Psychology* 37 (1979), pp. 822–32.
117. Latane et al., "Many Hands"; C.L. Jackson and J.A. LePine, "Peer Responses to a Team's Weakest Link: A Test and Extension of LePine and Van Dyne's Model," *Journal of Applied Psychology* 88 (2003), pp. 459–75; A. Sheppard, "Productivity Loss in Performance Groups: A Motivation Analysis," *Psychological Bulletin* 113 (1993), pp. 67–81.
118. C.E. Shalley, J. Zhou, and G.R. Oldham, "The Effects of Personal and Contextual Characteristics on Creativity: Where Should We Go from Here?," *Journal of Management* 30 (2004), pp. 933–58.
119. E. Miron-Spektor, M. Erez, and E. Naveh, "The Effect of Conformist and Attentive-to-Detail Members on Team Innovation: Reconciling the Innovation Paradox," *Academy of Management Journal* 54 (2011), 740–60.
120. G. Hirst, D. van Knippenberg, and J. Zhou, "A Cross-level Perspective on Employee Creativity: Goal Orientation, Team Learning Behavior, and Individual Creativity," *Academy of Management Journal* 52 (2009), pp. 280–93.
121. T. Kelley and J. Littman, *The Art of Innovation* (New York: Doubleday, 2001), p. 69.
122. A.F. Osborn, *Applied Imagination*, rev. ed. (New York: Scribner, 1957).
123. Ibid.
124. M. Diehl and W. Stroebe, "Productivity Loss in Brainstorming Groups: Toward a Solution of a Riddle," *Journal of Personality and Social Psychology* 53 (1987), pp. 497–509; B. Mullen, C. Johnson, and E. Salas, "Productivity Loss in Brainstorming Groups: A Meta-analytic Investigation," *Basic and Applied Social Psychology* 12 (1991), pp. 3–23.
125. Diehl and Stroebe, "Productivity Loss."
126. R.I. Sutton and A. Hargadon, "Brainstorming Groups in Context: Effectiveness in a Product Design Firm," *Administrative Science Quarterly* 41 (1996), pp. 685–718.
127. A.L. Delbecq and A.H. Van de Ven, "A Group Process Model for Identification and Program Planning," *Journal of Applied Behavioral Sciences* 7 (1971), pp. 466–92; H. Geschka, G.R. Schaude, and H. Schlicksupp, "Modern Techniques for Solving Problems," *Chemical Engineering*, August 1973, pp. 91–97.
128. B. Brehmer, and R. Hagafors, "Use of Experts in Complex Decision Making: A Paradigm for the Study of Staff Work," *Organizational Behavior and Human Decision Processes* 38 (1986), pp. 181–95; D.R. Ilgen, D. Major, J.R. Hollenbeck, and D. Sego, "Raising an Individual Decision Making Model to the Team Level: A New Research Model and Paradigm," in *Team Effectiveness and Decision Making in Organizations*, eds. R. Guzzo and E. Salas (San Francisco: Jossey-Bass, 1995), pp. 113–48.
129. J.R. Hollenbeck, A.P.J. Ellis, S.E. Humphrey, A.S. Garza, and D.R. Ilgen, "Asymmetry in Structural Adaptation: The Differential Impact of Centralizing Versus Decentralizing Team Decision-Making Structures," *Organizational Behavior and*

Human Decision Processes 114 (2011), pp. 64–74.
130. J.R. Hollenbeck, J.A. Colquitt, D.R. Ilgen, J.A. LePine, and J. Hedlund, "Accuracy Decomposition and Team Decision Making: Testing Theoretical Boundary Conditions," *Journal of Applied Psychology* 83 (1998), pp. 494–500; J.R.; Hollenbeck, D.R. Ilgen, D.J. Sego, J. Hedlund, D.A. Major, and J. Phillips, "Multilevel Theory of Team Decision Making; Decision Performance in Teams Incorporating Distributed Expertise," *Journal of Applied Psychology* 80 (1995), pp. 292–316.
131. S.E. Humphrey, J.R. Hollenbeck, C.J. Meyer, and D.R. Ilgen, "Hierarchical Team Decision Making," *Research in Personnel and Human Resources Management* 21 (2002), pp. 175–213.
132. Hollenbeck et al., "Multilevel Theory of Team Decision Making"; Hollenbeck, J.R.; D.R. Ilgen; J.A. LePine; J.A. Colquitt; J. Hedlund. "Extending the Multilevel Theory of Team Decision Making: Effects of Feedback and Experience in Hierarchical Teams," *Academy of Management Journal* 41 (1998), pp. 269–82.
133. Hollenbeck et al., "Extending the Multilevel Theory."
134. J. Hedlund, D.R. Ilgen, and J.R. Hollenbeck, "Decision Accuracy in Computer-Mediated vs. Face-to-Face Decision Making Teams," *Organizational Behavior and Human Decision Processes* 76 (1998), pp. 30–47.
135. D.G. Ancona, "Outward Bound: Strategies for Team Survival in an Organization," *Academy of Management Journal* 33 (1990), pp. 334–65.
136. Ancona, "Outward Bound"; J.A. Marrone, P.E. Tesluk, and J.B. Carson, "A Multilevel Investigation of Antecedents and Consequences of Team Member Boundary-Spanning Behavior," *Academy of Management Journal* 50 (2007), pp. 1423–39.
137. J.A. LePine, R.F. Piccolo, C.L. Jackson, J.E. Mathieu, and J.R. Saul, "A Meta-analysis of Team Process: Toward a Better Understanding of the Dimensional Structure and Relationships with Team Effectiveness Criteria," *Personnel Psychology* 61 (2008), pp. 273–307; M.A. Marks, J.E. Mathieu, and S.J. Zaccaro, "A Temporally Based Framework and Taxonomy of Team Processes," *Academy of Management Review* 26 (2001), pp. 356–76.
138. Marks et al., "A Temporally Based Framework," This section on teamwork processes is based largely on their work.
139. A.J. Villado and W. Arthur Jr., "The Comparative Effect of Subjective and Objective After-Action Reviews on Team Performance on a Complex Task," *Journal of Applied Psychology* 98 (2013), pp. 514–28.
140. C.M. Barnes, J.R. Hollenbeck, D.T. Wagner, D.S. DeRue, J.D. Nahrgang, and K.M. Schwind, "Harmful Help: The Costs of Backing-Up Behavior in Teams," *Journal of Applied Psychology* 93 (2008), pp. 529–39.
141. S.W.J. Kozlowski and B.S. Bell, "Work Groups and Teams in Organizations," in *Handbook of Psychology, Vol. 12: Industrial and Organizational Psychology*, eds. W.C. Borman, D.R. Ilgen, and R.J. Klimoski (Hoboken, NJ: Wiley, 2003), pp. 333–75.
142. K.J. Behfar, R.S. Peterson, E.A. Mannix, and W.M.K. Trochim, "The Critical Role of Conflict Resolution in Teams: A Close Look at the Links Between Conflict Type, Conflict Management Strategies, and Team Outcomes," *Journal of Applied Psychology* 93 (2008), pp. 170–88; C.K.W. De Dreu and L.R. Weingart, "Task Versus Relationship Conflict, Team Performance, and Team Member Satisfaction: A Meta-analysis," *Journal of Applied Psychology* 88 (2003), pp. 741–49.
143. K. Jehn, "A Multimethod Examination of the Benefits and Detriments of Intergroup Conflict," *Administrative Science Quarterly* 40 (1995), pp. 256–82.
144. De Dreu and Weingart, "Task Versus Relationship Conflict"; L.A. DeChurch, J.R. Mesmer-Magnus, and D. Doty, "Moving Beyond Relationship and Task Conflict: Toward a Process-State Perspective," *Journal of Applied Psychology* 98 (2013), pp. 559–78.
145. F.R.C. de Wit, J.L. Greer, and K.A. Jehn, "The Paradox of Intragroup Conflict: A Meta-analysis," *Journal of Applied Psychology* 97 (2012), pp. 360–90.
146. B.H. Bradley, A.C. Klotz, B.E. Postlethwaite, and K.G. Brown, "Ready to Rumble: How Team Personality Composition and Task Conflict Interact to Improve Performance," *Journal of Applied Psychology* 98 (2013), pp. 385–92.
147. L.L. Thompson, *Making the Team: A Guide for Managers*, 2nd ed. (Upper Saddle River, NJ: Pearson Prentice Hall, 2004).
148. L.A. DeChurch and M.A. Marks, "Maximizing the Benefits of Task Conflict: The Role of Conflict Management," *The International Journal of Conflict Management* 12 (2001), pp. 4–22; De Dreu and Weingart, "Task Versus Relationship Conflict"; E. Van de Vliert and M.C. Euwema, "Agreeableness and Activeness as Components of Conflict Behaviors," *Journal of Personality and Social Psychology* 66 (1994), pp. 674–87.
149. DeChurch and Marks, "Maximizing the Benefits"; Van de Vliert and Euwema, "Agreeableness and Activeness."
150. De Church and Marks, "Maximizing the Benefits."
151. A. Edmondson, "Psychological Safety and Learning Behavior in Work Teams," *Administrative Science Quarterly* 44 (1999), pp. 350–83; K. Kostopoulos and N. Bozionelos, "Team Exploratory and Exploitative Learning: Psychological Safety, Task Conflict and Team Performance," *Group and Organization Management* 36 (2011), pp. 385–415; E.W. Morrison, S.L. Wheeler-Smith, and K. Dishan, "Speaking Up in Groups: A Cross-level Study of Group Voice Climate and Voice," *Journal of Applied Psychology* 96 (2011), pp. 183–91.
152. K.D. Williams and S.A. Nida, "Ostracism: Consequences and Coping," *Current Directions in Psychological Science* 20 (2011), pp. 71–75.
153. M. Mach, S. Dolan, and S. Tzafrir, "The Differential Effect of Team Members' Trust on Team Performance: The Mediation Role of Team Cohesion," *Journal of Occupational and Organizational Psychology* 83 (2010), pp. 771–94.
154. L. Festinger, "Informal Social Communication," *Psychological Review* 57 (1950), pp. 271–82.
155. D.J. Beal, R.R. Cohen, M.J. Burke, and C.L. McLendon, "Cohesion and Performance in Groups: A Meta-analytic Clarification of Construct Relations," *Journal of Applied Psychology* 88 (2003), pp. 989–1004; B. Mullen and C. Copper, "The Relation Between Group Cohesiveness and Performance: An Integration," *Psychological Bulletin* 115 (1994), pp. 210–27.
156. I.L. Janis, *Victims of Groupthink: A Psychological Study of Foreign Policy Decisions and Fiascoes* (Boston, MA: Houghton Mifflin, 1972).
157. R. Hirokawa, D. Gouran, and A. Martz, "Understanding the Sources of Faulty Group Decision Making: A Lesson from the *Challenger* Disaster," *Small Group Behavior* 19 (1988), pp. 411–33; J. Esser and J. Linoerfer, "Groupthink and the Space Shuttle *Challenger* Accident: Toward a Quantitative Case Analysis," *Journal of Behavioral Decision Making* 2 (1989), pp. 167–77; G. Moorhead, R. Ference, and C. Neck, "Group Decision Fiascoes Continue: Space Shuttle *Challenger* and a Revised Groupthink Framework," *Human Relations* 44 (1991), pp. 539–50.
158. J. Stephens and P. Behr, "Enron Culture Fed Its Demise," *Washington Post*, June 27, 2002, pp. A1–A2.
159. G.P. Shea and R.A. Guzzo, "Groups as Human Resources," in *Research in Personnel and Human Resource Management*, Vol. 5, eds. K.M. Rowland and G.R. Ferris (Greenwich, CT: JAI Press, 1987), pp. 323–56.
160. K. Tasa, S. Taggar, and G.H. Seijts, "Development of Collective Efficacy in Teams: A Multilevel and Longitudinal Perspective," *Journal of Applied Psychology* 92 (2007), pp. 17–27.
161. S.M. Gully, K.A. Incalcaterra, A. Joshi, and J.M. Beubien, "A Meta-analysis of Team-Efficacy, Potency, and Performance: Interdependence and Level of Analysis as Moderators of Observed Relationships," *Journal of Applied Psychology* 87 (2002), pp. 819–32.
162. J.A. Concalo, E. Polman, and C. Maslach, "Can Confidence Come Too Soon?

Collective Efficacy, Conflict and Group Performance over Time," *Organizational Behavior and Human Decision Processes* 113 (2010), pp. 13–24.

163. Tasa et al., "Development of Collective Efficacy in Teams."
164. R.J. Klimoski and S. Mohammed, "Team Mental Model: Construct or Metaphor?," *Journal of Management* 20 (1994), pp. 403–37.
165. J.A. Cannon-Bowers, E. Salas, and S.A. Converse, "Shared Mental Models in Expert Team Decision Making," *Individual and Group Decision Making*, ed. N.J. Castellan (Hillsdale, NJ: Erlbaum, 1993), pp. 221–46.
166. D.M. Wegner, "Transactive Memory: A Contemporary Analysis of the Group Mind," in *Theories of Group Behavior*, eds. B. Mullen and G.R. Goethals (New York: Springer-Verlag, 1986), pp. 185–208.
167. A.B. Hollingshead, "Communication, Learning, and Retrieval in Transactive Memory Systems," *Journal of Experimental Social Psychology* 34 (1998), pp. 423–42.
168. Wegner, "Transactive Memory."
169. E. Sundstrom, K.P. De Meuse, and D. Futrell, "Work Teams: Applications and Effectiveness," *American Psychologist* 45 (1990), pp. 120–33.
170. Greg L. Stewart, Charles C. Manz, Henry P. Sims, and Kenneth G. Brown, *Team Work and Group Dynamics* (Hoboken, NJ: Wiley, 2000).
171. Stewart, "A Meta-analytic Review."
172. M.A. Campion, G.J. Medsker, and A.C. Higgs, "Relations Between Work Group Characteristics and Effectiveness: Implications for Designing Effective Work Groups," *Personnel Psychology* 46 (1993), pp. 823–49; M.A. Campion, E.M. Papper, and G.J. Medsker, "Relations Between Work Team Characteristics and Effectiveness: A Replication and Extension," *Personnel Psychology* 49 (1996), pp. 429–52.
173. LePine et al., "A Meta-analysis of Team Process."
174. M.R. Barrick, B.H. Bradley, A.L. Kristoff Brown, and A.E. Colbert, "The Moderating Role of Top Management Team Interdependence: Implications for Real Teams and Working Groups," *Academy of Management Journal* 50 (2007), pp. 544–57.
175. LePine et al., "A Meta-analysis of Team Process."
176. M.J. Stevens and M.A. Campion, "The Knowledge, Skill, and Ability Requirements for Teamwork: Implications for *Human Resource Management*," *Journal of Management* 20 (1994), pp. 503–30.
177. Ibid.; A.P.J. Ellis, B. Bell, R.E. Ployhart, J.R. Hollenbeck, and D.R. Ilgen, "An Evaluation of Generic Teamwork Skills Training with Action Teams: Effects on Cognitive and Skill-Based Outcomes," *Personnel Psychology* 58 (2005), pp. 641–72.
178. R.J. Stout, E. Salas, and J.E. Fowlkes, "Enhancing Teamwork in Complex Environments Through Team Training," *Group Dynamics: Theory, Research, and Practice* 1 (1997), pp. 169–82.
179. C.E. Volpe, J.A. Cannon-Bowers, E. Salas, and P.E. Spector, "The Impact of Cross-training on Team Functioning: An Empirical Investigation," *Human Factors* 38 (1996), pp. 87–100.
180. M.A. Marks, M.J. Sabella, C.S. Burke, and S.J. Zaccaro, "The Impact of Cross-training on Team Effectiveness," *Journal of Applied Psychology* 87 (2002), pp. 3–13.
181. E. Blickensderfer, J.A. Cannon-Bowers, and E. Salas, "Cross Training and Team Performance," in *Making Decisions Under Stress: Implications for Individual and Team Training*, eds. J.A. Cannon-Bowers and E. Salas (Washington, DC: APA Press, 1998), pp. 299–311.
182. D. Dotlich and J. Noel, *Active Learning: How the World's Top Companies Are Recreating Their Leaders and Themselves* (San Francisco: Jossey-Bass, 1998); M. Marquardt, "Harnessing the Power of Action Learning," *T&D* 58 (June 2004), pp. 26–32.
183. S. Carey, "Racing to Improve; United Airlines Employees Go to School for Pit Crews to Boost Teamwork, Speed," *The Wall Street Journal*, Eastern Edition, March 24, 2006, p. B1.
184. E. Salas, D. Bozell, B. Mullen, and J.E. Driskell, "The Effect of Team Building on Performance: An Integration," *Small Group Research* 30 (1999), pp. 309–29.
185. D. Berman, "Zap! Pow! Splat! Laser Tag and Paintball Can Enhance Teamwork, Communications, and Planning," *Businessweek*, February 9, 1998, p. ENT22. ProQuest Database, retrieved April 19, 2007.
186. M. Rasor, "Got Game? Bring It On: WhirlyBall Helps Workers Develop Drive, Teamwork," *Knight Ridder Tribune Business News*, April 3, 2006, p. 1. ProQuest Database, retrieved May 7, 2006.
187. M.P. Regan, "Team Players: From Drums to Daring Getaways, Workers Embark on Team-Building Exercises," *Gainesville Sun*, February 15, 2004, pp. 5G, 6G.
188. Salas et al., "The Effect of Team Building."
189. W.W. Chang, "Is the Group Activity Food or Poison in a Multicultural Classroom?," *T&D*, April 2010, pp. 34–37.
190. C. Moskowitz, "Farming on Mars? NASA Ponders for Supply for 2030 Mission," *FoxNews.com*, May 15, 2013, www.foxnews.com/science/2013/05/15/farming-onmars-nasa.
191. Novotney, "I/O Psychology Goes to Mars."
192. R. Plushnick-Masti, "NASA Builds Menu for Planned Mars Mission in 2030s," *AP Online*, July 17, 2012, bigstory.ap.org/article/nasa-builds-menu-planned-mars-mission-2030s.
193. Novotney. "I/O Psychology Goes to Mars."
194. Ibid.
195. Ibid.

Chapter 12

1. Canadian Pacific Railway Ltd. website, www.cpr.ca/en/about-cp/our-history, retrieved February 12, 2015; en.wikipedia.org/wiki/Canadian_Pacific_Railway, retrieved February 12, 2015.
2. Ibid.
3. Ibid.
4. Ibid.
5. Ibid.
6. Gordon Pitts, "Turnaround Ace: Inside the Hunter Harrison Era at CP Railway," *The Globe and Mail*, April 25, 2014, www.theglobeandmail.com/report-on-business/rob-magazine/hunter-harrison-cp-report-on-business-magazine/article18190120, retrieved February 15, 2015; Kristine Owram, "CP Rail's Hunter Harrison: 'We're Doing Things That People Didn't Think Were Imaginable,'" *Financial Post*, October 4, 2014, business.financialpost.com/2014/10/04/cp-rails-hunter-harrison-were-doing-things-that-people-didnt-think-were-imaginable, retrieved February 15, 2015.
7. Ibid.
8. Ibid.
9. Ibid.
10. Ibid.
11. V.V. McMurray, "Some Unanswered Questions on Organizational Conflict," *Organization and Administrative Sciences* 6 (1975), pp. 35–53; J. Pfeffer, *Managing with Power* (Boston: Harvard Business School Press, 1992).
12. J.L. Cotton, "Measurement of Power-Balancing Styles and Some of Their Correlates," *Administrative Science Quarterly* 21 (1976), pp. 307–19; R.M. Emerson, "Power-Dependence Relationships," *American Sociological Review* 27 (1962), pp. 29–41.
13. B.E. Ashforth and F.A. Mael, "The Power of Resistance," in *Power and Influence in Organizations*, eds. R.M. Kramer and M.E. Neal (Thousand Oaks, CA: Sage, 1998), pp. 89–120.
14. J.R.P. French Jr. and B. Raven, "The Bases of Social Power," in *Studies in Social Power*, ed. D. Cartwright (Ann Arbor: University of Michigan, Institute for Social Research, 1959), pp. 150–67; G. Yukl and C.M. Falbe, "The Importance of Different Power Sources in Downward and Lateral Relations," *Journal of Applied Psychology* 76 (1991), pp. 416–23.
15. G. Yukl, "Use Power Effectively," in *Handbook of Principles of Organizational Behavior*, ed. E.A. Locke (Madden, MA: Blackwell, 2004), pp. 242–47.
16. R.S. Tedlow, "The Education of Andy Grove," *Fortune*, December 12, 2005, pp. 117–38.
17. French and Raven, "The Bases of Social Power."
18. D.J. Hickson, C.R. Hinings, C.A. Lee, R.E. Schneck, and J.M. Pennings, "A Strategic Contingencies Theory of Intraorganizational Power," *Administrative Science Quarterly* 16 (1971), pp.

216–27; C.R. Hinings, D.J. Hickson, J.M. Pennings, and R.E. Schneck, "Structural Conditions of Intraorganizational Power," *Administrative Science Quarterly* 19 (1974), pp. 22–44; G.R. Salancik and J. Pfeffer, "Who Gets Power and How They Hold On to It: A Strategic Contingency Model of Power," *Organizational Dynamics* 5 (1977), pp. 3–21.

19. A. Somech and A. Drach-Zahavy, "Relative Power and Influence Strategy: The Effects of Agent/Target Organizational Power on Superiors' Choices of Influence Strategies," *Journal of Organizational Behavior* 23 (2002), pp. 167–79; A.J. Stahelski and C.F. Paynton, "The Effects of Status Cues on Choices of Social Power and Influence Strategies," *Journal of Social Psychology* 135 (1995), pp. 553–60.
20. G. Yukl, *Leadership in Organizations*, 4th ed. (Englewood Cliffs, NJ: Prentice Hall, 1998).
21. G. Yukl, C. Chavez, and C.F. Seifert, "Assessing the Construct Validity and Utility of Two New Influence Tactics," *Journal of Organizational Behavior* 26 (2005), pp. 705–25; G. Yukl, *Leadership in Organizations*, 5th ed. (Upper Saddle River, NJ: Prentice Hall, 2002).
22. G. Yukl, H. Kim, and C. Chavez, "Task Importance, Feasibility, and Agent Influence Behavior as Determinants of Target Commitment," *Journal of Applied Psychology* 84 (1999), pp. 137–43.
23. Yukl, *Leadership in Organizations*.
24. F. Manjoo, "The Quest: How New CEO Larry Page Will Lead the Company He Cofounded into the Future," *Fast Company*, April 2011, pp. 68–76.
25. Yukl et al., "Task Importance."
26. S.J. Wayne and G.R. Ferris, "Influence Tactics, Affect, and Exchange Quality in Supervisor–Subordinate Interactions: A Laboratory Experiment and Field Study," *Journal of Applied Psychology* 75 (1990), pp. 487–99.
27. H.C. Kelman, "Compliance, Identification, and Internalization: Three Processes of Attitude Change," *Journal of Conflict Resolution* 2 (1958), pp. 51–56.
28. Yukl et al., "Assessing the Construct Validity."
29. S. Levy, *In the Plex: How Google Thinks, Works, and Shapes Our Lives* (New York: Simon & Schuster, 2011).
30. R. Buderi, "The Talent Magnet," *Fast Company* 106 (2006), pp. 80–84.
31. M. Wong, "Guanxi Management as Complex Adaptive Systems: A Case Study of Taiwanese ODI in China," *Journal of Business Ethics* 91 (2010), pp. 419–32; C.C. Chen, Y.R. Chen, and K. Xin, "Guanxi Practices and Trust in Management: A Procedural Justice Perspective," *Organization Science* 15 (2004), pp. 200–209.
32. M.M. Yang, *Gifts Favors, and Banquets: The Art of Social Relationships in China* (Ithaca, NY: Cornell University Press, 1994).
33. P.P. Fu, T.K. Peng, J.C. Kennedy, and G. Yukl, "A Comparison of Chinese Managers in Hong Kong, Taiwan, and Mainland China," *Organizational Dynamics* 33 (2003), pp. 32–46.
34. Buderi, "The Talent Magnet."
35. Levy, *In the Plex*.
36. Y. Luo, Y. Huang, and S.L. Wang, "Guanxi and Organizational Performance: A Meta-analysis," *Management and Organization Review* 8 (2011), pp. 139–72.
37. Fu et al., "A Comparison of Chinese Managers."
38. R.Y.J. Chua, "Building Effective Business Relationships in China," *MIT Sloan Management Review* 53 (2012), pp. 27–33.
39. C.M. Falbe and G. Yukl, "Consequences for Managers of Using Single Influence Tactics and Combinations of Tactics," *Academy of Management Journal* 35 (1992), pp. 638–52.
40. Yukl, *Leadership in Organizations*.
41. Ibid.
42. Somech and Drach-Zahavy, "Relative Power and Influence Strategy"; Yukl, *Leadership in Organizations*; Yukl, "Use Power Effectively."
43. G.R. Ferris and W.A. Hochwarter, "Organizational Politics," in *APA Handbook of Industrial and Organizational Psychology*, Vol. 3, ed. S. Zedeck (Washington, DC: American Psychological Association, 2011), pp. 435–59; H. Mintzberg, "The Organization as Political Arena," *Journal of Management Studies* 22 (1985), pp. 133–54.
44. C. Bryan-Low and J. Singer, "Vodafone Group Life President Resigns over Management Flap," *The Wall Street Journal*, March 13, 2006, p. B3.
45. D. Ramel, "Protégé Profiles," *Computerworld* 39 (2005), p. 50.
46. S.B., Bacharach and E.J. Lawler, "Political Alignments in Organizations," in *Power and Influence in Organizations*, eds. R.M. Kramer and M.E. Neal (Thousand Oaks, CA: Sage, 1998), pp. 67–88.
47. K.M. Kacmar and R.A. Baron, "Organizational Politics: The State of the Field, Links to Related Processes, and an Agenda for Future Research," in *Research in Personnel and Human Resources Management*, Vol. 17, ed. G.R. Ferris (Greenwich, CT: JAI Press, 1999), pp. 1–39.
48. G.R. Ferris, D.C. Treadway, P.L. Perrewe, R.L. Brouer, C. Douglas, and S. Lux, "Political Skill in Organizations," *Journal of Management* 33 (2007), pp. 290–320; D.C. Treadway, G.R. Ferris, A.B. Duke, G.L. Adams, and J.B. Thatcher, "The Moderating Role of Subordinate Political Skill on Supervisors' Impressions of Subordinate Ingratiation and Ratings of Subordinate Interpersonal Facilitation," *Journal of Applied Psychology* 92 (2007), pp. 848–55.
49. M. Seldman and E. Betof, "An Illuminated Path," *T+D* 58 (2004), pp. 34–39.
50. G.R. Ferris, D.C. Treadway, R.W. Kolokinsky, W.A. Hochwarter, C.J. Kacmar, and D.D. Frink, "Development and Validation of the Political Skill Inventory," *Journal of Management* 31 (2005), pp. 126–52.
51. Ferris et al., "Political Skill in Organizations"; Ferris et al., "Development and Validation."
52. Ibid.
53. Ibid.
54. M.H. Bing, H.K. Davison, I. Minor, M.M. Novicevik, and D.D. Frink, "The Prediction of Task and Contextual Performance by Political Skill: A Meta-analysis and Moderator Test," *Journal of Vocational Behavior* 79 (2011), pp. 563–77.
55. G.R. Ferris, D.D. Frink, D.P.S. Bhawuk, J. Zhou, and D.C. Gilmore, "Reactions of Diverse Groups to Politics in the Workplace," *Journal of Management* 22 (1996), pp. 23–44.
56. C. Chang, C.C. Rosen, and P.E. Levy, "The Relationship Between Perceptions of Organizational Politics and Employee Attitudes, Strain, and Behavior: A Meta-analytic Examination," *Academy of Management Journal* 52 (2009), pp. 779–801; Kacmar and Baron, "Organizational Politics"; B.K. Miller, M.A. Rutherford, and R.W. Kolodinsky, "Perceptions of Organizational Politics: A Meta-analysis of Outcomes," *Journal of Business and Psychology* 22 (March 2008), pp. 209–22; W.A. Hochwarter, "The Interactive Effects of Pro-Political Behavior and Politics Perceptions on Job Satisfaction and Commitment," *Journal of Applied Social Psychology* 33 (2003), pp. 1360–78; M.L. Randall, R. Cropanzano, C.A. Bormann, and A. Birjulin, "Organizational Politics and Organizational Support as Predictors of Work Attitudes, Job Performance, and Organizational Citizenship Behavior," *Journal of Organizational Behavior* 20 (1999), pp. 159–74; L.A. Witt, "Enhancing Organizational Goal Congruence: A Solution to Organizational Politics," *Journal of Applied Psychology* 83 (1998), pp. 666–74.
57. K.M. Eisenhardt and L.J. Bourgeois, "Politics of Strategic Decision Making in High-Velocity Environments: Toward a Midrange Theory," *Academy of Management Journal* 31 (1988), pp. 737–70.
58. G. Atinc, M. Darrat, B. Fuller, and B.W. Parker, "Perceptions of Organizational Politics: A Meta-analysis of Theoretical Antecedents," *Journal of Managerial Issues* 22 (2010), pp. 494–513; G. Biberman, "Personality and Characteristic Work Attitudes of Persons with High, Moderate, and Low Political Tendencies," *Psychological Reports* 60 (1985), pp. 1303–10; Ferris et al., "Reactions of Diverse Groups"; W.E. O'Connor and T.G. Morrison, "A Comparison of Situational and Dispositional Predictors of Perceptions of Organizational Politics," *Journal of Psychology* 135 (2001), pp. 301–12.
59. E.H. O'Boyle, D.R. Forsyth, G.C. Banks, and M.A. McDaniel, "A Meta-analysis of the Dark Triad and Work Behavior: A Social Exchange Perspective," *Journal of*

Applied Psychology 97 (2012), pp. 557–79; M. Valle and P.L. Perrewe, "Do Politics Perceptions Relate to Political Behaviors? Tests of an Implicit Assumption and Expanded Model," *Human Relations* 53 (2000), pp. 359–86.

60. P.M. Fandt, and G.R. Ferris, "The Management of Information and Impressions: When Employees Behave Opportunistically," *Organizational Behavior and Human Decision Processes* 45 (1990), pp. 140–58; O'Connor and Morrison, "A Comparison of Situational and Dispositional Predictors"; J.M.L. Poon, "Situational Antecedents and Outcomes of Organizational Politics Perceptions," *Journal of Managerial Psychology* 18 (2003), pp. 138–55.
61. Atinc et al., "Perceptions of Organizational Politics."
62. R.J. Lewicki and J.A. Litterer, *Negotiations* (Homewood, IL: Irwin, 1985); K.W. Thomas, "Conflict and Negotiation Processes in Organizations," in *Handbook of Industrial and Organizational Psychology*, 2nd ed., Vol. 3, eds. M.D. Dunnette and L.M. Hough (Palo Alto, CA: Consulting Psychologists Press, pp. 651–717.
63. Weingart, L., and K.A. Jehn. "Manage Intra-Team Conflict Through Collaboration," *Handbook of Principles of Organizational Behavior,* ed. E.A. Locke. Madden, MA: Blackwell, 2004), pp. 226–38.
64. K.W. Thomas, "Toward Multi-dimensional values in Teaching: The Example of Conflict Behaviors," *Academy of Management Review* 2 (1977), pp. 484–90; C.K.W. de Dreu, A. Evers, B. Beersma, E.S. Kluwer, and A. Nauta, "A Theory-Based Measure of Conflict Management Strategies in the Workplace," *Journal of Organizational Behavior* 22 (2001), pp. 645–68.
65. J.L. Holt and C.J. DeVore, "Culture, Gender, Organizational Role, and Styles of Conflict Resolution: A Meta-analysis," *International Journal of Intercultural Relations* 29 (2005), pp. 165–96.
66. A. Schlareth, N. Ensari, and J. Christian, "A Meta-analytical Review of the Relationship Between Emotional Intelligence and Leaders' Constructive Conflict Management," *Group Processes and Intergroup Relations* 16 (2013), pp. 126–36.
67. C.K.W. de Dreu, "Conflict at Work: Basic Principles and Applied Issues," in *APA Handbook for Industrial and Organizational Psychology*, Vol. 3, ed. S. Zedeck (Washington, DC: American Psychological Association, 2011), pp. 461–93.
68. D. Balliet and P.A.M. Van Lange, "Trust, Conflict, and Cooperation: A Meta-analysis," *Psychological Bulletin* 139(5) (2013), 1090–1112.
69. G. Tett, "Billions of Children Could Be Transformed by Cheap Computers," *Financial Times*, March 5, 2011, p. 6.
70. One Laptop per Child website, one.laptop.org/map, retrieved June 17, 2013.
71. J. Fahey, "The Soul of a Laptop," *Forbes*, May 7, 2007, pp. 100–104.
72. S. Hamm, G. Smith, and N. Lakshman, "Social Cause Meets Business Reality: The Misadventures of One Laptop per Child," *Businessweek*, June 16, 2008, p. 48.
73. D. Malhotra and M.H. Bazerman, "Psychological Influence in Negotiation: An Introduction Long Overdue," *Journal of Management* 34 (2008), pp. 509–31.
74. M.H. Bazerman and M.A. Neale, *Negotiating Rationally* (New York: The Free Press, 1992); R.L. Pinkley, T.L. Griffeth, and G.B. Northcraft, "Fixed Pie a la Mode: Information Availability, Information Processing, and the Negotiation of Suboptimal Agreements," *Organizational Behavior and Human Decision Processes* 50 (1995), pp. 101–12.
75. Pinkley et al., "Fixed Pie a la Mode."
76. D.M. Kolb and J. Williams, "Breakthrough Bargaining," *Harvard Business Review*, February 2001, pp. 88–97.
77. Pinkley et al., "Fixed Pie a la Mode."
78. Based on D.G. Pruitt, "Achieving Integrative Agreements in Negotiation," in *Psychology and the Prevention of the Nuclear War*, ed. R.K. White (New York: Columbia University Press, 1986), pp. 463–78.
79. Thomas, "Conflict and Negotiation Processes."
80. Based on R. Shell, *Bargaining for Advantage: Negotiation Strategies for Reasonable People*, 2nd ed. (New York: Penguin Books, 2006).
81. R. Fisher and W. Ury, *Getting to Yes: Negotiating Agreement Without Giving In* (New York: Penguin Books, 1991).
82. Shell, *Bargaining for Advantage.*
83. M.J. Gelfand, A. Fulmer, and L. Severance, "The Psychology of Negotiation and Mediation," in *APA Handbook for Industrial and Organizational Psychology*, Vol. 3, ed. S. Zedeck (Washington, DC: American Psychological Association, 2011), pp. 495–554.
84. Ibid.
85. B. Barry and R.L. Oliver, "Affect in Dyadic Negotiation: A Model and Propositions," *Organizational Behavior and Human Decision Processes* 67 (1996), pp. 127–43.
86. Gelfand, "The Psychology of Negotiation and Mediation."
87. Ibid.
88. D.E. Conlon, H. Moon, and K.Y. Ng, "Putting the Cart Before the Horse: The Benefits of Arbitrating Before Mediating," *Journal of Applied Psychology* 87 (2002), pp. 978–84.
89. R. Donkin, "So What Do You Think You're Worth? The Evidence Seems to Support a New Book's Contention That If You Want a Good Salary, You Had Better Negotiate for It. But Recognize That It Takes Practice," *Financial Times*, November 18, 2004, p. 11.
90. R.L. Pinkley and G.B. Northcraft, *Get Paid What You're Worth: The Expert Negotiators' Guide to Salary and Compensation* (New York: St. Martin's Griffin, 2003).
91. B. Gerhart and S. Rynes, "Determinants and Consequences of Salary Negotiations by Male and Female MBA Graduates," *Journal of Applied Psychology* 76 (1991), pp. 256–62.
92. W.K. Roche and P. Teague, "The Growing Importance of Workplace ADR," *International Journal of Human Resource Management* 23 (2012), pp. 447–58.
93. P.S. Nugent, "Managing Conflict: Third-Party Interventions for Managers," *Academy of Management Executive* 16 (2002), pp. 139–54.
94. B.M. Goldman, R. Cropanzano, J. Stein, and L. Benson, "The Role of Third Parties/Mediation in Managing Conflict in Organizations," in *The Psychology of Conflict and Conflict Management in Organizations*, eds. C.K.W. de Dreu and M.J. Gelfand (New York: Erlbaum, 2008), pp. 291–319.
95. H.J. Bernardin, B.E. Richey, and S.L. Castro, "Mandatory and Binding Arbitration: Effects on Employee Attitudes and Recruiting Results," *Human Resource Management* 50 (2011), pp. 175–200.
96. Conlon et al., "Putting the Cart Before the Horse."

Chapter 13

1. Leander Kahney. "How Apple Got Everything Right by Doing Everything Wrong," *Wired Magazine*, March 18, 2008, www.wired.com/print/techbiz/it/magazine/16-04/bz_apple, retrieved August 23, 2011.
2. Steve Jobs, commencement speech, Stanford University, 2005, www.freerepublic.com/focus/chat/1422863/posts, retrieved August 23, 2011.
3. Ibid.
4. "Steve Jobs," Wikipedia. en.wikipedia.org/wiki/Steve_Jobs, retrieved August 23, 2011.
5. Steve Jobs, commencement speech.
6. Ibid.
7. "Steve Jobs," Wikipedia.
8. Ibid.
9. Ibid.
10. Ibid.
11. Ibid.
12. Peter Elkind. "The Trouble with Steve Jobs," *Fortune*, March 5, 2008, money.cnn.com/2008/03/02/news/companies/elkind_jobs.fortune/index.htm, retrieved August 23, 2011.
13. "Steve Jobs," Wikipedia.
14. Adam Satariano, "Apple Overtakes Exxon Becoming World's Most Valuable Company," *Bloomberg Businessweek*, August 10, 2011, www.businessweek.com/news/2011-08-10/apple-overtakes-exxon-becoming-world-s-most-valuable-company.html, retrieved August 23, 2011.
15. Laurie Segall and David Goldman, "Apple CEO Steve Jobs Resigns," *CNNMoney*, August 24, 2011, money.cnn.

com/2011/08/24/technology/steve_jobs_resigns/index.htm?hpt=hp_c1, retrieved August 24, 2011.
16. K. Blumenthal, *Steve Jobs: The Man Who Thought Different* (New York: Feiwel, 2012).
17. G. Yukl, *Leadership in Organizations*, 4th ed. (Englewood Cliffs, NJ: Prentice Hall, 1998).
18. Ibid.
19. Ibid.
20. Ibid.
21. F. Dansereau Jr., G. Graen, and W.J. Haga, "A Vertical Dyad Linkage Approach to Leadership Within Formal Organizations: A Longitudinal Investigation of the Role Making Process," *Organizational Behavior and Human Performance* 13 (1975), pp. 46–78; G. Graen, M. Novak, and P. Sommerkamp, "The Effects of Leader–Member Exchange and Job Design on Productivity and Satisfaction: Testing a Dual Attachment Model," *Organizational Behavior and Human Performance* 30 (1982), pp. 109–31; G.B. Graen and M. Uhl-Bien, "Relationship-Based Approach to Leadership: Development of Leader–Member Exchange (LMX) Theory of Leadership over 25 Years: Applying a Multi-level Multi-domain Perspective," *Leadership Quarterly* 6 (1995), pp. 219–47; R.C. Liden, R.T. Sparrowe, and S.J. Wayne, "Leader–Member Exchange Theory: The Past and Potential for the Future," in *Research in Personnel and Human Resources Management*, Vol. 15, ed. G.R. Ferris (Greenwich, CT: JAI Press, 1997), pp. 47–119.
22. G.B. Graen, and T. Scandura, "Toward a Psychology of Dyadic Organizing," in *Research in Organizational Behavior*, Vol. 9, eds. L.L. Cummings and B.M. Staw (Greenwich, CT: JAI Press, 1987), pp. 175–208.
23. Ibid.
24. Graen and Uhl-Bien, "Relationship-Based Approach to Leadership."
25. Ibid.
26. T.N. Bauer and S.G. Green, "Development of Leader–Member Exchange: A Longitudinal Test," *Academy of Management Journal* 39 (1996), pp. 1538–67; C.R. Gerstner and D.V. Day, "Meta-analytic Review of Leader–Member Exchange Theory: Correlates and Construct Issues," *Journal of Applied Psychology* 82 (1997), pp. 827–44; R.C. Liden, S.J. Wayne, and D. Stillwell, "A Longitudinal Study on the Early Development of Leader–Member Exchanges," *Journal of Applied Psychology* 78 (1993), pp. 662–74.
27. G.A. Ballinger, D.W. Lehman, and F.D. Schoorman, "Leader–Member Exchange and Turnover Before and After Succession Events," *Organizational Behavior and Human Decision Processes* 113 (2010), pp. 25–36.
28. Graen and Uhl-Bien, "Relationship-Based Approach to Leadership."
29. R. Ilies, J.D. Nahrgang, and F.P. Morgeson, "Leader–Member Exchange and Citizenship Behaviors: A Meta-analysis," *Journal of Applied Psychology* 92 (2007), pp. 269–77; J.H. Dulebohn, W.H. Bommer, R.C. Liden, R.L. Brouer, and G.R. Ferris, "A Meta-analysis of Antecedents and Consequences or Leader–Member Exchange: Integrating the Past with an Eye Toward the Future," *Journal of Management* 38 (2012), pp. 1715–759.
30. T. Rockstuhl, J.H. Dulebohn, S. Ang, and L.M. Shore, "Leader–Member Exchange (LMX) and Culture: A Meta-analysis of Correlates of LMX Across 23 Countries," *Journal of Applied Psychology* 97 (2012), pp. 1097–1130.
31. R.M. Stogdill, "Personal Factors Associated with Leadership: A Survey of the Literature," *Journal of Applied Psychology* 54 (1948), pp. 259–69.
32. D.N. Den Hartog and P.L. Koopman, "Leadership in Organizations," in *Handbook of Industrial, Work, and Organizational Psychology*, Vol. 2, eds. N. Anderson, D.S. Ones, H.K. Sinangil, and C. Viswesvaran (Thousand Oaks, CA: Sage, 2002), pp. 166–87.
33. Yukl, *Leadership in Organizations*; S.J. Zaccaro, "Trait-Based Perspectives of Leadership," *American Psychologist* 62 (1998), pp. 6–16.
34. D.S. DeRue, J.D. Nahrgang, N. Wellman, and S.E. Humphrey, "Trait and Behavioral Theories of Leadership: An Integration and Meta-analytic Test of Their Validity," *Personnel Psychology* 64 (2011), pp. 7–52.
35. V.H. Vroom, "Leadership and the Decision-Making Process," *Organizational Dynamics* 28 (2000), pp. 82–94; and Yukl, *Leadership in Organizations*.
36. A. Taylor, "Chrysler's Speed Merchant," *Fortune*, September 6, 2010, p. 82.
37. Vroom, "Leadership and the Decision-Making Process"; Yukl, *Leadership in Organizations*.
38. Ibid.
39. A. Bryant, *The Corner Office: Indispensable and Unexpected Lessons from CEOs on How to Lead and Succeed* (New York: Times Books, 2011).
40. Vroom, "Leadership and the Decision-Making Process"; Yukl, *Leadership in Organizations*.
41. Bryant, A. *The Corner Office*.
42. Ibid.
43. Vroom, "Leadership and the Decision-Making Process."
44. K.I. Miller and P.R. Monge, "Participation, Satisfaction, and Productivity: A Meta-analytic Review," *Academy of Management Journal* 29 (1986), pp. 727–53; J.A. Wagner III, "Participation's Effects on Performance and Satisfaction: A Reconsideration of Research Evidence," *Academy of Management Review* 19 (1994), pp. 312–30.
45. Vroom, "Leadership and the Decision-Making Process."
46. S.G. Rogelberg, D.J. Leach, P.B. Warr, and J.L. Burnfield, "'Not Another Meeting!' Are Meeting Time Demands Related to Employee Well-Being?," *Journal of Applied Psychology* 91 (2006), pp. 86–96.
47. J.L. Yang, "What's the Secret to Running Great Meetings?," *Fortune*, October 27, 2008, p. 26.
48. S. Terlep, "GM's Plodding Culture Vexes Its Impatient CEO," *The Wall Street Journal Online*, April 7, 2010.
49. Vroom, "Leadership and the Decision-Making Process"; V.H., Vroom and A.G. Jago, *The New Leadership: Managing Participation in Organizations* (Englewood Cliffs, NJ: Prentice Hall, 1988); V.H. Vroom and A.G. Jago, "Decision Making as a Social Process: Normative and Descriptive Models of Leader Behavior," *Decision Sciences* 5 (1974), pp. 743–69; V.H. Vroom and P.W. Yetton, *Leadership and Decision Making* (Pittsburgh, PA: University of Pittsburgh Press, 1973).
50. R. Adams and L.A. Schuker, "Time Inc. CEO Ousted After Six Months," *The Wall Street Journal Online*, February 18, 2011.
51. R.N. Aditya, R.J. House, and S. Kerr, "Theory and Practice of Leadership: Into the New Millennium," in *Industrial and Organizational Psychology: Linking Theory with Practice*, eds. C.L. Cooper and E.A. Locke (Malden, MA: Blackwell, 2000), pp. 130–65; R.J. House and R.N. Aditya, "The Social Scientific Study of Leadership: Quo Vadis?," *Journal of Management* 23 (1997), pp. 409–73; and Yukl, *Leadership in Organizations*.
52. V.H. Vroom and A.G. Jago, "On the Validity of the Vroom-Yetton Model," *Journal of Applied Psychology* 63 (1978), pp. 151–62. See also Vroom and Yetton, *Leadership and Decision Making*; Vroom and Jago, *The New Leadership*; R.H.G. Field, "A Test of the Vroom-Yetton Normative Model of Leadership," *Journal of Applied Psychology* 67 (1982), pp. 523–32.
53. Vroom and Yetton, *Leadership and Decision Making*.
54. Bryant, *The Corner Office*.
55. J.K. Hemphill, *Leader Behavior Description* (Columbus: Ohio State University, 1950). Cited in E.A. Fleishman, E.F. Harris, and H.E. Burtt, *Leadership and Supervision in Industry: An Evaluation of a Supervisory Training Program* (Columbus: Bureau of Educational Research, Ohio State University, 1955).
56. J.K. Hemphill and A.E. Coons, "Development of the Leader Behavior Description Questionnaire," in *Leader Behavior: Its Description and Measurement*, eds. R.M. Stogdill and A.E. Coons (Columbus: Bureau of Business Research, Ohio State University, 1957), pp. 6–38.
57. E.A. Fleishman, "The Description of Supervisory Behavior," *Journal of Applied Psychology* 37 (1953), pp. 1–6; Fleishman et al., *Leadership and Supervision in Industry*; Hemphill and Coons, "Development of the Leader Behavior Description Questionnaire"; A.W. Halpin and B.J. Winer, *Studies in Aircrew Composition: The Leadership Behavior of the Airplane Commander* (Technical

Report No. 3) (Columbus: Personnel Research Board, Ohio State University, 1952), cited in Fleishman et al., *Leadership and Supervision in Industry*.
58. Fleishman, "The Description of Supervisory Behavior"; Fleishman et al., *Leadership and Supervision in Industry*; and E.A. Fleishman and D.R. Peters, "Interpersonal Values, Leadership Attitudes, and Managerial 'Success,'" *Personnel Psychology* 15 (1962), pp. 127–43.
59. Yukl, *Leadership in Organizations*.
60. Fleishman, "The Description of Supervisory Behavior"; Fleishman et al., *Leadership and Supervision in Industry*; and Fleishman and Peters, "Interpersonal Values."
61. Yukl, *Leadership in Organizations*.
62. D. Katz, N. Maccoby, and N. Morse, *Productivity, Supervision, and Morale in an Office Situation* (Ann Arbor: Institute for Social Research, University of Michigan, 1950); D. Katz, N. Maccoby, G. Gurin, and L. Floor, *Productivity, Supervision, and Morale Among Railroad Workers* (Ann Arbor: Survey Research Center, University of Michigan, 1951); D., Katz and R.L. Kahn, "Some Recent Findings in Human-Relations Research in Industry," in *Readings in Social Psychology*, eds. E. Swanson, T. Newcomb, and E. Hartley (New York: Holt, 1952), pp. 650–65; R. Likert, *New Patterns of Management* (New York: McGraw-Hill, 1961); R. Likert, *The Human Organization* (New York: McGraw-Hill, 1967).
63. E.A. Fleishman, "Twenty Years of Consideration and Structure," in *Current Developments in the Study of Leadership*, eds. E.A. Fleishman and J.G. Hunt (Carbondale: Southern Illinois Press, 1973), pp. 1–37.
64. T.A. Judge, R.F. Piccolo, and R. Ilies, "The Forgotten Ones? The Validity of Consideration and Initiating Structure in Leadership Research," *Journal of Applied Psychology* 89 (2004), pp. 36–51.
65. Aditya et al., "Theory and Practice of Leadership"; Den Hartog and Koopman, "Leadership in Organizations"; House and Aditya, "The Social Scientific Study of Leadership"; A.K. Korman, "'Consideration,' 'Initiating Structure,' and Organizational Criteria—A Review," *Personnel Psychology* 19 (1966), pp. 349–61; Yukl, *Leadership in Organizations*; G. Yukl and D.D. Van Fleet, "Theory and Research on Leadership in Organizations," in *Handbook of Industrial and Organizational Psychology*, Vol. 3, eds. M.D. Dunnette and L.M. Hough (Palo Alto, CA: Consulting Psychologists Press, 1992), pp. 147–97.
66. Judge et al., "The Forgotten Ones?"
67. K.T. Greenfeld, "The Sharin' Huggin' Lovin' Carin' Chinese Food Money Machine," *Bloomberg Businessweek*, November 22, 2011, pp. 98–103.
68. P. Hersey, and K.H. Blanchard, "Life Cycle Theory of Leadership," *Training and Development Journal*, May 1969, pp. 26–34; P. Hersey and K.H. Blanchard, "So You Want to Know Your Leadership Style?," *Training and Development Journal*, February 1974, pp. 22–37; P. Hersey and K.H. Blanchard, "Revisiting the Life-Cycle Theory of Leadership," *Training and Development*, January 1996, pp. 42–47; P. Hersey and K.H. Blanchard, *Management of Organizational Behavior: Leading Human Resources*, 9th ed. (Upper Saddle River, NJ: Pearson, 2008).
69. Hersey and Blanchard, *Management of Organizational Behavior*.
70. Hersey and Blanchard, "Revisiting the Life-Cycle Theory of Leadership."
71. C.F. Fernandez and R.P. Vecchio, "Situational Leadership Revisited: A Test of an Across-Jobs Perspective," *Leadership Quarterly* 8 (1997), pp. 67–84.
72. C.L. Graeff, "Evolution of Situational Leadership Theory: A Critical Review," *Leadership Quarterly* 8 (1997), pp. 153–70.
73. R.P. Vecchio, "Situational Leadership Theory: An Examination of a Prescriptive Theory," *Journal of Applied Psychology* 72 (1987), pp. 444–51; W.R. Norris and R.P. Vecchio, "Situational Leadership Theory: A Replication," *Group and Organization Management* 17 (1992), pp. 331–42.
74. Vecchio, "Situational Leadership Theory"; Norris and Vecchio, "Situational Leadership Theory: A Replication"; W. Blank, J.R. Weitzel, and S.G. Green, "A Test of Situational Leadership Theory," *Personnel Psychology* 43 (1990), pp. 579–97.
75. Fernandez and Vecchio, "Situational Leadership Theory Revisited."
76. B.M. Bass and R.E. Riggio, *Transformational Leadership*, 2nd ed. (Mahwah, NJ: Lawrence Erlbaum Associates, 2006); B.M. Bass, *Leadership and Performance Beyond Expectations* (New York: The Free Press, 1985); L.M. Burns, *Leadership* (New York: Harper & Row, 1978).
77. Bass, *Leadership and Performance Beyond Expectations*.
78. B.M. Bass and R.E. Riggio, *Transformational Leadership*, 2nd ed. (Mahwah, NJ: Erlbaum, 2006); B.M. Bass, *Leadership and Performance Beyond Expectations* (New York: Free Press, 1985); L.M. Burns, *Leadership*.
79. Bass, *Leadership and Performance Beyond Expectations*.
80. Ibid.
81. Bass and Riggio, *Transformational Leadership*.
82. Ibid.; B.M. Bass and B.J. Avolio, *MLQ: Multifactor Leadership Questionnaire* (Redwood City, CA: Mind Garden, 2000).
83. Bass and Riggio, *Transformational Leadership*; Bass, *Leadership and Performance Beyond Expectations*; Burns, *Leadership*.
84. Bass and Riggio, *Transformational Leadership*.
85. Bass, *Leadership and Performance beyond Expectations*.
86. Bass and Riggio, *Transformational Leadership*; Bass and Avolio, *MLQ*.
87. Bass and Riggio, *Transformational Leadership*.
88. Ibid.; Bass and Avolio, *MLQ*.
89. Bass and Riggio, *Transformational Leadership*.
90. Ibid.; Bass and Avolio, *MLQ*.
91. Judge, T.A., and R.F. Piccolo. "Transformational and Transactional Leadership: A Meta-analytic Test of Their Relative Validity," *Journal of Applied Psychology* 89 (2004), pp. 755–68.
92. Ibid.
93. Y.I. Kane, "Jobs Quits as CEO," *The Wall Street Journal Online*, August 25, 2011; L. Friedman, "Steve Jobs Takes Medical Leave of Absence," *MacWorld*, April 2011, p. 12.
94. Ibid.; Bass and Avolio, *MLQ*.
95. Bass and Riggio, *Transformational Leadership*.
96. N.F. Koehn, "HIS Legacy," *Fortune*, November 11, 2009, pp. 110–14.
97. K. Blumenthal, *Steve Jobs: The Man Who Thought Different* (New York: Feiwel, 2012); W. Isaacson, *Steve Jobs* (New York: Simon & Schuster, 2011).
98. J.S. Young and W.L. Simon, *iCon: Steve Jobs—The Greatest Second Act in the History of Business* (Hoboken, NJ: Wiley, 2005).
99. R.J. House, P.J. Hanges, M. Javidan, P.W. Dorfman, and V. Gupta, *Culture (Leadership, and Organizations*. Thousand Oaks, CA: Sage, 2004); P.W. Dorfman, P.J. Hanges, and F.C. Brodbeck, "Leadership and Cultural Variation: The Identification of Culturally Endorsed Leadership Profiles," in *Culture, Leadership, and Organizations*, eds. R.J. House, P.J. Hanges, M. Javidan, P.W. Dorfman, and V. Gupta (Thousand Oaks, CA: Sage, 2004), pp. 669–720.
100. M. Javidan, R.J. House, and P.W. Dorfman, "A Nontechnical Summary of GLOBE Findings," in *Culture, Leadership, and Organizations*, eds. R.J. House, P.J. Hanges, M. Javidan, P.W. Dorfman, and V. Gupta (Thousand Oaks, CA: Sage, 2004), pp. 29–48.
101. Dorfman et al., "Leadership and Cultural Variation."
102. A.M. Johnson, P.A. Vernon, J.M. McCarthy, M. Molso, J.A. Harris, and K.J. Jang, "Nature vs. Nurture: Are Leaders Born or Made? A Behavior Genetic Investigation of Leadership Style," *Twin Research* 1 (1998), pp. 216–23.
103. T.A. Judge and J.E. Bono, "Five-Factor Model of Personality and Transformational Leadership," *Journal of Applied Psychology* 85 (2000), pp. 751–65.
104. Bass and Riggio, *Transformational Leadership*.
105. J.A. Conger, "Charismatic and Transformational Leadership in Organizations: An Insider's Perspective on these Developing Research Streams," *Leadership Quarterly* 10 (1999), pp. 145–79.

106. Bass and Riggio, *Transformational Leadership*; and Bass and Avolio, *MLQ*.
107. Young and Simon, *iCon*.
108. Ibid.
109. Bass and Riggio, *Transformational Leadership*.
110. Ibid.; Bass and Avolio, *MLQ*.
111. Isaacson, *Steve Jobs*.
112. Bass and Riggio, *Transformational Leadership*.
113. Ibid.; Bass and Avolio, *MLQ*.
114. Young and Simon, *iCon*.
115. K.B. Lowe, K.G. Kroeck, and N. Sivasubramaniam, "Effectiveness Correlates of Transformational and Transactional Leadership: A Meta-analytic Review of the MLQ Literature," *Leadership Quarterly* 7 (1996), pp. 385–425.
116. J.M. Howell and B.J. Avolio, "Transformational Leadership, Transactional Leadership, Locus of Control, and Support for Innovation: Key Predictors of Consolidated-Business-Unit Performance," *Journal of Applied Psychology* 78 (1993), pp. 891–902; J.M. Howell, D.J. Neufeld, and B.J. Avolio, "Examining the Relationship of Leadership and Physical Distance with Business Unit Performance," *Leadership Quarterly* 16 (2005), pp. 273–85; R.T. Keller, "Transformational Leadership, Initiating Structure, and Substitutes for Leadership: A Longitudinal Study of Research and Development Project Team Performance," *Journal of Applied Psychology* 91 (2006), pp. 202–10; D.A. Waldman, G.G. Ramirez, R.J. House, and P. Puranam, "Does Leadership Matter? CEO Leadership Attributes and Profitability Under Conditions of Perceived Environmental Uncertainty," *Academy of Management Journal* 44 (2001), pp. 134–43.
117. J.M. Howell and K.E. Hall-Merenda, "The Ties That Bind: The Impact of Leader–Member Exchange, Transformational and Transactional Leadership, and Distance on Predicting Follower Performance," *Journal of Applied Psychology* 84 (1999), pp. 680–94; R.F. Piccolo and J.A. Colquitt, "Transformational Leadership and Job Behaviors: The Mediating Role of Core Job Characteristics," *Academy of Management Journal* 49 (2006), pp. 327–40; H. Wang, K.S. Law, R.D. Hackett, D. Wang, and Z.X. Chen, "Leader–Member Exchange as a Mediator of the Relationship Between Transformational Leadership and Followers' Performance and Organizational Citizenship Behavior," *Academy of Management Journal* 48 (2005), pp. 420–32.
118. Judge and Piccolo, "Transformational and Transactional Leadership"; P.M. Podsakoff, S.B. MacKenzie, J.B. Paine, and D.G. Bachrach, "Organizational Citizenship Behaviors: A Critical Review of the Theoretical and Empirical Literature and Suggestions for Future Research," *Journal of Management* 26 (2000), pp. 513–63.
119. Judge and Piccolo, "Transformational and Transactional Leadership."
120. B.J. Avolio, W. Zhu, W. Koh, and P. Bhatia, "Transformational Leadership and Organizational Commitment: Mediating Role of Psychological Empowerment and Moderating Role of Structural Distance," *Journal of Organizational Behavior* 25 (2004), pp. 951–68; S.A. Kirkpatrick and E.A. Locke, "Direct and Indirect Effects of Three Core Charismatic Leadership Components on Performance and Attitudes," *Journal of Applied Psychology* 81 (1996), pp. 36–51; B. Shamir, E. Zakay, E. Breinin, and M. Popper, "Correlates of Charismatic Leader Behaviors in Military Units: Subordinates' Attitudes, Unit Characteristics, and Superiors Appraisals of Leader Performance," *Academy of Management Journal* 41 (1998), pp. 387–409.
121. P.M. Podsakoff, S.B. MacKenzie, and W.H. Bommer, "Transformational Leader Behaviors and Substitutes for Leadership as Determinants of Employee Satisfaction, Commitment, Trust, and Organizational Citizenship Behaviors," *Journal of Management* 22 (1996), pp. 259–98; P.M. Podsakoff, S.B. MacKenzie, R.H. Moorman, and R. Fetter, "Transformational Leader Behaviors and their Effects on Followers' Trust in Leader, Satisfaction, and Organizational Citizenship Behaviors," *Leadership Quarterly* 1 (1990), pp. 107–42; Shamir et al., "Correlates of Charismatic Leader Behaviors."
122. J.P. Meyer, D.J. Stanley, L. Herscovitch, and L. Topolnytsky, "Affective, Continuance, and Normative Commitment to the Organization: A Meta-analysis of Antecedents, Correlates, and Consequences," *Journal of Vocational Behavior* 61 (2002), pp. 20–52.
123. F.O. Walumbwa, B.J. Avolio, and W. Zhu, "How Transformational Leadership Weaves Its Influence on Individual Job Performance: The Role of Identification and Efficacy Beliefs," *Personnel Psychology* 61 (2008), pp. 793–825.
124. Judge and Piccolo, "Transformational and Transactional Leadership."
125. Piccolo and Colquitt, "Transformational Leadership and Job Behaviors," See also J.E. Bono and T.A. Judge, "Self-Concordance at Work: Toward Understanding the Motivational Effects of Transformational Leaders," *Academy of Management Journal* 46 (2003), pp. 554–71; S.J. Shin and J. Zhou, "Transformational Leadership, Conservation, and Creativity: Evidence from Korea," *Academy of Management Journal* 46 (2003), pp. 703–14.
126. J.E. Bono and R. Ilies, "Charisma, Positive Emotions, and Mood Contagion," *Leadership Quarterly* 17 (2006), pp. 317–34; and J.R. McColl-Kennedy and R.D. Anderson, "Impact of Leadership Style and Emotions on Subordinate Performance," *Leadership Quarterly* 13 (2002), pp. 545–59.
127. J. Bono, H.J. Foldes, G. Vinson, and J.P. Muros, "Workplace Emotions: The Role of Supervision and Leadership," *Journal of Applied Psychology* 92 (2007), pp. 1357–67.
128. S. Kerr and J.M. Jermier, "Substitutes for Leadership: Their Meaning and Measurement," *Organizational Behavior and Human Performance* 22 (1978), pp. 375–403.
129. J.P. Howell, P.W. Dorfman, and S. Kerr, "Moderator Variables in Leadership Research," *Academy of Management Review* 11 (1986), pp. 88–102.
130. Kerr and Jermier, "Substitutes for Leadership"; J.M. Jermier and S. Kerr, "'Substitutes for Leadership: Their Meaning and Measurement': Contextual Recollections and Current Observations," *Leadership Quarterly* 8 (1997), pp. 95–101.
131. J.P. Howell, D.E. Bowen, P.W. Dorfman, S. Kerr, and P.M. Podsakoff, "Substitutes for Leadership: Effective Alternatives to Ineffective Leadership," *Organizational Dynamics*, Summer 1990, pp. 21–38.
132. P.M. Podsakoff and S.B. MacKenzie, "Kerr and Jermier's Substitutes for Leadership Model: Background, Empirical Assessment, and Suggestions for Future Research," *Leadership Quarterly* 8 (1997), pp. 117–25; P.M. Podsakoff, B.P. Niehoff, S.B. MacKenzie, and M.L. Williams, "Do Substitutes for Leadership Really Substitute for Leadership? An Empirical Examination of Kerr and Jermier's Situational Leadership Model," *Organizational Behavior and Human Decision Processes* 54 (1993), pp. 1–44; Podsakoff et al., "Transformational Leadership Behaviors and Substitutes for Leadership"; and P.M. Podsakoff, S.B. MacKenzie, M. Ahearne, and W.H. Bommer, "Searching for a Needle in a Haystack: Trying to Identify the Illusive Moderators of Leadership Behavior," *Journal of Management* 21 (1995), pp. 422–70.
133. Howell et al., "Substitutes for Leadership: Effective Alternatives."
134. G. Kranz, "A Higher Standard for Managers," *Workforce*, June 11, 2007, pp. 21–26.
135. G. Kranz, "Wal-Mart Drafts Leaders for Military-Style Training," *Workforce*, June 12, 2013, www.workforce.com/article/20130612/NEWS02/130619994/0/topics.
136. M.E. Gist and D. McDonald-Mann, "Advances in Leadership Training and Development," in *Industrial and Organizational Psychology: Linking Theory with Practice*, eds. C.L. Cooper and E.A. Locke (Malden, MA: Blackwell, 2000), pp. 52–71.
137. N. Reardon, "Making Leadership Personal," *T+D*, March 2011, pp. 44–49.
138. M. Weinstein, "Farmer's Comprehensive Training Policy," *Training*, January/February 2013, pp. 42–44.
139. Ibid.; T. Dvir, D. Eden, B.J. Avolio, and B. Shamir, "Impact of Transformational Leadership on Follower Development and Performance: A Field Experiment,"

Academy of Management Journal 45 (2000), pp. 735–44; J. Barling, T. Weber, and E.K. Kelloway, "Effects of Transformational Leadership Training on Attitudinal and Financial Outcomes: A Field Experiment," *Journal of Applied Psychology* 81 (1996), pp. 827–32.
140. Barling et al., "Effects of Transformational Leadership Training."

Chapter 14

1. "Mike H.," Yelp.com, www.yelp.com/biz/the-cheesecake-factory-cheektowaga?hrid=MUgaFo_uf1fupvtndjSQOA.
2. "Lambert P.," Yelp.com, www.yelp.com/biz/the-cheesecake-factory-cheektowaga?hrid=qm7q71CLkwm_Wc-U2fVF_Q.
3. R. Alexander, "The Cheesecake Factory: A Great Place To Eat and Work," *Examiner*, November 12, 2012, www.examiner.com.
4. M. Robbins, "The Sweet Taste of Success," *Employee Benefit News*, January 2008, ebn.benefitnews.com/news/sweet-taste-success-522401-1.html.
5. A. Gawande, "Big Med," *The New Yorker*, August 13 and 20, 2012, pp. 52–63.
6. Ibid.
7. G. Ruiz, "Cheesecake Factory Cooks Up a Rigorous Employee Training Program," *Workforce Management*, September 7, 2011, www.workforce.com.
8. J.R. Hackman and G.R. Oldham, *Work Redesign* (Reading, MA: Addison-Wesley, 1980).
9. R.E. Silverman, "Who's the Boss? There Isn't One," *The Wall Street Journal*, June 20, 2012, p. B1.
10. H. Simon, *Administrative Behavior* (New York: Macmillan, 1947).
11. C. Edwards, "Shaking Up Intel's Insides," *Businessweek*, January 31, 2005, p. 35.
12. K.J. Meier and J. Bohte, "Ode to Luther Gulick: Span of Control and Organizational Performance," *Administration and Society* 32 (2000), pp. 115–37.
13. N.A. Theobald and S. Nicholson-Crotty, "The Many Faces of Span of Control: Organizational Structure Across Multiple Goals," *Administration and Society* 36 (2005), pp. 648–60.
14. J. Child and M. McGrath, "Organizations Unfettered: Organizational Forms in an Information-Intensive Economy," *Academy of Management Journal* 44 (2001), pp. 1135–48.
15. C. Hymowitz, "Today's Bosses Find Mentoring Isn't Worth the Time and Risks," *The Wall Street Journal*, March 13, 2006, p. B1.
16. C. Nuttal, "Intel Cuts 1,000 Management Jobs," *Financial Times*, July 14, 2006, p. 23.
17. J. Marquez, "Taking a Longer View," *Workforce Management*, May 22, 2006, pp. 18–22.
18. D. Michaels, "Airbus on Track to Double Profit Margin by 2015," *The Wall Street Journal*, June 17, 2013, p. B1.
19. S.M. Toh, F.P. Morgeson, and M.A. Campion, "Human Resource Configurations: Investigating Fit within the Organizational Context," *Journal of Applied Psychology* 93 (2008), pp. 864–82.
20. F. Walter and H. Bruch, "Structural Impacts on the Occurrence and Effectiveness of Transformational Leadership: An Empirical Study at the Organizational Level of Analysis," *The Leadership Quarterly* 21 (2010), pp. 765–82.
21. J. O'Brien, "Microsoft Reboots," *Fortune*, October 26, 2009, pp. 98–108.
22. B. Keats and H. O'Neill, "Organizational Structure: Looking Through a Strategy Lens," in *Handbook of Strategic Management*, eds. M.A. Hitt, R.E. Freeman, and J.S. Harrison (Oxford, UK: Blackwell, 2003), pp. 520–42.
23. J. Collins, *How the Mighty Fall* (New York: HarperCollins, 2009).
24. W.R. Scott and G.F. Davis, *Organizations and Organizing: Rational, Natural, and Open System Perspectives* (Englewood Cliffs, NJ: Pearson Prentice Hall, 2007).
25. Y.I. Kane and P. Dvorak, "Howard Stringer, Japanese CEO," *The Wall Street Journal*, March 3, 2007, pp. A1, A6; M. Singer, "Stringer's Way," *The New Yorker*, June 5, 2006, pp. 46–57.
26. M. Porter, *Competitive Strategy* (New York: The Free Press, 1980).
27. J. Woodward, *Industrial Organization: Theory and Practice* (London: Oxford University Press, 1965).
28. C.C. Miller, W.H. Glick, Y. Wang, and G.P. Huber, "Understanding Technology–Structure Relationships: Theory Development and Meta-analytic Theory Testing," *Academy of Management Journal* 34 (1991), pp. 370–99.
29. Gooding and Wagner, "A Meta-analytic Review"; see also A.C. Bluedorn, "Pilgrim's Progress: Trends and Convergence in Research on Organizational Size and Environments," *Journal of Management* 21 (1993), pp. 163–92.
30. E.E. Lawler III, "Rethinking Organizational Size," *Organizational Dynamics* 26 (1997), pp. 24–35.
31. Patrick J. Kiger, "Power of the Individual," www.questia.com/magazine/1P3-1008598621/power-of-the-individual, retrieved June 15, 2015.
32. R.E. Silverman, "Corporate Field Trip: Learning from Startups," *The Wall Street Journal*, March 27, 2013, p. B8.
33. Scott and Davis, *Organizations and Organizing*.
34. R.E. Miles and C.C. Snow, *Organizational Strategy, Structure, and Process* (New York: McGraw-Hill, 1978).
35. M. Singer, "Stringer's Way," *The New Yorker*, June 5, 2006, pp. 46–57.
36. D.B. Turban and T.L. Keon, "Organizational Attractiveness: An Interactionist Perspective," *Journal of Applied Psychology* 78 (1993), pp. 184–93.
37. J. Scheck, "HP Plans to Fuse Printer, PC Units," *The Wall Street Journal*, September 30, 2009; A. Lashinsky, "The Hurd Way: How a Sales-Obsessed CEO Rebooted HP," *Fortune*, April 17, 2006, pp. 92–102.
38. C. Salter, "Why America Is Addicted to Olive Garden," *Fast Company*, July/August 2009, pp. 102–8, 121.
39. D. Welch, D. Kiley, and C. Matlack, "Tough Love at Chrysler," *Businessweek*, August 24, 31, 2009, pp. 26–28.
40. C. Hosford, "Behind the Regus–HQ Merger: A Clash of Cultures That Wasn't," *Sales and Marketing Management*, March 2006, pp. 47–48.
41. "New IBM Delivery Center Opens in Costa Rica," *PR Newswire*, May 2012.
42. J. Galbraith, "The Multi-dimensional and Reconfigurable Organization," *Organizational Dynamics* 39, 2010, pp. 115–25.
43. Ibid.
44. S. Hamm, "Big Blue Shift," *Businessweek*, June 5, 2006, pp. 108–10.
45. C. Edwards, "Dell's Do-Over," *Businessweek*, October 26, 2009, pp. 37–40.
46. L.R. Burns and D.R. Wholey, "Adoption and Abandonment of Matrix Management Programs: Effects of Organizational Characteristics and Interorganizational Programs," *Academy of Management Journal* 36 (1993), pp. 106–38.
47. J.R. Hackman, "The Design of Work Teams," in *Handbook of Organizational Behavior*, ed. J.W. Lorsch (Englewood Cliffs, NJ: Prentice Hall, 1987), pp. 315–42.
48. E.W. Larson and D.H. Gobeli, "Matrix Management: Contradictions and Insight," *California Management Review* 29 (1987), pp. 126–38.
49. D.W. Rees and C. Porter, "Matrix Structures and the Training Implications," *Industrial and Commercial Training* 36 (2004), pp. 189–93.
50. R. Greenwood, T. Morris, S. Fairclough, and M. Boussebaa, "The Organizational Design of Transnational Professional Service Firms," *Organizational Dynamics* 39 (2010), pp. 173–83.
51. M. Derven, "Managing the Matrix in the New Normal," *T + D*, July 2010, pp. 42–47.
52. F. Gandolfi and M. Hansson, "Causes and Consequences of Downsizing: Toward and Integrative Framework," *Journal of Management and Organization* 17 (2011), pp. 498–521.
53. A. Taylor III, "GM and Me," *Fortune*, December 8, 2008, pp. 92–100; A. Taylor III, "GM Gets Its Act Together. Finally," *Fortune*, April 5, 2004, pp. 136–46.
54. C. Gopinath, "Businesses in a Merger Need to Make Sense Together," *Businessline*, June 26, 2006, p. 1.
55. J. Hamm, "The Five Messages Leaders Must Manage," *Harvard Business Review*, May 2006, pp. 114–23.
56. Lashinsky, "The Hurd Way"; B. Worthen, "H-P's Not-So-New Plan to Unite PC, Printer Units," *The Wall Street Journal*, March 20, 2012, p. B1.

57. D.M. Noer, *Healing the Wounds* (San Francisco: Jossey-Bass, 1993); K. Mishra, G.M. Spreitzer, and A. Mishra, "Preserving Employee Morale During Downsizing," *Sloan Management Review* 39 (1998), pp. 83–95.
58. M. Conlin, "The Big Squeeze on Workers: Is There a Risk to Wringing More from a Smaller Staff?," *Businessweek*, May 13, 2002, p. 96.
59. T.M. Amabile and R. Conti, "Changes in the Work Environment for Creativity During Downsizing," *Academy of Management Journal* 42 (1999), pp. 630–40; K.P. DeMeuse, M.L. Marks, and G. Dai, "Organizational Downsizing, Mergers and Acquisitions, and Strategic Alliances: Using Theory and Research to Enhance Practice," in *APA Handbook of Industrial and Organizational Psychology*, Vol. 3, ed. S. Zedeck (Washington, DC: APA, 2011), pp. 729–68; T.M. Probst, "Exploring Employee Outcomes of Organizational Restructuring—A Solomon Four-Group Study," *Group and Organization Management* 28 (2003), pp. 416–39.
60. J. Brockner, G. Spreitzer, A. Mishra, W. Hockwarter, L. Pepper, and J. Weinberg, "Perceived Control as an Antidote to the Negative Effects of Layoffs on Survivors' Organizational Commitment and Job Performance," *Administrative Science Quarterly* 49 (2004), pp. 76–100; T.M. Probst, "Countering the Negative Effects of Job Insecurity Through Participative Decision Making," *Journal of Occupational Health Psychology* 10 (2005), pp. 320–29.
61. J. Brockner, "The Effects of Work Layoffs on Survivors: Research, Theory and Practice," in *Research in Organizational Behavior*, Vol. 10, eds. B.M. Staw and L.L. Cummings (Berkeley: University of California Press, 1988), pp. 213–55; M.A. Campion, L. Guerrero, and R. Posthuma, "Reasonable Human Resource Practices for Making Employee Downsizing Decisions," *Organizational Dynamics* 40 (2011), pp. 174–80.
62. C. Tuna, "Many Companies Hire as They Fire," *The Wall Street Journal*, May 11, 2009, p. B6.
63. Ibid.
64. J.I. Porras and P.J. Robertson, "Organizational Development: Theory, Practice, and Research," in *Handbook of Industrial and Organizational Psychology*, Vol. 3, 2nd ed., eds. M.D. Dunnette and L.M. Hough (Palo Alto, CA: Consulting Psychologists Press, 1992), pp. 719–822.
65. Alexander, "The Cheesecake Factory."
66. Ruiz, "Cheesecake Factory."
67. Gawande, "Big Med."
68. Ibid.
69. Ruiz, "Cheesecake Factory."
70. Nicole Strong, "'Gamefying' Training with the Cheesecake Factory," Emgaming.com, June 2012, engaming.wordpress.com/2012/06/15/gamifying-training-with-the-cheesecake-factory, retrieved June 14, 2015.
71. V. Van Landinham, "MenuMasters 2012: The Cheesecake Factory," *Nation's Restaurant News*, April 2012, nrn.com/archive/menumasters-2012-cheesecake-factory.
72. Gawande, "Big Med."

Chapter 15

1. S. Hehn, "'Serendipitous Interaction' Key to Tech Firms' Workplace Design," NPR, March 13, 2013, www.npr.org/blogs/alltechconsidered/2013/03/13/174195695/serendipitous-interaction-key-to-tech-firms-workplace-design.
2. T.B. Lee, "Yahoo Can't Decide If It's a Media Company or a Tech Company," *Washington Post*, May 20, 2013, www.washingtonpost.com/blogs/wonkblog/wp/2013/05/20/yahoo-cant-decide-if-its-a-media-company-or-a-tech-company.
3. M. Moulton, "What Culture Means to Yahoo," Corvirtus.com, April 17, 2013, www.corvirtus.com/the-importance-of-company-culture-to-grow-yahoo.
4. K. Baskin, "Executive Privilege: Marissa Mayer's HR Decisions at Yahoo," *Boston Globe*, March, 17, 2013, www.bostonglobe.com/magazine/2013/03/16/marissa-mayer-why-yahoo-ceo-proves-changes-corporate-america-won-come-from-top/YSmDXsoLc1nhqmJuWMPNkJ/story.html.
5. N. Carlson, "Forget iPhones and Free Food, This Story Illustrates the Real Big Change Marissa Mayer Is Bringing to Yahoo," *Business Insider*, August 23, 2012, www.businessinsider.com/forget-iphones-and-free-food-heres-the-real-big-change-marissa-mayer-is-bringing-to-yahoo-2012-8.
6. Ibid.
7. D. Nordfors, "Mayer's Challenge: Merging the Cultures of Yahoo and Tumblr," *Xconomy*, May 23, 2013, www.xconomy.com/san-francisco/2013/05/23/mayers-challenge-merging-the-cultures-of-yahoo-and-tumblr.
8. W. Verbeke, M. Volgering, and M. Hessels, "Exploring the Conceptual Expansion within the Field of Organizational Behavior: Organizational Climate and Organizational Culture," *Journal of Management Studies* 35 (1998), pp. 303–29.
9. T.E. Deal, and A.A. Kennedy, *Corporate Cultures: The Rites and Rituals of Corporate Life* (Reading, MA: Addison-Wesley, 1982).
10. Adapted from C.A. O'Reilly III, J. Chatman, and D.L. Caldwell, "People and Organizational Culture: A Profile Comparison Approach to Assessing Person–Organization Fit," *Academy of Management Journal* 34 (1991), pp. 487–516; A.S. Tsui, Z. Zhang, W. Hui, K.R. Xin, and J.B. Wu, "Unpacking the Relationship Between CEO Leadership Behavior and Organizational Culture," *The Leadership Quarterly* 17 (2006), pp. 113–37.
11. C.A. O'Reilly and J.A. Chatman, "Culture as Social Control: Corporations, Cults, and Commitment," in B.M. Staw and L.L. Cummings, eds., *Research in Organizational Behavior*, Vol. 18 (Stamford, CT: JAI Press, 1996), pp. 157–200.
12. J.A. Chatman, "Matching People and Organizations: Selection and Socialization in Public Accounting Firms," *Administrative Science Quarterly* 36 (1991), pp. 459–84.
13. H.M. Trice and J.M. Beyer, *The Cultures of Work Organizations* (Englewood Cliffs, NJ: Prentice Hall, 1993).
14. I. Rowley, "What Put Honda in the Passing Lane," *Businessweek*, October 19, 2009, pp. 57–58.
15. S. Nicolas, "The Way We Do Things Around Here," *Director*, March 2011, pp. 56–59.
16. J. Hempel, "Bringing Design to Blue Chips," *Fortune*, November 12, 2007, p. 32; M. Stibbe, "Mothers of Invention," *Director* 55 (2002), pp. 64–68.
17. A. Vance, "Netflix, Reed Hastings Survive Missteps to Join Silicon Valley's Elite," *Bloomberg Businessweek*, May 9, 2013, www.businessweek.com/articles/2013-05-09/netflix-reed-hastings-survive-missteps-to-join-silicon-valleys-elite.
18. G. Rivlin, "The Problem with Microsoft," *Fortune*, April 11, 2011, pp. 45–51.
19. D.P. Shuit, "Yum Does a 360," *Workforce Management*, April 2005, pp. 59–60.
20. S. Berfield, "Howard Schultz Versus Howard Schultz," *Businessweek*, August 17, 2009, pp. 28–33.
21. S. Birk, "Creating a Culture of Safety: Why CEO's Hold the Key to Improved Outcomes," *Healthcare Executive*, March/April 2009, pp. 15–22.
22. "2007 Corporate Social Responsibility Report," TELUS Corporation website, csr.telus.com/content/pdf/telus_csr_2007-en.pdf, retrieved June 15, 2015.
23. A. Bryant, *The Corner Office: Indispensable and Unexpected Lessons from CEOs on How to Lead and Succeed* (New York: Times Books, 2011).
24. J.M. Higgins and C. McAllaster, "If You Want Strategic Change, Don't Forget to Change Your Cultural Artifacts," *Journal of Change Management* 4 (2004), pp. 63–74.
25. Enbridge Partners website, www.enbridge.com/AboutEnbridge/Values.asp, retrieved August 2014.
26. M. Gunther, "Marriott Gets a Wake-up Call," *Fortune*, July 6, 2009, pp. 62–66.
27. E.H. Schein, "Organizational Culture," *American Psychologist* 45 (1990), pp. 109–19.
28. E.H. Schein, *Organizational Culture and Leadership* (San Francisco: Jossey-Bass, 2004).
29. E.H. Schein, "What Is Culture?," in *Reframing Organizational Culture*, eds. P.J. Frost, L.F. Moore, M.R. Louis, C.C. Lundberg, and J. Martin (Beverly Hills, CA: Sage, 1991), pp. 243–53.

30. R. Goffee and G. Jones, *The Character of a Corporation* (New York: Harper Business, 1998).
31. Ibid.
32. Y. Hong, H. Liao, J. Hu, and K. Jiang, "Missing Link in the Service Profit Chain: A Meta-analytic Review of the Antecedents, Consequences, and Moderators of Service Climate," *Journal of Applied Psychology* 98 (2013), pp. 237–67; F.O. Walumba, C.A. Hartnell, and A. Oke, "Servant Leadership, Procedural Justice Climate, Service Climate, Employee Attitudes, and Organizational Citizenship Behavior: A Cross-level Investigation," *Journal of Applied Psychology* 95 (2010), pp. 517–29; B. Schneider, D.E. Bowen, M.G. Ehrhart, and K.M. Holcombe, "The Climate for Service: Evolution of a Construct," in *Handbook of Organizational Culture and Climate*, eds. N.M. Ashkanasy, C. Wilderom, and M.F. Peterson (Thousand Oaks, CA, Sage, 2000), pp. 21–36.
33. Hong et al., "Missing Link in the Service Profit Chain"; B. Schneider, M.G. Ehrhart, D.M. Mayer, J.L. Saltz, and K. Niles-Jolly, "Understanding Organization–Customer Links in Service Settings," *Academy of Management Journal* 48 (2005), pp. 1017–32.
34. "WestJet Culture," WestJet website. c5dsp.westjet.com/guest/media/investorMedia.jsp?id=Facts, retrieved February 16, 2009.
35. D. Zohar and G. Luria, "Climate as a Social-Cognitive Construction of Supervisory Safety Practices: Scripts as a Proxy of Behaviour Patterns," *Journal of Applied Psychology* 89 (2004), pp. 322–33.
36. D.A. Hofmann, F.P. Morgeson, and S.J. Gerras, "Climate as a Moderator of the Relationship Between Leader–Member Exchange and Content Specific Citizenship: Safety Climate as an Exemplar," *Journal of Applied Psychology* 88 (2003), pp. 170–78.
37. "2007 Sustainability Report (Health and Safety)," Syncrude Canada Ltd., syncrude.ca/sustainability2007/social/health, retrieved February 16, 2009.
38. Kim Mackrael and Grant Robertson, "Lac-Mégantic Report Blames Lax Oversight, Weak Safety Culture," *The Globe and Mail*, August 19, 2014).
39. Ibid.
40. RBC website, www.rbc.com, retrieved April 2008; Z. Hirji, "Growth and Innovation Rests on Diversity," *Canadian HR Reporter*, December 2006, p. 18; M. Shin, "Minority Report," *Corporate Knights: Cleantech Issue 2007* 6.2, pp. 34–42.
41. Ibid.
42. Anonymous, "Building a Better Workforce," *Profit* 30, March 2011, pp. 17–20.
43. L.D. McLean, "Organizational Culture's Influence on Creativity and Innovation: A Review of the Literature and Implications for Human Resource Development," *Advances in Developing Human Resources* 7 (2005), pp. 226–46.
44. D. Mattioli and K. Maher, "At 3M, Innovation Comes in Tweaks and Snips," *The Wall Street Journal Online*, March 1, 2010.
45. J. Seabrook, "How to Make It," *The New Yorker*, September 20, 2010, pp. 66–73.
46. T. Poulton, "Got a Creative Creative Process? Fostering Creativity in an ROI-Focused Cubicle-Ridden Environment Ain't Easy. Here's How to Get Your Team's Juices Flowing," *Strategy*, April 2006, p. 11.
47. C.A. O'Reilly, "Corporations, Culture, and Commitment: Motivation and Social Control in Organizations," *California Management Review* 31 (1989), pp. 9–25.
48. O'Reilly et al., "People and Organizational Culture."
49. E.H. Schein, "Three Cultures of Management: The Key to Organizational Learning," *Sloan Management Review* 38 (1996), pp. 9–20.
50. A. Boisner and J. Chatman, "The Role of Subcultures in Agile Organizations," in R. Petersen and E. Mannix, eds., *Leading and Managing People in Dynamic Organizations* (Mahwah, NJ: Lawrence Erlbaum Associates, 2003).
51. See J.A. Howard-Grenville, "Inside the 'Black Box': How Organizational Culture and Subcultures Inform Interpretations and Actions on Environmental Issues," *Organization & Environment* 19 (2006), pp. 46–73; J. Jermier, J. Slocum, L. Fry, and J. Gaines, "Organizational Subcultures in a Soft Bureaucracy: Resistance Behind the Myth and Façade of an Official Culture," *Organizational Science* 2 (1991), pp. 170–94.
52. B. Schneider, H.W. Goldstein, and D.B. Smith, "The ASA Framework: An Update," *Personnel Psychology* 48 (1995), pp. 747–73.
53. A.B. Graf, "Building Corporate Cultures," *Chief Executive*, March 2005, p. 18.
54. D. Foust, "Where Headhunters Fear to Tread," *Businessweek*, September 14, 2009, pp. 42–44.
55. For good summaries of socialization, see C.D. Fisher, "Organizational Socialization: An Integrative View," *Research in Personnel and Human Resource Management* 4 (1986), pp. 101–45; T.N. Bauer, E.W. Morrison, and R.R. Callister, "Organizational Socialization: A Review and Directions for Future Research," in *Research in Personnel and Human Resource Management*, Vol. 16, ed. G.R. Ferris (Greenwich, CT: JAI Press, 1998), pp. 149–214.
56. D.M. Cable, L. Aiman-Smith, P.W. Mulvey, and J.R. Edwards, "The Sources and Accuracy of Job Applicants' Beliefs About Organizational Culture," *Academy of Management Journal* 43 (2000), pp. 1076–85; M.R. Louis, "Surprise and Sense-Making: What Newcomers Experience in Entering Unfamiliar Organizational Settings," *Administrative Science Quarterly* 25 (1980), pp. 226–51.
57. G.T. Chao, A. O'Leary-Kelly, S. Wolf, H.J. Klein, and P.D. Gardner, "Organizational Socialization: Its Content and Consequences," *Journal of Applied Psychology* 79 (1994), pp. 450–63.
58. Ibid.; H. Klein and N. Weaver, "The Effectiveness of an Organizational-Level Orientation Training Program in the Socialization of New Hires," *Personnel Psychology*, Spring 2000, pp. 47–66; M.J. Wesson and C.I. Gogus, "Shaking Hands with a Computer: An Examination of Two Methods of Organizational Newcomer Orientation," *Journal of Applied Psychology* 90 (2005), pp. 1018–26.
59. M. Gravelle, "The Five Most Common Hiring Mistakes and How to Avoid Them," *The Canadian Manager* 29 (2004), pp. 11–13.
60. J. Van Maanen and E.H. Schein, "Toward a Theory of Organizational Socialization," *Research in Organizational Behavior* 1 (1979), pp. 209–64.
61. S.J. Ashford and J.S. Black, "Proactivity During Organizational Entry: The Role of Desire for Control," *Journal of Applied Psychology* 81 (1996), pp. 199–214; T. Kim, D.M. Cable, and S. Kim, "Socialization Tactics, Employee Proactivity, and Person–Organization Fit," *Journal of Applied Psychology* 90 (2005), pp. 232–241.
62. K. Lewin, *Field Theory in Social Science* (New York: Harper & Row, 1951); B. Burnes, "Kurt Lewin and the Planned Approach to Change: A Re-appraisal," *Journal of Management Studies* 41(6) (2004), pp. 977–1002.
63. D. MacMillan, "Can eBay Get Its Tech Savvy Back?," *Businessweek*, June 22, 2009, pp. 48–49.
64. Ibid.
65. M. Alvesson and S. Sveningsson, *Changing Organizational Culture: Cultural Change Work in Progress* (London: Routledge, 2008).
66. P. Mourier and M. Smith, *Conquering Organizational Change: How to Succeed Where Most Companies Fail* (Atlanta: CEP Press, 2001); P. Lawrence and K. White, "Leading Change: Why Transformation Efforts Succeed (and the Value of Systemic Coaching)," *Training & Development (1839–8561)* 40(2) (2013), pp. 10–12.
67. K.S. Cameron and R.E. Quinn, *Diagnosing and Changing Organizational Culture*, 3rd ed. (San Francisco: Jossey-Bass, 2011).
68. Ibid.
69. Ibid.
70. Ibid.
71. Ibid.
72. Ibid.
73. Ibid.
74. Ibid.
75. Ibid.
76. Mourier and Smith, *Conquering Organizational Change*; Lawrence and White, "Leading Change."
77. W.W. Burke, D.G. Lake, and J.W. Paine, *Organizational Change: A Comprehensive Reader* (San Francisco: Jossey-Bass, 2009).

78. Alvesson and Sveningsson, *Changing Organizational Culture*; Burke et al., *Organizational Change*.
79. Ibid.
80. B. Schneider, "The People Make the Place," *Personnel Psychology* 40 (1987), pp. 437–53; B. Schneider, H.W. Goldstein, and D.B. Smith, "The ASA Framework: An Update," *Personnel Psychology* 48 (1995), pp. 747–79.
81. "An Inside Look at Google's Data Driven Job Interview Process," www.washingtonpost.com/business/capitalbusiness/an-inside-look-at-googles-data-driven-job-interview-process/2013/09/03/648ea8b2-14bd-11e3-880b-7503237cc69d_story.html, retrieved September 14, 2014.
82. Ibid.
83. W.W. Burke, "Training and Development," in W. Warner Burke, Dale G. Lake, and Jill Waymire Paine, eds., *Organizational Change: A Comprehensive Reader* (San Francisco: Jossey-Bass, 2009), pp. 590–98.
84. "About Zappos," about.zappos.com, retrieved September 14, 2014.
85. "Zappos CEO: Training, Mentorship at the Core of Our Employee 'Pipeline Strategy,'" www.huffingtonpost.com/tony-hsieh/zappos-ceo-how-weve-built_b_812187.htm, retrieved September 14, 2014.
86. E.H. Schein, *Organizational Culture and Leadership* (San Francisco: Jossey-Bass, 2004).
87. E. Gubbins, "Nortel's New Execs Bring Cisco Experience," *Telephony*, April 11, 2005, pp. 14–15.
88. E. Glazer, J.S. Lublin, and D. Mattioli, "Penney Backfires on Ackman," *The Wall Street Journal*, April 10, 2013, p. B1.
89. Y. Weber, "Measuring Cultural Fit in Mergers and Acquisitions," in *Handbook of Organizational Culture and Climate*, eds. N.M. Ashkanasy, C. Wilderom, and M.F. Peterson (Thousand Oaks, CA; Sage, 2000), pp. 309–20.
90. D. Foust, "Pulling Delta out of a Nosedive," *Businessweek*, May 25, 2009, pp. 36–37.
91. S. Brahy, "Six Solution Pillars for Successful Cultural Integration of International M&As," *Journal of Organizational Excellence*, Autumn 2006, pp. 53–63.
92. Anonymous, "Shall We?," *The Economist*, February 9, 2013, www.economist.com/news/business/21571475-urge-merge-could-be-about-return-shall-we?zid=293&ah=e50f636873b42369614615ba3c16df4a; D. Anupreeta and G. Chon, "Deals Stage a Comeback," *The Wall Street Journal*, August 20, 2010, p. 1.
93. G. Edmondson, "Auf Wiedersehen, Mitsubishi," *Businessweek*, November 11, 2005, www.businessweek.com; B. Bremmer, "A Tale of Two Auto Mergers," *Businessweek*, April 29, 2004, www.businessweek.com.
94. N. Shirouzu, "Volvo's Search for Common Ground," *The Wall Street Journal Online*, June 6, 2011.
95. Gordon Pitts, "Turnaround Ace: Inside the Hunter Harrison Era at CP Railway," *The Globe and Mail*, April 24, 2014.
96. Ibid.
97. Ibid.
98. Ibid.
99. Alvesson and Sveningsson, *Changing Organizational Culture*.
100. C.A. Hartnell, A.Y. Ou, and A. Kinicki, "Organizational Culture and Organizational Effectiveness: A Meta-analytic Investigation of the Competing Values Framework's Theoretical Suppositions," *Journal of Applied Psychology* 96 (2011), pp. 677–94.
101. W. Arthur Jr., S.T. Bell, A.J. Villado, and D. Doverspike, "The Use of Person–Organization Fit in Employment Decision Making: An Assessment of Its Criterion-Related Validity," *Journal of Applied Psychology 91* (2007), pp. 786–801; A.L. Kristof-Brown, R.D. Zimmerman, and E.C. Johnson, "Consequences of Individuals' Fit at Work: A Meta-analysis of Person–Job, Person–Organization, Person–Group, and Person–Supervisor Fit," *Personnel Psychology* 58 (2005), pp. 281–342.
102. A.E. Barber, *Recruiting Employees: Individual and Organizational Perspectives* (Thousand Oaks, CA: Sage, 1998).
103. J.P. Wanous, *Organizational Entry: Recruitment, Selection, Orientation and Socialization of Newcomers* (Reading, MA: Addison-Wesley, 1992).
104. M. Gravelle, "The Five Most Common Hiring Mistakes and How to Avoid Them," *The Canadian Manager* 29 (2004), pp. 11–13.
105. N.R. Anderson, N.A. Cunningham-Snell, and J. Haigh, "Induction Training as Socialization: Current Practice and Attitudes to Evaluation in British Organizations," *International Journal of Selection and Assessment* 4 (1996), pp. 169–83.
106. Wesson and Gogus, "Shaking Hands with a Computer."
107. Ibid.; Klein and Weaver, "The Effectiveness."
108. M. Gunther, "Nothing Blue About This Airline," *Fortune*, September 14, 2009, pp. 114–18.
109. C.R. Wanberg, E.T. Welsh, and S.A. Hezlett, "Mentoring Research: A Review and Dynamic Process Model," *Research in Personnel and Human Resources Management* 22 (2003), pp. 39–124.
110. T.D. Allen, L.T. Eby, M.L. Poteet, E. Lentz, and L. Lima, "Outcomes Associated with Mentoring Protégés: A Meta-analysis," *Journal of Applied Psychology* 89 (2004), pp. 127–36.
111. G. Kranz, "More Firms Paying Mind to Mentoring," *Workforce Management*, January 2010, p. 10.
112. A. Efrati, "Google Seals Its Reputation for Minting Tech Executives," *The Wall Street Journal*, July 17, 2012, p. B7.
113. J. Surowiecki, "Face Time," *The New Yorker*, March 18, 2013, p. 26.
114. Ibid.
115. C. Tkaczyk, "Marissa Mayer Breaks Her Silence on Yahoo's Telecommuting Policy," *Fortune*, April 19, 2013, tech.fortune.cnn.com/2013/04/19/marissa-mayer-telecommuting.
116. D. Guthrie, "Marissa Mayer: Choosing Corporate Culture over Worker Independence," *Forbes*, March 8, 2013, www.forbes.com/sites/dougguthrie/2013/03/08/marissa-mayer-choosing-corporate-culture-over-worker-independence.
117. S. Hehn, "'Serendipitous Interaction' Key to Tech Firms' Workplace Design," *NPR*, March 13, 2013, www.npr.org/blogs/alltechconsidered/2013/03/13/174195695/serendipitous-interaction-key-to-tech-firms-workplace-design.
118. M. Maisto, "Yahoo CEO's Criticized Hiring Changes Suggest a Cultural Shift," *EWEEK*, March 21, 2013, www.eweek.com/mobile/yahoo-ceos-criticized-hiring-changes-suggest-a-cultural-shift.